DATE			

CHILD
PSYCHOLOGY
TODAY SECOND EDITION

ABOUT THE AUTHORS

ELIZABETH HALL is the co-author of *Developmental Psychology Today* (4th ed.), of *Sexuality* (both published by Random House), and of *Adult Development and Aging*. Before she turned to college textbooks, she was Editor-in-Chief of *Human Nature*, a magazine about the human sciences. She was on the staff of *Psychology Today* from the magazine's inception in 1967 and was Managing Editor of that magazine at the time she left to start *Human Nature*. As a science writer, Ms. Hall has interviewed many prominent psychologists, including Jean Piaget, Erik Erikson, Jerome Bruner, B. F. Skinner, Jerome Kagan, Sandra Scarr, and Bruno Bettelheim. She has also written a number of books for children; two of them, *Why We Do What We Do: A Look at Psychology* and *From Pigeons to People: A Look at Behavior Shaping*, received Honorable Mention in the American Psychological Foundation's National Media Awards.

MICHAEL E. LAMB is professor of psychology, psychiatry, and pediatrics at the University of Utah in Salt Lake City. A developmental psychologist by training, his research is concerned with social and emotional development, especially in infancy and early childhood; the determinants and consequences of adaptive and maladaptive parental behavior; and the interface of psychology and biology. His studies of the role and influence of the father helped break the limited focus of developmental psychology on the infant-mother dyad, and his research on attachment in Sweden, Japan, Israel, and the United States has led to reevaluations of the nature of that bond. Dr. Lamb is the co-author of *Socialization and Personality Development* and *Development in Infancy*, another Random House text. He is editor of *The Role of the Father in Child Development*, now in its second edition, and of *Nontraditional Families: Parenting and Childrearing*. Dr. Lamb is co-editor of the *Advances in Developmental Psychology* series, as well as more than a half dozen books on various aspects of child development, including infant social cognition, social and personality development, fatherhood and family policy, sibling influences, and attachment. He has also published widely in all the major psychology journals. In recognition of his contribution to developmental psychology, Dr. Lamb has received two national awards: The Young Psychologist Award (1976) and the Boyd McCandless Young Scientist Award (1978).

MARION PERLMUTTER is professor of psychology at the University of Michigan and research scientist at its Institute of Gerontology. She was formerly professor of psychology at the University of Minnesota, where she was also associate director of the Institute of Child Development, and a visiting professor at the Max Planck Institute for Psychological Study in Munich. A developmental psychologist, her major research interests concern cognitive development across the life span. Her research with infants and young children helped change developmental psychology's approach to memory by showing that youngsters' recall is organized and that in their daily lives infants demonstrate recall capabilities that escape laboratory inspection. Dr. Perlmutter is the co-author of *Adult Development and Aging*. She edited *Children's Memory* in the *New Directions in Child Development* series, and from 1981 to 1984, she edited the annual volumes in the *Minnesota Symposia on Child Psychology* series. She has published numerous articles on memory development in preschool children and the aging of memory in adults. She has also contributed many chapters to books on cognition and developmental psychology. In 1981, Dr. Perlmutter received the Boyd McCandless Young Scientist Award for Early Contributions to Developmental Psychology.

SECOND EDITION

CHILD PSYCHOLOGY TODAY

Elizabeth Hall
Michael E. Lamb *University of Utah*
Marion Perlmutter *University of Michigan*

Random House   New York

Second Edition
987654321
Copyright © 1982, 1986 by Random House, Inc.

Library of Congress Cataloging-in-Publication Data

Hall, Elizabeth, 1929-
    Child psychology today.

    Bibliography: p.
    Includes indexes.
    1. Child psychology.   I. Lamb, Michael E., 1953-
II. Perlmutter, Marion.   III. Title. [DNLM: 1. Child
Psychology.   WS 105 H175c]
BF721.H2175   1986   155.4   85-28205
ISBN 0-394-34285-2

Manufactured in the United States of America

Cover photo: Camilla Smith/Rainbow
Cover design: Katharine Urban

Chapter Opening Photo Credits

Chapter 1, Owen Kahn/Jeroboam; Chapter 2, Michael Hayman/Photo Researchers; Chapter 3, Joel Gordon; Chapter 4, Suzanne Arms/Jeroboam; Chapter 5, Alan Carey/ The Image Works; Chapter 6, Charles Harbutt/Archive; Chapter 7, Elizabeth Crews; Chapter 8, Frank Siteman/Taurus; Chapter 9, Joel Gordon; Chapter 10, Jerry Howard/Stock, Boston; Chapter 11, Hazel Hankin; Chapter 12, Suzanne Szasz; Chapter 13, Suzanne Arms/Jeroboam; Chapter 14, Elizabeth Hamlin/Stock, Boston; Chapter 15, Suzanne Arms/Jeroboam; Chapter 16, James Carroll/Archive; Chapter 17, Jane Scherr/Jeroboam

ACKNOWLEDGMENTS

Chapter 1:
P. 18: Reprinted with permission of *American Scientist* 68 [1980], W. K. Estes. "Is Memory Obsolete?"

Chapter 3:
P. 84: From Newton and Modahl, "Pregnancy, The Closest Human Relationship," *Human Nature*, March 1978, p. 47. Illustration by Everett Davidson.
P. 95: From J. G. Wilson. "Embryological Considerations in Teratology," in J. G. Wilson and J. Warkany (eds.), *Teratology: Principles and Techniques*. Chicago: University of Chicago Press, 1965, pp. 251–261.

Chapter 4:
P. 113: Reprinted with permission from E. Harms, *Problems of Sleep and Dreams in Children*. Copyright 1964, Pergamon Press.
P. 125: From W. Kessen and Salapatek, "Visual Scanning of Triangles by the Human Newborn," *Journal of Experimental Psychology*, Vol. 3, 1966, pp. 155–167.
P. 128: Graph after Friedman, "Differential Dishabilation as a Function of Magnitude of Stimulus Discrepancy and Sex of the Newborn Infant." (Unpublished paper)
P. 136: From A. R. Wisenfeld and C. Z. Malatesta. "Infant Distress: Variables Affecting Responses of Caregivers and Others," in L. W. Hoffman, R. J. Gandelman, and H. R. Schiffman. *Parenting: Its Causes and Consequences*. Copyright 1982 by Lawrence Erlbaum Associates, Inc.

Chapter 5:
P. 148: Adapted from *Biological Foundations of Language*, by E. H. Lenneberg. Copyright © 1967 John Wiley & Sons, Inc. Reprinted by permission of John Wiley & Sons, Inc.
P. 149: Adapted from C. N. Jackson (ed.), *Morris' Human Anatomy*, 7th Edition. Copyright © 1923, McGraw-Hill Book Company.
P. 151: Adapted from A. Prader, J. M. Tanner and G. A. Von Harnack, "Catch-up Growth Following Illness or Starvation," *Journal of Pediatrics*, Vol. 62, 1963, pp. 646–659.
P. 165: Adapted from R. C. Lewis, A. M. Duval, and A. Iliff, "Standards for the Basal Metabolism of Children from Two to Fifteen Years of Age," *Journal of Pediatrics*, Vol. 23, 1943.
P. 167: Adapted from J. M. Tanner, *Growth and Adolescence*.

Chapter 6:
P. 190: From S. Coren, C. Porac, and P. Duncan, "Lateral Preference Behaviors in Preschool Children and Young Adults," *Child Development*, Vol. 52, 1981, pp. 443–450. © The Society for Research in Child Development, Inc.

Chapter 7:
P. 211: From M. Schwartz, and R. H. Day, "Visual Shape Perception in Early Infancy," *Monographs of the Society for Researh in Child Development*, Serial no. 182, Vol. 44, 1979. © The Society for Research in Child Development, Inc.

Chapter 8:
P. 244: Adapted from J. W. Hagen, "The Effect of Distribution on Selective Attention," *Child Development*, Vol. 38, 1967. © The Society for Research in Child Development, Inc.
P. 252: Adapted from H. G. Furth, B. M. Ross and J. Youniss, "Operative Understanding in Reproduction of Drawings," *Child Development*, Vol. 45, 1974, pp. 63–70. © The Society for Research in Child Development, Inc.
P. 253: From *Studies in Cognitive Development: Essays in Honor of Jean Piaget*, edited by David Elkind and John H. Flavell. Copyright © 1969 by Oxford University Press, Inc. Reprinted by permission.

Chapter 9:
P. 272: From *NIM*, by Herbert Terrace. Copyright © 1979 by Herbert Terrace. Reprinted by permission of Alfred A. Knopf, Inc.
P. 275: From J. S. Bruner, "The Course of Cognitive Growth," *American Psychologist*, 19, 1964, pp. 1–15. Copyright 1964 by the American Psychological Association. Adapted by permission of the author.
P. 299: Paula Menyuk, *The Acquisition and Development of Language*, © 1971, p. 62. Adapted by permission of Prentice-Hall, Englewood Cliffs, New Jersey.

Chapter 10:
P. 327: From *The Growth of Logical Thinking: From Childhood to Adolescence*, by Barbel Inhelder and Jean Piaget. © 1958 by Basic Books, Inc., Publishers. Reprinted by permission of the publisher.
P. 329: From R. S. Siegler (ed.), *Children's Thinking: What Develops?* Copyright 1978 by Lawrence Erlbaum Associates, Inc.

P. 337: Adapted from Edward White, Bill Elson, and Richard Prawat, "Children's Conceptions of Death," *Child Development*, Vol. 49, 1978, pp. 307–310. © The Society for Research in Child Development, Inc.

Chapter 11:

P. 344: J. P. Guilford, "Theories of Intelligence" in *Handbook of General Psychology*, Benjamin B. Wolman, Editor, © 1973, p. 636. Reprinted by permission of Prentice-Hall, Englewood Cliffs, New Jersey.

P. 353: Terman, L. M., and M. A. Merrill. *Stanford-Binet Intelligence Scale: Manual for the Third Revision.* Boston: Houghton Mifflin Co., 1960. Copyright © 1949, 1960, by the Institute for Personality and Ability Testing, Inc. All rights reserved. Reproduced by permission.

P. 354: From R. B. McCall, M. I. Appelbaum, and P. S. Hogarty, "Developmental Changes in Mental Performance," in *Monographs of the Society for Research in Child Development*, Serial no. 150, Vol. 38, No. 3. © The Society for Research in Child Development, Inc.

P. 360: D. C. Rowe and R. Plomin. "The Burt Controversy: A Comparison of Burt's Data on IQ with Data from Other Studies," *Behavior Genetics*, 1978, Plenum Publishing Corporation.

P. 362: Adapted from M. Skodak and H. M. Skeels after M. Honzik, "Developmental Studies of Parent-Child Resemblance in Intelligence," *Child Development*, Vol. 28, 1957, pp. 215–228. © The Society for Research in Child Development, Inc.

P. 367: Adapted from C. T. Ramey, K. O. Yeates, and E. J. Short, "The Plasticity of Intellectual Drive: Insight from Preventive Intervention," *Child Development*, Vol. 55, 1984, pp. 1913–1926. © The Society for Research in Child Development, Inc.

P. 368: R. B. McCall, "Developmental Changes in Mental Performance: The Effect of the Birth of a Sibling," *Child Development*, Vol. 55, 1985, pp. 1317–1321. © The Society for Research in Child Development, Inc.

P: 369: From L. B. Miller and R. P. Bizzell, "Long-term Effects of Four Preschool Programs: Ninth and Tenth Grade Results," *Child Development*, Vol. 55, 1984, pp. 1570–1587. © The Society for Research in Child Development, Inc.

Chapter 12:

P. 377: Adapted from H. R. Schaffer and P. E. Emerson, "The Development of Social Attachment in Infancy," *Monographs of the Society for Research in Child Development*, Vol. 29, 1964. © The Society for Research in Child Development, Inc.

P. 388: T. Field, "Interaction Behaviors of Primary versus Secondary Caretaker Fathers," *Developmental Psychology*, 14, 1978, pp. 183–184. Copyright 1978 by the American Psychological Association. Adapted by permission of the author.

Chapter 14:

P. 445: After W. W. Hartup and B. Coates, *Child Development*, Vol. 38, 1967. © The Society for Research in Child Development, Inc.

P. 458: Adapted from P. R. Costanzo and M. E. Shaw, "Conformity as a Function of Age Level," *Child Development*, Vol. 37, 1966. © The Society for Research in Child Development, Inc.

P. 459: T. J. Berndt, "Developmental Changes in Conformity to Peers and Parents," *Developmental Psychology*, 15, 1979, pp. 606–616. Copyright 1979 by the American Psychological Association. Reprinted by permission of the author.

P. 465: Adapted from J. C. Condry and S. L. Dyer, "Behavioral Fantasy Measures of Fear of Success in Children," *Child Development*, Vol. 48, 1977. © The Society for Research in Child Development, Inc.

P. 469: B. G. Licht and C. S. Dweck. "Determinants of Academic Achievement: The Interaction of Children's Achievement Orientation with Skill Area," *Developmental Psychology*, Vol. 20, 1984, pp. 628–636. Copyright 1984 by the American Psychological Association. Reprinted by permission of the author.

Chapter 16:

P. 511: From Leon J. Kuczynski, 1983, p. 130. Copyright 1983 by the American Psychological Association. Reprinted/Adapted by permission of the author.

P. 524: From L. Peterson, "Role of Donor Competence, Donor Age, and Peer Pressure on Helping in an Emergency," *Child Development*, Vol. 19, 1983, p. 876. © The Society for Research in Child Development, Inc.

Chapter 17:

P. 547: Reproduced from *Children's Minds* by Margaret Donaldson, by permission of W. W. Norton & Company, Inc. Copyright © 1978 by Margaret Donaldson.

P. 560: Reprinted by permission of the publisher from H. G. Furth, *The World of Grown-Ups: Children's Conceptions of Society.* Copyright 1980 by Elsevier Science Publishing Co., Inc.

The success of the first edition of *Child Psychology Today* confirmed the need for a research-based, topic-oriented text that would hold the student's interest. As instructors who use this approach realize, the presentation of the content of development within a topical framework allows us to keep in sight the long-term, continuous processes that are at the heart of developmental psychology. The first edition of *Child Psychology Today* was a response to the need of these instructors, who felt that the chronological approach to child development, with its simultaneous focus on all aspects of every process, made it difficult for students to get a clear picture of the early basis of later development.

As we revised this text, we continued to find that arranging the story of development in a topical manner has many advantages. When a single topic is followed from infancy through adolescence, similarities as well as differences can be discussed without producing a redundant coverage. In addition, by placing the primary focus on aspects of development instead of on agencies of influence (such as the school), our account becomes more coherent and we can probe each area more deeply. Despite the book's depth, it is written with the assumption that students have no prior acquaintance with psychology. Theory, findings, and interpretations are explained clearly so that students at all levels can understand them. For example, our discussion of personality development in infancy (Chapter 12) attempts to show how infancy relates to later development rather than simply treating infancy as a fragmented stage of life. The treatment delves into the important influences on the infant and shows *why* they are important. It looks at the way later personality emerges from infancy.

This second edition of *Child Psychology Today* continues the firm basis in research, the readability, and the focus on processes of development that were the special strengths of the first edition. As with the first edition, our topical approach allows us to explore each topic analytically, focusing on theory. This increased concentration on theory places our discussion of research findings in the context of their implications so that the *whys* of development become clearer. In treating theory, we have again provided a fairly eclectic account, considering a number of perspectives and showing how each is useful and how each can explain certain aspects of development. This book presents the organismic, psychodynamic, and learning theories that have dominated the field of developmental psychology, but it discusses other approaches as well. Ethology, with its emphasis on our common heritage as members of the human species, is presented and given special emphasis in the discussion of attachment. Besides the customary consideration of Piagetian views, the coverage of cognitive development presents a thorough discussion of the increasingly important information-processing approach and its application to all cognitive processes (perception, attention, memory, and thought) as well as its usefulness in explaining such areas of development as sex roles and tendencies toward aggression. Finally, development is approached from the position of dialectical psychology, a view that has been rarely mentioned in introductory textbooks, despite the fact that its influence on developmental research has been growing steadily.

Once again the book's dominant theme is the interaction between heredity and environment. In fact, we have emphasized interaction more heavily in this edition than in the first. Throughout the text, interaction is stressed on two levels: first, the interplay of cognitive development, heredity, and experience; and second, the interaction between the growing child and other people. Always the stress is on the point that influence continually runs two ways: the child affects parents, siblings, and peers at the same time that these people affect the child. In Chapter 4, for example, we show how a child's temperament may affect the family atmosphere, and in Chapter 16, we present research showing how a child's actions can evoke the kind of discipline a parent uses.

Indeed, throughout the book the emphasis is on research. As students follow the development of each topic area, they are introduced to research that supports the facts presented or the conclusions drawn. They learn not only what researchers in child development know about the development of the child but how they have come to know it and what those findings mean.

In this edition, we have made several important changes that we believe strengthen the book and help increase the student's understanding of development:

¶ We have reorganized the introductory unit, dropping one chapter in order to get the student into content material more quickly. We have also emphasized developmental psychology's usefulness; for example, we focus on the adjustment of adopted children as an example of the way developmental research can be applied to real human problems (Chapter 2).

¶ We have reorganized the unit on cognitive development, providing a chapter on The Emerging Mind (Chapter 7) that parallels the chapter on The Emerging Self (Chapter 12) in the personality unit. This chapter gives students a thorough grounding in Piagetian ideas and research before they learn about development of basic cognitive processes—an area in which research is dominated by information-processing approaches. And we have merged the discussions of sensation, perception, and memory into one chapter. In the course of this reorganization, we have compressed the discussion of language into one chapter and inserted it into the unit on cognitive development. This change establishes students' understanding of basic cognitive processes before they encounter the development of language.

¶ We have reorganized the chapter on development within the family (Chapter 13) to take account of changes in the American family. In addition to discussions of maternal employment, father absence, and divorce, we now cover the effects of increased paternal involvement, maternal absence, living with a stepparent, and the postponement of parenthood until both parents are in their thirties or forties.

Child Psychology Today continues to differ from other topical texts in developmental psychology in the topics selected for chapter-length consideration:

¶ An entire chapter on brain development (Chapter 6) discusses traditional views of brain development in the light of new, contradictory research and presents a rigorous treatment of the research in hemisphere specialization.

¶ By allocating a full chapter to intelligence (Chapter 11), we have been able to widen our coverage beyond the traditional psychometric perspective to explore biological, structural, and information-processing views of intelligence. In addition to the expected discussion of what IQ tests can and cannot do, there is an explanation of the links between IQ and school success, success in life, and creativity—and *why* the link appears when it does. There is also a lengthy treatment of the way heredity, health, nutrition, and environment interact to affect both intelligence and IQ scores.

¶ A chapter on sex-role development (Chapter 15) allows us to place sex roles within the context of the life span, showing how their influence alternately tightens and loosens.

¶ A chapter on social cognition (Chapter 17) shows how understanding of others and of society grows naturally out of self-concept and the separation of self and world. We have heavily revised this chapter to take account of the massive research conducted over the last four years, much of it calling into question some of the earlier assumptions of developmental psychologists. Our reorganization of the section of self-understanding in terms of Piaget's developmental stages emphasizes the way that the study of social cognition weaves together strands of development that are usually seen separately.

¶ A chapter on language provides a full account of the increased emphasis on the role of pragmatics in children's speech, which reveals the intimate connection between language acquisition and social interaction.

¶ A chapter on self-control and morality gives us an opportunity to view moral development, aggression, and prosocial behavior in terms of the development of self-control.

Just as important as which chapters are singled out for special consideration is the way the text handles abnormal development and developmental controversies.

¶ Consistent with this book's emphasis on process, we consider aspects of abnormal development in the context of topical areas. Physical development provides a framework for the discussion of handicapped children; brain development provides a framework for the discussion of hyperactivity and developmental dyslexia; basic cognitive processes, a framework for the discussion of autism; family influence, a framework for the discussion of child abuse; peer relationships, a framework for the discussion of social isolation; and sex-role development, a framework for the discussion of gender disturbances.

¶ Current controversy in the field is met with a frank discussion that presents a balanced accounting of the evidence. For example, Chapter 4 presents two major controversies in the field of early development. The discussion of neonatal imitation considers the implication of such imitation (if newborns *do* imitate) alongside the problems of replicating this research. The review of research on early contact and bonding shows that the process may affect human development, but that its existence has yet to be established.

Covering the development of both sexes in the face of a sexist language can be a problem. We have chosen to eliminate the emphasis of our English language on the male by using plural subjects as often as possible and at other times have resorted to the admittedly ungraceful "his

or her," "girl or boy" approach. A further, less obvious but we hope more telling, strike against sexism has been our practice of giving the full name of the researcher whenever experiments are discussed in detail. This is done neither to flatter the investigators mentioned nor to add to the names students must remember, but to point out—without making an issue of it—that men have no monopoly on the field of developmental psychology and that much of the important research has been done by women.

We are deeply indebted to the editorial staff at Random House, whose hard work, attention to detail and enthusiasm helped speed our revision. Our special thanks goes to our editor, Mary Falcon; to Rochelle Diogenes and Alison Husting, who kept drafts and reviews flowing; to Carolyn Viola-John and Bob Greiner, who supervised the editing and production; to Lorraine Hohman, who developed the appropriate design; to Dorothy Sparacino, who assisted with layouts and graphics; to Lisa Haugaard, who caught our grammatical lapses; and to Kathy Bendo, who was always able to find the right photograph.

The final manuscript was greatly improved by our academic reviewers, whose careful readings led to many helpful suggestions. They include *Laura Berk*, Illinois State University; *Danuta Bukatko*, College of the Holy Cross; *D. Bruce Carter*, Syracuse University; *Marvin Daehler*, University of Massachusetts—Amherst; *James Greene*, Ricks College; *Wade F. Horn*, Michigan State University; *Kenneth D. Kallio*, State University of New York, College at Geneseo; *Daniel Kay*, University of California—Los Angeles; *Mary M. Kralj*, University of Maryland; *Stanley Kuczaj*, Southern Methodist University; *Gary B. Melton*, University of Nebraska—Lincoln; *Susan Nummedal*, California State University—Long Beach; *Frederick M. Schwantes*, Northern Illinois University; *Thomas D. Spencer*, San Francisco State University; *Judy Sugar*, Colorado State University; *Robert S. Tomlinson*, University of Wisconsin—Eau Claire.

Elizabeth Hall
Michael Lamb
Marion Perlmutter

OVERVIEW

PART 1   THE MEANING OF
          DEVELOPMENT   2
CHAPTER 1   Concepts and Theories of Development   5
CHAPTER 2   Studying Determinants of Development   41

PART 2   THE BEGINNING OF LIFE   72
CHAPTER 3   Prenatal Development   75
CHAPTER 4   The World of the Newborn   109

PART 3   PHYSICAL DEVELOPMENT   140
CHAPTER 5   Elements of Physical Growth   143
CHAPTER 6   The Developing Human Brain   173

PART 4   THE DEVELOPMENT OF
          COGNITION   202
CHAPTER 7   The Emerging Mind   205
CHAPTER 8   Basic Cognitive Processes   233
CHAPTER 9   Language Development   269
CHAPTER 10   The Development of Higher Cognitive
           Processes   309
CHAPTER 11   Intelligence and Intellectual Assessment   341

PART 5   SOCIAL AND PERSONALITY
          DEVELOPMENT   372
CHAPTER 12   The Emerging Self   375
CHAPTER 13   The Child Within the Family   403
CHAPTER 14   Social Competence in the Wider World: Peers and
           Teachers   435
CHAPTER 15   The Development of Sex Roles   473
CHAPTER 16   Self-Control and Morality   503

PART 6   REWEAVING THE STRANDS   536
CHAPTER 17   The Development of Social Cognition   539

C O N T E N T S

PART 1   THE MEANING OF
         DEVELOPMENT   2

CHAPTER 1   Concepts and Theories of Development   5
            LIFE STAGES: A HISTORICAL VIEW   6
            The Emergence of Childhood   7   /   The Emergence of
            Adolescence   8   /   Adulthood   9
            THE EMERGENCE OF DEVELOPMENTAL
               PSYCHOLOGY   10
            THEORIES OF DEVELOPMENT: THE HISTORICAL
               BACKGROUND   12
            MECHANISTIC THEORIES   13
            Behavior-Learning Theories   14   /   Information-Process-
            ing Theories   18
            PSYCHODYNAMIC THEORIES   20
            Freud's Psychosexual Theory   20   /   Erikson's Psychoso-
            cial Theory   22   /   Translating Freud into Learning The-
            ory   25
            ADAPTATION THEORIES   26
            ORGANISMIC THEORIES   28
            Piaget's Theory   29   /   Werner's Theory   33
            DIALECTICAL THEORIES   35
            Vygotsky's View   35   /   American Dialectical Psychology
            36
            THEORIES IN PERSPECTIVE   38
            SUMMARY   38

CHAPTER 2   Studying Determinants of Development   41
            EXPLAINING HUMAN DEVELOPMENT   42
            Contributions of Other Disciplines   43   /   Interpretation
            of Age Differences   46
            GENETIC DETERMINANTS   47
            Genetic Studies with Animals   48   /   Human Genetics
            49   /   Heritability   51
            ENVIRONMENTAL DETERMINANTS   51
            Physical Factors   52   /   Social Factors   53   /   Interac-
            tion of Determinants   59
            STUDYING HUMAN DEVELOPMENT   59

Sampling   59   /   Types of Studies   59   /   Research Approaches   62   /   Interpreting Statistics   70
SUMMARY   71

PART 2   THE BEGINNING OF LIFE   72

CHAPTER 3   Prenatal Development   75
HOW HEREDITY WORKS   77
The Production of Gametes   77   /   Genetic Transmission   78
PRENATAL GROWTH   79
The Germinal Period   81   /   The Embryonic Period   82   /
The Fetal Period   83
BRAIN DEVELOPMENT   84
PRENATAL BEHAVIOR   86
BIRTH   86
Labor and Delivery   87   /   Methods of Childbirth   89
DEVELOPMENTAL AND BIRTH
   COMPLICATIONS   89
Chromosomal Abnormalities   90   /   Genetic Diseases   91
NONGENETIC PATERNAL EFFECTS   94   /
Prenatal Environmental Hazards   94   /   Prematurity   99
PREVENTING DEVELOPMENTAL DEFECTS   101
Diagnosing Abnormalities   101   /   Genetic Counseling   102
TERMINATED PREGNANCIES   104
BECOMING A SEPARATE PERSON   104
SUMMARY   105

CHAPTER 4   The World of the Newborn   109
BIRTH: THE NEWBORN   110
BASIC FUNCTIONS AND RHYTHMS   111
Temperature   111   /   Sleep   112   /   Feeding   114   /
Sucking   115
REFLEXES   116
The Rooting Reflex   116   /   Grasping and the Moro Re-
flex   116   /   Walking Movements   117   /   Disappear-
ance and Reappearance of Responses   118
SENSORY CAPABILITIES   119
Vision   119   /   Hearing   120   /   Taste   121   /   Smell
121   /   Kinesthesis   123
PERCEPTION AND ATTENTION   123
Visual Attention   123   /   Auditory Attention   126
ADAPTING TO THE WORLD   126
Memory   127   /   Conditions for Learning   128
PERSONALITY AND SOCIAL RELATIONS   129
Temperament   129   /   Social Relations   132
SUMMARY   137

PART 3   PHYSICAL DEVELOPMENT   140

CHAPTER 5   Elements of Physical Growth   143
DIRECTIONS OF GROWTH   144
Cephalocaudal Development   145   /   Proximodistal De-
velopment   145   /   Differentiation and Integration   146

NORMS 147
Using Norms 147 / Individual Rates of Growth 149
ENVIRONMENTAL INFLUENCES ON GROWTH 154
Diet 154 / Illness 156 / Socioeconomic Status
156 / Ethnic Differences 157 / Stress 157
DEVELOPMENT OF MOTOR ABILITIES 158
Maturation and Experience 158 / Strength, Speed, and
Coordination 160 / Skill Development 161
SEX DIFFERENCES 162
Prepubertal Differences 163 / Sexual Maturation 165
SIZE AND MATURATIONAL TRENDS 167
SUMMARY 170

CHAPTER 6 The Developing Human Brain 173
EVOLUTION OF THE BRAIN 174
THE DEVELOPING BRAIN 175
Brain Growth and Development 175 / Cytoarchitecture
177 / Neurochemistry 179 / Electrical Activity 180
HEMISPHERIC SPECIALIZATION 181
Dividing the Work 181 / The Important Connection 184
LATERALIZATION 185
The Course of Lateralization 186 / Handedness 187 /
Sex Differences 190
PLASTICITY 193
Stimulation 193 / Recovery from Brain Damage 194
LEARNING DISORDERS 197
Developmental Dyslexia 197 / Hyperactivity 198
SUMMARY 200

PART 4 THE DEVELOPMENT OF
COGNITION 202

CHAPTER 7 The Emerging Mind 205
NATURE OF COGNITION AND COGNITIVE DEVELOPMENT 206
THE EMERGENCE OF SENSATION AND PERCEPTION 207
The Development of Auditory Perception 208 / The
Development of Visual Perception 209 / The Develop-
ment of Sensory and Sensorimotor Coordination 216
THE EMERGENCE OF LEARNING AND MEMORY 219
The Early Development of Attention 219 / The Early
Development of Learning and Memory 221
THE EMERGENCE OF THOUGHT 223
Substages of Sensorimotor Thought 224 / The Object
Concept 226 / Imitation 229
SUMMARY 230

CHAPTER 8 The Development of Basic Cognitive Processes 233
THE DEVELOPMENT OF PERCEPTION 234
The Development of Object Perception 234 / The De-
velopment of Picture Perception 236 / The Develop-

ment of Place Perception 239 / The Development of
Event Perception 240
THE DEVELOPMENT OF ATTENTION 241
Scanning 241 / Selectivity 242 / Television and Attention 245
THE DEVELOPMENT OF REPRESENTATION 247
Enactive Representation 247 / Imaginal Representation 248 / Linguistic Representation 248 / Categorical Representation 249 / Operative Representation 252
THE DEVELOPMENT OF MEMORY 254
Types of Remembering 255 / Strategies for Remembering 259 / Knowledge Factors 264
THE DEVELOPMENT OF METAMEMORY 265
SUMMARY 266

CHAPTER 9   Language Development   269
THE NATURE OF HUMAN LANGUAGE 270
The Properties of Human Language 270 / Analyzing
Language 271
THE PRIVATE FUNCTIONS OF LANGUAGE 274
Representation 274 / Thought 276 / Memory 277
THE COGNITIVE FOUNDATIONS OF LANGUAGE 277
THE PUBLIC FUNCTIONS OF LANGUAGE 278
THE SOCIAL FOUNDATIONS OF LANGUAGE 279
Intention 280 / The Role of the Caregiver 280 /
The Uses of Conversation 282 / The Importance of
Context 283
THEORIES OF ACQUISITION 285
Biological Theories 285 / Mechanistic Theories 286 /
Functional Theories 287
ACQUIRING A SYSTEM OF SOUNDS 288
Listening to Sounds 288 / Producing Sounds 289 /
Struggling with Sounds 291
ACQUIRING A SYSTEM OF MEANING 292
First Words 292 / The Structure of Meaning 293 /
The Use of Errors 296 / Meaning in First Sentences
297 / Expanding Vocabularies 297
ACQUIRING A SYSTEM OF STRUCTURES 298
First Syntactic Devices 298 / The Development of
Rules 302 / The Appearance of Error 303 /
Comprehending Complex Constructions 305
SUMMARY 305

CHAPTER 10   The Development of Higher Cognitive Processes   309
LEARNING 310
Learning Concepts 310 / Learning Rules 312
THE DEVELOPMENT OF THOUGHT 314
Preoperational Thought 315 / Concrete Operational
Thought 318 / Formal Operational Thought 325
UNDERSTANDING 330
Time 330 / Number 331 / Causality 333
METACOGNITION 335
SUMMARY 338

CHAPTER 11   Intelligence and Intellectual Assessment 341
THE NATURE OF INTELLIGENCE 342
Species Intelligence vs. Individual Intelligence 342 /
The Biological Perspective 346 / The Structuralist Per-
spective 347 / The Psychometric Perspective 347 /
The Information-Processing Perspective 348
THE MEASUREMENT OF INTELLIGENCE 351
THE STABILITY OF IQ SCORES 352
IQ Tests in Infancy 352 / IQ Tests in Childhood 353
WHAT CAN IQ SCORES PREDICT? 355
Success in School 355 / Success in Life 355 /
Creativity 358
MODIFIABILITY OF INTELLIGENCE 360
Heredity 360 / Health and Nutrition 362 / Environ-
ment 363
SUMMARY 370

PART 5   SOCIAL AND PERSONALITY
DEVELOPMENT 372

CHAPTER 12   The Emerging Self 375
ATTACHMENT 376
The Stages of Attachment 376 / The Function of At-
tachment 380 / Separation Distress 380 / Wariness
of Strangers 383
DIFFERENCES IN ATTACHMENT 384
IT'S NOT ALWAYS MOTHER 387
Fathers as Attachment Figures 387 / Multiple
Caregiving 389
CLASS, CULTURE, AND PERSONALITY 392
THE DEVELOPMENT OF SOCIABILITY 393
Self-Concept 393 / Striving for Competence 394 /
Autonomy 395 / Emotional Development 395
ATTACHMENT AND LATER PERSONALITY 396
EARLY EXPERIENCE 397
Types of Effects 397 / Limits on Effects 398
SUMMARY 400

CHAPTER 13   The Child Within the Family 403
THE PROCESS OF SOCIALIZATION 404
PARENTS 405
Style of Discipline 405 / Disciplinary Techniques 406 /
Predicting the Outcome 408
SIBLINGS 410
THE CHANGING AMERICAN FAMILY 412
Day Care 413 / When Mother Works 414 / In-
creased Paternal Involvement 416 / Father's Absence
416 / Mother's Absence 419 / Marital Discord and
Divorce 420 / Class and Cultural Differences 421 /
Black American Families 424
PHYSICAL CHILD ABUSE 427
The Abusing Parent 427 / The Abused Child 429 /

Socioeconomic Stress 430 / The Persistence of
Abuse 430
SUMMARY 431

CHAPTER 14   Social Competence in the Wider World: Peers and
              Teachers 435
              FROM PARENTS TO PEERS 436
              PRIMATES AND PEERS 436
              PEERS AND COMPETENCE 438
              Early Social Skills 438 / Play and Socialization 439 /
              Peer Reinforcement 442 / Peer Modeling / 444
              GETTING ALONG WITH PEERS 446
              Names and Appearance 446 / Social Skills 447 /
              Stability of Popularity 448
              SOCIAL ISOLATION 450
              CHANGING RELATIONSHIPS 453
              Friendship 453 / Peer Groups 455
              CONFORMITY 456
              SCHOOLS AND TEACHERS 460
              Effects of Desegregation 460 / Competence and
              Achievement 461
              SUMMARY 470

CHAPTER 15   The Development of Sex Roles 473
              THE PERVASIVENESS OF SEX ROLES 474
              ROLES AND IDENTITY 476
              THE DEVELOPMENT OF GENDER IDENTITY 476
              Learning One's Gender 476 / When Things Go
              Wrong 479
              THE DEVELOPMENT OF SEX ROLES 480
              The Influence of Biology 480 / The Influence of Cogni-
              tion 483 / The Influence of Parents 486 / The Influ-
              ence of Peers 488 / The Influence of Teachers 489 /
              The Influence of the Media 491
              SEXUALITY 492
              Reactions to Physical Change 492 / Retreat to Stereo-
              types 494 / Sex Roles and Sex Differences 495
              SEX ROLES AND THE LIFE SPAN 498
              ANDROGYNY 499
              SUMMARY 500

CHAPTER 16   Self-Control and Morality 503
              MORAL DEVELOPMENT 504
              Defining Moral Development 504 / Inconsistency in
              Moral Conduct 504
              DEVELOPING MORAL BEHAVIOR 506
              Establishing Guilt—The Psychoanalytic Approach 506 /
              Learning Moral Conduct—The Social-Learning
              Approach 507 / Empathizing with Others—The Motiva-
              tional Approach 513
              DEVELOPING MORAL REASONING—THE COGNITIVE AP-
                PROACH 515

Moral Judgment 515 / Stages in Moral Reasoning
516 / Consistency in Thought and Action   519
PROSOCIAL BEHAVIOR   519
Generosity 520 / Giving Aid 522 / The Influence of
Television 523
ANTISOCIAL BEHAVIOR   525
The Causes of Aggression 525 / The Development of
Aggression 528 / Sex Differences in Aggression 529 /
The Power of Television 530
SUMMARY 533

PART 6   REWEAVING THE STRANDS   536

CHAPTER 17   The Development of Social Cognition   539
UNDERSTANDING ONE'S SELF   540
The Sensorimotor Self 540 / The Preoperational
Self 541 / The Concrete Operational Self 541 / The
Formal Operational Self 542
UNDERSTANDING OTHERS   544
Understanding What Others Are Like 545 / Under-
standing What Others See 546 / Understanding How
Others Feel 549 / Understanding Friends 551 / Un-
derstanding and Communication 555
UNDERSTANDING SOCIETY   557
Understanding Social Roles 557 / Understanding How
Society Works 560
REWEAVING THE STRANDS   562
SUMMARY 563

References   565
Glossary   603
Name index   615
Subject index   625

CHILD PSYCHOLOGY TODAY SECOND EDITION

PART 1

The Meaning of Development

A person watching a baby girl gazing intently at her fist cannot possibly predict whether the woman she becomes will be honest or dishonest, rash or careful, confident or insecure. The direction a new life will take, the way the growing child will behave, what she will think, how she will feel, all are a mystery to the observer beside the crib. Development is an intricate process in which heredity, culture, and personal experience interact to produce the final pattern of a life. Developmental psychologists devote their lives to finding clues that will help solve the mystery

of development. Their goal is to explain the interaction of developmental influences; they seek to discover why a baby becomes one kind of adult and not another. The search has led to a number of theories of human development. No single theory has been able to explain all aspects of the process satisfactorily, but each has contributed to our understanding of human development. In this part of the book, we explore various theories and attempt to pinpoint the factors influencing the course of development.

Concepts and Theories of Development

LIFE STAGES: A HISTORICAL VIEW
The Emergence of Childhood
The Emergence of Adolescence
Adulthood
THE EMERGENCE OF DEVELOPMENTAL
    PSYCHOLOGY
THEORIES OF DEVELOPMENT: THE
    HISTORICAL BACKGROUND
MECHANISTIC THEORIES
Behavior-Learning Theories
Information-Processing Theories
PSYCHODYNAMIC THEORIES
Freud's Psychosexual Theory
Erikson's Psychosocial Theory
Translating Freud into Learning Theory
ADAPTATION THEORIES
ORGANISMIC THEORIES
Piaget's Theory
Werner's Theory
DIALECTICAL THEORIES
Vygotsky's View
American Dialectical Psychology
THEORIES IN PERSPECTIVE
SUMMARY

Only two hundred years ago people did not know that a human being developed from a fertilized cell. Most biologists believed that a preformed infant existed in either the mother's egg or the father's sperm. Those who contended the infant was in the egg said that the sperm simply stimulated the baby's growth. Those who argued that the infant was in the sperm maintained that the mother's role was to serve as an incubator. It was not until the middle of the eighteenth century that any scientist suggested that each human being began as a cluster of cells, and it was another fifty years before the theory was verified by the microscopic discovery of the mammalian egg cell. Today we can describe the development of the fertilized egg into a baby and the baby's development into an adult. But despite centuries of effort, we cannot say precisely how two babies, born within minutes of each other in the same hospital, become such radically different people.

Developmental psychologists are attempting to solve this puzzle. Their aim is to understand the processes involved in **development,** which refers to any age-related change in body or behavior from conception to death. It has become

5

clear that human development is the result of a complex interaction among multiple influences, and that virtually every aspect of development is affected by biology as well as by learning, by society as well as by family, and by historical events.

Although development continues throughout life, our exploration will be limited to that portion of the life span from conception to adolescence. This is a period of rapid development, and changes can be measured in a relatively short time. Psychologists who study the developing child investigate the ways in which children's physical growth, emotional life, intellectual skills, and social behavior change over time, and they seek to understand how these relate to one another.

In this chapter we look first at the life span itself, seeing how the concept of childhood as a separate stage of life emerged and how the social and economic structure of a society shapes the way its members view the life span. In order to provide a context of the study of development during childhood and adolescence, we examine the entire field of developmental psychology and its disparate origins. After exploring major historical influences on theories of development, we turn to the the theories themselves. We investigate theories that assume the environment is all-powerful, theories that spring from psychoanalytic insights into human motivation, theories that consider the evolutionary heritage of the human species to be a powerful force, theories that see the biological organism as the active creator of reality, and theories that set that organism within the framework of a dialectically changing society. Finally, we place theories in perspective, noting how they are used to guide research and explain development.

LIFE STAGES: A HISTORICAL VIEW

In the Middle Ages, childhood as we know it did not exist. According to Philippe Ariès (1962), there was a period of infancy, which lasted until a child was about seven years old. From that time on, however, people we would consider children were simply assimilated into the adult world. The art and social documents of the Middle Ages show children and adults mingling together in one unified community, wearing the same clothes and performing the same functions. Society made no distinction among them on the basis of age or phase of psychological development.

Today we take the periods of childhood, adolescence, adulthood, and late adulthood for granted, and we divide development into phases that are marked by *social* events: the beginning of meaningful speech (the end of infancy and the start of childhood, at about the age of two); the assumption of adult roles in employment, marriage, and parenthood (the end of adolescence and the start of adulthood, in the early twenties for many people); the loss of roles involved in retirement from work (the onset of late adulthood, generally in the sixties or early seventies). Other markers we attach to the life span are *biological:* birth (the end of the prenatal period and the start of infancy) and reproductive maturity at puberty (the end of childhood and the start of adolescence). We are not consistent in our choice of markers; nor are the markers we use to divide up the life span by any means universal. Other contemporary societies divide life into three periods—such as infancy, childhood, and adulthood; or only two—infancy and adulthood (Mead, 1968).

The way in which people in a society view the life span depends largely on that society's social and economic system. If the preparation for adult roles is gradual and continuous from early childhood and if the necessary technology can be acquired by apprenticeship, then adulthood is likely to begin shortly after a person reaches reproductive maturity. On the other hand, if full participation in the economic system depends on years of technical education, a period of adolescence is likely to be recognized. But that recognition cannot take place if the society cannot afford to support the additional stage. Toward the end of the life span, older adults may retire from their jobs, creating a period that some call "old age." The existence of a period when older, but still healthy, adults no longer participate in the economic system can occur only if society can afford to do without their labor. In a predominantly agricultural society, for example, older adults generally shoulder economic responsibilities as long as they are physically able.

The Emergence of Childhood

It was only in the seventeenth and eighteenth centuries that the concept of childhood as a separate stage of life evolved in Western societies. A new and sentimental view of childhood sprang up, along with new theories of education that were concerned with promoting children's moral and intellectual development, protecting them from the evils and corruptions of adult society, and preserving their real or imagined childhood virtues.

From historical evidence, it seems clear that childhood became a separate stage of life in Europe and North America only when large numbers of people entered the middle class, the amount of leisure time increased, and the rate of infant mortality decreased. As the middle class prospered, there was less need for their children to work in order to ensure the family's economic survival. The lowered rate of childhood mortality meant that more children would live to reach puberty; therefore, parents were less fearful of losing a child to disease. And the new mercantile capitalism required that a larger portion of the citizenry be literate and fluent with numbers; thus more children had to go to school.

Ariès' analysis of the emerging concept of childhood has had far-reaching implications for understanding the relationship between historical change and psychological development. Although his view has been criticized on the grounds that the special nature of childhood was recognized in earlier times (Kroll, 1977) and that

By the seventeenth century, the concept of childhood had begun to emerge. Although little girls still dressed like miniature women, little boys wore a long robe that distinguished them from adults. (Peter Paul Rubens, "Deborah Kip, Wife of Sir Balthasar Gerbier and Her Children." Courtesy, The National Gallery of Art, Andrew W. Mellon Fund, 1971)

his data are too fragmentary to justify his strong conclusions (Siegel and White, 1982), Ariès' contention that medieval children were assimilated into the adult world seems correct (Borstelmann, 1983). It also seems clear that the experience as well as the concept of childhood has changed over the centuries. In societies that placed little value on the individual life and viewed children as the property of their parents, survival could depend on parental whim. **Infanticide** was relatively common during antiquity; the usual victims, who were killed or allowed to die, were babies with birth defects, girl babies, and illegitimate babies. The practice continued into the Middle Ages, despite attempts by civil and religious authorities to halt the practice (Borstelmann, 1983). Among those who were allowed to live, at least half died before the age of six, victims of disease, neglect, or child abuse.

In many European societies, family life as we know it hardly existed before the eighteenth century. Among all but the poorest families, children spent the first few years away from their parents, living with wet-nurses. As late as 1780, only 1,400 of the 21,000 children born in Paris remained with their own parents (deMause, 1974). Children returned home from the wet-nurse some time between the ages of two and five, only to be apprenticed out or put to work by the time they were seven. Parents and masters often treated children with what we would consider a shocking lack of tenderness, protectiveness, attention, and care. Child abuse was widespread, even casual, and most advice on child rearing recommended severe beatings as the way to inculcate discipline. Parents seem to have invested little emotional energy in their children; children were not regarded as very important.

The experience of childhood has been strongly affected by society's need for schooled workers. During Middle Ages, the minimal schooling required to become a priest or clerk was received in ungraded schools, where children, adolescents, and adults learned together. As the concept of childhood began to emerge, schools came to be graded by age, and both the average length of schooling and the number of children who received formal education increased. This meant that an even larger proportion of those between the ages of six and fourteen were segregated into schools. Such segregation sheltered children from the demands of adult work. They found new freedom to play and to experiment, and had systematic opportunities to develop new interpersonal and technical skills.

In Western industrialized societies, the segregation of childhood is now virtually complete, but only in this century has it finally been extended to the working and lower classes. The mark of this full institutionalization of childhood is universal primary education. It has taken four centuries for us to move from an era in which childhood was unrecognized to an era in which we take it completely for granted and protect it with an array of legal, social, and educational institutions.

The Emergence of Adolescence

The concept of adolescence is of more recent origin—although adolescence as a stage of psychological growth existed before society formulated the concept. In previous centuries, many men and women passed through what would now be recognized as an adolescent experience. But it was only after childhood had been marked off from adulthood that adolescence could be interposed between them as the period between reproductive maturity and the assumption of adult responsibilities. In early Western societies, therefore, biological maturation largely went unmarked. When children were considered neither innocent nor importantly different from adults, the fact of puberty constituted neither a fall from innocence nor a change in status, and it had little special meaning.

The official emergence of adolescence was made possible by social, economic, and historical changes. Increasing industrialization freed most young people from the requirements of farm and factory labor. Indeed, rising standards of economic productivity made the adolescent, especially the uneducated adolescent, almost impossible to employ. New attitudes toward adolescence were expressed in laws that made full-time employment before the age of sixteen or eighteen illegal. Growing affluence provided most families and the larger society with the wealth needed to support these economically unproductive adolescents in school. All these changes have happened, on a mass scale, almost within living memory; most of our child labor laws were passed only in this century.

Today society sanctions and supports adolescence, buttressing it with educational, familial, institutional, and economic resources. These

For centuries, children and adolescents worked as hard as adults. Not until this century were adolescents like this girl freed from the drudgery of factory labor and given the opportunity for continuing psychological growth. (Lewis W. Hine/National Archives)

new resources, coupled with other changes in society, have protected an ever larger proportion of young people from adult responsibilities and have given them the possibility of continuing psychological growth during the years from thirteen to eighteen.

However, such generalizations overlook certain pockets of poverty in the society. Among migratory farm laborers, for example, financial considerations force children and adolescents to work, in defiance of the law. And in the inner cities there is a large pool of young people whose parents lack the resources to keep them in school. These adolescents, whose youth and lack of education make them unemployable, have no income, nothing to fill their time, and limited prospects for the future.

Adulthood

Adulthood has always been recognized as the normal phase of human existence. Traditionally, since it has been seen as the goal of development, it has been the yardstick by which other stages of life have been measured.

But our concept of adulthood has itself changed. Instead of regarding the person on the threshold of adulthood as having completed the course of human development, we now see the adult as a person who continues to develop. If the development goes on successfully, the person becomes mature. The mature adult makes commitments, takes on responsibilities, can relate intimately to another person, is productive, and can devote him- or herself to the welfare of others. Maturity also includes an awareness and realistic acceptance of the changes in life during the passage from young to middle adulthood. And it is during the middle years that people must cope with the realization that life will end. Until this century, most people died before they reached their seventies, so that few people were concerned about a lengthy old age. As the av-

An affluent society can afford to support a phase of adolescence, in which adult responsibilities are postponed in favor of a period of psychological growth. (Frank Siteman/Jeroboam)

erage life span increased, developmental psychologists began to pay special attention to the latter part of adulthood.

THE EMERGENCE OF DEVELOPMENTAL PSYCHOLOGY

Developmental psychology, as a discipline whose task is to describe and explain age-related changes in behavior over the life span, has only recently emerged as a separate branch of general psychology. Its origins go back to the turn of the century when there was a flurry of interest in studying the child. Later, after World War II, a spurt of studies on the problems connected with aging led some investigators to concentrate on the latter part of the life cycle. Finally, as the original subjects of studies that followed children over the years grew up, other researchers became interested in the processes of adult development (Charles, 1970). Although most developmental psychologists focus on small sections of the life span and the majority still deal

with infancy and childhood, their collective work is beginning to give us a clearer picture of the determinants and processes of development from birth to death.

One early influence on the study of child development came from the diaries kept by a number of ardent parents during the nineteenth century. Although these baby biographies were not objective or scientific descriptions, psychologists found them useful in describing sequences of development and differences in the ways that babies attained the various developmental milestones.

Another early influence came from the work of G. Stanley Hall, who established child and adolescent development as fields of study. Hall viewed development as being primarily determined by genetic and biological factors until adolescence, believing that from conception to birth, each developing individual passed through the evolutionary history of the species and that from birth to adolescence, each person repeated the social evolution of the species. This view, known as **recapitulation theory**, led him to suggest that efforts to curb the natural unruliness of children would be ineffectual until they were about twelve, when after allowing "the fundamental traits of savagery their fling," society would modify and control children's character (Hall, 1904). Hall supported his theories on human development by collecting information through questionnaires, and in 1904 he published an enormously influential two-volume work on adolescence. Hall or his students were responsible for early research in the areas of mental testing, early childhood education, adolescence, life-span developmental psychology, evolutionary influences on development, and child study (Cairns, 1983).

A third important influence, one that has been neglected until recently, came from the writings of James Mark Baldwin, who was professor at Johns Hopkins University until 1909. Baldwin's contributions were primarily theoretical, not experimental (Cairns, 1983). His view of development was important because it linked thought, the self, and the social order. Nevertheless, it influenced researchers in other countries and other disciplines before it influenced American psychologists. Although his view of intellectual development had an enormous influence on the thought of Jean Piaget, whose theories have dominated the study of cognitive development, it was only after Baldwin's ideas were translated by sociologists and biologists that they began to penetrate the thinking of American psychologists.

At the time that Baldwin was developing his theories, interest in developmental questions increased sharply. Child-guidance and psychological clinics began to be founded as a reaction to popular acceptance of the idea that children should be helped with emotional and intellectual problems so they would be able to lead constructive lives (Sears, 1975). This movement influenced the focus of developmental studies because it shifted attention from the general development of the species that was Hall's concern to the interests of the individual child (Charles, 1970). The study of the growing child brought together people from various groups, united in the idea that watching children would lead to an understanding of the principles of development. All wanted to know about the "normal" child and how he or she grew, but each for a different reason. Scientists hoped to establish laws of human behavior. Educators at the college level needed information for teacher training, while those at the elementary and secondary levels wanted to measure school performance, discover what could reasonably be expected from children, and establish the value of education. Social workers believed that information about normal development would help them in their work with handicapped children and those whose development was at risk. Clinical psychologists sought information about normal development in order to help children with developmental problems, and parents wanted guidance in child rearing (Siegel and White, 1982).

Perhaps because of this disparity of perspectives, during the first half of the twentieth century developmental psychology was frag-mented, with each topical area producing its own research and theories. Each subarea evolved along its own path, paying little attention to what was going on in other parts of the field (Cairns, 1983). One of the influential subareas focused on mental testing. This movement was pioneered by Lewis Terman, one of Hall's students. Terman studied one thousand children, ranging in age from three to eighteen, and provided standards for mental development during childhood and adolescence. By testing the same children over a period of years, psychologists could study the patterns of mental development.

As educators became convinced that both the content of schooling and the ways in which children are taught must take into account the nature of the growing child, they demanded research that would establish the nature of the child's interests and capabilities (Charles, 1970). This demand led to an increase in experimental studies of children, giving rise to educational psychology, which under the influence of E. L. Thorndike (1913) stressed the way that learning affects children's natural tendencies.

The influence of Thorndike, together with the early writings of J. B. Watson (1913), convinced both researchers and the general public that the scientific study and explanation of behavior was within grasp (Charles, 1970). Like Thorndike, Watson believed in the primacy of learning, and his research focused on the process of **conditioning,** a form of learning in which a person comes to respond in a specific manner to a specific object, action, or situation. As a result of public confidence, a number of child-development research centers were established at major universities across the country. These institutes were set up to carry out research, teach, and disseminate information on child development. They investigated all aspects of children's development and welfare, and their shared goal was to acquire a comprehensive understanding of development that could be used to help children and those who care for them. Many of these institutes are still active.

At some of these research centers, studies of

behavior over the life span were begun. At the University of California, for example, babies born in 1928 and 1929 were enrolled in a study of physical and intellectual development that still continues. At Fels Research Institute in Ohio, each year since 1929 another small group of infants has been added to a long-term study of intellectual and personality development. And at Stanford University, 1,500 gifted California children identified by intelligence testing have been followed since 1921, with investigators studying all phases of their development.

In the past thirty years, there has been a decided shift in the emphasis of developmental psychologists. They have moved from describing what people do at specific periods in life to emphasizing how circumstances affect development and what kind of developmental sequences occur. Along with this shift has come a greater sensitivity to differences among individuals and a renewed appreciation of the ways in which social and intellectual aspects of development interrelate.

THEORIES OF DEVELOPMENT: THE HISTORICAL BACKGROUND

Normal infants grow first into children and then into adults, and this progression implies several characteristics about developmental change: (1) it is orderly, (2) it is directional, (3) it is to a large extent cumulative, and (4) it is characterized by increasing differentiation and complexity of organization. To explain such changes, investigators construct sets of logically related statements, called **theories,** about the nature of development. These theories grow out of assumptions, often unstated, about human nature, which may focus on the existence of inborn differences among people, on how much human behavior can change in response to the environment, on the role of human beings in their own

development, on the existence of natural good or evil in humanity, and on the relationship of child to adult behavior.

Throughout history, assumptions about human nature have fluctuated, and the prevailing notions have tended to influence the way people reared their children. As long ago as the third century B.C., Plato stressed that there were innate differences in aptitude among human beings and that these individual differences should be recognized and used in child rearing and education. His pupil Aristotle, in turn, proposed that although people were the same at birth (because the human mind was a *tabula rasa*, or blank slate), there were also individual differences in natural inclinations and talents, and he suggested that education and training should be designed to fit these differences.

During medieval times, human beings were considered to be sinful and corrupt by nature. During their lengthy "infancy," children were regarded as self-centered and grasping. They were innocent only in that they had lacked the opportunity to do much sinning. Training designed to correct their supposedly depraved nature could be harsh or gentle, but those in charge of children were warned not to indulge them (Borstelmann, 1983).

By the seventeenth century, a different view had emerged. Human beings were thought to be born innocent and then corrupted by society. Childhood came to be distinguished from adulthood, and moral education—the way to train children to be trustworthy, disciplined, and rational human beings—was stressed.

In the latter part of the seventeenth century, John Locke (1690), a British philosopher, proposed another view. He stressed that all human beings are born equal in terms of inborn or native propensities. At birth, the human mind is a blank slate (as Aristotle had proposed), and ideas, concepts, and other human qualities are instilled as a result of training and experience. Although Locke realized that the needs and abilities of children differed, he firmly believed that early experience has powerful and lasting effects and that parents are responsible for the formation of their children's characters (Borstelmann, 1983).

Almost a century later, Jean Jacques Rousseau (1762), a French philosopher, reacting to the prevalent idea that human beings are inherently wicked, revived the view that human beings are born peaceful and compassionate, only to be turned from their good nature by an evil society. Their inborn propensities needed only to be allowed expression and given minimal guidance in order to bring about healthy and acceptable development.

The influence of Locke and Rousseau can be found in modern theories of development, which combine assumptions about human nature in various ways to explain different aspects of development. They fall into five broad but sometimes overlapping categories, which we shall call mechanistic theories, psychodynamic theories, adaptation theories, organismic theories, and dialectical theories. Each set of theories is based on different assumptions about human beings, and each generates testable hypotheses about the development of behavior.

Some of these theories, especially some mechanistic theories, see development as continuous, with the child gradually developing new understandings through a combination of maturation and experience but never making sudden jumps to new levels of functioning. The child grows as does a plant, from seedling to mature form, without showing sudden changes in form.

Psychodynamic, organismic, and dialectical theories agree that human development is continuous but see great discontinuities in the process as well. They point to the existence of radically different **stages,** in which the child thinks or feels about the world in such a changed manner that his or her behavior shows an accompanying qualitative change. Organismic theories, for example, see abrupt changes in the structure of a child's thought from one stage to the next. The change is so marked that it is as if a caterpillar had just become a butterfly.

Stage theories are useful because they give organization to development, making it easier to think about the process. But stage theories cannot be applied rigidly; we cannot place every child neatly into one of the stages. When children are classified as to their stage of intellectual development, for example, many children turn out to be in transition from one stage to another, exhibiting some characteristics of the lower stage and some belonging to the higher stage of thought. Indeed, in some areas of understanding the process of transition may take years (Flavell, 1977).

Whether development is continuous or discontinuous—or both—theories of all kinds, each with its own view of development, continue to flourish. They have managed to exist simultaneously largely because they concentrate on different phenomena and different developmental processes.

MECHANISTIC THEORIES

The machine is the basic metaphor in **mechanistic theories,** both for the universe and for human beings. Some years ago, the switchboard was a favorite model of the human mind; today, many psychologists prefer the computer. In this view, which goes back to John Locke's proposal that the infant mind is a blank slate, the child is passive. He or she receives stimulation from the environment but imposes no selectivity, so that the child's perceptions are true copies of the real world, which exists independently of the perceiver—a position called **naïve realism.** All causes are external, and the child acts in response to these external forces. Thus, if we had complete knowledge of the child's past history and present condition, we could—theoretically—predict how the child would act in any situation (Overton and Reese, 1973). Actually, no psychologist who adheres to the mechanistic view expects to be able to predict a person's every act because there is no way to discover every event in the person's history.

During development, thought and behavior

change as a result of accumulated knowledge and experience. The child becomes more competent, but this competence is the result of increased knowledge; there is no accompanying change in the structure of the child's mind. Development is gradual and continuous, and since there are no changes in mental processes or structure, any designation of "stages" in development is simply a convenient way to divide the life span in order to analyze the complex relationships involved in the child's passage to adulthood (Bijou, 1976).

Learning theories, which include reinforcement theory and social-learning theories, represent the major mechanistic view of development. Because the information-processing perspective, which relies on a computer model of the mind, shares a number of mechanistic assumptions, it is included in this section. However, certain aspects of this approach are nonmechanistic and some researchers (Kail and Bisanz, 1982) regard it as eclectic, drawing as it does from more than one world view.

Behavior-Learning Theories

Learning theorists see the human being as an organism that has learned to behave in uniquely human ways. The newborn baby is regarded as a malleable recipient of environmental stimulation. Most of what babies become is a matter of what they have experienced or learned, and learning begins even before birth. Although the idea that human beings learn or acquire much that characterizes them has been advanced by thinkers as diverse as Aristotle and Locke, formal learning theories date back only as far as the early part of this century and the establishment of behaviorism.

John B. Watson (1913, 1924), a founder of the behavioral school of psychology, believed that psychologists should limit themselves to the study of behavior—what people do or say—and forget the study of consciousness—what people feel or think. Watson studied behavior by ex-

amining the relationship between stimulus and response, defining a **stimulus** as anything within the body or in the world outside that evokes a response, and a **response** as anything a person does or says. Watson was so convinced of the power of experience that he once offered to take a group of infants and produce any kind of adult his critics specified. Although he became less certain about such sweeping early claims, his work left an indelible mark on American psychology. It was interpreted to mean that human behavior could be molded in almost limitless ways, and that human beings could be improved in any desired direction.

REINFORCEMENT THEORY Watson had explained his observations of learning in terms of **classical conditioning,** a process in which learning occurs through the association of one stimulus with another. Such a view disregards the consequences of a person's response, a position that troubled B. F. Skinner (1938), a psychologist at Harvard. Skinner agreed that Watson's view of conditioning explained some behavior, but he maintained that most learning was the result of **operant conditioning,** in which behavior is strengthened or changed as a result of the rewards or punishments that follow a person's actions. When some pleasant consequence follows an action, or when an action ends some unpleasant situation, said Skinner, that behavior is **reinforced**.

Because Skinner placed such great importance on the consequences of an organism's actions, theories of development that are based on his approach are sometimes called **reinforcement theory**. Although reinforcement was used to explain a wide range of behavior, from how the child acquires language and forms concepts to why the artist paints pictures—and why other people want to look at them (Skinner, 1972)—its acceptance by learning theorists did not mean that classical conditioning had been rejected. The process of classical conditioning continues to be used as an explanation for the establishment of emotional responses. For example, a year-old baby often begins to cry at the sight of a pediatrician who has been associated with painful injections. A child who has been bitten by a dog may come to fear the yard in which the attack occurred. A child may even generalize fear. Thus the infant who has been given injections by a pediatrician may come to fear all people in white coats or all rooms that look like pediatricians' offices. And the child bitten by a dog may come to fear all four-legged creatures.

Skinner never set forth a theory of child development based on his findings, but other psychologists have undertaken the translation. Sidney Bijou and Donald Baer (1961, 1965), who have used his approach, see the developing child as an "interrelated cluster of responses and stimuli." Because the child and the environment are interacting continuously, they suggest, the child's development consists of progressive changes in the ways of interaction, changes that are the result of opportunities and circumstances. These changes serve as the basis for their division of the life span into three stages. The first part of life is the *universal* stage, which begins before birth and lasts until about eighteen months, when a child begins to talk. The stage is universal because children in every society appear to develop similarly during this period. At this time the child, although learning rapidly, is less responsive to the environment than he or she will be later, when biological maturation plays a less powerful role in development.

The second, or *basic*, stage begins when a child starts to talk and lasts until the child enters school. The ability to talk obviously changes the way a child interacts with others. When a child starts school, the school environment is so different from the home that ways of interacting shift again, perhaps dramatically, and the child enters the *societal* stage of development, which occupies the rest of the life span. In Bijou and Baer's application of reinforcement theory, the child's developmental status affects what the child is able to do, but the process by which the child learns never changes (Stevenson, 1983).

Because school is so radically different from the home, when youngsters start school they enter a new stage of development, in which they begin to interact with others in new ways. (Peeter Vilms/Jeroboam)

Such early behavior-learning views seemed too narrow and inflexible for many mechanistic theorists, who proposed instead a social-learning view of development.

SOCIAL LEARNING According to **social-learning theories**, operant and classical conditioning account for only part of behavior and development, and theorists stress that many kinds of behavior are learned simply by observation. Seeing or hearing someone else act in a certain way can be a more effective form of learning than direct experience and reinforcement for both children and adults.

Thus the concept of imitation plays a key role in most social-learning accounts of human development. Studies and casual observation demonstrate the increasing resemblance of children's social behavior to that of adult models such as parents or teachers. Some researchers have discovered that if a child is rewarded for imitating a model, the child will tend to imitate the model on later occasions even if not rewarded (Bandura, 1969). And if the child sees that the model is rewarded for his or her actions, the child will tend to copy the rewarded behavior.

Interpretations of the role and importance of imitation have grown. In one of the first analyses, Neal Miller and John Dollard (1941) proposed that nurturance from parents becomes the motivating force for a child's imitations. That is, as parents satisfy the child's needs for food, warmth, and affection, the parents become associated with the satisfaction of those needs and take on reinforcing properties themselves. Because the parents' behavior has become reinforcing, the child imitates them to reward himself. Jerome Kagan (1958) and John Whiting (1960) added to the picture, pointing out that parents also have more power and control more possessions than the child does, and that the child envies their status and therefore copies both parents in the hope that the imitations will bring to the child their influence and status.

From this beginning, social-learning theory gradually shifted in a more radical direction. The work of Albert Bandura and his colleagues is representative of this shift. Bandura (1977) has restated many aspects of human learning and motivation in terms of **cognition**, or all the processes of sensing, perceiving, remembering, using symbols, and thinking that we use to gain knowledge about the world. According to Bandura, cognitive processes play a central role in regulating what children attend to, how they describe or think about what they see, and whether they repeat it to themselves and lodge it in memory. Short-lived daily experiences can have lasting effects because they are retained in memory. Learning from a model consequently is not simply a matter of imitation. As children and adults watch others, they form concepts about possible behavior that will later guide their own actions. As they then observe their actions and the consequences, they can change their concepts and act in a different way.

Children tend to copy complete patterns of behavior from models instead of slowly acquiring bits of a pattern in response to reinforcement. Exposure to a model can have one of three

When youngsters imitate their parents' actions, they are demonstrating social-learning theorists' belief that imitation plays an essential role in development. (Hella Hammid/Photo Researchers)

effects: (1) the child can learn a completely new pattern of behavior (trying out a new dance step); (2) the child can inhibit the performance of already learned behavior (ceasing to ride a bicycle on a busy street after seeing another child punished for it) or can indulge in previously learned behavior that has been forbidden (jumping a bicycle off a ramp after watching another child do so); or (3) the child can behave in previously learned ways that are recalled from memory by the model (playing a game that had been lying on the shelf but that the child just saw advertised on television) (Bandura and Walters, 1963). Not all children who watch a model later imitate the model's behavior. Children may observe a model and acquire the ability to copy the behavior they have just seen yet not perform it. Not all children, for example, who watch a television program filled with fistfights later go out and punch the first person who disagrees with them. They may never engage in a violent

Courtesy Dr. Albert Bandura

Albert Bandura (1925–   )

Albert Bandura received his doctorate in clinical psychology from Iowa State University in 1952. After completing a postdoctoral internship, he accepted a position at Stanford University, where he is professor of psychology. His research and writing on personality and social development reflect his background in clinical psychology and his strong interest in child development. Over the past two decades, his theories have had a major influence on the thought of developmental psychologists.

Early in his career, Bandura became dissatisfied with the gaps that existed between the concepts of clinical psychology and those of general psychology. He also believed that behavior-learning views, including social learning, were too narrow to account for socialization and the development of behavior.

To overcome these deficiencies, Bandura developed a broad, integrated sociobehavioral approach to human behavior. According to his view, direct experience is not the only teacher; human beings learn from infancy by simply observing what other people do and noticing what happens to them. Other symbolic models are provided by way of television, movies, books, or magazines; such models may teach unacceptable as well as acceptable behavior. Bandura emphasizes the importance of distinguishing between learning and performance. He stresses that although people learn to do many things, they are most likely to do the things that they or others consider acceptable or rewarding.

Bandura's work stresses the links between cognitive processes, learning, and performance. Thus, cognitive skills, information, and rules strongly affect what an individual does. And because people can think about what happened to them or what may happen to them, their behavior cannot be manipulated simply by reinforcement. Bandura sees people as freer to choose and to make changes in their lives than did the original behavior-learning theorists.

fight. But placed in a situation in which that behavior seems an appropriate response, say when a bully backs them into a corner in the schoolyard, they may indeed call upon the behavior they witnessed weeks or months ago.

In this new view, stimuli are no longer seen as purely external physical events that control behavior; instead they are signals—information that helps people decide what to do. The person's interpretation of a stimulus, not the stimulus itself, regulates behavior.

Cognitive social-learning theorists, as proponents of this stance are sometimes called, stress that people process and synthesize information from their experiences over long periods of time; consequently, they are not bound by what takes place in the immediate situation. On the basis of their past experiences, they decide what behavior may be effective. As human beings develop, they construct and reconstruct expectations about future events. They learn to estimate the possible positive and negative consequences of various actions, and accordingly set their own standards of behavior, which they use to evaluate their performance, reward their actions, and provide their motivation.

Unlike other behavior-learning theorists, cognitive social-learning theorists give human thought and knowledge central importance in explaining the development of human behavior. They see children as approaching, exploring, and dealing with things that they perceive are within their abilities. Children tend to avoid things that seem stressful or beyond their capabilities. Because other people become sources of information in this process, through their actions and words, they play a primary role in the development of children.

Information-Processing Theories

During the 1950s, the development of computers gave psychologists a new way of looking at the human mind; human beings could be seen as information-gathering, information-processing systems. This approach was spurred by A. M. Turing (1950), who proposed that if a person communicating with a computer could not say whether the responses were generated by the machine or by a human being, we would have to admit that machines could think. And if machines could think, we would have duplicated the human ability to manipulate information. Although no computer has yet been developed that can fool a person indefinitely, the possibility excited psychologists, many of whom believed that the decision-making powers of the human mind could not be explained by theories of reinforcement. They began to translate human cognitive processes into the computer model.

Computers and the human mind do have a lot in common: both take information from the outside world, encode it, combine it with other information, store it, retrieve it, and pass it out again to the world in a decoded form. As Earl Hunt (1971) describes it, we each have a slow, subtle computer in our heads, surrounded by a number of high-capacity, parallel-input trans-

mission lines. Regarding human thought as slow may conflict with our experience, but in comparison with a computer, the human mind is sluggish. (See Table 1.1.) Retrieving information from long-term memory requires from 180 microseconds to a full second, and getting information that is already in working memory takes 25 microseconds (Estes, 1980). But a computer can deliver information in a single microsecond.

The earliest information-processing theory was developed more than thirty years ago by Donald Broadbent (1954), who was especially interested in the way various situations affected people's attention to sounds. His work was not developmental, but most developmental psychologists have been guided in their studies by

Table 1.1 THE HUMAN COMPUTER

	Human Memory	Computer Memory
Preferred method of storage	Time-oriented	List-oriented
Retention of information	Graded	All-or-none
Efficiency (bits of information per second)	Low	High
Capacity	Dependent on experience	Independent of experience
Retrieval		
Relative to context	Strongly dependent	Independent
Relative to previous retrievals	Dependent	Independent
Purpose	General purpose; open set of functions	Special or general purpose; closed set of functions

This comparison of human and computer memories shows that the computer's speed and precision are offset by the adaptability and general-purpose capability of human memory. (Reprinted with permission of *American Scientist* 68 [1980], W. K. Estes. "Is Human Memory Obsolete?")

research with adults. For example, Broadbent's theory was used during the early 1970s for research on the development of attention (Hagen and Hale, 1973). As Robert Siegler (1983) has put it, "It simply is easier to understand any type of development when we know where the development is going" (p. 163). Siegler points out that knowledge of adult reasoning gained through an information-processing approach allowed researchers to determine that growth in the thoroughness with which children encode information is a major area of development.

How do researchers go about applying an information-processing approach to development? According to Siegler (1983), this framework has led researchers in two directions: toward the study of the basic capacities of the system and the processes used to control the flow of information, and toward investigations of the way the system interacts with various intellectual tasks.

Most researchers in the information-processing tradition assume that human thought and action, like the workings of a computer, are built out of a small set of simple processes (Kail and Bisanz, 1982). It is generally believed that these processes are present in some form from infancy and early childhood, but that they improve in speed and efficiency as children grow. These beliefs have led developmentalists to trace the development of basic processes from early infancy and to attempt to identify changes in control processes and the way they are used. A psychologist may study perception (information reception and coding), memory (information storage and retrieval), hypothesis testing (thinking), or evaluation (children's ability to assess their own thinking) (Ault, 1977). For example, studies (Hagen and Huntsman, 1971) have indicated that an eleven-year-old retarded child with a mental age of eight memorizes about as efficiently as does a nonretarded eight-year-old. With training, retarded children show improvement on specific memory tasks. This has been interpreted as indicating the possibility that the basic cognitive system of mildly retarded children may be intact and that the deficits may be confined to the way they use control processes to manipulate information, in this case the techniques they use to commit material to memory (Campione and Brown, 1977).

Other researchers have suggested that apparent changes in basic capacities and control processes may develop from an increase in children's knowledge base. For example, Michelene Chi, who earlier discovered that the memory for chess positions is better among ten-year-old chess players than among adults who do not play chess (Chi, 1978), taught a five-year-old girl a technique for remembering all her classmates' names. The girl quickly learned to use this control process with her classmates, but found it extremely difficult to use when trying to remember the names of people she did not know (Chi, 1982). Of course, although we know that possession of a store of knowledge affects the way the system works, we still do not understand exactly how this occurs (Siegler, 1983).

Studies of the way the information-processing system interacts with specific tasks has led some researchers to try to simulate human thought processes by reducing mental operations to computer operations. They often write programs for the computer that mimic complex cognitive functioning. For example, David Klahr and J. G. Wallace (1976) have produced programs that imitate the way children of different ages handle several mental tasks. One of the programs they developed describes the way children think when trying to decide whether a lump of clay that is squeezed into a ball contains the same amount of clay as a lump that is stretched into a long, narrow shape. Research into such cognitive functions promises practical payoffs that can be taken into the classroom, and researchers have been applying an information-processing view to reading, writing, and arithmetic. For example, D. P. Simon and Herbert Simon (1973) built a computer program that mimicked the way fourth-graders spell. The program included the complete spelling of some words, only the first and last few letters of other words, and a list that connected letters with sounds. The program enabled the computer to spell correctly the same words that most fourth-graders can spell and produced spelling errors like those found among the children. Their success enabled the researchers to come up with several techniques that children could use to improve their spelling.

The information-processing framework has become increasingly important in recent years; in fact, according to Siegler (1983), it has changed the way people think about development and seems to be the most popular approach to studies of cognitive development. Despite its successes, says Siegler, its greatest drawback is its failure to provide any insights into social, emotional, or personality development. This lack of success is probably inevitable, since computers do not feel love, hate, anger, fear, or joy. Such human feelings have been a major focus of psychodynamic theories of development.

PSYCHODYNAMIC THEORIES

Psychodynamic theories view human behavior as resulting from the interplay of active (dynamic) mental and biological forces with the environment. Although some theories regard the forces as benign, others see them as irrational forces that must be controlled by socialization. Most psychodynamic theorists, therefore, discuss and analyze human development in terms of confrontations between the growing individual and the social world. They stress that the individual must accommodate to the demands of society while gratifying basic human drives. Most also emphasize that children gradually develop a sense of self, an identity against which to judge their own behavior.

Psychodynamic theories have centered on the development of emotion and personality. The concern has been to understand and explain the development of rational as well as irrational feelings and behavior. To some extent, all psychodynamic theories describe human development in terms of early experiences that may influence later behavior.

Since Sigmund Freud developed the first psychodynamic theory, other psychodynamic theorists have constructed their own accounts of personality development. But because the other theories are either modifications of Freud's thought or reactions to it, this discussion is limited to Freud's views and those of Erik Erikson—a modifier of Freud's views whose theory has been widely used by developmental psychologists.

Freud's Psychosexual Theory

Sigmund Freud (1905) is the father of psychodynamic theories and the founder of **psychoanalysis**, a type of psychotherapy that attempts to give a patient insight into his or her unconscious conflicts. His theories of personality and development grew out of the insights that came from working with his patients.

As Freud saw it, from earliest infancy human beings are motivated by irrational urges toward pleasure, urges that are an expression of the **libido**, or "life force," that propels us all. Rational behavior develops out of conflict between social demands and the young child's instincts, which are **sublimated** (altered in socially acceptable ways) in the course of the child's adaptation to the environment.

Freud's **psychosexual theory** of personality described three conflicting aspects of human personality: the id, the ego, and the superego. In the **id** reside all of the unconscious impulses, or drives. The newborn baby is pure id. The **superego** is the conscience, which develops in early childhood as a child internalizes parental values and standards of conduct. The **ego** guides actual behavior and mediates the perpetual conflict between what the individual wants to do (the province of the id) and what the individual must or must not do (the province of the superego).

According to Freud, development proceeds through a series of stages in which instinctual impulses are expressed through various pleasure centers of the body. His theory of development describes human development as a series of con-

Archiv/Photo Researchers

Sigmund Freud (1856–1939)

Sigmund Freud's theories reflect his training in the biological sciences and his clinical experience. He specialized in physiology, received his M.D. degree in Vienna in 1881, and began lecturing and doing research in neuropathology. A grant enabled him to go to Paris and study under the famous neurologist Jean Martin Charcot, who was using hypnosis to treat hysteria—physical symptoms (such as paralysis or loss of sensation) caused by emotional stress.

Later, as Freud treated his patients, he developed the therapeutic methods of free association and dream interpretation. He found that his adult neurotic patients had repressed their memories of early childhood emotional experiences, which generally involved sex, aggression, or jealousy. Because these experiences were unpleasant, Freud proposed that they became lost to awareness because they were pushed into an unreachable area of the mind, the unconscious.

In his theory of psychosexual development, he interpreted what he learned from treating his patients in the light of embryology and physics. He proposed that the emergence of psychosexual stages was primarily determined by maturation and that mental life followed the law of conservation of energy, which states that energy cannot be created or destroyed, only transformed. People's mental and emotional lives, he believed, show a comparable transformation of psychic energy (libido) from one stage to the next. This energy motivates people's thinking, their perceptions, and their memories, and it remains constant even though it becomes associated with different regions of the body during development.

flicts between pleasure and discipline that a child must resolve in order to become a mature, well-adjusted adult. Unless the growing child successfully navigates each stage, Freud believed, he or she will become **fixated** at that stage; that is, the child's emotional growth will be stunted, and as an adult he or she will have an immature personality in which the characteristic traits of that stage predominate. This series of stages Freud labeled oral, anal, phallic, latency, and genital.

The first year of the child's life Freud designated the **oral stage**, because the lips and mouth are the focus of sensual pleasure. A baby busily sucking away at pacifier or thumb, breast or bottle, may not be hungry but simply enjoying the pleasurable feelings that arise when the mouth is stimulated. Although during the first few months babies lack the coordination to pick up an object and deliberately insert it into their mouths, whatever brushes cheek or lips goes in. Babies actively seek oral stimulation.

At about their first birthdays, babies enter Freud's second stage of psychosexual development, the **anal stage**. During this period, which lasts until they are about three, pleasurable feelings center around the rectum. The delights of oral stimulation do not fade completely away, but children now enjoy both expelling feces and retaining them. Toilet training may become a battle in which children learn to use their libidinal pleasures as a weapon against their parents.

The third, and in Freudian theory highly critical, period spans the years from three to five or six. During this **phallic stage**, the genitals become the focus, and children learn to derive pleasure from fondling them. Boys are said to fear castration and girls to be filled with penis envy. Boys are said to fall in love with their mothers and girls with their fathers. Powerless to push the parent of the same sex out of the way, both girls and boys resolve this conflict by identifying with that parent, boys assuming their fathers' masculine characteristics and girls the feminine characteristics of their mothers.

After the stormy phallic period, Freud believed, sexual feelings become less important in children. From about six until they reach puberty, children are in the **latency period**. Tenderness predominates over sexual feelings, and children learn to feel shame and guilt. With the mastery of their conflict with their parents, they have developed a superego. During the latency period, they also discover moral and esthetic interests.

The final period of psychosexual development, the **genital stage**, emerges with puberty. Among children who have successfully navigated all the earlier stages, primary sensual pleasure transfers to mature sexual relationships with members of the other sex.

Once Freud's theories found their way into academic and popular thinking, the field of human development changed. His theory was the first to consider the way biological, psychic, and environmental influences affect personality development and the first to realize that all children have sexual urges. Freud's direct influence is clearest in John Bowlby's (1969) influential theory of attachment, which is based in part on Freud's belief that rupturing the tie between a child and his or her mother during the early years can have harmful psychological consequences. Indirectly, Freud's influence has so pervaded Western thought that some of his insights—such as his focus on early experiences

and on the role played by a child's identification with the parent in the development of conscience—are used even by many researchers who reject his formal theory of development.

Erikson's Psychosocial Theory

Erik Erikson (1963), one modifier of Freud's analytic theory, has developed an elaborate stage theory that is unusual because it describes emotional development across the life span. His theory is called **psychosocial** because it focuses on the individual's interactions with society, instead of on sexual conflicts as does Freud's theory.

According to Erikson, personality develops in steps determined by the human organism's readiness to move toward, to be aware of, and to interact with a widening social world—a world that begins with a dim image of mother and ends with an image of humankind. Erikson saw development as the progressive resolution of conflicts between a person's needs and the demands of society. At each of eight stages, conflicts must be resolved, at least partially, before progress can be made on the problems of the next stage. But even when a person successfully resolves the conflict, the defeated quality remains part of the personality, so that Erikson expects no one to be completely free of mistrust, shame, guilt, and other conflicts (Erikson and Hall, 1983). (See Table 1.2.)

FROM TRUST TO INDUSTRY In the first stage, babies need to develop a relationship in which they can get what they require from a person who is ready to provide it—usually a mother. Constant, reliable care promotes the baby's sense of *trust*, enabling the infant to learn to tolerate frustrations and to delay immediate gratification. If a baby's needs are not consistently met, he or she can develop a sense of

Table 1.2 PSYCHODYNAMIC STAGES OF DEVELOPMENT

Freud's Psychosexual Stages	Erikson's Psychosocial Stages	Possible Outcomes
Oral	Infancy	Basic trust vs. mistrust
Anal	Early childhood	Autonomy vs. shame
Phallic	Play age	Initiative vs. guilt
Latency	School age	Industry vs. inferiority
Genital	Adolescence	Identity vs. role confusion
	Young adulthood	Intimacy vs. isolation
	Adulthood	Generativity vs. stagnation
	Maturity	Ego integrity vs. despair

Erikson's first five stages of development roughly correspond to Freud's five stages, but Erikson has elaborated on Freud's theory, adding three stages, each with its own developmental task.

mistrust and will react to frustration by becoming anxious and upset.

After infants begin to walk and to exercise some self-direction, they run into social restraints. During this second stage, they increasingly demand to control their own behavior ("Me do it!"), but because they have little judgment about their capabilities, they need to be protected from excesses while being granted *autonomy* in matters they can handle. It is particularly important at this stage, Erikson suggests, that parents not shame a child into feeling that he or she is incompetent. Shame can be a devastating experience for anyone, and it is particularly difficult for young children who are struggling for autonomy and who are not yet sure that they can develop competent self-regulation.

After children gain a relatively secure sense of autonomy, they enter the third stage of development and are ready to take the initiative in planning their activities. As Erikson sees it, *initiative* adds to autonomy the quality of undertaking a task for the sake of being active and on the move. In the preceding stage, self-will often inspired acts of defiance. In this stage, children are ready for positive, constructive activities under their own initiative. The potential problem at this period is guilt; a child may come to feel that his or her intrusiveness and activity have evil consequences. This is the period of sexual attraction to the opposite-sex parent, and as a child resolves this hopeless attraction, he or she identifies with the same-sex parent and develops a conscience. Harsh parental responses to a

This little boy is in Erikson's second stage of development, when his demands to do things himself reflect his struggle to control his own behavior. (Michael Hayman/Stock, Boston)

Olive R. Pierce/Black Star

Erik Erikson (1902–   )

Erik Erikson was born in Germany of Danish parents. He was graduated from art school and went to Florence, Italy, intending to become an art teacher. In Vienna, where he had gone to teach children of American families, he met Freud and other analysts, and soon entered psychoanalytic training.

When Hitler came to power in Germany, Erikson immigrated to America. He held a series of positions in child-guidance clinics and major universities while maintaining a private practice. During an appointment at Harvard University, Erikson developed an interest in anthropology and studied the Sioux and Yurok Indians. During a subsequent appointment at the University of California, Berkeley, he studied adolescents, using a technique in which the way young people played with dolls revealed their unconscious thoughts and feelings.

Erikson is one of the few theorists to describe emotional development across the life span. In his theory, personality develops through eight stages, from infancy to the final stage of life. As a person interacts with a widening social world, he or she moves from a universe of self and mother to an image of humankind. Each stage has its own conflict to be resolved, and the failure to resolve any of these conflicts can lead to psychological disorders. Erikson's psychodynamic theory is important because his emphasis is on the healthy personality instead of the disturbed individual, and because he includes society and history as well as the family among forces affecting emotional development.

child's initiatives and sexual overtures can lead to an overdeveloped conscience that may always plague the person with guilt.

Once children come to terms with their families by identifying with the same-sex parent, they enter the fourth stage and are ready to move into the larger world. About this time in our culture, children go to school. Before children can become adults, they must become workers, learning to gain recognition by producing things (industry), so at this stage they want to learn the technical skills that characterize adults. The potential problem in this period lies in a sense of inadequacy and inferiority, which can develop if children are not praised for their accomplishments. In Erikson's theory, this is a decisive stage in the child's preparation to assume effective adult roles.

FROM IDENTITY TO EGO INTEGRITY
In the fifth stage, adolescents question all their previous solutions to problems of trust, autonomy, initiative, and industry. Rapid body growth and genital maturity create a physiological revolution within them at the time that they face adult life. According to Erikson, adolescents search for continuity and sameness within themselves—a sense of *identity*—and in their search they must refight the battles of earlier

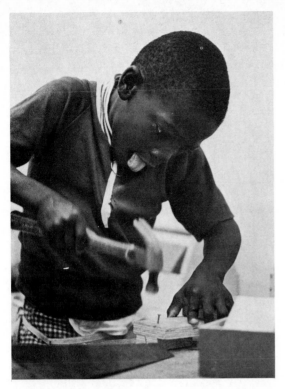

The schoolchild, who is in Erikson's fourth stage, has developed a sense of industry, learning the pleasure that comes when diligence and attention lead to the successful completion of a project. (Cary Wolinsky/Stock, Boston)

years, usually casting their parents in the role of adversaries. The potential problem at this period is that adolescents' identities will fail to become consistent and that they will be unable to develop a sense of who they are as people, as sexual beings, as adult workers, as potential parents. If this role confusion lasts into adulthood, they may never be able to make consistent decisions about who they are and where they are going in life.

Young adults, emerging from the search for identity, are eager and willing to fuse their own identities with those of others. In terms of Erikson's sixth stage, they are ready for *intimacy*— for relationships with others in which they are strong enough to make sacrifices for another's welfare without losing themselves in another's identity. It is at this point that true sexual love can emerge. The potential problem at this period is isolation from others—a failure to commit oneself to loving relationships because of fear or a need to compete.

Generativity characterizes the seventh stage and refers to the adult's concern with establishing and guiding the next generation. According to Erikson, productivity in work and creativity in one's life are important concepts in this period. The possible dangers of this period are self-absorption and a sense of stagnation, a sense of going nowhere, doing nothing important.

In Erikson's theory, the final stage of the life cycle should result in a sense of wholeness, of purposes accomplished and a life well lived. The potential problem in the final stage is regret and despair over wasted chances and unfortunate choices. A person in this stage who feels despair ironically fears death in a way that those with *ego integrity* do not. The despairing person, while expressing disgust with life, continues to yearn for another chance. The person with ego integrity accepts death as the end of a meaningful trip.

Translating Freud into Learning Theory

Although learning theory and psychoanalysis generally keep to their own sides of the street, an attempt has been made by John Dollard and Neal Miller (1950), two social-learning theorists, to translate Freudian theory into the language of learning theorists. Dollard and Miller proposed that the two theories are complementary. Where Freud talks about pleasure, they speak of reinforcement. Although their insistence on learning does not lend itself to the idea of a psyche divided into ego, id, and superego, they have little disagreement with Freud's belief in the existence of basic human drives, which they regard as strong stimuli.

They are comfortable with Freud's stages of psychosexual development and with his principle that a child's basic attitudes are formed in the early years. But instead of focusing on specific sites of libidinous pleasure, they concentrate on the child's typical experiences during these periods: the stimuli the child encounters, the responses made, the habits built up. They see disturbances not in terms of fixation but as learning that occurs in situations of conflict between drives and social pressures. For them, toilet training is important not because of the child's sensual pleasures but because it represents the child's first encounter with the culture's insistence on order and cleanliness. Similarly, Dollard and Miller see the identification that is established during the phallic period not as the child's way of overcoming incestuous desires but as the simple imitation of a powerful parent that is followed by reinforcement.

ADAPTATION THEORIES

Adaptation theories suggest that human behavior is the product of our evolutionary history. Human beings have evolved to behave in specifically human ways. Just as our internal organs and external limbs have evolved to certain forms, so our behavior has characteristic patterns that develop in interaction with the environment. The force behind this way of looking at development comes from **ethology,** which is the scientific study of animal behavior in evolutionary terms. Ethologists rely on rigorous observations of natural behavior and on studies carried out in natural settings—practices that have been increasingly adopted by developmental psychologists, including those who may not have been influenced by the emphasis on evolutionary significance.

In the view of adaptation theorists, the human species (like every other species) has evolved in environmental contexts that are as important to understand as the nature of humanity itself. The necessity for human beings to be in harmony with their environment leads ethologists of human behavior to look at development as adaptation. They see social behavior as related to

group cohesion, to the competition for mates, to survival of the young, and so forth. Intelligence is a prime mechanism for adaptation; during the course of human evolution, those individuals who solved problems related to their own survival were more likely to leave offspring for the next generation.

A good way to understand human behavior, therefore, is to look at the way it enables babies, children, or adults to survive and flourish in an environment like that in which our species evolved. For this reason, newborn infants, whose behavior is relatively little influenced by culture, human groups that live in conditions like those of our early ancestors, and apes and other primates are favorite subjects for developmental psychologists who have been influenced by ethology.

Researchers who wonder about infancy among our forebears often look at the !Kung San, a much-studied band of hunter-gatherers, who live a nomadic life in Africa's Kalahari desert under conditions that may be like those of our early ancestors. Observations of the !Kung San, says Melvin Konner (1977), indicate that in an environment like the one in which humanity evolved, a sensitive, immediately responsive mother is a regular part of child rearing. !Kung San babies spend most of their first year or two in close human contact, either on their mothers' laps or carried in a sling on their hips. The babies have continual access to the breast and nurse frequently. When they cry or fuss, their mothers' response is immediate, and the babies' whims are indulged. Yet when these indulged babies are two to five years old, they do not hang on to their mothers as observers from our own society might expect. Far from being spoiled or dependent, they show considerable independence, interacting less with their mothers and more with other children than English children of the same age.

Konner's observations suggest that human beings have evolved with close ties between mother and infant, and such seems to be the case. The bond between mother and infant is regarded by adaptation theorists as part of a behavioral system that evolved to protect the developing organism. Because human infants are helpless for so long, their survival depends on protection from mature members of the species, and the attachment of babies to their caregivers generally keeps the pair in close physical proximity (Bowlby, 1969). As will become clear in later chapters, although attachment is expressed in varying ways in different cultures, bonding between infant and caregiver has been present in every society studied.

Given the need of human infants for protection, we might expect that some sort of mechanism had evolved to ensure the establishment of the bond, and adaptation theorists point to the existence of two such devices: the baby's smile and the baby's "cuteness." These qualities are considered **releasing stimuli**, or events that regularly evoke certain behavior in all members of a species. Such stimuli help explain regularities in mating patterns, aggression, appeasement, and other typical behavior. In the case of the human infant's survival, the smile evokes a feeling of joy in the caregiver, an observation made long ago by Charles Darwin (1872). Studies of blind and deaf-blind infants have found that the babies smile in response to voice or touch, so it appears that the smile is as "natural" as walking, a part of our evolutionary heritage (Freedman, 1974). Blind babies have no model, hence their smiles cannot have been learned from watching the caregiver. In fact, most of the baby's expressions of emotion are seen as communication signals that have adaptive consequences, influencing the baby's survival (Plutchik, 1983). Certainly, the cry can also be regarded as a releasing stimulus, one that brings the caregiver to the baby's side, whether or not it affects the establishment of an emotional bond (Hinde, 1983).

Cuteness may be another releasing stimulus for human caregiving, a response that evolved because it improves the chance of adequate infant care and survival (Lorenz, 1942–1943). In every culture, most human beings find the physical appearance of babies and baby animals appealing. They respond to this cuteness by want-

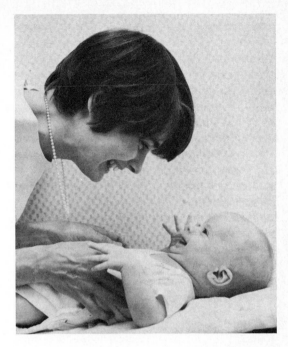

The baby's smile and cuteness may act as releasing stimuli, which evoke joy in adults and thereby establish the bond that ensures infant survival. (Suzanne Szasz/Photo Researchers)

ing to pick them up and cuddle them. In species other than humanity, the baby forms elicit caregiving from adult animals, whereas adult forms do not. Babies and young animals are cute because they have relatively large heads, particularly foreheads, and foreshortened facial features. The toy industry takes advantage of this appeal, generally making cute dolls with very small features embedded in large heads and small bodies.

In tracing development through childhood, psychologists have speculated on the evolutionary value of the long period of immaturity in the human species and suggested that evolution has guaranteed that during these years children will want to learn the skills required by adults, ensuring the species' survival. Babies and children yearn to explore and to learn, and they learn easily. In play, they practice skills without suffering adult consequences—as when they play house or doctor or soldier. According to

The preschoolers' play group is held together by friendships and dominance structures. Each youngster knows his or her own place in the hierarchy, as well as the places of the other children. (Laimute E. Druskis/Jeroboam)

Jerome Bruner (1972), language, playfulness, curiosity, and the need to master the environment appear to be evolved characteristics that make human development what it is.

Adaptation theorists have had other insights on human development from their observations of similarities in the social behavior of human beings and their nearest primate relatives. Although some ethologists (Hinde, 1983) are reluctant to make comparisons of adaptive behavior across species, investigators have found that "dominance hierarchies" in children's play groups are so similar to those that characterize monkey and ape troops that they may have the same evolutionary source (Rajecki and Flanery, 1981). Children climb the dominance ladder by means of physical attack, threats, or struggles over objects. Even among preschool play groups, most children know to which rung of the ladder each child belongs (Strayer and Strayer, 1976). In only a short time the roles of leader and follower are solidly established.

By enabling children to anticipate and avoid

aggressive encounters, the dominance hierarchy helps keep the group functioning smoothly. Children may not realize this, but researchers have found that when children fail to stay on their rung in the hierarchy, the entire group is likely to turn on them. Although these youngsters are neither extremely aggressive nor extremely submissive, they become scapegoats. Janet Strayer (1977), who studied several playgroups, proposes that the scapegoat either does not understand the group structure or else he or she knows it and deliberately violates it. But groups are not held together by dominance alone, either among children or monkeys. Friendships, coalitions, and subgroups are just as important (Hinde, 1983), and positive social bonds also appear in children's playgroups. Getting along in the playgroup is an important part of the development of social competence.

ORGANISMIC THEORIES

Like adaptation theories, organismic theories view human development from an evolutionary perspective; but **organismic theories** make no attempt to interpret development in terms of its evolutionary function. Instead, they look at the human infant as evolved to develop in certain ways along a path determined by the interaction of genetic maturation and experience.

The biological organism is the metaphor that dominates the view of organismic theorists (Reese and Overton, 1970). The individual is seen as a spontaneously active organism, and because some activity is not a response to external events, it is theoretically impossible ever to predict all of a person's acts.

Constructionism is the hallmark of the organismic view. Unlike learning theorists, who espouse the concept of naïve realism, organismic theorists assert that the world cannot be known objectively; instead, knowledge of it is actively constructed by the child. Change is not simply cumulative. As the child develops, his or her mind undergoes a series of reorganizations, each one moving the child into a higher stage of psychological functioning. In the organismic view, we can never understand a child's behavior apart from its purpose. Breaking up behavior into bits and studying it apart from its context, therefore, serves no purpose.

Organismic theories developed in Europe early in this century, and two of the foremost theorists were Heinz Werner (1948, 1957) and Jean Piaget (1952b, 1983). Both were affected by evolutionary theory and trained in the biological and natural sciences. This training led them to emphasize the adaptive functions of behavior in maintaining an equilibrium between the individual and the environment. Both emphasized that change in behavior and functioning result from the interaction of maturation and experience.

Werner and Piaget viewed cognition as a biological system of special importance. The function and characteristics of thought were like those of respiration or digestion—taking in, modifying, and using whatever elements were needed. Thought was particularly significant because it gave human beings extraordinary, highly flexible ways of dealing with the environment.

From birth, human beings actively engage and use their environment, and as time passes they gradually construct their own understanding of the world. At first, babies are **egocentric.** They make no distinction between themselves and the external world, or among feeling, thought, and the external world. As they develop, children gradually acquire **perspective**, a sense of themselves as people who are separate from the world, and develop objectively based concepts about the world that they share with others.

Werner and Piaget studied development at an everyday level, intervening in common situations and studying the effects of their experimental manipulations on a child's behavior. This approach was consistent with their belief that fragmenting natural patterns of behavior, as when memory is investigated by requiring children to memorize lists of words, leads to a limited understanding of development.

Piaget's Theory

Piaget's theory has had more influence in recent years than other organismic theories. It gives meaningful continuity to the development of human understanding, and it has strongly influenced research in the fields of perceptual and intellectual development. Piaget called his approach **genetic epistemology.** Epistemology is the study of knowledge—how we know what we know. The term "genetic" here means developmental. Piaget's theory covers the development of intelligence (ways of knowing).

For Piaget, knowledge came from action. Using **schemes,** or patterns of action, babies act on objects around them—they feel, turn, bang, or mouth them. Their knowledge of those objects grows neither from the objects themselves nor from the babies themselves, but from the interaction of the two, as the babies **assimilate,** or incorporate, new knowledge into their existing schemes and **accommodate,** or modify, their schemes to acquire knowledge that does not fit them. As a result of this process, children pass through a series of developmental stages as they mature, each stage representing an advance in their thinking, a qualitatively different way of understanding the world in which they live.

SCHEMES In Piagetian terms, a child's understanding of the world arises from the coordination of actions and the interrelationships of those actions with objects in the environment. The infant, in other words, is a **constructionist.** The baby constructs reality from the relationships of actions and objects, not simply from actions alone nor from the perceptual qualities of objects alone. For example, infants can throw a ball and roll it; they can apply those same actions to an orange. They learn that both objects roll (are round) but that when thrown, the ball bounces and the orange goes "thud." From their ordinary and simple actions on objects, infants come to know the effects of their actions and the properties of objects. They also learn to coordinate their actions—they cannot simultaneously

Anderson/Monkmeyer

Jean Piaget (1896–1980)

Jean Piaget was born and reared in Switzerland. As a boy he was a keen observer of animal behavior, and when he was only fifteen, published a paper on shells in a scientific journal. He came by his interest in knowledge and knowing (epistemology) as a result of studying philosophy and logic. Whereas most American psychologists have been influenced by the evolutionary theories of Charles Darwin, Piaget was influenced by the creative evolution of Henri Bergson, who saw a divine agency instead of chance as the force behind evolution. Another important influence on Piaget's thought was the cognitive theory of James Mark Baldwin.

After receiving his doctorate in biological science at the University of Lausanne in 1918, he became interested in psychology. In order to pursue his interest in abnormal psychology, he went to Paris and, while studying at the Sorbonne, secured a position in Alfred Binet's laboratory. During his work there, he began to pay more attention to children's wrong answers than to their right ones, realizing that the wrong answers provided invaluable clues to the nature of their thinking.

Piaget's interest in children's mental processes shifted and deepened when, in 1925, he began observing his own children. As he kept detailed records of their behavior, he worked at tracing the origins of children's thought to their behavior as babies. Later, he became interested in the thought of adolescents. Piaget's primary method was to present problems in a standardized way to children of different ages. He then asked each child to explain his or her answers and probed these explanations with a series of carefully phrased questions.

Soon after completing his work in Paris, Piaget accepted an appointment as director of research at the Jean Jacques Rousseau Institute in Geneva. Thereafter he lived in Geneva, conducting research and writing on cognitive development as professor of experimental psychology and genetic epistemology at the University of Geneva.

throw and roll the same object. These schemes, such as grasping or throwing, are the infant's forms of thought.

Older children and adults still think in the same kind of action patterns when they drive a car or play a piano or type a letter; but they also have internalized schemes derived from earlier concrete experiences, so that they can manipulate objects mentally, classifying them and understanding their relationships. They need not literally try out the solution to every problem. Mental arithmetic replaces the physical act of counting; logical sequences of thought, such as "if . . . then" statements, replace the younger child's concrete manipulations of cause-effect relations.

For example, most adults have come to understand the principle of gravity: when released from an elevated position, objects fall. But a ten-month-old baby explores gravity by dropping bits of dinner from the highchair tray and watching intently as each piece hits the floor.

(The baby also discovers that cups fall, spoons fall, cookies fall.) A baby's scheme of dropping objects in space soon incorporates information gleaned from dropping many objects. He or she no longer has to create the same mess again and again just to find out what will happen. And since dropping food is antithetical to eating it, a hungry baby comes to recognize that eating and dropping the same object are not compatible schemes.

ASSIMILATION AND ACCOMMODATION In Piaget's theory, children's thinking develops through the processes of assimilation and accommodation. For example, a baby can bang a large variety of objects, incorporating new knowledge through an existing "banging" scheme, assimilating to the scheme whether

In Piaget's view, to obtain the toy this baby first tries a familiar grasping scheme (assimilation) and then alters it with new knowledge (accommodation) to get the toy through the bars. (George S. Zimbel/Monkmeyer Press)

each object can be satisfactorily "banged." But if the baby has always picked up rigid objects and now reaches for a soft one, the same grasping scheme will not effectively hold the toy, so the baby must accommodate the grasping scheme, altering it to fit the qualities of the new object if banging is to be successful.

The processes of assimilation and accommodation work together in complementary fashion. To assimilate is to use what we already know how to do in order to do something new; to accommodate is to acquire a new way of doing something. Both processes continue to function throughout the life span. For example, in the United States we are being asked to convert our thinking to the metric system. In essence, we are being asked to restructure our existing schemes (accommodation). After we have learned the metric units of weight, volume, and linear measure, we will have to assimilate much of what we knew under the old scheme to the new one. Does one wear a sweater outdoors at 30°C? (No.) Is 80 kilometers per hour too fast a speed to drive on a freeway? (Probably not.) Is $3.50 per kilogram too much to pay for pork chops? (No.) In other words, the new knowl-

edge will have to be acquired by applying what we have already learned in a different way under other schemes.

At any given time, the developing person can make only limited changes in his or her cognitive structures. There must always be some continuity. Over the life span, the balance, or equilibrium, between assimilation and accommodation changes in the direction of greater balance. **Equilibration**, the most general developmental principle in Piaget's theory, describes the process by which the child restores balance between the world and his or her view of it. The organism always tends toward biological and psychological balance, and development is a progressive approximation to an ideal state of equilibrium that it never fully achieves. A child's equilibrium at any one stage may be upset by external events, such as new information he or she cannot readily assimilate, or by internal processes that bring the child to a new "readiness" to accommodate. In both cases, the child's previous temporary equilibrium is upset, and development advances to a new, higher level of organization.

STAGES According to Piaget, intellectual development goes through a series of stages, and the organization of behavior is qualitatively different at each stage. The two essential points of Piaget's stage theory are: (1) stages emerge in a constant order of succession, and (2) neither heredity nor environment independently explains the progressive development of mental structures. Piaget proposed four major stages of intellectual development: a sensorimotor period, a preoperational period, a concrete operational period, and a formal operational period.

The **sensorimotor stage** begins at birth and extends until the child is eighteen months to two years old. As a newborn, the baby's actions are rigid and inflexible. Soon, however, flexibility becomes apparent, and cognitive development progresses rapidly. Until they are about seven months old, babies repeat actions again and again because of the stimulation they pro-

vide. By about seven or eight months, these repetitive actions—shaking a rattle or banging a cup—are often meant to prolong interesting events. And by the time they are a year old, the repetitions are intelligent adaptations to specific situations. A similar progression appears in their development of the object concept: the six-month-old believes that an object that is out of sight no longer exists; the nine- or ten-month-old will look for a toy if he or she sees someone put a cloth over it; the year-old infant will look for a toy after observing it being hidden, but will give up the search if it is not in that place; and toward the end of the second year, the child will search in all the places a toy might have been hidden. By this time, toddlers form mental representations and store them; they can watch an adult and then imitate that behavior the next day. They have also become problem-solvers. No longer dependent on trial-and-error solutions, they have internalized schemes, solving problems in their heads and then applying the solutions. They are ready to move out of infancy and into the preoperational period.

The **preoperational stage** covers the preschool years and can last until a child is seven or eight. Although children at this stage can certainly form mental representations, those representations do not, for Piaget, qualify as mental operations because such children do not understand certain logical rules. For example, although they know that seven chocolate drops and five caramels are all candy, they will stoutly maintain that there are more chocolates than candy. Children's representations at this stage also fail in another way: they are not integrated. Because of these failures, children harbor some beliefs that adults might find amusing—such as the belief that everything in the world, including stones and rivers, was made by some person; or that their bicycles are alive. They also believe that putting a mask on an animal or person truly transforms that person. During this preoperational period, some of children's speech is not meant for communication but is addressed to themselves. When they think, they think out loud. They are also egocentric, according to Piaget, and believe that everyone sees the world exactly as they do. All in all, although this is an exciting period of cognitive development, when measured against the formal logical thought that Piaget saw as the goal of development, the thought of the preoperational child falls short on every count.

During the **concrete operational stage**, which lasts until a child is about eleven or twelve, children do indeed attain logical thought, but their schemes apply only to concrete objects. They now understand logical operations, including reversible transformations. They know that a string of beads that is stretched out straight is no longer than it was when it lay in a curve. They also know that when they have seven chocolate drops and five caramels, they have more candy than chocolate drops. They can reason about the solid, concrete objects in the world around them. Their speech is now intended for communication, because they now think silently. And they have put aside most of the childish beliefs that adults find so charming.

The stage of **formal operational** thought is the culmination of cognitive development. It can appear when a child is about eleven years old, although many children do not enter this stage until they are adolescents. Children can now use abstract reasoning and are capable of adopting artificial premises they know to be untrue. It is this ability to be flexible and to reason in the absence of observed fact—to use hypothetical or propositional schemes such as "if . . . then" statements—that marks the adult manner of thought.

During the past few years, Piaget's theory has been criticized on several counts. For example, Piaget apparently underestimated the ability of babies to extract information about the world (Harris, 1983). In an analysis of Piagetian theory, Rochel Gelman and Renée Baillargeon (1983) point out that development within particular cognitive areas, for example, the concrete operational ability to classify objects, does not progress in the precise manner that Piaget proposed and that his four major stages do not accurately reflect the course of cognitive devel-

opment. However, they conclude that Piaget's insistence on the active role played by the child in learning about the world and his basic idea that cognitive structures influence perceptions and memory and set limits to problem-solving have generally been substantiated and will continue to dominate the approach of many developmental psychologists.

Werner's Theory

Like Piaget, Heinz Werner emphasized the interacting roles of genetic maturation and environmental experience. He believed that psychological development resembles the development of the embryo; that is, all normal children pass through the same milestones of development in the same order. Yet Werner never set forth a general system of development, identifying each stage and its characteristics as did Piaget.

The major theme of Werner's developmental theory is the **orthogenetic principle** (Werner, 1948), for Werner tried to establish the principles of correct (ortho) development (genetic) in both physical and psychological growth. He saw the child as moving from a global, undifferentiated state to one of high differentiation and integration. Responses and skills are increasingly organized into hierarchies, a trend Werner called **hierarchic integration**. This is easy to see in the physical area, where the baby develops hierarchic patterns of movement that bring each separate motor capability into the service of others in a highly organized way. When a baby first learns to drink from a cup, for example, he combines and integrates a series of simple skills. First a little boy must be able to sit up and fix his eyes on the cup. Then he must be able to use visual information to reach out, find the cup, grasp it, and hold it upright. He must then combine visual information with kinesthetic information about the position of his head and mouth, arms and hands, in order to bring the cup to his mouth, tilt it at the correct angle, stop tilting it before it spills, and swallow. When the little boy drinks from a cup, he combines

Courtesy International Universities Press

Heinz Werner (1890–1964)

Heinz Werner was interested in formulating a comprehensive theory of cognitive development. He adopted principles and concepts from embryology, biology, and other natural sciences and applied them to mental development. Werner considered learning views of development wrong, because he believed development was much more than a gradual and continuous process of acquiring bits of behavior.

Because he was interested in explaining mental life, his approach was broad, eclectic, and comparative. He wanted his theory to explain the course of cognitive development over the life span and to account for differences in thought among species, among cultures, and among normal and abnormal groups.

He stressed that the development of human beings shows both change and stability. People go through an ordered sequence of stages, which are characterized by different organizations of cognitive structure and functioning. Each stage involves both adaptive change and organizational stability. Adaptive change means that with maturation there is a progressive development of specific, separate ways of doing and seeing things, and that these more advanced ways take precedence over early, simple forms. Organizational stability means that, even though changes occur, a person retains an essential and basic organization.

Werner showed that even as infants, human beings are organized and have some degree of competence, and this inborn organization is the basis for adaptive behavior and learning. Although movement, vision, thinking, and so on are always organized, they undergo progressive changes in a patterned order.

and integrates all these skills so smoothly that his parents never consider the number of simple abilities that are involved.

As babies become able to integrate perception and thought into hierarchies, they learn to distinguish parts from the whole, see relationships, and understand the difference between relevant and irrelevant qualities. They understand, for example, that Mother is still the same person, even though she has cut her hair and put a blond rinse on it. Gradually, the higher mental functions come to control the lower ones. Children use language to direct their behavior. By the time they are seven, they understand that the dreams they once thought arose from an external source originate within them and are private. They become less bound by the immediate situation and increasingly able to plan and to tolerate delay. Instead of interpreting the world entirely in terms of their own needs, children begin to appreciate the needs and goals of others.

Although Werner has not been the dominant figure Piaget has become, his concept of differentiation and hierarchic integration has been incorporated into general theories of child development, and his research in the field of perception has stimulated a good deal of theory. Some of the themes that occupy developmental psychologists today were apparent in Werner's approach (Pea, 1982). Among them are his insistence that any activity can be understood only in context, his belief that symbolic processes are central to an understanding of human functioning, his emphasis on assessing mental functioning with tasks that are significant to the individual, and his proposal of an "ordering function" that gives form to other cognitive activities—a way of looking at cognition that parallels contemporary interest in people's understanding of the way their minds operate.

DIALECTICAL THEORIES

Dissatisfaction with both mechanistic and organismic approaches to child development has given rise to yet another way of looking at the developing child: **dialectical theories**. With their roots in the philosophy of Hegel and Marx, these theories view development as a dialectical process. In a *dialectic*, each idea is seen as a thesis that interacts with its antithesis, or opposite, to form a synthesis on a new level. The synthesis becomes a new thesis that again interacts with its antithesis to form a new synthesis, and so on. In the dialectical view, human development proceeds in the same way; in each individual stage of development, a person interacts with society to reach a new level of functioning.

Although psychologists with differing theoretical views agree that the aim of developmental psychology is to understand the changing individual, dialectical psychologists believe that such an understanding is possible only when the individual is considered within the changing world. This perspective is unique because most psychologists fail to consider how historical-social changes affect behavior and its development. They seem to believe that if they can understand behavior as it was in 1900, they understand it as it is in the 1980s. In the dialectical view, however, knowledge is changing and social; it is created by a continually evolving society and transmitted to the individual. Dialectical psychologists have suggested that major cultural changes, such as television and com-

puters, can have an enormous impact on the nature of thought and its development.

The discomfort of dialectical psychologists with mechanistic psychology was summed up by Robert Wozniak (1975), who said that behavioral psychologists do not study change; instead, they analyze development into its elements and then recombine them into the whole, assuming that if they understand the elements and the way they are combined, they will understand development. Organismic psychologists come closer to the dialectical view, for they see development as arising out of the child's active operations on the environment. But their dialectic is incomplete. For Piaget, said Klaus Riegel (1975), the environment appeared to be an assemblage of things without activity or history; social interaction received little consideration in his theory. In addition, Piaget focused on equilibrium and believed that there is an endpoint to human development.

The dialectical view first became prominent when Soviet psychologists were searching for an approach to psychology that would fit comfortably within the Marxist framework. In recent years, American psychologists have reevaluated the methods of Soviet psychology, and many have come to regard dialectics as a helpful tool instead of as a dogmatic straitjacket.

Vygotsky's View

Shortly after the Russian Revolution, Lev S. Vygotsky became a leading Soviet psychologist. Society, he believed, was essential to human development. Instead of regarding intellectual development as primarily the result of maturation, he saw children as active organizers who used the tools and language of culture in a continual interaction with the social world, thereby changing both the world and themselves.

Everything that distinguishes the child's mind from that of a chimpanzee comes from the culture, he believed, and every facet of development begins between the child and another person. Vygotsky included voluntary attention, logical memory, the foundation of concepts, and language in his list of developmental facets. He saw each process as appearing twice in a child's development—first shared between the child and an adult (an interpersonal process) and then reappearing inside the child (an intrapersonal process) (Vygotsky, 1978). As the child reconstructs a process internally, he or she moves through an upward spiral of development and is increasingly able to control his or her behavior. Development is neither an accumulation of small changes in behavior nor a single upward line but a dialectical process. In each succeeding stage, the developing person creates new responses and carries them out in new ways under the influence of different psychological processes.

Because of his emphasis on the role of society in development, Vygotsky was especially interested in language. He saw language as the primary means used by society to affect a child's development and as the only way abstract thought could be transmitted. In addition, he believed that once a child developed the ability to think in words, the nature of development changed radically (Vygotsky, 1962).

At each stage, Vygotsky believed, the child is more capable than testing shows, and he urged educators to exploit this fact. Tests measure a child's developmental level, but there is also a zone of **proximal development,** which is the distance between the level at which a child can solve problems alone and the level at which the child can solve problems with the guidance of an adult or more capable peers. This zone can be extended by play and by learning, and its width varies among children. For example, one eight-year-old may, with cooperation, be able to solve problems designed for twelve-year-olds; another, with similar cooperation, may only be able to solve problems designed for nine-year-olds.

Vygotsky's influence has become increasingly strong over the past few years, affecting psychologists who are interested in comparing the way thought and language develop in various cultures, as well as the way in which social interaction may contribute to cognitive development.

American Dialectical Psychology

Among American developmental psychologists who have been influenced by dialectical views are Jerome Bruner (1983), who regards his research into the development of cognition and language as more in tune with Vygotsky's ideas than with those of Piaget, and Michael Cole (1978), whose research into various cultures has shown the ways in which culturally organized social patterns affect psychological development. Cole and his colleagues at the Laboratory of Comparative Human Cognition (1983) see thought as developing out of the child's activity in a social context—with the cultural and the immediate interpersonal contexts (what people are doing, when they are doing it, where they are doing it) playing equally important roles. That is, the kinds of contexts in which youngsters spend their time provide the building blocks of cognitive development.

This dialectical view leads developmental psychologists to focus on the meaningful goal of cognitive activity (remembering something important) instead of looking at cognitive processes as a goal in themselves (memory) (Rogoff, 1982). Thought and action are considered together, instead of as separate processes. And when these psychologists compare different age groups, or groups from different sociocultural backgrounds, they try to consider the context of any event as it *appears* to each group that is being studied.

Vygotsky's notion of the zone of proximal development, in which adult support helps children master problems they could not otherwise handle, has also been a fruitful area of research for developmental psychologists. For example, the concept has been used to construct programs that help children who have difficulty mastering the school curriculum (Palincsar and Brown, in press). These programs use social interaction to

Lev Semanovich Vygotsky (1896–1934)

Lev S. Vygotsky, who was born in Russia, was a contemporary of Piaget and Werner. He was graduated from Moscow University in 1917 and until 1923 taught both literature and psychology in Gomel. In 1924, just after Soviet psychology had officially adopted "reactology"—an approach to psychology that depended upon behavioral reactions in a Marxist framework (Cole and Scribner, 1978)—Vygotsky returned to Moscow to work at the Institute of Psychology. His views did not coincide with either of the major European approaches to psychology, which were either introspective or behavioristic (as was reactology). Nor did he find the Gestalt psychologists' attempts to study behavior and experience as wholes a satisfactory solution.

Vygotsky believed that psychologists should study processes and the way they change, for as people respond to a situation, they alter it. One of his complaints about Piaget's theory was that the Swiss psychologist did not give enough weight to the influence of the environment on the developing child. Vygotsky believed that the internalization of social and cultural activities was the key to human development and that it distinguished human beings from animals.

Vygotsky's primary interests were thought, language, memory, and play. Toward the end of his life, he worked on the problems of education. But Vygotsky was also trained as a physician and advocated the combination of neurology and physiology with the experimental study of thought processes and their development. Just before his death from tuberculosis in 1934, he had been asked to head the department of psychology in the All-Union Institute of Experimental Medicine.

Vygotsky died at thirty-eight, but his influence on Soviet psychology continued through his students, who hold major positions throughout the Soviet Union. For years after his death, Vygotsky's views were disregarded in this country; but in 1962, *Thought and Language* was translated, and his ideas entered the American psychological community. With each passing year, his notions about the relation of thought and language, the natures and uses of play, and the concept of proximal development have received more attention. In 1978, his essays, *Mind in Society*, were translated and published.

teach the sort of argument skills that help students understand—and remember—what they read in their textbooks.

As Vygotsky noted, some children can advance more rapidly with adult assistance than others. By measuring children's performance in this area, psychologists have been able to assess a child's learning potential more accurately than is possible with achievement or intelligence tests, which assess a child's ability to work without any kind of aid (Campione et al., 1984). In fact, this process often detects children who could profit from instruction in a particular area, but who might be denied the opportunity because standardized test scores show that they do poorly, left to their own devices.

THEORIES IN PERSPECTIVE

Although the groups of theories presented in this chapter may appear to have little in common, they are largely complementary. All suggest that human growth and development is regular, and all assume that a good deal of behavior is potentially predictable. But they often attend to different behavior (even if they give it the same label, such as "learning"), and they often explain different aspects of the developmental process.

When different theories look at the same process, they often talk about it in different ways. The relationship between baby and caregiver, called attachment, for example, is regarded by psychoanalytic theorists as an outgrowth of the caregiver satisfying the infant's need to suck that characterizes the oral period. Learning theorists see attachment as the result of conditioning; the primary caregiver both satisfies the infant's basic needs and provides interesting and satisfying stimulation. And ethological theorists view attachment as an evolved behavior pattern that increases the likelihood of the infant's—and therefore the species'—survival.

In recent years, the various viewpoints have begun to converge. Disagreements still run deep, but many proponents are beginning to see areas of compatibility where once there was only discord. All the theories have a common concern with identifying the processes involved in human growth and development. And they share the goal of synthesizing observations and experimental findings to explain how and why behavior originates and develops. As we have seen, social-learning theorists have modified early, narrow positions, and many use insights from cognitive theories to expand their explanations of human behavior and development. One theorist (Kegan, 1982) has attempted to extend Piaget's theories of cognitive development to explain all aspects of human development and believes that the result is compatible with psychodynamic theories. Another (Gholson, 1980) has attempted to reconcile information-processing views with organismic theories. And it has been suggested by a third (Lerner, 1978) that the dialectical approach might be used to integrate mechanistic and organismic world views into a compatible framework.

Because theories are made up of abstract statements that do not refer directly to what is observed, they can neither be verified nor disproved unless they lead to testable hypotheses or predictions about observable behavior. If the statements of a theory successfully predict a great deal of human behavior, then we say that the theory is a useful explanation of development. As we have seen, most theories are restricted in their view of development and none has given a satisfactory explanation for the entire developmental process. Perhaps it is this limited utility of most theories that has led to a situation in which many investigators do not link their research to the specifications of a single theory. Today's researchers are often eclectic, relying on ideas from a variety of theoretical perspectives and avoiding the restrictions of a single, rigid approach.

In the next chapter, we turn to the methods researchers use to test hypotheses. When studies lead to results that others can repeat and confirm, they may solidify an explanation of development or uncover omissions in the original formulation whose completion may begin to close the gaps among competing theories. But no matter what view a developmental psychologist adopts, his or her explanations involve an exploration and documentation of multiple, interacting causes, as the next chapter makes clear.

SUMMARY

The aim of developmental psychology is to understand the complex interaction among the multiple influences that determine development. Psychologists generally divide the life span after birth into infancy, childhood, adolescence, and adulthood. The concept of a separate childhood emerged with the rise of the middle class; adolescence, with growing industrialization; and late adulthood, with increased life expectancy.

The field of child psychology has disparate origins, including nineteenth-century baby biographies, evolutionary views of development, the foundation of child-guidance clinics, the mental-testing movement, the demands of educators for research on children, experimental psychology, and the foundation of institutes for child study.

Theories of child development are based on various assumptions about human nature. These differing assumptions focus on inborn differences among people, environmental influences, the role of human beings in their own development, the natural goodness or evil of humanity, and the relationship of child to adult behavior.

In behavior-learning theories, the major **mechanistic theory** of development, the individual is viewed as primarily passive, behavior is primarily the result of experience, and development is continuous. **Reinforcement theory**, based on the views of B. F. Skinner, assumes that most learning is the result of **operant conditioning**, although **classical conditioning** is also believed to play a role. **Social-learning theories** add to conditioning the role of observational learning (imitation) and have expanded their view to include the role of human thought and knowledge in development. In **information-processing theories**, human beings are information-gathering, information-processing systems, in which thought and action are built out of a small set of simple processes.

Psychodynamic theories see human behavior as motivated by various internal and external forces. For Freud, the child moves through a series of **psychosexual** stages, each characterized by the way psychic energy is expressed. For Erikson, personality develops according to steps determined by the organism's readiness to interact with the world. The stages are called **psychosocial** because interaction with society is the dominant factor, and in each stage a different developmental conflict must be resolved.

Adaptation theories, which have been heavily influenced by the field of **ethology**, view human behavior from an evolutionary perspective. Development is described in terms of its effect on human survival, and behavior in studied in the context of natural settings.

Organismic theories also see human development as evolved to develop in certain ways, but they concentrate on the interaction between person and environment. They stress an active organism that constructs an understanding of the world and a developmental progression in cognitive structures. In Piaget's theory, the child **assimilates** and **accommodates** new knowledge, approaching and then upsetting an equilibrium between internal **schemes** and the outside world. Intellectually, the child progresses through the **sensorimotor**, the **preoperational**, the **concrete operational**, and the **formal operational stages**. In Werner's theory, the child moves from a global, undifferentiated state to one of high differentiation and integration, in which responses and skills are organized into hierarchies.

Dialectical theories have much in common with organismic theories, but they stress the changing, social nature of knowledge. All knowledge is created by society and transmitted to the individual; therefore, major cultural changes can have profound impact on the nature and development of human thought.

Studying Determinants of Development

EXPLAINING HUMAN DEVELOPMENT
Contributions of Other Disciplines
Interpretation of Age Differences
GENETIC DETERMINANTS
Genetic Studies with Animals
Human Genetics
Heritability
ENVIRONMENTAL DETERMINANTS
Physical Factors
Social Factors
Interaction of Determinants
STUDYING HUMAN DEVELOPMENT
Sampling
Types of Studies
Research Approaches
Interpreting Statistics
SUMMARY

If a boy who is arrested for stealing a car has a brother with a prison record, people often say, "He's just like his brother. Criminality runs in the family." But the boy was slow to talk and has always done poorly in school; he has a quick temper and often gets into fights with his peers; his father cannot keep a job, and his family lives in a poverty area. Had any of these influences—intelligence, temperament, peer relations, father's continual unemployment, brother's example, or socioeconomic environment—been different, the boy might not have taken the car. Although finding a single cause for a developmental effect is attractive and easy, the relationship is invariably complicated. Few aspects of development or behavior can be understood by examining only one cause.

Developmentalists are aware that both genetic and environmental determinants are responsible for the changes that occur in the developing person. **Genes,** the microscopic elements that carry the blueprints of heredity, interact with the **environment,** the physical and social conditions that surround the child, to produce development. In the course of this **interaction,** genetic characteristics influence the environment, which in turn affects further development—and vice versa. Nearly every aspect of children's lives, including their concepts of themselves, their scores on intelligence tests, their heights, and the times at which they become sexually mature, are affected by such interaction.

In this chapter we move from theory to its application. No matter what theoretical assumptions researchers adopt, virtually all investigators accept in principle the concept of interaction in human development. This is true whether they are influenced by social-learning theory, adaptive theory, psychodynamic theory, organismic theory, or dialectical theory (Weisfeld, 1982). The differences among them arise in the emphasis each places on the various components of that interaction. The chapter begins with a look at information from other disciplines that is relevant to an understanding of human development, then moves to a broad consideration of the way individual differences are interpreted. Building on this base, we take up the various determinants of development. We look first at genetic determinants, discovering how research with animals helps us to understand the unfolding of heredity in human beings and exploring the role of genes in human development. We next examine various types of environments, seeing how each influences the developing person. Instances of interaction among various determinants will make clear the intertwining of genetic, physical, and social determinants in every aspect of development. Finally, we discuss the methods developmental psychologists use to investigate development, finding that each type of study has its particular strengths and weaknesses, and that none is superior in all situations.

EXPLAINING HUMAN DEVELOPMENT

The study of human development is the study of change—change within individuals over

hours, days, weeks, months, or years (Appelbaum and McCall, 1983). This change is generally reflected in **behavior**; that is, in observable acts that can be described or measured reliably. Behavior can be measured in many ways—sometimes simply by watching, at other times by using instruments of various kinds, such as questionnaires, films of children's interactions, or devices that record heart rates. The behavior that is seen, heard, or measured serves as a window through which psychologists can analyze children's or adults' underlying competencies, motives, and emotions. Since studying all possible human behavior is obviously impossible, and selecting any behavior at random has little purpose, psychologists select for detailed study behavior that is important for theoretical or practical reasons. Whether the goal is to describe age differences in development or to assess its determinants, the developmental psychologist must be aware of information and insights provided by other disciplines.

These psychologists are conducting an experiment in development. From the responses of this little girl and the other children in the experiment, researchers may be able to establish whether most youngsters of this age have developed some particular competency. (Frank Siteman/Stock, Boston)

Contributions of Other Disciplines

Developmental psychologists depend on information about the individual's biological history and maturation, about the organization of his or her society, and about the influences of culture—information that comes from other disciplines: biology, sociology, and anthropology. Such information is required to explain development because psychologists see the developing person as a changing system that integrates biological factors with individual and shared experience.

Biologists have emphasized the importance of humanity's evolutionary history and have provided detailed descriptions of embryological and later physical development, giving us models for understanding all development. The complex interaction of genetic and environmental influences across the life span, from the level of the single cell to that of the whole organism, has made psychologists aware of the need to consider genetic and biological influences on human development. A child's temperament, height, or intelligence may show the influence of genes or of such physical factors as hormones, nutrition, or disease.

Sociologists, who study age-related changes in social roles, have emphasized the importance of understanding development within the context of society. A child is always a member of a human group: a family, a neighborhood group, a school class, and so on. These settings influence most of children's behavior. Anthropologists, who study development in various cultures, provide information that keeps us from assuming that the developmental pattern of our own culture is simply the reflection of human nature (LeVine, 1982). As shown in the historical discussion of childhood and adolescence (Chapter 1), the ways in which a culture interprets the life span can have profound influences on the expectations that others have for a person's behavior at different times in life.

Although adequate explanations of development take all levels of influence into considera-

All development takes place within the context of society. The neighborhood group is one type of society; it influences how the children within it behave, what they learn, and what they value. (Eric A. Roth/The Picture Cube)

tion, this thoroughness is not always necessary. Psychological, biological, sociological, and anthropological factors continually interact, but at specified times, an aspect of development may be more heavily affected by one level of influence than another.

Suppose that psychologists are trying to explain sex differences in aggression. A study emphasizing biological factors might indicate that male hormones explain why eight-year-old boys act more aggressively than girls. Such research would be criticized because it reduces the causes of complex behavior to a single explanation, relying on a single biological factor. The concentration of male hormones may contribute (greatly or little) to sex differences in behavior, but by itself, it cannot explain most observed differences. Many factors that do not involve hormones—such as different parental responses to boys and girls, different rewards for appropriate sex-role behavior, and so forth—may also play important roles in making boys more ag-

Adoption: The Value of Research

The findings of developmental psychologists often provide the sort of knowledge that can be applied to daily life. Understanding how the very young acquire language may lead to more efficient ways of helping children with educational problems. And understanding how children develop their notions of male and female behavior can help prevent the growth of limiting and often destructive sexual stereotypes. No matter what the issue—day care, integrating the schools, the connection between television and aggression, child abuse, adjusting to divorce or a new stepparent—developmental psychologists are studying it. Recent research may also have given us information that can ease the adjustment of adopted children.

One of the tasks adoptive parents face is informing their children about their birth status and helping them come to terms with it. For years, personnel at adoption agencies have advised parents to begin telling their children about adoption when they are two or three years old, under the assumption that if the facts are broken down into simple bits, even a preschool child can understand the process.

After conducting a clinical study, researchers at Rutgers University concluded that the prevailing assumption is not true and that children's ability to understand their adoptive status is linked with their ability to understand the world. David Brodzinsky, Leslie Singer, and Anne Braff (1984), whose work reflects an organismic perspective, studied 100 adopted and 100 nonadopted children between the ages of four and thirteen, interviewing them in depth about the adoption relationship and asking them about the reasons people decide to adopt. The children's answers suggested that youngsters go through six levels of understanding, moving from a global, diffuse grasp of the concept to a knowledge that is increasingly differentiated, abstract, and hierarchically integrated.

Most preschoolers, even children who had been told they were adopted, confused the processes of biological birth and adoption. Part of the dialogue between five-and-a-half-year-old Alan and the interviewer illustrates this sort of confusion:

Alan: Adoption means you go to try to get a baby, and if you can't, you can't.
Interviewer: Where do you get the baby you adopt?
Alan: From your vagina or your tummy.
Interviewer: Whose vagina or tummy?
Alan: The baby's mommy.
Interviewer: Is the baby adopted?
Alan: Yes . . . cause the mommy has it now. It came out of her.
Interviewer: Are all babies adopted?
Alan: Yep.
Interviewer: If a man and a woman want to be parents, what do they have to do?
Alan: Adopt a child.
Interviewer: Is there any other way of becoming a parent—a mommy or a daddy—besides adopting?
Alan: I don't know. [pp. 871–872]

gressive than girls. To explain observed differences in aggression, we must consider the effects of hormones along with other prenatal and postnatal differences in environment. In this example, hormones are only one component in the behavioral system; whether they are an important influence can be determined by research that varies hormones and rearing conditions separately (Money and Ehrhardt, 1972). But if one is attempting to explain sex differences in be-

By the time they are six years old, most children know the difference between biological birth and adoption but have no understanding of the reasons that lead people to adopt. They are certain, however, that no one can take away an adopted child. Between the ages of eight and eleven, understanding deepens, and with it some appreciation of the complications. During this period, they begin to question the permanence of the relationship and begin to have fantasies about being reclaimed by a biological parent. As children move out of this period, they again accept the fact that adoption is forever, but not until they are adolescents do they grasp the legal transfer of parental rights and responsibilities that is involved.

Similar developmental changes were found in the children's understanding of the reasons for adopting a child and the reasons for placing a child for adoption. When young children in the study first understood the difference between adoption and birth, they tended to focus on emotional and nurturant needs of the parent ("Parents want to give love to a child." "Parents want to have someone to love them."). Older children tended to focus on infertility, family planning, and the welfare of children, although they did not eliminate parental needs as a consideration. For ethical reasons, the researchers did not ask the children why people would place a child for adoption. But the spontaneous comments of children indicated that younger children see it in terms of rejection (the child was bad, or the parents didn't want it) or lack of money to care for a child, whereas older children also talk about financial problems but

tend to add abuse, broken homes, death of a parent, and illegitimacy.

Brodzinsky and his colleagues believe that children's understanding of adoption is closely tied to cognitive development and the child's gradually developing knowledge about the social world. As they learn about reproduction, family roles and relationships, values, motives, and social institutions, children assimilate that knowledge to their understanding of adoption. Although telling two-year-olds they are adopted is not harmful, it does not seem to be very helpful, either. Children of this age simply don't understand what their parents have said.

Why should this be a problem? It can cause misunderstandings because adoptive parents assume that their child understands the information they have patiently doled out, bit by bit. As a result they harbor a false sense of security concerning the child's knowledge and adjustment. They are unaware that the six-year-old who stoutly maintained that no one could take away an adopted child ("because that's the way it is when you're adopted; my mommy said so") becomes the nine- or ten-year-old who sees the security of the relationship slipping away. But by now, the parents have stopped talking about the adoption and no longer are giving the child any reassurances. Brodzinsky and his colleagues urge that parents not stop the revelation process too soon. They point out that it is not the information given by parents, but the child's capacity for understanding it that is the key to successful adjustment to adoption.

havior among newborns in a hospital nursery, hormones might be expected to play a larger role—although not to the exclusion of the infants' prenatal environments and the circumstances of their deliveries. In the case of new-

borns, a biological level of explanation may help psychologists to look at an aspect of development in a new way. But focusing on any one influence—or even a pair of influences—can cause them to lose sight of the context in which all children live their lives. When drawing on findings from other fields, it is always essential to integrate the information into the picture of human development at the level at which behavior is influenced.

Interpretation of Age Differences

The major concern of developmental psychologists is to understand the process that accounts for age-related differences between people as well as age-related differences within a single individual (**intraindividual differences**). In addition, developmentalists are interested in differences between individuals of the same age (**interindividual differences**). As individuals go through life, such differences among them increase, so that the differences among seventy-year-olds are greater than the differences among forty-five-year-olds, who are in turn much less alike than twenty-year-olds. Why do people become less alike as they age? Paul Baltes, Hayne Reese, and Lewis Lipsitt (1980) have divided the factors responsible for age and individual differences into age-normative, history-normative, and non-normative influences. **Age-normative influences** affect almost everyone in a society at about the same time in life. They may be biological, such as starting to walk or reaching puberty, or social, such as education or retirement. Because they are highly associated with age, they contribute to age differences. Age-normative influences are strongest in infancy and childhood, probably because genetic programs are more powerful during those years.

History-normative influences are historical events that affect everyone who is alive at the time they occur, but that affect people of different ages in different ways. History-normative influences include wars, depressions, technological advances like television or the automobile, and medical improvements like vaccines or antibiotics. Because they affect all individuals who are at developmentally sensitive periods in their lives, they also contribute to age differences. Their influence is probably strongest on adolescents and young adults.

Finally, **non-normative influences** are specific to individuals and bear little relationship to age. They include physical influences, such as accidents and disease, and social influences, such as the divorce of a child's parents or a move from one state to another. Because non-normative events are unique to the individual, they bear a good deal of the responsibility for the widening of interindividual differences with age. Non-normative influences become increasingly powerful as individuals grow up and age, probably because these influences tend to pile up while age-normative influences are declining in strength.

Although individuals become less and less alike as they progress through life, most research reports deal only with differences among groups. Investigators generally summarize their work with general statements describing what was found to be true on the "average." But some children or adults in almost every experiment behave or develop in a way that is different from that of the majority. For example, William Rohwer's (1971) study of children's learning showed that categorically organized lists are easier to remember than randomly organized lists. That is, the list "car, boat, plane; chair, table, bed" is easier to remember than the list "car, bed, table; plane, chair, boat." Most elementary-school children will look at the first list and think "three things to ride in, three pieces of furniture," which helps them recall the individual items. Some children, however, do not use categories to help them remember and thus recall as few items from the first list as from the second.

Developmental psychologists acknowledge that the results shown for most people do not apply to all individuals. Thus one can say that elementary-school children are likely to use categories to help them remember lists, even if all children do not use the strategy. But individual differences are not simply annoyances that obscure the orderly, predictable behavior of a group. Differences may be the result of some inborn predisposition or of certain environmental influences or of a combination of the two effects, and learning the reason for their appearance can help us further understand the way development proceeds.

Studying individual variations in behavior may also provide clues about the many possible ways of behaving in the same situation. Children who learn to read successfully in the first grade seem to do so in a variety of ways. Choosing a single method to teach reading to less successful readers has been nearly impossible because no one method has been successful with all children who have reading problems. Studies of children with reading difficulties indicate that some of these children have trouble sounding out letters, some divide the words they are trying to read improperly, some are quite slow at recalling letter sounds or memorized words, and some have trouble blending letters they have sounded out individually (Farnham-Diggory, 1978). Individual differences in the way children approach reading are only one example of normal variation.

The existence of individual differences does not keep developmental psychologists from making general statements about their results. Although individual exceptions exist, general statements are useful in practical as well as theoretical ways. As we consider the effect of various determinants on development, it is helpful to keep the prevalence of individual differences in mind.

GENETIC DETERMINANTS

Our heredity is of two kinds: the general inheritance of our species that makes us into that peculiar primate *Homo sapiens*, and our specific inheritance from our parents, grandparents, and great-grandparents that makes each of us visibly and temperamentally different from other members of our species. Both inheritances are carried within our body cells, and in Chapter 3 we

This infant's resemblance to his grandmother demonstrates the transmission of specific genetic information that is not part of the general inheritance that accompanies membership in the human species. (© Michael Weisbrot & Family)

discuss in detail the ways in which genes transmit this hereditary information. Genes begin working on us at the moment of conception and continue their work until we die. They determine whether a child will be a boy or a girl; they determine the specific color of a person's eyes as well as the general fact that each member of the species has two eyes that can perceive various wavelengths of light; and they determine a person's susceptibility to certain types of diseases, such as diabetes.

Although the importance of genetic determinants is established, discovering specific genetic influences on behavior and development is a difficult task. Ethics forbids researchers to manipulate a human being's genetic structure. Nor is it ethical to select two people, ask them to mate and produce children, and subject their offspring to one environment or another in order to determine the kinds of behavior that might be attributed to genetic differences. How, then, do we know about the contribution of genetics to human behavior?

Genetic Studies with Animals

Most of our knowledge has come from research on lower animals, with which nearly ideal genetic research can be performed. Such studies can suggest general principles that alert us to possible genetic influences on human behavior.

By breeding genetically related animals, for example, researchers have discovered that genes go beyond dictating an animal's physical structure and play a role in its temperament and behavior. After testing rats on their ability to learn the path through a maze, R. C. Tryon (1940) interbred those rats that learned quickly. By repeating this process with the offspring, generation after generation, he developed a group of rats that were almost "purebred" for superior performance in mazes. And by interbreeding rats who had trouble finding their way through a maze, he developed another group that had enormous difficulty in learning the path. His research indicates that genes do indeed affect a rat's ability in maze learning. Similar studies have shown that genetic differences can also affect aggressiveness, hoarding, exploratory behavior, sex drive, alcohol preference, and a variety of other traits (McClearn, 1970).

Such inbred strains respond differently to events: an environment that will change the development of certain behavior in one strain of mice will have no effect on another strain, and the effect on a third strain will be opposite from its effect on the first strain (Scarr and Kidd, 1983). Since different strains of animals may respond differently to the same sort of experience, we know that it is impossible to predict the precise outcome of a particular learning experience for any animal or human being unless we know its genetic makeup—knowledge that is lacking outside the animal research laboratory.

Daniel Freedman's (1958) experiments on the connection between indulging or disciplining a young puppy and its later self-control provide an example of the effects of genes on experience. Freedman selected dogs from four different breeds: Basenji, Shetland sheepdog, wirehaired fox terrier, and beagle. The caretakers indulged some of the dogs from each breed between the third and eighth weeks of their lives by encouraging them to play, to be aggressive, and to engage in rough-and-tumble activities. In contrast, the caretakers disciplined other dogs from each breed by restraining them, teaching them to sit, stay, come on command, and so forth. After this training, each dog was tested. When it was hungry, its caretaker took it into a room containing a bowl of meat. For three minutes the caretaker prevented the animal from eating by hitting it on the rump with a rolled newspaper and shouting "No!" every time the dog approached the food. Then the handler left the room and the experimenter recorded the length of time that elapsed before the dog ate the meat.

Some theories of development might lead to the conclusion that an overindulged dog will not be able to inhibit its impulse to eat in such a test. But the results of eight days of testing indicate that such a prediction is not valid for dogs. In two breeds, the terriers and the beagles, the indulged animals waited longer before approaching the food than did their disciplined companions. Neither the indulged nor the disciplined Shetlands ever ate the food; but all the Basenjis dug right into the meal. Had Freedman studied only terriers and beagles, he would have assumed that environment determined self-control; had he studied only Shetlands and Basenjis, he would have assumed that genes determine it. But by using four breeds, he discovered that gene-environment interaction must always be considered, even in areas where our first assumption is that the environment is the overriding factor.

Momentary environmental circumstances may also affect the way that genetically influenced behavior is expressed or whether it appears at all. In many cases, hereditary behavior patterns appear only in the presence of a releasing stimulus. For example, Niko Tinbergen (1951) has observed that the male stickleback fish will attack a strange male stickleback only if the intruder is ready to mate, a condition revealed by a red belly. The fight that ensues looks natural and flexible, but the fish protecting its territory merely imitates the fighting characteristics of the intruder. If the intruder bites, the defender bites back; if it threatens, the defender threatens, and so on. The intruder's red belly releases the defender's attack, and each fighting thrust of the intruder releases a response that is identical to the stimulus. The result is an adaptive, natural, and flexible behavioral pattern, but its components are fixed patterns released by the specific stimuli of the intruder. Thus genetic behavior requires the appropriate environmental stimuli in order for it to appear. Although human behavior is unlikely to be influenced by such fixed patterns of action, some of our behavior that appears spontaneous may have genetic components. One such example is human caregiving, which, as we noted in Chapter 1, appears to be released by a baby's "cuteness."

We know, then, that genes may play a role in temperament and behavior, that their influence may extend to areas where we do not expect to find it, that it is impossible to predict the outcome of experience without knowing a person's genetic makeup, and that particular environmental circumstances are sometimes required for the appearance of genetically influenced behavior. Using such principles, researchers in **genetics,** the scientific study of the effects of heredity, have explored the role of genes in human development.

Human Genetics

Researchers ask two questions about the role of genes in human development: "How?" and "How much?" The question "How?" refers to the ways in which heredity interacts with the environment to produce development in all human beings. For example, how do genes combine with environmental factors, such as nutrition, to produce growth? Answers to the question "How?" come from studies of people in general. The question "How much?" refers to the sources of differences among individuals. How much of the differences in height among people in a developmental psychology class are dut to each student's different heredity (genetic effects) as distinguished from nutritional differences while the students were growing up (environmental effects)? Answers to the question "How much?" come from studies of the ways that people differ in their individual development. "How?" and How much?" are both important questions.

With our present knowledge, we cannot say exactly *how* genes affect behavior, but Sandra Scarr (1982; Scarr and McCartney, 1983) has proposed that the transmission could take the form of passive, evocative, and adaptive influ-

This child, who is growing up in a book-filled home, will probably enjoy reading. If so, his enjoyment may be the result of passive genetic influence. (Beryl Goldberg)

ences. **Passive genetic influence** exists in the home. Parents transmit genes to children, and they also provide environmental experience that is partly determined by parental genes. For example, some genetic influence has been found on reading ability. Parents who like to read and believe that reading is important are more likely to surround their children with books and read to them than parents who are uninterested in books. And because children share many of their parents' genes, the children of book-loving parents are more likely to be receptive to the books around them and to develop a love of reading themselves. Such passive genetic influence is strongest early in development. **Evocative genetic influence** refers to genetically influenced behavior on the part of the child that evokes particular responses from the social and physical environment that in turn influence the child. For example, temperament appears to be influenced by genetic makeup. A baby who likes to be cuddled, smiles a lot, and enjoys social interaction will be treated differently from a baby who is generally irritable, passive, or one who does not like to be cuddled. Evocative genetic influence is probably steady throughout the life span. Finally, **active genetic influence** refers to the sort of experiences people seek out. We cannot attend to all the stimuli in the world, so we actively ignore things we find boring, too easy, or too hard and select things that we find pleasant, interesting, or challenging. Our genetic makeup, believes Scarr, helps to determine those choices. Active genetic influence probably increases across the life span.

There are no genes that determine any specific behavior, so genes always influence behavior indirectly. They can work only by interacting with the environment through biochemistry and physiology. For example, genes may determine the structure of enzymes within individual cells (Scarr and Kidd, 1983). Hundreds of genes are probably involved in the development of any behavioral characteristic.

The timing of growth and aging and the sequence of development are, we know, related to gene action. Genes are "turned on" at some but not other points in development. The "turned-on" genes are active in producing substances within the body that create new structures, regulate their functions, or maintain their state. Many researchers in the field of biological aging believe that aging is also under the control of genes, whether due to a general developmental program that turns on genes responsible for physical aging, to gradual deteriorations in the genetic code, or to the programmed decrease of brain chemicals that may set off a hormonal imbalance (Walford, 1983).

Specifying just how heredity interacts with environment to affect growth and development in the human species is extremely difficult. The other important question, which asks *how much* genes affect the development of differences among individuals, is easier to answer. Although no one has yet been able to isolate a single gene that accounts for a substantial amount of the difference in normal behavior among people (Freedman, 1974), we do have conclusive answers for some abnormal physical traits caused by single genes, as will be clear in Chapter 3. In the case of such traits as height, we can get some idea of genetic influences by comparing the trait among related and unrelated people. The more closely people are related and the more similar the trait, the more likely it is that genetic factors have influenced the trait. Physical appearance is obviously influenced by genetic differences, because genetically related people resemble one another more than do unrelated people.

Yet even if two people have the same genes for a particular trait, it may not show itself in the same way. A person's genetic makeup, known as the **genotype,** is different from that same person's appearance and behavior, known as the **phenotype.** Each genotype has a unique range of possible phenotypic responses, called the **reaction range,** and the phenotype depends on the series of environments the person encounters over the course of development, beginning in the uterus. This means that different genotypes can produce phenotypes that are difficult to distinguish and that the same genotype will produce different phenotypes, depending on environmental conditions (Scarr and Kidd, 1983). Thus, the genotype specifies the reaction range, which limits the ways each of us can respond to specific environments, whether good or bad. In the case of height: good nutrition will make all of us taller than poor nutrition will, but given the same nutrition, some of us will be taller than others because of our genetic inheritance. The development of intellectual skills also has a reaction range: a stimulating environment will not make Albert Einsteins or Leonardo da Vincis of us all, nor will moderately deprived circumstances make us mentally retarded. In other words, genes do not specify a particular height or intelligence for anyone; they specify a range for development that depends on environmental factors. Our ultimate physical height and level of intellectual development depend on both genetic and environmental factors.

Heritability

We know that the individuals in any group have different genetic compositions as well as different life experiences. But how much of the variability in height or intellectual ability is associated with differences in their genetic makeup rather than with differences in their lives? The relative contribution of genetics to any trait in a given group is called the **heritability** of the trait. But heritability is only an estimate based on the number of cases in the particular group; it may or may not represent the heritability of that trait in the general population.

In general, the more restricted the environment, the higher the heritability of any trait. As environmental possibilities broaden, heritability decreases. Thus, because heritability depends on the specific characteristics of the sample, the heritability for a given trait may change from one year to the next, especially if the factors that produce that trait change. Years ago, for example, the heritability for tuberculosis was quite high. At that time, the bacillus for TB was widespread and nearly every individual

came into contact with it. Since all were exposed to the disease (same environment for this factor), whether one actually developed TB depended primarily on one's inborn biochemical susceptibility to that bacillus. In contrast, the TB bacillus is now present only in the most unsanitary circumstances, and many people who have a biochemical susceptibility to TB never come in contact with the bacillus. Thus the major determinant of whether one succumbs to TB is now exposure to the bacillus, not inborn susceptibility. Consequently, the heritability for TB is now quite low.

The cause of TB is the same today as it always was: the invasion of the TB bacillus in an individual with a biochemical susceptibility to that bacillus. But the heritability for TB has changed because getting the disease is now more closely associated with where one lives than with genetic predisposition. Therefore, the fact that a trait has a high heritability does not mean that genes cause it; nor does a low heritability mean that appearance of the trait is caused by environmental circumstances. Researchers (Scarr and Kidd, 1983) have suggested that the concept of heritability has so many limitations that it is difficult to apply in a meaningful way. It cannot tell us exactly what genetic influences are responsible for the appearance of the characteristic. It cannot predict how a person carrying the genetic predisposition will develop when placed in a different environment. And, depending on how the trait is defined, estimates of heritability will differ from study to study.

ENVIRONMENTAL DETERMINANTS

There is an old expression that genes set limits on development while environments determine what actually develops. This is only half the story. As we have seen, by responding to given environments in unique ways, genes help to determine the actual level of development. Environments are equally implicated in setting limits on development—by providing only certain opportunities and stimuli for a person to develop a particular characteristic or behavior. In an optimum environment, genetic factors are given full expression, unhindered by environmental constraints.

Even the most genetically oriented theorist would agree that environmental determinants play a powerful role in the development of the growing child. But the term "environment," which encompasses every influence, both physical and social, is too broad to have much scientific usefulness. It is always necessary to specify which features of any environment affect any particular behavior. To explain why some children achieve low scores on intelligence tests, for example, some environmentalists merely point to the obvious disparities between advantaged and disadvantaged homes, schools, and neighborhoods, claiming that (somehow) all the noticeable differences determine differences in test scores. However, there are various ways of defining the environment and of explaining how individual experience influences development. All such ways can sometimes be useful and sometimes inappropriate, depending on the behavior that we are trying to explain.

Physical Factors

It is obvious that all organisms must have sufficient air, water, food, and light to maintain life. Without these, there is biological deterioration and even death. What is not so obvious is the extent to which other features of the physical environment affect the course of development. For example, the environment of the mother's uterus is critical to the survival and development of the fetus, which requires an efficient exchange of oxygen and nutrients and the elimination of wastes. If the maternal environment is deficient in nutrients such as calcium or protein, the infant's development will be stunted. Or the maternal environment may be crowded: short mothers have small and prema-

ture babies more often than tall mothers do, and twins are often so crowded that they are born prematurely. As Chapter 3 explains, the maternal physical environment has other important effects on fetal development.

Once out of the uterus, children live in a physical environment that wraps them in a metaphorical rather than a literal capsule. The physical features of their world—both natural and man-made—limit and determine their development. Life in a nomad's tent and life in a city apartment have different effects on a growing child.

Just how potent the physical context can be is illustrated by a study of the effects of loud noise on children's development. Sheldon Cohen, David Glass, and Jerome E. Singer (1973) studied children who lived in a thirty-two-story apartment building located over a noisy expressway in Manhattan. As one went from the lower to the higher floors of the building, the noise level dropped. Cohen and his associates found that children who had lived at least four years on the lower, noisier floors were less able to tell the differences between subtle but contrastive speech sounds, such as "gear-beer" or "cope-coke," than children who lived on the higher, quieter floors. They also found that children who lived on the lower floors read less well than those on the higher floors. Both auditory discrimination and reading ability correlated highly with the noise levels in the apartments and the length of time the children had lived there. Although other factors may have been involved in the children's ability to hear or read well, the study seems to show that the physical environment can affect physical and mental abilities in a multitude of ways.

The physical environment comprises more than a child's home or the wider world he or she walks through. It includes the internal environment as well, with its changing body chemistry, which is continually altered by the intake of food or medication. A boy who has been diagnosed as hyperactive and who therefore takes a stimulant drug four times a day

The physical aspects of the environment have potent effects on the growing child; each of these environments offers some experiences to children and denies them others. (Michal Heron/ Woodfin Camp & Associates, above; Jim Anderson/Woodfin Camp & Associates, left)

reacts to experiences in a changed way and, as we shall see in Chapter 6, may not recall, when off the drug, what he learned under its influence. Hunger, thirst, pain, the presence of harmful bacteria or viruses, the malfunctioning of a gland or organ, can all affect the way a child responds to events, and serious disturbances of the internal environment can have lasting effects.

Social Factors

The social environment includes all those effects that people have on one another—in families, in peer groups, and in neighborhoods. It also encompasses the influences of social institutions, such as schools; cultural and subcultural values, attitudes, and beliefs; the media, such as newspapers and television; and technological innovations, such as computers. As children grow and develop, their social involvement with their environment increases, and as we shall see throughout this book, the nature of their social experience has an impact on the total developmental process.

THE FAMILY Most children grow up in the context of a family—father, mother, perhaps brothers and sisters. The family is generally the first social unit with which a child comes in contact, and it has been shown to influence many aspects of behavioral development: sex roles, self-concepts, and interpersonal and intellectual skills. Today the family is viewed as a system in which influences do not travel in a single direction. Instead they flow back and forth between family members. Over a long period of time the mutual influence, as child reacts

When fathers are highly involved in the care of their children, their sons tend to be quite masculine and daughters quite feminine. (Jane Scherk/Jeroboam)

to parent who reacts to child, can set up a cycle that can be either benign or destructive (Maccoby, 1984). In addition, the quality of the relationship between a child's parents affects a toddler's emotional and cognitive development, with the father's attitude toward the marriage perhaps having especially powerful effects upon daughters (Goldberg and Easterbrooks, 1984). Reviews of paternal impact suggest that fathers affect the development of sex roles in both boys and girls, leading boys to be more masculine and girls to be more feminine. Contrary to what we might expect, the most masculine boys and the most feminine girls tend to have nurturant fathers who participate extensively in child rearing (Lamb, 1981).

Siblings also play an important part in sex-role development, and again the effect may be different from what we might expect. For example, the more sisters there are in a family, the greater the masculinity of all the girls. And in families with only two children, a girl with an older brother tends to be more feminine than a girl with a younger sister. As for boys, a boy who has an older sister tends to be more masculine than a boy with a younger sister (Sutton-Smith, 1982). It has been suggested that these effects result from children's efforts to handle sibling rivalry (Schachter, 1982).

Families also provide a context for intellectual development. The opportunities that are available to children and the way that the parents respond to their curiosity affect what the children learn and how rapidly they learn it. If there are many children in the family, their intellectual skills tend to be less well developed than those of children in smaller families (Falbo, 1984). Birth order also has an effect: first-born children and those early in birth rank tend to have higher scores on intelligence tests than children born later. The effects of family size and birth order seem to come about in part because later-born children have fewer opportunities to act as teachers to younger siblings, a process that stimulates cognitive development in the child-teacher, and in part because parents of a large family provide a less stimulating intellectual atmosphere, perhaps because they pay less attention to any one child (Zajonc, Markus, and Markus, 1979). Although this explanation is controversial (Rodgers, 1984), a dilution of parental attention may be responsible for the lower intelligence test scores of twins as compared to those of single children. When there are twins to care for, the amount or quality of attention that parents can give to each one seems to diminish.

PEERS Peers affect behavior from early school age throughout the life span. When children go to nursery school, kindergarten, or first grade, they move partly out of the family world into the environment of the peer group. The peer group usually has its own values and rules of behavior, which may differ radically from those of the family. Especially important is the atmosphere of the peer group, which is relatively egalitarian and allows children to interact with equals instead of superiors (parents, teacher, older siblings) or inferiors (younger siblings) (Hartup, 1983).

Although peer influence is powerful from early childhood, by adolescence the peer group is especially important; it provides a sense of belonging that meets a child's social needs and facilitates his or her psychological growth (Newman, 1982). It also provides a central testing ground for becoming a person. Because one cannot go through life being "Mama's boy" or "Daddy's girl," one has to establish other identifications and goals. Adolescent peers are decidedly important in the development of a sense of identity (Erikson, 1968). Because peers share the problems of establishing independence and identity, they provide positive support in the often painful process of becoming an adult.

THE NEIGHBORHOOD Over the years it has been found that many features of a neighborhood influence its structure and function, affecting the development and behavior of the people who live there. In close-knit, active

The peer group plays a unique role in children's development; because all members are about the same age, children have an opportunity to interact with their equals. (Barbara Alper)

neighborhoods, children use the sidewalks to get acquainted, to meet their friends, and to play. Such neighborhoods provide a setting that encourages contacts. But if street traffic is dense and rapid, the sidewalks cannot be used as social areas and the neighborhood is less likely to be friendly. Similarly, unless the space near or around buildings is open to view and hence "defensible" (capable of supervision), people will not use it for play, recreation, or socializing.

In addition, the ethnic flavor, socioeconomic level, and age range of the inhabitants can radically affect the growing child. School-age children who live near a college, for example, are likely to have fewer playmates their own age than children who live farther from the campus. Similarly, for a young child, life in an area predominantly inhabited by retired people will be very different from life in an area inhabited by young families.

Although neighborhoods tend to shape the

development and activity of residents, residents also shape the activity of neighborhoods. If, for example, a major change occurs in the ethnic background, age, interests, or life style of neighborhood residents, major changes in neighborhood events or projects are likely to follow.

THE SCHOOL Schools socialize children in many of the same ways that families and peer groups do. Although for years the effects of schools on social and emotional development went unrecognized, today developmentalists generally agree that schools influence social skills, psychological growth, and children's feelings about the rules and regulations of society. Schools can be either a positive or a negative influence, depending on the child's early experience, classroom practices, and the structure of the general school environment (Busch-Rossnagel and Vance, 1982). When children enter school, they face new demands—demands that

By the time these children start school, they will have had six years of exposure to television, so that they will begin their academic careers with a very different background from that of six-year-olds of 1930, when preschool influence was largely limited to the family and neighborhood (© Camilla Smith)

they support their peers, reduce their pleasure, find satisfaction in the completion of tasks, and become industrious (Gump, 1978). Such requirements may have an important influence on their feelings of competence and on the way they regard themselves and others. As a result of their school experience, children may become self-directed, skillful in personal interaction, and able to accept group norms, or they may become increasingly passive, conforming, and dependent.

In addition, the school staff sets standards of conduct and values that may not be the same as those of the children's families and friends. Notable problems have arisen when the school represents an alien middle-class white world in the middle of a culturally different neighborhood. In large cities, ethnic groups have demanded more control over what their children are taught in school, because they believe that the established curriculum (and perhaps the staff) is irrelevant to their particular needs and values. In other places, fears that the curriculum's inclusion of certain subjects—such as sex education or evolution—threatens cherished values have led parents to demand similar control. In such circumstances, the influence of school may be different from that in communities that are content with the staff and curriculum and believe that success in school is a necessary prelude to success in life.

THE MEDIA All media affect behavior—for good or for bad. But the most pervasive medium in today's society is television; it is virtually impossible for a child to grow up without being exposed to heavy doses of it. Surveys indicate that 99 percent of all families with children own television sets, and most children spend from one-fifth to one-third of their waking hours before the flickering screen (Murray and Kippax, 1979).

Because young children are likely to get most of their information about the world from television, the medium has a powerful effect on social attitudes. It appears to socialize children as consumers, even when it does not carry commercials, perhaps because images on the screen of visible and tangible objects lead children to focus on consumption (what they will "have" in the future) (Greenfield, 1984). Television can also intensify sex-role and racial stereotypes or break them down, depending on the content of programs. The continuing controversy over the effects of televised violence has not been settled, although the majority of studies indicate a link between viewing violent television shows and later aggressive behavior in children (Rubinstein, 1983). Watching moderate amounts of violence on television may not trigger aggressive behavior in most children, but a heavy diet of violent television programs appears to influence violence-prone youngsters toward more aggression (Eron et al., 1983).

The structure of television programs may influence the way children process information. Researchers (Greenfield, 1984) have suggested that the quick changes of scene and continual movement require children to process information rapidly, without reflecting on it, and that television's reliance on images to convey most information may lead children to adopt a vague verbal style that is adequate for face-to-face conversation but can induce misunderstanding in written communication.

Certainly children learn from television, whether or not a program is explicitly educational, and educational programs have been particularly successful. "Sesame Streeet" and "The Electric Company" are designed to teach number and letter skills and reading to disadvantaged children, and studies consistently indicate that children who would have difficulty acquiring the skills at school do pick them up from these programs (Lesser, 1974). But the programs are unlikely to close the education gap between advantaged and disadvantaged children. Middle-class children also watch these programs, and they seem to benefit as much as the children for whom the programs were devised. As a result, widespread watching of educational television maintains the greater literacy of advantaged children over disadvantaged children.

TECHNOLOGY Technological advances can cause widespread changes in society and in the way children develop. Such history-normative events as the introduction of the printing press, the automobile, and television have had profound effects on individual development and on the way people experience the world. Computers appear to be causing another such revolution. Today's children are growing up in a world that is increasingly penetrated by computer technology, and more and more schools and homes have acquired personal computers. The adult lives of today's children may be as different from their grandparents' world as the automobile-dominated world of the mid-twentieth century differed from the horse-dependent world of the nineteenth.

The great difference between computers and television is the interaction that is basic to computer use. Instead of passively watching a program, the child can alter what is happening on the screen. However, if the computer is limited to learning software, in which education is carried on almost as usual, with the child following programmed instructions, change may be minimal. But if children are taught powerful programming languages, suggests Seymour Papert (1980), their way of processing information will change so drastically that it will affect the way all other learning takes place. There will be new possibilities for learning, thinking, and emotional as well as cognitive growth. Papert, whose work combines Piagetian theory with computer science, believes that children who learn a language like LOGO are placed in a new kind of relationship to the domain of mathematics, an alteration that puts ways of thought now available only to adolescents and adults within the grasp of children.

CULTURE It is easy to forget that what seems true or natural to an American may seem false or unnatural to people in other cultures, and vice versa. People raised in Baghdad or Botswana or Bolivia, for example, are very different from those raised in Boston.

When children use computers, they are interacting with the machine instead of passively watching, as they do when watching television. If they also write their own programs, they may make impressive cognitive gains. (Richard Sobol/Stock, Boston)

The influence of culture begins the moment a child is born, and it shapes much of human behavior—from the way people dress and relate to others to the way they think and solve problems and the things they believe and value. Even appropriate male and female behavior varies widely among cultures.

In some cultures, mothers and fathers have little to do with the rearing of their children; cultural practices and beliefs are passed on by others, such as brothers or sisters, or older unrelated children or adults who have been given the child-rearing function.

Also, within cultures there are subcultural variations related to ethnic background, social class, and economic status—all of which influence how a person develops. For example, in the United States, ethnic and social-class differences often predict an individual's wealth, education, and intelligence test scores. This relationship exists because there are class differences in parents' education and worklives, in neighborhoods and housing, and in the economic situation of families (Radke-Yarrow, Zahn-Waxler, and Chapman, 1983). Children in middle- or upper-class families are more likely to feel that they have the chance and ability to shape their own futures. But lower-class children and adolescents may be "street-wise" and better able than middle- or upper-class children to survive should they suddenly be cast out on their own resources.

Interaction of Determinants

All the influences we have discussed are powerful, but none of them works in isolation. Genetic, physical, and social factors are intertwined in every aspect of development. In an **ecological approach** to development, Urie Bronfenbrenner (1979) has highlighted this continually changing process. He proposes that descriptions of developmental influence must include the active, growing child, the child's changing physical and social settings, the relationship among those settings, and the way the entire process is affected by the society in which the settings are embedded. When reading about the influence of schools (or peers or parents or genes) on a child's development, we should recall that all of the other factors are simultaneously making a significant impact on the child. And we should also recall that the child's responses affect these determinants, altering their future influence.

STUDYING HUMAN DEVELOPMENT

Discovering just what factors affect any particular aspect of development is like solving an intricate puzzle. No single study in psychology—or any science for that matter—ever answers all relevant questions. A soundly designed and executed study can, at best, confirm or contradict our subjective judgment that a previous conclusion is correct. The best studies are objective, clear, reliable, and replicable. The final and most important test is **replication,** which establishes scientific findings by obtaining the same results in several investigations (the more, the better) conducted by different researchers in different places but using the same basic methods.

Sampling

The reliability of a study's results often depends on the nature of the **sample,** meaning the subjects of the study. If an investigator examines the development of concepts among children in a Kansas City suburb, for example, the results may show not what is typical for children in general but only how concepts develop in one group of middle-class American children. And if the investigator has limited his study to children in his own neighborhood, the results may not even be typical of middle-class American children. Similarly, the findings of a study about preschool development conducted at a private nursery school would not be equally valid for children who live in the inner city or in rural Appalachia.

Sex, age, ethnic background, and socioeconomic level are some of the factors that can bias the results of a study. In order to make sure that sex does not bias a study, for example, investigators either make sure they study an equal number of boys and girls or else study only girls or only boys, limiting generalization of their findings to one gender. Today, most researchers who study boys and girls together look at the responses of each gender separately and indicate in their reports whether major differences appeared that are related to gender.

Types of Studies

Any study, no matter what approach it utilizes, can study people once and then get out of their lives; or it can follow the same people over months or years, repeatedly observing or interviewing them, or subjecting them to various experiments. Each method has its own strengths and weaknesses.

CROSS-SECTIONAL DESIGN Much of the information we have concerning development comes from studies that compare different age groups, called **cross-sectional** studies. Such studies are common because they are relatively inexpensive and can be done quickly. Researchers generally assume that the differences found among such groups are the result of developmental change.

Often this is true. But the results obtained through a cross-sectional design may be invalidated by two major flaws. A cross-sectional design cannot detect the influence of history-normative experiences and it tells us nothing about changes within specific individuals. History-normative events affect members of each **cohort** (age group) differently, so that differences between age groups may not be the result of developmental change. For example, a cross-sectional study of the decline of intelligence test scores in later life might show a curve like that in Figure 2.1. The scores appear to decline with increasing age. Remember, however, that people studied at age eighty in 1975 were born in 1895, whereas those studied at age twenty in 1975 were born in 1955. Much happened to our cultural and social environment in the time between those two groups of cohorts, and sociocultural influences affect the development and maintenance of intellectual skills. In fact, there is good evidence that, as a nation, each new generation scores higher on intelligence tests—presumably because longer education and mass communications expose more people to the information and skills in abstract thinking required to score well on such tests. Younger cohorts score higher on the tests than older cohorts did at the same age. Thus what appears to be a dramatic decline in scores over age is in part an effect of the lower test scores for members of an older generation throughout their lives. Although age does affect test scores, it does not appear to have an influence that overshadows cohort effects until people are well past the age of eighty, when many abilities seem to decline in most people (Schaie, 1979).

Not all cross-sectional studies are flawed by cohort effects. If differences appear between close age groups—such as three- and four-year-olds, or even six- and ten-year-olds—it is unlikely that cohort effects are responsible, because the sociocultural environment generally changes slowly. With close age groups, it is more likely that differences are due to development.

The second limitation of cross-sectional studies is their inability to reveal changes within the individual. Because each person is tested only once, we are limited to information about differences between individuals. If we discover that the incidence of pretend play decreases

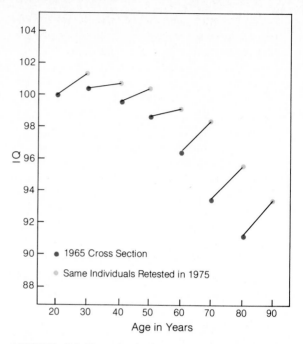

FIGURE 2.1 Hypothetical example illustrating apparent changes with age in IQ scores. The dots representing average scores of people at different ages tested in a cross-sectional study show a downward trend in IQ score with age. The dots representing average scores of these same samples of people tested again ten years later as part of a longitudinal study show a similar downward trend in IQ score with age, but each age group also shows an increase in the average score.

(Adapted from Nesselroade, J.R., K.W. Schaie, and P.B. Baltes. "Ontogenetic and Generational Components of Structural and Quantitative Change in Adult Behavior," *Journal of Gerontology*, 27, 1972, 222–228.)

after children reach the age of ten, we may have discovered an age-related developmental change, but we are dealing with group averages and still do not know how—or when—pretend play decreases in the case of a specific child (Baltes, Reese, and Nesselroade, 1977).

LONGITUDINAL DESIGN In contrast to cross-sectional studies, **longitudinal studies** follow people from the same cohort over time. The same people can be compared with themselves at ages twenty and eighty, so that the results are not affected by cohort differences and changes within the individual become apparent. One such study, begun in the 1920s by Lewis Terman, followed 1,528 gifted California school-children, reporting from time to time on how these extremely intelligent people developed and coped with life's problems. They were checked most recently in 1972, when the average age of the "children" was sixty-two (Sears, 1977).

Longitudinal studies may seem to be the answer to limitations in the design of cross-sectional studies, but they have their own problems. Long-term changes in behavior may be a response to historical changes in the culture as well as evidence of developmental change. Examples of recent shifts in the sociocultural environment are the changes wrought by movements devoted to establishing the civil rights of minorities, women, and homosexuals; the investigation of space; the dawning realization of the energy shortage; and the widespread acceptance of computers. Such historical shifts in social values, equality, and environment may have profound effects on some aspects of individual development.

Another serious problem is the fact that studying the same people repeatedly over many years may affect their development, and the continual testing may distort their behavior while taking part in the study—an influence known as the repeated testing, or **practice, effect.** In addition, when a study lasts for many years, not all participants are available until its end. Those who perform most poorly or are in frail health tend to drop out, so that the remaining individuals form a select group. Finally, longitudinal studies are expensive and time-consuming. Exploring developmental processes by this method requires a major commitment of time and funds by the researcher or sponsoring institution.

FINDING A MIDDLE GROUND Neither cross-sectional nor longitudinal studies alone can provide the basic data for developmental studies. Because of this, some researchers (Baltes, Reese, and Nesselroade, 1977) have proposed that the two designs be combined in what is known as a **sequential design.** Sequential designs may use either a cross-sectional or a longitudinal sequence as their basis. In the simpler, cross-sectional sequence, groups of two-, four-, six-, and eight-year-olds can be tested, then different groups of two-, four-, six-, eight-, and ten-year-olds are tested a number of years later. This procedure allows the researcher to estimate cohort and historical effects with some confidence that the performance of children in the second study is not influenced by practice. In addition, the problem of tracking down the children in the earlier sample is eliminated. In the longitudinal sequence, initial samples drawn at ages two, four, six, and eight can be followed for two years—until the two-year-olds are four, the four-year-olds are six, and so forth. And a final cross-sectional sample can be drawn at age ten to compare to the eight-year-olds in this longitudinal sequence, who would then be ten. (See Figure 2.2.) The effects of repeated testing, if any, will appear as differences between, for example, the starting scores for four-year-olds and the ending scores for the two-year-olds at age four. If the whole design is repeated some years later, cohort effects will appear; important shifts in the sociocultural environment will be revealed by higher or lower scores at all ages than the scores in the first study.

The advantage of combining the two designs becomes clear when we look at people's heights. Height measurements of a cross-sectional sample seem to indicate that people grow until middle adolescence and then begin to shrink. This "shrinkage" is due to cohort effects: people born a number of years ago are shorter on the average than people born more recently, and they were always shorter. A longitudinal study of people now in their seventies would show that they grew until late adolescence and then maintained their heights until late adulthood, when they may actually have shrunk a bit. A comparative longitudinal study of a younger cohort would find them reaching maximum growth at an ear-

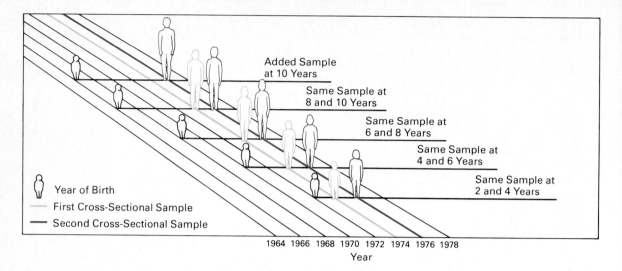

Added Sample
at 10 Years

Same Sample at
8 and 10 Years

Same Sample at
6 and 8 Years

Same Sample at
4 and 6 Years

Same Sample at
2 and 4 Years

Year of Birth

First Cross-Sectional Sample

Second Cross-Sectional Sample

1964 1966 1968 1970 1972 1974 1976 1978
Year

FIGURE 2.2 A research design that combines cross-sectional and longitudinal research. First, samples of children at each of four ages (two, four, six, and eight) are selected and studied. Two years later the same samples of children are studied again, and another sample of ten-year-olds is included. Using both methods on the same group of children offsets the weaknesses inherent in each type of study.

lier age; because of better nutrition, they are both taller and earlier-maturing than older cohorts. When studying height, it is necessary to separate developmental changes from pervasive historical changes. When studying other factors, it would also be important to separate developmental change from the effects of repeated measurements. Sequential designs can be so expensive and time-consuming that they are used infrequently. They are most likely to be selected for the study of babies or young children, when rapid development allows age-related changes to appear quickly. Because sequential designs are often impossible to apply, investigators who use cross-sectional or longitudinal designs can minimize the misinterpretation of their results by remaining sensitive to the factors that affect the study design they have chosen.

Research Approaches

The research approach selected by investigators depends upon the process being studied. Suppose we are interested in the relationship between chilren's play and the establishment of sex roles—that is, the culturally prescribed pattern of behavior for each gender. How would we go about discovering the connection? Jan Carpenter and Aletha Huston-Stein (1980) chose **naturalistic observation** to tease out the relationship. They watched nursery school children at play, noting the kind of activity (dolls, blocks, swings, play dough, etc.) children chose, when they complied with a teacher's suggestion, when they made novel use of play material, and how often the teacher guided or commented on a child's play. Many studies had shown that young children tend to play with toys designed for their own gender and that such play probably strengthened sex roles, but Carpenter and Huston-Stein believed that it was not the sex-role-related aspects of the toys but the structure that was responsible. For example, playing house is a highly structured activity, because children fit their play into structures provided by others. But sand box play is low in structure, for there are no guidelines; children provide their own structure. Sure enough, they found that girls spent more time than boys in play that

By using naturalistic observation, researchers discovered that children who prefer unstructured activities, such as sand box play, may become more independent than children who prefer highly structured play, such as playing house. (Alan Carey/The Image Works)

was highly structured, either by teachers' comments or by models at home whom they could imitate, and that boys spent more time in low-structure play, play that teachers generally ignored and that could not be patterned after the behavior of adults in the home. Further, the degree of compliance or originality in play bore a relation not to the children's gender but to the degree of structure in their play activities. Boys playing in highly structured situations tended to be compliant; girls playing in low-structured situations tended to find novel uses for toys. The investigators concluded that the degree of structure of their typical activities teaches boys and girls different skills, and that through such activities girls learn to be passive and boys to be aggressive and independent.

Carpenter and Huston-Stein could have sought their answers in other ways. For example, they might have interviewed the children and teachers; or they might have introduced some element into the nursery-school play situation and watched the children's responses; or they might have brought the children to a laboratory, where they had placed carefully selected toys, arranged so that children would have to respond in particular ways.

Distinctions among the methods for collecting information on human development center on how much **control** the investigator has over (1) the selection of subjects for study, (2) the specific experience the researcher wants to study, and (3) the possible responses subjects can give to that experience. At one extreme is the simple, naturalistic observation chosen by Carpenter and Huston-Stein, in which the children behaved naturally in their own environment without any interference from the investigators. At the other extreme is the **experiment,** which allows the investigator to control all three aspects of the study. Carpenter and Huston-Stein apparently felt that the advantages of watching children at natural play outweighed the advantages of having carefully selected subjects play-ing in a tightly controlled situation. Between the two extremes are **clinical studies** and types of **field studies,** where some but not other types of control are possible. Each research approach has its own place in the investigation of devel-opment.

EXPERIMENTATION An experiment gives the investigator the greatest amount of control over the situation, which can be contrived to eliminate influences that might be present in natural settings. Researchers examine the effect of selected factors or events on a child's behav-ior. These factors are called **variables,** and in an experiment, the researcher controls and manip-ulates the variable under study. The variable that is selected or changed in some way by the investigator is called an **independent variable.** The factor that changes as a result of the inde-pendent variable's introduction is called a **de-pendent variable.** For example, if we wanted to measure the effect of hunger on a baby's atten-tion, we would test the baby just before the next feeding was due. In this experiment, the independent variable would be the length of time since the last feeding; the dependent vari-able would be the length of time the hungry baby watched a display. If we then compared this time with the length of time the baby watched a display when *not* hungry, we would know something about the effects of hunger on attention.

Studying behavior through the experimental method has been used successfully in thousands of psychological studies. In one experiment, Lizette Peterson (1983) explored the factors that affect the likelihood of one child helping another in an emergency. The subjects were one hun-dred first-, fourth-, and sixth-graders who were taking part in a gambling game, in which each child played the game alone in a room with the researcher. Some of the children were told that the rotating wheels that selected the winning number often became stuck and that freeing them was a matter of simply loosening the cen-

ter bolt. While the researcher was out of the room, children heard the sounds of the wheels turning on a game in the next room, followed by cries of pain from a child who apparently had caught a finger in the wheel. Sometimes another child was supposedly in the room with the child in trouble; sometimes the distressed child was clearly alone. The older the child, the more likely he or she was to come to the aid of a peer in distress. Children who were perceived to be alone were aided more often than those who were believed to have a companion. And children who had been told about problems with the wheel and how to fix them were much more likely to help out than children who had not been instructed in how to free the mechanism. In this experiment, competency (instruction in manipulating the wheel) and the presence of an additional child were the independent variables; coming to the aid of the child in distress was the dependent variable. And in this study, the independent variables interacted, as factors af-fecting development often do. Competence had a very small influence on a child's decision to help when a third child was believed to be pres-ent, but a very large influence on a child's de-cision to help when the distressed child was believed to be alone. Peterson's results repli-cated findings in other experiments that, whether adult or child, a person is less likely to come to a person's aid when another possible source of aid is present. She also showed a de-velopmental trend in the tendency to give assis-tance, and the control provided by the experi-mental situation allowed her to discover the information in an efficient and convincing man-ner.

Despite their advantages, experimental stud-ies are not perfect. Because such studies are often conducted in laboratories, the subjects of the experiment may not respond to the situation as they would in a familiar setting. At one time, for example, it was widely believed that when they were about eight months old, all babies developed a fear of strangers. Later it was dis-covered that although babies might indeed be afraid of strangers in the unfamiliar surroundings of a laboratory, most babies showed much less fear when encountering a stranger in their own homes (Tracy, Lamb, and Ainsworth, 1976). In this case, the variable the researchers were changing in order to study infants' reactions (the stranger) had less influence on their subjects than the variable that remained constant (the laboratory itself). Unless investigators take seriously the systematic effect that surroundings have on children's responses, their experiments will demonstrate less about development than they believe.

The second pitfall in experimental studies comes from the rigid control that is also their virtue. Because the researcher designs the experiment so that he or she can control as many variables as possible, the situation may have no counterpart in the child's world. For example, the children who came to the aid of a peer in distress were in a situation in which they could hear, but not see, the hurt child, a situation that might lessen the tendency to help, and they had no other responsibilities at the time, a circumstance that might make them more likely to give aid. As Peterson (1983) points out, a study that was conducted in a familiar setting where the distressed youngster was clearly visible would be more applicable to children's behavior in daily life. When the experimental situation is too far removed from life, the results, although valid within the confines of the experiment, may be typical only of situations children never encounter in the world and thus bear little resemblance to their natural behavior.

Experimental studies often use animals because researchers can manipulate their subjects' environments in ways that are neither desired nor tolerated with human beings, and the knowledge derived can sometimes be applied to children. For example, raising baby monkeys in isolation has increased our understanding of the human baby's crucial need for close contact with a caregiver.

We cannot transfer the findings of animal research directly to the social development of children. However, social behavior among primates—including human beings—often seems to serve similar functions, just as the very different wings of butterflies and bats enable both to fly. Rhesus monkeys that had spent the first six months of their lives in total isolation and developed extremely abnormal behavior were rehabilitated by young monkey "therapists"— by the companionship of a monkey much younger than themselves (Suomi and Harlow, 1972); but isolated monkeys that were placed with peers or adult monkeys failed to show the same improvement. These studies show that early experiences of severe deprivation can be partially overcome, and they therefore hold out hope for human children who have been severely deprived—such as children who are occasionally discovered after having been shut away for years in prisonlike rooms by abusive parents. In a less severe situation, the example of the young monkey therapists was used to help socially withdrawn preschoolers (Furman, Rahe, and Hartup, 1979). Play sessions with younger children tended to bring withdrawn preschoolers out of their isolation and back into interaction with their peers.

Yet caution in applying the results of research with a single species of monkey directly to human beings was underscored by later research. When other species of monkeys were raised in total isolation, all showed some kind of behavioral disturbance, but the effect varied from one type of monkey to the next, making the interaction of genes and environment clear (Sackett et al., 1981). Pigtailed macaques who are raised in isolation show almost normal individual behavior but are extremely abnormal when placed with other monkeys, whereas crab-eating macaques show almost normal social behavior— although their individual behavior is aberrant.

If we are careful not to make direct applications, however, we can learn from animal studies where to look for possible effects in human situations. For example, another study with monkeys may aid researchers who study the effect of fathers on the development of young children. Stephen Suomi (1977) housed monkey families in cages that confined the parents to the family home but allowed the offspring to travel

The Ethics of Research with Children

When studying human behavior, researchers often intervene in people's lives in some way. Without such research, we would know little about human development and would be unable to test theories or to devise effective means of intervening when development goes awry. But developmental research is just as much an environmental experience as are incidents in daily life. Suppose a researcher wants to learn about the effects of repeated failure on children's self-concept. If children are subjected to situations in which they fail because of the researcher's manipulations, they are suffering the same consequences as a child who encounters failure in the outside world.

Aware that research can lead to invasions of privacy and sometimes to social, physical, and psychological risks, developmental psychologists, institutions, and the federal government have taken steps to ensure that developmental research has no harmful consequences for children. The National Commission for the Protection of Human Subjects of Biomedical and Behavioral Research (1977), Division 7 (Developmental Psychology) of the American Psychological Association (1968), and the Society for Research in Child Development (1975) have set guidelines for researchers that are meant to protect children who participate in any sort of study.

In addition, at most universities or hospitals an institutional review board reviews all proposed research to determine whether taking part in the research would place a child at risk. These review boards may approve the research or allow it to continue with some modification of procedure. Without the approval of the review board, researchers are unable to obtain government funding for their research.

The concerns of developmentalists and government alike are safety, consent, permission to withdraw, confidentiality, and full disclosure. In the matter of safety, any possible risk children might run must be acceptable in terms of probable benefits—either to the children themselves or to other children in the future. Where risk exists, procedures are devised to minimize it. For example, an investigator who subjected children to failure would, after gathering the data, place the children in situations that guaranteed success so that the experiment would not leave any child feeling helpless or incompetent.

Before children take part in studies, the consent of at least one parent or someone who serves in a parentlike role is required. If the child is at least seven years old, the child's consent is generally sought as well. And should a child of any age object to taking part, the child is excused—unless the research provides necessary and beneficial treatment that is unavailable elsewhere (Cooke, 1982). Permission to withdraw in the middle of the experiment must also be given, so that a child who becomes frightened or embarrassed can leave without fuss. Infants have an easy way of accomplishing withdrawal: they simply burst into tears, making further research impossible.

In order to maintain privacy, the researcher

freely from cage to cage. Monkey fathers played with both their sons and their daughters and with visiting young males; but they refused to play with visiting females. They were more hostile toward visiting monkeys of both sexes than toward their own offspring, and they showed least hostility toward their own daughters. The net effect of the fathers' behavior was to encourage the visits of male infants and to curtail the visits of female infants. If adult males in the

is expected to keep in confidence all information concerning children who participate in a study (and their parents). When discussing the project informally or making oral or written reports, the researcher conceals the identity of those who take part in the study. Such precautions protect the children and their families from embarrassment or legal complications.

The study is supposed to be carried out in an atmosphere of openness and honesty. The investigator is expected to tell the child's parents (and in some cases the child) about all aspects of the research that might affect their readiness to take part, and to answer all their questions so they can understand the consequences of their participation. When the study is complete, the investigator is expected to tell the parents (and in some cases the child) about the purpose and uses of the research and to clarify any misconceptions that may have arisen.

What about deception? Concealment or deception is permitted if the investigator can satisfy the review board (or a committee of peers if there is no official review board) that the practice is necessary, but participants must understand the reasons for the concealment or deception (Society for Research in Child Development, 1975). Most studies do not require deception; a survey indicated that children were told things that were not true in only 7 percent of behavioral studies (Cooke, 1982). In the study reported in this text that explored children's propensity to come to the aid of a child in distress, deception was used. No child was ever in distress; all the sobs and cries were coming from a tape recorder. But had the children known this, there would have been no experiment. When this study was completed, Lizette Peterson (1983) debriefed the children, talking about what had happened and discussing the reasons a child might or might not intervene in such a case. She had obtained previous written permission from the children's parents for the children to take part in the study and all children who participated had volunteered to do so.

The standards that have been established are meant to protect participants while still making possible the discovery of new knowledge about human beings. Not everyone agrees that children should take part in research meant simply to advance our knowledge of human development. The extreme position is that no research with children is ethically permissible unless it directly benefits the children who take part in it (Ramsey, 1977). In this view, children are never able to give informed consent, thus they cannot participate. But others (McCormick, 1976) believe that whenever research has any possible future benefits (such as research exploring developmental processes), children are obligated to take part, since such participation expresses basic human values. Neither position is held by a majority of researchers, and most believe that as long as children are protected, such research is ethical because it benefits all children and is usually without risk.

wild behave in a similar fashion, their actions would encourage males to be independent and free-ranging and girls to stay near their mothers, thereby establishing the nucleus for a stable social group. Suomi's findings may throw light on the work of researchers who are seeking to discover whether human fathers play a more important role in social development than traditional mother-oriented infant research has indicated.

NATURALISTIC OBSERVATION Human behavior is most appropriately studied by careful observation in natural settings, because people are more likely to behave naturally under these conditions. It was for this reason that Carpenter and Huston-Stein chose the method for exploring the connection between play and sex roles. In naturalistic observation, however, the investigator has less control than in any other method. Every variable is uncontrolled. Carpenter and Huston-Stein had no control over the socioeconomic level, ethnic group, or gender of children enrolled in the nursery school; nor could they control the toys that were available or the way the teachers interacted with the children or the children with each other.

The critical aspect of naturalistic observation is having explicit rules for categorizing and recording what the observer sees, so that the observations of two watchers will be comparable. If you have ever gone to a movie with several friends and disagreed afterward about the film's quality, plot, or motivation, you can appreciate the necessity of having observers in a research study see things the same way and record them in a like manner. If such a study is well conducted, valuable information can be gained about many aspects of child development.

Steve Sackin and Esther Thelen (1984) used naturalistic observation to study the way preschool children settled their conflicts. Half of the five-year-olds they observed were enrolled in a low-income day-care center, and the rest were from a middle-income day-care center. Their observations spanned a twelve-week period, in which they focused on a single child at a time, watching the youngster for thirty minutes during the free play period. Each child was observed for a total of five hours. In 200 hours of observation, the researchers recorded 215 conflicts and found that social class had no effect on the outcome. At both schools, most conflicts were settled with one child signaling submission and the pair of children then going their separate ways, a method of resolution likely to maintain the dominance hierarchy of the playgroup. This pattern characterized almost all the conflicts between boys and girls. But a substantial proportion of conflicts between children of the same sex were settled when one child made a conciliatory instead of a submissive gesture, and when this happened, the children continued to play peacefully together instead of separating. Because preschoolers tend to play in same-sex groups, suggest Sackin and Thelen, the conciliatory mode of settlement may be used when children need to keep amicable relations with youngsters who are their frequent companions. This study indicates that desirable social skills appear to develop in some children before they enter public school. The researchers suggest that further research be undertaken to determine whether children who learn conciliation early become popular with their peers.

The great advantage of naturalistic observation is, of course, its direct application to life. Its disadvantages lie in the lack of control. Variables investigators do not even consider can affect the results. One uncontrolled variable that may plague an observational study is the effect of the watching psychologist on the child's behavior. Children may behave differently if they know they are being observed. When children are studied in a laboratory, psychologists can watch through a one-way mirror; but outside the laboratory, it often becomes a matter of trying to be inconspicuous or of becoming so familiar to the children that one's presence is ignored.

FIELD STUDY Field studies also take place in natural social settings, but they differ from naturalistic observations in that the investigator introduces some factor into the natural situation that changes it. Field studies are not true experiments because the researcher can control only some aspects of the situation; but they are often more closely controlled than either observational or clinical studies.

In one field study, designed to explore the way group membership affects behavior, middle-class boys at a summer camp unwittingly participated in an elaborate situation (Sherif et al., 1961). The boys, who were placed in two groups, came to camp in separate buses and played, hiked, swam, and shared cabins only with members of their own group. After the boys had settled into the camp routine, psychologists pitted one group against the other, setting up tugs-of-war and baseball and football games. Soon the competition turned the groups into two warring tribes. They called each other names and raided each other's cabins. Fistfights broke out. Then the psychologists introduced two factors to change camp life. First, they cut the pipeline that brought water into the camp, so that all the boys had to work together to repair it. Next, they ran a truck loaded with food for an overnight hike into a ditch, so the boys had to pull together on a tow rope to get the vehicle back on the road. Cooperation dissolved the enmity between the two groups and the boys gradually became friends.

Few field studies are this complicated or this lengthy. For example, a researcher might simply introduce a highly unusual object into a play yard or have one child pretend to be in distress, then retire to observe how the children reacted to the strange sight or the unhappy child. Such control over the independent variable allows investigators to study important phenomena that cannot be brought into the laboratory, yet with more control than naturalistic observation permits. Except for this added control, however, field studies have the same advantages and disadvantages as naturalistic observation. The investigator may not have complete control over the experiences of the subjects or their reactions. Also, investigators generally cannot assign subjects randomly to one group or another. In order to interpret their results, they must be aware of ways in which comparison groups differ. And because they can never prove that all the differences between comparison groups have been identified, the results of field studies are often less certain than those of true experiments.

CLINICAL STUDY Clinical study often consists of in-depth interviews, frequently supplemented by observations and questionnaires. It may be controlled in a way that is not always possible in a field study; the same methods can be applied in a standardized way to each subject, or the psychologist can vary the approach with each subject. When a clinical study is designed with appropriate controls, it can yield interesting and important data. For example, a wealth of information on child rearing during infancy and the preschool years came from lengthy interviews with middle- and working-class mothers in New England. Robert Sears, Eleanor Maccoby, and Harry Levin (1957) studied how parents rear children, what effects different kinds of training have on youngsters, and what leads a mother to use one method rather than another. All mothers responded at length to seventy-two identical questions, but interviewers were free to probe deeply into any of the topics discussed.

Nearly four hundred mothers were interviewed in the New England study, giving researchers some confidence that they were not studying atypical families. A problem with many clinical studies is the small size of the sample. Exhaustive interviews are time-consuming and many clinical studies involve only a few subjects, so that generalization is often difficult.

The procedures for a controlled clinical study must be clearly and precisely defined; the investigator can improvise only in such matters as introducing the subject to the clinical situation or maintaining the subject's cooperation. Unless these actions are explicitly stated and controlled, they may bias the results of a study. For example, in his earlier studies, Jean Piaget (1952) talked freely with a child, asking whatever questions seemed necessary to reveal the child's concepts and thinking processes. Piaget was critical of standardized tests, but he later realized that differences in the way the questions were presented could affect his results. He chose an intermediate method, using a more standardized procedure in his later studies. By presenting the same questions to all children, Piaget gained a stronger basis for suggesting that the differences in children's responses at different ages are the result of actual changes in their cognitive activity.

Interpreting Statistics

Once investigators have obtained their results, they must interpret them. Various statistical measures have been devised for the purpose, and one commonly used tool is **correlation.** Correlation is a numerical expression of how closely two sets of measurements correspond. A correlation of .00 represents no direct relationship at all. For example, in the New England study of child rearing, the correlation between which parent established child-rearing policies and the family's general adjustment level was .00. This number implies that knowing which parent set policy tells nothing about the adjustment of the family.

The larger the correlation, the more closely two measures correspond, and the better one measure can predict the other. Correlations may vary from $+1.00$, a perfect positive relationship, to -1.00, a perfect negative relationship, but correlations generally fall at various places in between those figures. In the New England child-rearing study, for example, warmth on the part of the mother correlated $+.34$ with the amount of affectionate interaction with her baby and $+.37$ with a tendency to use reasoning in disciplining her child; but the correlation between maternal warmth and how highly she valued school achievement in her child was non-existent $(-.01)$. So we can say that a warm mother tends to be affectionate with her baby and to use reason as a disciplinary tool, but that she may or may not value school achievement. Although there was no correlation between which parent set child-rearing policies and the level of family harmony, the correlation between conflict over policies and level of family adjustment was $-.60$, indicating that when parents do not agree on these policies the family is rarely a harmonious one.

Correlations tell us what sorts of behavior go together, and the higher the positive correlation, the more confidently we can predict that one will be accompanied by the other. The higher the negative correlation, the more confident we can be that the two will not appear together. But correlation tells us nothing about causation. We do not know, for example, whether disagreement over discipline leads to an unhappy home or whether an unhappy home results in parents being unable to agree on discipline. In fact, both the unhappy home and the disagreement may be caused by a third factor we know nothing about.

A second frequently encountered statistic is that of **probability** (p), which indicates the likelihood that experimental findings are simply the result of chance. Probability is expressed in decimals, and a figure of .10 means that there is one chance in ten that the findings are meaningless; .50 means that the probability of a chance finding is one in two. When a researcher reports "significant" findings, it generally means the chances are not greater than one in twenty that they are the result of chance $(p \leq .05)$. In the New England study, 35 percent of the cold mothers had children with feeding problems, but only 11 percent of the exceptionally warm mothers had children with feeding problems. The probability that the link between coldness in a mother and feeding problems in her child was the result of chance was one in a hundred $(p \leq .01)$—a figure that researchers would feel warranted some attention. If researchers can get the measure of probability down to .001 (one chance in a thousand), they feel fairly certain of their results. However, results that are highly unlikely to have occurred by chance are not necessarily important. For example, when the sociability of eight-month-old infants was correlated with their performance on cognitive tests, the modest positive correlation was highly significant $(p \leq. 00001)$, but social responsiveness explained very few of the interindividual differences in cognitive scores (Lamb, Garn, and Keating, 1981).

As we follow the course of development from conception through adolescence, the information presented will be drawn from all the types of studies that have been considered. Some of these studies focus on one type of determinant and some on another, but few aspects of development depend on the influence of any single determinant. As the chapter has stressed, this continual interaction keeps simple explanations of development out of our grasp. Yet the intricate interplay of genes and environment, of the various levels of environment, and of the mutual influence between the child and other people provide a fascinating story that begins with conception.

SUMMARY

The study of human development is the study of change. In order to understand development, psychologists use information from biology, sociology, and anthropology as well as from psychology, integrating information at the appropriate level to explain any given behavior. Developmentalists are interested in differences between age groups, **interindividual differences,** and **intraindividual differences.** These differences may be the result of **age-normative, history-normative,** or **non-normative influences.**

Human development is the result of **interaction** between **genes** and the **environment.** Much of the research into the contribution of **genetics** to human behavior has focused on animals. Studies in animal genetics help establish general principles and provide important information on the effects of genetic and genetic-environmental interaction. Although they cannot provide specific details about the way such interactions affect human development, they can alert us to the fact that genes may affect temperament and **behavior,** that they may have influences in unexpected areas of development, that the same experiences have different effects on individuals with different genotypes, and that some genetically influenced behavior requires particular environmental circumstances for its expression.

Although we are uncertain exactly how genes affect behavior, the transmission may occur through **passive, evocative,** or **active influence.** Each **genotype** (individual genetic makeup) has a unique **reaction range,** and the **phenotype** (individual appearance and behavior) depends on the series of environments a person encounters during development. **Heritability,** which refers to the relative contribution of genetics to a trait or behavior, is at best an estimate applicable only to a limited group.

Environmental determinants of human development include physical and social factors. Physical factors include those ecological features that maintain life—air, water, food, and light—the interior environment of the body, and every feature of the surrounding world, whether natural or man-made. Social factors, which include all the effects of people on one another, are generally considered in terms of the family (parents, siblings), peers, neighborhoods, social institutions (including schools), cultural values, media, and technology. No determinant works in isolation. Genetic, physical, and social factors are implicated in every aspect of development. Physical growth, intelligence, personality, socialization, and hazards of birth all show the interaction of determinants.

Studies using a **cross-sectional design** in which different age groups are studied once and compared, may be difficult to interpret because of **cohort** effects. Cross-sectional studies also cannot detect change within individuals. Studies using a **longitudinal design** may be difficult to interpret because results have been affected by historical changes in the culture or by practice effects. **Sequential designs** escape some of the problems of other studies, but are often impossible to use.

A number of approaches are used to study development, each having its own advantages and disadvantages. Each approach permits a different degree of control over who is studied, the circumstances that are investigated, and the behavior that is examined. Approaches also vary in how closely they resemble life situations. **Experiments** are highest in control and lowest in correspondence to life, and **naturalistic observation** is lowest in control and highest in correspondence to life. Between these extremes are **field** and **clinical studies.**

When interpreting the results of studies, researchers often use **correlation** (how closely one measure corresponds with another) and **probability** (an estimate of the likelihood that the findings are simply the result of chance).

PART 2

The Beginning of Life

A newborn baby is both an end and a beginning. The thirty-eight weeks of growth within the mother's body suddenly ends with birth. No other developmental period will end so dramatically and so quickly. Birth is a time of separation and deprivation: the close relationship whereby the baby was automatically nourished and protected by the mother's body is suddenly ruptured. But birth is also a time of independence and the beginnings of self-reliance. Now the infant must develop his or her own physical, mental, and social capacities. By the moment of birth,

much that will distinguish the infant for the rest of his or
her life has already taken place. A baby's heredity, determined at conception, has had its initial expression in the
infant's physical form. An active, inquiring, responsive
being enters the world equipped with a growing body and
rapidly expanding motor, sensory, and mental capacities.
In this part of the book, we follow the baby's development
within the uterus and trace the first four weeks of independent life.

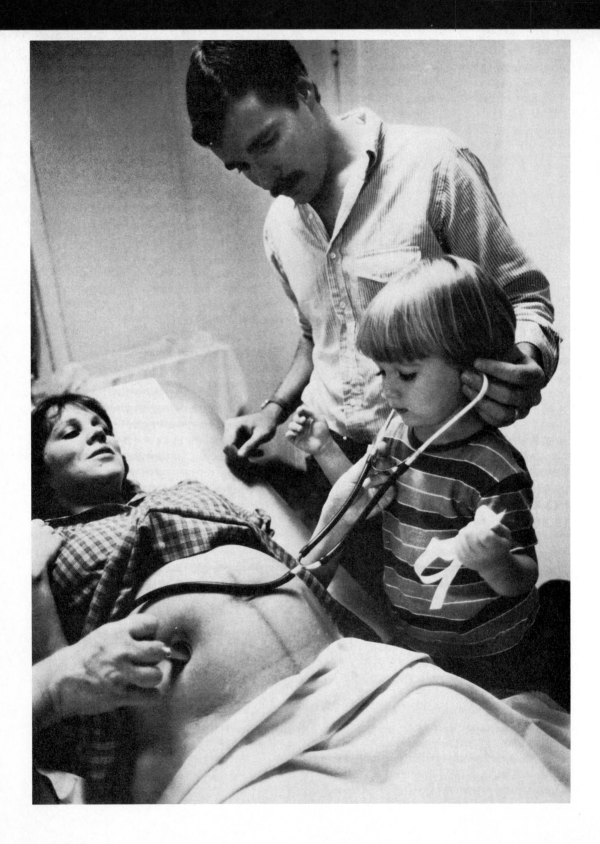

CHAPTER THREE

Prenatal Development

HOW HEREDITY WORKS
The Production of Gametes
Genetic Transmission
PRENATAL GROWTH
The Germinal Period
The Embryonic Period
The Fetal Period
BRAIN DEVELOPMENT
PRENATAL BEHAVIOR
BIRTH
Labor and Delivery
Methods of Childbirth
DEVELOPMENTAL AND BIRTH
   COMPLICATIONS
Chromosomal Abnormalities
Genetic Diseases
Nongenetic Paternal Effects
Prenatal Environmental Hazards
Prematurity
PREVENTING DEVELOPMENTAL DEFECTS
Diagnosing Abnormalities
Genetic Counseling
TERMINATED PREGNANCIES
BECOMING A SEPARATE PERSON
SUMMARY

Human development cannot be understood without examining the prenatal period. More growth and development take place during these thirty-eight weeks than in any comparable segment of life. The structures and functions that develop within the womb provide the basis of the new human being's body and behavior for the rest of life. Each baby has a unique inheritance, a genetic blueprint that specifies certain physical, mental, and personal charac- teristics. But the blueprint does not specify exactly how the new individual will look, function, or behave. From the moment of con- ception, environment interacts with heredity, affecting the way the blueprint is translated into flesh. During the prenatal period, the primary environmental influences are biological: nu- trients, oxygen, waste disposal, exposure to drugs, disease, or environmental contaminants. But there are psychological influences as well: a mother's emotional condition during pregnancy can influence the baby developing within her.

In this chapter we follow the development of the fertilized egg into a healthy, normal baby who is ready for life outside the mother's womb. We begin with the transmission of traits from

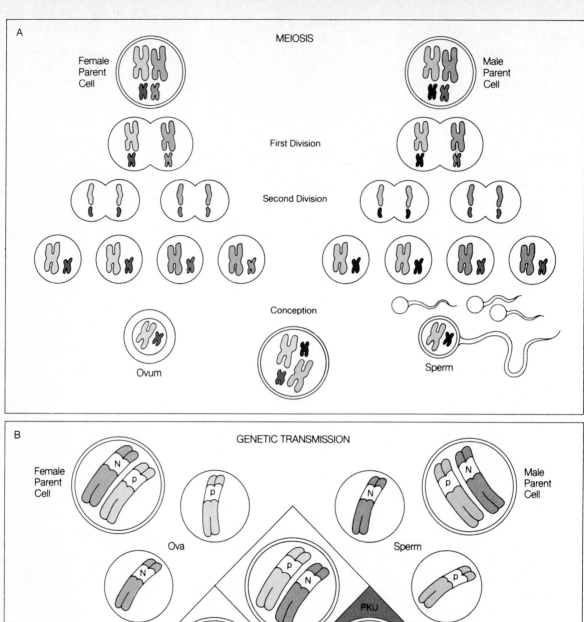

A

MEIOSIS

Female Parent Cell

Male Parent Cell

First Division

Second Division

Conception

Ovum

Sperm

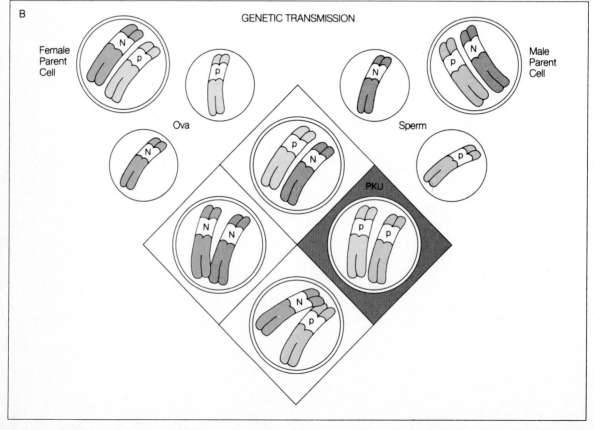

B

GENETIC TRANSMISSION

Female Parent Cell

Male Parent Cell

Ova

Sperm

PKU

FIGURE 3.1 *(A)* The production of sex cells. Certain cells in the ovaries of the mother and in the testes of the father divide twice in a special pattern of cell division called meiosis to produce gametes—ova and sperm—that have only half the number of chromosomes of the parent cells. The chromosomes occur in the parent cells in pairs, and each chromosome is itself a double strand. For simplicity, only two of the twenty-three pairs of human chromosomes are shown here. In meiosis, first the members of each pair split up *(first division)*, and then the chromosomes themselves split in half *(second division)*. They regenerate their missing halves in a subsequent step *(next line)*. The union of the gametes in conception results in a fertilized cell that has the full number of chromosomes, half from the mother and half from the father.

(B) Transmission of alleles in the inheritance of PKU. In this diagram only a single pair of chromosomes is represented. These chromosomes bear the alleles *N* and *p*. Both parents have both forms of the gene, and therefore they produce gametes with chromosomes bearing the *N* or the *p* gene in equal numbers. Depending on which gametes happen to unite in conception, the new cell may have the alleles *NN, Np, pN,* or *pp.* Because *p* is a recessive gene, only babies with *pp* will have PKU.

parent to child, a subject that was introduced in Chapter 2. After spelling out the behavior and capabilities of the growing fetus, we consider the problems that can arise in the course of its development. We also look at the link between the mother and her unborn child and discover the importance of maternal health, diet, habits, and emotions. Finally, we discuss the detection of fetal abnormalities and the role of genetic counseling in alerting prospective parents to possible defects in their unborn child.

HOW HEREDITY WORKS

The traits and dispositions that parents transmit to their offspring are coded in twenty-three pairs of **chromosomes**, which are present in every cell of the body. The chromosomes are composed of beadlike strings of *genes*, microscopic entities containing the instructions that guide the development of physical traits and behavioral dispositions. Whatever we pass on to our offspring is contained in approximately 250,000 genes composed principally of **deoxyribonucleic acid (DNA)**, a complex chemical code that guides the development of bones and eyes, brain and fingernails, and disposes the offspring toward certain behavioral patterns. All of that information is contained in a fertilized cell smaller than the period that follows this sentence.

The Production of Gametes

Most cells of the human body contain twenty-three pairs of chromosomes, direct copies of the original twenty-three pairs with which each person begins life. There is one major exception to this rule: the **gametes** (the sperm cell, or **spermatozoon,** of the father and the egg cell, or **ovum,** of the mother) that will eventually unite to produce a new human being each have twenty-three single chromosomes instead of twenty-three pairs. The difference arises because gametes and other body cells duplicate themselves in different ways. Other body cells divide through a process known as **mitosis,** in which the chromosomes first duplicate themselves and then the two complete sets move to opposite ends of the parent cell, which then divides to form two daughter cells. Each daughter cell has a full complement of forty-six chromosomes (twenty-three pairs). But gametes divide through a process called **meiosis,** in which the number of chromosomes in each daughter cell is halved. During division, members of each pair gravitate to opposite ends of the cell, which splits into two cells, each containing twenty-three single chromosomes. These cells then duplicate themselves and divide again, so that each original gamete produces four daughter cells containing twenty-three single chromosomes. Figure 3.1 illustrates meiosis in two pairs of chromosomes.

Chromosomes in the gamete are not always

duplicated exactly in the daughter cells. During meiosis, a pair of chromosomes may exchange corresponding sections, so that genes "cross over," mingling genes of paternal and maternal origin in the new chromosome and increasing possible genetic combinations (Scarr and Kidd, 1983). The exact combination of genes in any gamete is a matter of chance, with approximately half coming from the maternal side and half from the paternal side. At conception, when a sperm unites with an ovum, the result is a single cell having twenty-three pairs of chromosomes.

Genetic Transmission

Children sometimes resemble their parents in certain physical characteristics and sometimes do not. For example, a mother and father may both have brown hair, but one of their three children may be blond. How are physical characteristics passed on from parent to child?

Although hair color is a common and easily observed characteristic, its transmission is complicated, because hair color is determined by more than one gene. It is simpler to explain genetic transmission by examining a characteristic that depends on a single gene, such as **phenylketonuria,** or PKU, an inherited inability to metabolize phenylalanine, a component of some foods. If this metabolic abnormality is left untreated, the affected child will have fair skin and hair, a small head in proportion to body size, eczema, agitated and restless behavior, a stiff gait, and moderate to severe mental retardation.

In order to understand how PKU occurs, let N symbolize the gene corresponding to normal metabolic ability and p represent the gene for PKU. The related genes, N and p, are called **alleles.** Now look at Figure 3.1B, which illustrates the alleles in only one pair of chromosomes. The parent cells in the figure contain the alleles of interest, labeled N and p. In this example, the mother's and father's cells have a gene for both N and p. When the parent cells divide to form gametes, half of the father's

sperm cells and half of the mother's ova will contain a gene for PKU (p) and half will contain a gene for the normal metabolic condition (N). During conception, one of four possible combinations of these gametes will result. Depending on which male gamete unites with which female gamete, the new baby will have a genetic inheritance of NN, Np (which is the same as pN), or pp; these are shown in Figure 3.1B. If the selection process were perfectly random, one-fourth of the offspring of these parents would have the combination NN, one-fourth would have pp,and one-half would have Np.

But which of these offspring will be normal children, and which will show symptoms of PKU? In this example, the NN baby will be normal, and the pp baby will have PKU. These offspring are **homozygous,** which means that their cells have matching genes for this characteristic. But an Np baby is **heterozygous,** meaning that his or her cells have different genes for the same trait. Are these Np babies normal, or do they have PKU?

The answer depends on which gene is **dominant** and which is **recessive.** A dominant gene is one whose corresponding trait appears in the individual even when that gene is paired with a different gene for the trait. The paired gene whose corresponding trait fails to appear is recessive. In the case of PKU, the normal gene is dominant over the recessive PKU gene, and therefore Np individuals will be normal. That is, they will have normal metabolisms, although they will be able to transmit the PKU gene to their offspring.

Notice that there is not a perfect one-to-one correspondence between the genes a person carries and the traits that appear. This lack of correspondence illustrates the difference between genotype and phenotype, which was discussed in Chapter 2. The genotype is the specific combination of alleles that characterize one's genetic makeup, whereas the phenotype is the nature of the trait as it appears in the individual. The genes that produce PKU can combine to form three genotypes: NN, Np, pp. But there are only two phenotypes: normal and PKU. The genotypes *NN* and *Np* both produce the normal phenotype because *N* is dominant over *p*. There are, therefore, some differences between what we actually look like and how we behave (phenotype) and our genetic makeup (genotype).

For a variety of reasons, genetic transmission is rarely as simple as it is in the case of PKU. First, most traits, especially behavioral ones, are **polygenic,** which means that several genes have an equal and cumulative effect in producing the trait. Or, in other cases, some genes in the combination have more influence than others on the phenotype. Second, dominance is not always all-or-none. That is, there appear to be gradations of dominance, so that one allele for a trait is not totally dominant. The result may be somewhat an "average" of two extremes. In other instances, traits are **codominant,** so that the phenotype will show a combination of traits from the paired, but different, alleles. Third, one allele may not express itself unless an allele of quite different characteristic is also present. For example, although cataracts are caused by a single dominant gene, another gene determines the form the cataracts will take (Stern, 1960). Consequently, it is possible for a person to carry a dominant gene that does not affect his or her phenotype.

The example of PKU as a genetically transmitted trait reminds us of another important point about genetic transmission. A highly restricted diet can prevent most of PKU's effects, indicating that the expression of genetic traits is affected by the environment and that, as we saw in Chapter 2, all aspects of development are characterized by the interaction of heredity and environment.

One of the chromosomes in every gamete is a sex chromosome. Normal female gametes carry a female sex chromosome (X), and normal male gametes carry either a female sex chromosome (X) or a male sex chromosome (Y). When the gametes unite in the fertilized egg, either a female (XX—an X chromosome from each parent) or a male (XY—an X chromosome from the mother and a Y chromosome from the father) is produced. The same pair of sex chromosomes will appear in every cell of the new individual's body. Thus, it is the sperm that determines whether the fertilized ovum will develop into a male or a female.

The X chromosome is much larger than the Y chromosome and carries more genes, so that while girls receive the same number of genes from each parent, a boy receives more genes from his mother than from his father. In the case of genes for which there is no corresponding allele on the Y chromosome, the gene on the X chromosome will be free to express itself, even though it is recessive. These extra, unmatched genes are responsible for the predominance in males of such sex-linked conditions as hereditary baldness, color blindness, and hemophilia (a disease in which the blood does not clot). The possession of the second X chromosome also appears to protect females against some effects of physical deprivation and provides resistance against certain infectious diseases (Fryer and Ashford, 1972). Perhaps this protection is in part responsible for the fact that females have lower death rates than males at every age (U.S. Bureau of the Census, 1982).

PRENATAL GROWTH

At the moment of conception, the spermatozoon from the father unites with the ovum of the mother in one of the **Fallopian tubes,** the passages leading from the ovaries to the uterus. The ovum is the largest cell in the human body, and it can sometimes be seen without a microscope. Eggs mature in the female's ovaries, and one egg is released approximately every twenty-eight days during a woman's fertile years. The freed egg, which probably can be fertilized for less than twenty-four hours, travels down the Fallopian tube toward the uterus (see Figure 3.2).

As soon as sperm and ovum unite, **epigenesis,** or the course of development, begins. Only since the nineteenth century, when the ovum was identified under the microscope, have we had evidence that fetal development is epigenetic—that it begins with an undifferentiated

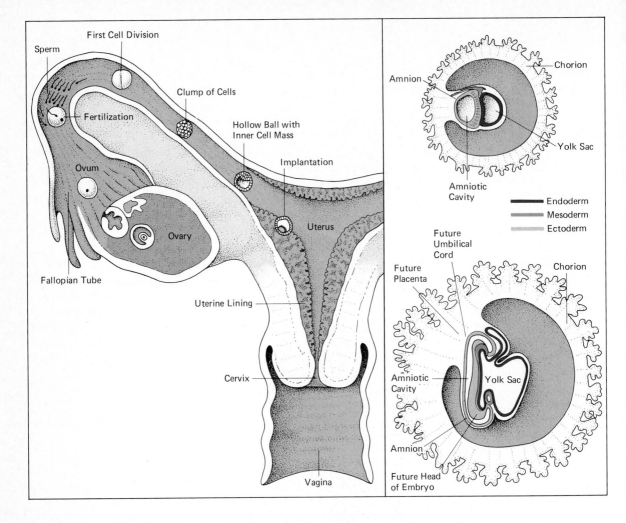

FIGURE 3.2 The early development of the human embryo. Fertilization occurs at the upper end of the Fallopian tube. By the time the fertilized ovum reaches the uterus, it has already divided many times. Within seven or eight days, it is securely implanted in the uterine wall, where the process of prenatal development continues.

structure. Without that evidence, biologists were free to speculate, and for centuries most believed that either the ovum or the sperm contained a preformed human being, which grew larger but did not change in form or feature during the prenatal period. **Preformation** was

challenged in the eighteenth century with the proposal that development consisted of continuing transformations that began with a cluster of globules, but this proposal was not verified for nearly seventy years. Today, developmentalists agree that development is epigenetic but disagree as to the nature of the process.

According to Gilbert Gottlieb (1983), the current controversy centers on whether epigenesis is predetermined or probabilistic. In **predetermined epigenesis,** development is a matter of preprogrammed maturation, in which genes determine the maturational processes that lead to structural and functional development. Prenatal development progresses in one predetermined direction. In **probabilistic epigenesis,** genes begin maturational processes that can then be affected by the functioning of the developing, but not fully established, system. Development is bidirectional, which means that the activity of brain cells, sensory stimulation, and feedback from motor movement can affect the course of subsequent development of these systems, perhaps altering the timing or sequence in which genes guiding further development turn on and off. The theory of probabilistic epigenesis emphasizes gene-environment interaction even at the prenatal level.

Whether epigenesis is predetermined or probabilistic, it progresses at a rapid rate. In approximately thirty-eight weeks, the total **gestation period**, the organism grows from one tiny cell to a newborn baby. Since most women do not know the precise date of conception, physicians commonly calculate fetal age from the beginning of the mother's last menstrual period, resulting in a gestation period of forty weeks (nine calendar months). However, we shall adopt the more accurate thirty-eight-week gestation period in discussions of prenatal life.

The course of prenatal development falls into roughly three periods. During the first two weeks after conception, called the **germinal period,** the fertilized egg is primarily engaged in cell division. In the next six weeks, the **embryonic period,** the organism begins to take shape, and its various organ systems begin to form. Thereafter, from approximately eight weeks after conception to birth, the developing organism is called a **fetus**.

The Germinal Period

Almost immediately after fertilization, the egg begins the process of cell division that will eventually produce a human body made up of many billions of cells. Although the cells of an adult are highly differentiated according to their location and function in the body (for example, nerve cells are quite different in form and func-

tion from muscle cells), the cells at this point in development are all identical.

The fertilized ovum takes approximately three days to progress through the Fallopian tube to the uterus, where it floats freely for another four or five days before becoming implanted in the uterine wall, which maternal hormones have prepared for the developing egg. The network of tiny roots that anchor the organism to the uterus will grow into the **placenta,** a pliable structure of tissue and blood vessels that stores nutrients and transmits nourishment and wastes between mother and fetus. At two weeks its primitive beginnings can be distinguished by microscope.

By the end of the first two weeks, the cells have multiplied greatly in number and have begun to differentiate. An outer membrane and an inner membrane form a sac that surrounds and protects the developing organism. Three primary layers of cells have formed: the **ectoderm**, which is the source of cells composing the skin, sense organs, and nervous system; the **mesoderm**, from which the muscular, circulatory, and skeletal systems will develop; and the **endoderm**, which will give rise to the lining of the intestinal tract and to related organs such as the liver, pancreas, and thyroid.

One phenomenon that needs explanation is how these cells become differentiated into nerve, muscle, fat, and blood. Some scientists have speculated that newly produced cells are essentially neutral, or undifferentiated. Somehow, these neutral cells are attracted to locations that need them, and then by some means, probably chemical, they are altered to serve the purpose required at that location.

The process may proceed in the same manner as a wound heals. For example, when skin is cut, neutral cells are sent to the wound, where they are transformed into specialized skin cells by chemicals apparently released by layers of tissue immediately below the skin. If the wound is not too deep, the cell differentiation is almost perfect, and there is no scar. However, if the cut is deep enough to destroy the layers that produce the differentiating chemicals, the body's repair job is incomplete, and a scar forms. It is possible that the fetus develops by similarly transforming neutral cells.

Other scientists have suggested that the process of cell differentiation is under the joint control of the mother and organism. It may be that both the mother's genes and the genes that are active early in the division of the fertilized egg reprogram the genes of embryonic cells, determining their proper sites and functions (Kolata, 1979).

The Embryonic Period

Four weeks after conception, the organism, now called an **embryo**, is about one-fifth of an inch long, 10,000 times larger than the original fertilized egg. In addition, its heart is pumping blood through microscopic veins and arteries, and there are a rudimentary brain, kidneys, liver, and digestive tract, and indentations that will eventually become jaws, eyes, and ears.

Organs along the central axis of the body develop first; the extremities develop later. Thus in the early weeks an embryo is literally all head and heart. Later, the lower part of the body begins to enlarge and to assume its newborn proportion and size.

By the end of the seventh week, the embryo is almost an inch long, and its appearance is clearly humanlike. What look like the gill slits of a fish are really rudimentary structures in the neck and lower face. What seems to be a primitive tail eventually becomes the tip of the baby's spine; the tail reaches its maximum length at about six weeks and then slowly recedes. The head is now clearly distinct from the rounded, skin-covered body and accounts for about half the embryo's total size. The eyes have come forward from the sides of the head and eyelids have begun to form. The face clearly contains ears, nose, lips, tongue, and even the buds of teeth. The knobs that will be arms and legs grow, and in a matter of weeks, they differentiate into hands and feet and then into fingers and toes. The **umbilical cord**, containing two

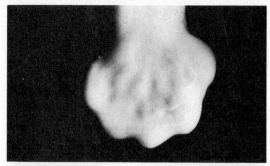
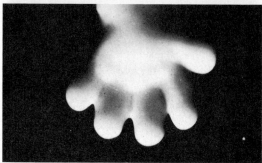
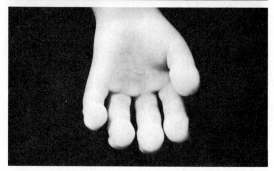

In the fifth week, hands are a "molding plate" with finger ridges. In the sixth week, finger buds form. In the seventh and eighth weeks, the fingers, thumbs, and fingerprints form, and the touch pads are prominent. (Courtesy Carnegie Institution of Washington)

arteries and one vein, has formed at the bottom of the tiny abdomen to connect embryo and placenta. Through the vessels in this flexible cord nourishment passes to the embryo and waste is taken from it.

In this early period, the brain sends out impulses that coordinate the functioning of other organ systems. The heart beats sturdily, the stomach produces some digestive juices, the liver manufactures blood cells, and the kidneys purify the blood. Testes or ovaries can be distinguished, and the endocrine system has begun to produce hormones. All these organs are in a primitive form, and it will be several months before they can be considered fully functional (Pritchard and MacDonald, 1976).

The Fetal Period

Approximately eight weeks past conception, when bone cells begin to develop, the organism is known as a fetus. Within twelve weeks it has begun to stretch out of its C-like posture, and the head is more erect. The limbs are nicely molded, and folds for fingernails and toenails are present. An external inspection could readily determine the sex of the fetus. The lips have separated from the jaws, crude teeth are apparent, the nasal passages have formed, the lungs have acquired their definitive shape, and the brain has attained its general structure; the eyes are organized, and the retina has become layered. The liver secretes bile, and the bone marrow has begun to produce blood. At this time, the fetus weighs about an ounce and is approximately three inches long.

By sixteen weeks, the fetus is approximately six to seven inches long and weighs about four ounces. Until now, its head has been enormous in relation to the rest of its body, but by sixteen weeks the lower part of the body has grown until the head is only about one-fourth of the total body size. The sixteen-week-old fetus looks like a miniature baby. Its face looks "human," hair may appear on the head, bones can be distinguished throughout the body, and the sense organs approximate their final appearance. All major internal organs have attained their typical shape and plan.

Nevertheless, the fetus could not survive if it were delivered at this point because it lacks the ability to breathe. A necessary component in this process is the liquid **surfactin**, which enables the lungs to transmit oxygen from the air

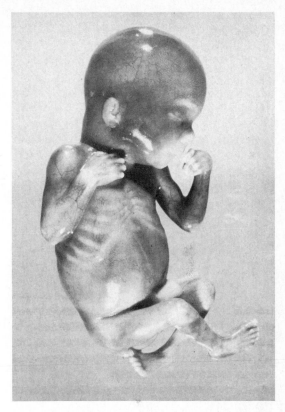

This sixteen-week-old fetus is about six inches long and weighs about four ounces. Its major bones and organs have formed, and for the first time, the fetus looks "human." (Martin M. Rotker/Taurus Photos)

to the blood. Around the age of twenty-three weeks, the fetus begins to produce surfactin, but if it is born at this time, it often cannot maintain the important liquid at the necessary levels and may develop **respiratory distress syndrome** and die. By about thirty-five weeks (sometimes earlier), the fetus develops a new system for maintaining surfactin, and this new method will allow it to live outside the uterus (Gluck and Kulovich, 1973).

Generally speaking, 161 days (twenty-three weeks, or about five and a half months) is regarded as the minimum possible age at which a fetus can survive (Kleiman, 1984). Babies born that early have lived, although it is only in re-

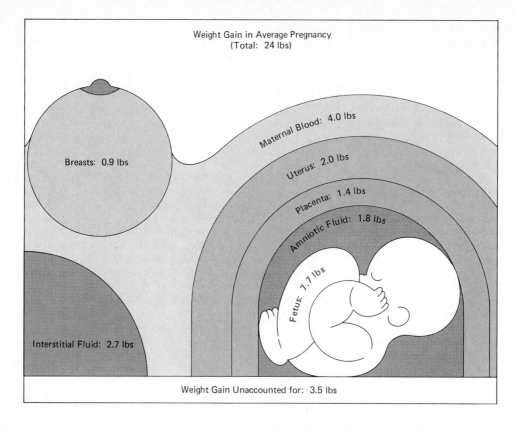

Weight Gain in Average Pregnancy
(Total: 24 lbs)

Maternal Blood: 4.0 lbs

Breasts: 0.9 lbs

Uterus: 2.0 lbs

Placenta: 1.4 lbs

Amniotic Fluid: 1.8 lbs

Fetus: 7.7 lbs

Interstitial Fluid: 2.7 lbs

Weight Gain Unaccounted for: 3.5 lbs

FIGURE 3.3 Of the twenty-four pounds recommended as the weight gain during a normal pregnancy, only about three and a half pounds is stored as fat and protein. This extra weight acts as a buffer against the stresses of the postnatal period.

(From Newton and Modahl. "Pregnancy, The Closest Human Relationship," *Human Nature,* March 1978, p. 47.)

cent years that such immature infants have survived. It requires a heroic medical effort to save such a young fetus, and its chances of a normal life are small, primarily because of its immature brain. In any case, the younger the fetus, the lower the likelihood that it will survive. Fetuses born after 252 days (thirty-six weeks) are considered to be of normal term, although unusual circumstances may still make special care necessary for the first few days or weeks of life.

During the final period of prenatal develop-

ment, at a time when the fetus could survive on its own, its organs step up their activity, and its heart rate becomes quite rapid. Fat forms over its entire body, smoothing out the wrinkled skin and rounding out contours. The fetus usually gains about half a pound a week during the last eight or nine weeks in the uterus. After its thirty-eight weeks in the uterus, the average full-term baby at birth is about twenty inches long and weighs a little more than seven pounds, although weight may vary from less than five to more than twelve pounds (see Figure 3.3 for average weight gain of *mothers* during pregnancy), and length may vary from less than seventeen to more than twenty-two inches.

BRAIN DEVELOPMENT

The **central nervous system** (brain and spinal cord) is of special interest to developmental psychologists because it is the brain that processes information, makes decisions, solves problems, and directs behavior. Its development is both intricate and extremely fast. It starts as a cluster of cells. As these cells continue to differentiate and multiply, they form a tubelike structure called the neural tube, which bends over at one end as it develops. This end eventually becomes the brain. By the end of the first four weeks of life, the embryo has a spinal cord and a recognizable brain with two lobes; by the sixteenth week the brain's major structures and shape resemble those of an adult. By this time, the **cortex**—a mantle of neural cells covering the cerebral hemispheres—has grown back over the lower parts of the brain.

The lower parts of the brain are primarily responsible for sustaining life, the coordination of reflexes, and other primitive behavior, but their development usually is not sufficient to maintain life outside the uterus much before twenty-eight weeks. By thirty-two to thirty-six weeks, the areas of the cortex governing motor and sensory behavior are reasonably mature, as are parts of the primary hearing areas. But at birth, the remaining and larger mass of the cortex is still very immature.

During the prenatal period, three major events mark development of the fetal brain. The first is the development of all the neural cells, or **neurons**, that make up the adult brain. Neurobiologists estimate that the average adult brain has 100 billion neurons (Hubel, 1979). Research indicates that these cells begin to develop when the fetus is about ten weeks old and that all 100 billion may be developed by about sixteen to twenty weeks. The second major event is cell death. Many more neurons are formed than the brain actually needs, and those that do not make contact with other cells die during the developmental stage (Cowan, 1979). In fact, the death of nerve cells appears to be a major basis of prenatal neural development. Studies suggest, for example, that cells connecting the eye with the brain's visual cortex multiply rapidly early in the prenatal period, reaching more than twice the number that will be present in the adult eye. As brain development progresses, great quantities of these cells begin to die. The loss soon

tapers off, but some cell loss may continue during early infancy (Rakic and Riley, 1983). The third major event involves the continuing growth of neurons and the growth of **glial cells**, which seem to play an essential role in the nourishment of neurons and in the development around each neuron of a sheath of **myelin**, a fatty substance that keeps nerve impulses channeled along the neural fibers and reduces the random spread of impulses from one fiber to another. This development begins at about twenty weeks and accelerates until the fetus is about twenty-eight to thirty-two weeks old. The glial cells continue to multiply until about the second year after birth, and myelination also continues for at least several years after birth. Indeed, in parts of the forebrain and in the reticular formation—an area of the brain that helps maintain attention and consciousness—myelination continues until adolescence (Tanner, 1978). As neurons move from the depth of the developing brain, where they are formed, to their final position, they appear to migrate along a path charted by special glial cells whose excessively long fibers extend to the outer surface of the brain (Cowan, 1979).

Despite its full complement of neurons, the fetal brain remains immature in other respects. For one thing, the adult cortex is composed of nine types of neurons arranged in six different layers. Not all these cells reach a mature form in the fetal cortex, nor are the cells distributed in the neat, layered arrangement of the mature cortex. Further, according to best estimates, each neuron in the adult brain has about ten thousand connections with other cells, whereas connections among cells in the fetal brain are, in comparison, sparse, and the fibers that extend from the neurons are short and stumpy; as the cells mature, many will be retracted (Cowan, 1979). The kind of connections a neuron makes appears to depend largely on which of the neurotransmitters (chemical substances that regulate brain activity) the neuron secretes and whether it can successfully compete with the fibers of other neurons (Marx, 1982). Although, as we shall see in the next chapter, the newborn infant has many capabilities, it takes time for the almost unbelievably massive and rich inter-connections to develop among the neurons.

PRENATAL BEHAVIOR

Movement, the major behavior that character-izes the fetus, begins long before the fetal neu-rons have developed. Mothers often report feel-ing movement when the fetus is approximately sixteen weeks old; but the muscles of the fetus are in fact capable of movement at about eight weeks.

Developmental psychologists are interested in how early the fetus responds to stimuli, what kinds of responses it makes, and what kinds of spontaneous behavior it shows. It is difficult to study prenatal behavior, but some years ago Davenport Hooker (1952) studied embryos and fetuses delivered by Caesarean section that were too immature to survive. His research shows that by twelve weeks after conception, the fetus can kick its legs, turn its feet, close its fingers, bend its wrists, turn its head, squint, frown, open and close its mouth, stick out its tongue, and respond to touch.

By twenty-three weeks the fetus shows a great deal of spontaneous activity, as many pregnant women report. It sleeps and wakes as a newborn does, but unlike the newborn infant, it also be-comes sluggish at times, perhaps because its rapid growth results in a reduced oxygen supply (Humphrey, 1970). By twenty-four weeks, it can cry, open and close its eyes, and look up, down, and sideways (Hooker, 1952). By this time it has also developed a grasp reflex and will soon be strong enough to support its weight with one hand. It may hiccup. During the final eight or nine weeks, the fetus is quite active, although its actions become limited by the in-creasingly snug fit of the uterus.

Behavioral development in the prenatal organ-ism corresponds to the development of its ner-vous system and of the muscles of its body. The earliest responses found in embryos appear at about five and a half weeks after conception (Humphrey, 1970). Stroking the area of the mouth with a fine hair causes the embryo to respond in a general manner, moving its upper trunk and neck. By nine weeks, the fetus will bend its fingers when the palm of its hand is touched and either curl or straighten its toes in response to a touch on the sole of the foot. By eleven weeks, the fetus can swallow. As the organism develops, more and more of its body becomes sensitive to stimulation, and the re-sponse eventually narrows to the area stimu-lated. Thus, when the mouth is touched, only reflexes about the mouth appear. Within the last few months before birth, the fetus behaves es-sentially as it does at birth, with grasping, suck-ing, kicking, and other typical infant reflexes.

It has long been known that a fetus in the third trimester can hear. By twenty-five weeks, the fetus responds to noise with a startled re-action, blinking its eyes, averting its head, mov-ing its arms, and extending its legs (Birnholz and Benacerraf, 1983). Such behavior is a reac-tion to immediate stimulation. Recent experi-ments suggest that a fetus may even register its mother's voice. Melanie Spence and Anthony DeCasper (1982) asked pregnant women to read the same simple children's story aloud each day for six weeks during the last trimester of their pregnancy. Three days after the babies were born, Spence and DeCasper took each baby into a quiet room and played a recording of his or her mother reading either the familiar story or a new one. The babies could turn the story on or off by sucking on a pacifier. The babies tended to adapt their sucking to deliver the fa-miliar story, clearly preferring it to the new one. Their behavior suggests that something about the sound pattern of the familiar story registered and that a fetus may be capable of a rudimentary kind of learning and remembering.

BIRTH

Near the end of pregnancy, the fetus normally lies head down in the uterus, which resembles a large sack opening into the vagina through the cervix. The exact mechanisms that begin labor

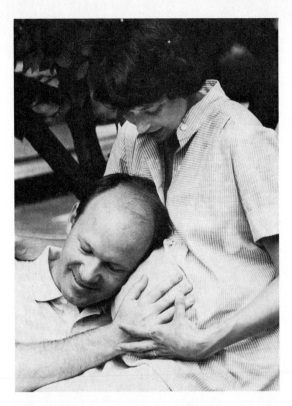

Within a month, this couple will become parents. By placing a hand or cheek against the abdomen, the father-to-be can easily detect the vigorous kicks of the fetus. From within the uterus, the fetus hears and reacts to many sounds of the outside world. (Joel Gordon)

more sensitive to oxytocin, and fetal-produced oxytocin passes from the amniotic fluid through the sac surrounding the fetus and stimulates the uterine wall (Fuchs et al., 1982). In the second procedure, some unidentified substance in the fetal urine passes into the amniotic fluid, stimulating prostaglandin production by fetal membranes and initiating uterine contractions (Strickland et al., 1983). Common to both explanations is the active role taken by the fetus in determining the onset of labor.

Labor and Delivery

Labor, or the birth process, progresses in three stages. For first-born infants, labor often lasts thirteen to fifteen hours, although its actual length varies greatly from mother to mother. The length of labor is markedly less for later-born children.

In the first stage of labor, which lasts until the cervix is completely dilated, the upper portion of the uterus contracts at regular and progressively shorter intervals. During this period, the lower part of the uterus thins out and the cervix dilates to permit the fetus to pass through the birth canal.

In the second stage of labor, which lasts until the fetus is born, the mother's abdominal muscles also contract in a bearing-down motion. Unless drugs deaden sensations, she usually pushes hard to get the baby out. During this period, the fetus passes head first through the birth canal and emerges from the mother's body, a process that lasts approximately eighty minutes in the birth of a first baby.

After the birth, the physician cleans the baby's nose and mouth with a suction apparatus to make breathing easier and to prevent mucus, blood, or the baby's own waste products from entering the lungs. Then the umbilical cord is tied and cut.

In the final stage of labor, uterine contractions expel the **afterbirth**—the placenta, its membranes, and the rest of the umbilical cord. This process lasts approximately five to twenty min-

are not well understood. They may involve changes in hormone levels in both mother and fetus. On the mother's side, her pituitary gland releases the hormone **oxytocin,** her uterus stretches, the relationship of other hormones within her uterus changes, and her body releases a substance that causes the uterus to contract. When the fetus is ready to be born, its adrenal gland produces cortisol and its pituitary gland produces oxytocin. Oxytocin is believed to stimulate the production of prostaglandin, a substance that is required for sustained uterine contractions. Two different procedures recently have been proposed as triggering the birth process. In the first, the mother's uterus becomes

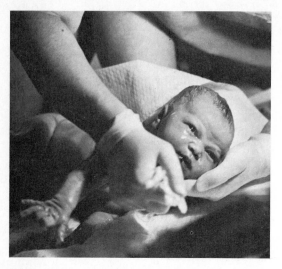

After thirty-eight weeks of growth, the moment of birth arrives. Before severing the umbilical cord, the physician removes mucus from the infant's nose and mouth. (Joel Gordon)

flexes and twenty-seven kinds of behavior, including alertness, cuddliness, motor maturity, and responses to stress and to environmental stimuli. The Brazelton scale was originally developed to provide a way of documenting differences in temperament among newborns, with the hope of predicting how those differences might affect the relationship between baby and caregiver (Als et al., 1979). It is more complicated than the Apgar and is not routinely administered, but it enables researchers to measure behavior that previously could not be assessed until babies were older. For example, the scale has been used to investigate such varied aspects of infancy as cross-cultural differences in the behavior of newborns, the effects on the newborn of maternal medication during delivery, and the condition of babies who are born prematurely or who suffer respiratory distress.

A third, increasingly popular measure is the Dubowitz scoring system, which uses physical

utes, and the afterbirth is immediately examined by the physician to determine whether it is complete and normal.

Not all deliveries proceed in this normal fashion. In a breech delivery, the baby's buttocks appear first, then the legs, and finally the head. Such deliveries can be dangerous because the baby may suffocate before the head emerges. Some babies must be delivered surgically, by Caesarean section, because the mother's pelvis is too small to permit her baby to pass through.

The newborn baby is assessed for appearance (color), heart rate, reflex irritability, activity, muscle tone, and respiratory effort to determine whether further medical help is needed. A much-used and practical scoring system for assessing these attributes is known as the **Apgar score** (Apgar and James, 1962). Each of the characteristics is rated 0, 1, or 2 (2 being best), and these scores are added together to obtain the baby's Apgar score, which may vary from 0 to 10. Another well-known measure is the Brazelton Neonatal Behavioral Assessment Scale (Brazelton, 1973), which consists of approximately thirty tests that score the baby on twenty re-

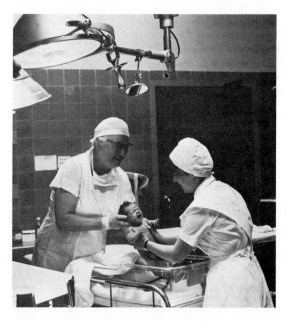

While a nurse holds the newborn, Dr. Virginia Apgar assesses the infant's condition, using the Apgar scale she devised to determine whether the new individual needs further medical help. (Ann Zane Shanks/Photo Researchers)

appearance and neurological signs to assess a newborn's gestational age (Dubowitz et al., 1970). This system takes less than five minutes to complete and appears to fix the infant's gestational age within a week (Self and Horowitz, 1979). The measure is particularly useful in separating babies who are born prematurely from those who have reached full term but are especially small.

Methods of Childbirth

For a good many years, American obstetrical practices were generally accepted by women and physicians alike as the best possible care for both mothers and babies. But over the past few decades a growing number of parents and medical personnel have seriously questioned the procedures in many American hospitals. In most of them, labor was regarded as difficult and painful, drugs were routinely given, and episiotomies (surgical incisions to enlarge the vaginal orifice) and forceps were used to speed the birth process.

Anthropologists have reported that childbirth varies dramatically around the world. In cultures that regard birth as fearful and something that should be hidden, women often had prolonged and difficult labors. But in cultures that regard birth as an open, easy process, women generally had short, uncomplicated labors (Mead and Newton, 1967).

Grantly Dick-Read (1944), a British physician who had noticed that some of his patients found childbirth a relatively peaceful, painless experience, believed that fear generated a tension that produced pain in most women. His urging of what he called "natural childbirth" met with some success, and his techniques, combined with the more recently introduced Lamaze method, have brought about changes in the way many obstetricians handle childbirth. In the Lamaze method, women learn to substitute new responses for learned responses of pain, and by concentrating on breathing, try to inhibit painful sensations (Chabon, 1966). Other methods of natural childbirth also have been introduced, and all share three characteristics. They emphasize the importance of parental knowledge about the birth process, the presence of a "coach" during labor, and the use of drugless techniques that diminish pain as they encourage the woman to become an active participant in the birth.

The rising popularity of natural childbirth has gradually led many American hospitals to change their procedures. The medical profession has come to realize that all family members benefit from sharing the experience of childbirth and has urged a more homelike hospital atmosphere, where older children can be with their mothers during the early stage of labor. In a joint position statement, the branches of the medical profession involved in childbirth have advocated the use of a birthing room for normal deliveries (Interprofessional Task Force, 1978). This combination labor and delivery room, where the father remains with the mother, is decorated like a bedroom instead of a hospital room, and the bed allows the mother to give birth in a semisitting position. A crib for the baby is in the room, and both breast-feeding and handling of the new baby are encouraged. In most cities where birthing rooms are not available, a husband is now permitted to accompany his wife into the delivery room, where he can offer her emotional support and can participate in the birth process. By the mid-1980s, most married American fathers were attending the births of their children. Further, some of the routine hospital procedures—from automatic medication to episiotomy—that can make birth an abnormal and unpleasant experience, have been eliminated for normal deliveries in a number of hospitals.

DEVELOPMENTAL AND BIRTH COMPLICATIONS

Most pregnancies follow a normal course of development, and most babies are normal and healthy. On occasion, however, a genetic abnor-

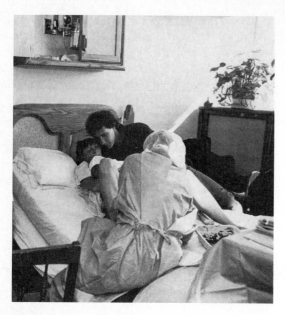

In hospital "birthing rooms" like this one, a woman can give birth in a relatively homelike setting, with her husband at her side to share the birth experience and provide her with emotional support. (Peter Menzel)

mality or an environmental factor, such as prenatal exposure to drugs or radiation, affects the developing fetus. Some of the resulting defects are minor, some respond to medical or surgical intervention, and others are so serious that they threaten the life of the baby.

No matter what the source of developmental or birth complications, their effects can range far wider than the physical malformations, the reduced birth weights, or the mental retardation that results. They may change the reactions of parents to their newborn so that the emotional tone of their relationship is never quite the same as it would have been had their baby been completely normal. Thus developmental complications form yet another strand in the intricate web of child development.

Chromosomal Abnormalities

Approximately one out of every hundred babies born has some sort of chromosomal abnormal-

ity, caused when cell division in the gamete goes wrong. During meiosis, a pair of chromosomes may fail to separate, so that one of the gametes has one chromosome too many and the other lacks a chromsome. Such cells, if they develop, produce individuals with an abnormal number of chromosomes in all their cells. Any abnormalities caused by such cell division are irreversible, and their consequences are often serious.

Sometimes the error in cell division is found in the sex chromosomes. Such errors may produce only a slight abnormality and be apparent only upon microscopic examination—as when a baby boy is born with an extra male sex chromosome (XYY). Such babies grow to be taller-than-average men. Claims that XYY males are extremely aggressive and violent have not been substantiated. Among men for whom records exist, behavior disturbances may be antisocial or impulsive, but there is a virtual absence of violent acts toward other human beings (Rubin, Reinisch, and Haskett, 1981).

When a baby boy is born with an extra female sex chromosome (XXY—two female and one male sex chromosomes), he will have **Klinefelter's syndrome.** The boy will be sterile, have rounded hips, will tend to develop breasts, and may be passive and somewhat retarded. Occasionally, however, an XXY male shows none of the typical signs, and in other cases treatment with male sex hormones often leads to a male body build and reverses many behavioral symptoms (Rubin, Reinisch, and Haskett, 1981).

Girls born with a missing female sex chromosome (XO—one female and no male sex chromosomes) suffer from **Turner's syndrome.** These girls often have a webbed or shortened neck, a broad-bridged nose, low-set ears, and short, chubby fingers. They are short and generally do not develop secondary sex characteristics unless given female hormones. Their verbal skills and reasoning ability are normal, but their spatial skills are significantly below normal (Reinisch, Gandelman, and Spiegel, 1979). This deficit in spatial skills has been attributed to the fact that Turner females, although shorter than normal, have periods of faster than normal growth (Rovet and Netley, 1982), a connection that will be explored in Chapter 6.

The extra chromosome is not always a sex chromosome. Each of the twenty-three pairs of chromosomes has been numbered by researchers. If the fertilized egg has an extra Chromosome 21 (three instead of two), the egg will develop into a baby who suffers from **Down's syndrome** (formerly called mongolism). These children tend to be short and stocky. They have a broad nose bridge; a large, protruding tongue; an open mouth; square-shaped ears; a broad, short neck with extra, loose skin over the nape; and large folds of skin above the eyes. Such children frequently have congenital heart disease and other problems, and often do not live past the teens. They have moderate to severe mental retardation, although the extent of retardation varies considerably from case to case.

Down's syndrome is caused in one of two ways. In one case, it arises when extra material from Chromosome 21 becomes attached to another chromosome. This process is extremely rare and the tendency is inherited. The other cause of Down's syndrome arises when an error in cell division produces an offspring with an extra Chromosome 21, a genetic makeup unlike that of either parent. This tendency is not inherited.

It was always assumed that the extra chromosome came from faulty cell division within the egg. But today it is possible to stain and compare chromosomes. When such comparisons have been made, from 20 to 30 percent of the cases of Down's syndrome have been traced to faulty cell division within the sperm (Gunderson and Sackett, 1982). The presumption that a defective egg was always responsible may be due to the fact that the likelihood of producing children with Down's syndrome through an error in cell division increases as a mother ages. Some studies show that the risk of producing a child with Down's syndrome is only about 1 in 2,500 for mothers less than twenty years old, 1 in 1,900 for mothers thirty to thirty-four years old, but 1 in 50 for forty-five-year-old mothers (Frias, 1975). However, older mothers are likely to be married to older men, and older men are more likely than younger men to produce faulty sperm.

Other abnormalities also occur more frequently in children born to older parents, especially disorders that are produced by a single dominant gene. In a review of the effect of parental age, Virginia Gunderson and Gene Sackett (1982) found that nonhereditary disorders, such as defects in the developing brain and spinal cord, are associated with paternal age, although not all studies indicate such a connection. Some studies that show no effect of paternal age on fetal malformation have indicated that such disorders are connected with the age of the mother. Taken together, these findings have led most geneticists to encourage couples to have their children before the mother reaches forty. The risks that may accompany teenage pregnancy are discussed in the accompanying box.

Genetic Diseases

Sometimes mutations in single genes produce new alleles that are transmitted to future generations. Some of these mutations lead to defects in body proteins that cause errors in metabolism, as is the case with PKU. Most mutations are caused by recessive genes, which must be paired with a similar gene to have a visible effect on the developing baby. Some, like PKU, are treatable; others are not.

In **Tay-Sachs disease**, the baby lacks Hex A, an enzyme that is required for the metabolism of certain fatty substances. Consequently, these substances accumulate throughout the body, including the brain, with lethal results. Such babies have convulsions, become blind or paralyzed or both, and undergo mental degeneration. They invariably die before they are seven years old.

Each year more than one hundred babies are born in the United States with Tay-Sachs disease, an affliction confined almost entirely to people whose Jewish ancestry can be traced back to an area in Eastern Europe between Russia

The Risks of Teenage Pregnancy

Both baby and mother seem to run special risks when the mother is a young adolescent. The statistics are sobering: The death rate among mothers younger than fifteen is 46.7 per 100,000 live births as compared with the average rate of 9.6 per 100,000, while the infant death rate is twice as high among mothers younger than sixteen as among mothers between the ages of twenty and thirty-four. (Bolton, 1980). A major complication among such young mothers arises from immaturity of the pelvis, where growth generally is not complete until a girl is sixteen or seventeen years old. Because of this immaturity, the pelvis is often too narrow to allow the fetal head to pass safely through, leading to a greater proportion of complicated deliveries and Caesarean sections among young teenagers (McCluskey, Killarney, and Papini, 1983).

Adolescent mothers of any age are more likely than other first-time mothers to have preterm or low birth weight infants (McKenry, Walters, and Johnson, 1979). The immediate risks to the baby do not seem to be the result of the mother's physical immaturity. Instead, they are apparently due to the fact that many pregnant adolescents have inadequate prenatal care—or none at all. When older adolescents get good prenatal care early in the first trimester, and when they follow medical advice on diet and on cigarette, alcohol, and

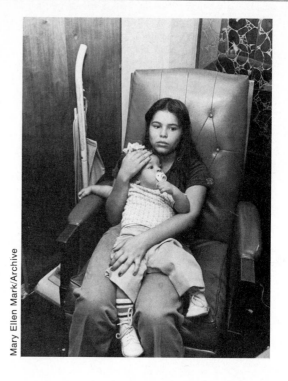

Mary Ellen Mark/Archive

drug use, their infants are as healthy as those of women in their twenties (Fielding, 1978).

Once the neonatal period is safely navigated, mother and infant continue to run additional risks. Researchers have found that adolescent mothers who breastfeed their babies may lose large amounts of calcium and other minerals from their bones, even when they take supplementary calcium and vitamin D and their diet contains as much calcium as

and Poland. Since Tay-Sachs is caused by a recessive allele, many people who show no symptoms are carriers of the disease. And since carriers have a level of Hex A far below that of the general population, a blood test can identify them. Only if both parents are carriers can the child be born with the disease.

In **sickle-cell anemia**, a genetic flaw affects the production of hemoglobin, a substance in red blood cells that combines with and releases oxygen. People with sickle-cell anemia have sickle-shaped blood cells that can clog the circulatory system, causing pain and tissue damage. Since these abnormal cells are rapidly destroyed by the spleen, the sufferer may develop severe anemia. Other destructive effects of the

needed to prevent mineral loss among lactating adults (Chan et al., 1982). Apparently, increased bone growth during adolescence, combined with milk production, requires much more calcium and phosphorus than most young mothers consume. Although the recommended daily allowance of calcium and phosphorus for lactating adolescents is higher than that for lactating adults, of the three lactating adolescents in this study whose diets met these recommendations, only one did not show mineral loss.

When the development of children with adolescent mothers was reviewed by Arthur Elster, Elizabeth McAnarney, and Michael Lamb (1983), it appeared that two hazards face these youngsters: child abuse and adverse cognitive development. Children of adolescent mothers are more likely than other children to be abused—but the abuse does not start while the mother is still an adolescent, leading the researchers to conclude that the increased abuse is probably the result of accumulated stress. The social and economic consequences of adolescent parenthood, which include low earning power, large families, and low marital satisfaction, do not go away. Without counseling and socioeconomic support, adolescent parents may find themselve as adult parents in situations they cannot handle.

Socioeconomic factors also seem to be the major influence on low school achievement and intelligence test scores among children of adolescent mothers (Belmont et al., 1981). There may be an additional effect from maternal age, since some studies that have controlled for socioeconomic factors have produced similar findings (Rinebold, Kehl, and Elster, 1982; Oppel and Royston, 1976). Just what is responsible for this additional effect is not known. However, adolescent and adult mothers do appear to behave differently with their children.

In a variety of studies reviewed by Elster, McAnarney, and Lamb (1983), adolescent mothers were less responsive to their newborn infants, talked less with their babies, seemed less sensitive to their needs, and punished them more. This less effective maternal behavior may be the result of several factors: the stress that accompanies a "problem" pregnancy, the adolescent mother's cognitive immaturity, unrealistic attitudes toward child rearing, an inaccurate knowledge of child development, and a lack of social support. Some adolescent mothers appear to believe that infants have only limited physical needs and limited mental capacities. No one knows whether these differences in maternal behavior have long-term consequences.

Yet many adolescents can become adequate parents. As Elster and his colleagues indicate, adequate social support can help solve many of the other problems. Social support can alleviate stress, provide practical assistance and information about children's capabilities, and enhance maternal self-esteem.

---

disease are rheumatism, pneumonia, kidney failure, and enlargement of the spleen. People with sickle-cell anemia often die before they are forty years old.

Sickle-cell anemia is largely confined to blacks; about one-fourth of 1 percent of American blacks have the disease, and another 5 percent carry a single allele. When a person is homozygous for this abnormal form of hemoglobin, sickle-cell anemia develops. When a person has only one abnormal allele, anemia does not develop, but because the alleles are codominant, the single allele manifests itself under certain conditions. Should such people go to very high altitudes, half their blood cells will sickle and they will become seriously ill. In tropical countries, however, such people are at an advantage, for possession of the allele protects them against malaria. Since people with sickle-cell anemia often live long enough to have children and since the gene protects against malaria, it tends to perpetuate itself. Indeed. although the possession of both alleles may be fatal, possession of a single allele confers a selective advantage in tropical areas where malaria is prevalent, because it represents a life-saving adaptation. In areas where malaria is not a problem, such as the United States, selection works against the transmission of the allele. It has been estimated that in about 2,000 years, the proportion of American blacks who carry the single allele may be reduced from 5 percent to 1 percent, greatly diminishing the incidence of sickle-cell anemia in the United States (Scarr and Kidd, 1983). Because a blood test can reveal the presence of the allele, couples can find out whether they carry the sickle-cell allele.

Nongenetic Paternal Effects

Fathers and mothers contribute equally to the development of many genetic diseases, and either can produce a gamete with chromosomal abnormalities. When we think of environmental hazards to infants, we generally assume that exposure within the uterus to some toxic substance is the source of danger. Yet it appears that when a man is exposed to such contaminants, subsequent children may be affected.

Unlike women, whose entire store of ova is present at birth, men produce sperm throughout their lives. Exposure to toxic substances may result in damage to developing gametes or to the chromosomes within them. In a review of paternal effects, Virginia Gunderson and Gene Sackett (1982) found that lead, alcohol, radiation, drugs, and industrial chemicals have been associated with reproductive damage. For example, studies with animals have shown that the offspring of lead-poisoned fathers are smaller, more likely to die soon after birth, and their learning ability is impaired compared with offspring of normal fathers. Such research confirms observations made seventy years ago (Weller, 1915), when it was noted that miscarriages and newborn deaths were more prevalent among families where the fathers were lead workers. More recently, fathers' occupational exposure to paints and solvents or their employment in the aircraft industry was associated with increased incidence of brain tumors in children younger than ten years old, even when such factors as diet, drug and alcohol use, and smoking were taken into account (Peters, Preston-Martin, and Yu, 1981).

Methadone, morphine, drugs used to treat cancer, cigarette smoke, and large doses of caffeine (more than eight cups of coffee per day) have been associated with abnormal sperm production in human males or excess fetal and infant mortality in animals, but deleterious effects on the human fetus have not been established. Because of the continual production of sperm, in many cases the likelihood of damage declines or disappears once exposure ceases. It is, of course, extremely difficult to isolate paternal effects from maternal, social, and other environmental influences. Yet once a healthy sperm and ovum meet, the possibility of problems does not end.

Prenatal Environmental Hazards

A fertilized egg that has a normal genetic makeup still faces many possible hazards before the course of pregnancy is completed. Although the environment within the uterus is usually stable, it is not proof against influences that can alter or kill the developing organism. At one time it was believed that the placental membranes, which filter all substances that pass between mother and fetus, acted as a barrier to any disease, drug, or antibody that might harm the fetus. Research and experience have destroyed this confidence, and a growing list of substances are now known to penetrate the barrier.

Even when fetal exposure to a destructive influence, called a **teratogen**, is known, there is no way to predict the precise influence the factor will have upon the developing organism. Timing is apparently a crucial factor in determining whether an environmental influence will produce an abnormality in the developing fetus. While the fertilized ovum is floating freely, it is unlikely to be affected, but once it has implanted itself and moved past the stage of simple cell division, its vulnerability increases. If some destructive agent is introduced at the time an organ is forming, that organ may never develop properly, and since organ systems do not develop simultaneously, the same teratogen can have different effects at different times. The brain is most vulnerable from the fifteenth to the twenty-fifth day of development, the eyes from the twenty-fourth to the fortieth day, the heart from the twentieth to the fortieth day, and the limbs from the twenty-fourth to the thirty-sixth day (Tuchmann-Duplessis, 1975). For example, more than twenty-five years ago, babies began to be born without arms or legs, their hands or feet growing like flippers from their bodies. It was discovered that these women had taken the drug thalidomide while the fetal limbs were forming. Teratogens may have less serious effects—or no effect at all—on organs already formed or those not yet ready to make their appearance. Most of the basic organ systems develop in the first third, or **trimester**, of pregnancy, so maternal health problems are likely to have a greater impact on the fetus at this time than later. In fact, it is during the embryonic period that the developing organism is at greatest risk (Figure 3.4).

In addition to timing, dosage may determine the destructiveness of a teratogen. Low levels of some substances, such as lead or mercury or radiation or alcohol, may have little or no effect on the fetus. Heavy dosages may lead to gross malformations.

Nevertheless, the same extent of exposure to a teratogen at the same point in development

FIGURE 3.4 Teratogens are most likely to affect major organ structures during the embryonic period, when the systems are forming. Although susceptibility to anatomic defects diminishes greatly as organ formation progresses, minor structural deviation is possible until late in the fetal period. During the fetal period teratogens usually affect an organ's growth or function rather than its structure because these are the predominant developmental features at the time.

(From J.G. Wilson. "Embryological Considerations in Teratology," in J.G. Wilson and J. Warkany, eds. *Teratology: Principles and Techniques.* Chicago: University of Chicago Press, 1965, pp. 251–261.)

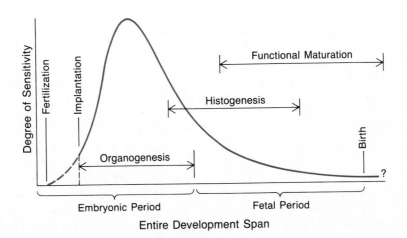

can affect two fetuses differently. The genetic susceptibility of the fetus and the mother's physical condition are factors that can limit or exaggerate the likelihood of fetal malformation (Tuchmann-Duplessis, 1975).

DISEASE A number of viruses, including mumps, influenza, and polio, pass through the placental barrier and may affect the fetus. One of the most common culprits is rubella (German measles). If a pregnant woman contracts rubella during the first trimester, her baby may be born blind, deaf, brain-damaged, or with heart defects. Not all babies born to mothers who have suffered from rubella are abnormal, but the earlier in the pregnancy the mother contracts the disease, the more likely it is that her baby will be affected. A study by Richard Michaels and Gilbert Mellin (1960) indicated that 47 percent of the babies born to mothers who had rubella during the first month of pregnancy were abnormal, whereas 22 percent of the babies whose mothers had the disease in the second month and 7 percent of those whose mothers had it in the third month were seriously affected.

Venereal diseases, such as syphilis, gonorrhea, and herpes simplex, can also seriously affect the fetus. In the case of syphilis, if a pregnant woman is in only the first or second stage of the disease, with symptoms of canker sore, rash, or fever, and if she receives treatment, her baby is likely to be born without ill effects. But if she remains untreated or if she is in a more advanced stage of the disease, the fetus may be deformed or die. If it survives, it is likely to be born prematurely and to have congenital syphilis, with all its debilitating consequences.

As the fetus moves down the birth canal, it can come into contact with *gonococcus*, the bacterium that produces gonorrhea. A number of years ago, many babies became blind when their eyes were infected during the birth process. Because many women have gonorrhea without showing any symptoms, it has become common practice to place drops of silver nitrate, erythromycin, or tetracycline in the eyes of all new-born babies. The practice has almost wiped out this kind of blindness.

The prospects are less hopeful for a herpes simplex infection, which represents a real danger for a fetus that picks up the virus in the birth canal. Since the incubation period for this virus is from four to twenty-one days, infected babies may not show any symptoms until after they go home from the hospital, when skin lesions may alert the parents. Up to half of the babies born to mothers with a genital herpes infection contract the disease, and only about half of them survive it (Babson et al., 1980).

NUTRITIONAL DEFICIENCIES Almost all vitamins, minerals, and nutrients are transported to the fetus through the placenta. Consequently, the nutritional state of the mother, especially during the first trimester, appears to be important for normal development.

Severely deficient maternal diets are associated with increased rates of abnormality (Robinson and Robinson, 1965). Diets deficient in calcium, phosphorus, and vitamins B, C, and D are associated with an increase in malformed fetuses. During the German occupation of the Netherlands in the 1940s, when food became extremely scarce, the rate of stillbirths and premature births increased among Dutch women, and the birth weight and birth length of their babies decreased. After the war, when food again became plentiful, these rates returned to normal (C. Smith, 1947). Additional data supporting the importance of adequate prenatal nutrition for fetal development come from depressed areas of the United States and from other countries where individuals customarily exist on relatively poor diets. In these regions, dietary supplements (both protein and calories) have led to improved maternal health, higher infant birth weight, and reduced levels of disease and death among infants (Pitkin, 1976). For example, pregnant Taiwanese women who had low-protein diets but were not malnourished took part in a double-blind study, in which half of the women received protein and vitamin supplements and the other half received calorie supplements (Joos et al., 1983). Babies born to the protein-supplemented mothers later performed better on tests of motor development than did babies born to mothers who got only additional calories.

It is less clear from findings in maternal nutrition how serious and widespread the effects of minor deficiencies in the mother's diet are on the developing fetus. Deficiency of a single element may sometimes have adverse effects. For example, animal research indicates that a lack of magnesium may be responsible for the development of *preeclampsia*, a serious disease of pregnancy that can result in maternal or fetal death, or growth retardation in the fetus. The animal results are paralleled by high infant mortality reported in geographic areas with low mineral content in water and magnesium-poor soil (Altura, Altura, and Carella, 1983). Such findings suggest that maternal and fetal well-being may be affected by isolated nutritional deficiencies.

DRUGS AND SMOKING A golden rule of obstetric practice has been to advise women to take as little medication during pregnancy as possible. Even aspirin has become suspect, and some researchers believe it can lengthen pregnancy and lead to bleeding in the newborn infant. The thalidomide tragedies of the 1960s vividly illustrate the consequences that heedless drug taking can have. Another example involves a drug given to maintain a pregnancy. Diethylstilbestrol (DES), a synthetic hormone that was widely prescribed during the 1950s, has been associated with vaginal cancer in women whose mothers received the drug. And prednisone, a drug prescribed for infertility, for the subsequent maintenance of pregnancy, and for such unrelated conditions as asthma or arthritis, has been associated with significantly reduced birth weights in full-term babies (Reinisch et al., 1979).

Heroin use creates an added problem. The newborn infant of a heroin or methadone user must often go through withdrawal, because both drugs pass through the placental barrier. Withdrawal symptoms usually appear about twenty-four hours after birth, and the baby may have tremors, vomiting, diarrhea, rapid breathing, high temperatures, and convulsions. In addition, almost half of these babies have low birth weights (Babson et al., 1980).

The seriousness of alcohol's effects on the fetus became apparent several years ago when a small group of pediatricians in the United States and Europe noticed that babies born to alcoholic mothers often suffered from what has become known as **fetal alcohol syndrome**. Studies in many countries have shown that a baby born to an alcoholic mother may have a low birth weight, an odd, conical-shaped head, and characteristic facial features and may be mentally retarded. Occasionally these infants have cleft palates, heart murmurs, hernias, kidney damage, and eye or skeletal defects (Streissguth et al., 1980). But a mother need not be an alcoholic for her baby to be affected. Infants born to heavy social drinkers may have low birth weights, abnormal heart rates, and low Apgar scores, and may suck weakly and perform poorly on tests of newborn behavior. Heavy drinkers also have about three times as many stillbirths as light drinkers. Not all these effects may be the result of alcohol by itself, because heavy drinkers often smoke, use both prescription and nonprescription drugs, and eat unwisely.

Researchers are still sorting out the effects of moderate social drinking. As yet, no serious effects have been found among women who take less than two drinks each day, although researchers have not ruled out the possibility of damage. In a recent study (Streissguth, Barr, and Martin, 1983), newborn infants of mothers who averaged five drinks per week during pregnancy seemed sluggish and had difficulty adjusting to stimuli. The effect remained even after researchers controlled for smoking, caffeine use, over-the-counter medication, street drugs, maternal age, nutrition during pregnancy, sex and age of infant, and medication during delivery. Once consumption reaches the two-drink per day level, the incidence of low birth weight increases (Kolata, 1981). And in another study (Streissguth et al., 1984), four-year-old children whose mothers averaged about fourteen drinks a week during pregnancy showed an impaired ability to pay attention and slower reaction time than the children of nondrinkers.

The woman who abstains six days a week and becomes intoxicated on the seventh probably places her fetus at greater risk than the woman who has a drink or two each day. Heavy doses of alcohol in the blood appear to cause the umbilical cord to collapse, sharply reducing the flow of oxygen to the fetus and possibly depriving the fetal brain of essential oxygen (Mukherjee and Hodgen, 1982). A single incident may have no effect on the fetus, but if such a pattern is maintained throughout pregnancy, there might be lasting consequences.

Cigarette smoking can also affect the fetus. Cigarette smoking by pregnant women who normally do not smoke produces an increase in fetal heart rate. Nicotine, tar, and carbon monoxide appear to be the noxious influences, and smoking appears to reduce the capacity of the blood to carry oxygen. Heavy smokers tend to miscarry more often than nonsmokers, to have smaller, lighter babies, and to have significantly more premature and low birth weight babies (Babson et al., 1980). Among 17,000 births in Britain smoking during the second half of pregnancy increased the rate of infant mortality by 30 percent and lowered the average birth weight of all babies by nearly eight ounces (Butler, 1974). When these children were seven years old, regardless of their social class, they were shorter than their peers, and lagged behind them in reading ability and social adjustment by a small but significant amount. Yet when ten-year-old children of mothers who had smoked during pregnancy were compared with the children of mothers who had not smoked, no differences could be found in growth, school achievement, or personality and social functioning (Lefkowitz, 1981). Although long-term effects cannot be ruled out, a smoker's child who

successfully weathers the newborn period does not appear to be at risk.

ANESTHETICS The fetus faces a final hazard in the delivery room. Since a number of studies (e.g., Bowes et al., 1970; Aleksandrowicz and Aleksandrowicz, 1974) have found that pain-relieving drugs given to women in labor can produce lingering effects on babies' behavior, some physicians have become increasingly reluctant to administer them. As Yvonne Brackbill (1979) has pointed out, the systems and organs most susceptible to drugs or most needed to clear drugs from the baby's system are also the most immature at birth. Her review of more than thirty studies revealed that in twenty of the studies drugs had substantial effects on a baby's behavior, in nine others there were significant but less substantial effects, and in only two did the effects seem negligible. In most studies, the drugged babies performed poorly on standard tests of infant behavior as compared with babies whose mothers received no drugs. The effects of drugs linger in babies after their mothers have recovered because the infant's metabolism is not as efficient at clearing the drug out of the system. Most discernible drug effects are gone within a few days, although subtle behavioral effects can still be detected when babies are ten days old (Lester, Als, and Brazelton, 1982).

In one of the studies that showed negligible results, Frances Horowitz and her colleagues (1977) found that medication during labor produced little effect on babies in Israel and Uruguay. The investigators point out that most American mothers who receive drugs—at least those in a group of Kansas births they studied—are more heavily sedated than women in Israel and Uruguay. Their data indicate that light dosage of pain-relieving medication has little effect on babies' behavior. However, Horowitz and her colleagues suggest that genetic and biological differences among the three groups, as well as the attitudes of women toward drugs, could magnify or diminish the effects of medication on their babies. The apathy of drugged babies can have a long-term effect on their relationships with their primary caregivers, as we shall see in Chapter 4.

EMOTIONAL CONDITION It is not far-fetched to suspect that a pregnant woman who is under considerable emotional stress is likely to find that her emotions have affected her newborn baby in some way. Stress causes chemical changes in the body, which can lead to gastric ulcers, high blood pressure, migraine headaches, cardiovascular disease, and neck pain (Selye, 1976), and women under emotional stress have more difficult pregnancies and deliveries than other women.

Some scientific investigations have suggested that a mother's emotional state can indeed influence her offspring. A number of researchers have demonstrated that stressful experiences in pregnant women and rats affect the activity level, birth weight, heart rate, motor development, and emotionality of their offspring (Joffe, 1965; Thompson, 1957). In human studies, high levels of anxiety during pregnancy have been associated with low scores by infants on various newborn assessment scales (Gunderson and Sackett, 1982). Among women studied by Lester Sontag (1966), sudden grief, fear, or anxiety invariably caused violent activity on the part of their fetuses. In one case, when a woman's husband threatened to kill her, her fetus kicked so violently that she was in pain. Subsequent recordings in this study showed a tenfold increase in activity over the levels at previous weekly checks. After these babies were born, they were irritable and hyperactive, and some had severe feeding problems.

Prematurity

Many of the environmental hazards discussed in the previous section can lead to premature birth, a term whose meaning has changed over the years. At one time "premature" simply referred to the baby that was born before **term,** a gestational age of thirty-eight weeks from conception. This definition proved to be inadequate, because some early babies were of normal weight and health, while some babies born late had serious weight deficiencies and reduced abilities to survive. As a result, prematurity came to be defined in terms of birth weight. Newborn babies who weighed less than 2,500 grams (about five and a half pounds) at birth, regardless of their gestational age, were labeled "low birth weight" and considered premature. This criterion also proved to be inadequate, because some newborns who weigh less than five and a half pounds—including those who are less than full term—may be completely normal.

Some babies are simply born small. Consider, for example, the cases of two babies whose birth weight is only four pounds. Both would have been labeled "premature," but their situations are different. The first was born substantially before term, and the younger gestational age explains the small size. Given proper premature infant care, the baby may show an accelerated "catch-up growth" once the weight of five pounds is reached. (Catch-up growth is discussed in greater detail in Chapter 5.) If so, by the time this child is three years old, he or she may be of average height and weight (Tanner, 1978). In contrast, the second baby has spent the full thirty-eight weeks in the uterus but is underweight for gestational age, that is, small-for-gestational age (SGA). In this case, it is likely that some aspect of development has gone awry and has inhibited fetal growth. This baby is likely to have physical problems. Whatever circumstances kept him or her from gaining weight also seems to inhibit catch-up growth. On the average, an SGA infant remains shorter than 75 percent of his or her cohort (Tanner, 1978).

Even if they are not SGA, babies who are born before they have completed thirty-three weeks in the uterus and those who weigh less

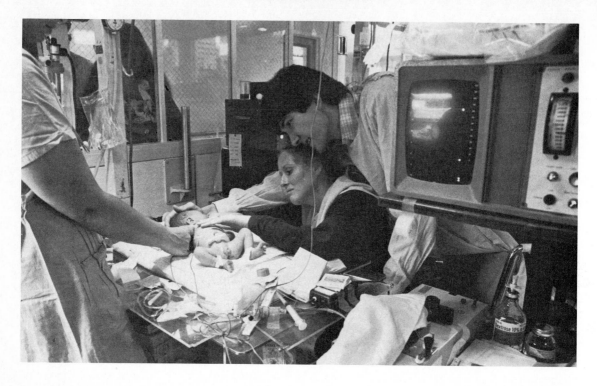

These parents watch as their tiny son, who is only thirty minutes old, receives special care in a premature nursery, where his vital signs will be monitored and he will receive intravenous feedings of water and milk. (Suzanne Arms/ Jeroboam)

than 2,000 grams (about four pounds seven ounces) are considered high-risk infants (Babson et al., 1980). If they are to survive, they need special care—and even then about 10 percent of them will not live. These babies receive intensive care in modern nurseries, where blood pressure, temperature, respiration, and heart rate can be continually monitored and where they can receive intravenous feedings of water and milk. These babies face additional hazards of development and lag behind normal babies in mental and motor skills. Although most catch up with other babies by the time they are four years old, about 15 percent of those who weigh less than 1,500 grams (three pounds five ounces)

at birth suffer some kind of intellectual impairment (Kopp and Parmalee, 1975). The prospects for preterm and high-risk infants are much brighter than they once were. Because of advances in medical technology and knowledge of development, their average intellectual development is higher and the likelihood of any motor handicap is lower than was the case only a generation ago. The best predictor of these infants' future is their home environment, and, as was the case with children born to teenage mothers, socioeconomic level is highly correlated with developmental outcome (Kopp, 1983).

Given an adequate environment, the high-risk infant's adaptive responses tend to resolve many of the physiological complications that accompany an untimely birth (Woodson, 1983). For example, high-risk infants tend to sleep more than full-term infants, allowing them to use more of their energy in catch-up growth. Thus, the baby's own adaptive behavior helps explain why most high-risk infants develop normally.

PREVENTING DEVELOPMENTAL DEFECTS

Some prospective parents who know of mal-formed children, mental retardation, or life-threatening diseases among their relatives are hesitant to produce children for fear their baby will be defective. Advances in prenatal diagnosis and the emergence of genetic counseling have made it possible for many of these people to have children without fear.

Diagnosing Abnormalities

Gross abnormalities of development can now be discovered by using ultrasound to look at the developing fetus. In an ultrasound examination, sound is bounced off the fetus and the echoes are transformed into thousands of dots that appear on a screen. The dots form a picture, called a **sonogram,** that shows details of fetus, **amniotic fluid** (the liquid in which the fetus floats), and placenta. Sonograms can find visible abnormalities, resolve confusion over the age of the fetus, and discover such conditions as a placenta that blocks the birth canal or the presence of more than one fetus.

Ultrasound is often used as a guide in performing another procedure that detects abnormalities. In this procedure, called **amniocentesis,** the physician inserts a hollow needle through the maternal abdomen and draws out a sample of amniotic fluid. The fetus sheds cells into this fluid, and if the fetal cells in the sample are grown in a culture, technicians can perform chromosomal analyses that will detect such abnormalities as Down's syndrome, Turner's syndrome, Tay-Sachs disease, sickle-cell anemia, and others. In addition, the chemical composition of the fluid frequently provides clues to other diseases and reveals whether the fetus can produce enough surfactin to avoid respiratory distress when it is born. Tests can also detect the blood group and sex of the fetus. This procedure can be done between the fourteenth and sixteenth weeks after conception, when enough cells are present in the fluid to make diagnosis possible. The procedure carries a slight risk for the fetus, however, so it is not used routinely.

Because amniocentesis cannot be performed until well into the second trimester and results are not known for several more weeks, the procedure leaves parents very little time to make major decisions concerning a defective fetus. A new diagnostic technique, **chorionic villus biopsy,** which can be performed between the eighth and tenth weeks of pregnancy, may replace amniocentesis for most purposes. In this test, a hollow tube is inserted into the uterus through the vagina and cells removed from the outer membrane that surrounds the fetus. After the twelfth week, the test no longer can be performed because the hairlike projections from which the cells are taken have disappeared (Kolata, 1983b). Because there is an abundance of cells, no culturing is necessary and diagnosis can be done immediately. Chorionic villus biopsy can detect the same range of conditions as amniocentesis.

One type of disorder that cannot be detected by chorionic villus biopsy is any neural tube defect. If the tube fails to close at the top, a condition known as **anencephaly,** the fetus will not develop a normal brain and usually dies soon after birth. If the opening is at the base of the skull, a portion of the brain will protrude, a condition known as **encephalocele.** Although the brain is normal, the only available treatment requires the removal of the protruding brain after birth, a procedure that generally leaves the infant blind and mentally retarded. An opening lower in the tube produces **spina bifida,** in which a bundle of nerves in the spinal cord protrude through the fetal back. This condition can be corrected surgically after birth, but the infant is generally paralyzed below the waist and has no bladder or bowel control. In about 70 percent of cases, spina bifida is accompanied by **hydrocephaly,** in which fluid accumulates within the skull, pressing on the brain. Although a device that drains excess fluid can be implanted into the newborn, the infant will often have learning disabilities or be mentally retarded (Leonard, 1981).

The incidence of neural tube defects is 1.2 per thousand live births in the United States. Women who are carrying a fetus with such a defect have high blood levels of alpha-fetoprotein (AFP), which appears in a simple blood test that can be given by the sixteenth week of pregnancy. The test can detect 90 percent of anencephalic fetuses and 80 percent of those with open spina bifida. In most cases, however, a high AFP level does not signify a neural tube defect. Among 1,000 pregnant women, 50 will have high AFP levels but only 1 or 2 will be carrying a defective fetus. A second blood test will show normal AFP levels in approximately 20 of these women, and ultrasound and amniocentesis can eliminate the remaining false positives. Routine AFP screening of all pregnant women has been proposed, a practice that is common in Britain. As the box on page 103 suggests, recent advances may one day make it possible to correct spina bifida before birth.

Genetic Counseling

As more ways are developed to detect abnormalities, genetic counseling takes on increased importance. The role of the genetic counselor is twofold: to provide information about the probability of fetal malformation before children are conceived, and to discuss the use of diagnostic techniques and explain the implications of test results with parents who have already conceived.

In the first role, the genetic counselor discusses probabilities. Couples who fear that they may carry a genetic disease can be tested, and often they can be reassured that their fears are groundless. For example, the Hex A level of their blood reveals whether the prospective parents are carriers of Tay-Sachs disease; if neither or only one of the couple is a carrier, the coun-

selor can assure them that their child will not have the disease. If both are carriers, the counselor can explain the probabilities (25 percent) that their child will be born with Tay-Sachs. The couple must then decide whether to go ahead with their plans to have a child. In the case of PKU, if both are carriers and the couple—knowing that there is a 75 percent probability that their child will be normal—decide to take the chance, the mother can be put on a diet that is low in phenylalanine before she conceives, thereby limiting any damage to the fetus.

With parents who have already conceived, the counselor explains the results of chorionic villus biopsy, sonograms, amniocentesis, and AFP tests. When the tests show a normal fetus—and most tests do, since the chances of normality are much greater than the chances of abnormality, even when both parents are carriers of a disease—the parents can look forward to the birth confidently, free from the worry and uncertainty that used to accompany such pregnancies. If the fetus proves to be abnormal, the counselor can discuss the extent of the possible damage and the kind of care the child will require, so that parents can decide whether to go ahead with the pregnancy or to terminate it. Many parents decide to go ahead, and forewarned that their baby will have Down's syndrome or sickle-cell anemia, are better able to handle the extra care the child will require and to establish emotional bonds with the baby without the hindrance of the sudden painful shock that used to accompany such discoveries.

Most genetic counselors see a couple after the fact. Either the woman is carrying a defective fetus or an afflicted child has already been born (Amato, 1980). When counseling occurs after the birth has taken place, the role of the counselor is to help the parents adjust to the disorder, ease any guilt feelings they might have, and provide information so they understand their child's probable future and the possible effects on any future pregnancies. But the efficacy of such counseling is still debatable. When researchers (Leonard, Chase, and Childs, 1972) studied sixty-one families in which parents of

Fetal Surgery

For more than a decade, physicians have been able to treat some fetal conditions in the uterus, administering drugs or, in some cases, transfusing blood. In 1978, researchers attempted to treat hydrocephaly by inserting hollow needles into the fetal skull and withdrawing fluid. The infant lived but was profoundly retarded; however, similar procedures with other hydrocephalic fetuses have been successful (Henig, 1982). In 1981, the practice of fetal medicine changed when researchers began to attempt procedures with the fetus that formerly had been carried out on the newborn.

In a survey of the major advances, Robin Henig (1982) reported that on December 9, 1981, Andrew Percival was born an apparently healthy, alert infant, two months after he had been diagnosed as hydrocephalic and one month after a brain shunt had been implanted in his skull to keep it drained of excess fluid while he was in the uterus. In another case, a catheter was placed within the bladder of a thirty-week-old fetus in order to relieve a life-threatening urinary-tract obstruction. The fetus, one of a pair of fraternal twins, was born at thirty-four weeks and later underwent a series of operations to construct and reroute his urinary tract. In an even more daring procedure, the uterus was opened, the fetus removed (without severing the umbilical cord), surgery performed on the urinary tract, and the fetus returned to the uterus for the remainder of the prenatal period.

A major obstacle to fetal surgery has been the fact that the procedure is likely to induce premature labor, resulting in the birth of a fetus too young to survive the dual hazards of surgery and a high-risk birth. Now that it is possible to prevent premature labor with drugs, fetal surgery has received increasing attention.

Researchers Gary Hodgen and Maria Michejda have been attempting to treat neural tube defects in the fetus. After developing a method of implanting a shunt in the skull of hydrocephalic fetuses, they began work on two other procedures that have not yet been tried on the human fetus (Kolata, 1983a). They are developing a treatment for encephalocele, in which they remove the protruding brain during fetal surgery, close the skull, and return the fetus to the uterus. (In monkeys, the fetal brain regenerates and the monkeys are born with full vision.) They are also developing a method of fetal surgery that will allow them to close the opening in cases of spina bifida and allow the nerves to regenerate, in the hope of avoiding paralysis and inability to control bladder and bowel function.

None of the fetal surgery techniques is yet standard medical procedure. By the end of 1981, twenty fetuses had undergone prenatal surgery. Nine were born healthy and appear to have been saved from lifelong disability; seven died before birth; and four were still within the uterus (Henig, 1982). It is still too early to tell whether the promise of fetal surgery will be fulfilled.

children with genetic disorders had had counseling, they found that decisions about future childbearing tended to be based on the burden involved in another defective birth—not on any realistic grasp of the probability that a future child might be affected. The families in this study subsequently had twenty-six children, and in only three instances did the parents carefully consider the odds as well as the possible burden and then take a calculated risk. Only about half of these parents understood the information they had been given, and a fourth of them learned almost nothing from genetic counseling. The greatest obstacle appeared to be such a lack of knowledge about genetics and human biology that the information they were given was meaningless. Apparently, if genetic counseling is to be effective, the public will have to be better informed.

TERMINATED PREGNANCIES

Sometimes pregnancies are terminated, and the developing organism is expelled or removed from the uterus. If this happens spontaneously and without deliberate interference on the part of the mother or a physician, it is called a **miscarriage,** or **spontaneous abortion,** when the fetus is less than twenty weeks old, and a **premature delivery** if the fetus is older. It has long been thought that miscarriages are nature's way of eliminating an abnormal fetus and that such an event, although sad, should be viewed as a blessing. Science supports this notion. Examinations of spontaneously aborted fetuses indicate that from 30 to 50 percent of all miscarried fetuses have chromosomal abnormalities. Some researchers believe that 95 percent of the embryos and fetuses with such abnormalities miscarry (Babson et al., 1980).

There is evidence that male fetuses are spontaneously aborted more often than female fetuses. Although it is difficult to verify such estimates, many researchers believe that approximately 130 to 150 males are conceived for every 100 females, but that only about 106 males are born for every 100 females (Beatty and Glueck-sohn-Waelsch, 1972). Consequently, it would appear that the prenatal death rate is higher for males than for females, a proposition that squares with the fact that the death rate for males is higher throughout life.

Not all terminations are spontaneous. Since the United States Supreme Court upheld the right of abortion, legal **induced abortions** have been more frequent. Physicians prefer to abort a fetus before it is twelve weeks old, because abortion is then relatively simple. The proce-

dure involves the use of suction to remove the embryo or fetus together with the uterine lining that sloughs off during a normal menstrual period. From twelve to twenty weeks after conception, an abortion usually requires injecting a substance into the amniotic fluid surrounding the fetus so as to make the uterus contract. This procedure is more difficult and carries a greater risk to the mother. After twenty weeks, induced abortion is not advisable because there is a chance of delivering a baby who has a remote possibility of surviving.

The decision to have an abortion, especially when the life or health of the mother is in no danger, presents complicated legal, psychological, social, and moral problems. From society's point of view, one important question is whether a fetus has a right to be born, and if so, at what point in development this right begins. Another important question is whether a woman has the right to determine how many children she will bear and when she will bear them. These issues are the focus of passionate debate and personal conflict.

BECOMING A SEPARATE PERSON

Our coverage of teratogens and birth complications may make pregnancy seem frightening and the delivery of a normal baby an unlikely event. Nothing could be further from the truth. Most babies come into the world healthy: The chances of producing a healthy, normal baby are greater than 94 percent. In 1980, out of every hundred American pregnancies that reached a gestational age of twenty weeks, one fetus died before term, one infant died in the first month of life, one had some kind of malformation (which was often correctable), and two and a half were mentally retarded because of pregnancy and birth complications (Babson et al., 1980). Since that time, medical care of the newborn has advanced and the newborn death rate has dropped even lower. For most parents, pregnancy is a time of hope and optimism, and the birth of their child is a joyous occasion.

As each baby emerges from the dark of the uterus, the most intimate human relationship ends. Within the womb, the child is dependent on the mother for the automatic satisfaction of every need; with birth, the child begins the process of learning to satisfy his or her own needs.

What happens during the prenatal period can affect the way the child will go about that process, and it can influence the entire course of the child's development. A fetus that experiences severe malnutrition, that has a genetic abnormality, or whose mother smokes heavily or drinks excessive amounts of alcohol will live in a different world from the fetus with normal genetic makeup whose prenatal existence was free from any of the environmental hazards the uterus can present. Compared to a normal baby, a baby who is deformed, sick, or thrust into the world prematurely will find that people react to him or her in altered ways. For example, the experience of spending the first several weeks of life in an intensive care nursery, separated from parents, can hamper the formation of affectional bonds between baby and caregivers. The sluggishness of a heavily sedated baby or the hyperactivity of a baby whose mother has been under severe emotional stress can alter the infant-parent relationship in subtle but sometimes important ways.

At birth, babies start life as separate individuals with all the advantages or disadvantages prenatal life has bestowed upon them. In the next chapter, we look at the beginnings of independent life—the world of the newborn child.

SUMMARY

Human development begins when the father's sperm cell, or **spermatozoon,** unites with the mother's egg, or **ovum.** These cells, called **gametes,** each have twenty-three single **chromosomes.** Chromosomes are made up of genes, which transmit traits and predispositions from parents to offspring.

The complex process of genetic combination determines the offspring's genotype, the unique combination of genes that he or she carries. The phenotype, or the actual expression of the genotype in physical appearance or behavioral disposition, is often different from the genotype, because some genes are **dominant** and some are **recessive.** Some characteristics, such as the inherited metabolic abnormality called **PKU,** appear only when two recessive **alleles** are paired. In all other cases, the dominant normal allele masks the abnormal allele.

Human development is **epigenetic:** it begins from an undifferentiated cell. During a thirty-eight-week **gestation period,** the organism rapidly progresses from a fertilized ovum engaged in cell division (**germinal period**) to an **embryo** with organ systems beginning to take shape (**embryonic period**) to a **fetus** that increasingly resembles a human being (**fetal period**).

The **central nervous system** starts as a cluster of cells and develops rapidly. By twenty weeks, all the **neurons** that make up the adult brain have formed. As brain development progresses, excess neurons begin to die. **Glial cells** develop and the fibers of neurons become **myelinated,** a process that continues for years after birth.

Behavioral development corresponds to development of the nervous system and muscles. At twelve weeks the fetus has developed many responses, and by twenty-eight weeks a rudimentary capacity for learning and remembering may be present. Twenty-three weeks is the minimum age at which a fetus can survive outside the uterus.

Birth begins with **labor,** in which strong uterine contractions push the infant and **afterbirth** through the birth canal. The physician then evaluates the baby's appearance and functioning, generally using the **Apgar method.** The experience of childbirth varies dramatically in different parts of the world, and the length and difficulty of labor seems culturally determined. In the United States, the popularity of natural methods of childbirth has led to changes in the way hospitals manage births.

Complications occasionally occur in prenatal development and birth. Abnormalities in cell division can result in a missing or extra chromosome, which creates such physical abnormalities as **Down's syndrome.** Mutations can result in genetic diseases, such as **Tay-Sachs** or PKU, which are caused by recessive genes. Some genetic diseases, such as **sickle-cell anemia,** are caused by **codominant genes,** in which the normally recessive gene expresses itself under certain conditions.

Prenatal development can also be affected when **teratogens** are present in the uterine environment. Disease, nutrition, drugs, and emotional stress are possible teratogens, but their influence depends on the timing and amount of the teratogen, fetal predisposition, and maternal health. Drugs administered during labor can also affect the fetus. Exposure to teratogens may lead to premature birth. When preterm infants are also small for their gestational age (SGA), they face additional hazards. Socioeconomic status is the best predictor of a preterm or high-risk infant's development, with babies in higher socioeconomic families generally developing in a normal fashion.

Chorionic villus biopsy, amniocentesis, and **sonograms** can detect many fetal abnormalities. AFP testing can detect the presence of neural tube defects. Such techniques allow the parents to prepare themselves to care for an abnormal baby; they may seek the advice of a genetic counselor as to the likelihood of such abnormalities and their meaning for the baby. Most genetically abnormal embryos and fetuses miscarry, and more males than females are spontaneously aborted. **Induced abortion,** a focus of continuing controversy, may sometimes be a choice for parents when a fetus has severe abnormalities.

CHAPTER FOUR

The World of the Newborn

BIRTH: THE NEWBORN
BASIC FUNCTIONS AND RHYTHMS
Temperature
Sleep
Feeding
Sucking
REFLEXES
The Rooting Reflex
Grasping and the Moro Reflex
Walking Movements
Disappearance and Reappearance of
   Responses
SENSORY CAPABILITIES
Vision
Hearing
Taste
Smell
Kinesthesis
PERCEPTION AND ATTENTION
Visual Attention
Auditory Attention
ADAPTING TO THE WORLD
Memory
Conditions for Learning
PERSONALITY AND SOCIAL RELATIONS
Temperament
Social Relations
SUMMARY

Only a few decades ago, newborn babies were considered to be helpless creatures with extremely limited sensory capacities who comprehended almost nothing of the chaotic world around them. Indeed, at one time the newborn infant was compared to a "decerebrate frog" and described as a "reflex being of a lower type." Nothing could be farther from the picture of the newborn infant as painted by today's developmental psychologists. Newborn infants can see and hear and smell; they can cry and feed and move their limbs. But they can do even more. Instead of being helpless creatures who are assailed by a barrage of meaningless stimuli, they are seen as active, searching, dynamic organisms who create much of their own experience. Newborns are now regarded as organisms constructed to acquire knowledge, and it is generally agreed that the acquisition begins almost immediately.

In this chapter, we discover that although newborn babies spend most of their time asleep, their bodies are remarkably prepared for life outside the womb, and that many of their basic functions—such as sleeping and waking, hunger and thirst, sucking, elimination, and body temperature—follow rhythmic biological schedules. The newborn's tasks of feeding and coping with

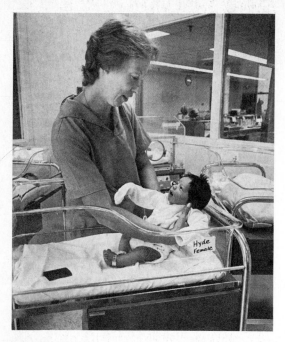

This newborn is alert and responsive; although she is only a day old, she can learn and remember and is already adapting to her environment. (Alan Carey/The Image Works)

would limit the neonatal period to the first week of life and others would limit it to the first two weeks, most researchers agree that we can refer to a baby as a neonate until the end of his or her first month of independent life (Pratt, 1954).

Why separate the study of this brief period from the rest of infancy? Most researchers make the distinction for two reasons. First, if we are to trace the development of behavior, we need to have a baseline, an understanding of the neonate's original condition before maturation and experience begin to affect it. Although these influences begin when the infant draws the first independent breath, behavior in the early weeks is least affected. Second, by understanding the capabilities of a "normal" newborn, we can more quickly detect any abnormal condition that might threaten development—or even life itself. For example, **Sudden Infant Death Syndrome (SIDS),** or crib death, in which a baby dies during sleep for no apparent reason, is rarely found among newborns. Most victims of SIDS are between two and four months old. But careful study of thousands of newborns has led researchers to detect signs, such as anemic mothers, low Apgar scores, low birth weight, respiratory problems, and jaundice, that identify newborns at risk for SIDS (Lipsitt, Sturner, and Burke, 1979). Once these infants are identified, appropriate early care might protect them from the disorder.

a strange environment are accomplished with the aid of reflexes—many of which are lost in a few weeks. Looking at the newborn's sense organs, we find that most of them are functional or soon will be, and that the baby uses them in an active and selective search of the world. From the results of experiments in hospital nurseries, it becomes clear that newborn infants are capable of learning and remembering and that certain conditions must be met for successful adaptation to the environment. We see that each infant has a distinctive temperament and the rudiments of a unique personality. Finally, we discover that the way newborns look and listen or the way they quiet when upset may provide the basis for individual differences in later social development.

The technical term for a newborn baby is **neonate,** a word derived from Greek and Latin terms, meaning "newly born." Although some

BIRTH: THE NEWBORN

To most of us, the thought of a little baby brings to mind images of a warm, roly-poly, cuddly, cooing bundle of softness and joy. Although this characterization will be apt in a few weeks, the sight of the newborn baby sometimes disappoints, if it does not shock, parents. Although most parents soon come to regard their own babies as beautiful, outsiders often disagree. One of America's earliest child psychologists, G. Stanley Hall (1891), described the neonate as arriving with a "monotonous and dismal cry, with its red, shriveled, parboiled skin . . . , squinting, cross-eyed, potbellied, and bow legged." Others have likened the physical appearance of the newborn to that of a defeated prize fighter—swollen eyelids, puffy, bluish-red skin, a broad flat nose, ears matted back at weird angles, and so forth. Considering the wet, cramped quarters of the uterus and the violent thrusting necessary for delivery, we should not regard this ragged appearance as surprising.

At the moment of birth, a newborn emerges blotched with maternal blood and covered with a white, greasy substance called **vernix,** which has facilitated passage through the birth canal. The baby's puffy, wrinkled appearance derives in part from the presence of fluid and small pads of fat under the skin. Some newborns still have fine hair, called **lanugo,** over parts of their body. When the baby emerges, the lanugo appears pasted to the skin by the greasy vernix, but after the baby is cleaned and dried, he or she may look quite furry for a few weeks until the lanugo disappears.

A newborn baby often looks somewhat battered. For example, the head may be oddly shaped—sometimes peaked rather than rounded—because the "bones" of the skull are not yet hard and consist of overlapping pieces of cartilage. This condition allows the head to compress, permitting passage through the mother's pelvis. As a result, the head is lumpy—hard in some places and soft in others. The soft areas at the crown of the head, which lack cartilage, pulsate up and down as blood is pumped about the brain. At the other end of the body, the legs are bowed and the feet cocked at a strange angle—a result of the legs having been tucked around the baby in the cramped quarters of the uterus.

Newborn babies look odd, and they often sound strange as well. In the uterus, they were suspended in liquid, and they arrive with nasal and oral passages filled with amniotic fluid and mucus. In Western hospitals, the physician cleans these passages with a suction bulb as soon as the baby's head has emerged from the uterus so that a newborn does not inhale this liquid into the lungs with the first gasping breath.

Sometimes a little remains, however, and bursts of rapid gasps, chokes, gags, coughs, and pauses can make the baby sound like a badly operating steam engine.

After the umbilical cord has been tied and cut, a nurse drops silver nitrate or antibiotics into the newborn's eyes to prevent infection, makes simple tests for certain diseases, and then swaddles the infant and allows him or her to sleep.

Although newborns occasionally jerk or cough up mucus, their first sleep is usually quite deep. They are difficult to arouse, and even a loud sound may fail to elicit any obvious response. During this sleep, their bodies are preparing to function on their own. In the uterus, the placenta linked the fetal circulatory, digestive, temperature regulation, and excretory systems with those of the mother; but now the infant's own physiological equipment must take over these necessary functions.

While these systems are being balanced and tuned, a baby frequently does not eat. Stores of fat and fluid will tide the neonate over until the first meal, which may take place within several hours of birth or may not occur for several days. As a result of this delay in feeding, most neonates lose weight during the first few days of life.

BASIC FUNCTIONS AND RHYTHMS

Although newborns are abruptly separated from their mothers' regulatory systems, they come into the world equipped with some mechanisms to keep their body systems in balance. A certain pattern or rhythm characterizes many of their basic body functions.

Temperature

The human being is a warm-blooded animal, which means that the body maintains its temperature within a narrow range. In the newborn, temperature regulation is important because the functions performed by most cells and organs are governed by enzymes that can act only within a limited range of temperature. If the baby's temperature is much lower than the optimum, several body functions might slow to dangerous levels. For example, the metabolic rate might decline so much that the infant dies. If body temperature is too high, the baby's physiological activity might be too rapid, triggering a mechanism that tends to shut down enzyme activity. Moreover, when newborns are too hot, they tend to breathe more rapidly, their blood becomes too acid, and several other biochemical and physiological systems are thrown out of balance. Consequently, the baby must maintain a relatively constant temperature.

When adults become overheated, their metabolism slows and their blood vessels dilate so that more blood can go to the body surface, where heat is dissipated into the air; they sweat and lose heat through evaporation, and they pant and release heat by exhalation. Conversely, when adults are too cold, they conserve heat by shunting blood away from the surface of the body, where it would cool, and they may move around or shiver, thus generating heat.

The newborn baby, in contrast, has a problem. In proportion to body weight, the newborn has more surface area exposed to cool air and less insulating fat than an adult. Together these factors mean that a newborn loses heat almost four times as fast as does an adult (Brück, 1961). The newborn rapidly develops mechanisms to cope with the problem. Within fifteen minutes of birth, babies—whether premature or full-term—respond to cold by constricting surface blood vessels and increasing their heat production. Two or three hours later, the newborn baby's metabolic response to cold is nearly as good as that of the adult, relative to the baby's body weight if not to body surface area. The problem is not that the newborn lacks the equipment to regulate body temperature but that the task is so great.

The efficiency of the newborn's temperature control is quickly put to the test in its first encounters in the hospital environment. The uterus generally remains at a constant 98.6°F., but the gaseous environment that greets the newborn is invariably colder: rarely over 80°F, and sometimes as low as 60°F. Because babies are born wet and are sometimes bathed, they lose considerable heat through evaporation and exposure of their skin to cool air. In fact, the drop in temperature may be so steep and rapid that the baby would have to produce twice as much heat energy per unit of body weight as the adult does in order to offset these conditions (Adamsons, 1966). Although many hospitals try to minimize this shock, life in the uterus is still considerably warmer than life in the delivery room or hospital nursery, and newborns need to be able to regulate their temperature to handle the transition. This is one reason that very small neonates often require a stay in an incubator.

Because the infant's body is so small, heat loss continues to be rapid during the neonatal period, and the problem of temperature regulation is not completely solved until the infant is between four and nine weeks old. Solving this problem is important because time and energy devoted to keeping warm reduce the infant's store, leaving fewer calories for growth. Two major ways in which infants handle thermoregulation are clinging to a caregiver, which transfers body heat to the infant, and lying quietly, which conserves heat (Rovee-Collier and Gekoski, 1979). When the temperature drops, infants draw up their limbs and curl their bodies, reducing their surface area and further decreasing heat loss (Woodson, 1983). Since activity increases metabolism, burning precious calories, newborn infants spend a lot of time sleeping.

Sleep

Newborn infants sleep approximately sixteen out of each twenty-four hours. Unfortunately for parents, most newborns package this sleep into seven or eight naps per day, with their longest single sleep averaging about four and a half hours. Consequently, newborns are roughly on a four-hour sleep/wake cycle, sleeping a little less than three hours in each four. By six weeks, however, their naps have become longer, and they take only two to four of them each day. Even newborns sleep a little more at night than during the day, and by approximately twenty-eight weeks, most babies sleep through the night without waking even once.

In addition to differences in the amount and phases of sleep, the quality of the newborn's sleep is also different from that of the adult. Studies of bodily activities during sleep indicate that there are two general kinds of sleep, distinguished principally by whether **rapid eye movement (REM)** occurs. During **REM,** or *active,* **sleep,** eye movements are accompanied by more rapid and changeable respiration, less muscular activity, and a more even pattern of brain waves. In Figure 4.1, the tube around the baby's stomach expands and contracts with each breath, the electrodes on the chest detect heart rate, and the stabilimeter that the baby lies on detects body movements. In addition, electrodes placed near the eyes detect eye movements, and other elec-

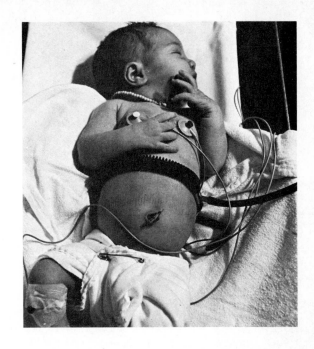

FIGURE 4.1 *(top)* This baby is in a stabilimeter crib, which measures muscular activity. The belt around the abdomen measures respiration, and the electrodes on the chest produce electrocardiographic records. When electroencephalographic recordings are made, electrodes are placed at the outer corners of the eyes. Although cumbersome, the apparatus is not uncomfortable for the baby. *(bottom)* Recordings showing the differences between thirty seconds of REM sleep and non-REM sleep in a newborn. Besides the heightened eye activity during REM sleep, note the absence of muscle activity, the rapid respiratory rate, and changing respiratory amplitude.

(Photograph by Jason Lauré; chart after Roffwarg, H.P., W.C. Dement, and C. Fisher. "Preliminary Observations of The Sleep-Dream Pattern in Neonates, Infants, Children, and Adults," in E. Harms, ed. *Monographs on Child Psychiatry,* No. 2. New York: Pergamon Press, 1964.)

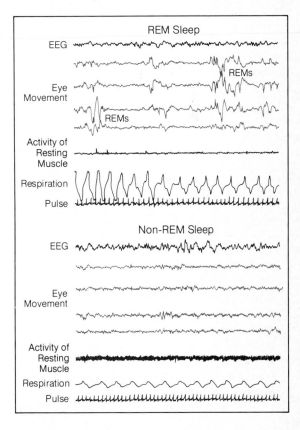

trodes placed on the head record brain waves on an electroencephalograph (EEG). The minute electrical changes that accompany muscular movements are amplified and written by a polygraph on a continuously flowing sheet of paper.

Newborns spend almost half of their sixteen hours of sleep in REM sleep. Not until children are almost five years old does this proportion drop to approximately 20 percent, which is the adult average. The amount of **non-REM,** or *quiet*, sleep changes little over the childhood years, indicating that much of the newborn's extra sleep is composed of REM sleep.

What do the rapid eye movements of REM sleep signify? Adults wakened during REM sleep often report that they have been dreaming. Consequently, some people have supposed that newborn babies (and perhaps pet dogs) dream during REM sleep. Physiologically, the REM sleep of neonates is not identical to that of dreaming adults and does not become so until infants are three to four months old (Parmelee and Sigman, 1983). It is unlikely that a newborn baby experiences anything like the integrated series of clear dream images that most adults report. The neurological activity of REM sleep apparently serves a physiological purpose, because most adults whose REM sleep is interrupted become nervous, anxious, and have trouble concentrating (Dement, 1960), and they make up for the loss of REM sleep by showing a higher percentage of it in subsequent sleep periods. Some scientists have suggested that the brain requires periodic neural activity, either from external or internal sources, and that REM sleep signifies self-generated activity in the absence of any external stimulus (Roffwarg, Muzio, and Dement, 1966). Others suggest that REM sleep reflects either a high metabolic rate or neural immaturity (Berg and Berg, 1979). Because newborns sleep so much and have less opportunity to respond to events in the world around them, they may require more of this neurological self-stimulation. In one study, neonates who spent a good deal of their waking time looking attentively at stimuli afterward showed a temporary decrease in REM sleep (Boismier, 1977). Premature babies show even higher percentages of REM sleep than do full-term infants, with those born as early as twenty-five weeks spending all their sleep time in a variety of REM sleep (Parmelee and Sigman, 1983). It is possible that such activity is necessary before birth if neurological development is to occur. Therefore, the first function of REM sleep may be to act as an internal stimulus to neurological development; later it will carry the visual patterns and integrated experiences that constitute the dreams of older children and adults (Roffwarg, Musio, and Dement, 1966).

An infant's physiological state fluctuates regularly. During the eight hours when babies are not asleep, they may be drowsy, alert, fussy, or crying. Obviously, a sleepy, fussy, or wailing baby is likely to be uncooperative and show little interest in tests devised to explore his or her capabilities. For that reason, most studies are performed when babies are alert—a state limited to about 11 percent of the first week outside the uterus (Wolff, 1963). But by the time babies are four weeks old, they are alert about 21 percent of the time.

Feeding

The newborn's sleep/wake cycle is closely tied to the need for nourishment. The typical neonate sleeps, wakes up hungry, eats, remains quietly alert for a short time, becomes drowsy, and then falls back to sleep. When unrestricted breast-feeding is practiced, in which babies are given the breast whenever they cry or fuss, they are likely to eat ten or more times a day during the first few weeks (Newton, 1979).

Books advising parents often suggest a four-hour feeding schedule. The four-hour schedule may have emerged from a study in 1900 of three newborns who were fed a barium-milk solution and then X-rayed periodically after they had swallowed it. The study showed that within four hours the stomach had emptied (Frank, 1966). Some years ago it was common practice

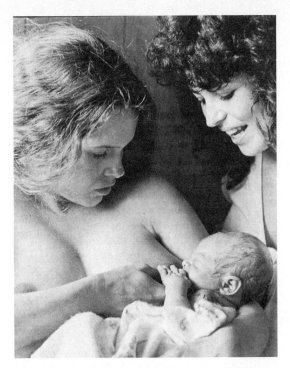

This newborn, who was born at home, is having the first meal. If allowed to eat on demand, the baby is likely to nurse more than ten times a day for the first few weeks. (Ed Buryn/Jeroboam)

to feed young babies on a strict schedule regardless of whether they appeared to be hungry. Parents even woke sleeping babies to feed them. If left to choose their own schedules, a practice called **self-demand feeding,** only about a fourth of them would adopt a four-hour regimen. C. Anderson Aldrich and Edith Hewitt (1947) studied one hundred babies who were allowed to establish their own feeding schedules during the first twelve months of life. At every age, different babies demanded different numbers of meals. For example, during the first month of life, 60 percent of the babies ate every three hours, 26 percent ate every four hours, and approximately 10 percent demanded a feeding every two hours. Most newborns begin by putting themselves on a three-hour schedule and reach three meals a day by the time they are ten months old. Although all babies show some

rhythm in their feeding patterns and all require progressively fewer daily feedings as they get older, there are marked differences among babies in the frequency of their meals. Because of studies like this, parents are now encouraged to feed their babies whenever they are hungry, while working toward fewer and fewer feedings as their babies grow.

Sucking

Being able to suck effectively is the foundation of feeding and therefore of survival. Consequently, it is one behavior that the newborn must perform competently and precisely, and it has been studied in great detail.

The young baby sucks rhythmically, in bursts separated by pauses. On the average, a baby puts together approximately five to twenty-four sucks in a single burst, sucking at a rate of approximately one to two and a half times each second, and then takes a brief rest. Although a baby's hunger, age, health, and level of arousal influence the pattern of sucking, individual babies also have their own characteristic patterns of sucking. Whether particular sucking patterns are innate is unknown, because sucking at birth is affected by drugs that pass through the placenta during labor. Several days later, when these drugs have worn off, sucking patterns may already have been affected by the behavior of the mother (Crook, 1979).

The neonate's feeding performance is often a little ragged during the first few days of life, but a baby quickly develops a fairly smooth coordination between sucking, swallowing, and breathing. The fact that a newborn can swallow almost three times faster than an adult, and can suck at the same time that he or she takes in air, aids in the accomplishment of this feat. Adults who sucked in a liquid and breathed at the same time would probably choke. Babies can manage simultaneous sucking and breathing because they extract milk from the nipple by pressing the nipple against the roof of the mouth instead of by inhalation.

REFLEXES

The reflexes of the newborn attracted the attention of neurophysiologists and pediatricians quite early, and their studies have provided us with an extensive catalog of reflexive behavior. The newborn comes equipped with a set of reflexes that are elicited by specific stimuli. Some are adaptive and may help the new baby avoid danger. For example, babies close their eyes to bright light and twist their bodies or move their limbs away from sources of pain. Other reflexes appear to be vestiges of the past, left over from our nonhuman ancestors. Still others are simple manifestations of neurological circuitry in the baby that later will come under voluntary command or will be integrated in more useful patterns of behavior. Most of these reflexes seem to disappear within a few weeks or months, perhaps because neurological development, especially in the cortex of the brain, allows the infant to control the responses so that a stimulus no longer evokes them (Zelazo, 1976).

When these reflexes fail to drop away, it may be a sign of abnormal neurological development, and when they are feeble, the infant may be at risk for SIDS. The unconditioned, defensive reflexes that babies use to clear their air passages may be weak in some infants. Unless these reflexes work properly during the neonatal period, suggests Lewis Lipsitt (1979), babies will not learn to clear obstructions by the time the reflexes drop away. Because the babies are weaker and not as visually alert, and engage their environment less, they may have fewer opportunities than other babies to learn the voluntary responses that could later save their lives. Indeed, babies who later died from SIDS have been found to react poorly just after birth to tests of their defensive reflexes in which cotton is placed over the nostrils and cellophane over the nose and mouth (Anderson and Rosenblith, 1971). The problem may be aggravated by modern living patterns, in which young infants sleep alone, away from the smell, sound, touch, and movement of their parents' bodies—stimulation that may help to regulate infant breathing

(McKenna, 1983). Among the prominent neonatal reflexes are the rooting reflex, the grasping and Moro reflexes, and the stepping and placing reflexes.

The Rooting Reflex

All newborns have a **rooting reflex**—a tendency to turn the head and mouth in the direction of any object that gently stimulates the corner of the mouth. Babies are most likely to show this at about a week or two of age when they are quietly awake with their eyes open, especially if they are somewhat hungry. If one strokes the corner of the baby's mouth with an index finger, moving sideways from the mouth toward the cheek, the baby may move tongue, mouth, or whole head toward the stimulated side. At first this reflex appears even when the cheek is stroked a long way from the mouth. As the baby gets older, the reflex will appear only when the stimulation is at the mouth, and only the baby's mouth will respond. The rooting reflex generally disappears at three to four months. This reflex has obvious adaptive significance because it helps a baby to place the nipple in the mouth. Babies sometimes learn to suck their thumbs while rooting, when a thumb and mouth accidentally make contact.

Grasping and the Moro Reflex

A baby in the first weeks of life has a strong **grasping reflex.** If one places a one-week-old baby on his or her back and places a finger in the infant's hand, the baby is likely to grasp that finger sturdily. Sometimes a grasping newborn can literally hang by one hand. Although the reflex becomes stronger during the first month, it then begins to fade, disappearing at three or four months.

Ernst Moro (1918) first described the **Moro reflex,** which consists of a thrusting out of the arms in an embracelike movement when the

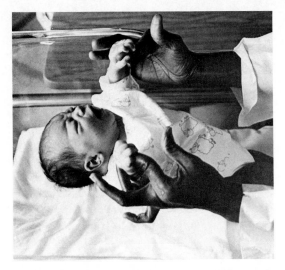

Newborns display the grasping reflex by tightening their fingers around anything placed in their hands. (Lawrence Frank)

In monkeys, who carry their young on their backs or stomachs, the grasping and Moro reflexes are still adaptive, for a loss of support is less likely to produce a fall if the youngster reaches out and grasps its mother's fur or skin.

Walking Movements

A one- or two-week-old baby shows behavior that resembles the movements required in walking. One of these is a **stepping** motion that can be elicited by holding a baby under the arms while gently lowering the infant to a surface until the feet touch and both knees bend. If the baby is slowly bounced up and down, he or she may straighten out both legs at the knees and hips as if to stand. Then, if the infant is moved forward, he or she may make stepping move-

baby suddenly loses support for the neck and head. It is easily seen after the first week when the baby is alert, with eyes open or barely closed. It can be elicited by holding a baby with one hand under the head and the other in the small of the back and then abruptly lowering one's hands, especially the hand holding the head. A second way to obtain the Moro reflex is to lay a baby on his or her back, with the head facing straight up, and then slap the mattress behind the head with enough force to jerk the head and neck slightly. Typically, the arms shoot out and upward and the baby's hands curl slightly as if preparing to grab something. In fact, if one places a finger in the baby's hand, having somebody else provide the stimulus for the Moro, one can feel the baby suddenly tighten his or her grip. The Moro reflex decreases as the baby gets older; it is difficult to elicit after the baby is three months old, and it is almost always gone by five or six months.

The meaning and purpose of the grasping and Moro reflexes are not clear. It has been suggested that this behavior is an adaptive response that has outlived its usefulness (Prechtl, 1982).

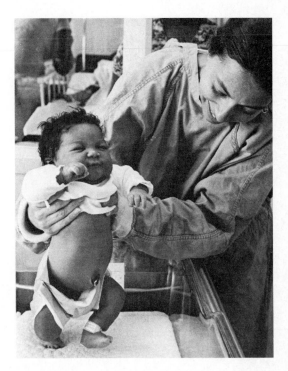

The stepping motion appears when a baby is lowered until the feet touch a surface; the baby responds by making walking movements. (Camilla Smith)

ments as if walking, although the baby can neither support his or her own weight nor maintain balance.

The second walking motion, a **placing** response, is simply the baby's propensity to lift the feet onto a surface. If held up and moved toward a surface until the top part of a foot touches the edge, the baby is likely to lift up the foot and place it on the surface.

Such behavior has relatively little practical utility in itself, because the one- or two-week-old baby possesses neither the strength nor the balance either to walk or to step. However, the two reflexes appear to indicate a certain inborn neurological organization that forms the basis for later standing and walking. These reflexes tend to disappear between the third and fourth month, and when stepping movements next appear, they will be voluntary acts from a baby who is getting ready to rise up and walk.

Disappearance and Reappearance of Responses

It seems odd that a newborn can make walking movements but an older baby cannot. Psychologists have puzzled over the disappearance and reappearance of this behavior and have come up with two possible explanations (Zelazo, 1976). In the first, reflexive walking is believed to be under the influence of the primitive areas of the brain. As the cortex matures, it takes over control, and the baby must actively learn the action he or she earlier performed as a reflex. Some data support this position. Anencephalic babies, who have no cortex at all, behave much like normal babies during the early weeks of life (Kessen, 1967). If this explanation is correct, practicing the reflex is unlikely to affect later behavior, since the disappearance and reappearance is solely the result of maturation.

The second explanation is that the reflexes do not actually disappear but instead are incorporated into a smooth pattern under cortical control (Zelazo, 1976). In this view, the reflexes

"disappear" when the baby develops the ability to inhibit them. If a baby found pleasure in exercising a reflex, then it might not disappear. Testing this supposition, researchers (Zelazo, Zelazo, and Kolb, 1972) gave babies practice in the stepping reflex for twelve minutes each day from one week until they were eight weeks old. At eight weeks, the time when the stepping response usually disappears, the stepping response of these infants was even stronger than it had been at one week, with the babies taking about thirty steps when placed on a flat surface. Babies who had been only passively exercised (their legs were pumped by their mothers as they lay in their cribs) took about seven steps, and those with no practice at all took less than one. The researchers believe that among the babies given daily practice, the stepping response had shifted from reflexive to voluntary, cortical control.

A third explanation, put forth by a developmental neurologist, is that another motor program develops, one that dominates the original program but does not incorporate it (Prechtl, 1982). In the case of walking, when the sole of the foot is placed on a smooth surface, a baby flexes the legs instead of stepping.

Walking is not the only response that appears, seems to disappear, then reappears later in development. Newborns have a reaching response and may move their hands toward objects they see, apparently without any intent to grasp the object but simply as part of their attentional response to it (von Hofsten, 1982). This sort of pattern, which appears in many areas of development, has been called **U-shaped behavioral growth** by Sidney Strauss (1982), who points out that when the behavior reappears it is not always identical with the original response. In early "prewalking," for example, the reflexive stepping takes a scissorlike pattern, in which the moving foot often gets caught on the other foot, that is not found in later walking. Yet the two forms of behavior apparently are related, for infants with early practice in the stepping response are likely to walk a bit earlier than the average baby (Zelazo, Zelazo, and Kolb, 1972).

SENSORY CAPABILITIES

Some years ago, many people believed that the newborn baby could not sense the physical energies in the environment. It was held that the baby could not see clearly, could not smell or taste, and could feel only pain, cold, and hunger. However, research has established that neonates' senses, although not as precise as those of adults, do inform them about their surroundings. Since the ability to learn, to think, and to become a social being depends upon our perceptions of the world, the newborn's sensory capabilities are important. If we know what newborns can see, hear, smell, and taste, we can discover which events in the environment might influence them.

Vision

When an infant is born, the retina (where focused light stimulates cells that pass signals along the optic nerve to the brain) is obviously immature. The peripheral area resembles the adult retina, but the center, which bears the major responsibility for detailed vision and color perception, is so poorly developed that it may be barely functional (Abramov et al., 1982). The optic nerve is both thinner and shorter than the adult's, but the sheath of myelin, which speeds transmission of signals, forms faster here than in other parts of the nervous system. The visual cortex—that part of the brain where visual signals are interpreted—is underdeveloped. All the neurons are present, but most are unmyelinated (Banks and Salapatek, 1983). Taken together, the condition of the visual system would lead us to expect that a newborn's vision is very different from that of an adult. Several such differences have been identified.

For example, if children or adults hold one finger a few inches from the nose and another at arm's length, they can quickly alternate their focus from one to the other, an ability called **visual accommodation.** Until recently, it was believed that the newborn did not possess this capability but instead operated like a fixed-focus camera, so that only objects about nine inches from the eye were in focus. Research now indicates that infants less than a week old have some ability to accommodate, but that it is quite limited (Braddick et al., 1979). Newborns do a better job of accommodating to an object that is seventy-five centimeters (about thirty inches) away than to an object that is one hundred fifty centimeters away (about sixty inches). Until they are well out of the newborn period, infants tend to overaccommodate for distant objects and to underaccommodate for near objects.

Despite the fact that such consistent errors in their attempts to focus suggest that newborns see some objects more clearly than others, clarity of vision does not seem to vary a great deal with distance (Banks and Salapatek, 1983). Seeing objects clearly and resolving their detail—an ability called **visual acuity**—is so poor among infants that most objects, near or distant, may be somewhat blurred. An object apparently must move a good distance toward or away from the infant before the sharpness of the image changes, indicating that newborns cannot tell whether an object is in focus or out of focus. Because acuity is generally poor, newborns do not seem to detect small objects or features. The week-old baby's acuity is so poor that an adult with the same vision would be considered legally blind. Vision improves rapidly, however; by six months the eyeball has become more spherical and a baby can see as clearly as the average adult. A six-month-old may even detect features so small that they escape the notice of the baby's parents (Banks and Salapatek, 1983). The newborn's limited focus is one mechanism that minimizes the confusion in a baby's world; the limitation sharply reduces the amount of distinctive visual stimulation that gets through. The newborn's peripheral vision is also quite limited. Whereas an adult's field of vision covers 180 degrees, the newborn's is only 60 degrees, shutting out two-thirds of the available stimulation and further minimizing possible confusion.

When adults look at an object, they focus both

eyes on it. Each eye sees a slightly different image, and by a mechanism called **convergence,** the two images come together until only a single object appears. If one holds a finger at arm's length, focuses on it, and then moves it toward the tip of the nose, one can feel the muscles of the eyes perform this function. The newborn does not possess this ability until the age of about seven or eight weeks. If, therefore, two objects are held nine inches in front of the baby's face, it is possible that the infant's right eye will look at the right object and the left eye at the left object (Wickelgren, 1967).

Because the newborn's eyes are not usually directed toward precisely the same point, the baby often looks wall-eyed (a condition known as **strabismus**) for the first month of so. Given their limited muscular ability, newborns are lucky if they move both eyes in the same direction half the time, let alone keep both trained on the same object. Although the newborn tries to converge both eyes on a target, success is so infrequent that images from the two eyes are probably misaligned most of the time, indicating that newborns do not perceive depth in their world—at least when using cues from both eyes. Whether they can use a single eye to tell when an object appears to have approached or receded is uncertain. Although some research (Bower, Broughton, and Moore, 1971) has indicated that very young infants can detect depth through cues of changing size and clarity, later studies have questioned these conclusions (Banks and Salapatek, 1983). It seems probable that some experience is required to appreciate depth.

For almost a century, scientists have been trying to determine whether newborn babies can see color. Babies easily tell the difference between objects that differ in brightness, but it is extremely difficult to separate brightness and hue in such a way as to test newborns for color vision (Banks and Salapatek, 1983). On the basis of physiological evidence, it appears that the color-sensitive cells in the eyes of newborns are functional but few in number and barely developed in structure. In addition, the central portion of the retina, where color-sensitive cells are packed closely together in adults, is immature in comparison with the rest of the retina (Abramov et al., 1982). This suggests that for at least the first several weeks of life the newborn may be colorblind.

Hearing

There is no question that newborn babies hear. Their ears operate four months before they are born; the basic neurology that enables them to discriminate between different tones and intensities is probably ready two months before birth; and approximately one month before birth they are prepared to direct their attention toward a sound. At first, the sounds reaching a neonate may be somewhat dampened, because for the first few days of life the middle-ear passages are filled with amniotic fluid, hindering the transmission of sound. Some receptor cells in the inner ear, especially those responsible for the transmission of high-frequency sounds, are immature at birth (Hecox, 1975). And although the auditory nerve is well myelinated at birth, the auditory cortex—that part of the brain where sound is interpreted—is quite immature. However, all normal newborns can hear, and some can hear very well. Most newborns will turn their heads in the direction of a shaking rattle, but instead of turning immediately, as an older infant would do, they take about two and a half seconds to respond (Muir and Field, 1979). Premature infants are even more sluggish in their response to sounds, not turning their heads toward the sound until about twelve seconds have passed (Aslin, Pisoni, and Jusczyk, 1983).

A major difference between adult and newborn hearing is the way they respond to the same sound coming from two different sources. When an adult hears a sound on the right, for example, followed a few microseconds later by the same sound on the left, the adult hears a single sound coming only from the first direction. This auditory illusion, called the **precedence effect,** apparently is not present in newborns, for they do not behave as if the first direction were the only source of the sound (Clifton et al., 1981). Since a five-month-old responds to the precedence effect just as adults do (Clifton et al., 1982), Rachel Clifton and her colleagues suggest that the suppression of the second sound occurs in the auditory cortex and that the newborn's failure to succumb to the illusion is evidence of the immaturity of the auditory cortex at birth.

One study suggests that the faintest sound that a baby can detect is about as soft as the faintest sound heard by the average adult (Eisenberg, 1970), but the detection depends upon the sound's frequency (sound cycles per second). At all frequencies, a sound may have to be more intense for a newborn to detect it. Although the newborn can hear a sound, as opposed to no sound, babies have difficulty in discriminating one sound from another. For example, the average newborn can only detect the difference between tones of 200 and 1,000 cycles per second—which is roughly comparable to the difference between a foghorn and a clarinet (Leventhal and Lipsitt, 1964). On the other hand, some exceptional infants have responded to tones that differ as little as 60 cycles per second, which is roughly equivalent to one step on a musical scale (Bridger, 1961).

Sounds are important to a newborn. A baby who is upset can often be soothed by the sound of a beating heart, the same sound that was a constant feature of the fetal world. Researchers have found that a metronome or other regular heartbeatlike sound is also an effective soother (Brackbill et al., 1966) and that newborns will suck vigorously at a nipple in order to prolong the sound of tape-recorded heartbeats (De-Casper and Sigafoos, 1983).

Taste

Like many of the newborn's other abilities, the sensitivity to taste is much more highly developed than was believed only a few years ago. When drops of various concentrated solutions are placed on their tongues, newborn babies respond with facial expressions much like those of adults. Jacob Steiner (1979) tested 175 full-term babies and found that an extremely sweet liquid brought forth smiles, followed by an eager licking and sucking. When they tasted a sour solution, most babies pursed their lips, wrinkled their noses, and blinked their eyes. When a bitter fluid was dripped into their mouths, the babies stuck out their tongues and spat. (See Figure 4.2.) Some even tried to vomit. Yet when Steiner placed distilled water on their tongues, the babies simply swallowed, showing no expression at all. A group of twenty premature infants, given plain water and a sour solution, responded just as the full-term infants had done. In a later study, Steiner (Ganchrow, Steiner, and Daher, 1983) found that these responses became more intense as the flavor intensified, indicating that newborns can tell the difference between "sweet" and "very sweet" and "bitter" and "very bitter."

Within several weeks after birth, a baby's taste sensitivity becomes more acute (Johnson and Salisbury, 1975). For example, when fed solutions of salt water, sterile water, artificial milk, or breast milk, a baby is likely to show a distinctly different pattern of sucking, swallowing, and breathing for each solution. Newborns also alter sucking patterns when the solution is sweet. Charles Crook and Lewis Lipsitt (1976) found that babies suck more slowly and their heart rate increases as solutions get sweeter. These results appear contradictory, because we might expect a baby to suck more vigorously when given a solution that tastes good. Crook and Lipsitt resolve this paradox by suggesting that because babies savor the taste of the sweeter solutions, they slow down to enjoy them, and that pleasurable excitement causes their hearts to speed up.

Smell

Newborns definitely react to strong odors. Babies less than twelve hours old responded in a

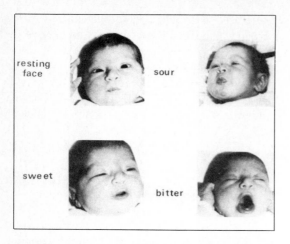

NEWBORN RESPONSES TO STRONG TASTES

Response	Percentage Responding	
	Less than 20 hours old (N = 75)	Three to seven days old (N = 100)
Sweets		
Retraction of mouth angle	81	87
Satisfied smile	77	73
Eager sucking and licking of upper lip	99	97
Sour		
Pursed lips	100	98
Wrinkled nose	77	73
Repeated blinking	89	70
Increased salivation	81	65
Flushing	76	64
Bitter		
"Arch-like" lips with depressed mouth angles	97	96
Protruding tongue	79	81
Salivation and spitting	76	87
Expression of "anger" & dislike	79	86
Vomiting	45	52

(*Source:* Adapted from Jacob E. Steiner, "Facial Expressions of the Neonate Infant Indicating the Hedonics of Food-related Chemical Stimuli," in *The Genesis of Sweet Preference,* by James M. Weiffenbach (ed.), National Institute of Dental Research, DHEW Publication No. (NIH) 77-1068, U. S. Department of Health, Education and Welfare, 1977.)

recognizable manner to synthetic odors of various foods (Steiner, 1979). When a cotton swab saturated with the odor of rotten eggs or concentrated shrimp was waved beneath their noses, the infants reacted as babies in Steiner's previous experiment had responded to bitter tastes. To the aroma of butter, bananas, vanilla, chocolate, strawberry, and honey, the babies responded with expressions of enjoyment and satisfaction.

In earlier experiments, newborns quickly turned away from the smell of ammonia or vinegar (Engen and Lipsitt, 1965). Studies have shown that within two or three days, newborns also recognize a strong odor they have smelled before. When first presented with the odor of anise oil, for example, a baby's activity increases and his or her heart rate and breathing pattern change. If the odor continues, the baby gradually stops responding to it. At this point, if a new odor, such as phenyl alcohol, reaches the baby's nose, the infant again becomes more active, and shows a changed heart rate and breathing pattern.

The keenness of the newborn's sense of smell was further suggested by the research of Aidan Macfarlane (1977) at Oxford University. He had noticed that when placed next to the mother's breast, a typical newborn turns his or her face toward it before seeing it or touching the nipple. Macfarlane wondered if this was because the baby could smell the milk beginning to drip from the nipple. To test this notion, he per-

FIGURE 4.2 Although it was once believed that newborn infants were unable to tell the difference between lemon juice and sugar, research has shown that they respond to strong tastes much as adults do. The facial expressions of the neonate resemble those of an adult who has just tasted similar solutions, and the accompanying table shows how widespread such reactions were among a group of 175 babies, whose ages ranged from several hours to a week.

(Photograph courtesy Jacob E. Steiner)

formed two simple experiments. First, he collected breast pads that mothers had used to absorb the small amount of milk that leaks between feedings. For the first experiment, he placed the mother's breast pad on one side of a baby's head and a clean pad on the other side next to the cheek. Because many babies prefer one side or the other, usually the right, care was taken to alternate the pads' placement. Babies spent more time with their heads turned toward their own mothers' milk-scented pads than toward the clean pads. But the babies' noses were sharper than Macfarlane had expected. In the second experiment, he substituted a milk-scented pad from another mother for the clean pad and compared the reactions. He found that babies turned their heads toward both pads for about the same amount of time during the first two days; but by the time they were six to ten days old, they turned most of the time toward their own mothers' pads. This sensitivity to the odor of human milk may help guide the newborn to the nipple, thus contributing to survival in early life.

Kinesthesis

A newborn apparently has a functioning **kinesthetic sense,** which provides information about body movement and position through nerve endings in the muscles, tendons, and joints. Kinesthesis is necessary for the regulation of body movement, and kinesthetic stimulation is necessary for normal development. Being rocked, jiggled, held up, and carried about provides a newborn with this essential stimulation, which has been associated with motor, cognitive, and social development. The pervasive effects of kinesthetic stimulation may come about because such activities seem to keep the infant in a quiet, alert state—stimulating an unaroused baby and calming a baby who is overaroused (Yarrow, Pedersen, and Rubenstein, 1977). The importance of kinesthetic stimulation was indicated by a study in which newborns were picked up and talked to whenever they were awake (Tho-

man, Korner, and Beason-Williams, 1977). This stimulation went on for five days. Compared with newborns that had only been talked to as they lay quietly in their cribs, the six-day-old newborns with extra kinesthetic stimulation were much more responsive to the sound of the human voice.

PERCEPTION AND ATTENTION

Because a newborn is not a passive recipient of whatever stimulation the environment presents, he or she pays attention to some stimuli and ignores others, actively selecting aspects of the world to notice and learn about. As Marshall Haith (1980) puts it, the neonate is biologically prepared to seek information and able to adapt to the consequences of information acquired in the search.

Visual Attention

As we have seen, the visual system is active at birth, and stimulation such as that found in contours and contrasts causes neurons to fire in the visual cortex of the brain. It appears probable, says Haith, that a single organizing principle underlies visual attention in the neonate: looking at objects in the world in order to maintain the firing of those cells at a high rate. Although babies are certainly not aware that this is their biological goal, the resulting activation of cells maintains established neural pathways and sets up new ones. Haith believes that this principle can explain the effect of illumination and contrast on the infant's visual system as well as neonatal visual search strategies.

When alert babies are in the light, they generally open their eyes, but objects that are too dim or too bright will not attract their gaze. Maurice Hershenson (1964) found that a baby who is two or three days old will look longer at objects of moderate brightness than at those that are either extremely bright or very dim, a discovery that confirms the experiences of parents that newborns shut their eyes and turn away from bright sunlight. Placed in the dark, these same babies open their eyes wide, as if straining to see, a technique that increases the chances of detecting visual stimulation, thereby increasing neural firing (Haith, 1980).

PATTERN AND CONTRAST A great deal of research has been devoted to a baby's attention to pattern. As early as 1944, Fritz Stirnimann found that babies only a day old would look longer at a patterned surface than at a plain one. In the first modern experiments on a baby's attention, Robert Fantz (1965) used a "looking chamber" with babies as young as two days old. Fantz placed the baby in a drawerlike carriage and slid the carriage into the looking chamber, where stimuli were placed directly above the infant. Using this procedure, he found that newborns look more at patterns than at homogeneous gray stimuli, a practice that increases stimulation of cells in the visual cortex.

Certain aspects of a pattern are more likely than others to attract an infant's gaze. By recording babies' eye movements, Philip Salapatek and William Kessen (1966) found that newborns do not devote an equal amount of attention to all parts of a figure. Shown a triangle, they concentrate their gaze on a corner and perhaps on the sides forming that corner. Here at the edges, black and white contrast is highest, providing peak stimulation, as shown in Figure 4.3. Once these newborns find a point of contrast, they are not likely to search the figure for another. However, later studies indicate that newborns sometimes scan a figure extensively, although not nearly so much as an older infant (Banks and Salapatek, 1983).

Two decades of experiments have not been able to demonstrate conclusively why some patterns are more attractive to newborns than others (Banks and Salapatek, 1983). Recently, Judith Gardner and Gerald Turkewitz (1982)

proposed that the infant's state plays an important part in determining preference for a pattern. They found that babies who are highly alert (hungry and free to move their arms and legs) are much less interested in visual patterns than hungry infants who are swaddled or full infants who are free to move about. The highest interest in patterns was shown by full, swaddled infants, who presumably were the least alert. All these babies were awake and quiet when tested. It would appear that visual preference and internal state interact to determine the sort of attention infants give to the world.

SEARCH STRATEGY AND MOVEMENT Babies respond early to movement. A five-day-old newborn who is sucking on a pacifier will stop this rhythmical sucking if a light moves across the visual field (Haith, 1966). Despite the fact that their right and left eyes do not always look at the same thing, newborns briefly pursue a slowly moving object with a smooth eye movement; but the movement soon becomes jerky (Kremenitzer et al., 1979). Not until babies are about three to six weeks old does their visual pursuit become coordinated and smooth. If the movement is not too rapid, newborns are more attracted to a moving object than to a stationary one.

Not all objects move, and when stimulation is stationary, newborns use some simple strategies to govern their visual searches. When in the dark they tend to scan the environment systematically in a horizontal rather than vertical direction, scanning rhythmically at the rate of approximately two scans per second (about the same as their sucking rhythm). This sort of search, says Haith (1980), maximizes the baby's chance of finding subtle shadows, edges, or any lit areas.

If light is available, the baby uses a different strategy, searching for edges with broad, jerky sweeps of the visual field. Once an edge is found, the baby stops the broad sweeps and stays in the region of the edge, as did the babies who looked at triangles in the earlier study. A

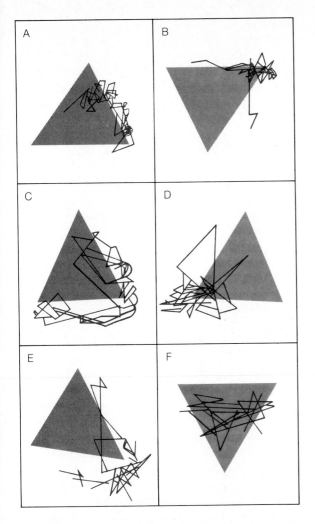

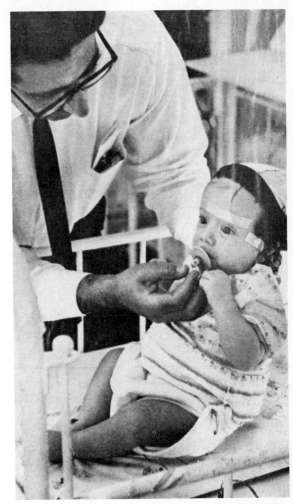

FIGURE 4.3 In this perception experiment, newborn babies were shown a large black triangle on a white field. *(left)* Infrared marker lights were placed behind the triangle and reflected in the baby's pupil, permitting the baby's eye movements to be traced and photographed. *(right)* Besides showing that the infants looked more toward the corners of the triangle, the six tracings illustrate the wide variation in patterns of scanning that occurs among babies.

(Photograph courtesy Dr. William Kessen; data from Salapatek and Kessen, 1966)

newborn's scanning strategy is mostly horizontal, probably because horizontal sweeps require only two eye muscles while vertical sweeps require six. As a result, babies are more likely to encounter a vertical edge than a horizontal one.

These patterns of search indicate that babies plan their looking patterns; small eye movements that cross edges are determined *before* the eye moves, and the size of the eye movement is not affected by the actual crossing of the edge. Such findings indicate that instead of being merely a reflexive organism that is captured by stimuli, the neonate has an organized information-gathering system, constructed to acquire knowledge (Haith, 1980).

Auditory Attention

It is difficult to discover whether neonates are as selective listeners to sounds as they are selective viewers of sights. By observing where a baby's eyes are turned, researchers find it relatively easy to determine when babies look at something or on what part of an object they focus. It is much harder to tell whether infants listen and even more problematical to tell what aspect of an auditory stimulus they listen to. However, some information has been gained by monitoring the heart rates, respiratory rates, brain waves, and sucking patterns of babies who are exposed to various sounds.

Babies do respond differently to sounds of contrasting frequencies or pitch. Low tones tend to quiet an upset baby, whereas high frequencies are likely to distress the infant and may even produce a kind of freezing reaction (Eisenberg et al., 1964). Some scientists have called attention to the parallel between the newborn's response to these sounds and the tendency among adults to use sounds of different frequencies to convey feelings of distress or calm. For example, the acoustical properties of musical instruments, alarm systems, and even some words that describe reactions to certain events use high frequencies to alert and to convey excitement or disturbance and low frequencies to communicate relative calm (Eisenberg, 1970).

There is some indication that newborns are especially responsive to sounds in the frequency of the human voice (200 to 500 cycles per second) and to sounds of moderate length, approximately five to fifteen seconds in duration (Eisenberg, 1970). In one study, three-day-old babies seemed to prefer their own mothers' voices over those of strange women (DeCasper and Fifer, 1980). Since these newborns had had no more than twelve hours' contact with their mothers during their postnatal existence, it has been speculated that a preference may have developed during the last trimester, when the mother's voice could be heard in the uterus (Aslin, Pisoni, and Juscyzk, 1983). This speculation is supported by the study reported in Chapter 3, indicating the newborn's apparent preference for a familiar story heard repeatedly during the last trimester (Spence and DeCasper, 1982). In Chapter 9 we will see how this response to the human voice plays a role in the development of language.

A neonate's response to a sound is also affected by illumination. Newborns who are in a dim room open their eyes to mild noises, as if they are trying to investigate the sounds (Kearsley, 1973). But babies in a bright room shut their eyes when they hear a noise; if their eyes are already shut, they will clamp the lids, shutting them even more tightly, perhaps in a defensive reaction.

As these examples of visual and auditory attention make clear, the newborn's perceptual world is less confusing than psychologists once thought. The sensory systems of newborns function, but their ability to detect stimuli or to discriminate among them is seriously limited, and a considerable amount of the visual environment simply is not accessible. Although some babies are quite good at discriminating between one kind of sound and another, many sounds that adults would detect as different are perceived by the average newborn as being the same. Finally, neonates are selective as to the stimuli that attract their attention or increase their responses; they tune some things in and tune other things out. As a result, the newborn neither detects nor pays attention to much of what adults perceive. The newborn's perceptual world is probably simpler and more orderly than we might guess.

ADAPTING TO THE WORLD

Given that babies have many ways of sensing events in the outside world and certain coordinated patterns of behavior for meeting situations that might arise, what are the mechanisms by which they adapt to the environment? How does the newborn come to know more about the world?

The neonate can learn—at least some things under some circumstances. For example, newborns learn to integrate sucking and breathing into an efficient feeding process, and they can learn to modify this behavior to fit the circumstances. In addition, they can form crude memories, remembering certain stimuli for several seconds. But they cannot learn by imitating others, although some researchers believe that newborns can imitate facial expressions (see box on page 130).

Memory

The newborn baby spends most of the time asleep, fussing and crying, or feeding. In fact the average newborn is rarely alert for longer than ten minutes at a time (Olson and Sherman, 1983). Is it possible that babies who are alert for such short periods can become familiar with the mobiles and other objects that parents put in their cribs? Can they form memories of these toys, retain the memories, and recognize an old mobile or detect the strangeness of a new one?

Steven Friedman explored this possibility with babies from one to four days old (Friedman, 1972; Friedman, Bruno, and Vietze, 1974). One of the checkerboards pictured in Figure 4.4 was shown to babies for sixty seconds at a time. The babies saw the checkerboard again and again until on two of its successive appearances, the baby looked a total of eight seconds less than he or she had looked at the board on the first two occasions. When this happened, an infant had *habituated*. The process of **habituation** is roughly analogous to becoming bored, and it implies that the baby has learned and remembered something about the stimulus. Such a decline in looking after repeated exposure may signify that the baby remembers the stimulus. Or it may not. Perhaps the baby is simply tired or fussy and does not remember it

at all. To find out whether a baby was showing memory or fatigue, Friedman changed the stimulus on a later test. If the baby looked longer at the new stimulus than at the last appearance of the checkerboard, the baby must have formed a memory that signaled the new stimulus was different. One neonate's pattern of looking under such a procedure is shown in Figure 4.4. Notice that during the familiarization phase, this neonate looked for about the same length of time again and again until suddenly the looking time dropped sharply on two successive occasions. When Friedman then introduced a new stimulus, the baby looked a long time (almost the entire sixty seconds), indicating that the neonate detected the new stimulus as being different from an earlier memory, and that fatigue had not been responsible for the earlier drop in looking time.

Given the stimuli used in this study, it was possible to find out whether newborns look longer at a new stimulus that is radically different from the familiar stimulus than at one that is only slightly different. The results suggest that the length of time the babies looked at the novel stimulus depended on how great the difference was. Apparently, newborns perform a crude perceptual analysis of the difference between the new stimulus and their memory of the old familiar one.

Habituation can also be used to study a newborn's memory for sounds. Three-day-old infants listened to the word *tinder* until they habituated, no longer turning their heads to hear it. When a new word (*beagle*) was played, they again turned their heads toward the sound, indicating the same sort of comparison between memory and perception found in studies of vision (Brody, Zelazo, and Chaika, 1984).

On the basis of such research, we can conclude that newborns can form a memory of a stimulus, retain that memory for five to ten seconds, retrieve the memory, and make some kind of analysis of the relationship between the memory and a new stimulus. But since almost no attempts have been made to find out if new-

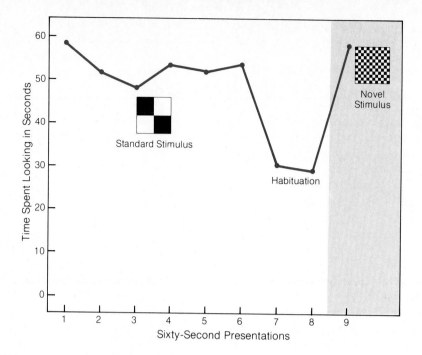

FIGURE 4.4 One newborn's response to familiar and unfamiliar checkerboard stimuli. After seven sixty-second exposures to the standard (familiar) stimulus, the baby became habituated. When the baby was then exposed to a novel (unfamiliar) stimulus on the ninth presentation, however, the infant immediately looked at it for an extended time.

(After Friedman, 1972)

borns' memories last for days or weeks (Olson and Sherman, 1983), we cannot say just how enduring these early memories are.

Conditions for Learning

It is clear that human newborns can learn. Just how much they actually do learn in their natural surroundings, however, is another question. We have seen that newborns have certain limitations; their environment may not satisfy the stringent conditions necessary before they are able to sense, perceive, attend, and learn.

One requirement of the learning situation is *timing*. Experimental studies have shown that there can be almost no delay of reward for the newborn; the baby who does not receive reinforcement (such as sweetened water, a smile, a sound, a touch) within one second is unlikely to learn (Millar, 1972). Another requirement is *repetition;* a stimulus must be presented over and over again with only short delays between each presentation in order for the young baby to form a memory of it (Lewis, 1969). As a baby grows older, however, learning proceeds in spite of delays between the infant's response and the reward or between the presentation of one stimulus and another.

Although scientists can construct a situation that satisfies the newborn's requirement for close timing, the baby's natural environment does not always meet that rigid standard. The delay between a baby's actions and their effects on people and objects nearby will often be longer than a second, making learning unlikely.

Even when the condition of timing is met, the condition of repetition may not be. For example, a push of the hand may immediately remove a blanket that has fallen across the baby's face, but the opportunity to repeat that action may not quickly recur. In a sense, then, there may be a period of "natural deprivation" (Watson, 1966), in which the baby is capable of learning but in which environmental conditions provide no opportunity to learn.

Yet, unless the laboratory task simulates a problem that infants are likely to encounter in the world and one that is important for them to solve, the infant's capabilities may be underestimated. As Carolyn Rovee-Collier and Marcy Gekoski (1979) have pointed out, most of the newborn's energy must be devoted to thermoregulation and growth. Requiring a newborn to kick vigorously is unlikely to be successful, even if the kicks produce some reward, such as movement in a mobile. But asking the neonate to suck vigorously, a reflexive act that uses little energy, is likely to show the baby's ability to learn. For example, preterm infants who were less than two weeks old quickly learned to suck hard on a nipple when their bursts of sucking illuminated a slide projector and allowed them to see a colorful red-and-white or green-and-white checkerboard (Werner and Siqueland, 1978).

Even among very young babies, there are individual differences in the ability to learn. For example, in the sucking study, high-risk babies with medical complications were less responsive than most preterm infants to the sight of a checkerboard, and preterm infants with higher birth weights and older gestational ages were most responsive of all. Investigators consistently find that some newborns can learn tasks that are difficult or impossible for other babies of the same age.

It also matters whether the response to be learned is one that the baby performs voluntarily or one that normally appears as an involuntary response. Learning to perform a naturally involuntary response in the absence of the stimulus that naturally evokes it—such as the blink of an eye at the sound of a buzzer—may be extremely difficult, whereas learning to perform a voluntary response—such as turning toward the buzzer—may be relatively easy. That is, babies learn responses that are operantly conditioned faster and more efficiently than they learn classically conditioned responses.

PERSONALITY AND SOCIAL RELATIONS

It is difficult to talk about the personality of a newborn. Adults think of personality in terms of verbal, cognitive, and emotional behavior displayed in a social context, and it is difficult for newborns to express their personalities in this way. However, newborn babies do differ in their behavior, and they can, and do, engage in primitive social relations.

Temperament

A visit to a hospital nursery would convince most casual observers that babies are not alike. Some newborns cry a lot; others do not. When they begin to cry, some babies are easy to soothe, and others are not. Some babies are restless sleepers and others sleep quietly and lie still while they are being dressed or changed. Each infant comes into the world with his or her own **temperament**—stable individual differences in the readiness to express emotions and in the intensity with which they are expressed (Campos et al., 1983). Temperamental predispositions are generally agreed to have a biological basis and to be heritable, but the way temperament is expressed is heavily influenced by experience. A temperamental characteristic may not remain stable throughout the life span—although some may. In addition, as development proceeds, the same characteristic may be expressed in different ways and in response to

Do Newborns Imitate Facial Expressions?

An alert newborn seems to watch intently as a man spends twenty seconds repeatedly sticking out his tongue, then stares impassively at the two-day-old infant for another twenty seconds, then repeats the tongue protrusions. This pattern goes on for twelve cycles, although the man may also open his mouth widely instead of sticking out his tongue. Using this procedure, Andrew Meltzoff and Keith Moore (1983) tested forty newborns, none older than seventy-two hours and one as young as forty-two minutes. Afterward another researcher acting as judge looked at a tape of the babies' reactions and decided that the newborns often imitated the actions of the experimenter.

After Meltzoff and Moore first reported such research in 1977, other investigators attempted to replicate the work. Some psychologists said their findings supported the concept of early infant imitation. The most spectacular report came from Tiffany Field and her colleagues (1983), who reported that healthy preterm newborns also imitated researchers and that the imitation went past tongue protrusion or mouth opening. The neonates studied by Field's group also seemed to detect facial expression, because they imitated the investigator's expressions or sadness, joy, and surprise. However, other psychologists reported that the newborns they tested showed no signs of imitation, no matter how closely they attempted to follow Meltzoff and Moore's methods.

Why should psychologists get so excited about claims of neonatal imitation? Primarily because the claims, if true, require a rethinking and revision of our concepts of cognitive development. Since a newborn is alert for such short periods, it seems unlikely that neonates have been conditioned to produce these facial actions by adult approval of their inadvertent tongue protrusions or mouth openings. Cognitive theory cannot explain the actions. According to Jean Piaget (1951), young infants cannot imitate actions they can neither see nor hear themselves perform. Such imitation, it is believed, would require the infants to form some mental representation of what they saw and match it to sensory information from their mouths, lips, and tongues. Given the immaturity of the infant's cortex, such actions seem impossible. And what of Field's claims that neonates imitate facial expressions? Is their visual acuity sharp enough to distinguish between a smile and a frown? Sandra Jacobson (1979), who studied six-week-old infants, reported that they indeed stuck out their tongues in response to an adult's tongue protrusion, but that they would do the same if she moved a small white ball or a felt-tip pen toward their mouths. Jacobson suggested that tongue protrusion was an unconditioned response that babies automatically make whenever an object moves toward their mouths. If so, the action is an adaptive response related to feeding, much like the young blackbird's gaping beak that automatically opens whenever any object is detected above eye-level, where the parent's food-laden bill would be located (Tin-

different events. A baby who sleeps fitfully and moves restlessly may become a toddler who incessantly climbs onto the furniture and a schoolchild who cannot sit still.

In fact, one relatively stable aspect of temperament is *activity*. Some newborns are more active than others; they frequently thrash about with their arms and legs and later bang toys and shake rattles with considerable gusto. Other babies are more placid, moving slowly and with

bergen, 1973).

Psychologists who have not been able to replicate Meltzoff and Moore's results believe that the way the experiments were carried out may have been responsible for the results. In the original experiments, both investigator and judge might have influenced the results. The investigator was allowed to repeat the modeling if he believed the baby had not been paying attention—a situation in which the investigator can keep protruding his tongue until the infant's behavior "happens" to match. In such a situation an investigator is not aware of his (or her) influence. The videotapes of the infant's responses were scored by a single judge. When Jean Koepke and her colleagues (1983) ran the study without giving the investigator discretion over its timing and used several judges, imitation disappeared.

The question has not been settled. Meltzoff and Moore (1983) believe that from the moment of birth, infants understand and can match the actions of others with their own unseen actions. In their view, infant development is built upon this foundation. Some (Maratos, 1982) believe that neonatal imitation is like the Moro or stepping reflexes, an unlearned response that drops out after a few weeks. Other psychologists believe that researchers who find imitation have simply demonstrated the way that an experimenter can, without being aware of it, influence the results of a study.

havior among children for at least two years (Walters, 1965). High activity levels have been associated with a variety of personality characteristics, including daring, competitiveness, self-assertion, lack of shyness, and a slowness to comply with parental demands (Buss, Block, and Block, 1980).

Another relatively stable characteristic of infant temperament is *irritability* (Korner et al., 1981). Highly irritable babies fret or cry a great deal, even after nursing. They have fits of irritability during sleep or wakefulness, fussing in circumstances that would not bother other babies. The highly irritable, hard-to-soothe infant is often perceived as "difficult."

Newborn babies also differ in *responsiveness*. Some babies are cuddlers. They are soft and snuggly and seem to enjoy being cuddled, kissed, and rolled about in their parents' arms. In contrast, other babies resist such affectionate play by stiffening their bodies when they are handled (Schaffer, 1971). It is easy to understand how such a rudimentary social response might have a substantial impact on parents who have been looking forward to hugging and kissing their newborn and then find themselves the parents of a noncuddler. They may falsely infer that their baby dislikes them or that they are inadequate parents, forming negative attitudes that can color the way they subsequently interact with their child.

Indeed, the newborn's temperament probably affects the pattern of interaction between infant and caregivers. Alexander Thomas and Stella Chess (1977) have suggested that the "goodness-of-fit" between infant temperament and parental caregiving style has important consequences for later development. When the two are in harmony, development is likely to proceed smoothly, but excessive conflicts between temperament and environmental demands may place a child under heavy stress.

Yet personality is more complex than these simple categories imply. A child's personality is a developing and evolving set of tendencies to behave in various ways, and parental-child interaction affects that evolution. When parental

less exaggeration. Mothers are sometimes aware of this kind of difference before their babies are born. Some fetuses kick and move about more than others, and there is some relationship between such fetal kicking and differences in be-

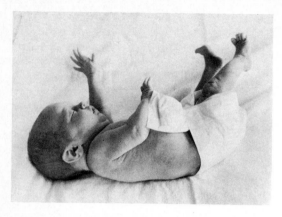

Newborns may turn their heads, move their hands, twitch or jerk, even while sleeping, but there are consistent individual differences in the amount of this low-intensity activity. (Suzanne Szasz)

demands and infant temperament clash, parents are likely either to change the environment so that a characteristic does not manifest itself or to condition the infant so that the characteristic is not expressed (Campos et al., 1983). For example, parents with a highly irritable infant are likely to make certain that feedings are not delayed. Parents of a highly active toddler are likely to schedule automobile trips so that the youngster does not have to sit in a car seat for eight hours. It is easy to see how the general tone of social interaction within the family could be influenced by a baby's consistent behavioral characteristics. It is also easy to see how such consistencies lead the same parents to treat one child differently from another.

The temperament a newborn displays may not always be an inborn disposition. For example, the level of responsiveness in the first few days may simply be an accident of birth or development. As noted in the last chapter, drugs administered during labor affect a baby's behavior (Brackbill, 1979). A baby born to a heavily sedated mother may be drowsy, sluggish, and slow to respond to her overtures. A malnourished baby also tends to be apathetic and sluggish. As Herbert Birch (1968) has pointed out, a baby's rate of development is affected by the

mother's responses to his or her actions, which in turn stimulate the baby. If babies are sluggish and apathetic, their mothers' responsiveness may diminish, setting an unfortunate pattern for their relationship.

Medication at delivery affected the subsequent relationship between Australian babies and their mothers studied by Ann Murray and her colleagues (1981). Epidural anesthesia, which blocks sensation in the legs and abdomen but leaves the mother alert, was the principal drug used in these deliveries. On the first day of life, the babies showed clear signs of being drugged. A month later, when they were again tested by researchers, the drug effects had vanished. But the mothers of the drugged babies were less responsive to their babies, fed them less often, and were less affectionate with them than were mothers in the control group who had had no anesthesia. The mothers themselves found the medicated babies difficult to care for, and their ratings of their babies at one month were similar to the ratings the researchers had made just after the infants were born.

Parents often interpret the smallest behavior as revealing their new baby's personality, and by the time an infant is two weeks old, a mother may develop a style of relating to her baby as well as an opinion of his or her personality (Osofsky and Connors, 1979). Murray and her colleagues speculate in their study that the unresponsive state of the drugged babies shortly after birth shaped the mothers' expectations and behavior, setting the tone for the future mother-infant relationship.

Social Relations

Social relations in the newborn are primitive by adult standards; yet as we have seen, they exist. Whenever there is communication between individuals, there is a social relation, and newborns and their parents certainly carry on a rudimentary sort of nonverbal communication. As the box on page 134 indicates, some researchers

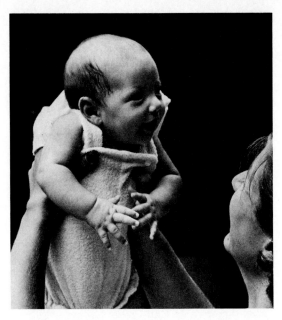

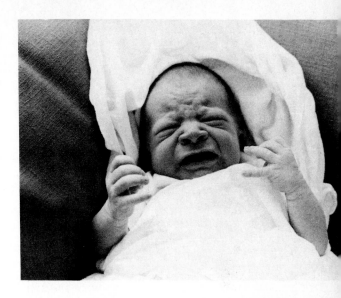

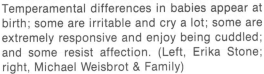

Temperamental differences in babies appear at birth; some are irritable and cry a lot; some are extremely responsive and enjoy being cuddled; and some resist affection. (Left, Erika Stone; right, Michael Weisbrot & Family)

have been concerned about parent-child relationships during the first few hours after birth.

EARLY INTERACTIONS Historically, the way in which a newborn was fed was thought to have major consequences for both the child's developing social relations and his or her personality. Such ideas stemmed from Freudian theory, which placed great emphasis on the possible impact of events early in the child's life. Because the newborn spends most of his or her waking hours feeding, it made good sense to assume that social relations begin in the feeding situation. The design of the human body ensures that nursing neonate and mother are placed in a situation that facilitates communication. A newborn being breast-fed for the first

time is cradled in the mother's arms with his or her face about nine inches from hers—the distance at which the baby's eyes can most easily focus.

Research by Kenneth Kaye and Anne Wells (1980) indicates that the feeding period may contain the seeds of turn-taking, a skill that is essential to language and social development. Mothers, whether breast- or bottle-feeding, tend either to jiggle the nipple in the baby's mouth or to stroke the baby about the mouth whenever sucking stops. But the baby does not resume sucking until the mother stops these actions. It appears that the infant's normal sucking pattern of bursts and pauses fits naturally into the turn-taking of human dialogue, and that a mother uses her child's natural feeding rhythm as a basis for early social communication.

Without realizing they are doing it, parents also tend to structure their interactions to fit their babies' capacities. According to Hanuš and Mechthild Papoušek (1978), analyses of films and video recordings reveal that mothers use the position of their babies' hands, small tests of muscle tone (such as touching the infant's chin), and eye contact as cues to the type and amount of stimulation they give their babies, thereby tailoring their own behavior to the baby's state.

Is There Magic in Early Contact?

Toward the close of the 1970s, many hospitals began to change their childbirth procedures to encourage early physical contact between the parents (especially the mother) and the newborn infant. The change was the medical establishment's response to Marshall Klaus and John Kennell's (1976) claim to have discovered a sensitive period just after birth when close, preferably skin-to-skin, contact between baby and parents was "necessary" if the baby were to develop properly.

This close contact was believed to create an emotional bond between mother and baby, increase the chances that a mother would breastfeed, and lessen the probability of child abuse or neglect (Lamb and Hall, 1982). **Bonding,** as the process was called, was seen as much like the bonding that develops in herd animals, such as sheep, goats, and cattle, within minutes after birth. Hormones present at birth set off the process, and once bonded, a mother can identify her own young. Timing is critical, because if mother and offspring are separated immediately after birth and kept apart for a few hours, the mother often rejects her offspring (Lamb and Hwang, 1982). (The bond formed by the *baby* with the mother, which is called attachment, develops later and will be discussed in Chapter 12.)

Since the human hormone balance changes sharply during labor and birth, Klaus and Kennell proposed a similar biological basis for human bonding and noted that human infants born preterm or with a life-threatening disease, who are separated at birth and placed in intensive care, run a greater risk of abuse during childhood than infants born full-term and healthy. Testing their hypothesis, Klaus and Kennell gave lower-class, inner-city women about an hour of skin-to-skin contact with their babies after delivery and an extra five hours of contact each day in the hospital. Five months later, these mothers seemed to be more affectionate with their babies and more concerned about them than similar mothers who lacked the early contact.

It looked as if an easy, natural way to increase maternal motivation had been discovered. As studies began to pile up, however, it became clear that Klaus and Kennell had been too optimistic. After a detailed review of bonding studies from Guatemala, Sweden, Brazil, Jamaica, and the United States, Michael Lamb and Carl-Philip Hwang (1982) concluded that there was no evidence of a special bonding period and no clear impact on the mother-infant relationship.

Whatever effects appeared in the studies were either fleeting or seemed to be the result of chance. If differences were due to early contact, they would tend to remain the same from one study to the next, but differences due to chance would shift from study to study. The differences that appeared in the study were apparently due to chance. It seemed possible to make almost any prediction and then find a study that supported it and another that refuted it. As Lamb wrote in another article:

Research can demonstrate that early contact influences only lower-class mothers, that it works only with mothers in "benign" circumstances, that mothers of boys are affected but not mothers of girls, that mothers of girls are affected but not mothers of boys, that contact affects only mothers of first babies but not

SOCIAL ASPECTS OF CRYING Crying is perhaps the most obvious means of communication available to the newborn. Crying appears to be a wired-in, autonomous activity. If earphones are placed on the crying newborn's head and sounds are played, the crying pattern shows no interruption, even though such competing stimulation would disrupt the speech of an adult

mothers of subsequent babies, that it affects only mothers whose pregnancies are planned, that mothers with early contact breastfeed longer and more successfully than mothers without it, that there is no effect on breastfeeding, or that mothers with early contact breastfeed less. Studies have found differences in mothers' behavior at thirty-six hours or at five weeks that disappear by ten days or by six weeks. Other studies have found no differences in behavior at six weeks but some differences at twelve weeks (Lamb and Hall, 1982, p. 22).

Early contact is certainly an emotionally satisfying experience for many new parents. But claims that it is necessary for an ideal relationship between parent and child can unnecessarily create feelings of guilt and failure among parents who do not have the experience. This group is largely made up of parents of premature or very ill babies and parents of babies delivered by Caesarean section, who already face complications as they are launched on parenthood.

In a new edition of their book, Klaus and Kennell (1982) have changed the concept of bonding from a process that must take place immediately after birth to a long-term process that begins at birth, but in which affectional bonds are established over a long period of time. Although it is possible that, given the lack of control and faulty design of most bonding studies, the concept of a sensitive bonding period simply has not been tested, it seems unlikely that human beings would retain a biological process that is found only in one other type of mammal—a herd animal with hooves.

(P. Wolff, 1976). Despite its automatic nature, a baby's cry is a signal of distress, saying, "Help me"; and the appeal is often successful. Although babies may not yet realize why their cries are followed by dry diapers and warm milk, they are communicating effectively, influencing the people around them.

Even quite young babies display different cries, depending on whether the crying is stimulated by hunger, pain, or anger. Each of these three basic cries can be distinguished by the pattern of pauses between bursts of crying, by the duration of the cry, and by its tonal characteristics (P. Wolff, 1967).

Are differences in crying detectable by parents or only by scientists armed with complex technical instruments? Complex instruments are superfluous, it seems. If a mother hears tape recordings of the cries of her own baby and the cries of four other babies, all responding to a slight pinprick on the foot, the mother readily picks out the cry of her own baby even when her infant is only a few weeks old (Lind, 1971). A mother's response to the hunger cry of her baby involves more than just making a mental note of the fact that her child is hungry. If she is breast-feeding her baby, she responds physiologically: an increased flow of blood and milk raises the surface heat of her breast (Lind, 1971). Many a lactating mother can relate occasions when her baby has given a hunger cry and she has discovered milk gushing from her breasts in response.

Crying is an effective means of communication because it evokes a range of physiological and emotional responses in parents—fathers as well as mothers. As Ann Frodi and her colleagues (1978a) discovered, mothers and fathers both react to a crying baby with an increase in blood pressure and the skin's ability to conduct electricity. This arousal is accompanied by feelings of annoyance, irritation, and distress. So when a parent picks up a wailing baby, one reason may be to stop the aversive sound.

However, studies with mothers indicate that the response of a mother to her own baby's cries may be primarily an empathic response, meant to relieve the baby's distress (Wiesenfeld and Malatesta, 1982). When mothers hear their own baby wailing with anger or pain, their hearts first slow, then speed up, seeming to indicate a readiness to cope with the problem. But when

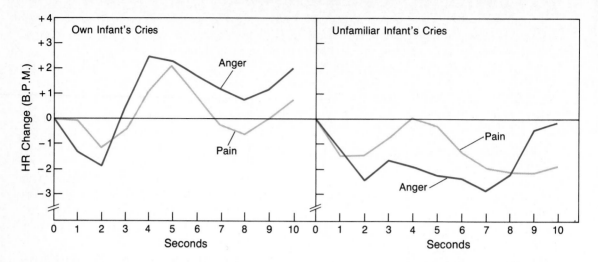

FIGURE 4.5 Mothers' responses to infant cries. When a mother's heartbeat is monitored for ten seconds as she listens to an infant's cries, her response varies dramatically depending on whether her own or an unfamiliar infant is crying.

(From A. R. Wisenfeld and C. Z. Malatesta. "Infant Distress: Variables Affecting Responses of Caregivers and Others," in L. W. Hoffman, R. J. Gandelman, and H. R. Schiffman, eds. *Parenting: Its Causes and Consequences.* Hillsdale, N.J.: Lawrence Erlbaum, 1982, 123–139.)

they hear the cries of an unfamiliar baby, their hearts do not speed up after the initial slowing; it is as if they had no intention of intervening—or felt no obligation to do so (Figure 4.5).

The quality of a baby's cry may also affect the nature of the parent-infant relationship. Researchers have found that cries of babies regarded as "difficult" by their parents have their own distinctive qualities. Compared with "average" and "easy" babies, difficult infants tend to pause longer between wails, and the pauses appear to communicate an urgent demand by the baby. Other mothers tend to interpret these "difficult cries" as "spoiled," and mothers with more experience are especially likely to interpret the cries as spoiled (Lounsbury and Bates, 1982).

The cries of a high-risk baby may pose an additional problem. Parents perceive the cries of at-risk babies (full-term babies whose birth involved obstetric complications) as more grating and aversive than the cries of normal newborns and say that the wails seem to indicate illness (Zeskind and Lester, 1978). Other researchers (Frodi et al., 1978b) have found that parents respond to the cries of an unfamiliar premature baby with faster heartbeat, higher blood pressure, and greater skin conductance than they show when listening to the cries of an unfamiliar normal baby. They also indicate that they are more annoyed and disturbed by the premature baby's cry. Such reactions appear to be associated with the baby's degree of medical risk, for the cries of low-risk preterm babies do not evoke the same aversion as the cries of medium- and high-risk babies (Friedman, Zahn-Waxler, and Radke-Yarrow, 1982).

If the cries of at-risk babies are especially unpleasant, speculate Ann Frodi and her colleagues, then the infants may become unpleasant objects to their parents. This process could make them targets for child abuse. Such conditioning may explain the results of a study by Frodi and Michael Lamb (1980), in which admitted child abusers responded with anger and physiological arousal to both crying and smiling babies. Apparently, child abusers have come to find *any* sort of social overture from an infant unpleasant.

Although the quality of a child's cry is not a sufficient explanation for child abuse, preterm babies may also seem less attractive to their parents, be slow to smile, and be separated from them for prolonged periods at a time when the parent-infant relationship is normally forming. Thus, when later environmental factors make abuse more probable, the premature infant with the aversive cry may run an increased risk of being an abused child.

Newborns are themselves responsive to the cries of other young babies. People who work in hospital nurseries often note that when one baby starts to cry, other babies in the nursery join in. Abraham Sagi and Martin Hoffman (1976) confirmed this contagion of crying and they suggested that it may be an inborn, early precursor to later forms of human empathy. In a later experiment, Grace Martin and Russell Clark (1982) discovered that newborns are able to distinguish between recordings of their own cries and those of another infant. When crying newborns heard tapes of another newborn's cry they wailed even louder, but when they heard their own cries, they fell silent. Calm newborns cried lustily at the sound of another crying newborn, but seem relatively unmoved by their own cries, the cries of an older baby, or the cries of a chimpanzee.

But not every baby cries at the sound of another's distress, nor does every baby quiet at the sound of his or her own recorded cries. As we have seen throughout this chapter, from the first moment of independent life, babies are different. They differ in their need for sleep, for food, for stimulation. Some learn quickly, some learn slowly. Some want to be cuddled, others do not like to be held. Some are placid, others are fussy. With such a wide span of individual differences at birth, it is no wonder that—given the additional influence of widely differing environments—no two children or adults are alike. From the time that babies draw their first breath, the differences among them become more and more pronounced—and the process continues throughout life. Yet despite these wide human differences, there are common themes in human development—similar tasks and challenges that each child will meet in his or her own way.

SUMMARY

Developmental psychologists study newborns for two reasons: in order to establish a baseline from which to trace the development of behavior, and to detect abnormal conditions that might threaten development, such as **Sudden Infant Death Syndrome (SIDS)**.

The **neonate** quickly develops functional patterns or rhythms. Body temperature becomes regulated, although the problem of thermoregulation is not completely solved until the infant is out of the neonatal period. Sleep, which is composed of both **REM** and **non-REM** patterns, evolves into a four-hour sleep/wake cycle for many newborns. Feeding, if left to the newborn's **self-demand**, occurs every three or four hours for most. Sucking, at which newborns must be competent in order to survive, is coordinated with swallowing and breathing into rhythmic bursts, separated by pauses.

From birth, the newborn is equipped with reflexive behavior that may be elicited by specific stimuli. These reflexes include the **rooting reflex,** the **grasping reflex,** the **Moro reflex,** and **stepping** and **placing responses.** When these reflexes fail to drop away after several months, it may be a sign of abnormal neurological development. Some apparently reflexive early behavior disappears, only to reappear later under conscious control. This **U-shaped behavioral growth** may reflect an actual disappearance due to cortical maturation, an incorporation of the reflex into a pattern under cortical control, or the domination of an early motor pattern by a later one.

The sensory capabilities of newborns keep them in touch with their environment, although both the visual and auditory cortex are still immature. Newborns have only a limited ability to focus both eyes on an object (**visual accommodation**) and both visual **acuity** and **conver-**

gence are poor. They probably lack depth perception and may be colorblind. By shutting out stimulation, these limits on vision reduce confusion in the newborn's world. Their auditory sense allows newborns to discriminate loudness and pitch, but their head-turning in response to a sound is slow. The **precedence effect,** an auditory illusion common to adults, is not present in newborns. The senses of taste and smell are functional at birth and become increasingly acute. Stimulation of the newborn's **kinesthetic sense** is essential to development, perhaps because it tends to put the infant in a quiet, alert state.

Newborns actively select visual and auditory stimuli, gathering information from the environment. Their patterns of visual attention and search appear aimed at increasing stimulation in the visual cortex, and in that quest, they attend to movement, pattern, and contrast. Their state of arousal may help determine what sort of pattern they prefer to look at.

In adapting to the world, the neonate forms short-term memories of certain stimuli and then compares new stimuli to them. Such learning has been demonstrated in studies using **habituation.** In order for newborns to learn, rewards must be immediate and the stimulus must be repeated frequently. The newborn may be more capable of learning than some laboratory research indicates, since most of his or her energy must be devoted to thermoregulation and growth. Responses that require the newborn to expend a great deal of energy, such as kicking, are unlikely to be repeated, making it appear that the newborn is unable to learn.

Newborn babies differ in **temperament,** and their predispositions to activity, irritability, and responsiveness to affection influence the tone of their social relationships. When there is "goodness-of-fit" between infant temperament and parental caregiving style, development is likely to proceed smoothly. The sluggishness of babies born to heavily sedated mothers may have a negative influence on the developing relationship between mother and infant. Feeding and the response of others to their cries offer neonates the first chances for social interaction. "Difficult" babies have a particular cry pattern that is perceived by others as "spoiled." All babies' cries are aversive, but the cries of a high-risk infant are perceived as especially unpleasant.

PART 3

Physical Development

Physical growth and maturation have vast psychological and social consequences. The world of an infant who can do nothing without assistance is very different from that of the competent child. As the baby's body grows, motions that were awkward and tentative become sophisticated, smooth probes into the workings of the world. Situations of "I can't" increasingly become opportunities for "I can," and the child's world widens. The rapidly maturing brain allows the child to understand the results of explorations and apply the lessons from one experience to new chal-

lenges and opportunities. But the obvious aspects of physical growth often cause us to forget that growth does not take place in a vacuum—the child's experiences can speed developing skills or hinder them; in fact, without appropriate experiences, some skills may never develop. As the child undergoes the major physical changes of puberty, the psychological and social consequences of events alter once again. The adolescent stands on the brink of adulthood, where new opportunities and new responsibilities await.

Elements of Physical Growth

DIRECTIONS OF GROWTH
Cephalocaudal Development
Proximodistal Development
Differentiation and Integration
NORMS
Using Norms
Individual Rates of Growth
ENVIRONMENTAL INFLUENCES ON
   GROWTH
Diet
Illness
Socioeconomic Status
Ethnic Differences
Stress
DEVELOPMENT OF MOTOR ABILITIES
Maturation and Experience
Strength, Speed, and Coordination
Skill Development
SEX DIFFERENCES
Prepubertal Differences
Sexual Maturation
SIZE AND MATURATIONAL TRENDS
SUMMARY

Rob, who is four, can turn a somersault with ease, his head tucked and his back rounded. Mark, who just turned six, cannot execute this simple maneuver, and when he sees Rob turning triumphant somersaults in the yard next door, he often feels jealous of the younger boy's skill and some anger at his own lack of physical ability. But children are not all alike, and although most learn to somersault proficiently when they are five, some learn the skill much earlier than the average child and others much later.

Marked structural differences develop among children soon after conception, and their individual environments tend to accentuate some of these differences. If Rob becomes fascinated with gymnastics, with practice he may develop into a champion, perhaps someday reaching the Olympics. But no matter how hard Mark tries, no matter how many hours he devotes to gymnastics, he will never make the Olympic team.

Growth is the result of a series of interactions between an organism and its environment. During this process, babies become larger, the structure and function of their bodies become increasingly complex, and they approach ever

Some children are highly skilled at jumping rope, while others are clumsy. Such variations in motor skills may be due to structural differences in their bodies, to differences in their environment opportunities—or both. (Kent Reno/Jeroboam)

more closely their adult size, organic structure, and body build.

Psychologists study the resulting physical changes to gain insight into the relationship between inherited factors and the child's environment, hoping to identify the conditions that lower a child's efficiency or hinder normal development. Once such interactions are understood, there is some possibility of controlling unwanted deviations from normal patterns of growth.

In this chapter, we follow a baby's physical development through childhood and adolescence. Basing our discussion on fundamental principles that govern all physical growth, we outline the ways in which psychologists summarize growth. Because each baby's combined environment and heredity are unique, we consider the ways in which physical development may differ from one child to the next, noticing that diet, illness, socioeconomic status, ethnic differences, and emotional stress can affect physical growth. A look at the development of motor skills shows us the part played by practice and instruction in their acquisition and refinement. We then explore the differences between boys and girls in motor and physical growth, and conclude by discussing historical trends toward an earlier onset of puberty.

DIRECTIONS OF GROWTH

The systematic study of any phenomenon, whether it be growth or gravity, usually begins with a description of the way that phenomenon ordinarily occurs. Thus the systematic study of physical development requires the observation of large numbers of infants and children over a considerable period of time. From such observations, scientists have formulated some basic principles of growth and outlined the general development of the average infant and child.

At the most general level of description, three basic principles underlie the growth and development of all body systems. These are cephalocaudal development, proximodistal development, and differentiation and hierarchic integration.

Cephalocaudal Development

The word *cephalocaudal* comes from the Greek word for *head* and the Latin word for *tail*, so **cephalocaudal development** refers to the literal direction of the body's physical growth. It is reflected in the order in which parts of the body become larger and in the order in which functions and structures become more complex. Physical growth progresses from head to foot; a baby's head develops and grows before the torso, arms, and legs. This pattern of growing seems to reflect the fact that the most rapid embryological development occurs in or near those cells destined to be parts of the brain and nervous system (Debakan, 1959).

At birth, a baby's head is nearer to its adult size than any other portion of the body. From birth to adulthood, a person's head doubles in size. In contrast, the trunk trebles, the arms and hands quadruple, and the legs and feet grow fivefold. Much of the increase in height that takes place in childhood is an increase in the length of the lower limbs. As a child grows, the head contributes proportionately less to total body length, shrinking from one-quarter of the total at birth to one-twelfth at maturity (Bayley, 1956). These changes in body proportions are shown in Figure 5.1.

Movement and motor ability also become more controlled and complex in a progression from head to toe. Babies first gain control over the muscles of the head and neck, then the arms and abdomen, and finally the legs. Thus babies learn to hold up their heads before they learn to sit; they learn to sit before they learn to walk;

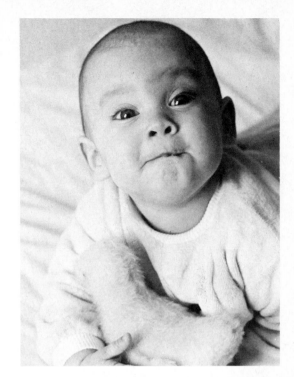

Babies first gain control over their head and neck muscles, learning to hold up their heads long before they can sit. (© Suzanne Szasz)

and long before they can walk or run steadily, they can make complicated, controlled movements of their arms and fingers, picking up even tiny specks of lint.

Proximodistal Development

Physical growth and motor development proceed also in a **proximodistal** direction. That is, growth and function progress from the center of the body toward the periphery. Babies learn to control the movements of their shoulders before they can direct their arms or fingers. In general, control over movement travels down a baby's arm as he or she becomes increasingly sophisticated in attempts to reach for and grasp an object.

During the first few weeks of life, a baby

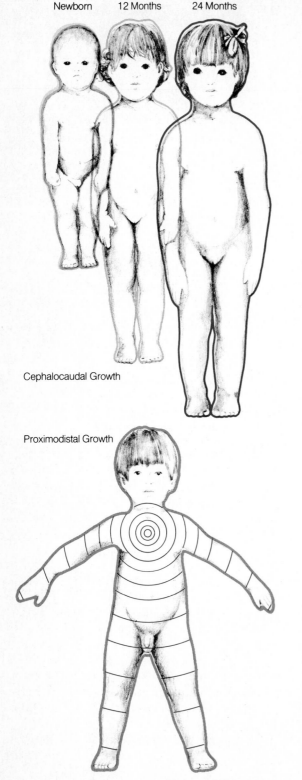

Newborn 12 Months 24 Months

Cephalocaudal Growth

Proximodistal Growth

FIGURE 5.1 Physical growth and motor abilities develop in two directions simultaneously: from top to bottom (cephalocaudal) and from center to periphery (proximodistal).

reaches for an object that comes into view but does not grasp it because the infant lacks control over hand and finger muscles. As we saw in Chapter 4, this reaching reflex does not represent learned control, and it disappears at the end of the neonatal period. Not until a baby is about twenty weeks old does he or she make crude attempts to grab an object, using both hands. Then, within a month, the infant develops a one-handed reach, usually managing to brush the object. In another four weeks the baby is able to flex the whole hand while reaching and, somewhat later, to poke at the object with an index finger. Finally, at about forty weeks, mature grasping appears, and the baby can oppose thumb and forefinger when trying to grab a toy. In the same manner, babies gain control over their upper legs before they can control the lower leg, foot, or toes.

Differentiation and Integration

The third principle of growth involves differentiation and integration. **Differentiation** means that infants' abilities become increasingly distinct and specific. They gain mastery of movement after movement. For example, when a baby is only a month old, the infant reacts to a shoe that is too tight with the whole body—wiggling, thrashing, crying, and generally creating a ruckus. As the baby grows older, movements become more specific, so that the response to a tight shoe is to thrash about with only the offending foot. Eventually the child learns to make specific and highly complex responses. The sensory stimulation that has traveled from the foot to the brain is now interpreted, and this interpretation takes the form of language, so that the child might say, for example, "Foot hurt."

Complex responses require the infant to combine and integrate many lesser skills. As noted in Chapter 1, Heinz Werner (1948) used the term *hierarchic integration* to describe this trend toward combining simple, differentiated skills into more complex skills. For example, after a baby has mastered the use of the arms as levers, the muscles of the abdomen as lifters of the upper body, and the neck muscles to gain control of the head, he or she develops hierarchic patterns of movement that bring each separate motor capability into the service of the others in a highly organized way. Thus, after each of these various simpler movements has been developed, the baby is able to put them all together and soon can sit up.

NORMS

The principles we have just discussed describe growth and development at a general level. Psychologists interested in the normal course of development have compiled detailed, specific descriptions of individual events in the growth process. A number of investigators (Bayley, 1956; Cattell, 1940; Gesell, 1925; Griffiths, 1954; Lenneberg, 1967) have analyzed the sequence in which physical characteristics and motor, language, and social skills emerge. Their investigations have resulted in **norms,** or typical patterns that describe the way in which important attributes and skills develop and the approximate ages at which they appear.

These norms allow us to summarize patterns of infant motor development (Figure 5.2). As these motor skills are developing, the rate of physical change is greater than at any other time after birth. During the first year of life, body length increases more than one-third, and weight almost triples. During the first two years, a child's head grows more slowly than the trunk and limbs, so that body proportions become more adultlike. In addition, the facial skeleton becomes relatively larger, so that a child's cranium is no longer so out of proportion with the face (see Figure 5.3).

Growth in early childhood is not as dramatic as it is during infancy. The velocity, or rate, of growth—in both height and weight—decelerates markedly during infancy and about the time a child is three or four, settles into a steady rate. Figure 5.4, which charts the average child's annual height increase, shows a velocity curve that flattens and remains about the same until just before the child enters puberty (Falkner, 1966). At that time, the plateau period of childhood growth ends and the adolescent growth spurt begins. Adolescence is virtually the only time in a person's life that this curve accelerates. Once the adolescent reaches the maximum point of growth velocity (in the case of height, "peak height velocity"), deceleration again occurs until the annual growth increment is zero and growth ceases.

Using Norms

When using norms to study child development, we need to understand that they are based on simple mathematical calculations that reflect average growth tendencies. They do not explain growth or development, they merely describe it, indicating what is most likely to appear in the development of children at various ages.

Norms can be useful in describing how most children develop. They can help in the assessment of the influence of environmental change on behavior—such as the effect of separating children from their mothers—or they can be useful in studying cross-cultural and subcultural variations. They have been used to examine the effects of institutionalization, gender, and birth order on a child's development. They have been helpful in studies of prematurity and early pathology (Kessen, Haith, and Salapatek, 1970).

The value of norms as a diagnostic tool for the individual child is, however, limited, because in every aspect of growth, normal children vary widely on each side of a norm. The wide range of individual differences in growth shows

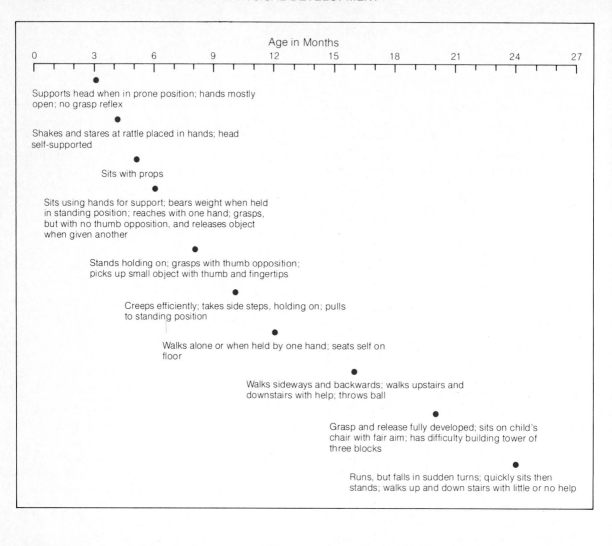

FIGURE 5.2 Some of the major milestones in motor development that occur over the first two years of life. Each dot indicates the approximate average age of occurrence. Individual infants may demonstrate these skills somewhat earlier or later than the average indicated.

(After Lenneberg, 1967, and Bayley, 1969)

clearly in a study Howard Meredith (1963) conducted among Iowa males. At the age of eighteen, the lightest boy in his study weighed no more than the heaviest boy had weighed when he was eight. The boy who was lightest at age eight weighed about the same as the heaviest boy had at age two.

The age at which normal children master motor skills shows similar variability. Some normal children never crawl or creep at all but go directly from sitting to standing and taking their first steps. The normal range for the onset of walking is itself large—from as early as eight months to as late as twenty months. And handicapped children, depending on the nature of their disability, may master various skills later than the average child—if they attain them at all (see accompanying box on page 152).

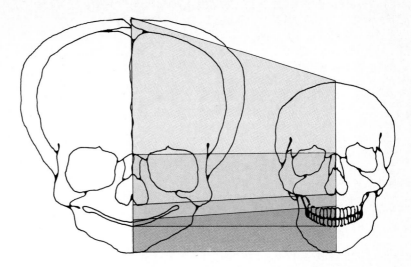

Individual Rates of Growth

FIGURE 5.3 Changes in skull and facial proportions with growth. The skull outlined at the left is that of a newborn, whereas the skull at the right is that of a mature adult.

(Adapted from C.M. Jackson, ed. *Morris' Human Anatomy.* 7th ed. Copyright © P. Blakiston's Sons & Co., 1923. Used by permission of McGraw-Hill Book Company.)

There are great individual differences in the velocity of growth, and some normal children mature much more slowly or more quickly than the mythical average child described by norms. Researchers have found that maturation rates seem to be related to body build. The child who is broadly built, large, and strong is likely to be a fast grower; whereas a slender, long-legged but small and lightly muscled child is likely to grow more slowly (Bayley, 1956). But this is another generalization. How can we assess the individual child's state of development?

Assessing a child's **developmental age,** or the progression toward physiological maturity, becomes easy in adolescence. Changes in appearance that accompany sexual maturity make it simple to pick out the early- and late-maturers. Before that time, however, there is no obvious guide to a child's progress. Height is notoriously unreliable, because a child who towers over his or her peers may be either an early maturer whose adult height will be average or an "on-time" child who will be a tall adult.

The rate at which teeth appear is one way to assess developmental age, but the most accurate measure is **skeletal maturity,** which reflects the shape and relative position of bones and their degree of calcification. Skeletal maturity can be assessed by X-raying the wrist and hand, a process that exposes the child to about the same increase in radiation that comes from moving from sea level to 2,000 feet for a weekend (Tanner, 1978). Although routine measurement of skeletal age is not recommended, it can at times be extremely helpful. Skeletal age and progress toward maturity are related, so that when **puberty,** or the attainment of biological sexual maturity, seems inordinately delayed, a hand X-ray can tell the physician whether the child is maturing slowly or whether some physiological problem is interfering with the onset of puberty.

Individual differences in the velocity of growth may be so wide that comparisons with norms are not always helpful. One possible way to resolve confusion about a child's developmental age is to assess an individual's growth only in relation to his or her own growth curve. For

FIGURE **5.4** Sample growth curves for children. *(top)* The growth curves of an early-maturing girl and a short boy are compared to similar curves depicting the rates of growth for an average boy and girl. *(bottom)* Averaged and smoothed curves for boys and girls show inches gained in height per year. After the initial growth spurt of infancy, the rate of growth (velocity) first declines and then remains relatively stable until puberty, when there is another temporary growth spurt, followed by a steady decline. When full height, is attained, growth ceases.

(Adapted from Bayley, 1956)

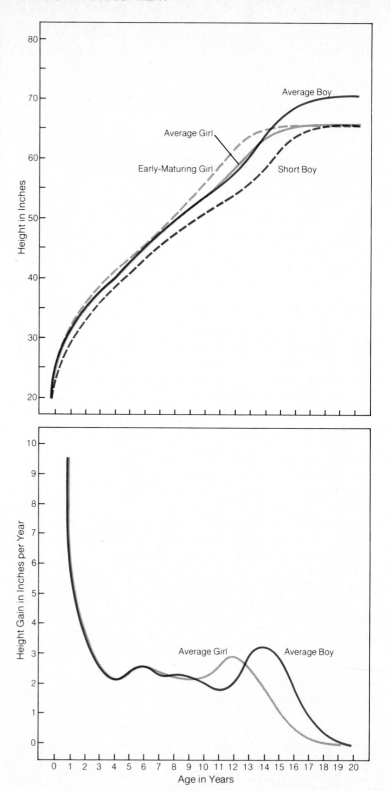

example, data taken on a child over long periods of time allow us to make a statement about that child's growth relative to him- or herself. This means that we take the child's status at a particular time (for example, height, weight, the closure of bones in the hand) and use it as the standard against which to compare his or her status at other times. Such individual growth rates can be compared to relevant norms in order to find indications of relative precocity or slowness in tempo of growth.

Although growth curves are relatively stable, severe dietary deficiencies and stress can affect them, temporarily slowing growth. When the condition responsible for the retarded growth is eliminated, a child often goes through a period of **catch-up growth.** This temporary deviation from the child's normal growth curve and the subsequent return results from canalization of growth (see Figure 5.5). **Canalization** describes a genetically determined predisposition that so strongly channels growth that the predisposition will appear in any natural human environment (Scarr, 1981). Thus, growth curves of individual children are genetically determined and self-stabilizing (Tanner, 1978). Illness or malnutrition may temporarily deflect a child's growth from this natural curve, as a stream can be temporarily deflected from its normal course by an obstruction, but once the impediment is removed and the environment becomes normal, the child caches up and development returns to its normal course.

Newborn babies show catch-up growth in both weight and height. From birth to six months or so, smaller babies gain more weight than larger ones (Tanner, 1978). This explains how small women can bear babies who become large adults. Such newborn catch-up growth is usually completed by the end of the third year. Because most babies have caught up by that time, if we know the height and weight of a three-year-old, our chances of predicting the child's approximate weight and height as an adult are quite good.

Genetic influence plays such a large part in determining growth curves that it is always important to compare children with their parents and older siblings before comparing them with the norm for the population. This comparison is especially necessary when a child appears to diverge greatly from the norm. According to J. M. Tanner (1978), by averaging the heights of both parents, it is possible to predict a seventeen-centimeter (6.7 inch) height range for each sex within which 97 percent of a specific couple's children will fall. Using such procedures, researchers have constructed growth charts that specify expected heights for offspring of parents of various heights. These charts can reveal whether a child's growth curve is normal and,

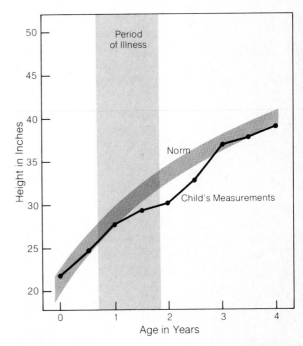

FIGURE 5.5 An illness in which food intake, greatly reduced for approximately one year, affected the growth of a young child. When the illness ended and food intake was restored to normal levels, the child caught up with his own time pattern in approximately two years, providing an example of canalization.

(Adapted from A. Prader, J.M. Tanner, and G.A. von Hamack, "Catch-up Growth Following Illness or Starvation: An Example of Developmental Canalization in Man," *Journal of Pediatrics*, vol. 62, 1963.)

A Handicapped Child in the Family

When a baby is born with Down's syndrome, spina bifida, cerebral palsy, mental retardation, or some other handicap, parents face a difficult adjustment. Having anticipated the birth of a normal infant, they discover they are the parents of a child with an incurable disorder. If the child has Down's syndrome, for example, he or she will have a characteristic physical appearance, moderate to severe mental retardation, and perhaps associated physical problems, such as poor vision, cardiovascular defects, or problems with respiration.

Robert Emde and Craig Brown (1978) have studied families who were adapting to the birth of a baby with Down's syndrome and have found that the adjustment is a complex process that goes through regular, predictable phases. Instead of building their feelings of love and caring on prenatal anticipations, parents go through an initial period of mourning, grieving over the loss of the normal baby who was not born. At the same time, they face adjustment to life with a baby who will always be different and who will require enormous amounts of medical, physical, and emotional care. Only after the first grief is over can parents begin to build bonds of affection to their real child. During the first few months, parents may deny their child's disability. The baby may turn over in the crib early, and this apparent physical precocity often gives parents hope that the diagnosis was mistaken.

When babies are about two months old, their social smiles and alert eye contact generally lead to an upsurge of positive emotion toward the child. But the first social smiles of the Down's infant are delayed, and when they come, they may diminish the parents' love and delight and set off a second wave of grieving. The baby's smiles are dampened. The cheeks and eyes fail to crinkle, the eyes never brighten, the arms and legs fail to move in the bicycling motion that conveys alertness and anticipation to parents. In addition, the baby generally shows poor eye contact. The alert, communicative gaze that leads parents to speculate about their child's feelings and thoughts is absent.

According to Rosalyn Darling (1983), two early critical events in the process of adjustment are telling friends and relatives about the baby's defect and taking the baby out in public for the first time. Once these hurdles have been passed, parents seem able to redefine their situation and find some meaning in their lives. However, many parents feel powerless because physicians often regard treatment of a condition that cannot be cured, such as Down's syndrome, as useless. Since parents have a need to help their child, this attitude turns many of them into researchers, who mine the library, contact national organizations, and seek second opinions, finding out everything they can about their child's condition. Once they discover a helpful program, the feeling of powerlessness generally fades.

By the end of the first year, most parents have adjusted to the situation. Their child responds to their attention, and that response is rewarding. The parents feel needed and their self-esteem increases. Some marriages even improve, says Darling, as wife and husband are drawn closer together by the shared social stigma of a handicapped child. However, the birth of a mentally retarded child often has a negative effect on a marriage, perhaps because many fathers tend to withdraw, leaving the mother to cope with the added emotional and physical burdens that go with rearing such a child (Lamb, in press). Some marriages may even break up. Most siblings seem to adjust to their situation, and studies indicate no major differences between siblings of normal and handicapped children. However, some siblings, especially older sisters who are expected to help care for the child, may have problems accepting this permanent change in the family.

In adjusting to their "different" child, parents of handicapped children tend to adopt one of three strategies: normalization, crusadership, or resignation (Darling, 1983). Normalization is the most common strategy and it generally works satisfactorily until the child reaches adolescence. In this approach, says Darling, the family establishes a life that resembles those of their friends. For normalization to be successful, the parents must find appropriate services, responsive medical care, satisfactory educational placement for their child, and acceptance by relatives and friends. Parents who adopt this strategy become less involved with support groups meant for families in their situation and turn instead to neighbors, the school system, and relatives.

As their child approaches adolescence, puberty may threaten the family's normalization. The child is seen to be growing up physically, yet remaining dependent. If the child is a daughter and she is mentally retarded, parents may fear that she will be sexually exploited. Their fears may lead them to overprotect their child, cutting her off from possible social interaction (Rosen and Hall, 1984). A larger fear is their worry about what will happen to the child should they die. The threat of institutionalization hangs over them, and parents may adapt to it by returning to their "researcher" role, looking for programs that will meet their child's future needs.

Parents who adopt the crusadership strategy are generally those whose child has multiple handicaps or can function only at a very low level. The crusader parent may write a book about the problem, initiate legal action against a school system, or picket for legislative changes. In contrast to parents who have opted for normalization, crusader parents become deeply involved in parents' associations and national organizations.

The least common and least successful adaption is resignation. Such parents resign themselves to the child's situation and make no effort to alleviate it. Their resignation makes them feel powerless, and their life seems to have no meaning. For some reason they never find their way to a parents' association, and they get no support from "normal" society. The resulting stress may be so severe that a parent breaks down. Resigned parents tend to be drawn from groups that already are isolated from the community. They may be foreign-born, in poor health, live in an isolated area, or the family may have other problems in addition to the child's disorder.

Only a few parents of handicapped children adopt a strategy of resignation, but early studies concentrated on this group. As a result, says Darling, this failure to adapt was regarded as typical, a misperception that is only now being corrected.

for children between the ages of two and nine years, can closely predict adult height.

ENVIRONMENTAL INFLUENCES ON GROWTH

A variety of environmental factors, including diet, general health, stress, and socioeconomic determinants, can either support normal growth and development or impede it. Exactly how or why environmental factors influence growth during childhood is uncertain. The internal mechanism that regulates growth includes hormones and chemical factors; their production and composition may be affected by nutrition, illness, and stress (Tanner, 1978).

Diet

Dietary deficiencies are a common cause of abnormal growth curves during infancy. In Chapter 3 we saw the effect of extreme dietary deficiency on the developing fetus. The importance of diet in growth and development continues after the baby is born. In general malnutrition, children simply do not get enough food to eat; their diets lack calories as well as protein, vitamins, and minerals. This near starvation sometimes occurs in developing countries (Waterlow and Payne, 1975). As the number of calories available to a young child drops dangerously near the level required for maintenance and growth, the child becomes sluggish and ceases to play or to explore the environment. When calorie intake drops below the minimum level, growth ceases.

Records of infants who have been exposed to wartime famine show delayed growth during periods of malnutrition (Tanner, 1978). Georg Wolff's (1935) study of Berlin children during World War I demonstrated that malnutrition at age five retards the development of height and weight. Once these children had a normal diet,

however, they began to overcome the adverse effects and by adolescence had caught up with their well-fed contemporaries. Studies of war children in Russia, Spain, France, Belgium, and Japan have shown the same general results as those in Berlin (Acheson, 1960).

If the episode of malnutrition is neither too severe nor too long, children can usually overcome the effects of acute malnourishment with periods of catch-up growth. However, a child who is chronically undernourished will suffer permanent effects. Such children generally grow to be smaller adults than they would have been had they eaten an adequate diet.

The probable effects of severe malnutrition on the human nervous system have been discussed by Neville Scrimshaw and John Gordon (1968). Head circumference shows no relationship to intelligence among well-nourished children or those who are only moderately malnourished (Pollitt, Mueller, and Leibel, 1982). It is, however, a reasonably good indicator of brain size and may reflect severe malnutrition. Scrimshaw and Gordon point out that children in Mexico, Guatemala, Peru, Uganda, and other developing countries who have had severely deficient diets from birth show smaller head circumference than children of the same ethnic group who have always been well fed.

Such speculation is supported by findings that severe malnutrition in laboratory animals, especially when the animals are very young, stunts brain growth. John Dobbing (1968) and others have shown that young pigs that suffer severe malnutrition during their first year of life never catch up with normal animals in brain development. Even after two and a half years of normal feeding, such animals show structural changes in their nervous systems, with certain cortical neurons, brain enzymes, and the cerebellum (a portion of the brain that controls muscular coordination) especially affected. The possible effects of severe malnutrition on human cognitive functioning will be discussed in Chapter 11.

Deficiencies of various nutrients can affect growth in different ways. Protein deficiency has

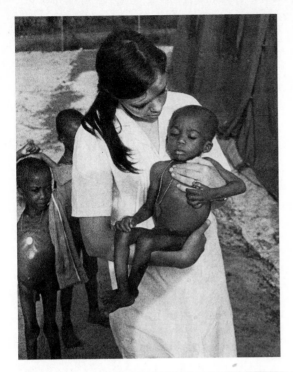

Severe protein deficiency can cause kwashiorkor, a disease resulting in a permanent stunting of growth and—when untreated—may even result in the child's death. (Roland Dourdin/Rapho-Photo Researchers)

widespread effects. If one group of average babies has a protein-deficient diet and the other eats protein-rich food, the deficient babies will grow to be shorter and less muscular, on the average, than the well-fed babies. If the two groups are compared to the norms of growth, it is apparent that the deficient babies are behind in development, while the well-fed babies are growing according to the average.

Severe, prolonged protein deficiency can lead to **kwashiorkor,** a serious, often fatal, disease found among infants in developing countries whose diets consist largely of breast milk after they are a year old (Scrimshaw, 1969; Waterlow, 1973). The symptoms of this disease include scaly skin, profound apathy, diarrhea, swollen limbs and abdomen, and liver degeneration. According to studies reported by Heinz Eichenwald and Peggy Crooke Fry (1969), when infants who are suffering from kwashiorkor eat adequate protein, they begin to grow rapidly but never catch up with normal children of their own age. This finding underlines the importance of diet as a central environmental determinant of normal physical growth.

Deficiencies of other nutrients can have specific effects. One of the most common disorders is anemia, which may develop when a child's diet lacks sufficient iron, folic acid, and vitamin B12. Such children may be listless, unable to pay attention, and have trouble sleeping (Kopp, 1983). Another nutrient, calcium, is crucial to the replacement of cartilage in the infant's skeleton with bone. A deficiency of vitamin D during infancy and childhood interferes with the metabolism of calcium and leads to a condition known as **rickets,** which is characterized by softening and bending of the bones, especially those that bear body weight. The condition is sometimes accompanied by cramps and muscle spasms.

Dietary excesses can upset normal growth patterns by making a child **obese,** or excessively fat. Although there appears to be a genetic contribution to obesity, genes interact with a variety of environmental factors to produce extreme overweight. In a longitudinal study, Judith Rodin and William Kessen (Rodin and Hall, 1984) are comparing children of normal-weight parents with children of two overweight parents. They have found three separate factors in newborns that predict obesity during the preschool years: obesity in the family, a heightened responsiveness to environmental stimuli on the first day of birth, and a heightened responsiveness to sweet tastes on the first day of birth. Some studies (e.g., Dwyer and Mayer, 1973) have suggested that overnutrition in infancy (often caused by a mother determined to have a large, healthy baby) may lead to a multiplication of extra-large fat cells. Fat cells have tiny nuclei in comparison with muscle cells, but each cell can expand to an enormous size with stored fat. Once formed, fat cells never disappear and are primed to store fat. This means that a baby with extra fat cells—

even if he or she lost weight—would be susceptible to later obesity. However, the transformation of fat babies into fat children has been questioned by Alex Roche (1981), whose review of various studies indicates almost no connection between obesity in infancy and obesity at age sixteen. After the age of six, however, childhood obesity is highly associated with obesity in adolescence. It was once believed that extra fat cells would form only during infancy, or perhaps early childhood, but mounting evidence suggests that excessive overeating can lead to the proliferation of fat cells at any time in life (Rodin, 1984). Once a child is past infancy, the danger of obesity appears to increase when parents who are anxious about their own weight either follow inconsistent feeding practices with their children or else restrain a child's eating so rigidly that the youngster never develops any internal psychological controls over eating (Rodin and Hall, 1984). Too much of even the healthiest food produces overweight children, and parents can also make their children obese by forcing food on a two- or three-year-old whose growth rate has settled into the childhood plateau, the period of relatively stable growth between infancy and puberty.

Illness

A child who escapes serious illness will show a more regular and satisfactory growth curve than one who is ill for any length of time, because severe illness tends to slow certain aspects of growth. Short illnesses have little effect, especially the communicable diseases common among children from two to six. Although a child's growth rate may slow slightly during an extended bout with illness, catch-up growth normally compensates for such slowing. Roy Acheson (1960) found that one year of severe, confining illness resulted in a height loss of only about one-fourth of an inch. When permanent underdevelopment results, it is not merely from the effect of the sickness but because a serious and protracted illness costs the child the periods of reasonably steady growth needed for adequate development.

Socioeconomic Status

Although many children who live in poverty are adequately nourished and show normal growth rates, setbacks to growth are most common among those in lower socioeconomic classes. Inadequate nutrition can have less dramatic but more insidious effects than severe malnutrition. Low energy levels produce sluggish children whose interest is hard to arouse. Undernourished children are also more vulnerable to infections, especially to diseases of the eyes, skin, and respiratory and gastrointestinal tracts. Because these children are unlikely to have regular medical care, they may suffer from additional nagging ailments, including badly decayed teeth.

The basis of these observations is the 1965 National Child Development Survey conducted in England, comparing all children born during a single week in 1958 (Tanner, 1978). This survey indicated that the more skilled the father's occupation, the more rapidly the children grew. Growth differences between the children of fathers in highly skilled and less skilled occupations became steadily larger with age among children between the ages of two and four and a half. Studies conducted in Scotland (E. Scott, Illsby, and Thomson, 1956) support the results of the English survey, as do studies conducted in the United States (Hamill, Johnston, and Lemeshow, 1972).

Children of higher socioeconomic backgrounds tends to be larger at all ages. Part of this difference in height among socioeconomic groups is probably a result of the fact that children of the wealthier classes generally have faster growth rates, reaching puberty earlier. As the more slowly developing children mature, however, they do not make up all of the height difference, which results in a socioeconomic difference in adult height.

Differences in nutrition and the availability

of medical care may be only partially responsible for these socioeconomic differences. Some researchers have suggested that class differences in habits of sleep, exercise, and general home life may contribute to the effect. For whatever reason, children from poor homes suffer more illnesses, are more vulnerable to accidents and disasters, and undergo more physical trauma than do middle-class children (Hess, 1970).

Meager resources and large families may combine to diminish the quality of maternal care, leading to retarded growth rates. When English researchers rated the "efficiency" of mothers (a measure that included how organized a mother seemed to be at meeting her child's basic needs), they found that the more efficient the mother, the taller her children (Acheson, 1960). When inefficiency was combined with poor socioeconomic conditions, the effect on growth was striking. In these same studies, birth order also correlated with height. First-born children tended to be taller than later-born children. The height advantage could be, at least in part, a result of the first-born's temporary status as an only child who receives the full attention of both parents.

Only one study has found no correlation between size and social status. Gunilla Lindgren (1976), who surveyed all urban schoolchildren in Sweden, found no relation between father's occupation and children's height at any age between seven and seventeen years. J. M. Tanner (1978), who adds that there is no longer any correlation between parental occupation and the height of Swedish military conscripts, suggests that a lack of discrepancy in children's growth on the basis of father's occupation might be a good measure of the classlessness of a society. Whether or not Sweden is actually a classless society, the nature of its welfare system has removed poverty as a cause of inadequate nutrition.

Ethnic Differences

Another influence on growth and development can be traced to ethnic differences in body proportions. Genetic differences in height are probably clearest when a group with an extremely tall average height, such as the Watusis of Africa, is compared with an extremely short group, such as the Ituri pygmies. Sometimes environment, in the form of diet, combines with genes so that height is expressed at the lower end of the possible reaction range. For example, at one time Japanese who grew up in Japan were considerably shorter than Japanese who grew up in the United States. Today, however, following widespread changes in the native Japanese diet, the difference has disappeared. Yet no matter how bountiful the diet, the average Japanese-American is still shorter than the average American of European or African descent. This disparity, says Tanner (1978), is genetic, and because Asiatics have faster growth velocity and earlier puberty, it is more pronounced among adults than among children.

When environment is alike, height is more similar than bodily proportions among Asiatics, Europeans, and Africans. The difference is primarily in leg length as compared with torso length. Seated Chinese, English, and Nigerian men may appear to be the same height, but when the three stand, the Chinese will be the shortest and the Nigerian the tallest. Tanner (Eveleth and Tanner, 1976) has also found that Africans have narrower hips in relation to shoulder width than Europeans and Asiatics, that African male body composition contains more muscle and heavier bone per pound of body weight than men of other ethnic groups, and that African men have leaner legs. He believes that such genetic differences give men of African descent the edge in some track events and Asiatic men (who have the shortest legs) the edge in gymnastics and weight-lifting.

Stress

Growth can also be retarded by severe emotional stress, apparently through its effect on hormonal secretions. Although a number of hormones have important roles in the regulation of growth, the growth hormone (GH) itself is one of the most interesting. At one time, children who lacked GH became midgets—perfectly proportioned adults about fifty inches tall. Today, such children receive injections of GH taken from human pituitary glands, which stimulate catch-up growth, enabling them to attain a height within the normal range. According to Tanner (1978), GH levels rise in the blood only a few times each day—about an hour or so after children go to sleep, after they have exercised, and when they are anxious. GH stimulates the liver to produce somatomedin, a hormone that acts on the growing cartilage cells at the end of bones, and probably on the muscle cells as well. A single dose of GH keeps somatomedin blood levels high for at least twenty-four hours.

Some children react to severe psychological stress not by increasing the amount of GH but by switching off its production. They simply fail to grow, just as do children whose bodies do not produce the hormone. Their skeletal structure is immature, with the bones exhibiting the shape and relation of those of a much younger child. This condition, called "psychosocial dwarfism," is associated with severe emotional distress in young children from homes in which family members are emotionally detached and there are no emotional bonds between parent and child (Powell, Brasel, and Blizzard, 1967; L. Gardner, 1972). If such children are removed from their disturbed environments, they show rapid catch-up growth.

Stress that is not quite so severe may sharply reduce the secretion of GH. For example, Elsie Widdowson (1951) found that children in an orphanage under the regime of a punitive and unfair teacher grew more slowly than orphanage children whose diet had 20 percent fewer calories but whose environment was less stressful. In some boarding schools, boys have been known to grow more slowly during the school term than when they were home for the holidays (Tanner, 1978). But it takes severe psychological or physical stress to affect a child's growth. The everyday stresses and illnesses encountered by most children have little impact.

DEVELOPMENT OF MOTOR ABILITIES

Some motor skills appear to develop in simple, orderly fashion, whereas others are complex and show little consistency in their development. Even simple sequences depend on an intricate interplay between maturational changes and experience.

Maturation and Experience

Maturation means simply an organism's progression toward physiological maturity. But when psychologists refer to maturation in relation to experience, they are stressing the effect on behavior of such factors as genes, hormones, nutrition, and metabolism, as opposed to the effect of learning.

As we saw in Chapter 4, certain motor skills appear to have a developmental sequence in which early, more primitive coordinations disappear and then reappear later in more advanced forms, a sequence known as U-shaped behavioral growth (Strauss, 1982). Although the causes of this sequence are not known, it is possible that some types of U-shaped behavioral growth are connected with maturational changes in brain and nervous system organization. Depending on the skill involved, the change can be influenced by stimulation, that is, learning. As we saw in Chapter 4, if babies are given practice in the stepping reflex for about ten minutes each day from one week until they are eight weeks old, they are likely to walk a bit earlier than the average baby (Zelazo, Zelazo, and Kolb, 1972).

The average age at which a child walks or crawls, for example, can be accelerated or slowed by cultural practices—but only about a month in each direction. Although this shift is statistically significant, the skill still appears during the normal age range for its mastery. Such general differences are not related to genetics, but depend upon the culture's way of caring for children. In one African culture, where babies walk early, about 80 percent of the mothers begin training their infants to walk when they are about seven months old. In another African culture, where babies crawl early, 93 percent of the mothers train them to crawl (Super, 1976). And Native American infants who spend their first year bound to cradleboards walk about a month later than American babies who have had more practice in muscular coordination.

Recently, researchers have been looking at motor development in another way, studying how babies put together the building blocks of basic motor skills. During the first year of life, infants often repeat rapid, rhythmical movements of their limbs, head, or torso. They kick, wave their arms, bang their heads, and rock, bounce, or sway their bodies. Infants obviously enjoy these movements, and Jean Piaget (1952) proposed that such repetition was the infant's way of affecting the environment, prolonging sensations that were interesting or pleasurable. According to Esther Thelen (1981), these movements are also adaptive and play an important role in the development of motor abilities. She believes that the repetitive motions, which appear before the infant has full voluntary control of the muscles involved, may be simple, unlearned activities that the baby later combines into postural control or coordinated movements. For example, the infant's rhythmical kicks may be a spontaneous forerunner of walking.

The amount of repetitive movement varies from one infant to the next. Babies who spend a good deal of time restricted to infant seats, cribs, and playpens spend more time rocking, swaying, and bouncing than do infants who are frequently rocked, jiggled, or carried by their caregivers. As we saw in Chapter 4, kinesthetic stimulation is vital for most development. Perhaps, says Thelen, infants who do not receive an appropriate amount of kinesthetic stimulation from caregivers provide their own stimulation in compensation.

One way to study the relative contribution of maturation and experience to motor control is the method of **co-twin control,** in which the experimenter gives one of a pair of twins some

Although cultural practices can speed up or retard a child's motor development, the effect is minimal. This Pueblo baby's lack of opportunity to practice walking will probably slow his first steps by no more than a month. (Roy Pinney/Monkmeyer)

experiences believed to be important in learning a skill and withholds or delays those same experiences for the other twin. In Myrtle McGraw's (1935, 1939) classic co-twin control study, one twin received practice in crawling and standing and the other was kept from all such opportunities. Despite the difference in their experience, both twins crawled and walked at the same age.

Deliberately restricting a child's movement has been used as a means of evaluating the roles of maturation and experience. For example, Wayne Dennis (1941) left a pair of female twins on their backs from birth to nine months, never allowing them to sit or to stand. Yet the sitting and standing of both twins emerged fully developed, with little or no practice. It should be noted that except for the experimental restriction, both girls had a fairly normal environment.

When the environment is both socially and physically impoverished, the development of motor skills may lag severely. In a series of studies conducted in institutions with such environments, Dennis and his associates (Dennis, 1960; Dennis and Najarian, 1957; Dennis and Sayegh, 1965) found that children who were neither attended to by adults nor surrounded by a stimulating environment showed retarded motor development from the time they were two months old. In one study, Dennis and Yvonne Sayegh (1965) worked with infants in The Creche, a foundling home in Lebanon. In that institution, infants spent most of their first year lying on their backs in cribs. Some of the infants who were more than one year old could not sit up. Infants in the experimental group were propped into a sitting position and allowed to play with such simple attractive objects as fresh flowers, pieces of colored sponge, and colored plastic disks strung on a chain, for as little as an hour each day. This seemingly small amount of stimulation caused the babies' developmental age to jump dramatically.

In a related study, Burton White and Richard Held (1966) investigated the effect of enriched stimulation on the development of grasping. They concluded that appropriate extra stimulation could accelerate the baby's acquisition of grasping. However, more detailed studies have suggested (White, 1971) that stimulation must be appropriate to both the age of a baby and his or her abilities. Too much stimulation, for example, may be irritating or confusing, at least temporarily, and fail to accelerate the development of the baby's motor skills.

It seems clear from such studies that even though a child's motor development may require only normal freedom for spontaneous activity, some environments promote development and others retard it.

The stimulation of an enriched environment may speed the development of motor skills, but too much stimulation can confuse the baby and thus be counterproductive. (Peter Vandermark/Stock, Boston)

Strength, Speed, and Coordination

As children develop new motor skills, their progress depends on several physiological factors. The ability to exert force is limited by the strength of the body muscles. The speed with which a child can execute a movement is influenced by the mass of the part of the body that is being moved. And the child's reactions depend on the type of stimuli, the nerves' transmission of impulses, the relative complexity of the movement, and the child's general physical and psychological condition. All mature activity is affected by these same aspects of motor abilities: strength, speed, and coordination.

As size and weight—particularly of muscle tissue—increase, strength is enhanced. A child's strength doubles between the ages of three and eleven. Speed is a sensorimotor function that first becomes important in the play of young children. A major factor in speed is **reaction time,** the interval of time that elapses between the instant a stimulus is presented and the individual's reaction to it. After reviewing studies of reaction time, Harold Fishbein (1976) concluded that the widest individual differences are found in young children. As children grow, individual differences narrow and reactions speed up. Before the age of four, reaction time is quite slow; between the ages of four and nine, speed increases sharply, stabilizing at about the age of ten. The more decision required in executing a motor skill, the more the performance of young children suffers. Teenagers execute simple skills requiring a single decision three times as fast as a four-year-old, but when several decisions go into a movement, the teenagers perform four times as fast as the younger children.

Many aspects of motor performance depend on coordination, which affects accuracy of movement, poise, smoothness, rhythm, and ease. Coordination involves more than strength and speed and is, therefore, a better index for determining a child's skill and agility. Children develop coordination more slowly than they acquire strength and speed, because coordination requires the interplay of sensory and motor skills that often depend on the maturation of small muscles and on practice. Since children are extremely conscious of their own and their playmates' degree of coordination, a child's relative mastery of any task that requires coordination can affect his or her self-confidence and self-esteem.

Skill Development

Maturation of muscles and bones plays a large part in the emergence of such skills as running, jumping, and skipping; but the opportunity to practice and the encouragement of others help to guarantee the smooth, speedy, confident mastery and refinement of such abilities. To master a particular motor skill, a child must pass through several stages of proficiency.

M. V. Gutteridge (1939), after studying more than 2,000 preschool children, constructed a scale of motor-skill development, which is reproduced in Table 5.1 and can be used to measure the specific skills of any child. The Gutteridge scale describes four general phases of motor development, within which are varying degrees of skill. The first ten degrees of skill mark the progressive acquisition of the ability; the final four degrees (A–D) measure the elaboration and use of the ability after the child has achieved competence.

When first developing a skill, a child requires external feedback: information from the environment about the relative success or failure of an attempt. The sight of the thrown ball's trajectory, the position of the dart hurled toward the target, the path of the bowling ball down the alley, the sight of the letters carefully printed on the page are necessary if the child's performance is to improve. With practice, internal feedback becomes enough to accomplish any motor skill. Kinesthetic information from muscles, joints, and tendons guide and correct movements (Fishbein, 1976). The skilled athlete knows from the feel of body position whether the ball just released from the hand is likely to hit its target.

There are, of course, large individual differences in the ages at which various children are able to do different things, as well as differences in the degree of their skill and coordination in each activity. For simple movement patterns, says Caroline Sinclair (1973), instruction and coaching are not necessary. All a child needs is time, space, equipment, and encouragement.

More complicated motor skills require formal instruction and special equipment. These include such sports as swimming, skating, skiing, tennis, and so forth. Many children are exposed to these skills during early childhood, and such early exposure and practice appear to give children an advantage in their performance. In Myrtle McGraw's (1935) co-twin study, for example, although one twin seemed to gain little from training in such skills as walking and stair-climbing, early training in swimming had some ad-

Table 5.1 GUTTERIDGE SCALE OF MOTOR SKILLS

PHASE	SCALE	DEGREE OF MOTOR SKILL
No attempt made	1	Withdraws or retreats when opportunity is given
	2	Makes no approach or attempt but does not withdraw
Skill in process of formation	3	Attempts activity but seeks help or support
	4	Tries even when not helped or supported but is inept
	5	Is progressing but still uses unnecessary movements
	6	Is practicing basic movements
	7	Is in process of refining movements
Basic movements achieved	8	Coordinates movements
	9	Performs easily with display of satisfaction
	10	Shows evidence of accuracy, poise, and grace
Skillful execution with variations in use	A	Tests skill by adding difficulties or taking chances
	B	Combines activity with other skill or skills
	C	Speeds, races, or competes with self or others
	D	Uses skill in larger projects such as dramatic play

(*Source:* Adapted from M. V. Gutteridge, ''A Study of Motor Achievement of Young Children,'' *Archives of Psychology* 244 [1939].)

Simple motor skills, such as running and jumping, depend primarily on the maturation of bones and muscles. This jumping game is easy enough for most preschoolers. (Elizabeth Crews)

vantages. Researchers began training one twin to swim at eight months, and when he was seventeen months old, he could swim up to fifteen feet without help while his twin could not swim at all. McGraw also had success in teaching the same twin diving and skating. Other studies have demonstrated that observation and verbal instruction increase a child's skill at throwing and catching, and of course, fine motor skills such as writing and drawing improve with practice.

SEX DIFFERENCES

Even before birth, girls and boys grow at different rates. By the time they are halfway through the fetal period, girls' skeletal development is three weeks ahead of boys'; and by the time they are born, girls have outstripped boys by four to six weeks in skeletal maturity, although not in size (Tanner, 1978). Some organ systems also are more developed in newborn girls, which may help explain why more newborn girls than boys survive.

If children are to learn a complicated motor skill, such as skiing, they need an opportunity to practice and the encouragement of others. (Phaneuf/ Gurdziel/The Picture Cube)

Prepubertal Differences

Baby girls have proportionately more fat and less muscle tissue and water than boys (Falkner, 1966). This difference exists throughout life. Young girls lose their fatty infant tissue at a far slower rate than do their male contemporaries (Stolz and Stolz, 1951).

Boys grow faster than girls during the first few months of life, but girls outstrip boys from seven months until they are four years old. Between four and puberty, there are no apparent differences in the velocity of growth, and differences in appearance are slight. Body proportions in both sexes are similar: straight and flat. Girls, however, remain ahead of boys in maturation. Until adolescence, the skeletal maturity (but not size) of boys is only 80 percent that of girls the same age (Tanner, Whitehouse, and Healy, 1962). And most girls reach sexual maturity about two years sooner than boys.

According to an old rule, children reach half their adult height by the end of their second year. However, differences discovered in the growth patterns of boys and girls make this old rule unreliable for girls. Since girls grow up faster than boys, they reach the halfway mark sooner, at about eighteen months (Acheson, 1966; Tanner, 1978). The old rule remains fairly reliable for boys, however.

Growth regulation is more efficient in girls than in boys. Girls catch up after a period of arrested growth more quickly than boys do, and placed under the same adverse circumstances, whether poor nutrition or exposure to atomic radiation, the growth of boys slows down more (Tanner, 1968).

Until they are four, girls have a slight advantage in the development of motor skills. Around the age of three, boys become more proficient than girls at tasks that require strength, such as throwing (Sinclair, 1973), and after age six, boys gain in strength more quickly than girls. By age seven, girls demonstrate about 10 percent less muscular strength than boys. Louis Govatos (1959) tested ten-year-old children and found no sex differences on tasks as diverse as jumping, reaching, the standing broadjump, the twenty-five-yard dash, or throwing a ball for accuracy. But boys were more proficient than girls in tasks that require superior strength in the arms and legs, such as soccer-style kicking or throwing a ball for distance. Among adolescents, boys consistently show more extensive muscle development, but until recently exercise patterns for older children and adolescents differed by sex. Whether the upsurge in the popularity of sports for girls will narrow the difference is uncertain (Petersen and Taylor, 1980).

Sex-related differences are also evident in brain development and function, a topic we shall discuss in Chapter 6, and in some involuntary physical functions as well (see Figure 5.6). In a measure of **vital capacity** (lung capacity), girls, when asked to inhale as much air as they could and then to expel it, demonstrated 7 percent less vital capacity than boys (Sherman, 1973). Vital capacity can be an important factor in tasks that require sustained energy output. However, females exhibit lower **basal metabolism** rates than males; that is, they require less energy while resting to maintain the same amount of body

Superstar Kids

Perhaps spurred by widespread television coverage of amateur sports and the financial rewards reaped by top athletes, a growing number of American children are taking athletics seriously. Aiming for the Olympics or the world of professional athletes, these youngsters spend their childhood in the pressure-filled world of competitive sports. If they stick with it, their adolescence will be spent in training and traveling—at the expense of friendships and any outside interests.

The constricted world of the adolescent athlete has been described by Emily Greenspan (1981), herself a former child member of the world of serious athletics. At fifteen, figure-skater Elaine Zayak was skating six and a half hours each day, seven days a week. Her school attendance was limited to two hours each morning, supplemented by a private tutoring session twice each week. During one several-week period, she skated in China, Canada, Boston, and Colorado Springs. Such a life has other drawbacks. It may create resentment among the athlete's brothers and sisters, who are expected to sacrifice for their superstar sibling. And it is expensive: Zayak's parents spent as much as $25,000 to finance their daughter's skating career each year.

Most sports psychologists take a dim view of this life for developing children. Physical injury is prevalent, especially when inexperienced coaches foster techniques that are unsuitable for a growing child's size, developmental age, or ability. Muscle, ligament, and tendon strains are common, and growth plates and cartilage at bone ends are often damaged. Most of us have heard of "Little League elbow" or "swimmer's shoulder," but few are aware that growth-plate injuries suffered in gymnastics or marathon running may permanently stunt growth. The younger the child, the greater the threat. A serious growth-plate injury may reduce the adult height of a fourteen-year-old by only a quarter inch, but the same injury in a seven-year-old can lead to a four- to five-inch height loss (Greenspan, 1981).

In addition to permanent physical injury, there is the possibility of psychological burnout. According to Thomas Tutko (cited in Greenspan, 1981), the organized competition of children's leagues generates too much pressure for many children. Promising young athletes are often burned out by the age of fifteen, no longer able to meet the demands of parents, coaches, fans—or their own personal obsessions. In a twelve-year longitudinal study, reports Greenspan (1981), Harrison Clarke found that only 25 percent of star athletes in elementary school continued as athletic stars in junior high school. For a handful, a childhood limited to athletics pays off in fame and immense wealth. For most children, however, there is neither fame nor wealth, only an immersion in a competition more intense than most adults will ever encounter.

---

tissue. Boys develop larger hearts and lungs than girls, and boys' hearts also beat more slowly (Hutt, 1972).

During early childhood, motor abilities and physical growth play an important part in the developing self-image of both boys and girls. When children are asked what they like and do not like about themselves, physical characteristics, appearance, and motor abilities play an important part in their answers (Jersild, 1952). Boys are more likely than girls to base their *social hierarchies*, or patterns of dominance and submission, on who is bigger, faster, and tougher. Children's social hierarchies, of course, also reflect their parents' values, and studies of sex-role behavior clearly show that adults value strength and athletic abilities more in males than in females (Sherman, 1973).

Some researchers speculate that extensive participation in traditionally masculine sports during later childhood and adolescence may narrow the gap in strength and muscular development between boys and girls. (Bruce M. Wellman/Stock, Boston)

Sexual Maturation

Adolescence begins as a biological phenomenon, with sexual maturation as its central theme. Long before emotional considerations and social conflicts become important in the course of adolescent growth, hormonal changes begin to affect the body. The main biological event of adolescence is puberty, when the reproductive glands begin to release sperm and ova. These glands are the **testes** in boys and the **ovaries** in girls. With the release of sperm or ova, the individual is, for the first time, capable of reproduction.

Both boys and girls produce male hormones (**androgens**) as well as female hormones (**estrogens**) in relatively equal amounts throughout their childhood. Hormones help to regulate growth at all stages, but it is only when a child reaches puberty that the hypothalamus of the brain signals the pituitary gland to begin the hormonal production found in adult men and

women. The pituitary gland stimulates other endocrine glands, the adrenals, ovaries, and testes (shown in Figure 5.7), to secrete hormones directly into the bloodstream, creating a balance that includes more androgens in boys and more estrogens in girls. These hormonal changes lead directly to the physical developments that emerge during puberty, although just how endocrine changes are related to the attainment of fertility is unknown (Petersen and Taylor, 1980).

During puberty, the ovaries and testes produce enough hormones to cause accelerated growth of the genitals and the appearance of **secondary sex characteristics,** which differen-

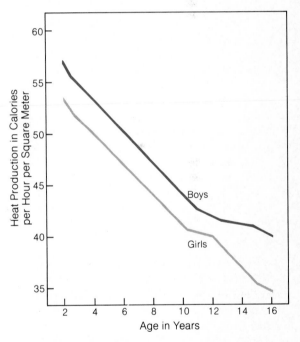

FIGURE 5.6 As this graph shows, the basal metabolic rate of boys is higher than that of girls, indicating that boys convert food and oxygen to various forms of energy faster than girls do. The difference is slight throughout childhood but increases somewhat during adolescence.

(Adapted from R.C. Lewis, A.M. Duval, and A. Iliff, "Standards for the Basal Metabolism of Children from Two to Fifteen Years of Age," *Journal of Pediatrics*, vol. 23, 1943.)

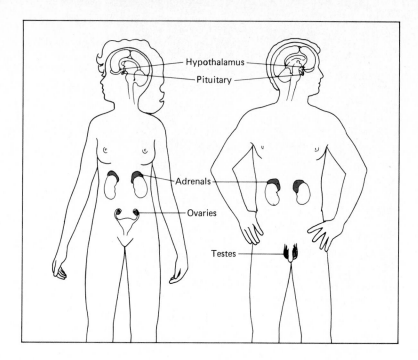

FIGURE 5.7 The endocrine system, showing only the major glands involved in pubertal changes. The hypothalamus (a part of the brain with neural and endocrine functions) signals the pituitary gland, which in turn stimulates hormonal secretions from other endocrine glands, resulting in many of the changes typifying adolescent and pubertal development.

tiate the genders but have no direct reproductive function. In girls, a cyclic secretion of estrogens anticipates the rhythm of the menstrual cycle well before **menarche**—the first incidence of menstruation—which is an obvious milestone in puberty.

The female adolescent growth spurt typically begins at around age ten, peaks just before twelve, and continues until about fifteen, although puberty varies so widely that a girl's growth spurt can start at any time between the ages of seven and thirteen (Faust, 1977). The appearance of secondary sex characteristics signals the onset of puberty in girls. The "breast buds" develop and pigmented pubic hair ap-

pears. Breast enlargement begins some time around the middle of the tenth year and continues for approximately three years until full size is reached. The entire breast enlarges and changes in its shape and appearance. At the same time, a girl's voice lowers somewhat and her vagina and uterus begin to mature.

In boys, the adolescent growth spurt generally occurs about two years later than in girls and peaks at about the age of fourteen. The onset of puberty typically occurs at about twelve among boys, and as is the case for girls, puberty includes more than one event. The appearance of live spermatozoa in the urine marks the onset of puberty, but because this event can be detected only by clinical tests, more observable changes are generally used. These changes include accelerated growth of the testes and scrotum, the pubertal height spurt, and nocturnal emissions. Secondary sex characteristics in boys include pubic hair, a deepened voice that results from an enlarged larynx and lengthened vocal cords, and the appearance of facial hair.

Although boys begin the pubertal growth

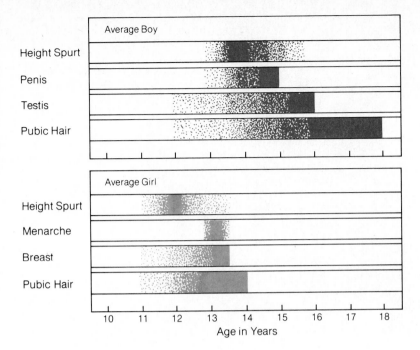

FIGURE 5.8 The pubertal development of an average boy and girl. Shaded areas represent the range of years during which such development usually occurs. Although individual growth and change patterns may vary widely from these norms, girls generally start and end such development earlier than boys.

(Adapted from J.M. Tanner. *Growth at Adolescence*, 2nd ed. Blackwell Scientific Publications, Oxford, 1962.)

spurt later than girls, their growth spurt lasts about three or four years longer than that of girls (see Figure 5.8). For this reason, girls between the ages of twelve and fifteen tend to be taller than boys; but the boys catch up as they enter puberty and end their growth spurt significantly taller, on the average, than girls.

Both sexes experience a growth characteristic called **asynchrony.** Asynchrony refers to the fact that different body parts mature at different rates. This means that at any given time during adolescence, certain body parts may be dispro-

portionately large or small in relation to the rest of the body. This disproportion may become pronounced with puberty, as legs begin to grow in length before the rest of the body does (Faust, 1977). Some girls complain that their hands and feet are too big, and boys may object that their jaws are too prominent or their noses too large. As growth progresses, body proportions become more harmonious; a girl gradually takes on the figure of a mature woman, while a boy develops the physique of a man.

SIZE AND MATURATIONAL TRENDS

Where records have been kept, they have indicated a trend toward earlier onset of puberty over the past century or more. Since the early nineteenth century, European girls have been reaching menarche earlier and boys' voices have been changing at an earlier age (Malina, 1979).

Adolescents often worry because their hands and feet seem too large for their bodies, but this asynchronism is a natural, temporary aspect of adolescent growth. (Bill Owens/Archive)

The data are more complete for girls than for boys, but according to choir records kept by Johann Sebastian Bach in eighteenth-century Leipzig, most boys' voices changed soon after their seventeenth birthday. Today, a boy's voice is likely to change when he is between 13.25 and 13.87 years old (Roche, 1979).

Until recently, it was commonly believed that the average age of menarche in the early nineteenth century was seventeen. Then an analysis of the data indicated that this late sexual maturation had been recorded for only one isolated Norwegian group, and that most nineteenth-century European girls reached menarche when they were about fifteen (Bullough, 1981). By the middle of the twentieth century, girls were beginning to menstruate at about the age of thirteen. Little nineteenth-century data exist for American girls, but a popular home medical

manual of the time set the date of first menstruation as between 12 and 14. Twentieth-century records show American girls reaching menarche somewhat earlier than Europeans. In 1910, the average age of menarche in the United States was about 14; by 1940, it was about 13.3; and by 1955, it had dropped to about 12.8. Since that time, there has been little change among American girls (Malina, 1979), and the age decrease also appears to have stopped in Norway and England, although it may be continuing in Holland and Hungary (Roche, 1979).

In addition to maturing earlier sexually, boys and girls today are taller and heavier before, during, and at the end of adolescence than they once were. Howard Meredith (1963) points out that at mid-century the average American boy was five and a quarter inches taller than a boy of the same age in 1870. Over the same period, the average weight for fifteen-year-old boys increased by thirty-three pounds.

Although adults also are taller than they were a century ago, the increase in height is less than among children and adolescents because of earlier maturation. In the past hundred years, the average height of young black American men has increased 5.3 centimeters (about 2 inches), and that of young white American men has increased 2.9 centimeters (just over an inch) (Meredith, 1976). Growth in height begins earlier today than it once did and both sexes now reach their adult height at an earlier age, suggesting that sexual maturation is completed earlier in life. The average boy now reaches his adult height at twenty-one, and the girl at about seventeen. Although no data document the age at which growth was completed in the last century, some authorities believe that men continued to grow until they were about twenty-six (Roche, 1979).

Accompanying this change in height and weight has been an alteration in body proprotions. This change was discovered when the student records of parents were compared with those of their children who attended the same college (Himes, 1979). The members of the younger generation were consistently taller and heavier than their parents. Among men, the length of the thigh had increased, as had chest, hip, thigh, arm, and wrist circumferences. However, sons' and fathers' waist measurements were about the same. Among women, thigh length showed no significant change, but younger women had longer trunks, larger waists, and broader chests than their mothers.

Changes in body size are not unique to the United States; many countries around the world report similar trends. The difference in height between the average British factory worker in 1830 and his contemporary counterpart, for example, is much greater than the present height difference between slum children in underdeveloped countries and affluent children in Western industrialized societies (Tanner, 1978). In Sweden, Holland, and Japan, similar increases have been found. During the first half of the twentieth century, for example, the average height of twenty-year-old Japanese men increased 4.6 centimeters (nearly 2 inches), and the height of twenty-year-old Japanese women increased 6.6 centimeters (more than 2.5 inches) (Roche, 1979).

There is no single explanation for these trends, which have resulted from the interplay of environmental and genetic factors. Better nutrition and sanitation and freedom from disease are usually credited with allowing human stature to approach the maximum of its reaction range. Today's children experience fewer severely debilitating diseases, and modern procedures prevent many diseases from exerting a negative influence. As a result, children are able to devote nutrients to growth and development instead of to overcoming disease (Malina, 1979). Since better living conditions play a crucial role in development and maturation, children from upper- and middle-class backgrounds generally become taller and heavier and reach puberty earlier than their lower-class peers do.

The improvement in living conditions has been especially striking in cities, and during the past thirty-five years urban living apparently has become healthier than it once was. Children and adolescents from urban areas are now taller and heavier than their rural counterparts (Meredith, 1982). This disparity represents a reversal of earlier findings, for between 1870 and 1915, young people who lived in the country tended to be taller and heavier than those who lived in the city. The change appears to be worldwide and has been found in a majority of ethnic groups studied.

Genetics may also have contributed to growth changes. Modern mobility has affected the breeding patterns of many populations, making it easier to marry outside the community. As animal breeders have known for centuries, such outbreeding is connected with increases in stature. For example, whether people in an Italian-speaking area in Switzerland immigrated to California or remained, children born to adults who married outside the community were two centimeters (about eight-tenths of an inch) taller, on the average, than children born to a couple in which both partners belonged to the Italian-speaking Swiss group (Hulse, 1957). But the power of environment became clear when children of immigrants were compared with their relatives in Switzerland. Children born in California (whether one or both parents were immigrants) were about four centimeters (just over an inch and a half) taller than children born in Switzerland (whether one or both parents belonged to the Italian-Swiss group).

The trends toward early maturity and increased height seem to have stopped in most industrialized countries, and in some developing countries there has been no increase in height. In the Oaxaca area of Mexico and on the Pacific island of Yap, people seem to be no taller than they were in the last century, while in India, Chile, and some areas of Africa, adults have been getting shorter (Roche, 1979). There is no guarantee that future generations of Americans, Europeans, and Japanese will be as tall or mature as early as those born today. Historical records indicate that sexual maturation arrived earlier in Classical Greece and Rome and in medieval Europe than it did during the nineteenth century. In fact, the average age at menarche was between 12 and 15 years, about what it is today in parts of Europe.

Why did Europeans begin to enter puberty later? According to Robert Malina (1979), a delay in growth and maturation developed about the time that large industrial cities were forming. Living conditions became crowded, health services were limited, sanitation was poor, and children were expected to work long hours. Malina speculates that the resulting combination of rampant disease, nutritional inadequacies, and social stresses was responsible for retarding growth and maturation. In recent years, concern has risen over the effects of pollution and increasing world population on the standard of living. Alex Roche (1979) has suggested that a deteriorating environment could reverse the increases in growth that have characterized developed countries for the past century.

For the present, however, earlier maturity has social consequences that are often overlooked. Childhood is shortened, and the social demands and urges associated with sexual maturity occur sooner. Society tends to attribute the rise in teenage birthrates to low income and less schooling, but the rate of teenage pregnancy has also

risen in higher socioeconomic groups (Zelnik, Kantner, and Ford, 1981). Yet the adolescent is regarded as socially and psychologically immature and often treated as an overgrown child. Although the shift toward early sexual maturity occurred thirty years ago, we seem not to have adjusted to its consequences.

SUMMARY

From the systematic study of physical development, scientists have formulated three basic principles that underlie the growth and development of all body systems: (1) **cephalocaudal development,** which means that growth progresses from the head downward; (2) **proximodistal development,** which means that growth progresses from the center to the periphery; and (3) the principle of **differentiation** and integration, which refers to the increasing specificity and complexity of growth and skills.

Psychologists have compiled descriptive summaries of important attributes and skills, called **norms,** which indicate average tendencies for a large number of children. Despite the nearly universal sequences of development described by norms, individual children may differ greatly from them. For this reason, **developmental age** is most accurately measured by **skeletal maturity,** not by chronological age or height.

A variety of environmental influences can either promote or impede a child's physical growth. These influences include diet, general health, and the type and quality of maternal care. In addition, severe emotional stress can switch off the production of growth hormones. Ethnic differences in growth are often due to a combination of genetic and environmental influences.

Early motor skills seem to require kinesthetic stimulation for development, and babies may supplement stimulation from their caregivers with repetitive movements that appear before full voluntary muscular control is established. Using several different methods of study, psychologists have learned that only minimal normal practice may be necessary for the development of most skills. The progress of motor skill development is influenced by a child's strength, speed, and coordination, with **reaction time** steadily becoming faster until about the age of ten. In order to become proficient in complicated motor skills, a child may require encouragement and some formal instruction.

During early childhood, physical growth and development differences between the sexes are relatively slight: the average boy is a little taller than the average girl, but girls are more advanced in some areas of motor development. Differences between the sexes have also been found in **vital capacity** and metabolic rate.

The physical and maturational changes that indicate increased hormone production are dramatically reflected in the adolescent growth spurt. Among the signs most often used to mark the attainment of sexual maturity, or **puberty,** are the first incidence of menstruation in girls and the appearance of pubic hair, nocturnal emissions, and enlarging sex organs in boys.

Size and maturational trends over the decades indicate an earlier onset of puberty, increases in size and weight, and the earlier attainment of final adult height than was the case in the last century. Improved nutrition and sanitation, more sophisticated medical care, and genetic effects are among the factors that appear to explain these changes across and variations within generations.

The Developing Human Brain

EVOLUTION OF THE BRAIN
THE DEVELOPING BRAIN
Brain Growth and Development
Cytoarchitecture
Neurochemistry
Electrical Activity
HEMISPHERIC SPECIALIZATION
Dividing the Work
The Important Connection
LATERALIZATION
The Course of Lateralization
Handedness
Sex Differences
PLASTICITY
Stimulation
Recovery from Brain Damage
LEARNING DISORDERS
Developmental Dyslexia
Hyperactivity
SUMMARY

Watch a two-year-old boy walk down a flight of stairs. He must integrate a host of sensory information and motor skills in order to move himself safely from the landing on the second floor to the hall below. Both visual information and kinesthetic feedback guide the way he places his feet, changes his posture, and shifts his weight as he makes his way down the steps. Not many months ago he could not have managed the job, but now the primary motor and sensory areas of his cortex have matured, and he has taken a giant step toward independence.

The development of the human brain is important to the study of human development because the brain is the seat of consciousness and of behavior. If we can understand how thought and behavior depend on the intricate connections and chemistry of the brain, we will have advanced our understanding of human limitations and possibilities. But even a thorough understanding of the brain will leave our understanding of the mind incomplete; for the mind is more than a collection of nerve cells and chemicals, just as a book is more than specks of black ink on paper.

173

In our explorations of the brain, we follow the cortical development that, for example, enables our toddler to descend safely from the second floor to the hall of his home and, when he gets there, to run to the kitchen and tell his mother that he wants a glass of milk and a cookie. After tracing the evolution of the human brain, we examine its growth and structure. Next we consider what we can learn from the presence of chemicals that pass messages along in the brain and the electrical activity that results when those messages are transmitted. A discussion of the brain's hemispheres will show that each has its own tasks, and that when the band of fibers that connects them is severed, it is almost as if two minds were living in a single body. We learn that signs of specialized function in each hemisphere are apparent from the time babies are born and that among the consequences of this specialization are right- or left-handedness and slightly different cognitive abilities in boys and girls. We then consider the effects of stimulation on the brain and its ability to recover from damage. Finally, we look at two common childhood problems that have been associated with brain functioning: developmental dyslexia and hyperactivity.

EVOLUTION OF THE BRAIN

The human brain is an intricate tissue composed of about a hundred billion highly specialized cells that pass electrical and chemical signals across perhaps a hundred trillion **synapses,** or connective spaces between the cells (Hubel, 1979). This mass of tissue, which weighs about three pounds when fully mature, has evolved from far simpler structures. As human beings evolved, both body and brain got larger; but the increase in the size of the brain was far greater than might be predicted from the increase in body size. It was the development of this extra brain tissue that allowed intelligence to develop (Jerison, 1973).

As brains evolved, few structures disappeared. Instead, as new ones developed, the old structures shrank in relative size and became less important (Rose, 1973). The maintenance of old structures deep within the human brain has led Paul MacLean (1970) to propose that human beings have a "triune brain," that is, a brain made up of three interconnected units that function in a coordinated fashion. The first to evolve, a reptilian brain, includes the brainstem and cerebellum. It maintains consciousness and alertness, and is responsible for such automatic functions as breathing, digestion, and metabolism. The second, or paleomammalian brain, includes the limbic system, thalamus, and hippocampus. This brain contains the "old cortex," and it plays a major part in emotions, scent, taste, and sexual behavior. Here we find control over such behavior as eating, fighting, drinking, and self-defense (Fishbein, 1976). The third brain, or neocortex, makes up 99 percent of the two cerebral hemispheres (Stephan, Bauchot, and Andy, 1970). This third brain is the seat of language, attention, memory, spatial understanding, and motor skills. In primates, and especially in human beings, an extremely large proportion of the cortex consists of **association areas,** regions that have neither motor nor sensory function and no direct connections outside the cortex (Rose, 1973). Association areas apparently act on information that has already gone through several stages of processing. Our logical thinking, then, comes from the neocortex; our emotions from older sections of the brain.

Dividing the brain in this way is probably too simplistic. Although human beings have retained the old structures, the functions have undergone changes (Rose, 1973). For example, although the limbic system is regarded as the source of emotions, parts of the cortex are heavily involved with emotional responses and with our recognition of emotions in others (Geschwind, 1979).

Psychologists who look at the evolution of intelligence as a gradual increase in learning capabilities ascribe increased human capabilities to the possession of large areas of uncommitted cortex (Rose, 1973). According to Harry Jerison (1973), intelligence is a natural development of the brain's work—which is the creation of a world to explain the mass of incoming and outgoing information processed by the brain. Part of this creation is the integration of different kinds of information about the same object—information derived from vision, hearing, smell, and touch. This integration is possible because of the evolutionary transfer of much of the sensory function to the new, large cortex, which gave the sensory systems access to one another.

One reason for the mental immaturity of newborns is the size of the human brain. If a baby's brain were any larger at birth, the skull would be too large to pass through the birth canal without injury. (Suzanne Szasz/Photo Researchers)

THE DEVELOPING BRAIN

The mature human brain is so large in proportion to the rest of the body that babies must be born with an exceedingly immature brain. If the brain were any larger at birth, a fetus could not pass uninjured through the birth canal, and further widening of the birth canal would impede a woman's ability to walk upright (Leakey and Lewin, 1977). Because the brain is not capable of complex functioning at birth, human babies are helpless for a much longer period than the young of other primates, and physical maturity also arrives later. This lengthy period of immaturity, which allows the brain to quadruple in size, makes human beings much more flexible and better able to adapt to environmental changes than other primates (Bruner, 1972).

Brain Growth and Development

At birth, the baby's brain has all its neurons, or nerve cells, but is only about 25 percent of its adult weight and size. Glial cells continue to form after birth. These cells seem to play an essential role in the nourishment of neurons and in the development around each neuron of a sheath of myelin, the fatty substance that keeps nerve impulses channeled along the neural fibers and reduces the random spread of impulses from one fiber to another. For the first two years the brain grows rapidly, reaching about 75 to 80 percent of its mature size. This rapid growth is due in part to increases in the sizes and shapes of existing glial cells, in part to the formation of new ones, in part to the continued formation of myelin around the neural fibers, and in part to development within the neuron. As neural fibers sprout spreading branches, small spines appear along them At these spines, synaptic connections develop with the **vesicles,** small, chemical-filled sacs that form on the bulging end-fibers of other neurons. Synapses proliferate so rapidly within the brain's frontal lobes that a two-year-old has far more neural connections than an adult. Once this peak is reached, there is a gradual reduction of synapses until about the age of sixteen, when the density has decreased to the adult level (Goldman-Rakic et al., 1983).

Although most of the myelination of fibers is complete after two years, some myelin sheaths continue to develop, and the nerve endings within and between cortical areas continue to grow in number and size at least until adolescence (Yakovlev and Lecours, 1967). When a child is about four, the fibers that connect the cerebellum to the cerebral cortex are mature. The cerebellum, as shown in Figure 6.1, is part of the brain stem, and the connecting fibers permit the fine control of voluntary movement involved in such skills as writing. Myelination continues in the reticular formation—the core of tissue that runs through the brain stem and filters incoming stimuli—and in some parts of the cortex as late as the third decade of life.

The course of brain growth proceeds in an orderly and patterned way. Although its prenatal development is genetically fixed, the program of postnatal development is affected by environmental circumstances. It has been suggested that many genes controlling development require environmental stimuli for their activa-tion, much as the genes that control sexual maturation are activated by hormones (Chaudhari and Hahn, 1983). The major pathways that connect parts of the nervous system and brain and are responsible for the sustenance of life are fully functional at birth. As other neural circuits develop, the cells show a great variety in shape and size, and their connecting fibers are relatively small and short. As these fibers spread, the distance between the cells of the infant's cortex increases, and the enlarged surface of the cortex continues to fold and become increasingly wrinkled (Rose, 1973).

The immature appearance of the cortex at birth indicates that much of a baby's behavior during the neonatal period may be primarily reflexive. Jesse Le Roy Conel's pioneering studies (1939–1963) of postnatal development of the cerebral cortex revealed the sequence of maturation during the first few years of life. Certain areas of the brain control particular sensory and motor functions, and these areas develop at different rates. As a specific cortical area develops, the corresponding functions appear in the infant's behavior. Yet this correlation cannot be relied on. For example, most studies focus on microscopic investigation of brain tissue, and any noted behavioral change could be related to development in some other portion of the nervous system, such as sensory receptors (Parmelee and Sigman, 1983). Nor is anatomical maturity a certain sign of functional maturity. Although neuronal connections may be established, the chemicals required for the transmission of nerve impulses may not yet be present (Goldman-Rakic et al., 1983). At any stage in development, brain functioning depends on seven factors:

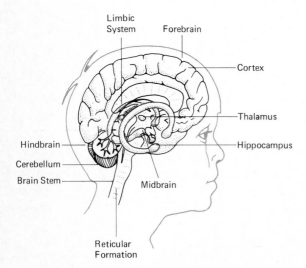

Limbic System
Forebrain
Cortex
Thalamus
Hippocampus
Hindbrain
Cerebellum
Brain Stem
Midbrain
Reticular Formation

FIGURE 6.1 The human brain evolved from simple structures into an organ consisting of three interconnected units: the hindbrain (or reptilian brain), the midbrain (or paleomammalian brain), and the forebrain (or neocortex). Without the forebrain, logical thought would be impossible.

1. the number and location of neurons
2. the neurons' maturity of structure and metabolism
3. the neurons' ability to generate nerve impulses
4. the number of connections between neurons
5. the development of synapses
6. the presence of chemicals that transmit nerve impulses

7. the organization of the neuronal network so that it can receive stimulation, process the information received, and respond to it (Parmelee and Sigman, 1983).

With these reservations in mind, we can follow the postnatal development of the cortex in two ways. One is the sequence in which the functional areas of the brain develop; the second is the advancement of body functions corresponding to each of these areas (Minkowksi, 1967). The early stages of development are characterized by an orderly sequence, in which the primary areas of the cortex begin to function efficiently. First, the primary motor area, in the precentral gyrus, develops; then the primary sensory area, in the postcentral gyrus (see Figure 6.2). Next, the primary visual area, at the back of the head in the occipital lobe, develops; and it is followed by the primary auditory area, at the side of the head in the temporal lobe. At first, these primary areas function at a simple level. For example, babies can control some of their basic body movements, and they can hear and see. However, the cortical association areas,

which must develop before babies can integrate and interpret the stimuli they encounter, lag behind the corresponding primary areas.

Cortical control of behavior develops sequentially. Whereas most of the cerebral cortex thickens during the baby's first three months, the primary motor area develops more rapidly. Again, the cephalocaudal and proximodistal developmental patterns hold true; cortical control of the head, upper trunk, and cortical control of arm movements appear before babies can use their hands skillfully. The other primary cortical areas also develop in sequence, and babies are capable of controlled movement and simple visual auditory functions.

When babies reach the age of six months, the primary motor and sensory areas are still the most advanced, but other areas of the cortex are beginning to catch up. There is marked growth in the cortical motor areas that control the hands, upper trunk, head, and legs. Between six and fifteen months, growth of these motor areas slows down. Infants can then control their hands and arms, but control over the legs is not nearly so well developed. In fact, some children still do not walk at fifteen months. During the period from six to fifteen months, the visual association areas of the cortex continue to be more advanced than the auditory association areas. By the time children are two, however, the primary motor and sensory cortical areas are well advanced and the cortical association areas have developed further. This continued cortical development enables two-year-olds to integrate their own movements with the information they get from the environment, resulting in complex patterns of behavior, as when the toddler walks down a flight of stairs.

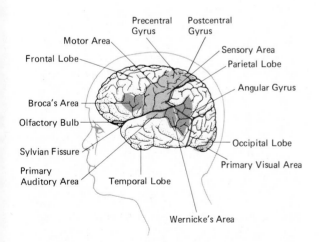

FIGURE 6.2 Language, attention, memory, spatial understanding, and motor skills are located in the cortex, which is immature at birth. This drawing shows the left hemisphere of the mature cortex, where—for most people—language is located in Broca's and Wernicke's areas.

Cytoarchitecture

Within each brain area, cells of various types are organized in particular patterns. This location and arrangement of cells, which is known as **cytoarchitecture,** appears to develop in a similar manner in all mammals. Because many studies cannot be conducted with human infants and

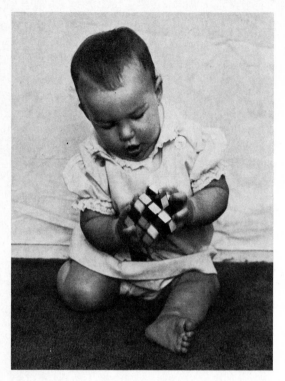

Because a baby's cortical control over the hands and fingers develops before control of the feet and legs, infants can manipulate objects long before they can walk. (Hazel Hankin)

children, much of our knowledge of developmental cytoarchitecture depends on animal studies. A good deal of this information comes from research with kittens and monkeys, whose nervous systems are immature at birth (Parmelee and Sigman, 1983). For example, the brain of a newborn kitten is similar in development to the brain of a twenty-four- to twenty-six-week-old fetus; the three-week-old kitten, to a newborn infant; and the six-week-old kitten, to a fifteen-week-old baby.

Animal and human studies indicate that the cortex is made up of six layers of cells, arranged in columns. It develops from the inside out, with the youngest, topmost layer maturing last. The mature cortex consists of horizontal layers of similar neurons and vertical columns, six lay-

ers deep, of many kinds of brain cells. The columns may differ in arrangement. In the visual cortex, for example, there are twice as many neurons in each column as in other cortical areas (Finlay and Slattery, 1983). Similarly constructed columns have different functions in different cortical areas, so that the function of any column appears to depend on its connections and the sort of stimuli it receives (Parmelee and Sigman, 1983). As we saw in Chapter 3, cell death is an important feature of brain development. Animal studies indicate that the major postnatal cell death occurs in cortical layers 2 and 3, with negligible death in the deep, oldest layers 5 and 6 (Finlay and Slattery, 1983). At birth, most of the frontal cortex is relatively immature, with few connections between neurons in layers 2, 3, and 5. During the first six months, connections within and among these areas multiply rapidly, then continue multiplying slowly for the next eighteen months or so of development, when the peak level of synaptic connections is reached (Goldman-Rakic et al., 1983).

Within specific sensory systems, neural connections in the cortex are distributed in an orderly fashion and correlate with function in a relatively straightforward manner (Goldman-Rakic et al., 1983). For example, the precedence effect, in which sounds separated by several milliseconds are heard as a single sound (see Chapter 4), is established at about the age of five months. As neurons become myelinated, they pass impulses more rapidly, and it has been suggested that the appearance of the precedence effect is probably connected with the faster transmission that follows myelinization of nerve fibers in the auditory cortex (Clifton et al., 1981).

In contrast with the cortex, development within the cerebellum, in evolutionary terms part of the oldest area of the brain, is much delayed. Although the cytoarchitecture of the cortex has reached a relatively advanced stage by the seventh prenatal month, such development in the cerebellum takes place only after birth (Parmelee and Sigman, 1983).

Neurochemistry

Neurons fire, transmitting an electrical impulse, or are kept from firing by the arrival of a **neurotransmitter.** About thirty of these chemicals act as messengers in the brain. When a nerve impulse travels along a neuron and arrives at a synapse, it triggers the release of a neurotransmitter, which travels to the adjacent neuron, where it changes the electrical activity of the nerve cell. Specific transmitters have specific effects. Depending on the nature of the receptor that picks up the transmitter, the change in electrical activity will either cause the neuron to fire or keep it from firing.

Most neurons can manufacture only one kind of neurotransmitter. Since these chemicals are not randomly distributed throughout the brain but located in specific areas and along pathways, investigators have been able to implicate specific transmitters in various kinds of behavior (Iverson, 1979). Norepinephrine, for example, is found in the brain stem, the hypothalamus, the cerebellum, and the forebrain. It is believed to be involved in arousal, brain reward, dreaming, and mood. Serotonin, found in a portion of the brain stem, the hypothalamus, and other areas, may influence temperature control, sensory perception, and the onset of sleep. Dopamine, which is concentrated in the midbrain and forebrain, is believed to play a part in the regulation of emotional response and complex movement.

Dopamine also has been implicated in performance or memory—or both. Thomas Brozoski and his colleagues (Brozoski et al., 1979) taught monkeys to solve a problem involving a delayed spatial response. When dopamine was removed from the association area of the cortex, the monkeys no longer could solve the problem. It was as if that area of their brains had been sliced away with a scalpel. But when dopamine was restored, the monkeys were again able to solve the problem.

Little is known about the development of neurotransmitter function, and most research is limited—for obvious reasons—to rats, monkeys, kittens, and lower animal forms. Research with kittens suggests that neurotransmitters not only send along neural impulses but also play a role in guiding neural development. In monkeys, dopamine is the first transmitter to reach mature concentrations, peaking at birth in the prefrontal cortex and at five months in the motor cortex. Norepinephrine levels increase steadily from birth until young adulthood. Serotonin reaches adult levels in some cortical areas at two months, in other areas at five months, and not until young adulthood in the prefrontal cortex (Goldman-Rakic et al., 1983). Whether neurotransmitters develop similarly in human children is not certain, but we do know that the protein composition of the brain changes as children grow (Gaitonde, 1969) and that the synthesis of protein is intimately involved with both the production and the storage of neurotransmitters. In fact, some amino acids—the building blocks of protein—are known to be neurotransmitters themselves (Iverson, 1979).

At one time, researchers believed that by untangling neurochemistry they would find the "memory molecule"—a single substance that was presumed to be responsible for the consolidation of memory. But the memory molecule has remained elusive, and as Dan Entingh and his associates (1975) point out, the physical basis of memory is probably a complex chain of metabolic reactions involving a number of substances. RNA (which carries the genetic information required for protein synthesis) and protein metabolism both seem to be involved in long-term memory storage. The appearance of a new stimulus, such as a flickering light, leads to changes in the metabolism of RNA, and learning a task leads to protein metabolism. When the synthesis of protein is inhibited, animals fail to form long-term memories. However, other substances have also been implicated in the process. Most research at present, say Entingh and his associates, focuses either on the control of gene expression within neurons or on biochemical reactions at the synapses between neurons.

An example of the latter research is a series of studies with lower animals by Eric Kandel

(1979) and his associates. Kandel's group studied a motor response and the habituation of the sensory neurons that control it. Habituation is a form of short-term memory that soon disappears. Kandel's work indicates that when an animal habituates to a stimulus, the neurons involved release a smaller quantity of transmitter, thereby decreasing the signal to the next neuron and leading to a temporary drop in the efficiency of the synapse. In the equivalent of long-term, or enduring, memory, synaptic connections were still inactive more than a week after the animal had habituated. Kandel concludes that long-term memory can be explained by an enduring change in synaptic effectiveness, that it requires surprisingly little training, and that short- and long-term memory both involve the same mechanism—a depression in the transmission of the impulses that cause cells to fire.

Electrical Activity

As neural connections develop and myelination progresses, changes also take place in the brain's electrical activity. This aspect of brain functioning can be studied in babies and children, since it is a relatively simple matter to attach electrodes to the scalp and record activity in various parts of the brain. As we saw in Chapter 4, at birth the brain shows characteristic electrical wave patterns when a baby is awake or sleeping. When babies are about three months old, their sleep patterns begin to resemble those found in adults, and they begin each sleep period with quiet sleep instead of going immediately into a form of REM sleep, as they do at birth.

Robert Emde and his colleagues (1976) have been trying to establish a connection between the development of infant wave forms and the appearance of certain emotional expressions, but so far their data show no close relationships. Alpha waves, which appear in adults when the eyes are closed and little information processing is going on, are not present at birth. At about four months, what seems to be a slowed form of alpha rhythm appears, gradually increasing

in frequency throughout childhood, and assuming the adult form by the time a child is sixteen years old. For this reason, alpha frequency has been used as a measure of brain maturation (Parmelee and Sigman, 1983).

Another form of electrical activity, called **evoked potential,** is a measure of the brain's response to a new sight or sound. Researchers study evoked potentials by recording many brain wave responses to the same stimulus, then use a computer to average the activity. In young infants, response to such events is delayed, apparently because nerve impulses travel more slowly over unmyelinated fibers and across immature synapses. After babies are three months old, the response begins to quicken, and by the time they are four years old, they are responding as rapidly as adults (Parmelee and Sigman, 1983). When Robert Hoffman (1978) recorded changes in brain activity evoked by showing either checkerboards or blank patterns to babies between the ages of six and ten weeks, he discovered that the control of such sights shifts from a subcortical location to the visual cortex at about two months.

Wave forms that appear in response to visual events take different forms as children mature, with the earliest wave pattern reaching maturity by the time babies are six months old, remaining prominent during middle childhood, waning during adolescence, and finally disappearing in nearly half of adults. The second wave pattern is first found in six-month-olds, remains prominent during middle childhood, and wanes during adolescence. The wave pattern that is the dominant response among adults is not found in infants but is clearly established by middle childhood. These various patterns are believed to reflect different cognitive processes (Courchesne, Ganz, and Norcia, 1981). As researchers have learned more about evoked potentials, it has become clear that they may represent a new way to study memory and decision making in infants and young children. Already, complex computer analyses of evoked potentials are being used to assess learning disabilities, and in Chapter 11, this approach will be examined.

HEMISPHERIC SPECIALIZATION

The two halves of the brain have specialized functions. Even the apparent physical symmetry of the two hemispheres turns out to be an illusion, as Norman Geschwind (1979) has demonstrated. Geschwind examined a hundred human brains and found that the length and direction of the sylvian fissure (the deep fold between the brain's temporal and frontal lobes) are different in the two hemispheres and that part of the language area on the left side of the brain is noticeably larger than that same area on the right. (See Figure 6.2). The difference is not a recent development: casts made from fossil skulls indicate that Neanderthal man had an asymmetrical brain; and the brains of great apes—but not monkeys—also show evidence of asymmetry in the sylvian fissues. The difference is also apparent in the human fetus, which indicates, says Geschwind, that the enlarged language area in the adult brain is not a response to the development of linguistic competence; rather, the left hemisphere's linguistic talents may have a solid anatomical base. As we shall see, the asymmetry of the brain has a bearing on handedness, language, differences in information processing, and cognitive differences between the sexes.

Dividing the Work

Each hemisphere of the brain receives sensations primarily from and controls the voluntary muscles primarily on the opposite side of the body (see Figure 6.3). For example, the left hemisphere controls the right hand and foot. Although each ear is connected to both halves of the brain, the strongest link is to the opposite hemisphere, which means that sounds from the right ear are interpreted by the left side of the brain. The eyes are more complicated. The visual field of each eye is split, so that images in the right half of each eye's field go to the left brain, and vice versa. So far, the division is symmetrical—each side of the brain handles half the body and half the visual field. The asymmetry appears when we move away from sensation and motor activities and examine complex forms of information processing, such as those involved in language, music, and spatial perception.

LANGUAGE In right-handed people, language is located in the left hemisphere. The two major sites are Broca's area, on the left side of the frontal lobe near the part of the motor cortex that controls the muscles used in speaking (face, tongue, lips, jaw, throat), and Wernicke's area, on the left side of the temporal lobe, between the auditory cortex and the angular gyrus—an area that seems to be involved in the connection of sounds and sights (Geschwind, 1979). A bundle of nerve fibers connects Broca's and Wernicke's areas.

The special role of this part of the brain was discovered through the study of victims of strokes, brain tumors, and head injuries. When Broca's area is damaged, people have trouble speaking but can make themselves understood; their words come out slowly, and their sentences are not grammatical, nor are they complex. These patients seem to understand language, but research has shown that their apparent understanding is based on context and redundancy of information. When they must decode a message by processing the structure of a sentence, they understand little (Gardner, 1978). When Wernicke's area is damaged, words flow freely and sentences are grammatical, but they often fail to make sense and generally include nonsense syllables. These patients have no trouble understanding the structure of sentences; their lack of comprehension comes in the area of meaning (Gardner, 1978).

Such language disruptions are called **aphasias.** A patient with Broca's aphasia, when asked what kind of work he had done, answered very slowly, "Me . . . build——ing chairs, no, no, cab——in——ets," taking forty seconds to get the words out. A patient with Wernicke's

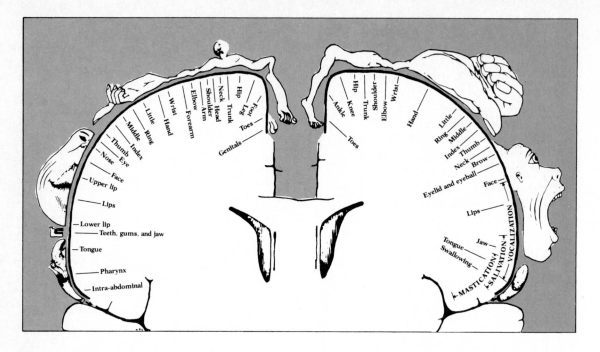

FIGURE 6.3 In this diagram, the right side of the brain is sliced through the motor and sensory areas of the cortex. The left side of the drawing locates areas that receive sensory information from various parts of the body; the right side of the drawing locates the relative amount of brain space devoted to various motor functions.

aphasia, asked the same question, replied, "We, the kids, all of us, and I, we were working for a long time in the . . . you know . . . it's the kind of space, I mean place, rear to the sped-wan" (Gardner, 1978).

There are, of course, problems in an understanding of normal brain function based on evidence from diseased or injured brains. Although such evidence is strong, it may be misleading (Kinsbourne and Hiscock, 1983). Brain-injured people may not be a representative sample of the population. Noticeable injury in one part of the brain may lead researchers to overlook small, but important, lesions in other areas. Tests may not be sensitive enough to pick up minor impairments or may not measure appropriate be-

havior. However, a technique in which a barbiturate is injected into the artery supplying one hemisphere with blood, thereby temporarily disabling that hemisphere, has confirmed the localization of language function. When the drug is injected into the blood supply for the left hemisphere, 95 percent of right-handed people cannot speak. Yet such patients continue to comprehend verbal instructions, indicating the right hemisphere's ability to understand some language (Rasmussen and Milner, 1975). Why, then, is the person with aphasia often unable to understand language? It has been suggested that in such cases either the damaged left hemisphere suppresses the limited language abilities of the right hemisphere, or else left-hemisphere damage adds so much "noise" to the system that it disrupts whatever abilities the right hemisphere retains (Kinsbourne and Hiscock, 1983).

Researchers studying the development of language have found that a baby's ability to speak follows the maturation of cortical tissue in the language areas, just as the ability to control his or her body follows maturation in the motor cortex. Brenda Milner (1976) has traced the maturation of Broca's area and indicates that the emergence of speech accompanies cell maturation and the growth of neuronal connections there. The area appears to mature from the bottom up, with the two deepest of the six cortical layers beginning to mature when babies are about a month old, and myelination begins to spread through the third layer about the time babies learn their first words. During this period, connections between neurons also are proliferating, with an especially rapid burst of growth about the time children learn to put two words together. Despite this close correlation of neuronal maturation and behavior, other factors, such as the loss of neuronal connections and the production of neurotransmitters, may be equally important in language development.

MUSIC AND SPATIAL PERCEPTION The right side of the brain also has its area of specialization. The perception of melodies and other nonspeech sounds—such as coughing, laughing, and crying—seems to be processed in the right hemisphere (Kimura, 1975). The perception and analysis of visual patterns also seem to be the work of this hemisphere. People who have had their left temporal lobes removed have trouble remembering words, but their memories of melodies, faces, spatial locations, and abstract visual patterns is as good as ever (Geschwind, 1979). People with damage to the right hemisphere have trouble drawing, finding their way from one place to another, and building models from a plan or picture (Kimura, 1975). They cannot detect emotion in the speech of others, being unable to tell, for example, whether a statement is made in a joking or angry fashion (Geschwind, 1979). Their own mood shifts radically, and they may seem inappropriately euphoric. Similarly, when the right hemisphere is inactivated by barbiturates, normal individuals seem euphoric or even maniacal. Because of this localization, right hemisphere damage often leads to inappropriate and disordered behavior, as if the patient's world had gone awry (Gardner, 1978). But emotion is not entirely the province of the right hemisphere. After damage to the left hemisphere, patients are often sad, and inactivation of the left hemisphere by barbiturates is accompanied by temporary depression (Kinsbourne and Hiscock, 1983).

Each hemisphere appears to be specialized for particular functions. Despite earlier conjectures that the hemispheres process material in different fashions, with the left hemisphere handling sequential, logical processing and the right handling simultaneous, intuitive processing (Ornstein, 1978), it appears that logic is not the property of one hemisphere nor creativity the property of the other. Instead, as Marcel Kinsbourne and Merrill Hiscock (1983) have pointed out, either hemisphere can operate in an analytic fashion, processing abstract as well as concrete material.

As research goes on, integrated behavior becomes difficult to explain in terms of hemispheric specialization. Each hemisphere appears to be more effective at processing certain kinds of material. According to Joyce Schwartz and Paula Tallal (1980), the left hemisphere's efficiency in language may come in part from its speed in processing rapidly changing events. They have found that when speech is slowed perceptibly it can be processed in the right hemisphere. Most tasks have components that draw on the skills of both hemispheres, and which side of the brain is more heavily involved may depend on the situation and the individual's way of approaching the task (Kinsbourne and Hiscock, 1983). For example, music is assumed to be the province of the right hemisphere, and when musically naïve individuals listen to music, the right hemisphere indeed does most of the processing. But among trained musicians, the left hemisphere seems heavily involved, apparently because of the tonal analysis musicians apply to the sounds (Henninger, 1981). Similarly, the signals of Morse code are processed in the right hemisphere by most people, but in the left by trained users of the code, to whom the dashes and dots are a language (Papcun et al., 1974). What we have been learning from research in the past decade is that the processing of information is more complicated than it seemed during the 1960s, and that some of the questions about hemispheric specialization that seemed settled as that decade drew to a close are open once again.

The Important Connection

The two halves of the brain are connected by the **corpus callosum,** a wide, arched band of myelinated fibers. The function of the corpus callosum is twofold: it keeps each hemisphere from interfering with the other's motor control of the opposite body side, and it transfers information from one hemisphere to the other (Den-

nis, 1977). If this connection is completely severed, as has been done surgically to stop seizures in some epileptics, the left brain literally does not know what the right brain is doing. (See Figure 6.4.) When a special apparatus flashes pictures or words to only the left visual field, for example, these split-brain patients will say they have seen nothing. The left hemisphere, which processes language, has not seen the material. If they handle an object, such as a spoon, with the left hand and are not allowed to look at it, they will deny that they have ever handled the spoon; but with the left hand, they will point out the spoon as the object they have handled (Gazzaniga, 1977).

At birth the corpus callosum is not completely

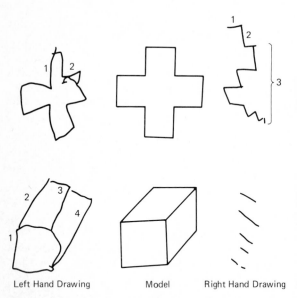

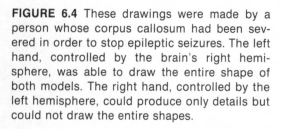

Left Hand Drawing   Model   Right Hand Drawing

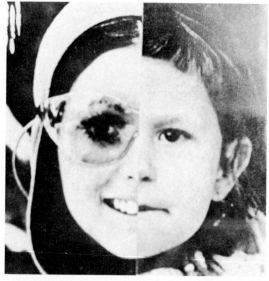

FIGURE 6.4 These drawings were made by a person whose corpus callosum had been severed in order to stop epileptic seizures. The left hand, controlled by the brain's right hemisphere, was able to draw the entire shape of both models. The right hand, controlled by the left hemisphere, could produce only details but could not draw the entire shapes.

(SOURCE: Courtesy of the Ross Loos Medical Group.)

When patients with a severed corpus callosum are shown this composite photograph of a woman and a little boy and asked to select the picture that they have seen from a group of six other photos, they say "the child"—which is the picture the left half of their brain has perceived. But asked to *point* to the picture they have seen, they will invariably select the photo of a woman with spectacles—the picture the right half of their brain has perceived.

(Photograph © Philip Daly 1967)

formed, and it matures very slowly, being one of the last systems to myelinate. Since myelination is not complete in this area until after a child is ten years old, say David Galin and his associates (1979), it is reasonable to wonder how integrated the world seems to a young child. Galin's group tested three- and five-year-old right-handed girls in order to discover how early certain kinds of information are transferred between the hemispheres. They covered small, two-inch-square pillows with various fabrics whose textures varied—such as rayon, wool, linen, and denim. With the child placed so that she could not see the pillow, they rubbed a fabric over one of her hands. Using either the same or a different fabric, they next rubbed either that same hand or the other hand. The child's job was to say whether the two fabrics were the same or not. Although five-year-olds made the same number of correct guesses whether the fabrics were rubbed on only one hand (sending messages to only one side of the brain) or on both hands (sending messages to both sides of the brain), three-year-olds found the judgment extremely difficult when both hands were involved. They did as well as the five-year-olds, however, when only a single hand was involved.

This study shows that although the hemispheres may function autonomously in very young children, communication between them improves greatly by the time the child is five years old. Galin's group tested only the sense of touch, which is a very simple kind of transfer, and they point out that the corpus callosum of five-year-olds may not be mature enough for the transfer of more complicated information—such as that involving evaluations and decisions.

LATERALIZATION

It was once thought that **lateralization** (the establishment of functions in one hemisphere or the other) had not begun at birth and that the brain was not completely lateralized until a child

reached adolescence. This view of brain development, known as **progressive lateralization,** was based on cases of childhood brain damage and its effect on language learning. It was assumed that at birth the sounds of language are processed by both hemispheres and that during the course of development, the ability of the right hemisphere to handle speech gradually shrinks until, by adolescence, it is incapable of processing language (Lennenberg, 1967).

Although some researchers still hold to the idea that lateralization is a gradual process, a growing number have adopted the position of **unchanging lateralization,** proposing that from birth the left hemisphere is specialized for some basic functions and the right hemisphere for others (Kinsbourne and Hiscock, 1983). In this view, although control may shift during development from subcortical areas to the cortex, there is no shift from the right hemisphere to the left for language, from the left to the right for spatial skills, and so forth. Apparent shifts of processing from one hemisphere to the other, as when trained musicians process music in the left hemisphere, do not indicate a change in brain organization. Instead, a different strategy is being used to process the material. If this is the case, say Kinsbourne and Hiscock (1983), then when studies of infants or young children show a lack of lateralization, it is because the neural mechanisms that are required for the function are still immature or else the lateral aspects of the task have not yet been integrated into the skill. The view that lateralization does not change after birth developed when studies began to find evidence of asymmetry as early as researchers chose to look for it.

In addition to referring to the localization of specific functions in each hemisphere (see Figure 6.5), lateralization includes the establishment of **cerebral dominance.** In people with left-hemisphere dominance, the right hand and the right ear become more proficient than the left; whereas in people with right-hemisphere dominance, the left hand and the left ear are generally more adept. But as we shall see, the division is not always as neat as theory would have it.

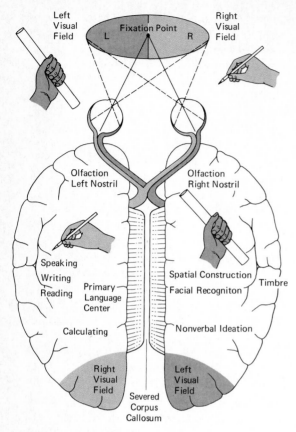

FIGURE 6.5 Each side of the brain controls half of the visual field; in addition, each hemisphere performs some tasks better than the other. When the corpus callosum is severed, as shown in the drawing, one half of the brain literally does not know what the other half is doing.

The Course of Lateralization

Differences in the way the brain processes linguistic and nonlinguistic auditory stimulation have been found in newborn babies, and even in preterm infants with an average conceptual age of thirty-six weeks (Molfese and Molfese, 1980). When infants hear consonant-vowel sounds or extended passages of speech, their brain-wave recordings show greater cortical activity over the left than over the right hemisphere. When they hear musical chords or bursts of noise in the range of speech frequency, the right hemisphere shows increased cortical

activity compared with the left hemisphere. In studies of newborn babies, Dennis Molfese and Victoria Molfese (1979) found special mechanisms within the left hemisphere that detect and analyze the sounds of human speech. The investigators played speech syllables while newborns slept and recorded the evoked potentials from each hemisphere. Upon analysis, it became clear that the two hemispheres were processing the sounds differently. Although both hemispheres had some capacity to process the sounds, the left was faster than the right and was the only hemisphere to process some types of sounds.

To establish which hemisphere handles the processing of spoken communication, researchers also use a **dichotic-listening technique,** in which two stimuli are presented at the same time, one to each ear. Although the test is also regarded as a measure of ear dominance, an individual is more likely to report hearing the stimulus that was transmitted to the hemisphere where language is processed (Studdert-Kennedy and Shankweiler, 1970). Studies using this technique indicate that right-ear superiority (indicating left-hemisphere activity) becomes established quite early in the majority of children. It has been found, for example, that when children hear such nouns as "ball," "cup," and "dog," they already show right-ear preference by three years, the youngest age tested (Ingram, 1975a). There is no indication of any increase in lateralization with age, even in a longitudinal study in which dichotic-listening tests were repeated on the same children after a long period of time (Bakker, Hoefkens and Van der Vlugt, 1979). In fact, among a group of three-year-olds, researchers found greater right-ear advantage than has been found in older children or adults (Kinsbourne and Hiscock, 1977). As language abilities improve, however, children are more likely to be able to report the stimuli directed simultaneously to both ears. Paul Mirabile and his colleagues (1978) found that the ability to report both words increased steadily until children were eleven years old, but that between eleven and fifteen there was no further improvement.

The visual field is also lateralized (see Figure

6.5), and a recent study by Kristine McKain and her colleagues (1983) may indicate a predisposition of the left hemisphere to recognize the connection between the sounds and the source of speech. Five-month-old infants looked more closely at a videotape of a speaking woman when the movements of her mouth were synchronized with the soundtrack than when the two did not match—but only when the video screen was in their right visual field. In adults, looking toward the right facilitates verbal, left-hemisphere processing.

Positive emotions have been connected to left-hemisphere activity in adults, and by the time they are ten months old, infants show greater activation of the left hemisphere when watching a laughing, smiling face (Davidson and Fox, 1982). In adults, the right hemisphere seems to be deeply involved in the perception of emotion in others. This specialization seems firmly established by the age of five. In a dichotic-listening study, kindergartners showed left-ear superiority (indicating right-hemisphere activation) in judging the emotions conveyed by speech intonation and a right-ear superiority (indicating left-hemisphere activation) when interpreting the verbal content of speech (Saxby and Bryden, 1984). The specialization of the right hemisphere for judging emotion was as strong in kindergartners as it was in high-school students.

Although some studies have indicated that spatial operations are established in the right hemisphere by the time a child is five years old (Carter and Kinsbourne, 1979), others indicate that spatial ability is lateralized between eight and ten years. In an experiment conducted by Randall Flanery and John Balling (1979), right-handed children and adults were asked to slip their hands beneath a curtain and feel geometric forms cut from a sheet of linoleum. First the children felt a form with one hand, then they felt either the same or a different form with the other hand. The task was to report whether they had felt the same or different forms. First- and third-graders were no better with their left than with their right hands, but beginning with the fifth grade, the left hand was clearly superior at discriminating the three dimensional forms.

Fifth-graders and adults were better at identifying forms with their left hands, even though they often said they could explore the shapes better with their right hands.

Handedness

A puzzle in the field of motor development is handedness. Only 5 to 10 percent of the world's adult population are left-handed, although a full 15 percent of preschoolers are "lefties." The frequency of left-handedness in both identical and fraternal twins is significantly higher than it is among single births (Hicks and Kinsbourne, 1976). There is no known genetic or physiological basis for handedness; however, Marian Annett (1978), a British researcher, proposes that right-handedness is influenced by the presence of a single allele in a gene pair (a concept discussed in Chapter 3), and that there is no corresponding allele for left-handedness. If the right-handed allele is not present, the use of the right or left hand will be randomly determined. Yet the facts suggest at least a partially experiential basis for handedness. Rhesus monkeys, who do not encounter human society, split half and half into left- and right-handers; and continued breeding of right-handed animals does not increase the percentage of right-handers among their offspring (Geschwind, 1979).

Handedness begins to become evident in the latter part of the first year. Almost as soon as infants can use their two hands independently, most of them prefer the right. Several findings suggest that this preference develops according to a timetable. Immediately after birth, a tendency to turn rightward is apparent in most babies (Kinsbourne and Swanson, 1979), and when young babies turn their heads, they will extend an arm in the direction in which the head is turned. This asymmetrical posture, called the **tonic neck reflex,** predicts which hand they will later prefer, because the arm they extend reflexively is likely to be that of the dominant side. By about three months, most infants tend to hold a toy longer when it is placed in the right hand than when it is placed in the left; and by

The cause of handedness is unknown, but the dominant right hand is usually accompanied by a dominant left hemisphere and often by a dominant right ear and right eye as well. The connection in left-handers is not as clear. (© Camilla Smith)

about six to nine months, most babies prefer to use the right hand when reaching for an object that is directly in front of them. However, many infants appear to go through phases when their preference for the right hand is either neutralized or overridden (Kinsbourne and Hiscock, 1983). From about twelve months, most infants begin to use their hands in coordination, adopting a consistent right- and left-hand strategy when faced with a task that requires both hands (Ramsay, Campos, and Fenson, 1979). In exploring toys with movable parts, right-handed babies are likely to hold the base of the toy in the left hand and manipulate its movable parts

with the right. There are wide individual differences in the timing of this preference, and it may develop as early as ten months or as late as seventeen months, about the time the baby begins to talk (see box on page 191). And by fifteen months, when a xylophone baton is placed in the left hand, babies tend to transfer it to the right in order to tap the instrument before them (Ramsay, 1979). Those who keep the baton in the left hand tap the xylophone more slowly than those who transfer the baton to the right hand.

As children grow, they continue to make definite improvements in the adeptness and accuracy of their preferred hands. When Donna Piazza (1977) asked three-year-olds to tap out a given sequence with their fingers, most showed greater ability with the right than with the left hand. This superior right-handed performance reflects greater experience and practice with the preferred hand; but it also indicates an increase in the dominance of the brain's left hemisphere

Hand preference develops in the last half of the first year, with babies first showing a consistent preference for one hand at about six months— at the time they begin to babble. (Elizabeth Crews)

and specialization in the serial organization of motor skills.

Although right-handed children show agility with their preferred hands, they are likely to perform certain skills better with the left. Dianna Ingram (1975b) found, for example, that by the time children are three, they do better with the left hand than with the right when they try to imitate hand postures modeled by another person. Blind children scan Braille better with the left hand than with the right (Hermelin and O'Connor, 1971); but this left-handed superiority is what we would expect, since the left hand is controlled by the brain's right hemisphere—the hemisphere that is superior at processing spatial information.

Research on left-handers has produced mixed findings, perhaps because only about 60 percent

of the people who think they are left-handed are solely left-handed when tested. The brains of most left- and right-handed people appear to be organized differently; although about 60 percent of left-handers process language in the left hemisphere, nearly all right-handers do. The rest use either the right hemisphere or both sides of the brain to process language. This apparent difference in brain organization showed up in a study by J. Lomas and Doreen Kimura (1976), who found that when right-handers tap with the right hand it interferes with speech, but when they tap with the left hand, it does not. However, no matter which hand left-handers use to tap with, their tapping interferes with speech.

Developmental research on **sighting dominance**—that is, which eye's muscles control the point on which both eyes focus—suggests that sighting dominance is established quite early. In studies of infants and children, Stanley Coren (1974) found that sighting dominance was established by one year in the majority of infants, and that the incidence of right-eye dominance did not change among older children. But not all right-handed adults are right-eyed; among adults, as among children, approximately 65 percent of the right-handed show right-eye dominance (Dziadosz and Schaller, 1977).

Most people show a consistent pattern of lateral preference, crushing an insect or a lighted cigarette with the right foot, sighting down a telescope with the right eye, and listening at a door with the right ear (Coren, Porac, and Duncan, 1981). However, a large minority of children and adults show a mixed pattern of dominance. In one study of three- to five-year-old right-handed children, only 60 percent showed a right-ear dominance when listening to numbers (Hiscock and Kinsbourne, 1977), and among another group of three- to five-year-old right-handers, there was no relationship between ear preference and the hand preferred for gesturing during speech (Ingram, 1975a). Yet a comparison of preschoolers and high-school students indicated that as individuals mature, they tend to show a more consistent pattern of laterality (Coren, Porac, and Duncan, 1981). Complete laterality (ear, eye, foot, and hand)

Table 6.1 DEVELOPMENT OF LATERAL PREFERENCES

	LATERALITY PREFERENCES (percent)	
	Preschool (n = 384)	High School (n = 171)
All right preference (hand, eye, foot, ear)	31.7	52.4
Three right	33.5	27.6
Two right	24.9	13.5
One right	8.3	3.5
All left preference	1.6	2.9

Lateral preference is not fixed. As children mature, their preference for the right side becomes stronger and more consistent. (Adapted from Coren, Porac, and Duncan, 1981.)

increased from 31.7 percent among the preschoolers to 52.4 percent among the high-school students (Table 6.1). Whether this greater consistency is the result of the culture's covert pressure toward the use of the right side or the result of increased neural maturation is uncertain. The fact that mixed patterns of dominance occur frequently among normal children and adults—and might even be associated with superior abilities in processing various types of information (Kershner, 1974)—indicates that interaction between the two hemispheres and the rest of the brain is quite complicated.

Sex Differences

Differences in the way boys and girls use their brains appear in nearly every study, but whether these differences reflect differences in lateralization has not been established. During the course of development, genes, hormones, and experience interact in an intricate fashion, and no one has yet been able to demonstrate that sex differences in cognitive strategies are biologically based (Kinsbourne and Hiscock, 1983).

As a result, descriptions of sex differences in brain development have been contradictory.

Early studies suggested that neural tissue matured earlier in the left hemisphere of girls and the right hemisphere of boys (Conel, 1963) and that the female brain matured more rapidly and showed left hemisphere dominance earlier than the male brain (Taylor, 1969). Later studies supported the opposite view, suggesting that the female brain never lateralized as completely as did the male brain, so that among women, most abilities tended to have some representation in both hemispheres (Springer and Deutsch, 1981).

Sex differences appear early in infancy, with one group of researchers (Shucard et al., 1981) reporting greater activation of the right hemisphere in boys and of the left hemisphere in girls, no matter whether the stimulus was words or music. In some studies, young children show small sex differences in spatial ability, with the size of the difference increasing with age, but in other studies sex differences remain stable (Kinsbourne and Hiscock, 1983). These sex differences in lateralization have been associated with sex differences in cognitive skills. Among older children, girls show an advantage in verbal abilities. The majority of studies indicate that girls are better at comprehending complex written material, understanding complex logical relations expressed in verbal terms, and carrying out tests of divergent thinking—a measure of creativity that involves the production of unusual verbal responses (Maccoby and Jacklin, 1974). Boys are generally better at tests of spatial ability, which include such tasks as the mental manipulation of objects in space, and at higher mathematics (but not at arithmetic)—a difference that is discussed in the box on page 194.

In one study of spatial ability, the results supported the view that boys show greater right hemisphere specialization for visual-spatial skills whereas girls show bilateral representation. Sandra Witelson (1976) had children explore by touch alone two differently shaped objects presented at the same time, one to each hand. The children then tried to identify the objects they had felt with each hand by selecting ones like them from a group of six variously shaped objects. Witelson found that by the time they were six, boys found it easier to identify shapes with

Handedness and Language: A Developmental Link?

The development of an unequivocal preference for the right hand appears to be connected with the development of speech. This conclusion has been put forward by several investigators (e.g., Bay, 1975) who believe that brain development follows a course of progressive lateralization. They propose that the fact that handedness is established at about the time speech makes its appearance is testimony to the progressive establishment of left-hemisphere dominance.

This position overlooks the infant's early preference for the right side, long before the first word emerges. However, a series of experiments has convinced Douglas Ramsay (Ramsay, 1984) that the baby's gradual control of speech sounds at the end of the first year is the result of successive levels of hemispheric specialization or asymmetrical brain organization. The first linkage of speech and handedness came in cross-sectional studies of five- to seven-month-olds. Five-month-olds neither babbled similar syllables ("dadada") nor showed any hand preference. Six-month-olds who had begun to babble showed a consistent hand preference; those who had not begun to babble showed no hand preference. And seven-month-olds, who were all babblers, also showed a consistent hand preference.

In a longitudinal study that followed infants from the age of five months until eight weeks after they began to babble, Ramsay (1984) found what appeared to be an example of U-shaped behavioral growth. During the week that they started babbling, babies began to show a preference for their right hand, only to lose it approximately three to four weeks after their babbling began. This temporary loss of handedness—or in some cases a temporary switch to a preference for the left hand—leads Ramsay to conclude that some sort of developmental change is taking place in either subcortical or hemispheric organization. Perhaps at a time when new connections for motor control are being established there is a temporary "disconnection" between the hemispheres, and the corpus callosum is failing to inhibit the right side of the brain from controlling the right side of the body. Or perhaps the emergence of new skills in the right hemisphere has disrupted motor control in the left side of the brain. Whatever the cause, the loss of right-hand preference is only temporary; four groups of nine-month-olds all showed strong, consistent preference for the right hand.

A further connection between speech and handedness appeared in a longitudinal study that began when babies were ten months old (Ramsay, 1980). Among these infants, the bimanual strategy for toy manipulation discussed in the text appeared either at the same time or just before babies first put together dissimilar syllables to form words ("daddy," "baby," "doggie," "pretty"). It may be that as neural control of the motor program for speech articulation develops, the left hemisphere's neural control over other motor programs becomes more firmly established.

As with other behavioral development, the joint appearance of two kinds of behavior does not prove that the two are related. Perhaps what Ramsay has found may not be hemispheric reorganization but the incorporation of a new strategy into an already established program.

their left hands, whereas girls identified shapes equally well with either hand. Since thirteen-year-old girls were still using both hemispheres in identifying objects by touch, Witelson concluded that girls use both hemispheres to process spatial information, at least until adolescence.

Somewhat different results appeared when

Joseph Cioffi and Gillray Kandel (1979) had boys and girls from six to fourteen years old identify three-dimensional objects—shapes like those used by Witelson, two-letter words (*TO*, *IT*), or paired consonants (*CM*, *HC*). In this study, boys and girls were generally equal in their ability to identify most stimuli, and the older the children, the more accurate their identifications. When Cioffi and Kandel looked closely at their results, however, they found some differences in the way each sex processed the material. Both boys and girls identified nonsense shapes better if they felt them with their left hands and words better if they felt them with their right hands, and neither sex showed an advantage at these tasks. When it came to the paired consonants, however, boys did better using the left hand, whereas girls did much better using the right hand. The boys apparently processed the consonant pairs as if they were shapes, the girls as if they were linguistic stimuli—a difference that could affect reading skills. This study supported the view that there are no sex differences in lateralization, but that differences exist in the strategies customarily used by each sex to process information (Bryden, 1978). In other words, the pattern of hemispheric specialization may well be identical in girls and boys, but the patterns of usage are different.

Among investigators whose research seems to support the view of progressive lateralization, Deborah Waber (1976, 1977) proposes that it is not biological differences at birth but the effects of sex hormones on the brain at puberty that account for general male superiority on spatial tasks. Boys and girls who reached puberty late were better at spatial tasks than those who matured early. But early puberty did not give the early maturers an advantage over late maturers on tests of verbal ability. Boys generally reach sexual maturity later than girls, and Waber suggested that later maturity was responsible for boys' tendency to perform better than girls at spatial tasks. Not all studies have supported Waber's proposal, and her own later research with boys (Waber et al., 1981) indicated that it held only among the middle class, suggesting that experience may be as important as biology.

Such an effect may help to explain the connection between late maturation and increased spatial skills among a group of girls studied by Nora Newcombe and Mary Bandura (1983). Although late maturers performed better on spatial tasks, tests that required the girls to identify objects by touch indicated no difference in lateralization between early and late maturers. However, late maturers tended to have less feminine interests than early maturers and favored typically masculine activities, such as building trains, model airplanes, and go-carts; mechanical drawing, carpentry, and using a compass. Since such activities have been shown to be correlated with spatial ability, the girls' experience with "boys' activities"—not the action of hormones on the brain—probably contributed to their high scores on spatial tasks.

Other attempts to establish a biological basis for these sex differences have focused on individuals with abnormal sex chromosomes. In a series of studies, Joanne Rovet and Charles Netley (1982) found that girls with Turner's syndrome, who have only a single X chromosome (XO), did as well as normal girls at processing verbal material, although they were somewhat slower. When processing spatial material, however, girls with Turner's syndrome did a much poorer job, and they had difficulty mentally rotating objects in space. Girls with an extra X chromosome (XXX) showed the opposite pattern: they were equal to normal girls at processing spatial material, but poor at processing verbal material (Rovet and Netley, 1983). Because girls with Turner's syndrome have periods of rapid growth and girls with the triple-X syndrome grow very slowly, Rovet and Netley believe that their research supports the view that early maturation favors verbal over spatial skills and that later maturation leads to greater lateralization, which favors spatial skills.

Whether or not reported sex differences in lateralization have a biological basis, customary differences appear to be modified by experience. When given training on visual-spatial tasks, which seem to be handled more efficiently by the right hemisphere, girls—but not boys—show improved performance (Connor, Serbin,

The brain appears to develop differently in boys and girls. The girl in this picture may use both hemispheres in visual-spatial tasks, while the two boys may rely on the right hemisphere. (Hazel Hankin)

and Schackman, 1977). Whatever sex differences do exist in lateralization or strategies, the cognitive differences seem relatively small and unimportant (Wittig and Peterson, 1979). The abilities of boys and girls, men and women, overlap, and some women show greater spatial skills than most men, just as some men show greater verbal skills than most women.

PLASTICITY

The developing brain is not rigid. As a child grows, functions that have been impaired as a result of brain damage tend to be restored or to become established in other parts of the brain. This plasticity of the nervous system means that experience itself can modify the tissue of the developing brain.

Stimulation

The relationship between growth of particular cortical areas and the development of motor

function is correlational. Since correlations do not tell us what is cause and what is effect, some authors have argued that the baby's use of his or her body and nervous system causes growth of appropriate brain areas, rather than brain growth leading to increased physical and mental control. Such a process would be an example of probabilistic epigenesis, which was discussed in Chapter 3. Steven Rose (1973) is among those who suggest that the barrage of sensory information that assails the newborn when the infant emerges from the shelter of the uterus leads the cortex to grow and neural connections to develop.

Experiments with animals indicate that stimulation—or the lack of it—can affect brain development. Mark Rosenzweig and his colleagues (1972) carried out a lengthy series of experiments in which they raised rats under conditions either of sensory enrichment (new toys every day, space, a view of the laboratory, and company) or of sensory deprivation (no toys, small cage, nothing to see, and a solitary existence). When the brains of these rats were later examined, Rosenzweig's group found that the brains of the privileged rats had heavier and thicker cerebral cortexes than the brains of the underprivileged rats, and they found a difference in the amount and activity of two enzymes. The cortexes of the privileged rats were heavier in relation to the rest of the brain and had fewer and larger neurons, and more glial cells. The privileged rats also had many fewer synapses in a particular area, but each synapse was larger and thicker, indicating increased activity. When Rosenzweig's group reared other rats in a large enclosure that resembled a natural environment, their brains had developed even more than those of their litter-mates who had been kept in the enriched laboratory environment. This finding could indicate that the cortical superiority of the "privileged" rats in the original experiment should be attributed to a less-deprived environment rather than to enrichment. In a different sort of study, David Hubel and Thorsten Wiesel (1963) found that prolonged rearing in the dark led not only to a failure of neuronal connections to develop in kittens' brains, but also to an atrophy of connections that were present at birth. Such visual deprivation is also followed by a shrinkage in the size of neurons and a decrease in the number of vesicles on their end-fibers. With fewer vesicles, synapses may lose part of their ability to manufacture or store neurotransmitters (Greenough and Juraska, 1979).

R. A. Cummins and his colleagues (1979) have suggested that some neurons are "environment-dependent" and will not develop if an animal's cortex is not generally aroused by experience. They go on to suggest that there is a developmental ceiling for brain development and that once that ceiling is reached, additional stimulation will not increase brain growth. Because these studies have been conducted with animals, no one is absolutely certain what happens in the developing human brain. For example, just how soon experience can modify the human brain has never been established. Arthur Parmelee and Marian Sigman (1983) believe that until about a month before term, the fetal brain adheres to a strict genetic program and is relatively unaffected by sensory stimulation. During the last four weeks in the uterus, neurons begin to respond to stimulation and environmental factors begin to have an increasingly important effect on brain organization and thus on behavioral and cognitive development. The shift from genetic to environmental domination of brain development may be gradual, take place at different times for different systems, or go through a series of major steps. According to Parmelee and Sigman, the unresponsiveness of the fetal brain may serve to protect a baby born considerably before term by shielding the brain from the continuous, unpatterned noise of incubators and the general clatter that accompanies hospital routine. It appears that such babies also have not reached the stage of neurological maturity that would allow them to process visual information, even when they make appropriate behavioral responses to it. Thus, a certain degree of maturation may be necessary before stimulation has its effects. Studies of premature infants show that they reach various motor milestones somewhat later than full-term babies do, despite their extra weeks of external stimulation.

Mathematical Genius, Sex, and the Brain

Tests among junior-high-school students regularly report that girls excel in computation, but boys excel on tasks requiring mathematical reasoning (Benbow and Stanley, 1980). At Johns Hopkins University, the longitudinal Study of Mathematically Precocious Youth has been supporting the proposition that males have superior mathematical ability. Each year, academically talented seventh-graders are encouraged to take the mathematical portion of the Scholastic Aptitude Test (SAT-M) generally given to high-school juniors and seniors. Between 1980 and 1982, nearly 40,000 seventh-graders took the SAT-M. Among these students, most of whom had never been exposed to algebra, geometry, or advanced mathematics, boys consistently outscored girls, and among the highest scorers, the proportions of girls dropped drastically.

A perfect score on SAT-M is 800; the mean among college-bound boys in their last year of high school is 493. Among seventh-graders who outscored the average college-bound high-school senior, boys outnumbered girls by more than two to one. But it was among the most talented youngsters that boys showed the greatest superiority. Among seventh-graders with scores of 700 or more, boys outnumbered girls by 13 to 1. Such a score indicates a level of mathematical reasoning ability achieved by only 1 in 10,000 seventh-

Recovery from Brain Damage

When infants are born with a malformed major brain tract, their nervous system may correct for it. In addition, when a baby suffers brain damage, the child often recovers quickly and shows no apparent aftereffects (Searleman,

graders and about 5 in 100 college-bound, twelfth-grade males (Benbow and Stanley, 1983).

Why do boys demonstrate such superiority at the highest ranges? The difference cannot be attributed to different classes in mathematics, because the students in this study have similar course backgrounds. Some researchers (Meece et al., 1982) believe that social learning is responsible. They point out that the expectations for boys and girls are different in this society, and that each sex is rewarded for different things. A girl who expresses an interest in mathematics is unlikely to be encouraged; in fact, such interests may be discouraged, if not ridiculed, by her friends and family.

Some research supports this view. In a study that followed children through the first three grades (Entwisle and Baker, 1983), the expectations of parents appeared to have a strong influence on their children's attitude toward school. In line with their parents' expectations, boys expected to do better in arithmetic than girls did, and the girls' expected to do worse than their test scores and grades indicated. But both expectations were wrong: there was no difference between boys and girls in either their test scores or grades in arithmetic. In reading, the girls expected to do better than the boys—and they did. These results matched parental expectations. The investigators speculate that years of parental expectation could lead boys and girls toward the pattern of SAT-M scores found in the Johns Hopkins Study. Other researchers (Novak and Ridley, 1984) have suggested an additional social influence. They believe that society teaches little girls to be compliant and that when the school pushes them toward rote learning, they are more likely than boys to comply. Although rote learning gives girls an advantage in school classrooms, it leads to progressively poorer performance when complex problem-solving is required.

Social learning may well explain most sex differences in mathematical ability, but another analysis has suggested that hormones may be partly responsible for those young mathematical "geniuses" who make extremely high scores. Norman Geschwind proposed that male hormones slow the growth of the left hemisphere, favoring development of the right side of the brain (Marx, 1982). He believed that such hormonal influences on brain tissue are responsible for the excess of left-handedness, learning disorders, and mathematical and other spatial talents among males. When Camilla Benbow and Julius Stanley, who are conducting the Johns Hopkins study, heard of Geschwind's proposal, they contacted all students who scored 700 or more on the SAT-M and discovered that 20 percent of them were left-handed—twice the level in the general population (Kolata, 1983). But Geschwind's proposal is still highly speculative and, even if it is true for the left-handers who scored above 700, it tells us little about the remaining 80 percent of the highest scorers.

1977). How does the brain compensate for the destruction of irreplaceable neurons? At least four ways have been suggested (Rosner, 1974):

1. Functions may be represented at several levels of the nervous system, and when tissue is damaged at a higher level, the lower levels may assume control.

2. Neurons may not be destroyed; instead, there may be only a temporary disruption of the nervous system when damage keeps intact brain areas from receiving stimulation.

3. Other areas of the brain may develop the same function that was handled by destroyed tissue.

4. Intact areas of the brain may be reorganized

so that the old function can be carried out in new ways. (The last two methods are possible only if brain tissue has a high degree of plasticity [Kinsbourne and Hiscock, 1983].)

The progress of a handful of children whose medical condition required the removal of an entire hemisphere indicates that the young child's brain is indeed highly plastic and may be able to transfer some functions to intact tissue (Dennis, 1980; Kohn and Dennis, 1974). Whether the right or left hemisphere was removed, the children developed adequate language and spatial skills. However, the ability of the brain to compensate for lost tissue was not perfect. Children with only a right hemisphere showed some deficiencies in language skills, and children with only a left hemisphere showed deficiency in some visual-spatial skills. Although the number of cases is extremely small, these children's experience would seem to indicate that the young can develop a function in an area of the brain that would not ordinarily have controlled that function.

The most extensively studied aspect of recovery from brain damage is in the area of language function. Eric Lenneberg (1967) studied twenty-five case reports of children who had suffered brain damage from accident or illness at ages ranging from twenty months to eighteen years. In children who were less than three when their brains were damaged, language learning came to an abrupt halt, only to start once again from the beginning. Children who were three or four went through a period when their language learning was disrupted, but they soon recovered. Children between the ages of four and ten suffered temporary aphasia, after which their grasp of language returned. Once children reached puberty, the picture changed. Their recovery was like that of adults, and in most cases some degree of permanent aphasia remained. Although Lenneberg explained the recovery of language in children as due to the fact that language was still represented in both hemispheres, an explanation that takes evidence of early lateralization into account would attribute the recovery to the children's brain plasticity (Kinsbourne and Hiscock, 1983).

More recent studies have indicated that Lenneberg was too optimistic about the plasticity of children's brains and too pessimistic about the plasticity of adult's brains. Eventual recovery from brain damage in children depends on the extent of the damage; its cause; the child's gender, maturational state, and early experience; and the quality of the child's environment following the damage. Because some types of deficiencies may not be detected by standard IQ tests or by clinical examinations, accounts of extreme plasticity in the immature brain may be exaggerated (Kinsbourne and Hiscock, 1983). In addition, experiments with monkeys indicate that apparent recovery in a young child may be followed by deficiencies that appear only when maturation calls for participation of the damaged area in a particular sort of behavior (Goldman-Rakic et al., 1983).

As for plasticity among brain-injured adults, their recovery potential appeared in Aaron Smith's (1978) study of eighty adult aphasics who had received therapy and fifteen who had received no therapy. Language function improved significantly in aphasics who had received therapy, although on tests of nonlanguage function they did not improve. The control cases showed either neglible gains or slight losses. Smith believes that patients who improve have transferred some degree of language function to the right hemisphere.

The position that the baby's brain is less plastic and the adult brain more plastic than most researchers have believed has also been taken by Ian St. James-Roberts (1979), who reviewed both animal and human studies—including the cases examined by Lenneberg. He suggests that the brain, like any other organ, tends to heal itself, and that disruptions of behavior immediately after an accident or disease tell us nothing about the nature of tissue damage. In many cases of apparent plasticity, he believes, there is only a temporary disruption of the central nervous system that involves little or no cell destruction. When cell destruction actually occurs, the brain may be able to repair itself by regenerating nerve fibers, so that old connections are reestablished or new connections are established on the other side of damaged tissue. St. James-Roberts also indicates that brain damage due to head injuries is much more likely to be temporary than injury due to disease, strokes, or other internal damage. In children, a head injury is likely to be the result of an accident; in adults, strokes are more common. This age-related cause of injury may well have contributed to our assumption about plasticity.

A condition that affects many more children than brain damage is some sort of learning disorder.

LEARNING DISORDERS

It has been estimated that 3 percent of the population cannot learn to read at all (Gardner, 1975). A much larger proportion experience difficulties in school, difficulties that seem related to central nervous system functioning, not to mental retardation. Two of these conditions are developmental dyslexia and hyperactivity.

Developmental Dyslexia

Dyslexia is a catch-all term for reading disabilities, and it appears to have several varieties. Children with developmental dyslexia have no trouble talking, recognizing numbers, and understanding instruction in mathematics, science, or history; but they have enormous difficulty trying to read, write, or spell. Their basic problem seems to be an inability to connect written symbols to the sounds they make. As a result, they are reduced to learning words as units; they simply cannot sound out a word from its letters (Gardner, 1975). Some dyslexic children try to read words from right to left or confuse letters that differ only in spatial position, such as *d*, *b*, *q*, and *p*.

Basing their studies on the belief that lateralization is a gradual process, many researchers have assumed that dyslexia is caused by a slowness or failure of language to lateralize to the left hemisphere. According to Kinsbourne and Hiscock (1983), however, evidence of lateralization from birth requires an adjustment of assumptions. Lateralization may be complete, for example, but a child may fail to adopt a verbal mental set when attempting to read, so that the left hemisphere is not activated. The failure may be due to physiological abnormality, to the child's assumption that he or she will fail, or to lack of motivation. An additional possibility is a neural immaturity; the brain is lateralized, but because of a slowness in development in the language area of the left hemisphere, the child has difficulty in learning to read.

Another explanation has been offered by Sandra Witelson (1979), who believes that dyslexia is the result of a different kind of brain organization. After testing dyslexics for lateralization, Witelson concluded that children with this affliction have developed spatial abilities in both

Dyslexia is a baffling disorder; many of the afflicted children, who seem unable to connect written symbols with the sounds of language, have no trouble understanding mathematics, science, or history. (Michael Siluk/EKM-Nepenthe)

hemispheres and that the processing of spatial information in the left hemisphere interferes with language ability. Among the battery of tests Witelson used with dyslexics was the identification of shapes by touch. She found that dyslexics are as good at identifying shapes with the right hand as with the left. This explanation assumes, as does Kinsbourne and Hiscock's, that lateralization is present from birth.

Some children with reading disabilities show no handicap of any kind—neurological, intellectual, emotional, or environmental. In many cases, the relatives of these children also have reading disabilities. After studying nine families, in which fifty of the eighty-four individuals tested had reading disabilities, a group of researchers (Smith et al., 1983) proposed that some specific reading disabilities have a genetic basis. Chromosomal analysis of these individuals turned up a site on Chromosome 15 that the researchers believe may carry the dominant allele responsible for one type of reading disability.

Just how any of these sources of dyslexia affect reading skills is uncertain. A number of studies indicate that dyslexic children have problems with specific stages of the reading process and that different children may have problems with different stages of the process (Farnham-Diggory, 1978). Some may have difficulty with auditory-linguistic aspects of reading and others with visual-spatial aspects (Kinsbourne and Hiscock, 1983).

Paul Rozin and Lila Gleitman (1977) have tried to solve the problems of dyslexic children by focusing on the apparent inability of some children to connect sight and sound. They have devised a system in which dyslexic children first learn to interpret pictures, then move to "reading" drawings that depict each word (a picture of a can for the word "can," for example). Gradually, they learn to build words in which each syllable is a different drawing, and then they learn to blend letters. Although Rozin and Gleitman developed their system on the assumption that reading disabilities are rare among children who read pictorially based lan-

guages, such as Chinese and Japanese, later studies indicate that their basic assumption was wrong. Reading disabilities are as common among Chinese and Japanese children as among American children (Stevenson et al., 1982). The picture-reading system is unlikely to be successful with all dyslexic children. Methods that will help dyslexic children to overcome their reading disabilities will probably come from research on specific aspects of the reading process.

Hyperactivity

Hyperactivity is a childhood disorder that afflicts five to nine times as many boys as girls. Between 1 and 5 percent of the population have been diagnosed as hyperactive, and it has been estimated that 600,000 American schoolchildren take drugs to control the condition (Weiss and Hechtman, 1979).

Most hyperactive children are extremely restless. As toddlers, they crawl, run, and climb incessantly; in middle childhood they find it difficult to sit still, and they fidget continually. But despite the disorder's name, not all hyperactive children are restless; instead, they are generally inattentive, easily distracted, and have difficulty sticking to a task (Kinsbourne, 1983). And they perform poorly in unsupervised situations. Hyperactive children are impulsive: they talk out of turn, interrupt others, have trouble playing games that involve taking turns, seem unable to tolerate frustration, and fight with other children.

As James Swanson and Marcel Kinsbourne (1979) point out, almost any child shows every symptom linked with hyperactivity at some time. In order to be labeled hyperactive, such behavior must occur constantly and in inappropriate situations. Because of the wide overlap between "normal" and "hyperactive" behavior, a principal problem is diagnosis. It has been suggested that the school situation, in which children are required to sit still for long periods of time, may be responsible for what appears to be a higher than normal incidence of hyperac-

Since all normal children show some symptoms linked with hyperactivity, diagnosing a child as hyperactive must be done with caution. (© Suzanne Szasz)

tivity in this country (up to 5 or 6 percent of children in some city schools) (McGuinness, 1979).

No one is sure just what causes hyperactivity. At one time, researchers thought it was the result of structural damage to the central nervous system, so many referred to it as *minimal brain damage* (MBD). Later it was decided that the brain's structure was probably intact, but that the way it processed information was faulty, so MBD came to mean minimal brain *dysfunction.* Others said children with hyperactivity suffered from learning disabilities and attached *that* tag to them. But while hyperactive children do often have learning problems, many learning disabilities have nothing to do with hyperactivity. The confusion in terms has led to a confusion in the search for a cause and even for an exact description of the disorder. Virginia Douglas and Kenneth Peters (1979) describe hyperactive children as impulsive creatures who have an unusual need for stimulation and difficulty in concentrating—especially on dull, repetitive tasks. The American Psychiatric Association (1980) no longer uses the term and instead calls the condition an "attention deficit disorder," one in which a child may or may not be hyperactive.

Hyperactivity has been attributed to genetic factors, brain damage, an imbalance of neurotransmitters (especially dopamine and norepinephrine), food additives, lead, and allergies. It has been suggested, on the one hand, that hyperactive children are simply extreme examples of an inherited temperamental type (Swanson and Kinsbourne, 1979), and on the other, that lagging brain development—as shown in EEGs that do not become normal until adolescence— is the basis of the disorder (Weiss and Hechtman, 1979). It may be that hyperactivity is a term covering a flock of disorders that manifest themselves in similar ways.

Treatment of hyperactivity varies. Among the methods used are diet, stimulant drugs (especially Ritalin and amphetamines), behavior modification, and cognitive training—in which children are taught skills that lessen their tendencies to act impulsively. All treatments appear to work for a short time, but none has been shown to have any long-term benefit (Swanson and Kinsbourne, 1979).

Although some parents and teachers say that as many as 90 percent of children show marked improvement in their behavior at school and at home after taking stimulant drugs (Whalen et al., 1979), researchers who have tested children in laboratories find that only between 60 and 70 percent show improved performance with drugs (Swanson and Kinsbourne, 1979).

It is generally supposed that the "normal" state of hyperactive children is one of under-arousal. In this view, the drugs work at subcortical levels, increasing the level of arousal and permitting children to sustain their attention and inhibit impulsive responses. When the stimulants are effective, hyperactive children who have taken one of them respond faster and make fewer unnecessary responses than those who have no drug in their systems (Douglas and Peters, 1979). However, Marcel Kinsbourne (1983) suggests that the problem is not underarousal, but underactivation in behavioral control mechanisms. He believes that the stimulant activates these mechanisms, enabling the children to make decisions about their actions.

Even when the drug is effective, it wears off rapidly and must be taken at least three times a day for its effect to be consistent (Swanson and Kinsbourne, 1979). The rapid dissipation of stimulant drugs from the system carries with it another problem, that of **state-dependent learning.** Both animal and human studies have indicated that what is learned under the influence of certain drugs, including alcohol and tranquilizers, tends to be forgotten when the drug wears off, although the information may be recalled if another dose of the drug is taken (Overton, 1969).

Drugs given for hyperactivity tend to have the same effect. Hyperactive children who take Ritalin make fewer errors while learning a task, but seem to forget what they have learned when the drug wears off (Swanson and Kinsbourne, 1979). Since hyperactive children are generally given sustaining doses of the drug, this tendency is rarely noticed by those about them.

Widespread drug treatment of hyperactivity has been noted with concern by Anne Pick (1983), who warns that, in addition to creating a state-dependent effect, the drugs may manipulate children's attention in a way that makes them tolerant of dull, boring, and meaningless tasks. She also warns that drugs apparently narrow children's attention so that they acquire little incidental information and knowledge. Pick urges that more attention be paid to environmental manipulations and exploration of educational approaches to the treatment of hyperactivity. For example, if hyperactive children's attention improves when background stimulation increases, as some researchers (Kinsbourne, 1983) have suggested, they may learn better in a noisy classroom, when walking around, or when a radio is playing. Such a course would seem prudent, particularly because no one knows the medical implications of long-term drug usage.

Hyperactive children whom researchers have followed into adolescence continue to deal with the world in an impulsive manner. In a longitudinal study (Weiss and Hechtman, 1979), hyperactive adolescents tended to have an impulsive life style, a year's less schooling, and a much higher involvement in motorcycle and automobile accidents than adolescents in a control group. Yet some of the problems of the hyperactive group seemed to ameliorate as they got away from school. Although their high-school teachers continued to rate them as inferior to individuals in the control group, employers found no difference between hyperactive adolescents and controls on any measure—an indication that the setting may have much to do with the judgment that hyperactive children are a problem.

SUMMARY

Human brains are larger in proportion to body mass than the brains of our early ancestors. As the brain evolved, the old structures shrank in relative size and new ones developed and assumed some functions of the old structure as well as taking on new ones. The newest part of the brain, the cortex, is responsible for language, attention, memory, spatial understanding, motor skills, and logical thought. Much of the cortex consists of **association areas,** which seem to act on information that already has gone through several stages of processing.

As specific areas in the cortex develop, the corresponding functions appear in a baby's behavior. The **cytoarchitecture** of the brain appears to develop similarly in all mammals, with the cortex made up of six layers of cells, arranged in columns. About thirty different chemicals have been identified as messengers in the brain, conducting nerve impulses from one neuron to the next. Little is known about the developmental course of such **neurotransmitters,** although we do know that brain protein changes as children grow and that protein plays a part in both the production of transmitters and their storage in **vesicles.** As children grow, electrical activity in the brain changes; studies of **evoked potentials** indicate that various brain-wave patterns reach adult forms during middle childhood and adolescence.

Each side of the brain primarily receives sensations from and controls the voluntary muscles on the opposite side of the body. Each hemisphere also appears to have specialized functions, with the left hemisphere more efficient than the right at language, and the right hemisphere more efficient at analyzing visual patterns, music, spatial locations, and emotions. The **corpus callosum,** which transfers information between the hemispheres and perhaps helps to integrate a person's world, is not fully myelinated until a child is ten years old.

There is disagreement as to whether the brain undergoes **progressive lateralization** during development or retains an unchanging degree of laterality. Evidence of lateralization is present at birth, but some aspects appear to increase during early and middle childhood. Handedness, which may be due to either genetic or experiential influences, begins to develop in the latter part of the first year. About 95 percent of right-handed people and 60 percent of left-handers process language in the left hemisphere. Damage to the language areas of the brain is often followed by some form of **aphasia.**

The brain develops somewhat differently in boys and girls, although evidence of differences in lateralization may actually reflect different strategies for processing information rather than physiological differences. Most studies show that girls are generally superior to boys in skills relating to language and boys are better at higher mathematics and spatial skills.

It may be that some neurons will not develop if a baby's cortex is not aroused by experience. A baby's and a young child's brain appear to be more plastic than the brain of an adult, although the adult brain is also capable of some repair. The brain may repair damage to tissue in several ways: by shifting control to lower levels, by switching functions to different areas, or by reorganizing function through the regeneration of portions of nerve cells and the establishment of new connections around damaged tissue. Sometimes an injury does not actually destroy tissue, but only disrupts function temporarily.

Children with developmental **dyslexia** have trouble connecting written symbols with the sounds they make, a condition that may be the result of a failure to activate the left hemisphere, a lag in development, or a different kind of brain organization. **Hyperactive** children, generally boys, are impulsive, seem to have an unusual need for stimulation, and often find it difficult to concentrate their attention. Treatment with stimulant drugs may lead to **state-dependent learning,** in which information learned while using the drug is forgotten when the drug wears off.

PART 4

The Development of Cognition

We cannot see cognition, hear it, or touch it, but we can see, touch, or hear its products: speech, intelligent action, human artifacts, music, art, literature, and science. We know of its existence in ourselves, but can only infer its existence in others from their actions. Perhaps the best way to describe cognition is to say that it encompasses all mental activity—from the perception of a pin prick to the creation of the Mona Lisa. In these chapters, we trace the emergence of the infant mind and follow the development of perception, attention, memory, and intelligent thought.

By the time we complete the tale of cognitive development, we shall have seen children as remarkably active organisms, curious about the world and about themselves and eager to make sense of both, constructing from their varied experiences new hypotheses about how its parts fit. We shall also see children as architects of time, space, and objects, and as designers and users of symbols. Cognition is the vehicle by which infants become intellectually accomplished adults.

CHAPTER SEVEN

The Emerging Mind

NATURE OF COGNITION AND COGNITIVE
  DEVELOPMENT
THE EMERGENCE OF PERCEPTION
The Development of Auditory Perception
The Development of Visual Perception
The Development of Sensory and
  Sensorimotor Coordination
THE EMERGENCE OF LEARNING AND
  MEMORY
The Early Development of Attention
The Early Development of Learning and
  Memory
THE EMERGENCE OF THOUGHT
Substages of Sensorimotor Thought
The Object Concept
Imitation
SUMMARY

Twenty-two-month-old Steven climbs onto a chair and, on his knees, bends over a piece of clean white paper. He picks up a fat green crayon and begins to scribble, making a series of continuous circles, then pauses and looks at his work. With a frown of concentration he repeatedly jabs at the paper, producing a random pattern of short green strokes that spread across the circles and into the margins. In just over a minute, he is finished. Steven lifts his head from his work and waves the paper in the air. "Picture!" he announces proudly to his father. Twenty-one months earlier, when Steven emerged from the neonatal period, such accomplishments were far beyond him. At that time, his major interests were warm milk, dry diapers, and contact with another comforting body. His cries of distress were unintentional signals to his parents, he had not yet smiled in a social fashion, and his actions were primarily reflexive. Held near paper and crayons, he could neither have formed the intent to scribble nor coordinated his hand and eye to grasp the crayon and pull it across the paper. In less than two years, Steven's mind has expanded at a prodigious rate; one goal of developmental psychologists is to explain such vast changes. Although all would say that maturation was heavily involved, their explanations concerning the nature and development of this cognitive transformation vary, depending on their theoretical orientation.

In this chapter, we trace the emergence of the toddler's mind, beginning with an exploration of the dominant world views that affect theory and research in cognitive development. We then turn to the mind itself, picking up the course of cognitive development where we left it at the close of Chapter 4. Since infants could not begin to organize the world without imposing some kind of order on the multitude of stimuli that surround them, we begin with sensation and perception. Next we examine the vast changes that take place in children's learning and memory during infancy, as they accumulate an ever-expanding store of information. Finally, we investigate the emergence of thought, focusing on the development of the object concept and the baby's ability to imitate others.

NATURE OF COGNITION AND COGNITIVE DEVELOPMENT

Cognition includes all mental activity—the processes of sensing, perceiving, remembering, using symbols, thinking, and imagining. As we saw in Chapter 4, the baby comes into the world with functioning sensory systems, and from the first days of independent existence works at the lengthy task of making sense out of the world. At first, memories are fleeting, symbols are nonexistent, and thought is not yet intelligent. But progress is swift, and by the close of infancy the baby will have become a competent youngster who uses symbols and reacts intelligently to people, animals, and objects in the world. After another decade, the baby will be an adolescent who reasons about the future and the past, handles hypothetical situations, and tests theories.

Despite this watching toddler's newly developed coordination, her own scribbles would probably look like tangles of spaghetti. The ability to draw simple shapes requires the maturation and experience of the preoperational child. (Laimute E. Druskis/Jeroboam)

Psychologists interpret this development in different ways, and the basic view a psychologist adopts leads him or her to view certain facts as more important than others and to impose a particular organization on the facts that are observed (Sameroff, 1983). It also determines the kinds of questions researchers ask and affects the form of their research. Whether psychologists see cognitive development as moving through a series of stages, in which the organization of thought changes radically from one stage to the next, or whether they see it as a gradual and continuous development, made possible by experience and accumulated knowledge, depends on the world view they adopt. As we saw in Chapter 1, organismic theorists take the former view, stressing reorganization of thought and behavior. Mechanistic theorists adhere to the latter view, stressing additions to thought and behavior.

Early research on cognition was primarily mechanistic and focused on perception and learning, paying little attention to thought. Impressed by the wide variety of individual differences in learning and memory, investigators looked for factors in the environment that could explain such differences. During the first half of the twentieth century, most researchers used classical or operant conditioning techniques, testing whether infants, who could not talk, responded and learned in the same ways as animals. Some researchers rejected this behavioral learning approach to perception. They argued that infants did not simply acquire new responses; instead, even without reinforcement, they became increasingly sensitive to the features of their environment. As infants encountered new kinds of stimuli, they worked at discriminating the various characteristics in order to resolve their uncertainty (Stevenson, 1983).

During the second half of the century, theories of social learning became increasingly important. Although researchers still pursued questions that assumed a mechanistic world view, they began to examine the role of observational learning. When considering the results of reinforcement, researchers began to talk about infants' and children's expectations instead of their automatic responses to stimuli.

Within the past twenty years, studies focusing on children's learning have declined. Although the results of such studies have been accepted and much of the methodology of learning theorists has been adopted by psychologists who adhere to other theories, researchers have become less interested in behavior and increasingly interested in what occurs between the stimulus and the infant's response. Today, most researchers use behavior as a clue to the way babies process information, and the information-processing approach has come to dominate studies of cognitive development (Siegler, 1983).

The other major approach to cognition is that of the organismic world view. Developmentalists who adopt an organismic view are not especially interested in perception or learning; they look instead at the acquisition of concepts and ideas, such as object permanence and causality. Their research focuses on universal aspects of cognitive development. The major organismic theorist was Jean Piaget, and his ideas have so dominated the study of cognitive devel-

opment that much of the research in the mechanistic tradition has involved attempts to test his theories.

THE EMERGENCE OF PERCEPTION

If researchers are to be able to interpret their investigations of cognitive processes, they must know how well babies' senses function and whether they perceive what is presented to them. It is through the senses that the raw material of stimulation is transformed into information. Children rely on their eyes, ears, mouths, hands, noses, and skin to extract information about the sights and sounds, the pains and pressures, the tastes and smells of their world. Young children can tell us whether two objects look the same, one note is higher than another, or a liquid is sweet or sour.

But this is not true of infants. In a test of vision, for example, a baby cannot say, "I see a red and yellow square." Researchers, therefore, must resort to careful monitoring of infants' behavior during an experiment. For example, in order to detect whether a baby perceives the red and yellow square, a researcher might monitor the baby's gaze, noting whether it strays from the stimulus. To do this, the researcher may rely on instruments that register reflections on the cornea, changes in the electrical potential of the retina, shifts in eye movements, or evoked potentials (see Chapter 6). When trying to determine an infant's reaction to sounds, researchers may use an obvious, but not always reliable, measure like head turning, or they may use recordings of more subtle reactions, such as patterns of sucking, evoked potentials, or changes in heart rate and skin resistance.

Except for the neonatal research reported in Chapter 4, few studies have been conducted on the development of smell, taste, temperature, touch, or pain during infancy. Most investigators have concentrated on the development of visual perception, although an increasing number have explored auditory perception. Some researchers have studied the development of co-ordination between senses, generally between vision and either touch or hearing.

The Development of Auditory Perception

One reason auditory research has lagged behind research in visual perception is our lack of knowledge about unique behavioral responses to sounds. There are no known characteristic responses, such as eye movements or gaze fixation, that tell a researcher when an infant has detected a sound. In addition, we know much less about the auditory system than we know about the mechanisms of vision (Aslin, Pisoni, and Jusczyk, 1983). Yet sound is a major source of environmental information for the developing infant. Auditory perception is important in learning to understand language and to speak it and in determining the location of people and objects.

It seems clear that babies do not hear as well as adults, and the difference is especially apparent when sounds are in the low-frequency range that characterizes the human voice. At these frequencies, sounds that are detected by adults must be considerably louder before babies detect them, although even this level is not much louder than a whisper. Between six and twenty-four months, infants become increasingly sensitive to low-frequency sounds.

Early research indicated that infants were relatively insensitive to shrill, high-frequency sounds and could not detect them unless they were extremely loud. However, in later studies, babies older than six months were relatively more sensitive to high-frequency sounds than to those of low frequencies, with the gap between adult and infant hearing narrowing sharply (Aslin, Pisoni, and Jusczyk, 1983). At extremely high frequencies, very close to the shrillest sound detected by adults, infants react very much as adults do—with both detecting only fairly intense sounds (Schneider, Trehub, and

Bull, 1980). Perhaps the auditory mechanisms responsible for frequency discrimination mature first at high frequencies (Olsho, 1984).

In some respects, babies show incredible sensitivity to sounds. William Kessen and his associates (1979) found that babies between three and five months old not only are responsive to pitch but can imitate it. Mothers coaxed their babies to vocalize, then followed the vocalizations with a musical note, which the babies soon began to imitate. Trained musicians who judged tape recordings of the musical "conversations" rated every baby as doing well, and some babies were within a quarter tone of the note they copied. The experimenters suggest that pitch matching is a natural ability that is often eroded or lost as children acquire language.

Babies can not only match pitch, they can perceive and later recognize melodies as well. Sandra Trehub and her colleagues (Trehub, Bull, and Thorpe, 1984) found that eight- to eleven-month-old infants could distinguish one melody from another. When a simple six-note tune was transposed into a different key (from C to E flat) and played after a fifteen-second delay, the babies treated it as the same tune, just as older children and adults do. However, when the transposed melody was played less than a second after the original melody, the infants treated it as a new tune—one they had never heard before. Presumably, when the transposed melody was played almost immediately afterward, the babies compared it with their immediate memory of the tune and detected the difference between original and transposed notes. But when they heard the transposed melody after a delay, they compared it to their memory of the melodic contour, which refers to the direction of change in note frequency and the relation between the frequency of adjoining notes. This is the way in which adults process melodies.

At a very early age, babies are sensitive to the sounds of language. As we shall see in the discussion of language development (Chapter 9), babies as young as a month can distinguish between the sounds "ba" and "pa." They appear to separate speech from nonspeech and to process the speech sounds in a way that supports the conjecture that the human organism is prepared to detect and decode spoken communication (Eimas, 1975).

Jerome Kagan and Steven Tulkin (1971) tested the extent to which eight-month-old boys could recognize familiar sounds. They read four sentences to each baby in the study. Two of the sentences used words, such as "smile" and "daddy," that parents frequently use in interactions with their babies, and the words were arranged in a meaningful way. The other two sentences were nonsensical ("Og, sesalk; lof perks mit sesalk?"). Kagan and his colleagues found that the babies responded differently to these different combinations of sounds. The meaningful sentences with familiar words brought about a higher rate of babbling in the babies than did the nonsensical ones, even when the nonsensical sentences were read with typical sentence intonation. This effect occurred even when the person who read the sentences was a male stranger, whose voice was unfamiliar.

Toward the end of the first year, infants have progressed considerably beyond their auditory capacities of the first few months, which even then were quite impressive. At that time they were sensitive to such things as the frequency, duration, and intensity of sounds. By the end of the first year, however, they are also sensitive to the differences between various combinations of sounds and they recognize certain words, becoming increasingly sensitive to the meanings of the sounds they hear.

The Development of Visual Perception

During the early months of life, vision may be babies' most important source of information about the environment. Through vision, infants learn to identify objects and guide their movements in the world (Banks and Salapatek, 1983). They learn to detect differences in pattern, color, or outline, and somehow they come to perceive a three-dimensional world, to perceive objects as the same size and shape even when their images cast different shapes on the retina, and to understand their physical relationship to a position in space. These changes are due to an interaction between the maturation of the baby's visual system and experiences in the world.

VISUAL CAPACITIES By the time they are six months old, babies can probably see as clearly as an adult. At first, the visual field is quite narrow; babies can see objects directly in front of them, but when an object is more than thirty degrees to either side, they are unable to detect it. By the time they are seven weeks old, however, their peripheral vision expands, so that they can detect an object as far as forty-five degrees to the side (Macfarlane, Harris, and Barnes, 1976); this gives them a visual field of ninety degrees, about half that of an adult's. In another five or six weeks, they will be able to tell the difference between two objects placed to the side, but the objects can be no more than thirty degrees off center (Maurer and Lewis, 1979). Adults use peripheral vision to guide eye movements and to decide what they will look at directly. Although by the time they are four months old babies can integrate peripheral and central vision to some extent, and both systems are mature by the time babies are six months old, no one is certain just how well the systems interact in a six-month-old (Cohen, DeLoache, and Strauss, 1979).

There is still some uncertainty as to how soon babies can perceive color. Since color is a significant source of information about the environment, and a better guide to an object's location than either size or shape, the development of color vision greatly increases the baby's ability to gather information about the world (Bornstein, 1981). As indicated in Chapter 4, newborn infants may be colorblind, but within a few months they seem to see all colors. In experiments that separated brightness from hue, infants as young as two months could apparently distinguish red, orange, blue-green, blue, and some purple stimuli from white. However, other purple and all yellow-green stimuli apparently looked the same to the babies (Teller, Peeples, and Sekel, 1978). A type of color-sensitive cell that is not functioning at two months apparently is present at three months, because further studies indicated that three-month-olds, but not two-month-olds, reacted as adults did to light in that part of the spectrum that is seen as green or blue (Pulos, Teller, and Buck, 1980). Perhaps by three, but certainly by four months, babies perceive colors as adults do, seeing blue, green, yellow, and red, as well as mixtures of these colors (Bornstein, 1981). These categories, and infants' perceptions of them, seem to correspond to the apparently universal and nonarbitrary psychological color categories used by older children and adults. We do not know what further changes occur in color vision, nor do we know precisely how infants can distinguish slight changes in hue; yet by about three months the fundamental aspects of color vision operate as they do in adults (Banks and Salapatek, 1983).

VISUAL SCANNING As human beings of any age look at the world, their eyes continually move, and their gaze shifts from one feature to another. Such scanning probably plays an important role in the process of learning about the environment, but it may not be essential to the infant's visual processing (Banks and Salapatek, 1983). As noted in Chapter 4, neonates demonstrate regular looking patterns, searching for the edges of objects with broad, jerky sweeps of the visual field. Often their attention is captured by a single feature, although they may scan an entire display (Banks and Salapatek, 1983). Even when there is something around they like to look at, babies seem unable to shift their eyes to it once their gaze encounters an edge. For example, Robert Fantz and Simon Miranda (1975) found that although the newborns in their experiment generally liked to look at bull's-eyes, they would not look at them if the target was

enclosed in a large white square. Apparently their eyes stopped when they found the edge of the square. By the time they were two months old, however, babies' eyes crossed the square in order to gaze at the bull's-eye.

The same sort of scanning takes place when babies have the opportunity to look at a human face. Daphne Maurer and Philip Salapatek (1976) found that month-old babies tended to look at the edges of a face, staring at an ear, the chin, or the line of the hair; but two-month-olds inspected internal features, such as an eye, the nose, or the mouth. Other researchers have found that by about two months, infants pay increased attention to the internal features of the face, especially the eyes (Hainline, 1978). Whether the face is moving slightly from side to side or remaining still, talking or silent, two-month-old infants concentrate their scanning around the eyes (Haith, Bergman, and Moore, 1977). Not even the extra mouth movements that accompany speech draw attention from the eyes to the mouth.

It may be that babies begin to look past the square to the bull's-eye and shift their gaze from the edge of the face to the eyes when visual control shifts from subcortical regions of the brain to the visual cortex, as it does at about two months of age (Hoffman, 1978). This maturation allows them to habituate to, or become bored with, the features that first catch their gaze, and then become receptive to features at the edge of the visual field (Salapatek, 1975). The reason may also be social; for at about two months, babies' first social smiles appear and they may have come to see the face as a meaningful entity instead of simply a collection of features. By this time, perhaps the eyes in a face have taken on social meaning, and babies have learned that fixing their attention on the eyes keeps the sound of a human voice going. Throughout the first year, the infant's perception of the face appears to go through a gradual discovery of its unchanging features and an integration of its parts into a meaningful configuration (Fagan, 1976).

As infants grow older, they scan more extensively, with their eye movements covering wider areas of a target. This change may indicate that instead of processing only parts of a target, they are now processing the entire stimulus (Banks and Salapatek, 1983). Such a shift is necessary if they are to be able to distinguish one object from another. Most research tracing the emergence of form discrimination has used geometric figures. For example, Marcelle Schwartz and Ross Day (1979) showed three-month-olds four Y-shaped stimuli. Two of the forms (A and B) were identical but oriented differently; the other two (C and D) differed in shape (see Figure 7.1). After babies habituated to Stimulus A, they were shown one of the other stimuli. The babies had apparently processed the original stimulus in terms of its form, for they responded to Stimuli C and D with renewed interest, but treated Stimulus B as if it were identical with Stimulus A. Although three-month-olds can recognize simple forms, the ability to discriminate among complex forms takes much longer to develop. When Holly Ruff (1978) showed babies objects that varied in color and size as well as in orientation, recognition was beyond the capabilities of six-month-olds, and even nine-month-olds had some trouble.

DEPTH PERCEPTION We live in a three-dimensional world, but the ability to perceive solidity and depth appears to emerge only gradually. Using technology that creates the illusion of depth by presenting a different image to each

FIGURE 7.1 After four-month-olds habituated to Stimulus A, they were tested with the other stimuli. They treated Stimulus B as if it were the same as Stimulus A, but reacted with renewed interest to Stimuli C and D.

(From Schwartz and Day, 1979)

eye, researchers have been able to determine that depth perception develops between the ages of three and six months. The technique is similar to one used with those 3-D films in which the audience views the screen through a pair of cardboard glasses, with one lens of red plastic and the other of green. Without the glasses, the image on the screen is blurred; with them, the picture appears to have solidity and depth. In order to study visual perception, Bela Julesz (1971) applied this technique using computers that generate paired displays of red and green dots, called *anaglyphs*. Viewing the two slightly different displays through a pair of glasses like those used with 3-D films fuses the images, and a three-dimensional form appears. The advantage of using the computer-generated dots lies in the fact that there are no familiar forms to give the viewer cues—only perception of the third dimension allows a shape to emerge in the display.

Applying this technique to the study of infant perception, Robert Fox and his associates (1980) showed two- to six-month-old infants a series of anaglyphs in which the solid forms changed position and seemed to move across the screen. As the anaglyphs appeared, the investigators tracked the babies' eye movements. The youngest babies' eyes followed the changing shapes no better than chance would allow; obviously they either saw nothing or were not interested in whatever they did see. But older babies did progressively better, and by six months, most babies were tracking the forms a good part of the time. When tested with anaglyphs that could not be fused to produce depth, babies' performance dropped to chance. Among these infants, depth perception emerged gradually, beginning at about three and a half months.

Earlier research had shown that by the time they are two or three months old, babies would rather watch a sphere than a flat disk (Fantz, 1966). Their preference suggests that these young babies were aware of a difference in depth, even if they could not appreciate it. Other findings confirm the results of Fox's experiment, indicating that some time between three and six months is the closest we can come at present to fixing a date for the emergence of depth perception. In an experiment with three-and-a-half- and five-month-old babies, for example, Albert Yonas and his colleagues (1978) used a projected image of another kind—a solid object that appears to come directly at the viewer—to establish the existence of depth perception. All infants looked intently at the image, their eyes converging on the illusory missile that seemed ready to strike them. But only the five-month-old infants either reached out toward the object or blinked and withdrew their heads as the object appeared to draw near.

Between the ages of five and seven months, babies become sensitive to depth cues that require the use of only one eye. One of these cues is *perspective*, the effect that makes a two-dimensional drawing appear to have depth. The emergence of this cue appeared when investigators placed infants in front of a trapezoidal window, which creates the illusion that one side is farther away than the other (Yonas, Cleaves, and Pettersen, 1978). The babies had a patch over one eye, so they were forced to rely on cues that could be processed using a single eye. Five-month-olds were not fooled; they believed both sides of the window were equally near, reaching as often to one side as to the other. But seven-month-olds succumbed to the illusion, reaching for the "near" side of the window much more often than the "distant" side. Other cues that babies seem to use from about the age of seven months are *familiar size*, in which they judge the distance of an object by its apparent size, and *interposition*, in which an object that blocks the view of another object is judged to be nearer (Banks and Salapatek, 1983).

Three-dimensional information can warn babies of imminent danger. For example, they use visual cues to save themselves from such dangers as falling off tables or chairs. In a novel experiment, Eleanor Gibson and Richard Walk (1960) studied infants' use of depth information by placing the infants on what appeared to be the edge of a cliff. Their experiments showed that

When placed on the "visual cliff," seven-month-old babies generally crawl across the glass covering the "shallow" side without hesitation. But faced with what appears to be a sudden drop, they balk and will not crawl over the glass covering the "deep" side, even to reach their mothers. (William Vandivert)

an infant who is old enough to crawl will not crawl over the edge of a visual cliff, even to reach his or her mother. Because the infants in these experiments were between eight and twelve months old, it is difficult to say whether the behavior simply represented a maturation of vision or whether some learning was also involved. Subsequently, however, Sandra Scarr and Philip Salapatek (1970), using the visual-cliff apparatus designed by Gibson and Walk, found that infants begin to use depth cues to avoid edges shortly after they reach seven months of age, but only if they have begun crawling before that time. When two-month-olds are placed on the deep side of the cliff, their hearts slow down, suggesting they notice something of interest. When nine-month-olds are placed on the deep side, however, their hearts speed up, suggesting they are afraid (Campos, 1976).

What causes the change in babies' reaction to depth from simply perceiving the drop to being actively afraid of it? Further research has indicated that the fear of depths emerges just after a baby develops the ability to move about (Campos et al., 1978). The perception of depth at an edge is inborn, according to Eleanor Gibson (1963), and emerges in almost any species as soon as locomotion is possible. The critical factor in the development of depth perception appears to be motion, which provides additional depth cues that require only one eye. This supposition was supported by an experiment in which a baby born with only one functioning eye responded to the visual cliff just as infants with two eyes do (Walk and Dodge, 1962).

PERCEPTUAL CONSTANCIES Objects stimulate the eye in very different ways, depending on their angle in relation to or distance from the viewer. Yet all human beings interpret the objects and people in their world as unchanging, no matter where in the visual field they happen to be. When, for example, a two-year-old boy walks through the aisle in the department store with his mother, he knows that the teddy bear seated on the distant counter is just the right size to cuddle in his arms, despite the fact that the image it casts on his retina indicates the toy is about the size of a peanut. And when he drops the quarter his mother has given him and it rolls on its side before coming to rest, he sees the coin as round, even though it casts an oval image on his retina. The invariant teddy bear is an example of **size constancy;** the rolling quarter, of **shape constancy.**

Although the year-old child perceives these constancies in the world, the reactions of younger infants make it clear that they do not. Developmental psychologists have devised ingenious experiments in their attempts to discover just how soon perceptual constancies develop.

Shape Constancy Shape constancy emerges at about three months, although researchers disagree as to its exact timing. Results appear to depend on the experimental techniques used. In one study, three-month-olds showed no indication of shape constancy. Albert Caron and his associates (1978) showed either a square or a trapezoid to the babies until they had habituated. Some babies saw the form in a vertical position; others saw it at a slant. After the infants had ceased to respond to the geometrical form, the experimenters showed all the babies a vertical square. The researchers reasoned that if the babies had developed shape constancy, both the babies who had originally watched the vertical square and those who had seen the same square tilted back would be bored and pay little attention to the square. But all the babies, except the ones who had seen the same vertical square, responded as if they were seeing something new. None showed shape constancy. When the same researchers presented squares or trapezoids at various angles, however, so that the infants would pay attention to an object's shape instead of its slant, three-month-olds clearly showed shape constancy (Caron, Caron, and Carlson, 1979).

In another experiment, three-month-old babies showed glimmerings of shape constancy. Michael Cook and his colleagues (1978) also used habituation, displaying either wooden forms painted white or photographs. They discovered that young babies could tell the difference between a cube and a photograph of a cube, and between a cube and an L-shaped block. But the babies appeared to see no difference between the cube and a trapezoid or between the cube and a wedge. In experiments with older babies, infants who were allowed to manipulate a complex wooden shape as well as look at it displayed shape constancy at nine months, but not at six (Ruff, 1978).

An experiment by Michael Cook and Rosemary Birch (1984) may help to clear the confusion. After testing three-month-olds with various geometrical shapes, they concluded that the infants apparently showed shape constancy, but only with simple shapes, such as rectangles or trapezoids. When shown irregularly shaped figures, the babies treated the tilted forms as if they were new. It may be that the irregular figures were simply too complicated for the babies to process, and that the complexity of the shapes explains why the six-month-olds who handled wooden shapes did not show shape constancy.

Looking for a way to test shape constancy that resembles the everyday situation of the rolling coin, Eleanor Gibson and her associates (1978) habituated babies to rotating foam-rubber disks. They discovered that five-month-old babies saw a disk as the same whether it rotated directly in front of them (either horizontally or vertically) or at an angle. But when the foam rubber was distorted so that it appeared to have a rippled surface, the babies reacted as if it were a new object, showing that they expected the object to be rigid in all conditions—constant not only in shape but also in texture.

Shape constancy may emerge at about three months, which would suggest that babies are beginning to perceive objects in a relatively objective manner instead of solely in relation to themselves (Banks and Salapatek, 1983). The fact that slight changes in the ways infants are tested produce conflicting results suggests that the development of this important event may be gradual, with certain environmental situations supporting the perception of constancy even before the ability is clearly established.

Size Constancy The size of the retinal image gives a viewer no clue as to the actual size of an object, yet by the time babies are a few months old, they appear to judge accurately the sizes of objects in their world. Somehow they realize that the farther away an object is, the smaller it will appear. The five-month-old babies who reacted to the illusory projectile as if it would strike them showed depth perception, but they showed size constancy as well.

In an experiment to test for size constancy, a team of Australian researchers used habituation techniques, showing colored models of human heads to infants of various ages (McKenzie, Tootell, and Day, 1980). For example, some babies saw a life-size head at a distance of sixty centimeters (about two feet). Next these babies saw a head half the size at a distance of thirty centimeters. (The smaller head at thirty centimeters stimulates the retina just as the larger head does at sixty centimeters.) If the baby is relying on retinal image, he or she will pay little attention to the smaller head; but if the baby has developed size constancy, the smaller head will seem like a new object and the infant will show renewed interest. The researchers found size constancy among six- and eight-month olds, but not among four-month-olds. Yet by changing their procedure slightly (using moving instead of stationary stimuli), they found clear evidence of size constancy among another group of four-month-olds (Day and McKenzie, 1981). According to Martin Banks and Philip Salapatek (1983), such results may illustrate the difference between a baby's *competence* and his or her actual *performance*. Babies may be capable of some action but fail to carry it out, either because they are bored, upset, or simply do not care to do it. After reviewing the research, Banks and Salapatek concluded that size constancy is certainly present by six months and may be present earlier. They point out that between four and six months, infants develop several skills that could affect the development of size constancy, such as the coordination of hand and eye in reaching for an object and the ability to comprehend such depth cues as perspective and familiar size.

Work with human babies and with the young of other species indicates that size constancy develops without the experience of moving around in the environment—at least as far as objects in motion are concerned (Rock, 1975). Peter Bryant (1974) believes that we establish size constancy for stationary objects by using the relation between the object and its background. Even though the retinal image of the teddy bear on the toy counter gets larger as the little boy approaches, its relation to the size of the counter, the clerk, and the other toys remains the same.

SPACE PERCEPTION If they are to get about confidently in the world, babies must understand that when they move, their position in relation to other objects around them changes. Basic to this understanding is the realization that while they are in motion, the world is stable. Infants must be prepared to cope with the consequences of their own movements (Acredolo and Hake, 1982).

These understandings begin with the infant's developing ability to orient him- or herself in space. According to Jean Piaget (1954), because babies first begin their orientation by locating objects in reference to themselves, moving the infants around will mix them up. For example, Linda Acredolo and Debra Evans (1980) placed six- to eleven-month-old babies in the center of a curtained space with windows on both the right and left sides. When a buzzer sounded, an experimenter appeared at one of the windows, called the baby's name, and entertained the infant. Babies soon learned to look at the window (which was always the same one) as soon as the buzzer sounded. Then the baby's chair was moved so that the exciting window was on the infant's opposite side. But when the buzzer sounded, six-month-old infants turned their heads just as they had before and wound up looking at the empty window. Even when Acredolo and Evans placed a large star beside the experimenter's window, infants who had learned to look to the right persisted in looking right and infants who had learned to look left persisted in looking left, despite the fact that they now had a landmark that told them where they could expect to see the entertainment. However, when landmarks were virtually impossible to ignore, such as flashing lights and stripes placed around the window where the experimenter appeared, about a sixth of the six-month-olds used the landmark instead of their bodies as a reference. By the time they were eleven months old, babies began to break out of the egocentric frame of reference. About half of them looked at the appropriate window—but only when they had a star to use as a landmark. Shown the flashing lights, nearly all the eleven-month-olds relied on the landmark. In an earlier experiment (Acredolo, 1978), nearly all of a group of sixteen-month-olds looked at the appropriate window when they had a star to guide them, and about a third looked in the correct direction even without a landmark. These studies indicate a gradual decrease in egocentrism and an increasing reliance on landmarks with increasing age.

Babies begin to crawl at about nine months and walk at about a year, so it is probable that their experiences in moving their own bodies around the world help infants learn to orient themselves in space. Babies apparently learn to orient themselves at home almost as soon as they can crawl, for Acredolo (1979) also found that whereas nine-month-old babies tested in a laboratory persistently used themselves as the only reference when looking for objects, tested at home they did as well as the sixteen-month-olds had done in the laboratory.

But babies find gravity even more of a help than their own bodies, as John Rieser (1979) discovered when he conducted an experiment similar to Acredolo's. This time six-month-olds were placed in a round room with four windows directly in front of them so that the babies had to look up, down, or to one of the sides. Even newborns are sensitive to cues that indicate their heads are tilted in respect to gravity (Prechtl and Beintema, 1964). With the baby seat tilted at a forty-five-degree angle, causing the babies to lean to one side, they would, Rieser presumed, be sensitive to the body cues that signified gravity. It appears that he was right, for babies in the tilted position used gravity to orient themselves, looking, for example, at the door that was in its original position relative to gravity rather than relative to their own bodies. Babies who were not tilted tended to act as they had in Acredolo's study.

In reviewing all of this research, Linda Acredolo and Janet Hake (1982) note that researchers

When they begin to crawl, babies learn to navigate around their homes. If tested at home, this infant would probably show that he can use landmarks to orient himself; but if tested in a laboratory, he would probably fail at the task. (Suzanne Szasz)

simply do not know what factors speed the baby's acquisition of spatial orientation. They suggest that advances in cognitive development, the freedom to explore in the home, and the presence of siblings may all be involved.

The Development of Sensory and Sensorimotor Coordination

Vision does not work in isolation; the senses and motor abilities of the healthy infant work as a team (Gibson, 1969). Jean Piaget showed that by the latter part of the first year, infants construct notions of objects in terms of their combined touchable, tastable, smellable, hearable, seeable, graspable, and reachable characteristics. Indeed, everything nine-month-old babies can reach enters the mouth, there to be explored

with tongue and lips. Babies are tireless reachers, graspers, and handlers of objects, which they study not only with their eyes but also with their fingers. For most babies the coordination of sound and touch with sight dominates the coordination of senses and motor abilities. But for blind infants, the task is to coordinate sound with touch (see accompanying box).

SIGHT AND SOUND Babies apparently come into the world prepared to learn about relations between sights and sounds, although at first they do not expect to find interesting sights at the source of a sound (Harris, 1983). But because most events or objects provide multiple kinds of stimulation, infants soon discover that one kind of sensation signals that sensations of other kinds are probably near them in space or in time. If they hear a sound, they learn that it pays to look because they may see some interesting sight.

Although newborns slowly turn their heads toward the sound of a shaking rattle, whether they expect to see anything is not known. Researchers have found that the turning is as frequent in darkness as it is in a lighted room (Muir et al., 1979). However, early signs of a connection between vision and hearing may have been found by Morton Mendelson and Marshall Haith (1976), who discovered that babies only a few days old kept their eyes wide, increased their eye control, looked more at the center of their visual field, and scanned with smaller movements when they heard a man's voice. The sound appeared to make the babies alert to possible visual stimulation. When the researchers played a repeating tape recording of a man reading an excerpt from a children's poem, the babies at first looked in the direction of the voice, but as the reading continued, their gaze gradually tended to wander from the source of the sound.

Head turning in response to a shaking rattle declines sharply during the second and third months, only to reappear at full strength when babies are about four months old (Muir et al.,

1979). Yet in an early study, Nancy Bayley (1969) noted that two-month-olds would move their eyes in apparent search when an unseen bell or rattle sounded. The babies she studied also failed to move their heads. It may be that coordination between vision and hearing is present at two months, but that babies have not yet developed the more precise coordination among ear, eye, and head required to turn the head and look in the correct direction.

However, young infants may simply be aroused by sounds instead of using them to locate objects. Katherine Lawson and Holly Ruff (1984) had infants sit on a researcher's lap while a brightly colored object moved across the infant's field of vision. Babies were more likely to follow the object with their eyes when it was accompanied by sounds, but they responded similarly whether the sound seemed to come from the object or whether it came from a stationary speaker placed to one side of the infant. The researchers suggest the sound apparently alerted the infants, making them more likely to pay attention to any obvious stimulus.

In other studies, two-month-old babies seemed able to use sounds to aid in visual search. This became apparent when Jeffery Field and his associates (1979) played a recording of a female voice reading poetry. If there was nothing to look at, the babies consistently turned their heads toward the voice. But at this early age, babies do not expect a correlation between what they see and what they hear. When Field played the recording but placed a female researcher in the baby's field of vision, so that the voice came from one side of the baby and the face from the other, babies ignored the voice, betraying no signs of surprise or disturbance at the displaced sound.

Slightly older babies may expect a synchrony between voice and lips. When three- to four-month-old babies heard nursery rhymes recited, they looked intently at the investigator when her lip movements were synchronized with the words of the rhyme; but when the two were out of synchrony, the babies' attention flagged and their gaze wandered (Dodd, 1979).

By the time babies are four months old, they have no trouble connecting sights and sounds and will search visually to locate a noisy object. (George Bellerose/Stock, Boston)

The association between sight and sound appears firmly established by four months, for an infant of this age searches visually for a parent whose tape-recorded voice is played in the infant's hearing, even when the face and voice are separated in space and are not synchronized (Spelke and Owsley, 1979). Four-month-olds clearly connect sound with action. Elizabeth Spelke (1979) gave four-month-old babies the choice of watching two films: a continuous game of peekaboo or a woman's hands playing toy percussion instruments. Although babies looked from one film to the other, whenever the accompanying soundtrack carried the music of the toy band, their gaze switched to the percussion instruments. In a similar study, babies of this age generally looked at film that was synchronized with the soundtrack and ignored the other (Bahrick, Walker, and Neisser, 1978).

Exploring the connection between sight and sound further, Spelke (1979) showed four-month-old babies movies of a yellow kangaroo and a gray donkey bouncing across the grass. The bounces of one were accompanied by thumps, the other by a clanging gong. The films and soundtracks were run in several combinations, both in and out of synchrony. It was apparent from the babies' visual searches that they detected the connection between simultaneous sound bursts and visible impacts. Spelke concluded that instead of experiencing a world of unrelated sounds and objects, infants immediately note the temporal relationship of motion and sound in a strange object, linking them together in a unified perceptual experience.

EYE-HAND COORDINATION Another important coordination that develops in the first half-year is that between the eyes and the hands. We take it for granted that our hands will reach out the proper distance to touch or grasp objects that appear in our line of sight. But it takes some time for infants to develop this skill. As we saw in Chapter 4, newborns often move their hands toward objects in their field of vision. However, this response is not a true attempt to grasp an object; it is simply an indication that they are paying attention to it (von Hofsten, 1982). It is not until babies are four and a half months old that half of them are able to touch a cube that is placed in front of them on a table, and not until they are six months old are virtually all infants that skilled.

Once babies can grasp and manipulate objects, enormous cognitive advances become possible. Infants with eye-hand coordination have some control over the information they extract from their explorations (Olson and Sherman, 1983). This eye-hand coordination is so important that many students of infancy and early childhood place the origins of intelligence in the sensorimotor experiences and developments of infancy. For example, Piaget's books (1952b, 1954) on infancy are full of vivid descriptions and perceptive interpretations of age changes in infants' sensorimotor coordination and of their link to concepts of objects, space, time, and causality.

COORDINATION OF SIGHT AND TOUCH By the time they are eight months old, babies can transfer information from touch to sight. Peter Bryant and his colleagues (1972) devised a pair of semiround objects that were identical except for a small square notch in the end of one. Both objects were shown to babies, who ranged in age from six to twelve months, while they sat in their mothers' laps. Then the objects were taken away. Without the baby being able to see the objects, one of them was placed in his or her hand. While the infant held it, it was made to bleep, then it was removed. When both objects were shown again, about two-thirds of the infants reached without hesitation for the particular object they had just handled, indicating their ability to translate information from a tactual to a visual mode.

Other studies in which babies must transfer information from touch to sight have led researchers to suggest that the ability is a good indication of cognitive development. Susan Rose and her colleagues (1978) have discovered that by the time they are a year old, full-term babies can make the transfer. If they are kept from seeing an object but allowed to explore it with their mouths or hands, they will later recognize the object by sight. But premature infants (even though they are tested a full year after their expected birth date) cannot manage the transfer; they cannot recognize on sight objects they have only touched. They do, however, recognize objects they have been allowed to look at but not touch. It may be that the full-term infants studied had processed the events in their world more rapidly and efficiently than the preterm babies had.

Some of the intersensory and sensorimotor coordinations that emerge during the first year of life clearly reflect the infant's experiences. For example, by the time she is a year old, a baby girl has learned that she must fully extend her arm to reach a stuffed animal one foot away, because in the past she has not been able to grab a toy at that distance without reaching for it. On the other hand, maturation of the visual and motor functions in the central nervous system also may contribute to the development of the four-month-old's visually directed grab for an object. All these coordinations improve during the second year of life, because infants have greater opportunities to use them on the diversity of objects and events they encounter.

THE EMERGENCE OF LEARNING AND MEMORY

As the infant's perceptual capacities improve, the range of available information expands by leaps and bounds. Like the rest of us, babies do not learn and remember all the information that is available to their senses. In order to understand the emergence of the infant mind, we must trace the development of attention, which determines what babies might learn; the development of learning, which determines what babies do learn; and the development of memory, which determines how much they draw on past learning.

The Early Development of Attention

Almost from birth, babies are selective about the sights they look at and the sounds they listen to. As noted in Chapter 4, this selectivity helps reduce the confusion in their strange new world. Researchers assume that babies look at what interests them most; for that reason, most studies focus on the length of time they gaze at various objects. Shifts in a baby's attention are important, for they often indicate learning or memory.

Given a choice, newborns look at patterns in preference to plain stimuli, but they are also willing to look at a blank panel for as long as fifty seconds. Within a few weeks, they will fuss, cry, or fall asleep when shown a solid black screen (Salapatek, 1975). The development of babies' preferences for various patterns has been studied carefully, but whether the ability to discriminate various patterns actually improves with age—and if so, how—is still unsettled (Banks and Salapatek, 1983). Some researchers believe that babies have an inborn preference for stimuli that are important to them, such as

a human face. Some believe that infants prefer to look at moderately discrepant stimuli (see Chapter 4). Others believe that physical characteristics of the stimuli—either the density of their contours or the degree of contrast in their patterns—explain the changes in preference that occur (Olson and Sherman, 1983). All that we can conclude with certainty is that the newborn is able to discriminate some patterns and that this ability changes with age (Banks and Salapatek, 1983).

Young infants prefer simple black-and-white patterns to color, movement, or a flickering light (Fantz, Fagan, and Miranda, 1975). This preference then declines rapidly. During the third month of life, significant changes occur in the visual world of the infant, and babies begin to watch strange objects in preference to familiar ones. For example, Joseph Fagan (1971) showed infants of five, seven, and ten weeks of age visual stimuli, some already familiar to the babies and others new to them. He found that seven-week-olds preferred the familiar stimulus, whereas ten-week-olds preferred the novel one.

The influence of biological maturation on these early preference changes was shown when Fagan, Robert Fantz, and Simon Miranda (1971) compared the visual preferences of infants born four weeks before they were due with others born at full term. At eleven weeks, the premature infants responded as the full-term infants had at seven weeks. Not until they were fifteen weeks old did the premature infants show the preference for novelty that appears in most infants by eleven weeks. Despite similar experiences, the premature infants could not respond to the familiar-novel dimension of visual information until their visual systems had reached a certain level of biological maturation, enabling them to remember that a stimulus had been seen before.

Novelty is sometimes not as attractive as discrepancy; some investigators have found that babies prefer objects or patterns that are somewhat similar to things they have seen before but are neither completely novel nor identical to the earlier sights (Kagan, 1978). By the time babies are three or four months old, they actively ex-

The Blind Infant's World

The baby who is born blind depends on smell, sound, taste, and touch for information about the world. Since visual stimulation provides so much of a sighted baby's knowledge, it is not surprising to find differences in development between sighted and blind infants. Like the sighted baby, the blind baby cries, laughs, and smiles spontaneously; but the appealing laughs and smiles of social interaction are much slower to develop.

When Daniel Freedman (1974) studied several blind babies, he discovered that their first social smiles come in response to voices, touch, or the squeaking of a familiar toy. These smiles are extremely fleeting and resemble the reflexive smile that appears in very young infants, whether they are sighted or blind. By the time the babies are six months old, their smiles are normal. At about three months, like sighted babies, blind babies wiggle their hands before their eyes as if they were observing them, but this response soon drops away. Instead of reaching for objects at about six months, as sighted babies do, blind babies reach for noisy objects at about eleven months (Fraiberg and Bayley, 1974). Blind infants are somewhat slow at walking, and generally do not take their first steps until they are more than fifteen months old.

Their lack of sight may give blind babies less reason to explore the world. Once they learn to move about on their own, they may develop the use of echolocation, in which they navigate by using the echo from sound bounced off the surroundings. Many blind adults make their way surely through the world in this manner, sometimes clicking their tongues or snapping their fingers to create echoes (Gibson, 1969). Thomas Bower (1977) discovered that a sixteen-week-old blind baby he studied was already beginning to develop this skill. The little boy made sharp, clicking noises with his lips and tongue and turned his head to follow a ball that Bower dangled soundlessly in front of him.

When imitative play begins, blind infants are limited to mimicking sounds in their world. Among sighted youngsters, the preschool period is a time filled with doll play and "let's pretend." Blind youngsters, however, show almost no imaginative play. Sound is an important source of play for blind children as well as their primary source of information. Instead of "feeding" their dolls or "driving" a car, young blind children tend to spend their time repeating conversations they have overheard or taken part in (Mogford, 1977).

A major hazard in the cognitive development of blind infants may be getting so little stimulation that they lose interest in exploring their environment (Reed, 1975). To guard against this, researchers have developed ways in which parents can help blind babies learn to connect sound and touch. For example, Selma Fraiberg (1977) suggests that parents keep up a flow of conversation while interacting with their blind infants—as they walk toward their babies, pick them up, dress them, feed them, bathe them, and the like. By keeping a supply of toys within reach, so that there is always something for the baby to explore with hands and mouth, parents can encourage the infants to learn about their world. In fact, most blind babies do develop normally. We have only to look at the example of Helen Keller, who was both blind and deaf, to realize that the lack of sight does not permanently impede cognitive development.

plore the world with their eyes, looking at objects for a shorter period and preferring increasingly complicated or meaningful patterns. The characteristics of a stimulus that first attract a baby's attention do not seem to change with age—loud noises, bold patterns, large objects, motion, and sudden changes of illumination are equally effective in catching the eye of a three-month-old and a six-month-old. But the effectiveness of an object in holding a baby's attention undergoes considerable change with age, with infants favoring increasingly complex stimuli (Olson and Sherman, 1983). Now the information a baby can glean from an event (indicated by its discrepancy or novelty) becomes as fascinating as its physical properties (such as content, movement, or complexity). This development was especially clear among four-month-olds studied by Judy DeLoache and her colleagues (DeLoache, Rissman, and Cohen 1978). Whenever a light blinked in front of these babies, they could see a slide by turning their heads. The babies turned their heads more rapidly to see an interesting, complicated slide than to see a simple one. In fact, when they were allowed to see interesting slides, they began to anticipate them. By behaving in such a manner, say the researchers, babies are actively attempting to control their visual experiences. From this point on, the infant's increasing store of knowledge is probably the major determinant of what holds his or her attention. For example, when eight- and twelve-month olds were given the opportunity to explore toys, they preferred new toys to ones they had played with before *unless* they had been interrupted in their earlier exploration of a toy (Hunter, Ames, and Koopman, 1983). Age did not affect this trend; babies seemed to play with a toy until they had learned all they could about it; once it had become familiar, they were ready for something new.

The Early Development of Learning and Memory

Stimuli that attract the attention of infants come to bore them after a while; the babies shift their attention to another stimulus or fall asleep. This tendency to habituate to familiar stimuli and to respond to novel stimuli is essential to the infant's ability to learn. It indicates that the infant remembers the earlier stimulus; unless such memory occurs, there can be no conditioning, no adaptation, no learning of any sort (McCall, 1971). Research on learning and memory in infants generally relies on attention, assuming that babies will pay more attention to unfamiliar objects or patterns than to those they have seen before, although operant conditioning has also been used.

Infants as young as five weeks old can learn quickly when their actions have an effect on the world. Ilze Kalnins and Jerome Bruner (1973) projected blurred movies of Eskimo family life onto a screen, positioned infants in front of the screen, and placed a pacifier in their mouths. Sucking on the pacifier rotated a plastic shield in front of the screen, making the picture sharp. The babies quickly learned to increase their sucking in order to keep the picture clear, averting their gaze whenever they paused and the picture blurred. However, some kinds of learning are easier than others. When conditions were reversed (a clear picture that blurred when the babies sucked on the pacifier) the babies were unable to learn to inhibit their sucking in order to enjoy the picture.

Habituation studies have shown that three-month-old infants can learn and remember such social stimuli as facial expressions and individual faces, solid objects, and shapes (Olson and Sherman, 1983). For example, three-month-olds studied by Allen Milewski (1979) recognized simple patterns even when those patterns changed in size or position. Infants who habituated to a pattern of three dots (either placed in a line or made to form a triangle) paid no attention to changes in the space between the dots (which changed the size of the pattern) or changes in the portion of the screen on which the pattern was displayed. Changes from one pattern to another, however, did attract renewed attention.

When sorting out the people in their world, babies apparently use age and sex as guidelines.

Given two thirty-second periods to study a photograph of a baby, five-month-olds recognized the photo when they saw it again along with the photo of a round-faced, bald man (Fagan and Singer, 1979). Since infants can recognize the difference between photographs of men and women, or babies and adults, psychologists assume that the babies remember features that define sex and age. But finer discriminations may still be too difficult: shown photographs of two male strangers, they cannot recognize the one they have seen. By seven months, however, they can make this distinction. The older babies apparently remember more distinguishing features. Such experiments may underestimate a baby's ability to tell one person from another. The perception of a flat, two-dimensional face, unmoving and silent, presents more problems than the perception of a three-dimensional, living, moving, and talking face.

When babies are tested in habituation studies, they demonstrate their ability to recognize stimuli shortly after they have learned about them. It is as if you were shown a group of pictures and, a few minutes later, asked which pictures in a second group were among those you had just seen. But knowing that babies can remember sights or sounds for twenty minutes or two hours tells us little about their ability to retain information long enough to make it useful in the future.

In habituation studies, when infants look at patterns for a specified length of time, gradual improvements appear with age in their ability to learn and to retain a memory. But when they are allowed to look at the patterns until they lose interest, two-month-old babies do as well as older babies at recognizing them. This suggests that, although it may take young babies more time to acquire information about stimuli, once they have acquired it, they are as good as older infants at retaining it.

After reviewing the research on infant memory, John Werner and Marion Perlmutter (1979) concluded that individual differences in processing visual information are present from birth. The researchers go on to point out that once

information is thoroughly processed, all babies appear to retain it. Individual differences no longer affect recognition when babies are allowed to look at a pattern until they are bored—a sign that they have represented the material in memory. Research has consistently indicated that babies begin forgetting almost immediately, probably within fifteen seconds, but that traces of a memory may last for hours or weeks, or even forever.

Several factors may contribute to developments in the ability of babies to learn and remember a stimulus. Gary Olson and Tracy Sherman (1983) suggest four candidates: (1) increases in sensory and perceptual sensitivity; (2) more rapid and more reliable processing of perceived stimuli; (3) changes in the way babies deploy their attention; and (4) growth in babies' store of knowledge. Whatever factors are responsible, between three and six months of age, babies become adept at extracting information from the world and quickly storing it in memory. Despite this increased proficiency, babies still require much more time than older children or adults to register a stimulus in memory so that they can remember it later.

Perhaps babies actually retain more information than we realize, but for some reason they cannot recall what they have learned. What sort of circumstances might aid infant memory? According to Carolyn Rovee-Collier (1984), babies are likely to remember when there are cues in the test situation that remind them of the original situation in which they learned the material. Attention is important; if the baby being tested does not notice the cues, he or she will fail to remember. Furthermore, if the testing situation includes novel cues that attract the baby's attention, the infant will not remember. Assuming that reminders of the original situation will later make memories more accessible, Janet Davis and Rovee-Collier (1983) trained eight-week-old babies to operate a mobile by kicking a foot that was attached to the mobile by a ribbon. When tested the following day, the babies clearly remembered how to operate the mobile, but two weeks later, they had forgotten how to work the toy. Such apparent forgetting is not necessarily permanent. Another group of two-month-olds learned to operate the mobile and seventeen days later were allowed to see (but not operate) it. The next day, given the opportunity, they immediately began working the mobile. The sight of the mobile the previous day had apparently reactivated their memory of the earlier encounter with the toy.

This research indicates that repeated exposure to stimuli may serve to keep information accessible in an infant's memory. Such reencounters are a regular part of most babies' daily life but are absent in most laboratory experiments. It therefore seems probable that laboratory studies have tended to underestimate the persistence of memory in young babies.

When older babies are observed in their homes, many show they remember objects or events. Daniel Ashmead and Marion Perlmutter (1980) collected examples of infant memory by having parents keep diaries of incidents in which their seven- to eleven-month-old babies showed that they recalled some object or activity that was not present. For example, at her father's suggestion, an eleven-month-old left the room, got her doll, brought it back to the living room, and played with it. The babies remembered the location of household items and conducted searches for missing objects. They remembered bathing and feeding routines, and they remembered social games, such as peekaboo. While her nine-month-old son was sitting in his highchair, one mother said, "Peekaboo." The baby immediately held his bib in front of his face. On another occasion, an eleven-month-old, on hearing the telephone ring, headed as fast as she could toward the phone and tugged on the cord. Apparently, this baby remembered the routine associated with answering the phone.

Familiar with such clear examples of intelligent actions in daily life, most parents find it difficult to believe that their clever baby may assume that a toy that has fallen off a highchair tray and rolled out of sight under a couch no longer exists. Yet, as the following consideration of infant thought makes clear, researchers take this proposition seriously.

This baby smiles delightedly at Grandfather, recognizing his face and probably remembering the fun of past games they have shared. (James Holland/Stock, Boston)

THE EMERGENCE OF THOUGHT

The study of cognitive development in infancy has been dominated by the ideas of Jean Piaget (1952b; 1954), which were discussed in Chapter 1. As an organismic theorist, he was interested in the changing structure of the infant mind. He saw the infant as acting on the world, observing what happens, and assimilating that knowledge to his or her existing schemes. A good many of these observations, however, cannot be assimilated without accommodation—altering existing schemes to incorporate the new information. When the conflict between the infant's schemes and observations is especially severe, or when the infant has problems coordinating conflicting schemes, his or her equilibrium is upset, thought is restructured, and the infant moves into the next stage of cognitive development. Although infancy is spent in a single stage of development, Piaget divided the sensorimotor period into six substages, each reflecting changes in the quality of thought.

Substages of Sensorimotor Thought

During the sensorimotor period, which covers approximately the first two years of life, a major task is that of separating self from the world. Babies cannot fully distinguish between their own bodies and the objects and people in the world around them until they are about a year old and have reached the fifth of Piaget's six sensorimotor substages (see Table 7.1). Piaget saw the glimmerings of a practical intelligence in the fourth substage, when babies begin to use their schemes to reach a goal, but he did not consider their behavior truly "intelligent" until they reached the fifth substage. At that point, there was, he believed, a systematic intelligence based on perceptions and motor skills, which he described as "sensorimotor intelligence."

SUBSTAGE ONE: REFLEX ACTS This first substage covers the newborn period, when the baby's actions are primarily based on reflexes and are rigid and inflexible. Inflexible as these innate actions are, they can be affected by experience. A baby learns to regulate sucking, for example, and will suck more slowly for sweetened than for unsweetened water, presumably in order to savor the flavor. During these first few weeks of life, the adaptive reflexes, such as vocalizing, grasping, and sucking, become more efficient with experience and practice.

SUBSTAGE TWO: PRIMARY CIRCULAR REACTIONS The second sensorimotor substage occupies the next two or three months of development. Its hallmark is the **primary circular reaction.** A circular reaction is any behavior—whether grasping, sucking, looking, or vocalizing—that the baby tends to repeat again and again because of the stimulation provided by it. These actions are based on reflexes; they are unlearned and involve parts of the babies' own body. Now babies look and listen to the sights and sounds of their world. They are beginning to coordinate their senses and will, for example, use their eyes to direct their grasp.

SUBSTAGE THREE: SECONDARY CIRCULAR REACTIONS In the third substage, which lasts until they are seven or eight

Table 7.1 **SENSORIMOTOR SUBSTAGES OF INFANCY**

Substage 1	Reflex Acts	Actions rigid and stereotyped
Substage 2	Primary Circular Reactions	Sensorimotor schemes based on reflexes
Substage 3	Secondary Circular Reactions	Learned sensorimotor schemes
Substage 4	Coordination of Secondary Schemes	Learning by observation; intentional acts toward goals
Substage 5	Tertiary Circular Reactions	Actions deliberately varied; problems solved through overt trial and error
Substage 6	Symbolic Thought	Mental representation; problems solved through mental trial and error

When this little girl repeatedly bangs the toy telephone on her high-chair tray, she is demonstrating what Piaget called a "secondary circular reaction." (Suzanne Szasz)

months old, babies rely on **secondary circular reactions.** Their repetitive acts—shaking a rattle or banging a cup on the highchair tray—are learned and involve objects in the external world. These action schemes are reinforced by the effects they have, and they are often meant to prolong events that interest babies. Sensorimotor coordination is improving, and babies are more proficient at grasping objects that attract them. Perceptions are so intertwined with actions that babies in this substage find it difficult to separate the two.

SUBSTAGE FOUR: COORDINATION OF SECONDARY SCHEMES

This substage often occupies the rest of the baby's first year.

During this period, babies work at coordinating their secondary circular actions into purposeful, larger schemes and developing adaptive schemes, which they apply to the world around them. They are busily engaged in solving problems and instead of simply prolonging interesting events, they intentionally use their schemes to attain some goal. This advance indicates that babies have begun to develop an idea of causality. Because they can now learn by watching others, they no longer have to stumble onto each new action. As the box on page 228 indicates, babies in this stage may be more advanced than Piaget supposed.

SUBSTAGE FIVE: TERTIARY CIRCULAR REACTIONS

The fifth substage may occupy a baby until he or she is eighteen months old. Babies in this substage are beginning to distinguish between themselves and the world. They now see objects and events as independent from their actions. Babies' schemes have become **tertiary circular reactions,** which are intelligent, systematic adaptations to specific situations. Faced with a problem, they will set about solving it by a process of trial and error. They may test various actions, just to see what happens. Their intelligence is, however, based on perceptions and movements rather than on words and concepts.

SUBSTAGE SIX: BEGINNING OF SYMBOLIC THOUGHT

The last substage of the sensorimotor period can extend until a baby is two years old. This is a period of significant cognitive advance. Now babies form mental representations of their own actions and of events in the world around them. They do not have to imitate an adult's actions immediately but can store the representation and imitate the person the next day. When solving problems, they no longer have to rely on overt trial and error. They have the ability to internalize schemes, which allows them to solve problems in their heads and then apply the solution. They are ready to move out of infancy and the stage of sensorimotor intelligence and into the preoperational period.

The Object Concept

Out of their sensory, perceptual, and motor interactions with the environment, babies gradually develop the **object concept.** This concept refers to the understanding that objects remain the same although they may move from one place to another (object identity) and that they continue to exist when out of sight (object permanence). These interrelated ideas of object identity and object permanence are not fully developed, Piaget believed, until the latter part of the second year, when the baby reaches the sixth and last substage of the sensorimotor period.

Piaget carefully traced the development of the object concept through the substages, using the baby's ability to find a hidden object as the basis for his conclusions. If an object being watched by a baby of less than four months (Substages One and Two) disappears from view, the baby tends to act as if the object had never been there. It is as though an object exists only when it is immediately perceived.

During the next four months or so, however, a baby in Substage Three often initiates a visual search for an object he or she has seen disappearing from view. At this point in the development of the object concept, the object seems to continue existing for the baby only if the infant sees the object starting to move away. When a cover is dropped over an object held in the grasp of a baby who is in Substage Three, the baby either withdraws the hand or behaves as if he or she did not know the object is still grasped in the hand.

Babies in Substage Three are able to track a moving object, and will, for example, follow an electric train as it moves along a rectangular track. But when the train goes into a tunnel, the baby does not shift his or her eyes to the tunnel exit; instead the infant gazes at the entrance until the reappearance of the train catches his or her attention. In laboratory studies, five-month-olds never seem to anticipate the emergence of the train, and only a few nine-month-olds seem to realize that it will reappear at the other end of the tunnel (Nelson, 1971). In fact, when one

At six months, babies have not developed the object concept. When the toy elephant that has captured this baby's attention (*left*) is hidden from view, the infant seems unaware that the fascinating toy is still on the tray before her (*right*). (George Zimbel/Monkmeyer Press)

object moving on a trajectory disappears behind a screen and a different object emerges, babies do not look back to see what happened to the original object but resume tracking the new object. Some babies, however, do frown at the sight of the new object (Meicler and Gratch, 1980).

In observations of his own children, Piaget (1952b, 1954) found that when they entered Substage Four, the infants searched with their hands for objects that they saw him place behind a screen, but they searched in a limited fashion. For example, Piaget moved a toy behind a screen while his child watched. The child retrieved it. Piaget made his move in the game again, and the child again responded appropriately. This was repeated several more times. Then Piaget, with his child attending to his actions, hid the toy behind a screen located in a different place. Yet the child insisted on searching for the toy in the original location. Piaget concluded that the child failed to search in the new location because of egocentrism. This egocentrism leads to an error because babies cannot separate the objects of the world from their own actions on them. They can remember a place only in terms of the movements they made when first retrieving the toy.

Because this reaction by the baby is basic to understanding the development of the infant mind, researchers have tested Piaget's explanation in an attempt to discover the nature of the baby's error. Some researchers have found that the error is more severe than Piaget supposed: babies continue to reach toward the original location even when the toy is not hidden but remains plainly visible at a new location (Butterworth, 1977). Others have found that under some conditions, as when the baby is allowed to search immediately (instead of after a delay of a second or more), the error disappears (Gratch et al., 1974).

After reviewing the mountainous and sometimes conflicting research on this point, P. L. Harris (1983) concluded that infants seem to link the toy with the place in which it was originally hidden and that, contrary to Piaget's belief, they

do not associate it with the movements that successfully retrieved it. He suggests that as babies begin to rely on landmarks instead of on their own previous positions to locate objects (Acredolo and Evans, 1980), they use the original landmark even if they have seen the object moved to a new location. In his view, this error lingers because babies in Substage Four may be confused by the world's complexity. Accustomed to seeing several oranges, spoons, blocks, or cups at the same time, each in a different location, babies may not yet understand that there is a lawful relationship between the successive positions of a single object as it is moved from one place to another. They may be slow in reaching this understanding because they retain information about an object's successive positions so briefly that they confuse earlier and later positions of an object.

Jerome Kagan (1984) agrees that memory is crucial to the development of the object concept, but doubts that infants believe hidden objects cease to exist. He contends that as memory develops, the baby is able to remember the location of the toy and use that knowledge to guide a reach for it. The fact that babies are not fooled by a switch in hiding places, provided they are allowed to search immediately, supports his suggestion.

Babies in Substage Five are not tricked when a toy hidden in one place is moved to another location, and yet another and another. They will search at the final location—but only if they have watched the toy being moved. Not until children reach Substage Six, at about eighteen months, do they seem to understand that an object can be moved without their seeing the relocation. Now they will search not only at the last place they saw the toy hidden, but in all possible places it might be found. They have developed the object concept. According to Bennett Bertenthal and Kurt Fischer (1983), this final search is not the systematic search that Piaget believed it to be, examining all places in the probable path of a hidden object. Instead, infants in this last substage understand that the actions of other people do not depend on the

Sorting Out the World

As babies work at understanding the world, one of their tasks is to develop categories, understanding that an older brother, a small cousin, and the child next door are all "boys" and that the oatmeal cookie, the chocolate chip cookie, and the peanut butter cookie are all "cookies." Dividing the world into categories this way seems natural to us, and in Chapter 8 we trace the development of this vital symbolic function. But before children have a language with which to label related but different objects, they begin sort their experiences into something that resembles categories.

Wondering just how soon this ability emerges, Barbara Younger and Leslie Cohen (1983) projected schematic drawings of animals on a screen before infants ranging in age from four to ten months. The drawings mixed animal features (body, tail, feet, ears, legs), with each feature appearing in several forms. For example, tails might be feathered, fluffy, or horselike, bodies shaped like giraffes, cows, or elephants. After habituating to four different animals from the same category (at least three correlated features), babies saw either another animal with familiar but uncorrelated features, or an animal with all new features.

All babies looked with renewed interest at the animal with entirely new features, but only the ten-month-olds found the animals with familiar but uncorrelated features new and interesting. Younger and Cohen suggest that the ten-month-olds were able to extract the correlations among the features and generalize this to a new situation—in short, they had formed a category. The younger infants apparently were not sensitive to the relationships among features in the original animal drawings and so found nothing unusual about a strange type of beast that bore familiar features. It was as if, having become familiar with antlers on deer, you paid no attention to the sight of a dog with antlers.

Roberta Golinkoff and Marcia Halperin (1983) studied one infant's view of the concept "animal." Golinkoff had noted that her eight-month-old son became excited and tried to pet nearly every dog, cat, or stuffed animal he encountered. So she and Halperin had observers rate the baby's reaction to various stuffed animals, dolls, and a fur coat. They discovered that he became excited and tried to pet stuffed dogs and a stuffed mouse, showed similar excitement when given teddy bears and a stuffed Big Bird—but did not try to pet them, and neither became excited nor tried to pet the dolls or the fur coat. No single feature seemed to determine the baby's reactions, so he was apparently reacting to some combination of features. The researchers suggest that the baby was forming a limited concept of animal around the features of a dog, since he had a pet dog and often encountered others. The reactions of this infant indicate once again that babies may often appear more advanced when placed in meaningful situations than when tested in the laboratory.

---

infant's own perceptions and actions. In an advance that is both social and cognitive, they understand that another person can surreptitiously move an object from one place to another.

Piaget's descriptions of the gradual development of the object concept have been supported by later research, and his belief that conceptual problems lie at the root of the infant's difficulty has held up. Where some later theorists disagree is on the nature of these conceptual problems. Piaget believed the infant was trying to solve the problem of whether hidden objects continue to exist, but Harris (1983) proposes that the infant is trying to solve the problem of where to search for an object. He sees the infant's reaction to the disappearance of an object as similar to the adult's reaction to the magician who has made an assistant vanish. The adult is puzzled, but does not believe that the assistant has ceased to exist. No matter what the explanation, once this basic problem has been solved, infants begin to regard people, places, and objects as existing separately from themselves and as not depending on their behavior.

Imitation

Although several researchers (Field et al., 1983; Meltzoff and Moore, 1983) believe that newborn infants can imitate facial expressions, other researchers have been unable to replicate their findings. In a study of babies between the ages of four and twenty-one weeks, Eugene Abravanel and Ann Sigafoos (1984) found that four- to six-week-old infants sometimes showed what appeared to be a reflexive tongue protrusion in response to a researcher who stuck out her tongue, but only when the researcher kept up the action for at least three minutes. After that age, responses dropped off, with infants between the ages of ten and twenty-one weeks failing to imitate the researcher's gestures.

Piaget (1951) believed that imitation was an activity dominated by accommodation, in which babies tended to imitate acts they did not fully understand as a way of grasping their meaning. He saw the ability to imitate the actions of another person as developing slowly during infancy, with a very simple kind of imitation first appearing in babies at Substage Two. If an observer imitates one of the baby's own actions just after the baby performs it, the infant may imitate the model. In Substage Three, babies can imitate an action that the observer first performs. However, the babies must be able to see themselves perform the action (such as hand or leg movements), it must be an act they already perform easily, and the imitation is possible only immediately after they see the act performed.

The sight or sound of the adult modeling the familiar action apparently has the same effect as the baby's own performance of primary circular reactions.

Toward the end of the first year, as babies reach Substage Four, they can imitate an action that is entirely new to them, opening up the possibilities of observational learning. For the first time, they can also imitate invisible actions, those they cannot see themselves perform, such as opening and shutting their mouths or sticking out their tongues. The imitation still must come immediately after babies see the model. Finally, in Substage Six, infants can imitate a model after a delay of hours or days, indicating they have developed mental images and are ready to acquire language, to engage in symbolic play, and to enter the preoperational stage of early childhood (see Table 7.2).

Not all acts are equivalent, and the meaningfulness of an act may affect an infant's tendency to imitate it. When researchers modeled acts for babies ranging in age from seven-and-a-half to

Table 7.2 DEVELOPMENT OF IMITATION

SENSORI-MOTOR SUBSTAGE	IMITATIVE ACTS
Substage 1	Reflexive imitation (e.g., crying in response to cries of other infants).
Substage 2	Babies can imitate an immediate imitation of their own action.
Substage 3	Babies can imitate an adult modeling one of their familiar actions, but must be able to see themselves to perform the action.
Substage 4	Babies can imitate an entirely new action. Imitations are of simple actions, such as banging a block.
Substage 5	As in Stage 4. Imitations are of conventional acts, such as drinking from a cup.
Substage 6	Babies can imitate after a delay of hours or days. Imitations of unconventional acts, such as "drinking" from a toy car.

(Information from Piaget, 1951. Additional data from Uzgiris, 1984.)

twenty-two months, infants imitated those acts they could understand (Uzgiris, 1984). The youngest babies imitated simple actions, such as banging a block or shaking a doll, whereas ten- to sixteen-month-old infants were most likely to imitate conventional acts such as drinking from a cup or brushing their hair. Only the oldest infants imitated unconventional acts as well. They would raise a toy car to their lips or stroke their hair with a cup. This last group of actions was uninteresting to seven-month-olds and, although ten-month-olds were interested, they did not imitate them, nor did sixteen-month-olds, who seemed to find the actions funny. Imitation by the oldest infants, who had reached the age of symbolic play, seemed to indicate that they were pretending the car was a cup or the cup was a hairbrush.

Immediate imitation usually involves some sort of social interaction, and Ina Uzgiris (1984) believes that the social function of imitation has not been sufficiently stressed. Observing mothers and infants interacting, she notes that spontaneous imitation by both mother and baby increases steadily between the ages of two and eleven months, and proposes that such social imitation serves as communication between the pair. Although Piaget (1951) emphasized the cognitive aspects of imitation, believing that older babies tended to imitate acts they did not fully understand, Uzgiris has found that babies also frequently imitate old, familiar activities. This sort of communication, which she believes conveys mutual feeling and understanding, serves an important social function.

SUMMARY

The world view adopted by psychologists determines the kind of questions they ask about cognitive development and the organization they impose on the facts they observe. In one major approach to development, the mechanistic view, cognitive development is seen as gradual and continuous, based on experience and accumulated knowledge. In the other major approach,

the organismic view, cognitive development is seen as moving through a series of stages, in which the organization of thought changes radically with each move to another stage.

Since babies cannot describe their sensations, investigators must monitor their reactions closely, often relying on instruments that measure physiological or behavioral change. Babies do not hear as well as adults, and although the difference is greatest in the range of human speech, infants are very sensitive to the sounds of language. Babies can imitate pitch and recognize melodies, even when they are transposed into another key.

By the time they are six months old, babies can probably see as clearly as adults. Color vision emerges by three months, with depth perception emerging gradually, sometime between three and six months. Once babies begin to crawl, most use depth cues to keep from falling over edges. Visual scanning patterns change with age: older infants scan wider areas of a target and probably process the entire stimulus. **Shape constancy** seems to emerge at about three months and **size constancy** by about six months. Babies first locate objects in reference to their own bodies, but once they begin crawling about, they start to use landmarks.

Young babies seem prepared to learn to connect sights and sounds, and by the time they are four months old, they can connect them appropriately. By six months, eye-hand coordination is smooth enough to enable babies to touch an object placed before them; this coordination gives them control over their environmental explorations and paves the way for cognitive advances. By eight months, they can make the transfer between touch and sight, visually recognizing objects they have handled but never seen.

Selective attention begins almost at birth, and the kinds of stimuli babies look at and the ways in which they look at them change in predictable ways. As babies' ability to discriminate among sights improves, they begin to watch strange objects in preference to familiar ones. Although the kind of stimuli that grab a baby's attention do not change with age, changes do occur in the kind of stimuli that hold attention.

The development of a baby's ability to learn and remember may depend on increases in sensory and perceptual sensitivity, more rapid and reliable processing of stimuli, changes in the way attention is deployed, and growth in the infant's store of knowledge. Babies may retain more information than some tests indicate. They can often recognize information they may not be able to recall. Reencounters with stimuli appear to improve a baby's ability to recall information over time.

Piaget divided the sensorimotor period into six substages, each reflecting changes in the quality of thought during infancy. After the first reflexive substage, the baby moves into a substage characterized by **primary circular reactions,** in which unlearned actions are repeated because of the stimulation they provide. In the third substage, babies use **secondary circular reactions,** which are learned. In the fourth substage, babies can learn by observation and act intentionally to reach a goal. By the fifth sub-

stage, babies have developed **tertiary circular reactions,** which are intelligent adaptations to specific situations. In the sixth substage, babies can solve problems through mental trial and error and represent events mentally.

During the sensorimotor period, babies gradually develop the **object concept.** Their earlier inability to find a hidden object appears to be due to conceptual limitations, but theorists disagree as to whether babies are trying to discover if hidden objects continue to exist or to figure out where to search for them.

The ability to imitate another person's actions also appears to develop gradually. At first only immediate imitation is possible; the observed action must be familiar, and babies must see themselves performing it. By the fourth substage of the sensorimotor period, babies can imitate new actions, making observational learning possible. Not until the sixth substage can infants imitate a model after delays of hours or days, a cognitive advance indicating that they have acquired mental images and can engage in symbolic play.

The Development of Basic Cognitive Processes

THE DEVELOPMENT OF PERCEPTION
The Development of Object Perception
The Development of Picture Perception
The Development of Place Perception
The Development of Event Perception
THE DEVELOPMENT OF ATTENTION
Scanning
Selectivity
Television and Attention
THE DEVELOPMENT OF REPRESENTATION
Enactive Representation
Imaginal Representation
Linguistic Representation
Categorical Representation
Operative Representation
THE DEVELOPMENT OF MEMORY
Types of Remembering
Strategies for Remembering
Knowledge Factors
THE DEVELOPMENT OF METAMEMORY
SUMMARY

An eight-year-old girl was being interviewed by a researcher studying what children know about memory. "What do you do when you want to remember a phone number?" he asked. The reply was immediate. "Say the number is 633-8854," said the girl. "Then what I'd do is—say that my number is 633, so I won't have to remember that, really. And then I would think, now I've got to remember 88. Now I'm eight years old, so I remember, say, my age two times. Then I'd say how old my brother is, and how old he was last year. And that's how I could remember that phone number." The researcher took a deep breath. "Is that how you would most often remember a phone number?" he asked. "Well," said the eight-year-old, "usually I write it down." This child's advocacy of sophisticated strategies quickly gave way to the practical external aid of pencil and paper, but her knowledge of the way the memory system works is impressive. Mary Anne Kreutzer, Catherine Leonard, and John Flavell (1975) received the child's advice in the course of an interview study of children and memory.

Memory makes life as we know it possible. Without memory, there would be no continuity to life. We would greet each new experience without information from the past to guide our actions, and we would be unable to plan for the future. Lacking memory, a mother would not recognize her own baby; indeed, without memory, human relationships could not exist.

Although the basic memory abilities develop during the first two years of life, a young child is not as adept as an adolescent or an adult at remembering things—primarily because young children have not yet developed efficient ways to put information into memory or to get it out again when they need it. Yet once a child has firmly committed something to memory, he or she will retain it as well as an adult.

Memory is a basic cognitive process that can be understood only in the context of other processes human beings use to gather and organize knowledge. In this chapter, we follow up on much that was introduced in the last chapter. We begin by looking at the way young children who have mastered the object concept learn to perceive objects, pictures, places, and events in their world. Next we follow the development of school-age children, examining how their ability to scan material becomes increasingly selective. Then we consider the various forms used to represent knowledge and the way these forms of representation—on which all other cognition depends—develop. Finally, we explore the verbal child's memory, considering its various developing forms, the strategies children use to help them remember, the importance of old knowledge in the acquisition of new information, and children's growing knowledge about the way their memory processes work.

THE DEVELOPMENT OF PERCEPTION

Children, like adults, are exposed to a continual flow of perceptual stimuli, but they do not perceive every stimulus, and their perceptions of the same stimuli change with age. According to Eleanor Gibson and Elizabeth Spelke (1983),

although perceptual development appears continuous rather than stagelike, five sorts of change can be seen. First, as children grow, their perception becomes more selective and more purposeful. Second, children become increasingly aware of the meaning of their perceptions—whether usefulness, pleasure, or danger may come from the various objects or events they perceive. Third, perception becomes more sensitive, as children begin detecting increasingly subtle aspects of stimuli. Fourth, children become more efficient in picking up critical information from stimuli. Fifth, children become more proficient at generalizing perceived meanings from one situation to another. Using their various senses, children monitor their world, obtaining information that guides their behavior. They perceive objects, pictures, places, and events.

The Development of Object Perception

In perceiving objects, we receive information about composition, texture, color, shape, size, and movement. Psychologists have offered several explanations of how we transform this information into the perception of objects. Traditional learning theorists believe that our perceptions of objects are learned, developed by associating the multiple sensations that an object evokes. Gestalt psychologists (Koffka, 1931) claim that we perceive objects by means of organizing principles that result from the brain's natural organizational processes. Although they agree that maturation and learning are involved in the development of perception, Gestalt theorists reject the idea that we learn to see objects by gradually building up associations. Instead, they claim that the perceptual process works by sudden reorganizations—mental rearrangements of the perceptual field along the lines of some innate organizing principles. A child sees an orange as a whole object, not a fragmented, rounded, dimpled contour with the quality of orangeness.

In this view, children interpret perceptual information according to these natural relationships. They group elements that are close together, the principle of *proximity*; they also group elements that are generally alike in form, the principle of *similarity*. They tend to expect the next element in a group to follow the line taken by the rest, the principle of *continuity*; they supply missing or broken elements, the principle of *closure*; and they see objects that move or change together as a unit, the principle of *common fate*. As a result of these principles, children—like adults—perceive an object as separate from its surroundings, separate from an object that lies next to it, and continuing behind an object that lies in front of it.

A different view of perception has been taken by Eleanor Gibson (1969), who says that perception is not simply organized along innate lines but is a matter of extracting increasingly differentiated information from sensory stimulation. We do this, she proposes, by selecting from the environment its permanent, unchanging features and the relationships among them; by filtering information so that irrelevant or changing features are ignored; and by visually exploring the environment, then selectively attending to various aspects of it. In this view, a child perceives an object when he or she detects its unchanging features, noting the arrangement and movement of its surfaces (Gibson and Spelke, 1983).

Although most basic perceptual processes function at an adult level during infancy, some aspects of visual perception continue to change during childhood. Researchers have looked for changes in size and shape constancy and have found that in some situations, children do better than adults. For example, when asked to estimate the size of a distant object, five-year-olds err by about 4 percent in their estimates, six- to eight-year-olds are off by only 1 percent, and adults may make estimates that are wrong by as much as 17 percent, tending to estimate the object's size as larger than it actually is (Gibson, 1969). It may be that the sophisticated realization of the difference between perceived and actual size tends to throw off adults who know the typical size of objects and who consciously try to allow for the discrepancy in such experiments.

When asked about an object's shape, four-year-olds seem to do as well as young adults when the object is close at hand. But if asked to compare the shapes of two objects when one object is five times as far from the viewer as the other, young children do the worst, and judgment improves steadily with age. According to Gibson and Spelke (1983), young children may pay less attention to distant objects or may be less competent when having to compare the shapes of objects that are presented at different distances.

Some aspects of shape perception appear to develop during childhood. When you work a jigsaw puzzle, you look at an array of possible pieces and select only those pieces whose shape is likely to match the hole in the puzzle. This ability to fit forms together was studied by having infants and young children try to obtain objects from behind a board (Zaporozhets, 1969). The openings in the board matched the shape of only one of the objects, so that only it could be drawn through the hole. Even if two-year-olds succeeded in withdrawing one object, they could not adapt when the shape of the opening was changed. They never learned to consider the relationship between the shape of the opening and the shape of the object. Preschool children begin to understand this relationship, and our appreciation of this development can be seen in the increasing complexity of jigsaw puzzles designed for various age levels.

A child's ability to coordinate information from sight and touch improves dramatically between the ages of three and six years. In one study, V. P. Zinshensko and A. G. Ruzskaya (see Zaporozhets, 1965) presented children between the ages of three and six with abstract forms that they were permitted to explore by touch but could not see. These researchers then tested the children's visual recognition of objects they had explored with their fingers. At about age five, there was a sharp improvement in per-

When this little girl is older, puzzles like this one will bore her. Her space perception will be so highly developed that only puzzles with much smaller pieces will present a challenge. (Will McIntyre/Photo Researchers)

formance, probably because the mental images of five- and six-year-olds have become increasingly detailed and precise as a result of their exposure to objects and their sophisticated methods of exploration.

When the object is another person, babies as young as five months old are able to distinguish between men and women, but not until they are adolescents will they find it easy to recognize people in photographs and short films. When distinguishing between two people who are similar in appearance, youngsters seem to base their identification on hairstyles, accessories, and facial expressions—all ephemeral aspects of the person. This was demonstrated by an experiment in which six- to ten-year-olds were shown colored photographs of two women and were asked which woman was in the one in a picture they had seen earlier (Carey and Diamond, 1977). In the test picture, the original model's hairstyle, expression, or dress had been

changed. Only older children paid attention to the configuration of facial features when judging the photographs.

The Development of Picture Perception

Our world has three dimensions; it is deep, solid, and filled with motion. But pictures—whether paintings, drawings, or photographs—are two-dimensional: motionless lines and colors on a flat surface. Psychologists have attempted to discover what mechanisms we use to recognize a drawing as a representation of reality and perceive three-dimensional depth in pictures.

Gestalt psychologists believe that perception is predetermined by the brain's innate organizing principles. Adults and children alike distinguish figures from the ground in which they are set, and when presented with an ambiguous figure, they will impose a form on it.

Young children's perceptions are controlled by these organizing principles, agreed Jean Piaget (1969), but not because perception is predetermined. Instead their attention is captured by dominant features in the picture, and these features are determined by innate organizing principles. As children grow older, he said, they develop new cognitive processes, so that by the time they are six or seven years old, their attention no longer is caught by dominant features. They can now act mentally upon the picture, exploring it visually, analyzing it, integrating its features, and reversing figure and ground at will.

By using ambiguous pictures, David Elkind (1977) and his associates tested which interpretation of picture perception was correct. Children from four to eleven years old looked at pictures that could be seen in two ways; for example, as a tree or a duck. (See Figure 8.1.) Adults see one element of the picture as the figure and the other as the ground, then see the reverse. Gestalt psychologists had argued that perceptual reorganizations should make the pictures reverse most rapidly and easily for young

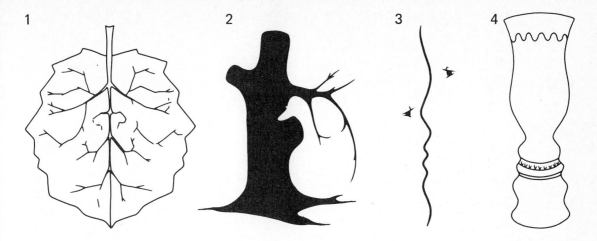

FIGURE 8.1 Ambiguous pictures such as these can be seen in two ways by reversing figure and ground. The older children are, the easier they find it to reverse figure and ground; for example, to switch back and forth from tree to duck, as in Number 2.

(From Elkind, 1977)

children (Köhler and Wallach, 1964). But if Piaget was right, the cognitive processes that emerge around the age of six or seven would make older children much more adept at seeing the reversal in such pictures. In this experiment, Piaget's prediction proved to be correct; Elkind and his associates found that the older the children, the more easily they reversed figure and ground.

Piaget (1969) found fault with Gestalt perceptual theory of predetermined perception on other grounds. He agreed that the first impression a child has of a picture (the figurative whole) is the result of innate organizing principles; but he argued that the final impression the older child derives after examining the picture carefully (the operative whole) was a reconstruction of pictorial elements based on the same cognitive processes that allow children to switch figure and ground. Once again his position was supported in a study by Elkind and his associates (1977), in which children looked at pictures that

consisted of large figures made up of smaller wholes (such as a man made from pieces of fruit or a scooter made from candy canes and lollipops). See Figure 8.2.

When they looked at the pictures, young children generally saw only the fruit or only the candy, although some saw only the larger figures. The young children lacked the cognitive development that would allow them to recognize that a picture could have more than one meaning. A four-year-old, therefore, tended to see apples, pears, grapes, and bananas; but a nine-year-old would describe the same picture as "a man made out of fruit." Some five- or six-year-olds could see both, but only one at a time. Such a child might say, "Some fruit. No, I mean a man." When asked to name the fruit they had mentioned, five-year-olds would deny there was any fruit in the picture. Nine-year-olds integrated the various aspects of the picture, constructing an operative whole that allowed them to see both fruit and man. From his studies, Elkind concluded that although the organizing principles described by Gestalt psychologists operate across the life span, cognitive development allows older children and adults to organize the visual field in other ways. These alternative methods of organization can become as automatic as the Gestalt principles.

According to Gibson and Spelke (1983), research with infants indicates that early picture

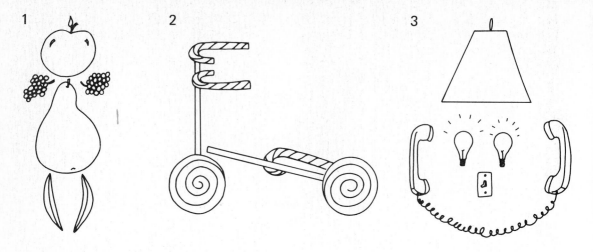

FIGURE 8.2 When young children look at pictures like these, they can see only the fruit, the candy, or the appliances. By the time children are nine, cognitive advances permit them to organize the shapes so that they can see, for example, both fruit and man in Number 1.

(From Elkind, 1977)

perception does not rely on the processes described by Gestalt psychologists, for infants show little tendency to group picture elements according to Gestalt principles. The perception of a realistic pictorial scene seems to require no special learning, and babies learn to differentiate pictured objects at the same time that they learn the distinctive features of real objects.

This view is supported by the study of a youngster who had seen neither pictures nor photographs, nor heard them referred to (Hochberg and Brooks, 1962). When the little boy was nineteen months old, he was shown his first pictures—line drawings of objects he had seen, such as shoes, skates, and airplanes. He had no trouble identifying the objects and afterward showed the same skill with photographs. Gibson argues that the little boy's accomplishments indicate that we do not need to learn to perceive pictures through associating them with real objects, and that as soon as babies learn to scan the edges of objects, they can apply that skill to drawings.

Judging depth in pictures does depend on learning, however, because the child must learn to disregard information that betrays the flat nature of the picture and to attend to cues that indicate depth. Although young children are sensitive to depth information in pictures, they do not interpret it as accurately as adults do. As they grow, their response to such information undergoes both qualitative and quantitative improvement (Gibson and Spelke, 1983). Young children use the depth cues discussed in Chapter 7 to perceive a three-dimensional scene. Three-year-olds can also use shading cues that indicate cast shadows as a portrayal of depth, but only when the pictured objects are lit from above and portrayed in their normal orientation (Yonas, Goldsmith, and Hallstrom, 1978). Children also have difficulty in interpreting the depth information in a picture unless they are positioned directly in front of it, at the "correct" viewing angle (Hagen and Jones, 1978). Yet adults can walk down the corridor in a museum and perceive the artist's rendition of a scene long before they reach the picture, while they are still viewing it at an oblique angle.

Finally, only older children seem aware of conventional techniques used to indicate movement in drawings (Friedman and Stevenson, 1975). Shown cartoon figures of a moving person, four- and six-year-olds perceived the figure as moving if it was portrayed in a running position with both legs off the ground. But they did not perceive motion when it was indicated by such conventions as clouds of dust or lines. Twelve-year-olds saw motion in both circumstances.

The Development of Place Perception

Adults take for granted their ability to find their way through the world to distant places and back again. The mental maps that make such navigation possible are the product of a perceptual skill that has its roots in infancy. As indicated in Chapter 7, babies apparently learn the spatial structure of their environment by using the information they glean from their own movements within it. How do children leap from looking in the appropriate place for a toy to navigating through the neighborhood and the wider world? The first step is in learning to rely on landmarks to guide the way (Siegel, Kirasic, and Kail, 1978).

Most studies of young children find that preschoolers are not very good at making their way around without significant landmarks (e.g., Acredolo, Pick, and Olsen, 1975), but in such studies children are usually tested after only one exposure to a strange environment. When they are familiar with a place, kindergartners move about as surely as fifth-graders. Given only a single walk through a model town, kindergartners could not reconstruct the layout nearly so well as fifth-graders, but when each group took three walks through the town, the five-year-olds were as accurate at reconstructing the layout as the ten-year-olds (Siegel, Kirasic, and Kail, 1978).

Once a child has learned to use landmarks, routes—series of landmarks—are the next step in the development of **cognitive maps**. Learning to follow a route through their neighborhood is much easier for kindergartners than reconstructing a layout. All children must do to make their way from home to school or to the store is to recognize the landmarks along the path. Alexander Siegel, Kathleen Kirasic, and Robert Kail describe routes as a kind of spatial glue that

As children grow older, their perception of places becomes more sophisticated. This boy's cognitive map of his neighborhood allows him to navigate surely through familiar streets. (Eric Kroll/Taurus)

connects the landmarks and gives shape to the spatial representation. The child progresses from knowing that a landmark is familiar to knowing where the landmark has been seen. If we put the development of cognitive maps into information-processing language, we can view the ability to recognize landmarks and associate them with places as part of the child's system of cognitive hardware; we would then view the ability to organize landmarks into routes through space and time as software—a map-making program.

Being able to map routes indicates an important cognitive advance, because the skill affects the way children think about, organize information for, and make inferences about problems that occur in large-scale environments. Linda Anooshian and her associates (1984) found that only preschoolers who had reached the route-mapping stage were able to figure out that an object "lost" by a researcher on a walk through a building and the surrounding lawn might be found somewhere between the last place it was used and the place where it was discovered missing.

Another skill involved in cognitive map making is the estimation of distance. Older children are as proficient at this skill as adults. Nine- and ten-year-olds at a boys' camp were as accurate as adults in estimating the distances between various locations in the hilly terrain of the camp (Cohen, Baldwin, and Sherman, 1978). Both children and adults overestimated distances when there were hills or barriers of some kind between locations and underestimated the distances when the land was flat and no barriers were present. Estimations of distance along a route appear to be linked with the ease of travel along the way.

Children are able to use landmarks before they can choose them efficiently. Gary Allen and his associates (1979) showed slides of a walk through a commercial neighborhood to children and adults. Asked to select scenes that would most help them remember where they went along the walk, second-graders tended to choose colorful awnings or shop displays that closely resembled other locations; fifth-graders did somewhat better, and adults picked critical landmarks, such as those indicating changes in bearing. When given a selection of slides chosen by their peers and asked to rank the pictures by their distances from a given point along the route, second-graders did poorly; and they made as many mistakes when adults chose the slides. Fifth-graders did little better than second-graders with slides chosen by their peers, but given slides picked by adults, they ranked the scenes as accurately as adults did (see Figure 8.3).

The ultimate skill in cognitive map making is to integrate various routes into a survey map of a larger area; for example, the routes from home to school, school to market, market to home, and movie to fast-food restaurant are integrated, and children can make their way from any one

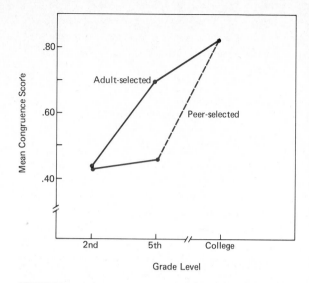

FIGURE 8.3 Regardless of whether they or adults selected critical landmarks, second-graders could not decide where along a familiar walk the markers belonged. Fifth-graders did poorly when peers selected the landmarks, but extremely well when they were selected by adults.

(From Allen et al., 1979)

point in the area to any other. The order in which children develop this ability is repeated by adults each time they must find their way around a new building, neighborhood, or city: first, landmarks; then, uncoordinated routes; finally, an integrated map that fits within an objective frame of reference. Siegel and his associates (1978) suggest that the ability to construct cognitive maps depends in part on the maturation of the child's nervous system but that the demands of the environment and the child's motivation for having the map are also extremely important.

The Development of Event Perception

Human beings get information about events as patterns of change in environmental stimulation.

During an event, part of the perceptual information changes, although the rest remains the same. Events may consist of activity, speech, or music, and the perceiver may be either an observer or an active participant (Gibson and Spelke, 1983).

Even infants are able to perceive events, but the way youngsters understand them changes with age. Some events, such as walking from the sandbox to the swings, are reversible; the child can turn around and retrace his or her steps. Other events, such as spilling a glass of milk, are irreversible; the child cannot return the milk to the glass. When shown movies of such events, four-year-olds distinguished between them (Megaw-Nyce, 1979). When the film of a reversible event was run backwards, children accepted it without comment, but when the film of an irreversible event (such as the breaking of egg) was run backwards, children were aware that the event had changed in some way that violated their understanding of it.

Events are perceived as meaningful and unified. An event's unity derives from certain unchanging stimuli, which designate its beginning and end, specify its properties, and indicate its meaning (Gibson and Spelke, 1983). In one study, the unchanging relationship of moving dots led children to perceive a meaningful event (Johansson, 1978). Schoolchildren watched the film of an actor who moved about in the dark. Although the man could not be seen, ten luminous dots attached to his major joints were visible on the screen. The children did not perceive the film as a group of moving dots. Instead, after seeing as little as 200 microseconds of the film, they said they saw a walking man.

Yet children do not perceive every event in their world. A little girl absorbed in play may not notice that her father is reporting yesterday's misbehavior to her grandmother, that a pot is boiling over on the stove, or that her mother is getting ready to go to the store. In order to perceive events, children must pay attention to them.

THE DEVELOPMENT OF ATTENTION

Attention is never haphazard, for it refers to our perceptions in relation to a task or goal—whether we are attending to a sight, a sound, a taste, a smell, or a touch (Gibson and Rader, 1979). As children grow, they deploy their attention more effectively and systematically, and the speed with which they pick up required information increases over childhood.

The efficient use of attention is a significant advance. Its importance was demonstrated by a study of young children at play (Krakow and Kopp, 1983). Some of the children in the study, who were developing normally, had just passed their second birthday. The others, who either had Down's syndrome or were developmentally delayed, were about three and a half years old. Although all children were judged to be at the same developmental level, the youngsters in the developmentally delayed group spent much more of their time doing nothing, had trouble making a transition from one play situation to another, and engaged in repetitive, regressive play typical of much younger children. The researchers believe that such behavior reflects differences in the quality of attention deployment, suggesting that the behavior of the developmentally delayed youngsters indicated a difficulty in processing stimuli and taking advantage of situations as they occur. Such behavior patterns may eventually increase a child's learning problems.

In studying attention, developmental psychologists generally focus on the way children scan new material and the selectivity of their attention.

Scanning

Children's scanning patterns reflect their interests, their expectations about the visual world, and their strategies for acquiring visual information (Day, 1975). Young children tend to scan unsystematically unless the display they are viewing has a pattern of its own. This tendency appeared when David Elkind (1977) and J. Weiss pasted pictures onto cards and showed them to children. On one card the pictures (which included such familiar objects as an ice-cream cone, a parrot, a chair, and a hat) were glued down randomly; on the other, the pictures formed a triangle. Given the random card and asked to name the objects, five-year-olds omitted some pictures and named others twice; they read off the objects in no particular order. Eight-year-olds, however, made no errors—either of omission or commission—and read off the objects from left to right and top to bottom. With the triangular picture, five-year-olds were just as accurate as the eight-year-olds. They began at the figure's apex and read off the objects, following the pattern of the triangle.

Young children not only fail to scan systematically when no structure is provided, but also tend to stop scanning before they have obtained all the information they need, so that their judgments are based on only a fragment of the available information. This was shown clearly when four- to nine-year-old children were given outline drawings of houses and asked to decide whether they were the same or different (Vurpillot and Ball, 1979). Some of the houses were identical, but others were not. The difference was always to be found in one of the windows: sometimes a window was curtained or had blinds or a birdcage hanging in it. When four-year-olds compared houses, they did not start at the top and compare each pair of windows in turn, nor did they look at every window. But nearly every one of the oldest children in the study did just that, scanning both systematically and exhaustively.

However, children do not develop in lockstep; researchers have found wide differences in scanning techniques. In a study similar to the window experiment, Eliane Vurpillot and William Ball (1979) report that one of the thirty-six five-year-olds scanned as effectively as a nine-year-old, and sixteen of the thirty-six six-year-olds were equally skilled.

Although older children scan more exhaustively, they are also more efficient and stop scanning once they have all the information they need for a task. As children grow older, they scan more rapidly—because they are processing visual information more rapidly, because they are integrating the information across glances, or because each fixation of their eyes picks up information from a wider field (Day, 1975).

All children scan downward, but until they are about five, their attention is caught by the focal point of a picture or pattern and they begin their downward scan from that point. Children who are more than five years old begin scanning from the top of a display, no matter where the main point of interest lies (Day, 1975). The context affects younger children's scanning patterns in other ways as well; when irrelevant information is added to a display, younger children find it difficult to identify figures or patterns.

All these changes in visual strategy, Mary Carol Day (1975) points out, are also found in the changing strategies children use to identify objects by touch—indicating that central cognitive processes direct children's acquisition of information through their senses.

Selectivity

Despite our wishes, some objects and events seize our attention: a building in flames, a pedestrian in a clown costume, the flashing light and siren of a patrol car, the roar of a subway train. Other sights and sounds we attend to by choice, filtering out stimuli that might distract us from our task. Young children's attention is not consciously selective; their attention seems to be captured by prominent characteristics of a stimulus. This inability to filter out what may be extraneous information may contribute to their inadequate scanning strategies. Between the age of five and seven, there appears to be a shift in the way children deploy their attention, and they begin to attend in a self-controlled, intentional, and systematic manner (Paris and Lindauer, 1982).

Their experiences in the classroom probably play a part in children's growing ability to focus their attention on a task and shut out distracting stimuli. (Tom Ballard/EKM-Nepenthe)

This shift in control may help explain why two- and three-year-olds tend to pay greater attention to the color of objects than to their form. Among four- to six-year-olds, most children pay greater attention to an object's shape (Stevenson, 1972). Such preferences may affect a child's ability to discriminate among objects and events. If asked to sort objects of various colors according to their shape, children who initially attend to shape find this task fairly easy, while those who attend to color find the task more difficult.

Not all researchers agree that the shift from color to shape matching reflects a developmental change in children's attentional preferences. After reviewing the research, Gordon Hale (1979) proposed that the shift instead reflects children's interpretation of the task they have been given. He believes that older children match by shape in part because they believe that it is what the experimenter wants them to do.

As children begin to control their attention, they are less likely to act impulsively and more likely to adapt their strategies to the nature of the task. When having children match animal pictures, researchers sometimes asked them to match the animals by size, sometimes by color, and sometimes by shape. If told about the standard for matching before they saw the pictures, sixth-graders completed the matching task more quickly and more accurately than if they received the information once the matching had begun. Apparently, they focused their attention on the prescribed task and ignored other aspects of the pictures. Second-graders, however, were no faster or more accurate when they had the information beforehand (Pick and Frankel, 1973).

As children grow older, their attention broadens, and they pick up an increasing amount of information from each stimulus. At the same time, as the matching study indicates, they develop the capability to narrow their attention, becoming increasingly selective when selective attention is necessary for the successful completion of a task (Hale, 1979). By contrast, younger children tend to respond to irrelevant cues, which hinders their performance when confronted with a problem that requires sustained attention to one or two properties and the deliberate ignoring of irrelevant aspects of the situation.

Children's performance on selective-attention tasks continues to improve with age. In one study of seven- to thirteen-year-olds, John Hagen and Gordon Hale (1973) assigned the children a simple learning task. The children were told that they would have to remember the location of some pictures that they would see. Then each child was shown a row of picture cards. On every card were two pictures, one of a common household object, such as a television set or a lamp, and one of an animal, such as a camel or a cat. The experimenter turned the cards face down and showed the child a "cue card" with one of the animals or one of the objects on it. Children were then asked to point to the one card in the set face down in front of them that pictured the same animal or object. The number of correct matches over a series of these trials was the measure of a child's **central learning**. After children were tested on picture location, which was the task given them, they were asked if they remembered which objects had been paired with which animals in the set of cards. The correct recall of the pairings measured a child's **incidental learning**.

Children who scored high on incidental learning must have paid attention to features that were irrelevant to the task described to them.

FIGURE 8.4 In Hagen and Hale's study of children's attention and learning, there was an increase with age in the average number of pictures identified correctly on the basis of their location (central-learning task). The inset (*top left*) is a sample of the cards used in the study. The average number of pictured pairings of animals and objects remained relatively constant until age thirteen, when it dropped sharply, indicating a decline in incidental learning. At about age twelve, children's selective attention becomes so powerful that they exclude extraneous material.

(Adapted from Hagen, J. W. "The Effects of Distraction on Selective Attention," *Child Development*, 38, 1967. By permission of The Society for Research in Child Development, Inc.)

Conversely, children who scored low on incidental learning must have paid little attention to the irrelevant aspects. It is reasonable to infer, therefore, that children who scored high on central learning and low on incidental learning are more selective in their attention. As instructed, they concentrated exclusively on location and hence learned little or nothing about the pairings.

As Figure 8.4 shows, there was a straightforward correlation between a child's age and his or her performance on the central-learning task. The older the child, the better his or her memory-for-position (central learning). Yet there were no significant differences in incidental-learning scores between seven- and eleven-year-olds. Among twelve- and thirteen-year-olds, the incidental-learning scores actually dropped. All children scored lower on incidental learning than on central learning.

The school experience surely plays some part in the development of selective attention, for when children enter school, they are continually presented with tasks that require them to pay sustained and formal attention to relevant parts

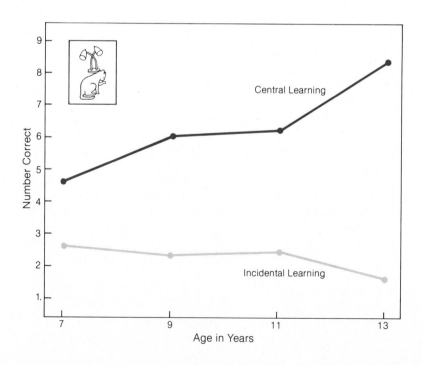

of material to be learned and to ignore irrelevant parts. For example, in learning to read, children must pay close attention to the shapes of letters and to their sequential order. The boldness of the print and the slant and size of the letters are usually irrelevant. A "p" is a "**p**," is a "*p*," but a "rose" is not a "sore" is not an "eros"; nor is an "o" identical to a "q" or a "c."

As children begin using various strategies to focus their attention, adapting them to the particular task at hand, they apparently become aware of factors that affect attention (Paris and Lindauer, 1982). This awareness in turn leads to more effective strategies. When first-graders were asked about their ability to pay attention, avoid distraction, and the like, they told researchers that the major influence on their attention was the noise level (Miller and Bigi, 1979). Fifth-graders had a more sophisticated view of attention; they said that motivation, mental effort, and being able to resist temptation were also extremely important.

As we have seen, even the youngest children are capable of directing their attention to a task at hand, and this capacity continually improves with age. As children mature, their past experiences lead them to concentrate on what they expect will be the relevant aspects of the situation, and they pick up more information, requiring less time to do so. According to Eleanor Gibson and Nancy Rader (1979), this development comes about in part because of children's increasing ability to find structure and order in what they perceive.

Television and Attention

Television is a powerful source of information that pervades the life of almost every American child. Since it is present in the child's environment almost from birth, psychologists have wondered just how soon youngsters begin to absorb information from it. To answer this question, they have studied the child's attention to television programs.

Most children do not begin to watch television in the sense of systematically following a program until they are about two and a half years old (Anderson, 1979). Before that time, they appear to have their attention captured for a minute or two at a time but soon return to their play or to interacting with their mothers. Daniel Anderson believes that until they are thirty months old, children simply lack the cognitive ability to grasp the meaning of related images and sound.

According to Anderson, once children begin following television programs, their viewing is a blend of passive and active cognitive activities, but probably more active than passive. Older children often play with their toys while they watch television, but they divide their attention, frequently glancing at the screen. Whether or not a child pays attention to the screen depends on the sound, camera techniques, and content of the program, and on the behavior of peers. Anderson has found that children's voices, peculiar voices, women's voices, sound effects, applause, laughter, and a change in the quality of the sound attract a preschooler's attention from toys to the screen. Such sounds tell children that the program is changing or that whatever is going on will interest them. They then watch until the program becomes incomprehensible or boring. Men's voices, on the other hand, seem to inhibit children's attention. They do not look up when a man's voice accompanies the picture, perhaps because they have learned that the adult male voice indicates a program that is abstract or of interest only to adults.

Camera techniques can also affect children's attention. Elizabeth Susman (1978) found that four-year-olds stop watching when the camera zooms in for a close-up, and she suggests that the zoom removes the focused material from the visual flow of events and interferes with the young child's processing of part-whole relationships.

Children control the attention they pay to television and seem to pick up information even when they do not watch the screen closely. Elizabeth Lorch, Anderson, and Stephen Levin (1979) had five-year-olds watch "Sesame Street" under two different conditions, either with their parents and a selection of attractive toys or just

Youngsters often divide their attention between television and their toys. Should a change in sound indicate that something worth watching may be on the screen, these youngsters will switch their attention from their book to the television program. (Mark Antman/The Image Works)

with their parents. The children with the toys watched the screen half as much as did the children who had nothing to play with, but subsequent tests indicated that both groups remembered about the same amount.

Five-year-olds are sensitive to the demands of a program: they watch the screen when the information being presented is primarily visual and play with their toys when the information is primarily auditory. Yet tests on the program content show that they are processing the auditory material even when their attention seems directed elsewhere (Pezdek and Hartman, 1983). Apparently, when placed in natural situations,

five-year-olds process information more efficiently than they do in laboratory studies when they are asked to match pictures.

Not all a child's television viewing is active. Anderson and his associates (1979) have found what they call "attentional inertia," in which the longer children watch a television program, the more probable it is that they will continue to do so. In this process, attention is not bound to content, for it does not change when a program made up of segments, such as "Sesame Street," switches from one segment to another. Anderson's group regard attentional inertia as the opposite of habituation, and they describe it as an involuntary response to a somewhat unpredictable, meaningful, dynamic stimulus. This sounds rather like the "plug-in drug" described by television's critics, but Anderson's group do not see children as the victims of hypnosis. Instead, they regard attentional inertia as a way for a child to keep processing material he or she does not understand, allowing the child to venture into unknown cognitive territory, perhaps to make an intellectual discovery.

THE DEVELOPMENT OF REPRESENTATION

In order for children to remember people, objects, and events, they must have some way to store the information so that they can retrieve it at the proper time. A six-year-old boy recognizes Aunt Ellen, remembers Mother's promise to go to the circus, and decides whether he would rather go and play at a friend's house or stay home and watch television by relying on his **representations**—the models he constructs to store information in memory. These representations form his understanding of the world, and without them he could not function socially, as the box on page 251 indicates.

We represent knowledge in various ways, and in thinking about various representational systems, suggests Jean Mandler (1983), it helps to consider the distinction between "knowing how" and "knowing that." "Knowing how" is the knowledge of procedures: we know how to drive a car or hit a baseball or find the square root of a number, just as a computer knows (from the instructions in its software) how to manipulate the data it is given. Knowledge that is represented in the form of procedures is embedded information; normally we are not conscious of it. Some **procedural knowledge** cannot be thought about at all (for example, knowledge about how our heart beats). And some of it can be brought to mind only by running through the procedure—either physically or mentally.

"Knowing that" is the knowledge of facts: we know that birds fly, that the name of the oldest president of the United States is Ronald Reagan, and that the square root of 9 is 3, just as the computer knows whatever facts have been included as part of its data base. We continually add new facts to our cognitive system, and call already stored facts to mind.

Piaget believed that infants are capable only of procedural knowledge until they reach the final substage of the sensorimotor period. He held this position because he believed that procedural knowledge is not based on representation. Piaget reserved the term *representation* for symbolic thought and conceptualization. As we have seen, researchers have been discovering that the infant's representational abilities may be more sophisticated than Piaget believed.

Representation may capture knowledge about actions (*enactive representation*), images (*imaginal representation*), symbols (*linguistic representation*), or categories (*categorical representation*), and representations may be changed after they are stored (*operative representation*). According to Jerome Bruner (1973), the enactive, imaginal, and linguistic systems develop consecutively as the child grows, each depending on the previous system for its emergence, and each demonstrating the child's increased ability to differentiate self from the environment. No system is ever discarded, and events that have been represented in one system can be translated into either of the other two. Although Piaget believed that representations undergo a structural change during childhood, many other developmentalists assume that the basic structures remain the same (Mandler, 1983). However, some changes in representation may occur; for example, representations may become more elaborate and more highly differentiated.

Enactive Representation

Young babies cannot separate themselves from the world and the objects within it. To them, "The world is what I do with it" (McCall, 1979b). For this reason, the earliest way of representing an event is through **enactive representation,** or motor responses. As Bruner puts it, the child literally defines events by the actions they evoke. Enactive representation is entirely procedural and limited to perception and motor action.

Perceptions and actions are so intertwined that during the middle of the baby's first year, the infant finds it difficult to separate them. When a seven-month-old girl drops her rattle, she continues to shake her fist as if it still clutched the toy, expecting the action to bring back the rattle. She relies on enactive representation, as did the babies in the last chapter who used their bodies as a guide when finding the window where they had seen the show. Enactive representation is used throughout life; adults rely on it for such skills as tying knots, typing, riding a bicycle, playing the piano, and the routine aspects of driving.

Imaginal Representation

As babies begin to distinguish between themselves and the world, they develop **imaginal representation,** or imagery, mentally visualizing objects that are out of sight. Perception and action can be separated; the infant can imagine a lost toy without going through the motions connected with it. The ability to form images greatly expands the infant's world.

Although Piaget believed that infants did not form images until the last stage of the sensorimotor period, Bruner believes that the ability develops toward the end of the first year. Both propose that imagery continues to dominate the thinking of young children, even after they have acquired language. In this view, children store most information in images, not words. This tendency makes their thought relatively inflexible. For example, although they can reorganize and reproduce three-dimensional arrangements, they cannot mentally manipulate them. If an experimenter asks them to reproduce a complicated arrangement of graduated blocks, they can do so exactly; but if asked to rearrange the display so that the tiny block that was on the left is on the right, they cannot do it.

Other theorists, among them Stephen Kosslyn (1978), believe that although preschoolers probably rely more on imaginal representation than older children and adults do, they use abstract representation as well. However, many young children apparently find it easier to think in images. Kosslyn (1983) asked six- and ten-year-old children to think about an animal, then asked them whether the animal possessed a particular feature (such as horns or a tail). Next he asked them to form an image of an animal and inspect the image to see if it had a particular

feature. After these instructions, some of the six-year-olds said, "Oh, you want me to do what I did last time again!" When asked to visualize the animals, both six- and ten-year-olds could answer questions about large features that were not highly associated with the animal (head on a cat; back on a mouse) more quickly than they could identify small features that were closely associated with the animal (claws on a cat; whiskers on a mouse). Presumably, the youngsters had to "zoom in" on their images to inspect small details. But when not told to visualize the animals, most ten-year-olds and a few of the six-year-olds identified the small, typical features more quickly, just as adults do. His research led Kosslyn to speculate that such information was stored abstractly and was easily available when the animal was brought to mind. Presumably, the rest of the children were still relying primarily on imaginal representation.

Like enactive representation, imaginal representation is used throughout life. When Kosslyn asks adults, "What shape are a Doberman pinscher's ears?" they tell him that in order to answer the question, they mentally picture the dog and then inspect its ears. However, if asked enough times about the dog's ears, they answer immediately and without visualizing the dog's head. Apparently, this bit of information eventually is stored in a more abstract form.

Linguistic Representation

Words and symbols are much more powerful forms of representation than motor patterns and imagery. Symbols are both arbitrary and remote; a word does not resemble the thing for which it stands, as does the visual image. Symbols can also be detached from the objects they represent and be manipulated, as they are in language.

Language is powerful because it is highly productive; its rules for the formation of sentences allow the child not only to represent experience but to transform it as well (Bruner, 1973). As we shall see in Chapter 9, two-year-olds know words but not the rules for combining them. Until children grasp a language's structure, words serve primarily as pointers, even though the pointing might be toward an unseen cookie in the kitchen.

With symbolic representation, children develop an increasing capacity to attend to multiple aspects of the environment and to track several sequences at one time (Bruner, Olver, and Greenfield, 1966). Symbols compress meaning so that much more can be held in the immediate consciousness at one time.

Bruner's belief in the power and primacy of language contrasts with Piagetian theory, for Bruner believes that language is at the root of the increase in problem-solving skills that appears in children around the age of six, whereas Piaget maintained that language is merely a symptom of that change and not its source.

When Bruner and Piaget first proposed their theories of representation, psychologists believed that most information was stored either in images or words. Today psychologists believe that information tends to be stored in more abstract forms, and that linguistic representations, instead of being stored as words, are stored as propositions—the abstract ideas underlying a concept. If this is true, young children—and perhaps even older infants—may use propositional storage as well as enactive and imaginal storage.

Categorical Representation

Without **concepts,** which are symbols with many examples, it would be difficult to deal with the world. Each instance of an object— every blade of grass, every pencil, every apple, every wristwatch—would have its own name. By conceiving of similar objects as a single concept, we economize on language and mental effort. Because we have concepts, the symbol "dog" stands for all the dogs in a little girl's world, but the symbol "Prince" refers only to her own puppy. Concepts allow children to divide the world into categories, simplifying its

overwhelming diversity and giving the child a way to deal with the unfamiliar. Once children have categorized scalloped potatoes as food or a dachshund as a dog, they can make inferences about them, in the expectation that the items share properties common to their class (Anglin, 1977). Food can be eaten and it is likely to taste good; dogs wag their tails, chase balls, and bark.

But how do children (and adults, for that matter) discover what objects belong to what category, and how do they place new members into the correct class? Eleanor Rosch (1973) suggests that each concept is built around a **prototype,** which consists of the very best examples of the concept. The prototype is surrounded by other members of decreasing similarity to those in the center. Thus, a robin or a canary is a central member of the bird category, closely resembling the prototypical bird, but a penguin or an ostrich is a peripheral member, having fewer of the prototype's attributes in the correct relationship.

As we saw in Chapter 7, concepts develop before babies can talk, indicating the nonlinguistic nature of their representation, at least during early development. Ten-month-old infants who saw schematic drawings of animals were able to abstract the relationship among the animal's features and recognize (in the sense of being bored with) another animal from the same category (Younger and Cohen, 1983). Although children this young are supposed to be limited to procedural knowledge, these infants displayed factually based knowledge—"knowing that." Jean Mandler (1983) believes that the ability to categorize the world is a natural by-product of assimilation and accommodation and that as babies form schemes they are also developing concepts.

As yet, psychologists are not sure how infants and children form prototypes. It is generally agreed that both the perceptual qualities and the function of objects are important in concept formation, but debate continues over which aspect is dominant. Katherine Nelson (1979) believes that children base the core of their concepts on function, grouping objects by their uses and actions. The process begins in infancy, and once a youngster has organized a concept in terms of its function (dogs run, bark, wag their tails, bite), he or she progresses to the next step: identifying the perceptual features that define it (dogs have furry coats, four legs, a tail). Only after the concept is developed in this way does the child attach a name to it.

Function continues to dominate among preschoolers (Nelson, 1978). Asked to respond to a word with "the first word you think of," four-year-olds will respond to "bread" with "eat." As children grow, their concepts cease to be dominated by function. Older children respond to word association requests as adults do, with other class members, synonyms, opposites, or the name of the class. To the word "bread," they might reply "food" or "butter"; to "apple," the response might be "fruit" or "pear."

Although they agree that function is often the essence of concept meaning, other investigators believe that perceptual features are more central than Nelson assumes. Jeremy Anglin (1977) speculates that young children initially rely on perceptual features, developing some sort of visual image of a concept such as "apple" or "dog" or "car," based on the first object in the class the child hears named. As they grow older, children supplement the imaginal representation with a propositional representation of the attributes that determine the concept. In the case of dog, the attributes might be furry coat, four legs, a tail, barks, wags its tail, bites. In this theory of concept formation, the child's original representation is never lost. It is simply supplemented with increasingly exact, abstract, and more highly differentiated descriptions.

Older children who know the attributes that determine a concept (food is edible, clothes are wearable) sometimes exclude peripheral items from it (such as lollipops and hats). Anglin believes that children often fail to coordinate their knowledge of category membership with the attributes that determine membership, and he points out that preschool children often have difficulty in specifying the critical attributes of a familiar concept.

Categories are arranged in a hierarchy, based on levels of abstraction: subordinate, basic, and superordinate. The **subordinate level** is most specific, consisting of such items as dachshunds, teaspoons, and coffee tables. At the **basic level** (dogs, spoons, and tables), category members are most like one another and most different from members of other categories. At this level, we can visualize the prototype. This is the most useful level for daily activities, and the one children learn first (Rosch et al., 1976). **Superordinate categories** (animals, eating utensils, and furniture) are highly generalized and rely more heavily on function than on appearance. The name of a superordinate category does not tell us enough about an object to allow us to visualize it.

The foundation for the later understanding of superordinate categories is laid down in infancy, as older infants observe such similarities as the similar usage of knives, forks, and spoons, the similar treatment of dogs and cats, and hear their parents or siblings refer to the superordinate category (Mandler, 1983). As children become more adept at language, they must figure out the relationships among dogs and cats and animals. Piaget (Inhelder and Piaget, 1964) believed that children did not understand superordinate categories until they were seven or eight years old and into the concrete operational period.

Yet a number of recent studies have indicated that younger children represent objects in superordinate as well as basic-level categories. When asked directly about superordinate categories, five-year-olds understand them, although they often either overgeneralize or undergeneralize their breadth (Mervis, 1980). Asked for examples of "furniture," they are likely to respond with anything that is found in the house (such as a broom), and asked for "animals," they are likely to confine their list to mammals. However, Mandler (1983) found that five-year-olds considered insects to be more similar to other animals than they were to plants. In one study, three-year-olds who were asked to put together pictures that are "all the same kind of thing" had no trouble sorting them at the basic level (cars), but could not sort them at

The Autistic Child's Mind

For more than forty years, researchers have been trying to solve the puzzle of the autistic child. **Autism,** a severe mental disorder that appears by the time a child is thirty months old, was first described by Leo Kanner in 1943. Autistic children seem unable to develop social relationships; for example, they do not even form a close bond with their parents. They show little social imitation, and they rarely engage in make-believe play. Their language development is retarded, and when they use speech, it is usually not to communicate; instead they repeat stereotyped phrases or the words of others. They engage in ritualistic or compulsive behavior, and many tend to make stereotyped, repetitive movements—such as flapping their arms, spinning about, or flicking their fingers (Rutter, 1978). Recent studies of twins suggest that the disorder has a genetic cause, one associated with a recessive gene (Goleman, 1985).

Although many autistic children are retarded, some are intelligent. Believing that the language problems of autistic children reflected deeper problems in information processing, Beate Hermelin (1978) compared autistic children with normal and with perceptually impaired children of similar intellectual levels. In one study, normal, deaf, and autistic children looked at a series of three letters that appeared one at a time in a series of horizontal windows—but never in a left-to-right order. All children recalled the letters equally well. The normal children treated the visually presented verbal material as if the letters had been spoken, recalling them in the order in which they had appeared (first to last). But the deaf children recalled the letters in a left-to-right order, indicating they had used a visual, spatially ordered code. They apparently had stored an image of the display, then read off the letters from left to right. Autistic children behaved like the deaf children.

In Hermelin's second study, autistic and normal children were blindfolded, then compared with blind children. The children extended two fingers of each hand, one in front of the other. Researchers taught them to associate a different word, such as "run" or "walk," with one finger on each hand. When the researcher touched the finger, the child was to respond with the word. Then children were told to reverse their hands, so that the "run" finger was now where the "walk" finger, had been and vice versa. Then the researcher again touched the fingers. Normal children tended to change their response, apparently relying on a visual code and associating the word with a spatial position. But blind children kept the original association between word and finger, responding exactly as they had before. In this study, autistic children behaved like the blind children.

Hermelin suggests that autistic children behave like blind and deaf children because they are unable to extract, code, and organize incoming information. Autistic children rely almost entirely on the information that is presented to them at any moment, failing to integrate current and past experiences. Such mental inflexibility, suggests Hermelin, may prevent them from forming representations of external events, so that autistic children are generally unable to use symbol systems, such as language.

---

the superordinate level (transportation). But four-year-olds knew that cars and trains were similar (Rosch and Mervis, 1977).

Perhaps youngsters find it difficult to draw on their hierarchical information in some situations. According to Ellen Markman (1981), the problem may lie in the possibility that young children assume that superordinate terms are collective nouns (like "orchestra" or "army"), which is a distortion of hierarchical categorization. For example, very young children may agree that a group of toys are "toys." Asked, "Show me a ball," the child picks up a ball from the group of assorted toys. Asked, "Show me a toy," the child will pick up a ball and a doll. If the researcher points to a ball and says, "Is this a toy?" the child will say, "No." In Chapter 10, we explore this aspect of categorization further.

Operative Representation

Once information is represented, proposed Jean Piaget and Bärbel Inhelder (1973), its representations may change as children undergo cognitive development and as their understanding of the world improves. In such cases, cognition and memory interact, and the representation improves. Because this changed representation is the result of the child's mental operations on stored representations, Piaget and Inhelder called it an **operative representation.** Most instances of operative representation seem to involve the improvement of imaginal representations.

To demonstrate this sort of change, Piaget and Inhelder showed children a group of ten sticks of various lengths and asked them to draw the arrangement from memory. After six months, the same children, asked to redraw the sticks, often produced copies that were closer to the original display than were their first drawings. Apparently, memory is not passive, simply serving up a faithful representation of original perceptions. Instead, as children's comprehension develops, their representations change to conform to their new understanding. According to Piaget and Inhelder, memory actively and selectively constructs the past, using schemes (or mental operations) borrowed from intelligence.

Some studies have supported Piaget and Inhelder's explanation. Hans Furth, Bruce Ross, and James Youniss (1974) showed children ranging in age from five through nine years a picture

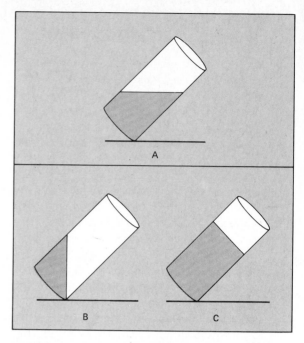

FIGURE 8.5 A tilted-glass experiment like that carried out by Furth, Ross, and Youniss. *(A)* Depiction of the actual angle of the level of liquid in a tilted glass. *(B* and *C)* Depiction of the angle reproduced by two children.

(Adapted from Furth, Ross, and Youniss, 1974)

of a glass tilted from the horizontal base to a forty-five-degree angle, as in Choice A of Figure 8.5. The children were told: "This is a glass with cola in it. It is tilted and on a table. Now draw this picture on your paper, just the way you see it here."

Many children do not realize that the level of liquid remains horizontal with respect to the table even though the glass is tilted. They have not yet acquired this particular understanding of spatial transformations, even though they have seen numerous tilted glasses of milk, water, juice, and cola. Piaget would say that they have not yet developed the operative scheme of spatial coordinates, referring to the mental operations of middle childhood's concrete operational period, in which children apply logical thought to concrete objects.

At varying intervals, the same children again drew the tilted glass from memory. Furth and his associates found that the oldest children always did better than the rest at reproducing the drawing. In sessions held six months later, twenty out of the one hundred and sixteen children drew more accurate pictures than they had drawn shortly after they saw the picture of the glass. Although only 17 percent of the children showed such improvement, the finding goes against our belief that representations either remain the same or else deteriorate over time. The investigators maintain that, during the six-month interval, these children had acquired a more sophisticated understanding of what happens to the level of contained liquids. As they developed the necessary operative schemes, they reconstructed their representations. Inhelder (1976) concludes that children do not represent what they see in their memories; instead, they represent their own understanding of the model before them. Apparently, advances in cognitive maturity actively modify the child's representations.

Yet not all children's representations improved with time. In many cases, children in both Piaget's and Furth's experiments did worse, not better, after six months had passed. For example, in one experiment children who had seen four matches in a straight row and, below them, another four matches arranged in the rough shape of a W (see Figure 8.6), sometimes added extra matches to their drawings (Type 1) or lengthened the matches that made up the W (Type 2) in order to make the two rows equal in length (Inhelder, 1976). Because their operative schemes for number and spatial systems were developing at different rates, suggests Inhelder, the two schemes were in conflict. Many of the children understood that each line has the same number of matches, but did not understand that the zig-zag line of matches was actually as long as the straight line. As a result, memory was dominated by a tendency to equalize the lines.

Operative representation may not always affect memory in the way that Piaget and Inhelder

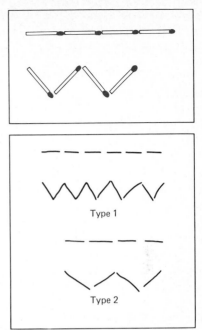

FIGURE 8.6 In a test of operative representation, children had to draw displays they had seen six months earlier (*top*). The performance of a number of children deteriorated as they attempted to equalize the lines. For example, some children added extra matches (Type 1) and others lengthened the matches in the bottom line (Type 2) (*bottom*).

(From D. Elkind and J. H. Flavell, eds. *Studies in Cognitive Development: Essays in Honor of Jean Piaget.* New York: Oxford University Press, 1969. Copyright © 1969 by Oxford University Press, Inc. Reprinted by permission.)

suggest. Although most studies have shown a correlation between children's understandings of the various physical principles involved in the models and their later drawings, Lynn Liben (1977) has found that some children reproduce the models accurately even if they have done poorly on previous tests of their understanding. Further, changes in understanding do not always result in improved drawings, nor do improved drawings always reflect changes in understanding. The operative theory of representation and memory, therefore, looks promising but is not yet completely understood.

THE DEVELOPMENT OF MEMORY

The retention and recall of past experience, which we call memory, forms the basis of cognition. Systematic investigations of its development in children have covered how information is acquired, stored, retained, and retrieved, as well as how much children understand about the workings of their memory processes (Kail and Hagen, 1977; Kail and Spear, 1984; Ornstein, 1978; Weinert and Perlmutter, in press). This research has generally been founded on assumptions based either on a Piagetian view or an information-processing view.

From Piaget's point of view, memory cannot be separated from the rest of intelligence, and the way to understand memory is to understand the development of cognition in general. In the preceding discussion of operative representation, we saw some implications that follow from his view of memory as an active construction of the mind that is tied to mental patterns of action.

From an information-processing point of view, memory is the transfer of information within the child's cognitive system. Researchers study the various processes involved in the transfer, expecting that an understanding of the mechanisms of memory will increase our understanding of cognition (Perlmutter, 1980).

Many information-processing theorists (e.g., Atkinson and Shiffrin, 1968), divide the hardware of the memory system into three types of memory storage: **sensory registers,** where information is recorded but decays within three to five seconds; **short-term store,** a temporary, working memory, where we are conscious of the active information; and **long-term store,** where information is held permanently. The strategies we use to help us remember information are part of the software that keeps information flowing through the system. Developmental differences in memory, according to this view, result from the techniques children use to make sure information does not get lost in the early stages of memory, and those they use to get it back out of long-term memory. These techniques are fairly well developed by the time children are twelve or thirteen years old (Naus, Ornstein, and Hoving, 1978).

Some information-processing theorists (e.g., Cermak and Craik, 1979) deemphasize various structures in memory and instead concentrate on stages of processing, from initial pattern recognition of stimuli to the extraction of meaning and the elaboration of relevant information. In this **levels-of-processing** approach, incoming information is thought to be processed at deeper and deeper levels of analysis, from a shallow perceptual level to deeper levels of meaning. Information that receives only a shallow analysis soon decays and is forgotten; information that is analyzed at a meaning level is retained. Researchers who adopt this approach attribute developmental differences in memory to increasingly skillful ways of storing material at deeper levels. As a child gets older, this ability improves (Naus, Ornstein, and Hoving, 1978).

Taken together, studies of children's memory seem to indicate that storage capacity does not change greatly with age. Once something is lodged in memory, a preschooler will probably remember it as well as an adult (Werner and Perlmutter, 1979). The young child's problem is in getting the material stored in the first place and then in recalling it from storage. Why is this procedure so difficult? Some researchers have considered the child's problem in terms of a processing limitation in short-term, or working, memory (Case, Kurland, and Goldberg, 1982). In their view, the actual amount of space in working memory does not increase with age, but a larger amount of holding space becomes available. When a young child tries to **encode** information (put it into memory) or **retrieve** information (get it back out again), most of the processing space in working memory may be taken up by the encoding or retrieval processes themselves. In the course of development, the child becomes more efficient at processing information, processing it faster and almost automatically. If less space is needed for carrying out basic processes, then more room will be available to hold information and manipulate it in complex ways. This allows children to develop increasingly sophisticated programs for encoding and retrieval.

Types of Remembering

Material that children (or adults) retain must be stored in some form, whether enactive, imaginal, linguistic, or some more abstract form of representation. No matter how the information is stored, children demonstrate their retention of material by recognition, reconstruction, or recall.

RECOGNITION **Recognition** requires only that we perceive an object as something that has been perceived in the past. It is the simplest form of remembering, for it takes place in the presence of the original object. Because of this simplicity, Piaget regarded recognition as a primitive process that is found in many lower animals, including frogs, fish, lizards, and birds (Piaget and Inhelder, 1973). A familiar example of recognition in action is a multiple-choice test. Given three possible answers, the task is to recognize the correct response, as opposed to recalling the answer on a completion test. According to Piaget, recognition is based on perception and on patterns of simple motor actions; therefore it is within the capacity of very young infants. Recognition is also the simplest form of memory from the standpoint of information processing. In order to recognize a person or a toy, a baby must only match a present perception with a representation in memory, a relatively simple operation (Perlmutter and Lange, 1978).

At any age, the more complex the stimulus, the longer it takes to become familiar with it (Werner and Perlmutter, 1979). In one study,

toddlers between the ages of twenty-nine and forty-four months looked at six pictures from a single category, such as animals, until they tired of watching them. Then the youngsters were shown the same six pictures, six additional pictures of animals, and six pictures from an entirely different group, such as fruit. The toddlers looked least at the familiar animal pictures, most at the fruit. Because the new animals seemed less interesting than the fruit, the researchers assumed that the toddlers not only remembered the animal pictures they had seen but also generalized their familiarity to other members of the same group (Faulkender, Wright, and Waldron, 1974). But as Perlmutter (1980) has pointed out, because the children were not asked about the pictures, there is no way to tell whether they realized they had seen the familiar pictures before. It is possible that differences in attention are automatic and do not reflect a conscious awareness of memory.

Toddlers can tell a researcher if they have previously seen an object, so Nancy Myers and Perlmutter (1978) studied the way recognition develops in preschoolers by showing youngsters eighteen small, attractive objects. Later the children looked at thirty-six objects: the eighteen they had seen before and eighteen new ones. Two-year-olds were correct in their judgments on 81 percent of the objects; four-year-olds on 92 percent. Both groups were extremely accurate at realizing they had never before seen an object; two-year-olds did about as well as four-year-olds. But four-year-olds were more accurate at recognizing familiar objects, an indication that during early childhood there is some improvement in children's ability to represent or to retain the memory of objects.

By the time children are ready for school, their recognition memory is very good, at least for simple stimuli. With more complex stimuli, requiring skilled scanning and registration of information, they generally do not do so well (Perlmutter, 1984). Children's lack of experience may also hinder their recognition skills, because some types of recognition depend on knowledge the child has already acquired (Brown et al.,

1983). Adults, with their vast store of knowledge, recognize abstract pictures that they have labeled better than five-year-olds do, but five-year-olds are as proficient as adults in recognizing pictures of realistic objects (Nelson and Kosslyn, 1976). As for retention itself, once information is processed, age may not have any effect on the length of time a memory is retained (Werner and Perlmutter, 1979).

RECONSTRUCTION Their studies of children led Jean Piaget and Bärbel Inhelder (1973) to suggest that there is an intermediate form of producing retrieved material, which they call **reconstruction.** This form of memory involves reproducing the form of information that has been seen in the past. Reconstructive memory, for example, allows children to take material (sticks, matches, checkers) and arrange it to resemble a model seen an hour, a week, or six months previously. Children's reconstructive memory is superior to their recall, said Piaget, because when children manipulate concrete objects, they intentionally repeat the natural order of events, calling their action schemes, or patterns of motor skills, into play. In the studies described in the earlier section on operative representation, for example, children who reconstructed the models they had seen, using sticks or matches, were more accurate than children who drew the models.

Even children younger than those Piaget tested show strong reconstructive memory. When toddlers were asked to reconstruct a display of eight small toys, replacing each toy in the correct compartment of a plain wooden box, both two- and three-year-olds did well. Each group got 75 percent of the toys in the right slot. But when researchers substituted an eight-room dollhouse for the plain wooden box, two-year-olds did worse and three-year-olds did better. The younger children may have been distracted by the interesting dollhouse, so that their attention was not on the original task of remembering where the toys were placed. The older children may have used the various locations in the dollhouse as an aid to memory (the ball goes in the kitchen) (Cohen, Perlmutter, and Myers, 1977).

In a similar experiment with older children, Susan Golbeck (1983) asked five- to nine-year-olds to replace furniture in a four-room "house," made by outlining the rooms on the floor with masking tape. The furniture in each room was identical except for its color and the pattern of chair cushions. No matter what their age, children who had earlier shown classification skills typical of Piaget's concrete operational level were most successful at putting the furniture back in its original arrangement.

RECALL **Recall,** the most complex of the ways people demonstrate memory, takes place in the absence of the material remembered. It is a goal-directed, cognitive skill that appears to be stimulated by environmental demands (Perlmutter and Lange, 1978). When a society requires well-organized recall, its members develop the skill, using supports provided by the culture—an example is the memorizing of epic poems that preserve the history of a nonliterate culture. Unlike recognition, which appears to be similar in all groups, recall varies according to the requirements of a culture (Cole and Scribner, 1977).

Piaget and Inhelder (1973) believed that recall is impossible in children who are less than a year old, because it depends on symbolic functions. (Unlike Bruner, Piaget includes mental imagery in the category of symbols.) Internalized images reinstitute the memory on a symbolic level rather than as action, as in reconstruction. For this reason, the emergence of recall is a significant step in cognitive development. Described in information-processing terms, recall requires children to generate material internally. Recall, if it is to be efficient, involves special skills to establish the material in memory so that it may be retrieved (Perlmutter, 1984).

Although preschoolers are beginning to organize their memories around concepts, their recall is poor. When playing a "remembering" game with a researcher, three- and four-year-olds had trouble recalling nine small, attractive objects even though they knew that they could keep each object they remembered (Perlmutter and Myers, 1979). Sometimes each object the children saw was from a different conceptual category (bell, clock, drum, flag, horse, leaf, pen, star, truck); the rest of the time there were three objects from each of three different categories (animals, utensils, transportation). After the researcher showed each object to the child, labeled it, and replaced it in a box, the child tried to recall what he or she had seen. Three-year-olds tended to remember about two items; four-year-olds remembered three or four items. Both groups did better on the list of related objects, indicating the conceptual organization of their memory. Moreover, when the experimenter provided conceptual cues ("Do you remember any more animals?"), their recall improved. Most children showed an "echo-box" effect; that is, they remembered the very last object they had seen, as if that were the only item stored in their immediate memory.

Their incompetence at recall may be due to a number of factors that affect memory. Preschoolers appear to be ignorant of strategies (such as rehearsal or clustering) that help register information in memory. They may be limited by their inappropriate search tendencies (such as their propensity to recall the last object shown). They may have difficulty in internally generating material. Finally, their limited verbal ability may limit their production of available information (Perlmutter, 1984).

Preschoolers are rarely required to engage in deliberate memorization of the sort demanded by laboratory studies. They all sing advertising jingles and nursery rhymes, however, and their recall of parental promises seems almost perfect. When three- and four-year-olds were studied in their homes, they showed an amazing amount of recall about their experiences (Todd and Perlmutter, 1980). These recollections were both spontaneous and in response to a researcher's questions. Most episodes were social, involving the preschoolers themselves or other people. Only 12 percent of the incidents they recalled

involved objects, the favorite focus of laboratory research, and 11 percent involved the antics of cartoon characters. Almost half the events the children recalled had taken place within the preceding month, although a third of them had happened more than three months before. Older children produced more spontaneous recollections than did the younger children, and those recollections were more likely to involve unusual events, as opposed to everyday occurrences that dominated the younger children's free recall.

In addition to studying memory in daily life, some researchers have begun to study social influences on memory—particularly the ways in which parents influence their children's memory. In one such study, Rebecca Eder and her associates (1984) had three- and five-year-olds work some puzzles on their own and work others with their mothers. Working a puzzle with his or her mother improved a three-year-old's memory of the puzzle, but had no effect on the memory of the five-year-old. Apparently, the five-year-olds already were competent puzzle solvers; they played skillfully with puzzles, even when they had to solve them on their own, and they remembered them quite well. Three-year-olds were at an earlier stage of puzzle-solving skill, and their mothers' comments as they worked together on the puzzles seemed to structure the activity in a way that improved their later retention. Many of the youngsters' everyday experiences may well be structured in a similar manner, with parents laying the framework for their children's independent encoding and retention of events in their world.

When children enter school, their recall continues to improve. When six- or seven-year-olds recall a story, for example, they recall it much as an adult would (Kail and Hagen, 1982). Most youngsters recall the important features of the stories but not incidental facts. They recall the meaning of the sentences they have heard but not their exact wording. And they often "recall" information that was not actually part of the story but that is consistent in meaning with what they have heard.

Among older children, this elaborated recall

Childhood Amnesia

Few of us have coherent memories from early childhood. Try as we might, all we can dredge up are a few fleeting, fragmentary memories of those early years—disconnected scenes or sensations. Researchers tend to agree that narrative memories of events go back no farther than the age of five or six years (White and Pillemer, 1979). Why is it virtually impossible to recall our experiences during those early years?

The most popular explanation comes from psychoanalysis. As children become socialized, they supposedly view their early sexual feelings and their incestuous impulses during the turbulent phallic period as perverse (see Chapter 1). These early feelings become so shameful that children repress all memories, locking them in the unconscious where they are no longer available.

Another explanation was offered by Ernest Schachtel (1947), who believed that childhood amnesia was an inevitable outcome of socialization. As children are molded into members of the culture, the forms of memory change. The acquisition of language changes the way events are represented and stored, a change that is accelerated by schooling, with its demands that thought be expressed in an organized fashion. Instead of storing events as they are experienced, in terms of their smells, tastes, sounds, and bodily sensations,

the child comes to store symbolic representations. The old memories are not compatible with the new forms of memory storage and retrieval. Trying to recall an incident from early childhood is rather like trying to run a BASIC program on a computer that was designed to handle FORTRAN.

This reorganization of memory processes may also be influenced by biological factors. When children are about five years old, an area of the brain known as the *hippocampus* matures (Rose, 1979). The hippocampus, which is located in a part of the brain that evolved before the cortex (see Chapter 6), is deeply involved in memory. When the hippocampus is damaged in adults, they can no longer lay down new memories of events (Hecaen and Albert, 1978). Neural maturation of this area may pave the way for the sort of memory reorganization that is responsible for childhood amnesia.

But how does this memory reorganization take place? Sheldon White and David Pillemer (1979) believe that it comes about through changes in the way youngsters process information. At about the age of five or six, children's information-processing capacity improves so that they can manipulate more than one idea or piece of information at a time. The assumed increase in available space allows children to process events at a deeper level, reorganizing them and storing them in a way that makes later retrieval pos-

goes further: they make inferences about the stories they are told, remembering actions and actors that were not mentioned in the story, but only implied. For example, if they are told that a nail was driven into a board, they will supply a hammer in their recall and someone to wield it. However, when told about an action, even adolescents rarely infer the consequences of the action. For example, if told that a light switch was turned off, adults are much more likely than

adolescents or children to "recall" that the room became dark (Kail and Hagen, 1982).

Much of the improvement in children's recall is not the result of an improved ability to retain information; recall improves because children acquire various strategies to help them remember (Hagen and Stanovich, 1977). As we shall see in the next section, children often develop the ability to use these aids before they actually employ them.

No matter how hard this little girl tries, she will not be able to remember the experiences portrayed in these snapshots of her babyhood. (Elizabeth Crews/Stock, Boston)

sible. Younger children can handle only one idea at a time, so that events are stored without adequate processing and cannot be recalled unless the child reencounters a situation (sound, sight, smell) or an emotion (fear, excitement, joy) that was associated with the event. White and Pillemer propose the existence of two memory systems for events: a private system that exists at birth and stores relatively unprocessed information; and a socialized system that develops with an increase in available working memory, storing highly processed information in retrievable form. In this information-processing view of childhood amnesia, White and Pillemer find the origin of the "censor" who shrouds our earliest memories in the increasing power of rational information-processing activities and our growing reliance on them.

Strategies for Remembering

When people know they must remember something—a telephone number, a name, the amendments to the Constitution—they use various **strategies** (such as rehearsal or mnemonic rhymes), either at the time they encode the material or at the time they retrieve it, or both. The importance of strategies cannot be overemphasized, because they are a major factor in the improvement of memory over the years. Young children do not use strategies, and in cases where strategies are not required for efficient performance on a memory task, preschoolers do almost as well as adults (Brown et al., 1983).

Such strategies are not used in isolation. As we saw in the section on attention, selectivity and scanning techniques can be very important in focusing attention. As children grow older and become more skilled at selecting important information and excluding what is unimportant, and as they learn to scan exhaustively and efficiently, they use memory strategies to better advantage.

ENCODING *Memory tasks* are problem-solving situations in which a strategy is used to recall specific information (Flavell, 1970). Memory strategies help move material from short- to long-term storage, or—from a levels-of-processing view—either maintain the information at a given level or else lead to its being reprocessed at a deeper level (Ornstein and Naus, 1978). The encoding strategies most studied by developmentalists are rehearsal, imagery, and organization.

Rehearsal **Rehearsal** is the repetition of material that is to be memorized; it can be done silently or aloud, and its use clearly increases with age. In their study of preschoolers' everyday recall, Christine Todd and Marion Perlmutter (1980) found that three- and four-year-olds engaged in a certain amount of rehearsal, which took the form of discussing events with their parents. But the strategy was not used intentionally.

Rehearsal increases rapidly during the school years. When told to remember words, objects, or pictures, five-year-olds do not rehearse the material, but ten-year-olds almost always do. The development of this strategy was first demonstrated in a study by John Flavell, David Beach, and Jack Chinsky (1966), in which they had five-, seven-, and ten-year-old children memorize pictures of common objects. The children looked at the pictures, then closed the visor on a "space helmet" for fifteen seconds. Afterward, the visor was lifted and the child selected from a group of pictures the ones he or she had been asked to recall. The visor did not obscure the children's lips, and during the fifteen-second interval, investigators watched and recorded any lip movements. A few five-year-olds and nearly all the ten-year-olds silently named the pictures

during the interval. Children who moved their lips remembered more pictures than children who did not.

The fact that a child does not use verbal rehearsal does not mean the child *cannot* use it. In a similar study, T. J. Keeney, S. R. Cannizzo, and Flavell (1967) found that when children who did not spontaneously move their lips were instructed to whisper the names of objects they were to remember, their performance improved. It appeared, said the investigators, that the memories of the non-lip movers were as good as those of the lip movers, but the non-lip movers suffered from a **production deficiency.** That is, they possessed the capability to rehearse material and to profit from the rehearsal, but they did not use it. Nor were they about to adopt the strategy. Given another test and allowed to memorize material in any way they liked, most of the young children who had rehearsed only when instructed to do so stopped using the strategy.

If shown a series of pictures and asked immediately or after a very short delay to recall as many as they can—in any order—children of almost any age generally recall the last picture they have seen. Since the test comes close on the heels of the pictures, the last picture is still lodged in short-term storage, so it is not surprising that children remember it. Older children are likely also to recall the first picture they saw, a tendency that indicates they have been rehearsing the list.

As children grow older, their rehearsal techniques change (Ornstein and Naus, 1978). For example, if given a series of words to remember, third-graders repeat a single word over and over. Older children repeat the series of words, as shown in Table 8.1. But when third-graders are instructed to repeat three different words at each rehearsal, they remember almost as many words as older children do. The difference that remains between the two groups is apparently due to the content of their rehearsal, as shown in Table 8.2. Third-graders cling to the same two words (generally the first two in the list) and change the third word in each repetition. Sixth-

Table 8.1   TYPICAL UNINSTRUCTED REHEARSAL

WORD PRESENTED	EIGHTH-GRADER	THIRD-GRADER
1. yard	yard, yard, yard	yard, yard, yard, yard, yard
2. cat	cat, yard, yard, cat	cat, cat, cat, cat, yard
3. man	man, cat, yard, man, yard, cat	man, man, man, man, man
4. desk	desk, man, yard, cat, man, desk, cat, yard	desk, desk, desk, desk

(Source: From P. A. Ornstein, M. J. Naus, and C. Liberty, "Rehearsal and Organizational Processes in Children's Memory," *Child Development,* 26 [1975], 818–830. Copyright by the Society for Research in Child Development, Inc. Reprinted by permission.)

graders mix up the words so that they rehearse the entire list.

Older children also use rehearsal time differently (Hagen and Stanovich, 1977). Given as long as they like, older children use more time than younger children do. They also often test themselves, deliberately looking away from the material they are to memorize and attempting to repeat the list. Even in adulthood, some people use rehearsal more effectively and in a more sophisticated manner than others do. By itself, rehearsal is not always the most efficient way to encode material, but as we shall see, it can be combined with other strategies.

Imagery As a memory strategy, **imagery** is the visual association of two or more things that must be remembered. Suppose a child must memorize a list of paired words: cat/ice cream, ball/moon, baby/statue, tree/fork. Later the experimenter will give the child the first word in the pair, and the child's job is to respond with the second. If the child connects the two words in a visual image—for example, imagines the cat licking an ice-cream cone, the ball bouncing high over the moon, the baby perched on the top of a statue, and a fork hanging from a tree— it will be much easier for the child to recall the second word of the pair. Children discover this

Table 8.2   TYPICAL INSTRUCTED REHEARSAL

WORD PRESENTED	SIXTH-GRADER	THIRD-GRADER
1. apple	apple, apple, apple	apple, apple, apple, apple
2. hat	hat, apple, hat, apple, hat, apple	hat, apple, hat, hat, apple
3. story	story, hat, apple, story, story, hat, apple	story, hat, apple, story, hat, apple
4. dog	dog, story, hat, dog, dog, story, story, hat	dog, hat, apple, dog, hat, apple
5. flag	flag, dog, story, flag, dog, story, flag, dog, story	flag, hat, apple, flag, flag, hat
6. dish	dish, flag, hat, dish, flag, hat, dish	dish, hat, apple, dish, dish, dish

(Source: From M. J. Naus, P. A. Ornstein, and S. Aivano, "Developmental Changes in Memory: The Effects of Processing Time and Rehearsal Instructions," *Journal of Experimental Child Psychology,* 23 [1977], 237–251. Reprinted by permission of Academic Press.)

strategy much later than they do other strategies (Flavell, 1977), and some may never arrive at it by themselves.

Like other strategies, however, imagery can be used by young children who would never use it spontaneously, unless they are instructed to do so. When preschoolers are shown drawings that connect the two objects for them, their memories improve sharply—but only if the researcher reminds the children to think back to the drawings and recall what object had been seen with the presented object (Pressley and Mac Fayden, 1983). Kindergartners do not have to be reminded; they recall the second object just as well when no one reminds them to think about the drawings. Today's youngsters seem better able to use images as memory aids than were preschoolers of the 1960s. Hayne Reese (1977) believes that television programs like "Sesame Street" may have accelerated children's cognitive growth, especially their ability to use imagery. Other studies have found that when the experimenter labels the pictures, preschoolers recall more of the paired words, but schoolchildren—even first-graders—do not (Means and Rohwer, 1974). The older children apparently label the pictures for themselves, so the experimenter's aid is unnecessary.

Imagery may be an effective memory aid because it strengthens the association between two things to be remembered. Or perhaps people who use it code the compound images two ways (in images and in words), thereby increasing the likelihood that material will be recalled. Or, from a levels-of-processing view, it may be that the elaboration required to form the compound images leads to processing at deeper levels of the memory system.

Organization One of the most effective memory strategies is **organization,** the grouping of items around some common element. Adults can hold approximately seven items in their short-term stores at a time. This can be seven elements ("bits" of information) or, if they organize the information, they can increase their access to seven groups (Miller, 1956). When memorizing a list, adults generally organize the words into semantic categories. If asked to recall the words, instead of retrieving each one separately, they recall them in groups—all of the furniture items, then the vehicles, then the musical instruments, and so on.

Despite the fact that even preschool children's memory is aided by semantically organized material, children this young do not spontaneously organize material as well as older children. Researchers test for organization by giving children a series of objects, pictures, or words, then asking them to recall items from the list in any order. Recalling words in groups that have a common feature indicates that the child has clustered the items. Sometimes researchers encourage children to sort items before they attempt to recall them. In these circumstances, the way young children divide the pictures or objects shows that their groupings often differ from those of older children or adults. Young children use a great many categories and place few items in any one category. They may take a long time to sort the items; they may group items according to a story line instead of by semantic category; and they sometimes find it difficult to explain why they assign items to certain groups (Moely, 1977).

With organization, as with rehearsal, preschoolers have a production deficiency. Items are presented one by one. When the items come in small blocks, a category at a time, they tend to remember by categories. But if the items are presented randomly, not even six-year-olds do much organizing, although there may be just a few items in each category (Furth and Milgram, 1973). Five-year-olds can sort items into categories when asked to do so, but they do not use the information to help them remember (Moely, 1977). When children are required to recall list items category by category, they remember more, but they will not use the same organizational technique to memorize a new list (Scribner and Cole, 1972).

Since young children who do categorize often use categories different from those an experimenter would choose, researchers have also studied how children organize unrelated material on their own. Faced with an array of objects, pictures, or words that have no semantic relation, children must impose their organization on the material. Garrett Lange (1978) points out that under these circumstances, children as old as twelve years show little inclination to organize their recall. Lange believes that most children fail to organize items when they are trying to learn them; and when they do organize the material, they do not use the organization extensively when trying to recall. As we shall see in the next section, children often know more than they recall.

RETRIEVAL Often a name or date that we know perfectly well is tucked away in memory becomes stuck in long-term storage. Try as we may, it will not transfer into working memory. Later, unbidden, it surfaces when we no longer need it. Such a commonplace event indicates that the ability to encode information does little good if we are unable to retrieve it. When children begin to use strategies, their ability to transfer material through the memory system improves. Strategies for retrieval can be simple (the resolution to keep searching for an item that does not immediately turn up in working memory) or complex (the planned use of intricate encoding strategies to simplify later retrieval).

An obvious strategy is the use of an external cue, such as the string tied around a child's finger as a reminder to ask a parent for lunch money or a senator's list of words to aid the recall of arguments to be made in a campaign speech. In a study that explored young children's ability to use external cues, 25 percent of the three-year-olds spontaneously used photographs to remind them of toys that had earlier been matched with the pictures, although they had to turn over the photographs that were lying face down on the floor; 75 percent of the five-year-olds did the same. But even after the experimenter showed the other children how to use the pictures, 30 percent of the three-year-olds could not manage to do it (Ritter et al., 1973).

A similar study with schoolchildren indicated that six-year-olds may still find the deliberate use of external cues difficult. Akira Kobasigawa (1974) showed children twenty-four pictures drawn from eight categories. Along with the pictures items in each category, the children saw a related card that could be regarded as a cue for the category. Three animal pictures, for example, were accompanied by the picture of a zoo. When the children were allowed to use the cue cards during the recall period, only a third of the six-year-olds elected to use them, and they did so inefficiently. They recalled one item from a cue card, then stopped searching their memory and moved on to the next card. Older children, on the other hand, tried to remember as many items as they could before moving on to the next card. But the younger children had stored more information than they could retrieve unaided. When the experimenter showed them each cue card and asked them specifically to recall all three items, the differences vanished. Six-year-olds recalled as many items from the list as did eleven-year-olds. In another study, when Kobasigawa (1977) placed three squares on the cue cards to remind children that there were three items in each category, six-year-olds improved dramatically, but eight-year-olds showed no difference. Apparently the older children were already applying the cue of number to their memories.

Eight-year-olds who spontaneously used number to help them remember the items in a category were generating their own internal retrieval cues. Other internal cues are category names. Lists that have been organized by category for encoding can be remembered as a group if the category name is generated. This technique was used by Harriet Salatas and John Flavell (1976) in an attempt to approach the way memory functions outside the laboratory. Except for shoppings lists and school exams, rote memorization is not common in daily life. Most of the information we recall is used in contexts different from those in which it was acquired. Therefore, Salatas and Flavell arranged a study in which children had to reorganize material they had learned but could do so by using category names as internal cues. First the children learned a list of words by category and were tested again and again until they could recall every item in each category. Then Salatas and Flavell asked them such questions as, "Which ones are small enough to fit in this box?" To answer the question, children had to retrieve each category, go through the items, decide which objects would fit, and list them aloud. Out of thirty-six six-year-olds, only one managed this complicated task; but nine out of thirty-two nine-year-olds could do it, and most of a group of college students automatically produced the requested items. When Salatas and Flavell told the children exactly how to go about the mental search, more than half the nine-year-olds could answer the question, but few of the six-year-olds could. Apparently most six-year-olds and many nine-year-olds are unable to conduct systematic searches of memory, and then report selectively concerning items that fit specific requirements (Kobasigawa, 1977).

Knowledge Factors

We all find it much easier to remember meaningful information than a meaningless collection of sounds, easier to remember a landscape painting than one that is completely abstract. Most of us would find it much easier to memorize four sentences about a picnic than about subatomic particles. We have been on picnics and have a vast store of information about them, but few of us have had much experience with subatomic particles. It is much easier to learn new information if it is related to something we already know. The relatively limited knowledge base possessed by young children, therefore, undoubtedly makes it more difficult for them to encode and retrieve information. The ease with which a child picks up new facts, new techniques, or new ideas depends in good part on the distance between the child's existing knowledge and the new information (Brown et al., 1983; Perlmutter, 1985).

With experience our store of concepts—and our knowledge of the relationships among them—grows ever larger. This knowledge base affects even the memorization of lists. In one study, older children learned word lists much more efficiently than younger children learned the same lists. But when the lists were varied, so that each group learned a list of words that were meaningful to them, younger children recalled as many words as older children (Richman, Nida, and Pittman, 1976). When words on a list were grouped by general category (furniture, animals, transportation), older children consistently remembered more of them; but when the categories were drawn from children's lives (television shows, teachers' names, books on the class reading list), younger children performed as well as older children (Linberg, 1980).

If children know more about a subject than adults do, they can outperform adults on recall tests. Michelene Chi (1978) showed chessboards to adults and children; on each board the pieces were arranged as if a game were in progress. The children, who were expert chess players, learned the positions more quickly and remembered them better than did the adults, who were indifferent chess players.

Even younger children can turn in impressive performances when they have a substantial knowledge base, as Chi discovered when she studied a four-year-old boy who had become fascinated with dinosaurs (Chi and Koeske, 1983). Asked to recall all the dinosaur names he could remember, over six sessions the youngster came up with no less than forty-six names. Some of the names were more familiar than others, and Chi discovered that the child's memory for the twenty names he found easiest to remember seemed to be organized in a complex and interrelated manner. For these dinosaurs, the youngster could connect each animal with a number of characteristics: habitat, appearance, size, diet, how it defended itself, the way it moved about, and its nickname.

There are, of course, individual differences in the way children use their existing knowledge to acquire and store new information. Some youngsters appear to draw on old knowledge almost automatically when presented with new information; others seem to make little use of their knowledge base (Brown et al., 1983). For example, John Bransford and his associates (1981) asked fifth-graders to learn the information in a paragraph about two kinds of robots. Children who were doing well in school could recall the various properties of each robot (suction feet on one type; spiked feet on another) and explain their significance. Children who were less successful students were unable to do so unless the significance of the various properties was explicitly stated in the paragraph. The good students apparently used information given earlier (the robots' functions) to understand the significance of the properties; the poor students did not draw on the information they had been given. As Ann Brown and her associates point out (1983), unless children are able to retrieve information they already have and apply it to new information, they will not be able to learn effectively on their own.

THE DEVELOPMENT OF METAMEMORY

Children are unlikely to make deliberate use of memory strategies unless they have some understanding of the way memory works. This understanding is called **metamemory,** and even three-year-olds show a glimmer of it. When told to remember where a toy is hidden, they look at or touch the hiding place and in some way make that place distinctive from the rest of the room. But when they are not given instructions to remember, they do nothing to single it out (Wellman, Ritter, and Flavell, 1975). Three-year-olds also know that noise makes remembering more difficult and that remembering a few items is easier than remembering many (Wellman, 1977).

Remembering where a toy is hidden and memorizing a list of words are very different tasks. In the former, the goal is retrieving an attractive toy; in the latter, the goal is recalling

a relatively uninteresting group of verbal labels. As John Flavell and Henry Wellman (1977) point out, the three- or four-year-old may not realize that being asked to memorize a list of words or a group of objects requires the child to do something special with those items and that the child's job is to do something now in anticipation of later use.

But by the time children are in kindergarten or first grade, they know what it means to learn, remember, and forget. Mary Anne Kreutzer, Catherine Leonard, and Flavell (1975) interviewed kindergarten and first-, third-, and fifth-grade children in order to discover their understanding of how memory works. Most of the youngest children were aware that events that happened a long time ago were hard to recall, that meaningless strings of items such as telephone numbers are quickly forgotten, and that once something is learned, it is easier to relearn the same material than to learn something new. These young learners realized that they could plan their study time to help their memory and even proposed deliberate schemes, such as careful inspection of the items to be learned. They also understood and proposed the use of external memory aids such as other people, tape recordings, written notes, or even a string on the finger to help them remember.

Third- and fifth-graders were firmer than younger children about what they knew and had acquired additional information about memory. They not only recognized that time affects memory, but they also understood that more study time helps recall and having to learn more items will hinder it. They realized that these two factors interact, so that a short study of a short list leads to better recall than long study of a long list.

Although the younger children studied by Kreutzer and her colleagues (1975) seemed to know that external memory aids were helpful, studies by William Fabricus and Henry Wellman (1983) indicate that it takes several years before youngsters understand how to take advantage of such cues. For example, many of the first-graders they studied believed that a cue was effective no matter where it was placed or when it was seen. They agreed that their school desk was a good place to keep a note reminding them to stop by a friend's house on the way *to* school. Gradually, children learned that cues were useless when seen *after* they were supposed to do a task. But not until they were in the fifth grade did children realize that a cue seen too far in advance was of little use to them.

A major difference between young and older children is the ability to plan. Older children are better at forming and maintaining a memory goal and using strategies to help them reach it (Flavell, 1977). But memory is more than knowing about strategies. As children learn more about the workings of memory, such stored knowledge can influence the way they handle material, leading them to integrate it with previous knowledge and process it at a deeper level, thereby increasing its availability (Cavanaugh and Perlmutter, 1982). For example, after a recall test in which they tried to remember pictured objects they had seen, first- and second-graders were asked what they did to help themselves remember (Fabricus and Hagen, 1984). Many of the children said they sorted the cards by category and that the sorting helped them remember the objects ("It's four things to wear" or "Cherry would remind me of other fruits").

Although we are learning more about children's memory, our understanding is far from complete. When research involves the memorization of lists, we may illuminate some important components of memory, but leave others, such as the child's knowledge base, in deep shadow. Taking memory out of its normal context may lead us to underestimate youngsters' capabilities. Soviet psychologists (e.g., Yendoviskaya, 1971) have proposed that the young child's memory is involuntary and depends on an understanding that is stimulated by cues in the surrounding world. Such a situation is extremely difficult to reproduce in a laboratory. Preschoolers approach a researcher's memory task in a different manner from schoolchildren, whose educational experience has accustomed them to structured memory tasks. A child who

has been memorizing spelling lists and multiplication tables may regard recall as a plausible end in itself and not only as a means to a goal. A child or adult who has never been to school may take a dim view of recall as a goal, and so perform far below his or her capabilities. As was pointed out earlier, the child's own history and the history of the child's culture have powerful effects on the development of memory.

SUMMARY

During childhood, perception becomes more selective and purposeful, more meaningful, more sensitive, more efficient, and can be generalized from one situation to another. In the Gestalt view of perception, children interpret what they see according to innate principles of organization. Perception develops not through gradual learning but through a series of insights—sudden reorganizations of the perceptual field. In Eleanor Gibson's view, children notice unchanging features in the environment and pay increasing attention to highly differentiated details. Children's perception of objects appears to develop through childhood, especially in the judgment of distant objects, the relationships of forms, and the ability to recognize people in photographs.

When young children look at pictures, their attention seems to be caught by dominant features, and they find it difficult, for example, to reverse figure and ground in ambiguous pictures. They also seem to rely on their first impression of a picture (figurative whole) instead of reconstructing its elements after examining the pictures (operative whole). Perceiving meaning in pictures does not appear to require special learning, but perceiving depth in them does. Learning to move about through the world depends on the use of **cognitive maps,** which develop from a reliance on landmarks, to the ability to follow a route, then to the integration of various routes into a mental map of a larger area. The way children perceive events also changes with age, but even four-year-olds are disturbed by films that show an irreversible event (such as spilling milk) reversing itself.

As they develop, children learn to deploy their attention more effectively, more systematically, and with increasing speed. Five-year-olds still scan unsystematically, tend to stop scanning before they have all the information they need, and have their attention grabbed by a picture's focus of interest. But eight-year-olds are efficient, rapid scanners, who scan patterns from the top down, regardless of where the picture's focus lies.

Young children find it difficult to ignore irrelevant information; but as children grow older, they learn to adapt to the task at hand, focusing intently on central information and ignoring anything irrelevant. Children begin watching television programs systematically before they are three years old. By the time they are five, they deploy their attention selectively while watching television, processing information efficiently even when they are playing with toys.

Children store information in memory by constructing a model, called a **representation.** Information consists of **procedural knowledge** ("knowing how") and factual knowledge ("knowing that"). Knowledge can be represented as actions (**enactive representation**), images (**imaginal representation**), or abstract symbols (linguistic representation). These systems develop consecutively, although none is ever lost, and events that have been represented in one system can be transferred to another.

By using **concepts,** children can divide the world into categories, grouping items with similar qualities. Concept formation may begin before children are a year old and may be a by-product of assimilation and accommodation. Many researchers believe that concepts are built around a **prototype,** which consists of the best example of the category. Both perceptual qualities and functional aspects of objects are important in the formation of concepts. Categories are arranged in a hierarchy, and children first learn **basic-level categories.** By the time they

are five years old, youngsters are also beginning to represent objects in **superordinate categories**.

During processing, information moves from **sensory registers** to **short-term store** (working memory) to **long-term store,** where it is held permanently. It may also be seen as passing through various **levels of processing,** from a shallow perceptual level to a deeper semantic level. **Recognition** is the simplest way of remembering, and once information is **encoded,** age appears to have no effect on the length of time a memory is retained. Children can also reconstruct models or patterns from memory; this type of memory, **reconstruction,** is more difficult than recognition, but easier than **recall,** the most complex demonstration of memory. Although preschoolers do poorly at laboratory tests of recall, their recollections of their own experiences are quite accurate.

One reason older children and adults seem to have more efficient memories is that they use memory **strategies,** both at the time they encode material and at the time they **retrieve** it from storage. Encoding strategies include **rehearsal, imagery,** and **organization.** Retrieval strategies consist of cues that may be either external or internal. Younger children often show a **production deficiency;** they are capable of using strategies before they tend to use them spontaneously. Another factor that makes it difficult for young children to encode and retrieve information is their relatively small knowledge base. It is easier to remember things that can be related to things already known.

Three-year-olds show traces of **metamemory,** which is a knowledge of how memory works. By the time they are in kindergarten, children know quite a bit about memory, although they may not take advantage of all their knowledge. As children learn more about the memory system, they begin forming memory goals and consciously using strategies. As a result, they integrate new material with old, process it at a deeper level, and remember more.

Language Development

THE NATURE OF HUMAN LANGUAGE
The Properties of Human Language
Analyzing Language
THE PRIVATE FUNCTIONS OF LANGUAGE
Representation
Thought
Memory
THE COGNITIVE FOUNDATIONS OF
    LANGUAGE
THE PUBLIC FUNCTIONS OF LANGUAGE
THE SOCIAL FOUNDATIONS OF LANGUAGE
Intention
The Role of the Caregiver
The Uses of Conversation
The Importance of Context
THEORIES OF ACQUISITION
Biological Theories
Mechanistic Theories
Functional Theories
ACQUIRING A SYSTEM OF SOUNDS
Listening to Sounds
Producing Sounds
Struggling with Sounds
ACQUIRING A SYSTEM OF MEANING
First Words
The Structure of Meaning

The Use of Errors
Meaning in First Sentences
Expanding Vocabularies
ACQUIRING A SYSTEM OF STRUCTURES
First Syntactic Devices
The Development of Rules
The Appearance of Error
Comprehending Complex Constructions
SUMMARY

A toddler who had learned to get between-meal snacks by saying, "I want a cookie," one day discovered that her requests, although perfectly phrased, no longer worked. "You don't need a cookie," her mother would say, handing her a carrot stick. After several days of futile attempts to get a mid-morning cookie, the little girl tugged at her mother's skirt and said plaintively, "Mommy, Mommy, I *need* a cookie." This small girl's utterance was a social act, designed to have a specific effect on the listener. As we shall see, language develops out of such social contexts, in which people use words to get things done.

By the time they are four years old, normal children all over the world have mastered the basic grammar of one or more of the world's thousands of different languages. Although each child hears a different set of sentences from the adults and children that he or she interacts with, all children exposed to a language learn to understand other speakers of that language. And the children end up with more or less the same pronunciation, grammar, and vocabulary as the rest of their speech community. This means that each child in a speech community arrives at the same basic linguistic rules.

In order to understand just how the infant who can only babble soon becomes a master of a complicated language, it is necessary first to know something about the nature and function of language. In this chapter, we begin by examining language, so we can see just how human language differs from animal communication. Next we see how the private and public functions of language differ—a dual discussion that also lets us explore the cognitive and social foundations of language. After reviewing various theories of language acquisition, we trace the child's gradual grasp of language, beginning with the system of sounds. We then look at the system of meaning, discovering how the meaning of some words may expand and contract, and observing how children expand their vocabularies. Finally, we examine the system of rules and structures, following children's developing mastery of the grammatical machinery of their language.

THE NATURE OF HUMAN LANGUAGE

Language is a system of communication used within a particular social group. Members of all societies—whether animal or human—have some way of communicating among themselves. A worker bee dances on the floor of the hive to tell its fellow workers how far and in what direction to fly for nectar (von Frisch, 1967). A father quail calls to warn his foraging family of approaching danger. Rats use chemical signals to communicate, aquatic insects use surface waves, land insects use vibrations, fish use electricity, and fireflies exchange light flashes. If all societies communicate, what is so special about human language?

The Properties of Human Language

Human language, suggests Roger Brown (1973), is set off from the communication systems of animals by three important properties: semanticity, productivity, and displacement. These properties are found in every human language, be it English, Russian, Chinese, or Urdu.

Semanticity refers to a language's meaningfulness—the fact that the symbols of the language represent an enormous variety of people, objects, events, and ideas. A mynah bird may mimic human speech perfectly, but it does not use these sounds in any meaningful way, so it cannot be said to possess language. And although the dance of the honeybee communicates meaning, the number of things that bees can "talk" about is quite small.

Productivity, the second property of language, is the ability to combine a finite number of words into an unlimited number of sentences. Except for common clichés, such as "How are you?" and "Have a nice day," almost every sentence we hear or speak is brand new (N. Chomsky, 1972). The productivity of language means that its speakers can communicate any kind of information about any topic in the world. Productivity appears to be limited to human beings. Although some chimpanzees have learned to use symbols to answer questions or ask for treats, none can pass such a test of their ability to communicate (see box, page 272).

Displacement, the last essential property of language, is the ability to communicate information about objects in another place or another time. Displacement is present in the child's language from the time he or she can ask for a cookie that is in the kitchen or for father, who is at the office. Displacement is the property that allows us to transmit information from one generation to another so that we do not have to rediscover all knowledge every thirty years or so. The bee's dance uses displacement in denoting the location of nectar, but as with semanticity, displacement in the communication of honeybees is limited to the subject of nectar.

Analyzing Language

Human language is system of social communication that uses sound to transmit meaning. As we have seen, it is also immensely productive, and can talk about near and distant places, past and future events, and abstractions. Developmental psychologists have generally approached language acquisition by looking at only one or another of these properties, and the one they choose to examine determines the sort of research they will do. These major avenues of language study are phonology, semantics, syntax, and pragmatics.

Phonology, or the study of speech sounds, concentrates on the sound patterns of language. Each language combines speech sounds, called *phonemes*, in some ways but not in others; and when a language fails to make a distinction between certain sounds, its native speakers do not notice the distinction themselves. The Japanese language, for example, makes no distinction between *r* and *l*, so that when Japanese speak English they generally confuse the two sounds, saying "Herro" for "Hello," or "butterfries" for "butterflies." Similarly, English speakers make no distinction between the *t* in "tar" and the *t* in "star," so that when they learn certain Indian or African languages, they consistently substitute one of these sounds for the other (Fry,

Psychologist Herbert Terrace, who is shown teaching Nim the signs for parts of the face, discovered that the chimpanzee knew much less about language than any of his trainers thought. (Susan Kuklin/Photo Researchers)

Do Chimpanzees Talk?

For centuries, scientists and ordinary citizens agreed that it was language that set human beings apart from the rest of the animal kingdom. From time to time, unconvinced researchers have worked diligently with chimpanzees, hoping to prove that the gulf between species is much narrower than had been assumed.

Perhaps the most famous "talking" chimpanzee is Washoe, who began her language lessons with Beatrice and Allen Gardner (1969) at the University of Nevada. Washoe learned a limited amount of ASL (American Sign Language), the language of hand signs used by deaf Americans to communicate. Washoe learned 132 signs, which she combined in strings such as "Please sweet drink" and "Key open please blanket" (at the bedding cupboard). Her use of words showed the overextension common to the language of young children. For example, taught the sign "hurt" for scratches and bruises, Washoe extended it to red stains, a tattoolike decal on the back of someone's hand, and her first sight of a human navel. But Washoe's words did not add up to language (Klima and Bellugi, 1973). The chimpanzee paid no attention to word order and apparently lacked the productivity that syntax gives to language.

Lana, a chimpanzee who was taught a computer-based language by Duane Rumbaugh (1977), "typed" her messages, which appeared on a lighted display as she struck the keys. The words she learned to "read" were geometric signs. Lana learned six stock sentences, into which she could insert the appropriate noun or verb, and she used them

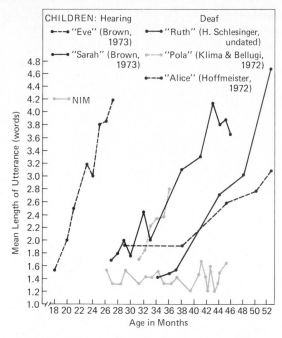

The difference between chimpanzee and human speech is shown clearly in this graph comparing the length of utterances of the chimpanzee Nim with those of two hearing and three deaf children.

(From *NIM*, by H. S. Terrace, 1979. Copyright © 1979 by Herbert Terrace. Reprinted by permission of Alfred A. Knopf, Inc.)

to converse about food, drink, and other desires.

Chimpanzees seemed to be getting closer and closer to real language—until Herbert Terrace (1979) worked with Nim and discovered that the chimpanzee knew less than his trainers thought. Nim learned 125 signs in ASL and put them together in two-word com-

1977). Because in these latter languages a change in the *t* sound changes meaning, English speakers often think they are saying one word when native speakers are hearing another.

Research in developmental phonology concentrates on the child's progress in detecting and producing the sounds of speech. Investigators study what sounds or combinations of sounds

binations. He even learned to substitute the signs "bite" and "angry" for physical aggression with trainers he had become attached to. But when Terrace analyzed videotapes of Nim with his trainers, the psychologist discovered that his chimpanzee could not qualify as a speaker of ASL. No matter how large Nim's vocabulary became, the average length of his utterances remained the same—between one and two words (see figure). A long string of words, upon analysis, seemed to be a simple pileup of all the words that might get the chimpanzee an orange ("give orange me give eat orange me eat orange give me eat orange give me you"). Nim rarely (less than 10 percent of the time) expanded upon what his trainers said. (Most three-year-old children expand on nearly half their parents' utterances.) Nim was primarily an imitator. What is more, Nim simply did not understand turn-taking, an essential nonverbal aspect of language that children learn long before they can talk.

The team that taught Lana threw additional cold water on the concept of chimpanzee language (Savage-Rumbaugh, Rumbaugh, and Boysen, 1980). They reviewed the major chimpanzee work and essentially agreed with Terrace, although their doubts ran even deeper than his. Both Lana and Washoe, they said, reached the linguistic level of a nine-month-old child, because they used their communication systems to control the behavior of their trainers. Nim, Washoe, and Lana used symbols to get contact, play, food, and a change of location. In contrast, a child in the two-word stage consistently uses language to comment on a situation. A human child may say, "More milk," but will also say,

"All gone," "Spill milk," "Pour juice," and "Pretty cup."

Sue Savage-Rumbaugh and her colleagues (1980) contended that chimpanzees used words primarily to get rewards and that none of these animals understood symbolization—they did not realize that objects have names. In producing words to get rewards, the chimpanzees accomplished no more than a pigeon that has learned to peck the proper key to get corn. In fact, using a similar but much simpler system than Lana's, other researchers taught pigeons to carry on a spontaneous "conversation" about hidden colors (Epstein, Lanza, and Skinner, 1980).

But Savage-Rumbaugh and her colleagues have not given up. They first trained two new chimpanzees, Sherman and Austin, to communicate with a keyboard like the one Lana used. Then they went on to teach the chimpanzees to use symbols to refer to objects (Savage-Rumbaugh et al., 1983). Through a series of games, Sherman and Austin learned to look at a table full of objects, go into another room, press the key that symbolized the object they had chosen, then return to the table, pick up the object, and carry it to the trainer in another room. Sherman and Austin had to work hard to grasp a referential principle that human infants learn easily, but the chimpanzees now have a base for language. If Sherman and Austin are to acquire language, they must now learn to combine true symbols according to rules of syntax. If they do, language will no longer be a uniquely human accomplishment.

children can detect; how their ability to detect various sounds changes with age and experience; and what sounds they produce, and when and in what order they produce them.

Semantics, or the study of meaning, reflects Roger Brown's first essential property of language; it focuses on the content of language and on the meaning of various words and combinations. Researchers who study semantic development are interested in the way children form concepts. Research in semantics also encompasses such topics as how children learn the meaning of prepositions ("under," "over," "on," "in," etc.), how they learn to distinguish between such words as "more" and "less," whether children understand more than they can say, and how adults' and children's meanings for words differ.

Syntax, or the structural principles that determine the form of sentences, reflects the second essential property of language—productivity. The syntax of a language is what makes the language productive, for it dictates the rules for combining words.

These rules vary from language to language. In English, for example, "Mommy kisses Baby" and "Baby kisses Mommy" have different meanings because the order of the words is different in the two utterances. But in Russian, the equivalent of "Mommy kisses Baby," with the three words in that order, could mean either that Mommy gets kissed or that Baby gets kissed, depending on whether "Mommy" or "Baby" has a particular sound on the end. So a Russian one-year-old must learn to pay special attention to the sounds that come at the end of words, whereas an American one-year-old must learn to pay special attention to word order.

Researchers who focus on syntax study the child's gradual grasp of grammar. They may be interested in the way a child forms the past tense or plurals, in the child's understanding of the passive sentence or the indirect object, or in the way a child comes to ask questions involving the use of auxiliary verbs ("Can cows fly?").

Pragmatics, or the study of language's social purposes, looks at the way language is used to get things done. When language is used for communication, each utterance is a social act, and the words are chosen because of assumptions and intentions on the part of the speaker. If the act is successful, the utterance will have the desired effect on the listener. The effect can be as simple as getting the salt at the dinner table or as complicated as persuading someone to

change his or her mind about an important issue.

Research in pragmatics centers on social interaction, examining the context of speech to see how the immediate situation affects both the expression and understanding of language. Researchers are especially interested in the way language emerges from earlier methods of communication, such as touching, pointing, and gazing.

THE PRIVATE FUNCTIONS OF LANGUAGE

Despite the emphasis of pragmatics, communication is not the only function of language. Human language serves an equally important private function by allowing us to translate our experiences into symbols, to remember experiences better, to think about abstractions, and to integrate our mental processes.

Representation

One of the ways human beings deal with the world is to represent experience in thought so that it may be used at a later date. We may think in images; but once we can translate our experiences into the symbols of language, our mental powers are greatly enhanced by the ease with which symbols can be processed and manipulated. Symbols give us the power of displacement; because they can be manipulated in the absence of whatever they represent, we can reason, remember, plan, and meditate, and we can solve complex problems quickly and efficiently.

According to Jerome Bruner (1964), the shared symbol system of language is conventionalized and transmitted by the culture, and the development of symbolic representation systems is a major component of cognitive growth. In one study by Bruner and his colleagues, five- to seven-year-old children were asked to

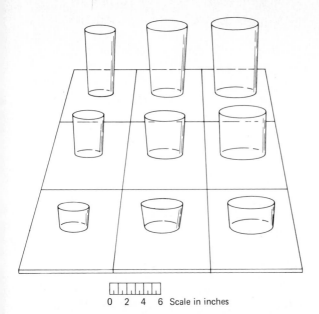

0 2 4 6 Scale in inches

FIGURE 9.1 The increased cognitive flexibility that accompanies language acquisition was illustrated in an experiment using these glasses. Five-year-olds had no trouble replacing them in their original arrangement, but when asked to transpose the arrangement, they always failed. Most seven-year-olds had little trouble with the new task, and their level of language facility predicted whether they would succeed.

(From J. S. Bruner, "The Course of Cognitive Growth." *American Psychologist*, 19 [1964], 1–15.)

rebuild a matrix of nine plastic glasses arranged by both height and diameter (as shown in Figure 9.1), after they had watched the experimenter remove all the glasses from the board. The five-year-olds rebuilt the matrix as easily as the seven-year-olds, although they took more time. When the matrix was transposed, however, so that the glass in the lower left corner was moved to the lower right, most seven-year-olds could rebuild it, but none of the five-year-olds could.

The key to whether a child would be able to rebuild the transposed matrix appeared in the child's language. When asked to tell how the glasses were originally arranged, children gave a dimensional (higher-shorter), a general percep-

tual (bigger-little), or a confused (higher-little) description. Regardless of age, those who confused terms from the two modes were twice as likely to fail at building the transposed matrix as those who used either the dimensional or the general description. The ability to manipulate symbols allowed the children to produce new structures based on the matrix's original organization.

Language also keeps children from being overpowered by the immediate perceptual attributes of their world. At first, children cannot separate words from the world they see around them. If a two-year-old who is seated on the carpet with her friend Jason is asked to say, "Jason is standing up," the little girl will say, "Jason is sitting down." The youngster reports the sight before her eyes instead of the words that contradict it, because meaning for a young child is fused with what he or she sees. But as language develops, it frees children from the immediate environment, allowing them to control and direct their own behavior (Vygotsky, 1962).

A study in which children were asked to say which of two glasses was fuller and which emptier demonstrated this effect. Two identical glasses were filled with the same amount of water and a tall, narrow glass was placed beside them. After Françoise Frank (1966) had screened the glasses from view, she poured the contents of one glass into the tall, narrow glass and then asked children to compare the amount of liquid in the two glasses. Four-year-olds who had said both glasses held the same amount of water changed their minds when the screen was removed; five-year-olds did not. According to Bruner, the four-year-olds relied heavily on perceptual attributes (the levels of liquid), whereas five-year-olds had a verbal formula based on action, not perception ("You only poured it"), to shield them from the overpowering appearance of the water levels before them.

A more radical notion about the power of language holds that language shapes and directs our thinking, rather than simply providing a means for representing our thoughts. This con-

These Eskimo children are much more aware of various snow conditions than are children in California, in part because their language has so many words to describe snow. (Sharon Fox/ The Picture Cube)

scribe it and the more precise and differentiated the perceptions of it by the speakers of the language. For example, Arabs have many words for camel; Eskimos, for snow; Americans, for car. The way a language carves up the world, then, may influence what we are likely to notice or do in a certain situation, but it does not limit the ways in which we *can* perceive it (Pollio, 1974).

Thought

Although we sometimes think in images, much of our thought is in the form of language—in that silent, condensed inner speech that consists of words turned into thought (Vygotsky, 1962). This inner speech helps us organize and integrate the processes of perception, memory, and problem solving, and allows us to understand and control our activities. Without it, our thought would be rudimentary and animalistic.

In fact, Lev Vygotsky believed that thought in infancy was like the thought of chimpanzees. He suggested that during the first part of life, speech and thought develop separately. Thought takes the form of images or of sensorimotor concepts such as those proposed by Jean Piaget (see Chapter 7); the child may know words, which are used to label objects, but not language. Around the age of two, speech and thought join, and children's behavior changes. Language gives children independence from the immediate situation, allowing them to plan solutions and carry them out, to search for new means to solve problems instead of being limited to objects already present. Language gives children control over their own behavior, freeing them from the impulsive, spontaneous movements of apes (Vygotsky, 1978).

Not until thought and speech meet can children understand syntax; and until children grasp the syntax of a language, Vygotsky believed, they cannot use the structure of thought. As he put it, "grammar precedes logic" (Vygotsky, 1962). Children learn to handle abstract

cept, called *linguistic relativity*, was proposed by Benjamin Lee Whorf (1956). According to Whorf, the vocabulary and grammar of a language in large part determine the way its speakers interpret their perceptions and experiences. In this view, then, language determines its speaker's ideas of time, matter, and space—even directing the form science takes in a culture.

The Whorfian hypothesis has not been generally accepted, but many researchers credit Whorf for calling attention to the complexity of social, cultural, linguistic, and cognitive interaction (G. Miller, 1978b). It is generally accepted that language influences our perception of the world, helping to determine what things in the world we notice and what we ignore. The more important a concept or category is for a culture, the more words a language has to de-

thought by first learning and using the language structures that express it. For example, children learn the structure of subordinate clauses (clauses that begin with such words as "because" and "although") long before they are able to grasp the structure of meaning indicated by those forms. But until children can express this scaffolding for thought, they cannot begin to understand and manipulate the kinds of relationships the clauses express.

Memory

Language can improve our ability to remember an object, an action, or an idea. Putting a concept into words seems to help us store the information in memory in a form that enables us to retrieve it. Most people have figured this out and repeat to themselves things they want to remember. Young children do not know this, but by telling them what to say, it is possible to make their memories more efficient, as Brian Coates and Willard Hartup (1969) have shown in their studies with four- and seven-year-olds. These investigators showed the children movies in which a man went through a series of twenty actions (such as building a tower of blocks, shooting a popgun at the tower, and whirling a hula hoop on his arm). Prior to running the film, Coates and Hartup told the children they would later have to imitate the model's actions. When asked to demonstrate the actions, four-year-olds who had watched the movie passively did worst. Those who had followed the experimenter's suggestion and described the man's actions in their own words as he performed them did better. But those who had repeated the words when the experimenter described the man's actions did best of all. Seven-year-olds did better than four-year-olds, no matter what technique was used. Apparently, they had already discovered that labeling is a good memory aid, and even when they appeared to be watching the movie passively, they were mentally harnessing the power of language to help them remember what to do.

THE COGNITIVE FOUNDATIONS OF LANGUAGE

A child's understanding of the world lays the basis for development of the ability to understand and to speak a language. It is obvious that a child who remained at the intellectual level of the neonatal period, when actions are primarily reflexive, would never learn to speak, and that a child who regarded the world as an extension of him- or herself would have little to talk about. Before children can use words meaningfully, they must have some notion that there is a world of enduring objects and people, and that people can act on objects. These notions develop during the first year of life, as we saw in Chapter 7.

A child's understanding of one aspect of causality, the use of tools, was related to the emergence of language among American and Italian babies studied toward the end of their first year by Elizabeth Bates (1979) and her associates. Babies who tugged at a supporting cloth in order to get an object they wanted, or who used sticks as tools to reach a desired toy, generally had larger vocabularies than babies who did not understand the use of tools to obtain a goal.

Imitation is also a good predictor of the baby's use of language. Before they celebrate their second birthdays, most babies are imitating events long after they have occurred. Jean Piaget (1951) reported many instances of such imitations among his own children. For example, when his daughter Jaqueline was sixteen months old, she was impressed by an eighteen-month-old boy's tantrum. As Piaget described it:

> He screamed as he tried to get out of a play-pen and pushed it backwards, stamping his feet. J. stood watching him in amazement, never having witnessed such a scene before. The next day, she

herself screamed in her play-pen and tried to move it, stamping her foot lightly several times in succession.

Piaget pointed out that because Jacqueline did not imitate the boy's behavior until the following day, she must have stored some representation of the event in her mind, acting it out in imitation much later. Just as toddlers can imitate events some time after they have experienced them, so they can use words some time after they have heard them. The abilities to imitate and to store internal images of sights and sounds are necessary prerequisites for the development of language.

A child's first words also emerge about the

These toddlers' imitation of adults they have seen cooking indicates that the youngsters have stored some representation of the act in their minds—an ability that is essential to the development of language. (© James R. Holland/Stock, Boston)

same time that he or she begins to use symbolic gestures and to engage in make-believe play. A baby girl who pushes a little stone along the table, pretending that it is a car, or rubs her hands together, pretending she is washing, has demonstrated symbolic play. Such play, as well as the sort of manipulative play in which babies build towers of blocks or stack wooden rings on a stick, is closely related to both the baby's use of words and his or her comprehension of others' speech (Bates, 1979). Later, when youngsters are about twenty months old, language and symbolic play again show a close kinship. At the same time that children connect two or more symbolic gestures in their play ("pouring" make-believe tea, "drinking" it, then wiping their mouths), they also begin to combine two or more words in a single utterance (Bates et al., 1982). This kinship is not surprising, because both language and symbolic play require the child to translate experience into symbols and then combine the symbols according to specific rules (Ungerer and Sigman, 1984).

Tool use, imitation, and both symbolic and manipulative play are related to the emergence of language. There is some evidence that when these capacities are absent, babies do not acquire language (Bates, 1979). Apparently, the same underlying intellectual capacities are necessary for any of this complex behavior to develop.

THE PUBLIC FUNCTIONS OF LANGUAGE

In the absence of other people, we could survive without language. Our utterances are meant to communicate meanings to others, and we learn to use language socially in many ways for many purposes. We express emotions, describe objects or events, exchange ideas, ask questions, give commands, and tell stories. And sometimes we lie. Communication, then, is the public function of language.

If communication is to be smooth, we must understand the purpose of others' speech. But speakers are not always direct in the way they phrase their requests, commands, or assertions. For example, if a small boy's mother wants him to pick up his blocks, instead of saying, "Pick up your blocks," she might use an indirect way of getting her son to clean up the living room floor. She might say, "I wish you'd pick up those blocks" or "Why not pick up those blocks?" or "Haven't you forgotten something?" Even two-year-olds respond appropriately to such indirect speech, but how much of it they understand is uncertain. Marilyn Shatz (1983) suggests that very young children may well take any comment addressed to them as a request for action, then act in a way that seems to fit the situation.

Children communicate as well as receive communications from others, and if they are to be effective, they must be able to fit their language to the immediate situation. As Jesse Delia and Barbara O'Keefe (1979) have indicated, children must know when to speak formally and when to speak colloquially. Once they can construct a sentence, they must know how to fit their utterances into the stream of conversation. They must learn how to interpret any violations of conversational rules. For example, if a person violates the turn-taking rule, is the interruption meant to communicate vital information or is the interrupter simply rude?

Finally, children must develop the ability to recognize the perspectives and the needs of others, realizing how much information the other possesses and what he or she expects from the conversation. As their facility for language manipulation grows, children begin to adapt their language to a specific audience or situation. When they are requested to do something they understand and are capable of doing, children as young as four can modify their language appropriately, as Rochel Gelman and Marilyn Shatz (1977) found when they asked four-year-olds to explain the workings of a toy to two-year-olds. The older preschoolers described the toy much as an adult would. They used repetition and simple, short sentences, modifying their messages to fit the limited capabilities of their pupils. They also adopted a "show-and-tell" approach, describing and demonstrating what the younger children were to notice and do. Yet when they explained the same toy to peers or adults, four-year-olds tended to use long sentences, to talk more about their own thoughts, and to ask the listener to provide information or clarification.

In another study, four-year-old boys went a step farther, adjusting their explanations of how a toy worked according to the individual responses of their two-year-old pupils (Masur, 1978). The more responsive the speech of the two-year-olds, the longer and more complex were the sentences of the four-year-old teachers.

The ability to adapt language to a listener's needs develops gradually during childhood; in Chapter 17 we trace the growth of this ability. When youngsters are unfamiliar with the demands of a situation, unable to understand the instructions, incapable of remembering what they are supposed to do, or preoccupied with figuring out an experimenter's wishes, they often cannot formulate an understandable message. They then make no allowances for a listener, appearing to assume that others see, hear, or feel exactly as they do.

THE SOCIAL FOUNDATIONS OF LANGUAGE

When language is a social act, that is, one in which the speaker is trying to accomplish something, its efficient use requires that both speaker and listener know more than the structure of the language and the meaning of its words; the social conventions that make communication possible also become important. Children learn these conventions as they acquire the language itself, in interactions with older human beings, usually their parents. In studying the development of this knowledge, researchers look at the emergence of intent in the baby's actions, at the context in which language is used, and at the social interaction in which the baby's understanding of the cultural context of language is forged. Long before children speak, they learn to manipulate the context of their actions according to rules they have acquired in activities with their caregivers.

Intention

Newborn infants communicate, but their messages are sent without intent. Their early cries are simply signals of distress, indicating that they are hungry, wet, uncomfortable, or in pain. Despite this lack of intent, the wails generally succeed in remedying the problem, and milk, a dry diaper, or cuddling customarily arrives in response to them.

After this successful, if unwitting, communication, babies develop clear intentions but do not try to communicate them to others. At about two or three months, for example, babies who see an attractive object dangled before them show their eagerness to grasp the object. They open and close their mouths, move their heads, and wiggle their bodies, behaving just as they would if they had the object. Within another month or so, if a toy is dangled before them, they will reach for it. In neither case, however, do babies make an attempt to get assistance from an adult. Similarly, when given a toy that requires adult assistance, babies will hit at the toy, push it, or throw it instead of indicating a need for help.

Somewhere around nine or ten months, babies who want a toy that is out of reach begin behaving in a very different way. They look at a nearby adult, then at the toy, then at the adult again. If there is no response, they may fuss loudly to attract the adult's attention. Very soon thereafter, the grasp toward the elusive toy becomes an intentional signal, perhaps a repetitive opening and shutting of the hand, and the fussing sound turns into short, regular noises that change in volume and insistence depending on whether the adult responds. This moment, says Elizabeth Bates (1979), is a great one in the dawn of language. It shows the child's intent to communicate as well as his or her realization that there are mutually agreed-on signals, such as pointing, that can be used for mutually agreed-on purposes. Earlier, the baby may have wanted to communicate but lacked any shared notion of conventional ways to express that intention. Now that the baby has grasped this notion, the way is open for the first words.

Seeking help is one of the major intentions that govern most of a baby's communication. At this age, Jerome Bruner (1983) proposes, babies' intentions are few, and it is to fulfill their intentions that they learn to use a language. Both the baby's job in learning to communicate and the parent's job in deciphering the baby's communication are simplified by the baby's limited intentions. In addition to seeking help, babies try to persuade adults to look at something with them; this achieves joint attention, with babies and parents attending to the same object. Babies also strive for friendly, affectionate interaction with their parents, enjoying the exchange of gestures, sounds, and facial expressions. Finally, babies try to induce others to join them in their games and experiences (Bruner, 1980). These intentions develop in a social context, with the caregiver playing an active role.

The Role of the Caregiver

Babies' knowledge of the cultural conventions that surround communication begins in the interaction of baby and caregiver. Almost from the beginning, parents treat their infants as if they were at least potentially competent social partners (Shatz, 1983). Parents attribute intent to their babies' gurgles and coos, and encourage babies to take their turn in "conversation." Much early learning of language convention takes place in dialogues between caregiver and infant, and at first the caregiver supplies both sides of the conversation. As a result, even though babies may not be trying to communicate, they are learning something about the nature of human communication. For example:

Infant: (*smiles*)
Mother: Oh, what a nice little smile! Yes, isn't that nice? There. That's a nice little smile.
Infant: (*burps*)
Mother: What a nice wind as well! Yes, that's better, isn't it? Yes. Yes.
Infant: (*vocalizes*)
Mother: Yes! There's a nice noise (Snow, 1977).

During such exchanges, parents pay close attention to the baby's reactions, and as the infant's competence increases, the conversations change. At first, a parent is content simply to call attention to an interesting object, perhaps saying, "Look!" But gradually, more and more participation is demanded from the baby—first babbling, then wordlike sounds, then labels for objects (Bruner, 1983).

Carrying on a conversation requires children to master other conventions as well: they must learn to take turns, speaking at the proper time and not interrupting their partners; they must learn to make eye contact and to indicate that they are paying attention. Turn-taking and other nonverbal conversational skills grow out of early games, such as peek-a-boo, in which baby and adult share experiences and exchange roles in ritualized and predictable ways. At about six or seven months, babies seem to learn that certain signals in adult speech mean that something the adult is attending to is worth looking at; from that moment joint attention becomes easier. Shortly thereafter, the baby learns to follow the adult's gaze to find the interesting object. In a study with Michael Scaife, Bruner (1983) found that between eight and ten months, two-thirds of the babies studied would follow an adult's gaze and look intently at whatever was the focus of the adult's attention. By the time they were a year old, all babies did this. Such shared gazing paves the way to shared linguistic reference and the acquisition of words.

Babies first begin learning about the conventions of communication in early dialogues with a parent, in which the parent provides both sides of the conversation. (Peter Menzel)

Parents also speak in special ways to their babies. In the early months, this altered manner of speaking consists of exaggerated pitch, loudness, and intensity, exaggerated facial expressions, extension of vowel length, and emphasis on certain words (Stern, 1977). At about ten months, just when the baby shows an intent to communicate, the early exaggerated talk shifts to a kind of speech that has been called "baby talk" or "motherese" (Gleason and Weintraub, 1978). In baby talk, adults typically speak more slowly, use simple sentences, replace difficult consonants with easy ones, substitute nouns for pronouns, and repeat words, phrases, or whole sentences. As in the earliest speech to infants, pitch and tone change, as the adult seems to be both conveying affection and capturing the child's attention for the task at hand. Baby talk appears in cultures around the world; its presence has been documented in at least fifteen cultures, and it is used by parents, childless adults, and older children alike (Ferguson, 1977; Jacobson et al., 1983).

Adults also talk to children primarily about the here and now. They comment on what they are doing or what the infant is doing or is about to do. They limit their vocabularies, and they select words that are most useful for the child—words that relate to what children are interested in. The adult is not trying to *teach* the child language; instead, the adult is trying to maintain interaction with the child (Shatz, 1984). As Roger Brown (1977) puts it, the adult is trying "to keep two minds focused on the same topic."

The result of baby talk is, however, anything but babyish. The content and the intonation of the communication is childish, but the dialogue pattern is strictly adult (Bruner, 1981). Researchers are not certain how much of this special interaction is necessary for language development to occur, or how much language acquisition is speeded by these patterns of interaction (Shatz, 1983). Yet without some degree of such assistance, children might never become competent users of language.

The Uses of Conversation

During the preschool years, children's conversation with their caregivers continues to be a major influence on their skill at communicating. Once they begin putting several words together, the children's side of the conversation grows, and instead of replying with "Yeah" or "Dat" or "Baby shoe," they make suggestions and bring up new topics.

Sometimes conversation goes well and a two-year-old maintains his or her side of the talk over twenty or more turns, always responding appropriately. At other times, conversation breaks down and the child either lapses into silence, resorts to repeated "Huhs," or makes an irrelevant comment—as when one thirty-month-old boy replied to "Which is your ball?" with "Drink copee" (Brown, 1980). After studying the transcripts of conversations between twenty-one young children and a pair of developmental psychologists, Brown concluded that the content of adult-child conversations was their least important aspect. As he points out, when an adult says, "What's this?" and the child replies, "A rabbit," the adult has learned nothing about the picture book they are sharing but a good deal about the little girl's assumptions and linguistic knowledge.

Children's relevant responses reassure the adult conversational partner that the pair share certain cultural beliefs, which form the background of the conversation. The child's contributions reveal his or her linguistic competence and knówledge, so that adults use these conversations as a running check on the child's progress. Research has shown that most parents are good at predicting their preschoolers' level of linguistic proficiency (Gleason and Weintraub, 1978).

How much do parents actively work at correcting their children's speech or indicating its accuracy? Parents often correct gross errors in a child's choice of words or pronunciation, but they show little concern for the syntax of a child's utterance. For example, in a longitudinal study of several children, when one girl wanted to indicate that her mother was also female and said, "He a girl," her mother replied, "That's right" (Brown and Hanlon, 1970). But when it comes to the truth of children's utterances, parents show an active concern. When another young girl in the same study said, using passable grammar, "There's the animal farmhouse," her mother corrected her, because the building was a lighthouse. In another study (Ninio and Bruner, 1978), mothers corrected every incorrect label their year-old children applied to a picture-book character, and made some sort of approving comment after most of the correct labels. Children also get another kind of feedback on their language: whether or not their requests and demands accomplish their intended purpose (Bruner, 1983). If their language does not succeed in getting them whatever they want, they know immediately, and try to adjust their language so that they reach their goals.

The Importance of Context

Every communication is affected by **context,** which includes the beliefs and assumptions of the speaker concerning the setting of his or her remarks; the prior, present, and future actions and remarks of both speaker and listener; and the knowledge and intentions of everyone involved (Ochs, 1979). Language itself can serve as context, as when the speaker's choice of a language style, whether formal, colloquial, distant, or affectionate, affects the way an utterance is interpreted. Both adult and child respond to context and use it to interpret the intentions of the conversational partner.

HOW ADULTS UNDERSTAND INFANTS Communication succeeds during the early stages of language because adults are good at guessing a child's intentions. Although children give some clues to their intentions in intonation and gesture, the ongoing context provides vital information, and early one- and two-word utterances can be understood only if their context is known. For example, on hearing a recording of the word "door" spoken with an emphatic intonation, we would not be able to tell whether the infant speaker wanted the door opened or closed or merely wanted us to pay attention to the door. But if we were watching a toddler stand in front of a closed door and knew that on the other side of the door her father was repairing a light switch, we would know immediately that the emphatic utterance, "Door," meant that we had been asked to open it.

The process of deciphering a child's language is made easier by the fact that children—like the adults who talk to them—speak about the here and now, so that immediate context provides a guide to meaning. Context plays such a dominant role in the infant's early speech that by relying on it, adults can frequently predict what children who are limited to one-word utterances will say next. These children often have more

When this little girl says "door," it is safe to assume that she wants the door opened, but without the context it would be impossible to decide whether she meant "Open the door," "Close the door," or "There's a door." (© Michael Weisbrot & Family)

than one word in their vocabularies that could apply to a situation, but they will select their word by the criterion of informativeness, according to Patricia Greenfield (1979). Information that is regarded as certain is not mentioned; whatever cannot be taken for granted will be the topic of conversation. "Certain" information is information that is certain to the child, not the adult, for children at this level of development generally assume that adults share their perceptions.

Suppose that an eighteen-month-old boy is playing with a toy car, running it across the top of a table. He would not say "car" because the car, being in his possession, is certain. Since the car can be taken for granted, he would direct his comment at its action, saying "hmmm" or "beep-beep" or whatever word he uses to imitate the sound of a car. Should the toddler's car fall off the table, he would say "car," because the car has suddenly become uncertain. However, having once mentioned the car, it becomes part of the context and therefore certain. Now he is free to comment on his elusive toy and might say "down" or "fall" or "gone."

When commenting on a person's actions, young children take the person for granted and talk about the action. Sitting on the kitchen floor and wishing to comment on the fact that his mother is fixing lunch, the same little boy would say "Lunch," not "Mommy." But if his mother left the room, she would become uncertain in the child's scheme of things and the comment would be "Mommy," no matter how interested he was in his mother's action. Since, as Greenfield points out, adults and children appear to analyze a situation similarly, the boy's mother understands his comments during play and responds appropriately, making communication possible.

HOW CHILDREN UNDERSTAND
ADULTS If children are to understand what others are trying to accomplish with language, they must be alert to the social, or pragmatic, meaning of the utterances they hear, and they must often disregard the literal meaning. As we saw earlier, children while still quite young show a comprehension of indirect utterances, quickly picking up their blocks when Mother says, "Haven't you forgotten something?"

According to Marilyn Shatz (1978), instead of decoding the language they hear according to the syntactical arrangement of the words and their meaning, very young children do whatever seems appropriate, given the immediate social context. When the context is ambiguous, they assume that language demands action. In her study, Shatz tested the comprehension of two-

year-olds with commands, questions, and simple declarative sentences spoken in a neutral fashion. She found, for example, that whether she said, "Fit the ball into the truck," "Can you fit the ball into the truck?" or "The ball fits into the truck," most children responded by putting the ball into the truck.

When she manipulated the context by setting up a situation that clearly demanded information from them, however, children responded appropriately. Using a toy telephone, she either steered the child toward action (saying such things as "Push the button" and "Ring the bell") or toward information (saying such things as "Who talks on the telephone in your house?" or "Can Daddy talk on the telephone?"). Asked the test question, "Can you talk on the telephone?" children in the action setting generally responded by talking on the play phone. Children in the information setting generally said "Yes" and left it at that, or else said "Yes" and then proceeded to demonstrate their ability. In other words, in the first situation, "Can you talk on the telephone?" was interpreted as a command; in the second situation, it was interpreted as a request for information. When words and actions work together to make simple action inappropriate and the giving of information appropriate, children will provide the information.

A child's interpretation of another's utterance may also depend on his or her status in relation to the speaker. When the words come from a parent, a teacher, or another adult, five-year-olds are likely to treat simple declarative statements or ambiguous questions about their ability to carry out an act as indirect commands. By the time they are in the second grade, however, they pay more attention to the form of an utterance and respond to requests, commands, ambiguous questions, and statements in different ways (Olson, 1980).

Context continues to guide children in other ways. From their experiences, they construct **scripts,** which are cognitive frameworks that describe the customary sequence of events for various activities. They develop scripts for meals, bedtimes, birthday parties, lunch at Mc-

Donald's, visits to Grandmother's house, and trips to the supermarket. These scripts shape a child's expectations about an event and help the youngster to infer the meanings and intentions of other people. According to Katherine Nelson and Janice Gruendel (1981), even three-year-olds—the youngest children they have studied—develop such scripts, which supply a context for their thought and action. Nelson and Gruendel believe that scripts not only help children interpret conversations but also aid them in learning language.

THEORIES OF ACQUISITION

The long path to language acquisition begins in the interactions between the baby and his or her caregiver. But exactly how cognitive development interacts with social experience to produce a competent speaker is a matter of debate. The debate centers on how a child manages to acquire syntax—that intricate system of grammar, intonation, and word order that makes language so productive. As yet, none of the explanations that have been advanced has satisfactorily accounted for this feat (Maratsos, 1983).

Biological Theories

According to Noam Chomsky (1975, 1979), language development is primarily a matter of maturation because the structure of language is laid down in our genes. All human languages, despite their surface differences, share an underlying deep structure, which he calls a *universal grammar.* This grammar consists of principles, conditions, and rules of sound, meaning, and structure. Since biological constraints characterize the grammar children will construct, they take the bits and pieces of language they hear, analyze them, and fit them to the universal grammar. Only in this way, says Chomsky, can we explain how children in a given community,

Although they have many fewer opportunities for verbal interaction, children who grow up on isolated farms develop language at the same time and in the same way as children who live in towns and cities. (© Jim Smith)

who each have entirely different—and mostly fragmentary—language experiences, come up with the same rich, complex language system. In this view, language is partly predetermined, in the same way that genes determine the pattern of sexual maturation, and—given experience—children will invariably acquire language.

When maturation is considered the determining factor in language acquisition, the reference is to maturation of the brain. Eric Lenneberg (1967), convinced that maturation is the key to language acquisition, believed that there is a sensitive period in human development when language can be learned. The period begins when children are about two years old and lasts until they reach sexual maturity. At that time the ability to learn a language declines, and by the late teens it is difficult—or even impossible—to acquire a first language. The end of the sensitive period, said Lenneberg (1973), coincides with the maturation of the brain; once brain tissue is fully differentiated, it loses plasticity and can no longer make the adjustments that the acquisition of language requires.

There is some evidence to support this view. Until they are sexually mature, most children who suffer damage to the brain's left hemisphere recover the ability to talk; but adolescents and adults who receive similar injuries do not. Since, as noted in Chapter 6, language is located in the left hemisphere for most people, this phenomenon points to maturation as a critical factor in the development of language. In children, said Lenneberg, even though the left hemisphere handles most language functions, the right is still involved in speech; and because the brain tissue is still plastic, it can assume all language functions when the left hemisphere is damaged.

Yet some researchers have questioned the concept of a sensitive period for language development. As we saw in Chapter 6, research indicates that brain lateralization is present at birth, and that a child is born with the left hemisphere more proficient than the right at processing language (Kinsbourne and Hiscock, 1983). Despite this early lateralization, is there any connection between brain maturation and language acquisition? The case of Genie, a California girl who grew up in almost total isolation, indicates that a first language *can* be acquired after sexual maturity. However, Genie's language is not the rich, fluent system spoken by other members of her speech community (Curtiss, 1977). Genie was discovered when she was nearly fourteen, and her social experience had been limited to spoonfeeding from her almost blind mother. No one spoke to her, and whenever she made a noise, her father beat her. Although Genie was severely disturbed and had no language, she acquired English. The acquisition was difficult, however, and Genie's language has remained abnormal. She understands normal language, but she does not produce some of its basic structures. Her speech is rule-governed and productive, however, and she speaks of people and objects that are not present. Genie's case may support a weak version of Lenneberg's theory

(Curtiss, 1977), but we cannot be certain. Language builds upon a cognitive foundation—a store of concepts and world knowledge. Surely Genie's sharply restricted childhood affected her cognitive development; this general cognitive restriction rather than a lack of exposure to language at a sensitive period may account for a good part of Genie's language problems.

If we apply Lenneberg's theory of language acquisition in a strict fashion, we would predict that children under twelve would find it easy to learn a second language, but that it would be a difficult task for their parents and adolescent siblings. Folklore keeps this idea current, but research has failed to support it. In a study of English-speaking families that had moved to the Netherlands, Catherine Snow and Marian Hoefnagel-Höhle (1978) found that preschoolers (who should have been star pupils) had the most trouble of any family members in picking up Dutch. In fact, learning the new language even caused a drop in the preschoolers' command of English. Among these families, adolescents learned Dutch the fastest, and parents did much better than their preschool children. There apparently is no sensitive period for acquiring a second language.

Mechanistic Theories

Noam Chomsky regards grammatical categories (such as subject, predicate, object, and verb) as innate, but mechanistic theorists see them as emerging gradually with experience (Whitehurst, 1982). According to B. F. Skinner (1957) and Sidney Bijou and Donald Baer (1965), who are behavior-learning theorists, language is simply verbal behavior that is reinforced by the action of another person. The random babbling of babies, which springs from a genetic predisposition, gradually changes to words through the process of shaping and conditioning. In this view, children make inferences and generalizations based on the reinforcement that follows language use. With experience, they begin to see analogies between situations and abstract rules to cover them; in the process, they gradually acquire syntax (Whitehurst, 1982).

Social-learning theorists would add that imitation plays a major role in the acquisition of speech. A child can learn by observing parents and other models; when a later occasion warrants it, the child imitates the language forms he or she has heard. Both comprehension and speech, says Albert Bandura (1977), are based on observational learning. Critics of mechanistic theories suggest that such learning is unlikely to lead to the acquisition of rules. When a small girl says "All-gone sticky" after washing her hands, or "I seed two mouses," she is not imitating forms she has heard. The latter sentence, say these critics, shows the child's attempt to force on language a rule-governed regularity it does not possess.

Social-learning theorists maintain, however, that children do imitate the structures they hear. Such sentences as "I seed two mouses," says Bandura (1977), simply indicate that children "model too well," slavishly applying the forms they have heard others use. This delayed selective imitation, argue Grover Whitehurst and Ross Vasta (1975), helps explain children's acquisition of language structure. By reinforcing four-year-olds each time the children indicated their understanding of sentences with both direct and indirect objects (e.g., "The boy gives the puppy the bone"), Whitehurst (1974) was able to get them to use similar constructions in their own speech.

In the information-processing view taken by some cognitive psychologists, children are indeed able to figure out the rules of language. These psychologists believe that children's general cognitive abilities provide the tools that enable youngsters to analyze the speech they hear and figure out a grammar. In order to demonstrate this proposal, John Anderson (1983) programmed a computer with general problem-solving rules, then began feeding it sentences. Each sentence was paired with an abstract structure of its meaning, just as a child hears an utterance within a meaningful context. Although the computer had been given no syntac-

tic rules, it quickly developed them. Soon the computer was generating completely new sentences with few grammatical errors. Then the same researcher attempted to simulate his young son's acquisition of language with the computer. This time the computer had to learn vocabulary as well as syntax. With fewer trials than a twenty-four-month-old would encounter, the computer had learned nearly 150 words and was generating such sentences as "No more apple juice" and "Please Mommy read book."

Functional Theories

Researchers who support functional theories of language acquisition agree with biological theorists that maturation is an important factor and that children cannot acquire language until they reach a certain cognitive level. They also agree with mechanistic theorists that social interaction is the place to look for the beginnings of language. But they believe that innate mechanisms cannot, by themselves, explain the child's grasp of language, and that the basis for linguistic competence goes beyond conditioning and observational learning to include all nonlinguistic aspects of human interaction: turn-taking, mutual gaze, joint attention, context, assumptions, and cultural conventions. The forms of language are acquired, says Elizabeth Bates (1979), in order to carry out communicative functions.

Pragmatics is seen as the key to language development, with the nonlinguistic aspects of interaction providing the prespeech bases of language. As we have seen, these aspects send children a long way on the path to human communication before they say their first words. Instead of the unfolding of preprogrammed behavior, language becomes the product of the child's active interaction with an environment provided by other human beings (Gleason and Weintraub, 1978). These other human beings are tuned to the child's linguistic needs, and their speech meshes precisely with those needs. Jerome Bruner (1983) agrees; he proposes that familiar adults provide the child with formats, structured patterns of adult-infant interaction with clearly marked roles. These formats structure the child's familiar routines. Children may begin their language acquisition by using the context of these routines to figure out what speakers are trying to accomplish. Later, the formats are generalized to other situations. In this view, language competence grows out of familiar situations, such as games or seeking help—situations that provide frameworks in which children learn to make their intentions plain and to interpret the intentions of others. As Jean Berko Gleason and Sandra Weintraub (1978) point out, the cognitive development of children can result from their interaction with the physical world, but in order to acquire language, they must interact with other human beings. Language would not develop if children were simply exposed to it as passive listeners.

ACQUIRING A SYSTEM OF SOUNDS

In order to acquire language, babies must first separate the sounds of the human voice from other noises in the environment. Then they must distinguish between the sounds of speech and the coughs, whistles, throat clearings, and other noises produced by the adults around them. Finally, they face the task of breaking down the stream of speech into meaning.

Listening to Sounds

The job of language acquisition is made easier by the fact that babies seem born prepared to attend to speech. Babies only a few days old prefer human voices to other sounds, as Earl Butterfield and Gary Siperstein (1974) discovered when they gave babies a chance to hear music. By sucking a pacifier, the babies could turn on tape-recorded music. The babies sucked to get musical reinforcement, and they sucked more to hear voices singing with music than to hear melodies without accompanying voices.

These babies were actively selecting sound over silence and human sounds over nonhuman ones. Within the first month of life, human sounds take on added significance; for the sound of a person talking will stop a baby's cries, but the sound of a bell or rattle will not (Menyuk, 1971).

The first specific sounds an infant notices may be those words that receive the heaviest emphasis and that often occur at the ends of utterances. By six or seven weeks, an infant can detect the difference between syllables pronounced with rising and falling inflections. Very soon, these differences in adult stress and intonation can influence a baby's emotional states and behavior. Long before babies understand the words they hear, they can sense when an adult is playful or angry, attempting to initiate or terminate behavior, and so on, merely on the basis of such cues as the rate, volume, and melody of the adult's speech.

Just as significant for language development as the response to intonation is the ability to make fine distinctions between speech sounds. From numerous studies, it is clear that young infants can hear the difference between most language sounds—both consonants and vowels (Aslin, Pisoni, and Jusczyk, 1983). Whether this ability is present at birth is uncertain, but by the time babies are a month old (the earliest age tested), they have no trouble making such distinctions. Many of these studies relied on the knowledge that babies will suck on a nipple at a constant rate as long as nothing new or startling strikes their senses, but that a sudden change in stimulation will cause them to suck at a more rapid rate. By giving babies a pacifier attached to electronic recording equipment, researchers are able to monitor a baby's rate and intensity of sucking. They repeatedly present a sound, such as "ba," to the baby until sucking reaches a stable rate; that is, until the baby has habituated to the stimulus. Then they switch to slightly different sound, such as "pa," and babies immediately suck faster, indicating their ability to distinguish between the two closely related sounds. Such studies suggest that babies come into the world prepared not only to attend to speech but also to make precisely those discriminations among human sounds that are necessary if they are to acquire language.

Babies also perceive language sounds the way adults do—by category. For example, some sounds, such as *b* and *p*, differ only in the time between the release of the lips and the onset of sound. Sound, or voice-onset time, is immediate with *b* and follows about .06 second later with *p*. There is a boundary between the two sounds: all sounds with a voice-onset time on one side of the boundary are heard as *b*; all sounds on the other side of the boundary are heard as *p*. At one time psychologists believed that this manner of perception indicated that the infant's hearing system was specialized for the processing of speech (Eimas, 1974). But later research showed that infants (as well as adults) perceive all sounds—not just the sounds of speech—in a categorical manner (Jusczyk et al., 1977). In fact, it is now clear that some other species, including chinchillas and macaques, also perceive sound categorically (Aslin, Pisoni, and Jusczyk, 1983).

Experience may change the way babies perceive some sounds. Months of listening to the speech of others can either sharpen the baby's distinction between two very close sounds, or it can broaden his or her perception so that the infant no longer notices differences that once were quite apparent (Aslin, Pisoni, and Jusczyk, 1983). For example, one- to four-month-olds who live in English-speaking homes have no trouble perceiving a sound distinction that is made in Czech but not in English. And they also readily perceive a sound distinction that is made in Polish and French but not in English (Trehub, 1976). With time, however, the babies will probably stop noticing these distinctions, for English-speaking adults find it difficult to hear them. Yet people do not permanently lose the ability to make such perceptual distinctions; in one study (Pisoni et al., 1982), adults quickly relearned to make a distinction they had stopped hearing.

Using sound differences to signal a difference in meaning develops later than the ability to detect differences between sounds heard in isolation, as Olga Garnica (1973) found in a study of eighteen-month-old infants. She gave the children colored blocks with features pasted on them, naming each block with a nonsense syllable, such as "bok" or "pok." When asked to put the "pok" under the blanket, few of the infants seemed to hear the difference between the *b* and *p* sounds that newborns notice. After several training sessions, however, three times as many children made the distinction between "bok" and "pok." Apparently, children can learn to pay attention to distinctions they do not ordinarily notice, when there is a reason to do so.

Producing Sounds

Despite their sharp discrimination, it usually takes nearly a year before babies can produce sounds that can be identified as words. It is much more difficult for them to acquire motor control over the muscles and organs involved in producing speech than it is for them to perceive auditory distinctions. The progression from crying to babbling to speech follows the same sequence in most infants, but many pass through the linguistic developments earlier or later than the ages suggested in Figure 9.2.

A baby's first sounds are cries. After about three weeks, his or her vocalizations gradually increase in frequency and variety. Some sounds are only physical and digestive mouthings and gurglings; but by the second month babies invent new noises, from squeals to Bronx cheers, and repeat them again and again in a circular fashion (Wolff, 1969). Sounds of joy, called *cooing*, also may appear at this time, usually when babies seem happy: after eating, while watching a smiling face, when listening to singing, and while looking at or handling objects.

Infants in institutions with few adults around make fewer spontaneous noises and may not even cry as much as other babies, because crying is part of a child's social interaction. If no one comes to answer a cry, crying becomes a useless vocalization. When adults respond to the sounds a baby makes in play, the frequency of those sounds increases.

Babbling begins around the age of five or six

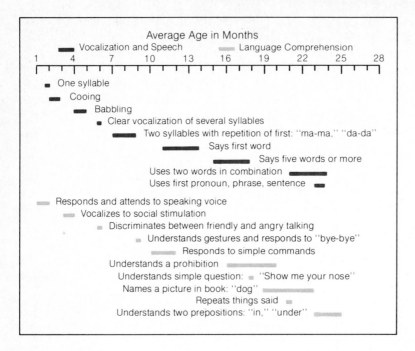

FIGURE 9.2 Highlights of language development during the first two years of life. Some infants may not show all the linguistic developments indicated. The average ages shown are approximations, and the length of the bars reflects the range in average ages that different researchers have reported for a particular linguistic development.

(Adapted from Lenneberg, 1967; McCarthy, D. "Language Development in Children," in L. Carmichael, ed., *Manual of Child Psychology*. 2nd ed. New York: Wiley, 1954, pp. 492–630; and Bayley, 1969)

months, when babies produce sequences of alternating vowels and consonants, such as "bababababa." These sound sequences give the impression that the baby is uttering a string of syllables. Such repetitions indicate that the baby's control over speech musculature has greatly improved. This control, along with the coordination of sound production with sound perception, is probably the primary function of babbling. When babies feel certain patterns of motor activity involving throat, tongue, and lip

muscles, they associate the movements with the sounds they hear themselves making. As babies gain motor control, babbling seems to follow the same rules and constraints that govern the development of words (deVilliers and deVilliers, 1978). As infants near the end of the first year, for example, they tend to babble consonants singly instead of in clusters, to put consonants at the beginning instead of at the end of a "syllable," and to drop final consonants. They also tend to switch the production of consonants from the back to the front of the mouth, shifting from babbles in which *g* and *k* sounds are frequent to those full of consonants formed with the tongue and lips—such as *b*, *p*, *d*, and *t*—the consonants that are found in children's early words (Oller et al., 1976).

Much early babbling appears to be sheer motor play, as indicated by the fact that deaf babies babble in the same way as babies who can hear. But because the babbling of normal six-month-old babies shows a greater diversity of sound than the babbling of deaf infants, we can suppose that hearing speech sounds stimulates the baby. Soon after six months, deaf infants stop babbling, whereas hearing infants go on to greater diversity and experimentation in their speech play (Lenneberg, 1967).

The early babbling of children from different language communities sounds alike. But toward the end of the first year, the infant's vocalizations change. Now the rising and falling pitch of his or her utterances becomes more and more like adult speech; the babblings of an English baby now sound like English, while the babblings of a Russian baby sound like Russian. At this time infants may produce long, complex sequences of meaningless sounds with the pitch contour of adult sentences. These sequences may appear when older infants are pretending to read or to talk to a doll.

Unlike babbling, first words do not sample a wide range of sounds. Indeed, when babies first begin to speak, they may be unable to imitate sounds they made earlier in playful babbling. First words tend to be short—one or two syllables—and each syllable generally consists of a consonant followed by a vowel. First syllables may be produced when infants simply release their lips while vocalizing. The first distinction among consonants that infants make is often between a sound such as "ma," which they produce by releasing air through the nose with the lips together and then opening the mouth, and "ba," which they produce by suddenly letting the air out between their lips. Once they have reached this point, they may be able to say "mama" and "ba" as distinct words; they are then ready to build a vocabulary.

The pronunciation of first words is not stable. If a baby's first word is something like "ba" for "ball," its pronunciation will vary from "bee" to "bow"; the consonant will also vary: it may be "pa," "va," "da," or "tha" (Ferguson and Farwell, 1975). Because a listener may expect to hear the sound "ball," he or she may believe the baby has a stable pronunciation of it. In fact, although babies can perceive the differences among sounds in adult speech, it takes a great deal of effort on their part to figure out how to produce the complex of sounds that correspond to adult words.

Because infants have few consonants at their command during the second year, their store of syllables is small and they often repeat them. For example, a year-old girl may say "pa-pa" or "bi-bi" or "car-car." Also, when she utters two words with different meanings, they may sound the same because her small collection of syllables offers few possibilities for different word forms. She may say "ba" to imitate the words "ball," "bird," and "flower." The first time she says "ba," her mother or father will probably say "ball" when a ball is nearby or "bird" when a bird flies by. Such auditory reinforcement helps the infant to shape her "ba" until at last she does say both "ball" and "bird."

Struggling with Sounds

The work of decoding and reproducing the sounds of speech does not end with the child's first words; many preschool children and some young schoolchildren have trouble articulating certain sounds. A common problem in English, for example, is the confusion between the consonants r and w, so that the child consistently says "west" instead of "rest" when it is naptime at nursery school.

Some children apparently do not notice any difference between the sounds they confuse, but they are in the minority. In an experiment John Locke (1979) conducted with three- to six-year-olds who confuse initial r's and w's, one-third of the group, when shown a picture of a common garden implement, agreed that it was indeed a "wake"—pronounced thus by an adult. But the rest of the children had no trouble distinguishing between the sound "rake" and the sound "wake" when an adult pronounced them, and they denied that a rake was a "wake"—although adults perceived them as saying exactly that in their speech.

Quite a few children who make speech errors respond in this way, often becoming indignant if adults substitute the children's sounds in their own speech. Such indignation is embodied in a conversation with a three-year-old girl reported by Wick Miller (1964). Miller began the conversation by asking the child her name:

Child: Litha.
Miller: Litha?
Child: No, *Litha*.
Miller: Oh, Lisa.
Child: Yes, Litha.

In some cases the child's exasperation can be explained by the fact that children *are* making a distinction in their speech that adults do not detect. When Judith Kornfeld (1971) subjected children's speech to spectrographic analysis, she found that two-year-olds who seemed to be saying "gwass" for both "glass" and "grass" were not producing a real *w* sound and that the sounds they made for *l* and *r* were consistently different from each other when analyzed by machine instead of by human ear.

Despite this actual difference in the child's production, tests have shown that when children hear their own recorded speech, most of them perceive it as adults do. In another study, John Locke (Locke and Kutz, 1975) showed five-year-olds pictures of a wing, a ring, and a king and asked them to point to the correct picture and label it when they heard the experimenter say the names. Later, as children heard their own naming of the objects played back, they again pointed to the pictures. All children could point to the correct picture when they heard the experimenter say the label, and children who customarily made the *l-r* distinction in their own speech also could identify the pictures from their own recorded labels. But children who had confused the sounds in their own speech pointed to the wing picture whether their taped voices were ostensibly saying "wing" or "ring." In other studies, Locke (1979) has found that children who say "wing" for "ring" when looking at a picture of a ring, if asked immediately, "Did you say 'wing'?" will reply, "No."

Children who confuse these sounds in their own production but not in their comprehension of them may be failing to process their own speech sounds. However, Locke thinks it more probable that the children do process their speech sounds but pay little attention to the auditory and kinesthetic feedback from them, relying instead on their knowledge of their own intentions and on the context of the situation.

ACQUIRING A SYSTEM OF MEANING

Some babies begin to use a variety of single words toward the end of their first year, but most will pass their first birthdays with a vocabulary of no more than three words. Before their second birthdays, their vocabularies begin to increase at an amazing speed. Between the ages of eighteen months and six years, the average child learns about nine words each day. By the time children are six, they have a vocabulary of about 14,000 words (Clark, 1983).

First Words

Babies' first words carry out the patterns of behavior and intent they have developed during the prespeech period. They use words to seek help, to initiate pleasant emotional interactions, and to persuade adults to play games or look at things with them (Bruner, 1980). Before they have separate labels for the objects and actions in their world, babies pass through a phase when a single sound performs many functions at once. This effect shows clearly in Table 9.1, which gives a child's first seven words. When this little girl said "uh," for example, and pointed to a toy that had fallen, she was simultaneously referring to the toy, expressing her concern that it had fallen, and requesting that it be given back to her. In this case, a single, undifferentiated utterance referred, expressed, and demanded at the same time. As we shall see, once a child can combine several words in one utterance, these functions will become differentiated in speech.

Table 9.1 THE FIRST SEVEN "WORDS" IN ONE CHILD'S LINGUISTIC DEVELOPMENT

Utterance	Age in Months	Meanings
uh?	8	An interjection. Also demonstrative, "addressed" to persons, distant objects, and "escaped toys."
dididi	9	Disapproval (loud). Comfort (soft).
mama	10	Refers vaguely to food. Also means "tastes good" and "hungry."
nenene	10	Scolding.
tt!	10	Used to call squirrels.
piti	10	Always used with a gesture, and always whispered. Seems to mean "interest(-ed), (-ing)."
deh	10	An interjection. Also demonstrative. Used with the same gesture as above.

(*Source:* Adapted from David McNeill, *The Acquisition of Language: The Study of Developmental Psycholinguistics.* New York: Harper & Row, 1970, p. 22. Based on material from Werner F. Leopold, *Grammar and General Problems in the First Two Years,* Vol. 3: Speech Development of a Bilingual Child: A Linguist's Record. Evanston, Ill.: Northwestern University Press, 1949, p. 6.)

An infant's first real words are related to the concepts he or she is acquiring, for, as Eve Clark (1983) says, learning the meaning of a word consists of learning which concept that word picks out. Often, these words are the names of objects, indicating the baby's recognition, first, that objects are worth talking about and, second, that they have names (Nelson and Nelson, 1978). The first object words include names of people (Dada), animals (dog), vehicles (car), toys (ball), food (juice), body parts (nose), clothing (shoe), and household implements (spoon). As we saw in Chapter 8, these words generally refer to concepts at the basic level; a baby learns "dog" but not "dachshund," "car" but not "Corvette," "flower" but not "daisy."

Soon children are learning situation words.

When they do, says Clark (1983), they focus on the outcome of actions. They may say "up," when talking about a toy that a parent has placed out of reach, or "off" to indicate that the nipple has come off the juice bottle. They also learn words that describe temporary states of objects or situations; many of these words focus on the outcome of actions, such as "broken," "dirty," or "wet." Words that describe permanent states, such as "big" or "red," usually come a little later, when the child is about two years old. According to Clark, these three kinds of words describe the first 50 to 200 words in a child's vocabulary.

The Structure of Meaning

No one is certain just how children go about structuring word meanings; and when children first learn a word, its meaning may be very different from the conventional meaning attributed to it by adults. Sometimes a word means much more to children than adults believe, and sometimes it means less. Such differences in word meaning go unnoticed unless a child's error makes the discrepancy obvious.

OVEREXTENSION Young children sometimes extend the meaning of a word in their small vocabularies to cover objects or actions for which they have no word. This widespread application of a word, called **overextension,** is logical; the child generally applies the word to objects that resemble one another in some way (Clark, 1983). Overextension is a fairly common practice, and analyses of parental diaries and observations of young children indicate that from 20 to 34 percent of a child's early words are extended in this fashion on some occasion (Nelson et al., 1978). For example, one little boy extended "fly" from a specific insect to all small insects, bits of dirt, specks of dust, the infant's own toes, crumbs of bread, and a toad. The vast majority of overextensions are based on shape, but a few are based on movement, size, taste, and texture. Even fewer overextensions refer to activities instead of objects (Clark, 1983).

As children acquire new words and have new experiences, they reorganize their early word meanings. Eve Clark (1973) charts this development for a single word, showing its course in a young boy's experiences with the word "bow-wow." He first learns to apply "bow-wow" to dogs, but he soon uses it to refer to many animals—dogs, cows, horses, sheep, and cats—perhaps basing his meaning of the word on shape and movement. When he learns the word "moo," the little boy distinguishes cows from other animals, apparently dividing the animal kingdom into two categories: cows ("moo") and other animals ("bow-wow"). As the boy learns more animal names, he keeps subdividing the general class, "bow-wow," so that eventually he has separate names for dogs, cows, horses, sheep, and cats.

Children's overextensions may not signify a true confusion of meaning. Perhaps, as Grover Whitehurst (1982) has suggested, overextension is based on the child's need to communicate. The child may know that the word does not actually apply to the new object he or she has just named, but lacking the correct word, the youngster reaches for the nearest label in the same semantic neighborhood. Children who overextend words in speaking often understand the same words in a much more restricted fashion. Janice Gruendel (1977) has found, for example, that youngsters who refer to all animals as "bow-wow" will always pick a dog from a group of animals when asked to point to the "bow-wow." These children never point to a cat or a sheep, even though they themselves use the term to refer to those animals. It is as if, she says, in comprehension a word denotes a single concept (such as dog), while in production it denotes the entire category of which the concept is a member (animals). In addition, overextensions may not always be examples of naming. Sometimes it appears as if the child is calling attention to similarities; as when a youngster calls a grapefruit a "moon" (referring to its roundness). If the child's grasp of language were firmer, he or she might say "It's like a moon" or "It's round" (Nelson et al., 1978).

"Bow-wow" may enter this baby's vocabulary as the word for dog, but until the child has words for the rest of the animal kingdom, "bow-wow" may be overextended to refer to horses, cows, goats, sheep, and cats. (Suzanne Arms/Jeroboam)

UNDEREXTENSION Another clue to the way children structure word meanings is a feature that is the opposite of the very young child's tendency to overextend meanings. Children also tend to **underextend** meanings of words, applying to a term only part of the meaning it has for adults. Children of all ages underextend words, and perhaps underextension is the first stage in the acquisition of any word (Clark, 1983). But the practice generally goes unnoticed, because detecting it requires us to notice the "non-use" of a word.

Underextension has been studied primarily among older children. A child may know the word "food" perfectly well, for example, and asked what it means, say in the functional sort of definition that is prevalent among children, "Food is to eat." Yet asked if a cookie or a lollipop or ketchup is food, the child will say no.

The child probably has never heard anyone refer to ketchup, cookies, and lollipops as food and may have established a central meaning for the term different from that held by adults. Food might mean, for example, "things to eat that are good for you," or "fruits, vegetables, meats, and cereal." The underextension arises when children come upon a poor example of a term—items that are a long way from the central meaning they have for the word (Anglin, 1977).

Children add verbs to their vocabularies more slowly than they add nouns, and for that reason, verbs are frequently underextended. Nouns are often concrete, and their meaning is bounded by their physical nature. In contrast, verbs express relationships that depend on abstract concepts; thus, learning the meaning of a verb requires a child to learn the abstract relations involved (Gentner, 1978). In the sentence, "The teacher gave Scott a gold star," for example, a child can see the teacher, the star, and Scott, but must deduce the abstract relationship between the teacher's initial possession of the star, Scott's final possession of it, and the way the star passed from one to the other (freely? by coercion?), and so forth.

According to Dedre Gentner (1978), children learn verbs in the order of their complexity and, until they know the meaning of a complex verb, will underextend it, representing just those aspects of it with which they are familiar. To test this proposal, she asked a group of children who were between three and eight years old to act out such sentences as, "Make Ernie buy a car from Bert," using dolls, toy cars, and play money. The youngest children could act out the meanings of "give" and "take"; children who were a little older could act out "pay" and "trade"; but only the oldest children could act out "buy," "sell," or "spend money." Younger children most frequently acted out "buy" as "take" and "sell" as "give." As Gentner points out, such children have acquired enough of the meaning of "buy" and "sell" to know that objects change hands in a certain direction, but they are unaware of the monetary nature of the transaction.

This sort of development could be traced in another study, in which John Miscione and his associates (1978) tested three- to seven-year-olds on their knowledge of "know" and "guess." Most three-year-olds simply have no knowledge of the words' distinct meanings, say the investigators. They use "know" and "guess" indiscriminately and either randomly choose one or else use the one that has been more common or regarded as more desirable in their experience. Sometime after four, the words begin to separate in meaning, and children use "know" to mean both "know" and "guess successfully," while using "guess" to mean "guess unsuccessfully." Next, they go through a phase in which "guess successfully" is added to the meaning of "guess" but not applied consistently. Finally, around five or later, they use both words correctly on all occasions. This development shows how closely language and cognition are linked, say the investigators, because in order to use "guess" correctly, children must have advanced to a level of abstraction where external appearances and physical outcome (the success or failure of the guess) no longer dominate their thoughts or the meaning of their words.

DEICTIC WORDS It is surprising enough that children master the underlying rules of language by the time they start school. It is nothing short of astounding that as toddlers they have already begun to learn the deictic function of words, a complicated aspect of semantics. **Deictic words** change their meaning because they locate things in reference to the speaker. "I" and "you," "my" and "your," "here" and "there," "this" and "that," "right" and "left," all reverse meaning depending on who is talking. Understanding this change would seem to be a perplexing task, but children pick it up—and without anyone explaining it to them.

Very early in the second year, they learn to discriminate between "I/you" and "my/your." This ability to shift perspective appears to grow out of the turn-taking and role interactions with primary caregivers (Bruner, 1980). Youngsters seem to learn first the term most closely associated with the speaker's position: this, here, near, and now. Later they learn the distant terms: that, there, far, then. But until both terms have been learned, children have not mastered the deictic system (Garvey, 1984).

From observation, Jill and Peter deVilliers (1978) decided that toddlers had some inkling of the distinction between such expressions as "here" and "there." As they point out, when a small boy is told from across the room by his mother that his toy truck is "over here," her son immediately trots to her vicinity to begin his search. But since in this case context might reveal meaning, the two researchers invented a game to test the discrimination. In this hide-and-seek game, children sat across from an experimenter. Between them was a low Styrofoam wall; on each side of the wall was an overturned cup. While children closed their eyes, candy was hidden under one of the cups. Then the experimenter told the children where the candy was concealed, using a deictic expression ("The M&M is on *this* side of the wall"). Even three-year-olds were adept at translating from the speaker's perspective into their own and had no trouble with "here/there," "my/your," and "this/that."

But other studies have found that children are slow to extend comprehension of "this/that" to all situations. For example, in one study, half of the seven-year-olds were not always sure of the distinction between "this" and "that," even though they had been using the words for years (Webb and Abrahamson, 1976).

The Use of Errors

Children's errors of comprehension and production are frequently used as clues to semantic knowledge, for researchers assume that errors indicate a child's lack of knowledge or the inability to retrieve a word from memory (Bowerman, 1978). In some studies, however, the reason for children's misunderstandings is unclear. For example, Margaret Donaldson and G.

Balfour (1968) found that young children confuse the words "less" and "more." The researchers constructed two apple trees from cardboard, on each tree putting six hooks from which red cardboard apples could be hung. After hanging a different number of apples on each tree, they asked three-year-olds which tree had more (or less) apples than the other. Preschoolers treated the two words as synonyms, answering every question as if both words meant "more." Donaldson and Balfour assumed that the children knew only that "more" and "less" had to do with amount, but not that they were opposites. Later research, however, indicated that children may not have gone by the meaning of the words but used context to decipher the researcher's questions. Susan Carey (1972) found that if she asked three-year-olds to "Make it so the glass has *tiv* in it," substituting a nonsense word for "more" or "less," the youngsters generally added water to the glass. Carey suggests that the context of the remark made during an obvious test led the children to understand that they were to do something with the amount of liquid in the glass. Adding water was a more typical response than pouring it out. In another study, three-year-olds did not know the meaning of "less," but they never confused it with "more" (Wannemacher and Ryan, 1978). Four-year-olds depended on context for their understanding of "less," and only five-year-olds had a clear understanding of the term. There appears to be a straightforward reason for the lag in the acquisition of "less": young children rarely hear the word. When Pamela Blewitt (1982) studied adults' speech to children in nursery school, she found only one use of "less" compared with 479 uses of "more."

But errors, especially errors of production, are not always instances of misunderstanding, believes Melissa Bowerman (1978, 1982). Instead, they may simply be slips of the tongue by knowledgeable children. When Bowerman recorded the speech of her preschool daughters, she found many examples of U-shaped behavioral growth (discussed in Chapter 4). The girls began to use words incorrectly weeks or even months after they had been using them properly. When Christy was three and a half, for example, she said at bedtime, "I don't want to go to bed yet. Don't *let* me go to bed," confusing "let" and "make." And two-year-old Eva, finding her big sister's juice glass empty, said, "Then *put* her some more," confusing "put" and "give."

The girls were insensitive to the errors they made and never tried to correct them, but sometimes used the same word correctly only a few minutes after they had used it improperly. They rarely confused nouns; most of their errors were confined to verbs, prepositions, and adjectives that bore some relation in meaning, such as "behind" and "after," or "take" and "put." Bowerman suggests that children learn individual words in specific contexts, without recognizing their similarity. Errors do not appear until youngsters become aware of the similarity, and their awareness forces them to work out how various aspects of meaning apply to related words. This may put a strain on children's ability to plan and monitor speech, so that when they search for a word, they select the wrong one from the same semantic neighborhood.

Meaning in First Sentences

Even when infants can speak only one word at a time, they appear to understand the longer utterances of their parents and older siblings. Their single-word utterances may also mean much more than they can say at one time. Toward the end of the one-word period, infants often produce a series of separate, one-word utterances that seem to relate to a larger meaning, although they speak each word with a falling intonation and pause between the words. For example, an eighteen-month-old girl described by Ronald Scollan (1979) held her foot above his tape recorder, looked up at him and said "tape" and then "step," as she threatened to step on the machine.

Within two months, this child was putting together two words with ease, saying such things as "drink soup" and "see Ron," with no pause between the words. The emergence of this two-word stage seems to be the result of an increase in neurological capacity, so that the child can process two words before forgetting the first. Now, although the child's level of understanding has not changed, he or she can put more information into a single statement.

The two-word stage is significant because it represents a striking advance in children's ability to code their understanding in linguistic terms and to project their ideas into the world of human interaction. Yet, with two-word sentences at their disposal, children still mean more than they can say in one utterance. For example, a small boy who wants his father to throw a ball cannot express the entire thought in a single statement. He can say "Daddy throw," "Throw ball," or "Daddy ball"; but he cannot say "Daddy throw ball." So youngsters again resort to stringing together short utterances to express a longer thought—as did the little girl in Scollan's study, who said such things as "Bathtub. Scrub it," and "Scary monster. Read dat."

Early language development has been studied in many different cultures, and everywhere the picture is the same. Sometime before their second birthday, children start to put two words together to express the same range of basic concepts that universally form the core of human language. Indeed, a large part of later language development is primarily a matter of elaborating and refining basic notions that are already present at this early age.

Expanding Vocabularies

Children's semantic development is a gradual process, and considering the speed with which new words are added to their vocabularies, it seems safe to assume that at any time there are many words whose relevance they roughly grasp, but whose precise meaning they have not worked out (Miller, 1978a).

But what sort of meaning do children focus on when they are in the process of expanding their vocabularies? According to Eve Clark (1983), as children become aware of a gap in their store of words, they begin looking for a new word that will fill it. This means that children will learn fastest words about aspects of the world that are of interest to them. Until they find the conventional word they are seeking, youngsters rely on overextension, on all-purpose words ("that" and "thing" for objects; "do," "make," and "go" for verbs) or on words they have coined themselves. For example, a little girl may call a gardener a "plant-man"; a little boy may use a noun as a verb, and ask his mother (who has been mending his jeans), "Is it all needled?"

In order to find out how a single word enters a child's vocabulary, researchers at the Rockefeller University nursery school set up an experiment with a new color term. Susan Carey and her associates painted a cup and tray an olive shade and introduced them into the school routine (see Miller, 1977). To make sure that none of these three-year-olds used learning from outside the school, they decided to call the color "chromium," Before the term was used, most children called the olive cup and tray "green." During the course of ordinary activities one day, an investigator used the term ("Please bring me the chromium cup") but made no attempt to teach it. The children had no trouble understanding the reference, because all that was needed to comply with the request was the knowledge "not the red one" or "not the blue one."

The word was not mentioned again. Six weeks after their single exposure to the word "chromium," the children were given a color test, in which they named color samples. One of the colors was olive. Eight of the fourteen children gave a response to the olive chip different from the one they had used before they heard the term chromium (two simply said they did not know the color's name; six used a new color term). After only one casual experience, more than half the children had learned that olive is not green and had begun to restructure their terminologies for the color domain. When

we consider that these children are mastering about nine words a day and are working on many other conceptual puzzles, it is difficult not to be amazed at their linguistic feat.

ACQUIRING A SYSTEM OF STRUCTURES

In order to become a competent speaker, a child must develop a command of syntax, especially of grammar. Grammar does not mean the schoolbook rules of how to speak "properly," but the rules that all of us know implicitly and use to organize our words into sentences. It is this knowledge of inflections, prepositions, word order, and so on that makes it possible for us to produce and understand sentences outside of any immediate physical context. The development of grammatical knowledge actively occupies the child from two to five, but some of the rudimentary grammatical tools are present before that time.

First Syntactic Devices

Early language acquisition, which lasts until the child breaks the two-word limit on his or her sentences, occupies approximately the first two years of life. Until a child can put together more than two words, he or she uses only a few syntactic devices, and these depend not only on the language the child is learning, but on the individual child as well. In the past decade or so, as Michael Maratsos (1983) points out, researchers have come to realize that this stage of language acquisition is not a "neatly packaged, universal, and clear period" of language development (p. 716).

INTONATION Infants at the one-word stage rely on intonation to communicate the intent behind a single word. When one-year-olds use intonation in this way, it is clear that they are not using their word simply to label an object, as Figure 9.3 indicates. Paula Menyuk and Nancy Bernholtz (1969) recorded the word "door" as spoken by an infant on three different occasions. When the tape was played, listeners had no trouble agreeing when the child made a declaration, made an emphatic statement, or asked a question. When the child used a falling pitch, listeners judged the utterance as simply referring to a door. When the word was uttered with a rising intonation, listeners interpreted it as a question. And when the intonation rose sharply and then fell, it was heard as an emphatic assertion or demand. Thus, the single word "door" could mean, "That's a door"; or it could mean, "Is that a door?" "Are you going to open the door?"; or it could mean, "Open the door!" or "Close the door!"

Toward the end of the two-word stage, another intonational device develops—the use of stress to convey meaning. When saying "Baby chair," for example, a child may emphasize the first word, saying "BABY chair" to indicate possession ("That is baby's chair"); or the child may emphasize the second word, saying "Baby CHAIR," to indicate location ("Baby is in the chair") or destination ("Put baby in the chair").

WORD ORDER In English and in many other languages, the order in which words are spoken partially determines their meaning. English sentences typically follow a subject-verb-object sequence, but this general concept of word order does not seem to develop until children are older. Children in the two-word stage do not fit their two words into the standard pattern, yet the child's two-word sentences generally follow the expected order: a twenty-month-old child does not say, "Throw Daddy" or "Ball throw." Instead of producing a random collection of words, using their two-word limit in any order, children appear to rely on semantics and context to establish permissible word combinations (Maratsos, 1983). At first, it seems, children develop many semantically based categories, such as actor, possessor, and location—each with its own small pattern. For example, one pattern is actor + action, which produces sentences like "Daddy throw." Another is action + patient (object or person receiving the force of the action); this pattern produces sentences like "Throw ball." Eventually, the small patterns come together and the child grasps general rules, but this does not happen until youngsters have left the two-word stage.

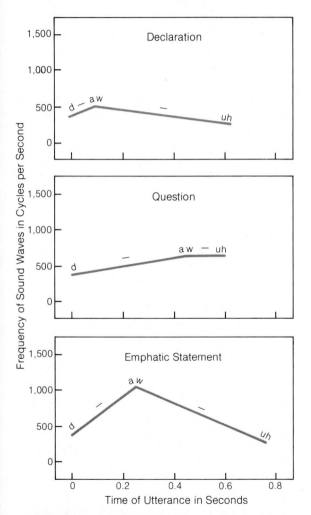

FIGURE 9.3 Three intonation patterns for the word "door" spoken by an infant at the one-word stage.

(After Menyuk, 1971)

This toddler constructs his two-word utterances according to the word patterns he has developed. He may say "Throw ball" or "Daddy throw," but he is unlikely to say "Ball throw." (Dave Schaefer/Jeroboam)

One influence on the patterns developed by young children seems to be the parents' language style (Nelson, 1981). When mothers use language mostly to teach, children seem to focus on the informational aspects of language; their two-word utterances are heavy with nouns. But when mothers use language mostly to get things done, telling their children what to do, children seem to focus on the social aspects of language; their two-word utterances are heavy with pronouns and they produce speech for many social routines.

To English speakers, it seems as if the subject-verb-object sequence is the natural form for language to take. But some languages do not follow this word order, and children learning those languages develop word patterns that correspond to the form of their own language. In Germany, for example, very young children consistently place the object *before* the verb in their two-word sentences, developing patient + action sequences that fit German word order (Roeper, 1973). Different or flexible word orders seem to pose no problem to children learning such languages; they acquire them as rapidly and as easily as English-speaking children acquire English (Maratsos, 1983).

When children first begin to combine two words, their sentences show wide individual differences. Martin Braine (1976) believes this variety shows that children have discovered different patterns of word order. One child may convey an object's location by naming the object first and the place second ("Baby chair"); another may first discover a pattern in which the place comes first ("Here baby," "There book"). A little boy in Braine's study developed a highly restricted pattern that consisted of only a part of the action + patient sequence. This child could say, "Eat cookie" or "Drink juice," but used the sequence only to describe the ingestion of food or drink. He did not produce such sequences as "Throw ball." Apparently, children do not follow a universal order in acquiring the various sequences (Maratsos, 1983).

INFLECTION Grammatical markers, such as the possessive "-'s" and the past tense "-ed," that are added to words to change their meanings are called **inflections.** Compared with other languages, English uses few inflections, and children do not learn them until they have left the two-word stage (Whitehurst, 1982). In some languages inflections are essential; they establish the contrasts in meaning that English expresses by word order. For example, in Turkish, where word order is highly flexible, an inflection is added to the object to make its role clear. If these inflections are clearly marked, as they are in Turkish, children acquire the endings during the two-word stage (Slobin, 1982). In fact, two-year-olds who are learning Turkish understand sentences like, "The cat chases the dog," but youngsters learning English or Italian usually

Crib Speech and Language Acquisition

About twenty-five years ago, Ruth Weir (1962) set up a tape recorder near her two-year-old son's bed. For several nights, she recorded Anthony's solitary talk just before he went to sleep. He seemed to be actively testing the language, trying out different combinations of words. On one occasion, the two-year-old said, "On the blanket—Under the blanket. . . . Berries—Not berries. . . . Too hot—Not too hot." Later, he tried, "Can bite—Bite— Have a bite. . . . Broke the vacuum—The broke—Get some broke—Alice broke the baby fruit" (p. 19).

Some psychologists wondered just how typical Anthony's experience was. Neither of Stan Kuczaj's (1983) two sons had produced any crib speech, so Kuczaj began to study fourteen children who did. He hoped to discover whether crib speech differs among children and whether it is an important aid in learning language. At the beginning of the study, the youngsters were from fifteen to twenty-four months old; each one was recorded every week until he or she stopped producing crib speech.

Crib speech, Kuczaj found, took a number of forms, and each child's crib speech had its own distinctive pattern. Sometimes children repeated the same word or phrase again and again; at other times, they built up word combinations, substituted single words in a phrase, began with fragments of words or phrases and then completed them, or broke down a phrase they had heard into its parts.

These children's crib speech was like An-

thony's in many ways. For example, it could be grouped in "paragraphs"—chains of related phrases in which a child varied the forms of crib speech. One youngster produced the following paragraph:

> He's in truck. He's in back. Miss Piggy in back. I put Miss Piggy in back. I put bunny rabbit in back. I put Miss Piggy in trunk. I put Miss Piggy in trunk first, first. I put Miss Piggy in back. Put bunny rabbit in the . . back (p. 169).

Kuczaj believes that crib speech may be intrinsically rewarding—children engage in it because it is fun—but he also believes that it helps them learn language. Learning language requires children to acquire new knowledge, categorize it, and relate it to old knowledge. Crib speech may give youngsters an opportunity to do just this. The process of breaking down an utterance may help them understand syntactic rules and categories (subject, object, verb). Building upon words and completing phrases may help them stretch their capacity to produce words.

When children hear a new language form, says Kuczaj, they first process it in short-term memory and store it. Later, they may recall the information, interpret it, and fit it into the information they already have. Crib speech gives them an ideal place for this sort of language practice. No one will laugh at the "cute baby" who mispronounces a word or misuses a verb. No one will interfere if a youngster makes a comment that is not "nice" ("You're bad") or issues a command ("Go to bed"). The child is alone and can test combinations of words without worrying about their consequences.

do not understand such sentences until they are about three years old. In such sentences, Turkish marks the direct object ("dog") with an inflection, but English relies on word order.

The Development of Rules

To discover children's knowledge of grammar, some developmental psychologists observe and record children's natural speech, noting well-formed utterances, omissions and errors, and utterances children produce that they probably have never heard. Others set up situations in which children must either produce certain language forms, such as passive constructions, or else demonstrate that they can understand them.

DEMONSTRATING RULES When observing young children, researchers use indirect evidence to infer a child's knowledge of linguistic rules. Each time children correct their own language, they show that they believe certain combinations of words are incorrect—revealing that they possess some grammatical standards. Their corrections also reveal that the children have been listening to their speech and evaluating it against those standards (Clark, 1982). Children correct their own pronunciation, choice of words, and syntax. When Eve Clark (1982) recorded the speech of three preschoolers over a period of several months, she found that most corrections made by the youngest child, who was just twenty-two months old when the study began, had to do with pronunciation. Syntactic corrections rose steadily from the beginning until the end of the study, when the oldest child was about three and a half years old. For example, at two years and eight months, Kate said, "The kittycat is—de—de spider's kissing the kittycat's back," switching the kittycat from subject to object of the sentence. In a study of older children, Mary Ann Evans (1985) found that second-graders correct their own speech more often than kindergartners do. Kindergart-

ners interrupted 7 percent of their utterances in order to correct them, but second-graders interrupted themselves 19 percent of the time. For example, one youngster said, "He felt like there's bells in his ears and he can't—couldn't hear."

In a major longitudinal study of language development, Roger Brown, Courtney Cazden, and Ursula Bellugi-Klima (1968) observed three children, whom they called Adam, Eve, and Sarah, over a period of three years. When the study began, the youngsters were just beginning to combine words into two-word utterances. In the recorded dialogues, it was easy to trace a child's gradual grasp of English syntax. For example, in a single dialogue between two-year-old Eve and her mother, both participants made requests, asked questions, and expressed positive and negative statements. On this occasion, certain elements that were systematically missing from Eve's speech were present in her mother's sentences. Eve's mother used auxiliary verbs (forms of "to be," "to do," and so forth) wherever English syntax requires them. These grammatical elements were not present in Eve's speech. Eve, for example, said, "It time," whereas her mother said, "It's time." Although the child's speech lacked the required auxiliary verb, it was understandable.

Within three months, Eve's language showed a dramatic change. She was using auxiliary verbs in negatives, questions, and statements. Her sentences were longer and more complex, and she was joining simple sentences together with such words as "when" and "and." She still made errors, of course, and some of these errors revealed that she was beginning to figure out the rules of English. For example, she said, "Then Fraser won't hear her too," where an adult would say, "Then Fraser won't hear her either." There is an odd rule in English that changes "too" to "either" in negative sentences (for example, it is correct to say, "Fraser will hear her too"). Eve had not figured out this rule for negative statements, but her use of "too" indicated that she understood the general function carried out by both "too" and "either."

FIGURING OUT RULES After studying research on language acquisition in many cultures, Dan Slobin (1973) concluded that children approach language with a set of seven beliefs that they apply to the words they hear. These beliefs, which Slobin calls **operating principles,** are strategies for processing language. Slobin proposed that these tendencies are universal among children and that linguistic constructions that follow them are easiest for a child to learn.

The first principle is, *Pay attention to the ends of words*. In languages Slobin studied, children learned suffixes (such as "-ed," "-ing," "-s," in English) more rapidly than they learned prefixes. This principle is essential in languages such as Russian, and it also plays a role in English. Its existence was demonstrated when Stan Kuczaj (1979) tested preschool children with a nonsense syllable, which he alternately placed at the beginning and end of words. For example, some children heard, "The boy drove the ip-car," while others heard, "The boy drove the car-ip." With some children, the syllable "ip" was always given the meaning "big"; with other children it was always given the meaning "red." Whether "ip" meant "big" or "red," children who heard the syllable as a suffix found its meaning easier to learn than children who heard it as a prefix. Either children process word endings better than initial sounds or they pay attention to endings because such attention has paid off in the past.

Another operating principle involved in Kuczaj's study was one that states, *The phonological form of words can be systematically modified*. In the study, the same suffix ("ip") was systematically added to nouns, altering their sounds, and most children found it comprehensible.

The remaining operating principles are:

Pay attention to the order of words; a principle we saw followed in the two-word stage.

Avoid interruption or rearrangement of linguistic units; children do not rearrange prepositional phrases; they say "on the table," not "table the on."

Mark underlying semantic relations clearly; children indicate the existence of two or more objects in a consistent way—by adding an "s" or "z" sound to the end of words.

Avoid exceptions; children tend to apply linguistic rules across the board, without making exceptions for irregular words, as we shall see in the next section.

The use of grammatical markers should make semantic sense. The last principle, Slobin believes, is demonstrated when a language violates it. Some languages assign gender to inanimate objects in an arbitrary fashion and insist that the ending of adjectives conform to the gender of the noun. In Spanish, for example, where pens are feminine and pencils are masculine, it is "una pluma blanca" (a white pen) but "un lapiz blanco" (a white pencil). Children have great difficulty learning these grammatical markers that denote gender, because they are arbitrary and make no semantic sense.

Not all of these operating principles have been tested in experimental situations, so there may be exceptions. For example, children do not always "mark underlying semantic relations clearly." If they did, they would say, "I will go" instead of "I'll go" (Maratsos, 1979). Slobin (1982) agrees, and he now suggests that some of his seven principles may not indicate the child's preset tendency, but rather factors that make the structure of a language easier to learn.

The Appearance of Error

As young children's grasp of the language increases, new errors sometimes appear in their speech. This is, of course, yet another example of U-shaped behavioral growth. It appears in semantic development, as we have seen, and it shows up in the development of syntax as well.

Many of children's language errors can be viewed as attempts to make the language more systematic than it is. Such errors often seem to catch a child following the principle, "Avoid exceptions," in which they overregularize the language. **Overregularization** is especially apparent in the past tense of verbs. The regular way to form the past tense for English verbs is to add "-ed": "walk, walked"; "ask, asked." However, many common verbs form their past tense in an irregular manner: "go, went"; "come, came"; "break, broke." Young children learn a number of these irregular past forms as separate words and produce correct sentences: "It broke"; "Daddy went out"; "I fell." After using these correct past tenses for many months, they discover the rule for forming regular past tenses. Suddenly, most of the irregular past forms disappear from their speech, to be replaced by overregularized forms. The child of three or four now may say, "It breaked"; "Daddy goed out"; "I falled." As children get older, a curious pattern of redundant usage develops. Five- and six-year-olds begin to drop such forms as "eated," "goed," and "marked," and in their place may use a doubled past form, like "ated," "wented," and "maded" (Kuczaj, 1978). By the time children are seven, they have abandoned the redundant form; most have ceased to overregularize common verbs in any way.

What looks like regression in younger children is actually a sign of progress in the child's analysis of English. Clearly, children have not heard the overregularized forms from their parents; instead, they have constructed the forms to conform with the regularities they have noticed in the speech of others. And so a change from "went" to "goed" indicates that children have, on their own, discovered a regular pattern in English and are using it in their speech. They are avoiding exceptions and, by insisting on indicating the idea of the past in a regular way, are also marking semantic relations clearly—another operating principle (Kuczaj, 1978).

During these periods of overregularization, a child's speech seems remarkably impervious to gentle efforts at correction, as the following conversation reported by Jean Berko Gleason (1967) shows:

Child: My teacher holded the baby rabbits and we patted them.

Mother: Did you say your teacher held the baby rabbits?

Child: Yes.

Mother: What did you say she did?

Child: She holded the baby rabbits and we patted them.

Mother: Did you say she held them tightly?

Child: No, she holded them loosely.

Although his mother substituted the correct verb form twice in this short dialogue, the little boy persisted in repeating "holded"—tenaciously clinging to his own linguistic structure. Apparently, regularity can be more powerful in its influence on children than are previous practice, reinforcement, and immediate imitation of adult forms. The child at this level of development seeks regularity and is deaf to exceptions (Bellugi, 1970).

As children gradually become aware of their overregularization errors, the correct form seems to filter in and out of consciousness. Dan Slobin (1978) reports a conversation with his young daughter, who was in the transitional phase. Slobin asked her if the baby-sitter had read a book the previous night and Heida replied, using first the correct past tense, "read," then switching to "readed." During the exchange, Slobin said, "That's the book she readed, huh?" His own overregularization alerted Heida to the correct form and she replied in an annoyed tone, "Yeah . . . *read!*" following up with the comment, "Dum-dum!" As Slobin persisted in using "readed," Heida finally protested, "Will you stop that, Papa?" Although Heida was shifting back to "read," she may still have been saying "goed" and "maked," because children eliminate their overregularization errors slowly. They must learn, word by word, that only a single past form exists for each irregular verb (Kuczaj, 1978).

The form of plurals is another area in which children tend to overregularize. Many common English words have irregular plural forms: "feet," "mice," "men," "children." These irregular forms must be learned as separate vocabulary items. From observations of free speech, researchers have found that the child who has been correctly using some irregular plural forms may, for a time, overgeneralize the newly discovered rules of formation and say "foots," "mans," "mouses." Here again, a child may keep the irregular form but apply the plural rule anyway, saying the redundant, "feets," "mens," "mices."

Comprehending Complex Constructions

Children often develop their own simple rules for figuring out the meaning of sentences, although these strategies sometimes lead a child into misinterpreting certain kinds of sentences, such as those using passive constructions. Children hear many simple declarative sentences, each containing an actor, an action, and the object of that action: "Mommy is eating soup"; "Jane feeds her doll"; "Scott spilled the milk." In each of these sentences, the relationship between the actor ("Scott"), action ("spilled"), and object of the action ("milk") is expressed by word order. In passive constructions, however, the word order is reversed, and in the sentence, "The milk was spilled by Scott," the object of the action ("milk") is the first noun in the sentence, and the actor ("Scott") the last.

Children's comprehension of sentences can be revealed by giving them objects to manipulate and asking them to act out the statements they hear. For example, the investigator may ask the child to act out "The truck follows the car." Using a toy truck and a toy car, most two- and three-year-olds can act out such declarative sentences; but when asked to demonstrate a passive sentence, such as "The truck is followed by the car," even four-year-olds are seldom correct. In fact, most four-year-olds carry out the opposite action each time, relying on word order.

Word order may not be the only cue children use. Henrietta Lempert (1978) found that young children also use the animateness of the nouns involved to judge the meaning of passive sentences. In her study, when both subject and object were either animate or inanimate, the question did not arise. But when the sentence mixed animate and inanimate forms ("The ball is hit by Mickey Mouse"), three- and four-year-olds systematically chose the inanimate noun as the subject (acting out the sentence as "The ball hits Mickey Mouse," but correctly acting out "Mickey Mouse is hit by the ball"). The five-year-olds in her study had given up this strategy, generally giving correct demonstrations of passive sentences. Other studies indicate that not until the school years do children understand passive constructions in which the verb involved is not an action verb ("Donald Duck was liked by Goofy") (Maratsos et al., 1979).

Passive sentences are not the only constructions that give children trouble. When active sentences are complicated, even nine-year-olds may resort to word order, interpreting the noun that most closely precedes the verb as the subject (C. Chomsky, 1969). For example, they may interpret "Sally promised Mother to wash the dishes" as meaning that Mother washed the dishes.

Children do not progress directly toward adult grammar but instead construct and discard a variety of provisional grammars as they go along. As a result of these changing strategies, sentences that are correctly interpreted at one age may be misinterpreted at a later age.

Although children have mastered much of their language's grammar by the time they are four, they will continue to add to their knowledge of complex syntactical structures during the school years (Palermo and Molfese, 1972). This seems to be true regardless of the language they are learning and regardless of the setting in which they have been exposed to it (Slobin, 1975).

SUMMARY

Human language is set off from animal communication systems by three important properties: **semanticity, productivity,** and **displacement.** Studies of the way children acquire language generally focus on one of language's four levels: **syntax** (structure), **phonology** (sound), **semantics** (meaning), or **pragmatics** (social use).

The private functions of language are representation, thought, and memory. Once children can represent events in the world with linguistic symbols, they can solve a greater range of problems, and their information-processing powers expand. A command of language also enhances memory and helps children understand and control their actions.

Language does not appear until a child reaches the appropriate level of cognitive development. Since tool use, imitation, symbolic play, and manipulative play emerge about the same time a child begins to speak, all apparently draw on the same underlying mental capacities.

Language acquisition begins in the social interactions of baby and caregiver, where babies learn the cultural conventions of language. The intent to communicate emerges at nine or ten months, when babies begin to seek adult help in reaching their goals. All communication is affected by **context,** and both children and adults rely on it when interpreting language. By the time they are three years old, children have developed **scripts** for customary events, which help children infer the meaning and intent of others.

The major explanations of language acquisition are biological, mechanistic, or functional. In biological theories, language is seen as the result of maturation, and the basic structure of human language is genetically determined, requiring only exposure to others' language to develop. In mechanistic theories, language development is perceived to be the result of experience, with conditioning and observational learning providing children with a basis for figuring out the rules of syntax. According to functional theories, language is a combination of maturation and social interaction, developing from the nonlinguistic communication between infant and adult.

Young babies can hear the difference between most language sounds, and they perceive language sounds the way adults do—by category.

Infants gradually acquire the muscular control to produce speech, and their production of sound progresses from crying to **babbling** to speech. By the end of the first year, a baby's babbling assumes the intonation patterns of his or her native language. The pronunciation of the first words is erratic, but gradually stabilizes.

The first words are related to the concepts an infant is acquiring; these words are often the names of objects. Soon children learn situation words and words that describe temporary states of objects or situations. Children **overextend** many of their first words in producing speech, but their actual understanding of the word seems relatively specific. Children also **underextend** the meaning of many words, applying only part of its accepted meaning. Early in the second year, children begin to discriminate their first **deictic words,** but they do not generally master the entire deictic system until after they start school. Children in the one-word stage may produce a series of clearly separate utterances that form a larger thought. As their information-processing capacity increases, they move into the two-word stage. While children are expanding their vocabularies they rely on overextension, on all-purpose words, and on words they coin themselves.

Until children are out of the two-word stage, they rely on intonation to help express meaning; because they do not understand the general rule of word order, they develop many small patterns for their utterances. Young children who are learning well-marked inflectional languages also acquire some **inflections** while they are in the two-word stage.

In acquiring language, children may rely on a set of **operating principles** that make it easier for them to learn syntax. Young children attempt to simplify language through **overregularization,** making it more systematic than it actually is. Over time, children appear to construct and discard a variety of provisional grammatical rules, and may not understand some forms of passive sentences or complicated active sentences until after they start school.

The Development of Higher Cognitive Processes

LEARNING
Learning Concepts
Learning Rules
THE DEVELOPMENT OF THOUGHT
Preoperational Thought
Concrete Operational Thought
Formal Operational Thought
UNDERSTANDING
Time
Number
Causality
METACOGNITION
SUMMARY

One four-year-old girl's favorite birthday present was an electric train, which came with a small, circular track. Later, her grandparents arrived for a visit bearing a big box filled with track—straight track, curved track, crossovers, and switches. There was also a large piece of plywood, on which her father screwed down the new layout securely so that the little girl could play with her train whenever she liked. As the last screw went into place, the child's mother said, "Later we'll get some little trees and houses and telephone poles and glue them down on the board. Then it'll look like a real little town." The little girl's eyes glowed. "Now?" she asked. "No, later," repeated her mother. The four-year-old accepted the postponement gracefully, but in less than fifteen minutes she came into the kitchen where her mother was preparing lunch. "Is it later enough yet?" she asked. The child's concept of time bore little resemblance to that of her mother, and as we shall see, it would be a number of years before she would be able to understand the relation between time and actions.

The development of children's concept of time is one example of the changing ways in which children think about the physical and social world—a subject that has been most extensively described by Jean Piaget, whose theory we first encountered in Chapter 1. Piaget saw the individual as progressing from the reflexive neonate who could not distinguish between self and world to the adolescent who could apply logical thought to abstract situations, solving problems in a rational, scientific manner. That progression, he believed, was the result of the child's spontaneous activity. In Chapter 7, we traced the emergence of mind in the sensorimotor period. As we now explore the development of children's thought processes, we can see that much research in cognitive development uses Piaget as a starting point, either refining his theory or attempting to challenge it.

In this chapter we explore changes in the way children think about the physical world. We begin with the way children learn concepts and how they build universal rules on the associations they learn in the first few years of life. As we examine the development of thought, we follow the progression of children through Piaget's preoperational, concrete operational, and formal operational stages. At each stage we take up the aspects of cognitive development that Piaget saw as the stage's essential developmental tasks. Because so many aspects of thought are not mastered during a single stage, we close by looking at the way time, number, and causality (the relationship between cause and effect) gradually develop during childhood.

LEARNING

In the course of cognitive development, a child grows from an infant whose memories last for a few fleeting seconds to an adolescent who tests hypotheses in a rigorous, scientific manner. Each year, the child seems to learn more rapidly and apply whatever he or she has learned more flexibly. These advances are obvious, but how do we explain them? Ann Brown and her associates (1983) have laid out the major factors involved:

1. *Interaction between the child and the environment.* The child's knowledge base, cognitive capacity, and activity in the learning task affect how rapidly he or she will learn. A ten-year-old who has never used a computer will learn how to operate a program more slowly than a seven-year-old who has a computer at home and plays with it every day. The environmental demands of the task, the materials, and the context also affect how rapidly a child will learn. A girl who wants to go to a friend's party and finds that her parents are too busy to drive her there will probably solve the transportation problem more quickly than she would solve a problem for a researcher—even though both problems require the same skills.

2. *The accessibility of the child's previous knowledge.* When children first learn a skill, it is limited to a specific task in a specific situation. A boy who has learned to do percentages at school may find that he cannot figure the tip on the family restaurant check. During development, isolated skills are gradually extended and joined so that the child can apply them in many situations.

3. *Conscious access.* When a child first learns a skill, he or she usually is not aware of it and cannot put it in words. In their speech, five-year-olds apply the grammatical rule for forming the past tense of verbs, but if asked to state the rule, they could not say what they do.

The task that faces developmental psychologists is explaining the way these mechanisms operate in cognitive growth. The search has led researchers to examine the ways in which children learn concepts, extract rules, and gradually gain understanding of the learning process.

Learning Concepts

Babies begin to learn concepts before they can talk, as we saw in Chapter 7. Concepts are essential to learning, because they are our basic cognitive tools. Without concepts we could not use the similarities we notice in the world about us or understand nonessential changes in objects and events (Fowler, 1980). Researchers have identified three different forms of concepts and have suggested that the most effective method of learning concepts may change as children grow (Farah and Kosslyn, 1982).

RULE-BASED REPRESENTATIONS Children seem to form some concepts around a rule; the rule specifies the attributes that are necessary and sufficient for any particular item to claim membership in a category. For example, a bird has feathers, wings, and a beak. When researchers study the way children form a rule-based concept, they generally have the children learn artificial concepts based on geometric figures. In a typical experiment (see Figure 10.1), children see two shapes (a large circle and a small triangle) and choose one of them. In this case, the large circle is the correct choice. The next pair of shapes is a small circle and a large triangle; the large triangle is correct. The child's task is to learn that the "big" shape, whether a circle or a triangle, is always correct. After the child has correctly chosen "big" ten times in a row, the experimenter abruptly shifts the rules; now the small triangle is correct, so that using either "small" or "triangle" as a basis of judgement is correct. After the child learns to choose the small triangle in the pair—which is shown again and again—the important part of the experiment begins. The investigator sets about

FIGURE 10.1 In the study of discrimination learning discussed in the text, children learn in the initial phase that "big" is correct and "small" is incorrect. In the shift phase, both "small" and "triangle" are correct. Whether a child's criterion shifts from "big" to "small" or from "big" to "triangle" is revealed in the test phase, and the choice helps indicate whether simple operant conditioning or thought was involved in the process.

(Adapted from Kendler, 1979. Reprinted by permission of the author and publisher)

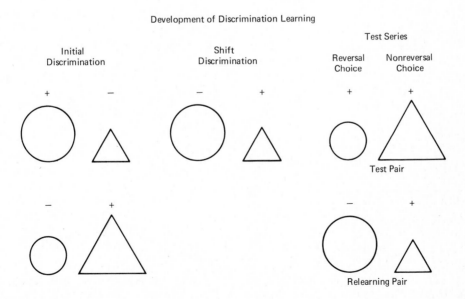

Development of Discrimination Learning

discovering whether the youngster has reversed the concept (now choosing the small stimulus instead of the large one) or whether the child has switched concepts and is now judging by shape instead of size (now choosing a triangle instead of a circle). Which course a child will take seems to be related to the child's age. Small children nearly always switch to the concept of shape. Why? Tracy Kendler (1979) believes that small children learn by a gradual strengthening of their tendency to choose whatever instances have been rewarded. Half of their rewards have come for choosing triangles, but they have never been rewarded for choosing small objects. So they find it extremely difficult to reverse their choice from big to small. Older children react differently; they usually stay with size, reversing their choice from big to small. They learn in a manner that allows them to think about the problem and the dimensions that have been reinforced. According to Kendler, this change in learning occurs shortly after children start school. Preschoolers form relatively direct associations between the stimuli in their world and their responses to them. But older children process stimuli as examples of a category. They first respond mentally to stimuli, then mentally generate a new cognitive stimulus that affects their response to the perceived stimulus. In short, they think about what they have seen. Because of this developmental difference in learning, we can use the results from animal conditioning experiments to predict the way a three-year-old child will learn, but if we try to apply the same rule to ten-year olds—or college students—our predictions will generally be wrong.

PROTOTYPICAL REPRESENTATIONS WITHOUT RULES

Some concepts seem to be formed around a prototype rather than around rules. In this sort of concept, children represent the "most typical" or generalized example of a concept and compare new examples to it, as we saw in Chapter 8. Researchers have also studied this method of concept formation, again by using geometric patterns. In this case, no single attribute is found in all the patterns, and each varies from the prototype in varying degrees. When shown such patterns, children and adults both seem to form a prototype for the concept (Lasky, 1974). However, six-year-olds seem to form the prototype more slowly than older children do, so that in most experiments, their prototype is generally incomplete.

EXAMPLE-BASED REPRESENTATIONS

The least sophisticated way of learning a concept is to learn a number of examples. Since all the examples are encoded, children compare a new category member with the examples they have seen in the past (Farah and Kosslyn, 1982). When concepts are complex, children may find learning examples the most efficient way to form a concept. This became apparent when Nancy Kossan (1981) had children learn rule-based and example-based concepts. She used pictures of imaginary animals and taught some children to divide the animals into categories by learning the distinctive features of each category. The rest of the children were asked to memorize individual examples from each animal category. Each child saw three examples from each animal category. When the categories were simple (only two features), second- and fifth-graders acquired the concepts easily through the rule-based method. But when the categories were complex, the children did much better when memorizing examples—and this was especially true of the second-graders. As children get older, their more efficient information-processing skills make the use of rule-based or prototypical concepts more likely. But when concepts are extremely complex or demand too many cognitive resources, people of any age may use the example-based method (Farah and Kosslyn, 1982).

Learning Rules

Concepts describe the way children organize their knowledge about the world, but just how do they figure out the rule on which a concept is based? And how do older children learn mental rules, which describe the way things work and how to work them and which tell the children how to organize and manipulate concepts (Fowler, 1980)? According to Kendler (1979), when children figure out the rule behind a rule-based concept, they test a series of hypotheses. They solve the problem by testing one dimension (shape, color, size) after another, using their errors to guide their search for the answer. The basic rule for hypothesis testing is simple: stay with your choice if you win, switch if you lose (Trabasso and Bower, 1968). Three- and four-year-olds do not use this rule, but most of them gradually learn to do so. Once a child masters the rule, he or she jumps from being generally wrong to being always right. The proportion of children who do this rises steadily until, by the time they are eighteen, nearly all use the win-stay, lose-switch rule.

Some children who do not use hypothesis testing on their own can be taught to do so. In one study, 26 percent of the kindergartners and 32 percent of the first-graders spontaneously used hypothesis testing to figure out concepts (Cantor and Spiker, 1979). But among children who were given direct instruction, 38 percent of the kindergartners and 75 percent of the first-graders used it. What enables a child to test hypotheses? Probably a combination of perceptual advances, an increase in the ability to scan and focus, and a broadening of the child's knowledge base.

Learning is generally considered an obvious specific change that takes place before our eyes. When a child figures out the rule for a concept, we can see the difference in the child's behavior. This rule, which is tied to a specific task, is considered a secondary rule. Children also learn basic rules, rules that extend across many tasks and many domains of knowledge (Fowler, 1980). When children learn one of these general rules, their capabilities seem to change; most psychologists consider this cognitive advance an example of development—not simply learning. For example, a four-year-old girl who watches her mother divide a bottle of cola will happily accept the tall, narrow glass in the belief that it contains more cola than the squat glass her older brother took. According to Piaget's theory, the child does not understand the concept of **conservation**; she does not realize that irrelevant changes in the physical appearance of objects do not affect their quantity. In another year or two, as a result of cognitive development, she will progress to a different stage of thinking and will no longer be fooled by the different shapes of glasses.

Some learning theorists believe that this change in a child's understanding is not the result of a movement from one stage of cognitive development to another, but the cumulative effect of learning. The distinction between learning and development is primarily one of time, believes Robert Gagné (1968), and slow, cumulative learning can explain a child's eventual grasp of basic rules such as those that govern irrelevant changes in the appearance of substances—whether glasses of cola, balls of clay, or rows of coins. Although Gagné is not proposing that basic rules are simply the result of conditioning, he does suggest that conditioning lies at the bottom of a great hierarchy of learning, and that changes in general capabilities take place when children learn new, complex rules.

The path to these rules begins with conditioning—associations between stimuli and their responses. These associations build up into chains—both motor and verbal—and the child learns to make discriminations. Objects have characteristic dimensions, textures, tastes, and smells, for example. They can be thrown, dropped, and manipulated in certain ways. Discriminations lead in turn to concepts—the concepts of "surface," "container," "liquid," and so on. From the concepts come simple rules, such as that one can pour liquid into a container, and that liquids assume the shapes of their containers. Simple rules lead to complex ones and eventually, by a lengthy process of recognition, recall, and the transfer of what the child learns from one situation to another, a developmental change occurs.

Each new association, concept, and rule, points out Gagné, is learned under different conditions, because as learning accumulates, the child has more and more information stored and available in memory. By the time a child is ten years old, most associations already have been established and much of the child's learning now consists of rules and concepts. The eventual learning of rules and concepts, of course, depends on the ability to recall all those discriminations, chains, and associations it took the child so many years to learn.

In Gagné's view, the understanding that irrelevant transformations in appearance can be reversed, which is basic to conservation and which Piaget regards as evidence of qualitative changes in the child's thinking, is evidence of accumulated concrete knowledge. In the case of liquids, it is knowledge the child has gradually piled up through years of experience with liquids and with containers of various widths and heights.

THE DEVELOPMENT OF THOUGHT

The thirteen-year-old laughs at the three-year-old's notion that the sun follows her around, that the tall, narrow glass holds more cola than the squat glass, and that the tomato seedling and vine are not the same plant. But ten years ago, the thirteen-year-old held the same views. Children everywhere seem to pass through a similar course of development. Because Piaget has given us the most comprehensive picture of cognitive development, we will organize our exploration of children's thought in terms of his system. However, Piaget's division of children's cognitive development into four major substages (sensorimotor, preoperational, concrete operational, and formal operational) is not as widely accepted as it was a few years ago. As noted in Chapter 1, Piaget believed that as children moved into a new substage, their thought underwent a general restructuring, but the accumulated research indicates that this general reorganization of thought probably does not occur (Gelman and Baillargeon, 1983). First, the preoperational child is a much more competent thinker than Piaget believed. Second, the concrete operational child's thinking seems to develop at widely different paces in different domains. Finally, in some areas of thought, preschoolers, older children, and adults reason about a problem in much the same way—although in other areas, their reasoning is quite different. As we trace the development of thought from the preschool years through adolescence, some of these discrepancies will become apparent. Yet Piaget's theories and research have not been discarded. Indeed, his view that thought is structured, that schemes guide behavior, and that thought develops through the processes of assimilation and accommodation remains as firmly entrenched as ever (Gelman and Baillargeon, 1983).

When Piaget described the development of thought, he maintained that a child is not capable of logical thought until the age of seven or eight. However, the logical thought of the school years does not suddenly spring into being. It is based on concepts laid down during the first two stages of life. It is hard to imagine, for example, that an eight-year-old could understand conservation without first developing the understanding that objects continue to exist when out of sight—a key task of the sensorimotor period of infancy. Or that the grasp of conservation could develop unless the child had first developed the understanding that people who change their clothes or hair color are the same individuals—a major developmental task of the preoperational stage of early childhood.

Yet the logic of the schoolchild is not the same as the logic of the adolescent or the adult. According to Piaget, the schoolchild uses logic only when thinking about tangible objects. For this reason, Piaget described the schoolchild's thought as concrete operational. And because the adolescent can apply formal logic and manipulate abstract relationships, Piaget applied the term "formal operational" to adolescent thought.

Preoperational Thought

Despite the obvious superiority of the preschooler's thought to that of the infant, the preoperational child lacks logic. Piaget saw thought at this period as intuitive, inflexible, focused on individual events, and contradictory. These qualities indicate that the cognitive processes are not **operations** (which are by definition flexible, rigorous, and logical thought), hence the period is called the **preoperational stage.**

The concept of **identity,** which develops during the preoperational period, is vital to the appearance of logical thought. It consists of understanding that objects and people remain the same, even if irrelevant properties are changed. A six-year-old girl understands that her friend can put on a gorilla mask and still be her friend, that her mother can change her hair color and still be Mother, and that a girl can have her hair cut and wear boys' clothes and still be a girl— a concept that is also important in the development of sex roles, which are discussed in Chapter 15. But when this same girl was only three, and firmly entrenched in preoperational thought, she would have believed that her friend in a gorilla mask was no longer her friend but some strange and terrible creature.

In order to test children's understanding that an animal cannot change its species, Rheta DeVries (1969) put masks made of fur and rubber on a cat's head. One mask was that of a dog, the other that of a rabbit. DeVries showed the cat to children whose ages ranged from three to six. Three-year-olds identified the cat as whatever species its head resembled. Whenever masks were put on or removed, these children believed that the animal's species had changed from cat to dog to rabbit and back. Children a little older would say that the cat would remain

A three-year-old who watches familiar children don their Halloween masks will be frightened by the terrifying monsters, because a child in the preoperational stage lacks the concept of identity and thinks that the masked children are no longer friends. (© Harvey Stein)

a cat, but once the mask was in place they would change their minds. The sight of a dog's head on a cat's body—even though the animal's body never left their field of vision—overwhelmed their earlier assertions that its species would remain unchanged. Only the five- and six-yearolds maintained that the cat was a cat no matter what kind of mask it wore.

Apparently, the concept of identity develops very slowly during the preoperational period.

How Do We Educate the Academically Precocious Child?

In every school there are a few children whose store of information amazes their teachers; these children acquire new knowledge with incredible speed and seeming ease. Their achievement scores show that they are at least three grade levels ahead of their classmates. Yet most of them sit in the same classroom, read the same textbooks and do the same assignments as the rest of the students.

A growing number of psychologists and educators have come to the conclusion that this practice may be harmful to the academically precocious child's future. Children learn when they meet problems that slightly exceed the levels they already have mastered. But the academic problems these children encounter, they have mastered months—if not years—before. It is no wonder, said Halbert Robinson (1983), that researchers who work with academically gifted children often note that they are bored or frustrated at school; most of their school time is wasted.

The ease with which these children sail through the normal curriculum may have an insidious effect (Robinson, 1983). The academically precocious child expends so little effort to get high grades that he or she may never develop good study habits, or learn to persevere in the face of difficulty. Instead the student spends twelve years daydreaming through class and skimming (or not even reading) textbooks. When he or she at last encounters the demands of higher education, the result may be anxiety or discouragement. The situation can become so severe that the student may even drop out of college or graduate school.

The conviction that these children need a radically changed educational program has led several universities to develop ways of identifying academically precocious youngsters and to design programs that allow them to develop their intellectual potential. At Johns Hopkins University, Julian Stanley established a search for seventh-graders whose mathematical reasoning outstripped most twelfth-graders (Benbow, Perkins, and Stanley, 1983). Once identified, these students took fast-paced mathematics classes on Saturday mornings that enabled them to complete the high-school and college precalculus curriculum over a fifteen-month period. In Illinois, the state used the Johns Hopkins program as a model for its own mathematical talent search (Van Tassel-Baska, 1983). At the University of Washington, Halbert Robinson (1983) developed a program to identify precocious five-year-olds, provide them with an accelerated education, and admit them to the university at about the age of fourteen. Both the Johns Hopkins and the Illinois programs have since been broadened to find verbal as well as mathematical talent.

Students from these programs either enter college several years early, take college courses for credit while they are in high school, or are given advanced placement when they enter college. Most of the researchers who have been involved with these programs believe that radical acceleration is probably the most effective and the least expensive method of meeting the needs of academically precocious children. For example, one student from the Johns Hopkins program had earned his Ph.D. and become an assistant professor in Northwestern University's Graduate School of Management by his twenty-second birthday. By the time she was eighteen years old, another had her B.A. in mathematics and had won a Rhodes Scholarship for advanced study at Oxford.

What happens to children who pass

(Martin M. Rotker/Taurus)

through school at such a rapid rate? Do they miss out on important knowledge that is generally taught in the grades they skip? Few gaps have appeared among accelerated students, and those that do can be handled by brief, targeted tutoring (Robinson, 1983). For example, some of the youngsters who entered the University of Washington's program had skipped the grades in which cursive writing was taught, and so they were still printing their work.

Do radically accelerated students suffer social isolation and emotional maladjustment because they are much younger than their academic peers? Apparently not. At least two hundred studies have been made of radically accelerated young people, and not a single one has found any sign of severe or permanent social or emotional harm (Daurio, 1979; Keating, 1979; Robinson, 1983). In a longitudinal study that matched radically accelerated adolescents with equally talented adolescents whose education was not accelerated, Lynn Pollins (1983) found no major differences between the groups. At the beginning of the study, when the youths were thirteen years old, both groups were found to be well adjusted, socially mature, and effective in interpersonal relations. Both preferred intellectual pursuits to social pursuits. Five years later, the radically accelerated youths had higher educational aspirations, participated to about the same extent in extracurricular activities, but had held fewer jobs. They felt that academic acceleration had had a positive effect on their social and emotional development, although they liked college somewhat less than the unaccelerated students, who were just entering.

Parents and teachers may worry about taking academically precocious children out of the age-graded educational pattern; it is more important, they say, that these students grow up "normal" and "happy." This argument, says John Feldhusen (1983), ignores the fact that forcing an academically gifted child to behave like an average child is forcing him or her to be abnormal. Feldhusen believes that these children are happiest when allowed to advance at their own rate.

Its beginnings can be seen fairly early. Preschool children do accept the identity of their own bodies; they realize that despite their increase in size, pictures of their younger selves are "still me" and that when they are big enough to go to school, the schoolchild will be "me." But in the case of a plant, they say, "It grew, but it isn't the same any more; here it's a little plant and there it's a big plant. It's not the same plant" (Piaget, 1968). By the time they are seven, however, they admit to the identity of the mature plant *and* the seedling.

Concrete Operational Thought

The child who crosses the threshold of the concrete operational period has come to what Piaget (Piaget and Inhelder, 1969) called the "decisive turning-point." For the first time, thought is logical, although only when applied to concrete objects and situations. Since children's cognitive processes are also flexible and rigorous, they qualify as operations. Among the operations that Piaget believed develop during this period are the principles of conservation, transitivity, and class inclusion.

CONSERVATION Once children understand that objects continue to exist and that superficial changes in the appearance of objects do not change their basic identity, they are ready to grasp the principle of conservation. Children who are "conservers" understand that irrelevant changes in the external appearance of objects have no effect on the object's quantity—its weight, length, mass, or volume.

In the best-known test of conservation, children watch an experimenter fill two glasses of the same size and shape to an equal level with colored water. The children are asked whether the two glasses contain the same amount of water. When the children assert that the amounts are the same, the researcher pours the water from one glass into a shorter, broader glass, so the levels of colored water in the glasses differ. A four-year-old boy, asked whether each glass now contains the same amount of water, says, "No! This one has more water in it because the water is higher." But a seven-year-old girl is not fooled. She points out that the squat glass is shorter, but that it is also broader; she understands the concept of conservation of quantity. She knows that if she pours the water back into the tall glass, the level will be just where it was before.

The seven-year-old has acquired what Piaget called the concrete operation of **reversibility:** the understanding that irrelevant changes in appearance can be reversed and that such changes tend to compensate one another. For example, as the water level falls in the short, broad glass its quantity also spreads out.

At one time, many developmental psychologists believed that children who gave erroneous replies in the experiment with the glasses of colored water had clearly demonstrated that they did not understand the conservation of quantity. But researchers now question this conclusion. For one thing, when children are allowed to pour the colored water themselves, more of them solve the problem correctly. For another, Margaret Donaldson (1979) has pointed out that the conditions of the experiment push the children toward the wrong answer. When the experimenter pours the water, he or she generally says, "Now watch what I do," indicating to the child that the change is important and will affect whatever follows.

The influence of the experimenter appeared when Susan Rose and Marion Blank (1974) conducted a version of the conservation experiment in which they did not ask the child about the quantity of the two items *before* they manipulated their appearance. They suspected that asking the same question both before and after the manipulation might suggest to children that they should change their answer. When they

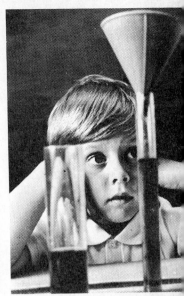

In a standard test of conservation, a boy watches carefully as water from one of two wide beakers is poured into a narrow container (*center*); then he is asked whether the squat and the narrow containers hold the same amount of water (*right*). Unless he understands that irrelevant changes in appearance can be reversed, the boy will say that there is more water in the narrow container. (Courtesy, *The New York Times*)

tested six-year-olds with only the final question, they found that the children not only made fewer errors on the task at hand but also scored much higher a week later when tested in the manner devised by Piaget.

It appears that changing the way a test is presented may allow additional children to demonstrate their grasp of conservation. In Piaget's view, however, not even the most skilled teacher can teach four-year-olds that pouring water into a short, squat glass does not change the amount of water, or that twisting a necklace into a curve does not affect its length. Although he agreed that learning takes place during cognitive development, Piaget maintained that all a child can learn is to apply cognitive structures (such as reversibility) he or she already has acquired to new contents (Brainerd, 1978), and since four-year-olds lack operations, they cannot learn to conserve. Yet many investigators have been able to teach three- and four-year-olds to pass conservation tests (e.g., Brainerd, 1977; Rosenthal and Zimmerman, 1978; Gelman, 1982). Their consistent success has led Rochel Gelman and Renée Baillargeon (1983) to conclude that preschoolers *do* have some of the reasoning structures necessary to understand simple forms of conservation, but that their capacity is limited.

Children's performance on the conservation of number supports this conclusion. In Piaget's test of this ability, the researcher places in front of a child two rows of seven checkers each. Then the researcher asks the child if one row has more, less, or the same amount of checkers as the other. The child usually says that the two rows have the same number of checkers. Next, while the child watches, the researcher either bunches together the checkers in one of the rows or else spreads them apart. Now when the child is asked about the two rows, the four- or five-year-old emphatically insists that there are more checkers in one row than in the other. The perceptual appearance of the rows apparently so dominates the child's thought that he or she believes that the number of checkers must vary. Within a few years, children's reactions change. Given the same problem, a seven-year-old responds to the posttransformation question with an equally emphatic, "Of course they are the same. You didn't add any or take any away, you just put them closer together." Some reply in a tone of surprise mixed with disdain at an experimenter who could ask such a silly question.

Researchers have found that under some conditions, preschoolers can handle problems in number conservation. When two- and three-year-olds are shown three checkers, and then a researcher surreptitiously adds a fourth or takes away one of the three, the children show surprise and point out that a checker has been added or subtracted (Gelman, 1977). One child said of a missing checker, "Jesus took it." And if the checkers are surreptitiously spread out without changing the number, the children again notice the change, but indicate that it is irrelevant. Their responses indicate that they understand some aspects of conservation. Preschoolers can also pass the standard conservation test in a special situation. If researchers use two rows of seven toy soldiers instead of checkers, carry out the transformation, and then ask the child, "Does your army have as many as my army?" a four-year-old answers correctly (Markman, 1979). The collective noun (army) apparently leads the child to think about the rows of objects as collections instead of classes (soldiers), and indicates that preschoolers are not as bound by perceptual features as Piaget supposed. Other researchers (Gelman, 1982) have shown that three- and four-year-olds can be trained to conserve number in standard experiments by giving them instruction and practice on small sets of three or four checkers.

Young children are much more likely to understand the conservation of number than the conservation of liquids or solids. For example, a three-year-old may understand that two rows of dimes still contain the same number of coins, even though the coins in one row have been spread widely apart by the researcher. But the same child may not understand that two balls of clay are still equal after one has been flattened. Both tasks involve the conservation of quantity. Why does the young child do better on one than on the other? Perhaps because children have more cues to guide them when judging discrete quantities (like dimes) than when judging continuous quantities (like clay). When judging two rows of coins, for example, a child can count the objects, mentally line up the rows in one-to-one correspondence, or notice just what the researcher did to transform one row (Siegler, 1981). When judging glasses of cola or balls of clay, children have only the manipulations of the experimenter as their guide.

Of course, in Piaget's view, the child who counts or uses one-to-one correspondence does not truly understand conservation. Some young children can use one-to-one correspondence when there are as many as ten dimes in a row (Gelman, 1982), but researchers have found that when the rows get much larger, children younger than five do not conserve (Halford and Boyle, 1985). Perhaps preschoolers who seem to understand simple forms of conservation are not mentally reversing the change in appearance, but simply maintaining their belief in the object's identity (Acredolo and Acredolo, 1979). For example, a four-year-old may say of the dimes, "You just spreaded them."

Such an explanation squares with the results of a study by Gilbert Botvin and Frank Murray (1975), which showed how children who fail to conserve weight, mass, and number on standard tests learn the concept from other children. Botvin and Murray put children in groups of five, each made up of three nonconservers and two conservers. A researcher first asked each child to answer the same series of questions about weight and mass conservation, so they heard one another's answers. The group then talked over their explanations and agreed on an answer to each conservation problem. After they had reached an agreement, the researcher questioned each child.

Most of the nonconservers, including an additional group of children who merely watched and listened to the group, learned to conserve mass, weight, and number. During the earlier group discussions, original conservers tended to explain conservation by talking about the reversibility of the change, whereas the new conservers tended to give "identity" explanations, noting that nothing had been added to or subtracted from the original amount, or that the change had been irrelevant. Botvin and Murray interpret the change as the result of modeling, suggesting that when the models gave correct answers, they produced mental conflicts in the other children, which prodded them into reorganizing their thinking. In this case, the first grasp of conservation relied on an understanding of identity, not of reversibility, which may be the way most children develop their comprehension.

Piaget's experiments (Piaget and Inhelder, 1969) on children's notions of conservation revealed that at first children grasp only part of the conservation concept. Seven-year-olds realize that the mass of an object, such as a piece of clay, does not change when the clay is stretched or compressed, but most fail to realize that its weight and volume also remain unchanged. Piaget found that children always acquire the various kinds of conservation in the same order. First a child understands conservation of quantity; then, at about the age of nine or ten, he or she grasps the notion of conservation of weight, and finally, at about ten or eleven, the child realizes that there is also conservation of volume, in the sense that the amount of water displaced by an object is not affected if its shape is changed (Piaget and Inhelder, 1941). Other researchers have confirmed Piaget's basic findings about the sequence of these acquisitions (Sigel and Mermelstein, 1966; Uzgiris, 1964).

Children as old as nine may not transfer their realization that changing the shape of an object does not affect its weight to other kinds of transformations. For example, many children who pass the weight conservation test when an object's shape is altered still think that butter loses weight as it melts and that water becomes heavier as it freezes (Lovell and Ogilvie, 1961).

Even without formal schooling, children constantly experience the heaviness or lightness of objects they lift, push, or pull. They "know" from their handling of objects, although they may not realize that they know, that things do not get heavier or lighter if their shape or color changes. Many children conserve weight in the sense of maintaining constant muscular pressure when they lift a ball of clay that has just been elongated, even though, if asked, they would state that its weight had changed. Thus they may demonstrate a working knowledge of conservation, just as they daily demonstrate their fluency as speakers of language. But they cannot explain their knowledge, just as they cannot explain the rules of syntax they use each time they speak.

TRANSITIVITY Another skill Piaget placed in the concrete operational period is one adults use often. We rely on it when we make a major purchase (comparing cars we have seen in various showrooms), choose a vacation spot (comparing airline prices), or decide how to vote (comparing several candidates in a primary election). This skill is **transitivity,** or the making of logical inferences based on separate related observations. No one asks children about cars or airline tickets or candidates, but concrete operational children show they have mastered the task when asked about children's ages. If told that Scott is older than Jennifer and that Jennifer is older than Mark, they infer that Scott must be older than Mark. This deduction requires a child to join two instances of the relational concept, "older than." Like conservation, transitivity does not suddenly appear full-blown. In order to handle the inferences the task requires, children must first understand **seriation,** or the

This boy's arrangement of graduated blocks indicates that he understands the concrete operation of seriation—an ability that Piaget believed was a first step toward more complex understanding. (Jean-Claude Lejeune/Stock, Boston)

ordering of objects by size or weight. In a seriation test, a child arranges a row of sticks in ascending or descending order of length, or places a row of coins in order of size, from dime to half-dollar, or threads different size beads on a string to make a necklace of graduated sizes. Although Piaget believed that younger children could not arrange objects in this way, researchers have found that many three- and four-year-olds understand the task, but can carry it out only with small groups of objects (Gelman and Baillargeon, 1983).

Once children can arrange objects in order of size, they are ready to develop the more sophisticated skill of transitivity, in which they arrange and compare objects in their heads. According to Piaget, this concept requires operational thought and is rarely found in children younger than seven. He tested children's grasp of the concept in the following manner:

We present two sticks to a child, stick A being smaller than stick B. Then we hide stick A and show him stick B together with a larger stick C. Then we ask him how A and C compare. Preoperational children will say that they do not know because they have not seen them together—they have not been able to compare them. On the other hand, operational children . . . will say right away that C is bigger than A, since C is bigger than B and B is bigger than A [Piaget, 1970, p. 30].

The reason young children fail the test may be because it also measures such factors as language ability and memory, which are unrelated to transitivity (Brainerd, 1978). Piaget required that a child not only give the correct answer but also explain each inference logically, a skill that may be beyond the scope of some children who otherwise would pass the test. The factor of memory may be even more critical. Young children may fail to infer the proper relationship between sticks A and C because by the time they reach the third (inferential) step of the experiment, they have forgotten the information given during the first two steps. (See Figure 10.2.)

Peter Bryant and Tom Trabasso (1971) decided to find out if memory played an important role in four-year-olds' failures to make correct inferences. Instead of asking the child about the relationship between three sticks, they used five. Bryant and Trabasso constructed four one-step comparisons (A and B, B and C, C and D, D and E) in which three of the sticks occur as both the larger and smaller members of pairs. This precaution ensured that a child could not pass the test simply by recalling that the word "bigger" was the only adjective connected with the larger stick in most of the comparisons.

In the initial training stage, children learned and remembered the four direct comparisons. When asked to compare B and D in their heads, 78 percent of the four-year-olds, 88 percent of the five-year-olds, and 92 percent of the six-year-olds made the correct inferences, indicating that memory is crucial to the task. This result

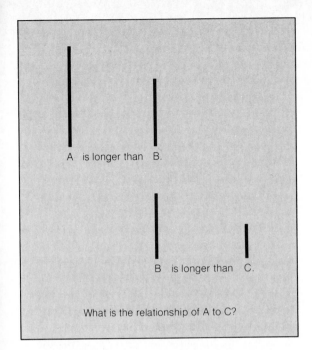

A is longer than B.

B is longer than C.

What is the relationship of A to C?

FIGURE 10.2 Example of a transitivity problem, which requires the joining together of two instances of the relational concept "longer than."

seems inconsistent with Piaget's belief that children cannot grasp the concept of transitivity until they have reached the concrete operational stage.

In subsequent research, Trabasso (1977) studied children to find out how they process the knowledge needed to solve the problem. He discovered that children (like adults) do not store the information the way they learn it—as four separate pairs. Instead, they recode the information, constructing an internal representation of the entire group of sticks, perhaps as a list, perhaps as a visual image. When asked to compare lengths, they "read" the answer off their representation. If children stored the information by pairs, they should be fastest at retrieving comparisons they had learned directly (B is longer than C), but they are not. The more widely separated the sticks, the faster children can answer questions about them. They can, for example, report the relation between B and D (an inference) more quickly than they can report the relation between B and C, which they memorized.

Although it takes a four-year-old much longer than it does a seven-year-old to learn the four comparisons, once the child understands and remembers them, the four-year-old is as accurate as an adult in making mental comparisons. Because their successes, their errors, and their comparative reaction times are similar, Trabasso (1975) concludes that the cognitive processes of adults and children are quite similar, and that memory and the young child's heavy dependence on linguistic context are responsible for the failures of young children on the traditional tests.

However, the results of Trabasso's research also indicate that the stick problem apparently does not require concrete operations for its solution. If children (and adults) are simply reading off the answers from a mental image, they are solving the problem without using inference (Flavell, 1977). Piaget may be wrong about the young child's ability to solve the stick problem but correct in maintaining that young children cannot reach such conclusions when inference is required. Children's ability to make other kinds of transitive inferences has not been studied extensively, but some research indicates that the ability develops about the time youngsters enter school (Braine and Rumain, 1983).

CLASS INCLUSION Children begin to categorize the world very early, beginning with basic-level concepts. And as we saw in Chapter 8, they show some understanding of superordinate classes by the time they are four or five years old. But if Piaget is correct, they do not understand **class inclusion,** a concrete operation that involves the child's knowledge that a superordinate class (animals) is always larger than any of its basic classes (cows, dogs). Most youngsters with eight lemon drops and five licorice drops agree that lemon drops are candy and that lic-

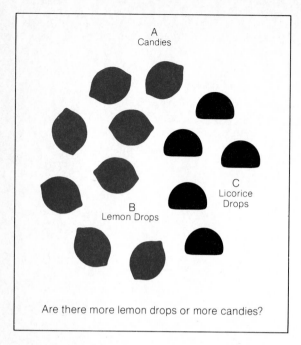

A
Candies

C
Licorice
Drops

B
Lemon Drops

Are there more lemon drops or more candies?

FIGURE 10.3 Young children are likely to have difficulty reasoning about the relation of a part or parts to a whole, and, if shown a collection of lemon drops and licorice drops, they are likely to say that they have more lemon drops than candy.

orice drops are candy. But unless a child has mastered class inclusion, he or she will also insist that there are more lemon drops than candy (see Figure 10.3). Piaget (1952a) explained this by saying that young children cannot think of both an entire class and a subclass at the same time; therefore, they cannot compare them. Presented this way, the problem is even more difficult than Piaget supposed. Some investigators (e.g., Winer, 1980) have discovered that many children are at least ten years old—not seven—before they can solve traditional class-inclusion problems.

A variation on the lemon and licorice drops experiment indicates that part of the children's problem may lie in language, not in concept. James McGarrigle (see Donaldson, 1979) tested forty-eight children, who were about six years

old, with four toy cows. Three of the cows were black and one was white. McGarrigle placed all the cows on their sides and told the children they were sleeping. When he asked the standard Piagetian question, "Are there more black cows or more cows?" only 25 percent of the children correctly answered, "More cows." But when asked, "Are there more black cows or more sleeping cows?" 48 percent of the children correctly said, "More sleeping cows." The inclusion of an object that encompassed the entire class enabled many more children to compare class with subclass. In another study, when all the classes involved were stated ("Are there more pets or more dogs or more cats?"), the number of children who answered correctly jumped from 5 percent to 55 percent (Ahr and Youniss, 1970). Finally, when the terms "more" and "less" are cast aside and the problem is rephrased in practical terms, even preschoolers do well at class inclusions. Shown three M&Ms and two jelly beans and asked, "Do you want to eat the M&Ms or the candy?" many three-year-olds showed they understood by promptly eating all the candy (Siegel et al., 1978).

Children also find it easier to compare class with subclass when researchers use collective nouns to refer to the class. For example, Ellen Markman (1973b) showed a picture of dogs to six- and eight-year-olds. She described the picture as a family of dogs, giving each of the dogs a family role (mother, father, and four babies). Then she asked the children who would have more pets, a person who owned the baby dogs or one who owned the family. Sixty percent of the children who heard the dogs described as a family said that someone who owned the family would have more pets. But almost all the children who had not heard the collective noun, "family," said that someone who had the four little dogs would have more pets. In a later study, Markman and J. Siebert (1976) found that using collective nouns (forest, band, crowd, pile) instead of class nouns (trees, musicians, people, bricks) increased from 45 to 70 percent the number of children who could answer class-inclusion questions about the groups. Why did this simple

If you asked this preschooler whether she had more brown horses or more horses in her farm set, she would confidently say, "More brown horses." (Peter Menzel)

change in language make it easier for children to compare class with subclass? As we saw in Chapter 8, using the collective noun makes it easier for children to form superordinate classes in the first place. Markman and Siebert believe the effect is due to the internal structure and psychological integrity of a collection. Members of a collection are related in some way, but there is no psychological connection among members of a class. This logic of classes allows children to focus on individual members, but the logic of collections forces them to focus on the entire collection.

The way children encode information about objects goes a long way in determining whether they can answer class-inclusion questions. Tom Trabasso and his colleagues (1978), who have approached class inclusion from an information-processing standpoint, explain that children can encode a display of five plastic cows and three horses as only the superordinate class (animals) or as two subordinate classes (cows and horses) or hierarchically (both as animals and as the

subordinates, cows and horses). Unless children use this last type of coding, they cannot solve the problem.

There are various ways to encourage hierarchical coding, and Trabasso's group mentions some of them. Labeling the superordinate and subordinate classes increases the number of first- and second-graders who pass the tests from 60 to 70 percent. Adding another superordinate class (fruit) with two subordinate classes (apples and oranges) to a display of animals (dogs and cats) also increases the number of children who know there are more animals than dogs and more fruit than apples. The sight of the fruit with the animals prompts the child to compare the two classes and to identify the superordinate sets, leading the youngster to encode all items hierarchically.

Trabasso's group believes that class-inclusion questions are not simply tests of logical ability or even of semantic knowledge, but that they mix hierarchical class concepts with language comprehension, counting ability, and decision making. If the child codes the information properly, the comparisons can be made by a three-year-old; if the child does not use a hierarchical coding, even a ten-year-old will find the going rough. However, the finding that encoding plays a major role does not conflict with Piaget's analysis, since only with hierarchical coding can a child think of the objects as being both class and subclass members, and only older children appear to use hierarchical coding spontaneously.

Formal Operational Thought

Children generally enter the stage of formal operations around the age of eleven or so, but Piaget (Inhelder and Piaget, 1958) believed that the abstract, scientific thought that characterizes the period and that he regarded as the culmination of cognitive development is not firmly established until children are about fifteen years old. The central feature of formal operational thought is the conception of possibilities that lie outside the immediate environment.

ARE FORMAL OPERATIONS
UNIVERSAL? Piaget often wrote as if all adolescents develop formal thought, but he agreed that in some cultures adult thinking might never develop beyond the level of concrete operations (Piaget, 1976). Indeed, studies suggest that formal thought is neither as inevitable nor as universal a step in development as is the concrete thought of childhood (Bullinger and Chatillon, 1983). However, some people in every society apparently develop the ability. It is difficult to see how the devices developed in ancient cultures to measure the changing position of the sun (such as Stonehenge in England or Fajada Butte in the southwestern United States) could have been designed without the application of formal operational thought (Neimark, 1982).

Yet abstract reasoning may not be an inevitable outcome of growing up; research in other countries indicates that formal education plays an important role in its development. In some societies few people develop the ability to reason from hypotheses. In Turkey, for example, formal thought appears in city dwellers but not in residents of primitive villages (Kohlberg and Gilligan, 1971). On the basis of numerous studies in Africa and Latin America, Michael Cole (1978) has concluded that formal education changes the mind in several ways: people group things into general categories according to formal rules (cow, dog, horse) instead of according to their function (cow, pasture, milk); they use these classes to solve problems and to organize their recall; and they treat problems in logic as hypothetical puzzles instead of as questions of fact or interpretation. Although literacy does not guarantee the development of formal thought, some children show these changes after as few as three years of schooling. Nine years of formal education, Cole discovered, will bring about the changes in most children.

Patricia Greenfield and Jerome Bruner (1966) attribute the greater evidence of formal thought in societies with schools to the fact that schooling promotes training in written language, a view that is similar to Cole's. Writing forces a child to separate thought from objects and thus may encourage children to let their symbolic processes run ahead of concrete fact, developing the capacity to think in terms of possibility instead of actuality. In modern societies with widespread school systems, more middle- and upper-middle-class adolescents show formal thought than do adolescents from working- and lower-class backgrounds, and adolescents in upper socioeconomic classes develop this thought earlier (Dulit, 1972; Peel, 1971).

Although formal thought is not a universal characteristic of adolescence, its development constitutes a change of primary importance for the individual. Because it allows adolescents to speculate about what might be instead of accepting things as they are, its appearance can signal profound changes in their identities and in their social relations.

TRACING THE DEVELOPMENT OF
FORMAL THOUGHT A child does not suddenly wake up one morning and begin to reason about hypothetical matters. In fact, Edith Neimark (1982) believes that the separate skills that go into formal operations probably begin developing early in the concrete operational period. But at this stage they are isolated; as a child nears adolescence, the various skills become coordinated; gradually the child is able to apply them in a more general fashion.

In a longitudinal study, Deanna Kuhn and Erin Phelps (1982) traced the slow emergence of one aspect of formal operations: the ability to isolate the variables responsible for some physical effect. Kuhn and Phelps used a group of five colorless liquids, which were mixed in various combinations by the researcher. Sometimes the mixture turned cloudy; sometimes it turned red; sometimes it remained colorless. The subjects in this experiment were nine- to eleven-year-olds who came to the lab every week for eleven weeks. On each of their visits, the researcher mixed the liquids in a different way and asked the children to discover what liquid— or combination of liquids—was responsible for the transformation they saw.

Over the eleven weeks, a number of the children gradually learned to test systematically for the potent liquid and to solve the problems. These children developed genuine hypotheses ("It could be either B or C that's making it red") and tested each liquid individually. But it took many weeks before children consistently followed this procedure. In most cases, children who solved the problem one week would try ineffective strategies the next week. Kuhn and Phelps concluded that discarding inadequate strategies was just as difficult for the children as consolidating their effective strategies.

A favorite problem used to test for formal operations is the pendulum problem. In this problem, children are given strings of different lengths and objects of different weights, which the children can attach to a rod so that they swing like pendulums (see Figure 10.4). Each of the possible pendulums swings through its arc at a different speed; the child's task is to explain the differences in speed. The four plausible causes are: (1) the weight of the object, (2) the length of the string, (3) the height from which the object is released, and (4) the force of the

initial push. Only the length of the string actually affects the speed of the pendulum. A child can find this solution either by methodically trying all possible combinations of the four factors (varying a single factor with each trial) or by imagining trials of all possible combinations of factors.

When Bärbel Inhelder and Piaget (1958) presented this problem to children between the ages of six and fifteen, they found that only fourteen- and fifteen-year-olds anticipated all possible combinations, tested them experimentally, and deduced not only what affects a pendulum's speed but also what factors are irrelevant. The youngest children (six- and seven-year-olds) ap-

FIGURE 10.4 Illustration of a pendulum problem. The child is given a set of weights (pictured at bottom) and a string that can be shortened or lengthened (as pictured at left). The task is to determine which factor or factors account for the speed with which a pendulum traverses its arc.

(After Inhelder and Piaget, 1958)

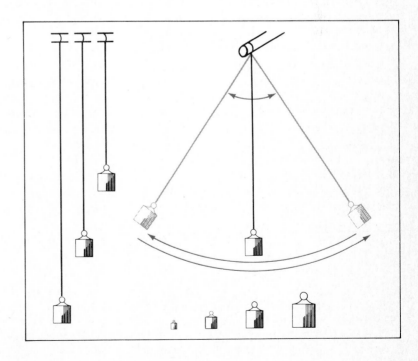

proached the problem unsystematically and seemed unable to vary the factors separately. They seemed unable to imagine that their own initial push had nothing to do with the pendulum's speed. Children between the ages of eight and thirteen were able to vary some of the factors, but they found it very difficult to exclude any of the factors. They were able to discover that the length of the string was involved, but not that it was the only factor.

Only the older children managed to solve the problem on their own. But younger children can be taught to solve the problem. Children as young as ten have been trained to carry out the necessary steps in the solution (Siegler, Liebert, and Liebert, 1973). After reviewing the training studies, Edith Neimark (1982) concluded that when such training is successful, the child has the necessary cognitive structures, but has not yet learned to apply them spontaneously. She points out that the same training procedure produces only slight improvements in young children, but major improvements in older children. However, age is not the only factor; among a group of ten- to twelve-year-olds, quick and accurate response, the use of systematic strategies on other tests, creativity, discipline in class, self-confidence, and initiative predicted formal operational ability (Cloutier and Goldschmid, 1976; Bereiter, 1978).

ROOTS OF SCIENTIFIC THOUGHT

When Siegler found that children in the concrete operational stage could learn to use the methods of formal thought, he searched for its origins in early childhood. Inhelder and Piaget (1958) acknowledged that the foundations of formal thought were laid in early childhood but took the position that young children could not reason in a scientific manner because they lacked the necessary logical structures and because their understanding of physical relationships was unsystematic.

In a series of studies that explored scientific reasoning, Siegler discovered that children could reason systematically much earlier than had been supposed. Presented with a simple problem in physics, the three-year-olds guessed randomly, but about half of the four-year-olds and nearly all of the five-year-olds consistently applied a single, simple rule (Siegler, 1978). For example, when asked to predict which arm of a balance scale would go down if the lever were released (see Figure 10.5), the rule these children applied was that if both sides of the scale have the same number of weights, the scale will be in balance; otherwise, the side with the greater number of weights will go down. (They did not realize that this rule will work only if the weights are the same distance from the fulcrum.) Siegler discovered that although eight-year-olds generally operate by the same simple rule, many of them develop more sophisticated rules when given problems that require them—but five-year-olds do not. The older children would, for example, learn to allow for the distance of the weights from the fulcrum except when the combination of weights and distance was so complicated it required arithmetical computation.

In another experiment with three- and four-year-olds who were random guessers, Siegler (1978) released the lever after each of their guesses. When the child's prediction was right, he said, "Very good. You were right." When it was wrong, he said, "No, that's not right. Look carefully at the balance scale to see if you can figure out what would have told you the right answer." Ten seconds later, he proceeded to the next problem. After a series of such problems, more than half the four-year-olds, but none of the three-year-olds, began to use the simple rule of weights to guide their predictions.

Siegler discovered that a major reason for the three-year-olds' failure to profit from their experience with the scale was the way they encoded the problem. In a test of their memories for the placement of the weights, he found that most of the four-year-olds, but none of the three-year-olds, could remember the number of weights placed on each arm of the scale. When he taught the three-year-olds to encode the weights, they too learned from their experience with the scale and began to use the simple rule so prevalent among five-year-olds. In the same way, Siegler taught five-year-olds to encode the

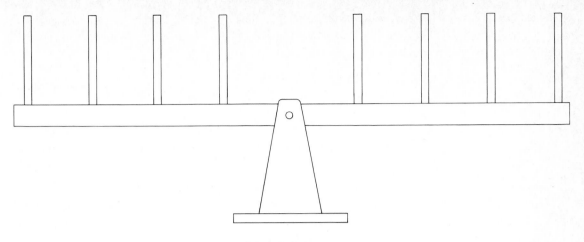

Balance Scale Apparatus

FIGURE 10.5 By using various weights on this balance scale and asking children which arm would go down if the lever were released, Robert Siegler discovered that children could reason systematically much earlier than had been supposed.

(From Siegler, 1978. Reprinted with permission of the editor and publishers)

distance of the weights from the fulcrum and found that they then performed as well on the scale problem as most eight-year-olds. But not until adolescence can children learn to use the most sophisticated rule, which requires computing the relation between weight and distance, and even then, Siegler found, they require both instruction and external memory aids. College students need only the instruction or the aid in order to adopt the rule.

As Siegler points out, something very important happens to children between the ages of three and five: when faced with new problem-solving situations, they begin to generate and apply systematic, rule-governed strategies. He divides scientific reasoning into two major phases: from birth to age five, and from age five to adulthood. As noted earlier, this is exactly the way Kendler divides human approaches to the learning of concepts.

ROOTS OF LOGICAL REASONING The sort of logical reasoning children and adults use in everyday life does not usually require formal thought. In daily life, the problem is set in context, background knowledge helps us toward a solution, and clues from any source may be helpful. But the logical reasoning studied by psychologists is the sort of formal logic you may have encountered in a philosophy or math class. Only the information contained in the problem can be used. This logical reasoning is also different from the scientific reasoning studied by Piaget in the pendulum problem (Braine and Rumain, 1983).

In a recent study, four- and five-year-olds showed that they could reason logically under certain conditions (Hawkins et al., 1984). Researchers gave the children two dozen reasoning problems. For example, the children were asked:

> Merds laugh when they're happy.
> Animals that laugh don't like mushrooms.
> Do merds like mushrooms? (p. 587)

When the problems were framed so that outside knowledge was unlikely to intrude into the solution, preschoolers were able to solve the problems and justify their answer to the researchers. The context of the problem also affected their performance. When the fantasy problems (about merds, bangas, and other imaginary animals and objects) were presented first, children could solve them. But when problems drawn from daily life were presented first (about glasses, bears, or books), children were unable to solve the fantasy problems. The "real" problems seemed to set the children up to reason about the real world and to draw on their outside knowledge, no matter what the problem. The researchers concluded that the children lacked control over their formal reasoning ability and did not yet understand when such hypothetical reasoning was appropriate. Their skills were still isolated and appeared only under highly constrained conditions.

Logical reasoning begins to emerge quite early, but the development of logical thought is not complete until children are into the formal operational period. Some types of logic problems can be solved by fourth-graders, others by sixth-graders, and some forms are understood only by boys and girl who are well into adolescence. After reviewing the research, Martin Braine and Barbara Rumain (1983) concluded that many of the problems schoolchildren have with logical reasoning can be traced to difficulty with language comprehension. They point out that even adults have problems handling some forms of logical reasoning, and that when adults run into trouble on a logic problem, they quickly resort to nonlogical strategies.

UNDERSTANDING

The adolescent in the stage of formal operations understands the concepts of time, number, and causality. Adolescents deal with past and future, manipulate negative numbers, and can predict the consequences of physical actions. They have no trouble thinking about the civilization of ancient Egypt; they are trying to decide which college to attend a few years hence; they solve problems involving distance, time, and speed; and they know just where to hit the cue ball to send a billiard ball spinning in any direction.

All these concepts developed slowly, and it is possible to trace their beginnings back to babyhood.

Time

The young infant with a memory of only a few seconds has no awareness of time, but within six months, the baby's repetitive shaking of a rattle or banging of a cup indicates that he or she is beginning to develop a primitive concept of duration. Toward the end of the sensorimotor period, as the baby's memory develops, the concept of time broadens.

It will be a good many years, however, before the baby's concept of time matches that of an adult. When Piaget (1971b) queried one- to five-year olds about age, for example, they believed that age could be determined by size and that when trees or people or dogs stop growing, they stop getting older. The children looked at a series of annual pictures of an apple tree and a pear tree. The pear tree was planted a year later but grew faster than the apple tree. By the fifth year, it was larger and bore more fruit. As long as the apple tree was larger, the children agreed that it was older; but as soon as the pear tree surpassed it, even the five-year-olds insisted the pear tree was older. A five-year-old might agree that the apple tree was five years old and the pear tree was four years old and that a five-year-old child is older than a four-year-old but still insist that the pear tree was older "because it had more pears."

The behavior of these five-year-olds seems to indicate that young children do not understand the concept of time as duration. Yet, in another study, five-year-olds were able to judge the simple passage of time. Iris Levin (1977) asked youngsters to decide which of two dolls "slept" longer. Five-year-olds judged correctly when both dolls went to sleep at the same time, but one woke up first; they were also correct when the dolls went to sleep at different times but woke up together. But when the situation became complex, the children had trouble. Few of them could solve the problem when neither the beginning nor the end of the dolls' naps were the same.

Understanding time as duration does not meet Piaget's definition of the time concept. Time, Piaget (1970) said, was an intellectual construction: the relation between an action and the speed with which it was accomplished. He believed that young children have a primitive intuition of speed, but that they cannot understand time because they confuse it with speed and distance. Because preoperational children do not understand the relationship between speed and action, they believe that "faster" means getting more done, and getting more done means they have to spend more time. For them, whether they walk briskly to school, run, or dawdle, it always takes the same time. In one of Piaget's (1970) experiments, the investigator took a little doll in each hand and—when the child said "Go!"—hopped them along the table, side by side. The dolls started at the same time and stopped at the same time. When they covered exactly the same distance, the preschoolers agreed that the dolls had stopped and started at the same time. But if one doll covered a greater distance than the other, the child denied that the dolls had stopped at the same time, saying that the doll that did not go as far had stopped first. The investigator could get the child to agree that one doll was not still going when the other stopped, but the child still argued that the dolls had not stopped at the same time because one of them had not gone as far as the other. Children only a little older said that both dolls had started at the same time and stopped at the same time, but still insisted that one had walked a longer time because it had gone farther.

After a lengthy series of experiments involving speed, time, and distance, Piaget concluded that children could not develop a mature concept of time until they had mastered three concrete operations: seriation, class inclusion, and a measurement of time. In seriation (discussed in the transitivity section), the child learns to order events in time. In class inclusion, the child learns that lunch follows breakfast and dinner follows lunch, and that the time from breakfast to dinner is longer than the time from breakfast to lunch. The child develops a measurement of time by synthesizing seriation and class inclusion.

In most studies, children are asked to choose which doll, train, or rabbit traveled farther, went faster, or took the most time to cover the ground. When Friedrich Wilkening (1981) had children judge the speed of only one animal—asking them to show how far a cat could run across a bridge while a dog barked—five-year-olds showed some understanding of time. When the dog barked eight seconds, for example, they decided the cat ran farther than when the dog barked for two seconds or five seconds. The children were not simply confusing time with distance, because when they were given the same problem, but were asked how far a turtle would run, they indicated that the turtle would never run as far as the cat in the same length of time. Apparently, having to compare two speed/distance/duration relationships is more than children can handle at this age.

In a later experiment, children were asked to judge whether a rabbit or a skunk ran faster, longer, or farther when a farmer's dog began to bark (Acredolo, Adams, and Schmid, 1984). Researchers varied the speed and time that each animal ran. In this more difficult problem, second-graders understood the relationship between speed and distance (the animal who runs faster goes farther), and between duration and distance (the animal who runs longer goes farther). But the relationship between speed and duration (the animals who runs faster gets there more quickly) was not understood by a majority of the children until they reached the third grade. These findings support Piaget's belief that eight-year-olds are developing mature concepts of speed and time.

Number

Young children do not understand the concept of number as Piaget defined it, although they may be efficient counters. Piaget (1952a) was not interested in whether children could count, add, or multiply; his definition of the number concept required that children be able to reason about number *without* counting. This kind of understanding does not develop until children reach the concrete operational stage, Piaget believed, because it goes hand in hand with the development of logic.

Much of Piaget's research about understanding number focused on conservation experiments. In tests of conservation, older children do not concern themselves with the exact number of items; instead, they reason without using any actual numbers. They look at the rows and consider the effect of the researcher's transformation apart from the specific number of items involved. Preschool children are just beginning to reason without counting; they can count no farther than five, but they can learn to conserve when each row has as many as ten checkers (Gelman, 1982). They succeed by using one-to-one correspondence, which does not involve counting, but they can do this only under special circumstances. And this is the only kind of nonnumerical reasoning they can do; they cannot handle the effects of transformations or the effects of a combination of arithmetical operations (Gelman and Baillargeon, 1983).

Young children do have a concept of number, and their understanding begins when they are as young as two years old—although many two-year-olds can count only as far as two. Rochel Gelman and Randy Gallistel (1978) believe that counting, like language, is a natural human function. Even young children who do not know the number words of their language count. Some use letters, some use their own words, others make up number sequences such as "one, two, three, eight, eleven" but always use them in the same way; that is, eight always functions as four, and eleven as five. When two-and-a-half-year-olds begin to count, they point at the objects they are counting or touch them and say their number words aloud. As they get older, they count to themselves and simply announce the result. Five-year-olds return to audible

This child is a skilled counter and is beginning to understand the structure of the number system. In order to add or subtract, he counts on his fingers, a technique that is common among preschoolers. (Suzanne Szasz)

counting, however, if they must count a large array of objects.

Preschoolers, say Gelman and Gallistel, are flexible about what they will count. As long as they can assign some superordinate term or can simply classify the objects to be counted as "things," they can count mixed groups (trees and flowers and chairs, or toys and books and candies) as easily, if more slowly, than they can count objects from the same group.

Children apparently learn how to count before they understand the principles that govern counting (Briars and Siegler, 1984). Over the preschool years, children slowly develop insight into these principles. Most three-year-olds seem unaware of the essential principle: that they must assign one (and only one) number word to each object. Four- and five-year-olds understand this principle, and most also know they can count objects in any direction. A good many have also learned that it is unnecessary to point at each object as they count it, but fewer have learned that they can start in the middle of a row and count in both directions. Not until they are five do a majority of children understand that they can skip around when counting; most believe that it is necessary to count adjacent objects. As Diane Briars and Robert Siegler (1984) point out, starting in the middle and skipping around are impractical in many instances (as when counting stairs) and impossible in others (as when counting the chiming of church-bells). So it is no wonder that young children have not grasped these principles.

In other experiments, researchers have used counting to trace the understanding of the number system in preschoolers. Robert Siegler and Mitchell Robinson (1982) found that in the early stages, children stop counting sometime before they reach 20. These children, who are usually three-year-olds, have memorized the numbers they use, and apparently do not realize the number system has a structure. At the next stage, children count beyond 20 but no farther than 99. When these children stop counting, it is almost always on a number that ends in 9 (29, 49), and if the experimenter starts them off with a higher decade (51, 52, 53), they can go on to the end of the decade (59). At this stage, children apparently understand the rule for combining digits with the various decades. Finally, some four- and five-year-olds can count beyond 100. These children understand an additional counting rule that allows them to combine hundreds, and generally stop counting when they get tired or bored. This usually occurs when they consider the job "complete"—with a number that ends either in 9 and 0.

Four- and five-year-olds can do more than count: they can handle equivalences, identity, addition, and subtraction. But they can do this only with very small numbers of objects (Gelman and Gallistel, 1978). Siegler and Robinson studied children's understanding of numerical magnitude (whether they knew that one number was larger than another) and of addition, and discovered that youngsters often failed to apply knowledge they had shown in one numerical area to another. They concluded that, like other skills, early mathematical skills seem to develop in isolation. Only after children become proficient in such skills do they begin to make use of the possible connections among them. Part of the failure to connect skills may be due to children's available memory span. In a study of four- and six-year-olds, Charles Brainerd (1983) found that memory failure, not processing errors, was responsible for 74 percent of the mistakes made by four- and five-year-olds, and for 65 percent of the mistakes made by six-year-olds. He believes this trend in the figures indicates a pronounced improvement in short-term memory among the six-year-olds.

Preschoolers clearly know more about number than researchers once believed they did. As Siegler and Robinson (1982) point out, even three-year-olds followed the experimenter's requests; they counted, compared, and added when asked to do so. But Siegler and Robinson do not know how the children knew to follow the instructions, what process they used in a particular situation, nor why they chose it. A child may use different processes in solving similar problems, and the selection is probably guided by the context of the problem.

Causality

The earliest ideas of causality arise out of the circular reactions of the sensorimotor period, as infants develop a sense first of themselves, then of other people, as causal agents. By the time babies are into their second year, they begin to connect events. Piaget (1954) described the way his thirteen-month-old son, Laurent, searched for the cause of his moving baby carriage. Peering over the edge, the infant saw Piaget's foot slowly pushing it and smiled with satisfaction. In another few months, Laurent would expand his notion of causality from actions that affected himself to actions between people and objects that had no direct effect upon him. During the sensorimotor period, said Piaget (1930), infants move from a belief in magical causes—in the sense that objects obey their desires—to an awareness that their own behavior can be affected by others.

According to Piaget, preschoolers have developed precausal thinking and simply do not believe in accidents. They search for a cause to explain every minor occurrence, and they ascribe thoughts, feelings, and life itself to inanimate objects, a type of belief known as **animism.** This aspect of children's thinking is reflected in many of their notions about the causes of such things as night and day, sun, moon, clouds, mountains, and rivers. Thread unwinds from a dropped spool because "it wants to." Slowly, over a period of several years, children develop more naturalistic explanations of causality. For example, Piaget (1930) described the way the explanation for cloud movements develops in children. Four- or five-year-olds, he said, believe they make the clouds move by walking. Six-year-olds believe clouds move because either God or adults make them move. Seven-year-olds believe the clouds move by themselves but at the command of the sun or moon. By this time, Piaget believed, there is at the back of the child's mind a motor scheme that prepares the way for the next development, when, at about the age of eight, children attribute the clouds' movements to the wind but explain that the wind rises out of the clouds ("They make air and the air chases the clouds"). Nine-year-olds do not know where the wind comes from, but they know that it pushes the clouds and that without it clouds cannot move.

But do children really believe that inanimate objects are alive? In one study, twelve-month-old infants seemed surprised when they saw a chair apparently move by itself (Golinkoff and Harding, 1980). Yet when inanimate objects were being shoved or pushed by adults, the same babies were unruffled. When preschoolers are simply asked to tell whether an object is alive or not, they do make many errors. However, when researchers ask them more detailed

questions (such as, "If there was a fire, could X run away?", "Can X grow bigger?", or "If we forget to give X food, will it get hungry?"), youngsters seem to have a much better grasp of the difference between animate and inanimate objects. These were some of the questions Merry Bullock (1985) asked preschoolers about another child, a live rabbit, a stack of wooden blocks, and a plastic wind-up worm. From their answers, it seemed clear that five-year-olds understand the difference between animate and inanimate objects. Three-year-olds are aware of the two categories but often make mistakes in deciding whether an object is alive or not. For example, nearly half the three-year-olds in Bullock's study thought that the wind-up worm was alive. Bullock concluded that preschoolers are not animistic, because they do not ascribe life to inanimate objects in general. Rather, they lack specific knowledge about some objects that would allow them to categorize them correctly. (See the box on p. 336 for a consideration of children's understanding of death.)

Piaget believed that such knowledge developed very slowly. As children interacted with machines, they came to understand that these objects were inanimate and gradually developed naturalistic explanations of causality. As they tried to make their toys function, produce physical effects, or overcome physical resistance in objects, they learned about the nature of physical causality. If Piaget was right, it is no wonder that children resort to animistic answers when asked about complex natural phenomena. Asking preschoolers about what causes wind and rain, why rivers flow, how bicycles and other machines work is asking them to talk about things they have had little experience with (Gelman, 1978). Since they lack the knowledge, they make up animistic but plausible answers. When Michael Berzonsky (1971) questioned children about remote events, asking, for example, "Why does the moon change shape?" they generally gave precausal answers. When asked about familiar events, such as tires going flat, or flying kites, however, they usually gave physical, mechanical answers.

Preschoolers usually understand the causes of

events in their daily lives. When three- and four-year-olds were given two pictures and asked to select a third that would complete the causal sequence of a familiar event, they solved the problem with no difficulty (Gelman, Bullock, and Meck, 1980). For example, when they were shown the picture of a cup and the picture of a hammer, they chose the picture of a broken cup to complete the sequence. No matter which part of the sequence was missing, the youngsters were able to complete it: shown the picture of a whole orange and a sliced orange, they chose the picture of a knife.

Young children also know that causes precede effects. In another study, Merry Bullock and Rochel Gelman (1979) showed three- and five-year-olds a box with two runways. The children watched the experimenter drop a ball in one runway; a few seconds later, a jumping jack popped up from a hole in the center of the box. Then the experimenter dropped an identical ball down in the other runway. When they were asked to explain what made the jack jump, the children almost always said it was the first ball. They chose the first ball even when the part of the box containing the runway for the first ball was separated physically from the rest of the box.

The child's knowledge that cause precedes effect is only a partial understanding of causation. A child must also understand the physical, mechanical force involved. Piaget (1974) believed that this understanding did not develop until children reached the stage of concrete operations. However, in a series of experiments with young children, Thomas Shultz (1982) found that two- and three-year-olds knew that physical events were caused by the transmission of some kind of force. The children were given problems involving wind, sound, and light. For example, in the wind problems, the children saw two mechanical blowers and a lit candle. When one blower was turned on and the other was off, they understood that the blower that was operating was responsible for blowing out the candle. The children also understood that the transmission of force was not effective if there was a barrier between the operating blower and the candle or if the blower was turned so that it faced away from the candle. In other experiments, three- and four-year-olds have understood the difference between relevant changes in causation (a wooden rod that knocked over a series of blocks was made too short to reach the first block) or irrelevant changes (a glass rod was substituted for the wooden rod) (Baillargeon, Gelman, and Meck, 1981).

How can we explain the discrepancy between Piaget's findings concerning children's knowledge of mechanical forces and the findings of other researchers? When Piaget (1974) studied children's grasp of causality, he insisted that they be able to explain why certain events occurred. Rochel Gelman and Renee Baillargeon (1983) believe that Piaget was not actually studying the child's understanding of causality; instead, he was studying the child's ability to *explain* causality. They believe that children develop an implicit understanding of the principles underlying causality before they *know* that they are using them. So young children can often discern causation when they cannot explain it. Their explanations of causality develop very slowly, and their understanding will not be complete for many years.

METACOGNITION

When asked if Merlin, a tic-tac-toe playing computer toy, was alive, six-year-old Alex said, "Oh, yes, this is not a regular toy. It is very mean" (Turkle, 1984, p. 48). Alex decided that Merlin was alive because it consistently won at tic-tac-toe, something it could not do unless it "cheated." Computers, points out Sherry Turkle (1984), do not fit neatly into the category of inanimate objects whose behavior can be described in physical terms. In fact, as children learn to program computers, they tend to talk about them in increasingly psychological terms. Among the four- to twelve-year-olds Turkle studied, children seem to think that computers are "sort of alive because they think but don't feel, because they learn but can't decide what to learn, because they cheat but don't know they

Understanding Death

Children who are younger than two or three appear to have no understanding of death. When Maria Nagy (1948) studied 378 children in Budapest, Hungary, she found that their concept of death fell into three phases. In the first phase, which characterized children between three and five, children saw death as a sleep or a journey—only a temporary separation. In the second phase, between the ages of five and nine, death was personified. For some children, it was an angel; for others, an evil, frightening monster or a "death man." Although children at this age saw death as final, they believed that their own deaths could be avoided—all they had to do was to outrun the death man. In the final phase, beginning around the age of nine or ten, children realized the final and inevitable nature of death, seeing it as a permanent, biological process that happens to everyone.

The older children in Nagy's study had lived in war-torn Europe, when soldiers died in battle and civilians died in air raids. Their experiences might have influenced the rate at which they grasped death's irrevocable, universal nature. Children who grow up in a protected environment might develop the concept more slowly, especially since most children's experience with death comes from its casual treatment in televised action shows. Edward White and his colleagues (White, Elson, and Prawat, 1978) examined the way five- to ten-year-old children in suburban American schools regard death. In this study, children's understanding of the universal nature of death was strongly linked to their cognitive development (see figure). More than 60 percent of the children who understood conservation believed that death came to everyone. But the idea that death was irrevocable and that it meant the end of bodily life showed no such connection. As the figure indicates, the big jump in understanding death's universality comes between the first and second grades, just where Piaget placed the transition from preoperational to operational thought. Nagy's children seemed to have a surer grasp of death's finality than these American children did. Since this aspect of the concept may not be strongly

are cheating" (p. 50). Younger children attributed emotion and malicious intent to the computer, but older children saw the computer differently. These children granted the machines intelligence, yet they drew the line between human beings and machines on the grounds of emotion.

Seymour Papert (1980), a mathematician and computer scientist, believes that as children come to understand how computers "think," they learn more about the mind. That is, they learn the difference between mechanical thought and creative thought. And they learn what kind of strategy or style of thought to apply to any problem. This kind of knowledge is known as **metacognition,** and it refers to a person's knowledge about mental states, mental abilities, and ways of regulating them. In Chapter 8, we explored metamemory, which is one kind of metacognition.

Another kind of metacognition is called **executive control;** this aspect of metacognition consists of the processes that regulate learning and problem solving: planning before starting to solve a problem, monitoring cognitive activities during learning, and checking the outcome (Brown et al., 1983). Children (or even adults) may not be able to put their knowledge of executive control into words, and the processes seem to vary from one task to the next. As executive control develops, children become more flexible in planning and executing solutions, and they learn to distribute their attention and effort more effectively.

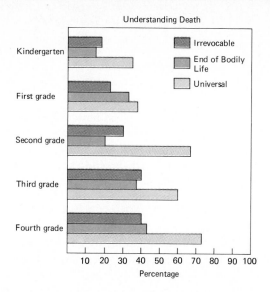

Understanding Death

Kindergarten

First grade

Second grade

Third grade

Fourth grade

■ Irrevocable
■ End of Bodily Life
□ Universal

10 20 30 40 50 60 70 80 90 100
Percentage

The sharp jump in the grasp of death's universality shows a connection with cognitive development; the slow growth in the grasp of death's finality indicates that the understanding is probably based on experience.

(Adapted from Edward White, Bill Elson, and Richard Prawat, "Children's Conceptions of Death," *Child Development*, 49:1978, 307–310.)

linked to cognitive development, the difference may lie in the gulf between the experience of the two groups of children.

It has proved difficult to settle the question. After reviewing thirty-five studies that explored children's understanding of death, Mark Speece and Sandor Brent (1984) found great discrepancies in the age at which the majority of youngsters in various studies understood the three aspects of death. Part of the problem lies in the different questions used by researchers to establish children's comprehension of death, but some of the discrepancy may lie in the fact that few researchers have investigated the relationship between children's understanding of death and their religious or personal experiences with it. Speece and Brent concluded that although few researchers have found strong connections between general cognitive development and an understanding of death, it seems likely that until children begin to develop concrete operational thought, they are unlikely to comprehend any of the basic aspects of death: its irrevocability, its universality, and its ending of bodily life.

This emergence of self-regulation can be seen among very young children trying to solve simple problems. Judy DeLoache, Susan Sugarman, and Ann Brown (1981) gave a set of nesting cups to youngsters between the ages of twenty-four and forty-two months. The youngest children (twenty-four to thirty months) frequently used brute force to try to assemble the set of cups. They twisted, banged, or pressed hard in an attempt to force a large cup inside a small one. When force failed, they tended to discard one of the cups and pick up another. Some children at this age used a costly strategy: after successfully nesting the first four cups, they tried to insert the final, large cup into the stack; when it did not fit, they dismantled the nearly completed set and began the task all over

again. Older children (thirty-one to forty-two months) showed more sophisticated strategies. If they had a cup that was too large to fit, they took apart the stack in the center and inserted it in its correct place. And if a cup they tried to fit inside another was too large, they simply reversed their strategy—they placed the bottom (small) cup inside the top cup.

Children gradually become more skilled in regulating their cognitive processes. For one thing, they know about planning and understand its value. After interviewing schoolchildren, Roy Pea (1982b) found that young and old alike defined planning as "thinking ahead about what to do in the future" (p. 15). All thought that planning took time, but eight- and nine-year-olds thought that, once completed,

Until they are about 30 months old, children's problem-solving strategies are relatively inflexible. As executive control develops, stacking a set of nesting cups changes from a frustrating problem to an easy game. (Peter Menzel)

plans were almost magical: good ones guaranteed success. Eleven- and twelve-year-olds were more sophisticated; they saw good plans as making it easier for them to achieve a goal, but not as guaranteeing it. Only the older children recognized that plans were tentative and could be changed along the way. These older children are apparently on the way to thinking about their strategies—able to step back and look at their solutions and use this thought to redirect their strategies (Brown et al., 1983). Piaget consider this ability to think about thinking as a hallmark of formal thought. Carla, an eleven-year-old girl in Turkle's (1984) study, not only thought about thinking; she thought about her own thinking in computer terms. Carla saw herself as programmed—programmed by her mother and her priest. But Carla also saw herself as different from the computer in a very important way: she could learn to change her own program.

SUMMARY

The major factors involved in a child's learning include interaction between the child and the environment, the accessibility of the child's previous knowledge, and the child's conscious access to his or her skills. Children seem to form some concepts around a rule; they learn others by building examples. Very young children appear to learn by associating stimuli and responses, but by the time they are five or six years old, children develop and test hypotheses. The development of basic mental rules, which allow children to organize and manipulate concepts, may simply be the cumulative effect of learning.

According to Piaget, the thought of preschoolers is intuitive, inflexible, focused on individual events, and contradictory. During this preoperational stage, children develop the concept of **identity,** which means that they understand objects and people remain the same even if some of their irrelevant properties are changed.

About the time a child starts school, he or she enters the concrete operational period, in which the child's cognitive processes become **operations;** that is, they are flexible, rigorous, and logical. Piaget believed that during this period, children developed the concept of **conservation,** the understanding that irrelevant changes in the physical appearance of objects do not affect their quantity. This understanding requires the child to first understand the concrete operation of **reversibility.** Piaget also believed that **transitivity,** or the making of logical inferences based on separate observations, first develops after children start school. To make these inferences, children must first understand **seriation,** or the ordering of objects by size or weight. Finally, concrete operational children are supposed to develop the concept of **class inclusion**—the understanding that a superordinate class is always larger than any of its basic classes. Research indicates that these concepts can be taught much earlier than Piaget supposed, and that the way children encode what they see determines their ability to solve problems involving these concepts.

In the formal operational period, children apply logical thought to abstractions, considering possibilities outside the immediate environment. Such scientific thought is not universal and may depend on formal education. When children are about five, they begin to generate and apply systematic, rule-governed strategies and can be taught to encode problems in a way that enables them to solve problems they normally could not handle. Logical reasoning also begins to appear about the age of five, but only when children are reasoning about fantasy situations and outside knowledge does not intrude into the problem. The development of logical thought is not complete until children are into the formal operational period.

The concept of time also develops slowly. In simple situations, five-year-olds appear to understand the concept of time as duration. But children are at least eight years old before they understand the time concept as the relation between an action and the speed with which it was accomplished. Although Piaget believed that children do not understand the concept of number until they reach the concrete operational stage, research indicates that preschoolers have mastered the concept. However, preschoolers cannot understand most forms of nonnumerical reasoning. Children learn how to count before they understand the principles involved in counting, and most five-year-olds also understand the structure of the number system.

From a period in which they believe in magical causes, very young children move into precausal thinking; at this stage they believe that nothing ever happens by accident. Piaget believed that the thinking of preschoolers is also **animistic:** they believe inanimate objects have thoughts, feelings, and life. Research indicates, however, that preschoolers may not be animistic but instead lack specific knowledge that would enable them to categorize some objects as inanimate. Preschoolers seem to understand physical causality before they can explain it. They know that causes precede effects, and they know that physical, mechanical forces are involved.

Children's understanding of **metacognition,** which refers to a person's knowledge of mental states, mental abilities, and how to regulate them, develops slowly. As **executive control,** the process that regulates learning and problem solving, develops, children become more flexible in planning and executing solutions, and they learn to allocate their attention and effort effectively.

Intelligence and Intellectual Assessment

THE NATURE OF INTELLIGENCE
Species Intelligence vs. Individual
  Intelligence
The Biological Perspective
The Structuralist Perspective
The Psychometric Perspective
The Information-Processing Perspective
THE MEASUREMENT OF INTELLIGENCE
THE STABILITY OF IQ SCORES
IQ Tests in Infancy
IQ Tests in Childhood
WHAT CAN IQ SCORES PREDICT?
Success in School
Success in Life
Creativity
MODIFIABILITY OF INTELLIGENCE
Heredity
Health and Nutrition
Environment
SUMMARY

Figan loved bananas, which were kept in a concrete box that fastened with a simple pin. Learning to pull the pin was an easy task for this chimpanzee, so Hassan, a member of the staff at the Gombe Stream Chimpanzee Reserve, cut threads in the pin and the handle so that the box would open only if the pin was unscrewed. Within a few months, Figan was deftly unscrewing the pin to get to the bananas. Next, Hassan put nuts on the ends of the screw. Now the nuts had to be removed before the pin could be unscrewed. In a short time, Figan had learned to remove the nuts in order to get to the pin. But problems remained. Once the lid was up, chimpanzees who ranked above Figan in the dominance hierarchy swarmed in for bananas, leaving him to go hungry. Figan soon learned not to open the box when other chimpanzees were in the vicinity. After removing the nuts and unscrewing the pin, he would sit, one foot holding the lid closed, and groom himself until all the high-ranking chimpanzees had gone. Jane Van Lawick-Goodall (1971) once timed a wait of more than half an hour, as Figan sat looking everywhere except at the banana box beneath his foot.

Such an anecdote provides a clear example of adaptive behavior, evidence—if any was needed—that human beings have no monopoly on intelligence. In this chapter, we temporarily set aside development and examine the concept of intelligence itself. We look at several ways of studying human intelligence: the biological approach, with its emphasis on evolution and adaptiveness; the structuralist approach, which emphasizes problem solving and logic; the psychometric approach, which focuses on individual differences; and the information-processing approach, which often uses artificial intelligence as a way of understanding human intelligence. After considering the many immediate influences that can affect a child's score on an intelligence test, we look at stability of these scores over the life span. Keeping in mind the fact that IQ scores often change, we investigate the use of the tests to predict success in school and success in life, and we consider the difference between IQ and creativity. Next we turn to the forces that influence a child's intelligence: heredity, health and nutrition, and factors in the environment. This allows us to investigate the possibility of modifying intelligence through early intervention and lets us examine specific environmental events that can affect children's test scores.

THE NATURE OF INTELLIGENCE

Establishing a definition of intelligence that satisfies everyone has been extremely difficult (Sternberg and Powell, 1983). Sixty-five years ago, psychologists filled an entire issue of the *Journal of Educational Psychology* with attempts to define the concept. Their definitions ranged from the ability to "carry on abstract thinking" through "an acquiring capacity," "a group of complex mental processes," "the power of good responses from the point of view of truth or fact," and the "ability to learn to adjust oneself to the environment" to a "a general modifiability

of the nervous system" (Resnick, 1976). The discussion continues today. One reason we lack a formal definition is that psychologists have focused on different aspects of intelligence. But no matter what approach psychologists take to intelligence, most would agree that intelligence is based on the ability to learn from experience and the ease with which a person can learn a new idea or new behavior. Even this working definition takes on different meanings, depending on whether we look at intelligence in the species as a whole or at individual differences.

Species Intelligence vs. Individual Intelligence

When Piaget spoke of intelligence, he referred to cognitive functions that are shared by the entire species; Piaget paid little attention to whether the speed, efficiency, or capacity of these functions differed among individuals. Like Piaget, many theorists are primarily interested in the ways in which people are alike, as well as the ways in which they are more intelligent than other species. Other theorists are primarily concerned with individual differences in cognitive functioning—a concern that leads them to look for ways to measure these differences.

SPECIES INTELLIGENCE When looked at from the standpoint of the species, intelligence is the disposition to behave adaptively when faced with the demands of the environment. The intelligence level of any species is the result of its evolutionary history, in which animals that could not adapt simply did not survive long enough to have any descendants. Among the various species, intelligence appears to fall along a continuum from simple pattern recognition through expectancy, understanding, intention, awareness, thought, and consciousness.

Donald Griffin (1976), who has studied birds, fish, and bats, believes that animals probably have significant mental experiences, and that the distance between human and animal intelligence is more one of quantity than of quality. Indeed, people seem to have little difficulty ranking species in terms of their intelligence. Knowing that an organism is an octopus, a dog, a chimpanzee, or a person, for example, tells us a good deal about its relative intelligence and provides a rough indication of what can be expected from it. As Donald O. Hebb (1949) points out, a dog shows superior intelligence by outstripping a rat or a hen in passing obstacles and reaching a goal by the shortest route. But a dog seems incredibly stupid when compared with a chimpanzee, who can use tools and will, for example, stack boxes in order to get food that is hung out of reach. And even the dullest human being who is able to earn a living is far more intelligent than the cleverest chimpanzee. Among members of any single species, however, differences in intelligence are slight.

INDIVIDUAL INTELLIGENCE When we look at human beings the concept of intelligence becomes exceedingly complex, although any normal twelve-year-old seems to understand the ordinary meaning of the term. In fact, ordinary people and psychologists pretty much agree on what intelligence is. Robert Sternberg and his colleagues (1981) gathered conceptions of intelligence from commuters in a train station, shoppers in a supermarket, and students in a college library, then compared them with conceptions put forth by experts in the field. All agreed on what kind of behavior describes an intelligent person. Ordinary people and the experts both described an intelligent person as possessing "a good vocabulary, making good decisions, planning ahead, and displaying interest in the world at large." David Wechsler (1975), who devised a widely used intelligence test, says that intelligence refers to behavior that is intentional, goal-directed, rational, and worthwhile. The last quality, he admits, means that judgments of intelligence are necessarily subjective and will change as the values of society change.

In fact, when psychologists look closely at individual differences, the picture of intelligence becomes fragmented and blurred. Alfred Binet, a French psychologist who practiced at the beginning of the twentieth century, supposed that intelligence is a general ability to understand the world and to reason about it. He believed that the best way to discover individual differences was to use three concepts: (1) there is a goal or direction to the mental processes involved; (2) intelligence involves an ability to show adaptable solutions; (3) intelligence involves a selectivity of judgment and a self-criticism of choices (Chaplin and Krawiec, 1974).

Charles Spearman (1927) agreed with Binet that there is a factor of general intelligence, which he called "g," and that it involves seeing and manipulating the relations among bits of information. He believed, however, that intelligence also includes specific abilities—"s" factors—and he used a system called *factor analysis* to detect them. In factor analysis, the scores people make on a variety of tests are correlated in the belief that when the scores show strong correlations, they are measuring a common mental ability. It is often further assumed that the mental abilities discovered through factor analysis are characteristic of human intelligence.

Over the years, the number of abilities thought to comprise intelligence has varied from 2 to 120. Louis Thurstone (1947), for example, used factor analysis to argue that intelligence consists of seven primary abilities: verbal comprehension, word fluency, number, space, memory, perceptual speed, and reasoning. According to J. P. Guilford (1973), intelligence is much more complicated than Thurstone's seven factors indicate. Guilford's structure-of-intellect model includes five kinds of intellectual processes (*operations*), which people use on four different classes of information (*contents*) to produce six different forms of information (*products*). (See Figure 11.1.) This means that there are 120 factors (5 × 4 × 6) involved in intelligence. Operations include cognition, memory, divergent production, convergent production, and evaluation; contents may be figural, symbolic, semantic, or behavioral; the products may be units, classes,

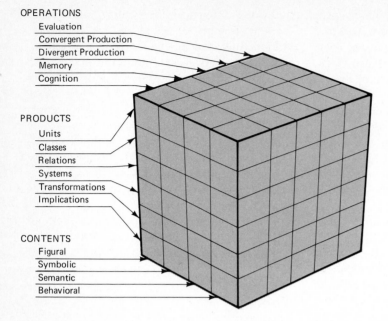

OPERATIONS
- Evaluation
- Convergent Production
- Divergent Production
- Memory
- Cognition

PRODUCTS
- Units
- Classes
- Relations
- Systems
- Transformations
- Implications

CONTENTS
- Figural
- Symbolic
- Semantic
- Behavioral

FIGURE 11.1 Guilford's structure-of-intellect model, in which intelligence is divided into 120 potential abilities; the three-dimensional arrangement shows the relationship of the abilities to one another.

(From Guilford, 1973, p. 636. Reprinted by permission of Prentice-Hall)

relations, systems, transformations, or implications.

Guilford's theory of intelligence goes beyond traditional academic skills. For example, divergent thinking—one of Guilford's operations, which he describes as "the generation of logical alternatives"—can lead to low scores on most intelligence tests, which measure convergent thinking, or "the generation of logical necessities." Divergent thinking involves remote associations and is often regarded as a measure of creativity. Convergent thinking produces conventionally accepted responses.

Another view of intelligence was proposed by Raymond Cattell (1968), who suggested that there were two major kinds of intelligence: fluid and crystallized. Fluid intelligence is relatively unaffected by cultural differences. A person who is high in fluid intelligence would be good in the strategy of games, solve puzzles quickly, and if placed in a new situation would perceive its complex relationships. Crystallized intelligence is a related group of abilities that are acquired through cultural experiences, especially through formal schooling. A person who is high in crystallized intelligence would have a large vocabulary, extensive mathematical skills, mechanical knowledge, and habits of logical reasoning. Cattell has tested deckhands and farmers who have for one reason or another missed schooling and finds that they sometimes score much higher than college professors on tests of fluid intelligence but do poorly on tests of crystallized intelligence, where professors excel.

Cattell used factor analysis in developing his approach and concluded that the two kinds of intelligence are made up of twenty-three different factors. John Horn (1970), who worked with Cattell in developing the distinction between the two kinds of intelligence, indicates that some of the twenty-three factors involved, such as figural relations and associative memory, primarily affect fluid intelligence. Others, such as verbal comprehension and mechanical knowledge, primarily affect crystallized intelligence; yet others, such as number facility and formal reasoning, are related to both kinds of intelligence.

Children who have not been adequately exposed to the majority culture are not likely to do well on traditional tests of intelligence, which focus heavily on crystallized intelligence. We would expect such children to do much better on a test of fluid intelligence, which is supposed to be "culture-fair" (see Figure 11.2). But our expectations would probably be wrong, since much of the material on a test of fluid intelligence is also learned. Although this learning is incidental and not directed by the culture, it turns out that supposedly "culture-fair" tests depend more on cultural background than theorists had expected. Children's scores on these tests, just as on more traditional tests of intelligence, generally increase with their socioeconomic level (Anastasi, 1982).

Another view of intelligence has recently come from Howard Gardner (1983), who has proposed a theory of "multiple intelligences." Gardner believes that human beings have seven different kinds of intelligence: linguistic, musical, logical-mathematical, spatial, bodily-kinesthetic, and two forms of personal intelligence—one involving access to a person's own feelings and the other involving the ability to notice and make distinctions among other people. Gardner takes a broader view of intelligence than most theorists, who tend to omit personal intelligence from their descriptions and to confine bodily intelligence to the period of infancy (Piaget's sensorimotor stage). These seven intelligences are supposed to be relatively independent, although they interact and build upon one another. Different cultures value different intelligences, says Gardner. For example, spatial skills are valued among the Eskimo, because they must be able to note slight cracks in the ice, to notice the angle and shape of snowdrifts, and to judge the weather from subtle cloud patterns. Eskimo would regard a person with highly developed spatial skills as much more intelligent

FIGURE 11.2 Culture-fair tests generally do not depend on verbal ability or formal schooling. From the IPAT Culture Fair Intelligence Test. Copyrighted by The Institute for Personality and Ability Testing. Used by permission.

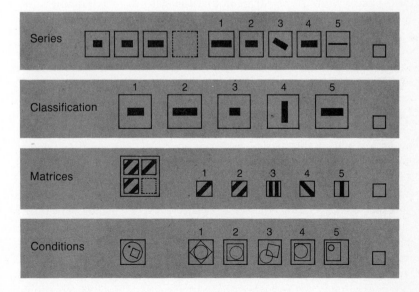

than a person with highly developed logico-mathematical skills.

Psychologists still argue about whether intelligence primarily reflects the operation of a general factor ("g") or many specific more-or-less independent abilities. The question is still open and still important. A look at the different approaches researchers have taken toward intelligence may help us see why the disagreement persists.

The Biological Perspective

It is impossible to study intelligence without raising biological questions, believed Piaget (1971a). His own research adhered to the **structuralist** approach, which means that he was engaged in a search for the cognitive structures that underlie intelligence. But he was aware of the biological underpinnings of thought and said that in the end knowledge must be interpreted in terms of biology, whether it was the development of knowledge in the individual or the evolutionary development of knowledge in the human species.

Biologically based approaches to the study of intelligence examine intelligence in terms of the species and its evolutionary history. For example, Sandra Scarr (1981) suggests that the sensorimotor intelligence of infancy evolved very early and that it has changed little since that time. To support her proposal, she notes the similarity between the abilities of ape and human babies. There are few intellectual accomplishments in the first eighteen months of a human infant's life that are not paralleled in the life of an infant chimpanzee.

As a result of the species' evolutionary history, human babies are genetically prepared to learn the typical sensorimotor schemes of infancy and to combine them in innovative and flexible ways. During the first eighteen to twenty-four months of life, cognitive growth appears to be highly canalized (a concept discussed in Chapter 5 in relation to physical growth), so that neither individual heredity nor minor environmental influences have much ef-

fect on its development (Scarr 1981; McCall 1979a). Intellectual development during this period appears to follow a path common to the entire species. Unless infants live in a severely deprived environment, one not typical of human life, they will develop similarly. And since early intellectual development is highly canalized, infants who suffer early deprivation will tend to catch up when placed in a normal environment, as has been found among babies who spent the first year or so in institutions or in, for example, a highly restricted environment in rural Guatemala (Kagan, 1978).

An adaptational view of intelligence is taken past infancy and applied to children by William Charlesworth (1976), who regards intelligence as the species' latest attempt to adapt to the everyday challenges of its evolutionary niche. Intelligence, according to Charlesworth, is a disposition—the result of evolved cognitive processes acting on a store of learned knowledge. He believes that although we can never measure intelligence directly, we can measure intelligent behavior, the behavior that is called forth when a child or an adult encounters a problem in daily life. Coping with life on an inner-city street requires intelligent, adaptive behavior, and behavior that has developed in response to life in a protected suburb might not be adaptive in city surroundings. In order to understand intelligence, we should—in Charlesworth's view—be applying to human beings the methods ethologists use with animals, especially field studies, which were described in Chapter 2.

Charlesworth has begun the spadework, observing toddlers at home and at school, in the hope of identifying the major cognitive processes used to deal with problems and discovering how contextual and emotional factors either hinder or aid the solutions. In one of his observations, for example, a toddler rides his tricycle along the sidewalk until he comes to an incline. The little boy tries to pedal up the slope, but begins to roll backward. He climbs off his tricycle, pushes it up the incline, climbs back on, and pedals off. The entire process from encounter to solution, took fifteen seconds. From such observations of behavior, suggests Charlesworth, it will be possible to discover how many problems children encounter as they go about their daily lives, the nature of the problems, how they deal with them, their rates of success or failure, and the extent to which other people help or hinder them in their solutions.

Charlesworth believes that data derived from ethological observations not only show the nature of a child's intelligence but also broaden the general study of intelligence, in which adaptive interactions with the environment have been generally ignored.

The Structuralist Perspective

Despite the biological strain in his own theory, Piaget was the major exponent of the structuralist approach to intelligence. Researchers who take this approach examine intelligence at the species level, focusing on the logic and the mental structures involved in problem solving. Piaget made no distinction between a child's level of cognitive development and his or her intelligence. He would probably have called Chapter 10 of this book "The Development of Intelligence," for he used the terms "intelligence" and "thought" interchangeably.

In Piaget's theory, babies develop intelligence through their interactions with the environment. This interaction involves maturation, experience with the physical environment, the influence of the social environment, and the child's own self-regulatory processes, which keep trying to reestablish an equilibrium (Piaget, 1983). Intelligence first appears in the third stage of the sensorimotor period, when the baby repeats actions in order to make interesting sights last. At first, a baby's intelligence is "empirical," because things in the environment, not deduction, control it. Toward the end of the sensorimotor period, when a baby's consciousness of the relation between his or her actions and the behavior of objects leads to the first deductions, intelligence becomes "systematic" (Piaget, 1952b). Once this happens, a baby uses mental combinations to invent ways of handling new

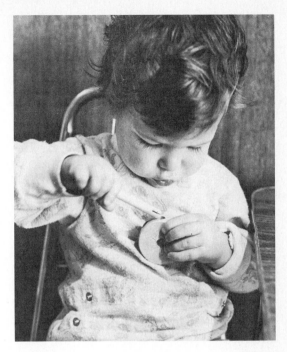

In Piaget's structuralist view, intelligence develops out of such simple interactions with the environment as discovering how to join Tinker Toys. (Sepp Seitz/Woodfin Camp & Associates)

situations. Without this sensorimotor experience, intelligence cannot develop.

In the structuralist approach to intelligence, the researcher's interest lies in the qualitative analysis of the structures that underlie intelligence; the purpose is to "discover the actual operational mechanisms that govern such behavior and not simply to measure it" (Piaget, 1953). Piaget was interested in intellectual competence, not intellectual performance—what is optimally possible for a person to do, not what that individual does in a specific situation (Boden, 1979).

The Psychometric Perspective

In contrast to the structural approach, which focuses on intelligence at the species level, researchers who take a psychometric view focus on individual differences. The field of **psycho-**

metrics, or mental testing, began when Alfred Binet tried to develop a test that would pick out children whose cognitive functioning made it impossible for them to learn in regular class-rooms. He hoped that his test would also indicate the sort of special instruction that would enable these children to profit from schooling. Psychologists in other countries saw these possibilities and adapted the test to their own societies. This marked the beginning of a strong movement centered on individual differences in intelligence.

The psychometric movement has no theory of human development, and intelligence tests are not designed to shed light on cognitive development. Instead, the tests are practical tools; they are constructed to accomplish two tasks: (1) to permit most children of a specific age to answer the questions specified for that age level; and (2) to produce scores that correlate highly with success at school.

At one time, psychologists in the field of psychometrics assumed that intelligence was a general capacity and that their tests measured a general aptitude. Today many psychologists believe that intelligence is made up of a host of abilities and that tests measure only a few of them. Ulric Neisser (1976) has suggested that the tests tap only academic skills and that we should be careful to distinguish academic intelligence from intelligence in general. Many academically talented people, he points out, behave stupidly in everyday life, and there is no evidence to indicate that they are better at conducting their lives than the academically dull. As the psychometric movement developed, factor analysis became one of its basic tools, and many measures of intelligence were constructed around it. Yet factor analysis has certain built-in problems (Sternberg and Powell, 1983). Factors are merely descriptive categories devised by researchers to identify individual differences that, for some reason, go together. On different tests, different factors emerge as components of intelligence. Reliance on factor analysis also leads to a narrow view of human intelligence—a view that has no place for the effect of moti-

vation or emotion on performance. In an attempt to relate factor analytic approaches to cognitive development, Robert Sternberg and Janet Powell (1983) suggested three possibilities. Perhaps the number of factors that make up intelligence increases with development. Or perhaps different factors contribute more heavily to intelligence at different ages. Or perhaps the number of factors and their contribution remain the same, but the skills that contribute to each factor develop separately and without any relationship to one another.

The Information-Processing Perspective

Psychologists who apply an information-processing approach to the study of intelligence believe that intelligence derives from the ways in which people mentally represent and process information (Sternberg and Powell, 1983). Many of these psychologists are interested in intelligence at the species level; for example they write computer programs that simulate the way children solve conservation problems. Other psychologists explore the possibility of applying information-processing theory to the investigation of individual differences in intelligence. They hope to simulate the kind of thought that is tapped by intelligence tests and to identify the differences in basic processes that account for variety in human performance.

INDIVIDUAL DIFFERENCES IN INFORMATION PROCESSING Earl Hunt (1976) proposes that individual differences may exist in the speed with which people can manipulate information in working memory or transmit it from place to place within the total system. Individuals may also differ in how efficient they are in shifting the burden of information processing from one component of the memory system to another or how rapidly a stimulus arouses codes stored in long-term memory. In his own work, Hunt has investigated the speed with which people can retrieve items from long-term memory. He has discovered that college students (all of whom have attained a certain level of verbal ability) can be divided into high-verbal and low-verbal groups. Although there is no difference in the amount of time it takes these students to detect similarity or difference between two stimuli, high verbal students are significantly faster in retrieving a conceptual code from memory. In another study reported by Hunt, both groups were asked to recall lists of "meaningless" syllables. When the syllables did not make up a word ("ark" "ler"), high- and low-verbal students performed similarly; but when syllables could form a word ("prob" "lem"), the high-verbal group was much more efficient, indicating that the conceptual nature of the code is important. And when the syllables were presented rapidly, the gap between high- and low-verbal students increased.

It has been suggested by John Carroll (1976) that information-processing theory be applied to the results of factor analysis, in an attempt to discover what specific processes underlie each of the various factors that make up intelligence. Individual differences, he suggests, can appear in the rules used by the information-processing system, in the speed with which information is handled, in the processing capacity, or in the contents of long-term memory. When Carroll analyzed twenty-four factors, he discovered that eight of them involved operations and strategies in either short-term memory or some kind of sensory buffer; for example, the visual search for specified items, the comparison of distances, and the mental rotation of figures in space. One factor involved storage and retrieval from intermediate-term memory, and fifteen involved long-term memory—its contents, search, or retrieval.

THE COMPONENTIAL ANALYSIS OF INTELLIGENCE Robert Sternberg (1984) has proposed that intelligence is best understood by breaking it down into various kinds of compo-

nents, or elementary information processes. There are three kinds of components and each has a different function. Metacomponents are higher order processes that correspond to executive control (see Chapter 10); they decide what problem to solve and how to solve it, and they monitor the progress toward a solution. There are two lower-order processes: performance components, which execute the plans and decisions of the metacomponents; and knowledge-acquisition components, which are involved in learning new information. Knowledge-acquisition components allow the individual to develop an ever-increasing knowledge base, which—as we saw in Chapter 8—makes it easier to pick up new facts, new techniques, or new ideas.

In Sternberg's theory, metacomponents can directly activate any of the other components and receive direct feedback from them. The lower order processes can activate other components or receive feedback from them only indirectly—by way of the metacomponents. Metacomponents are central to this theory of intelligence. They are so important to intelligent behavior that if they do not function efficiently, it makes no difference how efficient the performance or knowledge-acquisition components are.

Sternberg believes that the ability to solve analogies is a good measure of the performance components of intelligence. When such solutions are analyzed, individual differences among components in the solution process may appear. These differences become apparent when we trace the solving of a sample analogy:

WASHINGTON is to ONE as LINCOLN is to:
(a) FIVE (b) TEN (c) FIFTEEN (d) FIFTY.

There are, says Sternberg (1979), six performance components in the process used to solve problems, such as analogies, that involve reasoning from observed facts. First, the solver must *encode* the terms of the analogy, identifying each and retrieving relevant attributes from long-term memory. If he or she does not encode the names as those of presidents whose pictures appear on currency, the solution progresses no farther. Next, the solver must *infer* a relation between the attributes of WASHINGTON and ONE. Inferring that Washington is the first president instead of the portrait on the dollar bill ends the solution at this step. Third, the solver must *map* the relation that links the Washington half of the analogy with the Lincoln half (presidents of the United States whose pictures are on currency). The fourth step is to *apply* the relation between WASHINGTON and ONE to LINCOLN and each of the suggested answers, a step that requires recall of the information that Lincoln is portrayed on a five-dollar bill. If this analogy is given to a person from a different culture or to a young child, of course, that information is unlikely to be stored in long-term memory. The fifth step is to *justify* one of the four options as preferable to the other three. A person who did not encode the problem as one involving currency might look for SIXTEEN—Lincoln's position in the chronological list of presidents—and not finding that, settle for FIFTEEN on the grounds that his or her memory was slightly defective. Finally, the solver *responds* with the justified answer.

Individual differences can appear in the speed with which a person performs each of these steps, in the strategies the person uses, or in the contents of long-term memory. For example, Sternberg has found that people's strategies differ in the proportion of possible attributes that they encode and then compare during the later steps of the solution.

Assessing a person's solution of problem-solving tasks, such as analogies, offers a promising way to explore intelligence among older children and adults, but how successful are such approaches with young children? For example, Sternberg (Sternberg and Powell, 1983) believes that analogical reasoning first appears at about the age of seven and develops through three stages. Seven- to ten-year-olds can handle first-order relationships: they can understand the relationship between WASHINGTON and ONE and the relationship between LINCOLN and FIVE. But they cannot map the relationship

that links the two pairs of terms. Between the ages of nine and twelve years, they begin to see this relationship, but they are not very skillful. From about the age of eleven, children's ability to understand analogies is fully developed. In earlier research, Piaget (1977) had found similar stages in the development of analogical reasoning, and noted that the ability to map second-order relationships was a formal operation. However, he also found that when analogies were presented in the form of pictures, even five- and six-year-olds could understand first-order relationships, indicating that analogical reasoning can be assessed in relatively young children.

Children's strategies in carrying out each component also change with age. Younger children encode as few attributes as possible during the first step. As children grow older, they encode an increasingly greater proportion of attributes. Nine- to twelve-year-olds often solve analogies by association; they choose the answer that has the closest relationship to the key term. Adolescents rely on reasoning processes, solving analogies by inference (Sternberg and Nigro, 1980).

Other researchers have found that when the mapping relationship is very simple, four-year-olds can use analogies to solve problems (Holyoak, Junn, and Billman, 1984). In this case, children heard stories and transferred a method described in the story to a problem that confronted them. For example, Woodstock wanted to move her eggs from the top of Snoopy's doghouse to a nest in the tree. Snoopy rolled up a blanket, stretched it across to the tree branch, and rolled the eggs through the tube into the nest. Some of the four-year-olds directly applied the solution; they rolled a piece of paper into a tube and used it to transfer gumballs from one bowl to another. When asked, "Could the story help?", additional youngsters were able to use the analogy.

Analogies examine intelligence at the level of lower-order processes. Perhaps, suggests Sternberg (1979), intelligence tests do the same thing: their success is based on measuring the speed and accuracy of lower-order processes. When these tests fail to measure a person's intelligence accurately, the failure may be due to the tests' inability to measure the speed and accuracy of higher-order processes—the metacomponents.

THE MEASUREMENT OF INTELLIGENCE

If they are successful, says the author of the Wechsler series of intelligence tests, intelligence tests measure "the capacity of an individual to understand the world about him and his resourcefulness to cope with its challenges" (Wechsler, 1975). As we shall see, that is exactly what some psychologists believe that present ways of measuring intelligence fail to do.

Most of the innumerable tests a person takes over the course of a lifetime are not intelligence tests. Many are tests of achievement, and they measure what the person already has learned. Tests of intelligence are supposed to be aptitude tests—tests that measure the broad range of a child's ability to learn new scholastic skills. But most intelligence tests are heavily based on general cultural knowledge, so that the aptitude of some children is not fairly tested by them.

The results of a traditional intelligence test are generally given in terms of IQ, a number that represents a child's performance relative to the performance of numerous other children. Intelligence tests are constructed and standardized so that the average child's score is 100. Children who score above 100 are considered more intelligent than the average child; those who score below 100, less intelligent. This means that a child's IQ score is simply a descriptive statistic that relates his or her present performance to that of other children of the same chronological age.

Many factors determine a child's intellectual performance: biological change, general education, life experience, motivation, and personality. External influences at the time of the examination, including the manner of the examiner and the attitude of the child, can also affect the child's performance. It is risky, therefore, to make important decisions about a child's future based on only one assessment—or even several assessments—of his or her intellectual abilities (McCall, Appelbaum, and Hogarty, 1973).

Yet when properly used the IQ score is an efficient and accurate summary of the degree to which a child has learned the concepts and rules of middle-class Western society. The IQ score is useful because it predicts academic performance; for example, it does a fairly good job of telling us how easily a child of ten or eleven will master high-school courses in history or English. Tests are revised periodically to ensure that the questions contribute to the accuracy of this prediction. If questions predict school success, they are kept; it they do not, they are thrown out. Also, if questions distinguish between the sexes, generally being answered correctly only by boys or only by girls, they are discarded.

Because of the test's purpose, the eleven-year-old is asked to define "shilling" rather than "peso." The child is asked to state the similarity between a fly and a tree, rather than the similarity between "fuzz" and "Uncle Tom." The child is asked to copy a design, rather than to defend her- or himself against the neighborhood bully. As these examples indicate, present IQ tests are biased toward measuring skills that upper- and middle-class white Americans value and teach. But this bias is no reason to discard them. Instead, the parent and teacher should appreciate the arbitrary content of the test. If the primary objective is to predict a child's success in school subjects, then the IQ test is the best instrument psychologists have yet devised. But if the goal is to measure an individual's total cognitive functioning, it would be best to look elsewhere.

For many years psychologists thought that an IQ score measured practically everything of importance in cognitive development. Performance on an IQ test was taken as an index of creative abilities, productive thinking, and problem-solving abilities. Along with this faith in the IQ test

Many black children do poorly on group intelligence tests because the tests are biased toward measuring skills that are valued by upper- and middle-class white Americans. (Elizabeth Crews/ Stock, Boston)

went a belief that it was not possible to train mental capacities. Evidence and experience have modified these ideas about IQ, and attempts to develop new kinds of tests are under way. In Illinois, psychologists are developing procedures based on Vygotsky's zone of proximal development (see Chapter 1) to assess children's intelligence (Campione et al., 1984). Their initial experiments indicate the importance of such tests. After testing children to find areas of reasoning in which they perform poorly, these researchers placed the children in an interactive situation where they learned to apply a set of principles to similar reasoning problems. Later, the children were tested on other, similar problems, as well as on problems that required the use of a new principle—but one related to the set they had learned. Traditional IQ tests predicted the children's performance on the similar problems, but not on the problems requiring the new principle. Since some children learn more effectively than others in the zone of proximal development, their ratings on traditional IQ tests may underestimate their intellectual ability.

Despite the fact that present intelligence tests measure only certain aspects of cognitive functioning, they are as yet the only objective measures we have. For that reason, as we explore other areas of intelligence—its stability, its relationship to various aspects of life, and it susceptibility to modification—we shall use the results of such tests as our reference.

THE STABILITY OF IQ SCORES

If intelligence tests can predict a child's success at school, we might expect IQ scores to remain stable throughout life. Our expectations would often be wrong—especially when the scores come from tests given to infants.

IQ Tests in Infancy

Scores on intelligence tests given in infancy bear little resemblance to the results of tests given during the childhood or adult years. In the Berkeley Growth Study—a longitudinal study of sixty-one children—IQ testing began when the babies were a month old. As the year wore on, babies who scored low on early tests tended to catch up with the high-scoring babies (Bayley, 1955). There was no relation between test scores at the end of that year and those the babies made in the first few months. And when researchers looked at the results of four major longitudinal studies, they found that there was no way to predict later IQ scores from the results of intelligence tests given during the first eighteen months of a child's life (Wohlwill, 1980). Nancy Bayley (1955) explains this lack of connection between infant and childhood scores by pointing out that the abilities measured on infant tests—alertness, reaction to stimuli, sensorimotor coordination, vocalization, the recognition of differences—may reflect a baby's motor abilities more than they measure mental capacities. For example, on the Bayley Scale, a baby of 5.7 months is expected to pick up a cube skillfully, and a baby of 6.2 months is expected to respond playfully to a mirror (Bayley, 1969).

In fact, Sandra Scarr (1981) has proposed that sensorimotor intelligence is a different kind of intelligence from later intelligence. She believes that sensorimotor intelligence is independent of the cognitive skills that evolved later in human history. If this is so, the lack of any correspondence between scores on infant intelligence tests and later test scores becomes understandable. The tests themselves also differ in a major way: language is a relatively unimportant aspect of infant intelligence tests, but verbal ability plays an overwhelming role in child intelligence tests.

There may be one aspect of sensorimotor intelligence that persists into childhood—and perhaps remains important throughout life. After reviewing the research, Cynthia Berg and Robert Sternberg (in press) found that a baby's response to novel stimuli is a good predictor of cognitive functioning at age two and also predicts performance on verbal tests of intelligence at age three. Furthermore, the preference for novelty seems related to intelligence throughout life and is connected with seeking out and solving novel problems. The preference for novelty is related to educational success in fifth graders, and it reflects individual differences in intelligence. It distinguishes gifted children from children of average intelligence, children of average intelligence from mildly retarded children, and mildly retarded children from institutionalized retarded children. This preference is not assessed by traditional tests of infant intelligence.

Despite low correlations between scores on current infant intelligence scales and later IQ, infant tests can be valuable tools. They effectively detect severe mental retardation. Thus the correlation between infant and childhood IQ scores is somewhat better for retarded than for average or superior babies (McCall, 1979a). Infant IQ tests also identify babies who may need extra attention because of various factors connected with the fetal environment or with birth complications. Drawing an analogy between such uses and the practice of weighing a baby, Robert McCall points out that knowing a baby's weight at six months does not help us predict the infant's weight as an adult, but it does help a physician decide whether the baby needs medical assistance.

IQ Tests in Childhood

Once children have reached the toddler stage and begin to use symbols, they might be expected to show more stability in their IQ scores. And they do; as soon as children begin to talk, the stability of IQ scores does increase. Tests of older children rely heavily on verbal items and abstract-symbolic reasoning (see Table 11.1). Correlations between IQ scores at ages six and eighteen are at least .80 (1.00 would indicate that children who get high scores at age six always get high scores at age eighteen).

Nevertheless, many children show large changes in score. When the intellectual development of 140 typical mid-American children was followed at Fels Research Institute, investigators found that the IQ of the average child shifted over a range of almost thirty points between the ages of two and a half and seventeen years (McCall, Appelbaum, and Hogarty, 1973). One child out of seven showed a shift greater than forty points.

Table 11.1 THE STANFORD-BINET TEST FOR EIGHT-YEAR-OLDS

1. Defines eight words (such as *orange, straw, top*) from a standard vocabulary list.
2. Remembers most of the content of a simple story.
3. Sees absurdity in such statements as, "A man had flu (influenza) twice. The first time it killed him, but the second time he got well quickly."
4. Distinguishes such words as *airplane* and *kite, ocean* and *river.*
5. Knows what makes a sailboat move, what to do if you find a lost three-year-old.
6. Names the days of the week.

The average eight-year-old child can answer correctly all of these sample items from Form L-M, 1960 Stanford-Binet. (*Source:* Terman, L. M., and M. A. Merrill. *Stanford-Binet Intelligence Scale: Manual for the Third Revision.* Boston: Houghton Mifflin, 1960.)

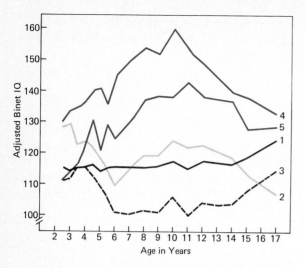

FIGURE 11.3 In the Fels Longitudinal Study of development, IQ scores over the years fell into five different groups, each with a characteristic pattern of change. The most nearly stable group (Group 1) contained the most individuals, but the average child showed a change of twenty-eight IQ points between ages two and seventeen.

(From McCall, Appelbaum, and Hogarty, 1973. Copyright © 1973 by the Society for Research in Child Development, Inc.)

In this group of children, investigators found five consistent patterns in IQ shifts over the years (see Figure 11.3). The largest group (45 percent of the children) showed relative stability in their scores, which tended to increase slightly as they grew. The rest of the children showed either general declines or general increases during the preschool years. What could have caused such dramatic changes?

When the researchers looked closely at the children, they discovered that the behavior of parents seemed to be connected to changes in IQ scores. Among these children, those whose parents used severe punishment (which may have caused fear and resentment) and those whose parents punished very lightly (so that punishments were inconsequential) both showed IQ declines. These children also received no particular encouragement to achieve; they were either left to "grow naturally" or else shielded from influences that might lead to increases in cognitive or motor skills. Children whose parents pushed them to achieve, were clear in their policies, and provided firm but not severe discipline showed general increases in IQ.

Yet the relationship is more complicated than it seems, because the siblings of these children did not necessarily show the same pattern of change. Apparently, when specific environmental events interact with the interest and skills of a child at a particular time in a particular family setting, the child's IQ may either rise or dip (McCall, Appelbaum, and Hogarty, 1973).

Sudden major shifts in IQ tended to come when the children were about six years old. As noted in Chapter 10, there appears to be a change in the way children learn at about this time, and there is also change in their learning situation—the formal classroom. Both may be factors in the shift. Among the brightest children (Group 4), another major shift appeared when they were about ten years old: their scores declined sharply. As we saw in Chapter 10, when academically precocious children are not challenged by school, they may grow bored and frustrated. The researchers suggested that this group of high-IQ children may have been turned off by the impersonal, regimented, slow pace of the regular classroom (McCall, Appelbaum, and Hogarty, 1973).

Apparently, the IQ score of many children varies almost as much during childhood as do scores among a group of unrelated people. But despite frequent changes in IQ scores over childhood, different tests given at fairly close intervals do produce similar scores; for example, tests given at age fifteen correlated .96 with tests given at age eighteen (Bayley, 1949). Although many IQ scores remain stable, others may go up or down, with changes continuing long into adulthood. For example, in several longitudinal studies, a number of people continued to show gains in their IQ scores at age fifty (Bayley, 1955).

WHAT CAN IQ SCORES PREDICT?

Given that IQ scores can change dramatically over time, can intelligence tests really predict performance? When scores from these tests are compared with what children and adults actually do in school, in life, and with their creative talents, the results are mixed.

Success in School

Tests that purport to measure intelligence are at their best when predicting success or failure in school. This should not be surprising, since such predictions are exactly what the tests were developed to make. IQ scores correlate about .70 with school grades (McClelland, 1973), making them the best single predictor of success in school for children of all socioeconomic levels (McCall, Appelbaum, and Hogarty, 1973). Tests predict success better in some academic areas than in others. For example, among high-school students, the Stanford-Binet scale correlates over .70 with reading comprehension but drops to just below .50 with geometry (Bond, 1940). The IQ test generally does the job of predicting, quickly and efficiently, how well a child can profit from regular classroom instruction. The tests are better at predicting elementary- and high-school performance than college or graduate-school success, because the farther a person moves up the educational ladder, the less varied the group that is competing for grades, and the more important such factors as personality, perseverance, and distraction may become. The correlation of less than 1.00 between school success and IQ scores warns us, however, that there will always be some errors in prediction; in the case of some children, the tests will not demonstrate their true potential.

There are some good things to be said about the use of IQ tests in school: they have saved many children from being placed in classes for the retarded; they have indicated whether a child's problems in school have behavioral or intellectual roots; they have selected gifted children who would otherwise have lost out on extra educational opportunities; and they have provided a way for children from disadvantaged families to move out of poverty (Hyman, 1979). In fact, Leona Tyler (1976) suggests that widespread use of IQ tests may have accelerated the breakdown of the class structure in society by identifying exceptionally able individuals in the lower socioeconomic classes.

There are also some bad things to say about the use of intelligence tests in the schools: they have been used to excuse bad education for minority groups; they have saddled children with a "retarded" label when all the children lacked was exposure to the dominant culture (Mercer, 1972); and they have set in motion self-fulfilling prophecies, by persuading teachers that certain children could not profit from instruction (Rosenthal, 1973).

Success in Life

IQ scores are not nearly as effective in predicting occupational success as they are at predicting success in school. Yet there is some relationship between IQ scores and success on the job. In one major longitudinal study, men with the highest IQ generally held professional or executive positions in middle adulthood (Clausen, 1981). And among white-collar workers there was a constant progression in IQ scores from men in lower-level jobs to men in top-level jobs.

Yet the connection is not as direct as it appears. Robert McCall (1977) compared childhood IQ scores of almost two hundred men and women from the Fels Study (see Figure 11.4) with their education and occupation at age twenty-six. He found that correlations got increasingly better until the children were about seven years old. At that time, they reached about .50, remaining fairly stable afterward. Although a correlation of .50 indicates some correspondence between whatever the tests measure and occupational success, it is not high enough to be used to predict an individual

A New Wave of Intelligence Tests?

If a new approach to the assessment of cognitive processing fulfills its developers' hopes, traditional intelligence tests will one day be obsolete. Their place will be taken by a computer that analyzes children's brain waves. Researchers at New York Medical College's Brain Research Laboratories (Karmel, Kaye, and John, 1978) use a forest of electrodes to gather information from throughout a child's brain as the child listens to and watches various types of computer-produced stimulation. As the child undergoes a battery of more than ninety tests, processing sensory, perceptual, and cognitive information, the computer evaluates the child's evoked potentials, comparing them with average reactions to the same measures. When a child's brain waves are significantly different from those of the average child of the same age, the computer print-out alerts the technician.

Behind the test is an attempt to unite information about perception and information processing developed by psychologists with a knowledge of brain function discovered by neuroscientists. E. Roy John and his colleagues call their approach **neurometrics,** as opposed to the psychometrics of the intelligence-test approach.

Cells in many parts of the brain, not simply cells in a specific region, are involved in all kinds of learning, says John (1976). Because the neurometric test averages information from all parts of the brain, it is much more sensitive than the ordinary EEG. For example, computer analysis of evoked potentials successfully identified twenty of a group of twenty-five epileptics (ten of whom showed no signs of epilepsy on an ordinary EEG), twenty-two of a group of twenty-five stroke patients (fifteen of whom had normal EEGs), and twenty-four out of twenty-five people with brain tumors (ten of whom had normal EEGs) (Goleman, 1976).

When used to diagnose school-related problems, the neurometric test may be faster and more accurate than traditional intelligence tests. John and his colleagues (Karmel, Kaye, and John, 1978) administered a two-minute portion of their fifty-three-minute Neurometric Battery to 172 boys between seven and eleven years old. Among the boys were sixty-two who had earlier been classified as "learning disabled." The computer analysis of only two minutes of data did as good a job of separating the learning-disabled boys from the normal boys as did the battery of intelligence tests that had taken several hours to administer. Both methods can distinguish between the two groups, but the psychometric method produces false diagnoses more often than does the neurometric method.

The Neurometric Battery does more than simply note whether a child's brain activity is normal; it can pinpoint specific disorders.

---

child's performance. According to McCall, 64 to 84 percent of the difference in these children's adult status was *not* accounted for by childhood IQ scores.

The correlation between years of schooling and IQ scores is generally about .55, indicating that the role of IQ in predicting occupational success may lie in its facility at opening the door to college enrollment. But in the Fels Study, children's IQ scores did not predict eventual educational level as well as did the factor of father's education, which correlated .62 with eventual educational levels. McCall suggests that bright but disadvantaged children often have no opportunity to continue their education, whereas upper-income children who are not as bright often go on to college.

IQ score, then, is no sure predictor of edu-

The test can also indicate whether a child's problem is sensory (he or she may simply need glasses) or involves information processing. Some of the items on the test battery, such as the spontaneous brain waves, provide a general measure of the brain's state. For example, Bernard Karmel, Herbert Kaye, and John believe that an abundance of delta waves (slow brain waves that—except among young children—appear only during sleep) indicate a maturational lag that manifests itself in general learning difficulties. Excessive theta waves (another slow brain wave) indicate a lag in the child's control over attention, which is manifested as a short attention span and perhaps an extra susceptibility to environmental stimulation—typical hallmarks of the hyperactive child. Other items measure specific functions, such as pattern perception, perception of complex relationships, short-term memory, spatial relations, attention, concept organization, representation of geometric forms, and word recall.

Some schools in New York State are now using the Neurometric Battery on an experimental basis. Should it prove as accurate as preliminary experiments have indicated, assessing the cognitive function of the next generation of schoolchildren may be simple. Each child would sit with the computer for an hour, listening to music and watching television programs that are accompanied by a series of flashes, clicks, and taps (Goleman, 1976).

cation or income; some farmers have IQ scores higher than those of most lawyers. What is more, correlation between IQ scores and proficiency on the job is as low as between .20 and .25 (Jensen, 1970). Although a minimum IQ is required for certain occupations, once that is attained, there is no indication that higher scores bring greater success. In a survey of mathematicians, for example, the IQs of those who were doing exceptionally fine research were no higher than the scores of other mathematicians (Helson and Crutchfield, 1970).

A look at the exceptionally gifted throws more light on the relative importance of IQ in a person's life. In the 1920s, Lewis Terman (1959) began studying more than 1,500 California schoolchildren with IQ scores of 135 or more (their average IQ was 150). As adults, this group of children ranked higher than average on almost any positive measure one could imagine: education, professional standing, social status, income, health, and happiness. Of the more than 800 males, 125 had earned either Ph.D.'s or M.D.'s. Their ranks included bankers, scientists, engineers, lawyers, physicians, corporate executives, journalists, writers, psychologists, and educators. One was a motion-picture director and one was a brigadier general, although some had less illustrious careers: one was a postman and another operated a sandwich shop. Their average income was more than four times the national average. In two areas of life, they ranked lower than the national average: mental illness and suicide.

In 1968, investigators separated the extremely successful and the least successful from the rest of this gifted group and found that those at the top had IQs that averaged six points higher than those at the bottom—not an impressive difference (Oden, 1968). The greatest difference between the top and bottom groups fell in the areas of personality and motivation, not intellect. General personality adjustment and a need to achieve were both much stronger in the top group. Despite high IQs, some of those in the bottom group failed college.

The group was checked again in 1972, when their average age was sixty-two (Sears, 1977; Sears and Barbee, 1978). This time, investigators wanted to know what had given these intellectually gifted people the most satisfaction in their lives. Both men and women rated the satisfaction derived from their family lives as most important to them. The men also found a great deal of satisfaction in their careers; fewer than half the women had followed careers, but career satisfaction was high among those who did

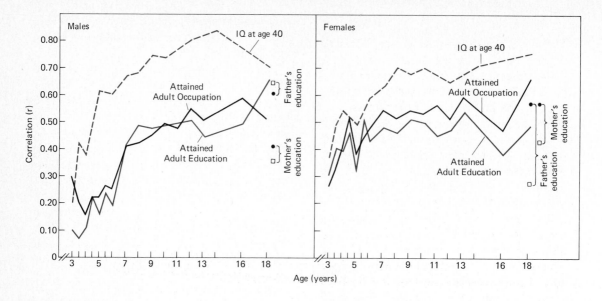

FIGURE 11.4 As children age, IQ scores become better predictors; IQ scores predict adult IQ much better than they predict occupational or educational status. Open squares show correlations with parental occupation; filled circles show correlations with parental education. Father's education is a better predictor of boys' occupations than IQ is.

(From McCall, 1977. Copyright © 1977 by the American Association for the Advancement of Science. Reprinted by permission of author and publisher.)

work. Investigators checked early records to see what factors predicted men's occupational and family satisfaction. In the area that gave these men their greatest satisfaction—their families—those who were most satisfied had good mental health, had been well adjusted as elementary-school students, and sociable as high-school students. They also admired their parents and scored high on a marital aptitude test.

As for occupational satisfaction, neither advanced degrees, occupational success, nor financial rewards were the important criteria. Instead, men who showed a general optimism about life, a zest for occupational combat (measured by ambition and liking for work), and a

feeling of self-worth were the ones who claimed to derive the greatest satisfaction from their careers. Robert Sears, who supervised the 1972 study, suggests that the men derived great satisfaction from their careers because their IQs probably made it possible for them to enter whatever profession they chose and to shape their careers in the way they wanted. Sears also notes that neither work nor intellectual pursuits was most important to these men; instead, they found their greatest satisfaction in their relations with other people.

Creativity

How closely is IQ related to creativity? By 1959, the men and women in Terman's study held 230 patents; they had written more than 130 books, including 38 novels, and 350 short stories and plays. From this abundance, we might suppose that a high IQ is necessary for creativity. That is true only in part. Once a certain minimum IQ is reached (and that IQ varies depending on the area of creativity), intelligence as measured by tests does not distinguish between highly creative and representative writers, architects, and scientists (Barron, 1968). Researchers at the Institute for Personality Assessment and Research studied such groups, comparing highly creative professionals in each occupation with professionals who were not especially distinguished. Although the men and women they studied were in the upper 5 to 10 percent of the general population in IQ, once they reached that level, there was absolutely no relationship (a zero correlation) between IQ and creativity. The average IQ of the novelists, poets, essayists, mathematicians, architects, research scientists, and engineers studied hovered between 135 and 140, but it varied by field. Generally, the more highly verbal a field, the higher the IQs of its practitioners.

Amy Lowell once subjected herself to a word-association test, and the psychologist who administered it reported that the poet "gave a higher proportion of unique responses than those of anyone outside a mental institution" (Bingham, 1953). This correlation has shown up in other situations. Among the architects studied by the Institute for Personality Assessment and Research, one of the best predictors of creativity was scores on a word-association test; unusual associations correlated .50 with creativity (MacKinnon, 1962).

Some areas of creativity seemed closed to the high-IQ subjects in Terman's study. Among the musicians and the painters in the study of the gifted, none was more than modestly successful in terms of critical recognition (Goleman, 1980). But as we have seen, IQ tests do not measure creativity. Neither do Piagetian tests of cognitive development. Children who are prodigies in music, chess, or some other area do not show formal operational thought on the standard Piagetian tests (Feldman, 1982).

Creativity is easier to understand in terms of Gardner's theory of multiple intelligences. We can see that the musician is high in musical intelligence and the artist is high in spatial intelligence. But in Gardner's (1983) view, no humanly valued skill depends solely on one of these forms of intelligence. The musician's musical intelligence is high relative to his or her other intelligences, but the successful musician must also have some kinesthetic, spatial, logico-mathematical, and personal intelligence.

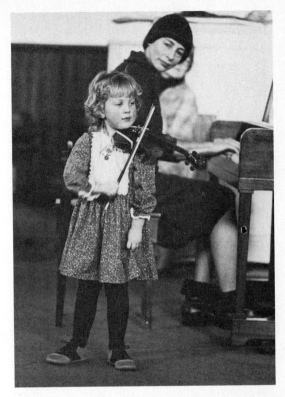

Although creative people are generally intelligent, intelligence does not guarantee creativity. No IQ test can tell us whether this little girl will become a musical prodigy. (Peter G. Aitken/ Photo Researchers)

What of the creative genius? How are the Mozarts, the Einsteins, the Darwins, and the da Vincis of the world different from the men and women studied by Terman or the academically precocious children discussed in Chapter 10? According to David Feldman (1982), creative talent is not enough to produce these towering geniuses. Four other forces are also important. First, the field itself must exist. The individual must be born at a time when there is a field that gives form to his or her particular talents. Second, the individual must be exposed to the field at the proper time. A potential Bobby Fischer who never sees a game of chess would never develop his talent. Third, the individual must have continuous, careful instruction—although it need not always be formal. Nurturance, training, and practice consistently appear in the background of such individuals (Bloom, 1985). Finally, the historical and cultural forces must be right. As Feldman (1982) notes, if Einstein had been reared as a Buddhist in Thailand, he probably would never have advanced Western physics. If Mozart had been born a tribal chieftain in Africa, he probably would never have composed great music. And if Gandhi had been born on a Kansas farm, he probably would never have transformed a whole society. Coincidence apparently plays a major role in the development of genius, and the process is so delicate that creative talent may only rarely be transformed into creative genius.

MODIFIABILITY OF INTELLIGENCE

Intelligence expresses itself in the ability to benefit from experience. It is generally assumed that each person has a ceiling, a point at which he or she will be unable to profit from experience in a particular activity, and that this ceiling is governed by environmental and hereditary factors.

Heredity

Heredity must play some role in intelligence. As we have seen, when compared with chimpanzees or dogs, people seem almost alike in their intelligence. Thus, there are genetic contributions to intelligence on the species level, just as there are genetic contributions to physical shape. None of us has a long tail or wings or retractable claws, and no amount of environmental variation can bring about such a radical restructuring of human shape. But what about the contribution of heredity to individual differences in intelligence?

The more closely two people are related, the more closely their scores on intelligence tests correspond. This correlation suggests some sort of genetic influence on the intelligence measured by the scores. Correlations between siblings, fraternal twins, and parents and children are all

similarly strong (see Table 11.2). In each of these cases, the two individuals involved share half their genes. Identical twins (twins developed from a single female egg cell) have identical genetic make up, so the often-demonstrated correspondence in their test scores has been taken to argue for a strong genetic component in the scores. The correlation between the IQ scores of two children who are unrelated and reared apart is essentially zero.

Yet genetic make-up is not the only determinant of a person's intellectual ability. As relatedness between individuals increases, so does the similarity of the environment in which they live. Brothers and sisters share half their genes. They also share some of their environment.

Some psychologists have suggested that because identical twins look alike, parents are apt to treat them alike; as a result, their similar scores on intelligence tests are due to similar environments. This notion has not been supported by research. In one twin study (Scarr and Carter-Salzman, 1979), researchers compared the intellectual similarities of nearly three-hundred-fifty pairs of twins who had been correctly or incorrectly classified by themselves, their parents, and others as identical or fraternal (twins developed from separate female egg cells). Forty percent of the twins had either been misclassified (as shown by blood tests) or else the twins disagreed about their status. When iden-

Table 11.2 CORRELATIONS OF INTELLIGENCE TEST SCORES

Correlations between:	
Unrelated children reared together	+.376
Siblings reared together	+.545
Fraternal twins reared together	+.534
Identical twins reared apart	+.741
Identical twins reared together	+.857

(Source: Correlations represent data from U.S. twin studies [and thus do not include data from Cyril Burt's English studies] as reported by Rowe, D. C., and R. Plomin. "The Burt Controversy: A Comparison of Burt's Data on IQ with Data from Other Studies," Behavior Genetics, 8 [1978], 81–84.)

tical twins were mistakenly classified as fraternal, their test scores corresponded as closely as scores of correctly identified identical twins. And when fraternal twins were mistakenly classified as identical, their test scores were no more similar than the scores of other fraternal twins.

Other researchers have studied the children of identical twins. The children of one identical twin are not simply ordinary first cousins of the other twin's children; genetically, they are half-siblings, because one of their parents has exactly the same genes. Studies of such families indicate that these children's IQs bear no resemblance to their unrelated uncles' or aunts' IQs (correlations are essentially zero) (Rose, 1979). Yet these same children's IQs correlate +.28 with the IQ of their own parent and +.23 with the IQ of their parent's twin.

Another way to examine genetic influences on IQ is to look at the test scores of adopted children. Studies of adopted children show that the IQ scores of adopted children and their biological parents correlate more closely (approximately +.35) than the scores of those same children and the parents who reared them (.00 in some studies; from .09 to .16 in others) (Honzik, 1957; Horn, 1983, 1979; Scarr, 1981; Skodak and Skeels, 1949). As Joseph Horn (1983) has put it, "The adopted children resemble strangers (their biological mothers) more than the lifelong providers and caretakers in their environment" (p. 273). In fact there is little difference between the correlations of adopted children and their biological parents and the correlations for children reared by their own parents (see Figure 11.5).

Do these findings mean that heredity overwhelmingly determines an individual's intellectual ability? Not at all. The power of the environment on intellectual skills becomes apparent when we look at the average IQ scores of these same children. Their average IQ scores are closer to the average scores of their upper-middle-class adoptive mothers than to the average IQ scores of their impoverished biological mothers. In one study, the average IQ score of the biological mothers was 86, but the average IQ score for the children was 106, a score near the

estimated IQ of the parents who reared them. Clearly, IQ scores are likely to improve if people are in a rich environment, for such surroundings allow intellectual abilities to develop near the upper limits of their reaction range, a concept discussed in Chapter 2.

Each person has a reaction range for IQ of about thirty points. A negative environment during childhood and the prenatal period can hinder the development of a child's IQ, keeping it in the lower end of the reaction range. But middle-class children, whose environment is culturally relevant to the tests, are likely to have IQs that fall in the middle of their reaction range—or even higher. Where nutrition and social factors are adequate, genes are allowed their full expression; where the environment is severely deprived, the effect of genes is depressed, decreasing heritability (see Chapter 2). Thus, it is probably safe to assume that genetic influences on IQ are much smaller among lower-class children than they are among middle-class children (Scarr, 1981).

Despite these findings, psychologists and ordinary citizens alike continue to argue about the genetic contribution to tested IQ performance. Nearly twenty years ago, Arthur Jensen (1969) heated up this nature-nurture controversy by claiming that 80 percent of the difference among the IQ scores of individuals can be traced to differences in their genetic backgrounds. Others countered that a close examination of the data reveals so many problems in untangling genetic and environmental influences that there is little evidence for any genetic component to IQ (Kamin, 1974; M. Schwartz and Schwartz, 1974).

When we look at Jensen's claim that the heritability for IQ is .80, we find a number of problems:

1. Jensen's statement implies that in a group of individuals, only about 80 percent of the *differences* in their scores—not 80 percent of their entire scores—is associated with differences in their genetic make up. No one has claimed that 80 percent of an individual's entire IQ score is "determined" by genetic make up and 20 percent by environment.

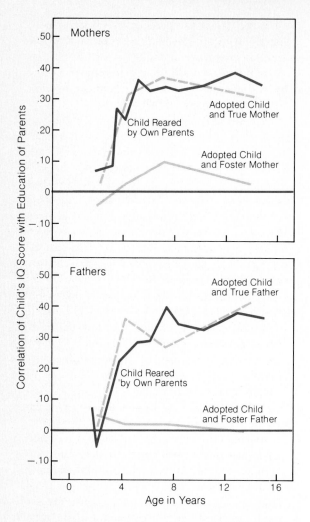

FIGURE 11.5 Correlations between children's IQ scores and estimated IQ scores of parents. Blue lines are based on Skodak and Skeels's research, and the other lines are based on research by Honzik. Note that in this research parents' educational level was used as a rough estimate of their IQ score because it was not possible to administer a test to each parent. The two top lines in each graph show that as children get older, their scores correlate more closely with their true parents' scores. The bottom line in each graph shows that there is little or no change with age in the low correlation between adopted children's scores and those of their adoptive parents.

(Adapted from Skodak and Skeels, 1949; after Honzik, 1957)

Most behavioral geneticists agree that it is impossible to put a number on the proportion of behavior that is inherited. In fact, as we saw in Chapter 2, some researchers have suggested that the concept of heritability has so many limitations that it is difficult to apply in a meaningful way (Scarr and Kidd, 1983). The child's test performance is the result of a complex and interdependent set of genetic and environmental circumstances.

2. A heritability estimate of .80 depends on the nature of the sample used to calculate it, as we saw in Chapter 2. Heritability is probably not the same among blacks as among whites, among upper-middle-class individuals as among the poor, among individuals tested in the 1930s as among those tested in the 1980s.

3. Jensen's estimate of heritability may be inaccurate, even in the specific samples tested. Because of the way genetic research must be done with human beings, both hereditary and environmental influences vary within any sample.

4. Even if human heritability for IQ were .80, attempts to stimulate or improve intellectual functioning could still be successful. It may not be as difficult as we might expect to change intellectual ability, once we discover which experiences are most important for its development. In a study of more than one hundred disadvantaged black infants who were adopted by white middle-class families, researchers found that as schoolchildren, their IQ scores were higher than the national average for both black and white children (Scarr and Weinberg, 1977).

Health and Nutrition

In earlier chapters, we saw that physical factors can retard intellectual development. One of the most damaging factors is fetal alcohol syndrome. When the syndrome was first detected in France, investigators reported that afflicted children did not outgrow the associated problems. By the time they were in school, they had short attention spans and were unable to continue an activity for very long (Lemoine et al., 1968). Their reported IQ scores indicated borderline mental retardation—about thirty points below average. Eight out of twelve children of alcoholic mothers studied at the University of Washington were retarded and three more had scores that indicated borderline retardation; only one had a normal IQ score (Streissguth, 1976). In a California study, 75 percent of the children of alcoholic mothers showed signs of mental retardation, compared with 22 percent of a control group (Jones et al., 1974).

The initial physical problems of babies with fetal alcohol syndrome are generally complicated by a poor environment that includes poverty and general disorganization in the home. Many factors interact to intensify or lessen the effects of fetal exposure to alcohol (Rosett and Sander, 1979). For example, middle-class children of alcoholic mothers seem less likely to show severe retardation, another indication of the powerful effect of a good environment, even on physical factors.

Severe malnutrition also can affect intellectual development. When such malnutrition occurs early in life, it may disturb brain growth, affecting connections between neurons and the development of neurotransmitters (Parmelee and Sigman, 1983). The consequences can be long-lasting. Babies suffering from kwashiorkor (discussed in Chapter 5) were tested on infant intelligence scales during and after their hospital treatment (Cravioto and Robles, 1965). Of the twenty babies tested, fourteen made higher scores after treatment; the six who failed to improve were the youngest babies in the group. If kwashiorkor is allowed to go untreated for more than four months among young infants, they may be severely retarded, and later treatment is unlikely to correct the condition (Cravioto and Delicardie, 1970). Some children are unable to absorb basic nutritional requirements from their food. This condition, called "failure to thrive," also affects IQ; seventeen out of nineteen infants who had the condition showed severe mental retardation in childhood (Pollitt and Granoff, 1967).

Some babies who are born "small-for-gesta-tional-age" suffer from malnutrition, but the effect on intellectual development apparently can be lessened by a good environment. In a survey of 17,000 births in Great Britain, babies whose birth weights were below the fifth percentile for their gestational age—regardless of the cause—had lower scores on tests when they were seven years old (Butler, 1974). First-born children of professional parents, however, showed only slight impairments, whereas later-born children of parents in low socioeconomic classes showed large impairments. Other studies have shown that children of diabetic mothers (who tend to have a higher rate of small-for-gestational-age births) showed significantly lower IQs on infant tests when they were eight months old and on standard IQ tests when they were four years old (Churchill and Berendes, 1969). Finally, when all the children born on the island of Kauai in Hawaii during 1954 and 1955 were followed, those who had suffered birth complications were twice as likely to have low IQ scores on tests given at twenty months and at ten years as babies whose births were uncomplicated (Werner, Bierman, and French, 1971). One reason may be that a baby who is born malnourished often is treated differently. As we saw in Chapter 4, the premature baby's features, cry, and lack of responsiveness in social interaction make such babies less attractive to adults. This lack of appeal may lead parents to be less responsive to their baby's needs and to interact less often with him or her.

Environment

Parents' degree of responsiveness may provide one kind of influence on intellectual development; another influence is the *way* in which parents interact with their children. Parents' style of discipline and teaching, for example, may affect a child's early intellectual development. In a recent study, the techniques a mother used in teaching her preschooler a task were correlated with the child's readiness for school at age five or six and with the child's achievement scores at age twelve (Hess and McDevitt, 1984). The consistent use of direct control

Differences in nutrition, sanitation, physical surroundings, and the quality of parent-child interaction probably combine to account for the social-class differences in IQ scores, a difference that is not present during the first eighteen months of life. (Left, Rick Smolan; right, UPI/ Bettmann Newsphotos)

seemed to have a negative impact on later academic achievement scores (which are closely related to IQ scores), and a teaching style that encouraged youngsters to generalize aloud about the problem seemed to have a later positive impact. This effect persisted even after the researchers controlled for the effect of socioeconomic class.

CLASS DIFFERENCES IN IQ Children from low socioeconomic classes consistently score ten to fifteen points below middle-class children on IQ tests. Psychologists have been trying to discover what causes lower scores among disadvantaged children and what sort of changes in the children's environment would enable them to develop their intellectual potential.

There are no class differences in intelligence scores among babies. For the first eighteen months of life, white and black, lower- and middle-class babies all score about the same on in-

fant intelligence tests (Golden and Birns, 1976). This is true whether the tests are the standard infant scales or newer tests based on Piagetian tasks. As noted earlier, tests given in infancy do not predict the IQ scores of children or adults, perhaps because sensorimotor intelligence is radically different from later intelligence.

Class differences in IQ scores begin to appear at about eighteen months, and may come from the child's physical surroundings, from the quality of parent-child interaction, from the level of nutrition and sanitation, or—as is most likely— from the interaction of all of these factors. The effects of malnutrition already have been mentioned.

A child's physical surrounding may affect IQ in several ways. The homes of disadvantaged preschoolers are often disorganized and unpredictable (Bradley and Caldwell, 1976). Lower-class infants are also more restricted; their mothers are more likely than middle-class mothers to confine them to a playpen instead of allowing them to explore their world (Tulkin and Kagan, 1972). This is understandable, in view of the fact that the homes of lower-class infants are more likely to be crowded, with more people and their possessions crammed into fewer rooms. The middle-class infant, on the other hand, often has his or her own room and is likely to live in a home where there is also space to place forbidden or dangerous objects safely out of an infant's grasp.

Theodore Wachs (1976) has found that freedom of exploration is very important in cognitive development, but that other home factors also play a role. One factor is noise. In most small, crowded, lower-class living quarters, there is a high level of background noise. Children who live in homes filled with inescapable noise tend to have lower IQs, an example of the negative effects of too much stimulation.

Too little stimulation, Wachs found, also has a negative effect on IQ. Three factors that provide cognitive stimulation had a positive effect on IQ: the availability of toys, papers, magazines, book, mobiles, and other items that provide visual and tactual-visual stimulation; the presence of a variety of objects a child can explore; and the presence of toys that produce interesting sounds and sights. Researchers have found that the availability of toys and reading materials in a child's home at twenty-four months is a good predictor of IQ and achievement scores in the first grade (Bradley and Caldwell, 1984).

The quality of interaction within the home is another possible source of social-class difference in IQ. The only clear-cut class difference in mother-infant interactions falls in the area of language. During the first year of a baby's life, middle-class mothers respond more to their babies' vocalizations with vocalizations of their own (Golden and Birns, 1976). Mark Golden and his associates (1974) found that lower-class infants tend to respond to their mothers' speaking with their own simultaneous babbling, whereas middle-class infants quiet and listen to what their mothers are saying. Other studies have found that middle-class infants differentiate between their mothers and other people, responding more to their mothers' words; whereas lower-class infants make no such distinction (Lewis and Freedle, 1973), perhaps indicating more advanced communication skills among the middle-class babies.

When asked to read books to their young children just "as you would at home," mothers in one study displayed another social-class difference related to language (Rossman et al., 1973). Middle-class mothers seemed to enjoy the project, read the whole story through before discussing it, and related the pictures to the story. Lower-class mothers often failed to finish the story and did not relate pictures and story. Compared with lower-class mothers, middle-class mothers used more complex, explicit language, explained more, asked their children more questions, and responded more often to their children's questions. Taken together, these studies indicate that the major component of IQ tests—language—is also the area of greatest class difference in maternal-infant interaction. Thus it is not coincidental that class differences in IQ appear just at the time that language starts to play its overwhelming role in development.

Other class differences add to these physical and social distinctions. If children are highly motivated to improve the quality of their intellectual skills and have a high standard for intellectual mastery, they are likely to score higher on tests than if they are not highly motivated or have low standards. Because middle-class children are more consistently encouraged than lower-class children to learn to read, spell, add, and write, a child's IQ, social class, and school grades all should be positively related. This is generally the case. In addition, the personality attributes of children who do well in school (persistence, lack of aggression, and responsible behavior) are similar to the characteristics of children from middle-class homes. In Chapter 13, we shall see other basic class differences in child rearing that may contribute to IQ differences.

EARLY INTERVENTION PROGRAMS
Early intervention programs are designed to help children overcome the effects of their early environment. At first, these effects are not apparent. As we have seen, not until about the age of eighteen months does any class difference in IQ begin to appear. Thus, the purpose of early intervention programs is to keep children's IQs from dropping. No matter how researchers intervene, children who are enrolled in these programs tend to benefit from them; when the pro-

gram closes, their scores on IQ and achievement tests are significantly higher than the scores of disadvantaged children who were not enrolled.

Many of these programs began as part of Project Head Start and were funded by the government. Some used day-care centers, some were carried on in infants' homes, some focused on children themselves, others worked primarily with parents. One of the simplest forms of intervention was the public television program, "Sesame Street," which was planned with the hope that it would help prepare disadvantaged children to do well in public schools (Lesser, 1974). Subsequent studies showed that the program may have had a pronounced effect on young children's developing cognitive skills and their symbolic representation. Preschoolers who regularly watched "Sesame Street" made large and important cognitive gains, as shown by tests that measured the children's knowledge of letters, numbers, geometric forms, and body parts, as well as their matching, sorting, and classification skills (Ball and Bogatz, 1972). The more often disadvantaged youngsters watched "Sesame Street," the more impressive their cognitive gains; three- and four-year-olds who watched regularly scored higher than five-year-olds who did not see the program.

Some programs intervened intensively. In a North Carolina program, babies were enrolled before birth (Ramey, Yeates, and Short, 1984). The mothers were young, black, mostly unmarried women; the majority had not completed high school. All the babies in the group received nutritional supplements, but only half participated in the early intervention program. These babies began attending a full-day program shortly after birth; the program was designed to foster intellectual development, and it stressed the sort of verbal interaction that generally occurs between middle-class mothers and their children. The program lasted until the children started kindergarten, and during the preschool years the children were systematically exposed to science, math, and music. At eighteen months, IQ differences began to appear between those who participated in the intervention program and those who did not. The differences

steadily widened; by the time the children were four years old, the IQs of program children were typical of a middle-class group, while the IQs in the control group were about fourteen points lower (see Table 11.3).

But how long will this effect last? Again and again, the comparative gains in IQ scores that are apparent at the end of the program begin to fade as children reach school age. When such IQ declines were first detected, researchers, educators, and taxpayers wondered whether the programs were worthwhile. Then a closer analysis of the children's progress made it clear that early intervention programs had lasting, positive effects.

In one analysis, Irving Lazar and Richard Darlington (1982) traced the graduates of twelve infant and preschool programs. The investigators compared children who had attended the program with other children from the same area who had not. Children who attended the program did much better in school: they were less likely than controls to be assigned to special education classes (13.8 percent as compared with 28.6 percent) or held back in school (25.4 percent as compared with 30.5 percent). But when it came to IQ scores, the programs failed to have permanent effects. Gains still faded gradually, until most had disappeared four years after a project's close. It would be surprising, however, if intervening for a few months in a child's life consistently overcame the influence of the twenty four-hour-a-day environment.

The programs had other effects that do not show on IQ scores: the children's attitudes and values seemed changed. They were much more likely than control children to be proud of themselves for accomplishments connected with school or work. And the older graduates (fifteen to nineteen years old) had higher opinions of their own school performance than did the controls. Finally, the mothers were more satisfied with their children's school performance and had higher aspirations for their children than did mothers of control children.

Children in the intervention programs have experienced less academic failure than other disadvantaged children. And the success has not

Table 11.3 NORTH CAROLINA PROJECT MEAN IQ SCORES

Age at Testing	Experimental Group (N = 42)	Control Group (N = 44)
Six months	106.26	101.36
Twelve months	112.14	105.73
Eighteen months	108.64	89.68
Twenty-four months	96.60	84.98
Thirty-six months	101.67	84.41
Forty-eight months	102.71	89.00

Disadvantaged children in the experimental group had significantly higher IQs than disadvantaged control children from the age of eighteen months. Children were given a test of sensorimotor intelligence on the first three occasions. When the children were twenty-four months old, researchers switched to the Stanford-Binet test. (Adapted from Ramey, Yeates, and Short, 1984.)

been expensive. Lazar and Darlington point out that the programs justified themselves financially. The cost of putting a child through a two-year preschool program is much less that the cost of special education classes or extra classroom years for children who are held back.

Some early intervention programs have had especially strong effects, and in the box on page 368 is a description of a program that had strong effects on boys. The Perry Preschool Program in Ypsilanti, Michigan, seems to have affected all aspects of children's lives (Schweinhart and Weikart, 1980; Clement et al., 1984). The children selected for this program as three-year-olds all had IQs between 70 and 85; their parents were poor, black; most had no more than nine years of schooling. The children attended the program half-days for two years; teachers also visited the home each week, where they tried to involve the mother and her child in educational activities. The program, which was based on Piaget's theories, focused on cognitive development. As in other programs, the children's IQ gains disappeared after the children entered public school. But as eighth-graders, the children who attended this program had significantly higher achievement scores in reading,

language, and arithmetic than control children. They were more competent in meeting school requirements: 13.8 percent were assigned to special education classes (14.9 percent of the control group), and only 4 percent were held back in school (compared with 29.4 percent of the control group). When they were nineteen years old, these children were also less likely to have dropped out of school or to have been arrested. And they were more likely to have attended college or job training courses, to be employed, and to be supporting themselves.

ENVIRONMENT AND THE INDIVIDUAL

Although socioeconomic factors provide a powerful pull in the same direction throughout childhood, we have seen that the same child may show a variation of thirty points between the ages of two and a half and seventeen. It may be that specific events interact with a child's skills and motivations to cause major changes in the abilities tapped by the tests (McCall, Appelbaum, and Hogarty, 1973).

Follow-up studies have found that although IQ gains from early intervention programs usually fade in about four years, children who attend such programs are less likely to fail in school than disadvantaged children who do not attend. (Joel Gordon)

Such events are responsible for part of the difference in IQ between siblings. Sometimes the process is negative. For example, the birth of a younger brother or sister seems to be followed by a temporary decline in IQ. When McCall (1984) examined the records of children in a longitudinal study, he found that during the two years after the birth of a sibling, the IQ of an older child dropped ten points compared with the IQ of an only child, and about six points compared to the IQ of last-born children with older siblings (see Figure 11.6). By the time children reached the age of seventeen, the differences were no longer significant. McCall speculates that when a new baby arrives, the older child suddenly gets less attention and finds relations with his or her parents strained by the demands of infant care.

Sometimes events can positively affect IQ. For example, a male teacher who has a deep interest in the space program has an eleven-year-

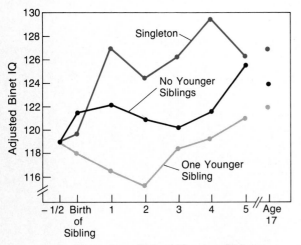

Years from Birth of Younger Sibling

FIGURE 11.6 The birth of a sibling is often followed by a temporary sharp drop in IQ, as a comparison of IQ scores for only children ("singleton"), children with no younger siblings, and children with one younger sibling shows. The scores have been controlled for sex, age at testing, and family size.

(From McCall, 1984, p. 1320)

Do Boys and Girls Respond Differently to Early Intervention Programs?

When Louise Miller and Rondeall Bizzell (1984) compared four different intervention programs, they found a curious sex difference in the programs' effects. By the time children were in the tenth grade, the average graduate of three of the programs had achievement scores that could not be distinguished from children in the control group. This was also true of girls in the fourth program—but not of the boys. The boys in the fourth program were doing well; their achievement scores were at grade level, although their IQ scores were slightly below average (see Figure 11.7). In this one program, intervention had a lasting effect on boys' achievement scores.

What made this fourth program different from all the other programs? It was a Montessori program that emphasized the physical manipulation of concept-oriented material. Miller and Bizzell are not certain why this hands-on method of intervention was so effective with boys, but they speculate that general developmental differences between boys and girls may have something to do with it. They point out that girls mature faster than boys during the preschool years. Around the age of four or five, when these children entered the prekindergarten program, the girls may have been better equipped to process information they gained through watching others and listening to verbal instructions. At this age, they suggest, the boys may have needed more kinesthetic methods of instruction. Perhaps boys were also more comfortable with the hands-on manipulation of objects—which is, as we shall see in Chapter 15, a characteristic of boys' play that is encouraged by parents and the culture.

Indeed, girls who attended the Montessori program did not do as well as girls who at-

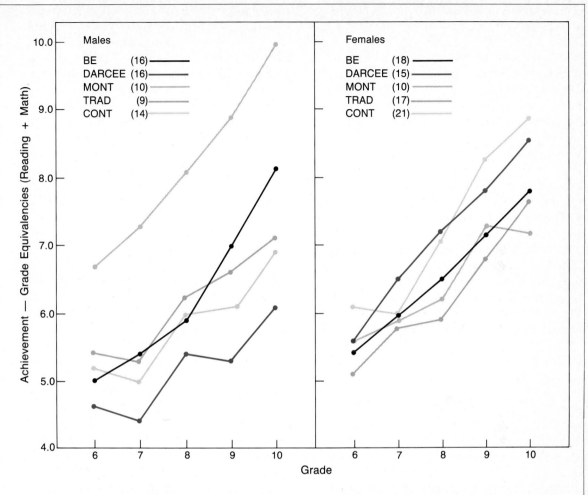

FIGURE 11.7 The strong effects of a Montessori-type early intervention program (MONT) on boys is still apparent in the tenth grade. The graphs compare the averaged reading and math achievement scores of boys and girls in four different early intervention programs (BE, DARCEE, MONT, TRAD) with one another and with children in a control group (CONT).

(From Miller and Bizzell, 1984, p. 1581)

tended programs that stressed verbal instruction and visual materials. In most cases, girls in each group scored higher on achievement tests than boys, but among the Montessori graduates, boys scored much higher than girls.

Did this difference come about by chance? The researchers do not think so. The children's initial assignment to the groups was done at random. And just as many of the Montessori children were available for tenth-grade testing as children from the other groups. All the children entered the program as four-year-olds; all attended for six and a half hours each day, five days a week, from September through May. Finally, it was not a

case of a special teacher whose talents were especially suited to young boys; for there were two Montessori classes included in the study. It seems as if the preschool boy is ready to profit from the Montessori method.

old boy for a pupil whose divorced father lives in another city. The boy identifies with the teacher, adopts the teacher's interests as his own, applies himself to mathematics and science, reads widely about the space program, and shows a large jump on an IQ test the following year. A ten-year-old girl, whose brother is captain of the football team, finds that she can get her own share of family attention by studying hard and making the honor roll; her IQ score soars. In the same quest for attention, she could have chosen to play the flute in the school orchestra or to rebel against family standards; but this year—perhaps because of a television program she saw, a book she read, or her observations of her parents' reactions to a scholarship winner—she chose to apply herself to academic subjects. A year or two earlier or later, the young boy and girl might have reacted differently. Different children may not respond to similar situations in the same way. McCall and his colleagues believe that such influences may be especially potent on children who are already making above average scores on IQ tests.

As we have seen in this chapter, intelligence is not a fixed quantity that can be measured at age six or eight or eighteen and then remains stable for the rest of life. Instead, it is flexible, develops out of the individual's interaction with the environment, and is responsive to physical, social, and emotional stimulation, and to motives, fears, and expectations. Intellectual ability reflects evolutionary history, genetic endowment, culture, and family circumstances, whereas IQ scores reflect only intellectual performance at a specific time under the influence of the immediate situation. It is no wonder that psychologists continue to argue over the concept of intelligence and how it relates to IQ tests.

SUMMARY

When looked at from the standpoint of the species, intelligence is the disposition to behave adaptively when faced with the demands of the environment. Differences in intelligence among individuals become negligible when compared with differences in intelligence among species. Human intelligence has been regarded both as a single, general capacity and—when dissected by factor analysis—as made up of as many as 120 factors.

Human intelligence has been considered from at least four perspectives. Biological analysis looks at the purpose of intelligence in species survival. **Structural** analysis focuses on problem solving and logic, examining how human beings think in the best of circumstances. **Psychometric** analysis is devoted to measuring individual differences in intelligence. And information-processing analysis applies computer models to human cognition, trying to identify the underlying process of thought and regarding individual differences as variations in the speed, content, or efficiency of specific parts of the information-processing system.

Intelligence tests, which produce a score in terms of IQ, measure a child's performance in relation to the performance of other children who have been tested under the same conditions. IQ tests measure how well a child has learned the concepts and rules of middle-class Western society, and any questions that do not predict school success are eliminated from the tests.

Scores on infant intelligence scales bear little resemblance to later IQ scores, perhaps because sensorimotor intelligence may be very different from later intelligence. Although IQ scores become more stable as children grow older, scores may shift by as many as thirty or forty points during childhood.

IQ tests do an efficient job of predicting school success. To a lesser degree, they also correlate with vocational success; although this correlation may be due to the fact that the higher a person's IQ, the more likely he or she is to receive advanced education. Certain professions require a minimum IQ, but once that level is reached, higher scores do not bring greater success. A similar relationship appears to exist with creativity, but great creative genius may require a delicate balance of environmental forces in order to flower.

Heredity plays a role in intelligence, but its full expression requires an optimal environment. It is likely that genetic influences on IQ are much smaller among lower-class than among middle-class children. Severe malnutrition, the fetal alcohol syndrome, low birth weight, and a disadvantaged environment can all depress IQ scores. Early intervention programs, such as Head Start, appear to lessen the rate of school failure among disadvantaged children. Specific environmental events may also interact, positively or negatively, with children's skills and motivation to cause changes in individual IQ scores.

PART 5

Social and Personality Development

Babies are social creatures from birth, and in these chapters we watch the expansion of the child's social world and the development of personality. In the tight world of the family circle, where they interact primarily with parents and siblings, infants develop emotional bonds with their caregivers, learning from them some of the constraints society will later impose. In these close first relationships, children may develop a sense of social competence that enables them to explore confidently the toddler's world of peers, teachers, and nursery school and later move into the wider

world of schoolchild and adolescent. They develop a sense of themselves as male or female, and they learn ways of handling conflicts with others as well as reasons for helping them. But throughout this process of development, influence runs both ways. From their earliest actions with their caregivers, babies are influencing others, contributing to the development of their parents, siblings, grandparents, and other people with whom they have contact. The process of personality and social development goes on as long as life itself.

The Emerging Self

ATTACHMENT
The Stages of Attachment
The Function of Attachment
Separation Distress
Wariness of Strangers
DIFFERENCES IN ATTACHMENT
IT'S NOT ALWAYS MOTHER
Fathers as Attachment Figures
Multiple Caregiving
CLASS, CULTURE, AND PERSONALITY
THE DEVELOPMENT OF SOCIABILITY
Self-Concept
Striving for Competence
Autonomy
Emotional Development
ATTACHMENT AND LATER PERSONALITY
EARLY EXPERIENCE
Types of Effects
Limits on Effects
SUMMARY

When Karen was a year old, her mother once took her to the university experimental room, where she played happily with toys. From time to time she looked up at her mother, who sat on a nearby chair, showed her a toy and, on one occasion, babbled at her. The door opened and a strange woman entered and sat beside Karen's mother. Karen smiled briefly at the stranger and continued to play, although she occasionally looked at the stranger. When her mother left the room, Karen got up, toddled toward the door, stopped, looked at her mother's empty chair and the handbag beside it, then sat down again. After some hesitation, she accepted a toy from the stranger and played with it, glancing from time to time at the closed door. When her mother returned, Karen greeted her with delight.

Karen behaved as many babies do in these circumstances, known as the Strange Situation. She was curious about the stranger but somewhat wary. Later, after the stranger departed, her mother again left the room and Karen found herself alone. The stranger reentered, and this time her presence tipped Karen's reaction from wariness to fear, bringing on tears. On her

375

mother's next return, Karen clung closely to her. Karen's reactions demonstrated a special bond between adult and infant that appears to be universal among human beings. The bond takes different forms, but its absence or unreliability signifies a major problem in social development.

In this chapter, we look at the baby's first social bond with primary caregivers and discover that there are wide differences in the form this attachment takes. We find that attachment plays an important role in the baby's developing trust in the world, in feelings of competence, and in a growing sense of self. Our investigation of early socioemotional development will show that early experiences lay the groundwork for the developing personality, but that these first experiences do not necessarily determine the course of future development. By the end of the chapter, the function of attachment in the development of the growing child's individuality will become apparent.

ATTACHMENT

A human baby arrives on the social scene prepared by millions of years of primate evolution to respond to the sights and sounds of people and to behave in ways that elicit responses from them. Ethologists (Bowlby, 1969; Ainsworth et al., 1978) have argued that by causing adults to stay nearby or to rush to the baby's side and provide necessary care, the baby's inborn tendencies play an active role in ensuring survival. Adults, in turn, have been prepared by evolution to respond to the baby's signals, providing care and giving the child early opportunities for social interaction. Adults have also been prepared to respond to the baby's cuteness, as we saw in Chapter 1.

These built-in biases are the building blocks for complex systems of social behavior that begin in the family. In most cultures, the closest relationship of all is between mother and infant. They are involved for a time in a close, symbiotic relationship in which the child is almost an extension of the mother's being. It is no sur-

prise, then, that investigators have taken a keen interest in the development of the special bond, called **attachment**, that a baby forms with his or her parents (see box on p. 382).

The Stages of Attachment

The development of attachment takes months to appear, requires a complex intermeshing of infant and caregiving behavior, and is subject to much variation. Attachment in human babies refers to the early love relationship between baby and caregiver (usually one or both parents), and developmental psychologists study it by examining the kinds of behavior associated with such a relationship. The signs of attachment include smiling and joyous greeting when the caregiver appears, and crying when he or she leaves. One of the most important aspects of behavior that signifies attachment is that it is directed toward some people and not toward others. According to ethologist John Bowlby (1969), in developing an attachment, the child passes through four stages. These stages begin with indiscriminate social responses that gradually become specific. In the first stage, which lasts until babies are about a month or two old, they respond to anyone; in the second, found in babies from two to about seven months old, babies prefer familiar people but do not protest when either parent leaves and can be comforted by others. In the third stage, which begins at about seven months and lasts until a baby is two or two and a half years old, attachment is strong, and separation from a caregiver leads to the baby's distress. Finally, in the fourth stage, as the child begins to understand the caregiver's feelings and motives, a partnership develops between them and they can work toward shared goals. Although attachment remains strong, the baby no longer becomes distressed each time a caregiver departs.

INDISCRIMINATE SOCIAL RESPONSIVENESS At first, newborn babies can summon

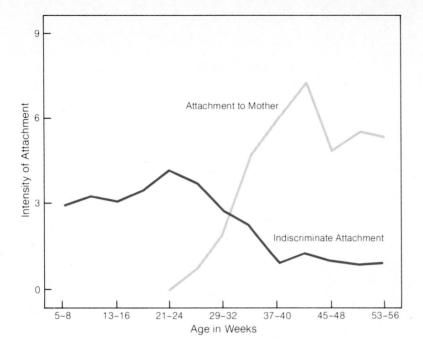

FIGURE 12.1 During the early weeks of life, most infants prefer not to be separated from the person they are with regardless of who that person is. Such "indiscriminate attachments" begin to decline about the same time that infants start to show preferences for specific persons, such as their mothers.

(Adapted from H. R. Schaffer and P. E. Emerson, "The Development of Social Attachment in Infancy," *Monographs of the Society for Research in Child Development*, vol. 29, 1964.)

aid only by crying. A baby's wails bring milk, dry clothes, an end to physical discomfort, and the pleasure of close human contact. Infants in this first stage of attachment will accept aid and comfort from anyone. Although Bowlby believed that the indiscriminate stage of responsiveness lasted for about two months (see Figure 12.1), there is some evidence that babies recognize some aspects of their mothers much earlier, for they seem to prefer the sound of their mother's voice and her odor (DeCasper and Fifer,

1980; Macfarlane, 1977). Toward the end of this stage, babies develop a social smile and at the same time often begin to coo.

This additional means of communication allows the baby to initiate, prolong, or end social interaction. A smile and a coo will often keep an adult near; by falling silent and turning away, a baby can shut off communication. If an infant can so influence the behavior of others, then babies have some control over their early social experiences. Karen, for example, came into the world with the predispositions common to all infants. But she also possessed her own bundle of individual characteristics, such as her levels of activity and general irritability. Her temperament interacted with her experiences to develop her own unique self.

DISCRIMINATE SOCIAL RESPONSIVENESS During the next few months of life, babies develop the ability to discriminate among the adults who come into contact with them. They continue to smile at familiar faces as often

or even more frequently than they did earlier, but the smiling at strange faces that was so prevalent at about two months drops off or even disappears. Harriett Rheingold (1969) has suggested that the talking, smiling human face, with its changing expression and movements, interests and attracts a young baby. Gradually, through a variety of experiences, the faces of principal caregivers come both to elicit positive emotional and social responses in the baby and to reinforce them.

For many years, both learning theorists and psychoanalysts assumed that babies develop close bonds with their caregivers because the caregivers feed them, satisfying the babies' physical needs. J. P. Scott (1962) has noted that this assumption can lead us to an unromantic conclusion: infants love us only because we feed them. Research with monkeys has demonstrated, however, that there is more to attachment than being fed. In one series of studies by Harry and Margaret Harlow (1966, 1969), infant monkeys were raised in cages with two surrogate mothers. One mother substitute was covered with soft terry cloth; the other was of hard wire mesh and was equipped with a feeding mechanism. If feeding were the most important factor in attachment, the infant monkeys would have spent more time expressing their attachment to the wire "mother," which fed them. But the monkeys spent much more time clinging to the cloth mother, which gave them no nourishment at all.

The monkeys seemed genuinely attached to the cloth mother. Given a choice of things to observe in a machine that allowed them to see various objects, they looked at the cloth mother much more often than they looked at the wire mother. Monkeys raised under normal conditions rarely chose to look at either artificial

When frightened by a toy bear (*top*), monkey babies in the Harlow experiment ran to the cloth-covered mother for comfort (*middle*), rejecting the wire mother that fed them (*bottom*). (Harry Harlow, University of Wisconsin Primate Center)

mother. When monkeys raised with artificial mothers were put in strange places or when frightening objects were placed near them, they ran to the security of the cloth, but not the wire, mother. At first the baby monkeys seemed terrified, but when allowed to cling to their cloth mother, they soon calmed down. Eventually, the monkeys used the cloth mother as a base for exploration, leaving to manipulate strange objects but returning frequently to cling to their soft, snuggly mother, as monkeys raised with real mothers do. The wire mothers were never used in this way.

Monkey babies may have become attached to the terry-cloth mothers because contact is important to the formation of attachment in monkeys. At birth young monkeys cling to their mothers; it seems as natural to them as scanning and vocalizing are to human infants. A soft, terry-cloth mother encourages clinging, but a cold, hard mesh mother does not, and the differences lead to lasting effects. After a year's separation, a monkey will run to embrace its terry-cloth mother, clinging passionately to its soft form. But after a similar separation from a wire mother, monkeys show no affection at all when they are reunited. Attachment in human beings and in monkeys follows a similar pattern, although the response of a human baby to his or her mother develops more slowly than the infant monkey's attachment to its mother. Similarly, the parent's feeling for the child develops more slowly than does the bond between some animal mothers and their infants (see Chapter 4).

Feeding undoubtedly can increase the development of attachment, but only if the feeding experience is pleasurable. Unless caregivers are sensitive to babies' signals and respond to them appropriately, feeding may give babies the physical nourishment their bodies require but withhold their social nourishment. Such a caregiver would function like a monkey's wire mother.

Although babies at this second stage of attachment are beginning to differentiate the world into the familiar and the strange, they have not yet developed a true attachment to any person. The seeds of attachment are probably present, however. As we saw in Chapter 4, picking up an infant generally places the baby in a state of quiet alertness, when learning about the environment takes place. This situation is most likely to occur when the caregiver responds to the baby's cries of distress. According to Michael Lamb (1981a), through this interaction the baby comes to recognize the person who consistently relieves the distress and may develop a concept of the caregiver as well as affection for him or her. Instead of responding to the caregiver's odor or voice, the baby responds to a unified perception, indicating the development of a generalized concept. Babies as young as three months old can tell their mothers from strangers. Nevertheless, if the baby is left with a sitter, the infant is unlikely to protest. Not until infants understand that other people continue to exist after they disappear from view (the concept of object permanence discussed in Chapter 7) will they develop the intense bond that signifies true attachment.

SPECIFIC ATTACHMENT Attachment to specific people may develop as early as six months, and most babies have formed their primary attachments by the time they are eight months old. By now they realize that the same people react to their needs in the same predictable ways. This realization is probably related to the baby's development of object permanence. Silvia Bell (1970) found that most babies are aware of their mothers as objects who continue to exist when out of sight slightly before they demonstrate such an awareness with physical objects. Although there is some question as to whether person permanence appears before object permanence in all situations (Levitt, Antonucci, and Clark, 1984), it may be that because the comings and goings of the parent are related to the satisfaction of the baby's needs, the baby pays special attention to the location of this very important "object." Bell also found that babies who developed secure attachments to their mothers were aware of their mothers as permanent objects earlier than babies with less secure attachments. Furthermore, babies who acquired the concept of person permanence early also developed the concept of physical object permanence early, suggesting that understanding in the social realm has positive effects on understanding in the physical realm.

An infant boy who knows that his mother exists even when she is out of the room can also creep across the floor, following her from living room to kitchen. He no longer must lie in his crib or sit in his playpen, waiting for his mother to respond to his cries. Because he can now seek out his mother and father, the infant can take on some of the responsibility for maintaining the close proximity to adults that helps ensure his survival.

The Function of Attachment

The biological function of attachment—its adaptive value—is to keep the infant alive. Important as this protective function is, attachment works in other ways to help the child develop essential social and cognitive skills. This secondary function becomes clear when one examines the four complementary systems that coordinate the behavior of child and environment (Lamb, 1978c). The first is the **attachment behavioral system,** which leads to the development of the attachment bond. The second, the **fear-wariness system,** which helps the baby avoid people, objects, or situations that might endanger life, is often called wariness of strangers; it is discussed later in this section. The third, the **affiliative behavioral system,** encourages a baby, once the initial wariness of strangers has been overcome, to interact with people outside the immediate family. This system promotes the baby's social development, a necessity in a social species like humanity. The fourth and last, the **exploratory behavioral system,** allows the baby to explore the surrounding world. Exploration of the environment is necessary if the growing child is to develop competence. The presence of a trusted and reliable attachment figure provides the baby

with emotional security, allowing the affiliative and exploratory systems to operate. If the attachment figure is missing or unreliable, the fear-wariness system takes over, and the distressed baby will refuse to investigate new people and new places, making it difficult for the child to develop a sense of competence or mastery.

Secure attachments between babies and caregivers appear to have influences that go far beyond the family circle. Perhaps the expectations about social relationships that develop out of interactions with their parents color the way babies approach or respond to other people. As babies learn that their parents are predictable and reliable, they may develop basic trust (Lamb, 1981a). Trust is usually assumed to be something a person possesses, an inner attitude; however, it reflects a system of interaction with the social world, in which social experiences have led to the expectation that parents can be counted on. When trust is generalized to other people, it helps determine the quality of a baby's future interactions with others. As noted in Chapter 1, the establishment of trust is seen by Erik Erikson as the baby's major developmental task, allowing the child to tolerate frustration and to delay gratification. The emotional warmth that accompanies a secure attachment makes parents more effective models and their approval a more potent reinforcer, increasing the likelihood that experience within the family circle will have the effects parents desire (Lamb, 1978c).

Separation Distress

After attachment has developed, a baby tends to cry and stop playing when left in an unfamiliar place. The child may reach out for the attachment figure when he or she leaves and later may crawl or walk in pursuit of the figure. This distinctly negative reaction to being parted from an attachment figure is called **separation distress,** and it can be studied by placing babies

Infants with secure attachments learn that their parents are predictable and reliable; the basic trust that develops in such relationships generalizes to other people. (Erika Stone)

and their mothers in the Strange Situation described at the beginning of the chapter. In this experimental situation, baby and mother are placed in a strange situation, and the mother goes out, leaving the baby behind. Separation distress is a familiar event to babysitters, who are not surprised when their year-old charges wail at their parents' departure.

Separation distress appears to be a universal phenomenon. Although Ugandan babies begin to protest as early as six months when separated from their mothers (Ainsworth, 1967), and most Guatemalan babies do not object to separation before they are nine months old (Lester et al., 1974), the form and timing of attachment are remarkably similar around the world. Among babies in all cultures that have been studied, whether in Europe, Africa, Latin America, Japan, or the United States, and whether the infants are growing up in nuclear families, kibbutzim, orphanages, or day-care centers, separation distress regularly appears by about eight or nine months, peaks at around twelve months, and remains high until about the middle of the second year, when it declines (Kagan, 1984).

Placed in a strange situation, most nine- to twelve-month-old babies are likely to show concern that their primary caregiver be present and nearby. For example, Mary Ainsworth and Barbara Wittig (1969) found that many babies in a strange situation first establish contact with their caregivers. Somewhat later they venture out on short forays into the strange environment, exploring bits of it but always returning to their caregivers between expeditions.

For example, when a mother brings her eighteen-month-old infant on a first visit to a friend's home, the infant clings to (indeed, hides behind) the parent. Only after the infant has become accustomed to the new setting is he or she likely to let go of the mother's leg. This reaction is similar to the way both cloth-surrogate-reared and normally reared young monkeys behaved in a strange environment.

By the time they are eighteen months old and separation distress has begun to decline, some babies are readier than others to accept their mother's departure. Two factors appear to affect a baby's willingness to be separated from an attachment figure: the security of the bond and the baby's previous experience with separation (Jacobson and Wille, 1984). Although securely attached twelve-month-olds may be extremely upset at parting, as eighteen-month-olds they may find separation easier to tolerate. And babies who are accustomed to a moderate amount of separation seem less distressed and spend more time playing than babies who are separated from their caregivers less than four hours a week or more than nineteen hours.

Caregivers are more than security bases. By staying near their attachment figures, babies maintain their emotional bonds, learn about the

Theories of Attachment

Psychoanalytic Theory

Sigmund Freud based his psychoanalytic theory of attachment on the infant's instinctual drives and saw the child as choosing the caregiver as a primary love object. In Freud's view, this relationship develops out of the infant's initial self-preoccupation, or *narcissism,* as the caregiver satisfies the baby's needs and gratifies the desire to suck that is the principal pleasure of infancy. Gradually, babies become attached to those who feed, care for, and protect them.

Adaptation Theory

John Bowlby is a British child psychiatrist who proposes a theory of attachment based on ethological thought, although he also draws on post-Freudian psychoanalytic views. He sees evolved predispositions on the part of both the infant and the adult caregiver as interacting to ensure the infant's survival. Bowlby suggests that certain stimulation (a human face, a human voice, a strange object) evokes specific behavior in the infant (smiling, alertness and scanning, crying). The infant's behavior, in turn, releases complementary behavior in the adult. Thus an infant's smile may trigger a smile in the adult and perhaps a strong attraction to the infant as well. Bowlby sees attachment as one of four behavioral systems that operate in infancy. The other three are the fear-wariness system, which helps the baby avoid life-threatening people or situations; the affiliative system, which encourages the baby to interact with people outside the immediate family; and the exploratory system, which allows the baby to explore the surrounding world.

Mary Ainsworth's view of attachment is heavily influenced by John Bowlby's theory. However, Ainsworth focuses not simply on behavioral systems and the nature of the bond that underlies those systems, but on individual differences in the quality of the attachment relationship that develops between infant and caregiver. Ainsworth argues that one can distinguish three different types of attachment (secure, ambivalent, and avoidant) and that the quality of interaction between mother and child determines what type of bond will form.

Behavior-Learning Theory

Sidney Bijou and *Donald Baer* are behavior-learning theorists who see attachment as complex behavior that is established and maintained through reinforcement. In this view, attachment develops because the adult caregiver and the infant each reinforce the other's behavior, thereby exerting some control over each other. The caregiver feeds and cares for the baby and provides interesting and satisfying stimulation, so that the caregiver's presence becomes reinforcing. In turn, the baby's responses—coos, gurgles, and smiles, and the cessation of cries—reinforce the caregiver's attention, communication, and other behavior connected with attachment.

world by observing the caregiver's actions, and exchange information they discover for themselves (Hay, 1980). For example, when Harriett Rheingold and Carol Eckerman (1970) placed infants in a new situation, the babies showed not distress but joy and excitement, leaving their mothers to explore their new surroundings and returning to share their fun. Babies apparently use attachment figures to reduce their fear and to share in the pleasures of life, and it seems that the same general pattern of behavior serves both purposes.

When they are taken to a strange place, most toddlers stay close to a parent, perhaps clinging to a leg until they become accustomed to the situation. (Ray Ellis/Photo Researchers)

Wariness of Strangers

Wariness of strangers, a manifestation of the fear-wariness system, usually develops a month or two after specific attachments begin. Babies appear to go through four phases in their reaction to strangers. At first they do not discriminate between strange and familiar persons. Later they respond positively to strangers, although less positively than to familiar people. Then they go through a period of reacting to strangers with fear if an attachment figure is present, looking back and forth between the stranger and the parent as though trying to decide how the parent is reacting to the stranger. At this time, babies merely become sober and stare at the stranger. It is not until they are around eight months old that some babies respond to strangers with fear

and withdrawal, looking away, frowning, whimpering, or even crying. This reaction is particularly intense when a baby's attachment figure is absent (Sroufe, Waters, and Matas, 1974).

George Morgan and Henry Ricciuti (1969) investigated the emergence of fear in the presence of strangers and the calming effect of a parent's presence. They found that at eight, ten, and especially at twelve months, a baby responds more positively to the approach of a stranger if seated on the mother's lap than if four feet away from her. At four or six months, however, a separation of four feet makes little or no difference; the baby responds positively to the stranger in either case.

The parent's reactions may exert a powerful effect on the infant's response to strangers. As the box on p. 385 indicates, babies appear to seek information about the situation from the caregiver, and in some situations the caregiver may be as wary as the infant. In a recent study of two dozen mothers and their babies, when a stranger approached a kneeling mother, she stopped smiling, became alert, and usually averted her gaze, showing less readiness to interact with the stranger than did her eight-month-old infant, who was seated in a nearby highchair (Kaltenbach, Weinraub, and Fullard, 1980). Kneeling placed the mother in a vulnerable position, showing how the context of an interaction helps set its tone.

The baby's prior information may also affect the response to a stranger. When babies had previously seen their mothers in pleasant, animated conversation with a stranger, the infants later responded positively to the stranger's approach. But when the stranger had simply been sitting quietly in the same room without talking to the mother, infants were less likely to smile and more likely to stop their play when the stranger approached (Feiring, Lewis, and Starr, 1984). As the box on social referencing would lead us to expect, babies watched intently while the stranger talked with the mother but paid little attention to a stranger who talked with the experimenter.

Before this baby decides whether to laugh or cry at the grinning clown, he will probably look at his mother, using her reactions as a guide to his own. (Michal Heron/Woodfin Camp & Associates)

Another influence on babies' reactions to strangers has to do with the manner of approach. As Mary Anne Trause (1977) found, if strangers pause before walking up to a year-old baby, the baby is more likely to smile and less likely to show distress than if the stranger walks rapidly over to the infant. Apparently, the slower approach gives babies time to judge whether the stranger presents a probable source of danger. In fact, most babies become fearful if a stranger touches them, reaches for them, or picks them up. When babies are given time to evaluate the stranger, their curiosity and affiliative tendencies can come into play.

The characteristics of the stranger may also have an effect. As Alison Clarke-Stewart (1978) has suggested, once the stranger acts—or fails to act—toward the child, the situation becomes social interaction, and the stranger's sex, appearance, and manner of behavior will influence the behavior of the child. She points out that in experiments in which strangers act out a rigid script, babies display more wariness or fear than in experiments that allow strangers to interact naturally.

Fear of strangers, like separation distress, appears sharpest when the baby is in an unfamiliar setting. Babies are much less likely to show wariness in their own homes than when they are observed in a laboratory. Russel Tracy and his colleagues (1976) studied babies from the time they were three weeks old until they were more than a year old. The babies were observed in their own home for four hours every three weeks. Tracy and his associates found that once babies began to crawl, they tended to follow their mothers from place to place and to play comfortably in the presence of strangers. Although no baby at any age ever followed a stranger, few cried or showed other distress at a stranger's approach. Babies also engage in more exploration and vocalize more freely at home than they do in the strange and perhaps frightening surroundings of the psychologist's laboratory.

DIFFERENCES IN ATTACHMENT

Not all infants develop the same kind of bond with their caregivers, but exactly what characteristics of the babies and their caregivers influence the sort of bond that develops has not been established. Mary Ainsworth and her colleagues (1978) discerned three major kinds of attachment bonds: secure, avoidant, and ambivalent. After a separation from their mothers and a meeting with a stranger, babies with *secure* attachments actively sought out their mothers when they returned, and contact with their mothers quickly ended the distress. Less securely attached infants fell into two major groups: *avoidant* infants, who shunned contact with their mothers upon being reunited, and *ambivalent* infants, who alternated between seeking contact

Social Referencing

When a stranger approaches, a baby often looks back and forth from caregiver to stranger before reacting. Joseph Campos and Craig Stenberg (1981) have proposed that this behavior is an instance of **social referencing,** a deliberate search for emotional information that helps the infant make sense out of an ambiguous event. The caregiver's expression, tone of voice, and gestures either reassure the baby or tell the infant to be wary.

For example, when the mothers of nine-month-old infants frowned at a stranger and said "Hello" in an abrupt and unfriendly tone, the babies' hearts speeded up, they stopped smiling, and some of them showed distress. But when the mother smiled at both baby and stranger and said "Hello" in a cheerful, friendly tone, the babies' hearts slowed, and they were more likely to smile, and less likely to show distress (Boccia and Campos, 1983).

In another study (Sorce and Emde, 1981), when the mothers of fifteen-month-old babies responded to their infants' play with smiles, flashes of their eyebrows, and reassuring pats, the babies tended to enjoy their play and to explore the area—making frequent visual checks of the mother's expression. When mothers remained impassive, reading a magazine without responding to their infants' bids for attention, the babies seemed to enjoy their play less, stay nearby, and to look less often at their mother's face.

Babies are not limited to caregivers when seeking emotional reassurance about a situation. When babies are in the same room with their mothers and a familiar adult, they will use the other adult as a social reference if the mother remains impassive. For example, if an ambiguous toy is placed in the room and the familiar adult smiles broadly and looks joyous, the baby is more likely to approach the toy and touch it than if the adult looks fearful (Klinnert et al., 1983b). In fact, after babies become accustomed to a stranger, they are almost as likely to refer to the stranger as to their mother in such situations (Zarbatany and Lamb, 1985).

Social referencing may explain why two-year-olds have been observed to desert attractive toys to be where they can see their mothers' face. When mothers sat facing the toys, youngsters played happily with them, indicating the toys' appeal for the children. Yet when mothers sat with their backs to the toys, half of another group of two-year-olds abandoned the toys and moved where they could see their mothers' faces—and thus be able to "read" their expressions (Carr, Dabbs, and Carr, 1975).

According to Mary Klinnert and her colleagues (1983a), social referencing does not develop until a child understands the emotions that accompany various expressions. It then comes into play when the infant's first cognitive appraisal of a situation fails. The object, person, or event is so ambiguous or uncertain that the infant does not know how to respond. In such a situation, emotions help to organize and regulate the baby's behavior. Social referencing is only one of several phenomena that indicate the importance of emotional communication in infancy (Feinman, 1983).

with their mothers and angrily squirming to get away from them.

Ainsworth's group, who studied only middle-class babies, found a connection between a year-old baby's attachment and a mother's style of caring for her baby, with securely attached babies having mothers who were highly responsive to their infants' cries, smiles, and other signals. These mothers were affectionate and accepting, helping their babies but not interfering with their efforts. Mothers of avoidant babies were relatively insensitive to their babies' signals, avoided bodily contact with their babies, and rarely expressed affection. Mothers of ambivalent babies were awkward as they held their babies and appeared to handle them primarily to attend to their needs.

After following middle-class infants from the indiscriminate stage of attachment (one month) until the attachment bond was established (nine months), Jay Belsky and his colleagues (1984), found a different relationship between maternal care and attachment. They speculated that the amount of stimulation provided by the mother may be important in determining what sort of attachment bond develops. Among these infants, babies who developed avoidant bonds had the highest level of interaction with their mothers and babies with ambivalent bonds had the least interaction. These researchers propose that overstimulation leads to avoidant attachment, understimulation to ambivalent attachment, and the optimal amount of stimulation to secure attachment.

In the only major study to look at poor, mostly unmarried mothers, Byron Egeland and Ellen Farber (1984) found that those with securely attached babies may have been more cooperative and sensitive with their infants than were mothers of insecurely attached babies. After reviewing many longitudinal studies, Michael Lamb and his colleagues (1984, 1985a) concluded that mothers who behave in socially desirable ways (warm, responsive, not intrusive, not abusive) consistently tend to have securely attached babies, whereas mothers who do not behave in this fashion are more likely to have insecurely attached babies. However, no one is certain just what aspects of the mother's behavior are most important, although many psychologists believe that responsiveness plays a crucial role. Apparently, researchers are missing some important factor, because only a small part of the difference in the quality of a baby's attachment is explained by identified variations in maternal behavior.

In all the studies described (Egeland and Farber, 1984; Belsky, Rovine, and Taylor, 1984;

Ainsworth et al., 1978), researchers found that babies appeared to be more influenced by their mothers' responsiveness than mothers were influenced by the characteristics of their babies. But various characteristics of an infant, including gender, activity level, cuddliness, responsiveness, physical attractiveness, alertness, affective expressiveness, susceptibility to illness, clarity of signaling, and regularity and predictability of behavior may affect a caregiver's reactions (Belsky and Tolan, 1981). Babies who actively resist cuddling may not find contact at all comforting, and they tend to develop attachments later than cuddlers do (Schaffer and Emerson, 1964). Cuddlers may develop a more intense attachment to their caregivers than noncuddlers do, but this difference seems to disappear during the second year, apparently as a result of infant and mother adapting to each other's styles. In Schaffer and Emerson's study, babies who actively resisted contact developed a system of social interaction with their parents that did not depend on physical contact.

When babies are especially fussy, they may be more likely to develop an insecure attachment, perhaps because of the effect their temperament has on parents (Belsky, Rovine, and Taylor, 1984). Studies show that parents of babies who fuss frequently are likely to wait longer before responding to their baby's cries than do parents of babies who fuss infrequently (Dunn, 1977). This may be analogous to the tale of the boy who cried wolf; parents of fussy babies may interpret their signals of distress as being simply bids for attention, or if the babies do not quiet easily, the parents may decide that since responding has little effect, they may as well ignore the babies' cries until they become too loud to disregard. Babies who quiet easily, on the other hand, are likely to reinforce their parents' attention and make them feel more secure as caregivers. Because parents need to feel they can respond to their baby's signals and satisfy his or her needs, the baby whose signs are easy to read enhances the parents' feelings of competence (Belsky, 1984). Thus the baby whose signals say clearly, "I'm hungry," "I'm bored," or "I'm wet," who sucks vigorously and smiles freely, is also the one who is most likely to make parents feel successful and important.

The quality of a baby's attachment can change. A baby who is avoidant or ambivalent at twelve months may be securely attached at eighteen months—and vice versa. Although the majority of babies retain the quality of their original bond, a good many do not. Among a group of middle-class babies, 47 percent showed a change over a seven-month period, with some securely attached babies developing avoidant or ambivalent attachments but a larger number of insecurely attached babies developing secure attachments (Thompson, Lamb, and Estes, 1982). Among the poor babies in Egeland and Farber's study (1984), over a six-month period the quality of attachment changed among 40 percent, with changes from insecure to secure attachments again more common than changes in the other direction. It appears that the quality of a baby's attachment is related to family circumstances, so that changes in the caregiving relationship—which may be affected by a variety of external circumstances—are often followed by changes in attachment (Lamb et al., 1984).

Another aspect of family circumstances that may affect the quality of attachment is the relationship between the baby's parents. In one study (Goldberg and Easterbrooks, 1984), parents of securely attached infants tended to be highly satisfied with their marriages, whereas parents of insecurely attached infants tended to be highly dissatisfied. It may be that when a marriage is good, parents tend to be more sensitive to their infants' needs, but when a marriage is bad, parents are so irritable or emotionally drained by the relationship that they tend to be less sensitive to their infants or pay less attention to them. As we shall see, the role of the father has been receiving increasing attention as well.

IT'S NOT ALWAYS MOTHER

Even in the same culture, no two sets of parents have precisely the same attitude toward their children, nor do they rear them in exactly the same way. As we have seen, the responsiveness of the parent to an infant's signals may have a powerful effect on the kind of bond the infant forms. An ambivalent or avoidant bond, however, is still a form of attachment.

Although most research on attachment has focused on the bond between infant and mother, babies become attached to more than one person. As we might expect, babies become attached to both parents at about the same time, whether or not the father takes an active role in child care (Lamb, 1981b). And babies in the Israeli kibbutzim become attached to mother, father, and *metapelet*, the primary caregiver in the kibbutz nursery (Sagi, Lamb, Lewkowicz, Shoham, Dvir, and Estes, 1985). Because each caregiver responds somewhat differently when relieving a baby's distress, the infant is likely to develop different relationships with each of them (Lamb et al., 1985a). The relationship with the primary caregiver seems stronger and more influential, and in stressful situations, it is to the primary caregiver that the infant turns.

Fathers as Attachment Figures

Although mothers and fathers do many of the same things with their infant, the attachment between babies and father might serve needs that are not met in the infant-mother relationship. In traditional nuclear families, fathers spend about a third as much time interacting with infants as mothers do (Lamb, Pleck, Charnov, and Levine, in press). The average father may spend as little as fifteen minutes a day caring for, playing with, or talking to an infant, or as much as ninety minutes. Although fathers have been regarded as relatively unimportant in their children's early social development, it appears that a father's function goes beyond the role of occasional mother substitute.

Fathers become as deeply attached to their infants as mothers do. As caregivers, they have been found to be nurturant and competent, and their involvement with their babies tends to complement that of the mother. During the first few days in the hospital, for example, middle-class fathers and mothers tend to spend an equal amount of time with their newborn babies. Both fathers and mothers look and smile at their babies, talk to and kiss them, explore their bodies, and give them their bottles. Given the opportunity, lower-class fathers also appear to be nurturant and competent with their newborn babies. When, for example, their baby shows distress during a feeding, both father and mother show their sensitivity in the same way; they stop the feeding, look at the baby, and pat the infant solicitously (Parke and Sawin, 1980).

Sensitivity to infant needs may be as important in fathers as in mothers. Among a group of twenty-month-olds, those who were securely attached and who did best at solving problems generally had fathers who were highly sensitive to their needs, were not aggravated by the child, and were unruffled by their lack of knowledge about child rearing (Easterbrooks and Goldberg, 1984).

Over the past twenty years, many fathers have become more involved with their young children, spending more time interacting with them, being accessible, and taking responsibility for a portion of child care (Lamb, Pleck, Charnov, and Levine, in press). Some fathers have taken primary responsibility for child care, and among a group of American fathers of four-month-old babies, those who played the role of primary caregiver reacted somewhat differently to their infants than did fathers who played the traditional role of secondary caregiver. When Tiffany Field (1978) videotaped parent-infant interactions, she found that all parents talked to their babies, wiped their noses, mopped up their burps, and attended to their needs. But primary caregivers—whether father or mother—laughed less and smiled more than did fathers who were secondary caregivers. They also imitated their baby's grimaces more and mimicked their vocalizations. In other respects, the primary caregiving fathers responded like traditional fathers with their infants (see Figure 12.2).

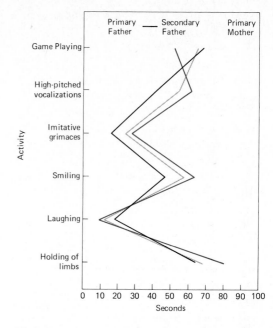

FIGURE 12.2 How fathers interact with babies.

(Adapted from Field, 1978)

As considerable research has shown (Lamb, 1981b), fathers tend to play with their babies, while mothers tend to care for their needs. Most of the time, mothers pick up their babies to feed, diaper, or comfort them; when fathers pick them up, it is generally to play. Mothers play such traditional games as peekaboo and pat-a-cake; fathers engage in rough-and-tumble play, regardless of the infant's sex. Perhaps because of this playful interaction, once boys are about thirteen months old, they begin to prefer their fathers. Girls show no preference for either parent. When the going gets rough, however, the preference for fathers disappears. Placed with both parents in a stressful situation, boys as well as girls will go to the mother for comfort.

This pattern of parent-infant relationship may be particularly American. Among Swedish families, no preference for the father develops among baby boys, even among boys whose fathers had spent at least a month as their primary caregiver. The researchers who studied these Swedish families (Lamb et al., 1983) point out

Fathers are deeply attached, competent caregivers, who engage in a great deal of rough-and-tumble play with their babies, whether they are boys or girls. (Jean Boughton/The Picture Cube)

but mothers clearly showed more affection, held the infants, and spent more time taking care of them than fathers did.

Although most infants prefer their mothers in time of trouble, some infants who have an insecure attachment with their mothers may develop a secure attachment with their fathers. Mary Main and Donna Weston (1981) found that although many infants develop secure bonds with both parents and some develop insecure bonds with both parents, others have an insecure attachment to one parent and a secure attachment to the other. Babies who were insecure with their mothers but secure with their fathers seemed more sociable with a stranger than babies who lacked a secure attachment with both parents, indicating that fathers can play an important role in social development.

Multiple Caregiving

In today's world, multiple caregiving is a frequent form of infant care even among babies who are not in institutions. Does the lack of an exclusive caregiver mean that a baby will suffer from discontinuous or inadequate interaction? After reviewing studies of such children, Alison Clarke-Stewart and Greta Fein (1983) concluded that when the main attachment figure shares caregiving with other people, as when mothers work or when the baby is part of an extended family, children will thrive as long as the other caregivers provide stable relationships.

Many children reared in Israeli kibbutzim show normal social and emotional development. In the majority of kibbutzim, a family arrangement is used, with infants joining their parents at four each evening and returning to the nursery early the next morning. In traditional kibbutzim, however, infants are moved into the residential nursery when they are between six and twelve weeks old. Their interaction with their parents is concentrated in a few hours each evening and on weekends, although parents often visit during the day (Lamb, Shoham, Dvir, and Lewkowicz, in press). *Metaplot* see to the

that Swedish parents play less with their infants than American parents do, and that the playful rough-and-tumble interaction that characterizes the American father-infant relationship is absent among Swedish fathers. During their babies' first year, even when Swedish fathers are primary caregivers, they touch, tickle, and kiss their babies less, smile less at them, and talk less to them than Swedish mothers do. Among families on Israeli kibbutzim, where neither parent is primary caregiver, a third pattern of parent-child relationships appeared (Sagi, Lamb, Shoham, Dvir, and Lewkowicz, 1985). At sixteen months neither boys nor girls showed a preference for either parent. Israeli fathers tended to engage in slightly more physical play and mothers to engage in conventional games,

These children in the day-care center at a carpet factory in Tietsin, China, will thrive as long as they can establish stable relationships with their day-care workers. (B. Salz/Monkmeyer)

daily needs and training of the infants, and the parents provide primarily emotional gratification. Again the conclusion emerges that parents may be absent for significant amounts of time without radically influencing attachment patterns as long as someone who cares is present (Rutter, 1981).

There is little evidence that infants reared by multiple caregivers develop differently from those reared by a single caregiver. In most non-industrial societies, a baby is reared by several caregivers, and even in many industrialized societies, infants are unlikely to spend the major part of their time alone with their mothers (Wer-

ner, 1984). Among such infants, the development of attachment and stranger wariness follows a course similar to that of infants reared by a single caregiver.

Studies of infants in day care have failed to find any evidence that such care interferes with the development of attachment to mothers or other primary caregivers. Infants in day care also form attachments to a supplementary caregiver, but when both caregivers are present, a youngster turns to the mother for help, stays closer to her, and interacts with her more often (Clarke-Stewart and Fein, 1983). When day-care and home-reared youngsters are compared, they show similar timing in the development of attachment and stranger wariness, but a difference appears in the quality of the attachment. Youngsters in day care tend to play farther away from their mothers, to spend less time in physical contact with them, and are more likely to ignore their mothers after a brief separation. This description resembles the avoidant attachment described by Ainsworth, but Clarke-Stewart and Fein (1983) suggest that not all these babies are insecurely attached. Some may be securely attached children who, perhaps through their day-care experiences, have developed independence early. Such children are sociable and cooperative, with their mothers and others; they simply are not bothered by their mothers' comings and goings. As noted earlier, babies who are accustomed to moderate amounts of separation tend to show little distress when their mothers leave.

As we shall see in the next chapter, most studies of day care have been undertaken in excellent centers, often those connected with universities. These day-care centers offer enriched programs and are not simply custodial institutions. In high-quality programs, infants develop normally, both emotionally and intellectually; the bond between mother and infant remains intact; and children have broad opportunities to interact with peers (Belsky, Steinberg, and Walker, 1982). However, university day-care centers, which have few infants per caregiver and programs designed to foster development, may not be typical of the center attended by most infants and toddlers.

A more serious challenge to an infant's well-being is loss or lack of mothering. Early studies of children reared in institutions found devastating effects on their social and intellectual development, but it is now clear that these unfortunate children suffered from a general lack of stimulation necessary to social and cognitive growth as well as from the absence of a single stable caregiver (Rutter, 1981). The babies in Lebanese institutions discussed in Chapter 5 showed gains in cognitive growth as well as in physical development when interesting objects were introduced into their lives for only a few minutes each day.

Research with monkeys suggests that while monkeys can partially overcome the absence of a parental relationship, the lack of attachment to an adult member of the species may be followed by some disturbances in social development (Suomi and Harlow, 1975). Although monkeys raised from birth with only other baby monkeys for company were more nearly normal than were monkeys raised with a surrogate mother, the monkeys who had grown up with only peer companionship became adults who were easily disturbed by the slightest stress and highly aggressive toward monkey strangers. The young monkeys' intense attachment for their cagemates did not seem to foster the same exploration and independence that grows out of the mother-infant attachment. Some monkeys seemed especially vulnerable to stressful events, breaking down in situations that had little effect on other monkeys (Suomi and Ripp, 1983).

A similar difference in vulnerability to stress appears to exist among human infants (Rutter and Garmezy, 1983). Not all infants who suffer maternal deprivation are able to cope with their loss. An infant whose attachment to a primary caregiver has been ruptured may develop depression, or extreme sadness. The British child psychiatrist John Bowlby (1973) has observed what he regards as depression in fifteen- to thirty-month-old healthy infants after they had been separated from their families and placed in a hospital or other residential institution. After an initial phase of active protest and crying, such an infant falls into a phase of despair. The baby becomes withdrawn and inactive, makes no demands of the environment, cries intermittently though without specific cause, and seems to feel increasing hopelessness and sadness. Later, the depressed infant gradually moves out of this phase into one of increased emotional distance. Now he or she interacts in a pleasant but shallow manner with institutional caregivers, and when parents visit, the baby responds in an aloof and detached way. If the separation is only temporary, such children when they return home may continue for a time either to treat their parents as strangers or to cling to them excessively and refuse to be left alone (Schaffer, 977).

Temporary ruptures of the attachment relationship rarely appear to have long-lasting effects, but some institution-reared babies who do not develop attachments to caregivers during infancy may have life-long difficulty in making close relationships. Although the rate of distorted social development seems to increase among children who grow up in institutions, only a vulnerable minority show intense problems with social relationships and many develop normal friendships and love relationships (Rutter and Garmezy, 1983).

CLASS, CULTURE, AND PERSONALITY

Although virtually all children, no matter what their social class or culture, become attached to their caregivers, parent-child relationships vary widely across classes and cultures. And differences in this basic relationship can have lasting effects on children's development.

A child's social class continually influences development, affecting even parents' belief in their infants' capabilities (Kaye, 1982). Jerome Kagan and Steven Tulkin (1971) have studied the influence of social class on maternal attitudes and behavior. Their observations of ten-month-old babies showed some similarities across classes: both middle- and lower-class mothers held, tickled, kissed, and bounced their babies. But other maternal behavior often differed. A middle-class mother was more likely than a lower-class mother to vocalize within two feet of her baby, imitate the baby's sounds, engage in prolonged "positive interaction," give verbal rewards, and encourage her baby to walk. About two-thirds of the lower-class mothers in the study used food to soothe their irritable babies, whereas less than one-third of the middle-class mothers solved problems with food.

When Kagan and Tulkin tested these babies in the laboratory, they found no class differences in the babies' levels of reactivity to meaningful and meaningless speech. However, middle-class babies quieted more dramatically to highly meaningful speech with a high degree of inflection than to other stimuli. In addition, they were more likely than lower-class children to look at a stranger after hearing such speech. Middle-class infants also quieted more to their mothers' voices than to strangers' voices, and they vocalized more than lower-class infants did after listening to recordings of their mothers' voices.

Parent-infant relationships also vary across societies. Urie Bronfenbrenner (1970) has described some of the differences between the Soviet Union and the United States in the parent-infant relationship and the socialization of children. He observed that Russian babies were held most of the time, even when not being fed. Although they seemed to get more hugging, kissing, and cuddling than American babies do, they were held tightly and allowed little freedom of movement. Russian mothers were generally solicitous and protective, and their efforts to protect the baby from discomfort, illness, or injury curtailed their babies' mobility and initiative.

Just the opposite tendency was found among German mothers, where there is a concerted effort to develop independence in babies at an early age. This effort may be responsible for the finding in a study of German mothers and babies that there was only a slight connection between a mother's sensitivity to her baby's needs and a secure attachment (Grossmann and Grossmann, 1982). Among German babies, the proportion of avoidant attachments was higher than in the United States. As noted earlier, some day-care children who show avoidant attachment may be developing independence early. Perhaps behavior that is assumed to indicate maternal sensitivity in American babies may reflect cultural expectations as much as the quality of mothering (Lamb et al., 1984; Lamb, Thompson, Gardner, and Charnov, 1985). This supposition is strengthened by findings from Japan, where a remarkably large proportion of resistant attachments was found among middle-class infants (Miyake, Chen, and Campos, 1985), and from Israel, where babies showed an increased proportion of anxious and avoidant attachments whether they grew up in kibbutzim or in city-dwelling nuclear families (Sagi, Lamb, Shohan,

Dvir, and Lewkowicz, 1985). Researchers who studied the Israeli infants suggest that the Strange Situation, in which attachment is assessed, may provide varying levels of stress, depending on the baby's cultural background. If so, a baby's behavior in the Strange Situation may mean different things in different cultures, and cultural differences in child rearing may have subtle but deep effects on personality development. Such findings remind us that the child-rearing practices we observe in our own culture are not necessarily universal or best for the baby.

THE DEVELOPMENT OF SOCIABILITY

Although attachment to parents is of primary significance in the life of the infant, the spectrum of significant relationships soon broadens. By the time a little girl reaches a year and a half she must contend with her older brother as a potential threat or aid to her well-being, just as she must contend with his playmates, her own peers, and possibly her younger siblings. It is within the first two years of life that we find the beginnings of sociability. During the development of this aspect of personality, babies regard other human beings with varying degrees of warmth, positive expectations, and trust, depending on their early experiences. The development of social skills begins with the emergence of a self-concept, efforts to achieve competence, and the demand for autonomy.

Self-Concept

From their early experience, infants appear to develop a first crude sense of "me" and "not me." These experiences begin in the first hours of life, for detailed studies of interactions of babies and their mothers reveal that a baby is a social creature from birth (Sander, 1977; Schaffer, 1977). Although they may not be aware of

their changing responses, most mothers quickly learn to read their babies' cues and adjust their own behavior so that the babies take the lead in their interactions. During these turn-taking experiences, babies control the rate, level, and nature of their experiences (Stern, 1977).

The infant's sense of self forms an increasingly noticeable and integral part of his or her sociability from the latter part of the first year. As a result of cognitive development, infants become conscious of themselves as separate and distinct persons. This blossoming self-awareness in turn influences their interest in others and how they relate to them.

The baby's developing sense of self has been explored in a series of studies by Michael Lewis and Jeanne Brooks-Gunn (1979). Using self-recognition as objective evidence of self-concept, they discovered that babies recognize themselves toward the end of the second year. Self-recognition was established by placing babies before a mirror after first surreptitiously dabbing rouge on their noses. No babies under a year seemed to recognize that the smudged nose in the mirror belonged to them, but among babies from fifteen to eighteen months, 25 percent immediately touched their noses, and by twenty-four months, 75 percent grabbed for their noses as soon as they looked in the mirror. When a similar study was carried out among children with Down's syndrome, most were nearly three years old before they reached for their noses (Mans, Cicchetti, and Sroufe, 1978). This delay in self-recognition among retarded children indicates that self-awareness is closely related to a child's level of cognitive development.

Self-recognition also shows in the reactions of infants as they look at videotapes of themselves and others. Lewis and Brooks-Gunn found that toward the end of the second year babies seemed to differentiate between themselves and others, looking longer, smiling more, and being more likely to move toward tapes of others. When they saw immediate videotapes of themselves, in which the images on the screen reflected their own actions of a moment before, they vocalized and imitated themselves much more than they imitated stock tape of themselves or of strange babies, making faces, sticking out their tongues, and playing peek-a-boo. This imitation of their own actions increased with age, and no babies younger than a year imitated any of the tapes. Lewis and Brooks-Gunn suggest that the babies may have become accustomed to seeing themselves through their experience with mirrors, for most infants are frequently held before a mirror by parents to "see the baby."

As babies begin to develop a concept of themselves, they probably use it as a reference point for their reactions toward others. If they do so, they should find unfamiliar children less threatening than adult strangers. When Lewis and Brooks-Gunn had various strangers approach babies between the ages of seven and nineteen months, the babies indeed seemed least disturbed by the approach of an unfamiliar child. Infants soon develop expectations about others in terms of height and facial features. In one experiment, babies as young as seven months stared with apparent surprise at a midget. Their eyes widened, their eyebrows arched, and their mouths rounded, as if they expected a small body to have a child's face.

How early do infants develop a more important self-concept—the sense of themselves as continuing psychological entities? This sort of awareness, which has been called *biographical self-awareness*, indicates that youngsters are aware of their personal history—in which they have experienced or caused some events, and have imagined others or been "told" of them—a category that would include memories of televised events. No one is certain when this important development occurs, and in fact there has been no research on this topic (Harris, 1983).

Striving for Competence

As infants' skills and sense of self develop, they find increasing satisfaction in acting on, exploring, and getting to know the social world. Rheingold and Eckerman (1970) point out that

As he explores the world on his own, this baby shows no sign of distress because he knows a parent is nearby. (Peter G. Aitken/Photo Researchers)

although infants show distress at being left by their parents, they show no distress when they themselves choose to leave attachment figures to explore. When Eckerman and Rheingold (1974) placed ten-month-old babies in an unfamiliar environmnent and gave each the opportunity to approach and touch an unfamiliar toy or person, babies promptly approached the toys and played with them. They rarely made physical contact with the strangers; instead, they looked at the strangers and smiled. These results suggest that looking and smiling at people serve an exploratory function similar to touching and manipulating toys.

When in a familiar situation, babies as young as nine months old may be unruffled by their mothers' departure, creeping after a moving toy even though they know their mothers are moving away from them in the opposite direction. Once children learn to walk, they begin to venture off on their own, sometimes passing and leading their mothers or toddling off in another direction to discover and explore the environment (Hay, 1980).

Early exploratory behavior becomes bolder with age, and girls explore as widely as boys. Rheingold and Eckerman (1970) recorded children's forays from their mothers, placing forty-eight children between one and five years old in an L-shaped yard behind a house, which allowed children to leave their mothers' field of vision. Although there were wide individual differences among the children who were two or older, researchers could generally predict from the age of the child how far a boy or girl would travel from his or her mother. The investigators suggest that during the second year of life there is a decline in the infant's need for physical contact, a decline that is motivated by the desire to be competent, to know the social and object world: to touch, take apart, put together, figure out toys and other objects, and to evoke responses (smiling or attention) from new people. Novelty, complexity, and change—interesting new stimulation—draw infants away from the comfortable familiarity of attachment figures. But this new independence does not signal the end of attachment. The desire to be close to familiar and loved people and the desire to try out new experiences and expand one's competence appear to coexist throughout the life of the individual. An infant who is secure in his or her attachments feels safe to explore and to develop a sense of self as an independent agent or a causer of effects in the world. From their explorations, infants bring back new knowledge and abilities that they may incorporate into increasingly differentiated and interesting interactions with familiar and cherished others.

Autonomy

The first concentrated push toward **autonomy,** or independence, appears toward the end of the second year, when infants enter a period of so-cial development that drives parents to despair. The baby becomes reluctant to agree with anything parents suggest and the consistent response to all questions or commands is "No!"

This "negativistic crisis" grows out of the infant's awareness of a mental distinction between self and others, a distinction between his or her own will and the will of others. Until now, infants have had to depend on caregivers for the satisfaction of most needs, in what David Ausubel (1958) has called **executive dependence:** the parent acts as an executive arm, instrumental to the infant's needs. As infants become aware of their own competence and effect on the world, they strive for **executive independence,** or autonomy. They want to do things for themselves. The negativistic infant is attempting to discover the limits of his or her center of activity and initiative: the self. Parents frequently note that the clash of wills seems to be conflict for conflict's sake; the infant is concerned not with a particular issue but with a principle.

This developing sense of control, competence, and autonomy will be important throughout children's lives. It appears to underlie what will later become their **locus of control,** the degree to which they believe that they or others control their fate. People with an internal locus of control generally believe that they are responsible for what they do and that they can affect what happens to them. People with an external locus of control generally believe that what they do makes little difference and that other forces—such as luck, fate, or powerful other people—determine what happens to them.

Emotional Development

Sociability is deeply affected by emotional development, because the expression of emotions affects all social relations. At one time, it was believed that babies came into the world with only a single emotion: general excitement. Under the influence of maturation and learning, negative emotions gradually appeared, in the following order: distress, at three weeks; anger, at four months; disgust, at five months; and fear, at six or seven months. Positive emotions developed more slowly: delight appeared at three months, with elation and affection absent until the baby was past six months old (Bridges, 1932). But it gradually became clear that neonates could feel a great deal more than distress, although the emotion felt by a neonate is very different from the same emotion as experienced by an older child or an adult.

Joseph Campos and his colleagues (1983) propose that before they are three months old, infants may be able to feel most of the major emotions: joy, surprise, anger, fear, disgust, interest, sadness, and perhaps sexual ardor. As we saw in Chapter 4, babies only a few hours old respond to pleasant or unpleasant tastes and smells with expressions that indicate the appropriate emotion. In this view, although all emotions have biological roots, some are heavily dependent on socialization. Emotional experiences change as the infant's perceptual and cognitive capacities develop, as his or her goals change, and as socialization shapes the expression and interpretation of the emotion. For example, to be afraid in the adult sense, babies must be able to hold the feared object in memory, and the sight of the object must call up the perceptual and emotional experiences that were connected with it in the past. Later, the mere mention of the object will be enough to evoke fear.

Changes in the nature of children's fears were reported by Sandra Scarr and Philip Salapatek (1970), who found that between the ages of five and eighteen months there was an increase in infants' fear of strangers, of a grotesque mask, and of heights (as measured by the visual-cliff technique described in Chapter 7). These fears could develop only after the infants learned about the familiar and safe aspects of their environments.

When researchers followed the emergence of anger, they found that with development the target of the emotion changed (Stenberg and Campos, 1983). When a four-month-old was frustrated, the infant directed anger at the immediate cause: the experimenter's restraining hands. At seven months, an infant directed anger at the experimenter himself. Other researchers have found that mothers tend to socialize anger differently in boys and girls (Malatesta and Haviland, 1982). When six-month-old boys showed anger, their mothers responded with knitted brows, as if to show sympathy for their sons' rage. But when six-month-old girls showed anger, their mothers often responded with angry expressions of their own, as if to express displeasure with their daughters' rage—perhaps discouraging its expression. Such responses might tend to socialize emotions along middle-class American standards, which give men greater freedom to express anger than women (Campos et al., 1983).

ATTACHMENT AND LATER PERSONALITY

As babies move into the second year of life, society begins to apply its pressures. In the next chapter we shall see that parents are the major socializing agents and that as toddlers show greater competence and increased independence, their parents will expect an accompanying growth of responsibility. Toward the end of the second year, for example, infants may find themselves subjected to toilet training.

If a secure attachment to parents allows infants a greater scope to explore the world and to interact comfortably with other people, this bond might influence later social development. Some investigators believe that they have found such a connection, indicating that babies with secure attachments become competent, independent toddlers.

Among one group of middle-class toddlers, the way two-year-olds approached and solved problems was related to the security of their attachment at the ages of twelve and eighteen months. Leah Matas, Richard Arend, and Alan Sroufe (1978) presented the two-year-olds with increasingly difficult problems, the last of which—weighting a lever to lift a piece of candy from a plastic box—was far beyond their capacity to solve. Most youngsters who had been judged as securely attached at both earlier assessments attacked the problems with an enthusiasm and persistence not generally present among children who had earlier been rated as either ambivalent or avoidant in their attachments. When they reached the insoluble problem, securely attached children were less likely to throw tantrums and more likely to accept help from their mothers than were the children with insecure attachments.

Differences in maternal behavior were just as pronounced. When their two-year-olds faced the difficult problem, mothers of securely attached children generally offered small hints that allowed the children to feel they had solved the problem themselves. Mothers of insecurely attached children, on the other hand, tended to allow their toddlers to become frustrated before they offered help, and then the mothers often solved the problem themselves.

In another study, children who had been rated on the quality of their attachments at fifteen months were observed in a nursery-school situation at three and a half years (Waters, Wippman, and Sroufe, 1979). The preschoolers who had been rated as having secure attachments were less hesitant and withdrawn than the insecurely attached children. They were also more likely to be leaders, to suggest play activities, to have their company sought by other children, and to be sympathetic to the distress of others. Striking differences in personal competence and other aspects of personality related to self-concept also appeared among the toddlers. Those who had been securely attached were more self-directed, displayed greater curiosity about new things, showed greater enjoyment in learning new skills, pursued their goals more forcefully, and were less likely to behave in a turned-off, "spaced-out" manner than were the insecurely attached children.

Yet earlier we saw that the quality of the attachment bond is related to family circumstances, and often changes. It is important to note that the children in both studies lived in stable, middle-class environments where both parents were present in the home, although both findings have recently been replicated with children from low-income families (Pastor, 1981; Sroufe, 1983). The attachment relationship may predict later behavior only for infants in stable environments (Lamb et al., 1984). If so, these findings may be reflecting a continuous pattern of parent-child interaction instead of the long-term effects of a bond established earlier. Similar studies of children whose parents are divorced or who live in families that have moved frequently or faced sporadic unemployment would probably uncover quite different patterns of personality, showing different degrees of continuity. As we shall see, early experiences do not irrevocably determine the course of a child's development.

EARLY EXPERIENCE

The notion that early experience is of primary importance for later life was popularized by Sigmund Freud (1917). His idea that certain experiences during infancy are crucial for personality development has been adopted by many developmental psychologists whose theoretical outlooks are otherwise quite different.

Types of Effects

Much of the evidence demonstrating the effects of early experience comes from studies of animals. Severe restriction or deprivation of experience in early infancy has striking effects on behavior in animals, and much of this behavior seems to persist into adulthood. These deprived animals are often quite different from normal animals in both social and emotional development. For example, puppies who spent their first few months in isolation from other puppies and from human beings showed "bizarre postures and a tendency to be unresponsive to playthings, people, and other puppies" (J. Scott, 1967). A less extremely deprived puppy will behave more normally but may have an intense fear of strange people and strange situations. Chimpanzees reared in a restricted environment also are more timid, especially in novel situations (Menzel, Davenport, and Rogers, 1963).

If impoverishment of the early environment can have such strong effects, we might expect that an enriched early environment would also have a major impact on animals. A variety of evidence suggests that this is so. Whereas restriction often produces fearful animals, extra stimulation at an early age often produces animals that are bolder than normal (Denenberg, 1966), even when the extra stimulation consists of mild electric shocks. In addition to being bold, animals raised in enriched early environments also tend to be curious in new situations (Forgus, 1954). Such evidence indicates that in some species, early experiences have important and enduring effects on the way animals respond to the world.

Limits on Effects

Although early learning can have pervasive effects on later development, some research suggests that the connection is more complicated than it appears. Early experiences of rodents, for example, do not necessarily determine the animals' later behavior, because later experiences modify the effects of earlier ones (Denenberg, 1984). As we saw in Chapter 2, determinants of development continually interact. A brief look at imprinting in animals and at the ability of human children to overcome what appear to be early disasters indicates that there are strong constraints on the effects of early experience.

SENSITIVE PERIODS Many animals form strong, long-lasting social attachments, but research has led some investigators to conclude that such attachments can form only during a sharply restricted period of life, called a **sensitive period.** In some species of birds, this attachment, called **imprinting,** forms when a baby

bird, fresh from the shell, sees and follows a moving object. In the normal course of events, the first thing a baby bird sees is its mother, so that the bird becomes imprinted on her; but birds also have become imprinted on human beings, rubber balls, and other objects. A bird overcomes substantial obstacles in order to follow this object (or others like it) and shows great distress when the object is out of sight (E. Hess, 1964). A young bird will try to feed the object on which it is imprinted and may even use it as a model for a suitable mate (an effect that has introduced complications into the lives of certain ethologists). But imprinting occurs only during a sensitive period shortly after the animal's birth, and the attachment can be changed. Ducklings that were imprinted on human beings have changed their attachment to mature ducks (E. Hess, 1972), and a young monkey's attachment, which supposedly develops only within the first few months of life, was changed from another monkey to a dog, even though the monkey was seven months old when the switch was made (Mason and Kenney, 1974).

Some theorists have suggested that the bond between human babies and their mothers develops in the same way that baby birds or goats or sheep become imprinted on their mothers. If this were true, it would have significant implications for child rearing. But as we saw in Chapter 4, the notion that mothers immediately bond to their babies as herd animals bond to their young has not been substantiated. Human attachment is far more complicated and diverse than animal bonding, which develops in species where it is vital for infant survival (Lamb and Hwang, 1982). For example, herd animals give birth only once a year, and most of these births take place during the same period. Because the newborn animals can move about from birth, bonding is necessary if mothers are to recognize their wandering infants and reject strange infants who try to nurse.

The importance of the imprinting phenomenon lies in two implications: first, that sensitive periods might exist in human beings during which certain kinds of learning, such as lan-

The first moving object these baby geese saw was ethologist Konrad Lorenz. As a result, they became imprinted on him, following Lorenz around as if he were their mother. (Thomas McAvoy/Time-Life Picture Agency, © Time, Inc.)

guage acquisition, must occur if they are to take place at all; and second, that experiences during infancy can have enduring effects on a child's later development, as Freud maintained. As we trace the social development of children, it will become clear that early experiences are important but do not irrevocably determine the way a child develops.

REVERSING EFFECTS In 1953, thirty-eight young refugee children were brought to the United States from various countries, with the majority arriving from Greece and Korea. The children, who ranged in age from five months to ten years, were either foundlings or illegitimate, and most had encountered the terrors of war. None could speak English, and about 20 percent of them showed signs of severe anxiety. Six years later the children were rated by psychologists, who reported that, on the average, they were socially competent, physically healthy, and had above-average IQs. None was having problems with schoolwork, and only two were regarded as clinically disturbed and in need of professional help (Clarke and Clarke, 1979). If the effects of early experience were as irrevocable as some theorists have proposed, most of these children would have had behavioral disorders and been failing in school.

The experience of these children is not especially unusual. The record is full of cases of children who have been isolated, deprived, abused, or abandoned, but who later develop into competent adults. Why do some children overcome such formidable obstacles while others, whose plight seems less severe, do not? When early experiences become strongly predictive of later development, it is usually because the child's environment does not change. Early experiences interact with later ones; instead of being simply the outcome of early experience, the individual's behavior is the result of continuing experience.

The early experiences of the children who were adopted from foreign countries failed to predict their development because their environment underwent a radical change. They were moved from a deprived or threatening environment to an environment that fostered development. They were given good food, adequate health care, good housing, and an above-average adoptive family that provided love, along with intellectual and social stimulation. Such a sweeping change in the environment has been called **ecological intervention** (Bronfenbrenner, 1979b).

When considering the effects of early experiences, we need to keep in mind the fact that an infant or child is not always open to the same learning experiences. Identical experiences may produce different effects, depending on the infant's genetic inheritance, maturational state, cognitive growth, past experiences, individual vulnerability, and present surroundings. As noted earlier, the quality of a child's attachment at twelve months predicts the quality of attachment at eighteen months only if the family circumstances remain stable (Lamb et al., 1984). If early experiences were irreversible, dramatic changes like those seen in the refugee children would not occur.

Similarly, a secure attachment does not protect a child against all future environmental insult, nor does an insecure attachment doom a child to become withdrawn and inept at solving life's problems. Yet it seems clear that a secure attachment gives a child an advantage at the starting line.

SUMMARY

In studying personality development, psychologists have paid special attention to the primary bond between infant and caregiver, known as **attachment.** This early love relationship takes months to develop, and ethologists have suggested that it passes through four stages, so that a baby who is initially comforted by anyone can finally be comforted only by specific attachment figures. The basic function of attachment is to keep the baby alive, but attachment is thought to be an expression of only one of four complementary behavioral systems, which are expressed in attachment, fear or wariness, affiliation, and exploration. As the infant develops a primary attachment, **separation distress** and wariness of strangers also appear.

The attachment bond differs in quality, with securely attached babies actively seeking out their mothers after a separation and being quickly comforted by them. Insecurely attached babies may shun contact with their mothers or else may be ambivalent, alternating between seeking contact and angrily squirming away. Exactly what determines the quality of attachment is not known, but the mother's responsiveness to her infant's needs and the amount of stimulation she provides may be important. The quality of the bond also seems related to family circumstances, with changes in the infant-caregiver relationship followed by changes in the nature of attachment.

Infants also become attached to other caregivers, and their attachment to their fathers may serve needs not met in the infant-mother relationship. Some babies have several caregivers, but as long as the relationships are stable, babies thrive and attachment develops along the same course seen among babies with a single caregiver.

Social class and culture affect the attitudes and behavior of primary caregivers. Consistent class differences appear in the way American mothers soothe and interact with their infants. Studies in Germany, Israel, and Japan indicate that behavior considered typical of a secure attachment in the United States may be partially a reflection of cultural expectations, and that some babies who might be rated "insecure" are actually developing independence early.

The infant's self-concept develops gradually, and toward the end of the second year most babies can recognize their images in a mirror. Yet how soon biographical self-awareness develops is not known. As they become motivated by a desire for competence, infants generally need less physical contact with their parents. The two-year-old's negativistic behavior represents a concentrated push for **autonomy.** Very young infants probably feel a rudimentary form of most emotions; however, emotional experiences change with development as cognitive, perceptual, and social influences shape the interpretation of each emotion.

Later personality may be affected by the quality of the attachment bond, with secure attachments leading to competence and independence among toddlers. However, this predictable relationship may hold true only for children in middle-class, stable environments.

Although early experience can have pervasive and enduring effects on later development, research indicates that there are strong constraints on the effects of early experience. These constraints may include **sensitive periods** in development, as well as maturational state, cognitive growth, and previous experiences. Predictions from early experience are likely to be valid only when environment remains stable, and with **ecological intervention,** even severely negative early experiences can often be reversed.

CHAPTER THIRTEEN

The Child Within the Family

THE PROCESS OF SOCIALIZATION
PARENTS
Style of Discipline
Disciplinary Techniques
Predicting the Outcome
SIBLINGS
THE CHANGING AMERICAN FAMILY
Day Care
When Mother Works
Increased Paternal Involvement
Father's Absence
Mother's Absence
Marital Discord and Divorce
Class and Cultural Differences
Black American Families
PHYSICAL CHILD ABUSE
The Abusing Parent
The Abused Child
Socioeconomic Stress
The Persistence of Abuse
SUMMARY

Three-year-old Jennifer pushed a chair to the kitchen cabinet, quietly climbed to the Formica counter, and stood on her tiptoes, stretching her hand up, up, toward the clock that hung on the wall. There was no crystal over the dial and her small fingers could just reach the hands. She was industriously pushing the minute hand around the dial when her mother entered the room. "Jennifer," said her mother, "just what are you doing?" Jennifer looked over her shoulder, slowly lowered her hand and said, "You should watch me." In three years, Jennifer had clearly built up a set of expectations—not only as to what was permitted but also as to the proper role for parent and child. She had also learned that a response that made her mother laugh was likely to eliminate— or at least ameliorate—any possible punishment.

In this chapter, we trace the development of the child within the family, exploring how children like Jennifer develop expectations about their families and the world. We examine the role of the family in socialization, the ways in which various styles of discipline affect children, and the influence of brothers and sisters on the growing child. The increasing participation of mothers in the labor force leads us to consider the effects of maternal employment and day care on the developing child, and the high divorce rate makes it important to explore the effects of a father's or mother's absence from the home, comparing it with the influence of marital discord. We also look at the powerful effect social class has on child-rearing practices and at the stresses and strengths typical of black American families. We close the chapter with a consideration of failed rearing in the form of child abuse, discussing the part that parents, children, and society play in this serious problem.

THE PROCESS OF SOCIALIZATION

The process of absorbing the attitudes, values, and customs of a society is called **socialization.** Slowly, the growing child is pressured to behave in approved ways and to conform to cultural standards. During the first few years of life, the family is the major agent of socialization. By encouraging appropriate behavior and discouraging behavior that is socially unacceptable, parents transmit the culture to their offspring. The family's power is considerable. Children depend on their parents for material wants: food, clothing, shelter, and other physical necessities. They also depend on them for attention, affection, physical contact, and play. Because the manner in which parents fulfill children's physical and psychological needs affects children's behavior, parental control exerts a strong influence on the kind of person a child becomes.

But parents are not the only agents of socialization. From the very beginning, television brings the wider world into the home, reinforcing or negating parental influence. Brothers and sisters also play an important role in early socialization, and as we shall see in the next chapter, once children start school the effect of parents and siblings is modified by peers, teachers, and other adults. In addition, children's appear-

Serving as playmate, teacher, and auxiliary caregiver, older siblings take an active role in the socialization of younger brothers and sisters. (Peter Menzel)

ance, health, and temperament will affect not only how they respond to others but also how others approach them. Socialization, like other aspects of development, grows out of the interaction of many influences.

The socialization process differs across cultures, but many psychologists believe that four basic mechanisms operate in all children in all cultures. These mechanisms are: (1) the desire to obtain acceptance, affection, regard, and recognition; (2) the wish to avoid the unpleasant feelings that follow rejection or punishment; (3) the tendency to imitate the actions of others; and (4) the desire to be like specific people whom the child has grown to respect, admire, or love (identification).

PARENTS

As babies approach the end of infancy, the role of parents changes. Instead of playing with them and attending to their needs, parents begin to demand that their children do certain things and refrain from doing others. By now, children's increasing mobility and sureness, their burgeoning mental powers, and their growing grasp of language make it possible for them to understand parental instructions and to follow parental suggestions. These new abilities also make it possible for children to refuse parental demands. The way the conflict between children's wishes and those of their parents is resolved has a profound effect on the behavior and personality of the growing child.

Style of Discipline

Few parents set out deliberately to "socialize" their toddlers; instead, their first demands and restrictions are aimed at making family life possible. Parents attempt to instill a sense of responsibility in their children in order to guard them from danger, to protect belongings from destruction, and to teach them to fit into family routines (Sears, Maccoby, and Levin, 1957). The way parents teach their children to stay out of the street, to refrain from scribbling on walls, and to eat with a fork instead of their fingers will in part depend on their attitude toward children. If they believe that children are full of dark urges that must be stamped out, they will use harsh, authoritarian measures of control. If, on the other hand, they believe that children are naturally good—perfect little buds that will unfold to form beautiful blossoms—they will abdicate attempts at discipline, allowing their child freedom for self-actualization. In truth, few parents are as extreme as either of these two examples would indicate, but styles of discipline do fall along that continuum.

No matter what approach parents take, they establish and maintain discipline by a system of rewards and punishment. In addition, parents serve as models of acceptable behavior. But despite years of study, psychologists' search for the most successful combination of disciplinary techniques has not resulted in the discovery of a foolproof method of socialization.

After reviewing a number of studies on child rearing, Eleanor Maccoby and John Martin (1983) suggested that most parents can be characterized by how demanding and how responsive they are. Demanding parents exert a good deal of control over their children; undemanding parents let children do pretty much as they please. Responsive parents tend to accept their children and to see their children's needs as primary; unresponsive parents tend to reject their children and to see their own needs as primary.

These parental characteristics were found to be extremely important by Diana Baumrind (e.g., 1968, 1972) and her associates, who have spent more than twenty years studying disciplinary styles among parents of preschool children in an attempt to discover the connection between the way children are reared and their personalities. The investigators gathered information on parents from lengthy interviews, standardized tests, and observations in the home. They also watched the children in nursery school and talked to teachers and parents. The styles of most parents, Baumrind found, fit one of four patterns: authoritarian, permissive, noncomformist, or authoritative (Lamb and Baumrind, 1978).

THE AUTHORITARIAN STYLE **Authoritarian** parents are highly demanding, but not very responsive. They stress obedience, and when a child's actions or beliefs conflict with the parent's view of right conduct, the child is punished forcefully. Respect for authority, work, and the preservation of order are important. The child must accept without question the parent's word on matters of right and wrong. As preschoolers, children of such parents tend to be overprotected and dependent. Daughters tend to set low goals for themselves and to withdraw in the face of frustration, whereas sons tend to be hostile.

THE PERMISSIVE STYLE The **permissive** parent tends to be responsive and undemanding, avoiding control and relying on reason and consultations with children about policy decisions. These parents are nonpunitive, accepting, and affirmative, and make few demands for household responsibility and orderly behavior. Children are allowed to regulate their own activities and are not encouraged to obey externally defined standards. Despite this difference in disciplinary style, children of permissive parents resemble children reared by authoritarian parents, and tend to be dependent. Again, daughters set low goals, withdrawing in the face of frustration, and sons tend to be hostile.

Baumrind (Lamb and Baumrind, 1978) speculates that the children of permissive and authoritarian parents turn out similarly because both types of parents tend to shield their children from stress, thereby inhibiting the development of assertiveness and the ability to tolerate frustration. Passive permissiveness on the one hand and overprotectiveness on the other both produce dependent children.

THE NONCONFORMIST STYLE The approach of the **nonconformist** parent shares the opposition to authority that characterizes the permissive parent, but the nonconformist exerts more control than the permissive parent and may demand high performance in selected areas. As preschoolers, daughters of nonconformist parents are like the daughters of permissive and authoritarian parents: dependent children who set low goals for themselves and cope with frustration by withdrawing. The sons, however, are much more independent than sons of permissive and authoritarian parents, and they tend to set high goals for themselves.

THE AUTHORITATIVE STYLE The **authoritative** parent is demanding but accepting. These parents agree that control is necessary but use reason as well as power to achieve it. When directing the child's activities, the authoritative parent uses a rational, issue-oriented method and encourages verbal give-and-take, which the authoritarian parent does not tolerate. As a result, children experience firm control, in which necessary rules are enforced, their own demands are resisted, and they receive guidance. But in addition, their individuality is encouraged, and they have ample opportunity to try out new skills. The aim is responsible conformity to group standards without the loss of independence (Baumrind, 1972). Daughters of authoritative parents tend to be independent and socially responsible; the sons are also socially responsible, but no more independent than average. According to Baumrind, the children's social responsibility develops because the parents impose clearly communicated, realistic demands on their children.

THE INDIFFERENT STYLE Maccoby and Martin (1983) have identified another group of **indifferent** parents, who are undemanding and unresponsive. Their involvement with their children is minimal, and these parents try to spend as little time and effort as possible interacting with their children. Such parents are likely to pay little attention to any aspect of the parental role that inconveniences them, such as setting standards concerning aggression or establishing and enforcing rules about homework. The effect of this parental style is not known, although studies suggest that their toddlers and preschoolers may be more demanding, less compliant, and more aggressive than the offspring of involved parents.

Disciplinary Techniques

Most parents, believes Baumrind (Lamb and Baumrind, 1978), want to produce **instrumen-**

tally competent children—children who are "self-assertive, friendly with peers, and not intrusive with adults," showing a combination of social responsibility and independence. In their attempts to produce such children, parents use different disciplinary styles, but all of them implement their styles with similar techniques: punishment, rewards, and modeling.

Regardless of disciplinary style, parents who produce instrumentally competent children punish them often. Parents punish by scolding, social isolation, withholding expected rewards, and the withdrawal of affection. With toddlers, the withdrawal of affection appears to be the most effective disciplinary technique. Although it is rarely used alone, no matter what other technique it bolsters, compliance generally follows (Maccoby and Martin, 1983). Some parents also use physical punishment—including many authoritative parents in Baumrind's studies (who were the most effective at producing instrumental competence). This aspect of authoritative child-rearing may be a cohort effect. The children in Baumrind's original studies were toddlers during the 1950s, when physical punishment was generally accepted and widely practiced. Today's authoritative parents may be less inclined to resort to spankings.

To be effective, any kind of punishment should come immediately after the child's misbehavior, and the child should know exactly why he or she is being punished. If, for example, a three-year-old girl is spanked when her mother catches her smearing fingerprints on the wall, she should be told clearly that the spanking is for disfiguring the wall, not for using her brother's fingerpaints without permission. Discipline should also be consistent; to punish for painting the wall one day and to ignore it the following week only confuses a child.

Again regardless of disciplinary style, punishment from a generally warm parent may be more effective than punishment from a parent who is cold. Baumrind found that warmth, when associated with the firm control of authoritative parents, appears to produce socially

As most parents know, their hugs of approval bolster children's good behavior and serve as an effective disciplinary technique. (Peter Vandermark/Stock, Boston)

responsible children. In a large study of five-year-olds, Robert Sears and his associates (Sears, Maccoby, and Levin, 1957) found that although most mothers rated as "warm" did not use frequent physical punishment, those who did claimed that it worked. Relatively cold mothers who relied on physical punishment were much less likely to say that it was effective. Both studies, then, point to the importance of parental warmth.

Punishment is applied when children misbehave. But children are often good, and parents can support good behavior with reinforcement. Rewards for good behavior need not be tangible. Dimes, cookies, and special treats may be effective, but so are smiles, nods, pats, praise, hugs, or even a certain tone of voice. In the study by Sears and his associates, warm mothers were especially likely to use lots of praise and tangible rewards with their children. However, praise and rewards apparently are most effective when used sparingly. If not, youngsters adapt to the customary level and parents must keep increasing its amount or lavishness to get the same effect. And if children believe they are being manipulated with rewards, the rewards may lose their effectiveness (Maccoby and Martin, 1983).

In addition to rewards and punishment, an extremely powerful influence on children's behavior is what they see their parents do. In Chapter 1, we noted that children imitate models; parents are permanent models for their growing children. They are powerful dispensers of rewards and punishment, and when they are warm and nurturant as well, they are precisely the kind of model that researchers have found to be most effective. Children who have been allowed time to develop a rewarding relationship with an adult model engage in far more imitation than children who have not (Bandura and Huston, 1961). When parents encourage their children's identification with them and approve of their attempts to imitate them, the modeling becomes even more effective. As we shall see in Chapter 15, identification with the parent of the same sex is a factor in children's learning of sex roles; in Chapter 16, we shall examine the role of identification in the development of morality and aggression.

In their investigations of child rearing, both Baumrind and Sears studied young children, with Baumrind concentrating on preschoolers and Sears on five-year-olds. To see if different methods of rearing had lasting effects, both researchers followed up the children they had studied. Baumrind found that by the time her preschoolers were nine years old, the differences in social competence among the groups had narrowed, so that although the distinctions remained, they were not nearly so striking (Baumrind, 1975). When Sears checked up on the children he had studied after a lapse of seven years, he found that twelve-year-old high achievers with high self-concepts generally had warm parents who had used reason and discussion with their young children instead of authoritarian control (Sears, 1970). These parents were also likely to discipline their children by using social isolation or withholding expected rewards, rather than by spanking or the withdrawal of their love. However, the high-achieving girls—but not the boys—tended to have permissive mothers, a finding that contradicts the results among Baumrind's preschoolers.

In a longitudinal study of Finnish children, an authoritative parental style was found to be clearly the most effective (Pulkkinen, 1982). Parents who used this style had established child-centered homes: they were highly involved with their children, demanding but democratic, and rarely used physical punishment. Six years after the study started, when the children were fourteen, they were judged to be generally responsible, socially competent, achievement-oriented, and had good relationships with their parents. In contrast, children from parent-centered homes, whether parents were authoritarian or indifferent, tended to be impulsive, uninterested in school, and to begin drinking, smoking, and dating at earlier ages.

Predicting the Outcome

Placing the results of long-term studies side by side shows how difficult it is to single out the precise parental traits that lead to competent children and then write a prescription for successful child rearing. Perhaps as children develop, they require different sorts of responses from their parents, so that the kind of parental behavior that encourages competence at eight months would not encourage its development at three years. If we look again at infants who are developing attachments, we find that neither warmth nor firmness nor permissiveness but sensitivity may be the single most important factor in producing a secure bond. To be sensitive to a baby's needs, a parent must be able

Warm, authoritative parents, who discuss the effects of a misdeed with their children and explain any punishment, seem to have found the most effective style of discipline. (Christy Park/Monkmeyer)

to interpret the baby's signals and respond effectively.

PARENTAL BEHAVIOR Perhaps sensitive parents behave differently with their children over the course of childhood. If preschoolers are to become socially competent, for example, the last thing they need is to have every desire met. In the studies of toddlers, we saw that sensitive mothers who responded quickly to their babies' needs encouraged their two-year-olds to solve problems by themselves (Matas, Arend, and Sroufe, 1978; Bates, Maslin, and Frankel, 1985). It was the mothers of insecurely attached babies who stepped in and solved their toddlers' problems. This indicates that parental sensitivity probably consists not in instant responsiveness but in empathic understanding of a child's needs. If that is the case, then parental behavior would change as the child developed; empathic parents would understand when their children

needed guidance and when they should be allowed to strike out on their own (Lamb, 1981a).

In a longitudinal study of California children (Roberts, Block, and Block, 1984), researchers found that many parental attitudes and practices were consistent over a nine-year period. Parents who had strict rules for their three-year-olds had strict rules when the children were twelve. However, as children grew older, parents put much heavier emphasis on achievement and independence and were much less likely to show physical affection for their children. Parents also switched from physical punishment or isolating a naughty child to the withdrawal of privileges, and now believed that praise was more effective than punishment. Many parents, it seems, are responsive to their child's cognitive and social development, changing their methods to correspond with their child's relative maturity.

Another important factor may be continuity in caregiving arrangements. As we saw in Chapter 12, when family circumstances lead to changes in the relationship between infant and caregiver, the nature of the attachment bond changes (Lamb et al., 1984). Divorce, marital discord, sporadic losses of employment by either parent, or a mother's unwilling entry into the labor force—any kind of stress—may be followed by changes in child-rearing practices. When under stress, mothers of preschoolers become more likely to use physical punishment, more likely to respond negatively to their youngsters in play situations or when teaching them some task, and less likely to dispense praise or other rewards (Feshbach, in press). In some cases, a parent's preoccupation with solving a personal problem provides enough stress to change the way he or she interacts with a preschooler (Maccoby and Martin, 1983).

THE CHILD'S TEMPERAMENT Yet no matter how empathic, consistent, and reasonable parents are, there is no guarantee that their methods will produce a socially competent child. A child's personality results from an interaction between his or her own temperament, parental style and personality, and influences from the rest of the culture, which become progressively stronger after the child starts school. When studying rhesus monkeys, Stephen Suomi (1983) found that those with fearful or anxious temperaments tended to be at a disadvantage if their mothers were punitive or if the social environment of the group was unstable. As adults, they were chronically anxious and fearful. However, a fearful, anxious monkey whose mother was competent and sensitive and whose social environment was stable and supportive became an adult who could not be distinguished from monkeys who showed little fear or anxiety as infants. Similar interactions between a child's temperament and parental or social influences may well affect human development.

The methods a parent uses may be a response to the child's temperament, not a cause of it. "Difficult" toddlers may not get into trouble more than other youngsters, but once they begin to misbehave they are more persistent and less likely to pay attention to their parents' prohibitions and warnings. Their parents respond by saying "no" often, stepping up their warnings, taking things away from the youngsters, and exerting power directly (Maccoby and Martin, 1983). One study that followed children from birth found that difficult children were more likely than others to develop behavior problems, but that such problems were most likely to develop when children's temperaments did not match their parents' styles. The goodness-of-fit between a child's temperament and a parent's style may also change. When a youngster begins school, characteristics that were in harmony with a toddler's home environment may no longer fit parental demands and expectations, placing the child under heavy stress (Thomas and Chess, 1981).

As noted earlier, the best that psychologists can do in describing the effects of various child-rearing techniques is to point out what patterns of parental behavior are connected with what characteristics in children. They cannot, however, establish any sort of cause-effect relationship.

SIBLINGS

Until many children start school, their brothers and sisters are their primary, if not their sole, playmates, and even afterward their interaction with siblings remains high. This steady companionship probably plays a major role in children's socialization, for the patterns of interaction that develop are likely to affect their expectations about people outside the home and their interactions with them.

Whether a child is surrounded by siblings of the same or opposite sex or has one or many siblings may have a profound influence on personality development. The birth of a second child changes family roles. The first-born child is no longer "baby," the focus of parental concern and attention. For the first time, the youngster is interacting with a human being who is not only unconcerned with the child's wants or needs, but is helpless as well. Little wonder that among forty working-class youngsters studied by Judy Dunn and Carol Kendrick (1982), almost every child was disturbed and unhappy when a new baby arrived in the family. The children, who were between eighteen months and forty-three months old, were also interested in their new sibling and most showed affection for the baby, but they clearly had trouble getting used to a shrinking share of parental attention. Most began demanding attention from their mother, misbehaved, and were especially jealous when their father played with the baby. But the birth spurred most youngsters to new shows of independence. Many began insisting on dressing or feeding themselves, going to the toilet alone, and played by themselves for longer intervals.

Children showed wide differences in the way they accommodated the new family member. Some were friendly and affectionate in 94 percent of their approaches to the baby; others were

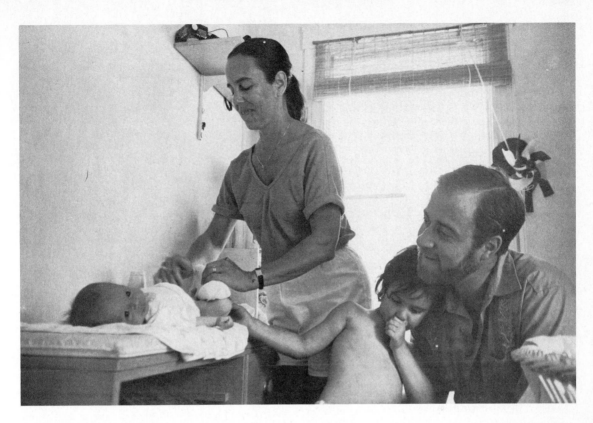

The arrival of a new sister or brother is usually a distressing time for a youngster, no matter how affectionately the older child greets the baby. (Randy Matusow/Monkmeyer)

hostile on every single approach. After fourteen months, those with the friendliest relationships had mothers who talked about the baby as a person during the very first weeks, explaining the baby's needs, discussing the care with the older child, and encouraging the older child to help. Other factors that contributed to later friendly sibling relations were an initial positive reaction by the older child and the children's gender—siblings of the same sex were much more congenial than siblings of different sexes. These factors interacted, so when more than one was present, the chances of siblings becoming friends increased markedly. Age differences be-

tween the siblings had no effect on the relationship that developed.

Siblings clearly play an important part in one another's social lives. When preschoolers were observed at play with their eighteen-month-old siblings, the youngsters tussled over toys and teased and threatened each other, but they also shared toys, helped, hugged, and comforted each other, and indicated their approval (Abramovitch, Pepler, and Corter, 1982). The youngsters also imitated their siblings; most of the imitation was done by the eighteen-month-olds, but the older children sometimes imitated their younger siblings, banging play dough on the table, blowing cake crumbs, or dancing around in imitation of the infants. When these pairs were again observed after a lapse of eighteen months, the overall pattern of interaction remained the same, although the boys—who had done more hitting, kicking, biting, and pinching during the first study—now showed no more physical aggression than the girls, and all children shared and cooperated more. In other studies, babies seemed to have learned from older brothers and sisters that force was not always effective. Toddlers with older siblings were less likely than only children to grab toys from peers and squabble with them (Easterbrooks and Lamb, 1979).

A thread of aggression has run through all studies of younger siblings. Fights between siblings seem to be typical of American families. In a national survey, 82 percent of the children between three and seventeen years old had taken some kind of violent action against a sibling in the previous year (Straus, Gelles, and Steinmetz, 1980). Most pushed, slapped, shoved, or threw things, but 42 percent also kicked, bit, or punched a sibling. Aggressive acts went down over the years, from 90 percent among preschoolers to 64 percent among teenagers, and the rate of violent acts was consistently higher in all-boy families.

Are sibling quarrels a sign of deep sibling rivalries? In most cases, probably not. Studies of younger children indicate that sibling rivalry is not a dominant feature of their relationships (Lamb, 1978a; 1978b). However, many children in middle childhood are ambivalent about their siblings, and when they perceive that parents are meeting the needs of one sibling and not the other, each child is likely to harbor ill will toward the other (Bryant, 1982). In their relationships, siblings develop social skills they will need in other situations. They learn to give help and to accept it; they find ways to settle differences. Younger siblings may have to learn to negotiate, to accommodate, and to lose gracefully in order to get along with their older, more powerful brothers and sisters.

In many societies, older siblings are responsible for much of the caregiving, once a younger sibling is a year or so old (Weisner, 1982). In these societies, children learn to be both charge and caretaker, with a six-year-old watched by an older sibling but also taking some responsibility for the care of a younger sibling. Such

These siblings will help each other develop social skills that they will need to get along with people outside the family. (Suzanne Szasz)

arrangements are believed to make siblings interdependent, peer-oriented, and perhaps slower to learn adult understandings of various social norms, simply because they are not exposed to them. As children become adults in these societies, the interdependence continues, so that brothers and sisters remain closely involved in one another's lives. This pattern differs from the American pattern, in which sibling relationships generally take on less importance as children grow up and leave home, although many retain close ties throughout life (Cicirelli, 1982; Ross and Milgram, 1982).

THE CHANGING AMERICAN FAMILY

Most research on personality development has focused on children in intact, white, middle-class families in which the father is the primary breadwinner. Such families, although they may conform to an American ideal, are now a minority in this society. Children from varied ethnic groups and social classes live in a variety of family arrangements. A majority of mothers are employed, and an increasing number of fathers are involved with the care of their young children. Some children live with one parent, some have stepparents, some spend most of their waking hours in day care, some live amid continual marital conflict, and some are reared in nontraditional families. All these variations on the familiar theme provide experiences for the growing child that can affect the socialization process.

Day Care

A child in day care is both separated from primary caregivers for most of the day and subjected to the influence of many peers and substitute caregivers. It seems logical to assume that these circumstances influence the socialization process in some way.

The number of children in day care is growing, and the proportion of children under two that are enrolled is increasing at a rapid rate. In 1978, 2.5 million infants and toddlers, 3.7 million preschoolers, and 4.9 million schoolchildren spent a considerable portion of their day in some form of substitute care (Belsky, Steinberg, and Walker, 1982). Most of these children are not in day-care centers. Nursery schools and day-care centers together account for only 15 percent of the children in full-time substitute care. The best government estimates indicate that 29 percent of children whose mothers work all day are cared for by a babysitter in their own homes and another 47 percent are taken to someone else's home (Scarr, 1984). We are just beginning to find out about the quality and effects of these kinds of care.

In a six-year study of children in Bermuda, where 90 percent are in substitute care by the time they are two years old, Sandra Scarr and her colleagues (Scarr and Hall, 1984) found that the intellectual and emotional development of youngsters who spent their first two years in day-care homes or with babysitters was like that of youngsters who spent their first two years at home with their mothers. However, children who were placed in day-care centers before they

were two years old tended to be slower intellectually, less cooperative, and more aggressive than children who entered day-care after their second birthday. The researchers attribute this difference primarily to the ratio in centers of one adult to eight children, which apparently is adequate for toddlers but may not give infants the sort of attention they need. Children who were placed in day-care centers at the age of three or four did better than those who remained at home with their mothers, and those who were fortunate enough to be placed in a structured day-care center, with planned educational activities, did best of all on social and intellectual measures.

This sort of longitudinal study, which followed virtually the entire population of Bermudan children until they were eight years old, may give us a better view of day care's effects than most research. Most comparisons of American children in day care with those who are reared at home are generally invalid because parents who put their children in day care and parents who do not usually differ in their attitudes—toward day care, toward the maternal role, perhaps even toward children themselves. Finally, most research has consisted of testing children—usually in laboratories. Few researchers have explored the possible effects of day care on the family as a whole.

Bearing these limitations in mind, Jay Belsky, Laurence Steinberg, and Ann Walker (1982) reviewed American day-care research and concluded that it is impossible to judge the effects of day care on the basis of the scant evidence that is available. In addition to possible differences between the parents of children at home and those placed in day care, most studies probably do not reflect the effect of typical day-care centers. As noted in Chapter 12, research has been confined largely to high-quality care in centers connected with universities, where the daily program is designed to foster cognitive, emotional, and social development.

When only high-quality day care is considered, there appear to be no lasting effects—good or bad—on the cognitive development of most children. Even the intellectual gains stimulated by the highly enriched curricula generally seem to vanish soon after a child leaves the program. Disadvantaged children, however, do appear to profit from these programs, as the discussion in Chapter 11 indicated. Such children do not show the decline in IQ that generally appears among poor preschool children.

In most cases, children's emotional development does not seem to suffer as a result of day-care experience, and there appear to be no long-range effects on the mother-child relationship. In the area of socialization, day care appears to have both positive and negative effects. Children in day care seem to get along with their peers better than home-reared children do, and they are more socially competent and cooperative with unfamiliar children than either children in day-care homes or those who remain with their mothers. In some cases children in day care are more aggressive and impulsive than other children, being more hostile as kindergartners and less cooperative with adults (Belsky, Steinberg, and Walker, 1982; Clarke-Stewart and Fein, 1983). However, children in day care who refuse to comply with some parental demands are also more helpful and comforting to their mothers and cooperate better with them when playing games (Clarke-Stewart and Fein, 1983). Such results seem to be program-specific, report Belsky and his colleagues (1982), and are most likely to appear when caregivers adopt a permissive child-rearing style.

The superior social competence of children in day-care programs is still apparent among children in the first few years of elementary school. Because the gap generally lessens with time, some researchers (Clarke-Stewart and Fein, 1983) believe that it is partly the result of accelerated development, although there may be some permanent enhancement of social skills.

Researchers agree that children in day care suffer when each adult is responsible for too many youngsters. Some suggest that an adult should care for no more than three infants or toddlers (Kagan, Kearsley, and Zelazo, 1978) or six preschoolers (Clarke-Stewart, 1982), but in one survey of day-care centers, the average number of children per staff member was 3.9 for infants under seventeen months and 5.9 for toddlers from eighteen to twenty-four months (Connell, Layzer, and Goodson, 1979). In fact, some licensed day-care centers had as many as ten infants or fourteen toddlers assigned to each caregiver. Few researchers have examined the effects of day care under such conditions.

Most studies have focused on the children themselves, but the change in routine that follows when an infant or preschooler is removed from the home for a good part of the child's waking hours undoubtedly has some effects on family life. Research is scanty, but it appears that when day care frees a parent who finds full-time child care dissatisfying or when it enables a family to have a more comfortable life through a second income, the marital relationship will improve (Belsky, Steinberg, and Walker, 1982). When this happens, children also benefit. And by affecting the behavior of the children, day care may improve the parent-child relationship. Bouts of play between three-year-olds in day care and their mothers lasted twice as long as bouts of play between home-reared youngsters and their mothers, and the children in day care made more active attempts to influence their mother's behavior (Farran and Haskins, 1980). Day-care experience also seems to change parental attitudes, for when two groups of mothers were compared, those whose kindergartners had been in day care since infancy felt they had more power to influence the school and were more likely to say that parents had some teaching responsibilities and that the future was more important than the present, than mothers of home-reared kindergartners (Ramey, Dorval, and Baker-Ward, 1981). Such attitudes are likely to affect parents' participation in their children's school experience and the expectations they hold for their children.

When Mother Works

Traditionalists have warned that the movement of mothers into the labor force threatens the foundation of the family; others have been equally loud in claims that a mother's employment has no effect on the growing child. Research indicates there is no clear answer.

Employed mothers of preschoolers obviously spend less time with their children than do mothers who are at home, but the quality of the time together differs. Employed mothers, especially those with high levels of education, appear to make a special effort to compensate for their absence, so that the time with their children often includes direct or intense interaction (Hoffman, 1984). During much of the time preschoolers share with their homebound mothers, the mothers are doing household chores, watching television, or eating.

Whether a mother's job has benign or harmful influences on her child's socialization depends on the interaction of other factors: the nature of child care for infants and preschoolers, social class, whether the mother works steadily or sporadically, how she feels about her job, and the father's involvement with his children. One of the strongest influences is the mother's satisfaction, a factor that seems so important that some researchers have speculated that a child is probably better off with an employed mother who is satisfied than with a dissatisfied mother who is at home all day but yearns to be working (Scarr and Hall, 1984). Some studies have found insecure attachment among infants whose mothers were employed, yet this effect seems to be linked with a mother's attitudes, values, and circumstances (Lamb, 1982). We might speculate that a mother who is committed to her vocation, who enjoys her job, who does not feel guilty about working, and whose husband supports her decision to work is likely to have a securely attached infant. Insecure attachments are more likely to develop when a mother is forced to work by economic circumstances and dislikes her job, and when her husband also believes that a mother's place is in the home and the father should provide for the family. Since working-class parents tend to be more conservative in their views of the family, such dissatisfaction is most likely to be found among the working class, where many men believe that a

wife's employment signals a husband's failure to provide.

Class differences appeared when Dolores Gold and David Andres (1978) studied more than two hundred ten-year-old children, half of whose mothers had worked steadily since their offspring entered elementary school. Children of employed mothers were less bound by sex-role stereotypes than children of mothers who did not work. The effect was strongest among girls and weakest among working-class boys, although even they were less stereotypical in their views than working-class boys whose mothers did not work.

In general, children's psychological adjustment was not affected by their mothers' employment. As groups, children of employed and unemployed mothers did not differ. Any problems that did appear were limited to boys. More working- than middle-class fathers whose wives worked reported problems with their sons' behavior in school; these fathers rarely described their sons as cooperative or ambitious. Middle-class sons of working mothers were generally described as confident. Among children of employed mothers, relations between working-class fathers and sons seemed strained, and the boys respected their fathers less.

A number of studies have found that girls generally benefit intellectually when their mothers are employed but that boys sometimes suffer. In an attempt to discover why this should be so, Urie Bronfenbrenner, William Alvarez, and Charles Henderson (1984) studied more than one hundred fifty families with three-year-old children. They discovered that the mother's employment and education affected the way both parents perceived their child. When the mother was employed and had at least some college education, both parents had highly favorable views of their daughter. The more hours the mother worked, the more favorably the daughter was perceived. But in a similar situation, both parents tended to have unfavorable views of their sons. The researchers suggest that this effect arises because boys, who tend to have higher levels of activity and aggression, require more supervision and parental control than girls.

The more hours a mother works, the less time she has to supervise her children. Once such parental perceptions are established, they affect the way parents treat the child. Thus they could have indirect effects on children's behavior. For example, when parents see a three-year-old daughter as lovable and helpful, but a three-year-old son as "ornery," their treatment of the child may lead him or her to respond in ways that match the label.

No matter whether they are boys or girls, children of employed mothers are generally more independent and have more responsibilities than children of mothers who stay at home. Such responsibilities may help to increase self-esteem in a society where children may feel they are "not needed."

Increased Paternal Involvement

Along with the entry of mothers into the labor force has come pressure for increased paternal involvement in home and family. Whether many fathers have responded is doubtful. Although studies have shown a general trend for fathers in families with two employed parents to be relatively more involved in child rearing and household chores than fathers in families where they are the sole wage earners (Hoffman, 1983), the change usually means that mothers are doing less, so that the proportion of fathers' involvement in the total rises (Lamb, Pleck, Charnov, and Levine, in press). The children are often in some form of child care, and working mothers tend to cook simpler meals, use clothes that need no ironing, and adopt other shortcuts in household chores.

The effects of increased paternal involvement on the developing child are uncertain, and it remains an area that few researchers have explored. As we saw in Chapter 12, fathers have a much more important influence on infant development than was once assumed, and any in-

crease in their participation is likely to be followed by shifts in the roles of all family members. In addition to possible direct influences on the child, there may also be indirect influences arising from effects on the mother and on the marital relationship.

It is probable that when fathers become involved in child care and household responsibilities, children will develop more flexible ideas about appropriate male and female roles and attitudes, learning that a man can be nurturant as well as powerful. From preliminary studies (Sagi, 1982), it seems possible that children with highly involved fathers will show increased empathy with others, increased cognitive skills, increased independence and motivation to achieve, and a belief that they can control their own lives. The relationship between fathers and children may become closer, and fathers' enjoyment in their children may deepen (Russell and Radin, 1983).

Because satisfied parents tend to have well-adjusted children, the way mothers and fathers feel about increased paternal involvement will probably have a greater effect than any actual increase in responsibility (Lamb, Pleck, and Levine, 1985). The possible benefits of paternal involvement are likely to appear only when parents agree about the division of responsibility, when there is relatively little conflict in the marital relationship, and when parents' values concerning the family and sex roles coincide. When either father or mother are ambivalent about the father's involvement, the resulting dissatisfaction may create an atmosphere that does more harm than good.

Father's Absence

Although the lengthening life span means that fewer parents are lost by death, the increased divorce rate and the growing number of unwed mothers has led to more and more children being reared in single-parent homes. As a result, their early socialization escapes much of the influence of the missing parent's gender. In this century, custody has almost always been given to the mother, so that research has focused on the consequences of life without father.

Differences regularly turn up between groups of children who have fathers and those who do not, but how much of the discrepancy is due to the father's absence and how much to other factors is unknown. Perhaps child rearing goes more smoothly when there are two parents to share the task. If so, any effects may be the result of one person trying to do a two-person job. Perhaps the presence of a male model is essential for children's social, emotional, or cognitive development, indicating that it is the lack of masculine influence that is most important (Lamb, in press). Perhaps the causes are economic; the father's absence removes the major breadwinner and produces financial hardship. Perhaps it is not the absence of a father at all, but the emotional stress caused by the circumstances of the divorce. Or, most likely, all of these factors may contribute to the effects that have been found.

The area of most intensive study has been sex-role development. Although many factors affect the child's developing sex role, experimenters have been concerned that a growing boy's masculinity or girl's femininity might be impaired by an absent father. A study that looked only at first-born, lower-class boys—both black and white—indicated that the permanent loss of a father after a boy was six years old had little effect on his independence, his dependency on adults, his aggression, or his sex-role preference (Hetherington, 1966). But boys who lost their fathers before they were four were not aggressive and tended to get feminine scores on a sex-role test. They also liked nonphysical, noncompetitive activities (reading, working puzzles, watching television, collecting things) and preferred checkers, cards, or Monopoly to physical sports. A subsequent review of the effects of father absence agreed that early father absence appears to slow—but not prevent—the acquisition of characteristics that typify the masculine role (Biller, 1981). By the time

When no father is present during their early years, boys seem to take longer to develop the male sex role. (Joel Gordon)

boys are adolescents, there is little difference in sex-role development between fatherless boys and boys whose fathers have always been present. Yet in late adolescence, men who grew up without fathers may have difficulty establishing a long-term heterosexual relationship.

Evidence on the effects of a father's absence on a girl's sex-role development is scant. Henry Biller's (1981) review turned up conflicting conclusions. Some studies found that girls are less affected than boys by the absence; others found that girls from broken homes tend to reject the role of wife and mother or have difficulties in achieving satisfactory sexual relationships. It may be that the father's early departure affects girls as it does boys but that the influence does not show until girls reach adolescence. Mavis Hetherington (1972) found that working-class adolescent girls who had lost their fathers before they were five seemed uncertain about their actions around males. When taking part in an interview, they were either painfully shy (if their fathers had died) or excessively seductive (if their parents had been divorced). But middle-class college women who had lost their fathers before they were five did not show the same inappropriate responses to males (Hainline and Feig, 1978). Either middle-class girls have wider opportunities than working-class girls to learn how to behave with the opposite sex or else practice in socialization during high school helps most girls overcome the problem. We will return to the topic of sex-role development in Chapter 15.

The effect of a father's absence on a child's cognitive development varies, depending on the child's sex and the family's socioeconomic level and ethnic background. Boys' intellectual development and academic performance suffers more than that of girls. Some studies of divorced families that report detrimental effects on children's school performance are carried out shortly after the divorce and may simply be reflecting the immediate impact of a father's departure, not the lasting influence.

After reviewing the research, Norma Radin (1981) concluded that early absence appears to have the deepest effects on cognitive development, as it does on sex-role development. With boys, the damage is heightened if they are younger than five at the time the father leaves, although no signs of difficulty usually appear before the boys are about eight years old. In American groups with Hispanic or Oriental backgrounds, in which the father is extremely powerful, children tend to be most adversely affected.

Socioeconomic level and the effect of a father's absence interact, so that among middle-class and upper-middle-class families, children who grow up without fathers show little cognitive impairment, and in some areas—such as verbal ability—fatherless youngsters may show superior achievement (Radin, 1981). For example, in a study of Harvard students, a father's absence appeared to affect scores in mathematics but not in verbal aptitude (Carlsmith, 1964). When fathers were present throughout boyhood, math scores were generally higher than verbal scores—a typically masculine pattern.

When fathers were absent early—and for a long time—verbal scores tended to be higher than math scores, a typically feminine pattern. The earlier a father stepped out of a boy's life and the longer he was gone, the lower the student's math aptitude score in relation to his verbal score. A late, brief absence, however, was associated with zooming math scores.

Radin (1981) found that among youngsters in black families or those whose families are below the poverty level, the effect of a father's absence on cognitive development is difficult to discern, perhaps because these children already contend with many factors that retard development. The absence of a father appears most detrimental among all children in working-class families and among very bright children in lower-class families.

Some studies find that boys without fathers also run the risk of becoming juvenile delinquents; other studies find no connection. The available figures are simply too confused for us to be able to say with any certainty that children in fatherless homes are more likely than other children to become delinquent. According to Elizabeth Herzog and Celia Sudia (1973), who reviewed the studies, a father's absence is less of a factor in juvenile delinquency than are the climate and tone of the home and the kind of supervision the child receives. They agree that there is probably a greater frequency of delinquent behavior among boys without fathers but contend that the increase is so small as to have little social significance.

Growing up without a father obviously leaves some mark on a child, but no one can say how long the effects last. A myriad of other factors can heighten or ameliorate the impact of the absence. The age of the child at the time of the father's departure, the reason for the departure, the length of the absence, the presence or absence of siblings, whether siblings are younger or older, and of the same or different sex, the presence or absence of a stepfather, the socioeconomic level of the home, the mother's reactions to the father's departure, the ability of the mother to exercise supervision, and community standards—all these factors are inextricably woven together in such a way that makes it impossible to tease out the single strand of socializing influence marked "father's absence."

Mother's Absence

More and more fathers are gaining custody of their children, providing examples of socialization in the absence of a mother. The single-father family, however, has received little attention from psychologists. Although boys are more likely to have problems when the father is absent, one study indicates that girls are more likely to have problems when the mother is gone (Santrock, Warshak, and Elliott, 1982). Among the children in this study of custodial fathers, girls' social development tended to lag. They were less mature, less sociable, and more dependent than boys, a picture that was reversed among children living with their divorced mothers, where the boys' social development suffered.

Sex roles are another area of development where the absence of a mother might be expected to affect development. Unless there is an older sister (or some other woman) with whom she can identify, a girl whose mother is absent will lack a feminine role model. However, in the same study of custodial fathers and their children, researchers (Santrock, Warshak, and Elliott, 1982) noted that the way a father interacted with his daughter had powerful effects on her behavior. When fathers were attentive to their daughters, the girls tended to behave in masculine ways, but when fathers were authoritarian, their daughters tended to behave in a highly feminine manner. In addition, a daughter who is reared by her father may be expected to assume some maternal responsibilities in the family, giving her an opportunity to learn the feminine role (Lamb and Bronson, 1980). She will, as will a son, miss the chance to see suc-

After divorce, boys may do best when their father has custody, but girls' social development may suffer. (Inger McCabe/Rapho-Photo Researchers)

cessful interaction between men and women, but this deficit also characterizes the single-mother household.

Puberty is likely to be a difficult time when a single father rears a daughter. Almost all fathers expect their wives to discuss matters of sexuality and menstruation with daughters, and they are extremely uncomfortable at the prospect of having to assume that responsibility. Girls, therefore, are likely to be without any individual adult counsel and guidance in the area of sexuality, and some evidence indicates that these girls are more likely than others to have an illegitimate pregnancy (Fox, 1978).

On the positive side, single fathers tend to encourage their daughters toward competence and success in careers. In addition, because the father is highly involved with the children, performing the duties that traditionally fall to the mother, both sons and daughters are likely to develop flexible views of masculinity and femininity (Lamb, Pleck, and Levin, in press).

Marital Discord and Divorce

Growing up amid marital strife also affects the socializing process and may be more damaging to children than growing up in a one-parent home. According to Michael Rutter (1981), family discord and disharmony have been strongly linked with delinquency and severe behavior problems in children. Divorce, which often follows a stormy marriage, is also a common factor in the background of delinquent children, but the death of a parent is not. The implication is that the loss of the parent is not so critical, but that discordant, tense relationships may create more stress than some children can handle.

Ending a bad marriage ultimately seems to benefit the children. Following a divorce, children's problems tend to get worse, but two years after a divorce most children have fewer problems than children who continue to live in an atmosphere of marital strife (Hetherington, Cox, and Cox, 1982). In cases where the mother has custody, the effects linger longer with boys than with girls. Within two years, girls are functioning as well as their counterparts in intact families where there is little conflict. Boys, although they are doing better than boys who live with marital discord, are not doing as well as their counterparts in intact families with little conflict. However, when the father has custody, boys seem to adjust better than girls (Santrock, Warshak, and Elliott, 1982).

This difference has led researchers to suggest that most children may do better when living with a parent of the same sex (Santrock, Warshak, and Elliott, 1982). When interviewed, boys who were living with their fathers and girls who were living with their mothers impressed investigators as being more honest than father-custody girls and more appealing than mother-custody boys. These same researchers discovered that, no matter which parent has custody, when children are reared in an authoritative style, they seem to do better in many ways. This parental style, which is marked by parental warmth, clear rules for behavior, and a good deal of verbal give-and-take, seems to increase a child's self-esteem, maturity, sociability, and social conformity, while it apparently decreases a child's level of anger and demands on the parent. By contrast, when the custodial father or mother uses a permissive or authoritarian style, the children tend to be less socially competent. A custodial mother's permissive style was associated with daughters who were warm but angry, demanding, and unsociable. A custodial father's authoritarian style was associated with sons who were anxious, dependent, and socially immature. How strongly a child's own behavior evoked these differing parental styles is of course, impossible to determine. (See the box on p. 422 for the effect of living with a step-parent.)

There is one circumstance in which discord is better for children than divorce (Hetherington, Cox, and Cox, 1982). When intense conflict exists between a child and one parent (but not the other), that child would probably be better off in the conflicted family than in the custody of the parent with whom the child is in conflict. It seems that a good relationship with one parent acts as a protective buffer against the adverse impact of conflict with the other parent.

Among juvenile delinquents, those from intact but strife-ridden homes are much more likely to relapse into delinquency than children from intact homes without serious problems. The influence extends into later life, for people from unhappy homes have a higher-than-average rate of poor marital adjustment and divorce. In addition, boys appear to be more vulnerable than girls to the effects of marital discord, as they are more vulnerable to the effects of divorce. Boys with delinquency and behavior problems are more likely than girls to come from families characterized by marital conflict.

By itself, marital discord is not likely to damage a child. Rutter (1981) points out that studies of general populations show that children in families suffering only from marital discord show no higher rates of psychiatric disorders than children who live in harmonious families. But if another stress (such as unemployment or imprisonment of a parent) is added to the discord, the risk of a child from a strife-ridden home developing some psychiatric disorder is four times as great.

Class and Cultural Differences

Differences in social class and ethnic group within a single society, as well as differences among cultures, further complicate attempts to make concise statements about the way the family socializes the growing child. The values and life styles of families in various subcultures differ, as do their resources and financial security. As a result, families live in such different worlds that, as Melvin Kohn (1979) has said, they develop "different conceptions of social reality, different aspirations and hopes and fears, different conceptions of the desirable." And what parents believe is desirable will strongly influence their child-rearing practices. As the box on p. 426 indicates, the parents' age is another factor that influences the way children are reared.

CLASS AND CHILD REARING Parents at all social-class levels, says Kohn, want their children to be honest, happy, considerate, obedient, and dependable. But there is a definite class split when it comes to autonomy. Parents in higher social classes generally want their children to be responsible, self-controlled, and interested in how and why things happen. Parents in lower social classes tend to want their children to be neat, clean, and good students. The effect is to encourage autonomy in one social class and conformity to authority in the other.

Children from different classes may not start life differently, but they are treated differently by their parents. Working-class mothers talk less to their toddlers than do middle-class mothers, intrude more into their activities, and tend not to explain punishments and prohibitions. In a study of ninety first-born Caucasian children, Jerome Kagan (1978) and his associates watched the children at home with their mothers on several occasions. They found that lower-class mothers issued a prohibition every five minutes, whereas "No" or "Don't touch that" came only every ten minutes from the middle-class mothers. Although this difference may sound trivial, it indicates that lower-class children hear twice as many prohibitions as do middle-class children, and the cumulative effect could be substantial. Kagan suggests that this sort of difference in training is one element that helps middle-class children become more autonomous.

By the time youngsters enter nursery school, the lessons in autonomy and conformity have taken hold. Middle-class children are likely to believe that they have some control over what happens to them; lower-class children tend to believe that their efforts will have little effect (Stephens and Delys, 1973). The middle-class child is developing an internal locus of control, whereas the lower-class child is developing an external locus of control.

All parents punish their children, but the conditions of punishment differ from one social class to another. Working-class parents tend to punish their children on the basis of the consequences of the child's misbehavior, whereas middle-class parents generally punish on the basis of the child's intent (Kohn, 1979). Working-class parents, for example, who usually punish for fighting may not punish brothers and sisters for arguing. Middle-class parents, however, are likely to treat fighting with a neighborhood child and arguing with a sibling similarly. Such differences appear about the time the child is six years old. Distributing punishment in this manner is in line with parental values. A parent who values autonomy will judge misbehavior in terms of the reasons a child misbehaves. Parents who value conformity to authority, on the other hand, will judge misdeeds in terms of whether the act violates the rules that have been laid down.

By the time they are adolescents, middle-class children are likely to believe that they can achieve occupational status and other external

(Alice Kandell/Photo Researchers)

Living with a Stepparent

An increasing number of American children live in homes with a stepparent, a situation that puts children through another major transition. Young children and older adolescents seem most willing to accept a stepparent, but children between the ages of nine and fifteen tend to reject the stepparent, no matter how loving and attentive he or she is (Hetherington, Cox, and Cox, 1982).

Because most children live with their mothers, the new parent is generally a stepfather. When Mavis Hetherington and her colleagues (Hetherington, Cox and Cox, 1982) studied stepfather families, they found that stepfathers tended either to be disengaged, paying little attention to the children and giving the mother little support in child rearing, or to be

extremely involved and often restrictive. Yet when the stepfather used an authoritative style of child rearing and his involvement was welcomed by the mother, children did better than those in divorced, one-parent families or in intact families filled with marital discord. In these families, relationships between the children and their biological mother also improved. The presence of a stepfather was especially beneficial to young boys, who often developed warm attachments to their new fathers. In another study of stepfathers (Santrock et al., 1982), stepsons were found to be more socially competent than sons in intact families, but stepdaughters were more anxious than girls in intact families. Among these families, the presence of a stepfather seemed to disrupt the relationship between mother and daughter.

It appears that relationships in remarried families are much smoother and less conflict-ridden when the stepparent and the child are of the same gender. In a study of stepmothers (Santrock, Warshak, and Elliott, 1982), boys with stepmothers showed less social competence than boys living in one-parent homes with their own fathers or girls living in families with stepmothers.

Relationships in remarried families are often complicated by the fact that each parent has children from a former marriage. In such cases, families with stepfathers tend to be less happy, even if the stepfather does not have custody of his own children (Clingempeel, 1981). When the stepfather brings his

symbols of success through their personal efforts. But the middle class splits in an important respect. The experiences of adolescents from upper-middle-class families (professional and managerial occupations) are likely to have prepared them for careers, and they grow up believing in the importance of delaying gratification in the interest of future success (Mischel,

1966). They are also likely to value their cognitive competencies, because the social roles they are being socialized for involve using the head more than the hands (R. Hess, 1970).

For the most part, adolescents from lower-middle-class families (semiprofessional, semimanagerial, white-collar, and skilled-craft occupations) look forward to jobs, not careers.

own children into the new family, problems often develop over child rearing, each spouse's parental role, and family members' belief that each parent gives preferential treatment to his or her own children (Hetherington, Cox, and Cox, 1982).

The amount of contact with the former spouse also affects the atmosphere in stepfather families (Clingempeel, 1981). When former spouses are seen once a week or more often, the new marriage seems to be under such stress that it fails to solidify. Yet when former spouses are seen less than once a month, problems also develop. It may be that children's resentment over infrequent contact with their biological father spills over into the new family and erodes their relationship with their stepfather. In stepfamilies that were happiest, the former spouse was seen two or three times a month.

Life with stepparents introduces many new factors into a child's life. Exactly how a child will be affected depends on the child's age and gender, the gender of the stepparent, the parental style used by the stepparent, the child's relationship with the noncustodial parent, the feelings of the biological parents toward each other and toward the former spouse of the stepparent, and the presence—or availability—of grandparents and other members of the extended family. As with the effects of a father's or mother's absence, the web of influences is complex, and individual outcomes are impossible to predict.

Both upper- and lower-middle-class adolescents tend to share the attitudes and beliefs that correspond to those demanded by schools and colleges (Douvan, 1956). Thus the idea of prolonged schooling is likely to make sense to both groups.

Prolonged schooling is less likely to find favor with adolescents from working-class families (semiskilled and unskilled blue-collar workers) or from lower-class families that depend on irregular employment in marginal work roles or on welfare funds. Going to college, thereby delaying immediate gratification in the interest of future success, is not likely to make much sense to these adolescents. Adolescents from lower-class families tend to adjust their occupational plans to what they think they can hope to achieve; when they look around them, they are unlikely to expect much from life.

Among many working-class families, employment is valued as a means of providing goods and services to the extended family, and family loyalty may stand in the way of any action, such as going away to school, that may weaken family bonds. Fathers of working-class families take pride in their regular employment, but they rarely move up; the tasks they perform are simple, specialized, circumscribed, and repetitive. If they work in a factory, the pace and rhythm of work are imposed from above by supervisors and technicians. The worker on the assembly line is rewarded for following orders and coordinating his work with the rest of the line, not for showing self-direction, individuality, or innovative techniques (Blau, 1972). It is not difficult to see how conforming to authority came to be an important aspect of working-class life.

They value individualism and take an activistic stance toward the world and their future in it. However, lower-middle-class adolescents and their parents are likely to see that future in terms of the security, stability, and respectability that jobs bring rather than in terms of opportunities for development, intrinsic satisfaction, or self-actualization.

CULTURE AND CHILD REARING Child-rearing practices also vary from culture to culture, and the influence of a society's general economy on its values shows most clearly in agricultural, fishing, and hunting societies. In a study of 104 societies, most of them nonliterate, Herbert Barry, Irvin Child, and Margaret Bacon (1959) found that knowing whether a culture tends to accumulate and store food surpluses or to consume the food as it is obtained allowed them to predict what qualities would be inculcated in children. Societies based on animal husbandry, for example, train children to be responsible and obedient; they do not stress achievement, self-reliance, and independence. Carelessness in animal management or innovation in herding techniques can threaten a family's food supply for months ahead. Hunting and fishing societies, where few means exist to store the day's catch, stress achievement, self-reliance, and independence; they place little stress on responsibility and obedience. In these societies, innovation carries no penalties and initiative pays off immediately.

In the Soviet Union, obedience and discipline are highly valued. Parents use a combination of reason and praise, backed up by the withdrawal of love, to instill these qualities in their children. According to Urie Bronfenbrenner (1970), the difference between American and Russian discipline lies in the "emotional loading" of the parent-child relationship in the USSR. Russians are more demonstrative than Americans and quick to withdraw affection when a child misbehaves. As a result, the child feels that he or she is ungrateful and has betrayed an affectional bond.

Black American Families

Many children in black American families face stresses that are not considered in studies of white, middle-class family life—stresses that may result in different patterns of socialization. Black children are more likely to live in the central city (80 percent live in urban areas, 60 percent in the inner city); more likely to be poor (black adult unemployment is two and a half times that of whites); more likely to have both parents working at low-paying, precarious jobs; less likely to be living with both parents (only 43 percent have both mother and father in the home); less likely to have a father at home (46 percent of black families are headed by women);

and more likely to be illegitimate (illegitimacy rates are six times as high among blacks as among whites) (U.S. Bureau of the Census, 1982; Cummings, 1983). Economic pressures are intense, for half of all black families headed by women have incomes below the poverty level. Stresses apparently interact, each additional stress greatly increasing the strain on growing children. Added to all these burdens on black children is the burden of racism.

Most black parents report that race has had an impact on the way they bring up their children, with many mothers feeling that they must focus on developing self-esteem and self-confidence in their children so that they will be able to handle the racism they encounter (Peters, 1981). Black children are socialized to live in two worlds—in the world of the black community, where they must be accepted if they are to have friends, and the world of the white community, where they must be accepted if they are to survive.

Despite these hazards, many black families are healthy, cope effectively with their problems, and rear competent children. Robert Hill (1971) has identified a number of strengths that enable black families to overcome negative social and economic conditions. First, kinship bonds, by tradition, are especially strong. In times of trouble, the extended family steps in with money, advice, and services; and both child and adult relatives are accepted into the extended family. Second, both husbands and wives have a strong work orientation and both participate in decision making; when the husband is present, the black family is not a matriarchy. Third, all members of the black family are characterized by a strong desire to achieve: to get a better education, better job, more income. This urge is not, however, generally matched by the conviction that improvement is possible. Finally, many black families rely on the church, which helps maintain the values of respectability, perseverance, and achievement.

Albert McQueen (1979) studied black families in Washington, D.C., to see how these strengths affected them and to determine just what strat-

Although black children face additional stresses, the black family has developed unique strengths that help it deal with social and economic problems. (Hazel Hankin/Stock, Boston)

egies distinguished those who coped successfully from those who did not. All the families were poor or near poor, but some, whom he called the *troubled poor*, had difficulty feeding and clothing their children and paying the rent. The others, the *future-oriented poor*, seemed able to handle their economic problems. The future-oriented families were more likely than the troubled poor to be headed by males: 85 percent compared with 65 percent. Both types of families aimed at improving their economic lot, wanted to rear their children well, and wanted

good family relations, but the future-oriented devoted more of their resources to family goals. Although all the families wanted to improve the quality of their lives, not one of the mothers was striving to get into a higher socioeconomic bracket for herself. Mothers in future-oriented families had higher aspirations for their sons than mothers in troubled poor families, being much more likely to want their sons to finish college and to believe that their sons would do so.

Most studies that compare black and white families confuse class differences with racial differences, often using a white middle-class group and a disadvantaged black group. Researchers have found that when they correct for socioeconomic differences, only small differences remain in the attitudes of black and white women toward marriage and the family (Heiss, 1981). For

(Erika Stone/Photo Researchers)

Parental Age and Child Development

Older women are having more babies. In only three years, the birth rate for women in the thirty- to thirty-five-year-old group increased 15 percent (*New York Times,* 1984). Having a baby at thirty-five is a different experience from having a baby at twenty—different for both parents and child. The most obvious difference is economic. Older parents generally have assets—savings, perhaps a home of their own—and one or both are established in their careers. With money for the extras that make life easier, there is less pressure on both parents and less strain on the marital relationship. As we have seen, satisfied parents tend to have well-adjusted children.

In a study of parenthood timing, Pamela Daniels and Kathy Weingarten (1982) found that when the first child arrived after the mother was thirty, fathers were more likely to assume part of the household duties and to become involved in child care. In addition, fathers were likely to be highly nurturant and solicitous of the mother's emotional needs. By contrast, when women gave birth in their late teens or early twenties, they found themselves having to mother both baby and husband.

Other studies (Ragozin et al., 1982) have shown that the older the mother of a first baby, the more she enjoys the experience. Mothers in their thirties reported much more gratification from interacting with their babies than did young mothers; the general emotional tone of the baby-mother relationship was more positive; and the mother was more sensitive to her baby's needs. As noted earlier, such sensitivity has been associated with secure attachments and social competence. The difference between younger and older mothers was even more pronounced when the baby was premature.

In Chapter 3, we saw that adolescent mothers not only seem to be less sensitive to their infants' needs than older mothers, but also talk less with their babies, and punish them more. Their babies are also more likely than the babies of older mothers to be slow in cognitive development and to be abused in later years (Elster, McAnarney, and Lamb, 1983). Given such disparity in effects, are there any disadvantages to postponing birth? No research can give us the answer, but Daniels and Weingarten (1982) asked older parents if they had found any drawbacks. These parents, who were in their thirties and forties when their first child was born, said they often felt they lacked the energy needed to keep up with active children and some wondered if their age would make them a burden to their children. Others wondered if they would live to see their grandchildren. However, 75 percent of the couples who had postponed parenthood were enthusiastic about their decision, and more than 50 percent of those whose first child had been born while they were in their early twenties wished they had waited at least a few years.

example, the way mothers of any race interact with their young children and how much they talk to the youngsters can generally be predicted on the basis of socioeconomic level alone (Peters, 1981). When John McAdoo (1981) observed a group of black middle-class fathers with their young children, he discovered that the fathers behaved similarly toward boys and girls, except that they tended to talk more to their young sons and to rely more on facial expressions, touches, and gestures with their daughters. Most of the fathers seemed to be using an authoritative parental style; they were warm and loving and encouraged independent, assertive behavior in their children. A smaller group seemed to be authoritarian, noticing only behavior that required parental control and paying no attention to their children's good behavior. Most of the men in this study were consciously breaking with tradition; 84 percent said they were rearing their children differently from the way they had been reared—most being less strict than their own parents had been.

PHYSICAL CHILD ABUSE

Sometimes the rearing process goes dreadfully wrong, and instead of successfully socializing their children, parents may beat, maim, or even kill them. According to the accepted definition, an abused child is one who has been physically injured because of intentional acts or failures to act on the part of his or her caregiver; and the acts or omissions violate the community's standards concerning the treatment of children (Parke and Collmer, 1975). Some years ago, few cases of child abuse were reported to authorities; but once the problem received public recognition, many states passed laws requiring the reporting of child abuse. As a result, the magnitude of the problem became clear. According to the records of the American Humane Association (1983), during 1981 there were 850,000 reported cases of child abuse or neglect—an increase of 100,000 cases over the number

The prevalence of child abuse has led to the formation of groups of former child abusers who counsel one another, just as alcoholics come to each other's aid through Alcoholics Anonymous. (Joan Menschenfreund)

reported in 1978. Some researchers (Straus, Gelles, and Steinmetz, 1980) believe that the incidence of child abuse probably has not risen appreciably, but that greater public awareness, less toleration of cruelty to children, and the enactment of laws requiring abuse to be reported are responsible for the apparent increase.

Like any other outcome of child rearing, child abuse has no single cause. It appears to result from the interaction of many factors: the personality characteristics of the parents, the socioeconomic strains on the family, the patterns of family interaction, the personality characteristics of the children, the isolation of the family, and the cultural acceptance of violence (Starr, 1979).

The Abusing Parent

It was once thought that child abuse had a simple explanation: psychotic parents beat or murdered their children. As more and more cases were investigated, however, it became clear that psychosis was rarely a factor in child abuse (Spinetta and Rigler, 1972). Studies that have focused on parental personality characteristics have come up with a number of traits that have been found in abusing parents; the only problem is that different studies have found different clusters of traits (Parke and Collmer, 1975). Child abusers have been found to possess one or more of nineteen traits, including a tendency to be rigid, domineering, impulsive, immature, self-centered, hypersensitive, low in self-esteem, or lacking in impulse control. That they cannot always control their aggressive impulses is obvious; the existence of child abuse is ample testimony to that defect. But most people who have never abused a child possess at least one of the remaining eighteen traits, so that the list adds little to our understanding of the problem (Steele and Pollock, 1968).

Some investigators believe that child abusers had wretched childhoods. They may themselves have been abused or neglected and deprived of basic mothering. As children, they learned from their own parents to be aggressive; and they learned, too, that parents criticize and disregard their young children while making demands on them (Parke and Collmer, 1975).

But most people who show the various personality traits discovered in abusing parents do not batter their children. In fact, some researchers reject the idea of a "cycle of abuse." Not all people who were abused as children become child abusers; nor were all child abusers abused by their own parents. Among monkeys, for example, females who are taken from their mothers and raised with peers or with cloth or wire surrogate mothers often neglect or abuse their infants. Yet not all these monkeys who were never mothered become abusive mothers themselves. Stephen Suomi and Chris Ripp (1983) found that other factors, combined with the lack of mothering, tipped the scales toward abuse. Monkeys who were kept from social contact until they were a year old, who gave birth before they were eight years old (about thirty years in human terms), and whose offspring was male were more likely to abuse their first infant. Even among these "motherless mothers," those who kept their first infant for at least forty-eight hours before abusing it were much less likely to abuse a subsequent infant. Other factors that

contributed to infant abuse among monkeys were social isolation around the time of the infant's birth and a history of reacting with depression to brief social separations during adolescence. Apparently, adequate mothering depends on the interaction of the mother's previous social experience, her current social environment, her emotional state at the time of birth, and the characteristics of her infant. If the causes of child abuse are this complicated among monkeys, they are probably even more complex among human beings.

In a Colorado study, the way parents of full-term babies behaved in the labor and delivery room separated those who would not abuse their babies from those who *might* (Kempe and Kempe, 1978). Potential child abusers seemed either indifferent or hostile to their babies and unloving toward their spouse. By the time the infants were eighteen months old, several in the high-risk group had been hospitalized for abuse or neglect and 44 percent had had at least one accident requiring medical attention. Not one of the babies in the low-risk group was hospitalized and less than 15 percent had had an accident. Yet despite the fact that researchers had found a factor that may be involved in child abuse, they grossly overpredicted the likelihood of abuse. In fact, they were wrong more often than they were right. Unless other factors are present, the marked lack of affection apparently does not get translated into abuse.

The same problem has plagued other attempts to locate potential child abusers. For example, researchers have developed a Child Abuse Potential Inventory, which detects 94 percent of the parents who already have abused their children (Milner et al., 1984). Parents respond to 160 statements, which include 77 items describing abusive individuals. These items cover distress, rigidity, the presence of a child with problems, problems with the family and with others, unhappiness, loneliness, negative self-concept, and negative concepts of the child. However, when used to screen parents in an attempt to identify potential abusers, it also overpredicts the likelihood of abuse, selecting more parents who do not abuse their children than parents who later abuse them.

The Abused Child

The child may play a part in bringing about or maintaining abuse from parents. A child's appearance or temperament may somehow increase the chances that a parent will be abusive. For example, among monkeys, male infants are four times as likely to be abused as females, perhaps, say Suomi and Ripp (1983), because male offspring seem to be more demanding and difficult to care for than females. Among human beings, boys are more likely than girls to be seriously injured by a parent (Straus, Gelles, and Steinmetz, 1980). Whether this is because boys are more likely to be "difficult" or because violence is more likely to be approved in connection with males is unknown. Appearance and temperament are not the only aspects of the child that can contribute to abuse. The child may learn, from parents or siblings, to act in ways that evoke abuse, or the experience of being battered may alter his or her behavior in such a way as to make future episodes of battering more likely.

As noted in Chapter 4, the premature baby may run a special risk. Babies with low birth weights have particularly aversive cries, they are less attractive than full-term babies, they require more parental care at home, they develop slowly, and their relationship with their parents may suffer because the babies' precarious condition requires them to be separated from their parents and placed in special-care nurseries. Although most premature babies are not abused, they do seem to be at increased risk.

Studies have shown that abused infants are more likely than other babies to develop avoidant attachments, and the proportion of such insecure attachments is higher among abused infants who are living with their abusing mothers than with those who have been placed in a foster home (Lamb, Gaensbauer, Malkin, and Schultz, 1985; Schneider-Rosen and Cic-

chetti, 1984). The avoidant attachment seems related specifically to the abuser, for when a baby is abused by someone other than the mother, the infant's attachment to his or her mother remains secure.

Not surprisingly, the experience of abuse affects a child's behavior. Infants who have been abused or neglected tend to react to events with dampened emotions—whether the emotion evoked is pleasure, interest, sadness, or fear (Gaensbauer, 1982). Sometimes their reactions seem inappropriate. When abused nineteen-month-olds had their noses smudged with rouge and were then placed in front of a mirror, they tended to react negatively or not at all to the baby with the dirty face (Schneider-Rosen and Cicchetti, 1984). Nineteen-month-olds who have not been abused tend to react with pleasure to the same sight; only much younger normal babies are impassive or react negatively to the baby in the mirror.

Abuse also affects a youngster's reactions to other people. Carol George and Mary Main (1979) watched ten abused toddlers and ten toddlers from families under stress the first time they attended a day-care center. The two groups of children differed only in the fact that one group had been abused and the other had not. The battered toddlers were more aggressive than the other children; only the abused toddlers assaulted or threatened to assault the caregivers. Seven of the abused children but only two of the children who had not been abused harassed the caregivers, behaving in malicious ways that were intended to distress the caregiver. There is, of course, no way to tell whether the abused toddlers' aggression and harassment were a cause or a result of their parents' abuse.

Although the abused children approached their peers, they were much less likely to approach the caregiver. They frequently avoided the friendly advances both of other children and of the caregiver, and often showed *approach-avoidance*—that is, in response to a friendly overture, they would crawl toward the caregiver, then suddenly veer away. Or they would creep toward the caregiver, carefully keeping their heads averted. Ann Frodi and Michael Lamb's study (1980) showing that abusive parents react with aversion to smiling, friendly babies might provide a clue here. The apparent apprehensiveness of the abused babies may have developed from their having learned that *any* adult attention is sometimes followed by blows. Their negative responses to friendliness, however, might in turn help to maintain their parents' abuse.

Socioeconomic Stress

The family's social setting is a third factor that affects the incidence of child abuse. In two California counties, increases in the unemployment rate were followed by jumps in the reported cases of child abuse (Steinberg, Catalano, and Dooley, 1981). Careful studies in New York and Nebraska (Garbarino, 1976; Garbarino and Crouter, 1978) show that where socioeconomic support for mothers is poor, child abuse increases. Children are more likely to be abused or neglected when incomes and educational levels are low, when mothers head the household, when the neighborhood is unstable, and when day care is not available.

For example, when two neighborhoods with similar socioeconomic and racial composition but with radically differing rates of child abuse were compared, sharp differences were found between them (Garbarino and Sherman, 1980). Given their socioeconomic makeup, each area should have had between 65 and 70 cases of child abuse during the year. Yet one neighborhood reported 130 cases while the other reported only 16. In the low-risk neighborhood, a parent was usually present when a child came home from school, families assisted one another, neighborhood children played together, and residents kept up their homes and cared for their families. In the high-risk neighborhood, there were many "latchkey" children, families were socially isolated, and both houses and families were run down. When parents are under economic and social stress, when they have no relief from child care, when they have no support from friends, and when—from lack of education—they do not know where to turn for help, the impulse to strike out in response to a crying, whining, or aggressive child may be overpowering. But wiping out poverty would not eliminate child abuse. Although the rate of child abuse is higher among the poor, prosperous parents also abuse their children. Marital discord, employment worries, and other stresses of the affluent can result in a battered child.

The Persistence of Abuse

For years, psychologists assumed that child abuse was part of a family cycle. Abused children grew up to become abusive parents. It seemed that child abusers learned as children that violence works. As adolescents, some were either beaten by their own parents or they grew up in a family where the parents hit each other (Straus, Gelles, and Steinmetz, 1980). Some studies have found this connection. Men and women with such a history are more likely than others to hit their spouses and abuse their children. The childhood home lesson that violence is an appropriate outlet for anger and a reasonable way to enforce rules or to reach one's goals is reinforced by three-quarters of the programs seen on television (Gerbner, 1972). Having learned this lesson, abusive parents apply it inconsistently. One study found that abusive families lack guidelines for children's behavior and any consistency in discipline (Young, 1964). As a result, children never know when they will be punished or why. Since erratic punishment is not effective, abusive parents are likely to intensify their use of force. According to Parke and Collmer (1975), abusive parents often justify their violence as necessary discipline, forget the harmful effects of abuse, blame the child for provoking them, label the child as incorrigible, "crazy," or "dumb," react to the child's pain with intensified aggression, and are encouraged in their attacks by approval or indifference on the part of their spouses.

In a study of abused children and their parents, both the abused children and children who had not been abused behaved similarly with their families when building with Tinker Toys, tossing bean bags, or discussing how they would spend lottery winnings (Burgess and Conger, 1978). Mothers of abused children, however, showed 77 percent more negative behavior than mothers in the control group. They also spoke less often to their children and had less positive contact with them. Fathers of abused children were much less likely to comply with the requests of either the mother or the children than fathers of children in the control group.

Ruth and Henry Kempe (1978), who work with the National Center for the Prevention and Treatment of Child Abuse and Neglect, have found that most abused children are excessively compliant, passive, and obedient. They seem stoical and accept whatever happens. Others are negative, aggressive, and sometimes hyperactive. A third small group swerves between sweet, compliant behavior and unprovoked disruption and impulsiveness. These researchers believe that the abused children they have seen have failed to develop the basic sense of trust that Erik Erikson believes is the major developmental task for young children. Such children find it hard to trust adults, make only superficial friendships, and discard their new friends at the slightest hint of rejection. In school they are underachievers, generally poor at communication, lonely and friendless. If the "cycle of abuse" view is correct, these children are candidates to become child abusers.

How likely is it that these children will grow up to abuse their children? Some researchers believe the connection has been overstated (Potts and Herzberger, 1979). Although abused children may be more likely to become child abusers than children who have never been abused, the connection seems to be much weaker than has generally been assumed. In fact, one study has found that mothers who abuse their children are no more likely to have been abused as children than other mothers (Fisher, 1984). This is just one more example of the fact that, as Richard Gelles and Claire Cornell (1985) suggest, most factors related to child abuse are still unexplained.

SUMMARY

Socialization is the process by which the growing child slowly absorbs the attitudes, values, and customs of society. Parents and siblings play an important role in this process, although their influence interacts with that of media, peers, school, and relatives and other adults.

Connections have been found between the disciplinary styles of parents and the personalities of their children, although it is impossible to say definitively that any particular type of child rearing has a specific effect on children. **Authoritarian** and **permissive** parents both are likely to produce dependent children, perhaps because both kinds of parents tend to shield their children from stress. **Nonconformist** parents often produce dependent girls and independent, high-achieving boys. **Authoritative** parents, who are firm but not repressive, tend to produce independent, socially responsible girls and socially responsible boys with average levels of independence. **Indifferent** parents may produce demanding, less compliant, aggressive children, although the link has not been established by research. The techniques parents use in the hope of producing **instrumentally competent** children include punishment, reinforcement, and modeling. Among other factors believed to affect child rearing positively are consistent parental behavior that responds to changes in children's cognitive and social development, continuity in caregiving arrangements, and the child's temperament.

Most toddlers and preschoolers are disturbed and unhappy when a younger sibling is born. The way a mother talks about the new baby, whether she encourages the older child to help with infant care, and the older child's initial interest in the new baby interact, affecting whether the siblings later become friends. Siblings help socialize one another and, although most siblings fight, sibling rivalries do not seem to dominate their relationships.

High-quality day care does not seem to harm the cognitive, social, or emotional development of children. No long-term effects on the mother-child relationship have appeared, and children in day care tend to get along better with peers than children who stay home—although this may simply be accelerated development of social skills. The ratio of staff to children in any day-care center is critical. The effect of maternal employment on children appears to depend on the interaction of many factors, but the strongest influence may be the mother's level of satisfaction. Daughters generally benefit when their mothers work, but sons sometimes suffer. Increased paternal involvement in child rearing probably benefits children when both parents are favorably disposed toward the father's increased participation.

Growing up without a father has some effect on children's personalities and socialization, but the depth of the impact depends on a host of factors: the age of the child at the time of the loss, the presence of siblings, the sex of the child, the socioeconomic level of the home, the mother's reaction to the loss, and community standards. Growing up without a mother also affects children, and it may be that when the only parent is a father, girls will be competitive and career-oriented, and both sons and daughters will have flexible views of masculinity and

femininity. Studies suggest that the gender of the child is especially important. Despite the problems of one-parent homes, marital discord may be worse in its impact on the child than the loss of either parent by death or divorce.

Parents in different social classes tend to treat their children differently, and the major effect is to encourage conformity to authority among working-class children and autonomy among middle-class children. The economy of a culture plays a major part in determining which values are stressed during socialization.

Many black mothers feel they must work at developing self-esteem and self-confidence in their children so that they will be able to handle racism. Although black families face extra stresses, they have strengths that are not found in most middle-class white homes. Most studies of black families confuse class and race; when socioeconomic differences are corrected for, there are only small differences in the attitudes toward children of black and white mothers.

Child abuse has no single cause; it seems to result when personality characteristics of parent and child interact with socioeconomic stress, patterns of family interactions, and social isolation. Whether the pattern of abuse tends to be handed down, so that the lonely, friendless, isolated, abused child is likely to grow up to become a child abuser, has not been clearly established.

CHAPTER FOURTEEN

Social Competence in the Wider World: Peers and Teachers

FROM PARENTS TO PEERS
PRIMATES AND PEERS
PEERS AND COMPETENCE
Early Social Skills
Play and Socialization
Peer Reinforcement
Peer Modeling
GETTING ALONG WITH PEERS
Names and Appearance
Social Skills
Stability of Popularity
SOCIAL ISOLATION
CHANGING RELATIONSHIPS
Friendship
Peer Groups
CONFORMITY
SCHOOLS AND TEACHERS
Effects of Desegregation
Competence and Achievement
SUMMARY

One afternoon after school, Jan and Debby stopped at a local variety store. "Watch me," whispered Jan, as her hand snaked out, grabbed a handful of pencils from the counter, and dropped them into her schoolbag. Eleven-year-old Debby's eyes widened, but she said nothing. "Try it," Jan said. "It's easy." Debby hesitated. "Go ahead," Jan whispered, "are you a scairdy-cat?" Debby looked nervously over her shoulder, grabbed a pencil, thrust it under her sweater, and walked quickly out the door. Debby did not need the pencil; she did not even want it, but the demands of her peer were stronger than her wishes or her own sense of right or wrong.

The influences of a child's peers can be extremely important in shaping development. Some years ago, peers had little impact until a child skipped off to elementary school. Until then, brothers, sisters, and perhaps cousins, the boy next door and the girl across the street provided a youngster's only sustained contacts with other children. Today, about a third of all three- and four-year-olds meet their peers in regular, organized contact at nursery school. The power of the peer group has also increased

435

at the other end of childhood. Fifty years ago, only about half of American adolescents attended high school; today nearly 95 percent are enrolled.

This chapter traces the development of children as they move into the wider world, concentrating on the growth of social competence. First, we examine the role that peers play in the development of competence, looking at their part in the social development of other species as well as in human children. Next the importance of early social skills, the role of play, and the techniques peers use to influence one another are investigated. We then consider the qualities that cause a child to be welcomed into the peer group, a topic that leads us to explore the reasons some children become isolated from the peer group—and what can be done to end this isolation. Next, the chapter traces the changing course and increasing importance of peers in a child's life and the waxing and waning pressures toward conformity encountered by children. Moving from the peer group to the school, we investigate the effects of desegregation on children, as well as the various influences of educational models and teachers. Finally, we look at the development of competence within the child, examining the way a child's assessment of his or her own competence influences academic achievement.

FROM PARENTS TO PEERS

Until children enroll in school, parents are the most important socializing force in their lives. When children develop and maintain a secure attachment to their parents (a concept discussed in Chapter 12), they become competent, independent toddlers. Some of the skills they develop within the family are transferred to their contacts with others. As a result, they enjoy learning new things, play well with other children, and plunge into the day at nursery school with enthusiasm.

At the age of four, children with a history of secure attachment are more popular with their nursery-school peers than are insecurely attached children (Sroufe, 1983). The securely attached youngsters are also more adept at social skills, friendlier, cry less, and are less likely to be aggressive. Such a course of development does not reflect the influence of early infant experiences on later social competence. Instead, as noted in Chapter 12, it reflects a continuity in the child's background, which maintains the development of social skills (Lamb et al., 1984).

Despite their greater social competence, securely attached infants do not make up a uniform group. Differences in social competence appeared among a group of securely attached eighteen-month-olds (Easterbrooks and Lamb, 1979). Those who used their mothers as a base from which to explore the environment, maintaining contact with smiles, looks, and vocalizations, were more likely to play with an unfamiliar baby than were babies who seemed to need to stay near their mothers.

The transition from family to nursery school takes children from a world populated almost entirely by giants to one in which a far greater number of people are near their own size and share their interests. The child for the first time has a real peer group, and the importance of that group steadily increases.

Much of what young children learn about their world they learn from other children, and most of what they learn, from whatever source, they practice and rehearse within the peer group. Thus, the peer group is the place where children perfect the roles that they will play in later years. During early childhood, a child's dependence on adults often decreases while dependence on peers (such as in seeking approval or asking for help) increases. In fact, well-adjusted youngsters tend to have a comfortable reliance on their peers (Emmerich, 1966).

PRIMATES AND PEERS

The role of peers as agents of socialization is not uniquely human. Students of primate behavior are generally convinced, both from laboratory studies and from studies conducted in the wild, that early contact with peers is necessary for the normal development of most primates. In fact, it is almost impossible to conceive of socialization among rhesus monkeys or chimpanzees in the absence of peer interaction. Because of this similarity across species, primate social interaction can provide insights that help clarify the role of peers in the socialization of the human child.

In many primate species, young animals spend much of their time in a play group consisting of other infants and juveniles. Within this group, young primates practice the behavior they will later be expected to perform as adults. It is here that primates perfect the intricate patterns of facial gestures and social threat. And it is here, by approach and mounting during play, that young primates learn adult sexual behavior. Rough-and-tumble play within the peer group also develops the aggressiveness that primates use both to maintain status and to defend the group against predators.

The animal research of Harry and Margaret Harlow (1969) and their associates helps us understand the role of peers in socialization. Infant monkeys raised in total isolation never learned to play the usual monkey games, and they never had the opportunity to acquire the social roles that they would need in later life. After six to twelve months of such isolation, these monkeys found it almost impossible to fit into a group when, as adolescents, they were introduced to others of their kind. They tended to remain isolated from the rest of the group; they rarely engaged in social play, and when they did, it was with other isolates. Even individual play was infrequent among monkeys that had been isolated for twelve months.

Such isolated monkeys encountered great difficulties when they became sexually mature. Males did not know how to approach young females (or even that it was females that they should approach), and the females did not know how to entice and yield to the males. Both males and females were abnormally aggressive. They attacked and bit young monkeys, which normally reared animals almost never do. They also launched attacks against the largest and most

Monkeys raised without their mothers and with only their peers for company at first developed strange patterns of behavior, such as clinging together in a "choo-choo" pattern, but the monkeys soon went on to normal play. (Harry Harlow, University of Wisconsin Primate Laboratory)

dominant adult males, an extraordinarily maladaptive action for an adolescent.

Clearly, these monkeys had severe social problems (Suomi and Harlow, 1975). To try to pinpoint the cause of the problems, researchers raised more monkeys, but each group was raised in a different manner. Some monkeys spent the first few months of their lives with their mothers but had no contact with any other monkeys. Another group spent the first few months of life only with other infant monkeys. The infants raised with only their mothers behaved in a far less abnormal manner than did the monkeys raised earlier in isolation. They were, however, less affectionate with peers and more aggressive than monkeys raised in a normal manner, and they tended to avoid social play. Furthermore, the longer the baby monkeys were isolated with their mothers, the more abnormal their behavior.

Researchers had suspected that the peer-raised animals would show severe social problems, and for the first several days it appeared that their suspicions were correct. The infants simply clung together in a "choo-choo" pattern, as shown in the photograph (p. 437). This pattern soon broke up, however, and the monkeys established normal play. The later development of peer-raised monkeys was relatively normal. They showed affection and played normally, and they demonstrated only normal aggression toward monkeys in their rearing group. They were, however, aggressive toward other monkeys.

In view of the important role of parents in the rearing of both infant monkeys and human infants, these results are surprising. They seem to indicate that at least among rhesus monkeys, peers teach certain social skills that are not learned from parents.

PEERS AND COMPETENCE

The world of peers is different from the rest of a child's experience because it is a world of egalitarian interaction between individuals of approximately equal developmental level (Hartup, 1983). Interacting with another person of the same age allows even young children to test their skills and enhances a growing sense of self. As children grow, peers serve a number of important functions in their lives. They provide emotional security, set norms for behavior, teach cognitive, motor, and social skills, stimulate and encourage play, and help children adjust to life (Asher, 1978). Peers carry out these functions in two major ways: by reinforcement and by modeling. Even babies are affected by this social interaction.

Early Social Skills

In the past, many investigators simply did not look for social interaction between infants, perhaps because of the general belief that young babies are too egocentric for such sociability. Yet as early as three or four months, one infant will reach for and touch another, and by the time babies are six months old, these actions are accompanied by smiles and vocalizations (Hartup, 1983). When Dale Hay and colleagues (1983) placed six-month-old strangers together, they found that the babies' interaction was harmonious. Babies tugged at one another's hair, poked at one another's eyes, mouths, and ears, and touched one another's toys without setting off frowns, fussing, resistance, or withdrawal.

Babies are clearly interested in one another but seem to lack the social skills that are needed for sustained interaction (Hartup, 1983). Perhaps for this reason, the presence of toys generally decreases infant sociability, with the babies exploring toys instead of interacting. If this is so, experience with other babies might develop social skills and thus increase interaction between babies. Indeed, infants are more sociable with acquaintances than with strangers (Field and Roopnarine, 1982). Nine-month-olds who played in pairs for a total of ten sessions paid more attention to each other than to toys or to their mothers. As the sessions went on, reports Jacqueline Becker (1977), the babies became increasingly involved with each other and played with each other more; their play also became more complex. But the increased play and its greater complexity seemed unaffected by peer reinforcement. Behavior that was not rewarded increased as much as behavior that was.

This finding has appeared in other studies. Among six-month-olds, a baby who failed to get a toy (and thus was not reinforced) was the one who first reached for a toy in the next bout of interaction (Hay, Nash, and Pedersen, 1983). It may be that one baby serves as a model for the other or that sustained social contact with another child may stimulate social behavior that is natural to the species (K. Bloom, 1974).

In Becker's study, the babies' increased social competence was not confined to their specific partners. They apparently learned general social skills, because they transferred their competence to a new situation. When babies had an opportunity to play with an unfamiliar infant, those who had previously played with a peer for ten sessions played more with the unfamiliar baby than did babies who had previously played with a peer for only two sessions.

Most studies of infant social interaction take place in laboratories, where two baby strangers confront one another for the first time, almost always in the presence of both mothers. Tiffany Field and Jaipaul Roopnarine (1982) point out that that such situations are not typical of most natural infant interaction, which takes place between acquaintances either at home or in day-care situations. The highly social infants studied by Becker, for example, were studied in the babies' homes. Infants studied in nursery-school situations became increasingly social over the months, until fourteen-month-old infants were watching their peers more, smiling and vocalizing at them more, and making more physical contact with them than did twenty-four-month-olds in other studies (Field and Roopnarine, 1982).

During the second year, social interaction becomes more complex, with sustained social exchanges appearing toward the end of the second year (Hartup, 1983). Squabbles over toys are frequent. Among pairs of twenty-one-month-old infants, the average number of conflicts during a fifteen-minute play period was 2.3, although some pairs of youngsters did not fight at all and others fought 14 times during the brief period (Hay and Ross, 1982). Toddlers in this study often found discarded toys attractive as soon as their play-partner picked them up.

Once toddlers have resolved their conflicts over play materials, they attend positively to peers. For the eighteen- to twenty-four-month-old, toys and playmates are more successfully integrated and social interactions begin to predominate. Infants modify their behavior to adjust to playmates' activities. For example, Judith Rubenstein and Carollee Howes (1976) found that seventeen- to twenty-month-old playmates who met regularly with each other in their own homes not only played freely and made few demands on the adults present but also seldom squabbled over toys. Play between a pair of playmates was also more intricate and constructive than solitary play by either member of the pair or play by a single baby and his or her mother.

Play and Socialization

Although youngsters' play is determined primarily by their cognitive level, social experience also affects its development. As we shall see, different kinds of play contribute in different ways to cognitive and social development. At first, social play does not exist. Infants begin with solitary play, then most move on to **parallel play**—in which two children play side by side, each intent on his or her own toy and each perhaps keeping up a running commentary that amounts to thinking aloud. Only later, when children become less egocentric, does truly social and group play develop. Social play increases throughout the preschool years, but solitary play does not disappear. Four-year-olds often play alone, engaging in functional activity such as running around the room, cognitive activity such as drawing or modeling with playdough, or solitary dramatic play (Hartup, 1983).

Among toddlers and preschoolers between the ages of eighteen and forty-three months, not age but experience with their peers was the best predictor of a child's level of play (Howes, 1980). Toddlers with less than six months' experience spent more time than other youngsters in parallel play, without making eye contact or any social overtures to the child playing beside them. All toddlers engaged in simple social play, in which one child indicates an awareness of the other—by smiling, vocalizing, touching, offering a toy, or stealing one. But toddlers with more than six months of peer interaction were more likely to engage in full-blown social play, in which children's actions are responsive and centered on the same toy or action.

Some children may skip the stage of parallel play altogether. When Peter Smith (1978) observed preschoolers at play over a nine-month period, he found that many children went directly from playing alone to playing with a

True social play is beyond the capabilities of very young children. Instead, most enjoy some type of parallel play, in which each youngster is aware of the other but involved with his or her own toy. (Ray Ellis/Photo Researchers)

group. This pattern of behavior was especially typical of three- and four-year-olds, perhaps because their level of cognitive development or their experiences before entering nursery school (or both) made the parallel play experience unnecessary. Two-year-olds in this study often went through a period of parallel play before they ventured into group play. Children who did engage in parallel play kept it up throughout the preschool period, although it occupied an ever-diminishing proportion of playtime.

Cognitive development is obviously related to the development of symbolic play, as we saw in Chapter 7. The infant's earliest play is with objects; at first the baby uses objects indiscriminately, perhaps banging, waving, or chewing on them. Then, at about nine months, he or she begins to use two objects together, banging a cup with a spoon. Some time after a child is a year old, symbolic play abruptly appears. Now the youngster pretends to drink out of the cup, and some time between fifteen and twenty-one months the child begins feeding a doll with a bottle or even holding the bottle in the doll's hand so it can feed itself. According to Kenneth Rubin and his colleagues (1983), once pretend play develops, it probably fosters the development of a child's self-confidence and self-regulation. It also may alleviate boredom, maintain the child's arousal at an optimum level, promote exploration, and develop creative, flexible thought.

Pretend play becomes increasingly dominant throughout the preschool years, and children do not confuse reality and pretense. Their in-

The pretend play of these five-year-old girls allows them to test various social roles without any of the consequences that accompany the actual roles. (Alice Kandell/Photo Researchers)

creased cognitive abilities allow them to play roles while retaining a personal identity and to switch back and forth between roles at will (Rubin et al., 1983). When playing *Star Wars*, the child who takes the role of Han Solo knows that he is really Mark Smith; when playing house, children never actually eat a mud pie. The context of dramatic play encourages socialization. As they play house, doctor, bus driver, or take any adult role, children are indoctrinating themselves into the culture, testing what they have learned about social roles without any of the physical, emotional, or economic consequences that accompany mistakes made when engaging in the real thing (Bruner, 1972). As

with the earliest social play, dramatic play occurs more often and at a more sophisticated level when three-year-olds are playing with friends than among youngsters who are meeting for the first time, perhaps because playmates build up a share of stored meaning that makes it easy to begin such activity (Doyle, Connolly, and Rivest, 1980).

Socially competent children are especially likely to be fond of pretend play. Among preschoolers, those who frequently engaged in pretend play with their peers were more popular and higher in social skills than other children, even when researchers allowed for the effects of age, sex, IQ, and activity level (Connolly and Doyle, 1984). Their bouts of pretend play were highly verbal, lasted for extended periods, and other children happily joined them.

As children practice a variety of roles and deal with the inevitable conflicts that arise, their egocentrism decreases and their skill in understand-

ing others increases. Children begin to comprehend the effects of their actions on others and
to see their playmates more as individuals and
less as objects of play. As they differentiate
among people, children's specific attachments
increase and they form friendships that may be
remarkably durable. Smith (1977) believes that
one of the basic functions of rough-and-tumble
play is that it serves to form and maintain friendships.

Adults watching rough-and-tumble play may
believe that a fight is in progress, but the laughter, the expression on the faces of the children
involved, the wrestling, and the jumping tell
ethologists that the struggle is not aggressive and
that there is no hostility involved. According to
Nicholas Blurton-Jones (1976), such play—more
common among boys than among girls—is similar to play among rhesus monkeys, where it is
important in the development of the monkeys'
social and sexual behavior. Like Smith, Blurton-
Jones indicates that such violent play appears to
gain friends more often than it loses them.

All play is governed by rules. Even rough-
and-tumble play is not totally aimless. Blows do
not actually land, for example, and the fist is
never closed, as it is during a fight. The basic
rules of children's pretend play allow youngsters
to take appropriate roles (mother, father, baby)
and to maintain the context of their make-believe world (Rubin, Fein, and Vandenberg,
1983). These rules leave children free to change
the framework ("Now let's play doctor") or the
roles ("It's my turn to be mommy") at any time.
As children grow older, pretend play declines
in favor of games. Now the rules are rigid and
cannot be changed in midplay; any variation
must be decided before the play begins. As we
shall see in Chapter 16, the rules children develop in play have given psychologists an opportunity to study the development of moral
thought.

Peer Reinforcement

One important way in which children influence
one another is through actions that support or
encourage behavior. When children praise another child's behavior, join in the activity, imitate the first child, comply with his or her requests, or simply watch attentively, the
likelihood that the first child will repeat the behavior is increased. The kinds of responses that
reinforce an activity such as aggression, however, differ from those that reinforce an activity
such as sharing. And because of differences in
past experience, one child may respond to a sort
of encouragement that has no effect on another.
Nevertheless, such responses as praise and affection reinforce most children in most situations.

The way a child initiates social interaction
helps determine whether the overture will be
reinforced (Leiter, 1977). When a child approaches others in a friendly manner, smiling or
pleasantly suggesting an activity, most other
children will agree. But if the child uses demands or coercion, the amount of compliance
drops sharply; many children will threaten, hit,
or shove the child instead of agreeing to his or
her requests. Others simply ignore the child.
Sometimes, however, coercive children do get
reinforced, as when other children agree to their
demands or plead with them, crying or begging
them to stop. Children who whine, beg, or cry
when making requests generally get ignored.

The way children distribute social reinforcers
seems to be strongly related to their popularity
within the peer group. Popular youngsters approach others in a friendly manner and are generous with praise and approval. Rosalind
Charlesworth and Willard Hartup (1967) found,
for example, that popular young children who
were frequently supportive of other children
tended to distribute their approval among nearly
all their peers. This study also found a strong
positive correlation between the amount of reinforcement children gave and the amount they
received.

Yet in another study, Hartup (1964a) found
that young children performed simple better
tasks when they disliked the child who praised
their performance than when they liked the
youngster. This connection between dislike and

approval showed when Hartup had children carry out a task that required them to drop marbles through holes. Periodically, either the child's best friend or a child the marble dropper disliked expressed approval. Children dropped marbles faster when the disliked child applauded their skill than when the praise came from a friend.

The effectiveness of approval from a disliked child may have something to do with expectations. Joanne Floyd (1965) found that children who received unexpectedly large or small rewards in a sharing task changed their patterns of sharing more radically than children who got rewards they had more or less expected. Because children may expect their friends to approve their actions, the support merely meets the expectation. A child may expect disliked children to disapprove of his or her actions, however, so that approval from such children exceeds expectations and has a powerful influence on performance.

Children's responses can also affect a playmate's level of aggressiveness. Gerald Patterson, Richard Littman, and William Bricker (1967) describe just how this process worked in a nursery school. When attacked, 97 percent of the beleaguered children responded in one of two general ways: they either reinforced their attacker—by becoming passive, crying, or assuming a defensive posture; or else they punished the offending child—by telling the teacher, retrieving their property, or retaliating with an aggressive act of their own. When a physical attack met with passiveness, crying, or defensiveness, before long the young attacker generally tried new acts of aggression against the original victim. The most effective way to alter the attacker's behavior was with counteraggression. A young offender whose aggressiveness met with attack usually acted in a changed manner toward the former victim, picked a different victim, or both.

Punishment also plays a role in peer-group interaction. In one study, three- to seven-year-olds regularly punished their peers for playing with toys belonging to the other sex. Sometimes they criticized the offending child or complained loudly about a boy's "sissy" behavior; at other times they stopped playing with a youngster or else physically intervened to stop the play. Regardless of the kind of punishment inflicted, the offending child stopped his or her play almost immediately. The researchers (Lamb and Roopnarine, 1979) believe that children who receive such punishment are not learning anything new; they are already aware that boys and girls are not supposed to play with toys designated for the other sex. Instead, the punishment merely reminds youngsters that they have crossed the boundary of permissible behavior.

Unpopular children who are frequently punished by their peers are often the first to break the peer group's standards. Apparently, their low status within the group makes the group's standards less attractive to them. Among groups of four- and five-year-olds, youngsters who had been consistently punished by peers were more likely to go ahead and play with a toy when they had been told that the other children had agreed not to play with it than when told that an adult had forbidden them to play with it (Furman and Masters, 1980). Among children who were not accustomed to peer punishment, the peer prohibition was as strong as the adult prohibition.

Other studies of the ways in which children encourage one another's behavior have shown how closely children's actions are linked to reinforcement. For example, Robert Wahler (1967) selected five nursery-school children whose behavior was related in some way to encouragement from their peers. He then enlisted the aid of the children's friends. Wahler asked them to ignore their friend whenever he or she acted in a certain way. Within a few days, the selected behavior—whether talking, shouting, fighting, or cooperating—dropped. When Wahler told the children's friends to resume their usual treatment, the five children went back to behaving just as they had before the experiment began. Studies such as this one indicate that by remaining alert to established patterns of peer reinforcement, parents and teachers may be able

Children learn many things by watching their playmates model new activities. A child who has never thought of perching on the handlebars with "no hands" may try it after seeing a peer accomplish the feat without mishap. (Charles Gatewood/The Image Works)

to use peers to help solve problems within the group.

Peer Modeling

Reinforcement and punishment are not the only ways in which children influence one another's behavior; modeling is also powerful. Seeing another child behave in a certain way can affect the behavior of a child for at least three different reasons (Bandura, 1977). First, the watching child may learn how to do something new that he or she previously either could not do (such as working a puzzle) or would not have thought of doing (such as riding a bicycle with "no hands"). Second, the child may learn what happens when one acts in a certain way—for example, that fighting gets children into trouble or that disobeying does not always bring pun-

ishment. As a result of this knowledge, the child's own behavior may change. Third, a model may suggest possible ways of behaving in a strange situation. For example, a child may stand around nervously at a birthday party until another child begins throwing cake. Immediately, the ill-at-ease child and others join the game. As we saw in Chapter 13, even babies imitate the behavior of their older siblings.

Preschoolers are most likely to imitate the behavior of a model immediately after they have observed it; but such immediate imitation declines sharply as children reach the school years, becoming rare among nine- to eleven-year-olds. In a study by Rona Abramovitch and Joan Grusec (1978), however, no matter what the age group, the more a child was looked at, the more the child was imitated. Children high in the dominance hierarchy were imitated most, and these children also imitated others. It may be, say the investigators, that imitating others is a good way of establishing and maintaining influence.

Since children often learn a new response and save it for an appropriate occasion, imitation of models is likely to be much higher than Abramovitch and Grusec found. The decline in immediate imitation among older children could have two causes: first, they may have other ways of gaining influence; second, they may be more likely than younger children to store a response until later. Being called a copycat is no compliment among children in elementary school.

Models can establish a situation that encourages compliance or disobedience, as Thomas Wolf (1972) found when he told young boys not to play with an attractive toy and then had another boy comment on the prohibition. Some children heard the boy say that he expected most boys would not play with the toy; others heard him say that he expected most children would play with the forbidden toy. The model's statements about probable disobedience apparently made playing with the toy an appropriate thing to do, for children who heard the model say that he expected disobedience disobeyed more often than the others.

Additional research has shown that the consequences received by a model affect watching children as if they had received those rewards or punishments themselves (Walters, Leat, and Mezei, 1963). If the model is reinforced, as when an aggressive child gets to keep a toy he or she has grabbed, children are likely to imitate the model themselves, grabbing another child's toy at the first opportunity. But if the model is punished, as when the grabber is scolded and made to return the toy, the watching children are unlikely to grab a toy themselves.

Peer models can induce positive behavior as well as aggression and disobedience. In one study by Hartup and Brian Coates (1967), while four- and five-year-old children watched, one of their classmates solved a series of maze-drawing problems and then shared the prizes he received with a mythical child from another class. The model was actually the experimenter's confederate and had been coached to give away most of his trinkets to the "other child." After the altruistic model had left the room, the ex-perimenter asked the watching children to complete the same maze-drawing task, rewarding their solutions with trinkets and giving them an opportunity to divide their prizes with the "other child." As Figure 14.1 shows, children

FIGURE 14.1 The results of Hartup and Coates' study of children's altruistic behavior. Children had six trinkets that they could give away in each trial. In all four of the experimental conditions, children saw an altruistic model, and in each case they shared more trinkets in comparison with the children in the control group, who saw no model. In addition, popular children gave away more trinkets when the model they saw was a child who usually reinforced them, whereas unpopular children tended to give away more trinkets when the model they saw was a child who had never before shown them attention or approval.

(After Hartup and Coates, 1967)

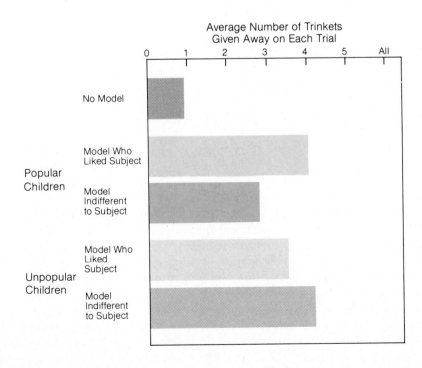

who had watched the altruistic model gave away many more trinkets than did children in the control group who had not seen the model, providing straightforward evidence that peer models can influence a socially approved activity.

The effectiveness of a peer model varies, and in the Hartup and Coates study, two factors seemed responsible: the nature of a child's previous experience with the model and the nature of the child's interactions with the peer group. Popular children (who are accustomed to receiving reinforcement) imitated a child who had previously reinforced them more often than they imitated a child who had never given them attention or approval. But unpopular children (who are rarely reinforced) were readier to imitate a child who had never paid them any attention than a child who had reinforced them in the past.

Although modeling often establishes the appropriateness of actions children are unsure about, children are unlikely to imitate a peer when they regard his or her actions as clearly inappropriate or "awful" (Hicks, 1971). Imitation seems most likely to occur when the modeled actions are clearly "good" in the eyes of watching children.

Since adults and peers can both serve as models, we might wonder which model a child is likely to follow when the examples conflict. Hartup (1964b) has noted that children who imitate models tend to do so whether the model is an adult or another child. But when it comes to learning new ways to express aggression, young children are more likely to imitate other children than adults (Hicks, 1965).

GETTING ALONG WITH PEERS

Whether children are comfortable with their peers will depend on what they bring to the social system and the way others treat them. As we saw, children who emerge from secure and rewarding home relationships tend to be trust-ing and confident. They are also interested in and capable of initiating rewarding interactions and of receiving overtures from others. These characteristics correlate with a child's popularity as measured by **sociometric analysis,** a method that charts how often a child is chosen by peers as a preferred friend or companion (Campbell and Yarrow, 1961).

Children's behavior, the responses of others to them, and the expectations of all the persons involved form an interlacing web, so that it is difficult to say which comes first or to establish a cause-effect relationship between a child's behavior and the responses of others to him or her. A number of additional factors over which children have no control—such as their appearance, their names, and their social skills—help determine their experiences within the group and their acceptance or rejection by their peers.

Names and Appearance

Even among preschool children, physical attractiveness is an asset and unattractiveness is a liability. Karen Dion (1973), for example, found that young boys and girls prefer attractive peers as potential friends and expect them to be friendly and nice, but they reject unattractive peers and expect them to be unfriendly and mean. These same views are generally held by kindergartners and fourth-graders. Judith Langlois and Cookie Stephan (1977) found, for example, that black, Anglo, and Mexican-American children see attractive peers, regardless of their race, as being more likeable, smarter, more friendly, and more willing to share than unattractive peers. Attractive Anglo children are particularly likely to benefit from shared social stereotypes, since they are likely to be perceived by all children, regardless of their race, as being the smartest, kindest, and happiest, and as doing the best in school. Attractiveness was, however, more important than ethnic background in determining the children's responses. As children reach middle childhood, once they know a child, attractiveness may become less important for boys, perhaps because unattractive boys seem to develop an assertive, aggressive stance that appeals to other males (Hartup, 1983).

Physical attractiveness continues to affect popularity in late adolescence, but then extreme attractiveness is no help when it comes to popularity with one's own gender, as Dennis Krebs and Allen Adinolfi (1975) discovered when they investigated friendship and dating choices of sixty male and sixty female residents of a student dormitory. Each resident chose the persons they liked and disliked most. The most liked persons were students who were attractive but not stunning. The most attractive students were most frequently rejected by members of their own sex; the least attractive students were chosen neither as the most nor as the least liked—they were simply ignored.

An attractive first name is similarly an asset, whereas an unattractive first name is likely to be a liability (McDavid and Harari, 1966). Children with first names considered attractive, such as John or Karen, are more likely to be popular with their peers than children with unattractive or unusual names such as Horace or Adele. In view of the expectations that names carry, it is understandable that a child's name may affect his or her self-concept. Among sixth-grade boys, those with desirable names had a more positive view of themselves, their abilities, and their interpersonal relations than boys with undesirable names (Garwood, 1976). Boys with desirable names also believed they could do better work and get along better with others in more situations, and they made significantly higher scores on a standardized achievement test.

Social Skills

Name and appearance are not the only determinants of popularity. A child's skill in relating to his or her peers also plays a major role in determining popularity. Popular children are both friendly and skilled in initiating and then maintaining new relationships (Hartup, 1983).

When elementary-school children pretended for researchers that they were meeting a strange child, popular children greeted the newcomer, gave or requested information, or invited the child to join in activities. Unpopular children were much less likely to do so (Gottman, Gonso, and Rasmussen, 1975). If the first meeting with a strange child goes badly, children who believe the rebuff is due to a misunderstanding will try again when they meet new children; children who believe they were rebuffed because they simply do not know how to make friends may avoid a new encounter (Dweck and Goetz, 1977).

Steven Asher (1978) has compiled a list of maintenance skills that children use to keep a friendship going. They include the ability to sustain informative communications with another child, to analyze the effectiveness of their own communications and adjust their messages accordingly, to tell another child when his or her message is ambiguous, to interact in a positive manner, and to manage interpersonal conflict. As already noted, popular children are friendly, and generous with praise and approval. Among nursery-school children, they also tend to go along with the wishes of another child and often spontaneously offer their playmates toys or food (Hartup, Glazer, and Charlesworth, 1967). Popular children also help their peers—but they do it in accepted ways. Gary Ladd and Sherri Oden (1979) found that third- and fifth-graders who suggested highly unusual ways of helping other children tended to be disliked.

Children may be aggressive and still have friends; but if their blows or verbal abuse are seen as inappropriate by their peers, they will be disliked (Moore, 1967). Among nursery-school children, as was reported in Chapter 1, the child on the top of the dominance ladder is rarely the most aggressive child in the group. A study of adolescent boys (Olweus, 1977) indicates that the popularity of bullies is average; they are neither leaders nor are they rejected. At nursery school, the scapegoats are children who do not remain on their rung of the dominance ladder; but among adolescents, the scapegoats are social isolates who do nothing to provoke the attacks of bullies. In Olweus's study of Swedish adolescents, the bullies were physically strong, the scapegoats physically weak.

The importance of social skills on peer acceptance becomes clear when researchers observe children attempting to enter the peer group. Unpopular children seem not to understand how to insinuate themselves into a group of playing youngsters. Unlike popular children, when unpopular children attempt to enter a group they use devices that call attention to themselves—asking questions, speaking about themselves, disagreeing, and stating their opinions and feelings in a way that disrupts the flow of group play (Putallaz and Gottman, 1981). As a result, the group tends to ignore their efforts. However, these disagreeable tactics are apparent primarily in free-play situations, where their negative behavior tends to increase over time. When placed in a task-oriented situation with one other child, unpopular children often became cooperative and agreeable, leading researchers (Markell and Asher, 1984) to speculate that the context of play has a good deal to do with the way children's interactions progress.

The personal and social consequences of popularity can have a wide effect on children's actions. Herbert Harari and John McDavid (1969), for example, recruited both a popular and an unpopular child as collaborators and had them carry out prohibited acts in the classroom, such as stealing money from the teacher. The other children in the class, who had watched what took place, were later called into the principal's office and asked what had happened. Half the children came in by themselves; the rest were accompanied by another child.

The principal questioned all the children, insisting that they tell on the culprit. When children were interrogated alone, all identified the guilty child. When the children were questioned in pairs, however, they refused to tell on the popular child but without hesitation told on the unpopular culprit. Children apparently realize that their actions in the presence of another child are likely to get back to their peers. Informing on a popular child could lead to their own rejection, whereas informing on an unpopular child is unlikely to have adverse personal consequences.

Popularity is also highly related to conformity to peer-group norms, customs, and fads. During adolescence, as in childhood, the characteristics having most to do with peer acceptance are those that define appropriate sex-typed behavior in our society (Hartup, 1970). Athletic participation and skill, standing up for one's rights, sexual prowess, and sometimes drinking prowess, are valued in the adolescent boy. The popular girl is one who is fun to be with and has interpersonal skills. Because these characteristics bring with them the positive consequences of peer acceptance, they are in turn strengthened. Thus, behavior that helps make adolescents popular with their peers also reinforces sex-role learning, which in turn tends to keep adolescents' popularity stable.

Stability of Popularity

Children's popularity is generally established by asking children to rate one another—choosing their best friends, children they would like to play with, children they dislike—or even by asking children to cast their classmates in stereotypical roles in a fictitious play. When ranked in this manner, children's popularity generally remains stable from one day to the next or even one month to the next, but over periods of several years, the classification of many children may change. Age also has a good deal to do with the stability of a child's popularity. The younger the child, the less stable his or her ranking. Popularity also is less stable among children who are not well acquainted; as groups are established, rankings begin to solidify (Hartup, 1983).

The context of relationships also affects a child's popularity. Andrew Newcomb and William Bukowski (1984) followed more than three hundred youngsters for two years, checking their popularity ratings over the fifth-, sixth-,

Mixing Age Groups

Most studies of peer interaction focus on children of a single age, yet outside the classroom youngsters of a wide variety of ages play together. The age structure of a neighborhood peer group depends on chance; the children may be within a year or two of one another, or there may be a large gap between the youngest and oldest members—especially if a younger sibling is tagging along.

Unlike day-care centers, which generally group youngsters by age, day-care homes often give infants, toddlers, and preschoolers an opportunity to interact. After comparing toddlers in the two environments, Carollee Howes and Judith Rubenstein (1981) reported that although play was similar in both groups, there was much more vocalizing in the day-care home. They suggest that older children in these small, mixed groups talk to younger toddlers, promoting their use of speech. Earlier studies have found that when interacting with toddlers, children as young as four adjust their speech to the level of the younger child, and that eighteen-month-olds vocalize much more when interacting with twenty-four-month-olds than when with agemates (Hartup, 1983).

An experimental program involving three- to eight-year-olds gave Jaipaul Roopnarine and James Johnson (1984) an opportunity to study a mixed-age group. Kindergartners and school-age children preferred to socialize with their agemates, but preschoolers sought out kindergartners in preference to agemates. In most cases, age, not sex, determined the way children paired off, a finding that squares with many parents' observations of neighborhood playmate choice.

Children soon learn what sort of behavior to expect from youngsters of different ages. First- and third-grade youngsters studied by Doran French (1984) were in agreement on this issue. Older children provide leadership, assistance, and sympathy to younger children. Youngsters do not instruct children older than themselves, or give them visible sympathy. Children's expectations are reflected in their descriptions of other youngsters. Among another group of first- and third-graders, younger children were regarded as "dumb," "worst," "silly," and "weak," whereas children older than themselves were described as "best," "strong," "smart," and "fast"—as well as "mean," "bossy," and "show-off" (Graziano, Musser, and Brody, 1980). After reviewing the research, Hartup (1983) concluded that mixed-age groups probably help socialize children to seek assistance from others and to be assertive—in both positive and negative ways.

---

and seventh-grade school years. At the end of the fifth grade, these children moved from five different elementary schools to a single consolidated middle school, allowing peer ratings to be resorted and reestablished. The largest group of children, those of average popularity, tended to remain relatively stable across the two-year period. Highly popular children tended to slip in and out of the average group. Only about a third of the popular fifth-graders were popular as seventh-graders, and many of them had gone through temporary periods of waning popular-

ity. Similar patterns appeared among rejected children, many of whom made their way into the average group. Children who remained in the popular group tended to be socially mature and academically competent; children who remained in the rejected group tended to be socially immature and highly aggressive. Isolated children showed no particular pattern, and their ratings tended to be least stable of any, with only about one in five of the fifth-graders still characterized as isolates two years later.

Exactly how much effect the move to a new,

larger school had on the popularity rating of these children is difficult to determine. However, when more than 15,000 nine- to twelve-year-olds who remained in the same school were followed for several years, rankings of highly popular children were fairly stable (Roff, Sells, and Golden, 1972).

SOCIAL ISOLATION

Not all children are accepted by their peers. Several studies conducted over a thirty-year period (Bonney, 1943; Gronlund, 1959; Hymel and Asher, 1977) have shown that when children are asked to designate their friends, about 10 percent of the children in a group are not named at all. Rejection or neglect by their peers may have greater consequences for children than simply unhappiness. Isolates tend to drop out of school (Ullman, 1957); they are also more likely than the accepted child to have later emotional problems or to become juvenile delinquents. When researchers checked back eleven years after they had studied a group of third-graders, they found that children who had been disliked by their peers were more likely to have developed emotional problems than the rest of the group (Cowen et al., 1973). Another study (Roff, Sells, and Golden, 1972) found that rejected middle-class and upper-middle-class children tended to become juvenile delinquents. Social isolation did not predict delinquency among lower-class children, and it has been suggested that because gang membership accompanied by delinquency is common at low socioeconomic levels, it washes out the connection between isolation and delinquency (Asher, 1978). That is, in a group where delinquent acts are considered part of normal social activities, peer acceptance may demand them.

Until recently, educators and psychologists did little to bring isolated children back into the group. After all, the withdrawn child does not disrupt the classroom, and teachers—who most often witness peer interaction—tend to be con-

Children become social isolates when they are either neglected or rejected by their peers; children who are simply neglected have a much better chance of later being taken into the peer group. (Chester Higgins, Jr./Rapho-Photo Researchers)

cerned about the child who interferes with classroom or playground activities, not about the social isolate. Realization of the possible social consequences of isolation has changed the picture, and various programs are now under way that attempt to bring unpopular children into the group.

However, past research with unpopular children has tended to lump neglected and rejected children together under the label of "rejected" or "social isolate." Today, researchers are separating them on the grounds that, when placed in a new group of children, rejected children often remain rejected but neglected children sometimes are accepted or even become popular (Asher, Hymel, and Renshaw, 1984). Rejected children are probably at greater risk for later adjustment problems. They are generally described by their peers as restless, talkative, and not likeable, and their attempts at interaction are regarded as aversive. Rejected children seem inflexible in their interactions; when they try to enter a group and fail, they are unable to devise new strategies and persist in their assertive or aggressive techniques (Rubin and Krasnor, in press). Neglected children are described by their peers as quiet, and when they do interact, they may be competent and agreeable (Asher, Markell, and Hymel, 1981). When their attempts at social interaction fail, neglected children, who apparently lack social confidence, tend to ask for adult intervention (Rubin and Krasnor, in press).

Perhaps the best way to discover if children are lonely is to ask them. Most youngsters know when they are having problems with their peers. When more than five hundred elementary-school children were given a twenty-four item questionnaire, more than 10 percent reported feelings of loneliness and social dissatisfaction (Asher, Hymel, and Renshaw, 1984). These feelings correlated significantly with their popularity ratings among their classmates, and the more best friends a child had, the less likely he or she was to report being lonely. Some children with low popularity ratings were not especially lonely, but such children typically reported playing with siblings or neighborhood friends.

Perhaps lonely, isolated children have never learned the social skills they need to get along with other children. Researchers have designed programs to teach such skills, in the hope of bringing isolates back into the group. Such programs generally use behavior modification, modeling, or coaching.

Approaches based on behavior modification teach social skills by reinforcing children's attempts at social interaction. Sometimes a child already possesses these skills, but does not use them. That was the case with Ann, a four-year-old who entered nursery school and found that the other children were not impressed by her physical and linguistic skills and creativity.

Within a few weeks, Ann retreated from group play and spent most of her time seeking attention from adults. Eileen Allen and her colleagues (1964) discovered that the techniques that brought Ann adult attention isolated her from her peers. The team had teachers reinforce Ann only when she interacted with other children and ignore her when she was alone or seeking adult attention. Ann's behavior changed immediately, and she began spending much of her time interacting with other children. The children responded, and after a few weeks, the teachers slowly phased out their reinforcement for peer activities, putting Ann on an intermittent schedule of reinforcement. Ann continued playing with the other children and seemed accepted by the peer group.

Ann's case is unusual because she already had learned social skills. With children who have never learned how to interact successfully with others, teachers can reinforce social interaction and ignore (thereby extinguishing) actions that interfere with it. Allen and her colleagues (1964) say that when this procedure is used, children generally take several weeks to reach the level of social interaction that Ann achieved on the first morning of the program. If rewards for social interaction are ended abruptly, however, children tend to retreat to their original isolation. But if teachers switch to intermittent reinforcement, then gradually fade the rewards, the natural reinforcement of group play builds up, as it did in Ann's case.

When modeling techniques are used, children watch filmed models who approach children at play and join in their activities. After withdrawn children have seen the filmed model, they may engage in role-playing, rehearsing the actions they have seen on the film. Modeling techniques have led to increased social interaction by withdrawn children; when observed a month later, children are still interacting at a higher level (Evers and Schwartz, 1973).

In a program that combined social reinforcement with modeling techniques, however, the reinforcement seemed more powerful and longer lasting than the modeling (Weinrott, Corson,

Bringing Low-Achieving Rejected Children into the Peer Group

Most programs that have been designed to help rejected children make friends have concentrated on social skills. This approach assumes that it is a child's lack of social competence that causes him or her to be rejected. For many isolated children, this is true, but some children are doubly handicapped: they have serious academic problems and they are unlikable youngsters whose attempts to interact with others are rebuffed.

In an experiment designed to discover what sort of program would bring these children back into the group, John Coie and Gina Krehbiel (1984) tried three different approaches with black fourth-graders in the Durham, North Carolina, public schools. One group of youngsters received individual tutoring in reading and mathematics; a second group received direct instruction in social skills, using the program described in the text (Oden and Asher, 1977); a third group received both academic tutoring and social skills training; and a fourth group served as a control.

The academic tutoring began in October and lasted until April; social skills training began with six weeks of individual tutoring during the fall and another six weeks of group instruction the following January. In May, the children's social acceptance was checked by administering sociometric tests in the classrooms. And the following May, when the children were in fifth grade, the tests were repeated.

To the investigators' surprise, both groups that were tutored in academic skills, whether or not they had been trained in social skills, made great strides toward social acceptance—improvements that were still apparent a year later. The youngsters had moved from the "rejected" to the "average" category in peer rankings, and they were significantly more likely to be chosen as "liked most" by their classmates than either children whose training had been limited to social skills or children in the control group. All three groups that received training showed large decreases in nominations as "liked least," but the improvement shown by children who received only social skills training had disappeared by the following year.

The children who received academic tutoring also showed lasting, significant improvement in reading, as well as improvement in mathematics that disappeared by the following year. Coie and Krehbiel (1984) speculate that improved academic skills, greater participation in classwork, and positive attention from the teachers helped to increase these children's self-esteem and positive attitude toward school. They did fewer things to annoy their classmates and spent more classtime working at their desks. In addition, changes in the teachers' behavior may have led other children to see these youngsters in a new light, giving them an opportunity to be accepted.

Although the social skills program had been successful with other rejected children, its gains were shortlived with these doubly burdened children. It may be that when children have both academic and social problems, focusing only on social problems is unlikely to pay off, given the unpleasantness of their classroom experiences. Or, say Coie and Krehbiel, the extra hours of individual attention that were involved with the academic program may have been instrumental in its lasting success.

and Wilchesky, 1979). This study used peer re-inforcement and group rewards in addition to rewards for the isolated children. By the end of the program, these first- to third-grade isolates were involved in as much social interaction as other children, and their peer activities extended to lunchroom and playground contacts. The formerly isolated children began to visit friends and to invite them to their own homes. Teachers said the children seemed happier, more alert, and eager to assume responsible tasks, although they did not show as much altruistic or cooperative behavior as other children, nor did they pay as much attention to others.

Coaching, the third approach to social isolation, directly instructs children in social skills. Sherri Oden and Steven Asher (1977) taught third- and fourth-grade children how to start playing a game; how to pay attention; how to take turns; how to share materials; how to reward other people by looking at them, smiling, offering help or encouragement. The children practiced the skills they had learned in play sessions with their peers. Afterward, the coaches met again with the children and went over the skills they had been taught. After a six-week program, the isolated children appeared to be accepted by their peers; a follow-up one year later showed that the acceptance had increased. The program's only visible failure was that it did not increase the number of "best friends" the isolates had.

No matter what kind of approach is used, the earlier the intervention, the better for the isolated child. It may be harder to change established patterns of withdrawal in older children; in addition, isolated children's peers may be slower to change their opinion of a withdrawn child (Asher, 1978).

CHANGING RELATIONSHIPS

As children develop, the nature of their interaction with peers changes. The infant plays be-

side and with another baby, making simple social overtures. When children enter nursery school or kindergarten, peers increase in importance. Children find a large number of schoolmates of their own age and, in elementary school, many others of slightly different ages. The new peer group includes children from different neighborhoods, children who would have remained strangers without the school setting.

Friendship

A wider group of acquaintances, however, does not necessarily lead to an increase in the number of close friends. During early childhood, children tend to draw close to an increasing number of their peers; but during later childhood, their friendships increase in intensity rather than in number. They spend more time with their friends than they used to, playing after school at friends' houses or spending the night with friends. As they move into adolescence, the relation with their peers changes, and so do their friendships, moving from the congenial sharing of activities to psychological sharing and intimacy. Asked what they like best about a friend, young children mention play; they expect their friends to be entertaining. Adolescents and adults, however, expect their friends to be useful (Reisman and Shorr, 1978).

Like adults, children make friends with individuals who resemble them. Most childhood friends are similar in age (a tendency that is accentuated by the age-graded structure of the schools) and are usually of the same gender and ethnic background. To a lesser degree, friends resemble each other in attitudes and behavior. For example, friends tend to have similar levels of sociability (Hartup, 1983). Resemblances in behavior and attitudes tend to increase with age. Among nearly two thousand New York State adolescents, best friends were usually the same age, sex, and ethnicity; they tended to do the same things; their use or rejection of drugs was similar; and their attitudes and personality characteristics tended to be similar, although resem-

These young friends value their relationship for the fun they get from playing together, and each expects the other to be entertaining company. (Alan Carey/The Image Works)

blance in these areas were weakest (Kandel, 1978b). Over the period of a year, friends became more alike in behavior and attitudes, and those who did not were likely to sever their friendships (Kandel, 1978a).

We would expect children to spend more time with their best friends than with acquaintances, and this is generally the case among children and adolescents. When together, friends tend to act in ways that set them apart from acquaintances. Eight-year-olds who attempted a block-building task were equally successful with friends or acquaintances, but when working with friends they showed more emotion, interacted more, paid closer attention to rules of fairness, and were more likely to work out natural strategies than when working with acquaintances (Newcomb, Brady, and Hartup, 1979). The nature of the task also affects the way children interact with friends. When property rights are clear, children are more competitive with friends than with acquaintances, but on tasks that do not provide concrete rewards, children share more with friends than with acquaintances (Hartup, 1983).

Friendships are not always forever. Either party can decide to end the relationship. Friendships among preschoolers are especially unstable, and Robert Selman (1980) has suggested that they have such a short duration because preschoolers are generally unaware of the attitudinal and behavioral similarity that underlies most enduring friendships, choosing best friends on the basis of physical characteristics or transitory play. In Chapter 17, we shall see how cognitive development affects children's understanding of others and the quality of their friendships.

A cooling in most children's friendships was observed by Thomas Berndt (in press) when he followed fourth- and eighth-grade pairs of friends for six months. Although 69 percent of the autumn friendship pairs were still "best friends" in spring, most children were less positive about the friendship and about their friend's personality. They had more negative things to say about each other in the spring, and most were seeing each other less. This tendency appeared in both age groups and in both sexes.

Although boys' and girls' friendships are alike in most respects, as girls move into adolescence their friendships become much more intimate than those of boys (Berndt, in press). Girls' friendships appear to progress from activity-centered pairs in childhood to interdependent, emotional, and conflict-resolving relationships by middle adolescence, finally becoming relationships that are less emotional, less an instrument for reducing conflict, and more a sharing of personalities, talents, and interest (Douvan and Adelson, 1966). Boys in junior- and senior-high school appear to be less concerned with the intimacy that characterizes girls' friendships. Their friendships are more like those found among preadolescent girls, involving a congenial companion with whom one shares activities (Douvan and Adelson, 1966). This gender difference is part of a larger pattern of sex-role differences in American society. Close interpersonal relationships are a major factor in the formation of female identity, while males are more likely than females to spend their adolescent

These nine-year-old best friends do "everything" together; if their friendship lasts until adolescence, its basis will shift from shared activities to shared feelings and emotional support. (Joel Gordon)

social lives in cliques and gangs instead of in pairs.

Peer Groups

Although nursery-school and kindergarten children form peer groups with structures that are visible to observers, the youngsters themselves are often unaware of them and have little sense of belonging to a group. In tracing the development of the peer group, Hartup (1983) notes that children in the primary grades see the group as made up of a series of unilateral relations; by preadolescence, they view it as a series of interlocking pairs. Not until children move into adolescence do they view the peer group as a community of like-minded people. During adolescence, the structure of the peer group changes to accommodate young people's sexual maturation and heterosexual activities. What begins as a clique of adolescents of the same sex becomes a group made up of both sexes, and

each member tries to establish a significant relationship with a member of the other sex (Dunphy, 1963).

Two patterns are characteristic of the peer groups of later childhood and adolescence. The first is the elaboration of an ingroup-outgroup sense of belonging that is supported by special group activities and rituals and the exclusion of outsiders. Each group develops its own norms, some reflecting the norms of the larger culture and some peculiar to the specific group. These latter norms are often highly visible and may govern items as trivial as whether shirt cuffs are buttoned or rolled or what brand of soft drink is consumed. Children learn to define their own special qualities and ways of behaving in relation to the group and, frequently, in contrast to the ways outsiders act. Fortunately, group membership is not rigid, and many such cliques break up and reform, so that temporarily and arbitrarily excluded children may later slip into the fold. The impact of the peer group on a child's life is determined by the strength of his or her identification with the group and the depth of the child's desire to belong to it (Hartup, 1983).

A second pattern of group interaction that soon emerges is the development of hierarchies. The dominance hierarchy, which was discussed in Chapter 1, is present among nursery-school children, even when they are not able to say who is the "strongest" or "toughest" group member (Strayer, Chapeskie, and Strayer, 1978). As children get older, their awareness of the various hierarchies increases, so that the typical fifth-grader can rattle off an ordered list of the smartest, most athletic, and most popular. Children show surprising agreement about such orderings.

Social power within the group depends on which members have the attributes needed to reach group goals. Unless aggression will serve this end, it will not provide the basis for the dominance hierarchy. In some groups, aggressiveness or assertiveness does mark the leader; in others, it is social sensitivity and the ability to manipulate others; in groups that form in hazardous environments, the leader may have to be the most knowledgeable concerning survival skills (Hartup, 1983).

The requirements that characterize leaders also tend to change with age (Hartup, 1983). Group leaders in early childhood tend to be children who can keep possessions and know how to use them. In middle childhood, the ability to direct and play games becomes important. By early adolescence, athletic and social skills characterize leaders, who also tend to be early maturers. Finally, in late adolescence, the group chooses intelligent, well-liked peers to lead them. These changing guidelines are flexible, and children tend to be discriminating in their assignment of leadership roles. During middle childhood, for example, when children organize a baseball game, they generally listen to an athletically skilled child; when they are staging a play, they turn to an imaginative child. Among a larger number of six- to eleven-year olds, leaders tended to be more intelligent, active, aggressive, achieving, and socially adept than children who rarely led (Harrison, Rawls, and Rawls, 1971). A child's position in peer-group activities provides training for the later assumption of adult social roles, and the ranking of children in their dominance hierarchies seems to predict their general social competence (Hartup, 1979).

Group members often deny the existence of a hierarchy within the group, but in some groups the hierarchies are open. For example, in a study of twelve- to fourteen-year-olds at a summer camp, Ritch Savin-Williams (1979) found that boys frankly recognized the dominance hierarchies in their cabins, but in only two of the four girls' cabins did the girls agree on the ranking of leaders and followers. Leaders among both sexes were self-confident, "cool," mature, athletic, intelligent, and popular. Boy leaders asserted themselves physically, argued with others, and tended to threaten and displace their cabinmates. Girl leaders controlled by recognizing the status of their cabinmates, giving unsolicited advice and information to some and shunning or ignoring others. Leaders took the biggest pieces of cake at dinner, the preferred seats at discussions, and the best sleeping sites near the campfire at campouts. Leaders also took on group obligations; dominant girls, for example, often intervened in squabbles and patched interpersonal relationships. This made them useful to the group. As Savin-Williams suggests, the rankings appear to add stability and predictability to social relationships and to reduce group friction and overt aggression.

CONFORMITY

No matter what status children hold in a group, group solidarity exercises a great deal of influence on their behavior. Competition within a group may decrease solidarity (Stendler, Damrin, and Haines, 1951), but Muzafer and Carolyn Sherif (1953, 1964) have found that evenly balanced competition between groups results in greater cohesiveness within each group. Although occasional rancor may appear just after a competitive defeat, group members generally become much closer to one another in competitive situations. Because competition between groups produces a cooperative atmosphere within an individual group, it is not surprising that it should promote group solidarity. However, in a field study of unbalanced competition among boys in a summer camp, when one group consistently lost, the losing group threatened to collapse in disharmony (Sherif and Sherif, 1953). Apparently, when the unpleasantness generated by defeat becomes constant, it simply overcomes any tendency within the group for members to cooperate.

Whether competition was balanced or unbalanced, it produced a considerable amount of friction between groups. The boys looked down on members of the other group, and the situation eventually exploded into open hostility. This intergroup hostility further strengthened group cohesiveness and increased the influence of the group over the behavior of its members. Further, boys who were not normally hostile participated in intensively aggressive acts for the

Peer pressure is at its height in early adolescence; if traveling alone, none of these youths would dare to perform acrobatics in a subway car. (Joel Gordon)

sake of the group. In such a case, it seems that the structured group has the ability to overpower any tendency children have developed toward self-judgment and leads them to engage in behavior they would normally avoid.

The strong influence that peers can have on a child's behavior was clearly demonstrated in a study by Philip Costanzo and Marvin Shaw (1966), who asked children to compare the lengths of a pair of lines and identify the longer one. One line was obviously longer than the other, but all except one of the children were confederates of the investigators, and they chose the incorrect line. If the child denied the evidence of his or her senses and agreed with the obviously incorrect judgment of the group, the child had altered a personal judgment to conform to that of peers. As Figure 14.2 shows, a child's susceptibility to this form of peer influence increases with age, reaches its peak during the preadolescent years, and then gradually declines.

The behavior of children in such a contrived situation may not accurately reflect their conformity to peer pressure, points out Hartup (1983). Conformity—or lack of it—apparently depends on the child's understanding of social rules, his or her motives, and the nature of the peer group. After reviewing the research, he concluded that on easy tasks, children become progressively less likely to conform to peer judgment with age, but that on difficult or insoluble tasks, they may continue to rely on the suggestions or judgment of their peers.

Instead of asking youngsters to defy their senses, Thomas Berndt (1979) gave them thirty different situations and asked them how they would respond to peer pressure in each. Their

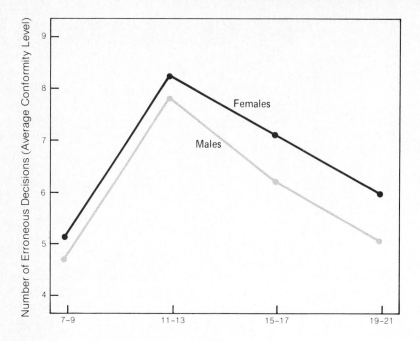

FIGURE 14.2 Children's conformity to the judgments of a peer group. Both females and males show increased susceptibility to peer influence with age, until early adolescence; then it gradually declines.

(After Costanzo and Shaw, 1966)

answers supported Costanzo and Shaw's finding that conformity to peers declines during adolescence (see Figure 14.3). Berndt found that children's tendencies to conform to their parents' wishes decrease from the third through the ninth grade, and that conformity to antisocial pressure from peers increases sharply from the third to the ninth grade, then declines during the high-school years. Among third-graders, parents' wishes outweigh those of peers; where there is conflict, third-graders generally conform to their parents' desires. Although peer influence increases among sixth-graders, there seems to be no conflict between family standards and those of the peer group. Children apparently live in two worlds, each with its own standards. Conflict between those worlds is sharp among ninth-graders, perhaps because the push toward antisocial behavior is strongest among these children. But among eleventh- and twelfth-graders, the conflict has eased; adolescents no longer feel as compelled to conform to their peers' wishes. In addition, they are beginning to accept conventional adult standards for their behavior.

These findings conflict with the popular belief that conflict between peer and parental standards inevitably accompanies adolescence. However, no available evidence demonstrates that the onset of adolescence necessarily means any decrease in conformity to parental demands. Adolescents conform to peers in matters pertaining to choice of friends, music, language fads, and clothes, but they conform to parental values in matters pertaining to achievement, such as academic performance and job or career aspirations (Hartup, 1983).

Studies by Denise Kandel and Gerald Lesser (1972) in the United States and Denmark indicate that in both countries parental influence on an adolescent's life goals is much stronger than peer influence. Although they confirmed earlier findings that adolescents rarely reward intellec-

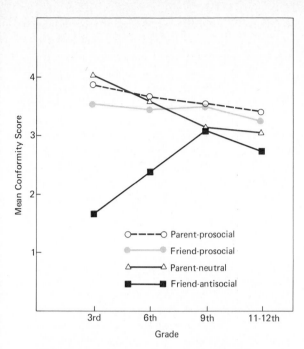

FIGURE 14.3 The course of antisocial peer pressure on children follows a characteristic course, rising sharply from third to sixth grade, then declining during the high-school years as adolescents begin to accept conventional standards.

(From Berndt, 1979. Copyright © 1979 by The American Psychological Association. Reprinted by permission.)

tual achievement in their peers, they also found that peers have less influence than parents on adolescents' future educational goals.

The continuing link between adult and adolescent standards is illustrated by studies of adolescent alcohol use. Every study of alcohol use has found that the drinking patterns of teen-agers directly reflect those of their parents and the community in which they live. About two-thirds of all adults in the United States drink on occasion, and drinking is more prevalent among persons of higher social status than among those of lower social status. Margaret Bacon and Mary Brush Jones (1968) found that most adolescents who drink tend to drink mod-

erately, to begin drinking at home with their parents, and to follow rules of alcohol consumption that their parents set. They also found that drinking among adolescents varies from 86 percent in Nassau County, New York, to 44 percent in rural Kansas. Other studies show that teen-age drinking patterns imitate adult drinking patterns: boys drink more than girls, city adolescents drink more than country adolescents; middle- and upper-middle-class adolescents drink more than working- or lower-class adolescents.

Because adolescents have learned from their parents and other adults to perceive drinking as an explicitly social activity, peer-group norms for acceptable drinking behavior tend to keep such behavior in line. Thus when adolescents drink in the secrecy of the peer group, social control is still present.

Smoking is one area where parental admonitions appear to have little effect, and most psychologists believe that peer pressure is a primary cause of adolescent smoking. Adolescents know about the risks connected with cigarettes, but since the effects do not appear for decades, they are not gravely concerned about the personal consequences (Evans, 1976). If peer pressure is indeed an important factor in adolescent smoking, then self-confident individuals should be the most resistant and therefore the least likely to smoke. A study sponsored by the American Cancer Society showed that this was true among boys but not among girls. Boys who smoked were less self-confident than boys who did not smoke, but girls who smoked were more self-confident than girls who did not. The girl smokers were also heavier smokers and more socially outgoing than the boy smokers, but the girls did not regard smoking as a social asset. Like many women, girls believe that by keeping them from eating, smoking helps them control their weight.

Adolescent use of other drugs alarms parents, but as with alcohol, adult behavior serves as a model. Adolescents have had more than a decade of exposure to adults whose behavior—whether legal or illegal—has been a model for their own experimentation and for the control of group behavior. But adults who smoke, drink alcohol, or take tranquilizers or barbiturates tend to ignore these connections and consider drugs as a purely adolescent problem. Studies consistently show that the use of cigarettes, alcohol, marijuana, and other drugs is significantly lower among children of nonusing parents (Hartup, 1983).

The experience of other cultures shows that conflicts between parent and peer standards are not necessary; the peer group can function as a representative of adult society. Urie Bronfenbrenner's (1970) observations and studies in the Soviet Union indicate that Soviet children are brought up in a series of "nested social units" that carry the responsibility for a child's behavior, each concerned with a progressively larger number of children. For example, in the school, the units include the row of double-seated desks, the classroom, and the entire school; youth organizations are composed of similar units. Because the group is held responsible for the individual's behavior and administers formal rewards and punishments, children soon learn to adhere to society's standards and to subordinate their own interests to those of the group. The Soviet peer group functions under the guidance of the adult society. Bronfenbrenner points out that an earlier American experiment—similar to the line experiment discussed earlier (Costanzo and Shaw, 1966)—shows how the process works. Morton Deutsch and Harold Gerard (1955) discovered that when a person's behavior affects only him- or herself, conformity in the line experiment runs about 33 percent. But when the entire group is rewarded for making the fewest errors, thereby intensifying group feelings, twice as many people conform to the obviously incorrect judgment.

SCHOOLS AND TEACHERS

Although the original focus of the schools was literacy, the scope of the school's influence ex-tends far beyond the content of the curriculum. As a major, long-term setting for social experience, schools interact with the influence of parents, peers, religion, and media to affect all aspects of socioemotional development. An adolescent leaves high school with a propensity to approach situations in particular ways, a propensity that has been shaped in part by what takes place at school (Minuchin and Shapiro, 1983). Two areas in which the school is especially involved are children's attitudes toward other ethnic groups and children's sense of competence and achievement.

Effects of Desegregation

When schools were first desegregated, many people hoped that daily classroom contact would lead to children's increasing acceptance of other races. But sociometric analysis, in which children were asked to name their best friends, indicated that blacks almost invariably chose blacks and whites chose whites—even in schools that had been integrated for some time (Bartel, Bartel, and Grill, 1973). As we have seen, children tend to choose as friends children who are similar to themselves, so this result conforms to other research concerning friendship formation.

Instead of looking at "best friends," Louise Singleton and Steven Asher (1979) later used acceptance as an appropriate measure of integration among children in a midwestern city. Singleton and Asher asked third-graders to rate each of their classmates (on a scale of 1 to 5) as to how much they liked to play with them and how much they liked to work with them. Three years later, when the children were in the sixth grade, the test was repeated. All the children had been in integrated classrooms since kindergarten.

Although both black and white children rated their own race higher, each indicated a sturdy acceptance of the other race, producing similar ratings for play and for work (see Figure 14.4). Gender played a larger role than race in the ratings. Boys rated boys of another race high,

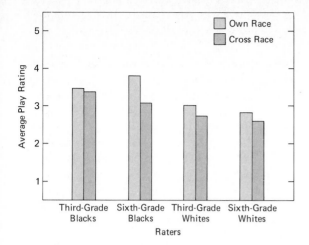

FIGURE 14.4 Black and white children attending integrated schools said they liked to play with children of the opposite race, although both showed a slight preference for their own race.

(From Singleton and Asher, 1979. Copyright © The Society for Research in Child Development, Inc. Reprinted by permission.)

and girls low; girls showed the same pattern, with white children showing stronger cross-gender rejections of the other race than black children. As children moved from the third to the sixth grade, cross-gender rejection dropped among all boys but increased among white girls.

White children showed no greater preference for their own race in the sixth grade than they had in the third, but sixth-grade blacks were not as comfortable playing and working with whites as they had been earlier. Singleton and Asher suggest that by the time they are eleven or twelve, blacks have become much more aware of their minority status and so make ingroup-outgroup distinctions, redrawing friendship lines with a greater emphasis on race.

In another study, children showed little tendency to allow race to affect their sense of fair play (Graziano et al., 1982). Black and white children in a large, integrated rural school in Georgia were asked to distribute prizes to other children on the basis of towers that had been built from blocks. In each case, one of the tower builders was a black child and the other was white. As first-graders, not race but the physical size of the tower builder affected children's judgments, but four years later all children tended to give the most prizes to the child who built the best tower, regardless of race or size.

The effect of attending a desegregated school may depend in good part on other aspects of the school environment. Among elementary-school students, positive attitudes toward other races have developed when the curriculum promotes concepts of racial equality and teachers assign children to integrated groups within the classroom where assignments cannot be completed without cooperative action. Among high-school students, the use of multiethnic texts or courses in minority history seems to have little effect, but when students are assigned to work together or when they participate in integrated sports teams, race relations generally show strong improvement (Minuchin and Shapiro, 1983).

Competence and Achievement

Children's feelings about themselves affect the decisions they make, the way they meet challenges and opportunities, and the impacts of rewards and punishments along the way. Often it is not what happens to a child that bolsters or diminishes the sense of competence, but the way the child explains the event to him- or herself. A child who feels incompetent will not be motivated to succeed. Interactions with peers and with teachers deeply affect a child's feelings of competency and attitudes toward achievement. However, these experiences interact with early home influences, so that before examining the power of teachers, we need to trace the birth of a child's need to achieve, or **achievement motivation,** to the family circle.

FAMILY INFLUENCE Both mother and father influence a child's urge to succeed, but

Children are most likely to develop positive attitudes toward other races when their school assignments cannot be completed without cooperative action within an integrated group. (Elizabeth Crews)

each plays a different role. When Marian Winterbottom (1958) studied mothers, looking for a link between achievement motivation and child rearing, she found certain clear differences between the mothers of boys with strong achievement motivation and mothers of boys whose achievement motivation was weak. The first group of mothers make more demands on their sons before they are eight years old and place more restrictions on them before they are seven—but the demands made are greater than the restrictions imposed. They expect their sons to do such things as hang up their clothes, make their beds, do well in competition with other children, attempt difficult undertakings without asking for help, cut their own meat, make their own friends, and select their own clothes earlier than do mothers of boys with weak achievement motivation. Mothers of boys with high achievement motivation also evaluate their sons' accomplishments higher and reward them more profusely then do mothers of boys with low achievement motivation. The mothers' expec-

tations for their sons indicate that they train their children for both independence and achievement and certainly there is likely to be some connection between doing things well and doing things by oneself.

But simply training a boy to be independent will not motivate him to succeed, report Bernard Rosen and Roy D'Andrade (1959), who watched parents interact with their sons. Mothers of boys with high achievement motivation stressed achievement at the expense of independence and became emotionally involved as their sons worked at difficult tasks. They showed significantly more warmth—but also more rejection following a poor performance—and were more dominant than mothers of boys with low achievement motivation. They pushed their sons to succeed.

Fathers of boys with high achievement motivation stressed independence rather than achievement in their sons. They sat back and gave the boys hints instead of becoming involved as the mothers did. They were less rejecting, less pushing, and less dominant than fathers of boys with weak achievement motivation, who tended to be relatively rejecting, dominating parents.

Both the parents of boys with high achievement motivation had high aspirations for their sons, expected them to do well, believed they were competent problem solvers, and were interested in and concerned with their sons' performance. They also tended to be competitive and involved and to enjoy the problem-solving part of the study themselves. They showed more affection for their sons than did the parents of boys with weak achievement motivation, and they rewarded successful performance with warmth and approval.

Parents' views of their children's abilities appear to have a powerful influence on children's expectations concerning their own success in school, and may be partly responsible for the typical sex-linked differences in mathematical aptitude and achievement that begin to show up during adolescence, and for the tendency of girls to avoid advanced mathematics classes. Jacquelynne Parsons and her colleagues (Parsons, Adler, and Kaczala, 1982) discovered that when parents expected their children to do well in math, their fifth- to eleventh-grade children had similar expectations. But when parents held a dim view of their children as mathematicians, the children expected to do poorly. Parents' expectations followed stereotypical views of male and female ability: they believed that math would be relatively difficult for their daughters and easy for their sons and that advanced mathematics was more important for sons. Their children echoed these beliefs, even though the boys and girls had similar scores on math achievement tests and had performed similarly in the previous year's math classes. Although children were aware of their parents' personal use and enjoyment of math, this knowledge had no effect on the children's expectations about their own performance, leading Parsons and her colleagues to conclude that a child's achievement motivation is not affected by the parent's power as role model.

Although Robert Sears (1970) did not look specifically at achievement motivation, he found that among twelve-year-old boys whose early years were marked by warm parents and non-dominant fathers, self-concept and school achievement in reading and arithmetic tended to be high. For girls, there was no relation between father dominance and self-concept, but school achievement was linked to parental warmth.

Girls generally receive more warmth from their parents than boys do, but this extra warmth may not be the best recipe for producing a girl whose achievement extends outside the classroom. Aletha Stein and Margaret Bailey (1973) reviewed studies of achievement in girls and concluded that girls are most likely to become independent high achievers when their parents are only moderately warm and moderately to highly permissive, and when they both reinforce and encourage the girls' attempts. Excessive maternal warmth, say Stein and Bailey, may produce a dependent girl, and some studies (e.g., Baumrind, 1968; 1972) have shown that

If these parents believe in their son's academic capabilities, expect him to achieve, and punish his failures, he probably has developed a strong need to achieve. (Myron Wood/Photo Researchers)

early protectiveness on the part of parents produces girls who are passive and withdraw from situations that demand achievement motivation. Achievement is also encouraged when girls have high-achieving mothers as role models.

Expecting achievement from boys and girls, then rewarding their successes and punishing their failures appears to be intimately bound up with the development of achievement. Middle-class parents generally have higher expectations for their children than do lower-class parents. Asked how their four-year-olds would perform on four tasks, middle-class parents consistently predicted higher scores for their children than lower-class parents predicted for their children (Marcus and Corsini, 1978). Middle-class parents expected their children to make average scores, but lower-class parents believed their children would perform less well than the average child. In fact, middle-class and lower-class children made similar, average scores on the tasks. The low expectations held for their children by lower-class parents may be one reason that lower-class children tend to be low achievers in school.

Most research on achievement motivation has been done on boys, but research on another aspect of achievement has focused on what was originally considered a female phenomenon: the fear of success.

FEAR OF SUCCESS Concerned because research into achievement motivation seemed unable to explain its development adequately in girls and women, Matina Horner (1969) suggested that women learn to fear success. They learn early that achievement in the world is aggressive and therefore masculine; if they compete, they may become less feminine (Tavris and Offir, 1977). And if they defeat males in competition, they may be punished. When women discover that aversive social consequences follow when they expend effort, persist in the face of obstacles, or compete and actually succeed, they may learn to withdraw from achievement situations—or avoid them. At the very least, they may learn to play down their accomplishments. They withdraw, then, not because they are afraid of failure but because they are afraid of success. Subsequent research has shown that the situation is not quite that simple. Men and boys frequently show as much evidence of "fear of success" as girls and women do. And male college students who feel threatened by female competence score high on tests that measure fear of success, but their girlfriends do not (Tresemer, 1974).

Believing that fear of success might reflect a girl's or woman's attempt to avoid expected punishment for outperforming a male, John Condry and Sharon Dyer (1977) studied the impulse among fifth- to ninth-grade children in an actual competitive situation. Boys and girls, working by themselves but seated in pairs opposite each other, unscrambled anagrams as part of an "intelligence test." Afterward, they were taken to another room, one at a time, ostensibly for another test but actually to be told that they had "won" over their partner of the other sex. Then they returned to the testing room, where they were seated opposite the same partner and asked to unscramble more anagrams. If they feared success, they would not do as well on their second try with anagrams.

Fifth-grade girls and boys both improved on the second anagram test, and by about the same amount. The scores of seventh-grade girls plummeted, however, while the scores of seventh-grade boys improved (see Figure 14.5). Among ninth-graders, boys' scores went up substantially and girls' average scores improved, but only by a slight amount. Placed in direct competition, neither girls nor boys in the fifth grade nor boys in the seventh and ninth grades showed any fear of success. But told they were outperforming a male, seventh-grade girls retreated. Their achievement was severely affected, despite the fact that they understood they were taking an intelligence test that might be expected to affect their academic futures. These girls simply withdrew from competition. When ninth-grade girls' scores were analyzed, a curious pattern appeared: half the girls improved as much as the boys did, and half showed disastrous declines.

Condry and Dyer believe the results of this study are in line with sex-role development. Most seventh-grade girls have just entered puberty, and as we shall see in the next chapter, at this time adolescents show increased adherence to stereotypical views of appropriate male and female behavior. Within a few years, many may be less uncertain about themselves and less restricted by stereotypes.

As we have seen, fear of success is not inevitable and is not restricted to women. There can be many reasons for a person to fear success, which as originally conceived was a fear of the social repercussions of success—disapproval, rejection, rivalry, jealousy. Carol Dweck and Elaine Elliott (1983) suggest that some people's fear of success may actually be a fear that if they succeed, they will be unable to maintain or exceed the new standard on later occasions. However, others may fear the increased responsibility that sometimes accompanies success—the

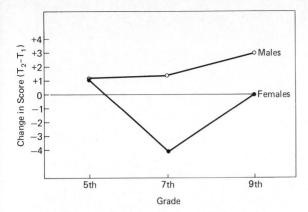

FIGURE 14.5 When children discover they have defeated a member of the other sex in an anagram game, adolescent boys and girls react differently to the news, and on a similar game seventh-grade girls show a pronounced fear of success.

(From Condry and Dyer, 1977. Copyright © The Society for Research in Child Development, Inc. Reprinted by permission.)

more children learn to do for themselves, the fewer things parents or teachers or older siblings will do for them.

THE EFFECT OF CLASSROOMS AND TEACHERS

A child's attitude toward learning, achievement, and self may be influenced by the educational model on which the school is established. Most schools are considered traditional; they emphasize the academic body of knowledge they are passing on and the values, attitudes, and behavior of the culture. Teachers are seen as authorities, determining the content, sequence, and pacing of instruction. Other schools are called "open schools," a quality that is sometimes reflected in their architecture, which does away with walls between classrooms. Open schools balance the content of the curriculum and societal standards against the needs of the individual child. Teachers share authority with children as they are able to han-

dle it, and both contribute to the curriculum (Minuchin and Shapiro, 1983).

An assumption behind the open school is that children will develop higher self-esteem there than children in traditional classrooms, because the open classroom is more supportive and allows children to experience greater satisfaction in mastering the curriculum. Although students in open classrooms generally have more positive feelings toward school, Patricia Minuchin and Edna Shapiro's (1983) review of the research found that in most cases the educational model has no effect on self-esteem. However, in open schools girls and boys tend to socialize on the playground and choose each other for friends more often than youngsters in traditional schools, where play is generally segregated by gender. There are also fewer highly popular "star" children and fewer scapegoats and social isolates in open classrooms, with children often selecting friends from outside their own classes. Finally, children in open classrooms are more likely than children in traditional classrooms to work cooperatively with others and seem more self-reliant. No difference has been found in curiosity, creativity, or a child's sense of locus of control (an aspect of personality discussed in Chapter 12).

Such analyses of classroom effects assume that all teachers have comparable influence on all children in the class. Yet each child in a class forms a different relationship with the teacher and thus has a different social experience. Research has consistently shown that teachers respond to the characteristics of children in specific ways. For example, children who conform to school routine, are high achievers, and who make few demands are generally favored by teachers. Children who continually demand inappropriate attention are usually rejected, and withdrawn or silent children may be ignored (Minuchin and Shapiro, 1983).

Teachers' expectations about children's academic achievement also affect teacher-student interactions. When teachers expect students to do well in class, the students usually succeed; when teachers expect students to fail, they often

This teacher's expectations concerning her individual students will affect the way she treats them in class, and that treatment will in turn affect each student's classroom behavior and success. (David S. Strickler/The Picture Cube)

do. This effect was first noted by Robert Rosenthal and Lenore Jacobson (1968), who picked students at random and told elementary-school teachers that tests showed the children would show unusual intellectual development during the school year. Among first- and second-graders, the researchers' predictions came true, with first-grade "bloomers" gaining about fifteen IQ points during the year. Among older children, the prediction had little effect, perhaps because teachers had lengthy school records for these youngsters that may have contradicted the predictions.

Researchers have concluded that teachers' expectations affect the behavior of children by affecting the teachers' own behavior (Cooper, 1979). When a teacher expects a child to be a high achiever, the teacher gives the child more chances to participate in class activity and more time to respond to questions. When the child is correct, he or she gets extra praise, and when wrong, the child is praised for trying and not scolded unless the teacher believes the child has not tried. When a teacher expects a child to be a low achiever, the teacher assumes that the child will rarely know the answer and may avoid calling on the youngster to keep from embarrassing him or her. When low-achieving children are praised or criticized, it is not for effort—or lack of it—but often for some extraneous reason, such as neatness.

Children also develop expectations concerning their teachers. A teacher's reputation spreads quickly through the school, and youngsters may tremble with fear or jump for joy when they discover who their teacher will be the following year. According to Minuchin and Shapiro (1983), little research has been done into the effect of children's expectations about their teachers and how they interact with teachers' expectations about the children. It would be unusual, however, if children's expectations did not affect their reactions to school and thereby influence their development.

EXPLAINING ACHIEVEMENT Children's reactions to the world vary depending on whether they expect to succeed or fail at various tasks and on the values that they attach to particular goals and activities. By the time they are in kindergarten, most children have developed consistent explanations for the results of their efforts and social interactions. These explanations are likely to depend in part on their intelligence and socioeconomic level. Toni Falbo (1975) found, for example, that five-year-old middle-class children were more likely than working-class children to stress the causal relationship between a person's effort and success or failure at a task. Bright children generally explained success as being due to personal ability and failure as due to the difficulty of the task. Less bright children tended to explain success as being due to the ease of the task but used lack of personal ability to explain failure. Falbo points out that the bright children's explanations encourage them to perceive themselves as responsible for success ("I'm smart") and not responsible for failure ("It was too hard"). In contrast, less-bright children's explanations encourage them to perceive themselves as responsible for failure ("I'm dumb") and as deserving no credit for their success ("It was just easy").

It is not success or failure that determines attitudes and expectancies, but the causes to which children attribute the success or failure. The causes can be inside the child (effort, ability, characteristics, mood) or outside in the environment (conditions under which a task is performed, difficulty). The causes can be stable (ability) or unstable (mood, unfamiliarity with task). The causes can be controllable (effort) or uncontrollable (ability); they can be global, affecting everything the child does (intelligence), or specific (learned skill). When a child views a task as influenced by stable, controllable, and global positive factors, the task is approached with expectations of success; when a child believes the task is influenced by stable, uncontrollable, and global negative factors, the task is either avoided or worked at half-heartedly, with no expectation of success. If Larry believes that he is inherently lazy and his effort is impossible to change, he is unlikely to work very hard at his clarinet lessons. But if Rob believes that he is musically talented and no lazier than the next person, he may practice hard every night in order to win first chair in band.

When children encounter a new achievement situation, say Carol Dweck and Elaine Elliott (1983), their beliefs, emotional state, and various situational cues combine to determine their expectations and values. Some children are more likely to attempt a task in order to learn; they ask themselves, "How can I do it?" or "What will I learn?" These children's goal is to increase their competence. Their standards are likely to be personal, and they judge their relative success in relation to their level of skill before they undertake the task. They see intellectual competence as a collection of skills that can be expanded by their own efforts and accept errors as part of the learning process.

Other children attempt a task in order to be rated for their performance; they ask, "Can I do it?" or "Will I look smart?" Their goal may be to seek a positive judgment of their competence or to avoid a negative evaluation. Their standards are likely to be normative, and they judge their success in relation to other children. They see intellectual competence as a fixed trait and errors as a sign of failure.

In any situation, children may have mixed goals, but when children develop low expectations of success and consistently approach a task with the aim of avoiding negative evaluations of their performance, their achievement motivation may suffer. According to Dweck and Elliott (1983), such children generally fall into two different patterns when placed in achievement situations. Those in one group, who tend to have a history of low achievement scores, IQ scores, and grades, may become highly anxious, hang on every cue they can get from the person who will evaluate them, and be unable to devise strategies for solving whatever problems they face (Wine, 1982). If pressure is eased ("This test won't count on your grade"), the anxious child may perform much better than when pressure is intense ("This test will determine your grade").

The other group of children, who have average or better IQs and no history of low test scores, have developed **learned helplessness,** a reaction to frustration or failure that leaves them with the belief that nothing they can do will enable them to succeed. Because of this belief, they respond to difficulties with diminished effort and concentration. They may refuse to try even when situations are such that they can succeed. Many researchers believe that learned helplessness develops when people are consistently placed in negative situations where their own efforts have no effect on the outcome.

Girls are especially vulnerable to learned helplessness. Although they do at least as well as boys through elementary school, they are much more likely than boys to interpret the news that they have made a mistake as indicating their own lack of ability. They may respond to such news from a teacher by failing at a task they had performed easily in the past.

Dweck and her colleagues (1978) believe that the school experiences of girls are especially likely to promote learned helplessness, whereas school failure has little effect on boys. When observing in the classroom, the researchers noted that when teachers criticize boys, they frequently criticize them for not following instructions, for being messy, and for not trying hard enough. Yet when teachers criticize girls, it is usually for inaccuracies in their work.

Reasoning that these differences in feedback were responsible for the tendency of girls to show learned helplessness, Dweck and her colleagues (1978) divided fifth-grade children into groups that received "boy" or "girl" criticism for mistakes in solving anagrams. Children who got "boy" criticism heard negative remarks that were devoted half the time to the inaccuracy of the child's solution and the rest of the time to their lack of neatness. The other children were given "girl" criticism; that is, all critical comments were devoted to the inaccuracies of the child's answers. Then each was given another task, which was halted three times and the child criticized for not working fast enough. After the third criticism, the children were asked to fill out a slip on which they checked the reason for their failure (I did not try hard enough; The man was too fussy; I am not very good at it). So that they would not end the experiment on a note of failure, all the children worked additional problems, for which they received considerable praise.

The results exactly followed Dweck's conjectures. Few of the boys and girls in the "boy" criticism group thought their own ability had anything to do with their mistakes: 80 percent of the girls and 50 percent of the boys said they had not tried hard enough, 20 percent of the boys said the man was too fussy. Both boys and girls in the "girl" criticism group reacted similarly: most attributed their failure to lack of ability, only a few thought they had failed because they did not try hard enough, none of the children blamed the experimenter.

Dweck believes that boys hear so much criticism directed at their sloppiness or laziness that they may discount past failures and expect that if they persevere on a new task they will succeed. Girls, who take criticism as an indication of a general lack of ability, may embark on a new task with fewer expectations of success. If so, such experiences may add to parental expectations in explaining why, after years of outscoring boys on math tests, girls begin to fall behind when they reach junior high school.

Other researchers believe that boys and girls do not receive different kinds of feedback, but

Table 14.1   CHILDREN' ATTRIBUTIONS AND MASTERY OF NEW MATERIAL

Attributional Style	Learning Condition	
	No confusion	Confusion
Material Mastered on First Attempt		
Helpless	29.51%	5.04%
Mastery-oriented	34.16%	24.43%
Material Mastered on Final Attempt		
Helpless	76.57%	34.65%
Mastery-oriented	68.36%	71.88%

When introductory material was confusing, children who had developed learned helplessness learned much less than mastery-oriented children. Yet when all the material was clear, helpless and mastery-oriented children learned approximately the same amount. (From Licht and Dweck, 1984.)

different amounts. Jacquelynne Parsons and her colleagues (1982) found that teachers' expectations concerning a child's performance determined the amount of praise that was dispensed. When teachers had expected boys to do well, they loaded them with praise, but when they had expected girls to do well, teachers were stingy with praise for their work. Perhaps because it reflected the teachers' expectations, boys who were highly praised were confident of their abilities. Praise had no effect on girls' view of their abilities, probably because it was so infrequent that it gave the girls no information about the teachers' expectations.

Children who have developed learned helplessness tend to attribute their failures to factors outside their control, whereas mastery-oriented children, who react to a difficult problem with increased effort, attribute their failures to unstable, controllable factors—such as insufficient effort. Learned helplessness appears to affect the way children evaluate their own performances. For example, when helpless and mastery-oriented children perform equally well, helpless children generally underestimate their successes (such as the number of problems they have solved correctly) and overestimate their failures, as compared with mastery-oriented children. And when asked how other children performed on the same task, the estimates of helpless children are significantly higher than the esti-

mates of mastery-oriented children (Diener and Dweck, 1978).

The belief of helpless children that success or failure is outside their control may lead them to give up when faced with difficult material, as Barbara Licht and Carol Dweck (1984) discovered when they altered the style of academic material. When sections near the beginning of a simple booklet on psychology required children to deal with confusing concepts, helpless children did poorly throughout the session, learning much less than mastery-oriented children, even on later material that was clearly written. But when all the material was clearly written, the helpless children did just as well as the mastery-oriented children in learning and understanding the material (see Table 14.1). The children were equally able to understand the material, but when the initial encounter promised to be difficult, children with learned helplessness stopped trying.

Young children appear to be less susceptible to learned helplessness than older children. Five- and six-year-olds tend to overestimate their abilities, and most children believe they are near the top of their class—even though their estimates of other children's ability are fairly accurate (Stipek, 1981). When they are placed in a situation in which they fail repeatedly, as when they are given an insoluble puzzle, kindergartners and first-graders tend to keep trying, but fifth-graders soon decide the situation is hopeless and give up (Rholes et al., 1980). Perhaps young children may be so accustomed to failure because of their limited abilities and lack of coordination that a failure or two at solving puzzles just does not bother them. After all, they face many situations—such as learning to ride a bicycle or tie their shoes—in which a long series of failures ends with a sudden breakthrough (Dweck and Elliott, 1983).

The scarcity of learned helplessness among the youngest children may also be related to their inability to distinguish between the effects of luck and skill. After playing a game of chance, kindergartners said that if they were older, smarter, practiced, or tried harder, they would win more at the game (Weisz et al., 1982). They gave similar answers for a game of skill, where their replies were more logical. Although fourth-graders understood the difference between chance and skill, they still believed that effort and practice would increase their winnings in a game of chance. Among eighth-graders (where learned helplessness becomes apparent) and college students, the majority understood that effort and practice did not affect the outcome in a game of chance, although a large minority continued to predict that effort, practice, or intelligence could increase their winnings.

Women seem more likely than men to attribute all success to luck, no matter what the situation. Whether this tendency is related to the greater incidence of learned helplessness in girls or to the style of criticism found by Dweck and her colleagues (1978) in the classroom is not known. If women believe they lack ability, they will tend to seek other explanations for their success. Kay Deaux (1976) has found that at state and county fairs, men seek out games of skill (such as tossing coins into dishes) but women seek out games of chance (such as bingo). What is more, men and women have similar expectations of success when they begin a game of luck; but when they start to play a game of skill, men's expectations go up and women's come down. As we move on to the

discussion of sex roles, we shall see that gender affects every aspect of peer relationships and achievement.

SUMMARY

Boys and girls transfer to their contacts with other children the social skills they develop within the family. As children grow older, the importance of the peer group steadily increases, and it is here that children practice and perfect the roles they will play in later years.

Studies with primates show that contact with peers is necessary for normal development. Peers appear to teach one another certain social skills that are not learned from parents.

Interaction and play with peers begin before babies are a year old, although babies lack the social skills needed for sustained interaction. Experience seems to help, because infants are more sociable with acquaintances than with strangers and play between familiar playmates goes on at a more intricate and constructive level. Sustained social interactions are apparent toward the end of the second year. The earliest play is with objects, which moves from indiscriminate manipulation to symbolic play when infants are about a year old. Solitary play is often followed by **parallel play,** but some youngsters seem to move directly from solitary to group play. Children influence one another by acting as models and by reinforcing and punishing one another's behavior. Through these means, peers can encourage or discourage such actions as aggression, disobedience, sharing, cooperation, or adherence to sex roles.

A child's popularity is influenced by many factors over which he or she has no control, such as physical appearance or name. Social skills, something a child can learn, are also important determinants of popularity, and they enable children to enter new relationships and then to sustain them. The stability of children's popularity, as measured by **sociometric analysis,** increases as they grow older, but many children's popularity fluctuates over the years, with highly popular children moving in and out of the average category, and isolated children making their way into the average group.

Not all children are accepted by their peers. Some are neglected children, who are not especially disliked but simply ignored; others are rejected children, unlikeable and restless, whose overtures tend to disrupt the play of their peers. Behavior modification, modeling, and coaching youngsters in social skills have all been used to bring isolates back into the group, with varying degrees of success.

Children tend to make friends with peers who are like themselves in age, gender, ethnic background and, as children get older, they tend to choose friends with similar attitudes and behavior. Friendships among preschoolers are highly unstable, and among older children, they often become more distant over time. Although boys' and girls' friendships are alike in most respects, the friendships of girls become much more intimate than those of boys as youngsters enter adolescence.

In later childhood and adolescence, the peer group provides a special sense of belonging, and hierarchies develop within the group. Children generally conform to peer standards in matters of friendship, language, and clothing, but they retain parental values concerning their future goals. The tendency to conform to peers rises throughout the elementary-school years, peaking in the ninth grade, then declines during high school.

Although desegregation is rarely followed by the formation of "best friends" across racial lines, each group accepts the other, playing and working with them. The effects of school desegregation depend on the interaction of many factors, including the nature of the curriculum and whether youngsters are required to engage in cooperative action.

A child's **achievement motivation** is affected by parental expectations, rewards, and punishment. Girls may learn to withdraw from competition because success makes them appear less feminine, although fear of success in boys as well as girls may reflect children's fear of social repercussions, an inability to maintain a new standard, or a reluctance to assume new responsibilities.

Open classrooms apparently encourage positive feelings toward school, cross-gender socialization, cooperation, and self-reliance, but their effect on self-esteem, curiosity, creativity, and a child's sense of locus of control is like that of traditional classrooms. Teachers respond to different children in different ways, often treating girls and boys differently, and their expectations may affect a child's achievement. Children's attitudes toward their successes or failures depend on the causes to which they attribute the outcome. If children fail repeatedly and believe their failures are due to enduring factors they cannot control, they may develop **learned helplessness.**

CHAPTER FIFTEEN

The Development of Sex Roles

THE PERVASIVENESS OF SEX ROLES
ROLES AND IDENTITY
THE DEVELOPMENT OF GENDER IDENTITY
Learning One's Gender
When Things Go Wrong
THE DEVELOPMENT OF SEX ROLES
The Influence of Biology
The Influence of Cognition
The Influence of Parents
The Influence of Peers
The Influence of Teachers
The Influence of the Media
SEXUALITY
Reactions to Physical Change
Retreat to Stereotypes
Sex Roles and Sex Differences
SEX ROLES AND THE LIFE SPAN
ANDROGYNY
SUMMARY

Four-year-old Tommy walked into the nursery-school playroom for the first time. While waiting for the morning's activities to begin, he strolled over to the doll corner and picked up a doll similar to the one that belonged to his sister. Tommy had three older sisters; he had often played house with them, and the familiar doll made him feel less uncomfortable in the strange surroundings. Just then a pair of boys burst through the door, stopped, and stared. Still carrying his doll, Tommy walked over to them. "Hi!" he said, smiling. There was no answering grin. "Look at the sissy," one of the boys said to the other; then the pair turned their backs and started toward the block corner.

Tommy will soon learn that boys play only with boy toys—especially at nursery school. Although he plays with dolls at home, he knows that he is a boy. He loves rough-and-tumble play and wears with pride his jeans and western shirt that are "just like Daddy's." Tommy is becoming a male psychologically by a complex process that is still incomplete. He is acquiring aspects of the male sex role and will rapidly learn that his peers have rigid ideas about permissible masculine behavior, ideas that he will soon adopt himself.

The shaping of a baby girl or boy into a firmly female or male adult is a lengthy and complex process involving hormones, learning, identification, imitation, and cognition. It is carried out by parents, friends, teachers, books, television, and most of the institutions of society. And it is helped along by the growing child, who seeks out and acquires behavior that seems appropriate to his or her gender. But the development of sex roles is not simply a cumulative process; the importance of being masculine or feminine ebbs and flows. Despite all the furor over sexist attitudes and behavior in our society, there are times in life when sex roles are not very important.

This chapter considers the importance of sex roles and examines the biological and social forces that shape them. After establishing the pervasiveness of sex roles in every society and every aspect of life, we explore the difference between sex role and gender identity, and examine the consequences of an insecure gender identity. In turn, we take up the interacting influences of biology, cognition, parents, peers, teachers, and the media on the development of sex roles. We then look at the relationship of sex roles to a person's life situation and, finally, consider the topic of androgyny.

THE PERVASIVENESS OF SEX ROLES

Every culture has established acceptable and unacceptable patterns of behavior and psychological standards for the sexes, and these sex-role standards are imposed at an early age. Sex roles pervade every aspect of life, and most of our activities reinforce the distinction between the sexes. In all societies, men and women have different duties, different responsibilities, and often different pleasures. Together, they make up a culture's **sex roles,** which include aspects that are inseparable from gender (the potential to bear a child or impregnate another person) and aspects that have nothing to do with it (in some cultures only men plant crops; in others,

only women). Sex roles ignore many inherent sex differences. If they did not, most brain surgeons would be women, since females generally are superior to males when it comes to the delicate motor control required in neurosurgery.

Sex roles are inevitably interwoven with the status that society attaches to each role. Thus male dominance was one of the earliest bases of discrimination among human beings, presumably because survival among hunting and gathering tribes depended on the ability to move about unencumbered by childbearing and nursing. The burden of advanced pregnancy or of carrying a small child would make it impossible for a woman to throw a spear accurately or to run after game (Friedl, 1978). Male children have always been valued, and many cultures have regularly killed excess female babies at birth (Johansson, in press).

The superiority of the male sex role has been perpetuated by incorporating it into the customs, laws, and socialization practices of successive generations. A cross-cultural survey of tribal societies by Herbert Barry, Margaret Bacon, and Irvin Child (1957) disclosed that the more its economy requires physical strength, the more strongly a society emphasizes sex differences in socialization. In most societies, whether ancient, primitive, or modern, the prestige of the task determines whether it is assigned to males or to females, with women often treated as if they were members of a minority group.

Somehow sex roles get translated into **sex-role stereotypes**—simplified, fixed concepts about the behavior and traits typical of each sex. Slight differences between the sexes, which are magnified by sex roles, become full-blown gender traits in the public mind. Stereotypical women talk and cry a lot; they are sociable, submissive, dependent, and timid. Stereotypical men, on the other hand, are silent and stoic; they are aggressive, competitive, and independent, with an itch to achieve. Men and women who fit these stereotypes are rare, but as we shall find, young children readily acquire the concepts however militantly nonsexist their parents may be.

Society prescribes the duties, responsibilities, and pleasures of each sex, and the resulting sex roles may have nothing to do with the biological aspects of gender. These Indian women would never think of joining the men in their evening social hour. (Above, Marc & Evelyne Bernheim/ Woodfin Camp & Associates; below, Thomas Hopker/Woodfin Camp & Associates)

ROLES AND IDENTITY

A sex role is like an outer garment. It is the visible and socially prescribed manifestation—in speech, dress, behavior—of one's gender. A woman, for example, is not likely to settle an angry dispute with a right to her opponent's jaw, nor is a man likely to burst into tears when distressed. Sex roles vary from culture to culture and from time to time in the same culture. Thirty years ago, closely cropped hair was a symbol of masculinity; today, hair length has no necessary connection with sex role. Seventy-five years ago, femininity and skirts were inseparable; today, women wear jeans as often as dresses. But before children can wrap themselves in society's sex roles, they must establish a sense of gender identity—a quite different concept.

Gender identity is invisible. It is the inner experience of gender, the unchanging sense of oneself as male or female (Money and Ehrhardt, 1972). Most developmental psychologists believe that gender identity is secure when a child not only understands the fact of his or her gender but also feels comfortable in the role. In this view, a person's degree of masculinity or femininity would be signified by the amount of satisfaction derived from being male or female (Lamb and Urberg, 1978).

In the view held by cognitive theorists, on the other hand, satisfaction has nothing to do with gender identity; it is largely intellectual, limited to the understanding of one's gender (Kohlberg, 1966). If gender identity is defined in this way, a male who had accepted the fact of gender but did not feel masculine would still have achieved gender identity. An eleven-year-old boy, for example, might know he is now and always will be male, but he might feel distinctly unmasculine because he does not care for football and finds the rough-and-tumble horseplay of his schoolmates distasteful.

Gender identity and sex role are the same in most cases; but sometimes there is little correspondence between the two. A woman who lacks a secure gender identity might, for that reason, adopt a highly stereotypical sex role.

She may, for example, know she is female but take little comfort in the fact and not "feel" feminine. In compensation, she might go in for ruffles and timidity, play the cuddly, clinging vine, and never under any circumstances behave in an "unfeminine" way. On the other hand, those who flout prescribed sex roles, as in the case of the working wife and the househusband, may nevertheless have secure gender identities.

THE DEVELOPMENT OF GENDER IDENTITY

Before babies learn to think of themselves as girls or boys, they must discover what a "girl" or a "boy" is. The voyage of discovery begins before they are aware they have embarked on it, for they are wrapped in pink or blue blankets in the hospital nursery and surrounded with sex-typed clothes and toys at home.

Learning One's Gender

Around the time they are eighteen months old and begin to acquire language, children learn gender labels and begin to apply them, generally relying on hair and clothes as clues. Two-year-olds can identify females as "girl" or "mommy" even when the pictured models have short hair or wear long pants. But as Spencer Thompson (1975) found, most two-year-olds are not convinced of their own gender. The children he studied did not always sort their own pictures appropriately by gender (as they did pictures of stereotypical males and females), nor did they always answer correctly when asked, "Are you a boy?" or "Are you a girl?" As we saw in Chapter 9, children are still learning the meaning of concepts long after they have a word for them. To a two-year-old, the label "girl" may be as idiosyncratic as "Susan" or "Lauren"; it is a name that applies to a lot of people, just as the child's caregiver and the caregiver of the little boy next door are both called "mommy."

By the time they are thirty months old,

This child has developed a sense of gender identity; he knows that he is a boy and he seeks out male models and imitates them. (Karen Collidge/Taurus Photos)

Thompson found, most youngsters know their own gender, although 25 percent of them are still likely to have trouble sorting their pictures and answering gender questions about themselves. Three-year-olds have no trouble with questions about the gender of themselves or others. They seem to realize that they—and all other people—are either male or female.

According to Lawrence Kohlberg (1966), this rudimentary sense of gender identity is only the first step. He believes the process is not complete until the child realizes that gender is constant: boys always become men and girls always become women, and maleness or femaleness cannot be changed. When Kohlberg asked children if a girl could become a boy if she wanted to, most four-year-olds said that she could. All she had to do was to cut her hair and wear boys'

clothes. Kohlberg reports that one young boy, just two months short of four years old, told his mother, "When you grow up to be a Daddy, you can have a bicycle, too [like his father]."

The sense of **gender constancy** develops between the ages of five and seven, when the child is also developing an understanding of physical conservation—a concept that was discussed in Chapter 10. As children come to understand that the amount of clay remains constant whether it is squeezed into a lump or rolled into a long string, so they understand that gender does not change—by dress or by magic. Because these concepts develop about the same time, says Kohlberg, a stable gender identity is primarily an intellectual accomplishment. A number of recent studies have explored this assertion.

In one such study, Dale Marcus and Willis Overton (1978) tested five- to eight-year-olds with the standard Piagetian conservation tasks involving clay of various shapes and the transfer of soybeans from a squat to a narrow container. Then, on another test, each child's sense of gender constancy was rated. For example, children looked at pictures of girls and boys and were asked whether the pictured children's gender remained constant as their clothes and hair styles were transformed. Marcus and Overton found that for most children, conservation preceded gender constancy. They also found that although the older a child, the firmer his or her assertion of gender constancy, brighter children developed the concept before less bright children did—an indication that a certain level of cognitive development, not simply a specific number of years of experience, is required for its understanding.

In a similar experiment, gender constancy showed a U-shaped course of development, with four-year-olds more likely to show gender constancy than five- or six-year-olds. According to Walter Emmerich (1982), the four-year-olds were apparently showing a "pseudo-constancy," because when asked to explain their judgments, they either could give no reason or else resorted to emotional justification ("I don't *want* him to be a girl"). Among seven-year-olds, youngsters' explanations reflected concrete operational thought ("She was born a girl"). Among children in another study (Ulian, 1976), six-year-olds who lacked gender constancy believed that unless one adhered rigidly to sex-typed activities, one's gender might change. Indeed, Emmerich (1982) has suggested that the pseudo-constancy of four-year-olds reflects the child's anxiety at the prospect of a boy behaving in a femininely stereotypical way—or vice versa.

If Emmerich is correct, such anxiety may have accounted for some responses of a group of four- to six-year-olds studied by Diane Ruble and her colleagues (Ruble, Balaban, and Cooper, 1981). These children watched television commercials for a sexually neutral toy, a Fisher-Price movie viewer. Half the children saw a commercial portraying the movie viewer as a boy's toy; the rest saw it portrayed as a girl's toy. When later given an opportunity to play with the toy, only children who understood that their gender would never change consistently shunned the move viewer when it was depicted as belonging to the other sex.

As children get older, they are more flexible about sex-role stereotypes. Eight-year-olds, who have an unshakeable sense of gender constancy, have become more relaxed and believe it is all right for males and females to engage in activities typed for the other sex (Ulian, 1976). Despite their new flexibility, boys' preferences, behavior, and attitudes become increasingly masculine throughout middle childhood. Yet girls do not show a corresponding trend; instead, they begin to prefer masculine activities and become aware of their own masculine attributes (Huston, 1983).

The development of gender constancy does not appear to be speeded by having seen people unclothed. Kohlberg (1966) reports that four- to seven-year-olds who had no trouble explaining "how you could tell [naked] boys from girls" were no more advanced in their understanding of gender constancy than were children who lacked an awareness of anatomical differences.

But cognitive development cannot by itself explain children's understanding of the concept.

This little girl knows about the obvious physical differences between the sexes and understands that boys always become men and girls always become women. But the acquisition of gender constancy apparently is not speeded by early exposure to naked individuals. (Barbara Rios/ Photo Researchers)

In another study of preschool children, Ronald Slaby and Karin Frey (1975) found children as young as three who understood that boys always become men and girls always become women, and children as young as three and a half who understood that gender could never be changed. In fact, in a group of children ranging from twenty-six to sixty-seven months, 25 percent understood the first concept and another 40 percent understood the second—an indication that children may develop a sense of gender constancy earlier than suggested by Kohlberg.

Once a child develops a sense of gender constancy, Kohlberg believes, the child seeks out sex-typed models, identifying with the opposite-sex parent and choosing same-sex friends and sex-typed clothes, games, and behavior. Slaby and Frey did find that as children developed gender constancy, they paid increased attention to models of their own sex. In Marcus and Overton's study, however, children who understood gender constancy did not show Kohlberg's predicted increase in preference for sex-typed games and same-sex friends and television characters; the preferences were already firmly established by the time they entered kindergarten.

Gender constancy may not be necessary for the child to acquire a sturdy sense of gender identity, as Kohlberg had suggested. The rudimentary realization that one is a girl or a boy (a knowledge that children develop around age two) may be the crucial foundation. But the meaning this knowledge has for the child will indeed change over the years, and perhaps what Kohlberg has been studying are these shifts in meaning.

When Things Go Wrong

Not all children develop an appropriate sense of gender identity. A child whose gender identity does not coincide with his or her anatomical sex faces a miserable childhood, and the situation rarely improves with maturity. People who grow up believing they have been trapped in the body of the other sex are known as **transsexuals.** The vast majority are men; male transsexuals are believed to outnumber female transsexuals by about six or eight to one (Levine and Lothstein, 1981). Often they request surgery so as to change their exterior anatomy to conform to their inner feelings. And for every tennis-playing physician who has had such surgery and is written up in the press, there are thousands of other transsexuals living in a world gone wrong.

A transsexual is not a homosexual; homosexuals rarely have disturbed gender identities. As yet, no one is sure just how the transsexual's inappropriate gender identity develops. It is not simply a matter of biology, wrong chromosomes, or inappropriate hormones. In fact, the hormonal level of adult transsexuals is within the normal range (Ehrhardt, Grisanti, and McCauley, 1979). Socialization has a powerful influence on gender identity. John Money and Anke Ehrhardt (1972) report case after case in which children born with ambiguous genitalia have been assigned to one sex or the other and reared with secure gender identities. Also, after appropriate surgery or hormonal treatment, genetic boys have been reared successfully as girls, and girls as boys.

Nor is a confused gender identity simply a matter of the child's lacking a parent of the same sex with whom he or she can identify. Although the lack of a male role model may impede a young boy's development of masculine behavior, single parents generally rear boys and girls with appropriate gender identities. Nor does having a homosexual parent as a model seem to interfere with the development of gender identity. A study comparing the sons and daughters of lesbian mothers with children of heterosexual single mothers showed no difference between the two groups (Kirkpatrick, Smith, and Roy, 1979). Even growing up with a transsexual seems to have little influence on gender identity. Richard Green (1978) has been following the development of sixteen children between the ages of three and twenty years old who are being reared by or have grown up with transsexual parents. All but four of the children are aware of their parent's unusual status. All sixteen children are heterosexually oriented and not one has developed gender identity problems.

Learning one's gender begins early—so early that Money and Erhardt believe it is a risky business to reassign a child to the other sex after the baby is eighteen months old. They believe that the critical period in the establishment of gender identity is from eighteen months, when a child begins to develop language, until three or four years. To switch a baby's sex during this period, they say, means the child will never be comfortable with his or her gender, and to switch gender after the age of four is to risk serious disturbance. Other researchers believe such restrictions do not apply to children with disturbed gender identities and believe that when children are in a supportive environment, gender identity can be safely changed at a much later date (Zucker, in press).

Just how children come to develop an inappropriate gender identity is not known. The process apparently involves some unusual interaction among child, family, and social environment. Green (1974), who has worked with many transsexual boys, notes that in almost every case he has studied, the young boy's first attempts at cross-dressing and behaving in highly feminine ways were tolerated, if not encouraged, by the parents. In most cases, the father either was not present or did not object. About the time he was four, certainly by the time he was six, the boy habitually dressed in high heels, jewelry, cosmetics, and improvised dresses. In Green's hypothetical pattern for the development of a male transsexual, such a boy, perhaps because of low hormonal levels, shows little interest in rough-and-tumble play. This alienates the father, who labels him "mama's boy." The child prefers to play with girls instead of rough boys. His behavior becomes increasingly feminine, and he is teased by his peers. When he is about seven—generally at the instigation of a neighbor or teacher—his mother brings him to a professional for help.

Although gender-disturbed girls have not been studied so extensively, Anke Ehrhardt and her colleagues (1979) have studied female transsexuals who were considering surgery and reassignment as men. Most of these transsexuals recalled cross-dressing as children, wanting desperately to be boys, and feeling disgust at the body changes that accompanied puberty. As their breasts began to grow, some began binding them tightly to their bodies.

Kenneth Zucker (in press) stresses that disturbed gender identity does not develop in isolation. Most parents and siblings of these children show signs of behavioral disorder in areas of life that are unrelated to gender, as does the child him- or herself. Yet these children stand out from their siblings. Zucker has found that gender-disturbed children consistently play more with toys and clothes belonging to the other sex than do their brothers and sisters with normal gender identities. Because children play an active role in developing their own gender identity, a child with a disturbed gender identity apparently has developed the wrong gender "rules" for him- or herself.

It appears that a disturbed gender identity develops when biological, constitutional, and social forces combine to push a child into the role of the other sex. Not only is the young child reinforced for cross-sex behavior, but he or she feels more comfortable with it, perhaps because of hormonal or temperamental predispositions.

Whether the disturbed gender identity will result in a transsexual adulthood is uncertain. Adult transsexuals, who report feeling trapped in the body of the other sex since childhood, may have rearranged their memories to conform with their adult life style. Nothing is known about the fate of children with disturbed gender identities who never receive therapy. After reviewing the adolescent or adult psychosexual status of seventy-six males who had been treated for disturbed gender identity, Zucker (in press) found that only four had become transsexuals and that thirty had become homosexuals. (The outcome in twenty-five cases was uncertain.) He concluded that either few children with disturbed gender identity become adult transsexuals or therapy alters the natural course of transsexualism.

THE DEVELOPMENT OF SEX ROLES

Gender identity is closely connected with a child's sex role. As indicated, although the two may be at odds, generally they are the same. The influences that shape sex roles come from biology, parents, peers, teachers, the media—and the development of gender identity itself.

The Influence of Biology

In the absence of contrary instructions, the fertilized egg develops into a female. The information that turns the egg into a male is carried by the Y chromosome, which causes the neutral gonads of the fetus to develop into testes. The testes, in turn, produce the hormones that develop male sexual organs and keep female organs from developing. Male hormones also affect the developing fetal brain. Without their presence, the hypothalamus (a part of the midbrain close to the pituitary) will develop as female—that is, set to produce hormones cyclically, so as to maintain the female reproductive cycle, instead of continually, as in the male brain.

Some of the differences in male and female intellectual functioning were discussed in Chapter 6; here, the question is whether male hormones also leave permanent traces on the developing personality. It seems clear that they do, although the traces are neither as many nor as deep as once was thought.

Ovarian hormones are not required for stereotypical female behavior to develop. Babies with Turner's syndrome—in which there is a single X (female) chromosome but neither a second X (as in normal girls) nor a Y (as in boys)—look like girls when they are born. But they have no ovaries and therefore no ovarian hormones. They are, of course, reared as girls. Such children seem, if anything, more feminine than normal girls; they show less interest in athletics, fight less as children, and are more interested in such personal adornments as jewelry, perfume, and hair styling. The interest in other sex-typed activites and the anticipations of marriage and motherhood of such children are similar to those of normal girls (Money and Ehrhardt, 1972).

But even a girl with a full complement of female hormones tends to show traces of masculine behavior when she has been inadvertently exposed to the male hormone androgen before birth. Anke Ehrhardt and Susan Baker (1975) studied seventeen girls who had received prenatal doses of androgen. The girls were genetically female, with normal female internal organs, but at birth their external genitalia appeared masculine and had to be surgically corrected. Although the girls were no more aggressive than their normal sisters, most were

tomboys—they showed a much higher level of rough, outdoor play and a disinterest in dolls, babies, and marriage. Ehrhardt and Baker speculate that fetal exposure to androgens results in a temperamental inclination to the rough-and-tumble, high-energy play regarded as "natural" for boys. But they believe that for the inclination to become manifest, the environment must be one that permits—or encourages—such play, because it did not develop in all the androgenized girls. All the girls developed secure female gender identities.

Some researchers (Eccles-Parsons, 1982) have suggested that any behavioral differences in these girls are the result of others' reactions to the appearance of the girls' genitalia at birth. However, in a study of both boys and girls whose mothers took male hormones during pregnancy, the boys had a much stronger tendency to be aggressive than their brothers who had not been exposed to the additional hormones, although additional hormonal exposure has no effect on the appearance of a baby boy (Reinisch, 1981). The girls in this study also had stronger tendencies to be aggressive than their unexposed sisters. Neither age nor birth order affected the children's tendency toward aggression, which was measured by asking them how they would respond in situations involving conflict with other people. Yet environment was clearly important. Two girls and one boy who had been exposed to prenatal androgens were *less* aggressive than their unexposed siblings, again indicating that if the conditions that encourage the expression of aggression are absent, it may not appear.

One way to search for the influence of biology on sex-role development is to study infants in the first few days of life, before the culture has had any chance to begin training boys to be masculine or girls to be feminine. In a study of newborn infants, Sheridan Phillips, Suzanne King, and Louise DuBois (1978) had observers who did not know the babies' gender watch them several times over a two-day period. Although boys and girls cried about the same amount, there were significant differences in their behavior. Boys were awake significantly

The Dominican Challenge

The most serious challenge to the idea that gender identity is primarily learned has come from the Dominican Republic, where researchers discovered thirty-eight male Dominicans with a rare inherited enzyme deficiency. Babies born with the disorder are male (XY chromosomes), their brains are exposed to male hormones during the prenatal period, and their internal sex organs are male. But because of the enzyme defect, their external sex organs appear to be female. At puberty the picture changes. Under the influence of male hormones, their voice deepens, their muscle mass increases, their testes enlarge and descend, and their inconspicuous penis grows. Their external appearance now matches their chromosomes; they are men. Although the condition is extremely rare, it was fairly common in this rural area.

Verifying the gender identity of these individuals would appear to decide whether society or biology determines gender identity. Researchers discovered that half of them had been reared "unambiguously" as girls and managed to get information about nearly all of this group after they reached puberty (Imperato-McGinley et al., 1979). They found that sixteen had developed a male gender identity at puberty and were living as men, and another had developed a male gender identity but was living as a woman. Only one had maintained a female gender identity.

At first glance, the example of these Dominican men seemed to establish the primacy of biology in determining gender identity. Male hormones appeared to overturn fourteen years of socialization as a female. As we have seen, Money and Ehrhardt (1972) maintain that switching gender identity after age four is virtually impossible to do successfully, although Zucker (in press) believes that it can be done if gender identity is already disturbed.

After sifting through the evidence, Robert Rubin, June Reinisch, and Roger Haskett (1981) concluded that these cases did not disprove Money's contention. They pointed out that, even though these individuals were reared as girls, their exterior genitals had never appeared to be those of a normal female. They grew up in a rural culture with little individual privacy, where their physical abnormalities would have been noted, especially since everyone bathed in the river. Although reared as girls, they were probably treated somewhat differently by others. In addition, from about the age of six, Dominican society is highly segregated by sex. After that time, boys and girls no longer play together, girls stay close to home, and boys roam freely. Among adults, women's lives are highly restricted, while men's lives are rela-

---

more than girls. Boys grimaced more—that is, they raised their eyebrows, winced, wrinkled their brows, or contorted their faces without making any sound. And boys showed more low-intensity activity; they turned their heads, waved their hands slowly, twitched, or jerked. Since these boys had not been circumcised, their behavior indicates that male infants may be slightly more irritable and prone to distress than females, a conclusion that was supported by another study, which found that three-month-old boys fuss more than girls (Moss, 1974).

Other studies (Yang and Moss, 1978) have found more behavioral stability over the first three months in boys than in girls, suggesting that girls are more responsive to environmental influences.

Whether or not such early differences are important, society certainly prescribes different roles for boys and girls. It is difficult, therefore, to gauge the strength of any biological component of sex roles. After reviewing more than one-thousand-four-hundred studies of sex differences, Eleanor Maccoby and Carol Jacklin

tively free. Rubin and his associates note that the individuals studied said they first realized they were "different from other girls" some time between the ages of seven and twelve—after their lives became restricted. The researchers suggest that social customs may have caused this realization; the prenatal male hormones probably resulted in a preference for rough-and-tumble play, one that was curtailed by a society that has no place for tomboys. And in a society where women's lives are so curtailed, puberty may have presented these individuals with a passport to the freedom of the male life style. Finally, these individuals lived in a society where this hereditary disorder was well known. They knew of others whose sex had been transformed at adolescence.

Rubin and his colleagues speculate that the abnormal appearance of their genitals probably led the individuals to experience some confusion about their gender identity during childhood, a confusion that would ease any transfer of gender identity. They point out that eight cases of this disorder have been found in the United States, and that the individuals, who were reared as girls, developed female gender identities, which they retained after puberty. Gender identity still seems to result from the interaction between biology and society.

(1974) concluded that when it came to personality, the only clear-cut difference between the sexes was in aggression. Males were definitely more aggressive than females in every culture studied; they were more aggressive from the beginnings of social play as toddlers, and they expressed it by word and deed. Because male aggressiveness appears to be universal, because it is affected by hormone levels, because differences in aggression were established before the age of six, and because they saw no sign that boys were reinforced for aggression, Maccoby

and Jacklin (1980) argue that this one aspect of behavior indeed has a biological component, although it also interacts with sociocultural factors and cognitive development.

Other traditional behavioral differences between the sexes—activity, competitiveness, and dominance for boys; timidity, compliance, and nurturance for girls—were not resolved by the researchers' review. Some studies found the expected sex differences, others did not. Jeanne Block (1976) has suggested that the failure to find additional sex differences may have been due to the fact that pertinent studies were omitted, many were inappropriate to the age of the group studied, others did not properly sample the expected differences in behavior, and yet others were inadequate because the children studied were too young to detect differences in behavior. However, it does seem unlikely that these differences have a biological basis, although it is possible that activity, competitiveness, and dominance are linked to aggression, and timidity and compliance to its absence.

For all of these sex differences, however, the behavior of boys and girls overlaps. The findings describe only the average behavior of a group, and some girls may be more active or aggressive than the average boy while some boys may be more compliant or nurturant than the average girl. Differences between the sexes in aggression, while well established, are not large (Hyde, 1984), although highly aggressive children are more likely to be boys than girls (Maccoby and Jacklin, 1980). It appears that prenatal hormones may predispose children toward certain kinds of behavior. In addition, the babies' anatomy and their temperamental predispositions lead others to treat them in ways that reinforce the behavior society expects from their gender.

The Influence of Cognition

The way children perceive the world and process the information they receive also contributes to the development of sex roles. Developmentalists have accounted for the influence of

In every culture that has been studied, boys are more aggressive than girls—even as toddlers. There is apparently some biological basis for this difference, although it is magnified by sex roles and society's expectations. (Peter Vandermark/Stock, Boston)

cognition on sex-role development either in terms of gender constancy or gender schema.

THE IMPLICATION OF GENDER CONSTANCY

The sure knowledge that one's gender is unchangeable has, believes Kohlberg (1966), a tremendous influence on the development of sex roles. Before gender constancy develops, says Kohlberg, the two- or three-year-old likes objects and toys associated with his or her own sex because of previous toys, playmates, and reinforcement provided by parents, which build on whatever innate tendencies exist. A girl likes dresses and dolls because she associates them with herself; a boy likes toy trucks and masculine clothes for the same reason.

Once children know their gender will never change, most decide they are happy with it—whatever the gender is. They believe the positive things they hear about their own sex and the negative things they hear about the other sex. They identify with the parent of their own sex and seek out—from all available sources—the behavior and attitudes that go along with that gender.

Parents are not the only models, however, as a study by David Perry and Kay Bussey (1979) made clear. Eight- and nine-year-old children watched a group of men and women choose one item from pairs that had no connection with gender—between a plastic cow and a plastic horse, for example. Afterward the children were given a chance to choose for themselves. The more often models of their own sex had selected an item, the more likely children were to choose it. In a second study, children watched adult models make choices that were either sex-appropriate or sex-inappropriate; afterward, the models chose items that had no connection with gender. When later choosing from the latter set of items, children imitated according to the sex appropriateness of the models' first set of choices. That is, boys and girls imitated adults of their own sex who had earlier made sex-appropriate choices; they also imitated models of the opposite sex who had earlier made sex-inappropriate choices. Children apparently imitate adults whom they believe provide good examples of their own sex roles. However, youngsters absorb information about both roles. As they learn what the other sex does, they also learn what they are *not* supposed to do, feel, or think (Money, 1977). Among the six-year-olds studied by Slaby and Frey (1975), those who had developed gender constancy spent more time watching a movie character of their own sex than one of the opposite sex when, on one side of the movie screen a woman built a fire, popped corn, played a musical instrument, and drank juice, and on the other side of the screen a man did the same thing. But boys watched the man more than girls watched the woman.

Girls' tendency to watch the male as well as the female may be explained by their realization of where power lies. As children develop their sense of gender constancy, they are also becoming aware of the power and competence associated with the male sex role. Now girls no longer like their own sex better, but they continue to believe that girls are "nicer" and "prettier" than "bad" boys. So they decide, says Kohlberg, to go after the only kind of power they think society offers girls—the power one can wield through being attractive and good.

Children also make a moral judgment: compliance with sex-role stereotypes is good; flouting of stereotypes is bad. Whether they are middle-class or lower-class, white or black, have traditional or liberated parents, children adhere to this judgment. So despite enormous differences in adult behavior—and despite the wide overlap in male and female behavior—children gravitate to the narrow stereotypical examples.

THE IMPLICATION OF GENDER
SCHEMAS Although Kohlberg's description is persuasive, it places the development of a stable gender identity at a far later age than other theories. A number of studies have shown that at four—sometimes as early as three—many children have already developed gender constancy and the attitudes that go along with it. Long before this time, they have begun to behave in a stereotypical fashion. Noting this trend, Sandra Bem (1983) has proposed that the child's early associations are channeled into sex roles because the child develops an appropriate gender schema.

A **gender schema** is a cognitive network of sex-related associations that allows the child to impose meaning and structure on any new information encountered, organizing it according to the culture's definition of maleness and femaleness. Parents, friends, teachers, and the media alert the child to the importance of gender by labeling the world in gender-related terms, tagging even abstract shapes with femininity (roundness) or masculinity (angularity). Children absorb this labeling system and eventually begin to evaluate new information in its terms. They develop a male gender schema and a female gender schema and, once they pattern their own self-concept in terms of the appropriate schema, they have developed a sex role. The thoroughness with which children learn to code events as "masculine" or "feminine" showed clearly when Aletha Huston and her colleagues (1984) had children watch pseudocommercials, which were identical in content but varied in formal features. Commercials with masculine formal features had rapid action, frequent cuts, loud music, sound effects, and frequent scene changes. Commercials with feminine formal features had background music, many fades and dissolves, and female narration. The voice-over in commercials was in Persian so that children could not use verbal information as a guide. Six-year-olds, the youngest age tested, had no trouble distinguishing between commercials aimed at girls and those aimed at boys.

Children apparently learn to sex-type toys and activities before they learn to sex-type personality attributes, probably because toys and activities can be observed and attributes, such as strength, intelligence, fear, kindness, speed, or quietness, must be abstracted from behavior. Most studies have found that children younger than five are not aware of the personal attributes of each sex role, although Aletha Huston (1983) suggests that such findings may reflect the absence of an opportunity to judge a concrete situation. When preschoolers were asked to judge the attributes of a baby they watched in a videotape, they assigned the infant sex-typed attributes according to whether the researchers labeled the baby a "boy" or a "girl"—regardless of the baby's actual gender (Haugh, Hoffman, and Cowan, 1980). Bem (1983) notes that attributes are taught early; children rarely hear girls described as strong or boys described as nurturant, yet they often hear adults tell little boys how strong they are becoming and little girls what good mothers they are.

Once gender schemas develop, children begin matching their own attributes, preferences, attitudes, and behavior against the schema prototype, judging their own adequacy in its terms (Bem, 1983). If the child does not measure up, self-esteem may be damaged. Gender schemas are so powerful that when children see others behaving in gender-inappropriate ways, they generally do not notice, forget what they have seen, or transform the sex of the model to fit their schema (Huston, 1983). For example, when children were shown commercials in which boys and girls behave in unstereotypical ways, about half of them switched the gender of the child actor when recalling the commercial. And when they watched a film showing a physician and a nurse, more than half the children later said they saw a male physician and a female nurse, no matter what the sex of the actor portraying either role. It was more difficult for them to recall watching a male nurse than a female physician (Cordua, McGraw, and Drabman, 1979).

The Influence of Parents

For the first few years, parents are the primary influence on a child's development. Whether the child is cared for full-time at home or left in day care, the bonds of attachment described in Chapter 12 are forged. If parents treat boys and girls differently, then a powerful force within the family pushes children into the appropriate sex role.

If we assume that parents treat their own children as they do the children of other people, the push begins early. When Caroline Smith and Barbara Lloyd (1978) videotaped mothers of first-born babies playing with an unfamiliar six-month-old, they discovered that adult behavior changed with the baby's gender label. Told the baby was a boy, mothers encouraged "him" with words to crawl, walk, and behave vigorously; if "he" did, they were likely to reinforce the behavior with their own activities. If they were told the baby was a girl, there was no verbal encouragement for motor activity, and the toy of choice was never a hammer.

Additional differences in adult behavior turned up in a study conducted by Hannah Frisch (1977). When fourteen-month-old infants were identified as boys, most adults encouraged

them to engage in large motor activity by putting them on a tricycle and choosing blocks for further play. When the babies were called girls, adults talked more to them and chose a doll or a baby bottle for play. Adults whose scores on an "Attitudes toward Women Scale" indicated their sympathy with feminism were likely to get out the tricycle for "girls" or to play blocks with them; but they did not encourage "boys" to play with the doll or the baby bottle. The infants, for their part, showed no sex differences in behavior.

It is possible, of course, that when adults play with strange babies, they respond to the only information they have: gender and age. Mothers and fathers may be more likely to respond to their own infants on an individual basis, encouraging motor activity in girls who have shown they like it and talking quietly to boys who prefer that. After reviewing the research, however, Huston (1983) concluded that from the beginning, fathers play more boisterously with baby boys, being rougher and playing more active physical games with them. As babies become toddlers, mothers seem to change their behavior in a way that encourages boys to be more independent and less affectionate. Mothers interacting with their twelve-month-old youngsters were more likely to touch their sons than their daughters. Six months later, the same mothers were more likely to touch their daughters, a change that resulted entirely from a decrease in physical contact between mothers and sons (Clarke-Stewart and Hevey, 1981).

How much of this change is due to the mothers' initiative and how much to their sons' higher activity level is unknown. When Peter Smith and Linda Daglish (1977) watched English babies at home, they found sex-typed differences in play were already apparent at twelve months and did not change appreciably over the next year. Girls tended to play more with dolls and soft toys, and boys with transportation toys. The boys were more active in their play and more likely than girls to do forbidden things, such as playing with wall plugs and climbing on the furniture. There was only one major difference in parents' behavior—a tendency to discourage or punish boys more than girls.

But by the time children are two years old, Beverly Fagot (1978a) found, parents react in predictable ways to specific behavior. She watched twenty-four single-child families whose children were between the ages of twenty and twenty-four months. Each family was watched on five different occasions for a period of an hour, while Fagot closely observed the ways parents responded to the actions of boys and girls. Girls and boys were often reinforced or punished differently for the same behavior. Girls, she found, were never encouraged when they played with blocks; and only girls tended to be discouraged by parents when they manipulated objects. As a result, while boys explored the physical world freely, girls might get criticized for it. Girls were encouraged to be helpers and to ask for assistance when they tried to do things. The differences in parents' responses were subtle, and these mothers and fathers were unaware that they were training their girls to be dependent and their boys to be independent.

The same push toward early independence for boys showed in another study, in which Fagot (1974) found that mothers discouraged their toddler sons from following them around the house. Their daughters, on the other hand, were encouraged to stay near them. Other studies show that boys are allowed to investigate wider areas of the community without parental permission (Saegert and Hart, 1976) and that they are expected to run errands at an earlier age. Boys are generally given greater freedom in all areas of life, with girls kept under closer surveillance so that they lead a more sheltered existence. This difference in treatment, although apparently meant to protect daughters, pushes girls toward a greater conformity to adult standards (Huston, 1983).

Whether researchers asked parents to describe the way they rear their children or asked young adults to recall the way their parents treated them, the reports from northern European countries and the United States were similar

Mothers are usually more relaxed than fathers about children's activities that violate sex roles, such as this little boy's attempt to learn to bake bread. (Jean-Claude Lejeune/Stock, Boston)

(Block, 1978). Boys were taught to hide their feelings, encouraged to compete, and pushed toward social conformity. Girls were more likely to be trusted, to get warmth and affection from their parents, and to be closely supervised. Although cultural expectations probably colored both the adults' recollections and the parents' reports, the pattern is consistent with that of the independent, aggressive male and the dependent, helpful female that emerges from studies of young children.

Fathers appear to be more active than mothers in steering preschoolers into traditional sex roles and may even become upset when their young sons engage in girlish games. Judith Langlois and Chris Downs (1980) observed parents interacting with their three- and five-year-old children as the children played with toys that were highly sex-typed for boys (a gas station with many cars; an army set with soldiers; cowboy outfits) or for girls (a toy stove with pots, dishes, and utensils; a dollhouse; women's dress-up clothes). Mothers showed no strong inclinations to push their children into traditional sex roles. They rewarded their daughters no matter which type of toy they played with, but tended to praise them more and show more affection when they played with girls' toys. A different pattern appeared when mothers interacted with their sons: they actively praised them for playing with girls' toys, showing affection and sharing the toys with them.

Fathers turned out to be the guardians of traditional sex roles. They rewarded daughters for playing with girls' toys and sons for playing with boys' toys. When either a son or a daughter played with a toy meant for the other sex, the father tended to punish them by talking negatively, ridiculing the play, or suggesting the child play with some other toy. Sons came in for much more punishment than daughters, and daughters were rewarded much more than sons. Fathers apparently play a more decisive role than mothers in perpetuating traditional sex roles.

The pressure on boys to be "real boys" may translate into rigid sex roles during childhood. When more than a hundred preschool children were tested for their absorption of sex-role stereotypes and their knowledge of sex-appropriate behavior, boys tended to choose stereotypical toys and behavior for children but to be somewhat more relaxed about what adults did (Edelbrock and Sugawara, 1978). Girls were more relaxed about the present, choosing a wide range of toys and behavior for children. However, they were more restrictive when they described acceptable adult behavior. The investigators suggest two reasons for these discrepancies. Because boys are ridiculed for "sissy" behavior but girls are permitted to be tomboys, young boys may be more reluctant to engage in or to condone cross-sex activities. (Although mothers rewarded such behavior in Langlois and Downs' study, fathers ridiculed it.) Regarding adult behavior, since more primary caregivers are mothers, girls have much more experience with women than boys have with men, so that girls are more likely to be aware of the range of women's behavior. Fathers and adult males are around so little that young boys may be less certain about the appropriate behavior of men.

Yet fathers are around enough to demonstrate the "appropriate" social display of emotions in men. Among 1,500 parents living in the Cleveland area, 75 percent of the fathers said they never—or rarely—hugged their close male friends, but 60 percent of the mothers said they often hugged their female friends (Roberts, 1982). Boys and girls quickly learn which sex expresses affection and which sex keeps its emotions under control.

The Influence of Peers

As we saw in Chapter 14, peers play an important role in the social development of young children. Now that an increasing number of youngsters are enrolled in some kind of day care, the influence of peers is more important than it traditionally has been. By the time they are three, children know "what boys do" and "what girls do," and they pressure one another to conform.

Children as young as two are more responsive to peers of the same sex and pay more attention to them than to children of the other sex. Their same-sex peers also have more power over their behavior, for two-year-olds continue an activity if a same-sex peer responds favorably and stop it if the peer seems upset. Yet reactions from a peer of the other sex are generally ignored (Fagot, 1982).

As children grow, these responses steer children into traditional sex roles. When three- and four-year-old boys played with dolls or played dress-up at a nursery school studied by Fagot (1977), they were criticized by their peers. And boys who persisted in such play were criticized five or six times as often as other children, even when the boys later played with neutral toys or boys' toys. Occasionally girls would allow such a boy to join them in the play kitchen, but they too were mostly negative in their reactions. Boys who persisted in cross-gender play played alone almost three times as often as other children. Girls who played with boys' toys fared better. They were generally ignored by the other chil-

Preschool boys who play with girls' toys are usually punished by their friends, who either criticize them or simply stop playing with them. (David S. Strickler/Monkmeyer)

perhaps simply indicating a lack of interest. Five- to seven-year-olds, however, let their disapproval be known; they often make direct attempts to change the offending child's behavior. But for most children, the physical presence of peers is unnecessary to make a child avoid cross-gender play; simply believing that an activity is typed for the other sex is often enough (Thompson, 1975; White, 1978).

The Influence of Teachers

In their role as instructor in sex differences, children's schoolmates are joined by another ally—the teacher. Even in nursery school, teachers unobtrusively push children into traditional sex roles—and most of them do not know they are doing it. Lisa Serbin and her associates (1973), for example, observed teachers in fifteen nursery-school classrooms and recorded how they behaved toward boys and toward girls. They found that teachers were helping to shape traditional sex roles, often unwittingly, by prompting and reinforcing independent, assertive behavior in boys and dependent, passive behavior in girls. In one classroom, for example, the children were making party baskets, a task that required them to staple a paper handle in place. The teachers provided instruction as the boys manipulated the staple gun and attached the handle. The teacher, however, was likely to take the basket from a girl, staple the handle to it, and hand it back. Serbin's group points out that most teachers do not realize that they demonstrate things and explain them more to boys than to girls and that they give boys more directions that require them to accomplish things on their own. From such findings, the investigators conclude that most girls learn to be submissive, to remain near an adult, and to be rewarded with affectionate hugs, whereas most boys learn to be assertive and to receive praise for being independent problem solvers.

dren and allowed to continue their play; when they returned to girls' activities, they were welcomed back into the group.

Preschoolers who played with boys' or girls' toys in the presence of a parent also played with the toys while a peer was in the room (Langlois and Downs, 1980). Girls and boys alike were punished by their peers for playing with toys belonging to the other sex, with peers using ridicule and even interfering with the play. No matter what sort of punishment is inflicted, the punished child generally stops playing with the "wrong" toy. As children get older, they tend to change the way they punish other children who engage in cross-gender play (Lamb, Easterbrooks, and Holden, 1980). Three-year-olds are likely to stop playing with a boy who plays with a doll or a girl who begins hammering—

When nursery-school children engage in play that is regarded as the province of the opposite sex, teachers sometimes join peers in making the children feel uncomfortable (Fagot, 1977). Boys who dress up or girls who play outside in the sandbox are criticized. But when girls dress up, or boys hammer or play with blocks, the teacher joins in, suggests additional activities along the same line, or makes favorable comments. On the other hand, teachers are kindly disposed toward art activities and shower boys with approval when they cut, paste, or draw—although such activities are overwhelmingly favored by girls. This may be, says Fagot, who observed more than two-hundred nursery-school children, because teachers see art activities as appropriate academic tasks.

When children's free play is observed, girls prefer playing with art materials, looking at books, inspecting objects, and watching people, whereas boys gravitate to wagons, tricycles, trucks, sandboxes, and rough-and-tumble play. As a result, when teachers steer children to the "cultural enrichment" of the nursery-school curriculum, they are pushing boys to do things that they would not choose on their own. Observations of nursery-school teachers indicate that the more experienced the teacher, the stronger such pressure on boys (Fagot, 1978b). Experienced teachers reinforce both boys and girls more than 80 percent of the time for doing what girls prefer to do. The mismatch between early school curriculum and boys' inclinations toward active play may help explain why girls make better students early in their academic careers—and why more little boys than girls dislike school.

But as school progresses, teachers take a hand in redressing the balance—again without knowing it. Experiments in the classroom indicate that the behavioral cues and reinforcement provided by teachers have a strong influence on the degree of sex-typed behavior shown by young children (Huston, 1983). Among older children, boys are praised more than girls in math classrooms, where boys are expected to succeed (Parsons, Kaczala, and Meese, 1982). In regular classrooms, boys and girls get the same amount of praise. As pointed out in the last chapter, when boys do fail, teachers generally criticize them for not trying. In contrast, when girls fail,

teachers almost always criticize them for having the wrong answer. Because the criticism that girls receive focuses on the content of their work, they are likely to attribute their failure to lack of ability and may come to believe that their successes are simply lucky. Boys fail, hear that they should try harder, and may do so. As a result, teachers may also be teaching some girls to fail and some boys to persevere in academic tasks, perhaps preparing both sexes to expect that males will solve problems for helpless females.

Over the years, teachers' expectations guide students' behavior, which in turn confirms the teachers' expectations. When high-school teachers were given almost identical descriptions of excellent students, those identified as boys were tabbed by teachers to go on to successful careers, but those identified as girls were not even expected to go to college (Gaite, 1977). The structure of the school itself may mold students' expectations along the lines of traditional sex roles. As Patricia Minuchin and Edna Shapiro (1983) have suggested, the clustering of female teachers in the early grades and male teachers in high school, the preponderance of men in science and math teaching, and the overwhelming gender imbalance in the staff (men are concentrated in administration and women in classroom teaching and clerical positions) may directly affect student perceptions of the gender-related way in which the adult world distributes power.

Even when an effort is made to break down sex-typed activities in junior high and high school, the students' sex-role schemas may diminish the impact. In one school that integrated formerly all-male shop classes, girls' concerns about the reactions of their male classmates apparently interfered with the attention and effort girls applied to course content. In another school, initial gains in girls' feelings of competence in the male domain of shop and boys' feeling of competence in the female domain of the kitchen diminished over the school year. Minuchin and Shapiro (1983), who reviewed the studies, believe that the return of sex-typed attitudes resulted from the interaction of subtle sex discrimination within the integrated classes, stereotypical language and examples in course materials, and remnants of old attitudes on the part of students and teachers, which colored their behavior.

The Influence of the Media

In nonliterate cultures, children hear the exploits of heroes and heroines in song and story. The folksinger and the storyteller, with their tales of brave deeds and weaknesses, of loyalty and love, describe ideal models. In a media-saturated culture, models continually assault the child from every side. Television, books, movies, magazines, radio, and newspapers portray—in words or pictures—the approved sex roles for the society.

When two-year-olds turn the glossy pages of their mothers' magazines, pointing to the kitty in the catfood ad or the baby advertising paper diapers, they see in the pitches for soaps, floor waxes, canned soups, cigarettes, and cosmetics what boys and girls, mommies and daddies are supposed to do. Mommies are young and beautiful and spend most of their time at home or in the supermarket; daddies play tennis and ride horses through Marlboro country. What children see in magazines may help develop the sex-role stereotypes that are found in preschoolers; but those ads are a minor influence compared to the impact of the omnipresent television set.

TELEVISION Children at play often enact social roles they have taken from television, and they have plenty of time to absorb them. On the average, American children between the ages of two and eighteen years watch more than three hours of television each day (Nielsen Television Index, 1982). Many children spend more time watching television than they do going to school. Television often serves as an unpaid babysitter, keeping preschoolers occupied while their parents are busy.

For the most part, television is a purveyor of stereotypes. As Carol Tavris and Carole Offir (1977) have pointed out, when Wonder Woman was not saving the world, she worked as a secretary; and the Bionic Woman taught school. Most television heroines unmask villains by luck or accident. In children's programs, men tend to be aggressive, constructive, and helpful; their activities bring them tangible rewards (Sternglanz and Serbin, 1974). Women in the same programs tend to be deferential, passive, and ignored; if they are too active, they are punished. Despite the development of some competent, assertive heroines, the old stereotype-laden programs are in almost perpetual rerun during hours that are outside network control. This practice may be linked to the findings of one study (Greer, 1980), in which prime-time viewing had no relation to stereotypical views of sex roles, but heavy TV viewing after school and on Saturday mornings did show such correlations.

Few commercials shatter sex-role stereotypes. Researchers who analyzed 300 commercials reported that the difference between female and male sex roles in these commercials was far greater than it is in society (Mamay and Simpson, 1981). Except for the occasional woman bank manager and traveling sales representative, women in commercials either do housework or are sex objects. They defer to men's needs, wishes, and preferences. Men are the authorities, confronting women shoppers with twelve-hour cold capsules, correcting their choices of detergents, and delivering the smooth, authoritative voice-over pitches in most commercials.

Placed among the mass of sex-typed commercials and programs, the occasional series or sales pitch that goes against the traditional tide is unlikely to make a major impression. As we saw in the discussion of gender schemas, children simply tend to "forget" or "transform" material that runs counter to traditional sex roles, recalling what they see along sex-typed lines. Andrew Collins (1981) reports that when third-graders watched two programs, one with a stereotypical female character and one with an untraditional female character, children who held conventional views of sex roles recalled both programs in a way that reflected sex-role stereotypes, while children who held less conventional views of sex roles recalled both programs in a far less stereotypical manner.

BOOKS The other heavy media influence on children is the printed word—primarily readers and other textbooks, but also books a child reads for pleasure or for book reports. Children no longer grow up in the white, middle-class world of Dick and Jane, who once dominated American readers; but the stories still tend to be boy-centered, and the main character, when an adult, is generally a male. Even animal characters, from Peter Rabbit and the Three Little Pigs to Stuart Little and Ferdinand the Bull, are usually male.

When Women on Words and Images (1972) examined 134 anthologies compiled as children's readers, they found five boy-centered stories for every two that featured a girl, and 147 occupations described as possible for boys but only 26 for girls. One reason boys predominate in such collections may be that, given the penalties from parents, peers, and teachers for cross-sex behavior, boys object vigorously to reading books that feature female heroines. As librarians know, boys will not read them and find it nearly impossible to identify with a heroine. But girls have no difficulty reading about Robin Hood or Johnny Tremaine.

Female characters are scarce in prize-winning picture books for young children. Over a five-year period, eleven times as many males as females were depicted in Caldecott medal winners and honor books, ninety-five male animals were portrayed for every female animal, and there were eight obviously male characters in the title for every three females (Gagnon, 1977). Things do change as children progress to books for older children. In the same five-year period, female heroines outnumbered males in Newbery medal winners and honor books. And from Jo March to Caddie Woodlawn to Karana, there are many resourceful girls to be found. In books that fea-

ture boys as protagonists, however, girls tend to be easily frightened, incompetent followers, whose problems are solved by resourceful, intelligent brave boys. Heroines in fairy tales have the same problem; they rarely succeed on their own—a handsome prince, a fairy godmother, or a passing woodcutter generally rescues them from sorrow or disaster.

SEXUALITY

With the onset of puberty, biology again becomes a strong force in development. Hormones, a sudden growth spurt, the development of secondary sexual characteristics, a new interest in sexuality and the opposite sex, and changed expectations from family, peers, and society come together to produce uncertainty and self-consciousness. Adolescents' bodies are changing rapidly—and in a way that dramatically announces their sexual maturation to the world. No longer "sexless" children moving through the placid latency period, they find themselves suddenly thrust into the genital period and beset by new role demands. In response, most children retreat to the safety of sex-role stereotypes.

Reactions to Physical Change

Understandably, physical changes of the magnitude experienced by adolescents have a significant effect on how they feel about themselves. Peer and social attitudes influence both boys' and girls' reactions to these changes. In the midst of their uncertainty, they may overconform to sex roles, confining themselves to rigid conceptions of masculinity or femininity. These attempts can lead to **sex-role strain,** in which adolescents feel anxiety when they do not live up to stereotypical sex roles and may develop unhealthy personality characteristics (such as dependency in women and aggression in men) when they do (Pleck, 1981).

One important influence on adolescent self-esteem is the myth of the **body ideal,** the body type defined by the culture as "attractive" and sex-appropriate. Peer and family expectations and portrayals in the mass media teach these ideal characteristics. William Schonfeld (1963) has pointed out that movies, television, advertising, and the worship of sports heroes perpetuate the reverence for the ideal body and encourage the disparagement of those whose bodies do not conform to the ideal.

Adolescents of both sexes are especially sensitive to any body characteristic that might be interpreted as sex-inappropriate. From childhood, boys and girls learn which physical attributes are feminine and which are masculine, and they show deep concern over any deviations from those stereotypes (Schonfeld, 1964). Adolescent boys are particularly concerned about such characteristics as a circle of fat around the hips and thighs, underdeveloped external genitalia, or the development of subcutaneous tissue in the breast region. Although such developments as fatty hips and breast growth are normal and usually soon disappear, they are often a source of great embarrassment to a boy.

Herbert and Lois Stolz (1951) have identified certain physical characteristics that adolescent girls consider unfeminine. These include large hands and feet, a figure that is much too full or too thin, pigmented facial hair, and a large body. Thus many of the normal temporary changes of adolescents may seem "unfeminine" to a girl. She grows body hair, her voice becomes lower, her hands and feet grow, and so forth. Eventually, however, a girl may be comforted by the fact that her friends are experiencing the same changes.

The developing adolescent whose body conforms to the cultural ideal has a social advantage. But extremely tall, skinny adolescents and extremely short, fat ones are likely to evoke negative reactions from their peers. For example, J. Robert Staffieri (1967) found that classmates more often chose well-muscled and thin adolescents as friends than fat ones. Such evaluations by others generally have a strong influence on an adolescent's social relations and behavior.

Pressure to conform to the body ideal is felt more strongly by girls. When adolescents in four countries were interviewed, well over 80 percent of boys and girls alike reported that they felt strong and healthy (Offer, Ostrov, and Howard, 1981). But the sexes split when asked about their bodies: 77 percent of younger boys (ages thirteen to fifteen) and 80 percent of older boys (ages sixteen to eighteen) were proud of their bodies, whereas only 57 percent of younger girls and 51 percent of older girls felt that way. The discrepancy was also apparent when asked about their attractiveness. Among the boys, 26 percent of younger adolescents and 21 percent of older adolescents agreed that, "I frequently feel ugly and unattractive," but 46 percent of the younger girls and 42 percent of the older girls agreed with that statement. Judith Rodin and her colleagues (in press) believe that the unnatural thinness of the female ideal body is responsible for this kind of reaction on the part of girls. These researchers speculate that girls' concern with their weight may be linked with the higher rate of eating disorders like bulimia (in which an individual alternately goes on food binges, then takes laxatives or vomits) and anorexia nervosa (in which an individual diets to emaciation) among adolescent girls and young women.

Girls' reactions to menstruation vary, and most have developed expectations about the process by the time they are in the fifth or sixth grade. The typical girl finds menstruation much less painful and distressing than she had anticipated. However, expectations appear to set a self-fulfilling prophecy in motion, so that girls who expect premenstrual symptoms and painful periods are more likely than other girls to develop them (Brooks-Gunn and Ruble, 1982).

The timing of puberty appears to influence the social course of adolescence. Developmental psychologists Mary Cover Jones and Nancy Bayley (1950) and their colleagues have followed groups of boys from early adolescence through the fourth decade of life. During early adolescence, early-maturing boys were taller, stronger, more attractive, and better coordinated than later maturers, and they tended to have well-muscled bodies. Late maturers tended to be thin and were more talkative, active, busy, and un-inhibited, yet they also tended to be tenser and bossier than the early maturers. These findings suggest that late maturers possess less social maturity and that they use negative behavior to get attention, thereby compensating for their physical disadvantages. Additional studies support this interpretation. Late maturers also show a greater need for social acceptance, greater anticipation of rejection, heightened dependence, and negative self-concepts (Mussen and Jones, 1957).

Schonfeld (1964) points out that many of the physical characteristics of late-maturing boys, which the boys themselves may regard as evidence of inadequate masculinity, fall within the normal range of development. When such is the case, a late-maturing boy need only wait until he catches up with his peers. But in the meantime, the values placed on athletic prowess and manly appearance (by boys and girls alike) may make him feel inferior to those who mature early.

The early maturer is more active in athletics and student government and has greater visibility in the school social system. The social advantages of early maturity also appear to continue into adulthood, when differences in physique no longer exist. In their thirties, early maturers tended to have higher occupational status, were more likely to work in supervisory or managerial positions, and reported more active social lives in clubs, organizations, and business (Jones, 1957). The differences that became apparent when the groups were in their late thirties suggest that early maturers achieve in a conforming way, whereas later maturers' achievements are more likely to be idiosyncratic. Early maturers are likely to be conventional in both thought and attitude; they continue to have social poise and to show responsibility. Late maturers appear to be more flexible and adaptive; they tolerate ambiguity better than early maturers (Jones, 1965). Thus, as Harvey Peskin (1967) suggests, it appears that the greater social advantage of early maturers may lead them to fix on their identity early in life, thereby producing conventionality.

Studies of early- and late-maturing girls suggest that the early-maturing girl has less prestige than other girls in early adolescence but that as the growth process continues, she comes to enjoy the same social advantages as the early-maturing boy (Faust, 1960). At first, the early-maturing girl is somewhat conspicuous and is likely to be far out of step developmentally with boys of her own age. However, early maturity may be a source of satisfaction if a girl's favorite companions are also early maturers. At seventeen, girls who have matured early may have a more favorable view of themselves and may rate higher in popularity than they rated earlier in their teens. However, studies that follow early- and late-maturing girls into adulthood have not been especially revealing, presumably because in the past a woman's social life, status, and opportunities for achievement have depended on the status of her husband (Eichorn, 1963). These studies have not been repeated since recent changes in society and sex roles, but Willard Hartup (1983) believes that the correlations between maturation rates and standing in the peer group remain valid.

Retreat to Stereotypes

At about the age of fourteen, the adolescent retreats to sex-role stereotypes. A boy or girl who once was comfortable with activities and attitudes typical of the other sex suddenly becomes rigidly stereotypical in behavior. How much of this change is directly attributable to hormones and how much to adolescent uncertainty in the face of new social pressure is unknown, but both presumably have some part in the process.

Despite their changed behavior, individual adolescents see themselves as less stereotypical than does the rest of the world. In Katheryn Urberg's (1979) study of sex-role development, when twelfth-graders described themselves, there was only one significant difference in their portrayals: girls saw themselves as more dependent than boys did. But when adolescents described the ideal person, stereotypes abounded

Many girls find that adhering to stereotypical sex-role activities makes the physical changes of adolescence and its accompanying social pressures less threatening. (Alan Carey/The Image Works)

for both sexes. And their descriptions of the opposite gender were always more stereotypical than were their descriptions of their own gender. The pattern of sex-role stereotype development showed clearly in Urberg's study. Seventh-graders and adults—whether twenty or sixty-five—had a similar and much less stereotyped view of males and females than did twelfth-graders.

One place where the retreat to stereotypes shows clearly is in adolescents' responses to babies. Shirley Feldman, Sharon Nash, and Carolyn Cutrona (1977) watched eight- and nine-year-old children and fourteen- and fifteen-year-old adolescents react to a baby who was playing on the floor near them. The younger girls and boys showed a similar degree of interest, both in the playing baby and later in pictures of babies. But among adolescents, girls paid more attention to the live baby, and they looked longer at pictures of babies and liked them more than did boys. Other studies have shown that

this sex difference disappears by late adolescence (Nash and Feldman, 1981).

The sex difference in attention to infants does not, however, reflect an increase among adolescent girls. All adolescents pay less attention to a baby than younger children do; interest in babies declines more among boys than girls. Other studies (Frodi et al., 1984) indicate that girls' interest in interacting with infants declines between late childhood and adolescence, with interest lowest among girls who have been menstruating for at least a year. Yet during this same period, girls' preference for pictures of babies increases while boys' preference drops (Goldberg, Blumberg, and Kriger, 1982). Increased interest among girls is not related to their attitude about menstruation, their knowledge about it, or their interest in motherhood. Researchers are not certain whether a girl's increased interest in baby pictures reflects her feeling that she *should* show such interest or whether the reluctance to approach a baby reflects the older girl's greater self-consciousness in the presence of the baby's mother (Frodi et al., 1984).

This conflicting pattern of interest does not appear in physiological measures, for children and adolescents of both sexes react identically to crying and smiling babies (Frodi and Lamb, 1978). When a baby cries, heart rate and skin conductance increase and young people feel distressed, irritated, and unhappy. When a baby smiles, their heart rates slow and they feel good about it. Perhaps, suggest Ann Frodi and her colleagues (1984), responsiveness to babies is not a good measure of sex-role differences in adolescence, whether the change is due to biology or learning, for at this period in life, interest in babies has no relevance for sex roles. As we shall see, heightened interest in babies appears in new mothers, when it bears obvious relevance to sex roles, but not in childless women.

Sex Roles and Sex Differences

Traditional childhood and early-adolescent socialization generally provide girls with a greater

The Impact of Puberty

In Western societies, adolescence is an awkward period. Physical changes signal to the world that boys and girls no longer are children, but despite their obvious sexual maturity, they are still regarded as psychologically and socially immature (Miller and Simon, 1980). Within the family, patterns of interaction change to accommodate the adolescent's new status, and the changes may usher in a period of conflict.

When conflict arises, it seems to follow a typical pattern in families with adolescent boys. For a year, Lawrence Steinberg (1981) followed thirty-one intact, middle-class families in which the oldest child was a boy on the brink of puberty. He discovered that changes within the family were related to the boy's physical maturation, not to the development of formal reasoning, and that mothers and fathers reacted to their sons' sexuality in different ways.

As physical signs of puberty appeared, mother and son entered a period of conflict, with the pair interrupting each other with increasing frequency during family discussions, and the son steadily becoming less deferential. Both parties became less likely to explain the reasons behind their decisions to the other. The conflict appeared to be initiated by the son. Once the boy had clearly reached sexual maturity, the conflict subsided somewhat, although his behavior did not change. Instead, the mother backed off and began to defer to her son.

The pattern of a son's relationship with his father showed less overt conflict. Like the mother, the father began interrupting his son more and explaining his decisions less, but the son showed his father none of the assertiveness or defiance that characterized the mother-son relationship. Instead the son became more deferential to his father and interrupted him less. The pattern did not change when the boy reached full sexual maturity.

Among these families, male puberty ushered in a clear change in the family hierarchy. During the boy's childhood, both parents had roughly equal influence in family decisions. When the son became sexually mature, the mother's influence waned and the balance of power shifted. The father became dominant, exerting most influence on decisions, and the son moved into second place, stripping the mother of much of her former power.

Steinberg notes that this shift in influence parallels the pattern of relationships seen in many species, in which females are deferential to all adult males, young adult males are deferential to older males but assertive toward females, and older males dominate both groups. Whether or not this parallel is significant, interactions within these thirty-one families demonstrate that male puberty is accompanied by social and psychological consequences.

---

degree of competence than boys in interpersonal relationships. For most girls, sexual behavior involves incorporating sexuality into a social role and an identity that already included capacities for tenderness and sensitivity. For most boys, on the other hand, the pathway to mature heterosexual behavior involves sexuality first; only secondarily does the capacity for concerned, tender, and loving sexual relationships develop.

Thus cultural stereotypes and parental and peer socialization emphasize, to use Ira Reiss' (1973) terms, "body-centered" sexuality for the male and "person-centered" sexuality for the female.

There is a connection between this formulation and the pattern of sex differences that should not go unnoticed. Boys reach the peak of their sexual powers earlier than girls, even though girls reach menarche earlier than boys reach a corresponding level of development. Boys desire orgasm more often than girls; they resort more than girls to sexual fantasies; they are more responsive to sexual symbols; they reach a sexual climax in dreams more often; they require less constant physical stimulation to remain aroused; they have more often had sexual relations with more than one partner; they do not tend to insist, as many girls do, that there should be a feeling of affection between sexual partners; and they prefer to go steady less often than girls do (Kinsey et al., 1948, 1953; Sorenstein, in press).

Alfred Kinsey and his colleagues tended to explain differences in male and female sexual behavior in biological terms—by assuming, for example, a more urgent male sex drive. A more balanced view suggests that these differences are the result of a complex interaction among neurological, hormonal, psychological, and cultural factors. It seems clear that male and female sexual behavior is influenced by sex-role stereotypes and expectations just as much other behavior is.

These stereotypes are reflected in American standards for dating. Usually the girl plays a passive but friendly role, and the boy takes the initiative in petting. The girl assents, but if the approach threatens to go beyond the limits she sets, she is expected to serve as a calming influence for both (Brooks-Gunn and Matthews, 1979). Although our culture's sex-role stereotypes are changing, few adolescents have escaped the social pressures that dictate appropriate sexual behavior for each gender. Among one group of older adolescents, whether the young people rated themselves as "liberal" or "conservative" in their view of sex roles, they reported that their behavior on dates followed this stereotypical pattern (La Plante, McCormick, and Brannigan, 1980). As society has become more open about sexuality, adolescents' sexual worries have begun to increase. Twenty years ago, 7 percent of American teenagers thought their sexual experience was behind that of their peers; ten years later, 21 percent felt that way (Offer, Ostrov, and Howard, 1981).

American culture encourages boys to develop a body-centered sexuality, and boys encourage one another for their responsiveness to erotic stimuli. (Joel Gordon)

Among their peers, groups of girls are likely to support and encourage one another for interpersonal competence and romantic interests, whereas groups of boys are likely to support and encourage one another for erotic interests, responsiveness to erotic stimuli, and proclaimed erotic activity. Although girls and boys now have roughly similar rates of premarital intercourse, their first experiences are very different (Miller and Simon, 1980). A boy's first sexual experience is most likely to be with a partner he does not love, and he will either not repeat the experience with her or will have intercourse with her no more than a few times. He will probably boast about it afterward to his male friends. A girl's first experience is likely to be with a partner she loves and intends to marry. She will probably say nothing about it to her friends.

Adolescent peer groups are also likely to reward popularity with the opposite sex with status (Schwartz and Merten, 1967). Thus during adolescence, both boys and girls learn to incorporate sexual behavior into their gender roles, but the experiences each brings to his or her relationships are likely to be quite different.

Further, as William Simon and John Gagnon (1969) suggest, adolescent dating and courtship can be seen as a training process in which boys train girls and girls train boys in the meaning and context of each sex's commitment to the heterosexual relationship.

The evolutionary changes in American sexual behavior and attitudes can be seen as part of a more general movement toward egalitarianism and, therefore, may affect traditional gender roles. For example, after surveying these changes, Reiss (1973) concludes that the human sexual relationship is changing from an occasion for male satisfaction of body-centered sexuality to an egalitarian relationship that involves more than physical attraction. He notes that although people will continue to pursue sexuality for pleasure, the pleasure is more likely to be mutual and egalitarian.

SEX ROLES AND THE LIFE SPAN

We might expect that a child begins life completely ignorant of the components of a sex role, then—as the rewards and punishments of society pile up—the constraints of gender become tighter and tighter, so that people over sixty-five adhere to the most rigid stereotypes of all. But that is not the case. In fact, once developed, the degree of conformity to sex roles does not even remain stable. Already we have seen that the stereotypes so dear to the heart of the four-year-old loosen during the latency period of middle childhood, only to tighten again during adolescence.

What appears to happen is that during certain periods of life it becomes useful for most people to live within the traditional sex roles. And during those times when a traditional sex role is useful for a person, there is also an accompanying societal pressure for him or her to conform. During adolescence, when boys and girls are uncertain about their sex roles, conformity helps ease the uncertainty. The same ebb and

flow of adherence to sex roles appears to be a characteristic of the entire life span.

In a series of studies, Shirley Feldman, Sharon Nash, and their colleagues (Feldman, Biringen, and Nash, 1981; Nash and Feldman, 1981) have shown that as their life situations change, men and women modify their attitudes toward sex roles and even their own self-concepts in regard to them. If this is the case, one would expect childless adults to be less interested in babies than parents are. When adults in their twenties and thirties were placed in a situation similar to that Feldman, Nash, and Cutrona used with adolescents, the responses to a live baby and the interest in baby pictures were almost identical in all groups: single men and women who were cohabiting, childless couples, and couples who were expecting their first child. But mothers of babies showed a high interest in the baby who was playing in the waiting room and spent a lot of time looking at baby pictures, although fathers did not. In addition, when tested on a sex-role inventory (which measures a person's degree of masculinity or femininity), mothers scored higher in femininity than did childless women, and fathers scored higher in masculinity than did childless men.

Parenthood usually makes sweeping changes in a couple's life, and during their child's infancy, parents tend to conform to stereotypical roles. As we saw in Chapter 12, mothers and fathers respond similarly to their newborn infants, but since mothers are expected to take primary responsibility for their babies, they spend more time with them than fathers do—and less time with their husbands than they did before the baby's arrival. Fathers, on the other hand, often become more preoccupied with the economic necessities of life, because although the mother may plan to return to work eventually, for the present the father bears the responsibility of supporting three lives. For most fathers, interest in their own babies does not extend to infants in general. However, among a group of fathers who were highly involved in caregiving, interest in babies did become generalized, and they responded to babies in the laboratory as strongly as did their wives (Nash and Feldman, 1981).

Similar connections between people's situations and their interest in babies continue throughout life. Parents of adolescents and parents whose grown children have left home display similar (minimal) interest in babies, although mothers always show slightly more interest than fathers. The level of interest rises sharply among grandparents, and grandmothers show the most interest of all. Again, when sex differences serve no purpose, they diminish.

Changes in self-concept are similarly linked with a person's stage of life (Nash and Feldman, 1981; Feldman, Biringen, and Nash, 1981). When women are compared on autonomy, an attribute usually considered masculine, new mothers score lowest and grandmothers score highest. On compassion, an attribute usually considered feminine, men's ratings increase steadily as they move through the life cycle, being lowest among single men and higher among grandfathers. These attributes are included on the sex-role inventory, where self-ratings place grandmothers as high in femininity as other women, but higher in masculinity. Similarly, grandfathers are as high in masculinity as other men, but show increases in their femininity scores. This change in self-concept to include qualities of the opposite sex conforms to the proposal of David Guttman (1975). On the basis of studies in several cultures, he believes that the responsibilities of parenthood play an overwhelming role during much of adulthood, requiring men to become assertive and dominant and women to become nurturant and passive. But once their family responsibilities have been completed, older adults may indulge those qualities that have been suppressed in the interest of their children, with both sexes moving toward the middle ground of androgyny.

ANDROGYNY

In recent years there has been a trend away from stereotypical notions of masculinity and femininity for adults. In their place has come the concept of **androgyny,** a term that describes people who embrace the characteristics of both sexes. Their self-concepts allow them to be masculine or feminine, assertive or yielding, depending on the appropriateness of a reaction to a specific situation (Bem, 1974).

If androgynous people are defined as those who are high in *both* masculinity and femininity—both competently assertive and securely sensitive to other people—we might expect androgyny to lead to fuller human functioning. Janet Spence (1979) has found that androgynous people have the highest self-esteem of any group. She speculates that they are individuals with multiple talents. Because they are flexible, they can take on any role they choose or that their life situation demands. This may well be so, for some studies (Hammer, 1964; Helson, 1966) have shown that highly creative men and women tend to incorporate attributes of the other sex. However, among adolescents, there is little difference between the high self-esteem of androgynous and masculine individuals—in either sex (Lamke, 1982). Adolescents who are high only in feminine attributes, as well as those who are undifferentiated (high only in neutral attributes such as being adaptable, friendly, sincere, and tactful), tend to have equally low self-esteem. Some researchers (Lerner, Sorell, and Brackney, 1981) have explained this pattern by proposing that today's society rewards only those attributes traditionally associated with masculinity (assertiveness, self-reliance, ambition, dominance).

Androgynous people, believes Sandra Bem (1979), differ from traditionally masculine and feminine people in their beliefs about basic differences between the sexes. These beliefs influence both how they behave and how they interpret the sex-role behavior of others. Since androgynous people see little basic psychological difference between the sexes, they process gender-related information differently. If gender schemas do not dominate an individual's view of the world, he or she becomes less likely to interpret variations in people's behavior as attributable to gender.

Given the barrage of gender-related information that children encounter, how does anyone develop androgyny? Researchers have just begun to explore this question. When college students were asked about their families, androgynous men said their fathers had been highly involved in their lives, that they felt rejected by neither parent, and that they felt relatively close to their mothers (Orlofsky, 1979). But masculine men reported similar family relationships. Androgynous women tended to be moderately close to their fathers and to differ from traditional women by having mothers who modeled—and encouraged—achievement, curiosity, and intellectual values. The recollections of college students, which may be transformed to fit the student's present view of self and world, may not tell us a great deal about the developmental course of androgyny. As we have seen, sex roles are determined by so many influences—parents, peers, teachers, media, and society—that parents' efforts to counteract stereotypical sex roles are unlikely to have a great influence.

It is unlikely that society will either abolish or reverse gender roles. Although many formal obstacles to the advancement of women in economic and legal areas have been overcome, most women will continue to be responsible for primary child care. The effect of recent changes has been limited to giving women freedom to work and to share the chores with their husbands and (primarily female) day-care workers. Given this situation, most men will continue to bear primary financial responsibility while the children are very young. But the edges of stereotypes are likely to blur, with both sexes feeling less hemmed in by rigid restrictions than in former times.

SUMMARY

Sex roles pervade every aspect of life, and in every culture men and women have different duties, different responsibilities, and different pleasures. Slight differences between the sexes become magnified into **sex-role stereotypes,** simplified concepts about sex differences that resemble few people in the culture.

Sex roles, which refer to the socially prescribed manifestations of gender, may vary over time. **Gender identity** is one's inner experience of the self as male or female. Although the two usually correspond, sometimes they do not, as in the case of the househusband with a secure male gender identity.

Gender identity develops in the early preschool years, but **gender constancy**—the knowledge that one's gender will never change—may not develop until a child understands the concept of conservation. A pseudo-constancy may develop among nonconserving four-year-olds. Children whose gender identity is different from their anatomical sex are called **transsexuals,** a disorder that may result from a combination of biological, constitutional, and social forces.

Prenatal hormones may dispose male and female infants toward different kinds of behavior, but the way they are treated by others has an extremely powerful influence on gender identity and on sex-role development. Slight sex differences in behavior are apparent during the first few days of life, yet their importance has not been established. For any sex difference, however, the behavior of boys and girls overlaps.

Cognition affects the development of sex roles through gender constancy, which leads youngsters to seek out information about sex roles and attitudes, and **gender schemas,** cognitive networks of sex-related associations used by the child in processing new information. Gender schemas are so powerful that conflicting information is either unnoticed, "forgotten," or transformed to fit the schema.

Parents appear to encourage independence in boys and nurturance and dependence in girls, and the work they begin is furthered by teachers. Peers also play an important role by reinforcing appropriate sex-role behavior and punishing behavior they see as inappropriate. Through their portrayal of sex-role stereotypes, the media also have a powerful influence.

With the onset of puberty, adolescents retreat

to the shelter of sex-role stereotypes, perhaps influenced by both hormones and social pressures. Overconforming to sex roles may lead to **sex-role strain.** Adolescents, especially girls, feel pressure to conform to the culture's **body ideal.** Sexual behavior itself is influenced by stereotypes, so that adolescent boys and girls bring quite different backgrounds and expectations to sexual experiences.

Conformity to sex roles is not stable. During certain periods of life—the preschool years, when children are developing their sex roles; the adolescent years, when they are learning to cope with the role demands of sexual maturation; and the years of early parenthood—traditional sex roles are useful and most people conform to them. When one's life no longer is built around the implications of gender, the strictures of sex roles drop away. Older adults appear to move toward **androgyny,** with men expressing feminine and women expressing male qualities that have been suppressed.

Androgynous people embrace the characteristics of both sexes, being assertive or yielding as the situation demands. People who score high on androgyny see little psychological difference between the sexes and may process gender-related information differently, since their view of the world may not be dominated by gender schemas. Although society is unlikely to abolish gender roles, both sexes face fewer restrictions today than they once did.

CHAPTER SIXTEEN

Self-Control and Morality

MORAL DEVELOPMENT
Defining Moral Development
Inconsistency in Moral Conduct
DEVELOPING MORAL BEHAVIOR
Establishing Guilt—The Psychoanalytic
    Approach
Learning Moral Conduct—The Social-
    Learning Approach
Empathizing with Others—The Motivational
    Approach
DEVELOPING REASONING—THE
    COGNITIVE APPROACH
Moral Judgment
Stages in Moral Reasoning
Consistency in Thought and Action
PROSOCIAL BEHAVIOR
Generosity
Giving Aid
The Influence of Television
ANTISOCIAL BEHAVIOR
The Causes of Aggression
The Development of Aggression
Sex Differences in Aggression
The Power of Television
SUMMARY

Paul and Michael, both fifteen months old, were struggling desperately over a toy. First Michael, then Paul, tugged at the attractive plaything, each trying to capture it for himself. Suddenly Paul began to cry. At the sound of his friend's distress, Michael let go of the toy. But possession did not end the tears; Paul kept on sobbing. Michael studied his friend for a moment, then gave his teddy bear to Paul. Paul cried on. After another pause, Michael ran from the room and came back with Paul's security blanket. He offered it to his friend, who took it, then stopped crying. Somehow this infant realized that just as his prized teddy bear could comfort his own distress, Paul's security blanket would end his friend's unhappiness. This anecdote, reported by Martin Hoffman (1976), indicates that even an infant can be empathic and correctly assess and minister to another's needs. Empathy, which underlies much of the behavior that we consider moral, has been the basis of one approach to moral development.

In considering moral development, which is the topic of this chapter, we distinguish between moral behavior and moral reasoning, and look

503

at the effect of the immediate situation on moral behavior. After describing psychoanalytic, social-learning, and motivational approaches to moral behavior, the discussion turns to cognitive approaches to moral reasoning. Comparing Piaget's theory of moral judgment with the system developed by Lawrence Kohlberg, we consider the application of both to moral behavior. Next we look at prosocial and antisocial behavior as examples of self-control. Altruism is examined as it appears in generosity and coming to the aid of others. The discussion of aggression examines its origins, the situations that evoke it, and the influence of television on aggressive behavior and its acceptance.

MORAL DEVELOPMENT

Children who learn to abide by the rules of their culture are generally considered "good." But how do they come to carry out rules that uphold their culture's values and to avoid breaking its prohibitions? And what is good? If being good simply means conforming to social standards, then a good Nazi was a moral human being in the Germany of the 1930s and 1940s. The valuation we place on human life and on justice will not allow us to accept such a totally relative position, one that requires us to regard slavery or genocide as moral if it is practiced and condoned by a culture. But whether right or wrong is whatever a culture says it is or whether there are universal moral principles or whether certain human moral predispositions take different forms in different cultures, children learn the rules of their own culture in basically the same way. Many psychologists agree that (1) babies come into the world as amoral beings, (2) they are active learners, (3) they acquire their first personal moral values and standards from their parents, (4) early moral edicts are tied to specific situations, (5) a child's early moral concepts and understandings differ from those of adults, and (6) a person's moral concepts and understandings change with increasing cognitive sophistication and social experience.

Defining Moral Development

When researchers talk about moral development, they are often talking about two different things. By moral development, psychoanalysts and social-learning theorists mean just what parents, policemen, and the average citizen mean—behavior. These researchers focus on what children do and how that behavior changes as children grow. Much of their research involves lying, cheating, stealing, resisting temptation, and being willing to share possessions or to assist people in need. In contrast, cognitive theorists pay little attention to what children do. They are interested in how children think about moral problems and the kinds of judgments they make. Most of their research involves presenting stories that center on some kind of transgression or moral dilemma and asking children to judge the actors and explain why the children in the story are good or bad and whether they should be punished.

The basic problem is that the connection between what children or adults say is right in tests of moral reasoning and what they actually do is slight. Whenever researchers have found a relationship between moral reasoning and moral behavior, it has been modest. Walter and Harriet Mischel (1976) surveyed the existing research and concluded that it is difficult to justify claims of strong links between moral reasoning and individual action. They suggest that knowing people's moral reasoning allows one to predict only 10 percent of the variation in their behavior in different situations. For example, it is often possible to predict moral behavior just as accurately from a child's need for achievement or need for affiliation as from the child's level of moral reasoning. And the problem of prediction is complicated by the fact that a child will cheat in one situation and will not cheat in another.

Inconsistency in Moral Conduct

Although people continue to talk about moral conduct as a class of reactions that go together and are governed by some central controlling process such as conscience, it is plain that most of us behave inconsistently in situations involving moral problems. After surveying the research, Douglas Graham (1972) concluded that people are likely to show highly consistent moral conduct only when the range of situations that confronts them is restricted or when a high level of abstract thinking allows them to apply general principles over many varied situations.

More than fifty years ago, Hugh Hartshorne and Mark May (1928) conducted a landmark study of children's consistency in moral conduct and disappointed all those who would like to divide the world into moral and immoral people. In the course of their research, Hartshorne and May tested 11,000 schoolchildren for many types of moral behavior (such as cheating, lying, and stealing) in different contexts (such as tests, games, and contests) in widely varied settings (such as home, church, and playground). They found that children's moral judgments remained consistent provided that the questionnaires that measured them were administered in the same setting. When the setting was moved—for example, from a church to a clubhouse—the correlations between the two scores dropped drastically, making it appear that the children's basic moral codes changed when a given situation changed.

The children's moral behavior was even less consistent than their moral judgments. Hartshorne and May found that almost all children cheat some of the time and that knowing a child has cheated in one situation does not make it possible to predict whether the child will cheat in another. Expediency appeared to determine the decision. When it seemed safe and easy to cheat or when it appeared that other children cheated or approved of cheating, a child was more likely to cheat. For example, in some classrooms, many children cheated; in others, almost no one cheated. It also appeared that the child who cheats in the classroom is not necessarily the same child who tells lies there; nor is the child who lies to the teacher the same child who lies to peers. Finally, the relationship between children's moral judgments and their actual be-

Circumstances often determine behavior in situations involving morality. This child will steal if he thinks he won't get caught; another child might steal only if the payoff is enormous; and a third, only if the theft is easy. (Sepp Seitz/ Woodfin Camp & Associates)

havior was virtually nonexistent. Their results convinced Hartshorne and May that it was foolish to try to categorize children or adults as moral or immoral. The crucial question was not whether an individual would behave morally or immorally but rather when he or she would do so.

The children studied by Hartshorne and May did not, however, cheat at random. According to Roger Burton (1976), who reanalyzed these classic studies, they did establish individual predispositions to be honest or dishonest. Burton believes that children's learning experiences lead some of them to be relatively consistent in their honesty or dishonesty and others to be relatively inconsistent. Yet even when a child develops a general tendency to resist or to succumb to temptation, the conditions surrounding each moral choice will have a strong effect on the child's final decision.

Inconsistency in moral conduct should not be surprising. Moral situations involve strong and conflicting pressures, and only a slight change in these pressures may shift a course of action from moral to immoral in a person's judgment. By changing the consequences for individuals involved, William Sobesky (1983) was able to change people's judgment of a situation. Circumstances also influence people in different ways. For one person, the chances of getting caught may determine his or her behavior. For another, the magnitude of the payoff may be the determining factor. A third person's behavior may depend on the amount of effort involved. Although moral reasoning may become increasingly unified and consistent as a person develops, his or her behavior often depends on situational constraints. Moreover, moral conduct in one situation (resistance to temptation) is a behavior pattern different from moral conduct in another (the donation of money to charity). Both are examples of moral behavior, but they are not necessarily governed by the same processes, nor do they necessarily manifest themselves in a consistent fashion across individuals.

DEVELOPING MORAL BEHAVIOR

However inconsistently people behave, at times "conscience" keeps them from breaking moral codes. When they speak of conscience, however, people are referring to their feelings when they remember or anticipate some transgression. These feelings develop gradually during childhood, and babies who come into the world without any sense of right or wrong become eight-year-olds who "feel bad" when they disobey parents or teachers. In fact, the language of morality is full of terms that relate to feelings—terms such as "guilt," "shame," "anxiety"—and how people come to feel about their actions is a critical factor in the development of moral conduct.

Psychoanalytic theory describes *what* children learn in the process of developing a conscience; social-learning theory describes *how* they learn moral actions and under what conditions they are likely to put that learning into action. The two approaches to moral development, then, are complementary—one concentrates on content, the other on process (Hogan and Emler, 1978).

Establishing Guilt—The Psychoanalytic Approach

According to Freudian theory (see Chapter 1), the child's conscience, or superego, develops out of the oedipal struggle. Fearing the loss of parental love, children identify with the parent of the same sex. They strive to be like that parent in every way, copying behavior and incorporating moral standards and values. Once this is accomplished (at about six, or the beginning of the latency period), whenever children are tempted to violate a parental prohibition, they experience guilt—a form of self-punishment. The rules that once had to be enforced by the parent are now enforced by the child because they have become the child's own values.

If the psychoanalytic view is correct, then disciplinary techniques that keep the child uncertain about a parent's love (withdrawal of love, denial of rewards, and threats of ostracism) are likely to produce children who feel guilty when they violate parental standards. In a study of seventy-five cultures, John Whiting and Irvin Child (1953) found that societies in which parents used these love-oriented techniques of discipline were indeed more likely to produce guilty children than were societies in which parents used physical punishment or ridicule. The relation, however, was weak.

Further support for identification with parents as the basis of conscience turned up in the study by Robert Sears, Eleanor Maccoby, and Harry Levin (1957). They found that five-year-olds who were disciplined with love-oriented techniques tended to develop strong consciences—but only if they had warm mothers whose love, acceptance, and enthusiasm for their children were apparent to interviewers. Children of cold mothers who relied on the withdrawal of love were less likely to develop strong consciences. However, the relationship among parental identification, guilt, and moral behavior is not as straightforward as Freud believed. When Martin Hoffman (1984) reviewed a number of studies, he found that, as predicted, identification with parents appeared to be linked with some forms of moral behavior. But contrary to expectations, parental identification was not correlated with children's guilt. Hoffman also discovered that love-oriented disciplinary techniques were more likely to be connected with a tendency to inhibit anger than with the development of a conscience.

When a strong conscience does develop, the guilt that accompanies it is unpleasant. Most children soon learn one or more ways of avoiding or reducing their guilt. As children's ability to understand and to think increases and as they gain additional social experience, they learn new ways to manage guilt. And, although individual differences in this aspect of moral development are large, most children appear to develop somewhat similar ways of managing guilt (McMichael and Grinder, 1966).

One of the most obvious ways to avoid guilt is through self-control. For example, children can resist temptation and refuse to do something that is forbidden. If, however, they believe that they will succumb to temptation, they may learn to avoid guilt by not even thinking about forbidden things, because the thoughts themselves provoke guilt feelings. In the box on page 508, we can see the power of children's thoughts over their ability to resist temptation.

As their cognitive sophistication increases, however, most children learn elegant ways of avoiding the guilt produced by their thoughts or actions. For example, if a boy hurts another person, he may define his actions in benevolent terms, saying, "I just did it for his own good." Or he may learn to avoid guilt and self-condemnation by telling himself that the other person is a "tattletale" or a "cheater." Other learned ways of reducing the unpleasantness of guilt appear equally effective. A boy may learn to confess his transgressions or to apologize for what he has said or done. Or he may learn to reduce his guilt by saying that his misbehavior was only half as bad as it could have been or as what others have done.

Some of these ways in which children and adults learn to handle their feelings of guilt and responsibility appear strikingly similar to what has been called the "just world hypothesis" (Fein, 1976). In general, people want to see the world as working in a consistent and just fashion, so that evil is punished and good is rewarded. Adopting this perspective allows people to see themselves as caring, helpful, and concerned human beings, no matter what happens to others. They have, therefore, a way to escape feelings of guilt or responsibility when someone else is the victim of an obvious wrong; if the world is just, the person must have deserved it.

Learning Moral Conduct— The Social-Learning Approach

Social-learning theorists agree that parents are important in the development of moral behavior, but instead of focusing on the child's identification with one parent, they see both parents as models and dispensers of rewards and punishment. Social-learning theorists believe that children learn moral behavior as they learn any other behavior. Children discover that when they do or say things their parents approve of, they generally receive affection, and through conditioning, this affection becomes coupled with their feelings of self-approval. They also discover, however, that when they do or say things their parents disapprove of, withdrawal of affection or punishment of some kind is likely to follow, and through conditioning, this punishment becomes coupled with their feelings of guilt and self-reproof. As a result of this kind of

How Children Postpone Pleasure

An important aspect of moral behavior is the ability to postpone immediate gratification. For example, an adolescent who cannot postpone pleasure may steal an appealing record, sweater, television set, or a car because he or she is not able to pay for it immediately and cannot endure waiting until the required money has been saved. Although most young children want what they want immediately, research indicates that even three- or four-year-olds are capable of postponing their pleasure. However, research shows that their ability to do so varies with such factors as their mood and what they do while waiting.

Most studies of young children's self-control involve their desires for snacks or small toys, and their moods apparently affect their ability to wait for them. Bert Moore, Andrea Clyburn, and Bill Underwood (1976) asked some preschoolers to talk and think about things that made them happy; others were told to talk and think about things that made them sad. Afterward, each child was given a choice between a less-valued treat (a pretzel) to eat immediately or a more-valued treat (a lollipop) to be eaten several hours later. Children who were told to talk and think about sad things more often chose the pretzel, and those who were told to talk and think about happy things more often chose the lollipop. This suggests that negative moods may increase children's tendency to be impulsive, whereas positive moods may increase their willingness to be patient.

What children do while they wait affects how long they can delay gratification. In a series of studies, Harriet and Walter Mischel (1983) traced the development of children's strategies for postponing pleasure. Four-year-olds prefer to look at the promised rewards while they wait, although many know that the sight of them makes waiting difficult.

They apparently overestimate their ability to resist temptation. By the time children are six, they prefer to have the rewards covered. They have learned to distract themselves by doing or thinking about something else, often singing, whistling, or playing games with their hands. Some have learned to keep their thoughts trained on the task of waiting, saying to themselves such things as, "If you wait, you get two marshmallows; if you don't, you only get one."

Some time around the third grade, the realization emerges that the way one thinks about the rewards affects the ability to delay gratification. Understanding that focusing on the abstract qualities of the reward is more effective than dwelling on its delicious taste allows children to delay gratification even if the reward is in front of them. This development may explain why it makes little difference to older children whether rewards are covered or exposed during the wait. The timing of this advance in understanding leads Mischel and Mischel to speculate that it may require the emergence of concrete operational thought.

Although they do not spontaneously arrive at the strategy of thinking about the reward abstractly, younger children can use the technique if instructed in it. Walter Mischel and Nancy Baker (1975) gave children a choice of eating one pretzel or marshmallow immediately or getting two pretzels or marshmallows if they waited. Children who followed instructions and thought about the pretzel sticks in front of them as "little brown logs" or "crayons," or who thought about the marshmallows as being "cotton balls" or "clouds," managed to wait for a relatively long time— an average of fourteen minutes. But those who thought about the "crunchy, salty, toasty taste" of pretzels or the "chewy, sweet, soft taste" of marshmallows gave up and took their single pretzel or marshmallow after an average wait of less than five minutes.

learning, children eventually may behave morally even though their parents or other people are not present. Gradually, their own thoughts and feelings replace rewards and punishments administered by others, and they come to regulate their own moral conduct. They are also likely to keep learning various ways of reacting to their guilt over actual or contemplated transgressions.

DISCIPLINE Studies have shown that the nature of the parental relationship, the explanation of the reasons for discipline, and the timing of punishment are all important factors in the establishment of guilt and self-regulation in moral conduct. According to Justin Aronfreed (1976), punishment (which includes rejection and disapproval) is an inevitable part of child rearing, and without it socialization probably cannot take place—as we saw in Chapter 13. Mild physical punishment, coupled with a mild withdrawal of love, appears to establish guilt and self-regulation much more efficiently than does severe physical punishment (M. Hoffman, 1977a). A child can always avoid the brief unpleasantness of physical punishment merely by avoiding the punisher, but if a normally loving parent also withdraws his or her love, the punishment lasts until the love is restored. Children disciplined by severe and unexplained punishment are unlikely to develop an effective sense of guilt or self-regulation and instead only learn to behave so that they will not get caught. Yet, as the box on p. 512 indicates, a parent's choice of discipline may be partly determined by the child.

Studies by Martin Hoffman and Herbert Saltzstein (1967), Aronfreed (1969), and others suggest that reasoning with children and pointing out the effects of their wrongdoing are at least as important as withdrawing love—possibly more so. Such verbal explanation and reasoning do two things: they encourage a child to take the role of others, and they help a child to internalize moral standards by providing thoughts to associate with his or her feelings and with the reward or punishment. As a girl (or

Whether parental discipline is effective may be determined by the nature of the parent-child relationship, the way the parent explains the disciplinary action, and the timing of the punishment. (Tom Carter/Jeroboam)

boy) comes to understand how her behavior affects others and how their behavior affects her, and as she comes to adopt the moral thoughts and attitudes of her parents, she soon responds with self-approval to what are now her own correct thoughts and actions. She learns to use self-instruction and self-praise. And when faced with a temptation, such as a dazzling display of dials and push buttons on a color television set, the child may regulate her conduct by telling herself, "No. Don't touch. That's a good girl. I'm a good girl for not touching."

The effectiveness of reasoning may depend in part on the sort of explanation parents give their children. Nine- and ten-year-olds were told that a toy manufacturer was testing the durability of various toys, and that the children had been selected to test the durability of a toy crank. Behind them was an array of attractive toys, including a model railroad set, in which the electric train was running through a village; an electric bowling game, a pinball game, a puppet, and a toy car. Leon Kuczynski (1983) told the children that they were not to look at the toys, but instead must keep rotating the crank. Some of the children were simply prohibited from looking at the toys ("Listen, don't look at those toys again until I let you"); the rest were given reasons for the prohibition. Half were told that if they looked at the toys, they would have to work so much longer there would be no time to play with the toys. The rest were told that if they looked at the toys, the experimenter would be unhappy and would have to do additional work later on his own. When the experimenter left the room, children who had been given a reason that described the consequences to the experimenter continued to work at a fairly stable rate, but compliance began to drop in the other two groups. Then the experimenter returned for a moment, saying that he had to be away awhile and would understand if the children didn't work steadily or if they looked at the toys. Now the differences widened significantly; children who had been told that disobedience would place a hardship on the experimenter worked almost as steadily as they had before, but most children in the other groups seemed to feel little obligation to continue working (see Figure 16.1).

Kuczynski suggests that reasons focusing on consequences to the child were perceived by children as blatant attempts to control their behavior, and that such reasoning by parents is likely to be effective only as long as the parents are present. Reasons focusing on consequences to another may have aroused concern about the experimenter, so that the children's empathic reactions motivated them to continue their work. This sort of reasoning by parents, believes Kuczynski, not only arouses empathy but leads children to attribute their compliance to their own dispositions, which may lead them to internalize the standard. As we shall see, some theorists believe that the development of empathy is vital to morality.

The timing of parental discipline appears to be especially important in the development of guilt and self-regulation. Aronfreed (1976) found that a majority of children who were punished as they reached for a toy did not touch the forbidden toy when they were left alone

with it. Those who did pick it up succumbed only after a lengthy period. But children who were not punished until after they had picked up the toy began playing with the forbidden toy as soon as the experimenter left the room. Aronfreed suggests that when a child is punished early in the course of transgression, enormous anxiety becomes associated with the *anticipation* of doing wrong, allowing the child's inner monitors to exercise control over behavior.

In a second study, Aronfreed found that children who were given a verbal reason (that the toy was "only for older boys") along with the delayed punishment resisted temptation much longer than children who simply experienced delayed punishment without a reason for it. And when the late punishment was accompanied by an explanation that focused on the child's intentions (the experimenter realized that the child "had wanted" to play with the toy) along with the reason it was not to be played with, resistance to temptation was as strong as when children were punished as they reached for the toy.

It is, of course, often impossible to punish children just before they begin to do something that is forbidden, but as Aronfreed's studies show, delayed punishment can be effective. Along with providing punishment, the parent must use words to recreate the transgression as fully as possible, sensitizing the child to his or her intention as well as to the consequences of the act. In this way, when the child is later tempted, anxiety will be generated *before* any transgression takes place, greatly increasing the chances that the child will resist temptation. By using this sort of approach, Donald Meichenbaum and Joseph Goodman (1971) have taught impulsive children with a history of getting into trouble to talk to themselves when they are tempted to do something forbidden. Using this kind of self-regulation, children end up modifying their own behavior.

MODELS As earlier discussions of modeling indicated, if models are warm, powerful, and

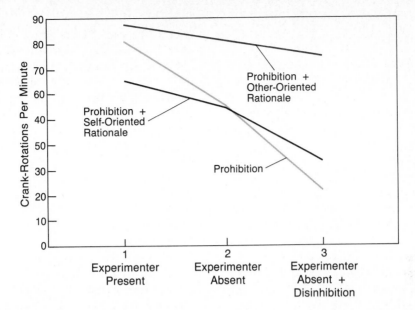

FIGURE 16.1 The mean rate at which children worked steadily in the presence of inviting toys was affected by the type of reasoning used by the experimenter in prohibiting them from looking at the toys. The difference was striking when children were told the experimenter would understand if they disobeyed (Condition 3).

(From Kuczynski, 1983)

competent (and in early childhood that is just the way parents are likely to seem), a child may well copy their behavior. But as we also saw in earlier discussions, what happens to the models a child sees also affects the probability that a child will imitate them. If the model is rewarded, the child is likely to copy the model and to expect a reward for behaving in the same way. If the model is punished, the child is unlikely to copy the behavior because he or she would expect to receive similar punishment. And if a model resists moderate temptation—especially if the model explains why he or she resisted—a child will be likely to forgo temptation, even when it means having to continue to work on a boring task (Grusec et al., 1979).

One of the most important findings to come out of research on the observational learning of moral conduct is that watching an unpunished transgression appears to have the same effect on a child as watching a transgression followed by rewards. Children who see peers playing freely with forbidden toys are more likely to play with the toys than children who see no such transgression (Grosser, Polansky, and Lippitt, 1951). Apparently, when a child sees other children breaking a prohibition and getting away with it, the consequences the child anticipates for violating that prohibition change.

An experiment by Richard Walters and Ross Parke (1964) supports the idea that the absence of expected punishment may act as a reward. They showed films of a model playing with forbidden toys to several groups of children. Some of the children saw the model rewarded; some saw the model punished; others saw nothing—either good or bad—happen to the model. When these children were later placed in a situation similar to that depicted in the film, both those who had seen the transgression rewarded and those who had seen it go unpunished were more likely to play with the forbidden toys than children who had seen the model's actions punished or those in a control group who had seen no film.

All the children who saw the films learned

Reason or Power—Not Always the Parents' Choice

The sort of discipline parents use with their children apparently affects children's behavior—including their moral development, as the discussions in Chapter 13 and in this chapter have indicated. For example, the use of reasoning with children has been linked with the development of altruism (Hoffman, 1984). But what if the influence runs both ways? An experiment by Barbara Keller and Richard Bell (1979) indicates that a child's behavior may go a long way toward determining techniques parents use to instill codes of morality.

Keller and Bell trained three nine-year-old girls to behave in two entirely different ways. The first style was "person-oriented": the girls looked at adults' faces, smiled, and answered questions promptly. In the second, "object-oriented" style, the girls kept their attention on the materials before them (beads, small toys, etc.) and counted silently to five before answering adults' comments. Each girl learned both styles of behavior.

Twenty-four undergraduate college women, who were the subjects, were each instructed to interact with one of the two girls in an attempt to get her to show some consideration for others. In order to give the stu-

dent power over the child, the experimenter handed her a stack of poker chips, which could be exchanged for toys or books after the session. The student could award the child chips or take away chips the child already had.

Before the twenty-minute interaction period began, the student watched one of the girls through a one-way mirror as she ran through a memorized script with the experimenter. During this enactment, the girl behaved in either a person- or an object-oriented style. During the following session with the college student, the girl (while continuing to behave in the person- or object-oriented style) impeded whatever altruistic task the student was urging her to do. For example, she spent more time working on a pillow for herself than on one for a handicapped child.

When the videotaped sessions were scored, it was plain that the girls' manner of behaving had a profound effect on the college students. When speaking to a girl who behaved in a person-oriented manner, the students relied on reason, often referring to the consequences of the child's behavior. When speaking to a girl who behaved in an object-oriented manner, the students fell back on the only kind of power they had—references to the poker chips that they could give or take away. The girls' behavior also affected the students' impressions of them. On a questionnaire they answered after the

the model's behavior, for when the experimenter indicated that no one would be punished for playing with the forbidden toys, children who had seen any of the films were more likely to play with the toys than children who had not seen the films. Thus it is apparent that those who did not copy the model's transgression were trying to avoid expected punishment.

Subsequently, Richard Walters, Ross Parke, and Valerie Cane (1965) also found that in certain conditions, only the prospect of punishment

can keep a child from transgression. Once again, they showed children films of a model playing with forbidden toys, but this time the toys were so enticing that punishing the model was the only consequence that affected children's transgressions. The rest—children who had seen the model rewarded, those who had seen nothing happen to the model, and those who had no film—could not resist the tempting toys.

When children watch a model go unpunished,

session, students rated the girls as significantly more attentive, responsive, attractive, cheerful, intelligent, and physically active when they had behaved in a person-oriented manner than when they had used the object-oriented style.

The results of this experiment indicate that children play an important part in determining the ways in which they are socialized. The apparent attentiveness of person-oriented children may reinforce a parent's attempts to use reason with them, while the seeming inattentiveness of object-oriented children may either fail to reinforce (thereby extinguishing) or even punish their parents' attempt at reason. And when a parent believes that reason is ineffective, power is the only remaining tool.

The process of parent-child interaction is surely a circular one. As noted in Chapter 3, the infant's initial responsiveness may set the tone for parent-child interaction, and the discussion in Chapter 12 pointed out the importance of a mother's responsiveness to her child. What combination of inborn tendencies, rewards and punishment, and level of cognitive understanding—in both child and parent—develops a highly person-oriented child is unknown. It appears, however, that the choice of disciplinary techniques is not arbitrary but dictated in part by the child's behavior.

two things happen. First, the punishment-free transgression suggests to them that the usual negative sanction does not apply in this situation, and they modify their own thinking accordingly. Second, the children then copy the model's violations because transgression is safe and because playing with the forbidden toys is rewarding. Consequences to a model can also affect other aspects of moral conduct. When children see a model go unrewarded for moral behavior, such as altruism, they will also fail to copy the model (Staub, 1975). Thus in a paradoxical sort of way, seeing moral behavior go unrewarded may decrease the rate at which it occurs, just as if the behavior were immoral and therefore punished.

Children who develop high standards of moral conduct, says Albert Bandura (1977), are likely to be children whose parental models keep high standards themselves, have reaped rewards because of their standards, demand that their children adhere to the same standards, and protect their children from different standards that might be held by their peers.

Empathizing with Others— The Motivational Approach

Motivation is crucial to any theory of moral development, for it provides the reason for moral behavior. Moral behavior often requires us to endure hardship or to sacrifice our own interest. Some theorists believe that **empathy,** or the vicarious identification with another's emotions, is a basic motive impelling us to do good deeds even when they require sacrifice or to refrain from bad deeds because they might harm another. Many theorists believe that empathy develops through conditioning as the child comes to associate the pain or distress of another with his or her own painful past experience. But Martin Hoffman (1984) believes that although simple conditioning plays a part in the development of empathy, the cognitive components are also vital. Hoffman believes that a child progresses through four stages in developing the ability to empathize with others.

In the first stage, which lasts most of the first year, an infant does not distinguish between the self and the person in distress. Hoffman describes an eleven-month-old girl who saw another baby fall and begin to cry. The baby girl, looking as if she were about to cry herself, put her thumb in her mouth and buried her face in her mother's lap—her customary reaction to her own distress or injury. In the second stage, which depends on the development of person permanence, infants realize that the other person is physically distinct from them and that the observed distress is not their own. However, infants assume that the person in distress feels exactly as they do. In the anecdote about Paul and Michael that began the chapter, Michael's first response to Paul's tears was to assume that his own teddy bear would have as much meaning and comfort for Paul as it did for him. As youngsters move from the first to second stage, they go through an intermediate period in which they feel sad, so that they attempt to comfort both the victim and themselves.

In the third stage of empathy, which is reached sometime after the second birthday, children develop an awareness that other people may have responses to a situation that differ from their own. Now children have a rudimentary ability to put themselves in another's place. The final stage of empathy, which develops late in childhood, includes an appreciation of others' feelings that goes beyond the immediate situation. The child becomes aware that giving a single meal to a starving person, for example, does not end that person's want.

Hoffman believes that empathy may build upon an inborn predisposition that often leads babies in a hospital nursery to cry when they hear the wails of another infant (Sagi and Hoffman, 1976), but that it is developed primarily by parental disciplinary actions. As we saw earlier, social-learning theorists have described how disciplinary techniques may arouse feelings of guilt within a child at the thought of transgressing. According to Hoffman, when reasoning is used in disciplining a child, the child's attention is drawn to the effect of his or her actions on others. In ambiguous situations, reasoning also makes clear to the child that he or she caused another's distress. Eventually the child comes to feel empathy and empathy-based guilt whenever he or she contemplates acting in a manner that would harm others.

The purely cognitive accompaniment of empathy is role taking. Until children reach Hoffman's third stage, they will have difficulty in assuming the role of another, because most preschool children tend to be egocentric. But just

as fifteen-month-old Michael managed to take Paul's role to the extent that he realized his friend's security blanket would comfort him, young children may be more capable of role taking than laboratory tests would indicate. Most research tasks that young children fail put a premium on verbal and cognitive skills, which they may lack, thereby masking their actual role-taking capabilities (Hoffman, 1976).

Morality based on empathy may not cover all moral situations. In situations involving justice, a major concern of cognitive theorists, empathic morality may be of little guidance unless someone has been treated unfairly (Hoffman, 1984). And when confronted with moral dilemmas, in which competing claims to right or wrong must be balanced, empathy may impede a person's judgment.

Jerome Kagan (1984), who agrees with Hoffman that empathy provides a basis for morality, views morality as an expression of the capacity to evaluate acts as good or evil. In his view, empathy is only one of the strands involved in the development of such standards. As children empathize with others, coming to understand that others are distressed by actions that distress themselves, they begin to treat such actions as a violation of standards. Another important strand is the child's realization that adults disapprove or punish acts that violate standards, an understanding that appears after children are about eighteen months old. At this time, reports Kagan, children are first upset at a broken toy or a missing button, and their concern about damaged objects emerges as they begin to make inferences about the causes of events.

The third strand in the development of standards is the child's realization that in some cases he or she is not competent to reach a desired goal. When the child tries to meet a standard and knows that he or she is incapable of doing so, the child becomes distressed; but when the child meets a self-imposed standard, he or she shows signs of pleasure. As we shall see in the discussion of prosocial behavior, other researchers have also seen competence as an integral part of moral behavior.

Finally, the child comes to see him- or herself as "bad" for committing antisocial acts. Kagan believes that this development does not occur until a child is three or four years old. Now the impulse to hit another child or to take a toy or to violate parental standards is inhibited not only by fear of punishment but by self-condemnation. The belief that it is good to be obedient provides the child with a motive to obey.

DEVELOPING MORAL REASONING—THE COGNITIVE APPROACH

Cognitive theorists pay little attention to whether people's conduct is moral or immoral or to how people feel about their actions; instead, cognitive theorists focus on how people reason about moral issues and how they justify their moral judgments. Just as social-learning theorists regard the development of moral behavior as a case of learning applied to a single realm, so cognitive theorists regard moral reasoning as a kind of thought that is subject to the same developmental constraints as the rest of cognition. In this view, until a child reaches an appropriate level of cognitive development, certain types of moral reasoning are impossible. The child in the sensorimotor stage, for example, lacks even a rudimentary appreciation of morality. Once the child moves into the preoperational stage and begins to use symbols, the beginnings of moral reasoning appear. Not until a child acquires formal operational thought are the highest levels of moral reasoning possible—and even then, there is no guarantee they will develop. The dominant theorists in the area of moral thought have been Jean Piaget and Lawrence Kohlberg.

Moral Judgment

Jean Piaget (1932) believed that, since morality is embodied in a system of rules, the best place

As children get older, their belief that changing the rules of a game is naughty disappears. By the time they are ten, they respect the rules but are willing to change them if all the players agree. (Frank Siteman/EKM-Nepenthe)

to watch moral development is in children's games. Consequently, he spent a good deal of time watching children play marbles and talking to them at length about the rules of the game. He discovered that until children are two, there are no rules because there is no game; children simply handle marbles as they wish. From two until they are five or so, children imitate rules but do not try to win. Rules are regarded as interesting but not obligatory. From about six until they are ten, there is an attempt to agree on rules, but each child seems to play by a different set. Despite their contradictory accounts of the rules and their general laxity in following them, children of this age regard the rules as imposed from the outside by authorities. Rules are sacred, eternal, and untouchable; even to consider changing them is naughty. From ten to twelve, everybody knows the same rules and there is a regulation for every detail of the game. Although children respect the rules, they know that they may change them. Any change however, must be the result of a consensus and also be consistent with the spirit of the game.

Piaget proposed that as children move from

confidence in the eternal nature of rules to a belief in their mutability, they also tend to move from one major stage of morality to another. In the first stage, called the **morality of constraint,** duty consists of obedience to authority. Transgressors are punished by imminent justice, that is, wicked deeds inevitably bring punishment, even if it takes time or appears in the form of accidental injury. If a boy steals a quarter from his mother's purse and later cuts himself on a broken cola bottle, the cut is seen as punishment for the theft. Children operating under the morality of constraint judge an act by its consequences, not by the intentions of the actor.

The second stage, the **morality of cooperation,** develops from children's interactions with their peers. In judging transgressions, children believe the intentions of the actor are more important than the consequences of the act. Punishment is not inevitable, and when it comes, it should not be arbitrary. The wrongdoer should receive a similar injury (a punch in the nose for a child who hits another), suffer the natural consequences of the action, or make restitution for the wrong.

Piaget realized that both these moralities can exist side by side—that a child may apply the morality of constraint to one action and the morality of cooperation to another—but he believed that as children grow older, they tend increasingly to judge in terms of the morality of cooperation.

Since Piaget first advanced this theory of moral development, researchers have found that in some situations young children may show much more advanced moral reasoning than Piaget found. They can distinguish between accidental and intended actions, between good and bad intentions, and they can weigh both intention and consequence in making moral judgments (Surber, 1977). Even five- and six-year-olds can weigh the circumstances surrounding a misdeed and adjust the punishment accordingly (Darley, Klosson, and Zanna, 1978). They are also likely to distinguish between harm to human beings and other types of damage, and to judge the former more harshly (Elkind and Dabek, 1977).

As Piaget found, however, when young children are fully aware of the intentions behind an action, they still may base their moral judgments primarily on the result of an act. Rachel Karniol (1978) suggests that young children appear to learn, first, that acts based on bad intentions are naughty regardless of their outcome and therefore deserve punishment. But when a well-intentioned act does greater harm than an act with bad intentions, children may give the consequences greater weight than intentions in assessing punishment. This interpretation, according to Karniol, is consistent with the common socialization experiences of young children. That is, parents are more likely to punish consequences than to reward good intentions, so children are likely to learn early what others consider wrong; they learn to distinguish good behavior later and more slowly.

Stages in Moral Reasoning

Building on Piaget's ideas about the nature and development of moral reasoning, Lawrence Kohlberg (1976) has proposed a series of six developmental stages of moral reasoning, with each succeeding stage consisting of a more complex and balanced way of looking at the moral-social world. These stages were originally developed on the basis of the responses made to a series of moral dilemmas by fifty-eight boys between the ages of ten and sixteen, with their statements providing information about the nature of a person's moral reasoning. For example, they might have to decide whether a poor man whose wife was near death from cancer should steal a life-saving drug from a pharmacist who insisted on full cash payment.

In developing the stages, Kohlberg was not interested in the decision concerning the theft of the drug, but the form of its justification. A person at any stage may decide either way in a given situation. The stages differ in the reasons a person gives for making a decision and in the type of concerns that are indicated for self, authority, and society.

Children progress through these stages in an

unvarying progression, never skipping a stage. The move from one stage to another occurs when cognitive conflict leads to a reorganization of thought patterns, so that in each stage children look at moral issues in a new and different way, although they continue to understand the reasoning of previous stages.

The proposed six stages form three basic developmental levels of moral reasoning, distinguished by what defines right or moral action. The first two stages form what is called the **premoral level,** because value is placed not in persons or social standards but in physical acts and needs. In Stage 1, people behave morally to keep from being punished or because the authorities have the power to compel obedience. In Stage 2, people behave morally when following the rules is in their own interest. The next two stages form the **conventional level,** with value placed on maintaining the social order and fulfilling the expectations of others. In Stage 3, people behave morally in order to appear good in the eyes of themselves and others, or because they care for other individuals. In Stage 4, people behave morally because they believe rules and obligations are necessary for a stable society. The final two stages form the **principled level,** where values reside in principles and standards that have a universal logical validity and therefore can be shared. In Stage 5, people behave morally because the social contract (which provides for everyone's welfare and protects their rights) demands it. In Stage 6, people behave morally because they are following self-chosen, internalized principles, which they believe are universal. Because it has sometimes proved difficult to distinguish between the stages at any single level (Kurtines and Greif, 1974), our focus will be primarily on the levels of moral reasoning.

INFLUENCES ON MORAL REASONING
The levels appear to be related to age. Kohlberg and his colleagues (Colby et al., 1983) have now followed the boys in the original study for twenty years and report that the use of premoral reasoning decreased steadily after the age of ten. Conventional reasoning continued to dominate most of these individuals' moral judgments, with the less advanced Stage 3 declining toward the end of adolescence. Principled reasoning did not appear until the boys reached young adulthood and was never seen in more than 10 percent of these working- and middle-class individuals. Experience as well as cognitive growth appears necessary for the acquisition of higher-level moral concepts and attitudes, because socioeconomic level was related to the emergence of more advanced stages. Each stage appeared several years earlier among the middle class, and only one of the working-class men in the study ever reasoned on the principled level.

The ties between moral judgment and formal education are also close. In Kohlberg's final analysis of the study (Colby et al., 1983), every individual who reached the principled level of reasoning had graduated from college. Studies by other researchers (Rest, Davison, and Robbins, 1978), using a more objective and simpler version of the test, indicate that moral judgment generally stops developing when people leave school. Among these adults, no more than a third of high-school graduates reasoned at the principled level, but among those who continued with advanced study in philosophy, political science, and theology, a majority reached the principled level of reasoning.

Among children, the level of moral reasoning combines with relative intelligence to produce unexpected effects. In one study (Krebs, 1968), among children who were at an opportunistic, premoral level of reasoning, those who were bright and attentive enough to see that they could cheat jumped at the chance. Among those children who were at a rule-oriented, conventional level of reasoning, however, the ones who cheated seemed to be those who were not bright or attentive enough to succeed by understanding and following the rules.

CRITICISMS OF THE THEORY Kohlberg's theory has been criticized on several counts. Its most fundamental problem, according to Hoffman (1984), is its basic assumption that there is a universal principle of justice or fairness. If this principle is not accepted, there are no grounds for assuming that moving toward a morality based on justice represents higher stages of moral reasoning. Elizabeth Simpson (1974) believes that Kohlberg's theory is culturally biased and not universal, since it is based on a social organization and values that fit only Western culture. She argues that because Kohlberg's approach focuses on issues of equality, rights, and justice, moral reasoning at a principled level fits only a constitutional democracy. In addition, the abstract thinking involved at this level is probably beyond most of the people in the world. In a study of Bahamian children and adolescents, for example, not a single one reached the principled level of reasoning (White, Bushnell, and Regnemer, 1978). It may be that like formal, abstract reasoning, principled moral reasoning requires formal thought for its development.

A built-in male bias in Kohlberg's stages has been found by Carol Gilligan (1982), who points out that no females were included in Kohlberg's research and that most women who respond to the moral dilemmas are placed in Stage 3, where morality is cast in interpersonal terms. Women traditionally have been taught to equate goodness with helping others and tend to see moral problems as arising from conflicting responsibilities. In Kohlberg's scheme, which equates moral development with the acceptance of justice, moral problems arise from competing rights, so that women who base their reasoning on the values of compassion, responsibility, and obligation are automatically classified at a lower level of moral development. According to Gilligan, women place different priorities on human experience and may see a morality of rights and noninterference as frightening because it seems to justify indifference and unconcern. She believes that moral development should incorporate an ethic of care as well as an ethic of justice.

Even if these problems are resolved, however, other problems remain in Kohlberg's theory (Hoffman, 1984). Some people have been found to regress to earlier stages of reasoning, indicating that an unvarying progression through the stages is not universal. Cognitive conflict over moral decisions is not necessarily followed by movement to a higher stage of reasoning. People's moral judgments are not consistently at the same stage, tending to vary from one moral dilemma to the next (Fishkin, Keniston, and MacKinnan, 1973). Finally, there is no direct relationship between the level of moral reasoning and a person's behavior.

REVISIONS OF THE THEORY   In response to such criticisms, Kohlberg and his associates (Colby et al., 1983) have revised the scoring system, switching its emphasis from the content of people's reasoning to its structural moral features. One effect of this shift is to move many people (usually women) who focus on interpersonal concerns from Stage 3 to a higher stage. It also drops the rating of the Archie Bunker law-and-order mentality, originally considered an example of Stage 4 morality, to Stage 3, because, Kohlberg says, Bunker is more concerned with the small group ("people like us") than with society (Muson, 1979). These changes may eliminate part of the sex-related bias that appears to be built into the proposed sequence of stages.

In the new scoring, Stage 6 has been dropped from the system, in part because the dilemmas did not distinguish between Stages 5 and 6 and in part because none of the people in Kohlberg's study reach that stage under the new scoring system (Colby et al., 1983). The new scoring system is also more stringent, reducing the proportion of individuals who reach principled reasoning from 40 percent in the original system (Rest, 1983) to 10 percent in the revised system.

This latest revision, says Kurt Fischer (1983), has cleared up some of the theory's problems. It produces results that support Kohlberg's first five stages as reflecting the development of moral judgment among white lower- and middle-class males. However, development through the stages remains extremely slow, individuals still tend to be inconsistent in their reasoning, and test scores do not translate to moral behavior—or even to moral judgments made outside the context of the dilemmas.

Consistency in Thought and Action

Looking at the evidence, the pessimist is tempted to say that high levels of moral reasoning simply allow sophisticated excuses for dubious conduct. It is certainly true that principled reasoning does not guarantee honesty or loyalty, nor does it rule out deceit. The consistency of a child's conduct, and the link between conduct and reasoning, will depend on the way that intellectual, social, and emotional factors combine during the course of moral development. At present, there is no way to predict the consistency of any individual's moral thoughts, feelings, and actions.

Some connection does exist between the way we think about moral issues and our actions. In a review of seventy-five studies, Augusto Blasi (1980) found that moral judgment and behavior were related in 76 percent of the studies, but that the relationship, while significant, was not strong, indicating a good deal of inconsistent behavior. The studies ranged over a wide variety of situations and covered both antisocial (juvenile delinquency, cheating) and prosocial (helping someone in distress) behavior.

Inconsistencies between moral reasoning and behavior should be no more surprising than the inconsistencies noted earlier in moral behavior. If behavior is not consistent from one situation to the next, then reasoning and behavior are unlikely to be perfectly matched. As James Rest (1983) reminds us, moral judgment is but one element in moral behavior, and people at the same level of reasoning differ in the way they apply it in specific situations and in the extent to which religious or ideological doctrines may take precedence over moral judgment.

PROSOCIAL BEHAVIOR

The discussion thus far has focused on keeping the rules, making moral decisions, discipline, and guilt. But there is another side to morality—acts that go beyond simply adhering to the rules and enter the realm of prosocial behavior. **Prosocial behavior** includes all actions that promote or benefit another person, so that it covers a wide span of activities, including obeying the law, helping, generosity, sacrifice, rescue, fairness, honesty, cooperation, sharing, sympathizing, comforting, and nurturing (Radke-Yarrow, Zahn-Waxler, and Chapman, 1983). In this section, however, our focus is on **altruism,** which encompasses prosocial acts that are done by intent, not accident, so that they involve an unselfish concern for the welfare of others. Altruistic action often involves some sort of risk, cost, or self-sacrifice on the part of the actor.

The purposeful nature of altruism makes it an example of **self-regulation,** which, Charlotte Patterson (1984) says, involves the "achievement, through intentional action, of personally selected aims and goals" (p. 374). Any act that is carried out freely in order to fulfill an intention is self-regulated behavior, so that altruism is only one of its forms. Such a view means that many forms of prosocial behavior are not altruistic. A child who carries out the garbage or sets the table without complaining may be behaving altruistically (to help) or may be trying to avoid punishment (no allowance). An observer may often find it difficult to distinguish altruism from other prosocial behavior, especially when the actor is a young child, because intent is not visible. Yet when children are asked about their apparently altruistic actions, even those as young as four years old are likely to explain them in terms of altruistic intent (Eisenberg, 1982).

The insistence that intent is essential to altruism means that altruism requires a certain level of cognitive development. Before a child can behave altruistically, he or she must be able to distinguish between self and other, know that others might need help, what action might help them, and how to carry it out.

Generosity

The earliest instances of generosity are found when toddlers attempt to share toys or other objects. When toddlers in Germany were observed in play situations, researchers noted many instances of spontaneous sharing and gift-giving (Stanjek, 1978). Altruistic intent probably was absent in the case of the youngest, who seemed to use their presents of a stone or a piece of wood as a way to initiate or maintain social contact. Although much of the older children's generosity seemed genuine, some of the five- and six-year-olds appeared to be motivated by selfish reasons, for they used their gifts to attain a position of social dominance.

DOES GENEROSITY INCREASE WITH AGE? If we rely on laboratory experiments, we would conclude that, for the most part, children become more generous as they get older. In controlled experiments, older children are usually more willing than youngsters to share with others, whether they are sharing candy, toys, or money (Radke-Yarrow, Zahn-Waxler, and Chapman, 1983).

In a typical laboratory study, children are asked to carry out a task or play a game and then are given an opportunity to donate part of their earnings or prizes to "poor children" or to "children who didn't get a chance to play." When William Froming, Leticia Allen, and Bill Underwood (1983) tested children between the ages of five and ten in such a situation, the youngsters' donations of M&Ms or pennies increased steadily from the youngest to the oldest except that second-graders gave less than first-graders. Similar results appeared when the researchers repeated the experiment among children at another school, and when they retested

the youngsters two years later, the formerly stingy second-graders had become as generous as older children in the previous study, and the former kindergartners had become miserly second-graders. An earlier study (Underwood, Froming, and Moore, 1977) had also found the dip in generosity among second-graders, and researchers are at a loss to explain it.

Several explanations have been offered for the increased trend in generosity that appears in most such studies. First, older children may find it easier to part with possessions simply because they do not seem quite so valuable. At the age of three, a child regards a dime as a huge sum that will bring the pleasures of bubble gum, candy or some trinket. Consequently, he or she will be reluctant to part with it. In contrast, the ten-year-old sees a dime as such an inconsequential sum that it can easily be given to others.

Second, older children have had more opportunities to learn that people are supposed to help others. They may have seen their parents donate to charities or do volunteer work in hospitals. They may have rung doorbells on Halloween to collect money for UNICEF. They may have heard people say that "A friend in need is a friend indeed" and that "It is better to give than to receive." Such experiences generally make it clear to children that their society places a premium on helping other people.

Third, as the last section indicated, older children are likely to be less egocentric than young children. Many have learned to take the perspective of others and to empathize with people who need help. Kenneth Rubin and Frank Schneider (1973) measured the egocentrism of their seven-year-old subjects and then gave them an opportunity to donate candy to poor children and to help a younger child complete a task. The children who were better able to see things from another's viewpoint were more likely both to donate candy and to assist the younger child.

The generosity that appears in the laboratory may diminish on the playground. Most studies that have observed children in naturalistic situations, where sharing is spontaneous and not contrived by the researcher, have shown no trend toward increased generosity with age (Yarrow and Waxler, 1976; Dyan-Hudson and Van Dusen, 1972). When Nancy Eisenberg-Berg and Randy Lennon (1980) rated children on empathy and then observed them at play over a ten-week period, they found that children who indicated strong empathy with characters in a story shared less than children who had shown lower levels of empathy. Research reviewed by James Bryan (1975) indicates that in competitive situations, ten-year-olds become less willing to sacrifice. When looking at the conflicting research, Marian Radke-Yarrow and her colleagues (Radke-Yarrow, Zahn-Waxler, and Chapman, 1983) suggest that there is as yet no basis for any conclusions on the connection between generosity and age.

ARE GIRLS MORE GENEROUS THAN BOYS? Although theorists have often supposed that girls are more generous and empathic than boys, most laboratory studies show no differences in the frequency or amount of sharing (Radke-Yarrow, Zahn-Waxler, and Chapman, 1983), although when differences do appear in empathy, they favor girls (Hoffman, 1977b). When Carol Shigetomi, Donald Hartmann, and Donna Gelfand (1981) compared the reputation and behavior of fifth- and sixth-graders, they found that both teachers and classmates believed the girls were more friendly, helpful, and generous. Yet when given an opportunity to display their generosity, girls were more generous than boys only with time and effort. Boys were more generous than girls in donating material objects. Both sexes gave equal amounts of money to charity. Girls' greater reputation for generosity may be the result of cultural expectations, since girls are more likely than boys to be taught to express their emotions, to be sensitive to the feelings and needs of others, and to be assigned responsibility for child care.

GENEROSITY AND MOOD Wide individual differences in generosity exist among children. One factor that may influence generosity is a child's mood, an influence that has been studied by inducing children to think about happy, sad, or neutral events and then giving them an opportunity to contribute money, toys, candy, or other prizes. At first it appeared that the happier the child, the more he or she would donate, but further research failed to support this position (Radke-Yarrow, Zahn-Waxler, and Chapman, 1983). Then a pair of studies, one with children (Barnett, King, and Howard, 1979) and one with adults (Thompson, Cowan, and Rosenhan, 1980) came up with similar findings: When sad thoughts are connected with the self, children and adults both become close-fisted; but when sad thoughts are connected with other people's distress, both children and adults become generous. People who are filled with happy thoughts give more than people who are feeling sad about themselves.

The way that individual differences in empathy interact with sadness to affect altruism was clarified by a later study. After asking teachers and peers to rate classmates on altruism, Mark Barnett and his colleagues (1982) had children recall a sad experience from their own lives. Afterward, the children all showed a similar degree of altruistic behavior, whether or not they were generally empathic. But after dwelling on a sad experience in another child's life, children who were not especially empathic were less likely to be altruistic than when they thought about themselves, but highly empathic children showed an enormous surge in altruistic behavior.

GENEROSITY AND EXPERIENCE A child's general tendency to donate money, toys, time, or effort can be affected by various sorts of experiences. Obviously, anything that causes children to become less egocentric will be likely to increase generosity, but seeing another person act in a generous manner will have the same effect. For example, Joan Grusec and Sandra Skubiski (1970) found that children who watched an adult donate to charity were more generous in their own donations. However, when the adult simply said that the children should share their money with the charity, donations were markedly smaller than when the adult actually gave money. Verbal exhortations had strong effects on children's giving only among girls who had previously had a warm relationship with the adult who urged generosity.

Similarly, J. P. Rushton (1975) and other investigators have noted that exhortations increase only children's statements that people should be altruistic; they do not affect children's behavior. The lesson from these studies seems clear. If we want children to talk altruistically, we should talk altruistically ourselves. However, if we want them to behave altruistically, we should act in an altruistic manner. Children can learn hypocrisy just as they learn altruism.

When combined with a warm relationship, exhortations to donate can induce generosity, as previously mentioned. Apparently, adult nurturance increases the effectiveness of other methods as well. In one study of young children, Marian Yarrow, Phyllis Scott, and Carolyn Waxler (1973) found that although any adult model could affect children's immediate behavior, children who saw a warm, nurturant model were still generous two weeks after they watched the generous adult. It seems that models who have strong, lasting effects on children are likely to be those who have close, rewarding relationships with the children—such as parents. Without such a relationship, examples are likely to have only a fleeting effect.

Giving Aid

Coming to the aid of another child in distress is a form of altruism that is quite different from generosity. While generosity is usually clearly defined, the circumstances in which aid may be appropriate are usually confusing and unclear. It may not be obvious to a child that an emergency exists, that responsibility for help rests on him or her, or even that the child is competent to help. As one might expect, this kind of altruistic behavior follows a different developmental course from that taken by generosity.

DEVELOPMENTAL CHANGES As the discussion on empathy indicated, children in their second year may respond to the distress of others. For a period of nine months, Zahn-Waxler and Radke-Yarrow (1982) followed the development of such responses in infants between the ages of ten and twenty months and found that they corresponded to the early stages of empathy described by Hoffman (1984). Before a child was a year old, another's emotional distress brought either a frown, crying, or social referencing with the caregiver among about half of the infants studied. But about a third of infants this young either showed no response or else simply watched the upset person. During the next eight months, children seemed less agitated but began to reach out to people in distress, often patting them consolingly.

Once children reached the age of two, they tried to do something for the distressed person, protecting them, bringing help, making suggestions, or verbally expressing sympathy. When one tactic failed, they tried another, and their persistence may indicate the emergence of altruistic intent. But not all two-year-olds try to offer aid; some flee the scene, avoid the distressed person, or even attack them.

In a naturalistic study, in which Douglas Sawin (1979) observed three- to seven-year-olds on playgrounds, nearly every youngster showed some sort of response to a crying child. Just under 50 percent of the children showed visible concern, and 32 percent either came to the youngster's aid, asked an adult to help, or threatened the child who was responsible for the tears. However, 12 percent of the watching children walked away from the scene and 2 percent responded in ways that showed a complete lack of sympathy.

As children get older, distress need not be quite so obvious to evoke an altruistic response. When a child has clearly been hurt, is visibly upset, or in apparent danger, a four-year-old is as likely to give aid as an eight-year-old. But when the cues are subtle, the four-year-old might not realize that the other child is in distress (Pearl, 1979).

Most children are concerned when another child is in trouble, and many will come to the distressed child's aid—especially if they believe they are able to help. (Alan Carey/The Image Works)

INFLUENCES ON THE DECISION TO HELP Various factors affect a child's decision to give aid in an emergency. In an experiment with first- to sixth-graders, Lizette Peterson (1983) instructed the children in a simple gambling game that used three interlocking wheels to determine winning numbers. Half the children were told that fingers could become caught in the spokes and were instructed in how to dismantle the wheels (turning a nut) should the device become stuck. The rest of the children were simply told how to play the game. The children were then taken to another area and given a simple task while, they believed, another child was playing the game.

The children then heard the sound of the turning wheels, followed by the tape-recorded cries of a child in distress, who sobbed and appealed for help to disentangle a caught finger from the machinery. The older the waiting child, the more likely he or she was to go to the victim's aid. Like adults, children were more likely to give aid when under the impression that the distressed child was alone rather than with another child. Children who had been instructed in how to dismantle the game, so that they felt more competent to help, rescued the victim more often than children who had received no instruction—but only when they believed the distressed child was alone. Apparently, when they believed another bystander was present, children felt less responsibility to help and so their own competence did not affect their decision. But when they believed they were the only source of aid, whether or not they felt competent to help was a powerful consideration in their decision to attempt a rescue (see Figure 16.2).

As with moral conduct, altruistic behavior depends on the interaction of the immediate situation with the child's level of cognitive maturity, his or her competence, and his or her predisposition to help—which itself depends, in great part, on previous experiences. Children with strong, solidly established prosocial dispositions, suggest Paul Mussen and Nancy Eisenberg-Berg (1972), may donate to charity or come to the aid of a child in distress regardless of the immediate situation. Children with weaker tendencies toward prosocial action may donate or help only when the immediate situation makes altruistic behavior easy.

The Influence of Television

When children watch television designed for them, they generally understand the prosocial messages embodied in the programs. For example, children who watched four episodes of "Big Blue Marble" (a program designed to show youngsters how children live in other countries)

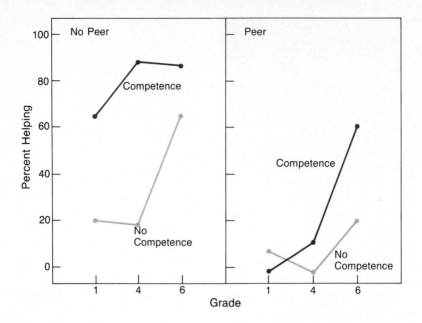

FIGURE 16.2 When children hear the cries of a child in distress, the likelihood that they will go to the aid of the distressed child is affected by their own age, their belief that they are competent to help, and whether they are alone *(left)* or in the company of another child bystander *(right)*.

(From Peterson, 1983)

showed changes in attitude toward the rest of the world. They perceived children in other countries as more like themselves and were less likely to endorse ethnocentric statements extolling the superiority of the United States over every other country (Roberts et al., 1974). In another study, 90 percent of the children who watched an episode of "Fat Albert" recalled at least one prosocial message from the program (Columbia Broadcasting System, 1974).

Aletha Stein and Lynette Friedrich (1975) have found, however, that recalling the message does not necessarily mean that it influences behavior. They showed four episodes of "Mr. Rogers' Neighborhood" to kindergarten children. The programs attempted to teach children to understand others, to express sympathy, and to help others and share with them. After viewing each episode, some children spent time with an adult, hearing a story that covered the material in the program and explicitly labeled it, and then answered questions. Other children replayed the story they had seen with hand puppets. A third group carried out both activities, and a fourth had activities with no connection to the program's themes. A control group saw neutral films.

All children who had seen the Mr. Rogers program learned from their experiences; they knew more about prosocial themes than children who saw neutral films. But when placed with a child who needed assistance, most children were no more helpful than children who had seen neutral programs. Only those children who had used the puppets and thus had experience in taking another's role were likely to translate their learning into action.

Supposing that longer exposure to prosocial television might increase the likelihood that children will act on its messages, researchers showed children twenty episodes of Mr. Rogers over a period of eight weeks (Friedrich-Cofer et al., 1979). Once again, simply watching the programs had no effect on children's altruistic behavior, but children who watched the programs and also had play material related to them (books, records, puppets, a dress-up corner) were significantly more likely to be sympathetic, affectionate, considerate, and cooperative with their peers and to engage in positive interchanges with adults. Yet in another study, simply viewing the programs changed behavior. Preschoolers who watched prosocial episodes of commercial children's programs, such as "Lassie," "I Love Lucy," "Gilligan's Island," and "The Brady Bunch," every school day for four weeks were significantly more likely to help their peers than children who watched episodes of the same program that lacked the prosocial content (Ahammer and Murray, 1979). None of these children had supporting play material. Although a number of similar studies have shown small increases in altruism after viewing prosocial television, none of the increases have been dramatic or long-lasting (Radke-Yarrow, Zahn-Waxler, and Chapman, 1983).

Once children enter elementary school, their major source of knowledge about the world is the television newscast. Each night they may see people in need or danger, as well as individual and community responses to their distress. Yet, as Radke-Yarrow and her associates (Radke-Yarrow, Zahn-Waxler, and Chapman, 1983) point out, these incidents are sandwiched in a flow of commercials, entertainment, and action programs that show little concern for distressed individuals. These researchers wonder whether this juxtaposition might not desensitize children to the needs of others and reduce their tendencies to be altruistic.

ANTISOCIAL BEHAVIOR

Antisocial behavior is a concern of parents everywhere. Earlier we dealt with such antisocial behavior as cheating, lying, and stealing; in this section we explore the problem of aggression. The amount of aggression that societies tolerate differs and their rules regarding its expression vary, but an important aim of socialization in every society is to teach youngsters how to manage feelings of hostility and anger.

It may be easier to understand the development and expression of aggression if we look at it as an example of self-regulation, as was the case with altruism. Once again, the child is intentionally acting to achieve personally selected aims, but the intent is hostile (Patterson, 1984). When intent is regarded as an essential part of aggression, many of the child's acts that are violent or that others find aversive are no longer considered aggressive, although they are certainly antisocial. The insistence on intent also makes the appearance of aggression an event of developmental importance, for it signifies an understanding on the child's part that harming another (psychologically or physically) is one way to reach a goal. It also marks the emergence of the child's ability to regulate his or her activity. As with altruism, the problem with a focus on intent is that intentions are invisible and must be inferred by the observer.

The Causes of Aggression

Most developmentalists see aggressive behavior as resulting from the interaction of many factors, but their attempts to explain the prevalence of human aggression have given rise to a variety of theories, each emphasizing a different aspect of aggression. Little recent research has been done under the influence of psychoanalytic theories (Parke and Slaby, 1983); among the approaches that guide present research are the adaptation view, the frustration-aggression hypothesis, the learning view, and the information-processing view.

THE ADAPTATION VIEW There is a continuing debate over whether human beings have an inherent drive toward aggression. Konrad Lorenz (1966) believes that aggression is instinctual and that aggressive energy builds up in a person until a releasing stimulus allows its expression. In this view, aggressive behavior is therefore inevitable. But as Karl Moyer (1971) points out, what we know about human physiology tells us that, even if people have an inborn aggressive drive, the expression of aggression is not inevitable. An inborn drive would presumably be governed by the level and balance of hormones in the bloodstream; and the same mechanisms that strengthened impulses toward aggression would also lessen them. For example, hormone levels first rise, then fall; and once hormone levels drop, the impulse to behave aggressively passes. Such an explanation indicates that if socialization can teach people to control aggressive impulses during the peak period, aggression will not have to be expressed.

Whether aggression must be expressed or not, in Lorenz's view human violence is a distortion of a useful innate behavior that evolved to space human beings out over the vast available territory on this planet. Lorenz sees the defense of territory and the existence of dominance hierarchies as expressions of the aggressive drive. With the human invention of lethal weapons, the instinct became maladaptive, leading to mutilation, murder, and war in the "defense" of mates, property, and territory. Some psychologists have adopted a version of this theory to study dominance hierarchies in children (Strayer, 1980), adolescents, and adults.

THE FRUSTRATION-AGGRESSION HYPOTHESIS

Some researchers reject the idea of an innate aggressive force but believe in the existence of an aggressive drive. According to this **frustration-aggression hypothesis,** which was proposed by John Dollard and his colleagues (1939), the aggressive drive is the result of a child's or an adult's frustration when someone or something interferes with their activity toward a goal. In its original form, this theory assumes that all aggression is the result of frustration, although frustration may be displaced on another person or object. When a child is punished by a parent, he or she may yank the cat's tail; or an adolescent who has been refused use of the family car may chop wood with a vengeance.

The frustration-aggression hypothesis was modified by Seymour Feshbach (1964) to distinguish between hostile aggression and instrumental aggression, a distinction that has been widely accepted. In this view, **hostile aggression** fits our definition of aggression, for it aims at hurting another person. Most cases of **instrumental aggression,** which are violent or aversive acts aimed at retrieving or acquiring an object, territory, or privilege, do not meet our definition of childhood aggression, for their goal is nonaggressive. A child's instrumental aggression appears to be undertaken without any anticipation that others may be hurt in the process; however, instrumental aggression on the part of an adult (who is aware of the consequences) would still be aggressive (Patterson, 1984). Only hostile aggression is thought to involve frustration, and it is often not the injury itself that is the goal, but the victim's pain. The sight of the suffering victim restores the aggressor's self-esteem. Children learn specific aggressive responses, but whether they will be expressed or inhibited depends on the environment, as we saw in studies of modeling.

THE LEARNING VIEW

Psychologists who accept behavior-learning theory reject the idea of an aggressive drive. They believe that aggression is conditioned behavior, which, like any other behavior, is controlled by the environment. The assumption is that, for example, a boy's habitual fighting is a response to the actions of others just before the act of hitting; and the immediate consequences of the blows will have a strong effect on whether the child will hit again in the same situation (Patterson and Cobb, 1973). If the victim cries, leaves the scene, or hands over the object of dispute, the aggressor is likely to hit again the next time he wants his own way. The boy's fighting is also reinforced by other responses: the victim's obvious pain, the attention the aggressive boy may get from his nursery-school teacher, or the sudden cessation of his sister's teasing. In this view, much aggression is under the control of aversive stimuli, such as being ignored by a teacher or

Behavior-learning theorists believe that the immediate consequences of a young fighter's blow will help determine whether the aggressor will hit out in his next playground argument; information-processing theorists believe that the selective encoding of social cues and a child's expectations are equally important. (Robert Eckert/EKM-Nepenthe)

and how effective these methods have been (Bandura, 1973). One child might seek help, another might try harder, a third might give up, a fourth might hit. Frustration or anger might increase the chances that a child will respond aggressively, but neither is necessary for aggression to occur. According to Albert Bandura, a culture that keeps frustration limits low, values aggressive accomplishments, provides aggressive models who are successful, and rewards aggressive actions will produce aggressive children who become highly aggressive adults.

THE INFORMATION-PROCESSING

VIEW In recent years, an information-processing view of aggression has been emerging, which stresses the way a child processes situational cues. According to Kenneth Dodge (1981), on entering a social situation, a child first perceives social cues from the environment, then interprets them in the light of remembered information and his or her present goals. This interpretation requires the child to determine the intent of the other person, which is accomplished by matching the cues and recollected information with a series of rules ("If Tim laughs after hitting me, he meant to hurt me").

Once the situation has been interpreted, says Dodge, the child generates possible responses and matches them against the rules governing a response ("If Tim meant to hurt me, I can hit him back"). In the next step, the child evaluates the probable consequences of each response and chooses the best possible action. Finally, the child carries out the chosen response.

In this information-processing approach to aggression, the aggressive child is seen as having stored the expectation that peers are generally hostile. Because of these expectations, the child may attend selectively to social cues, encoding only those that confirm his or her expectations. Selective encoding increases the probability that the aggressive child will interpret a peer's actions as hostile, behave aggressively toward the peer, and encounter an aggressive response. The peer's retaliation, says Dodge (1982), reinforces the aggressive child's expectations that others

parent, being teased or laughed at, or being refused a toy or companionship. But if the environment changes so that a child no longer experiences the aversive stimuli, or if the aggression is no longer reinforced, aggressive responses will cease.

Most contemporary research into the causes of aggression is based on social-learning theory, which agrees that the environment is powerful but also takes into consideration the influence of models and cognitive control. In this view, aversive stimuli lead to emotional arousal. Whether a child responds with aggression will depend on how the child has learned to cope with stress

This squabble over a tricycle is an example of instrumental aggression. Because neither child intends physical harm to the other, it is not a true example of childhood aggression. (Chester Higgins, Jr./Rapho-Photo Researchers)

are hostile, increasing the probability that the child will interpret future situations as hostile.

The Development of Aggression

The earliest expressions of anger are the result of physical discomfort or are demands for attention (Goodenough, 1931). Most early outbursts are not aimed at a particular person. The infant probably lacks the capacity for aggression and most toddlers' tantrums lack aggressive intent (Patterson, 1984). However, as soon as young children begin to throw tantrums, to hit, or to hurl toys about, parents generally impose restraints, and the socialization of aggression begins. In a study of 200 nursery-school quarrels, H. C. Dawe (1934) found that a shift in children's antisocial behavior appeared with age. The youngest children were heavily involved in conflict, but among eighteen-month-olds, 78 percent of the interpersonal squabbles were cen-

tered on the possession of toys or other objects, and only 8 percent began with blows, bites, or hair-pulling. Any harm involved in instrumental aggression is generally inadvertent, as when a toddler grabs a toy from a peer, knocking the youngster down in the process. When preschoolers quarreled, however, 27 percent of the conflicts began with physical violence and only about 38 percent of their squabbles were over possessions.

This shift reflects the child's cognitive development. As indicated in earlier discussions, children younger than six generally find it difficult to make inferences about people (Flavell et al., 1968). If aggression depends on attributing negative intentions to people who frustrate them, then younger children would be less likely to show aggression. And younger children would also be less likely to regard frustration as a threat to their self-esteem.

Using this rationale, Willard Hartup (1974) tested and extended the earlier findings of Dawe. He observed children at play over a ten-week period and found that older children (from six to eight years old) fought less than younger children (four to six years), and that the difference was due primarily to the preponderance of quarrels over possessions among younger children. As he had expected, older children showed a higher proportion of hostile aggression. Hartup also found, as had Goodenough, that children shifted from physical to verbal aggression as they got older, confirming a change in both the form and the amount of aggression as children develop. As they get older and their acts of physical aggression are punished, children find more subtle ways of expressing aggression.

The socializing influences that lead children to be generous or helpful also teach them to behave aggressively. Watching someone behave in a violent or aggressive manner tends to make children behave aggressively, but it does not always do so. The situation itself helps decide whether a child will imitate such a model, as Marian Martin, Donna Gelfand, and Donald Hartman (1971) found in a study of 100 children. The children watched a model go through a series of aggressive acts. During a later play period, children were most aggressive when a peer of the same sex was present. When an adult was present, a child at first showed little aggression; but if the adult failed to disapprove of the child's aggressive acts, the child became more and more aggressive. Apparently, the presence of an adult tends to inhibit aggression, but the inhibitions disappear if children become aware that their aggressive acts are acceptable, or at least neutral, in adult eyes.

According to the information-processing view of aggression, children's interpretation of another's intent often determines whether a conflict will erupt. As children grow older, they make increasingly fine distinctions concerning others' intentions. In one study, Tamara Ferguson and Brendan Rule (1980) asked children to judge the actions of a child in stories that resulted in such consequences as broken arms. Second-graders tended to judge by the consequences of an act, making little distinction among situations, although they assigned somewhat less blame for accidental damage. Eighth-graders made clear distinctions, judging intentional aggression or foreseeable damage as much worse than accidental damage or injuries that resulted from intentional but justified acts, such as a broken arm that resulted when a child was pushed out of a treehouse that was on fire. Older boys and girls apparently believe that children should consider the consequences before they act and that those who do not are responsible for any consequences. Other studies (Rule, Nesdale, and McAra, 1974) have shown that even first-graders believe that violent or aversive acts done to help another person are not as "naughty" as similar acts intended to hurt another or to gain some possession.

When another person's intentions are clear, aggressive and nonaggressive boys tend to respond similarly to a peer's actions; but when the situation is ambiguous, aggressive boys tend to attribute hostile intentions to others and to respond aggressively. This difference became apparent when Kenneth Dodge (1980) placed boys in a situation where damage was either clearly intended, clearly accidental, or ambiguous. Both groups responded aggressively to intentional damage and benignly to accidental damage, but when the situation was ambiguous, aggressive boys responded with aggression and nonaggressive boys responded benignly, giving the other person the benefit of the doubt.

Actions are not the only cue children use to interpret another's actions; they rely on reputation as well. Ken Rotenberg (1980) found that most children between the ages of five and ten described a child who intentionally caused harm as "mean." Asked about that child's probable future actions, kindergartners were unlikely to predict that the child would be "mean" in other circumstances. But from the time children are in the second grade, they attribute enduring personality characteristics to others, and so they expect peers who are aggressive or unhelpful in one situation to behave similarly in the future. Such findings lead Ross Parke and Ronald Slaby (1983) to suggest that as children develop reputations among their peers, other children's attitudes and behavior toward them may solidify. Even if aggressive children behave in a friendly manner, others may interpret their actions as hostile.

Sex Differences in Aggression

Although sex differences in aggression among younger children are clear, the picture becomes complicated as boys and girls grow older. Recent analyses of research indicate that before they enter first grade, boys are more aggressive than girls, in both word and deed (Maccoby and Jacklin, 1980). This difference is apparent at all socioeconomic levels. Boys as young as two appear to be more physically aggressive and more negativistic than girls. The largest proportion of nursery-school fights occur between two boys, and the smallest between two girls. Boys' victims are usually other boys, particularly those who give in (Maccoby, 1976). When observed in play, preschool boys initiated 26 percent more attacks on other children than girls did, with four-year-olds clearly more aggressive than three-year-olds (Darvill and Cheyne, 1981). In response to physical attack, boys' aggressiveness became even more apparent. When hit by another child, boys counterattacked, hitting back more often than girls by 116 percent.

Among children in primary school, fights between boys—whether verbal or physical—continue to be more prevalent than fights between girls. Boys and girls are equally aggressive when the opponent is another girl. When attacked physically by another boy, boys are more likely than girls to counterattack, but when the attacker is a girl, girls are more likely to respond with blows. Attacked verbally, boys and girls are equally likely to respond with harsh words (Barrett, 1979).

The consistency of findings that males are, on the average, more physically aggressive than females suggests possible biological contributions to such behavior, or other constitutional factors linked with gender that might predispose boys toward physical aggressiveness. Seymour Feshbach (1970) has suggested that the greater physical strength and more vigorous motor impulses of males may lead to different social experiences. Boys, for example, have greater success than girls in getting what they want by hitting. Also, parents more often frustrate a boy's impulsive acts, thereby stimulating his aggressive reactions. To such influences can be added all the sex differences in parental practices noted in Chapter 15, from sex-typed toys and the encouragement of independence in boys to discipline practices, with boys getting the major share of physical punishment and girls more likely to be disciplined with reason (Block, 1978).

Although girls and boys may differ in the extent to which they find aggression a useful and accepted way to solve a problem, girls are just as capable of aggression as boys. Differences may even be narrowing. Although five times as many adolescent boys as girls are arrested for violent crimes, the percentage of violent crime committed by women has been rising (Parke and Slaby, 1983).

A highly aggressive child generally becomes a highly aggressive adult, although the link is stronger for boys than for girls. When more than 600 children were followed from the age of eight until they were thirty years old, the most aggressive children remained the most aggressive adults (Huesmann et al., 1984). Aggression in boys at age eight correlated .50 with their aggression at age thirty, while aggression in girls at age eight correlated .35 with their aggression at age thirty. High aggressiveness in children of both sexes was frequently followed by criminal behavior, physical aggression, and the practice of child abuse during adulthood. For example, 23 percent of the highly aggressive boys, but only 10 percent of the nonaggressive boys, were convicted of a crime by their thirtieth birthday. Girls were considerably less aggressive, but the relationship held: 6.3 percent of the highly aggressive girls and none of the nonaggressive girls were convicted of a crime. In addition, when these highly aggressive individuals became parents, their own children tended to display high levels of aggression. The investigators believe that constitutional factors probably interacted with continual development in an environment that encouraged aggressive behavior.

The Power of Television

Over the past thirty-five years, American society has undergone a major shift in the way it introduces its young to the world. Before 1950, young children's exposure to adult society was usually filtered by their parents. The young child knew about the culture from experience with the family, the neighbors, the occasional shopping trip, and perhaps from Sunday school or picture books. Now, most children witness televised murder, arson, muggings, and warfare almost from birth. By the age of sixteen, the average adolescent has seen more than 18,000 murders on television.

In reporting these figures, Sally Smith (1985)

notes that although the level of violence has remained fairly steady for nearly two decades, its quality has changed: what violence is shown is more intense and realistic, violent acts are interspersed with humor, the line between heroes and villains is becoming blurred, and more violent acts are committed by people with psychological problems. In addition, rock videos—which make up the entire broadcasting schedule of some cable channels—often exude images of menace and cruelty as well as detached violence against people and property, portrayed without any dramatic context that might justify it or indicate its consequences. Even when parents regulate their children's viewing habits, the network news and the Saturday morning cartoons deliver a dependable diet of murder and mayhem, presenting models who not only transmit new behavior but also may reduce inhibitions on antisocial behavior the child has already learned.

Researchers have not yet established how changes in the quality of televised violence, such as the detached cruelty that is often a feature of rock video, will affect children. (Tequila Minsky)

THE IMMEDIATE EFFECTS OF TELEVISED VIOLENCE Numerous experiments have been conducted to assess the effects of television on children. Early studies by Albert Bandura (1973) and his associates showed that children can learn new ways to express aggression from television and similar media. D. Keith Osborn and Richard Endsley (1971) went further, investigating children's emotional reactions to various sorts of television programs. Children in this study saw four films depicting either human violence, cartoon violence, human nonviolence, or cartoon nonviolence and then talked about what they liked best and what was the scariest. The two violent films produced the most emotional reactions; the children remembered details of the violent films the best, and they found the human violence the scariest. But the film they liked best was the nonviolent cartoon. This study shows that watching television violence evokes emotional responses in children and that they are likely to remember the details of depicted violence.

Moving closer to the central question of whether television violence affects the way that children behave, the Office of the Surgeon General (1972) commissioned an exhaustive study of the effects of television violence but failed to reach any definitive conclusions. Within a decade, however, an analysis of subsequent research for the National Institute of Mental Health (1982) indicated that the causal link between televised violence and hostile aggression had become obvious.

Specific studies give some clues as to how television may affect behavior. For example, Robert Liebert and Robert Baron (1972) investigated whether watching television aggression would make children more willing to hurt another child. Liebert and Baron showed brief excerpts taken directly from regular television shows to boys and girls from five to nine years old. The excerpts were either violent and aggressive (a fist fight or a shooting) or exciting but nonaggressive (a tennis match). After they saw one of these programs, the children were given a series of opportunities either to hurt or to help another child by pushing a button. Each child was told that pushing one button would help another child (who was not actually present) to win a prize, but that pushing the other button would hurt the child. They were also told that the longer they pressed either button, the more the other child would be helped or hurt.

Despite their brief exposure to these television shows, children who had observed the violent television sequence chose to hurt the other child for a significantly longer period of time than those who had watched the nonaggressive scenes. Obviously, this study uses a specialized definition of aggression, but it demonstrates that watching one kind of aggression may lead to aggression of a very different sort. It suggests that television programs depicting aggression may remove or reduce some children's inhibitions against committing violence—at least immediately after a child sees the program. Additional studies support this position (Leifer and Roberts, 1972).

The younger the child, the more likely he or she is to respond to a televised violent act as if it were an isolated event, stripped of any motivation or consequences (Parke and Slaby, 1983). In one study, Andrew Collins and his colleagues (1974) found that when an aggressive act was separated from its motivation and consequence by commercials, kindergartners and second-graders tended to remember the violence but to forget both its motivations and consequences. When there was no separation, these children judged the aggressor only in terms of the act's consequences; they made no allowance for motivation. By the time children were in the fifth grade, the insertion of commercials did not affect their recollection of an act's motivation and consequences, and these youngsters took motives as well as consequences into consideration when judging an aggressor. In another study (Collins and Zimmerman, 1975), only consistently negative motives and consequences surrounding violence led to a reduction in aggressive behavior among watching children. When either motives or consequences were portrayed

as a mixture of good and bad, watching children responded with increased levels of aggression.

THE EFFECTS OF HABITUAL VIEWING ON AGGRESSION

Studies that focus on the immediate or short-term effects of televised violence shed little light on the cumulative effects of years of television viewing. The long-term effects of television violence may have been detected by Leon Eron and his colleagues (1972), who followed a group of children for eleven years. At the beginning of the study, they found a significant relationship between the amount of television violence that third-grade boys watched and their aggression as rated by their peers. Even more impressive is their finding of a relationship between the amount of television violence that boys watched in the third grade and their later aggression, at age nineteen. The investigators concluded that it was not merely that children who commit aggressive acts watch more television violence, but that a preference for watching televised violence contributes to the development of aggressive behavior.

A decade later the same investigators (Huesmann, Lagerspetz, and Eron, 1984) conducted sequential longitudinal studies with 758 American children and 220 Finnish children, following three waves of first- and third-graders in each country for three years. In both countries, heavy viewing of televised violence was linked with later aggression in daily life, but with some changes. In the original study, the connection had not appeared among girls. This time, American girls' television viewing (but not Finnish girls' viewing) was linked with future aggression, leading the investigators to suggest their study may be reflecting recent changes in American socialization practices to emphasize greater assertiveness and physical activity for girls. Rowell Huesmann and his associates stress that television alone does not make a child aggressive. After analyzing their data, they found that the most aggressive children also believed the shows accurately portrayed life, tended to identify strongly with the aggressive characters they watched, had frequent aggressive fantasies, had aggressive mothers, had parents with low education and social status, performed poorly in school, and were unpopular with their peers. In addition, aggressive girls preferred boys' activities.

HABITUAL VIEWING AND THE ACCEPTANCE OF AGGRESSION Steady viewing of televised violence may make a child relatively indifferent to violence in daily life. Youngsters who watched a violent television program and were then asked to supervise other children were significantly slower to intervene or to call for assistance when a fist fight broke out than child supervisors who watched a nonviolent program (Drabman and Thomas, 1976). Parke and Slaby (1983) suggest that television may indeed have this effect and propose that steady viewing of televised violence may lead a child to change his or her standards concerning the appropriateness, acceptability, and prevalence of aggression in daily life. Parke and Slaby believe this change is most likely to occur when children see violence as rewarded, justified, realistic, and commonplace; when their own environment supports such an interpretation; and when they have little experience against which to judge television standards for violence.

Years of heavy television viewing may sometimes take children beyond the acceptance of violence to a passivity in the face of aggression. George Gerbner and Larry Gross (1976) believe that television may teach people to play the role of victim. Their research has shown that, regardless of age, people who watched four or more hours of television each day tended to be significantly more suspicious of others and afraid of being involved in violence themselves than people who watched television two hours or less each day. (They also discovered that nearly half of the twelve-year-olds in their study watched at least six hours of television each day.)

At present, our knowledge of television's power to increase violence is confused. We know that aggressive children and adolescents are attracted to violent television programs, but we are not certain that the habitual viewing of violent programs causes aggression (Freedman, 1984). Part of the confusion that comes from conflicting findings in the fields of moral development can probably be traced to a point that has been made again and again: the developing child's behavior is a product of continuous interaction between constitutional forces and the child's own social environment. The older the child, the greater the accumulation of different experiences. And for this same reason, no two children will react to the same experience in precisely the same way.

SUMMARY

Although moral conduct is often viewed as a group of related actions governed by some central process such as conscience, research indicates that most people are inconsistent in what they say, feel, and do. Individual predispositions toward honesty or dishonesty appear to exist, but the aspects of each situation have powerful effects both on people's judgment of an action's morality and on their behavior.

Psychoanalysts believe that moral behavior results from children's attempts to avoid the guilt that arises when they violate prohibitions imposed by parents with whom they identify. Social-learning theorists believe that children learn moral behavior through a combination of rewards, punishment, and the observation of models. Developmentalists who take the motivational approach see **empathy,** or the vicarious identification with another's emotions, as the basic motive for moral behavior. Empathy appears to develop through four stages, and its cognitive accompaniment is role taking.

Cognitive theorists believe that moral judgments depend on cognitive development. Piaget saw childhood morality as passing through two major stages: the **morality of constraint,** which predominates among young children, and the **morality of cooperation,** which is found among older children. After assessing boys' reactions to posed moral dilemmas, Lawrence Kohlberg proposed that moral reasoning goes through six stages, forming a progressive series of developmental levels: the **premoral level,** the **conventional level,** and the **principled level.** The levels seem related to age and formal education, and may describe the development of moral judgment only among white males. The relationship between levels of moral reasoning and moral behavior is not strong.

Altruism consists of **prosocial** acts that are done by intent and that involve an unselfish concern for the welfare of others. Because altruistic acts require **self-regulation,** children must attain a certain level of cognitive development before they are possible. Although generosity increases with age in laboratory experiments, the same trend does not appear in naturalistic situations. Mood appears to interact with empathy to affect altruism. Age, competence, and the belief that they are the only source of aid increase a child's tendency to assist a person in distress. Watching prosocial television slightly increases a child's tendency to behave altruistically, but the results are not long-lasting.

Like altruism, **aggression** is an example of self-regulation, but the aim is to harm another person. According to the adaptation view, human beings have an inherent drive toward aggression. According to the **frustration-aggression hypothesis,** aggression is the result of a drive that is caused by the frustration of activity toward a goal. Only **hostile aggression** is believed to be the result of frustration; frustration does not cause **instrumental aggression,** which is an attempt to retrieve or acquire something that is valued. In the learning view, aggression is conditioned behavior, and children who are reinforced for aggressive acts or who observe others being reinforced for them will continue to commit them. How a child responds to situations likely to evoke aggression will depend on how the child has learned to cope with stress and how effective these methods have been. In the information-processing view, aggressive behavior depends on the way a child processes situational cues.

Most conflicts among infants and toddlers lack aggressive intent, and the emergence of such intent reflects an advance in cognitive development. Studies consistently show that young boys are more aggressive than girls. Biological predispositions may well exist among males, but the social environment has a powerful influence on whether or how aggression is expressed. The causal link between televised violence and hostile aggression has been established, but other environmental factors, as well as the child's predispositions, interact with television in determining levels of aggression. Televised violence may also increase the acceptance of violence among children who are not especially aggressive.

PART 6

Reweaving the Strands

The time has come to reweave the strands of cognition and personality that were unraveled in Parts 4 and 5. Although the results of a child's cognitive processing are heavily dependent on motivations, emotions, attitudes, and past experiences, and although the effect of experiences depends on the level of a child's cognitive development, much of the discussion has proceeded as if the two strands of development progress in isolation. One place where the

close weaving of strands is most apparent is in the general area of social cognition. In order to understand self, others, and society, the child must apply cognitive processes to personal relationships, to groups, and to highly emotional events and situations. By concluding the book with a consideration of an area in which the strands are so tightly knit, we emphasize for a final time the interactive nature of human development.

CHAPTER SEVENTEEN

The Development of Social Cognition

UNDERSTANDING ONE'S SELF
The Sensorimotor Self
The Preoperational Self
The Concrete Operational Self
The Formal Operational Self
UNDERSTANDING OTHERS
Understanding What Others Are Like
Understanding What Others See
Understanding How Others Feel
Understanding Friends
Understanding and Communication
UNDERSTANDING SOCIETY
Understanding Social Roles
Understanding How Society Works
REWEAVING THE STRANDS
SUMMARY

Come on, I want a television for my room. Come on. Please. Daddy, come on. Buy me a television. I want one for my room. Come on. Come on, Daddy, I want you to. There!"

"Say, Dad, a lot of kids at school I know are getting televisions for Christmas. Can I have one? Gee, I know a lot of kids that want one, gee. I could really use it, you—for some of the educational programs, you know, that are on TV, and they're real good, and for homework at night some of our teachers want us to watch 'em, and—you know, Johnnie always wants to watch cowboys and . . . and everything, and I—I'll never get a chance to watch it down there, so why can't I have it in my room? C'mon, Dad, please."

The first plea came from a third-grader, the second from a child in the seventh grade. Both had been asked by John Flavell and his associates (1968) to show how they would persuade their fathers to buy them their own television sets. The third-grader's simple pleading becomes the seventh-grader's triple pitch of education, family harmony, and what Flavell called the bandwagon approach (everybody's doing it).

The growth in understanding that makes this

539

development possible forms the major part of this chapter on social cognition, which explores the way children come to know the social world. The process has many parallels with the general development of children's cognition, but here the understanding is of people and society instead of the physical world. The baby who sees the world as an extension of the self becomes the adolescent who understands the workings of social institutions and realizes that each person is unique, with his or her own, probably different, feelings and opinions. That development is a lengthy one, but it begins with the understanding of the self. Consequently, we begin this chapter by looking at the development of self-concept during childhood and adolescence. Next we examine children's understanding of others, tracing their dawning realization that others neither see nor feel exactly as they do. After exploring changes in the meaning that friendship holds for children, the chapter follows their deepening understanding of communication—including the realization that their inability to understand another's message is not always their own fault. Finally, we watch the growth of children's understanding of family roles and of society, noting that this understanding, too, develops in a regular sequence, building on the child's understanding of others.

UNDERSTANDING ONE'S SELF

The discussion of such concepts as identity and self-knowledge in a chapter on social cognition might seem surprising. But the domains of self and other cannot be totally separated. Our interpretation of others' behavior comes from our knowledge of how they have acted in the past, from cues in the immediate environment, and from what we know about ourselves. For ultimately, most of what we know about others' feelings and intentions comes from inferences based on our own perceptions, emotions, and

knowledge. Yet much of what we know about ourselves comes in turn from our interactions with others (Lewis and Brooks-Gunn, 1979). Children's self-concepts develop through the interaction of cognition and experiences with the world and other people. Susan Harter (1983) sees this self-understanding as progressing through stages that roughly parallel Piaget's stages of cognitive development.

The Sensorimotor Self

During the sensorimotor period, the infant concentrates on developing a sense of self. It begins very early—when the baby begins to distinguish him- or herself from the world. The first signs appear when babies seem to recognize and behave differently toward different people—at about two or three months (Lamb, 1981). According to Harter, the baby then develops a sense of self as "I"—an active, independent agent who can cause his or her own movements in space. This concept emerges by the time a baby is twelve to fifteen months old. Only then does the baby develop a sense of self as "me"— a recognizable object that the baby can know about, an object with unique features, a baby, a girl, and so on. As we saw in Chapter 12, this aspect of self-concept emerges gradually between the ages of fifteen and twenty-four months. At that time, babies consistently touch a spot of rouge on their noses when they see their reflections in a mirror (Lewis and Brooks-Gunn, 1979). Babies' ability to recognize themselves in a mirror appears to develop along with the concept of object permanence. The two concepts are highly correlated (+.84); although they usually emerge about the same time, sometimes object permanence runs ahead of self-recognition (Bertenthal and Fischer, 1978). There is good reason for the parallel development of these concepts. Without an awareness that objects and other people continue to exist when out of their sight, babies could not develop a sense of their own continuing identities.

The Preoperational Self

Between the ages of two and six, the concept of self as "me" continues to develop. A child comes to understand whether he or she is a boy or a girl, big or small, capable or not capable. Throughout early childhood, children perceive themselves in terms of concrete attributes, such as sex, age, activities, personal appearance, and possessions. Asked to describe themselves, they reply in terms of such attributes: "I'm Lauren" (name), "I'm four" (age), "I have a brother" (kinship), "I'm little" (size), "I have a kitty" (possessions). Most frequent, however, are replies concerning activities, in terms of habitual actions ("I sit and watch TV"), acts of competence ("I wash my hair myself"), and helpful acts ("I help mommy") (Keller, Ford, and Meacham, 1978).

At this age, says Harter (1983), children see attributes in an all-or-nothing fashion. At first, they believe that if they are good at one thing (say, puzzles) they are good at everything. Toward the end of the preoperational period, children begin to understand that they may be good at one thing, but not very skillful at something else (good at puzzles, but not very good at numbers).

Children seem to understand emotions early. In one study, youngsters only twenty-eight months old correctly attributed emotional states to themselves or to others (Bretherton and Beeghly, 1982). For example, they talked about anger, fear, disgust ("yucky"), sadness, and love. Three- and most four-year-olds can define the major emotions—happy, sad, mad, scared, worried—but they do not seem to understand the emotions of pride and shame. Most five-year-olds say that being ashamed is a "bad" feeling and being proud is a "good" feeling, but not until toward the close of this period do children talk about how others might be proud (or ashamed) of them ("Dad was proud of me when I took out the trash") (Harter, 1983). Preschoolers also have no trouble acting out the major emotions, but when they were asked how they knew they were feeling a particular emotion,

the children resorted to situational cues (Carroll and Steward, 1984). For example, they knew they were "happy" if they had a party, or if they smiled, or if someone told them. Only a few children talked about inner experience. Preschoolers see emotions as they do attributes—in an all-or-nothing fashion. They deny that they can feel happy and sad, or loving and mad, at the same time (Harter, 1983).

The Concrete Operational Self

When children reach the concrete operational stage, personal qualities begin to enter their self-descriptions. A child might say, "I'm shy," or "I'm a hard worker," or "I'm dumb." This change from describing themselves in terms of specific behavior to listing general traits indicates a cognitive advance. The child has begun to see him- or herself as having qualities that persist over situations; the child who says, "I'm shy," is one who is generally reticent when meeting adult strangers or who dislikes reciting in class. This shift was reflected in a study of schoolchildren. When Don Mohr (1978) asked them, "What would you have to change about yourself for you to become your best friend?" first-graders talked about such external attributes as their name, age, or possessions. But third-graders talked about traits and other regularities in behavior. As we saw in Chapter 15, first-graders have just come to understand another aspect of enduring qualities: the permanency of gender.

At the beginning of the concrete operational period, children who see themselves as shy, or smart, or hard-working, or dumb apply the trait in the same all-or-nothing fashion as the younger child applied self-descriptions (Harter, 1983). Even if the child who is shy when meeting adult strangers or when asked to recite in class is relaxed and outgoing when meeting unfamiliar children, the youngster will see her- or himself as all shy. Toward the end of this period, children begin to see that they can be shy in some situations and outgoing in others.

In the early years, a child's relative lack of ability in any area may not affect his or her self-concept; it is not until children are seven or eight years old that they begin to evalute themselves by comparing their own and others' behavior. In a series of studies, Diane Ruble and her associates (1980) had children carry out a task, then let the children know how well their peers had done on the same task. In judging themselves, first-graders paid no attention to information about the performance of others. The information affected the judgment of a few second-graders, but only fourth-graders allowed information from social comparisons to affect their self-evaluations in any consistent way. Ruble and her associates suggest that younger children are aware of their limited abilities and are not particularly interested in self-evaluation. Their concern is in making some correct answer and getting their fair share of the rewards. Yet as we saw in Chapter 14, children's concepts of their own abilities may come to have a profound effect on their achievement.

About the time they reach the age of eight, children's understanding of emotions deepens. Now children understand how they can be ashamed or proud of themselves. They talk about being ashamed of themselves for throwing milk at someone or hurting someone's feelings, and about being proud of themselves for passing a test or doing a good deed (Harter, 1983). Such understanding appears to parallel the development of concrete operational thought. Youngsters in the transitional stage, whether they are five or eight years old, tend to talk about emotions in terms of specific actions ("stomping my feet") or expressions ("when I laugh") (Carroll and Steward, 1984). By the time they are firmly into the concrete operational period, they also understand the inner feelings that accompany an emotion; they know that it is possible to feel more than one emotion at a time; and they know how to hide an emotion. They also have strategies for changing their emotions: children suggest cuddling up to a stuffed animal in order to combat fear or thinking of something to do to make themselves happy.

The Formal Operational Self

Adolescents take a far less simplistic view of themselves than children do. Around the age of thirteen or fourteen, a qualitative change appears in children's self-descriptions. W. J. Livesley and D. B. Bromley (1973) found that adolescents use descriptive terms more flexibly and precisely than younger children do, often adding subtle qualifying and connecting terms. They tend to describe themselves in terms of their ambitions, wants, expectations, fears, wishes, beliefs, attitudes, and values, and by comparing themselves to others. Adolescents also try to combine or integrate various traits into a single abstraction, such as "intelligence" (Harter, 1983). These changes reflect the adolescent's grasp of formal thought.

As the concept of self develops, so does self-consciousness, a concern with what others think of one. This heightened self-consciousness, suggests David Elkind (1980), is the result of the young adolescent's belief that other people share the adolescent's own preoccupations with him- or herself and hence are always noticing the adolescent's appearance, behavior, and actions. Elkind and Robert Bowen (1979) studied children in fourth, sixth, eighth, and twelfth grades and found that self-consciousness shows a developmental trend. They asked children to consider themselves in a number of situations in which they would have to reveal either their "transient selves" (momentary appearance or behavior, such as soiled clothing or inadvertent acts, which people do not regard as reflecting their true selves) or their "abiding selves" (mental ability or personality traits that people regard as permanent aspects of the self). The imaginary situations involved either the transient self (a red, scraped, swollen face on the day class pictures are taken) or the abiding self (being watched while at work). In all situations, eighth-graders were much more self-conscious than either younger children or older adolescents—except for fourth-grade boys, who were just as reluctant to reveal their transient selves as were the eighth-grade boys. An eighth-grader who went to a dress-up party in soiled clothing, for example, would either "stand in a dark place," "hold a hand over the stain," or arrange "to spill something" on the soiled clothing. Younger or older children were likely to say the stain would not bother them. This may indicate that self-consciousness peaks among children who are just making the transition into formal operational thought. Most children were more reticent about exposing their "real" than their transient selves, perhaps because only aspects of the abiding self were linked with a child's self-esteem on another test. **Self-esteem,** which is the value a person puts on the self, is a judgment of the "me" aspect of self by the "I" aspect of self.

Girls in this study were more self-conscious than boys in every age group. An eighth-grade girl, placed in the stained clothing situation, might say that she would simply refuse to go to the party. In a similar study of sixth- to twelfth-graders, William Gray and Lynne Hudson (1984) found somewhat similar results, except that boys' concern about revealing their abiding selves peaked in the tenth grade. Gray and Hudson point out that although they found the same greater self-consciousness among girls, the progress of boys' scores toward diminishing self-consciousness tended to lag behind the girls' pattern. This may indicate that the ability to reason about people progresses more rapidly among girls.

Self-consciousness in early adolescence seems to go hand-in-hand with the tendency to feel that one's own experiences are historically unique (Harter, 1983). The adolescent may believe that no one has ever thought, felt, or experienced the world in the way that he or she is experiencing it. For example, the young adolescent in love often insists that no one else has ever loved as deeply, as totally, or as intensely (Lerner and Spanier, 1980). And when the relationship breaks up, the adolescent suffers as no one else has ever suffered.

The eighth-graders who were so hesitant about revealing themselves had just entered adolescence, when developmental changes often bring about a disruption of the concept of self. For this reason, Erik Erikson (1968) believes that establishing a concept of **identity** is the major developmental task of this period. This identity is a self-constructed organization of drives, abilities, beliefs, and individual history (Marcia, 1980). When it is well developed, adolescents have a consistent, unified self; they are aware of their strengths as well as their weaknesses, of their uniqueness as well as their similarity to other people. This sort of identity structure becomes possible in adolescence because the child's physical development, cognitive skills, and social expectations have reached the necessary level of maturity.

In order to construct a consistent, unified self, the adolescent must select a series of suitable roles, making a commitment to an occupation, a religious view, a political ideology, a sexual orientation, and the like. After studying adolescents, James Marcia (1980) found four different types of identity structures:

identity achievement, in which the adolescent has made these decisions and is pursuing occupational and ideological goals;

foreclosure, in which the adolescent is committed to an occupation or an ideology, but the positions have been chosen by his or her parents;

identity diffusion, in which the adolescent has no occupational goal or ideological commitment but is not particularly concerned about the situation, although he or she may have gone through a decision-making period; and

moratorium, in which the adolescent is still struggling with occupational or ideological issues—or both. Only adolescents in this group are considered to be in an "identity crisis."

When adolescents are followed through college, the proportion of young people in the identity

This girl's experience as a reporter during a political convention may help her make a commitment to an occupation, a commitment that is necessary if the adolescent is to achieve a new identity structure. (Jim Anderson/Woodfin Camp & Associates)

ology, so that the commitments involved in their construction of an identity may differ. Despite the increasing number of adolescent girls who commit themselves to careers, girls are still reared in a way that emphasizes relationships and responsibilities (Gilligan, 1982). This sex difference continues to appear in studies. For example, among a group of nineteen-year-old college students, women were higher than men in the development of intimacy (Erikson's developmental task of young adulthood), as we might expect. But women were also higher in identity achievement—a difference that disappeared among students a few years older (Schiedel and Marcia, 1985). The researchers do not understand why women seem to forge an identity earlier than men, but perhaps women who pursue an occupationally oriented life (as opposed to a traditional homemaker's life) grapple with the identity problem at a younger age.

UNDERSTANDING OTHERS

Once babies learn that objects and people have an existence of their own, they can begin to develop an understanding of others. The discussion of empathy in the last chapter indicated that children only gradually come to understand that the needs, wants, and beliefs of other people are different from their own. Until they achieve this understanding, they find it difficult to comprehend the behavior and emotions of another individual. Such understanding requires children to infer another's response by taking the other's role, that is, mentally putting themselves in the place of the other.

Piaget (1926) believed that the young child is trapped by egocentrism. Even after the young boy (or girl) can distinguish himself from the rest of the world, for example, he still believes that others see the world exactly as he does and

achievement and identity diffusion categories increases as more and more young people move out of the moratorium category, a position that is generally characterized by some anxiety. By a few years after college, the moratorium category is further reduced, but now the identity diffusion category has also shrunk, indicating a general tendency toward a relatively stable identity (Harter, 1983).

Marcia (1980) suggests that identity formation may be different for girls than for boys. Girls are traditionally more concerned with interpersonal relations than with career choices and ide-

that they experience his thoughts and feelings. Slowly, during both the preoperational and the concrete operational stages, the boy's (or girl's) social interactions with adults and with other children make him aware that his perceptions and reactions are not theirs. It is not until children are about nine or ten, said Piaget, that they escape from this sort of egocentric thought. A new sort of egocentrism appears in early adolescence. As we have seen, the adolescent boy (or girl) develops an intense self-consciousness and the belief that his experiences are totally *different* from those of other people.

Children's egocentrism may not be entirely due to children's unawareness of others' reactions. Much of their apparent egocentrism may be due to their lack of information, inadequate memory, or still developing language skills, which keep them from communicating their understanding. Robert Selman (1980) suggests that preschoolers may be capable of recognizing that others have their own feelings and thoughts, but usually do not make such a distinction. About the time they start school, youngsters begin to realize that others not only have distinctive thoughts and feelings, but that they may react differently in a similar situation. Sometime between the age of six and twelve, children become able to put themselves in another person's place and look at their own action through his or her eyes. As they learn to understand others, children must comprehend what others are like, what others see and know, and how others feel.

Understanding What Others Are Like

Children's understanding of others is influenced by their own characteristics—the way they deploy their attention and their mental representations (Shantz, 1983). It comes as no surprise, then, that when children are asked to describe others, their descriptions follow the same general course as their self-perceptions.

Until they are about eight years old, children describe others in terms of their appearance, behavior, possessions, family, and home. Carolyn Shantz (1983) suggests that the young child seems unable to distinguish between inner and outer characteristics: a person *is* what he or she owns, where he or she lives, how he or she looks. In addition, the young child does not understand that others might have different conceptions of the person, or that a person might have both good and bad qualities. These tendencies, she says, are similar to the way the young child thinks about the physical world during the preoperational period, when appearance and reality are the same.

In middle childhood, concrete attributes give way to personal qualities; now children describe others in terms of traits, abilities, and regularities of behavior. This trend parallels the development of conservation. Clothing, hair styles, and possessions may change, as the level of cola changes when poured into the tall, narrow glass, but a person's values, beliefs, and inner qualities are likely to remain relatively steady despite surface alterations.

By adolescence, children show a greater ability to analyze and interpret the behavior of others and an increased concern with making their descriptions convincing (Livesley and Bromley, 1973). In describing another person, only adolescents report an impression and then hastily add a qualifier. For example, a fifteen-year-old girl might say of a friend, "He is shy—but not anxious." The statement indicates that she considered other people's possible misinterpretation of her description, revealing reflective thought. Adolescents also show their understanding that a person's feelings or actions differ depending on the situation, indicating their realization that situations and personal characteristics interact.

How do children decide about the personal qualities of other people? In an attempt to find out, William Rholes and Diane Ruble (1984) showed younger (five- and six-year-olds) and older (nine- and ten-year-olds) children four videotaped sequences in which child actors displayed either generosity or stinginess, bravery or fearfulness, high or low athletic ability, and the ability to solve problems or the lack of it. Even the younger children had no trouble labeling the sort of behavior they saw; they could tell the difference between generous and stingy behavior. But only the older children expected the actors to show stability of behavior across situations; for example, only the nine- and ten-year-olds expected a child who shared her lunch with a hungry child to give up her playtime to help another child rake leaves. Yet the younger children did expect consistency in the same situation across time: they expected that a child who liked to look at picture books on Thursday would also like to look at picture books on Friday. Note that these children were describing consistencies of behavior, not inner qualities. Young children apparently can make limited generalizations about people, but they do not always do so. Rholes and Ruble explain this by pointing out that individual acts are generally separated from one another by considerable periods of time. In most cases, picking such incidents out of the stream of behavior and relating them may be beyond the child's information-processing skills. And so young children may not become aware of consistent patterns in other people's behavior. As a result, they may not have developed the concept of abiding personal characteristics.

Yet younger children are aware of some stability in others. Although nearly half of the five-year-olds in another study described others in such terms, many of their statements referred to stability of behavior ("He hits everyone") rather than to inner personal qualities ("He's mean") (Ferguson et al., 1984). And some of their descriptions were purely external ("He's eight years old") or referred to a specific situation ("He's mean to Erik"). All of the older children described the person in terms of enduring qualities. However, there was a difference with age in the sort of information children relied on in making their judgments. Five- and six-year-olds depended most on the frequency of a particular behavior, but older children

(eleven- to thirteen-year-olds) depended most on the consistency of a person's behavior across situations.

Understanding What Others See

When Piaget said that young children believe others see exactly as they do he meant it literally. It sometimes seemed as if not even putting a blindfold on the other person interfered with the child's belief that others saw everything he or she did. Yet researchers have found that by the close of infancy, children are aware of *what* another person sees or does not see (Shantz, 1983). A two-year-old will turn a cup on its side so that another person can see a picture glued into the bottom. And two-and-a-half-year-olds will hide a Snoopy doll behind a tabletop screen so that the experimenter cannot see Snoopy from where she is sitting. John Flavell and his associates (Flavell, Shipstead, and Croft, 1978), who conducted the Snoopy experiment, are convinced that the young children they studied could distinguish what they saw from what another person might see, could think about what the other person saw, and could both produce and recognize some physical situations in which the other person could not see some object.

Preschoolers can even figure out what others can see when playing a complicated "hide-from-the-policeman" game. Martin Hughes (1975) built two small walls that intersected to form a cross and placed them on a table. Then he added a policeman doll and a boy doll to the display. Three- and four-year-olds had no trouble hiding the boy doll from the policeman's sight when the policeman was placed so he could see two of the areas (see Figure 17.1). They could also hide the doll when Hughes added additional policemen to the display and only one area was hidden from the policemen's sight.

But young children—and even many older children—seem to have trouble understanding exactly *how* objects appear to another person

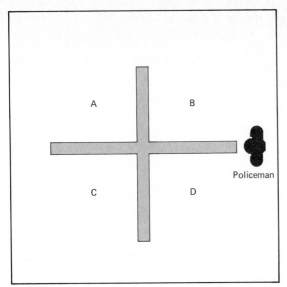 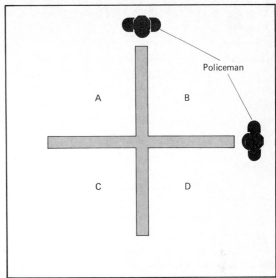

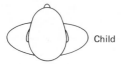 

FIGURE 17.1 Although preschoolers are considered egocentric, they have little trouble hiding a doll in this display so that it is invisible to a policeman doll, even when there are two policemen and the only area out of a policeman's sight (Area C) is in full view of the child.

(From Donaldson, 1978. Reprinted by permission of W. W. Norton & Company, Inc. Copyright © 1978 by Margaret Donaldson.)

(Shantz, 1983). A well-known demonstration of the young child's inability to realize that others do not perceive the world as they do involves a three-dimensional model of a landscape. Three cardboard cones of varying sizes (one red, one blue, and one yellow) stand on a piece of green cardboard, and a little clay man is placed beside them. The experimenter tells the child that the man is going to walk around the mountains and take pictures of them with his camera. As the little man moves around the model, the experimenter shows the child cards that illustrate the display from various perspectives. The child's job is to pick the card that shows the display as the little man would see it. In a second section of the study, the child looks at a card and places the little man where he would have to stand in order to see the scene on the card.

Using this display, Monique Laurendeau and Adrian Pinard (1970), who have been closely associated with Piaget, found that children are very slow in developing the ability to choose the correct picture or place the little man in the right position. Four-year-olds are often "preegocentric": they completely fail to understand the task and may choose a picture because "it's the prettiest." Among children who seem to understand the task, those in the first stage of egocentrism consistently choose the picture that represents the mountains from their own position. Those in the transitional stage show an awareness that the scene would look different to the little man, but they either cannot select the right picture or cannot explain their choice. Those who can successfully complete both tasks are considered to have freed themselves from egocentrism. But only 28 percent of the twelve-year-olds tested by Laurendeau and Pinard were not egocentric—in terms of this test.

Perhaps the mountaintop study is not actually a test of egocentrism. When they can rotate the display to produce the view the other person sees, most three-year-olds can solve the problem (Borke, 1975). Sometimes children simply seem to be selecting the "best" view of the display. When Lynn Liben and Beverly Belknap (1981) constructed a display out of colored blocks and asked children to pick the card that showed their *own* view, preschoolers frequently chose cards showing all the blocks when some of them were hidden from their view. In such cases, children apparently are overpowered by what they know exists, and so they have trouble deciding what they actually see themselves.

Much of the child's failure on the mountaintop test may have to do with the way he or she mentally represents information about space. In one study, Janellen Huttenlocher and Clark Presson (1979) asked eight-year-olds two different types of questions. In *appearance* questions, children had to point to the picture that showed how the display would look from another posi-

tion. This is the problem set by Piaget and by Laurendeau and Pinard. In *item* questions, children had to point to the part of the display that would be in a particular position from another viewpoint (in back, in front, on the red side [right], or on the green side [left])—that is, if the display were rotated instead of the viewer. Children found the first question extremely difficult; the eight-year-olds were wrong 56 percent of the time, and 80 percent of their errors were egocentric. The second question was much easier; this time only 20 percent of the answers were wrong and 49 percent of the wrong answers egocentric.

Huttenlocher and Presson believe that children as old as ten may make apparently egocen-

FIGURE 17.2 Children's errors in the mountaintop display problem may occur because they code each mountain in reference to the room *(right)*, so that visualizing the display from another's viewpoint requires them to recode each mountain. Adults code the display as a unit, with the mountains in relation to one another *(left)*.

(From Huttenlocher and Presson, 1979. Reprinted by permission.)

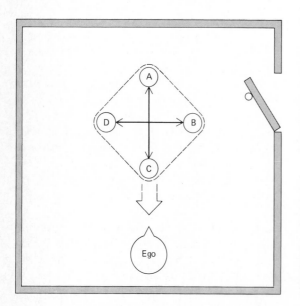
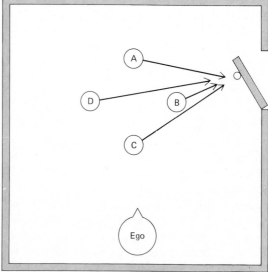

tric errors in Piaget's problem because of the way they code the mountaintop display. In Chapter 8, we noted that toddlers often use landmarks to remember where an object is hidden. With the mountaintop display, children apparently use the surrounding room in the same manner (as depicted in Figure 17.2). They do not code the display as a unit, with the three mountains in relation to one another; instead, they code each of the three mountains in relation to the larger room. When they are asked to visualize where a particular item would be if they stood in a different position, they have to recode the position of only one object. But when they are asked to visualize the appearance of the entire display from another perspective, they must recode the viewer's position in respect to both the array and its framework, a much more difficult task. The researchers suggest that an increase in information-processing abilities, such as the ability to hold the original coding of the entire display and the viewer's position in working memory while examining possible solutions, may help explain why children get better at this task as they get older.

After reviewing a number of studies in which the demands of the task varied, Carolyn Shantz (1983) concluded that the mountaintop test is a test of the child's spatial representations as well as a test of social cognition. It is the most cognitive and the least social aspect of a child's understanding of others.

Understanding How Others Feel

When children understand how others feel, they are inferring the motivations and reactions of other people. This understanding develops gradually throughout childhood; some researchers believe that the process builds on an inborn human predisposition (Sagi and Hoffman, 1976). As we saw in Chapter 16, empathy seems to develop through four stages, from infancy— when the baby does not distinguish between him- or herself and another person—to late

When preschoolers try to comfort a baby sibling in distress, they show that they are beginning to understand how others feel. (Erika Stone)

childhood (Hoffman, 1984). In empathizing, children respond vicariously to an event, feeling an emotion that is more appropriate to the other person's situation than to their own. Not until children reach the third stage of empathy, when they are about two or three years old, do they begin to understand that another person's feelings may differ from their own.

Children as young as three years old have shown an appreciation for the feelings of others. In one study, Robert Stewart and Robert Marvin (1984) placed preschoolers and their infant siblings in the Strange Situation described in Chapter 12. When the mother left the room and the preschooler (three to five years old) and his or her sibling were alone in an unfamiliar place, half of the preschoolers tried to alleviate the infant's distress. They hurried to the infant's side, hugged him or her, and said that mother would soon be back. Often the older child carried the baby to the center of the room and tried to distract him or her with toys. Such behavior on the part of the older child seemed to be part of an ongoing family relationship, because babies with responsive older siblings showed that they were attached to their big brother or sister. Babies whose older siblings ignored them showed no signs of attachment to them.

What distinguished the preschoolers who comforted their younger siblings from those who did not? It was not age. Three-year-olds were as likely to reassure their baby brothers or sisters as five-year-olds. But the responsive preschoolers were much more likely than nonresponsive preschoolers to understand other people. Before the experiment began, researchers tested the preschoolers' ability to understand another person. (The test included such questions as, "Brent likes loud noises; would he rather bang on a drum or put together a puzzle?") Most of the caregiving children (72 percent) showed they understood other people, while most of the noncaregiving children (64 percent) did not.

How do children know what another person is feeling? One clue is the person's facial expression. As we saw in Chapter 12, older babies not only seem able to pick up emotional information from other people, but use that information to guide their own reactions. The process, known as social referencing, seems to develop as soon as a child comes to understand the emotions that accompany various expressions— as early as eight or nine months (Campos et al., 1983). In social referencing, of course, babies have the context of the situation, as well as the other person's gestures and tone of voice, to help them interpret and respond to the emotion being displayed. Laboratory studies of children's ability to interpret emotional expressions often require children to identify an expression from the face alone, which removes other possible cues. Four- and five-year-olds are pretty good at interpreting emotional expressions from such photographs (Felleman et al., 1983). They are best at recognizing happy expressions, not quite so good at recognizing sadness, and find anger somewhat harder to interpret.

Many psychologists believe that young children generally infer emotional reactions from the situation itself instead of interpreting the other person's reaction to it (Gove and Keating, 1979). The child looks at the context and decides how he or she would feel in a similar situation. This procedure has been regarded as an egocentric response, indicating that youngsters assume all people react the same way to the same situation. But recent research indicates that children of all ages can use either cue, and that younger children are more likely to rely on a person's emotional expression than on the situation, while older children tend to go by the situation (Gnepp, 1983). In this study, when preschoolers saw conflicting cues in a picture (a frightened child eating an ice-cream cone), they often invented a new situation to explain the emotion, or else attributed some idiosyncratic reaction to the pictured child. (The idiosyncratic explanation indicates that many preschoolers understand that others' reactions may differ from their own.) Sixth-graders tended to reinterpret the emotional expression, perhaps suggesting that the pictured child was either feeling an emotion that differed from the pictured expression or masking his or her emotions. This reliance on situation is not egocentric, but probably indicates that older children have come to realize that people often do not express the emotions they feel.

When there is no conflict between facial expression and context, children of all ages judge emotions from contextual cues rather than from emotional expressions (Reichenbach and Masters, 1983). However, when the cues are inconsistent, preschoolers tend to rely on facial expressions while third-graders tend to use the situation. Among the children in this study, those from intact homes were more accurate at judging emotions than children from single-parent homes. The researchers suggest that the children's own emotional experience may have disrupted their ability to infer the emotions of other people. These children tended to see less happiness and more anger in the situations they judged.

Children who understand another's emotions can take that person's role. Some children are more adept at role taking than others. In an attempt to develop this ability, Ronald Iannotti (1978) had six- and nine-year-olds assume the roles of characters in a story, acting out, for example, the behavior of children who have found a billfold bulging with money. The trainer asked questions that encouraged role taking ("Why did you do what you did?" "Why do you feel that way?") and emphasized facial expression, tone of voice, conversation, and behavior, as well as the children's role-taking skills and reasoning. Some of the children had to switch roles, changing the character they played every five minutes. When these children subsequently were given tests of role-taking ability, both groups showed improvement compared with children in a control group. The ability to take another's role, however, did not affect the children's empathy. When asked to describe the feelings of characters in a story or the way they would respond in situations involving aggression, they were no more empathic or no less aggressive than children without role-taking experience. But role taking did increase altruistic behavior among the younger children (see Chapter 16). Six-year-olds who had training in role playing voluntarily shared more raisins or M&M's with a "poor boy" than six-year-olds without such experience.

Understanding Friends

In their friendships, children apply what they know about others in a practical way. Their ability to make and keep friends depends on how well they understand what others are like, what they intend, and how they feel. As children develop, the way they think about their friends changes. A child's view of friendship changes in certain predictable ways:

from a purely behavioral relationship (playing together and giving each other things) to an emotional relationship (caring for each other, sharing thoughts and feelings, and comforting each other);

from a self-centered view, in which the friend satisfies the child's wants and needs, to a relationship in which friends satisfy each other's wants and needs; and

from a smooth, transient relationship to a sometimes bumpy, enduring relationship (Shantz, 1983).

In fact, Robert Selman (1981) believes that until children are about four years old, their peer relationships are "playmateships," not friendships. They think about a "friend" as someone who lives nearby or someone they play with; they rarely see affection as having anything to do with the relationship. Selman believes the concept of friendship develops at different rates among children. In the first stage, which begins sometime between the ages of four and nine, friendship is "one-way assistance." A friend is someone with known likes and dislikes who does what the child wants. The second stage, called "fairweather cooperation," develops sometime between the ages of six and twelve. Children adjust themselves to their friends' likes and dislikes, coordinating them with their own, but any argument can rupture such relationships. Finally, when children are between the ages of nine and fifteen, they move into the stage of intimate relationships, characterized by mutual sharing.

When Thomas Berndt (in press) interviewed nearly a hundred kindergartners, third-graders, and sixth-graders, he found somewhat similar changes in their conceptions of friendship. Across all ages, playing together was the most important aspect of friendship. But none of the kindergartners regarded loyalty as an aspect of friendship or saw disloyalty as a reason to break off a relationship; a few third-graders and many of the sixth-graders did. Similar trends appeared in children's view of intimacy. As we saw in Chapter 14, intimacy is especially important in the friendships of older girls. And in this study, half the girls but only about a fifth of the boys said that they would break off a friendship if their friend was disloyal. Berndt concluded that the most important developmental change in

Understanding Television

If young children only gradually acquire role-taking abilities, how well do they understand what goes on in television dramas? If a five-year-old watches "The Dukes of Hazzard," for example, does he or she understand why the main characters periodically pile into cars and go on wild chases?

Understanding "The Dukes of Hazzard," or any other television program, is not limited to role-taking ability; it involves several processing tasks. Before children can understand a television program, they must recognize the essential pieces of information and then make inferences that go beyond what has been explicitly presented on the screen. But as Andrew Collins (1979) has pointed out, in most programs, motives and consequences are portrayed subtly, never made explicit, and they may be separated from each other and from the act they surround by several commercial breaks.

One factor that affects comprehension is the use of formal features of television to transmit meaning. These visual features, such as cuts, zooms, pans, and fades, may either mark significant content or transmit meaning. They seem to assume a degree of information-processing skills we would not expect to find in young children, but studies with four-year-olds have shown that preschoolers are indeed able to make many of the necessary inferences involving time, space, implied action, and character perspective (Anderson and Smith, 1984). For example, many of these youngsters were able to take the visual per-spective of a TV character when the camera revealed it, a social cognitive skill that some researchers might think was beyond four-year-olds. Daniel Anderson and Robin Smith, who conducted these studies, believe that youngsters rely on scripts for various activities to help them interpret much of what they see. As we saw in Chapter 9, scripts are cognitive frameworks that describe the customary sequence of events for various activities.

When the situation becomes complex, however, scripts are not enough. When schoolchildren watched an action-adventure program, second-graders could make only simple inferences about why a character was carrying out some action or what would happen next in the program (Collins et al., 1978). When the inferences required intermediate inferential steps, second-graders were overwhelmed, while fifth-graders had no problem. Andrew Collins (1979) believes that second-graders have difficulty in comprehending television programs because of memory limitations and a failure to integrate what they are seeing now with what they remember. Second-graders are not very good at selecting information from the program for storage or at retrieving the information they need to make inferences. Sometime between the second and fifth grades, there seems to be a pronounced change in information-processing skills. When fifth-graders were wrong in their prediction of actions or motives, it was generally because they had made a wrong inference from the material they successfully recalled.

Why should four-year-olds do so well in one

---

friendship is the emergence of the adolescent's concern with intimacy and loyalty.

Berndt found this trend reflected in children's behavior. When friends worked together on a structured, competitive task, in which the children had a choice between sharing with a part-ner or working for their own rewards, fourth-graders were more competitive when working with friends than when working with acquaintances. But eighth-graders shared more with friends and were more competitive with acquaintances. Berndt attributes the competition

study while seven-year-olds were doing so poorly in another? Anderson and Smith (1984) believe that children understand more of what they see than most studies reveal. They propose that some of the poor performance children show can be traced to language difficulties. In their study, they had four-year-olds act out the answers to questions, using doll characters on a small set. If these children had been asked to respond verbally to the questions, researchers might have believed they had not understood what they saw. In addition, if children rely on their scripts to interpret a program, a regular viewer of "The Dukes of Hazzard" probably understands more of an episode (which fits into the stereotypical "Dukes of Hazzard" plot) than a first-time viewer who is a year or two older.

A store of knowledge derived from previous experience certainly helps young children to interpret what they see on television. Andrew Newcomb and Collins (1979) showed edited episodes from network comedies to middle- and lower-class black and white children. One episode centered around a white, middle-class family; the father was a supervisor and the family of four lived in the suburbs. The other featured a black, working-class family; the father worked at a loading dock and the family of four lived in a housing project. After the children, who were again in second, fifth, and eighth grades, had seen one of the episodes, they were asked questions about the plot, the actors, the actors' feelings, and the reasons for their behavior. As in the earlier study, recall, understanding,

and inference all got progressively better with age. Ethnic background made no difference to comprehension at any age. Among fifth- and eighth-graders, social class also had no effect on their understanding of either program; but among second-graders, social class had a strong influence. Middle-class second-graders understood the program about the middle-class family much better than did lower-class second graders, doing significantly better at comprehending the story and on inferring an actor's feelings and the cause for his or her behavior. But the picture was reversed when it came to second-graders' understanding of the working-class program; those from the lower socioeconomic class did significantly better at both comprehension and inference.

When younger children's previous social experiences bear some relation to the dramatic content of programs, Newcomb and Collins (1979) found, their understanding of all aspects of those programs is improved. The finding that there is an improved understanding in children who can draw on their knowledge base and cognitive scripts is in line with the conclusion reached by Anderson and Smith, as well as with the research on knowledge factors presented in Chapter 8, where we met the four-year-old with a prodigious knowledge of dinosaurs.

between younger friends to the spontaneity of their relationship; he sees the cooperativeness of the older friends as further evidence of the sensitivity and mutual responsiveness that is part of adolescent friendships.

Among the children studied by Berndt,

friendships often foundered on the aggressive behavior of one of the friends. Solving conflicts without overt aggression involves social cognition; in Chapter 16 we saw how children's interpretations of others' actions determine whether hostilities will occur. In an attempt to discover

Most of these children are in the "fairweather cooperation" stage of friendship, when any argument can destroy the relationship. (Elizabeth Crews/Stock, Boston)

how children solve social conflicts, Kenneth Rubin and Linda Krasnor (in press) conducted a series of studies, with preschoolers, kindergartners, and first-graders. They found that children at play encounter a variety of social problems, some as simple as getting another child's attention or obtaining information and others as tricky as persuading a child to stop doing something or gaining possession of some object. They found that there were individual differences in the way children set about solving their problems. The most successful children had the greatest variety of strategies and adapted them to their goal and to other children's age and sex. When their first attempts at solving a problem failed, children who attributed their failures to themselves tended to be flexible and to devise alternate solutions, but children who attributed their failures to some external cause often tended to give up.

Rejected and neglected children differed markedly from popular children in their peer interactions, as we saw in Chapter 14. This difference showed clearly in their approach to social problems (Rubin and Krasnor, in press). Children who were rejected by their peers seemed to have trouble thinking about their problems. They tended to use aggressive or assertive strategies; when they could not solve a problem they either persisted with their old strategy or else gave up. It was as if failure caused the thought processes involved in problem solving to break down. Neglected children had no difficulty in thinking about their problems, but they seemed to lack confidence in their ability to solve them. Often they did not even try to work out their conflicts, but instead appealed to an adult for a solution.

Kenneth Dodge (in press) has further analyzed the way children think about social conflicts. He believes that any child's response depends on the way the child processes information regarding the situation. First the child encodes the social cues in the environment; the next step is to integrate the cues with memories of past situations. This integration de-

The way children try to solve social conflicts may depend on how they process information concerning the situation and what sort of responses are provided by their cognitive script for settling disputes. (Ken Gaghan/Jeroboam)

termines the way the child interprets the situation. If the child fails to interpret the cues correctly or does not use them, or if the child attends only to negative cues, he or she is likely to respond unsuccessfully. As we saw in Chapter 16, the processing of highly aggressive boys breaks down at this point. Once the child has interpreted the situation, he or she generates a possible response, evaluates the consequences, and decides whether to execute it. It is at this point that younger children may fail, because they cannot hold the necessary material in working memory long enough to consider the consequences. A young child may simply carry out the first response that enters his or her mind. Indeed, this seems to be the way the rejected children behaved in Rubin and Krasnor's study; their reactions often seemed impulsive. After the child carries out a selected response, he or she monitors its effect. If the response did not succeed, the child uses the new social cues (the other child's behavior) and repeats the entire process. In this information-processing view of conflict resolution, the behavior of one child affects the thoughts and actions of the other child involved.

In most cases this processing takes place outside the child's awareness. Dodge points out that when the processing is conscious, the effect may be disastrous—as when an anxious adolescent carefully considers the meaning of every social cue he or she perceives. Often the child relies on cognitive scripts for a guide to the proper response. Children have scripts not only for birthday parties and trips to the dentist, but also for settling disputes and for making friends. In fact, habitual strategies come from their scripts for particular kinds of social interactions.

Children who generally carry out this process successfully, obtaining their goals and keeping their friends, are considered socially competent. As children develop, Dodge notes, they become increasingly skilled at this process. For example, five-year-olds are not as competent as older children at noticing and interpreting neutral or friendly cues, and thus are more likely to notice hostile social cues, a practice that leads to squabbles and ruptures friendships. And six-year-olds tend to move on to the process of searching for an appropriate response more quickly than ten-year-olds, basing their solutions on fewer cues than older children use. This haste may lead to ineffective solutions.

Understanding and Communication

When studying the child's ability to take another's place, researchers often ask the child to describe geometric figures or the rules of a game to someone who is blindfolded or from whom a display is hidden. Descriptions that seem to depend on the other person's ability to see what the child is describing supposedly indicate egocentrism. When John Flavell and his associates (1968) asked children to tell a blindfolded person how to play a game that involved rolling a cube that had sides of various colors, then moving a man along a board to a square of the appropriate color, most second-graders made no effort to adjust their descriptions of the game for people who could not see. Yet we saw in Chapter 9 that some researchers have found little connection between visual perspective taking and children's ability to adjust their communication to the listener. Four-year-olds adjust their instructions to the level of younger children when showing them how to work a new toy. And a child's role and goals also affect his or her communication: four-year-olds talk differently when they are playing informally with two-year-olds than when they are acting as teacher (Shatz and Gelman, 1977). Such studies have led most researchers to conclude that inadequate communication by preschoolers cannot be used as evidence of egocentrism, but is more likely a lack of some communicative skill or a gap in the child's knowledge base (Shatz, 1983).

In a recent study, however, Ralph Roberts and Charlotte Patterson (1983) found that in some situations a child's ability to take the perspective of another was indeed related to the way he or she communicated with others. If so, there is more to effective communication than knowledge and skill. Roberts and Patterson suggest that there are two levels of perspective-taking skill involved on the part of the speaker. First, the child must know that although he or she has the necessary information, the other person does not. Most of the four- and five-year-olds they tested showed this level of understanding. Second, the child must understand exactly what information is necessary for the other person to identify whatever the child is describing. Few of the younger children showed this level of understanding, but most of the six-year-olds did. And all the children who passed a test of visual perspective gave the needed information to the other person, indicating that young children's problems in adjusting their communication are related to their deficiency in perspective taking.

Most research in children's communicative ability today focuses on the other side of the task: the child's ability to understand communications and to detect when a communication is faulty. In a typical study of effective listening, the child plays a communication game in which he or she tries to select the card being described by the experimenter, who is sometimes delib-

erately ambiguous. The children are told to ask questions if they do not have enough information. In one such study, most kindergartners seemed to have trouble detecting ambiguity in the messages (Ironsmith and Whitehurst, 1978). Second-graders could tell when a message lacked necessary information, but they seemed unable to isolate the information they needed to know. Their questions tended to be general and not very helpful. Even sixth-graders asked appropriate questions only about half the time.

However, other investigators (Patterson, Cosgrove, and O'Brien, 1980) have found that much younger children do realize, at some level, when messages are ambiguous and indicate their realization by nonverbal behavior. When a message lacks essential information, preschoolers seek eye contact, move their hands, and are slow to respond. Kindergartners and second-graders are also slow to respond to ambiguous messages, and they move their bodies as well as their hands. Other researchers have found that, despite this reaction, five-year-olds are likely to blame themselves for not understanding an ambiguous message. But if their failure at a task is called to their attention, six-year-olds will blame the speaker—as long as the speaker is another child (Whitehurst, 1981).

By studying kindergartners as they played a game, James Speer (1984) detected two strategies young children use to figure out ambiguous instructions. The kindergartners were acting as policemen who—with the help of a puppet police chief—were trying to keep the Grinch from stealing a Christmas present Santa had hidden in one of the buildings on the game board. Speer played the police chief, who told them which building to guard. When his instructions were vague, the children first relied on the context—obvious physical cues and the experimenter's gestures. When that strategy failed, they simply guessed and, if the guess was not corrected, assumed that they were right. But if the children thought that the experimenter was not being cooperative, they no longer assumed that an uncorrected guess was right. Speer suggests that when five-year-olds blame the speaker, it is because they have concluded that he or she is being uncooperative.

Another skill required for successful communication is the speaker's ability to evaluate the listener's understanding at various points in a conversation. Carole Beal and John Flavell (1983) studied this skill by having children give messages to a puppet that were either complete, incomplete, or ambiguous. Even when preschoolers and kindergartners knew that a message was inadequate, they seemed not to understand that the puppet would not have enough information to carry out its task. This finding supports earlier studies indicating that young children do not understand that their problems of comprehension are often due to the poor quality of the messages they receive. First-graders were more competent communicators. They understood when the puppet could not carry out the task and said so, even if the puppet said it had enough information. Beal and Flavell concluded that younger children probably accept speakers' statements about their comprehension uncritically—even when their own knowledge should make them skeptical.

Perhaps, suggest Susan Sonnenschein and Grover Whitehurst (1984), young children do not blame the speaker for inadequate instructions because they do not yet know all the rules that govern communication. They found that many children who did not blame the speaker already possessed speaking skills (they could describe an object to a person who could not see it) and listening skills (they realized that they did not understand an ambiguous message), but still lacked the ability to criticize the communications they received. Criticism skills, which are used to handle inadequate communication, seem to emerge at about the age of nine or ten, although Sonnenschein and Whitehurst found that five-year-olds could learn them. They gave children feedback on their responses to inadequate instructions and also stressed that the youngsters should ask for clarification when they did not understand. The five-year-olds not only learned this criticism skill, but they also transferred it to other situations.

Children's understanding of others develops gradually, as does their ability to communicate. Preschoolers, who are in the preoperational stage, see others in terms of concrete attributes. They understand that others have different visual experiences but seem to have trouble understanding how those differences manifest themselves. They infer emotions from expressions and contextual cues, and sometimes seem to believe that other people always react as they do to an event. By middle childhood, when they are in the concrete operational stage, children are seeing people in terms of inner qualities. They understand how a scene may appear to another person, and they can understand differing reactions to the same event. The adolescent, who has moved into the formal operational stage, is proficient at all these skills and sees subtleties and complexities that are missing from the view of children. The adolescent not only infers another's reactions but attempts to explain them. Children's views of society develop in parallel with their views of other people, because their understanding of the larger groups is built upon their understanding of individuals.

UNDERSTANDING SOCIETY

Children's understanding of the way society works and the role of law and government develops slowly. They build this understanding from knowledge gleaned during their daily experiences—at school, at the shopping mall, at the physician's office, at restaurants, at the homes of friends, and from the world displayed to them on television. Before they can understand how society functions, they must grasp the notion of social roles.

Understanding Social Roles

A child begins by understanding the concept of roles within his or her immediate family:

Children's knowledge of social roles develops slowly. Only after youngsters start school do they realize that a person can be both a mother and a grandmother at the same time. (Michal Heron/Monkmeyer)

mommy, daddy, brother, sister, grandmother, grandfather. But this understanding is limited. One six-year-old boy who was struggling with the concept said, "Daddy, why do you call Grandpa dad? How can he be your dad and my grandpa at the same time?" (Watson and Amgott-Kwan, 1983). Within a few weeks he had moved to a higher level of understanding; he said that when he grew up and had children of his own, his father would be their grandpa but still be his own father.

This understanding of social roles seems to go through a regular series of steps. In a series of studies, Malcolm Watson (Watson and Fischer, 1980; Watson and Amgott-Kwan, 1983; Watson and Amgott-Kwan, 1984) has traced this progress. Two-year-olds understand that other people are active agents, independent of the child. By the time they are four, children understand some of the behavior connected with a role, and they can combine information from at least two representatives of the role (Sally's mother and their own mommy). But for some months, they do not understand parental roles as complementary roles (created by the relation between parent and child). When four-year-olds reach this stage, they know that not all men are fathers and that when a man has a child he becomes a father.

The next step, usually among five- or six-year-olds, is the understanding that a person can

Detecting Lies and Sarcasm

If young children have problems understanding ambiguous statements, how soon can they detect a lie? How soon can they interpret an adult's sarcastic remark? These are sophisticated skills that draw on a child's knowledge of language, situations, and people. Before children can detect either sort of statement, they must understand that the speaker's intentions are at cross-purposes with his or her words. How soon do children learn to detect deliberately false statements? Preschoolers are trusting; they assume that people are sincere. When they notice a discrepancy between the facts and what a person says, they decide either that the facts are wrong or that the person made an unintentional mistake (Ackerman, 1981; Wimmer and Perner, 1983).

In a recent study, Ann Demorest and her associates (1984) traced the development of children's ability to detect false statements by presenting them with a series of twelve stories that differed in the facts surrounding the statement and in the speaker's intonation. In one story, for example, a boy had his hair cut and then encountered another boy who said, "That new haircut you got looks terrific." In some versions of the story, the haircut was "the best he had ever had"; in other versions, it was "the worst he had ever had." When the speaker lied, he smiled deceptively. And in the version that tested the child's abil-ity to appreciate sarcasm, the speaker laughed and pointed derisively at the terrible haircut as he praised it.

By the time they are six years old, children are beginning to understand deception—about half of them detected deliberately deceptive remarks. And where the speaker intended sarcasm, these youngsters also saw deception. But more than a third of the six-year-olds were still trusting; they saw even the sarcasm as a sincere compliment. Nine- and thirteen-year-olds were better at detecting deception—about three-quarters of them recognized deliberate falsehoods. However, they, too, were unable to appreciate sarcasm and called it deception. They used the speaker's words to decide his intent; although they could tell that the laughter and pointing finger did not match his statement, they ignored it in making their judgment.

The detection of lies and sarcasm requires the listener to figure out the speaker's motivation. As children get older, they become better at this skill. They are good at detecting deception, perhaps because the motives behind it are often obvious. But sarcasm is more complicated; it involves language play and indirection—saying one thing while intending the opposite. This, say Demorest and her associates, makes sarcasm difficult to detect. In fact, when they gave the same series of stories to a group of adults, they discovered that nearly half of the adults could not recognize sarcasm.

change to a new role and still remain the same person: a girl can grow up and become a mommy; a mommy can become a grandmother. This step seems linked to the preoperational child's grasp of the identity concept. However, these children are unable to understand that a person can occupy two roles simultaneously. They deny that a person can be *both* a mother and a grandmother, or that a mother who goes out to the office is still a mother. A child may be seven or eight years old before he or she reaches the stage where he or she accepts this concept, which seems to be related to the child's grasp of conservation.

Even then, however, children may be unable to handle role concepts under certain kinds of transformations. An eight-year-old who knows that a father can also be a physician will deny that a father can become a drunkard or that a good baseball player can become a liar. The child will probably maintain that the baseball player who becomes a liar can no longer play baseball well. Children have somewhat less trouble with transformations that do not change the person's valuation (a mother can become a lawyer) or those that transform the person from "bad" to "good" (a thief can become a sales representative) (Shantz, 1983).

Until they are about the age of ten, children seem to have trouble conserving family roles when the family is transformed by death or divorce (Watson and Amgott-Kwan, 1984). They are likely to have trouble seeing a divorced person as a parent and may see divorce as destroying the family. This view may affect the way a child interprets a divorce; if parents are aware of their children's probable reactions, they may be able to provide the reassurance and explanations that will ease the transition.

Understanding How Society Works

Children seem to go through four different stages as they sort out the various aspects of the social system, such as money and work. In a series of interviews with British schoolchildren, Hans Furth (1980) found that children go through these stages at their own pace and that the movement follows the same Piagetian processes that characterize other aspects of cognitive development (see Figure 17.3).

Thinking in Stage I is dominated by accommodation, in which the child submissively accepts the results of social actions as an end in themselves. Five- and six-year-olds saw no need to explain the workings of the social system they observed. Five-year-olds believed that money was freely available. They noticed that money accompanies transactions in a store, but they believed that merchants give the goods to the purchasers and also present them with money (change). Almost uniformly, five- and six-year-olds said that change from purchases is the

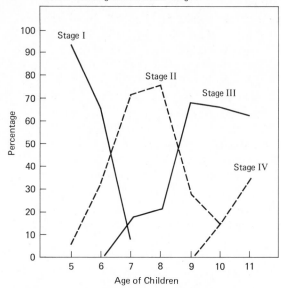

Thinking About Society:

Percentage of Children in Each Age Group That Adhered to the Thinking of a Particular Stage

FIGURE 17.3 Children progress steadily through the stages of understanding society, from the submissive acceptance of Stage I, to the concrete understanding of Stage IV, with most primary-school children in one of the transitional stages.

(From Furth, 1980. Reprinted by permission of the publisher. Copyright © 1980 by Elsevier-North Holland, Inc.)

source of money, although one boy added that a shopkeeper bought a store by finding money in the mud. Other children in this stage indicated that garbage men live on the presents they get at Christmas and that telephones are free, a gift from friends who have more than they need.

In Stage II, children's thinking is characterized primarily by assimilation, in which children elaborate playfully on social actions, creating a childish form of reality in which play and actuality are not easily distinguished. Children in Stage II understood many of the social functions they observed or experienced directly. These seven- and eight-year-olds understood the difference between paying for an item in the store and giving money as change. Yet many continued to believe that merchandise is free to the shopkeeper and that the money paid for purchases is then given to the blind or the poor.

Most nine- and ten-year-olds had reached Stage III, in which children begin to interpret parts of society with which they have no contact. This is a transitional stage, when children search for logical and factual consistency but construct incomplete explanations for aspects of society that conflict. Many of the children were aware of this cognitive gap and handled the conflict in one of two ways. Either they refused to push their interpretations beyond the immediate situation (which Furth calls *reluctant thinking*), or else they made compromise solutions, in which they came up with a logically possible, but incorrect, explanation. One young reluctant thinker said that libraries ran on the fines they got from overdue books. Asked if fine money would pay for all the books in the library, he replied, "Yes. You can tell if they do, because if they didn't, you wouldn't have all the books." A compromise solution to the workings of society was advanced by Nick, who indicated that the government gets all the money paid into the system in economic transactions and in turn pays all wages, builds all schools, and provides goods for all stores.

Children who had found real solutions to the conflicts of the third stage had achieved a temporary equilibrium and moved into Stage IV. At this level, boys and girls make sense out of the system, and their ideas of society begin to approximate an adult viewpoint. The understanding of these ten- and eleven-year-olds was concrete and, for the first time, logical—corresponding to Piaget's concrete operational thought. Although a knowledge of the abstract system escaped them, these children understood the way profit functions and knew that shopkeepers sell goods for more than they pay for them.

Children in the fourth stage are aware of personal motivations and individual differences. Asked if any particular job required a certain kind of person, for example, one ten-year-old

boy said that being a good clown at a circus called for a "jolly, jumpy person," and being a teacher of small children required "patience." He also said that one needed training to become a policeman, and that teachers could also be students. Another child advanced five reasons for working: money, national need, keeping fit, satisfying ambitions, and controlling anger.

Children's thinking about government itself develops slowly, with preadolescents viewing law and government as primarily coercive institutions. Not until their late teens do most children come to see government as a cooperative venture—an institution that is more or less capable of keeping society running smoothly, instead of a giant policeman. This difference, says Judith Gallatin (1980), appears in children's answers to social questions. When eleven-year-olds are asked how to eliminate poverty, they say that lazy people should be forced to work. When eighteen-year-olds are asked the same question, they are likely to suggest increased government spending.

The view of eleven-year-olds is highly concrete and resembles the social views of children in Furth's Stage IV. These children are functioning on a concrete operational level and do not seem to grasp abstractions. As Joseph Adelson (1975) has put it: "The young adolescent can imagine a church but not the church, the teacher and the school but not education, the police and the judge and the jail but not law, the public official but not government."

By the time they are thirteen and entering the formal operational stage, adolescents can reason about the political system and envision long-range social consequences of political acts, but not in any consistent way, often sliding back into the concrete, present-bound view of the concrete operational child. Fifteen-year-olds seem solidly into the formal operational stage and deal easily with the abstract concepts of government and politics. Adelson and his colleagues found few qualitative differences between fifteen- and eighteen-year-olds. Eighteen-year-olds have a greater store of knowledge and are more fluent in expressing their ideas, but their basic understanding is similar to that of fifteen-year-olds.

REWEAVING THE STRANDS

Children's knowledge of self, of others, and of society progresses together, and in each case, the child is applying cognition to the psychological and social world (see Table 17.1). Social

cognition shows the intertwined nature of cognitive and social development more clearly than any other sphere of life, but in earlier chapters we have seen the way aggression, moral behavior, and the understanding of gender also depend on a child's level of cognitive development.

We have seen how children's knowledge about the social world deepens as cognitive development progresses. Their experiences with others affect the way children think about that world, and the way they think about others undoubtedly affects the way they behave. How does a

Table 17.1 DEVELOPMENT OF SOCIAL COGNITION

	Understanding Self	Understanding Others	Understanding Friends	Understanding Social Roles	Understanding Society
Preoperational Period (About age 2–7)	Understands concrete attributes Understands major emotions, but relies on situation	Understands concrete attributes, including stability of behavior	One-way assistance (age 4–9)	Can generalize role (age 4) Understands person can change role and remain same person	Feels no need to explain system (age 5–6)
Concrete Operational Period (About age 7–12)	Understands personal qualities Relies on inner feelings as guide to emotions Understands shame and pride	Understands personal qualities	Fairweather cooperation (age 6–12)	Understands that people can occupy two roles simultaneously	Understands social functions observed or experienced (age 7–8) Provides fanciful explanations of distant functions (age 9–10) Has acquired concrete knowledge of society
Formal Operational Period (After about age 12)	Capable of complex, flexible, precise description Understands abstract traits Establishes identity	Capable of complex, flexible, precise description	Intimate sharing (age 9–15)		Can deal with abstract conception of society, government, and politics (by age 15)

(*Sources:* Adelson, 1975; Carroll and Steward, 1984; Erikson, 1968; Ferguson et al., 1984; Furth, 1980; Harter, 1983; Selman, 1981; Watson and Amgott-Kwan, 1983.)

child apply this social knowledge to his or her understanding of others? Shantz (1983) has suggested four possible ways:

A child can make inferences about another by knowing what most people in that category or social role (boy, girl, teacher, mother, father, friend, enemy, physician) do;

a child can make inferences about another by knowing what that person has done in similar situations in the past;

a child can generalize from the self in an egocentric manner, assuming that others think, feel, and behave as he or she does; and

a child can generalize from the self in a nonegocentric manner, inferring the other's reactions by role taking—either putting the self in that position ("What would I do in that case?") or taking that individual's role ("What would I do if I were that person?").

But no matter which aspect of understanding we have considered, whether understanding the self, others, or the workings of society, the same developmental process has appeared—progressing from the self to the wider world, from the concrete to the abstract. The baby who could not distinguish between self and world has become, through the interaction of genetic inheritance, cognitive development, and individual experiences, the adolescent who can see the complexities inherent in a world of unique individuals.

SUMMARY

A child's self-understanding progresses through stages that roughly parallel Piaget's stages of cognitive development. In the sensorimotor period, babies' development of one aspect of self-concept (the self as "me") and the ability to recognize themselves in the mirror are correlated with the concept of object permanence. In the preoperational period, children perceive themselves in terms of concrete attributes. Preschool-

ers take an all-or-nothing view of attributes, but toward the end of this period, the kindergartner or first-grader realizes that he or she can be good at one task but not very good at another. In the concrete operational period, children begin to see themselves in terms of personal qualities— again moving from an all-or-nothing view to a later perspective that takes varied situations into account. In the formal operational period, adolescents see themselves as having a more flexible and integrated combination of traits. Early in this period, adolescents are highly self-conscious and are reluctant to reveal abiding aspects of themselves, which are linked with their **self-esteem.** Establishing an **identity** is the major developmental task for adolescents; they may successfully achieve an identity structure, have their identity **foreclosed,** develop a **diffuse** identity, or enter a period of **moratorium.**

Children's understanding of what others are like develops gradually, generally following the same path as the development of self-concept. Although young children understand that others do not see exactly what they see, they have trouble understanding exactly how objects appear to another person. The ability to understand how another feels develops from the toddler's assumption that everyone feels as he or she does to the realization that people can have different reactions to the same event. Children seem to infer others' emotions from facial expressions, gestures, tone of voice, and the situation, with younger children paying more attention to the other person's emotional expression and older children tending to rely on the situation.

A child's view of friendship changes from a purely behavioral relationship to an emotional relationship; from a self-centered relationship to a mutually satisfying relationship; and from a smooth, transient relationship to a bumpy, enduring relationship. Aggression can disrupt friendships at any age, but only among older children does disloyalty break up friendships.

Inadequate communication by preschoolers is not always a demonstration of egocentrism; it may simply indicate that a child lacks some communicative skill or some essential knowledge. Preschoolers generally know when another person lacks some information that they need to complete a task, but they may not understand exactly what information is required. Most young children blame themselves when they do not understand another's message, but by the time they are about nine years old—and have learned the rules that govern communication—they are ready to blame the speaker for misunderstandings.

Children's understanding of social roles begins in the immediate family. Two-year-olds can see others as independent, active agents; four-year-olds can combine information from different representatives of a role; five- or six-year-olds know that people can assume a new role and remain the same person; and children in the concrete operational stage can understand that a person may occupy two roles simultaneously. Children's understanding of society seems to go through at least four stages. At age five, young-

sters accept but do not attempt to explain what they see in the world around them; seven- and eight-year-olds can interpret and understand social functions within their experience; nine- and ten-year-olds try to explain parts of society with which they have no contact, but are aware of the inadequacies of their explanations; and by the time they are eleven, children begin to make sense out of the system, viewing it in a concrete fashion. However, not until they are about fifteen and well into the formal operational period are they able to deal with abstract concepts of government and politics.

When trying to understand others, children may apply their knowledge of the social world, using any of these four methods: making inferences from the person's social role or category; making inferences from the person's past behavior in similar situations; generalizing from the self in an egocentric manner; or generalizing from the self in a nonegocentric manner, making inferences through role taking.

REFERENCES

Abramov, I., J. Gordon, A. Hendrickson, L. Hainline, V. Dobson, and E. LaBossiere. "The Retina of the Newborn Human Infant," *Science*, 217 (1982), 265–267. (Ch. 4)

Abramovitch, R., and J. E. Grusec. "Peer Imitation in a Natural Setting," *Child Development*, 49 (1978), 60–65. (Ch. 14)

———, D. Pepler, and C. Corter. "Patterns of Sibling Interaction Among Preschool-Age Children," in M. E. Lamb and B. Sutton-Smith (eds.), *Sibling Relationships: Their Nature and Significance Across the Lifespan*. Hillsdale, N. J.: Lawrence Erlbaum Associates, 1982, pp. 61–86. (Ch. 13)

Abravanel, E., and A. D. Sigafoos. "Exploring the Presence of Imitation During Early Infancy," *Child Development*, 55 (1984), 381–392. (Ch. 7)

Acheson, R. M. "Effects of Nutrition and Disease on Human Growth," in J. M. Tanner (ed.), *Human Growth*. New York: Pergamon Press, 1960, pp. 73–92. (Ch. 5)

———. "Maturation of the Skeleton," in F. Falkner (ed.), *Human Development*. Philadelphia: Saunders, 1966, pp. 465–502. (Ch. 5)

Ackerman, B. "Young Children's Understanding of a Speaker's Intentional Use of a False Utterance," *Developmental Psychology*, 17 (1981), 472–480. (Ch. 17)

Acredolo, C., and L. P. Acredolo. "Identity, Compensation, and Conservation," *Child Development*, 50 (1979), 524–535. (Ch. 10)

———, A. Adams, and J. Schmid. "On the Understanding of the Relationships Between Speed, Duration, and Distance," *Child Development*, 55 (1984), 2151–2159. (Ch. 10)

Acredolo, L. P. "Development of Spatial Orientation in Infancy," *Developmental Psychology*, 14 (1978), 224–234. (Ch. 7)

———. "Laboratory Versus Home: The Effect of Environment on the 9-Month-Old Infant's Choice of Spatial Reference System," *Developmental Psychology*, 15 (1979), 666–667. (Ch. 7)

———, and D. Evans. "Developmental Changes in the Effects of Landmarks on Infant Spatial Behavior," *Developmental Psychology*, 16 (1980), 312–318. (Ch. 7)

———, and J. L. Hake. "Infant Perception," in B. B. Wolman (ed.), *Handbook of Developmental Psychology*. Englewood Cliffs, N. J.: Lawrence Erlbaum Associates, 1982, pp. 244–283. (Ch. 7)

———, H. L. Pick, Jr., and M. G. Olsen. "Environmental Differentiation and Familiarity as Determinants of Children's Memory for Spatial Location," *Developmental Psychology*, 11 (1975), 495–501. (Ch. 8)

Adamson, K., Jr. "The Role of Thermal Factors in Fetal and Neonatal Life," *Pediatric Clinics of North America*, 13 (1966), 599–619. (Ch. 4)

Adelson, J. "The Development of Ideology in Adolescence," in S. Dragastin and G. H. Elder (eds.), *Adolescence in the Life Cycle*. Washington, D.C.: Hemisphere Books, 1975, pp. 63–78. (Chap. 17)

Ahammer, I. M., and J. P. Murray. "Kindness in the Kindergarten: The Relative Influence of Role-Playing and Prosocial Television in Facilitating Altruism," *International Journal of Behavioral Development*, 2 (1979), 133–157. (Ch. 16)

Ahr, P. R., and J. Youniss. "Reasons for Failure on the Class Inclusion Problem," *Child Development*, 41 (1970), 131–143. (Ch. 10)

Ainsworth, M. D. S. *Infancy in Uganda: Infant Care and the Growth of Love*. Baltimore: Johns Hopkins University Press, 1967. (Ch. 12)

———, M. C. Blehar, E. Waters, and S. Wall. *Patterns of Attachment: A Psychological Study of the Strange Situation*. Hillsdale, N. J.: Lawrence Erlbaum Associates, 1978. (Ch. 12)

———, and B. A. Wittig. "Attachment and Exploratory Behavior of One-Year-Olds in a Strange Situation," in B. M. Foss (ed.), *Determinants of Infant Behavior*, Vol. 4. London: Methuen, 1969, pp. 111–136. (Ch. 12)

Aldrich, C. A., and E. S. Hewitt. "A Self-Regulating Feeding Program for Infants," *Journal of the American Medical Association*, 135 (1947), 340–342. (Ch. 5)

Aleksandrowicz, M. M., and D. R. Aleksandrowicz. "Obstetrical Pain-Relieving Drugs as Predictors of Infant Behavioral Variability," *Child Development*, 45 (1974), 935–945. (Ch. 3)

Allen, G. L., K. C. Kirasic, A. W. Siegel, and J. F. Herman. "Developmental Issues in Cognitive Mapping: The Selection and Utilization of Environmental Landmarks," *Child Development*, 50 (1979), 1062–1070. (Ch. 8)

Allen, K. E., B. Hart, J. S. Buell, F. R. Harris, and M. M. Wolf. "Effects of Social Reinforcement on Isolate Behavior of a Nursery School Child," *Child Development*, 35 (1964), 511–518. (Ch. 14)

Als, H., E. Tronick, B. M. Lester, and T. B. Brazelton. "Specific Neonatal Measures: The Brazelton Neonatal Behavior Assessment Scale," in J. D. Osofsky (ed.), *Handbook of Infant Development*. New York: Wiley-Interscience, 1979, pp. 185–215. (Ch. 3)

Altura, B. M., B. T. Altura, and A. Carella. "Magnesium Deficiency—Induced Spasms of Umbilical Vessels: Relation to Preeclampsia, Hypertension, Growth Retardation," *Science*, 221, (1983), 376–377. (Ch. 3)

Amato, S. S. "Is Genetic Counseling Intervention?" in R. R. Turner and H. W. Reese (eds.), *Life Span Developmental Psychology: Intervention*. New York: Academic Press, 1980, pp. 185–196. (Ch. 3)

American Humane Association. *Annual Report, 1981: Highlights of Official Child Neglect and Abuse Reporting*. Denver: American Humane Association, 1983. (Ch. 13)

American Psychiatric Association. *Diagnostic and Statistical Manual of Mental Disorders*. 3rd ed. Washington, D. C.: American Psychiatric Association, 1980. (Ch. 6)

Anastasi, A. *Psychological Testing*. 5th ed. New York: Macmillan, 1982. (Ch. 11)

Anderson, D. R. "Active and Passive Processes in Children's Television Viewing." Paper presented at the Annual Meeting of the American Psychological Association. New York, September 1979. (Ch. 8)

————, L. F. Alwitt, E. P. Lorch, and S. R. Levin, "Watching Children Watch Television," in G. Hale and M. Lewis (eds.), *Attention and Cognitive Development*. New York: Plenum Press, 1979, pp. 331–361. (Ch. 8)

————, and R. Smith. "Young Children's TV Viewing: The Problem of Cognitive Continuity," in F. J. Morrison, C. Lord, and D. P. Keating (eds.), *Applied Developmental Psychology*. Vol. 1. New York: Academic Press, 1984, pp. 115–163. (Ch. 17)

Anderson, J. R. *The Architecture of Cognition*. Cambridge, Mass.: Harvard University Press, 1983. (Ch. 9)

Anderson, R. B., and J. F. Rosenblith. "Sudden Unexpected Death Syndrome: Early Indicators," *Biology of the Neonate*, 18 (1971), 395–406. (Ch. 4)

Anglin, J. M. *Word, Object, and Concept Development*. New York: Norton, 1977. (Chs. 8, 9)

Annett, M. "Genetic and Nongenetic Influences on Handedness," *Behavior Genetics*, 8 (1978), 227–249. (Ch. 6)

Anooshian, L. J., V. U. Pascal, and H. McCreath. "Problem Mapping Before Problem Solving: Young Children's Cognitive Maps and Search Strategies in Large-Scale Environments," *Child Development*, 55 (1984), 1820–1824. (Ch. 8)

Apgar, V., and L. S. James. "Further Observations on the Newborn Scoring System," *American Journal of Diseases of Children*, 104 (1962), 419–428. (Ch. 3)

Appelbaum, M. I., and R. B. McCall. "Design and Analysis in Developmental Psychology," in P. H. Mussen (ed.), *Handbook of Child Psychology*. 4th ed. Vol. 1: W. Kessen (ed.), *History, Theory, and Methods*. New York: Wiley, 1983, pp. 415–476. (Ch. 2)

Aries, P. *Centuries of Childhood: A Social History of Family Life*. New York: Vintage, 1962. (Ch. 1)

Aronfreed, J. "The Concept of Internalization," in D. A. Goslin (ed.), *Handbook of Socialization Theory and Research*. Chicago: Rand McNally, 1969, pp. 263–323. (Ch. 16)

————. "Moral Development from the Standpoint of a General Psychological Theory," in T. Lickona (ed.), *Moral Development and Behavior*. New York: Holt, Rinehart and Winston, 1976, pp. 54–69.

Asher, S. R. "Children's Peer Relations," in M. E. Lamb (ed.), *Social and Personality Development*. New York: Holt, Rinehart and Winston, 1978, pp. 91–113. (Ch. 14)

————, S. Hymel, and P. D. Renshaw. "Loneliness in Children," *Child Development*, 55 (1984), 1456–1464. (Ch. 14)

————, R. A. Markell, and S. Hymel. "Identifying Children at Risk in Peer Relations: A Critique of the Rate-of-Interaction Approach to Assessment," *Child Development*, 52 (1981), 1239–1245. (Ch. 14)

Ashmead, D. H., and M. Perlmutter. "Infant Memory in Everyday Life," in M. Perlmutter (ed.), *New Directions in Child Development*. No. 10. *Children's Memory*. San Francisco: Jossey-Bass, 1980, pp. 1–16. (Ch. 7)

Aslin, R. N., D. B. Pisoni, and P. W. Jusczyk. "Auditory Development and Speech Perception in Infancy," in P. H. Mussen (ed.), *Handbook of Child Psychology*. 4th ed. Vol. 2: M. M. Haith and J. J. Campos (eds.), *Infancy and Developmental Psychobiology*. New York: Wiley, 1983, pp. 573–687. (Chs. 4, 7, 9)

Atkinson, R. D., and R. M. Shiffrin. "Human Memory: A Proposed System and Its Control Processes," in K. W. Spence and J. T. Spence (eds.), *The Psychology of Learning and Motivation*. Vol. 2. New York: Academic Press, 1968. (Ch. 8)

Ault, R. L. *Children's Cognitive Development*. New York: Oxford University Press, 1977. (Ch. 1)

Ausubel, D. P. *Theories and Problems of Child Development*. New York: Grune & Stratton, 1958. (Ch. 12)

Babson, S. G., M. L. Pernoll, G. I. Benda, and K. Simpson. *Diagnosis and Management of the Fetus and Neonate at Risk: A Guide for Team Care*. 4th ed. St. Louis: C. V. Mosby, 1980. (Ch. 3)

Bacon, M., and M. B. Jones. *Teenage Drinking*. New York: Crowell, 1968. (Ch. 14)

Bahrick, L., A. Walker, and U. Neisser. "Infants' Perception of Multimodal Information in Novel Events." Paper presented at the meeting of the Eastern Psychological Association. Washington, D.C., March 1978. (Ch. 7)

Baillargeon, R., R. Gelman, and E. Meck. "Are Preschoolers Truly Indifferent to Causal Mechanisms?" Paper presented at the biennial meeting of the Society for Research in Child Development. Boston, April 1981. (Ch. 10)

Bakker, D. J., M. Hoefkens, and H. Van der Vlugt. "Hemispheric Specialization in Children as Reflected in the Longitudinal Development of Ear Asymmetry," *Cortex*, 15 (1979), 619–625. (Ch. 6)

Ball, S., and G. A. Bogatz. "Summative Research of *Sesame Street*: Implications for the Study of Preschool Children," in A. D. Pick (ed.), *Minnesota Symposia on Child Psychology*. Vol. 6. Minneapolis: University of Minnesota Press, 1972, pp. 3–17. (Ch. 11)

Baltes, P. B., H. W. Reese, and L. P. Lipsitt. "Life-Span Developmental Psychology," in *Annual Review of Psychology*. Vol. 31. Palo Alto, Calif.: Annual Reviews, 1980, pp. 65–110. (Ch. 2)

————, H. W. Reese, and J. R. Nesselroade. *Life-Span Developmental Psychology: Introduction to Research Methods*. Monterey, Calif.: Brooks/Cole, 1977. (Ch. 2)

Bandura, A. "Social-Learning Theory of Identificatory Processes," in D. A. Goslin (ed.), *Handbook of Socialization Theory and Research*. Chicago: Rand-McNally, 1969, pp. 213–262. (Ch. 1)

————. *Aggression: A Social Learning Analysis*. Englewood Cliffs, N. J.: Prentice-Hall, 1973. (Ch. 16)

————. *Social-Learning Theory*. Englewood Cliffs, N. J.: Prentice-Hall, 1977. (Chs. 1, 9, 14, 16)

————, and A. C. Huston. "Identification as a Process of Incidental Learning," *Journal of Abnormal and Social Psychology*, 63 (1961), 311–318. (Ch. 13)

————, and R. H. Walters. *Social Learning and Personality Development*. New York: Holt, Rinehart and Winston, 1963. (Ch. 1)

Banks, M. S., and P. Salapatek. "Infant Visual Perception," in P. H. Mussen (ed.), *Handbook of Child Psychology*. 4th ed. Vol. 2: M. M. Haith and J. J. Campos (eds.), *Infancy and Developmental Psychobiology.* New York: Wiley, 1983, pp. 435–571. (Chs. 4, 7)

Barnett, M. A., J. A. Howard, E. M. Melton, and G. A. Dino. "Effect of Inducing Sadness about Self or Other on Helping Behavior in High- and Low-Empathic Children," *Child Development,* 53 (1982), 267–277. (Ch. 16)

——, L. M. King, and J. A. Howard. "Inducing Affect About Self or Other: Effects on Generosity in Children," *Developmental Psychology,* 15 (1979), 164–167. (Ch. 16)

Barrett, D. E. "A Naturalistic Study of Sex Differences in Children's Aggression," *Merrill-Palmer Quarterly,* 25 (1979), 193–207. (Ch. 16)

Barron, F. "The Dream of Art and Poetry," *Psychology Today,* 2 (December 1968), 18–23 +. (Ch. 11)

Barry, H., M. K. Bacon, and I. L. Child. "A Cross-Cultural Survey of Some Sex Differences in Socialization," *Journal of Abnormal and Social Psychology,* 55 (1957), 327–332. (Ch. 15)

——, I. L. Child, and M. K. Bacon. "Relation of Child Training to Subsistence Economy," *American Anthropologist,* 61 (1959), 51–63. (Ch. 13)

Bartel, H. W., N. R. Bartel, and J. J. Grill. "A Sociometric View of Some Integrated Open Classrooms," *Journal of Social Issues,* 29 (1973), 159–173. (Ch. 14)

Bates, E. *The Emergence of Symbols: Cognition and Communication in Infancy.* New York: Academic Press, 1979. (Ch. 9)

——, I. Bretherton, M. Beeghly-Smith, and S. McNew. "Social Bases of Language Development: A Reassessment," in H. W. Reese and L. P. Lipsitt (eds.), *Advances in Child Development and Behavior.* Vol. 16. New York: Academic Press, 1982, pp. 7–75. (Ch. 9)

Bates, J. E., L. A. Maslin, and K. A. Frankel. "Attachment Security, Mother-Child Interaction, and Temperament as Predictors of Behavior Problem Ratings at Age Three Years," in I. Bretherton and E. Waters (eds.), "Growing Points of Attachment Theory and Research," *Monographs of the Society for Research in Child Development,* 50 (1985), entire no. 209, 167–193. (Ch. 13)

Baumrind, D. "Authoritarian vs. Authoritative Parental Control," *Adolescence,* 3 (1968), 255–272. (Chs. 13, 14)

——. "Socialization and Instrumental Competence in Young Children," in W. W. Hartup (ed.), *The Young Child: Reviews of Research.* Vol 2. Washington, D.C.: National Association for the Education of Young Children, 1972, pp. 202–224. (Chs. 13, 14)

——. "The Contribution of the Family to the Development of Competence in Children," *Schizophrenia Bulletin,* 14 (1975), 12–37. (Ch. 13)

Bay, E. "Ontogeny of Stable Speech Areas in the Human Brain," in E. H. Lenneberg and E. Lenneberg (eds.), *Foundations of Language Development: A Multidisciplinary Approach.* Vol. 2. New York: Academic Press, 1975. (Ch. 6)

Bayley, N. "Consistency and Variability in the Growth of Intelligence from Birth to Eighteen Years," *Journal of Genetic Psychology,* 75 (1949), 165–196. (Ch. 11)

——. "On the Growth of Intelligence," *American Psychologist,* 10 (1955), 805–818. (Ch. 11)

——. "Individual Patterns of Development," *Child Development,* 27 (1956), 45–74. (Ch. 5)

——. *Manual for the Bayley Scales of Infant Development.* New York: Psychological Corporation, 1969. (Chs. 7, 11)

Beal, C. R., and J. H. Flavell. "Young Speakers' Evaluations of Their Listener's Comprehension in a Referential Communication Task," *Child Development,* 54 (1983), 148–153. (Ch. 17)

Beatty, R. A., and S. Gluecksohn-Waelsch. *Edinburgh Symposium on the Genesis of the Spermatazoan.* Edinburgh/New York: 1972. (Ch. 3)

Becker, J. M. "A Learning Analysis of the Development of Peer-Oriented Behavior in Nine-Month-Old Infants," *De-*

velopmental Psychology, 13 (1977), 481–491. (Ch. 14)

Bell, S. M. "The Development of the Concept of Object as Related to Infant-Mother Attachment," *Child Development,* 41 (1970), 291–311. (Ch. 12)

Bellugi, U. "Learning the Language," *Psychology Today,* 4 (December 1970), 32–35 +. (Ch. 9)

Belmont, L., P. Cohen, J. Dryfoos, et al. "Maternal Age and Children's Intelligence," in K. G. Scott, T. Field, and E. Robertson (eds.), *Teenage Parents and Their Offspring.* New York: Grune & Stratton, 1981, pp. 177–197. (Ch. 3)

Belsky, J. "The Determinants of Parenting: A Process Model," *Child Development,* 55 (1984), 83–96. (Ch. 12)

——, M. Rovine, and D. G. Taylor. "The Pennsylvania Infant and Family Development Project, III: The Origins of Individual Differences in Infant-Mother Attachment: Maternal and Infant Contributions," *Child Development,* 55 (1984), 718–728. (Ch. 12)

——, L. D. Steinberg, and A. Walker. "The Ecology of Day Care," in M. E. Lamb (ed.), *Nontraditional Families: Parenting and Child Development.* Hillsdale, N. J.: Lawrence Erlbaum Associates, 1982, pp. 71–116. (Chs. 12, 13)

——, and W. J. Tolan. "Infants as Producers of Their Own Development: An Ecological Analysis," in R. M. Lerner and N. A. Busch-Rossnagel (eds.), *Individuals as Producers of Their Development: A Life-Span Perspective.* New York: Academic Press, 1981, pp. 87–116. (Ch. 12)

Bem, S. L. "The Measurement of Psychological Androgyny," *Journal of Consulting and Clinical Psychology,* 42 (1974), 155–162. (Ch. 15)

——. "Theory and Measurement of Androgyny: A Reply to the Pedazur-Tetenbaum and Locksley-Colten Critiques," *Journal of Personality and Social Psychology,* 37 (1979), 1047–1054. (Ch. 15)

——. "Gender Schema Theory and Its Implications for Child Development: Raising Gender-Aschematic Children in a Gender-Schematic Society," *Signs,* 8 (1983), 598–616. (Ch. 15)

Benbow, C. P., S. Perkins, and J. C. Stanley. "Mathematics Taught at a Fast Pace: A Longitudinal Evaluation of SMPY's First Class," in C. P. Benbow and J. C. Stanley (eds.), *Academic Precocity: Aspects of Its Development.* Baltimore, Johns Hopkins University Press, 1983, pp. 51–78. (Ch. 10)

——, and J. C. Stanley. "Sex Differences in Mathematical Ability: Fact or Artifact? *Science,* 210 (1980), 1262–1264. (Ch. 6)

——, and ——. "Sex Differences in Mathematical Ability: More Facts," *Science,* 222 (1983), 1029–1031. (Ch. 6)

Bereiter, C. "An Error of Interpretation in Cloutier and Goldschmid's 'Individual Differences in the Development of Formal Reasoning,' " *Child Development,* 49 (1978), 251–252. (Ch. 10)

Berg, C. A., and R. J. Sternberg. "Response to Novelty: Continuity Versus Discontinuity in the Developmental Course of Intelligence," in H. W. Reese and L. P. Lipsitt (eds.), *Advances in Child Development and Behavior.* Vol. 19. New York: Academic Press [in press]. (Ch. 11)

Berg, W. K., and K. M. Berg. "Psychophysiological Development in Infancy: State, Sensory Function, and Attention," in J. D. Osofsky (ed.), *Handbook of Infant Development.* New York: Wiley-Interscience, 1979, pp. 283–343. (Ch. 4)

Berndt, T. J. "Developmental Changes in Conformity to Peers and Parents," *Developmental Psychology,* 15 (1979), 608–616. (Ch. 14)

——. "Children's Comments about Their Friendships," in M. Perlmutter (ed.), *Minnesota Symposia on Child Psychology.* Vol. 18. Hillsdale, N. J.: Lawrence Erlbaum Associates [in press]. (Chs. 14, 17)

Bertenthal, B. I., and K. W. Fischer. "Development of Self-Recognition in the Infant," *Developmental Psychology*, 14 (1978), 44–50. (Ch. 17)

———, and ———. "The Development of Representation in Search: A Social-Cognitive Analysis," *Child Development*, 54 (1983), 846–857. (Ch. 7)

Berzonsky, M. "The Role of Familiarity in Children's Explanations of Physical Causality," *Child Development*, 42 (1971), 705–715. (Ch. 10)

Bijou, S. W. *Child Development: The Basic Stage of Early Childhood*. Englewood Cliffs, N. J.: Prentice-Hall, 1976. (Ch. 1)

———, and D. M. Baer. *Child Development*. Vol. 1: *A Systematic and Empirical Theory*. New York: Appleton-Century-Crofts, 1961. (Ch. 1)

———, and ———. *Child Development*. Vol. 2: *Universal Stage of Infancy*. New York: Appleton-Century-Crofts, 1965. (Chs. 1, 9)

Biller, H. D. "Father Absence, Divorce, and Personality Development," in M. E. Lamb (ed.), *The Role of the Father in Child Development*. 2nd ed. New York: Wiley-Interscience, 1981, pp. 489–552. (Ch. 13)

Bingham, M. T. "Beyond Psychology," in *Homo Sapiens Auduboniensis: A Tribute to Walter Van Dyke Bingham*. New York: National Audubon Society, 1953, pp. 5–29. (Ch. 11)

Birch, H. G. "Field Measurement in Nutrition, Learning, and Behavior," in N. S. Scrimshaw and J. E. Gordon (eds.), *Malnutrition, Learning, and Behavior*. Cambridge, Mass.: MIT Press, 1968. (Ch. 4)

Birnholz, J. C., and B. R. Benacerraf. "The Development of Human Fetal Hearing," *Science*, 222 (1983), 516–518. (Ch. 3)

Blasi, A. "Bridging Moral Cognition and Moral Action: A Critical Review of the Literature," *Psychological Bulletin*, 88 (1980), 593–637, (Ch. 16)

Blau, Z. S. "Maternal Aspirations, Socialization, and Achievement of Boys and Girls in the Working Class," *Journal of Youth and Adolescence*, 1 (1972), 35–37. (Ch. 13)

Blewitt, P. "Word Meaning Acquisition in Young Children," in H. W. Reese (ed.), *Advances in Child Development and Behavior*. Vol. 17. New York: Academic Press, 1982, pp. 139–195. (Ch. 9)

Block, J. H. "Issues, Problems, and Pitfalls in Assessing Sex Differences: A Critical Review of *The Psychology of Sex Differences*," *Merrill-Palmer Quarterly*, 22 (1976), 283–308. (Ch. 15)

———. "Another Look at Sex Differentiation in the Socialization Behaviors of Mothers and Fathers," in J. Sherman and F. L. Denmark (eds.), *The Psychology of Women: Future Directions of Research*. New York: Psychological Dimensions, 1978. (Chs. 15, 16)

Bloom, B. S. *Developing Talent in Young People*. New York: Ballantine, 1985.

Bloom, K. "Eye Contact as a Setting Event for Infant Learning," *Journal of Experimental Child Psychology*, 17 (1974), 250–263. (Ch. 14)

Blurton-Jones, N. "Rough-and-Tumble Play Among Nursery School Children," in J. S. Bruner, A. Jolly, and K. Sylva (eds.), *Play—Its Role in Development and Evolution*. New York: Basic Books, 1976, pp. 352–363. (Ch. 14)

Boccia, M., and J. Campos. "Maternal Emotional Signalling: Its Effect on Infants' Reaction to Strangers." Paper presented at the biennial meeting of the Society for Research in Child Development. Detroit, April 1983. (Ch. 12)

Boden, M. *Jean Piaget*. New York: Viking, 1979. (Ch. 11)

Boismier, J. D. "Visual Stimulation and Wake-Sleep Behavior in Human Neonates," *Development Psychobiology*, 10 (1977), 219–227. (Ch. 4)

Bolton, F. G., Jr. *The Pregnant Adolescent: Problems of Premature Parenthood*. Beverly Hills, Calif.: Sage, 1980. (Ch. 3)

Bond, E. A. *Tenth-Grade Abilities and Achievements*. New York: Columbia University Teachers College, 1940. (Ch. 11)

Bonney, M. E. "Values of Sociometric Studies in the Classroom," *Sociometry*, 6 (1943), 251–254. (Ch. 14)

Borke, H. "Piaget's Mountains Revisited: Changes in the Egocentric Landscape," *Developmental Psychology*, 14 (1975), 240–243. (Ch. 17)

Bornstein, M. H. "Psychological Studies of Color Perception in Human Infants: Habituation, Discrimination and Categorization, Recognition, and Conceptualization," in L. P. Lipsitt and C. K. Rovee-Collier (eds.), *Advances in Infancy Research*. Vol. 1. Norwood, N. J.: Ablex, 1981, pp. 1–40. (Ch. 7)

Borstelmann, L. J. "Children Before Psychology: Ideas About Children from Antiquity to the Late 1800s," in P. H. Mussen (ed.), *Handbook of Child Psychology*. 4th ed. Vol. 1: W. Kessen (ed.), *History, Theory, and Methods*. New York: Wiley, 1983, pp. 1–40. (Ch. 1)

Botvin, G. J., and F. B. Murray. "The Efficacy of Peer Modeling and Social Conflict in the Acquisition of Conservation," *Child Development*, 46 (1975), 796–799. (Ch. 10)

Bower, T. G. R. *The Perceptual World of the Child*. Cambridge, Mass.: Harvard University Press, 1977. (Ch. 7)

———, J. M. Broughton, and M. K. Moore. "Infant Responses to Approaching Objects: An Indicator of Responses to Distal Variables," *Perception and Psychophysics*, 9 (1971), 193–196. (Ch. 4)

Bowerman, M. "Systematizing Semantic Knowledge Changes Over Time in the Child's Organization of Word Meaning," *Child Development*, 49 (1978), 977–987. (Ch. 9)

———. "Starting to Talk Worse: Clues to Language Acquisition from Children's Late Speech Errors," in S. Strauss (ed.), *U-Shaped Behavioral Growth*. New York: Academic Press, 1982, pp. 101–145. (Ch. 9)

Bowes, W. A., Y. Brackbill, E. Conway, and A. Steinschneider. "The Effects of Obstetrical Medication on Fetus and Infant," *Monographs of the Society for Research in Child Development*, 35 (1970), whole no. 137. (Ch. 3)

Bowlby, J. *Attachment and Loss*. Vol. 1: *Attachment*. New York: Basic Books, 1969. (Chs. 1, 12)

———. *Attachment and Loss*. Vol. 2: *Separation*. New York: Basic Books, 1973. (Ch. 12)

Brackbill, Y. "Obstetrical Medication and Infant Behavior," in J. D. Osofsky (ed.), *Handbook of Infant Development*. New York: Wiley-Interscience, 1979, pp. 76–125. (Chs. 3, 4)

———, G. Adams, D. Crowell, and L. Gray. "Arousal Level in Neonates and Preschool Children under Continuous Auditory Stimulation," *Journal of Experimental Child Psychology*, 4 (1966), 178–188. (Ch. 4)

Braddick, O., J. Atkinson, J. French, and H. C. Howland. "A Photorefractive Study of Infant Accommodation," *Vision Research*, 19 (1979), 1319–1330. (Ch. 4)

Bradley, R. H., and B. M. Caldwell. "The Relation of Infants' Home Environments to Mental Test Performance at Fifty-Four Months: A Follow-Up Study," *Child Development*, 47 (1976), 1171–1174. (Ch. 11)

———, and ———. "The Relation of Infants' Home Environments to Achievement Test Performance in First Grade: A Follow-Up Study," *Child Development*, 55 (1984), 803–809. (Ch. 11)

Braine, M. D. S. "Children's First Word Combinations," *Monographs of the Society for Research in Child Development*, 41 (1976), whole no. 164. (Ch. 9)

———, and B. Rumain. "Logical Reasoning," in P. H. Mussen (ed.), *Handbook of Child Psychology*. 4th ed. Vol. 3: J. H. Flavell and E. M. Markman (eds.), *Cognitive Devel-*

opment. New York: Wiley, 1983, pp. 263–340. (Ch. 10)

Brainerd, C. J. "Feedback, Rule Knowledge, and Conservation Learning," *Child Development*, 48 (1977), 401–411. (Ch. 10)

——. *Piaget's Theory of Intelligence*. Englewood Cliffs, N. J.: Prentice-Hall, 1978. (Ch. 10)

——. "Young Children's Mental Arithmetic Errors: A Working-Memory Analysis," *Child Development*, 54 (1983), 812–830. (Ch. 10)

Bransford, J. D., B. S. Stein, T. S. Shelton, and R. A. Owings. "Cognition and Adaptation: The Importance of Learning to Learn," in J. Harvey (ed.), *Cognition, Social Behavior, and the Environment*. Hillsdale, N. J.: Lawrence Erlbaum Associates, 1981. (Ch. 8)

Brazelton, T. B. *Neonatal Behavioral Assessment Scale*. Philadelphia: Lippincott, 1973. (Ch. 3)

Bretherton, I., and M. Beeghly. "Talking about Internal States: The Acquisition of an Explicit Theory of Mind," *Developmental Psychology*, 18 (1982), 906–921. (Ch. 17)

Briars, D., and R. S. Siegler. "A Featural Analysis of Preschoolers' Counting Knowledge," *Developmental Psychology*, 20 (1984), 607–618. (Ch. 10)

Bridger, W. H. "Sensory Habituation and Discrimination in the Human Neonate," *American Journal of Psychiatry*, 117 (1961), 991–996. (Ch. 4)

Bridges, K. M. "Emotional Development in Early Infancy," *Child Development*, 3 (1932), 324–341. (Ch. 12)

Broadbent, D. E. "The Role of Auditory Localization in Attention and Memory Span," *Journal of Experimental Psychology*, 47 (1954), 191–196. (Ch. 1)

Brody, L. R., P. R. Zelazo, and H. Chaika. "Habituation-Dishabituation to Speech in the Neonate," *Developmental Psychology*, 20 (1984), 114–119. (Ch. 4)

Brodzinsky, D. M., L. M. Singer, and A. M. Braff. "Children's Understanding of Adoption," *Child Development*, 55 (1984), 869–878. (Ch. 2)

Bronfenbrenner, U. *Two Worlds of Childhood: U.S. and U.S.S.R.* New York: Russell Sage Foundation, 1970. (Chs. 12, 13, 14)

——. *The Ecology of Human Development*. Cambridge, Mass.: Harvard University Press, 1979a. (Ch. 2)

——. "Is Early Intervention Effective? Facts and Principles of Early Intervention: A Summary," in A. M. Clarke and A. D. B. Clarke (eds.), *Early Experience: Myth and Evidence*. New York: Free Press, 1979b, pp. 247–256. (Ch. 12)

——, W. F. Alvarez, and C. R. Henderson, Jr. "Working and Watching: Maternal Employment Status and Parents' Perceptions of Their Three-Year-Old Children," *Child Development*, 55 (1984), 1362–1378. (Ch. 13)

Brooks-Gunn, J., and W. S. Matthews. *He & She: How Children Develop Their Sex Role Identity*. Englewood Cliffs, N. J.: Prentice-Hall, 1979. (Ch. 15)

——, and D. N. Ruble. "The Development of Menstrual-Related Beliefs and Behaviors During Early Adolescence," *Child Development*, 53 (1982), 1567–1577. (Ch. 15)

Brown, A. L., J. D. Bransford, R. A. Ferrara, and J. C. Campione. "Learning, Remembering, and Understanding," in P. H. Mussen (ed.), *Handbook of Child Psychology*. 4th ed. Vol. 3: J. H. Flavell and E. M. Markman (eds.), *Cognitive Development*. New York: Wiley, 1983, pp. 77–166. (Chs. 8, 10)

Brown, R. *A First Language: The Early Stages*. Cambridge, Mass.: Harvard University Press, 1973. (Ch. 9)

——. Introduction to *Talking to Children: Language Input and Acquisition*, C. Snow and C. Ferguson (eds.). New York: Cambridge University Press, 1977, pp. 1–27. (Ch. 9)

——. "The Maintenance of Conversation," in D. R. Olson (ed.), *The Social Foundations of Language and Thought*. New York: Norton, 1980, pp. 187–210. (Ch. 9)

——, C. Cazden, and U. Bellugi-Klima. "The Child's Grammar from I to III," in J. P. Hill (ed.), *Minnesota Symposia on Child Psychology*. Vol. 2. Minneapolis: University of Minnesota Press, 1968, pp. 28–73. (Ch. 9)

——, and C. Hanlon. "Derivational Complexity and Order of Acquisition in Child Speech," in J. R. Hayes (ed.), *Cognition and the Development of Language*. New York: Wiley, 1970. (Ch. 9)

Brozoski, T. J., R. M. Brown, H. E. Rosvold, and P. S. Goldman. "Cognitive Deficit Caused by Regional Depletion of Dopamine in Prefrontal Cortex of Rhesus Monkey," *Science*, 205 (1979), 929–932. (Ch. 6)

Brück, K. "Temperature Regulation in the Newborn Infant," *Biologia neonatorum*, 3 (1961), 65–119. (Ch. 4)

Bruner, J. S. "The Course of Cognitive Growth," *American Psychologist*, 19 (1964), 1–15. (Ch. 9)

——. "Nature and Uses of Immaturity," *American Psychologist*, 27 (1972), 687–708. (Chs. 1, 6, 14)

——. *Beyond the Information Given*. New York: Norton, 1973. (Ch. 8)

——. "The Social Context of Language Acquisition." The Witkin Memorial Lecture. Presented at Educational Testing Service. Princeton, N. J. May 1980. (Ch. 9)

——. "Intention in the Structure of Action and Interaction," in L. P. Lipsitt and C. K. Rovee-Collier (eds.), *Advances in Infancy Research*. Vol. 1. Norwood, N. J.: Ablex, 1981, pp. 41–56. (Ch. 9)

——. *Child's Talk: Learning to Use Language*. New York: Norton, 1983a. (Ch. 9)

——. *In Search of Mind*. New York: Harper & Row, 1983b. (Ch. 1)

——, R. R. Olver, and P. M. Greenfield. *Studies in Cognitive Growth*. New York: Wiley, 1966. (Ch. 8)

Bryan, J. H. "Children's Cooperation and Helping Behaviors," in E. M. Hetherington (ed.), *Review of Child Development Research*. Vol. 5. Chicago: University of Chicago Press, 1975, pp. 127–182. (Ch. 16)

Bryant, B. K. "Sibling Relationships in Middle Childhood," in M. E. Lamb and B. Sutton-Smith (eds.), *Sibling Relationships: Their Nature and Significance Across the Lifespan*. Hillsdale, N. J.: Lawrence Erlbaum Associates, 1982, pp. 87–122. (Ch. 13)

Bryant, P. E. *Perception and Understanding in Young Children*. New York: Basic Books, 1974. (Ch. 7)

——, P. Jones, V. C. Claxton, and G. M. Perkins. "Recognition of Shapes Across Modalities by Infants," *Nature*, 240 (1972), 303–304. (Ch. 7)

——, and T. Trabasso. "Transitive Inferences and Memory in Young Children," *Nature*, 232 (1971), 456–458. (Ch. 10)

Bryden, M. P. "Strategy Effects in the Assessment of Hemispheric Asymmetry," in G. Underwood (ed.), *Strategies of Information Processing*. London: Academic Press, 1978. (Ch. 6)

Bullinger, A., and J.-F. Chatillon. "Recent Theory and Research of the Genevan School," in P. H. Mussen (ed.), *Handbook of Child Psychology*. 4th ed. Vol. 3: J. H. Flavell and E. M. Markman (eds.), *Cognitive Development*. New York: Wiley, 1983, pp. 231–262. (Ch. 10)

Bullock, M. "Animism in Childhood Thinking: A New Look at an Old Question," *Developmental Psychology*, 21 (1985), 217–225. (Ch. 10)

——, and R. Gelman. "Preschool Children's Assumptions About Cause and Effect: Temporal Ordering," *Child Development*, 50 (1979), 89–96. (Ch. 10)

Bullough, V. L. "Age at Menarche: A Misunderstanding," *Science*, 213 (1981), 365–366. (Ch. 5)

Burgess, R. L., and R. D. Conger. "Family Interaction in Abusive, Neglectful, and Normal Families," *Child Development*, 49 (1978), 1163–1173. (Ch. 13)

Burton, R. V. "Honesty and Dishonesty," in T. Lickona

(ed.), *Moral Development and Behavior*. New York: Holt, Rinehart and Winston, 1976, pp. 173–197. (Ch. 16)

Busch-Rossnagel, N. A., and A. K. Vance. "The Impact of Schools on Social and Emotional Development," in B. B. Wolman (ed.), *Handbook of Developmental Psychology*. Englewood Cliffs, N. J.: Prentice-Hall, 1982, pp. 452–467, (Ch. 2)

Buss, D. M., J. H. Block, and J. Block. "Preschool Activity Level: Personality Correlates and Developmental Implications," *Child Development*, 51 (1980), 401–408. (Ch. 4)

Butler, N. "Late Postnatal Consequences of Fetal Malnutrition," in M. Winick (ed.), *Current Concepts of Nutrition*. Vol. 2: *Nutrition and Fetal Development*. New York: Wiley-Interscience, 1974. (Chs. 3, 11)

Butterfield, E. C., and G. N. Siperstein. "Influences of Contingent Auditory Stimulation upon Non-Nutritional Suckle," in *Proceedings of the Third Symposium on Oral Sensation and Perception: The Mouth of the Infant*. Springfield, Ill.: Charles C. Thomas, 1974. (Ch. 9)

Butterworth, G. "Object Disappearance and Error in Piaget's Stage IV Task," *Journal of Experimental Child Psychology*, 23 (1977), 391–401. (Ch. 7)

Cairns, R. B. "The Emergence of Developmental Psychology," in P. H. Mussen (ed.), *Handbook of Child Psychology*. 4th ed. Vol. 1: W. Kessen (ed.), *History, Theory, and Methods*. New York: Wiley, 1983, pp. 41–102. (Ch. 1)

Campbell, J. D., and M. R. Yarrow. "Perceptual and Behavioral Correlates of Social Effectiveness," *Sociometry*, 24 (1961), 1–20. (Ch. 14)

Campione, J. C., and A. L. Brown. "Memory and Metamemory Development in Educable Retarded Children," in R. V. Kail, Jr., and J. W. Hagen (eds.), *Perspectives on the Development of Memory and Cognition*. Hillsdale, N. J.: Lawrence Erlbaum Associates, 1978, pp. 73–96. (Ch. 1)

———, A. L. Brown, R. A. Ferrara, and N. R. Bryant. "The Zone of Proximal Development: Implications for Individual Differences and Learning," in B. Rogoff and J. V. Wertsch (eds.), *New Directions for Child Development*. Vol. 23: *Children's Learning in the "Zone of Proximal Development."* San Francisco: Jossey-Bass, 1984, pp. 77–92. (Chs. 1, 11)

Campos, J. J. "Heart Rates: A Sensitive Tool for the Study of Emotional Development," in L. Lipsitt (ed.), *Developmental Psychobiology: The Significance of Infancy*. Hillsdale, N. J.: Lawrence Erlbaum Associates, 1976. (Ch. 7)

———, K. C. Barrett, M. E. Lamb, H. H. Goldsmith, and C. Stenberg. "Socioemotional Development," in P. H. Mussen (ed.), *Handbook of Child Psychology*. 4th ed. Vol. 2: M. M. Haith and J. J. Campos (eds.), *Infancy and Developmental Psychobiology*. New York: Wiley, 1983, pp. 783–915. (Chs. 4, 12, 17)

———, S. Hiatt, D. Ramsay, C. Henderson, and M. Svejda. "The Emergence of Fear on the Visual Cliff," in M. Lewis and L. Rosenblum (eds.), *The Origins of Affect*. New York: Plenum Press, 1978. (Ch. 7)

———, and C. Stenberg. "Perception, Appraisal, and Emotion: The Onset of Social Referencing," in M. E. Lamb and L. R. Sherrod (eds.), *Infant Social Cognition: Empirical and Theoretical Considerations*. Hillsdale, N. J.: Lawrence Erlbaum Associates, 1981, pp. 273–314. (Ch. 12)

Cantor, J. H., and C. C. Spiker. "The Effects of Introtacts on Hypothesis Testing in Kindergarten and First-Grade Children," *Child Development*, 50 (1979), 1110–1120. (Ch. 10)

Carey, S. "Are Children Little Scientists with False Theories of Amounts?" Doctoral dissertation. Harvard University, 1972. (Ch. 9)

———. "Cognitive Competence," in K. Connolly and J. S. Bruner (eds.), *The Growth of Competence*. New York: Academic Press, 1974, pp. 169–193. (Ch. 10)

———, and R. Diamond. "From Piecemeal to Configurational Representation in Faces," *Science*, 195 (1977), 312–315. (Ch. 8)

Carlsmith, L. "Effect of Early Father Absence on Scholastic Aptitude," *Harvard Educational Review*, 34 (Winter 1964), 3–21. (Ch. 13)

Caron, A. J., R. F. Caron, and V. R. Carlson. "Do Infants See Objects or Retinal Images? Shape Constancy Revisited," *Infant Behavior and Development*, 1 (1978), 229–243. (Ch. 7)

———, ———, and ———. "Infant Perception of the Invariant Shape of Objects Varying in Slant," *Child Development*, 50 (1979), 716–721. (Ch. 7)

Carpenter, C. J., and A. Huston-Stein. "Activity Structure and Sex-typed Behavior in Preschool Children," *Child Development*, 51 (1980), 862–872. (Ch. 2)

Carr, S., J. Dabbs, and T. Carr. "Mother-Infant Attachment: The Importance of the Mother's Visual Field," *Child Development*, 46, (175), 331–338. (Ch. 12)

Carroll, J. "Psychometric Tests as Cognitive Tests: A New 'Structure of Intellect,' " in L. B. Resnick (ed.), *The Nature of Intelligence*. Hillsdale, N. J.: Lawrence Erlbaum Associates, 1976, pp. 27–56. (Ch. 11)

Carroll, J. J., and M. S. Steward. "The Role of Cognitive Development in Children's Understandings of Their Own Feelings," *Child Development*, 55 (1984), 1486–1492. (Ch. 17)

Carter, G. L., and M. Kinsbourne. "The Ontogeny of Right Cerebral Lateralization of Special Mental Set," *Developmental Psychology*, 15 (1979), 241–245. (Ch. 6)

Case, R., D. M. Kurland, and J. Goldberg. "Operational Efficiency and the Growth of Short-Term Memory Span," *Journal of Experimental Child Psychology*, 33 (1982), 386–404. (Ch. 8)

Cattell, P. *The Measurements of Intelligence of Infants and Young Children*. New York: Psychological Corporation, 1940. (Ch. 5)

Cattell, R. B. "Are IQ Tests Intelligent?" *Psychology Today*, 1 (March 1968), 56–62. (Ch. 11)

Cavanaugh, J. C., and M. Perlmutter. "Metamemory: A Critical Examination," *Child Development*, 53 (1982), 11–28. (Ch. 8)

Cermak, L. S., and F. I. M. Craik (eds.). *Levels of Processing in Human Memory*. Hillsdale, N. J.: Lawrence Erlbaum Associates, 1979. (Ch. 8)

Chabon, I. *Awake and Aware: Participation in Childbirth through Psychoprophylaxis*. New York: Delacorte, 1966. (Ch. 3)

Chan, G. M., N. Ronald, P. Slater, J. Hollis, and M. R. Thomas. "Decreased Bone Mineral Status in Lactating Adolescent Mothers," *Journal of Pediatrics*, 101 (1982), 767–770. (Ch. 3)

Chaplin, J. P., and T. S. Krawiec. *Systems and Theories of Psychology*. 3rd ed. New York: Holt, Rinehart and Winston, 1974. (Ch. 11)

Charles, D. C. "Historical Antecedents of Life-Span Developmental Psychology," in L. R. Goulet and P. B. Baltes (eds.), *Life-Span Developmental Psychology: Research and Theory*. New York: Academic Press, 1970, pp. 24–52. (Ch. 1)

Charlesworth, R., and W. W. Hartup. "Positive Social Reinforcement in the Nursery School Peer Group," *Child Development*, 38 (1967), 993–1002. (Ch. 14)

Charlesworth, W. R. "Human Intelligence as Adaptation: An Ethological Approach," in L. B. Resnick (ed.), *The Nature of Intelligence*. Hillsdale, N. J.: Lawrence Erlbaum Associates, 1976, pp. 147–168. (Ch. 11)

Chaudhari, N., and W. E. Hahn. "Genetic Expression in

the Developing Brain," *Science*, 220 (1983), 924–928. (Ch. 6)

Chi, M. T. H. "Knowledge Structure and Memory Development," in R. S. Siegler (ed.), *Children's Thinking: What Develops?* Hillsdale, N. J.: Lawrence Erlbaum Associates, 1978, pp. 73–96. (Chs. 1, 8)

———. "Knowledge Development and Memory Performance," in M. Friedman, J. P. Das, and N. O'Connor (eds.), *Intelligence and Learning*. New York: Plenum Press, in press. (Ch. 1)

———, and R. D. Koeske. "Network Representation of a Child's Dinosaur Knowledge," *Developmental Psychology*, 19 (1983), 29–39. (Ch. 8)

Chomsky, C. *Acquisition of Syntax in Children from 5 to 10.* Cambridge, Mass.: MIT Press, 1969. (Ch. 9)

Chomsky, N. *Language and Mind.* Enl. ed. New York: Harcourt Brace Jovanovich, 1972. (Ch. 9)

———. *Reflections on Language.* New York: Pantheon, 1975. (Ch. 9)

———. *Language and Responsibility.* New York: Pantheon, 1979. (Ch. 9)

Churchill, J. A., and H. W. Berendes. "Intelligence of Children Whose Mothers Had Acetonuria During Pregnancy," in *Perinatal Factors Affecting Human Development, Proceedings.* Pan American Health Organization. Scientific Publication No. 185, 1969. (Ch. 11)

Cicirelli, V. G. "Sibling Influences Throughout the Lifespan," in M. E. Lamb and B. Sutton-Smith (eds.), *Sibling Relationships.* Hillsdale, N. J.: Lawrence Erlbaum Associates, 1982, pp. 267–284. (Ch. 13)

Cioffi, J., and G. L. Kandel. "Laterality of Sterognostic Accuracy of Children for Words, Shapes, and Bigrams: A Sex Difference for Bigrams," *Science*, 204 (1979), 1432–1434. (Ch. 6)

Clark, E. V. "What's in a Word? On the Child's Acquisition of Semantics in His First Language," in T. E. Moore (ed.), *Cognitive Development and the Acquisition of Language.* New York: Academic Press, 1973, pp. 65–110. (Ch. 9)

———. "Language Change during Language Acquisition," in M. E. Lamb and A. L. Brown (eds.), *Advances in Developmental Psychology.* Vol. 2. Hillsdale, N. J.: Lawrence Erlbaum Associates, 1982, pp. 171–195. (Ch. 9)

———. "Meanings and Concepts," in P. H. Mussen (ed.), *Handbook of Child Psychology.* 4th ed. Vol. 3: J. H. Flavell and E. M. Markman (eds.), *Cognitive Development.* New York: Wiley, 1983, pp. 787–840. (Ch. 9)

Clarke, A. D. B., and A. M. Clarke. "Studies in Natural Settings," in A. M. Clarke and A. D. B. Clarke (eds.), *Early Experience: Myth and Evidence.* New York: Free Press, 1979, pp. 69–96. (Ch. 12)

Clarke-Stewart, K. A. "Recasting the Lone Stranger," in J. Glick and K. A. Clarke-Stewart (eds.), *The Development of Social Understanding.* New York: Gardner Press, 1978, pp. 109–176. (Ch. 12)

———. *Day Care.* Cambridge, Mass.: Harvard University Press, 1982. (Ch. 13)

———, and G. G. Fein. "Early Childhood Programs," in P. H. Mussen (ed.), *Handbook of Child Psychology.* 4th ed. Vol. 2: M. M. Haith and J. J. Campos (eds.), *Infancy and Developmental Psychobiology.* New York: Wiley, 1983, pp. 917–1000. (Chs. 12, 13)

———, and C. M. Hevey. "Longitudinal Relations in Repeated Observations of Mother-Child Interaction from 1 to 2½ Years," *Developmental Psychology*, 17 (1981), 127–145. (Ch. 15)

Clausen, J. A. "Men's Occupational Careers in the Middle Years," in D. H. Eichorn, J. A. Clausen, N. Haan, M. P. Honzik, and P. H. Mussen (eds.), *Present and Past in Middle Life.* New York: Academic Press, 1981, pp. 321–351. (Ch. 11)

Clement, J., L. J. Schweinhart, W. S. Barnett, A. S. Epstein, and D. P. Weikart. *Changed Lives: The Effects of the Perry Preschool Program on Youths Through Age 19.* Ypsilanti, Mich.: High/Scope Press, 1984. (Ch. 11)

Clifton, R. K., B. A. Morrongiello, J. W. Kulig, and J. M. Dowd. "Newborns' Orientation toward Sound: Possible Implications for Cortical Development," *Child Development*, 52 (1981), 833–838. (Chs. 4, 6)

———, ———, ———, ———. "Developmental Changes in Auditory Localization in Infancy," in R. Aslin, J. Alberts, and M. Peterson (eds.), *The Development of Perception: Psychobiological Perspectives.* Vol. 1. *Audition, Somatic Perception, and the Chemical Senses.* New York: Academic Press, 1982. (Ch. 4)

Clingempeel, W. G. "Quasi-Kin Relationships and Marital Quality in Stepfather Family," *Journal of Personality and Social Psychology*, 41 (1981), 890–901. (Ch. 13)

Cloutier, R., and M. L. Goldschmid. "Individual Differences in the Development of Formal Reasoning," *Child Development*, 47 (1976), 1097–1102. (Ch. 10)

Coates, B., and W. W. Hartup. "Age and Verbalization in Observational Learning," *Developmental Psychology*, 1 (1969), 556–562. (Ch. 9)

Cohen, E., M. Perlmutter, and N. A. Myers. "Memory for Location of Multiple Stimuli by 2- to 4-Year-Olds." Unpublished manuscript. University of Massachusetts, 1977. (Ch. 8)

Cohen, L. B., J. S. DeLoache, and M. S. Strauss. "Infant Visual Perception," in J. D. Osofsky (ed.), *Handbook of Infant Development.* New York: Wiley-Interscience, 1979, pp. 393–438. (Ch. 7)

Cohen, S., D. C. Glass, and J. E. Singer. "Apartment Noise, Auditory Discrimination, and Reading Ability," *Journal of Experimental Social Psychology*, 9 (1973), 407–422. (Ch. 2)

Coie, J. D., and G. Krehbiel. "Effects of Academic Tutoring on the Social Status of Low-Achieving, Socially Rejected Children," *Child Development*, 55 (1984), 1465–1478. (Ch. 14)

Colby, A., L. Kohlberg, J. Gibbs, and M. Lieberman. "A Longitudinal Study of Moral Judgment," *Monographs of the Society for Research in Child Development*, 48 (1983), whole no. 200. (Ch. 16)

Cole, M. "How Education Affects the Mind," *Human Nature*, 1 (April 1978), 50–59. (Chs. 1, 10)

———, and S. Scribner. "Cross-Cultural Studies of Memory and Cognition," in R. V. Kail, Jr., and J. W. Hagen (eds.), *Perspectives on the Development of Memory and Cognition.* Hillsdale, N. J.: Lawrence Erlbaum Associates, 1977, pp. 239–271. (Ch. 8)

———, and ———. Introduction to *Mind in Society*, by L. S. Vygotsky. Cambridge, Mass.: Harvard University Press, 1978, pp. 1–14. (Ch. 1)

Collins, W. A. "Children's Comprehension of Television Content," in E. Wartella (ed.), *Children Communicating.* Beverly Hills, Calif.: Sage, 1979, pp. 21–52. (Ch. 17)

———. "Schemata for Understanding Television," in H. Kelly and H. Gardner (eds.), *New Directions for Child Development.* No. 13: *Viewing Children Through Television.* San Francisco: Jossey-Bass, 1981, pp. 31–46. (Ch. 15)

———, T. V. Berndt, and V. I. Hess. "Observational Learning of Motives and Consequences for Television Aggression: A Developmental Study." *Child Development*, 45 (1974), 799–802. (Ch. 16)

———, H. Wellman, A. Keniston, and S. Westby. "Age-Related Aspects of Comprehension and Inferences from a Televised Dramatic Narrative," *Child Development*, 49 (1978), 389–399. (Ch. 17)

———, and S. A. Zimmerman. "Convergent and Divergent Social Cues: Effects of Televised Aggression on Children," *Communication Research*, 2 (1975), 331–346. (Ch. 16)

Columbia Broadcasting System. *A Study of the Messages Received by Children Who Viewed an Episode of Fat Albert and the Cosby Kids*. New York: CBS, 1974. (Ch. 16)

Condry, J. C., and S. L. Dyer. "Behavioral and Fantasy Measures of Fear of Success in Children," *Child Development*, 48 (1977), 1417–1425. (Ch. 14)

Conel, J. L. R. *The Postnatal Development of the Human Cerebral Cortex*. 7 vols. Cambridge, Mass.: Harvard University Press, 1939–1963. (Ch. 6)

Connell, D. B., J. I. Layzer, and B. D. Goodson. "National Study of Day Care Centers for Infants: Findings and Implications." Paper presented at the Annual Meeting of the American Psychological Association. New York, September 1979. (Ch. 13)

Connelly, J. A., and A.-B. Doyle. "Social Fantasy Play and Social Competence," *Developmental Psychology*, 20 (1984), 797–806. (Ch. 14)

Connor, J. M., L. A. Serbin, and M. Schackman. "Sex Differences in Children's Response to Training on a Visual-Spatial Task," *Developmental Psychology*, 13 (1977), 293–294. (Ch. 6)

Cook, M., and R. Birch. "Infant Perception of the Shapes of Tilted Plane Forms," *Infant Behavior and Development*, 7 (1984), 389–402. (Ch. 7)

———, J. Field, and K. Griffiths. "The Perception of Solid Form in Early Infancy," *Child Development*, 49 (1978), 866–869. (Ch. 7)

Cooke, R. A. "The Ethics and Regulation of Research Involving Children," in B. B. Wolman (ed.), *Handbook of Developmental Psychology*. Englewood Cliffs, N. J.: Prentice-Hall, 1982, pp. 149–172. (Ch. 2)

Cooper, H. M. "Pygmalion Grows Up: A Model for Teacher Expectation, Communication and Performance Influence," *Review of Educational Research*, 49 (1979), 389–410. (Ch. 14)

Cordua, G. D., K. O. McGraw, and R. S. Drabman. "Doctor or Nurse: Children's Perceptions of Sex Typed Occupations," *Child Development*, 50 (1979), 590–593. (Ch. 15)

Coren, S. "Development of Ocular Dominance," *Developmental Psychology*, 10 (1974), 302. (Ch. 6)

———, C. Porac, and P. Duncan. "Lateral Preference Behaviors in Preschool Children and Young Adults," *Child Development*, 52 (1981), 443–450. (Ch. 6)

Costanzo, P. R., and M. E. Shaw. "Conformity as a Function of Age Level," *Child Development*, 37 (1966), 967–975. (Ch. 14)

Courchesne, E., L. Ganz, and A. M. Norcia. "Event-Related Brain Potentials to Human Faces in Infants," *Child Development*, 52 (1981), 804–811. (Ch. 6)

Cowan, W. M. "The Development of the Brain," *Scientific American*, 241 (September 1979), 88–133. (Ch. 3)

Cowen, E. L., A. Pederson, H. Babijian, L. D. Izzo, and M. A. Trost. "Long-Term Follow-up of Early Detected Vulnerable Children," *Journal of Clinical and Consulting Psychology*, 41 (1973), 438–446. (Ch. 14)

Cravioto, J., and E. Delicardie. "Mental Performance in School Age Children," *American Journal of Diseases of Children*, 120 (1970), 404. (Ch. 11)

Cravioto, J., and B. Robles. "Evolution of Adaptive and Motor Behavior during Rehabilitation from Kwashiorkor," *American Journal of Orthopsychiatry*, 35 (1965), 449. (Ch. 11)

Crook, C. K. "The Organization and Control of Infant Sucking," in H. W. Reese and L. P. Lipsitt (eds.), *Advances in Child Development and Behavior*. Vol. 14. New York: Academic Press, 1979, pp. 209–253. (Ch. 4)

———, and L. P. Lipsitt. "Neonatal Nutritive Sucking: Effects of Taste Stimulation upon Sucking Rhythm and

Heart Rate," *Child Development*, 47 (1976), 518–522. (Ch. 4)

Cummings, J. "Breakup of Black Family Imperils Gains of Decades," *The New York Times*, November 20, 1983, A1+. (Ch. 13)

Cummins, R. A., P. J. Livesey, J. G. M. Evans, and R. N. Walsh. "Mechanism of Brain Growth by Environmental Stimulation," *Science*, 205 (1979), 522. (Ch. 6)

Curtiss, S. R. *Genie: A Psycholinguistic Study of a Modern-Day 'Wild Child.'* New York: Academic Press, 1977. (Ch. 9)

Daniels, P., and K. Weingarten. *Sooner or Later: The Timing of Parenthood in Adult Lives*. New York: Norton, 1982. (Ch. 13)

Darley, J. M., E. C. Klosson, and M. P. Zanna. "Intentions and Their Contexts in the Moral Judgment of Children," *Child Development*, 49 (1978), 66–74. (Ch. 16)

Darling, R. B. "The Birth Defective Child and the Crisis of Parenthood: Redefining the Situation," in E. J. Callahan and K. A. McCluskey (eds.), *Life-Span Developmental Psychology: Nonnormative Life Events*. New York: Academic Press, 1983, pp. 115–147. (Ch. 5)

Darvill, D., and J. A. Cheyne. "Sequential Analysis of Responses to Aggression: Age and Sex Effects." Paper presented at the meeting of the Society for Research in Child Development. Boston, April 1981. (Ch. 16)

Darwin, C. *The Expression of the Emotions in Man and Animals*. New York: The Philosophical Library, 1955 [orig. pub. 1872]. (Ch. 1)

Daurio, S. P. "Educational Enrichment versus Acceleration: A Review of the Literature," in W. C. George, S. J. Cohn, and J. C. Stanley (eds.), *Educating the Gifted: Acceleration and Enrichment*. Baltimore: Johns Hopkins University Press, 1979, pp. 13–63. (Ch. 10)

Davidson, R. J., and N. Fox. "Asymmetrical Brain Activity Discriminates between Positive versus Negative Affective Stimuli in Ten-Month-Old Infants," *Science*, 218 (1982), 1235–1236. (Ch. 6)

Davis, J. M., and C. K. Rovee-Collier. "Alleviated Forgetting of a Learned Contingency in 8-Week-Old Infants," *Developmental Psychology*, 19 (1983), 353–365. (Ch. 7)

Dawe, H. C. "An Analysis of Two Hundred Quarrels of Preschool Children," *Child Development*, 5 (1934), 139–157. (Ch. 16)

Day, M. C. "Developmental Trends in Visual Scanning," in H. W. Reese (ed.), *Advances in Child Development and Behavior*. Vol. 10. New York: Academic Press, 1975, pp. 154–193. (Ch. 8)

Day, R. H., and B. E. McKenzie. "Infant Perception of the Invariant Size of Approaching and Receding Objects," *Developmental Psychology*, 17 (1981), 670–677. (Ch. 7)

Deaux, K. "Ahhhh, She Was Just Lucky," *Psychology Today*, 10 (March 1976), 70–75. (Ch. 14)

Debakan, A. *Neurology of Infancy*. Baltimore: Williams and Wilkins, 1959. (Ch. 5)

DeCasper, A. J., and W. P. Fifer. "Of Human Bonding: Infants Prefer Their Mothers' Voices," *Science*, 208 (1980), 1174–1176. (Chs. 4, 12)

———, and A. D. Sigafoos. "The Intrauterine Heartbeat: A Potent Reinforcer for Newborns," *Infant Behavior and Development*, 6 (1983), 19–26. (Ch. 4)

Delia, J. G., and B. J. O'Keefe. "Constructivism: The Development of Communication in Children," in E. Wartella (ed.), *Children Communicating*. Beverly Hills, Calif.: Sage, 1979, pp. 157–185. (Ch. 9)

DeLoache, J. S., M. W. Rissman, and L. B. Cohen. "An Investigation of the Attention-Getting Process in Infants," *Infant Behavior and Development*, 1 (1978), 11–25. (Ch. 7)

———, S. Sugarman, and A. Brown. "Self-Correction Strategies in Early Cognitive Development." Paper presented at the biennial meeting of the Society for Research in Child Development. Boston, April 1981. (Ch. 10)

deMause, L. (ed.), *The History of Childhood*. New York: Harper & Row, 1974. (Ch. 1)

Dement, W. "The Effect of Dream Deprivation," *Science*, 131 (1960), 1705–1707. (Ch. 4)

Demorest, A., C. Myers, E. Phelps, H. Gardner, and E. Winner. "Words Speak Louder Than Actions: Understanding Deliberately False Remarks," *Child Development*, 55 (1984), 1527–1534. (Ch. 17)

Denenberg, V. H. "Animal Studies on Developmental Determinants of Behavioral Adaptability," in O. J. Harvey (ed.), *Experience, Structure, and Adaptability*. New York: Springer, 1966. (Ch. 12)

———. "Stranger in a Strange Situation: Comments by a Comparative Psychologist," *Behavioral and Brain Sciences*, 7 (1984), 150–152. (Ch. 12)

Dennis, M. "Impaired Sensory and Motor Differentiation with Corpus Callosum Agenesis: A Lack of Callosal Inhibition During Ontogeny?" *Neuropsychologia*, 14 (1977), 455–459. (Ch. 6)

———. "Capacity and Strategy for Syntactic Comprehension after Left and Right Hemidecortication," *Brain and Language*, 10 (1980), 287–317. (Ch. 6)

Dennis, W. "Infant Development under Conditions of Restricted Practice and of Minimum Social Stimulation," *Genetic Psychology Monographs*, 23 (1941), 143–191. (Ch. 5)

———. "Causes of Retardation among Institutional Children: Iran," *Journal of Genetic Psychology*, 96 (1960), 47–59. (Ch. 5)

———, and P. Najarian. "Infant Development under Environmental Handicap," *Psychological Monographs*, 71 (1957), 436. (Ch. 5)

———, and Y. Sayegh. "The Effect of Supplementary Experiences upon the Behavioral Development of Infants in Institutions," *Child Development*, 36 (1965), 81–90. (Ch. 5)

Deutsch, M., and H. G. Gerard. "A Study of Normative and Informational Social Influence Upon Individual Judgment," *Journal of Abnormal and Social Psychology*, 51 (1955), 629–636. (Ch. 14)

deVilliers, J. G., and P. A. deVilliers. *Language Acquisition*. Cambridge, Mass.: Harvard University Press, 1978. (Ch. 9)

DeVries, R. "Constancy of Generic Identity in the Years Three to Six," *Monographs of the Society for Research in Child Development*, 34 (1969), whole no. 127. (Ch. 10)

Dick-Read, G. *Childbirth without Fear: The Principles and Practice of Natural Childbirth*. New York: Harper & Bros., 1944. (Ch. 3)

Diener, C. I., and C. S. Dweck. "An Analysis of Learned Helplessness: Continuous Changes in Performance, Strategy, and Achievement Cognitions Following Failure," *Journal of Personality and Social Psychology*, 36 (1978), 451–462. (Ch. 14)

Dion, K. K. "Young Children's Stereotyping of Facial Attractiveness," *Developmental Psychology*, 9 (1973), 183–188. (Ch. 14)

Division on Developmental Psychology of the American Psychological Association. "Ethical Standards for Research with Children," *Newsletter*, 1968, 1–3. (Ch. 2)

Dobbing, J. "Effects of Experimental Undernutrition on Development of the Nervous System," in N. S. Scrimshaw and J. E. Gordon (eds.), *Malnutrition, Learning, and Behavior*. Cambridge, Mass.: MIT Press, 1968, pp. 181–202. (Ch. 5)

Dodd, B. "Lip Reading in Infants: Attention to Speech Presented in and out of Synchrony," *Cognitive Psychology*, 11 (1979), 478–484. (Ch. 7)

Dodge, K. A. "Social Cognition and Children's Aggressive Behavior," *Child Development*, 51 (1980), 162–170. (Ch. 16)

———. "Behavioral Antecedents of Peer Rejection and Isolation." Paper presented at the meeting of the Society for Research in Child Development. Boston, April 1981. (Ch. 16)

———. "Social Information Processing Variables in the Development of Aggression and Altruism in Children," in C. Zahn-Waxler, M. Cummings, and M. Radke-Yarrow (eds.), *The Development of Altruism and Aggression: Social and Sociobiological Origins*. New York: Cambridge University Press, 1982. (Ch. 16)

———. "A Social Information Processing Model of Social Competence in Children," in M. Perlmutter (ed.), *Minnesota Symposia on Child Psychology*. Vol. 18. Hillsdale, N. J.: Lawrence Erlbaum Associates [in press]. (Ch. 17)

Dollard, J., and N. E. Miller. *Personality and Psychotherapy*. New York: McGraw-Hill, 1950. (Ch. 1)

———, L. W. Doob, N. E. Miller, O. H. Mowrer, and R. R. Sears. *Frustration and Aggression*. New Haven, Conn.: Yale University Press, 1939. (Ch. 16)

Donaldson, M. *Children's Minds*. New York: Norton, 1979. (Ch. 10)

———, and G. Balfour. "Less Is More: A Study of Language Comprehension in Children," *British Journal of Psychology*, 59 (1968), 461–472. (Ch. 9)

Douglas, V. I., and K. G. Peters. "Toward a Clearer Definition of the Attentional Deficit of Hyperactive Children," in G. A. Hale and M. Lewis (eds.), *Attention and Cognitive Development*. New York: Plenum Press, 1979, pp. 173–248. (Ch. 6)

Douvan, E. "Social Status and Success Strivings," *Journal of Abnormal and Social Psychology*, 52 (1956), 219–223. (Ch. 13)

———, and J. Adelson. *The Adolescent Experience*. New York: Wiley, 1966. (Ch. 14)

Doyle, A., J. Connolly, and L. Rivest. "The Effect of Playmate Familiarity on the Social Interactions of Young Children," *Child Development*, 51 (1980), 217–223. (Ch. 14)

Drabman, R. S., and M. H. Thomas. "Does Watching Violence on Television Cause Apathy?" *Pediatrics*, 57 (1976), 329–331. (Ch. 16)

Dubowitz, L. M. S., V. Dubowitz, and C. Goldberg. "Clinical Assessment of Gestational Age in the Newborn Infant," *Journal of Pediatrics*, 77 (1970), 1. (Ch. 3)

Dulit, E. "Adolescent Thinking *a la* Piaget: The Formal Stage," *Journal of Youth and Adolescence*, 1 (1972), 281–301. (Ch. 10)

Dunn, J. *Distress and Comfort*. Cambridge, Mass.: Harvard University Press, 1977. (Ch. 12)

———, and C. Kendrick. *Siblings: Love, Envy, and Understanding*. Cambridge, Mass.: Harvard University Press, 1982. (Ch. 12)

Dunphy, D. C. "The Social Structure of the Urban Adolescent Peer Groups," *Sociometry*, 26 (1963), 230–246. (Ch. 14)

Dweck, C. S., W. Davidson, S. Nelson, and B. Enna. "Sex Differences in Learned Helplessness. II: The Contingencies of Evaluative Feedback in the Classroom;" and "III: An Experimental Analysis," *Development Psychology*, 14 (1978), 268–276. (Ch. 14)

———, and E. S. Elliott. "Achievement Motivation," in P. H. Mussen (ed.), *Handbook of Child Psychology*. 4th ed. Vol. 4: E. M. Hetherington (ed.), *Socialization, Personality, and Social Development*. New York: Wiley, 1983, pp. 643–691. (Ch. 14)

———, and T. E. Goetz, "Attributions and Learned Helplessness," in J. W. Harvey, W. Ickes, and R. F. Kidd (eds.), *New Directions in Attribution Research*. Vol. 2. Hillsdale, N. J.: Lawrence Erlbaum Associates, 1977. (Ch. 14)

Dwyer, J., and J. Mayer. "Overfeeding and Obesity in Infants and Children," *Bibliotheca Nutritio et Dieta*. no. 18

(1973), 123–152. (Ch. 5)

Dyan-Hudson, R., and R. Van Dusen. "Food Sharing Among Young Children," *Ecology of Food and Nutrition*, 1 (1972), 319–324. (Ch. 16)

Dziadosz, G. M., and M. J. Schaller. "Acuity and Sighting Dominance in Children and Adults," *Developmental Psychology*, 13 (1977), 288. (Ch. 6)

Easterbrooks, M. A., and W. A. Goldberg. "Toddler Development in the Family: Impact of Father Involvement and Parenting," *Child Development*, 55 (1984), 740–752. (Ch. 12)

———, and M. E. Lamb. "Relationship Between Infant-Mother Attachment and Infant Competence in Initial Encounters with Peers," *Child Development*, 50 (1979), 380–387. (Chs. 13, 14)

Eccles-Parsons, J. "Biology, Experience and Sex Dimorphic Behaviors," in W. Gove and G. R. Carpenter (eds.), *The Fundamental Connection Between Nature and Nurture: A Review of the Evidence*. Lexington, Mass.: Lexington Books, 1982. (Ch. 15)

Eckerman, C. O., and H. L. Rheingold. "Infants' Exploratory Responses to Toys and People," *Developmental Psychology*, 10 (1974), 252–259. (Ch. 12)

Edelbrock, C., and A. I. Sugawara. "Acquisition of Sex-Typed Preferences in Preschool-Aged Children," *Developmental Psychology*, 14 (1978), 614–623. (Ch. 15)

Eder, R., C. Parks, C. Todd, and M. Perlmutter. "Effects of Mother-Child Interaction on Young Children's Memory." Paper presented at Infancy Meeting. New York, 1984. (Ch. 8)

Egeland, B., and E. A. Farber. "Infant-Mother Attachment: Factors Related to Its Development and Change Over Time," *Child Development*, 55 (1984), 753–771. (Ch. 12)

Ehrhardt, A. A., and S. W. Baker. "Hormonal Aberrations and Their Implications for the Understanding of Normal Sex Differentiation," in P. H. Mussen, J. J. Conger, and J. Kagan (eds.), *Basic and Contemporary Issues in Developmental Psychology*. New York: Harper & Row, 1975, pp. 113–121. (Ch. 15)

Ehrhardt, A. A., G. Grisanti, and E. A. McCauley. "Female-to-Male Transsexuals Compared to Lesbians: Behavioral Patterns of Childhood and Adolescent Development," *Archives of Sexual Behavior*, 8 (1979), 481–490. (Ch. 15)

Eichenwald, H. F., and P. C. Fry. "Nutrition and Learning," *Science*, 163 (1969), 644–648. (Ch. 5)

Eichorn, D. *Biological Correlates of Behavior*. Chicago: National Society for the Study of Education, 1963. (Ch. 15)

Eimas, P. D. "Auditory and Linguistic Processing of Cues for Place of Articulation by Infants," *Perception & Psychophysics*, 16 (1974), 513–521. (Ch. 9)

———. "Speech Perception in Early Infancy," in L. B. Cohen and P. Salapatek (eds.), *Infant Perception: From Sensation to Perception*. Vol. 2: *Perception of Space, Speech, and Sound*. New York: Academic Press, 1975, pp. 193–231. (Ch. 7)

Eisenberg, N. "The Development of Reasoning Regarding Prosocial Behavior," in N. Eisenberg (ed.), *The Development of Prosocial Behavior*. New York: Academic Press, 1982. (Ch. 16)

Eisenberg, R. B. "The Development of Hearing in Man: An Assessment of Current Status," *Journal of the American Speech and Hearing Association*, 12 (1970), 245–269. (Ch. 4)

———, E. J. Griffin, D. B. Coursin, and M. A. Hunter. "Auditory Behavior in the Human Neonate: A Preliminary Report," *Journal of Speech and Hearing Research*, 7 (1964), 245–269. (Ch. 4)

Eisenberg-Berg, N., and R. Lennon. "Altruism and the Assessment of Empathy in the Preschool Years," *Child Development*, 51 (1980), 552–557. (Ch. 16)

Elkind, D. "Perceptual Development in Children," in I. Janis (ed.), *Current Trends in Psychology*. Los Altos, Calif.: Kaufmann, 1977, pp. 121–129. (Ch. 8)

———. "Strategic Interactions in Early Adolescence," in J. Adelson (ed.), *Handbook of Adolescent Psychology*. New York: Wiley-Interscience, 1980, pp. 432–446. (Ch. 17)

———, and R. Bowen. "Imaginary Audience Behavior in Children and Adolescents," *Developmental Psychology*, 15 (1979), 38–44. (Ch. 17)

———, and R. F. Dabek. "Personal Injury and Property Damage in Moral Judgments of Children," *Child Development*, 48 (1977), 518–522. (Ch. 16)

Elster, A. B., E. R. McAnarney, and M. E. Lamb. "Parental Behavior of Adolescent Mothers," *Pediatrics*, 71 (1983), 494–503. (Chs. 3, 13)

Emde, R. N., and C. Brown. "Adaptation to the Birth of a Down's Syndrome Infant," *Journal of the American Academy of Child Psychiatry*, 17 (1978), 299–323. (Ch. 5)

———, T. J. Gaensbrauer, and R. J. Harmon. *Emotional Expressions in Infancy: A Biobehavioral Study*. New York: International Universities Press, 1976. (Ch. 6)

Emmerich, W. "Continuity and Stability in Early Social Development. II: Teacher Ratings," *Child Development*, 37 (1966), 17–27. (Ch. 14)

———. "Nonmonotonic Developmental Trends in Social Cognition: The Case of Gender Identity," in S. Strauss (ed.), *U-Shaped Behavioral Growth*. New York: Academic Press, 1982, pp. 249–269. (Ch. 15)

Engen, T., and L. P. Lipsitt. "Decrement and Recovery of Responses to Olfactory Stimuli in the Human Neonate," *Journal of Comparative and Physiological Psychology*, 59 (1965), 312–316. (Ch. 4)

Entingh, D., A. Dunn, E. Glassman, J. E. Wilson, E. Hogan, and T. Damstra. "Biochemical Approaches to the Biological Basis of Memory," in M. S. Gazzaniga and C. Blakemore (eds.), *Handbook of Psychobiology*. New York: Academic Press, 1975, pp. 201–240. (Ch. 6)

Entwisle, D. R., and D. P. Baker. "Gender and Children's Expectations for Performance in Arithmetic," *Developmental Psychology*, 19 (1983), 200–209. (Ch. 6)

Epstein, R., R. P. Lanza, and B. F. Skinner. "Symbolic Communication Between Two Pigeons (*Columba livia domestica*)," *Science*, 207 (1980), 543–545. (Ch. 9)

Erikson, E. H. *Childhood and Society*. 2nd rev. ed. New York: Norton, 1963. (Ch. 1)

———. *Identity: Youth and Crisis*. New York: Norton, 1968. (Chs. 2, 17)

———, interviewed by E. Hall. "A Conversation with Erik Erikson," *Psychology Today*, 17 (June 1983), 22–30. (Ch. 1)

Eron, L. D., L. R. Huesmann, M. M. Lefkowitz, and L. O. Walder. "Does Television Cause Aggression?" *American Psychologist*, 27 (1972), 253–263. (Ch. 16)

———, ———, P. Brice, P. Fischer, and R. Mermelstein. "Age Trends in the Development of Aggression, Sex Typing and Related Television Habits," *Developmental Psychology*, 19 (1983), 71–77. (Ch. 2)

Estes, W. K. "Is Human Memory Obsolete?" *American Scientist*, 68 (1980), 62–69. (Ch. 1)

Evans, M. A. "Self-Initiated Speech Repairs: A Reflection of Communicative Monitoring in Young Children," *Developmental Psychology*, 21 (1985), 365–371. (Ch. 9)

Evans, R. I. "Smoking in Children: Developing a Social Psychological Strategy of Deterrence," *Journal of Preventive Medicine*, 5 (1976), 122–127. (Ch. 14)

Eveleth, P. B., and J. M. Tanner. *Worldwide Variation in Human Growth*. London: Cambridge University Press, 1976. (Ch. 5)

Evers, W. L., and J. C. Schwartz. "Modifying Social Withdrawal in Pre-Schoolers: The Effects of Filmed Modeling and Teacher Praise," *Journal of Abnormal Child Psychology*, 1 (1973), 248–256. (Ch. 14)

Fabricus, W. V., and J. W. Hagen. "Use of Causal Attributions About Recall Performance to Assess Metamemory and Predict Strategic Memory Behavior in Young Children," *Developmental Psychology*, 20 (1984), 975–987. (Ch. 8)

———, and H. M. Wellman. "Children's Understanding of Retrieval Cue Utilization," *Developmental Psychology*, 19 (1983), 14–21. (Ch. 8)

Fagan, J. F., III. "Infants' Recognition Memory for a Series of Visual Stimuli," *Journal of Experimental Child Psychology*, 11 (1971), 244–250. (Ch. 7)

———. "Infants' Recognition of Invariant Features of Faces," *Child Development*, 47 (1976), 627–638. (Ch. 7)

———, R. L. Fantz, and S. B. Miranda. "Infants' Attention to Novel Stimuli as a Function of Postnatal and Conceptual Age." Paper presented at the Biennial Meeting of the Society for Research in Child Development. Minneapolis, 1971. (Ch. 7)

———, and L. T. Singer. "The Role of Simple Feature Differences in Infants' Recognition of Faces," *Infant Behavior and Development*, 2 (1979), 39–46. (Ch. 7)

Fagot, B. I. "Sex Differences in Toddlers' Behavior and Parental Reaction," *Developmental Psychology*, 10 (1974), 554–558. (Ch. 15)

———. "Consequences of Moderate Cross-Gender Behavior in Preschool Children," *Child Development*, 48 (1977), 902–907. (Ch. 15)

———. "The Influence of Sex of Child on Parental Reactions to Toddler Children," *Child Development*, 49 (1978a), 459–465. (Ch. 15)

———. "Reinforcing Contingencies for Sex-Role Behaviors: Effect of Experience with Children," *Child Development*, 48 (1978b), 30–36. (Ch. 15)

———. "Adults as Socializing Agents," in T. Field, A. Huston, H. Quay, L. Troll, and G. Finley (eds.), *Review of Human Development*. New York: Wiley, 1982, pp. 304–315. (Ch. 15)

Falbo, T. "Achievement Attributions of Kindergartners," *Developmental Psychology*, 11 (1975), 529–530. (Ch. 14)

——— (ed.). *The Single Child Family*. New York: Guilford, 1984. (Ch. 2)

Falkner, F. T. (ed.). *Human Development*. Philadelphia: Saunders, 1966. (Ch. 5)

Fantz, R. L. "Visual Perception from Birth as Shown by Pattern Selectivity," *Annals of the New York Academy of Science*, 118 (1965), 793–814. (Ch. 4)

———. "Pattern Discrimination and Selective Attention as Determinants of Perceptual Development from Birth," in A. H. Kidd and J. E. Rivoire (eds.), *Perceptual Development in Children*. New York: International Universities Press, 1966, pp. 181–224. (Ch. 7)

———, J. F. Fagan III, and S. B. Miranda. "Early Visual Selectivity," in L. B. Cohen and P. Salapatek (eds.), *Infant Perception: From Sensation to Cognition*. Vol. 1: *Basic Visual Processes*. New York: Academic Press, 1975, pp. 249–345. (Ch. 7)

———, and S. B. Miranda. "Newborn Infant Attraction to Form of Contour," *Child Development*, 46 (1975), 224–228. (Ch. 7)

Farah, M. J., and S. M. Kosslyn. "Concept Development," in H. W. Reese and L. P. Lipsitt (eds.), *Advances in Child Development and Behavior*. Vol. 16. New York: Academic Press, 1982, pp. 125–167. (Ch. 10)

Farnham-Diggory, S. *Learning Disabilities*. Cambridge, Mass.: Harvard University Press, 1978. (Chs. 2, 6)

Farran, D., and R. Haskins. "Reciprocal Influence in the Social Interactions of Mothers and Three-Year-Old Children from Different Socioeconomic Backgrounds," *Child Development*, 51 (1980), 780–791. (Ch. 13)

Faulkender, P. J., J. C. Wright, and A. Waldron. "Generalized Habituation of Conceptual Stimuli in Toddlers," *Child Development*, 45 (1974), 351–356. (Ch. 8)

Faust, M. S. "Developmental Maturity as a Determinant in Prestige of Adolescent Girls," *Child Development*, 31 (1960), 173–184. (Ch. 15)

———. "Somatic Development of Adolescent Girls," *Monographs of the Society for Research in Child Development*, 42 (1977), whole no. 169. (Ch. 5)

Fein, D. "Just World Responding in 6- and 9-Year-Old Children," *Developmental Psychology*, 12 (1976), 79–80. (Ch. 16)

Feinman, S. "How Does Baby Socially Refer? Two Views of Social Referencing: A Reply to Campos," *Merrill-Palmer Quarterly*, 29 (1983), 467–471. (Ch. 12)

Feiring, C., M. Lewis, and M. D. Starr. "Indirect Effects and Infants' Reaction to Strangers," *Developmental Psychology*, 20 (1984), 485–491. (Ch. 12)

Feldhusen, J. F. "Eclecticism: A Comprehensive Approach to Education of the Gifted," in C. P. Benbow and J. C. Stanley (eds.), *Academic Precocity: Aspects of Its Development*. Baltimore: Johns Hopkins University Press, 1983, pp. 192–204. (Ch. 10)

Feldman, D. H. "A Developmental Framework for Research with Gifted Children," in D. H. Feldman (ed.), *New Directions for Child Development*. Vol. 17: *Developmental Approaches to Giftedness and Creativity*. San Francisco: Jossey-Bass, 1982, pp. 31–60. (Ch. 11)

Feldman, S. S., Z. C. Biringen, and S. C. Nash. "Fluctuations of Sex-Related Self-Attributions as a Function of Stage of the Family Life Cycle," *Developmental Psychology*, 17 (1981), 24–35. (Ch. 15)

———, S. C. Nash, and C. Cutrona. "The Influence of Age and Sex on Responsiveness to Babies," *Developmental Psychology*, 13 (1977), 675–676. (Ch. 11)

Felleman, E. S., R. C. Barden, C. R. Carlson, L. Rosenberg, and J. C. Masters. "Children's and Adult's Recognition of Spontaneous and Posed Emotional Expressions in Young Children," *Developmental Psychology*, 19 (1983), 405–413. (Ch. 17)

Ferguson, C. A. "Baby Talk as a Simplified Register," in C. E. Snow and C. A. Ferguson (eds.), *Talking to Children: Language Input and Acquisition*. New York: Cambridge University Press, 1977, pp. 219–236. (Ch. 9)

———, and C. Farwell. "Words and Sounds in Early Language Acquisition: English Consonants in the First 50 Words," *Language*, 51 (1975), 419–439. (Ch. 9)

Ferguson, T. J., T. Olthof, A. Luiten, and B. G. Rule. "Children's Use of Observed Behavioral Frequency versus Behavioral Covariation in Ascribing Dispositions to Others," *Child Development*, 55 (1984), 2094–2105. (Ch. 17)

———, and B. G. Rule. "Effects of Inferential Set, Outcome Severity, and Basis of Responsibility on Children's Evaluations of Aggressive Acts," *Developmental Psychology*, 16 (1980), 141–146. (Ch. 16)

Feshbach, N. "Chronic Maternal Stress and Its Assessment," in J. N. Butcher and C. D. Spielberger (eds.), *Advances in Personality Assessment*. Vol. 5. Hillsdale, N. J. Lawrence Erlbaum Associates [in press]. (Ch. 13)

———. "The Function of Aggression and the Regulation of Aggressive Drive," *Psychological Review*, 71 (1964), 257–272. (Ch. 16)

———. "Aggression," in P. H. Mussen (ed.), *Carmichael's Manual of Child Psychology*. 3rd ed. Vol. 2. New York: Wiley, 1970, pp. 159–259. (Ch. 16)

Field, J., D. DiFranco, P. Dodwell, and D. Muir. "Auditory-Visual Coordination in 2½-Month-Old Infants," *In-*

fant Behavior and Development, 2 (1979), 113–122. (Ch. 7)

Field, T. M. "Interaction Behaviors of Primary Versus Secondary Caretaker Fathers," *Developmental Psychology*, 14 (1978), 183–184. (Ch. 12)

———, and J. L. Roopnarine. "Infant-Peer Interactions," in T. M. Field, A. Huston, H. C. Quay, L. Troll, and G. E. Finley (eds.), *Review of Human Development*. New York: Wiley-Interscience, 1982, pp. 164–179. (Ch. 14)

———, R. Woodson, D. Cohen, R. Greenberg, R. Garcia, and K. Collins. "Discrimination and Imitation of Facial Expression by Term and Preterm Neonates," *Infant Behavior and Development*, 6 (1983), 485–490. (Chs. 4, 7)

Fielding, J. "Adolescent Pregnancy Revisited," *New England Journal of Medicine*, 299 (1978), 893–896. (Ch. 3)

Finlay, B. L., and M. Slattery. "Local Differences in the Amount of Early Cell Death in Neocortex Predicts Adult Local Specialization," *Science*, 219 (1983), 1349–1351. (Ch. 6)

Fischer, K. W. "Illuminating the Processes of Moral Development," in A. Colby, L. Kohlberg, J. Gibbs, and M. Lieberman, "A Longitudinal Study of Moral Judgment," *Monographs of the Society for Research in Child Development*, 48 (1983), whole no. 200, pp. 97–107. (Ch. 16)

Fishbein, H. D. *Evolution, Development, and Children's Learning*. Santa Monica, Calif.: Goodyear, 1976. (Chs. 5, 6)

Fisher, K. "Family Violence Cycle Questioned," *APA Monitor*, December 1984, 30. (Ch. 13)

Fishkin, J., K. Keniston, and C. MacKinnon. "Moral Reasoning and Political Ideology," *Journal of Personality and Social Psychology*, 27 (1973), 109–119. (Ch. 16)

Flanery, R. C., and J. D. Balling. "Developmental Changes in Hemispheric Specialization for Tactile Spatial Ability," *Developmental Psychology*, 15 (1979), 364–372. (Ch. 6)

Flavell, J. H. "Developmental Studies of Mediated Memory," in H. W. Reese and L. P. Lipsitt (eds.), *Advances in Child Development and Behavior*. Vol. 5. New York: Academic Press, 1970, pp. 182–211. (Ch. 8)

———. *Cognitive Development*. Englewood Cliffs, N.J.: Prentice-Hall, 1977. (Chs. 1, 8, 10)

———, D. R. Beach, and J. M. Chinsky. "Spontaneous Verbal Rehearsal as a Memory Task as a Function of Age," *Child Development*, 37 (1966), 283–299. (Ch. 8)

———, P. T. Botkin, C. L. Fry, Jr., J. W. Wright, and P. E. Jarvis. *The Development of Role-Taking and Communication Skills in Children*. Huntington, N.Y.: Krieger, 1975 (orig. pub. 1968). (Chs. 16, 17)

———, S. G. Shipstead, and K. Croft. "Young Children's Knowledge about Visual Perception: Hiding Objects from Others," *Child Development*, 49 (1978), 1208–1211. (Ch. 17)

———, and H. M. Wellman. "Metamemory," in R. V. Kail, Jr., and J. W. Hagen (eds.), *Perspectives on the Development of Memory and Cognition*. Hillsdale, N. J.: Lawrence Erlbaum Associates, 1977, pp. 3–33. (Ch. 8)

Floyd, J. M. "Effects of Amount of Reward and Friendship Status of the Other on the Frequency of Sharing in Children," *Dissertation Abstracts*, 25 (1965), 5396–5397. (Ch. 14)

Forgus, R. H. "The Effects of Early Perceptual Learning on the Behavioral Organization of Adult Rats," *Journal of Comparative Physiological Psychology*, 47 (1954), 331–336. (Ch. 12)

Fowler, W. "Cognitive Differentiation and Developmental Learning," in H. W. Reese and L. P. Lipsitt (eds.), *Advances in Child Development and Behavior*. Vol. 15. New York: Academic Press, 1980, pp. 163–206. (Ch. 10)

Fox, G. L. "The Family's Role in Adolescent Sexual Behavior." Paper presented to the Family Impact Seminar. Washington, D.C.: October 1978. (Ch. 13)

Fox, R., R. N. Aslin, S. L. Shea, and S. T. Dumais.

"Stereopsis in Human Infants," *Science*, 207 (1980), 323–324. (Ch. 7)

Fraiberg, S. *Insights from the Blind*. New York: Basic Books, 1977. (Ch. 7)

———, and N. Bayley. "Gross Motor Development in Infants Blind from Birth," *Child Development*, 45 (1974), 114–126. (Ch. 7)

Frank, F. "Perception and Language in Conservation," in J. S. Bruner, R. R. Olver, P. M. Greenfield et al., *Studies in Cognitive Growth*. New York: Wiley, 1966. (Ch. 9)

Frank, L. K. *On the Importance of Infancy*. New York: Random House, 1966. (Ch. 4)

Freedman, D. G. "Constitutional and Environmental Interactions in Rearing of Four Breeds of Dogs," *Science*, 127 (1958), 585–586. (Ch. 2)

———. *Human Infancy: An Evolutionary Perspective*. Hillsdale, N. J.: Lawrence Erlbaum Associates, 1974. (Chs. 1, 2, 3)

Freedman, J. L. "Effects of Television Violence on Aggression," *Psychological Bulletin*, 96 (1984), 227–246. (Ch. 16)

French, D. C. "Children's Knowledge of the Social Functions of Younger, Older, and Same-Age Peers," *Child Development*, 55 (1984), 1429–1433. (Ch. 14)

Freud, S. "Three Essays on the Theory of Sexuality," in *The Standard Edition of the Complete Psychological Works of Sigmund Freud*. Vol. 7. London: Hogarth, 1953, pp. 125–245 [orig. pub. 1905]. (Ch. 1)

———. *Psychopathology of Everyday Life*. New York: Macmillan, 1917. (Ch. 12)

Frias, J. L. "Prenatal Diagnosis of Genetic Abnormalities," *Clinical Obstetrics and Gynecology*, 18 (1975), 221–236. (Ch. 3)

Friedl, E. "Society and Sex Roles," *Human Nature*, 1 (April 1978), 68–75. (Ch. 15)

Friedman, S. "Habituation and Recovery of Visual Response in the Alert Human Newborn," *Journal of Experimental Child Psychology*, 13 (1972), 339–349. (Ch. 4)

Friedman, S., L. A. Bruno, and P. Vietze. "Newborn Habituation to Visual Stimuli: A Sex Difference in Novelty Detection," *Journal of Experimental Child Psychology*, 18 (1974), 242–251. (Ch. 4)

Friedman, S. L., and M. B. Stevenson. "Developmental Changes in the Understanding of Implied Motion in Two-Dimensional Pictures," *Child Development*, 46 (1975), 773–778. (Ch. 8)

———, C. Zahn-Waxler, and M. Radke-Yarrow. "Perceptions of Cries of Full-Term and Preterm Infants," *Infant Behavior and Development*, 5 (1982), 161–174. (Ch. 4)

Friedrich-Cofer, L. K., A. Huston-Stein, D. M. Kipnis, E. J. Susman, and A. S. Clewett. "Environmental Enhancement of Prosocial Television Content: Effects on Interpersonal Behavior, Imaginative Play, and Self-Regulation in a Natural Setting," *Developmental Psychology*, 15 (1979), 637–646. (Ch. 16)

Frisch, H. L. "Sex Stereotypes in Adult-Infant Play," *Child Development*, 48 (1977), 1671–1675. (Ch. 15)

Frodi, A. M., and M. E. Lamb. "Sex Differences in Responsiveness to Infants: A Developmental Study of Psychophysiological and Behavioral Responses," *Child Development*, 49 (1978), 1182–1188. (Ch. 15)

———, and ———. "Child Abusers' Responses to Infant Smiles and Cries," *Child Development*, 51 (1980), 238–241. (Chs. 4, 13)

———, ———, L. A. Leavitt, and W. L. Donovan. "Fathers' and Mothers' Responses to Infant Smiles and Cries," *Infant Behavior and Development*, 1 (1978a), 187–198. (Ch. 4)

———, ———, ———, ———, C. Neff, and D. Sherry. "Fathers' and Mothers' Responses to the Faces and Cries of Normal and Premature Infants," *Developmental Psychol-*

ogy, 14 (1978b), 490–498. (Ch. 4)

———, A. D. Murray, M. E. Lamb, and J. Steinberg. "Biological and Social Determinants of Responsiveness to Infants in 10- to 15-Year-Old Girls," *Sex Roles*, 10 (1984), 639–649. (Ch. 15)

Froming, W. J., L. Allen, and B. Underwood. "Age and Generosity Reconsidered: Cross-Sectional and Longitudinal Evidence," *Child Development*, 54 (1983), 585–593. (Ch. 16)

Fry, D. *Homo Loquens: Man As a Talking Animal.* New York: Cambridge University Press, 1977. (Ch. 9)

Fryer, J. G., and J. R. Ashford. "Trends in Perinatal and Neonatal Mortality in England and Wales, 1960–1969," *British Journal of Preventive and Social Medicine*, 26 (1972), 1–9. (Ch. 3)

Fuchs, A.-R., F. Fuchs, P. Husslein, M. S. Soloff, and M. J. Fernstrom. "Oxytocin Receptors and Human Parturition: A Dual Role for Oxytocin in the Initiation of Labor," *Science*, 215 (1982), 1396–1398. (Ch. 3)

Furman, W., and J. C. Masters. "Peer Interactions, Sociometric Status, and Resistance to Deviation in Young Children," *Developmental Psychology*, 16 (1980), 229–236. (Ch. 14)

———, D. F. Rahe, and W. W. Hartup. "Rehabilitation of Socially Withdrawn Preschool Children through Mixed-Age and Age Socialization," *Child Development*, 50 (1979), 915–922. (Ch. 2)

Furth, H. G. *The World of Grown-Ups: Children's Conceptions of Society.* New York: Elsevier, 1980. (Ch. 17)

———, and N. A. Milgram. "Labeling and Grouping Effects in the Recall of Pictures by Children," *Child Development*, 44 (1973), 511–518. (Ch. 8)

———, B. M. Ross, and J. Youniss. "Operative Understanding in Reproductions of Drawings," *Child Development*, 45 (1974), 63–70. (Ch. 8)

Gaensbauer, T. J. "Regulation of Emotional Expression in Infants from Two Contrasting Caretaker Environments," *Journal of the American Academy of Child Psychiatry*, 21 (1982). (Ch. 13)

Gagné, R. M. "Contributions of Learning to Human Development," *Psychological Review*, 75 (1968), 177–191. (Ch. 10)

Gagnon, J. *Human Sexualities.* Glenview, Ill.: Scott, Foresman, 1977. (Ch. 15)

Gaite, A. J. H. "Teachers' Perceptions of Ideal Male and Female Students: Male Chauvinism in the Schools," in J. Pottker and A. Fishel (eds.), *Sex Bias in the Schools: The Research Evidence.* Cranbury, N. J.: Associated University Presses, 1977. (Ch. 15)

Gaitonde, M. K. "Report on Meeting of Neurochemical Group of the Biochemical Society," *Nature*, 221 (1969), 808. (Ch. 6)

Galin, D., J. Johnstone, L. Nakell, and J. Herron. "Development of the Capacity for Tactile Information Transfer Between Hemispheres in Normal Children," *Science*, 204 (1979), 1330–1332. (Ch. 6)

Gallatin, J. "Political Thinking in Adolescence," in J. Adelson (ed.), *Handbook of Adolescent Psychology.* New York: Wiley-Interscience, 1980, pp. 344–382. (Ch. 17)

Ganchrow, J. R., J. E. Steiner, and M. Daher. "Neonatal Facial Expressions in Response to Different Qualities and Intensities of Gustatory Stimuli," *Infant Behavior and Development*, 6 (1983), 473–484. (Ch. 4)

Garbarino, J. "A Preliminary Study of Some Ecological Correlates of Child Abuse: The Impact of Socioeconomic Stress on Mothers," *Child Development*, 47 (1976), 178–185. (Ch. 13)

———, and A. Crouter. "Defining the Community Context for Parent-Child Relations: The Correlates of Child Mal-

treatment," *Child Development*, 49 (1978), 604–616. (Ch. 13)

———, and D. Sherman. "High-Risk Neighborhoods and High-Risk Families: The Human Ecology of Child Maltreatment," *Child Development*, 51 (1980), 188–198. (Ch. 13)

Gardner, H. *The Shattered Mind.* New York: Knopf, 1975. (Ch. 6)

———. "The Loss of Language," *Human Nature*, 1 (March 1978), 76–84. (Ch. 6)

———. *Frames of Mind: The Theory of Multiple Intelligences.* New York: Basic Books, 1983. (Ch. 11)

Gardner, J. M., and G. Turkewitz. "The Effect of Arousal Level on Visual Preference in Preterm Infants," *Infant Behavior and Development*, 5 (1982), 369–385. (Ch. 4)

Gardner, L. "Deprivation Dwarfism," *Scientific American*, 227 (1972), 76–82. (Ch. 5)

Gardner, R. A., and B. T. Gardner. "Teaching Sign Language to a Chimpanzee," *Science*, 165 (1969), 664–672. (Ch. 9)

Garnica, O. K. "The Development of Phonemic Speech Perception," in T. E. Moore (ed.), *Cognitive Development and the Acquisition of Language.* New York: Academic Press, 1973, pp. 215–222. (Ch. 9)

Garvey, C. *Children's Talk.* Cambridge, Mass.: Harvard University Press, 1984. (Ch. 9)

Garwood, S. G. "First-Name Stereotypes as a Factor in Self-Concept and School Achievement," *Journal of Educational Psychology*, 68 (1976), 482–487. (Ch. 14)

Gazzaniga, M. S. "One Brain—Two Minds?" In I. L. Janis (ed.), *Current Trends in Psychology.* Los Altos, Calif.: Kaufmann, 1977, pp. 7–13. (Ch. 6)

Gelles, R. J., and C. P. Cornell. *Intimate Violence in Families.* Beverly Hills, Calif.: Sage, 1985. (Ch. 13)

Gelman, R. "How Young Children Reason About Small Numbers," in N. J. Castellan, D. P. Pisoni, and G. R. Potts (eds.), *Cognitive Theory.* Hillsdale, N. J.: Lawrence Erlbaum Associates, 1977, pp. 219–238. (Ch. 10)

———. "Cognitive Development," in M. R. Rosenzweig and L. W. Porter (eds.), *Annual Review of Psychology.* Vol. 29. Palo Alto, Calif.: Annual Reviews, 1978, pp. 297–332. (Ch. 10)

———. "Accessing One-to-One Correspondence: Still Another Paper on Conservation," *British Journal of Psychology*, 73 (1982), 209–220. (Ch. 10)

———, and R. Baillargeon. "A Review of Some Piagetian Concepts," in P. H. Mussen (ed.), *Handbook of Child Psychology.* 4th ed. Vol. 3: J. H. Flavell and E. M. Markman (eds.), *Cognitive Development.* New York: Wiley, 1983, pp. 167–230. (Chs. 1, 10)

———, M. Bullock, and E. Meck. "Preschoolers' Understanding of Simple Object Transformations," *Child Development*, 51 (1980), 691–699. (Ch. 10)

———, and C. H. Gallistel. *The Child's Understanding of Number.* Cambridge, Mass.: Harvard University Press, 1978. (Ch. 10)

———, and M. Shatz. "Appropriate Speech Adjustments: The Operation of Conversational Constraints to Talk in Two-Year-Olds," in M. Lewis and L. A. Rosenblum (eds.), *Interaction, Conversation, and the Development of Language.* New York: Wiley, 1977, pp. 27–61. (Ch. 9)

Gentner, D. "On Relational Meaning: The Acquisition of Verb Meaning," *Child Development*, 49 (1978), 988–998. (Ch. 9)

George, C., and M. Main. "Social Interactions of Young Abused Children: Approach, Avoidance, and Aggression," *Child Development*, 50 (1979), 306–318. (Ch. 13)

Gerbner, G. "The Violence Profiles: Some Indicators of the Trends in the Symbolic Structure of Network Television Drama, 1967–1970." Unpublished manuscript. Annenberg School of Communications, University of Pennsylvania, 1972. (Ch. 13)

———, and L. Gross. "Living with Television: The Violence Profile," *Journal of Communication*, 26 (1976), 173–199. (Ch. 16)

Geschwind, N. "Specialization of the Human Brain," *Scientific American*, 241 (September 1979), 180–201. (Ch. 6)

Gesell, A. L. *The Mental Growth of the Pre-School Child: A Psychological Outline of Normal Development from Birth to the Sixth Year, Including a System of Developmental Diagnosis.* New York: Macmillan, 1925. (Ch. 5)

Gholson, B. *The Cognitive-Developmental Basis of Human Learning.* New York: Academic Press, 1980. (Chs. 1, 10)

Gibson, E. J. "Development of Perception: Discrimination of Depth Compared with Discrimination of Graphic Symbols," in J. C. Wright and J. Kagan (eds.), "Basic Cognitive Processes in Children," *Monographs of the Society for Research in Child Development*, 28 (1963), whole no. 86. (Ch. 7)

Gibson, E. J. *Principles of Perceptual Learning and Development.* Englewood Cliffs, N. J.: Prentice-Hall, 1969. (Chs. 7, 8)

———, C. J. Owsley, and J. Johnston. "Perception of Invariants by Five-Month-Old Infants: Differentiation of Two Types of Motion," *Developmental Psychology*, 14 (1978), 407–415. (Ch. 7)

———, and N. Rader. "Attention: The Perceiver as Performer," in G. A. Hale and M. Lewis (eds.), *Attention and Cognitive Development.* New York: Plenum Press, 1979, pp. 1–21. (Ch. 8)

———, and E. S. Spelke. "The Development of Perception," in P. H. Mussen (ed.), *Handbook of Child Psychology.* 4th ed. Vol. 3: J. H. Flavell and E. M. Markman (eds.), *Cognitive Development.* New York: Wiley, 1983, pp. 1–76. (Ch. 8)

———, and R. D. Walk. "The Visual Cliff," *Scientific American*, 202 (April 1960), 64–71. (Ch. 7)

Gilligan, C. *In a Different Voice: Psychological Theory and Women's Development.* Cambridge, Mass.: Harvard University Press, 1982. (Chs. 16, 17)

Gleason, J. B. "Do Children Imitate?" *Proceedings of the International Conference on Oral Education of the Deaf*, 2 (1967), 1441–1448. (Ch. 9)

———, and S. Weintraub. "Input Language and the Acquisition of Communicative Competence," in K. E. Nelson (ed.), *Children's Language.* Vol. 1. New York: Gardner Press, 1978, pp. 171–222. (Ch. 9)

Gluck, L., and M. V. Kulovich. "Fetal Lung Development: Current Concepts," *Pediatric Clinic of North America*, 20 (1973), 367–379. (Ch. 3)

Gnepp, J. "Children's Social Sensitivity: Inferring Emotions from Conflicting Cues," *Developmental Psychology*, 19 (1983), 805–814. (Ch. 17)

Golbek, S. L. "Reconstructing a Large-Scale Spatial Arrangement: Effect of Environmental Organization and Operativity," *Developmental Psychology*, 19 (1983), 644–653. (Ch. 8)

Gold, D., and D. Andres. "Developmental Comparisons Between Ten-Year-Old Children with Employed and Unemployed Mothers," *Child Development*, 49 (1978), 73–84. (Ch. 13)

Goldberg, S., S. L. Blumberg, and A. Kriger. "Menarche and Interest in Infants: Biological and Social Influences," *Child Development*, 53 (1982), 1544–1550. (Ch. 15)

Goldberg, W. A., and M. A. Easterbrooks. "Role of Marital Quality in Toddler Development," *Developmental Psychology*, 20 (1984), 504–514. (Chs. 2, 12)

Golden, M, and B. Birns. "Social Class and Infant Intelligence," in M. Lewis (ed.), *Origins of Intelligence.* New York: Plenum Press, 1976, pp. 299–352. (Ch. 11)

———, W. H. Bridger, and A. Montare. "Social-Class Dif-

ferences in the Ability of Young Children to Use Verbal Information to Facilitate Learning," *American Journal of Orthopsychiatry*, 44 (1974), 86. (Ch. 11)

Goldman-Rakic, P. S., A. Isseroff, M. L. Schwartz, and N. M. Bugbee. "The Neurobiology of Cognitive Development," in P. H. Mussen (ed.), *Handbook of Child Psychology.* 4th ed. Vol. 2: M. M. Haith and J. J. Campos (eds.), *Infancy and Developmental Psychobiology.* New York: Wiley, 1983, pp. 281–344. (Ch. 6)

Goleman, D. "A New Computer Test of the Brain," *Psychology Today*, 9 (May 1976), 44–48. (Ch. 11)

———. "1,528 Little Geniuses and How They Grew," *Psychology Today*, 13 (February 1980), 28–53. (Ch. 11)

———. "Rigorous Study of Autism Points to a Genetic Factor," *The New York Times*, January 29, 1985, C1 + . (Ch. 8)

Golinkoff, R. M., and M. S. Halperin. "The Concept of Animal: One Infant's View," *Infant Behavior and Development*, 6 (1983), 229–233. (Ch. 7)

———, and C. Harding. "Infants' Expectations of the Movement Potential of Inanimate Objects." Paper presented at the International Conference on Infant Studies. New Haven, Connecticut, 1980. (Ch. 10)

Goodenough, F. L. *Anger in Young Children.* Minneapolis: University of Minnesota Press, 1931. (Ch. 16)

Gottlieb, G. "The Psychobiological Approach to Developmental Issues," in P. H. Mussen (ed.), *Handbook of Child Psychology.* 4th ed. Vol. 2: M. M. Haith and J. J. Campos (eds.), *Infancy and Developmental Psychobiology.* New York: Wiley, 1983, pp. 1–26. (Ch. 3)

Gottman, J. M., J. Gonso, and B. Rasmussen. "Social Interaction, Social Competence, and Friendship in Children," *Child Development*, 46 (1975), 709–718. (Ch. 14)

Govatos, L. A. "Relationships and Age Differences in Growth Measures and Motor Skills," *Child Development*, 30 (1959), 333–340. (Ch. 5)

Gove, F. L., and D. F. Keating. "Empathic Role-Taking Precursors," *Developmental Psychology*, 14 (1979), 594–600. (Ch. 17)

Graham, D. *Moral Learning and Development: Theory and Research.* New York: Wiley, 1972. (Ch. 16)

Gratch, G., K. J. Appel, W. F. Evans, G. K. LeCompte, and N. A. Wright. "Piaget's Stage IV Object Concept Error: Evidence of Forgetting or Object Conception?" *Child Development*, 45 (1974), 71–77. (Ch. 7)

Gray, W. M., and L. M. Hudson. "Formal Operations and the Imaginary Audience," *Developmental Psychology*, 20 (1984), 619–627. (Ch. 17)

Graziano, W. G., L. M. Musser, and G. H. Brody. "Children's Social Cognitions and Preferences Regarding Younger and Older Peers." Unpublished manuscript. University of Georgia, 1980. [cited in Hartup, 1983] (Ch. 14)

———, ———, S. Rosen, and D. R. Shaffer. "The Development of Fair-Play Standards in Same-Race and Mixed-Race Situations," *Child Development*, 53 (1982), 938–947. (Ch. 14)

Green, R. "Children's Quest for Sexual Identity," *Psychology Today*, 7 (February 1974), 44–51. (Ch. 15)

———. "Sexual Identity of 37 Children Raised by Homosexual or Transsexual Parents," *American Journal of Psychiatry*, 135 (1978), 692–697. (Ch. 15)

Greenfield, P. M. "Informativeness, Presupposition, and Semantic Choice in Single-Word Utterances," in E. Ochs and B. B. Schieffelin (eds.), *Developmental Pragmatics.* New York: Academic Press, 1979, pp. 159–166. (Ch. 9)

———. *Mind and Media: The Effects of Television, Video Games, and Computers.* Cambridge, Mass.: Harvard University Press, 1984. (Ch. 2)

———, and J. S. Bruner. "Culture and Cognitive Growth,"

International Journal of Psychology, 1 (1966), 89–107. (Ch. 10)

Greenough, W. T., and J. M. Juraska. "Experience-Induced Changes in Brain Fine Structure: Their Behavioral Implications," in M. E. Hahn, C. Jensen, and B. C. Dudek (eds.), *Development and Evolution of Brain Size: Behavioral Implications*. Academic Press, 1979, pp. 295–320. (Ch. 6)

Greenspan, E. "Little Winners," *New York Times Magazine*, April 26, 1981, pp. 59–60+. (Ch. 5)

Greer, L. D. "Children's Comprehension of Formal Features with Masculine and Feminine Connotations." Unpublished master's thesis. Department of Human Development, University of Kansas, 1980. [cited in Huston, 1983] (Ch. 15)

Griffin, D. R. *The Question of Animal Awareness*. New York: Rockefeller University Press, 1976. (Ch. 11)

Griffiths, R. *The Abilities of Babies*. New York: McGraw-Hill, 1954. (Ch. 5)

Gronlund, N. E. *Sociometry in the Classroom*. New York: Harper, 1959. (Ch. 14)

Grosser, D., N. Polzansky, and R. Lippitt. "A Laboratory Study of Behavior Contagion," *Human Relations*, 4 (1951), 115–142. (Ch. 16)

Grossmann, K., and K. E. Grossmann. "Maternal Sensitivity to Infants' Signals During the First Year as Related in the Year Old's Behavior in Ainsworth's Strange Situation in a Sample of Northern German Families." Paper presented at the International Conference on Infant Studies. Austin, Texas, 1982. (Ch. 12)

Gruendel, J. M. "Referential Overextension in Early Language Development," *Child Development*, 48 (1977), 1567–1576. (Ch. 9)

Grusec, J. E., L. Kuczynski, J. P. Rushton, and Z. M. Simutis. "Learning Resistance to Temptation Through Observation," *Developmental Psychology*, 15 (1979), 233–240. (Ch. 16)

———, and S. L. Skubiski. "Model Nurturance, Demand Characteristics of the Modeling Experiment and Altruism," *Journal of Personality and Social Psychology*, 14 (1970), 352–359. (Ch. 16)

Guilford, J. P. "Theories of Intelligence," in B. B. Wolman (ed.), *Handbook of General Psychology*. Englewood Cliffs, N. J.: Prentice-Hall, 1973, pp. 630–643. (Ch. 11)

Gump, P. V. "School Environments," in I. Altman and J. F. Wohlwill (eds.), *Children and the Environment*. New York: Plenum Press, 1978, pp. 131–174. (Ch. 2)

Gunderson, V., and G. P. Sackett. "Paternal Effects on Reproductive Outcome and Developmental Risk," in M. E. Lamb and A. L. Brown (eds.), *Advances in Developmental Psychology*. Vol. 2. Hillsdale, N. J.: Lawrence Erlbaum Associates, 1982, pp. 85–124. (Ch. 3)

Gutteridge, M. V. "A Study of Motor Achievements of Young Children," *Archives of Psychology*, no. 244 (1939). (Ch. 5)

Guttman, D. "Parenthood: A Key to the Comparative Study of the Life Cycle," in N. Datan and L. H. Ginsberg (eds.), *Life-Span Developmental Psychology: Normative Life Crises*. New York: Academic Press, 1975, pp. 167–184. (Ch. 15)

Hagen, J. W., and G. A. Hale. "The Development of Attention in Children," in A. D. Pick (ed.), *Minnesota Symposia on Child Psychology*. Vol. 7. Minneapolis: University of Minnesota Press, 1973, pp. 117–140. (Chs. 1, 8)

———, and N. Huntsman. "Selective Attention in Mental Retardates," *Developmental Psychology*, 5 (1971), 151–160. (Ch. 1)

———, and K. G. Stanovich. "Memory Strategies of Acquisition," in R. V. Kail, Jr., and J. W. Hagen (eds.), *Perspectives on the Development of Memory and Cognition*.

Hillsdale, N. J.: Lawrence Erlbaum Associates, 1977, pp. 89–111. (Ch. 8)

Hagen, M. A., and R. K. Jones. "Differential Patterns of Preference for Modified Linear Perspective in Children and Adults," *Journal of Experimental Child Psychology*, 26 (1978), 205–215. (Ch. 8)

Hainline, L. "Developmental Changes in the Visual Scanning of Face and Nonface Patterns by Infants," *Journal of Experimental Psychology*, 25 (1978), 90–115. (Ch. 7)

———, and E. Feig. "The Correlates of Father Absence in College-Aged Women," *Child Development*, 49 (1978), 37–42. (Ch. 13)

Haith, M. M. "The Responses of the Human Newborn to Visual Movement," *Journal of Experimental Child Psychology*, 3 (1966), 235–243. (Ch. 4)

———. *Rules That Babies Look By: The Organization of Newborn Visual Activity*. Hillsdale, N. J.: Lawrence Erlbaum Associates, 1980. (Ch. 4)

———, T. Bergman, and M. J. Moore. "Eye Contact and Face Scanning in Early Infancy," *Science*, 198 (1977), 853–855. (Ch. 7)

Hale, G. A. "Development of Children's Attention to Stimulus Components," in G. A. Hale and M. Lewis (eds.), *Attention and Cognitive Development*. New York: Plenum Press, 1979, pp. 43–64. (Ch. 8)

Halford, G. S., and F. M. Boyle. "Do Young Children Understand Conservation of Number?" *Child Development*, 56 (1985), 165–176. (Ch. 10)

Hall, G. S. "Notes on the Study of Infants," *The Pedagogical Seminary*, 1 (1891), 127–138. (Ch. 4)

———. *Adolescence*. 2 vols. New York: Appleton, 1904. (Ch. 1)

Hamill, P. V., F. E. Johnston, and S. Lemeshow. *Height and Weight of Children: Socio-Economic Status: United States*. Rockville, Md.: U.S. Department of Health, Education and Welfare. Pub. no. HRA 73–1601, 1972. (Ch. 5)

Hammer, E. F. "Creativity and Feminine Ingredients in Young Male Artists," *Perceptual and Motor Skills*, 19 (1964), 414. (Ch. 15)

Harari, H., and J. W. McDonald. "Situational Influences on Moral Justice: A Study of 'Finking,'" *Journal of Personality and Social Psychology*, 3 (1969), 240–244. (Ch. 14)

Harlow, H. F., and M. K. Harlow. "Learning to Love," *American Scientist*, 54 (1966), 244–272. (Ch. 12)

———, and ———. "Effects of Various Mother-Infant Relationships on Rhesus Monkey Behaviors," in B. M. Foss (ed.), *Determinants of Infant Behavior*. Vol. 4. London: Methuen, 1969, pp. 15–36. (Chs. 12, 14)

Harris, P. L. "Infant Cognition," in P. H. Mussen (ed.), *Handbook of Child Psychology*. 4th ed. Vol. 2: M. M. Haith and J. J. Campos (eds.), *Infancy and Developmental Psychobiology*. New York: Wiley, 1983, pp. 27–94. (Chs. 1, 7, 12)

Harrison, C. W., J. R. Rawls, and D. J. Rawls. "Difference between Leaders and Nonleaders in Six- to Eleven-Year-Old Children," *Journal of Social Psychology*, 84 (1971), 262–272. (Ch. 14)

Harter, S. "Developmental Perspectives on the Self-System," in P. H. Mussen (ed.), *Handbook of Child Psychology*. 4th ed. Vol. 4: E. M. Hetherington (ed.), *Socialization, Personality, and Social Development*. New York: Wiley, 1983, pp. 275–385. (Ch. 17)

Hartshorne, H., and M. A. May. *Studies in Deceit*. New York: Macmillan, 1928. (Ch. 16)

Hartup, W. W. "Friendship Status and the Effectiveness of Peers As Reinforcing Agents," *Journal of Experimental Child Psychology*, 1 (1964a), 154–162. (Ch. 14)

———. "Patterns of Imitative Behavior in Young Children," *Child Development*, 35 (1964b), 183–191. (Ch. 14)

———. "Peer Interaction and Social Organization," in P.

H. Mussen (ed.), *Carmichael's Manual of Child Psychology.* 3rd ed. Vol. 2. New York: Wiley, 1970, pp. 361–456. (Ch. 14)

———. "Aggression in Childhood: Developmental Perspectives," *American Psychologist,* 29 (1974), 336–341. (Ch. 16)

———. "The Social Worlds of Childhood," *American Psychologist,* 34 (1979), 944–950. (Ch. 14)

———. "Peer Relations," in P. H. Mussen (ed.), *Handbook of Child Psychology.* 4th ed. Vol. 4: E. M. Hetherington (ed.), *Socialization, Personality, and Social Structure.* New York: Wiley, 1983, pp. 102–196. (Chs. 2, 14, 15)

———, and B. Coates. "Imitation of a Peer as a Function of Reinforcement from the Peer Group and Rewardingness of the Model," *Child Development,* 38 (1967), 1003–1016. (Ch. 14)

———, J. A. Glazer, and R. Charlesworth. "Peer Reinforcement and Sociometric Status," *Child Development,* 38 (1967), 1017–1024. (Ch. 14)

Haugh, S. S., C. D. Hoffman, and G. Cowan. "The Eye of the Very Young Beholder: Sex Typing of Infants by Young Children," *Child Development,* 51 (1980), 598–600. (Ch. 15)

Hawkins, J., R. D. Pea, J. Glick, and S. Scribner. " 'Merds That Laugh Don't Like Mushrooms': Evidence for Deductive Reasoning by Preschoolers," *Developmental Psychology,* 20 (1984), 584–594. (Ch. 10)

Hay, D. F. "Multiple Functions of Proximity Seeking in Infancy," *Child Development,* 51 (1980), 636–645. (Ch. 12)

———, A. Nash, and J. Pedersen. "Interaction Between Six-Month-Old Peers," *Child Development,* 54 (1983), 557–562. (Ch. 14)

———, and H. S. Ross. "The Social Nature of Early Conflict," *Child Development,* 53 (1982), 105–113. (Ch. 14)

Hebb, D. O. *Organization of Behavior.* New York: Wiley, 1949. (Ch. 11)

Hecaen, H., and M. L. Albert. *Human Neuropsychology.* New York: Wiley-Interscience, 1978. (Ch. 8)

Hecox, K. "Electrophysiological Correlates of Human Auditory Development," in L. B. Cohen and P. Salapatek (eds.), *Infant Perception: From Sensation to Cognition.* Vol. 2: *Perception of Space, Speech, and Sound.* New York: Academic Press, 1975, pp. 151–191. (Ch. 4)

Heiss, J. "Women's Values Regarding Marriage and the Family," in H. P. McAdoo (ed.), *Black Families.* Beverly Hills, Calif.: Sage, 1981, pp. 186–198. (Ch. 13)

Helson, R. "Personality of Women with Imaginative and Artistic Interests: The Role of Masculinity, Originality, and Other Characteristics in Their Creativity," *Journal of Personality,* 34 (1966), 1–25. (Ch. 11)

———, and R. S. Crutchfield. "Mathematicians: The Creative Researcher and the Average Ph.D." *Journal of Consulting and Clinical Psychology,* 34 (1970), 250–257. (Ch. 11)

Henig, R. M. "Saving Babies Before Birth," *New York Times Magazine,* February 28, 1982, 18–21+. (Ch. 3)

Henninger, P. "Problem-Solving Strategies of Musically Trained and Untrained Subjects and Hemisphere Activation." Doctoral dissertation. University of Toronto, 1981. [cited in Kinsbourne and Hiscock, 1983] (Ch. 6)

Hermelin, B. "Images and Language," in M. Rutter and E. Schopler (eds.), *Autism: A Reappraisal of Concepts and Treatment.* New York: Plenum Press, 1978, pp. 141–154. (Ch. 8)

———, and N. O'Connor. "Functional Asymmetry in the Reading of Braille," *Neuropsychologia,* 9 (1971), 431–435. (Ch. 6)

Hershenson, M. "Visual Discrimination in the Human Newborn," *Journal of Comparative and Physiological Psychology,* 58 (1964), 270–276. (Ch. 4)

Herzog, E., and C. E. Sudia. "Children in Fatherless Families," in B. M. Caldwell and H. N. Ricciuti (eds.), *Review of Child Development Research.* Vol. 3. Chicago: University of Chicago Press, 1973, pp. 141–232. (Ch. 13)

Hess, E. H. "Imprinting in Birds," *Science,* 146 (1964), 1128–1139. (Ch. 12)

———. "Imprinting in a Natural Laboratory," *Scientific American,* 227 (1972), 24–31. (Ch. 12)

Hess, R. D. "Social Class and Ethnic Influences on Socialization," in P. H. Mussen (ed.), *Carmichael's Manual of Child Psychology.* 3rd ed. Vol. 2. New York: Wiley, 1970, pp. 457–557. (Chs. 5, 13)

———, and T. M. McDevitt. "Some Cognitive Consequences of Maternal Intervention Techniques: A Longitudinal Study," *Child Development,* 55 (1984), 2017–2030. (Ch. 11)

Hetherington, E. M. "Effects of Paternal Absence on Sex-Typed Behaviors in Negro and White Preadolescent Males," *Journal of Personality and Social Psychology,* 4 (1966), 87–91. (Ch. 13)

———. "Effects of Father Absence on Personality Development in Adolescent Daughters," *Developmental Psychology,* 7 (1972), 313–326. (Ch. 13)

———, M. Cox, and R. Cox. "Effects of Divorce on Parents and Children," in M. E. Lamb (ed.), *Nontraditional Families: Parenting and Child Development.* Hillsdale, N. J.: Lawrence Erlbaum Associates, 1982, pp. 233–288. (Ch. 13)

Hicks, D. J. "Imitation and Retention of Film-Mediated Aggressive Peer and Adult Models," *Journal of Personality and Social Psychology,* 2 (1965), 97–100. (Ch. 14)

———. "Girls' Attitudes Toward Modeled Behaviors and the Content of Imitative Private Play," *Child Development,* 42 (1971), 139–147. (Ch. 14)

Hicks, R. E., and M. Kinsbourne. "Human Handedness: A Partial Cross-Fostering Study," *Science,* 192 (1976), 908–910. (Ch. 6)

Hill, R. B. *Strengths of Black Families.* New York: Emerson Hall, 1971. (Ch. 13)

Himes, J. H. "Secular Changes in Body Proportions and Composition," in A. F. Roche (ed.), "Secular Trends in Human Growth, Maturation, and Development," *Monographs of the Society for Research in Child Development,* 44 (1979), whole no. 179, pp. 28–58. (Ch. 5)

Hinde, R. A. "Ethology and Child Development," in P. H. Mussen (ed.), *Handbook of Child Psychology.* 4th ed. Vol. 2: M. M. Haith and J. J. Campos (eds.), *Infancy and Developmental Psychobiology.* New York: Wiley, 1983, pp. 27–94. (Ch. 1)

Hiscock, M., and M. Kinsbourne. "Selective Listening Asymmetry in Preschool Children," *Developmental Psychology,* 13 (1977), 217–224. (Ch. 6)

Hochberg, J. E., and V. Brooks. "Pictorial Recognition as an Unlearned Ability: A Study of One Child's Performance," *American Journal of Psychology,* 75 (1962), 624–628. (Ch. 8)

Hoffman, L. W. "Increased Fathering: Effects on the Mother," in M. E. Lamb and A. Sagi (eds.), *Fatherhood and Family Policy.* Hillsdale, N. J.: Lawrence Erlbaum Associates, 1983, pp. 167–190. (Ch. 13)

———. "Maternal Employment and the Young Child," in M. Perlmutter (ed.), *Minnesota Symposia on Child Psychology.* Vol. 17: *Parent-Child Interaction and Parent-Child Relations in Child Development.* Hillsdale, N. J.: Lawrence Erlbaum Associates, 1984, pp. 101–128. (Ch. 13)

Hoffman, M. L. "Empathy, Role Taking, Guilt, and the Development of Altruistic Motives," in T. Lickona (ed.), *Moral Development and Behavior.* New York: Holt, Rinehart and Winston, 1976, pp. 124–143. (Ch. 16)

———. "Moral Internalization: Current Theory and Research," in L. Berkowitz (ed.), *Advances in Experimental Social Psychology.* Vol. 10. New York: Academic Press,

1977a, pp. 85–133. (Ch. 16)

——. "Sex Differences in Empathy and Related Behaviors," *Psychological Bulletin*, 84 (1977b), 712–722. (Ch. 16)

——. "Moral Development," in M. H. Bornstein and M. E. Lamb (eds.), *Developmental Psychology*. Hillsdale, N. J.: Lawrence Erlbaum Associates, 1984, pp. 279–324. (Chs. 16, 17)

——, and H. D. Saltzstein. "Parent Discipline and the Child's Moral Development," *Journal of Personality and Social Psychology*, 5 (1967), 45–57. (Ch. 16)

Hoffman, R. F. "Developmental Changes in Human Infant Visual-Evoked Potentials to Patterned Stimuli Recorded at Different Scalp Locations," *Child Development*, 49 (1978), 110–118. (Chs. 6, 7)

Hogan, R., and N. P. Emler. "Moral Development," in M. E. Lamb (ed.), *Social and Personality Development*. New York: Holt, Rinehart and Winston, 1978, pp. 200–223. (Ch. 16)

Holyoak, K. J., E. N. Junn, and D. O. Billman. "Development of Analogical Problem-Solving Skill," *Child Development*, 55 (1984), 2042–2055. (Ch. 11)

Honzik, M. P. "Developmental Studies of Parent-Child Resemblances in Intelligence," *Child Development*, 28 (1957), 215–228. (Ch. 11)

Hooker, D. *The Prenatal Origins of Behavior.* Lawrence, Kans.: University of Kansas Press, 1952. (Ch. 3)

Horn, J. L. "Organization of Data on Life-Span Development of Human Abilities," in L. R. Goulet and P. B. Baltes (eds.), *Life-Span Developmental Psychology: Research and Theory.* New York: Academic Press, 1970, pp. 423–466. (Ch. 11)

Horn, J. M. "The Texas Adoption Project: Adopted Children and Their Intellectual Resemblance to Biological and Adoptive Parents," *Child Development*, 54 (1983), 268–275. (Ch. 11)

Horner, M. "Fail: Bright Woman," *Psychology Today*, 3 (November 1969), 36–38. (Ch. 14)

Horowitz, F. D., J. Ashton, R. Culp, E. Gaddis, S. Levin, and B. Reichmann. "The Effects of Obstetrical Medication on the Behavior of Israeli Newborn Infants and Some Comparisons with Uruguayan and American Infants," *Child Development*, 48 (1977), 1607–1623. (Ch. 3)

Howes, C. "Peer Play Scale as an Index of Complexity of Peer Interaction," *Developmental Psychology*, 16 (1980), 371–372. (Ch. 14)

——, and J. L. Rubenstein. "Toddler Peer Behavior in Two Types of Day Care," *Infant Behavior and Development*, 4 (1981), 387–394. (Ch. 14)

Hubel, D. H. "The Brain," *Scientific American*, 241 (September 1979), 44–53. (Chs. 3, 6)

——, and T. N. Wiesel. "Receptive Fields of Cells in Striate Cortex of Very Young, Visually Inexperienced Kittens," *Journal of Neurophysiology*, 26 (1963), 994–1002. (Ch. 6)

Huesmann, L. R., L. D. Eron, M. M. Lefkowitz, and L. O. Walder. "Stability of Aggression Over Time and Generations," *Developmental Psychology*, 20 (1984), 1120–1134. (Ch. 16)

——, K. Lagerspetz, and L. D. Eron. "Intervening Variables in the TV Violence-Aggression Relation: Evidence from Two Countries," *Developmental Psychology*, 20 (1984), 746–775. (Ch. 16)

Hughes, M. "Egocentrism in Pre-School Children." Doctoral dissertation. Edinburgh University, 1975. (Ch. 17)

Hulse, F. S. "Exogamie et Heterosis," *Archives Suisse d'Anthropologie General*, 22 (1957), 103–124. (Ch. 5)

Humphrey, T. "The Development of Human Fetal Activity and Its Relation to Postnatal Behavior," in H. W. Reese and L. P. Lipsitt (eds.), *Advances in Child Development and Behavior.* Vol. 5. New York: Academic Press, 1970, pp.

2–59. (Ch. 3)

Hunt, E. "What Kind of Computer Is Man?" *Cognitive Psychology*, 2 (1971), 57–98. (Ch. 1)

Hunt, E. "Varieties of Cognitive Power," in L. B. Resnick (ed.), *The Nature of Intelligence*. Hillsdale, N. J.: Lawrence Erlbaum Associates, 1976, pp. 237–260. (Ch. 11)

Hunter, M. A., E. W. Ames, and R. Koopman. "Effect of Stimulus Complexity and Familiarization Time on Infant Preferences for Novel and Familiar Stimuli," *Developmental Psychology*, 19 (1983), 338–352. (Ch. 7)

Huston, A. C. "Sex-Typing," in P. H. Mussen (ed.), *Handbook of Child Psychology.* 4th ed. Vol. 4: E. M. Hetherington (ed.), *Socialization, Personality, and Social Development.* New York: Wiley, 1983, pp. 387–467. (Ch. 15)

——, D. Greer, J. C. Wright, R. Welch, and R. Ross. "Children's Comprehension of Televised Formal Features with Masculine and Feminine Connotations," *Child Development*, 20 (1984), 707–716. (Ch. 15)

Huttenlocher, J., and C. C. Presson. "The Coding and Transformation of Spatial Information," *Cognitive Psychology*, 11 (1979), 375–394. (Ch. 17)

Hyde, J. S. "Gender Differences in Aggression," *Developmental Psychology*, 20 (1984), 722–736. (Ch. 15)

Hyman, I. A. "Psychology, Education, and Schooling," *American Psychologist*, 34 (1979), 1024–1029. (Ch. 11)

Hymel, S., and S. R. Asher. "Assessment and Training of Isolated Children's Social Skills." Paper presented at the Biennial Meeting of the Society for Research in Child Development. New Orleans, March 1977. (Ch. 14)

Ianotti, R. J. "Effect of Role-Taking Experience on Role-Taking, Empathy, Altruism, and Aggression," *Developmental Psychology*, 14 (1978), 119–124. (Ch. 17)

Imperato-McGinley, J., R. E. Peterson, T. Gautier, and E. Sturia. "Androgens and the Evolution of Male-Gender Identity among Male Pseudohermaphrodites with 5α-Reductase Deficiency," *New England Journal of Medicine*, 300 (1979), 1233–1237. (Ch. 15)

Ingram, D. "Cerebral Speech Lateralization in Young Children," *Neuropsychologia*, 13 (1975a), 103–105. (Ch. 6)

——. "Motor Asymmetries in Young Children," *Neuropsychologia*, 13 (1975b), 95–102. (Ch. 6)

Inhelder, B. "Memory and Intelligence in the Child," in B. Inhelder and H. H. Chipman (eds.), *Piaget and His School.* New York: Springer-Verlag, 1976, pp. 100–120. (Ch. 8)

——, and J. Piaget. *The Growth of Logical Thinking From Childhood to Adolescence.* New York: Basic Books, 1958. (Chs. 1, 10)

——, and ——. *The Early Growth of Logic in the Child.* London: Routledge & Kegan Paul, 1964. (Ch. 8)

Interprofessional Task Force on Health Care of Women and Children. *The Development of Family-Centered Maternity/Newborn Care in Hospitals.* Chicago: Interprofessional Task Force, 1978. (Ch. 3)

Ironsmith, M., and G. J. Whitehurst. "The Development of Listener Abilities in Communication: How Children Deal with Ambiguous Information," *Child Development*, 49 (1978), 348–352. (Ch. 17)

Iverson, L. I. "The Chemistry of the Brain," *Scientific American*, 241 (September 1979, 134–149. (Ch. 6)

Jacobson, J. L., D. C. Boersma, R. B. Fields, and K. L. Olson. "Paralinguistic Features of Adult Speech to Infants and Small Children," *Child Development*, 54 (1983), 436–442. (Ch. 9)

——, and D. E. Wille. "Influence of Attachment and Separation Experience on Separation Distress," *Developmental Psychology*, 20 (1984), 447–484. (Ch. 12)

Jacobson, S. "Matching Behavior in the Young Infant," *Child Development*, 50 (1979), 425–430. (Ch. 4)

Jensen, A. R. "How Much Can We Boost IQ and Scholastic Achievement?" *Harvard Educational Review*, 39 (1969), 1–123. (Ch. 11)

———. "Another Look at Culture Fair Testing," in J. Hellmuth (ed.), *The Disadvantaged Child (Compensatory Education: A National Debate)*. Vol. 3. New York: Bruner-Mazel, 1970. (Ch. 11)

Jerison, H. J. *Evolution of the Brain and Intelligence*. New York: Academic Press, 1973. (Ch. 6)

Jersild, A. *In Search of Self: An Exploration of the Role of the School in Promoting Self-Understanding*. New York: Columbia University Press, 1952. (Ch. 5)

Joffe, J. M. "Genotype and Prenatal and Premating Stress Interact to Affect Adult Behavior in Rats," *Science*, 150 (1965), 1844–1845. (Ch. 3)

Johansson, G. "Visual Event Perception," in R. Held, H. W. Leibowitz, and H.-L. Teuber (eds.), *Handbook of Sensory Physiology: Perception*. Berlin: Springer-Verlag, 1978. (Ch. 8)

Johansson, S. R. "Neglect, Abuse, and Avoidable Deaths among Children: Suggestive Observations on the European Experience, from Medieval to Modern Times," in R. Gelles and J. B. Lancaster (eds.), *A Biosocial Perspective on Child Abuse and Neglect*. Chicago: Aldine [in press]. (Ch. 15)

John, E. R. "How the Brain Works—A New Theory," *Psychology Today*, 9 (May 1976), 48–52. (Ch. 11)

Johnson, P., and D. M. Salisbury. "Breathing and Sucking during Feeding in the Newborn," in *Parent-Infant Interaction*. Amsterdam: CIBA Foundation Symposium 33, new series, ASP, 1975. (Ch. 4)

Jones, K. L., D. W. Smith, A. P. Streissguth, and N. C. Myrianthopoulos. "Outcome in Offspring of Chronic Alcoholic Women," *Lancet*, 1 (1974), 1076–1078. (Ch. 11)

Jones, M. C. "The Later Careers of Boys Who Were Early- or Late-Maturing," *Child Development*, 28 (1957), 113–128. (Ch. 15)

———. "Psychological Correlates of Somatic Development," *Child Development*, 39 (1965), 899–911. (Ch. 15)

———, and N. Bayley. "Physical Maturing Among Boys as Related to Behavior," *Journal of Educational Psychology*, 41 (1950), 129–248. (Ch. 15)

Joos, S. K., E. Pollitt, W. H. Mueller, and D. L. Albright. "The Bacon Chow Study: Maternal Nutritional Supplementation and Infant Behavioral Development," *Child Development*, 54 (1983), 669–676. (Ch. 3)

Julesz, B. *Foundations of Cyclopean Perception*. Chicago: University of Chicago Press, 1971. (Ch. 7)

Jusczyk, P. W., B. S. Rosner, J. E. Cutting, F. Foard, and L. B. Smith. "Categorical Perception of Non-Speech Sounds by Two-Month-Old Infants," *Perception & Psychophysics*, 21 (1977), 50–54. (Ch. 9)

Kagan, J. "The Concept of Identification," *Psychological Review*, 65 (1958), 296–305. (Ch. 1)

———. *The Growth of the Child*. New York: Norton, 1978. (Chs. 7, 11)

———. *The Nature of the Child*. New York: Basic Books, 1984. (Chs. 7, 12, 16)

———, R. B. Kearsley, and P. R. Zelazo. *Infancy: Its Place in Human Development*. Cambridge, Mass.: Harvard University Press, 1978. (Ch. 13)

———, and S. R. Tulkin. "Social Class Difference in Child Rearing During the First Year," in H. R. Schaffer (ed.), *The Origins of Human Social Relations*. New York: Academic Press, 1971, pp. 164–186. (Chs. 7, 12)

Kail, R. V., Jr., and J. Bisanz. "Information Processing and Cognitive Development," in H. W. Reese (ed.), *Advances in Child Development and Behavior*. Vol. 17. New York: Academic Press, 1982, pp. 45–81. (Ch. 1)

———, and J. W. Hagen. Introduction to R. V. Kail, Jr., and J. W. Hagen (eds.), *Perspectives on the Development of Memory and Cognition*. Hillsdale, N. J.: Lawrence Erlbaum Associates, 1977, pp. xi–xiii. (Ch. 8)

———, and ———. "Memory in Childhood," in B. B. Wolman (ed.), *Handbook of Developmental Psychology*. Englewood Cliffs, N. J.: Prentice-Hall, 1982, pp. 350–366. (Ch. 8)

———, and N. E. Spear (eds.). *Comparative Perspectives on the Development of Memory*. Hillsdale, N. J.: Lawrence Erlbaum Associates, 1984. (Ch. 8)

Kalnins, I. V., and J. S. Bruner. "The Coordination of Visual Observation and Instrumental Behavior in Early Infancy," *Perception*, 2 (1973), 307–314. (Ch. 7)

Kaltenbach, K., M. Weinraub, and W. Fullard. "Infant Wariness Toward Strangers Reconsidered: Infants' and Mothers' Reactions to Unfamiliar Persons," *Child Development*, 51 (1980), 1197–1202. (Ch. 12)

Kamin, L. J. *The Science and Politics of IQ*. Potomac, Md.: Erlbaum Associates, 1974. (Ch. 11)

Kandel, D. B. "Homophily, Selection, and Socialization in Adolescent Friendships," *American Journal of Sociology*, 84 (1978a), 427–436. (Ch. 14)

———. "Similarity in Real-Life Adolescent Friendship Pairs," *Journal of Personality and Social Psychology*, 36 (1978b), 306–312. (Ch. 14)

———, and G. S. Lesser. *Youth in Two Worlds*. San Francisco: Jossey-Bass, 1972. (Ch. 14)

Kandel, E. R. "Small Systems of Neurons," *Scientific American*, 241 (September 1979), 134–149. (Ch. 6)

Kanner, L. "Autistic Disturbances of Affective Contact," *Nervous Child*, 2 (1943), 217–250. (Ch. 8)

Karmel, B. Z., H. Kaye, and E. R. John. "Developmental Neurometrics: The Use of Quantitative Analysis of Brain Electrical Activity to Probe Mental Functioning Throughout the Life Span," in W. A. Collins (ed.), *Minnesota Symposia on Child Psychology*. Vol. 11. Hillsdale, N. J.: Lawrence Erlbaum Associates, 1978, pp. 141–198. (Ch. 11)

Karniol, R. "Children's Use of Intention Cues in Evaluating Behavior," *Psychological Bulletin*, 85 (1978), 76–85. (Ch. 16)

Kaye, K. *The Mental and Social Life of Babies*. Chicago: University of Chicago Press, 1982. (Ch. 12)

———, and A. J. Wells. "Mothers' Jiggling and the Burst-Pause Pattern in Neonatal Feeding," *Infant Behavior and Development*, 3 (1980), 29–46. (Ch. 4)

Kearsley, R. B. "The Newborn's Response to Auditory Stimulation: A Demonstration of Orienting and Reflexive Behavior," *Child Development*, 44 (1973), 582–590. (Ch. 4)

Keating, D. P. "The Acceleration/Enrichment Debate: Basic Issues," in W. C. George, S. J. Cohn, and J. C. Stanley (eds.), *Educating the Gifted: Acceleration and Enrichment*. Baltimore: Johns Hopkins University Press, 1979, pp. 217–220. (Ch. 10)

Keeney, T. J., S. R. Canizzo, and J. H. Flavell. "Spontaneous and Induced Verbal Rehearsal in a Recall Task," *Child Development*, 38 (1967), 953–966. (Ch. 8)

Kegan, R. *The Evolving Self: Problem and Process in Human Development*. Cambridge, Mass.: Harvard University Press, 1982. (Ch. 1)

Keller, A., L. H. Ford, Jr., and J. A. Meacham. "Dimensions of Self-Concept in Preschool Children," *Developmental Psychology*, 14 (1978), 483–489. (Ch. 17)

Keller, B. B., and R. Q. Bell. "Child Effects on Adult's Method of Eliciting Altruistic Behavior," *Child Development*, 50 (1979), 1004–1009. (Ch. 16)

Kempe, R. S., and H. C. Kempe. *Child Abuse*. Cambridge, Mass.: Harvard University Press, 1978. (Ch. 13)

Kendler, T. S. "The Development of Discrimination Learning: A Levels-of-Functioning Explanation," in H. W.

Reese and L. P. Lipsitt (eds.), *Advances in Child Development and Behavior*. Vol. 13. New York: Academic Press, 1979, pp. 83–117. (Ch. 10)

Kershner, J. R. "Ocular-Manual Laterality and Dual Hemisphere Specialization," *Cortex*, 10 (1974), 293–302. (Ch. 6)

Kessen, W. "Sucking and Looking: Two Organized Congenital Patterns of Behavior in the Human Newborn," in H. W. Stevenson, E. H. Hess, and H. L. Rheingold (eds.), *Early Behavior: Comparative and Developmental Approaches*. New York: Wiley, 1967, pp. 147–180. (Ch. 4)

———, M. M. Haith, and P. H. Salapatek. "Human Infancy: Bibliography and Guide," in P. H. Mussen (ed.), *Carmichael's Manual of Child Psychology*. 3rd ed. Vol. 1. New York: Wiley, 1970, pp. 287–445. (Ch. 5)

———, J. Levine, and K. A. Wendich. "The Imitation of Pitch in Infants," *Infant Behavior and Development*, 2 (1979), 93–100. (Ch. 7)

Kimura, D. "The Asymmetry of the Human Brain," *Scientific American*, (1975), 70–78. (Ch. 6)

Kinsbourne, M. "Toward a Model for the Attention Deficit Disorder," in M. Perlmutter (ed.), *The Minnesota Symposia on Child Psychology*. Vol. 16: *Development and Policy Concerning Children with Special Needs*. Hillsdale, N. J.: Lawrence Erlbaum Associates, 1983, pp. 137–166. (Ch. 6)

———, and M. Hiscock. "Does Cerebral Dominance Develop?" in S. J. Segalowitz and F. A. Gruber (eds.), *Language, Development and Neurological Theory*. New York: Academic Press, 1977. (Ch. 6)

———, and ———. "The Normal and Deviant Development of Functional Lateralization of the Brain," in P. H. Mussen (ed.), *Handbook of Child Psychology*. Vol. 2: M. M. Haith and J. J. Campos (eds.), *Infancy and Developmental Psychobiology*. New York: Wiley, 1983, pp. 157–280. (Chs. 6, 9)

———, and J. M. Swanson. "Developmental Aspects of Selective Orientation," in G. A. Hale and M. Lewis (eds.), *Attention and Cognitive Development*. New York: Plenum Press, 1979, pp. 119–134. (Ch. 6)

Kinsey, A. C., W. B. Pomeroy, and C. E. Martin. *Sexual Behavior in the Human Male*. Philadelphia: Saunders, 1948. (Ch. 15)

———, ———, ———, and P. H. Gebhard. *Sexual Behavior in the Human Female*. Philadelphia: Saunders, 1953. (Ch. 15)

Kirkpatrick, M., K. V. R. Smith, and R. Roy. "Adjustment and Sexual Identity of Children of Lesbians and Heterosexual Single Mothers." Paper presented at the Annual Meeting of the American Psychological Association. New York, September 1979. (Ch. 15)

Klahr, D., and J. G. Wallace. *Cognitive Development: An Information-Processing View*. Hillsdale, N. J.: Lawrence Erlbaum Associates, 1976. (Ch. 1)

Klaus, M. H., and J. H. Kennell. *Maternal-Infant Bonding*. St. Louis, Mo.: Mosby, 1976. (Ch. 4)

———, and ———. *Parent-Infant Bonding*. St. Louis, Mo.: Mosby, 1982. (Ch. 4)

Kleiman, D. "When Abortion Becomes Birth: A Dilemma of Medical Ethics Shaken by New Advances," *New York Times*, February 15, 1984, B1+. (Ch. 3)

Klima, E. S., and U. Bellugi. "Teaching Apes to Communicate," in G. A. Miller (ed.), *Communication, Language, and Meaning: Psychological Perspectives*. New York: Basic Books, 1973, pp. 95–106. (Ch. 9)

Klinnert, M. D., J. J. Campos, J. F. Sorce, R. N. Emde, and M. Svejda. "Emotions as Behavior Regulators: Social Referencing in Infancy," in R. Plutchik and H. Kellerman, (eds.), *Emotion: Theory, Research and Experience*. Vol. 2: *Emotions in Early Development*. New York: Academic Press, 1983a, pp. 37–86. (Ch. 12)

———, R. N. Emde, P. Butterfield, and J. J. Campos. "Emotional Communication from Familiarized Adults Influences Infants' Behavior." Paper presented at the biennial meeting of the International Conference on Infant Studies. Austin, Texas, March 1983b. (Ch. 12)

Kobasigawa, A. "Utilization of Retrieval Cues by Children in Recall," *Child Development*, 45 (1974), 127–134. (Ch. 8)

———. "Retrieval Strategies in the Development of Memory." In R. V. Kail, Jr., and J. W. Hagen (eds.), *Perspectives on the Development of Memory and Cognition*. Hillsdale, N. J.: Lawrence Erlbaum Associates, 1977, pp. 177–201. (Ch. 8)

Koepke, J. E., M. Hamm, M. Legerstee, and M. Russell. "Neonatal Imitation: Two Failures to Replicate," *Infant Behavior and Development*, 6 (1983), 97–102. (Ch. 4)

Koffka, K. *The Growth of the Mind*. 2nd ed. New York: Harcourt, 1931. (Ch. 8)

Kohlberg, L. "A Cognitive-Developmental Analysis of Children's Sex Role Concepts and Attitudes," in E. E. Maccoby (ed.), *The Development of Sex Differences*. Stanford, Calif.: Stanford University Press, 1966, pp. 82–173. (Ch. 15)

———. "Moral Stages and Moralization: The Cognitive-Developmental Approach," in T. Lickona (ed.), *Moral Development and Behavior*. New York: Holt, Rinehart and Winston, 1976, pp. 31–53. (Ch. 16)

———, and C. Gilligan. "The Adolescent as a Philosopher: The Discovery of the Self in a Post-Conventional World," *Daedalus*, 100 (1971), 1051–1086. (Ch. 10)

Köhler, W., and H. Wallach. "Figural Aftereffects," *Proceedings of the American Philosophical Society*, 88 (1944), 269–357. (Ch. 8)

Kohn, B., and M. Dennis. "Selective Impairments of Visuo-Spatial Abilities in Infantile Hemiplegics after Right Cerebral Hemidecortication," *Neuropsychologia*, 12 (1974), 505–512. (Ch. 6)

Kohn, M. "The Effects of Social Class on Parental Values and Practices," in D. Reiss and H. A. Hoffman (eds.), *The American Family: Dying or Developing*. New York: Plenum Press, 1979, pp. 45–68. (Ch. 13)

Kolata, G. B. "Developmental Biology: Where Is It Going?" *Science*, 214 (1981), 642–645. (Ch. 3)

———. "Fetal Surgery for Neural Defects?" *Science*, 221 (1983a), 441. (Ch. 3)

———. "First Trimester Prenatal Diagnosis," *Science*, 221 (1983b), 1031–1032. (Ch. 3)

———. "Math Genius May Have Hormonal Basis," *Science*, 222 (1983c), 1312. (Ch. 6)

Konner, M. "Infancy Among the Kalahari San," in P. H. Leiderman, S. R. Tulkin, and A. Rosenfeld (eds.), *Culture and Infancy: Variations in the Human Experience*. New York: Academic Press, 1977, pp. 287–328. (Ch. 1)

Kopp, C. B. "Risk Factors in Development," in P. H. Mussen (ed.), *Handbook of Child Psychology*. 4th ed. Vol. 2: M. M. Haith and J. J. Campos (eds.), *Infancy and Developmental Psychobiology*. New York: Wiley, 1983, pp. 1081–1188. (Chs. 3, 5)

———, and A. H. Parmelee. "Prenatal and Perinatal Influences on Behavior," in J. D. Osofsky (ed.), *Handbook of Infant Development*. New York: Wiley-Interscience, 1979, pp. 29–75. (Ch. 3)

Korner, A. F., C. A. Hutchinson, J. A. Koperski, H. C. Kraemer, and P. A. Schneider. "Stability of Individual Differences of Neonatal Motor and Crying Patterns," *Child Development*, 52 (1981), 83–90. (Ch. 4)

Kornfield, J. R. "Theoretical Issues in Child Phonology," *Proceedings of the Seventh Annual Meeting of the Chicago Linguistic Society (CLS 7)*, University of Chicago, 1971, pp. 454–468. (Ch. 9)

Kossan, N. E. "Developmental Differences in Concept Acquisition Strategies," *Child Development*, 52 (1981), 290–298. (Ch. 10)

Kosslyn, S. M. "The Representation-Development Hypothesis," in P. A. Ornstein (ed.), *Memory Development in Children*. Hillsdale, N. J.: Lawrence Erlbaum Associates, 1978, pp. 157–190 (Ch. 8)

———. *Ghosts in the Mind's Machine*. New York: Norton, 1983. (Ch. 8)

Krakow, J. B., and C. B. Kopp. "The Effects of Developmental Delay on Sustained Attention in Young Children," *Child Development*, 54 (1983), 1143–1155. (Ch. 8)

Krebs, D., and A. A. Adinolfi. "Physical Attractiveness, Social Relations, and Personality Style," *Journal of Personality and Social Psychology*, 31 (1975), 245–253. (Ch. 14)

Krebs, R. L. "Some Relationships Between Moral Judgment, Attention, and Resistance to Temptation." Doctoral dissertation. University of Chicago, 1968. (Ch. 16)

Kremenitzner, J. P., H. G. Vaughan, Jr., D. Kurtzberg, and K. Dowling. "Smooth-Pursuit Eye Movements in the Newborn Infant," *Child Development*, 50 (1979), 442–448. (Ch. 4)

Kreutzer, M. A., C. Leonard, and J. H. Flavell. "An Interview Study of Children's Knowledge About Memory," *Monographs of the Society for Research in Child Development*, 40 (1975), whole no.159. (Ch. 8)

Kroll, J. "The Concept of Childhood in the Middle Ages," *Journal of the History of the Behavioral Sciences*, 13 (1977), 384–393. (Ch. 1)

Kuczaj, S. A., II. "Children's Judgments of Grammatical and Ungrammatical Irregular Past-Tense Verbs," *Child Development*, 49 (1978), 319–326. (Ch. 9)

———. "Evidence of a Language-Learning Strategy: On the Relative Ease of Acquisition of Prefixes and Suffixes," *Child Development*, 50 (1979), 1–13. (Ch. 9)

———. *Crib Speech and Language Play*. New York: Springer-Verlag, 1983. (Ch. 9)

Kuczynski, L. "Reasoning, Prohibitions, and Motivations for Compliance," *Developmental Psychology*, 19 (1983), 126–134. (Ch. 16)

Kuhn, D., and E. Phelps. "The Development of Problem-Solving Strategies," in H. W. Reese (ed.), *Advances in Child Development and Behavior*. Vol. 17. New York: Academic Press, 1982, pp. 1–44. (Ch. 10)

Kurtines, W., and E. B. Greif. "The Development of Moral Thought: Review and Evaluation of Kohlberg's Approach," *Psychological Bulletin*, 8 (1974), 453–470. (Ch. 16)

Laboratory of Comparative Human Cognition. "Culture and Cognitive Development," in P. H. Mussen (ed.), *Handbook of Child Psychology*. 4th ed. Vol. 1: W. Kessen (ed.), *History, Theory, and Methods*. New York: Wiley, 1983, pp. 295–356. (Ch. 1)

Ladd, G. W., and S. L. Oden. "The Relationship Between Children's Ideas About Helpfulness and Peer Acceptance," *Child Development*, 50 (1979), 402–408. (Ch. 14)

Lamb, M. E. "Interactions Between Eighteen-Month-Olds and Their Preschool-Aged Siblings," *Child Development*, 49 (1978a), 51–59. (Ch. 13)

———. "The Development of Sibling Relationships in Infants: A Short-Term Longitudinal Study," *Child Development*, 49 (1978b), 1189–1196. (Ch. 13)

———. "The Development of Social Expectations in the First Year of Life," in M. E. Lamb and L. R. Sherrod (eds.), *Infant Social Cognition: Empirical and Theoretical Considerations*. Hillsdale, N. J.: Lawrence Erlbaum Associates, 1981a, pp. 155–176. (Ch. 17)

———. "Developing Trust and Perceived Effectance in Infancy," in L. P. Lipsitt (ed.), *Advances in Infancy Research*. Vol. 1. Norwood, N. J.: Ablex, 1981b, pp. 101–130. (Chs. 12, 13)

———. "The Development of Father-Infant Relationships," in M. E. Lamb (ed.), *The Role of the Father in Child Development*. 2nd ed. New York: Wiley-Interscience, 1981c, pp. 459–488. (Ch. 12)

———. "Fathers and Child Development: An Integrative Overview," in M. E. Lamb (ed.), *Fathers and Child Development*. 2nd ed. New York: Wiley-Interscience, 1981d, pp. 1–70. (Ch. 2)

———. "Maternal Employment and Child Development: A Review," in M. E. Lamb (ed.), *Nontraditional Families: Parenting and Child Development*. Hillsdale, N. J.: Lawrence Erlbaum Associates, 1982, pp. 45–70. (Ch. 13)

———. "Fathers of Exceptional Children," in M. Seligman (ed.), *A Comprehensive Guide to Understanding and Treating the Family with a Handicapped Child*. New York: Grune & Stratton [in press a]. (Ch. 5)

———. "The Father's Role in a Changing World," in M. E. Lamb (ed.), *The Father's Role: Applied Perspectives*. New York: Wiley [in press b]. (Ch. 13)

———, and D. Baumrind. "Socialization and Personality Development in the Preschool Years," in M. E. Lamb (ed.), *Social and Personality Development*. New York: Holt, Rinehart and Winston, 1978. (Ch. 13)

———, and S. K. Bronson. "Fathers in the Context of Family Influences: Past, Present, and Future," *School Psychology Review*, 9 (1980), 336–353. (Ch. 13)

———, M. A. Easterbrooks, and G. W. Holden. "Reinforcement and Punishment Among Preschoolers: Characteristics, Effects, and Correlates," *Child Development*, 51 (1980), 1230–1236. (Ch. 15)

———, M. Frodi, C.-P. Hwang, and A. M. Frodi. "Effects of Paternal Involvement on Infant Preference for Mothers and Fathers," *Child Development*, 54 (1983), 450–458. (Ch. 12)

———, T. J. Gaensbauer, C. M. Malkin, and L. A. Schultz. "The Effects of Abuse and Neglect on Security of Infant-Adult Attachment," *Infant Behavior and Development* [in press]. (Ch. 13)

———, S. M. Garn, and M. T. Keating. "Correlations between Sociability and Cognitive Performance among Eight-Month-Olds," *Child Development*, 52 (1981), 711–713. (Ch. 2)

———, and E. Hall. "Bonding," *Childbirth Educator*, 2 (Fall 1982), 19–23. (Ch. 4)

———, and C.-P. Hwang. "Maternal Attachment and Mother-Neonate Bonding: A Critical Review," in M. E. Lamb and A. L. Brown (eds.), *Advances in Developmental Psychology*. Vol. 2. Hillsdale, N. J.: Lawrence Erlbaum Associates, 1982, 1–40. (Chs. 4, 12)

———, J. H. Pleck, and J. Levine. "The Role of the Father in Child Development: The Effects of Increased Paternal Involvement," in A. Kazdin (ed.), *Advances in Clinical Child Psychology*. Vol. 8. New York: Plenum Press [in press]. (Ch. 13)

———, ———, E. L. Charnov, and J. A. Levine. "A Biosocial Perspective on Paternal Behavior and Involvement," in J. B. Lancaster, J. Altmann, A. Rossi, and L. Sherrod (eds.), *Parenting Across the Lifespan: Biosocial Perspectives*. Chicago: Aldine [in press]. (Chs. 12, 13)

———, and J. L. Roopnarine. "Peer Influences on Sex-Role Development in Preschoolers," *Child Development*, 50 (1979), 1219–1222. (Ch. 14)

———, R. A. Thompson, W. P. Gardner, and E. L. Charnov. *Infant-Mother Attachment*. Hillsdale, N. J.: Lawrence Erlbaum Associates, 1985. (Ch. 12)

———, ———, ———, ———, and D. Estes. "Security of Infantile Attachment as Assessed in the 'Strange Situation': Its Study and Biological Interpretation," *The Behavioral and Brain Sciences*, 7 (1984), 127–171. (Chs. 12, 13, 14)

———, and K. A. Urberg. "The Development of Gender Role and Gender Identity," in M. E. Lamb (ed.), *Social and Personality Development*. New York: Holt, Rinehart and Winston, 1978, pp. 178–199. (Ch. 15)

Lamke, L. K. "The Impact of Sex-Role Orientation on Self-Esteem in Early Adolescence," *Child Development*, 53 (1982), 1530–1535. (Ch. 15)

Lange, G. "Organization-Related Processes in Children's Recall," in P. A. Ornstein (ed.), *Memory Development in Children*. Hillsdale, N. J.: Lawrence Erlbaum Associates, 1978, pp. 101–128. (Ch. 8)

Langlois, J. H., and A. C. Downs. "Mothers, Fathers, and Peers As Socializing Agents of Sex-Typed Play Behaviors in Young Children," *Child Development*, 51 (1980), 1237–1247. (Ch. 15)

———, and C. F. Stephan. "The Effects of Physical Attractiveness and Ethnicity on Children's Behavioral Attributions and Peer Preferences," *Child Development*, 48 (1977), 1694–1698. (Ch. 14)

LaPlante, M. N., N. McCormick, and G. G. Brannigan. "Living the Sexual Script: College Students' Views of Influences in Sexual Encounters," *Journal of Sex Research*, 16 (1980), 338–355. (Ch. 15)

Lasky, R. E. "The Ability of Six-Year-Olds, Eight-Year-Olds, and Adults to Abstract Visual Patterns," *Child Development*, 45 (1974), 626–632. (Ch. 10)

Laurendeau, M., and A. Pinard. *The Development of the Concept of Space in the Child*. New York: International Universities Press, 1970. (Ch. 17)

Lawson, K. R., and H. A. Ruff. "Infant Visual Following: Effects of Size and Sound," *Developmental Psychology*, 20 (1984), 427–434. (Ch. 7)

Lazar, I., and R. Darlington. "Lasting Effects of Early Education: A Report from the Consortium for Longitudinal Studies," *Monographs of the Society for Research in Child Development*, 47 (1982), whole no. 195. (Ch. 11)

Leakey, R. E., and R. Lewin. *Origins*. New York: Dutton, 1977. (Ch. 6)

Lefkowitz, M. M. "Smoking During Pregnancy: Long-Term Effects on Offspring," *Developmental Psychology*, 17 (1981), 192–194. (Ch. 3)

Leifer, A., and D. F. Roberts. "Children's Responses to Television Violence," in J. P. Murray, E. A. Rubenstein, and G. A. Comstock (eds.), *Television and Social Behavior*. Vol. 2: *Television and Social Learning*. Washington, D.C.: U.S. Government Printing Office, 1972, pp. 43–180. (Ch. 16)

Leiter, M. P. "A Study of Reciprocity in Preschool Play Groups," *Child Development*, 48 (1977), 1288–1295. (Ch. 14)

Lemoine, P., H. Haronsseau, P.-P. Borteryu, and J.-C. Menuet. "Les Infants et Parents Alcooliques: Anomalies Observées à propos de 127 Cas," *Ouest Medical*, 25 (1968), 476–482. (Ch. 11)

Lempert, H. "Extrasyntactic Factors Affecting Passive Sentence Comprehension by Young Children," *Child Development*, 49 (1978), 694–699. (Ch. 9)

Lenneberg, E. H. *Biological Foundations of Language*. New York: Wiley, 1967. (Chs. 5, 6, 9)

———. "Biological Aspects of Language," in G. A. Miller (ed.), *Communication, Language, and Meaning*. New York: Basic Books, 1973, pp. 49–60. (Ch. 9)

Leonard, C. O. "Serum AFP Screening for Neural Tube Defects," *Clinical Obstetrics and Gynecology*, 24 (1981), 1121–1132. (Ch. 3)

———, G. A. Chase, and B. Childs. "Genetic Counseling: A Consumers' View," *New England Journal of Medicine*, 287 (1972), 433–439. (Ch. 3)

Lerner, R. M. "Nature, Nurture, and Dynamic Interactionism," *Human Development*, 21 (1978), 1–20. (Ch. 1)

———, G. Sorell, and B. Brackney. "Sex Differences in Self-Concept and Self-Esteem of Late Adolescents: A Time-Lag Analysis," *Sex Roles*, 7 (1981), 709–722. (Ch. 15)

———, and G. Spanier. *Adolescent Development*. New York: McGraw-Hill, 1980. (Ch. 17)

Lesser, G. S. *Children and Television: Lessons from Sesame Street*. New York: Random House, 1974. (Chs. 2, 11)

Lester, B. M., H. Als, and T. B. Brazelton. "Regional Obstetric Anesthesia and Newborn Behavior: A Reanalysis Toward Synergistic Effects," *Child Development*, 53 (1982), 687–692. (Ch. 3)

———, M. Kotechuck, E. Spelke, M. J. Sellers, and R. E. Klein. "Separation Protest in Guatemalan Infants: Cross-Cultural and Cognitive Findings," *Developmental Psychology*, 10 (1974), 79–84. (Ch. 12)

Leventhal, A. S., and L. P. Lipsitt, "Adaptation, Pitch Discrimination, and Sound Localization in the Neonate," *Child Development*, 35 (1964), 756–767. (Ch. 4)

Levin, I. "The Development of Time Concepts in Children," *Child Development*, 48 (1977), 435–444. (Ch. 10)

LeVine, R. "Culture, Context, and the Concept of Development," in W. A. Collins (ed.), *Minnesota Symposia on Child Psychology*. Vol. 15: *The Concept of Development*. Hillsdale, N. J.: Lawrence Erlbaum Associates, 1982, pp. 162–166. (Ch. 2)

Levine, S. B., and L. M. Lothstein. "Transsexualism or the Gender Dysphoria Syndrome," *Journal of Sex and Marital Therapy*, 7 (1981), 85–113. (Ch. 15)

Levitt, M. J., T. G. Antonucci, and M. C. Clark. "Object-Person Permanence and Attachment: Another Look," *Merrill-Palmer Quarterly*, 30 (1984), 1–10. (Ch. 12)

Lewis, M. "A Developmental Study of Information Processing within the First Three Years of Life: Response Decrement to a Redundant Signal," *Monographs of the Society for Research in Child Development*, 34 (1969), whole no. 133. (Ch. 4)

———, and J. Brooks-Gunn. *Social Cognition and the Acquisition of Self*. New York: Plenum Press, 1979. (Chs. 12, 17)

———, and R. Freedle. "The Mother-Infant Dyad," in P. Pliner, L. Kranes, and T. Alloway (eds.), *Communication and Affect: Language and Thought*. New York: Academic Press, 1973. (Ch. 11)

Liben, L. S. "Memory in the Context of Cognitive Development: The Piagetian Approach," in R. V. Kail, Jr., and J. W. Hagen (eds.), *Perspectives on the Development of Memory and Cognition*. Hillsdale, N. J.: Lawrence Erlbaum Associates, 1977, pp. 297–332. (Ch. 8)

———, and B. Belknap. "Intellectual Realism: Implications for Investigations of Perspective Taking in Young Children," *Child Development*, 52 (1981), 921–924. (Ch. 17)

Licht, B. G., and C. S. Dweck. "Determinants of Academic Achievement: The Interaction of Children's Achievement Orientation with Skill Area," *Developmental Psychology*, 20 (1984), 628–636. (Ch. 14)

Liebert, R. M., and R. A. Baron. "Some Immediate Effects of Televised Violence on Children's Behavior," *Developmental Psychology*, 6 (1972), 467–475. (Ch. 15)

Lind, J. "The Infant Cry," *Proceedings of the Royal Society of Medicine*, 64 (1971), 468. (Ch. 4)

Lindberg, M. "The Role of Knowledge Structures in the Ontogeny of Learning," *Journal of Experimental Child Psychology*, 30 (1980), 401–410. (Ch. 8)

Lindgren, G. "Height, Weight, and Menarche in Swedish Urban Schoolchildren in Relation to Socioeconomic and Regional Factors," *Annals of Human Biology*, 3 (1976), 510–528. (Ch. 3)

Lipsitt, L. P. "Critical Conditions in Infancy," *American Psychologist*, 34 (1979), 973–980. (Ch. 4)

———, W. Q. Sturner, and B. Burke. "Perinatal Indicators and Subsequent Crib Death," *Infant Behavior and Development*, 2 (1979), 325–328. (Ch. 4)

Livesley, W. J., and D. B. Bromley. *Person Perception in Childhood and Adolescence*. New York: Wiley, 1973. (Ch. 17)

Locke, J. *An Essay Concerning Human Understanding*. Oxford: Clarendon Press, 1894 [orig. pub. 1690]. (Ch. 1)

Locke, J. L. "The Child's Processing of Phonology," in W. A. Collins (ed.), *Minnesota Symposia on Child Psychology*. Vol. 12: *Children's Language and Communication*. Hillsdale, N. J.: Lawrence Erlbaum Associates, 1979, pp. 83–120. (Ch. 9)

———, and K. J. Kutz. "Memory for Speech and Speech for Memory," *Journal of Speech and Hearing Research*, 18 (1975), 176–191. (Ch. 9)

Lomas, J., and D. Kimura. "Intrahemispheric Interaction Between Speaking and Sequential Manual Activity," *Neuropsychologia*, 14 (1976), 23–33. (Ch. 6)

Lorch, E. P., D. R. Anderson, and S. R. Levin. "The Relation of Visual Attention to Children's Comprehension of Television," *Child Development*, 50 (1979), 722–727. (Ch. 8)

Lorenz, K. "Die Angeborenen formen möglicher Erfahrung," *Zeitschrift für Tierpsychologie*, 5 (1942–1943), 239–409. (Ch. 1)

———. *On Aggression*. New York: Harcourt, Brace and World, 1966. (Ch. 16)

Lounsbury, M. L., and J. E. Bates. "The Cries of Infants of Differing Levels of Perceived Temperamental Difficultness: Acoustic Properties and Effects on Listeners," *Child Development*, 53 (1982), 677–686. (Ch. 4)

Lovell, K., and E. Ogilvie. "A Study of the Conservation of Weight in the Junior School Child," *British Journal of Educational Psychology*, 31 (1961), 138–144. (Ch. 10)

Maccoby, E. E. "Sex Differentiation During Childhood Development," in *Master Lecture Series*. Washington, D.C.: American Psychological Association, 1976. (Ch. 16)

———. "Socialization and Developmental Change," *Child Development*, 55 (1984), 317–328. (Ch. 2)

———, and C. N. Jacklin. *The Psychology of Sex Differences*. Stanford, Calif.: Stanford University Press, 1974. (Chs. 6, 15)

———, and ———. "Sex Differences in Aggression: A Rejoinder and Reprise," *Child Development*, 51 (1980), 964–980. (Chs. 15, 16)

———, and J. A. Martin. "Socialization in the Context of the Family: Parent-Child Interaction," in P. H. Mussen (ed.), *Handbook of Child Psychology*. 4th ed. Vol. 4: E. M. Hetherington (ed.), *Socialization, Personality, and Social Development*. New York: Wiley, 1983, pp. 1–102. (Ch. 13)

Macfarlane, A. *The Psychology of Childbirth*. Cambridge, Mass.: Harvard University Press, 1977. (Chs. 4, 12)

———, P. Harris, and I. Barnes. "Central and Peripheral Vision in Early Infancy," *Journal of Experimental Child Psychology*, 21 (1976), 532–538. (Ch. 7)

MacKinnon, D. W. "The Nature and Nurture of Creative Talent," *American Psychologist*, 17 (1962), 484–495. (Ch. 11)

Maclean, P. D. "The Triune Brain, Emotion, and Scientific Bias," in F. O. Schmitt (ed.), *The Neurosciences: Second Study Program*. New York: Rockefeller University Press, 1970. (Ch. 6)

Main, M., and D. R. Weston. "The Quality of the Toddler's Relationship to Mother and to Father: Related to Conflict Behavior and the Readiness to Establish New Relationships," *Child Development*, 52 (1981), 932–940. (Ch. 12)

Malatesta, C., and J. Haviland. "Learning Display Rules: The Socialization of Emotion Expression in Infants," *Child Development*, 53 (1982), 991–1003. (Ch. 12)

Malina, R. M. "Secular Changes in Size and Maturity: Causes and Effects," in A. F. Roche (ed.), "Secular Trends in Human Growth, Maturation, and Development," *Monographs of the Society for Research in Child Development*, 44 (1979), whole no. 179, pp. 59–102. (Ch. 5)

Mamay, P. D., and R. L. Simpson. "Three Female Roles in Commercials," *Sex Roles*, 7 (1981), 1223–1232. (Ch. 15)

Mandler, J. M. "Representation," in P. H. Mussen (ed.), *Handbook of Child Psychology*. 4th ed. Vol. 3: J. H. Flavell and E. M. Markman (eds.), *Cognitive Development*. New York: Wiley, 1983, pp. 420–494. (Ch. 8)

Mans, L., D. Cichetti, and L. A. Sroufe. "Mirror Reaction of Down's Syndrome Infants and Toddlers: Cognitive Underpinnings of Self-Recognition," *Child Development*, 49 (1978), 1247–1250. (Ch. 12)

Maratos, O. "Trends in the Development of Imitation in Early Infancy," in T. G. Bever (ed.), *Regressions in Mental Development: Basic Phenomena and Theories*. Hillsdale, N. J.: Lawrence Erlbaum Associates, 1982, pp. 81–102. (Ch. 4)

Maratsos, M. "How to Get from Words to Sentences," in D. Aaronson and R. Rieber (eds.), *Perspectives in Psycholinguistics*. Hillsdale, N. J.: Lawrence Erlbaum Associates, 1979. (Ch. 9)

———. "Some Current Issues in the Study of the Acquisition of Grammar," in P. H. Mussen (ed.), *Handbook of Child Psychology*. 4th ed. Vol. 3: J. H. Flavell and E. M. Markman (eds.), *Cognitive Development*. New York: Wiley, 1983, pp. 707–786. (Ch. 9)

———, S. A. Kuczaj II, D. E. C. Fox, and M. A. Chalkley. "Some Empirical Studies in the Acquisition of Transformational Relations: Passives, Negatives, and the Past Tense," in W. A. Collins (ed.), *Minnesota Symposia on Child Psychology*. Vol. 12: *Children's Language and Communication*. Hillsdale, N. J.: Lawrence Erlbaum Associates, 1979, pp. 1–46. (Ch. 9)

Marcia, J. E. "Identity in Adolescence," in J. Adelson (ed.), *Handbook of Adolescent Psychology*. New York: Wiley-Interscience, 1980, pp. 159–187. (Ch. 17)

Marcus, D. E., and W. F. Overton. "The Development of Cognitive Gender-Constancy and Sex Role Preference," *Child Development*, 49 (1978), 434–444. (Ch. 15)

Marcus, T. L., and D. A. Corsini. "Parental Expectations of Preschool Children as Related to Child Gender and Sociometric Status," *Child Development*, 49 (1978), 243–246. (Ch. 14)

Markell, R. A., and S. R. Asher. "Children's Interactions in Dyads: Interpersonal Influence and Sociometric Status," *Child Development*, 55 (1984), 1412–1424. (Ch. 14)

Markman, E. M. "The Facilitation of Part-Whole Comparisons by Use of the Collective Noun 'Family,'" *Child Development*, 44 (1973b), 837–840. (Ch. 10)

———. "Classes and Collections: Conceptual Organization and Numerical Abilities," *Cognitive Psychology*, 11 (1979), 395–411. (Ch. 10)

———. "Two Different Principles of Conceptual Organization," in M. E. Lamb and A. L. Brown (eds.), *Advances in Developmental Psychology*. Vol. 1. Hillsdale, N. J.: Lawrence Erlbaum Associates, 1981, pp. 199–236. (Ch. 8)

———, and J. Siebert. "Classes and Collections: Internal Organization and Resulting Holistic Properties," *Cognitive Psychology*, 8 (1976), 561–577. (Ch. 10)

Martin, G. B., and R. D. Clark III. "Distress Crying in Neonates: Species and Peer Specificity," *Developmental Psychology*, 18 (1982) 3–9. (Ch. 4)

Martin, M. F., D. M. Gelfand, and D. P. Hartmann. "Effects of Adult and Peer Observers on Boys' and Girls' Responses to an Aggressive Model," *Child Development*, 42 (1971), 1271–1275. (Ch. 16)

Marx, J. L. "Autoimmunity in Left-Handers," *Science*, 217 (1982a), 141–144. (Ch. 6)

———. "Transplants as Guides to Brain Development,"

Science, 217 (1982b), 340–342. (Ch. 3)

Mason, W. A., and M. D. Kenney. "Redirection of Filial Attachment in Rhesus Monkeys: Dogs as Mother Surrogates," *Science*, 183 (1974), 1209–1211. (Ch. 12)

Masur, E. F. "Preschool Boys' Speech Modifications: The Effect of Listeners' Linguistic Levels and Conversational Responses," *Child Development*, 49 (1978), 924–927. (Ch. 9)

Matas, L., R. A. Arend, and L. A. Sroufe. "Continuity of Adaptation in the Second Year: The Relationship Between Quality of Attachment and Later Competence," *Child Development*, 49 (1978), 547–556. (Chs. 12, 13)

Maurer, D., and T. L. Lewis. "Peripheral Discrimination by Three-Month-Old Infants," *Child Development*, 50 (1979), 276–279. (Ch. 7)

———, and P. Salapatek. "Developmental Changes in the Scanning of Faces by Infants," *Child Development*, 47 (1976), 523–527. (Ch. 7)

McAdoo, J. L. "Black Father and Child Interaction," in L. E. Gary (ed.), *Black Men*. Beverly Hills, Calif.: Sage, 1981, pp. 115–130. (Ch. 13)

McCall, R. B. "Attention in the Infant: Methods of Study," in D. N. Walcher and D. L. Peters (eds.), *Early Childhood: The Development of Self-Regulatory Mechanisms*. New York: Academic Press, 1971, pp. 107–140. (Ch. 7)

———. "Childhood IQ's as Predictors of Adult Educational and Occupational Success," *Science*, 197 (1977), 482–483. (Ch. 11)

———. "The Development of Intellectual Functioning in Infancy and the Prediction of Later IQ," in J. D. Osofsky (ed.), *Handbook of Infant Development*. New York: Wiley-Interscience, 1979a, pp. 707–741. (Ch. 11)

———. "Stages in Play Development Between Zero and Two Years of Age," in B. Sutton-Smith (ed.), *Play and Learning*. New York: Gardner Press, 1979b, pp. 35–44. (Ch. 8)

———. "Developmental Changes in Mental Performance: The Effect of the Birth of a Sibling," *Child Development*, 55 (1984), 1317–1321. (Ch. 11)

———, M. I. Appelbaum, and P. S. Hogarty. "Developmental Changes in Mental Performance," *Monographs of the Society for Research in Child Development*, 38 (1973), whole no. 150. (Ch. 11)

McClearn, G. E. "Genetic Influence on Behavior and Development," in P. H. Mussen (ed.), *Carmichael's Manual of Child Psychology*. 3rd ed. Vol. 1. New York: Wiley, 1970, pp. 39–76. (Ch. 2)

McClelland, D. C. "Testing for Competence Rather Than for Intelligence," *American Psychologist*, 28 (1973), 1–14. (Ch. 11)

McCluskey, K. A., J. Killarney, and D. R. Papini. "Adolescent Pregnancy and Parenthood: Implications for Development," in E. J. Callahan and K. A. McCluskey (eds.), *Life-Span Developmental Psychology: Nonnormative Life Events*. New York: Academic Press, 1983, pp. 69–113. (Ch. 3)

McCormick, R. A. "Experimentation with Children: Sharing in Sociality," *Hastings Center Report*, 6 (1976), 41–46. (Ch. 2)

McDavid, J. W., and H. Harari. "Stereotyping of Names and Popularity in Grade School Children," *Child Development*, 37 (1966), 453–459. (Ch. 14)

McGraw, M. B. *Growth: A Study of Johnny and Jimmy*. New York: Appleton-Century-Crofts, 1935. (Ch. 5)

———. "Later Development of Children Specially Trained during Infancy: Johnny and Jimmy at School Age," *Child Development*, 10 (1939), 1–19. (Ch. 5)

McGuinness, D. "How Schools Discriminate Against Boys," *Human Nature*, 2 (February 1979), 82–88. (Ch. 6)

McKain, K., M. Studdert-Kennedy, S. Spieker, and D. Storm. "Infant Intermodal Speech Perception Is a Left

Hemisphere Function," *Science*, 219 (1983), 1347–1349. (Ch. 6)

McKenna, J. J. "Sudden Infant Death Syndrome in an Anthropological Context: Model and Hypothesis." Paper presented at the World Congress of Infant Psychiatry. Cannes, April 1983. (Ch. 4)

McKenry, P. C., L. H. Walters, and C. Johnson. "Adolescent Pregnancy: A Review of the Literature," *The Family Coordinator*, 28 (1979), 17–28. (Ch. 3)

McKenzie, B. E., H. E. Tootell, and R. H. Day. "Development of Visual Size Constancy During the 1st Year of Human Infancy," *Developmental Psychology*, 16 (1980), 163–174. (Ch. 7)

McMichael, R. E., and R. E. Grinder. "Children's Guilt After Transgression: Combined Effect of Exposure to American Culture and Ethnic Background," *Child Development*, 37 (1966), 425–431. (Ch. 16)

McQueen, A. J. "The Adaptation of Urban Black Families: Trends, Problems, and Issues," in D. Reiss and H. A. Hoffman (eds.), *The American Family: Dying or Developing*. New York: Plenum Press, 1979, pp. 273–295. (Ch. 13)

Mead, M. *Coming of Age in Samoa: A Psychological Study in Primitive Youth for Western Civilization*. New York: Dell, 1968. (Ch. 1)

———, and N. Newton. "Cultural Patterning of Perinatal Behavior," in S. A. Richardson and A. F. Guttmacher (eds.), *Childbearing: Its Social and Psychological Factors*. Baltimore: William & Wilkins, 1967. (Ch. 3)

Means, B. M., and W. D. Rohwer, Jr. "A Developmental Study of the Effects of Adding Verbal Analogs to Pictured Paired Associates." Unpublished paper. University of California, Berkeley, 1974. (Ch. 8)

Meece, J., J. Parsons, C. Kaczala, S. Goff, and R. Futterman. *Psychological Bulletin*, 91 (1982), 324. (Ch. 6)

Megaw-Nyce, J. S. "Perception of Reversible and Irreversible Events by Pre-Schoolers." Paper presented at the Meeting of the Society for Research in Child Development. San Francisco, March 1979. (Ch. 8)

Meichenbaum, D. H., and J. Goodman. "Training Impulsive Children to Talk to Themselves: A Means of Developing Self-Control," *Journal of Abnormal Psychology*, 77 (1971), 115–126. (Ch. 16)

Meicler, M., and G. Gratch. "Do 5-Month-Olds Show Object Conception in Piaget's Sense," *Infant Behaviour*, 3 (1980), 265–282. (Ch. 7)

Meltzoff, A. N., and M. K. Moore. "Imitation of Facial and Manual Gestures by Human Neonates," *Science*, 198 (1977), 75–78. (Ch. 4)

———, and ———. "The Origins of Imitation in Infancy: Paradigm, Phenomena, and Theories," in L. P. Lipsitt and C. K. Rovee-Collier (eds.), *Advances in Infancy Research*. Vol. 2. Norwood, N. J.: Ablex, 1983, pp. 265–301. (Chs. 4, 7)

Mendelson, M. J., and M. M. Haith. "The Relations between Audition and Vision in the Human Newborn," *Monographs of the Society for Research in Child Development*, 41 (1976), whole no. 167. (Ch. 7)

Menyuk, P. *The Acquisition and Development of Language*. Englewood Cliffs, N. J.: Prentice-Hall, 1971. (Ch. 9)

———, and N. Bernholtz. "Prosodic Features and Children's Language Production," *M.I.T. Research Laboratory of Electronics Quarterly Progress Reports*, no. 93 (1969), 216–219. (Ch. 9)

Menzel, E. W., Jr., R. K. Davenport, Jr., and C. M. Rogers. "The Effect of Environmental Restriction upon the Chimpanzee's Responsiveness to Objects," *Journal of Comparative and Physiological Psychology*, 56 (1963), 78–85. (Ch. 12)

Mercer, J. R. "IQ: The Lethal Label," *Psychology Today*, 6 (September 1972), 44–47+. (Ch. 11)

Meredith, H. V. "Change in the Stature and Body Weight of North American Boys during the Last 80 Years," in L.

P. Lipsitt and C. C. Spiker (eds.), *Advances in Child Development and Behavior*. Vol. 1. New York: Academic Press, 1963, pp. 69–114. (Ch. 5)

———. "Findings from Asia, Australia, Europe, and North America on Secular Change in Mean Height of Children, Youths, and Young Adults," *American Journal of Physical Anthropology*, 44 (1976), 315–326. (Ch. 5)

———. "Research between 1950 and 1980 on Urban-Rural Differences in Body Size and Growth Rate of Children and Youths," in H. W. Reese (ed.), *Advances in Child Development and Behavior*. Vol. 17. New York: Academic Press, 1982, pp. 83–138. (Ch. 5)

Mervis, C. B. "Category Structure and the Development of Categorization," in R. J. Spiro, B. C. Bruce, and W. F. Brewer (eds.), *Theoretical Issues in Reading Comprehension: Perspectives from Cognitive Psychology, Linguistics, Artificial Intelligence, and Education*. Hillsdale, N. J.: Lawrence Erlbaum Associates, 1980, pp. 279–307. (Ch. 8)

Michaels, R. H., and G. W. Mellin. "Prospective Experience with Maternal Rubella and the Associated Congenital Malformations," *Pediatrics*, 26 (1960), 200–209. (Ch. 3)

Milewski, A. E. "Visual Discrimination and Detection of Configural Variance in 3-Month Infants," *Developmental Psychology*, 15 (1979), 357–363. (Ch. 7)

Millar, W. S. "A Study of Operant Conditioning under Delayed Reinforcement in Early Infancy," *Monographs of the Society for Research in Child Development*, 37 (1972), whole no. 147. (Ch. 4)

Miller, G. A. "The Magical Number Seven, Plus or Minus Two: Some Limits on Our Capacity for Processing Information," *Psychological Review*, 63 (1956), 81–96. (Ch. 8)

———. *Spontaneous Apprentices*. New York: Seabury Press, 1977. (Ch. 9)

———. "The Acquisition of Word Meaning," *Child Development*, 49 (1978a), 999–1004. (Ch. 9)

———. "Reconsiderations: *Language, Thought, and Reality*," *Human Nature*, 1 (June 1978b), 92–96. (Ch. 9)

Miller, L. B., and R. P. Bizzell. "Long-Term Effects of Four Preschool Programs: Ninth- and Tenth-Grade Results," *Child Development*, 55 (1984), 1570–1587. (Ch. 11)

Miller, N. E., and J. Dollard. *Social Learning and Imitation*. New Haven, Conn.: Yale University Press, 1941. (Ch. 1)

Miller, P. H., and L. Bigi. "The Development of Children's Understanding of Attention," *Merrill-Palmer Quarterly*, 25 (1979), 235–250. (Ch. 8)

Miller, P. Y., and W. E. Simon. "The Development of Sexuality in Adolescence," in J. Adelson (ed.), *Handbook of Adolescent Psychology*. New York: Wiley-Interscience, 1980, pp. 383–407. (Ch. 15)

Miller, W. R. "The Acquisition of Formal Features of Language," *American Journal of Orthopsychiatry*, 34 (1964), 862–867. (Ch. 9)

Milner, B. "CNS Maturation and Language Acquisition," in H. Whitaker and H. A. Whitaker (eds.), *Studies in Neurolinguistics*. Vol. 1. New York: Academic Press, 1976. (Ch. 6)

Milner, J. S., R. G. Gold, C. Ayoub, and M. M. Jacewitz. "Predictive Validity of the Child Abuse Potential Inventory," *Journal of Consulting and Clinical Psychology*, 52 (1984), 879–884. (Ch. 13)

Minkowski, A. (ed.), *Regional Development of the Brain in Early Life*. Oxford: Blackwell, 1967. (Ch. 6)

Minuchin, P. P., and E. K. Shapiro. "The School as a Context for Social Development," in P. H. Mussen (ed.), *Handbook of Child Psychology*. 4th ed. Vol. 4: E. M. Hetherington (ed.), *Socialization, Personality, and Social Development*. New York: Wiley, 1983, pp. 197–274. (Chs. 14, 15)

Mirable, P. J., R. J. Porter, Jr., L. F. Hughes, and C. I. Berlin. "Dichotic Lag Effect in Children 7 to 15," *Devel-*

opmental Psychology, 14 (1978), 277–285. (Ch. 6)

Mischel, H. N., and W. Mischel. "The Development of Children's Knowledge of Self-Control Strategies," *Child Development*, 54 (1983), 603–619. (Ch. 16)

Mischel, W. "Theory and Research on the Antecedents of Self-Imposed Delay of Reward," in B. A. Maher (ed.), *Progress in Experimental Personality Research*. Vol. 3. New York: Academic Press, 1966, pp. 85–132. (Ch. 13)

———, and N. Baker. "Cognitive Appraisals and Transformations in Delay Behavior," *Journal of Personality and Social Psychology*, 31 (1975), 254–261. (Ch. 16)

———, and H. N. Mischel. "A Cognitive Social-Learning Approach to Morality and Self-Regulation," in T. Lickona (ed.), *Moral Development and Behavior*. New York: Holt, Rinehart and Winston, 1976, pp. 84–107. (Ch. 16)

Miscione, J. L., R. S. Marvin, R. G. O'Brien, and M. T. Greenberg. "A Developmental Study of Preschool Children's Understanding of the Words 'Know' and 'Guess,' " *Child Development*, 49 (1978), 1107–1113. (Ch. 9)

Miyake, K., S.-J. Chen, and J. J. Campos. "Infant's Temperament, Mother's Mode of Interaction, and Attachment in Japan: An Interview Report," in I. Bretherton and E. Waters (eds.), "Growing Points in Attachment Theory and Research," *Monographs of the Society for Research in Child Development*, 50 (1985), whole no. 209, 1985, 276–297. (Ch. 12)

Moely, B. E. "Organization Factors in the Development of Memory," in R. V. Kail, Jr., and J. W. Hagen (eds.), *Perspectives on the Development of Memory and Cognition*. Hillsdale, N. J.: Lawrence Erlbaum Associates, 1977, pp. 203–236. (Ch. 8)

Mogford, K. "The Play of Handicapped Children," in B. Tizard and D. Harvey (eds.), *Biology of Play*. Philadelphia: Lippincott, 1977, pp. 170–184. (Ch. 7)

Mohr, D. M. "Development of Attributes of Personal Identity," *Developmental Psychology*, 14 (1978), 427–428. (Ch. 17)

Molfese, D. L. and V. J. Molfese. "Hemisphere and Stimulus Differences as Reflected in the Cortical Responses of Newborn Infants to Speech Stimuli," *Developmental Psychology*, 15 (1979), 505–511. (Ch. 6)

———, and ———. "Cortical Responses of Preterm Infants to Phonetic and Nonphonetic Speech Stimuli," *Developmental Psychology*, 16 (1980), 574–581. (Ch. 6)

Money, J. "Determinants of Human Gender Identity/Role," in J. Money and H. Musaph (eds.), *Handbook of Sexology*. Amsterdam: Elsevier/North Holland Biomedical Press, 1977, pp. 57–79. (Ch. 15)

———, and A. A. Ehrhardt. *Man and Woman, Boy and Girl*. Baltimore: Johns Hopkins University Press, 1972. (Chs. 2, 15)

Moore, B. S., C. Clyburn, and B. Underwood. "The Role of Affect in Delay of Gratification," *Child Development*, 47 (1976), 273–276. (Ch. 16)

Moore, S. G. "Correlates of Peer Acceptance in Nursery School Children," in W. W. Hartup and N. L. Smothergill (eds.), *The Young Child*. Washington, D.C.: National Association for the Education of Young Children, 1967. (Ch. 14)

Morgan, G. A., and H. N. Ricciuti. "Infants' Responses to Strangers During the First Year," in B. M. Foss (ed.), *Determinants of Infant Behavior*. Vol. 4. London: Methuen, 1969, pp. 253–272. (Ch. 12)

Moro, E. "Das Erste Timenon," *Münchener Medizinische Wochenschrift*, 65 (1918), 1147–1150. (Ch. 4)

Moss, H. A. "Early Sex Differences and Mother-Infant Interaction," in R. C. Friedman, R. N. Richard, and R. L. Van de Wiele (eds.), *Sex Differences in Behavior*. New York: Wiley, 1974. (Ch. 15)

Moyer, K. E. *The Physiology of Hostility*. Chicago: Markham,

1971. (Ch. 16)

Muir, D., W. Abraham, B. Forbes, and L. Harris. "The Ontogenesis of an Auditory Localization Response from Birth to Four Months of Age," *Canadian Journal of Psychology*, 33 (1979), 320–333. (Ch. 7)

———, and J. Field. "Newborn Infants Orient to Sounds," *Child Development*, 50 (1979), 431–436. (Ch. 4)

Mukherjee, A. M., and G. D. Hodgen. "Maternal Ethanol Exposure Induces Transient Impairment of Umbilical Circulation and Fetal Hypoxia in Monkeys," *Science*, 218 (1982), 700–702. (Ch. 3)

Murray, A. D., R. M. Dolby, R. L. Nation, and D. P. Thomas. "The Effects of Epidural Anesthesia on Newborns and Their Mothers," *Child Development*, 52 (1981), 71–82. (Ch. 4)

Murray, J. P., and S. Kippax. "From the Early Window to the Late Night Show: International Trends in the Study of Television's Impact on Children and Adults," in L. Berkowitz (ed.), *Advances in Experimental Social Psychology*. Vol. 12. New York: Academic Press, 1979, pp. 322–352. (Ch. 2)

Muson, H. "Moral Thinking: Can It Be Taught?" *Psychology Today*, 12 (February 1979), 48–68 + . (Ch. 16)

Mussen, P., and N. Eisenberg-Berg. *Roots of Caring, Sharing, and Helping: The Development of Prosocial Behavior in Children*. San Francisco: Freeman, 1977. (Ch. 16)

———, and M. C. Jones. "Self-Conceptions, Motivations, and Interpersonal Attitudes of Late- and Early-Maturing Boys," *Child Development*, 28 (1957), 243–256. (Ch. 15)

Myers, N. A., and M. Perlmutter. "Memory in the Years From Two to Five," in P. A. Ornstein (ed.), *Memory Development in Children*. Hillsdale, N. J.: Lawrence Erlbaum Associates, 1978, pp. 191–218. (Ch. 8)

Nash, S. C., and S. S. Feldman. "Sex Role and Sex-Related Attributions: Constancy and Change Across the Family Life Cycle," in M. E. Lamb and A. L. Brown (ed.), *Advances in Developmental Psychology*. Vol. 1. Hillsdale, N. J.: Lawrence Erlbaum Associates, 1981, pp. 1–36. (Ch. 15)

National Commission for the Protection of Human Subjects of Biomedical and Behavioral Research. *Report and Recommendations: Research Involving Children* (DHEW Publication [OS]77-0004). Washington, D.C.: U.S. Government Printing Office, 1977. (Ch. 2)

National Institute of Mental Health. *Television and Behavior: Ten Years of Scientific Progress and Implications for the Eighties*. I: *Summary Report*. Washington, D.C.: Department of Health and Human Services, 1982. (Ch. 16)

Naus, M. J., P. A. Ornstein, and K. L. Hoving. "Developmental Implications of Multistore and Depth-of-Processing Models of Memory," in P. A. Ornstein (ed.), *Memory Development in Children*. Hillsdale, N. J.: Lawrence Erlbaum Associates, 1978, pp. 219–232. (Ch. 8)

Neimark, E. D. "Adolescent Thought: Transition to Formal Operations," in B. B. Wolman (ed.), *Handbook of Developmental Psychology*. Englewood Cliffs, N. J.: Prentice-Hall, 1982, pp. 486–502. (Ch. 10)

Neisser, U. "Academic and Artificial Intelligence," in L. B. Resnick (ed.), *The Nature of Intelligence*. Hillsdale, N. J.: Lawrence Erlbaum Associates, 1976, pp. 135–144. (Ch. 11)

Nelson, K. "Semantic Development and the Development of Semantic Memory," in K. E. Nelson (ed.), *Children's Language*. Vol. 1. New York: Gardner Press, 1978, pp. 39–80. (Ch. 8)

———. "Explorations in the Development of a Functional Semantic System," in W. A. Collins (ed.), *Minnesota Symposia on Child Psychology*. Vol. 12. Hillsdale, N. J.: Lawrence Erlbaum Associates, 1979, pp. 47–82. (Ch. 8)

———. "Individual Differences in Language Development," *Developmental Psychology*, 17 (1981), 170–187. (Ch. 9)

———, and J. Gruendel. "Generalized Event Representation: Basic Building Blocks of Cognitive Development," in M. E. Lamb and A. L. Brown (eds.), *Advances in Developmental Psychology*. Vol. 1. Hillsdale, N. J.: Lawrence Erlbaum Associates, 1981, pp. 131–158. (Ch. 9)

———, L. Rescorla, J. Gruendel, and H. Benedict. "Early Lexicons: What Do They Mean?" *Child Development*, 49 (1978), 960–968. (Ch. 9)

Nelson, K. E. "Accommodation of Visual-Tracking as an Index of the Object Concept," *Journal of Experimental Child Psychology*, 12 (1971), 182–196. (Ch. 7)

———, and S. M. Kosslyn. "Recognition of Previously Labeled or Unlabeled Pictures by 5-Year-Olds and Adults," *Journal of Experimental Child Psychology*, 21 (1976), 40–45. (Ch. 8)

———, and K. Nelson. "Cognitive Pendulums and Their Linguistic Realization," in K. E. Nelson (ed.), *Children's Language*. Vol. 1. New York: Gardner Press, 1978, pp. 223–286. (Ch. 9)

Newcomb, A. F., J. E. Brady, and W. W. Hartup. "Friendship and Incentive Condition as Determinants of Children's Task-Oriented Social Behavior," *Child Development*, 50 (1979), 878–881. (Ch. 14)

———, and W. M. Bukowski. "A Longitudinal Study of the Utility of Social Preference and Social Impact of Sociometric Classification Schemes," *Child Development*, 55 (1984), 1434–1447. (Ch. 14)

———, and W. A. Collins. "Children's Comprehension of Family Role Portrayals in Televised Dramas: Effects of Socioeconomic Status, Ethnicity, and Age," *Developmental Psychology*, 15 (1979), 417–423. (Ch. 17)

Newcombe, N., and M. M. Bandura. "Effect of Age at Puberty on Spatial Ability in Girls: A Question of Mechanism," *Developmental Psychology*, 19 (1983), 215–224. (Ch. 6)

Newman, P. R. "The Peer Group," in B. B. Wolman (ed.), *Handbook of Developmental Psychology*. Englewood Cliffs, N. J.: Prentice-Hall, 1982, pp. 526–536. (Ch. 2)

Newton, N. "Key Psychological Issues in Human Lactation," in L. R. Waletzky (ed.), *Symposium on Human Lactation*. (No. HSA 759-5077). Rockville, Md.: U. S. Department of Health, Education, and Welfare, 1979, pp. 25–37. (Ch. 4)

The New York Times. "Study Shows Births Up in Women in Their 30's," May 9, 1984, C8. (Ch. 13)

Nielsen Television Index. *National Audience Demographics Report, 1982*. Northbrook, Ill.: A. C. Nielsen Co., 1982. (Ch. 15)

Ninio, A., and J. S. Bruner. "The Achievement and Antecedents of Labeling," *Journal of Child Language*, 5 (1978), 1–15. (Ch. 9)

Novak, J. D., and D. R. Ridley. "Achievement in Mathematics," *Science*, 223 (1984), 1248. (Ch. 6)

Ochs, E. "Introduction: What Child Language Can Contribute to Pragmatics," in E. Ochs and B. B. Schieffelin (eds.), *Developmental Pragmatics*. New York: Academic Press, 1979, pp. 1–17. (Ch. 9)

Oden, M. H. "The Fulfillment of Promise: 40-Year Follow-Up of the Terman Gifted Group," *Genetic Psychology Monographs*, 77 (1968), 3–93. (Ch. 11)

Oden, S., and S. R. Asher. "Coaching Children in Social Skills for Friendship Making," *Child Development*, 48 (1977), 495–506. (Ch. 14)

Offer, D., E. Ostrov, and K. I. Howard. *The Adolescent: A Psychological Self-Portrait*. New York: Basic Books, 1981. (Ch. 15)

Office of the Surgeon General. *Television and Growing Up: The Impacts of Televised Violence*. Washington, D.C.: U.S.

Government Printing Office, 1972. (Ch. 16)

Oller, D. K., L. A. Wieman, W. J. Doyle, and C. Ross. "Infant Babbling and Speech," *Journal of Child Language*, 3 (1976), 1–12. (Ch. 9)

Olsho, L. W. "Infant Frequency Discrimination," *Infant Behavior and Development*, 7 (1984), 27–37. (Ch. 7)

Olson, D. R. "Some Social Aspects of Meaning in Oral and Written Language," in D. R. Olson (ed.), *The Social Foundations of Language and Thought*. New York: Norton, 1980, pp. 90–108. (Ch. 9)

Olson, G. M., and T. Sherman. "Attention, Learning, and Memory in Infants," in P. H. Mussen (ed.), *Handbook of Child Psychology*. 4th ed. Vol. 2: M. M. Haith and J. J. Campos (eds.), *Infancy and Developmental Psychobiology*. New York: Wiley, 1983, pp. 1001–1080. (Chs. 4, 7)

Olweus, D. "Aggression and Peer Acceptance in Adolescent Boys: Two Short-Term Longitudinal Studies of Ratings," *Child Development*, 48 (1977), 1301–1313. (Ch. 14)

Oppel, W. E., and A. B. Royston. "Teenage Births: Some Social, Psychological, and Physical Sequelae," *American Journal of Public Health*, 61 (1976), 751–756. (Ch. 3)

Orlofsky, J. L. "Parental Antecedents of Sex-Role Orientation in College Men and Women," *Sex Roles*, 5 (1979), 495–512. (Ch. 15)

Ornstein, P. A. (ed.), *Memory Development in Children*. Hillsdale, N. J.: Lawrence Erlbaum Associates, 1978. (Ch. 8)

———, and M. J. Naus. "Rehearsal Processes in Children's Memory," in P. A. Ornstein (ed.), *Memory Development in Children*. Hillsdale, N. J.: Lawrence Erlbaum Associates, 1978, pp. 69–99. (Ch. 8)

Ornstein, R. E. "The Split and Whole Brain," *Human Nature*, 1 (May 1978), 76–83. (Ch. 6)

Osborn, D. K., and R. Endsley. "Emotional Reactions of Young Children to TV Violence," *Child Development*, 41 (1971), 321–331. (Ch. 16)

Osofsky, J. D., and K. Connors. "Mother-Infant Interaction: An Integrative View of a Complex System," in J. D. Osofsky (ed.), *Handbook of Infant Development*. New York: Wiley-Interscience, 1979, pp. 519–548. (Ch. 4)

Overton, D. "High Education," *Psychology Today*, 3 (November 1979), 48–51. (Ch. 6)

Overton, W. F., and H. W. Reese. "Models of Development: Methodological Implications," in J. R. Nesselroade and H. W. Reese (eds.), *Life-Span Developmental Psychology: Methodological Issues*. New York: Academic Press, 1973, pp. 65–86. (Ch. 1)

Palermo, D. S., and D. L. Molfese. "Language Acquisition From Age Five Onward," *Psychological Bulletin*, 78 (1972), 404–428. (Ch. 9)

Palincsar, A. S., and A. L. Brown. "Reciprocal Teaching of Comprehension-Fostering and Monitoring Devices," *Cognition and Instruction* [in press]. (Ch. 1)

Papcun, G., S. D. Krashen, D. Terbeek, D. Remington, and R. Harshman. "Is the Left Hemisphere Specialized for Speech, Language, and/or Something Else?" *Journal of the Acoustical Society of America*, 55 (1974), 319–327. (Ch. 6)

Papert, S. *Mindstorms: Children, Computers, and Powerful Ideas*. New York: Basic Books, 1980. (Chs. 2, 10)

Papoušek, H., and M. Papoušek. "Interdisciplinary Parallels in Studies of Early Human Behavior: From Physical to Cognitive Needs, From Attachment to Dyadic Education," *International Journal of Behavioral Development*, 1 (1978), 37–49. (Ch. 4)

Paris, S. G., and B. K. Lindauer. "The Development of Cognitive Skills During Childhood," in B. B. Wolman (ed.), *Handbook of Developmental Psychology*. Englewood Cliffs, N. J.: Prentice-Hall, 1982, pp. 333–349. (Ch. 8)

Parke, R. D., and C. W. Collmer. "Child Abuse: An Inter-disciplinary Analysis," in E. M. Hetherington (ed.), *Review of Child Development Research*. Vol. 5. Chicago: University of Chicago Press, 1975, pp. 509–590. (Ch. 13)

———, and D. B. Sawin. "The Family in Early Infancy: Social Interaction and Attitudinal Analyses," in F. A. Pedersen (ed.), *The Father-Infant Relationship*. New York: Praeger, 1980. (Ch. 12)

———, and R. G. Slaby. "The Development of Aggression," in P. H. Mussen (ed.), *Handbook of Child Psychology*. 4th ed. Vol. 4: E. M. Hetherington (ed.), *Socialization, Personality, and Social Development*. New York: Wiley, 1983, pp. 547–641. (Ch. 16)

Parmelee, A. H., Jr., and M. D. Sigman. "Perinatal Brain Development and Behavior," in P. H. Mussen (ed.), *Handbook of Child Psychology*. 4th ed. Vol. 2: M. M. Haith and J. J. Campos (eds.), *Infancy and Developmental Psychobiology*. New York: Wiley, 1983, pp. 95–156. (Chs. 4, 6, 11)

Parsons, J. E., T. F. Adler, and C. M. Kaczala. "Socialization of Achievement Attitudes and Beliefs: Parental Influences," *Child Development*, 53 (1982), 310–321. (Ch. 14)

———, C. Kaczala, and J. L. Meece. "Socialization of Achievement Attitudes and Beliefs: Classroom Influences," *Child Development*, 53 (1982), 322–339. (Chs. 14, 15)

Pastor, D. L. "The Quality of Mother-Infant Attachment and Its Relationship to Toddlers' Initial Sociability with Peers," *Developmental Psychology*, 17 (1981), 326–335. (Ch. 12)

Patterson, C. J. "Aggression, Altruism, and Self-Regulation," in M. H. Bornstein and M. E. Lamb (eds.), *Developmental Psychology*. Hillsdale, N. J.: Lawrence Erlbaum Associates, 1984, pp. 373–403. (Ch. 16)

———, J. M. Cosgrove, and R. G. O'Brien. "Nonverbal Indicants of Comprehension and Noncomprehension in Children," *Developmental Psychology*, 16 (1980), 38–48. (Ch. 17)

Patterson, G. R., and J. A. Cobb. "Stimulus Control for Classes of Noxious Behaviors," in J. F. Knutson (ed.), *The Control of Aggression*. Chicago: Aldine, 1973, pp. 145–200. (Ch. 16)

———, R. A. Littman, and W. Bricker. "Assertive Behavior in Children: A Step Toward a Theory of Aggression," *Monographs of the Society for Research in Child Development*, 32 (1967), whole no. 113. (Ch. 14)

Pea, R. D. "Werner's Influence on Contemporary Psychology," *Human Development*, 25 (1982a), 303–308. (Ch. 1)

———. "What Is Planning Development the Development of?" in D. L. Forbes and M. T. Greenberg (eds.), *New Directions for Child Development*. No. 18: *Children's Planning Strategies*. San Francisco: Jossey-Bass, 1982b, pp. 5–28. (Ch. 10)

Pearl, R. A. "Developmental and Situational Influences on Children's Understanding of Prosocial Behavior." Paper presented at the meeting of the Society for Research in Child Development. San Francisco, March 1979. (Ch. 16)

Peel, E. A. *The Nature of Adolescent Judgment*. New York: Wiley-Interscience, 1971. (Ch. 10)

Perlmutter, M. "Development of Memory in the Preschool Years," in R. Greene and T. D. Yawkey (eds.), *Childhood Development*. Westport, Conn.: Technemic Publishing, 1980, pp. 3–27. (Ch. 8)

———. "Continuities and Discontinuities in Early Human Memory Paradigms, Processes, and Performances," in R. V. Kail, Jr., and N. E. Spear (eds.), *Comparative Perspectives on the Development of Memory*. Hillsdale, N. J.: Lawrence Erlbaum Associates, 1984, pp. 253–287. (Ch. 8)

———. "A Life-Span View of Memory," in P. B. Baltes, D. Featherman, and R. Lerner (eds.), *Life-Span Development and Behavior*. Vol. 7. New York: Academic Press,

1985. (Ch. 8)

————, and G. Lange. "A Developmental Analysis of Recall-Recognition Distinctions," in P. A. Ornstein (ed.), *Memory Development in Children*. Hillsdale, N. J.: Lawrence Erlbaum Associates, 1978, pp. 243–258. (Ch. 8)

————, and N. A. Myers. "Development of Recall in 2- to 4-Year-Old Children," *Developmental Psychology*, 15 (1979), 73–83. (Ch. 8)

Perry, D. G., and K. Bussey. "The Social Learning Theory of Sex Differences: Imitation Is Alive and Well," *Journal of Personality and Social Psychology*, 37 (1979), 1699–1712. (Ch. 15)

Peskin, H. "Pubertal Onset and Ego Functioning," *Journal of Abnormal Psychology*, 72 (1967), 1–15. (Ch. 15)

Peters, J., S. Preston-Martin, and M. Yu. "Brain Tumors in Children and Occupational Exposure," *Science*, 213 (1981), 235–237. (Ch. 3)

Peters, M. F. "Parenting in Black Families with Young Children: A Historical Perspective," in H. P. McAdoo (ed.), *Black Families*. Beverly Hills, Calif.: Sage, 1981, pp. 211–224. (Ch. 13)

Petersen, A. C., and B. Taylor. "The Biological Approach to Adolescence," in J. Adelson (ed.), *Handbook of Adolescent Psychology*. New York: Wiley-Interscience, 1980, pp. 117–155. (Ch. 5)

Peterson, L. "Role of Donor Competence, Donor Age, and Peer Presence on Helping in an Emergency," *Developmental Psychology*, 19 (1983), 873–880. (Chs. 2, 16)

Pezdek, K., and E. F. Hartman. "Children's Television Viewing: Attention and Comprehension of Auditory versus Visual Information," *Child Development*, 54 (1983), 1015–1023. (Ch. 8)

Phillips, S., S. King, and L. DuBois. "Spontaneous Activities of Female versus Male Newborns," *Child Development*, 49 (1978), 590–597. (Ch. 15)

Piaget, J. *The Language and Thought of the Child*. New York: Harcourt, Brace, 1926. (Ch. 17)

————. *The Child's Conception of Physical Causality*. London: Kegan-Paul, 1930. (Ch. 10)

————. *The Moral Judgment of the Child*. New York: Free Press, 1965 [orig. pub. 1932]. (Ch. 16)

————. *Play, Dreams, and Imitation in Childhood*. New York: Norton, 1951. (Chs. 4, 7, 9)

————. *The Child's Conception of Number*. New York: Humanities Press, 1952a. (Ch. 10)

————. *The Origins of Intelligence in Children*. New York: International Universities Press, 1952b. (Chs. 1, 2, 5, 7, 11)

————. *Logic and Psychology*. Manchester: Manchester University Press, 1953. (Ch. 11)

————. *The Construction of Reality in the Child*. New York: Basic Books, 1954. (Chs. 7, 10)

————. *On the Development of Memory and Identity*. Barre, Mass.: Clark University Press, 1968. (Ch. 10)

————. *The Mechanics of Perception*. New York: Basic Books, 1969. (Ch. 8)

————. *Genetic Epistemology*. New York: Columbia University Press, 1970. (Ch. 10)

————. *Biology and Knowledge*. Chicago: University of Chicago Press, 1971a. (Ch. 11)

————. *The Child's Concept of Time*. New York: Basic Books, 1971b. (Ch. 10)

————. *Understanding Causality*. New York: Norton, 1971c. (Ch. 10)

————. "Need and Significance of Cross-Cultural Research in Genetic Psychology," in B. Inhelder and H. H. Chipman (ed.), *Piaget and His School*. New York: Springer-Verlag, 1976, pp. 259–268. (Ch. 10)

————. *The Development of Thought: Equilibration of Cognitive Structures*. New York: Viking, 1977. (Ch. 11)

————. "Piaget's Theory," in P. H. Mussen (ed.), *Handbook of Child Psychology*. 4th ed. Vol. 1: W. Kessen (ed.), *History, Theory, and Methods*. New York: Wiley, 1983, pp. 103–128. (Chs. 1, 11)

————, and B. Inhelder. *Le Developpement des Quantités Chez L'Enfant; Conservation et Atomisme*. Neuchâtel: Delachaux et Niestle, 1941. (Ch. 10)

————, and ————. *The Psychology of the Child*. New York: Basic Books, 1969. (Ch. 10)

————, and ————. *Memory and Intelligence*. New York: Basic Books, 1973. (Ch. 8)

Piazza, D. S. "Cerebral Lateralization in Young Children as Measured by Dichotic Listening and Finger Tapping Tasks," *Neuropsychologia*, 15 (1977), 417–425. (Ch. 6)

Pick, A. D. "Comments on Kinsbourne's Chapter," in M. Perlmutter (ed.), *Minnesota Symposia on Child Psychology*. Vol. 16: *Development and Policy Concerning Children with Special Needs*. Hillsdale, N. J.: Lawrence Erlbaum Associates, 1983, pp. 167–174. (Ch. 6)

————, and G. W. Frankel. "A Study of Strategies of Visual Attention in Children," *Developmental Psychology*, 4 (1973), 348–357. (Ch. 8)

Pisoni, D. B., R. N. Aslin, A. J. Percy, and B. L. Hennessy. "Some Effects of Laboratory Training on Identification and Discrimination of Voicing Contrasts in Stop Consonants," *Journal of Experimental Psychology: Human Perception and Performance*, 8 (1982), 297–314. (Ch. 9)

Pitkin, R. M. "Nutritional Support in Obstetrics and Gynecology," *Clinical Obstetrics and Gynecology*, 19 (1976), 489. (Ch. 3)

Pleck, J. H. *The Myth of Masculinity*. Cambridge, Mass.: MIT Press, 1981. (Ch. 15)

Plutchik, R. "Emotions in Early Development: A Psychoevolutionary Approach," in R. Plutchik and H. Kellerman (eds.), *Emotion: Theory, Research, and Experience*. Vol. 2: *Emotions in Early Development*. New York: Academic Press, 1983, pp. 221–257. (Ch. 1)

Pollins, L. D. "The Effects of Acceleration on the Social and Emotional Development of Gifted Students," in C. P. Benbow and J. C. Stanley (eds.), *Academic Precocity: Aspects of Its Development*. Baltimore: Johns Hopkins University Press, 1983, pp. 139–159. (Ch. 10)

Pollio, H. R. *The Psychology of Symbolic Activity*. Reading, Mass.: Addison-Wesley, 1974. (Ch. 9)

Pollitt, E., and D. Granoff. "Mental and Motor Development of Peruvian Children Treated for Severe Malnutrition," *Review of Interamericana Psicologia*, 1 (1967), 93. (Ch. 11)

————, W. Mueller, and R. L. Leibel. "The Relation of Growth to Cognition in a Well-Nourished School Population," *Child Development*, 53 (1982), 1157–1163. (Ch. 5)

Potts, D., and S. Herzberger. "Child Abuse: A Cross-Generational Pattern of Child Rearing." Paper presented at the meeting of the Midwestern Psychological Association. Chicago, May 1979. (Ch. 13)

Powell, G. F., J. A. Brasel, and R. M. Blizzard. "Emotional Deprivation and Growth Retardation Simulating Idiopathic Hypopituitarism. I: Clinical Evaluation of the Syndrome," *New England Journal of Medicine*, 276 (1967), 1271–1278. (Ch. 6)

Pratt, K. C. "The Neonate," in L. Carmichael (ed.), *Manual of Child Psychology*. 2nd ed. New York: Wiley, 1954, pp. 215–291. (Ch. 4)

Prechtl, H. F. R. "Regressions and Transformations during Neurological Development," in T. G. Bever (ed.), *Regressions in Mental Development: Basic Phenomena and Theories*. Hillsdale, N. J.: Lawrence Erlbaum Associates, 1982, pp. 103–116. (Ch. 4)

————, and D. Beintema. "The Neurological Examination of the Full Term Newborn Infant," *Clinics in Developmental*

Medicine. No. 12. London: Spastic Society with Heinemann Medical, 1964. (Ch. 7)

Pressley, M., and J. MacFayden. "Mnemonic Mediator Retrieval at Testing by Preschool and Kindergarten Children," *Child Development*, 54 (1983), 474–479. (Ch. 8)

Pritchard, J. A., and P. C. MacDonald. *Obstetrics*. 15th ed. New York: Appleton-Century-Crofts, 1976. (Ch. 3)

Pulkkinen, L. "Self-Control and Continuity from Childhood to Late Adolescence," in P. B. Baltes and O. G. Brim, Jr. (eds.), *Life-Span Development and Behavior*. Vol. 4. New York: Academic Press, 1982, pp. 63–105. (Ch. 13)

Pulos, E., D. Y. Teller, and S. Buck. "Infant Color Vision: A Search for Short Wavelength-Sensitive Mechanisms by Means of Chromatic Adaptation," *Vision Research*, 20 (1980), 485–493. (Ch. 7)

Putallaz, M., and J. M. Gottman. "An Interactional Model of Children's Entry into Peer Groups," *Child Development*, 52 (1981), 986–994. (Ch. 14)

Radin, N. "The Role of the Father in Cognitive, Academic, and Intellectual Development," in M. E. Lamb (ed.), *The Role of the Father in Child Development*. 2nd ed. New York: Wiley-Interscience, 1981, pp. 379–428. (Ch. 13)

Radke-Yarrow, M., C. Zahn-Waxler, and M. Chapman. "Children's Prosocial Dispositions and Behavior," in P. H. Mussen (ed.), *Handbook of Child Psychology*. 4th ed. Vol. 4: E. M. Hetherington (ed.), *Socialization, Personality, and Social Development*. New York: Wiley, 1983, pp. 469–546. (Chs. 2, 16)

Ragozin, A. S., R. B. Basham, K. A. Crnic, M. T. Greenberg, and N. M. Robinson. "Effects of Maternal Age on Parenting Role," *Developmental Psychology*, 18 (1982), 627–634. (Ch. 13)

Rajecki, D. W., and R. C. Flanery. "Social Conflict and Dominance in Children: A Case for a Primate Homology," in M. E. Lamb and A. L. Brown (eds.), *Advances in Developmental Psychology*. Vol. 1. Hillsdale, N. J.: Lawrence Erlbaum Associates, 1981, pp. 87–130. (Ch. 1)

Rakic, P., and K. P. Riley. "Overproduction and Elimination of Retinal Axons in the Fetal Rhesus Monkey," *Science*, 219 (1983), 1441–1444. (Ch. 3)

Ramey, C., B. Dorval, and L. Baker-Ward. "Group Day Care and Socially Disadvantaged Families: Effects on the Child and the Family," in S. Kilmer (ed.), *Advances in Early Education and Day Care*. JAI Press, 1981. (Ch. 13)

Ramey, C. T., K. O. Yeates, and E. J. Short. "The Plasticity of Intellectual Development: Insights from Preventive Intervention," *Child Development*, 55 (1984), 1913–1926. (Ch. 11)

Ramsay, D. S. "Manual Preference for Tapping in Infants," *Developmental Psychology*, 15 (1979), 437–441. (Ch. 6)

————. "Beginnings of Bimanual Handedness and Speech in Infants," *Infant Behavior and Development*, 3 (1980), 67–78. (Ch. 6)

————. "Onset of Duplicated Syllable Babbling and Unimanual Handedness in Infancy: Evidence for Developmental Change in Hemispheric Specialization?" *Developmental Psychology*, 20 (1984), 64–71. (Ch. 6)

————, J. J. Campos, and L. Fenson. "Onset of Bimanual Handedness in Children," *Infant Behavior and Development*, 2 (1979), 69–76. (Ch. 6)

Ramsey, P. "Children as Research Subjects: A Reply," *Hastings Center Report*, 7 (1977), 40–41. (Ch. 2)

Rasmussen, T., and B. Milner. "Clinical and Surgical Studies of the Cerebral Speech Areas in Man," in K. J. Zulch, O. Creutzfeldt, and G. Galbraith (eds.), *Otfrid Foerstersymposium on Cerebral Localization*. Heidelberg: Springer-Verlag, 1975. (Ch. 6)

Reed, E. "Genetic Anomalies in Development," in F. D. Horowitz (ed.), *Review of Child Development Research*. Vol.

4. Chicago: University of Chicago Press, 1975, pp. 59–100. (Ch. 7)

Reese, H. W. "Imagery and Associative Memory," in R. V. Kail, Jr., and J. W. Hagen (eds.), *Perspectives on the Development of Memory and Cognition*. Hillsdale, N. J.: Lawrence Erlbaum Associates, 1977, pp. 113–175. (Ch. 8)

————, and W. F. Overton. "Models of Development and Theories of Development," in L. R. Goulet and P. B. Baltes (eds.), *Life-Span Developmental Psychology: Research and Theory*. New York: Academic Press, 1970, pp. 116–145. (Ch. 1)

Reichenbach, L., and J. C. Masters. "Children's Use of Expressive and Contextual Cues in Judgments of Emotion," *Child Development*, 54 (1983), 993–1004. (Ch. 17)

Reinisch, J. M. "Prenatal Exposure to Synthetic Progestins Increases Potential for Aggression in Humans," *Science*, 211 (1981), 1171–1173. (Ch. 15)

————, R. Gandelman, and F. S. Spiegel. "Prenatal Influences on Cognitive Abilities: Data from Experimental Animals and Human Genetic and Endocrine Syndromes," in M. A. Wittig and A. C. Peterson (eds.), *Sex-Related Differences in Cognitive Functioning*. New York: Academic Press, 1979, pp. 215–239. (Ch. 3)

————, N. G. Simon, W. G. Karow, and R. Gandelman. "Prednisone Therapy and Birth Weight," *Science*, 206 (1979), 97. (Ch. 3)

Reisman, J. M., and S. I. Shorr. "Friendship Claims and Expectations Among Children and Adults," *Child Development*, 49 (1978), 913–916. (Ch. 14)

Resnick, L. B. "Introduction: Changing Conceptions of Intelligence," in L. B. Resnick (ed.), *The Nature of Intelligence*. Hillsdale, N. J.: Lawrence Erlbaum Associates, 1976, pp. 1–10. (Ch. 11)

Rest, J. R. "Morality," in P. H. Mussen (ed.), *Handbook of Child Psychology*. 4th ed. Vol. 3: J. H. Flavell and E. M. Markman (eds.), *Cognitive Development*. New York: Wiley, 1983, pp. 556–629. (Ch. 16)

————, M. L. Davison, and S. Robbins. "Age Trends in Judging Moral Issues: A Review of Cross-Sectional, Longitudinal, and Sequential Studies of the Defining Issues Test," *Child Development*, 49 (1978), 263–279. (Ch. 16)

Rheingold, H. L. "The Social and Socializing Agent," in D. A. Goslin (ed.), *Handbook of Socialization Theory and Research*. Chicago: Rand McNally, 1969, pp. 779–791. (Ch. 12)

————, and C. O. Eckerman. "The Infant Separates Himself from His Mother," *Science*, 168 (1970), 78–83. (Ch. 12)

Rholes, W. S., J. Blackwell, C. Jordan, and C. Walters. "A Developmental Study of Learned Helplessness," *Developmental Psychology*, 16 (1980), 616–624. (Ch. 14)

————, and D. N. Ruble. "Children's Understanding of Dispositional Characteristics of Others," *Child Development*, 55 (1984), 550–560. (Ch. 17)

Richman, C. L., S. Nida, and L. Pittman. "Effects of Meaningfulness on Child Free-Recall Learning," *Developmental Psychology*, 12 (1976), 460–465. (Ch. 8)

Riegel, K. F. "Adult Life Crises: A Dialectic Interpretation of Development," in N. Datan and L. H. Ginsberg (eds.), *Life-Span Developmental Psychology: Normative Life Crises*. New York: Academic Press, 1975, 99–128. (Ch. 1)

Rieser, J. J. "Spatial Orientation of Six-Month-Old Infants," *Child Development*, 50 (1979), 1078–1087. (Ch. 7)

Rinebold, S., T. Kehl, and A. Elster. "The Effects of Maternal Age and Family Income on Children's Cognitive, Academic and Psychosocial Competence." Paper presented at meeting of the National Association of School Psychologists. Toronto, March 1982. (Ch. 3)

Ritter, K., B. H. Kaprove, J. P. Fitch, and J. H. Flavell. "The Development of Retrieval Strategies in Young Children," *Cognitive Psychology*, 5 (1973), 310–321. (Ch. 8)

Roberts, D. F., C. Herold, M. Horby, S. King, D. Sterne, S. Whiteley, and T. Silver. "Earth's a Big Blue Marble: A Report of the Impact of a Television Series on Children's Opinions." Unpublished manuscript. Stanford University, 1974. (Ch. 16)

Roberts, E. J. "Children's Sexual Learning: A Report on the Project on Human Sexual Development, 1974–1980." Doctoral dissertation. Harvard University, 1982. (Ch. 15)

Roberts, G. C., J. H. Block, and J. Block. "Continuity and Change in Parents' Child-Rearing Practices," *Child Development*, 55 (1984), 586–597. (Ch. 13)

Roberts, R. J., Jr., and C. J. Patterson. "Perspective Taking and Referential Communication: The Question of Correspondence Reconsidered," *Child Development*, 54 (1983), 1005–1014. (Ch. 17)

Robinson, H. B. "A Case for Radical Acceleration: Programs of the Johns Hopkins University and the University of Washington," in C. P. Benbow and J. C. Stanley (eds.), *Academic Precocity: Aspects of Its Development*. Baltimore: Johns Hopkins University Press, 1983, pp. 139–159. (Ch. 10)

———, and N. M. Robinson. *The Mentally Retarded Child: A Psychological Approach*. New York: McGraw-Hill, 1965. (Ch. 3)

Roche, A. F. "Secular Trends in Stature, Weight, and Maturation," in A. F. Roche (ed.), "Secular Trends in Human Growth, Maturation, and Development," *Monographs of the Society for Research in Child Development*, 44 (1979), whole no. 179, pp. 3–27. (Ch. 5)

———. "The Adipocyte-Number Hypothesis," *Child Development*, 52 (1981), 31–43. (Ch. 5)

Rock, I. *An Introduction to Perception*, New York: Macmillan, 1975. (Ch. 7)

Rodgers, J. L. "Confluence Effects: Not Here, Not Now!" *Developmental Psychology*, 20 (1984), 321–331. (Ch. 2)

Rodin, J. "Insulin Levels, Hunger, and Food Intake: An Example of Feedback Loops in Body Weight Regulation." Unpublished manuscript. Yale University, 1984. (Ch. 5)

———, interviewed by E. Hall. "A Sense of Control," *Psychology Today*, 18 (December 1984), 38–45. (Ch. 5)

———, L. Silberstein, and R. Striegel-Moore. "Women and Weight: A Normative Discontent," in T. B. Sonderegger (ed.), *Nebraska Symposium on Motivation* [in press]. (Ch. 15)

Roeper, T. "Connecting Children's Language and Linguistic Theory," in T. E. Moore (ed.), *Cognitive Development and the Acquisition of Language*. New York: Academic Press, 1973, pp. 187–196. (Ch. 9)

Roff, N., S. B. Sells, and M. M. Golden. *Social Adjustment and Personality Development in Children*. Minneapolis: University of Minnesota Press, 1972. (Ch. 14)

Roffwarg, H. P., J. N. Muzizo, and W. C. Dement. "Ontogenic Development of the Human Dream Cycle," *Science*, 152 (1966), 604–619. (Ch. 4)

Rogoff, B. "Integrating Context and Cultural Development," in M. E. Lamb and A. L. Brown (eds.), *Advances in Developmental Psychology*. Vol. 2. Hillsdale, N. J.: Lawrence Erlbaum Associates, 1982, pp. 125–170. (Ch. 1)

Rohwer, W. D., Jr. "Learning, Race, and School Success," *Review of Educational Research*, 41 (1971), 191–210. (Ch. 2)

Roopnarine, J. L., and J. E. Johnson. "Socialization in a Mixed-Age Experimental Program," *Developmental Psychology*, 20 (1984), 828–832. (Ch. 14)

Rosch, E. M., "On the Internal Structure of Perceptual and Semantic Categories," in T. E. Moore (ed.), *Cognitive Development and the Acquisition of Language*. New York: Academic Press, 1973, pp. 111–144. (Ch. 8)

———, and C. B. Mervis. "Children's Sorting: A Reinterpretation Based on the Nature of Abstraction in Natural Categories," in R. C. Smart and M. S. Smart (eds.),

Readings in Child Development and Relationships. 2nd ed. New York: Macmillan, 1977. (Ch. 8)

———, ———, W. D. Gray, D. M. Johnson, and P. Boyes-Braem. "Basic Objects in Natural Categories," *Cognitive Psychology*, 8 (1976), 382–439. (Ch. 8)

Rose, D. *Dentate Granule Cells and Cognitive Development*. New York: Columbia University Press, 1979. (Ch. 8)

Rose, R. J. "Genetic Variance in Non-Verbal Intelligence: Data from the Kinship of Identical Twins," *Science*, 205 (1979), 1153–1155. (Ch. 11)

Rose, S. *The Conscious Brain*. New York: Knopf, 1973. (Ch. 6)

Rose, S. A., and M. Blank. "The Potency of Context in Children's Cognition: An Illustration through Conservation," *Child Development*, 45 (1974), 499–502. (Ch. 10)

———, A. W. Gottfried, and W. H. Bridger. "Cross-Modal Transfer in Infants: Relation to Prematurity and Socioeconomic Background," *Developmental Psychology*, 14 (1978), 643–652. (Ch. 7)

Rosen, B. C., and R. D'Andrade. "The Psychological Origins of Achievement Motivation," *Sociometry*, 22 (1959), 185–218. (Ch. 14)

Rosen, R., and E. Hall. *Sexuality*. New York: Random House, 1984. (Ch. 5)

Rosenthal, R. "The Pygmalion Effect Lives," *Psychology Today*, 7 (September 1973), 56–63. (Ch. 11)

———, and L. Jacobson. *Pygmalion in the Classroom: Teacher Expectation and Pupils' Intellectual Development*. New York: Holt, Rinehart and Winston, 1968. (Ch. 14)

Rosenthal, T. L., and B. J. Zimmerman. *Social Learning and Cognition*. New York: Academic Press, 1978. (Ch. 10)

Rosenzweig, M. R., E. L. Bennett, and M. C. Diamond. "Brain Changes in Response to Experience," *Scientific American*, 226 (February 1972), 22–29. (Ch. 6)

Rosett, H. L., and L. W. Sander. "Effect of Maternal Drinking on Neonatal Morphology and State Regulation," in J. D. Osofsky (ed.), *Handbook of Infant Development*. New York: Wiley-Interscience, 1979, pp. 809–836. (Ch. 11)

Rosner, B. G. "Recovery of Function and Localization of Function in Historical Perspective," in D. G. Stein, J. J. Rosen, and N. Butters (eds.), *Plasticity and Recovery of Function in the Nervous System*. New York: Academic Press, 1974. (Ch. 6)

Ross, H. G., and J. I. Milgram. "Important Variables in Adult Sibling Relationships: A Qualitative Study," in M. E. Lamb and B. Sutton-Smith (eds.), *Sibling Relationships*. Hillsdale, N. J.: Lawrence Erlbaum Associates, 1982, 225–250. (Ch. 13)

Rossman, E., M. Golden, B. Birns, A. Moss, and A. Montare. "Mother-Child Interaction, IQ, and Social Class." Paper presented at the biennial meeting of the Society for Research on Child Development. Philadelphia, March 1973. (Ch. 11)

Rotenberg, K. J. "Children's Use of Intentionality in Judgments of Character and Disposition," *Child Development*, 51 (1980), 282–284. (Ch. 16)

Rousseau, J. J. *Emile*. New York: Dutton, 1971 [orig. pub. 1762]. (Ch. 1)

Rovee-Collier, C. K. "The Ontogeny of Learning and Memory in Human Infancy," in R. V. Kail, Jr., and N. E. Spear (eds.), *Comparative Perspectives on the Development of Memory*. Hillsdale, N. J.: Lawrence Erlbaum Associates, 1984, pp. 103–134. (Ch. 7)

———, and M. J. Gekoski. "The Economics of Infancy: A Review of Conjugate Reinforcement," in H. W. Reese and L. P. Lipsitt (eds.), *Advances in Child Development and Behavior*. Vol. 13. New York: Academic Press, 1979, pp. 195–255. (Ch. 4)

Rovet, J., and C. Netley. "Processing Deficits in Turner's Syndrome," *Developmental Psychology*, 18 (1982), 77–94.

(Chs. 3, 6)

———, and C. Netley. "The Triple X Chromosome in Childhood: Recent Empirical Findings," *Child Development*, 54 (1983), 831–845. (Ch. 6)

Rozin, P., and L. R. Gleitman. "The Structure and Acquisition of Reading," in A. S. Reber and D. Scarborough (eds.), *Reading: Theory and Practice*. Hillsdale, N. J.: Lawrence Erlbaum Associates, 1977. (Ch. 6)

Rubenstein, J., and C. Howes. "The Effects of Peers on Toddler Interaction with Mothers and Toys," *Child Development*, 47 (1976), 990–997. (Ch. 14)

Rubin, K. H., G. G. Fein, and B. Vandenberg. "Play," in P. H. Mussen (ed.), *Handbook of Child Psychology*. 4th ed. Vol. 4: E. M. Hetherington (ed.), *Socialization, Personality, and Social Development*. New York: Wiley, 1983, pp. 693–774. (Ch. 14)

———, and L. R. Krasnor. "Social-Cognitive and Social-Behavioral Perspectives on Problem Solving," in M. Perlmutter (ed.), *Minnesota Symposia on Child Psychology*. Vol. 18. Hillsdale, N. J.: Lawrence Erlbaum Associates [in press]. (Chs. 14, 17)

———, and F. W. Schneider. "The Relationship Between Moral Judgment, Egocentrism, and Altruistic Behavior," *Child Development*, 44 (1973), 661–665. (Ch. 16)

Rubin, R. T., J. M. Reinisch, and R. F. Haskett "Postnatal Gonadal Steroid Effects on Human Behavior," *Science*, 211 (1981), 1318–1324. (Chs. 3, 15)

Rubinstein, E. A. "Television and Behavior: Research Conclusions of the 1982 NIMH Report and Their Policy Implications," *American Psychologist*, 38 (1983), 820–825. (Ch. 2)

Ruble, D. N., T. Balaban, and J. Cooper. "Gender Constancy and the Effects of Sex-Typed Television Commercials," *Child Development*, 52 (1981), 667–673. (Ch. 15)

———, A. K. Boggiano, N. S. Feldman, and J. H. Loebl. "Developmental Analysis of the Role of Social Comparison in Self-Evaluation," *Developmental Psychology*, 16 (1980), 990–997. (Ch. 17)

Ruff, H. A. "Infant Recognition of the Invariant Form of Objects," *Child Development*, 49 (1978), 293–306. (Ch. 7)

Rule, B. G., A. R. Nesdale, and M. J. McAra. "Children's Reactions to Information About the Intentions Underlying an Aggressive Act," *Child Development*, 45 (1974), 794–798. (Ch. 16)

Rumbaugh, D. M. (ed.). *Language Learning by a Chimpanzee: The Lana Project*. New York: Academic Press, 1977. (Ch. 9)

Rushton, J. P. "Generosity in Children: Immediate and Long Term Effects of Modeling, Preaching, and Moral Judgments," *Journal of Personality and Social Psychology*, 31 (1975), 755–765. (Ch. 16)

Russell, G., and N. Radin. "Increased Paternal Participation: The Fathers' Perspective," in M. E. Lamb and A. Sagi (eds.), *Fatherhood and Family Policy*. Hillsdale, N. J.: Lawrence Erlbaum Associates, 1983, pp. 139–166. (Ch. 13)

Rutter, M. "Diagnosis and Definition," in M. Rutter and E. Schopler (eds.), *Autism: A Reappraisal of Concepts and Treatment*. New York: Plenum Press, 1978, pp. 1–26. (Ch. 8)

———. *Maternal Deprivation Reassessed*. 2nd ed. Harmondsworth, England: Penguin, 1981. (Chs. 12, 13)

———, and N. Garmezy. "Developmental Psychopathology," in P. H. Mussen (ed.), *Handbook of Child Development*. 4th ed. Vol. 4: E. M. Hetherington (ed.), *Socialization, Personality, and Social Development*. New York: Wiley, 1983, pp. 775–911. (Ch. 12)

Sackett, G. P., G. C. Rupenthal, C. E. Fahrenbruch, R. A. Holm, and W. T. Greenough. "Social Isolation Rearing Effects in Monkeys Vary with Genotype," *Developmental Psychology*, 17 (1981), 313–318. (Ch. 2)

Sackin, S., and E. Thelan. "An Ethological Study of Peaceful Associative Outcomes to Conflict in Preschool Children," *Child Development*, 55 (1984), 1098–1102. (Ch. 2)

Saegert, S., and R. Hart. "The Development of Sex Differences in the Environmental Competence of Children," in P. Burnett (ed.), *Women in Society*. Chicago: Maaroufa Press, 1976. (Ch. 15)

Sagi, A. "Antecedents and Consequences of Various Degrees of Paternal Involvement in Child Rearing: The Israeli Project," in M. E. Lamb (ed.), *Nontraditional Families: Parenting and Child Development*. Hillsdale, N. J.: Lawrence Erlbaum Associates, 1982, pp. 289–314. (Ch. 13)

———, and M. L. Hoffman. "Empathic Distress in Newborns," *Developmental Psychology*, 12 (1976), 175–176. (Chs. 4, 16, 17)

———, M. E. Lamb, K. S. Lewkowicz, R. Shoham, R. Dvir, and D. Estes. "Security of Infant-Mother, -Father, and -Metapelet Attachments among Kibbutz-Raised Israeli Children," in I. Bretherton and E. Waters (eds.), "Growing Points of Attachment Theory and Research," *Monographs of the Society for Research in Child Development*, 50 (1985), whole no. 209, 257–275. (Ch. 12)

———, ———, R. Shoham, R. Dvir, and K. S. Lewkowicz. "Parent-Infant Interaction in Families on Israeli Kibbutzim," *International Journal of Behavioral Development*, 1985. (Ch. 12)

St. James-Roberts, I. "Neurological Plasticity, Recovery from Brain Insult, and Child Development," in H. W. Reese and L. P. Lipsitt (eds.), *Advances in Child Development and Behavior*. Vol 14. New York: Academic Press, 1979, pp. 254–320. (Ch. 6)

Salapatek, P. "Pattern Perception in Early Infancy," in L. B. Cohen and P. Salapatek (eds.), *Infant Perception: From Sensation to Cognition*. Vol. 1: *Basic Visual Processes*. New York: Academic Press, 1975, pp. 133–248. (Ch. 7)

———, and W. Kessen. "Visual Scanning of Triangles by the Human Newborn," *Journal of Experimental Child Psychology*, 3 (1966), 155–167. (Ch. 4)

Salatas, H., and J. H. Flavell. "Retrieval of Recently Learned Information: Development of Strategies and Control Skills," *Child Development*, 47 (1976), 941–948. (Ch. 8)

Sameroff, A. J. "Developmental Systems: Contexts and Evolution," in P. H. Mussen (ed.), *Handbook of Child Psychology*. 4th ed. Vol. 1: W. Kessen (ed.), *History, Theory, and Methods*. New York: Wiley, 1983, pp. 237–294. (Ch. 7)

Sander, L. W. "The Regulation of Exchange in the Infant-Caretaker System and Some Aspects of the Context-Content Relationship," in M. Lewis and L. Rosenblum (eds.), *Interaction, Conversation, and the Development of Language*. New York: Wiley, 1977, pp. 133–156. (Ch. 12)

Santrock, J. W., R. A. Warshak, and G. L. Elliott. "Social Development and Parent-Child Interaction in Father-Custody and Stepmother Families," in M. E. Lamb (ed.), *Nontraditional Families: Parenting and Child Development*. Hillsdale, N. J.: Lawrence Erlbaum Associates, 1982, pp. 289–314. (Ch. 13)

———, C. Lindberg, and L. Meadows. "Children's and Parents' Observed Social Behavior in Stepfather Families," *Child Development*, 53 (1982), 472–480. (Ch. 13)

Savage-Rumbaugh, E. S., J. L. Pate, J. Lawson, S. T. Smith, and D. Rosenbaum. "Can a Chimpanzee Make a Statement?" *Journal of Experimental Psychology: General*, 112 (1983), 457–492. (Ch. 9)

———, D. M. Rumbaugh, and S. Boysen. "Do Apes Use Language?" *American Scientist*, 68 (1980), 49–61. (Ch. 9)

Savin-Williams, R. C. "Dominance Hierarchies in Groups of Early Adolescents," *Child Development*, 50 (1979), 923–

935. (Ch. 14)

Sawin, D. B. "Assessing Empathy in Children: A Search for an Elusive Construct," in D. B. Sawin, *Empathy in Children: Conceptual and Methodological Issues in Current Research.* Symposium presented at the meeting of the Society for Research in Child Development. San Francisco, March 1979. (Ch. 16)

Saxby, L., and M. P. Bryden. "Left-Ear Superiority in Children for Processing Auditory Emotional Material," *Developmental Psychology,* 20 (1984), 72–80. (Ch. 6)

Scarr, S. *Race, Social Class, and Individual Differences in I.Q.* Hillsdale, N. J.: Lawrence Erlbaum Associates, 1981. (Chs. 5, 11)

———. "On Quantifying the Intended Effects of Interventions: A Proposed Theory of the Environment," in L. A. Bond and J. M. Joffe (eds.), *Facilitating Infant and Early Childhood Development.* Hanover, Vt.: University Press of New England, 1982, pp. 466–484. (Ch. 2)

———. *Mother Care/Other Care.* New York: Basic Books, 1984. (Ch. 13)

———, and L. Carter-Saltzman. "Twin Method: Defense of a Critical Assumption," *Behavior Genetics,* 9 (1979), 527–542. (Ch. 11)

———, interviewed by E. Hall. "What's a Parent to Do?" *Psychology Today,* 18 (May 1984), 58–63. (Ch. 13)

———, and K. K. Kidd. "Developmental Behavioral Genetics," in P. H. Mussen (ed.), *Handbook of Child Psychology.* 4th ed. Vol. 2: M. M. Haith and J. J. Campos (eds.), *Infancy and Developmental Psychobiology.* New York: Wiley, 1983, pp. 345–434. (Chs. 2, 3, 11)

———, and K. McCartney. "How People Make Their Own Environments: A Theory of Genotype → Environmental Effects," *Child Development,* 54 (1983), 424–435. (Ch. 2)

———, and P. Salapatek. "Patterns of Fear Development in Infancy," *Merrill-Palmer Quarterly,* 16 (1970), 53–90. (Chs. 7, 12)

———, and R. A. Weinberg. "Intellectual Similarities Within Families of Both Adopted and Biological Children," *Intelligence,* 1 (1977), 170–191. (Ch. 11)

Schachtel, E. G. "On Memory and Childhood Amnesia," *Psychiatry,* 10 (1947), 1–26. (Ch. 8)

Schachter, F. F. "Sibling Deidentification and Split-Parent Identification," in M. E. Lamb and B. Sutton-Smith (eds.), *Sibling Relationships: Their Nature and Significance Across the Lifespan.* Hillsdale, N. J.: Lawrence Erlbaum Associates, 1982, pp. 123–152. (Ch. 2)

Schaffer, H. R. *The Growth of Sociability.* Baltimore: Penguin, 1971. (Ch. 4)

———. *Mothering.* Cambridge, Mass.: Harvard University Press, 1977. (Ch. 12)

———, and P. E. Emerson. "Patterns of Response to Physical Contact in Early Human Development," *Journal of Child Psychology and Psychiatry,* 5 (1964), 1–13. (Ch. 12)

Schaie, K. W. "The Primary Mental Abilities in Adulthood: An Exploration in the Development of Psychometric Intelligence," in P. B. Baltes and O. G. Brim, Jr. (eds.), *Life-Span Development and Behavior.* Vol. 2. New York: Academic Press, 1979, pp. 67–115. (Ch. 2)

Schiedel, D. G., and J. E. Marcia. "Ego Identity, Intimacy, Sex Role Orientation, and Gender," *Developmental Psychology,* 21 (1985), 149–160. (Ch. 17)

Schneider, B., S. E. Trehub, and D. Bull. "High-Frequency Sensitivity in Infants," *Science,* 207 (1980), 1003–1004. (Ch. 7)

Schneider-Rosen, K., and D. Cicchetti. "The Relationship Between Affect and Cognition in Maltreated Infants: Quality of Attachment and the Development of Visual Self-Recognition," *Child Development,* 55 (1984), 648–658. (Ch. 13)

Schonfeld, W. A. "Body-Image in Adolescents: A Psychi-

atric Concept for the Pediatrician," *Pediatrics,* 31 (1963), 845–855. (Ch. 15)

———. "Body-Image Disturbances in Adolescents with Inappropriate Sexual Development," *American Journal of Orthopsychiatry,* 34 (1964), 493–502. (Ch. 15)

Schwartz, G., and D. Merten. "The Language of Adolescence: An Anthropological Approach to the Youth Culture," *American Journal of Sociology,* 72 (1967), 453–468. (Ch. 15)

Schwartz, J., and P. Tallal. "Rate of Acoustic Change May Underlie Hemispheric Specialization for Speech Perception," *Science,* 207 (1980), 1380–1381. (Ch. 6)

Schwartz, M., and R. H. Day. "Visual Shape Perception in Early Infancy," *Monographs of the Society for Research in Child Development,* 44 (1979), whole no.182. (Ch. 7)

———, and J. Schwartz. "Evidence Against a Genetical Component to Performance on IQ Tests," *Nature,* 248 (March 1974), 84–85. (Ch. 11)

Schweinhart, L. J., and D. P. Weikart. *Young Children Grow Up: The Effects of the Perry Preschool Program on Youths Through Age 15.* Ypsilanti, Michigan: High/Scope Press, 1980. (Ch. 11)

Scollan, R. "A Real Early Stage: An Unzippered Condensation of a Dissertation on Child Language," in E. Ochs and B. B. Schieffelin (eds.), *Developmental Pragmatics.* New York: Academic Press, 1979, pp. 215–227. (Ch. 9)

Scott, E. M., R. Illsby, and A. M. Thomson. "A Psychological Investigation of Primigravidae. II: Maternal Social Class, Age, Physique, and Intelligence," *Journal of Obstetrics and Gynaecology of the British Empire,* 63 (1956), 338–343. (Ch. 5)

Scott, J. P. "Genetics and the Development of Social Behavior in Mammals," *American Journal of Orthopsychiatry,* 32 (1962), 878–893. (Ch. 12)

———. "The Development of Social Motivation," *Nebraska Symposium on Motivation,* 15 (1967), 111–132. (Ch. 12)

Scribner, S., and M. Cole. "Effects of Constrained Recall Training on Children's Performance in a Verbal Memory Task," *Child Development,* 43 (1972), 845–857. (Ch. 8)

Scrimshaw, N. S. "Early Malnutrition and Central Nervous System Function," *Merrill-Palmer Quarterly,* 15 (1969), 375–388. (Ch. 5)

———, and J. E. Gordon (eds.). *Malnutrition, Learning, and Behavior.* Cambridge, Mass.: MIT Press, 1968. (Ch. 5)

Searleman, A. "A Review of Right Hemisphere Linguistic Capabilities," *Psychological Bulletin,* 84 (1977), 503–528. (Ch. 6)

Sears, P. S., and A. H. Barbee. "Career and Life Satisfaction Among Terman's Gifted Women," in J. C. Stanley, W. C. George, and C. H. Solano (eds.), *The Gifted and the Creative: Fifty-Year Perspective.* Baltimore: Johns Hopkins University Press, 1978. (Ch. 11)

Sears, R. R. "Relation of Early Socialization Experiences to Self-Concepts and Gender Role in Middle Childhood," *Child Development,* 41 (1970), 267–290. (Chs. 13, 14)

———. "Your Ancients Revisited: A History of Child Development," in E. M. Hetherington (ed.), *Review of Child Development Research.* Vol. 5. Chicago: University of Chicago Press, 1975, pp. 1–73. (Ch. 1)

———. "Sources of Life Satisfaction of the Terman Gifted Men," *American Psychologist,* 32 (1977), 119–128. (Chs. 2, 11)

———, E. E. Maccoby, and H. Levin. *Patterns of Child Rearing.* Stanford, Calif.: Stanford University Press, 1976 [orig. pub. 1957]. (Chs. 2, 13, 16)

Self, P. A., and F. D. Horowitz. "The Behavioral Assessment of the Neonate: An Overview," in J. D. Osofsky (ed.), *Handbook of Infant Development.* New York: Wiley-Interscience, 1979, pp. 126–164. (Ch. 3)

Selman, R. L. *The Growth of Interpersonal Understanding.* New

York: Academic Press, 1980. (Chs. 14, 17)

———. "The Child as a Friendship Philosopher," in S. R. Asher and J. M. Gottman (eds.), *The Development of Friendships*. New York: Cambridge University Press, 1981. (Ch. 17)

Selye, H. A. *The Stress of Life*. New York: McGraw-Hill, 1976. (Ch. 3)

Serbin, L. A., K. D. O'Leary, R. N. Kent, and I. J. Tonick. "A Comparison of Teacher Response to the Pre-Academic and Problem Behavior of Boys and Girls," *Child Development*, 33 (1973), 796–804. (Ch. 15)

Shantz, C. U. "Social Cognition," in P. H. Mussen (ed.), *Handbook of Child Psychology*. 4th ed. Vol. 3: J. H. Flavell and E. M. Markman (eds.), *Cognitive Development*. New York: Wiley, 1983, pp. 495–555. (Ch. 17)

Shatz, M. "On the Development of Communicative Understandings: An Early Strategy for Interpreting and Responding to Messages," *Cognitive Psychology*, 10 (1978), 271–301. (Ch. 9)

———. "Communication," in P. H. Mussen (ed.), *Handbook of Child Psychology*. 4th ed. Vol. 3: J. H. Flavell and E. M. Markman (eds.), *Cognitive Development*. New York: Wiley, 1983, pp. 841–889. (Chs. 9, 17)

———. "Contributions of Mother and Mind to the Development of Communicative Competence: A Status Report," in M. Perlmutter (ed.), *Minnesota Symposia on Child Psychology*. Vol. 17: *Parent-Child Interaction and Parent-Child Relations in Child Development*. Hillsdale, N. J.: Lawrence Erlbaum Associates, 1984, pp. 33–60. (Ch. 9)

———, and R. Gelman. "Beyond Syntax: The Influence of Conversational Constraints on Speech Modifications," in C. E. Snow and C. A. Ferguson (eds.), *Talking to Children*. New York: Cambridge University Press, 1977, pp. 189–198. (Ch. 17)

Sherif, M., O. J. Harvey, B. J. White, W. R. Hood, and C. W. Sherif. *Intergroup Conflict and Cooperation. The Robbers Cave Experiment*. Norman, Okla.: Institute of Group Relations, 1961. (Ch. 2)

———, and C. W. Sherif. *Groups in Harmony and Tension: An Integration of Studies on Intergroup Relations*. New York: Harper & Row, 1953. (Ch. 14)

———, and ———. *Reference Groups: Explorations into Conformity and Deviation of Adolescents*. New York: Harper & Row, 1964. (Ch. 14)

Sherman, J. A. *On the Psychology of Women: A Survey of Empirical Studies*. Springfield, Ill.: Charles C. Thomas, 1973. (Ch. 5)

Shigetomi, C. C., D. P. Hartmann, and D. M. Gelfand. "Sex Differences in Children's Altruistic Behavior and Reputations for Helpfulness," *Developmental Psychology*, 17 (1981), 434–437. (Ch. 16)

Shucard, J. L., D. W. Shucard, K. R. Cummins, and J. J. Campos. "Auditory Evoked Potentials and Sex Related Differences in Brain Development," *Brain and Language*, 13 (1981), 91–102. (Ch. 6)

Shultz, T. R. "Rules of Causal Attribution," *Monographs of the Society for Research in Child Development*, 47 (1982), whole no. 194. (Ch. 10)

Siegel, A. W., K. C. Kirasic, and R. V. Kail, Jr. "Stalking the Elusive Cognitive Map: The Development of Children's Representations of Geographical Space," in I. Altman and J. F. Wohlwill (eds.), *Children and the Environment*. New York: Plenum Press, 1978, pp. 223–258. (Ch. 8)

———, and S. H. White. "The Child Study Movement: Early Growth and Development of the Symbolized Child," in H. W. Reese (ed.), *Advances in Child Development and Behavior*. Vol. 17. New York: Academic Press, 1982, pp. 233–285. (Ch. 1)

Siegel, L. S., A. E. McCabe, J. Brand, and J. Matthews.

"Evidence for the Understanding of Class Inclusion in Preschool Children: Linguistic Factors and Training Effects," *Child Development*, 49 (1978), 688–693. (Ch. 10)

Siegler, R. S. "The Origins of Scientific Reasoning," in R. S. Siegler (ed.), *Children's Thinking: What Develops?* Hillsdale, N. J.: Lawrence Erlbaum Associates, 1978, pp. 109–149. (Ch. 10)

———. "Developmental Sequences Between and Within Concepts," *Monographs of the Society for Research in Child Development*, 46 (1982), whole no. 189. (Ch. 10)

———. "Information Processing Approaches to Development," in P. H. Mussen (ed.), *Handbook of Child Psychology*. 4th ed. Vol. 1: W. Kessen (ed.), *History, Theory, and Methods*. New York: Wiley, 1983, pp. 129–211. (Chs. 1, 7)

———, D. E. Liebert, and R. M. Liebert. "Inhelder and Piaget's Pendulum Problem: Teaching Preadolescents to Act as Scientists," *Developmental Psychology*, 9 (1973), 97–101. (Ch. 10)

———, and M. Robinson. "The Development of Numerical Understandings," in H. W. Reese and L. P. Lipsitt (eds.), *Advances in Child Development and Behavior*. Vol. 16. New York: Academic Press, 1982, pp. 241–312. (Ch. 10)

Sigel, I. E., and E. Mermelstein. "Effects of Nonschooling on Piagetian Tasks of Conservation." Unpublished paper. (Cited in J. H. Flavell, "Concept Development," in P. H. Mussen [ed.], *Carmichael's Manual of Child Psychology*. 3rd ed. New York: Wiley, 1970, pp. 983–1060). (Ch. 10)

Simon, D. P., and H. A. Simon. "Alternative Uses of Phonemic Information in Spelling," *Review of Educational Research*, 43 (1973), 115–137. (Ch. 1)

Simon, W. E., and J. H. Gagnon. "On Psychological Development," in D. A. Goslin (ed.), *Handbook of Socialization Theory and Research*. Chicago: Rand McNally, 1969, pp. 733–752. (Ch. 15)

Simpson, E. L. "Moral Development Research: A Case Study of Scientific Cultural Bias," *Human Development*, 17 (1974), 81–106. (Ch. 16)

Sinclair, C. B. *Movement of the Young Child: Ages Two to Six*. Columbus, Ohio: Merrill, 1973. (Ch. 5)

Singleton, L. C., and S. R. Asher. "Racial Integration and Children's Peer Preferences: An Investigation of Developmental and Cohort Differences," *Child Development*, 50 (1979), 936–941. (Ch. 14)

Skinner, B. F. *The Behavior of Organisms: An Experimental Analysis*. New York: Appleton-Century-Crofts, 1938. (Ch. 1)

———. *Verbal Behavior*. New York: Appleton-Century-Crofts, 1957. (Ch. 9)

———. *Cumulative Record: A Selection of Papers*. 3rd ed. New York: Appleton-Century-Crofts, 1972. (Ch. 1)

Skodak, M., and H. M. Skeels. "A Final Follow-Up Study of One Hundred Adopted Children," *Journal of Genetic Psychology*, 75 (1949), 85–125. (Ch. 11)

Slaby, R. G., and K. S. Frey. "Development of Gender Constancy and Selective Attention to Same-Sex Models," *Child Development*, 46 (1975), 849–856. (Ch. 15)

Slobin, D. I. "Cognitive Prerequisites for the Development of Grammar," in C. A. Ferguson and D. I. Slobin (eds.), *Studies of Child Language Development*. New York: Holt, Rinehart and Winston, 1973, pp. 175–208. (Ch. 9)

———. "On the Nature of Talk to Children," in E. H. Lenneberg and E. Lenneberg (eds.), *Foundations of Language Development: A Multidisciplinary Approach*. UNESCO-IBRO, 1975. (Ch. 9)

———. "A Case Study of Early Language Awareness," in A. Sinclair, R. J. Jarvella, and W. J. M. Levelt (eds.), *The Child's Conception of Language*. New York: Springer-Verlag, 1978, pp. 45–54. (Ch. 9)

———. "Universal and Particular in the Acquisition of Language," in L. R. Gleitman and E. Wanner (eds.), *Language*

Acquisition: The State of the Art. New York: Cambridge University Press, 1982. (Ch. 9)

Smith, A. "Lenneberg, Locke, Zangwill, and the Neuropsychology of Language and Language Disorders," in G. A. Miller and E. Lenneberg (eds.), *Psychology and Biology of Language and Thought.* New York: Academic Press, 1978, pp. 133–150. (Ch. 6)

Smith, C. "Effects of Maternal Undernutrition upon the Newborn Infant in Holland (1944–1945)," *Journal of Pediatrics,* 30 (1947), 1263–1265. (Ch. 3)

————, and B. Lloyd. "Maternal Behavior and Perceived Sex of Infant Revisited," *Child Development,* 49 (1978), 1263–1265. (Ch. 15)

Smith, P. K. "Social and Fantasy Play in Young Children," in B. Tizard and D. Harvey (eds.), *Biology and Play.* Philadelphia: Lippincott, 1977, pp. 123–145. (Ch. 14)

————. "A Longitudinal Study of Social Participation in Preschool Children: Solitary and Parallel Play Reexamined," *Developmental Psychology,* 14 (1978), 517–523. (Ch. 14)

————, and L. Daglish. "Sex Differences in Parent and Infant Behavior in the Home," *Child Development,* 48 (1977), 1250–1254. (Ch. 15)

Smith, S. B. "Why TV Won't Let Up on Violence," *The New York Times,* January 13, 1985, Section 2, 2+. (Ch. 16)

Smith, S. D., W. J. Kimberling, B. F. Pennington, and H. A. Lubs. "Specific Reading Disability: Identification of an Inherited Form Through Linkage Analysis," *Science,* 219 (1983), 1345–1347. (Ch. 6)

Snow, C. E. "The Development of Conversation Between Mothers and Babies," *Journal of Child Language,* 4 (1977a), 1–22. (Ch. 9)

————, and M. Hoefnagel-Höhle. "The Critical Period for Language Acquisition: Evidence from Second Language Learning," *Child Development,* 49 (1978), 1114–1128. (Ch. 9)

Sobesky, W. E. "The Effects of Situational Factors on Moral Judgments," *Child Development,* 54 (1983), 575–584. (Ch. 16)

Society for Research in Child Development (Developmental Interest Group). *Ethical Standards for Research with Children.* 1975. (Ch. 2)

Sonnenschein, S., and G. J. Whitehurst. "Developing Referential Communication: A Hierarchy of Skills," *Child Development,* 55 (1984), 1936–1945. (Ch. 17)

Sontag, L. "Implications of Fetal Behavior and Environment for Adult Personalities," *Annals of the New York Academy of Science,* 134 (1966), 782. (Ch. 3)

Sorce, J. F., and R. N. Emde. "Mother's Presence Is Not Enough: The Effect of Emotional Availability on Infant Exploration," *Developmental Psychology,* 17 (1981), 737–745. (Ch. 12)

Sorenstein, F. "Sexual Activity among Adolescent Males," in A. B. Elster and M. E. Lamb (eds.), *Adolescent Fatherhood.* Hillsdale, N. J.: Lawrence Erlbaum Associates, [in press]. (Ch. 15)

Spearman, C. *The Abilities of Man.* New York: Macmillan, 1927. (Ch. 11)

Speer, J. R. "Two Practical Strategies Young Children Use to Interpret Vague Instructions," *Child Development,* 55 (1984), 1811–1819. (Ch. 17)

Spelke, E. S. "Perceiving Bimodally Specified Events in Infancy," *Developmental Psychology,* 15 (1979), 626–636. (Ch. 7)

————, and C. J. Owsley. "Intermodal Exploration and Knowledge in Infancy," *Infant Behavior and Development,* 2 (1979), 13–27. (Ch. 7)

Spence, M. J., and A. J. DeCasper. "Human Fetuses Perceive Maternal Speech." Paper delivered at International Conference on Infant Studies. Austin, Texas, March 1982. (Chs. 3, 4)

Spinetta, J. J., and D. Rigler. "The Child-Abusing Parent: A Psychological Review," *Psychological Bulletin,* 77 (1972), 296–304. (Ch. 13)

Springer, S. P., and G. Deutsch. *Left Brain, Right Brain.* San Francisco: W. H. Freeman, 1981. (Ch. 6)

Sroufe, L. A. "Infant-Caregiver Attachment and Patterns of Adaptation in Preschool: The Roots of Maladaptation and Competence," in M. Perlmutter (ed.), *Minnesota Symposia on Child Psychology.* Vol. 16: *Development and Policy Concerning Children with Special Needs.* Hillsdale, N. J.: Lawrence Erlbaum Associates, 1983, pp. 41–84. (Chs. 12, 14)

————, E. Waters, and L. Matas. "Contextual Determinants of Infant Affective Response," in M. Lewis and L. Rosenblum, *The Origins of Fear.* New York: Wiley, 1974. (Ch. 12)

Staffieri, J. R. "A Study of Social Stereotype of Body Image in Children," *Journal of Personality and Social Psychology,* 7 (1967), 101–104. (Ch. 15)

Stanjek, K. "Das Überreichen von Gaben: Funktion und Entwicklung in den ersten Lebensjahren," *Zeitschrift für Entwicklungpsychologie und Pädagogische Psychologie,* 10 (1978), 103–113. (Ch. 16)

Starr, R. H., Jr. "Child Abuse," *American Psychologist,* 34 (1979), 872–878. (Ch. 13)

Staub, E. *The Development of Prosocial Behavior in Children.* New York: General Learning Press, 1975. (Ch. 16)

Steele, B. F., and D. Pollock. "A Psychiatric Study of Parents Who Abuse Infants and Small Children," in R. E. Helfer and C. H. Kempe (eds.), *The Battered Child.* Chicago: University of Chicago Press, 1968. (Ch. 13)

Stein, A. H., and M. M. Bailey. "The Socialization of Achievement Orientation in Females," *Psychological Bulletin,* 80 (1973), 345–366. (Ch. 14)

————, and L. K. Friedrich. "The Effect of Television Content on Young Children," in A. D. Pick (ed.), *Minnesota Symposia on Child Psychology.* Vol. 9. Minneapolis: University of Minnesota Press, 1975, pp. 78–105. (Ch. 16)

Steinberg, L. D. "Transformations in Family Relations at Puberty," *Developmental Psychology,* 17 (1981), 833–840. (Ch. 15)

————, R. Catalano, and D. Dooley. "Economic Antecedents of Child Abuse and Neglect," *Child Development,* 44 (1973), 670–674. (Ch. 13)

Steiner, J. E. "Facial Expressions in Response to Taste and Smell Stimulation," in H. W. Reese and L. P. Lipsitt (eds.), *Advances in Child Development and Behavior.* Vol. 13. New York: Academic Press, 1979, pp. 257–296. (Ch. 4)

Stenberg, C., and J. J. Campos. "The Development of the Expression of Anger in Human Infants," in M. Lewis and C. Saarni (eds.), *The Socialization of Affect.* New York: Plenum Press, 1983. (Ch. 12)

Stendler, C., D. Damrin, and A. C. Haines. "Studies in Cooperation and Competition. I: The Effects of Working for Group and Individual Rewards on the Social Climate of Children's Groups," *Journal of Genetic Psychology,* 79 (1951), 173–197. (Ch. 14)

Stephan, H., R. Bauchot, and O. J. Andy. "Data on the Size of the Brain and of Various Brain Parts in Insectivores and Primates," in C. R. Noback and W. Montagna (eds.), *The Primate Brain.* New York: Appleton-Century-Crofts, 1970. (Ch. 6)

Stephens, M. W., and P. Delys. "External Control Expectancies Among Disadvantaged Children at Preschool Age," *Child Development,* 44 (1973), 670–674. (Ch. 13)

Stern, C. *Principles of Human Genetics.* 2nd ed. San Francisco: Jossey-Bass, 1960. (Ch. 3)

Stern, D. N. *The First Relationship: Infant and Mother.* Cambridge, Mass.: Harvard University Press, 1977. (Chs. 9, 12)

Sternberg, R. J. "Stalking the IQ Quark," *Psychology Today,* 13 (September 1979), 42–54. (Ch. 11)

———. "Mechanisms of Cognitive Development: A Componential Approach," in R. J. Sternberg (ed.), *Mechanisms of Cognitive Development.* New York: W. H. Freeman, 1984, pp. 163–186. (Ch. 11)

———, B. E. Conway, J. L. Ketron, and M. Bernstein. "People's Conceptions of Intelligence," *Journal of Personality and Social Psychology: Attitudes and Social Cognition,* 41 (1981), 37–55. (Ch. 11)

———, and G. Nigro. "Developmental Patterns in the Solution of Verbal Analogies," *Child Development,* 51 (1980), 27–38. (Ch. 11)

———, and J. S. Powell. "The Development of Intelligence," in P. H. Mussen (ed.), *Handbook of Child Psychology.* 4th ed. Vol. 3: J. H. Flavell and E. M. Markman (eds.), *Cognitive Development.* New York: Wiley, 1983, pp. 341–419. (Ch. 11)

Sternglanz, S. H., and L. A. Serbin. "Sex Role Stereotyping in Children's Television Programs," *Developmental Psychology,* 10 (1974), 710–715. (Ch. 15)

Stevenson, H. W. *Children's Learning.* New York: Appleton-Century-Crofts, 1972. (Ch. 8)

———. "How Children Learn—The Quest for a Theory," in P. H. Mussen (ed.), *Handbook of Child Psychology.* 4th ed. Vol. 1: W. Kessen (ed.), *History, Theory, and Methods.* New York: Wiley, 1983, pp. 213–236. (Chs. 1, 7)

———, J. W. Stigler, G. W. Lucker, S. Lee, C. Hsu, and S. Kitamura. "Reading Disabilities: The Case of Chinese, Japanese, and English," *Child Development,* 53 (1982), 1164–1181. (Ch. 6)

Stewart, R. B., and R. S. Marvin. "Sibling Relations: The Role of Conceptual Perspective-Taking in the Ontogeny of Sibling Caregiving," *Child Development,* 55 (1984), 1322–1331. (Ch. 17)

Stipek, D. J. "Children's Use of Past Performance Information in Ability and Expectancy Judgments for Self and Other." Paper presented at the Meeting of the International Society for the Study of Behavioral Development. Toronto, August 1981. (Ch. 14)

Stirnimann, F. "Uber das Farbempfinder Neugeborener," *Annales Paedriatrici,* 163 (1944), 1–25. (Ch. 4)

Stolz, H. R., and L. H. Stolz. *Somatic Development of Adolescent Boys: A Study of the Growth of Boys During the Second Decade of Life.* New York: Macmillan, 1951. (Chs. 5, 15)

Straus, M. A., R. J. Gelles, and S. K. Steinmetz. *Behind Closed Doors: Violence in the American Family.* Garden City, New York: Doubleday, 1980. (Ch. 13)

Strauss, S. "Ancestral and Descendant Behaviors: The Case of U-Shaped Behavioral Growth," in T. G. Bever (ed.), *Regressions in Mental Development: Basic Phenomena and Theories.* Hillsdale, N. J.: Lawrence Erlbaum Associates, 1982, pp. 191–220. (Chs. 4, 5)

Strayer, F. F. "Social Ecology of the Preschool Peer Group," in W. A. Collins (ed.), *Minnesota Symposia on Child Psychology.* Vol. 13: *Development of Cognition, Affect, and Social Relations.* Hillsdale, N. J.: Lawrence Erlbaum Associates, 1980, pp. 165–196. (Ch. 16)

———, T. R. Chapeskie, and J. Strayer. "The Perception of Preschool Social Dominance," *Aggressive Behavior,* 4 (1978), 183–192. (Ch. 14)

———, and J. Strayer. "An Ethological Analysis of Social Agonism and Dominance Relations Among School Children," *Child Development,* 47 (1976), 980–989. (Ch. 1)

Strayer, J. "Social Conflict and Peer-Group Status." Paper presented at the Biennial Meeting of the Society for Re-

search in Child Development. New Orleans, March 1977. (Ch. 1)

Streissguth, A. P. "Psychologic Handicaps in Children with Fetal Alcohol Syndrome. Work in Progress on Alcoholism," *Annals of the New York Academy of Science,* 273 (1976), 140–145. (Ch. 11)

———, H. M. Barr, and D. C. Martin. "Maternal Alcohol Use and Neonatal Habituation Assessed with the Brazelton Scale," *Child Development,* 54 (1983), 1109–1118. (Ch. 3)

———, S. Landesman-Dwyer, J. C. Martin, and D. W. Smith. "Teratogenic Effects of Alcohol on Humans and Laboratory Animals," *Science,* 209 (1980), 353–361. (Ch. 3)

———, D. C. Martin, H. M. Barr, B. M. Sandman, G. L. Kirchner, and B. L. Darby. "Intrauterine Alcohol and Nicotine Exposure: Attention and Reaction Time in 4-Year-Old Children," *Developmental Psychology,* 20 (1984), 533–541. (Ch. 3)

Strickland, D. M., S. A. Saeed, M. L. Casey, and M. D. Mitchell. "Stimulation of Prostaglandin Biosynthesis by Urine of Human Fetus May Serve as a Trigger for Parturition," *Science,* 220 (1983), 521–522. (Ch. 3)

Studdert-Kennedy, M., and D. Shankweiler. "Hemispheric Specialization for Speech Perception," *Journal of the Acoustical Society of America,* 48 (1970), 579–594. (Ch. 6)

Suomi, S. J. "Adult Male-Infant Interaction Among Monkeys Living in Nuclear Families," *Child Development,* 48 (1977), 1255–1270. (Ch. 2)

———. "Social Development in Rhesus Monkeys: Consideration of Individual Differences," in A. Oliverio and M. Zapella (eds.), *The Behavior of Human Infants.* New York: Plenum Press, 1983. (Ch. 13)

———, and H. Harlow. "Social Rehabilitation of Isolate-Reared Monkeys," *Developmental Psychology,* 6 (1972), 487–496. (Ch. 2)

———, and ———. "The Role and Reason of Peer Relationship in Rhesus Monkeys," in M. Lewis and L. A. Rosenblum (eds.), *Friendship and Peer Relations.* New York: Wiley, 1975, pp. 153–185. (Chs. 12, 14)

———, and C. Ripp. "A History of Motherless Mother Monkey Mothering at the University of Wisconsin Primate Laboratory," in *Child Abuse: The Nonhuman Primate Data.* New York: Alan R. Liss, 1983, pp. 49–78. (Chs. 12, 13)

Super, C. M. "Environmental Effects on Motor Development: The Case of 'African Infant Precocity,'" *Developmental Medicine and Child Neurology,* 18 (1976), 561–567. (Ch. 5)

Surber, C. F. "Developmental Processes in Social Inference: Averaging of Intentions and Consequences in Moral Judgment," *Developmental Psychology,* 13 (1977), 654–655. (Ch. 16)

Sussman, E. J. "Visual and Verbal Attributes of Television and Selective Attention in Preschool Children," *Developmental Psychology,* 14 (1978), 565–566. (Ch. 8)

Sutton-Smith, B. "Birth Order and Sibling Status Effects," in M. E. Lamb and B. Sutton-Smith (eds.), *Sibling Relationships: Their Nature and Significance Across the Lifespan.* Hillsdale, N. J.: Lawrence Erlbaum Associates, 1982, pp. 153–166. (Ch. 2)

Swanson, J. M., and M. Kinsbourne. "The Cognitive Effects of Stimulant Drugs on Hyperactive Children," in G. A. Hale and M. Lewis (eds.), *Attention and Cognitive Development.* New York: Plenum Press, 1979, 249–296. (Ch. 6)

Tanner, J. M. *Fetus into Man: Physical Growth from Conception to Maturity.* Cambridge, Mass.: Harvard University Press,

1978. (Chs. 3, 5)

———, R. H. Whitehouse, and M. J. R. Healy. *A New System of Estimating Skeletal Maturity from the Hand and Wrist*. Parts I and II. Paris: Centre International de l'Enfance, 1962. (Ch. 5)

Tavris, C. A., and C. W. Offir. *The Longest War: Sex Differences in Perspective*. New York: Harcourt Brace Jovanovich, 1977. (Chs. 14, 15)

Taylor, D. C. "Differential Rates of Cerebral Maturation Between Hemispheres," *Lancet*, 2 (1969), 140–142. (Ch. 6)

Teller, D. Y., D. R. Peeples, and M. Sekel. "Discrimination of Chromatic from White Light by Two-Month-Old Human Infants," *Vision Research*, 18 (1978), 41–48. (Ch. 7)

Terman, L. M. (ed.). *Genetic Studies of Genius*. Vol. 5. Stanford, Calif.: Stanford University Press, 1959. (Ch. 11)

Terrace, H. S. *Nim: A Chimpanzee Who Learned Sign Language*. New York: Knopf, 1979. (Ch. 9)

Thelen, E. "Rhythmical Behavior in Infancy: An Ethological Perspective," *Developmental Psychology*, 17 (1981), 237–257. (Ch. 5)

Thoman, E. B., A. F. Korner, and L. Beason-Williams. "Modification of Responsiveness to Maternal Vocalization in the Neonate," *Child Development*, 48 (1977), 563–569. (Ch. 4)

Thomas, A., and S. Chess. *Temperament and Development*. New York: Brunner-Mazel, 1977. (Ch. 4)

———, and ———. "The Role of Temperament in the Contribution of Individuals to Their Own Development," in R. M. Lerner and N. A. Busch-Rossnagel, *Individuals As Producers of Their Own Development*. New York: Academic Press, 1981, pp. 231–256. (Ch. 13)

Thompson, S. K. "Gender Labels and Early Sex Role Development," *Child Development*, 46 (1975), 339–347. (Ch. 15)

Thompson, W. C., C. L. Cowan, and D. L. Rosenhan. "Focus of Attention Mediates the Impact of Negative Effect on Altruism," *Journal of Personality and Social Psychology*, 38 (1980), 291–300. (Ch. 16)

Thompson, W. P. "Influence of Prenatal Maternal Anxiety on Emotionality in Young Rats," *Science*, 125 (1957), 698–699. (Ch. 3)

Thorndike, E. L. *Educational Psychology*. Vol 1. New York: Columbia University, 1913. Vols. 2 and 3. New York: Teachers College, 1913. (Ch. 1)

Thurstone, L. I. *Multiple-Factor Analysis*. Chicago: University of Chicago Press, 1947. (Ch. 11)

Tinbergen, N. *The Study of Instinct*. Oxford: Clarendon Press, 1951. (Ch. 2)

———. *The Animal in Its World*. Vol. 2. Cambridge, Mass.: Harvard University Press, 1973. (Ch. 2)

Todd, C. M., and M. Perlmutter. "Reality Recalled by Preschool Children," in M. Perlmutter (ed.), *New Directions in Child Development*. No. 10: *Children's Memory*. San Francisco: Jossey-Bass, 1980, pp. 69–86. (Ch. 8)

Trabasso, T. "Representation, Memory, and Reasoning: How Do We Make Transitive Inferences?" in A. D. Pick (ed.), *Minnesota Symposia on Child Psychology*. Vol. 9. Minneapolis: University of Minnesota Press, 1975, pp. 135–172. (Ch. 10)

———. "The Role of Memory as a System in Making Transitive Inferences," in R. V. Kail, Jr., and J. W. Hagen (eds.), *Perspectives on the Development of Memory and Cognition*. Hillsdale, N. J.: Lawrence Erlbaum Associates, 1977, pp. 333–366. (Ch. 10)

———, and G. H. Bower. *Attention in Learning Theory and Research*. New York: Wiley, 1968. (Ch. 10)

———, A. G. McLanahan, A. M. Isen, C. A. Riley, P. Dolecki, and T. Tucker. "How Do Children Solve Class Inclusion Problems?" in R. S. Siegler (ed.), *Children's Thinking: What Develops?* Hillsdale, N. J.: Lawrence Erlbaum Associates, 1978, pp. 151–180. (Ch. 10)

Tracy, R. L., M. E. Lamb, and M. D. Ainsworth. "Infant Approach Behavior as Related to Attachment," *Child Development*, 47 (1976), 571–578. (Chs. 2, 12)

Trause, M. A. "Stranger Response: Effects of Familiarity, Strangers' Approach, and Sex of Infant," *Child Development*, 48 (1977), 1657–1661. (Ch. 12)

Trehub, S. E. "The Discrimination of Foreign Speech Contrasts by Infants and Adults," *Child Development*, 47 (1976), 466–472. (Ch. 9)

———, D. Bull, and L. A. Thorpe. "Infants' Perceptions of Melodies: The Role of Melodic Contour," *Child Development*, 55 (1984), 821–830. (Ch. 7)

Tresemer, D. "Fear of Success: Popular But Unproven," *Psychology Today*, 7 (March 1974), 82–85. (Ch. 14)

Tryon, R. C. "Genetic Differences in Maze Learning in Rats," *Thirty-Ninth Yearbook, National Society for the Study of Education*. Part 1. Bloomington, Ill.: Public Schools Publishing Co., 1940, pp. 111–119. (Ch. 2)

Tuchman-Duplessis, H. *Drug Effects on the Fetus*. Sydney: ADIS Press, 1975. (Ch. 3)

Tulkin, S. R., and J. Kagan. "Mother-Child Interaction in the First Year of Life," *Child Development*, 43 (1972), 31–41. (Ch. 11)

Turing, A. M. "Computing Machinery and Intelligence," *Mind*, 59 (1950), 433–460. (Ch. 1)

Turkle, S. *The Second Self: Computers and the Human Spirit*. New York: Simon and Schuster, 1984. (Ch. 10)

Tyler, L. E. "The Intelligence We Test—An Evolving Concept," in L. B. Resnick (ed.), *The Nature of Intelligence*. Hillsdale, N. J.: Lawrence Erlbaum Associates, 1976, pp. 13–26. (Ch. 11)

Ulian, D. Z. "The Development of Conceptions of Masculinity and Femininity," in B. Lloyd and J. Ascher (eds.), *Exploring Sex Differences*. London: Academic Press, 1976. (Ch. 15)

Ullman, C. A. "Teachers, Peers, and Tests as Predictors of Adjustment," *Journal of Educational Psychology*, 48 (1957), 257–267. (Ch. 14)

Underwood, B., W. F. Froming, and B. S. Moore. "Mood, Attention, and Altruism: A Search for Mediating Variables," *Developmental Psychology*, 13 (1977), 541–542. (Ch. 16)

Ungerer, J. A., and M. Sigman. "The Relation of Play and Sensorimotor Behavior to Language in the Second Year," *Child Development*, 55 (1984), 1448–1455. (Ch. 9)

U.S. Bureau of the Census. *Statistical Abstract of the United States, 1982–83*. 103rd ed. Washington: U.S. Government Printing Office, 1982. (Chs. 3, 13)

Urberg, K. A. "Sex Role Conceptualizations in Adolescents and Adults," *Developmental Psychology*, 15 (1979), 90–92. (Ch. 15)

Uzgiris, I. C. "Situational Generality of Conservation," *Child Development*, 35 (1964), 831–841. (Ch. 10)

———. "Imitation in Infancy: Its Interpersonal Aspects," in M. Perlmutter (ed.), *Minnesota Symposia on Child Psychology*. Vol. 17: *Parent-Child Interaction and Parent-Child Relations in Child Development*. Hillsdale, N. J.: Lawrence Erlbaum Associates, 1984, pp. 1–32. (Ch. 7)

Van Lawick-Goodall, J. *In the Shadow of Man*. Boston: Houghton Mifflin, 1971. (Ch. 11)

Van Tassel-Baska, J. "Statewide Replication in Illinois of the Johns Hopkins Study of Mathematically Precocious Youth," in C. P. Benbow and J. C. Stanley (eds.), *Academic Precocity: Aspects of Its Development*. Baltimore: Johns Hopkins University Press, 1983, pp. 179–191. (Ch. 10)

von Frisch, K. *The Dance Language and Orientation of Bees*.

Cambridge, Mass.: Belknap/Harvard University Press, 1967. (Ch. 9)

von Hofsten, C. "Eye-Hand Coordination in the Newborn," *Developmental Psychology*, 18 (1982), 450–461. (Chs. 4, 7)

Vurpillot, E., and W. A. Ball. "The Concept of Identity and Children's Selective Attention," in G. A. Hale and M. Lewis (eds.), *Attention and Cognitive Development*. New York: Plenum Press, 1979, pp. 23–42. (Ch. 8)

Vygotsky, L. S. *Thought and Language*. Cambridge, Mass.: MIT Press, 1962. (Chs. 1, 9)

———. *Mind in Society*. Cambridge, Mass.: Harvard University Press, 1978. (Chs. 1, 9)

Waber, D. P. "Sex Differences in Cognition: A Function of Maturation Rates?" *Science*, 192 (1976), 572–573. (Ch. 6)

———. "Sex Differences in Mental Abilities, Hemisphere Lateralization, and Rate of Physical Growth in Adolescence," *Developmental Psychology*, 13 (1977), 29–38. (Ch. 6)

———, M. Bauermeister, C. Cohen, R. Ferber, and P. H. Wolff. "Behavior Correlates of Physical and Neuromotor Maturity in Adolescents from Different Environments," *Developmental Psychobiology*, 14 (1981), 513–522. (Ch. 6)

Wachs, T. "Utilization of a Piagetian Approach in the Investigation of Early Experience Effects: A Research Strategy and Some Illustrative Data," *Merrill-Palmer Quarterly*, 22 (1976), 11–30. (Ch. 11)

Wahler, R. G. "Child-Child Interactions in Free Field Settings: Some Experimental Analyses," *Journal of Experimental Child Psychology*, 5 (1967), 278–293. (Ch. 14)

Walford, R. L. *Maximum Life Span*. New York: Norton, 1983. (Ch. 2)

Walk, R. D., and S. H. Dodge. "Visual Depth Perception of a 10-Month-Old Monocular Human Infant," *Science*, 137 (1962), 529–530. (Ch. 7)

Walters, C. E. "Prediction of Postnatal Development from Fetal Activity," *Child Development*, 36 (1965), 801–806. (Ch. 4)

Walters, R. H., M. Leat, and L. Mezei. "Response Inhibition and Disinhibition Through Empathetic Learning," *Canadian Journal of Psychology*, 17 (1968), 235–243. (Ch. 14)

———, and R. D. Parke. "Influence of Response Consequences to a Social Model on Resistance to Deviation," *Journal of Experimental Child Psychology*, 1 (1964), 260–280. (Ch. 16)

———, ———, and V. Cane. "Timing of Punishment and the Observation of Consequences to Others as Determinants of Response Inhibition," *Journal of Experimental Child Psychology*, 2 (1965), 10–30. (Ch. 16)

Wannemacher, J. T., and M. L. Ryan. "'Less' Is Not 'More': A Study of Children's Comprehension of 'Less' in Various Contexts," *Child Development*, 49 (1978), 660–668. (Ch. 9)

Waterlow, J. C. "Note on the Assessment and Classification of Protein-Energy Malnutrition in Children," *Lancet*, 2 (1973), 87–89. (Ch. 5)

———, and P. R. Payne. "The Protein Gap," *Nature*, 258 (1975), 113–117. (Ch. 5)

Waters, E., J. Wippman, and L. A. Sroufe. "Attachment, Positive Effect, and Competence in the Peer Group: Two Studies in Contrast," *Child Development*, 50 (1979), 821–829. (Ch. 12)

Watson, J. B. "Psychology As the Behaviorist Views It," *Psychological Review*, 20 (1913), 158–177. (Ch. 1)

———. *Behaviorism*. New York: Norton, 1970 [orig. pub. 1924]. (Ch. 1)

Watson, J. S. "The Development and Generalization of 'Contingency' Awareness in Early Infancy: Some Hypotheses," *Merrill-Palmer Quarterly*, 12 (1966), 123–135. (Ch. 4)

Watson, M. W., and T. Amgott-Kwan. "Transitions in Children's Understanding of Parental Roles," *Developmental Psychology*, 19 (1983), 659–666. (Ch. 17)

———, and ———. "Development of Family-Role Concepts in School-Age Children," *Developmental Psychology*, 20 (1984), 953–959. (Ch. 17)

———, and K. W. Fischer. "Development of Social Roles in Elicited and Spontaneous Behavior during the Preschool Years," *Developmental Psychology*, 16 (1980), 483–494. (Ch. 17)

Webb, P. A., and A. A. Abrahamson. "Stages of Egocentrism in Children's Use of 'This' and 'That': A Different Point of View," *Journal of Child Language*, 3 (1976), 349–367. (Ch. 9)

Wechsler, D. "Intelligence Defined and Undefined," *American Psychologist*, 30 (1975), 135–139. (Ch. 11)

Weinert, F., and M. Perlmutter. *Memory Development: Individual Differences and Universal Changes*. Hillsdale, N. J.: Lawrence Erlbaum Associates, 1986 [in press]. (Ch. 8)

Weinrott, M. R., J. A. Corson, and M. Wilchesky. "Teacher-Mediated Treatment of Social Withdrawal," *Behavior Therapy*, 10 (1979), 280–294. (Ch. 14)

Weir, R. H. *Language in the Crib*. The Hague: Mouton, 1962. (Ch. 9)

Weisfeld, G. E. "The Nature-Nurture Issue and the Integrating Concept of Function," in B. B. Wolman (ed.), *Handbook of Developmental Psychology*. Englewood Cliffs, N. J.: Prentice-Hall, 1982, pp. 208–229. (Ch. 2)

Weisner, T. S. "Sibling Interdependence and Child Caretaking: A Cross-Cultural View," in M. E. Lamb and B. Sutton-Smith (eds.), *Sibling Relationships: Their Nature and Significance Across the Lifespan*. Hillsdale, N. J.: Lawrence Erlbaum Associates, 1982, pp. 305–328. (Ch. 13)

Weiss, G., and L. Hechtman. "The Hyperactive Child Syndrome," *Science*, 205 (1979), 1348–1354. (Ch. 6)

Weisz, J. R., K. O. Yeates, D. Robertson, and J. C. Beckham. "Perceived Contingency of Skill and Chance Events: A Developmental Analysis," *Developmental Psychology*, 18 (1982), 898–905. (Ch. 14)

Weller, C. "The Blastophthoric Effect of Chronic Lead Poisoning," *Journal of Medical Research*, 33 (1915), 271–293. (Ch. 3)

Wellman, H. M. "Preschoolers' Understanding of Memory-Relevant Variables," *Child Development*, 48 (1977), 1720–1723. (Ch. 8)

———, K. Ritter, and J. H. Flavell. "Deliberate Memory Behavior in the Delayed Reactions of Very Young Children," *Developmental Psychology*, 11 (1975), 780–787. (Ch. 8)

Werner, E. E. *Child Care: Kith, Kin, and Hired Hands*. Baltimore: University Park Press, 1984. (Ch. 12)

———, J. M. Bierman, and F. E. French. *The Children of Kauai*. Honolulu: University of Hawaii Press, 1971. (Ch. 11)

Werner, H. *Comparative Psychology of Mental Development*. New York: International Universities Press, 1948. (Chs. 1, 5)

———. "The Concept of Development from a Comparative and Organismic Point of View," in D. B. Harris (ed.), *The Concept of Development: An Issue in the Study of Human Behavior*. Minneapolis: University of Minnesota Press, 1957, pp. 125–148. (Ch. 1)

Werner, J. S., and M. Perlmutter. "Development of Visual Memory in Infants," in H. W. Reese and L. P. Lipsitt (eds.), *Advances in Child Development and Behavior*. Vol. 14. New York: Academic Press, 1979, pp. 1–56. (Chs. 7, 8)

———, and E. R. Siqueland. "Visual Recognition Memory in the Preterm Infant," *Infant Behavior and Development*, 1 (1978), 79–94. (Ch. 4)

Whalen, C. K., B. Henker, B. E. Collins, S. McAuliffe,

and A. Vaux. "Peer Interactions in a Structured Communication Task: Comparisons of Normal and Hyperactive Boys and of Methylphenidate (Ritalin) and Placebo Effects," *Child Development*, 50 (1979), 388–401. (Ch. 6)

White, B. L. *Human Infants: Experience and Psychological Development*. Englewood Cliffs, N. J.: Prentice-Hall, 1971. (Ch. 5)

——, and R. Held. "Plasticity of Sensorimotor Development in the Human Infant," in J. F. Rosenblith and W. Allinsmith (eds.), *The Causes of Behavior. II: Readings in Child Development and Educational Psychology*. 2nd ed. Boston: Allyn & Bacon, 1966, pp. 60–70. (Ch. 5)

White, C. B., N. Bushnell, and J. L. Regnemer. "Moral Development in Bahamian School Children: A 3-Year Examination of Kohlberg's Stages of Moral Development," *Developmental Psychology*, 14 (1978), 58–65. (Ch. 16)

White, D. G. "Effects of Sex-Typed Labels and Their Source on the Imitative Performance of Young Children," *Child Development*, 49 (1978), 1266–1269. (Ch. 15)

White, S. H., and D. B. Pillemer. "Childhood Amnesia and the Development of a Socially Accessible Memory System," in J. F. Kihlstrom and D. B. Pillemer (eds.), *Functional Disorders of Memory*. Hillsdale, N. J.: Lawrence Erlbaum Associates, 1979, pp. 29–73. (Ch. 8)

Whitehurst, G. J. "The Role of Comprehensive Training in the Generative Production of Direct-Indirect Object Sentences by Preschool Children." Unpublished paper. State University of New York, Stony Brook, 1974. (Ch. 9)

——. "Commentary," in J. H. Flavell, J. R. Speer, F. L. Green, and D. L. August, "The Development of Comprehension Monitoring and Knowledge about Communication," *Monographs of the Society for Research in Child Development*, 44 (1981), whole no. 192, pp. 58–65. (Ch. 17)

——. "Language Development," in B. B. Wolman (ed.), *Handbook of Developmental Psychology*. Englewood Cliffs, N. J.: Prentice-Hall, 1982, pp. 367–386. (Ch. 9)

——, and R. Vasta. "Is Language Acquired Through Imitation?" *Journal of Psycholinguistic Research*, 4 (1975), 37–59. (Ch. 9)

Whiting, J. W. M. "Resource Mediation and Learning by Identification," in I. Iscoe and H. W. Stevenson (eds.), *Personality Development in Children*. Austin: University of Texas Press, 1960, pp. 112–126 (Ch. 1)

——, and I. L. Child. *Child Training and Personality: A Cross-Cultural Study*. New Haven: Yale University Press, 1953. (Ch. 16)

Whorf, B. L. *Language, Thought, and Reality*. Cambridge, Mass.: MIT Press, 1956. (Ch. 9)

Wickelgren, L. W. "Convergence in the Human Newborn," *Journal of Experimental Child Psychology*, 5 (1967), 74–85. (Ch. 4)

Widdowson, E. M. "Mental Contentment and Physical Growth," *Lancet*, 260 (1951), 1316–1318. (Ch. 5)

Wiesenfeld, A. R., and C. Z. Malatesta. "Infant Distress: Variables Affecting Response of Caregivers and Others," in L. W. Hoffman, R. J. Gandelman, and H. R. Schiffman (eds.), *Parenting: Its Causes and Consequences*. Hillsdale, N. J.: Lawrence Erlbaum Associates, 1982, pp. 123–139. (Ch. 4)

Wilkening, F. "Integrating Velocity, Time, and Distance Information: A Developmental Study," *Cognitive Psychology*, 13 (1981), 231–247. (Ch. 10)

Wimmer, H., and J. Perner. "Beliefs about Beliefs: Representation and the Constraining Function of Wrong Beliefs in Children's Understanding of Deception," *Cognition*, 13 (1983), 103–128. (Ch. 17)

Wine, J. D. "Evaluation Anxiety: A Cognitive-Attentional Construct," in H. W. Krohne and L. Laux (eds.), *Achievement, Stress, and Anxiety*. Washington, D.C.: Hemisphere

Books, 1982. (Ch. 14)

Winer, G. A. "Class-Inclusion Reasoning in Children: A Review of the Empirical Literature," *Child Development*, 51 (1980), 309–328. (Ch. 10)

Winterbottam, M. "The Relation of Need for Achievement to Learning Experiences in Independence and Mastery," in J. Atkinson (ed.), *Motives in Fantasy, Action, and Society*. Princeton, N. J.: Van Nostrand, 1958, pp. 453–478. (Ch. 14)

Witelson, S. F. "Sex and the Single Hemisphere: Specialization of the Right Hemisphere for Spatial Processing," *Science*, 193 (1976), 425–427. (Ch. 6)

——. "Developmental Dyslexia: Research Methods and Interferences," *Science*, 203 (1979), 201–203. (Ch. 6)

Wittig, M. A., and A. C. Petersen (eds.). *Sex Differences in Cognitive Performance*. New York: Academic Press, 1979. (Ch. 6)

Wohlwill, J. F. "Cognitive Development in Childhood," in O. G. Brim, Jr., and J. Kagan (eds.), *Constancy and Change in Human Development*. Cambridge, Mass.: Harvard University Press, 1980, pp. 359–444. (Ch. 11)

Wolf, T. M. "A Developmental Investigation of Televised Modeled Verbalizations on Resistance to Temptation," *Developmental Psychology*, 6 (1972), 537. (Ch. 14)

Wolff, G. "Increased Bodily Growth of School-Children Since the War," *Lancet*, 228 (1935), 1006–1011. (Ch. 5)

Wolff, P. H. "Observations on the Development of Smiling," in B. M. Foss (ed.), *Determinants of Infant Behaviour*. Vol. 2. London: Methuen, 1963. (Ch. 4)

——. "The Role of Biological Rhythms in Early Psychological Development," *Bulletin of the Menninger Clinic*, 31 (1967), 197–218. (Ch. 4)

——. "The Natural History of Crying and Other Vocalizations in Early Infancy," in B. M. Foss (ed.), *Determinants of Infant Behaviour*. Vol. 4. London: Methuen, 1969, pp. 81–109. (Ch. 9)

Women on Words and Images. *Dick and Jane as Victims: Sex Stereotyping in Children's Readers*. Princeton, N. J.: Women on Words and Images, 1972. (Ch. 15)

Woodson, R. H. "Newborn Behavior and the Transition to Extrauterine Life," *Infant Behavior and Development*, 6 (1983), 139–144. (Chs. 3, 4)

Wozniak, R. H. "A Dialectical Paradigm for Psychological Research: Implications Drawn from the History of Psychology in the Soviet Union," *Human Development*, 18 (1975), 50–64. (Ch. 1)

Yakovlev, P. I., and A. R. Lecours. "The Mylogenetic Cycles of Regional Maturation of the Brain," in A. Minkowski (ed.), *Regional Development of the Brain in Early Life*. Oxford: Blackwell, 1967. (Ch. 6)

Yang, R. K., and H. A. Moss. "Neonatal Precursors of Infant Behavior," *Developmental Psychology*, 14 (1978), 607–613. (Ch. 15)

Yarrow, L. J., F. A. Pedersen, and J. Rubenstein. "Mother-Infant Interaction and Development in Infancy," in P. H. Leiderman, S. R. Tulkin, and A. Rosenfeld (eds.), *Culture and Infancy: Variations in the Human Experience*. New York: Academic Press, 1977, pp. 539–564. (Ch. 4)

Yarrow, M. R., P. M. Scott, and C. Z. Waxler. "Learning Concern for Others," *Developmental Psychology*, 8 (1973), 240–260. (Ch. 16)

——, and C. Z. Waxler. "The Emergence and Functions of Prosocial Behavior in Young Children," in M. S. Smart and R. C. Smart (eds.), *Infants, Development and Relationships*. 2nd ed. New York: Macmillan, 1978. (Ch. 16)

Yendovitskaya, T. V. "Development of Memory," in A. V. Zaporozhets and D. Elkonin (eds.), *The Psychology of Preschool Children*. Cambridge, Mass.: MIT Press, 1971. (Ch. 8)

Yonas, A., W. Cleaves, and L. Pettersen. "Development of Sensitivity to Pictorial Depth," *Science*, 200 (1978), 77–79. (Ch. 7)

———, L. T. Goldsmith, and J. L. Hallstrom. "Development of Sensitivity to Information Provided by Cast Shadows in Pictures," *Perception*, 7 (1978), 333–341. (Ch. 8)

———, C. Oberg, and A. Norcia. "Development of Sensitivity to Binocular Information for the Approach of an Object," *Developmental Psychology*, 14 (1978), 147–152. (Ch. 7)

Young, L. *Wednesday's Children: A Study of Child Neglect and Abuse.* New York: McGraw-Hill, 1964. (Ch. 13)

Younger, B. A., and L. B. Cohen. "Infant Perception of Correlations Among Attributes," *Child Development*, 54 (1983), 858–867. (Chs. 7, 8)

Zahn-Waxler, C., and M. Radke-Yarrow. "The Development of Altruism: Alternative Research Strategies," in N. Eisenberg-Berg (ed.), *The Development of Prosocial Behavior.* New York: Academic Press, 1982. (Ch. 16)

Zajonc, R. B., H. Markus, and G. B. Markus. "The Birth Order Puzzle," *Journal of Personality and Social Psychology*, 37 (1979), 1325–1341. (Ch. 2)

Zaporozhets, A. V. "The Development of Perception in the Preschool Child," in P. H. Mussen (ed.), "European Research in Cognitive Development," *Monographs of the Society for Research in Child Development*, 30 (1965), 82–101. (Ch. 8)

———. "Some of the Psychological Problems of Sensory Training in Early Childhood and the Preschool Period," in M. Cole and I. Maltzman (eds.), *A Handbook of Contemporary Soviet Psychology.* New York: Basic Books, 1969. (Ch. 8)

Zarbatany, L., and M. E. Lamb. "Social Referencing as a Function of Information Source: Mothers versus Strangers," *Infant Behavior and Development* [in press].

Zelazo, P. R. "From Reflexive to Instrumental Behavior," in L. P. Lipsitt (ed.), *Developmental Psychobiology: The Significance of Infancy.* Hillsdale, N. J.: Lawrence Erlbaum Associates, 1976, pp. 87–104. (Ch. 4)

———, N. Zelazo, and S. Kolb. " 'Walking' in the Newborn," *Science*, 177 (1972), 1058–1059. (Ch. 5)

Zelnik, M., J. F. Kantner, and K. Ford. *Sex and Pregnancy in Adolescence.* Beverly Hills, Calif.: Sage, 1981. (Ch. 5)

Zeskind, P. S., and B. M. Lester. "Acoustic Features and Auditory Perceptions of the Cries of Newborns with Prenatal and Perinatal Complications," *Child Development*, 49 (1978), 580–589. (Ch. 4)

Zucker, K. J. "Cross-Gender Identified Children," in B. W. Steiner (ed.), *Gender Dysphoria: Development, Research, Treatment.* New York: Plenum Press [in press]. (Ch. 15)

GLOSSARY

accommodation In Piaget's theory, the modification of schemes to incorporate new knowledge that did not fit them. In terms of visual perception, the change in the lens of the eye to keep an image in sharp focus.

achievement motivation The need to accomplish something of value, to overcome obstacles, or to meet standards of excellence.

active genetic influence Influence that comes from experiences people seek out, choices that are partially determined by genetic makeup.

active sleep *See* REM sleep.

acuity The ability to see objects clearly and to resolve detail.

adaptation theories Theories of human development that see human behavior as the product of evolutionary history, so that behavior is best understood by looking at the way it enables human beings to survive and reproduce in an environment like that in which the species evolved.

affiliative behavioral system According to Bowlby, a behavioral system that encourages babies to interact with people outside the immediate family, promoting social development.

afterbirth The placenta, its membranes, and the remainder of the umbilical cord, delivered in the final stage of labor.

age-normative influence An influence that affects almost every individual in a given society at about the same point in the life span.

allele The alternative form of a gene found at a given site on a chromosome.

altruism An unselfish concern for the welfare of others.

amniocentesis A way to detect fetal abnormalities by drawing out a sample of amniotic fluid and performing chromosomal analyses.

amnion The inner membrane of the sac that surrounds and protects the developing fertilized ovum.

amniotic fluid The liquid within the uterus in which the fetus floats.

anal stage The second of Freud's stages of psychosexual development, covering the second and third years of life. During this period, a child's primary sensual pleasure is in expelling and retaining feces.

androgens Male hormones.

androgyny A development characterized by a self-concept that incorporates characteristics considered typical of both sexes.

anencephaly A condition in which the fetal brain fails to develop because the top of the neural tube does not close.

animism The belief that inanimate objects have thoughts, feelings, and life.

Apgar score A common system for assessing the newborn's physiological condition; it rates color, heart rate, reflex irritability, muscle tone, and respiratory effort.

assimilation In Piaget's theory, the incorporating of new knowledge into existing schemes.

association areas Regions in the human cortex that have neither motor nor sensory function and no direct connections outside the cortex.

asynchrony The maturation of different body parts at different rates, a growth characteristic typical of adolescence.

attachment The primary social bond that develops between infant and parent or caregiver.

attachment behavioral system According to Bowlby, a behavioral system of infancy. It develops in four stages: indiscriminate social responsiveness, discriminate social responsiveness, specific attachments, and partnership.

authoritarian A style of child rearing in which unquestioning obedience, respect for authority, work, and the preservation of order are paramount.

authoritative A style of child rearing in which parents exert firm control, but use reason as well as power to achieve it.

autism A severe mental disorder that manifests itself early in childhood; it is characterized by an inability to develop social relationships.

autonomy A feeling of self-control and self-determination; also called executive independence.

babbling Sound sequences of alternating vowels and consonants, such as "bababa," that the infant produces and that may be a form of motor practice which facilitates language development.

baby talk The simplified speech adults typically use with infants who are acquiring language; also called "motherese."

basal metabolism The rate of energy required to maintain body functions while resting.

basic level category The level at which category members are most like one another and most different from members of other categories (dogs, tables).

behavior An observable act that can be described or measured reliably. Many psychologists include everything an individual experiences (dreams, thoughts, sensations) in the category of behavior, although these experiences can be measured only indirectly, for example, by recording brain waves or eye movements.

body ideal The body type defined by a culture as ideally attractive and sex-appropriate.

bonding The process by which the mother develops a close emotional bond with her infant. (The infant's feeling for the mother is known as attachment.)

canalization The tendency for development to return to a normal, genetically influenced pattern after a temporary deviation.

catch-up growth A period of rapid growth found in most children after a condition that has been retarding growth has been eliminated.

central learning Learning of material selected and attended to by an individual.

central nervous system The brain and the spinal cord.

cephalocaudal development The progression of physical and motor growth from head to foot. For example, a baby's head develops and grows before the torso, arms, and legs.

cerebral dominance The greater proficiency of one hemisphere of the brain over the other in the control of body movements, as in handedness.

chorion The outer membrane of the sac that surrounds and protects the developing fertilized ovum.

chorionic villus biopsy A way to detect fetal abnormalities by examining cells taken from the chorion; the test must be performed before the twelfth week of pregnancy.

chromosomes Beadlike strings of genes present in every cell of the body. Except in the gametes, they occur in pairs that reproduce and split during cell formation.

circular reaction Any behavior the baby tends to repeat because of the stimulation it provides. There are three levels of circular reactions (primary, secondary, tertiary), each more sophisticated than the last.

classical conditioning The association of one stimulus with another, so that the first evokes the response that normally follows the second stimulus. It is a simple form of learning, sometimes called respondent conditioning.

class inclusion The knowledge that a superordinate class (fruit) is always larger than any of its subordinate classes (apples).

clinical study A study consisting of in-depth interviews and observations, sometimes supplemented by questionnaires and tests.

closure In Gestalt psychology, the innate perceptual tendency to supply any broken or missing lines in a figure.

codominant genes Genes that are not recessive but that require the existence of another like themselves before a trait can be expressed.

cognition All intellectual processes, including sensing, perceiving, remembering, using symbols, thinking, and imagining.

cognitive map Mental representation of the environment (school, neighborhood, etc.) consisting of organized routes and landmarks.

cohort The members of a certain age group; a group of people of the same age.

common fate In Gestalt psychology, the innate perceptual tendency to see objects that move or change together as a unit.

componential analysis An approach to intelligence that analyzes both the lower-order processes required to solve a problem and the higher-order processes that exert executive control.

concept A symbol with many examples. "Jennifer" is a symbol, but "girl" is a concept.

concrete operational stage The third stage in Piaget's theory; it begins when children are about age six or seven and lasts until around age eleven. In this stage, thought is logical, but only in regard to concrete objects and situations.

conditioning A form of learning in which a person comes to respond in a specific manner to a specific object, action, or situation.

conservation The understanding that irrelevant changes in the physical appearance of objects do not affect their quantity, mass, weight, or volume. Conservation is one of Piaget's concrete operations.

constructionism The view that the world cannot be known objectively, but is actively constructed by the perceiver.

constructionist Piaget's term that describes the child's understanding of reality. By acting on objects, the child discovers the effects of his or her actions and the properties of objects; this knowledge leads to a construction of an understanding of the world.

context The situation surrounding an act or utterance, including beliefs, assumptions, actions, knowledge, and intentions.

continuity In Gestalt psychology, the innate tendency to expect the next element in a group (such as dots forming a curve) to follow the line taken by the rest.

control The intentional modification of any condition of a study, including the selection of subjects, the experiences they have in the study, and the responses they can give to that experience.

conventional level The level of moral reasoning (according to Kohlberg) in which value is placed on maintaining the social order and the expectations of others.

corpus callosum A wide band of myelinated fibers that connects the two halves of the brain, ensuring the exchange of information.

correlation A numerical expression of how closely two sets of measurements correspond. Correlations range from $+1.00$ (perfect positive correlation) to -1.00 (perfect negative correlation).

cortex A mantle of neural cells that covers the cerebral hemispheres; the cortex is the seat of language, attention, memory, spatial understanding, and motor skills.

co-twin control A method of study in which one of a pair of twins undergoes some experience that is withheld or delayed in the other twin.

cross-sectional study A study that compares the performance of different age groups on a single occasion.

cytoarchitecture The location and arrangement of cells within the brain.

decoding *See* retrieval.

deictic words Words whose meaning changes because they locate things in reference to the speaker. Among common deictic words are "I" and "you," "this" and "that," "right" and "left."

deoxyribonucleic acid (DNA) The complex chemical containing the genetic code that guides development.

dependence Reliance on others for comfort, nurturance, or assistance in accomplishing a task. In executive dependence, the parents act as an executive arm instrumental to the baby's needs.

dependent variable A factor that changes as the result of the introduction of an independent variable.

development Any age-related change in body or behavior from conception to death.

developmental age A child's progression toward physiological maturity.

dialectical theories Theories of human development that see development as proceeding in a dialectic between the individual and society, with each new interaction leading to a higher level of functioning.

dichotic-listening technique A method of research in which two stimuli are presented at the same time, one to each ear.

differentiation The developmental trend in which an infant's abilities become increasingly distinct and specific.

displacement The ability to communicate information about objects in another place or another time; one of language's formal properties.

dominant gene The allele whose corresponding trait appears in an individual when the allele is paired with a different allele for the same trait.

Down's syndrome A condition that results when an extra Chromosome 21 is present in the fertilized ovum, or when extra material from Chromosome 21 becomes attached to another chromosome. It produces various physical abnormalities and mental retardation in the afflicted child.

dyslexia A catch-all term for reading disabilities of all varieties.

ecological approach A view of human development that sees the growing individual as influenced by the relationship among various physical and social settings, as well as by the influence of the entire society.

ecological intervention Sweeping changes in environment as opposed to intervention that focuses solely on the child or the parent-child relationship.

ectoderm The layer of cells in the embryo from which the skin, sense organs, and nervous system develop.

ego The conscious self, which in Freudian theory guides behavior and mediates the perpetual conflict between id and superego.

egocentric Among babies, the inability to distinguish

between the self and the external world; among older infants and young children, the belief that everyone sees the world and responds to it exactly as the child does.

embryo The individual from the second to the eighth week of development within the uterus.

embryonic period The six weeks after the germinal period; during this period the organism begins to take shape, and organ systems begin to form.

empathy The vicarious identification with another's emotion.

enactive representation Motor responses that serve as models for information in memory. They may be the only form of representation during most of the first year of life.

encephalocele A protrusion of the brain through the base of the skull or back caused by the failure of the neural tube to close during development.

encode To put information in memory.

endoderm The layer of cells in the embryo from which the visceral organs and digestive tract develop.

environment The physical and social surroundings of any organism or part of an organism; this includes the prenatal environment of the individual before birth and the internal environment of cells within the body.

epigenesis The course of development, which begins when sperm and ovum unite.

equilibration Piaget's developmental principle, which states that the organism always tends toward biological and psychological balance, and that development consists of progressive approximations to an ideal state of balance between assimilation and accommodation that is never fully achieved.

estrogens Female hormones.

ethology The scientific study of animal behavior in evolutionary terms.

evocative genetic influence Genetically influenced behavior that evokes particular responses from the social and physical environment; these responses in turn influence the child.

evoked potential A characteristic electrical response in the brain that is evoked by a new stimulus, such as a sight or a sound.

executive control The cognitive process that regulates learning and problem solving.

executive dependence *See* dependence.

executive independence *See* autonomy.

experiment A type of study designed to control the arrangement and manipulation of conditions so that researchers can systematically observe particular phenomena.

exploratory behavioral system According to Bowlby, a behavioral system that allows the child to explore the surrounding world; this promotes competency.

factor analysis A system of analyzing experimental results by correlating scores on a variety of tests, in the belief that strong correlations among scores indicate the influence of a common factor.

Fallopian tube The passage leading from an ovary to the uterus.

fear of success The purported tendency of women to withdraw from competition with men or to avoid it because of social reprisal.

fear-wariness system According to Bowlby, a behavioral system that helps a baby avoid potentially dangerous situations; often called wariness of strangers.

fetal alcohol syndrome A serious condition involving various physical defects and mental retardation that often appears in infants born to alcoholic mothers.

fetus The developing organism from eight weeks after conception to birth.

field study A study in which the investigator introduces some factor into a natural setting that changes the setting.

fixated In Freudian theory, to become stalled emotionally at an immature level of personality development, so that in adulthood the characteristic traits of that immature level dominate behavior.

foreclosure A type of identity structure in which the adolescent is committed to an occupation or ideology, but the positions have been chosen by his or her parents.

formal operational stage The final stage in Piaget's theory; it begins when children are about age eleven, and it represents the culmination of cognitive development. Thought is logical and fully abstract and can be applied to hypothetical situations.

frustration-aggression hypothesis The belief that aggression results when someone or something interferes with the activity toward a goal.

gamete Mature reproductive cell; the sperm or the ovum.

gender constancy The understanding that gender will never change, that boys always become men and girls always become women.

gender identity The inner experience of gender; the unchanging sense of self as male or female.

gender schema A cognitive network of sex-related associations for each gender, which organizes a person's perceptions of the world and determines the way new information will be organized.

genes Microscopic particles of DNA that are carried by the chromosomes. Genes contain instructions that guide the development of physical traits and behavioral dispositions.

genetic epistemology Piaget's basic approach to development, focusing on the development of intelligence (genetic = development; epistemology = how we know the world).

genetics The scientific study of the effects of heredity.

genital stage The final stage in Freud's theory of psychosexual development; it begins at puberty. Primary sensual pleasure transfers to mature sexual relationships with members of the other sex.

genotype The specific combination of alleles that make up an individual's genetic inheritance.

germinal period The first two weeks after conception; during this period the fertilized ovum is primarily engaged in cell division.

gestation period The period of prenatal development, calculated from fertilization (thirty-eight weeks) or from the date of the last menstruation (forty weeks).

gestational age The age of the fetus, calculated from the date of conception.

glial cells Supporting and connecting cells in the brain that play an essential role in the nourishment of neurons.

grammar The structural principles of a language, made up of phonology and syntax.

grasping reflex The baby's tendency to clutch any small object placed in his or her hand; it disappears within a few months.

guilt A negative feeling that arises when a person deviates from his or her own internalized moral standards.

habituation Reduced response to a stimulus after repeated or continuous encounters with it; analogous to becoming bored with the stimulus.

heritability An estimate, based on a sample of individuals, of the relative contribution of genetics to any trait in that group.

heterozygous The condition in which alleles at a given chromosome site are different. In such cases, the dominant gene generally determines the appearance of the affected trait.

hierarchic integration In Werner's theory, the tendency for the child's developing responses and skills to become increasingly organized into hierarchies.

history-normative influence Influence that results from circumstances that exist at a particular historical moment and that affect all individuals in the society.

homozygous The condition in which the alleles at a given chromosome site are identical.

hostile aggression Aggression aimed at hurting another person (*see* instrumental aggression).

hydrocephaly A condition in which fluid accumulates within the skull, pressing on the brain.

hyperactivity A disorder in which children have difficulty in sustaining attention; it is usually accompanied by extreme restlessness.

id That aspect of the personality which, in Freudian theory, contains all the unconscious impulses or drives.

identity In Piaget's theory, the understanding that objects and people remain the same even if irrelevant properties are changed. In Erikson's psychosocial theory, a combination of self-esteem and the relation between self-concept and the description of the self by others; its achievement is the crucial developmental task of adolescence.

identity achievement A type of identity structure in which the adolescent has committed him or herself to an occupation, a religious view, a political ideology, a sexual orientation, and the like, and is pursuing occupational and ideological goals.

identity diffusion A type of identity structure in which the adolescent has no occupational goals or ideological commitment, but is not particularly concerned about the situation.

imagery An encoding strategy in which a person uses visual images to associate two or more things that must be remembered.

imaginal representation Visual images that serve as models for information in memory. They seem to develop toward the end of the first year of life.

imitation Copying or reproducing observed behavior.

imprinting A phenomenon that characterizes the development of some birds, in which the newly hatched chick follows a moving object (generally the mother) and forms a strong, enduring attachment to it.

incidental learning Learning of material that is irrelevant to the task that is the focus of attention.

independent variable In a study, a factor that is selected or changed in some way by the investigator.

indifferent A style of child rearing in which parents are undemanding, unresponsive, and minimally involved with their children.

induced abortion The premature removal of a fetus by deliberate interference.

infanticide Killing an infant, or allowing it to die by withholding care, a common practice during antiquity.

inflection A grammatical marker, such as the past tense "-ed," that is added to words in a regular way in order to change their meaning.

information-processing theories Theories of cognition that see human beings as information-gathering, information-processing systems, who process information much as computers do.

instrumental aggression Aggression aimed at retrieving or acquiring an object, territory, or privilege (*see* hostile aggression).

instrumental competence A combination of independence and social responsibility; instrumentally competent children are self-assertive, friendly with peers, and not intrusive with adults.

instrumental conditioning *See* operant conditioning.

interaction A developmental process in which genetic characteristics influence the environment, which in turn affects further development—and vice versa.

interindividual differences Differences in patterns of change among individuals.

intraindividual differences Changes that occur within the individual.

kinesthetic sense The sense that provides information about body movement and position through nerve endings in the muscles, tendons, and joints.

Klinefelter's syndrome A condition resulting from the presence in boys of an extra female sex chromosome (XXY). The boys are sterile, have rounded bodies, and may be somewhat retarded.

kwashiorkor A severe, often fatal, disease caused by prolonged protein deficiency.

labor The birth process. It begins with the first contraction of the uterus, and does not end until both the infant and the placenta have been delivered.

lanugo Fine hair appearing on some newborns' bodies; it disappears within a few weeks.

latency period In Freudian theory, the fourth period of psychosexual development; it lasts from about age six until puberty. Libidinal pleasures become less important and children discover moral and esthetic interests.

lateralization The establishment of functions in one hemisphere of the brain, such as the establishment of language in the left hemisphere of most right-handed people.

learned helplessness A condition in which repeated failure in situations over which a person has no control leads to a refusal to try.

levels of processing The view that information is processed at increasingly deeper levels of analysis, with retention depending on the depth of the analysis.

libido The life force, including all mental energy.

locus of control The perceived location of control over an individual's life. If the locus is internal, individuals believe they control their own lives; if the locus is external, individuals believe their lives are controlled by forces outside themselves.

longitudinal study A study that follows the same subjects over time, comparing their performance at different ages.

long-term store Permanent memory; where information is held indefinitely.

mechanistic theories Theories of human development that see people as being like machines, so that development follows regular laws; development is generally seen as gradual and continuous.

meiosis The form of cell division followed by gametes, in which four daughter cells, each containing twenty-three single chromosomes, are produced.

menarche The first incidence of menstruation.

menstrual age The age of the fetus when calculated from the beginning of the mother's last menstrual period.

menstrual cycle The discharge of blood and tissue from the uterus; it occurs monthly from puberty to menopause, except during pregnancy and lactation.

mesoderm The layer of cells in the embryo from which the muscular, circulatory, and skeletal systems develop.

metacognition A person's knowledge about mental states, mental abilities, and ways of regulating them.

metamemory An understanding of the workings of the memory system; one aspect of metacognition.

miscarriage A spontaneous abortion; the expulsion from the uterus of a fetus less than twenty-eight weeks old.

mitosis The form of cell division followed by all body cells except gametes, in which two daughter cells, each with forty-six chromosomes (twenty-three pairs), are produced.

morality of constraint According to Piaget, the first stage of morality, in which duty consists of obedience to authority.

morality of cooperation According to Piaget, the second stage of morality, in which children believe that the intentions of an actor are more important than the consequences of his or her act.

moratorium A type of identity structure generally characterized by some anxiety; the adolescent is still struggling with occupational or ideological issues and may be in an "identity crisis."

Moro reflex The baby's tendency to thrust out the arms and curl the hands when support for the neck and head is removed; disappears after about three months.

myelin A fatty substance that keeps nerve impulses channeled along neural fibers and reduces the random spread of impulses from one fiber to another.

naïve realism The view that our perceptions are true copies of the world, which exists independently of the perceiver.

naturalistic observation A form of study in which behavior is observed in natural settings with no interference from the investigator.

neonate A baby during the first month of independent life.

neurometrics Mental testing with computers. Evoked potentials and brain waves are analyzed by the computer in order to assess cognitive functioning and to identify specific disorders.

neuron One of the neural cells in the central nervous system.

neurotransmitter One of the thirty or more chemicals that act as messengers in the brain, causing neurons to fire or keeping them from firing. Among the neurotransmitters are norepinephrine, serotonin, and dopamine.

nonconformist A style of child rearing in which parents tend to be permissive but may demand high performance in some areas.

nonnormative influence A factor that influences a specific individual but does not affect all members of society or all members of any cohort.

non-REM sleep Sleep during which there is no movement of the eyes, when respiration is slowed, and brain waves show an uneven pattern; also called quiet sleep.

norm A pattern of growth or achievement that describes the way in which important attributes and skills develop and the approximate ages at which they appear.

obese Extremely fat.

object concept The understanding that objects remain the same although they may move from one place to another (object identity) and that they continue to exist when out of sight (object permanence).

object identity *See* object concept.

object permanence *See* object concept.

operant conditioning A form of learning in which a response is strengthened or changed as a result of rewards or punishments (the consequences of the response); sometimes called instrumental conditioning.

operating principles A set of beliefs that children may apply to the language they hear and that may determine which linguistic constructions are easiest to learn.

operations Flexible and rigorous cognitive processes that first appear during the concrete operational stage.

operative representation A stored representation in memory that changes as the result of mental operations.

oral stage In Freud's theory, the earliest stage in psychosexual development. It consists of the first year of life when the lips and mouth are the focus of sensual pleasure.

organismic theories Theories of human development that see people as active organisms whose changes are due to the interaction of genetic maturation and experience with the environment; development is usually seen as progressing through a series of stages.

organization An encoding strategy in which a person groups items to be remembered around a common element.

orthogenetic principle The major theme of Werner's developmental theory; it holds that the child moves from a global, undifferentiated state to one of high differentiation and integration.

ovaries The female reproductive glands, which mature and release ova.

overextension A generalization in the child's meaning of a word so that it includes a number of dissimilar objects or events.

overregularization A temporary error in language acquisition in which the child makes the language more regular than it actually is, as when a child says "breaked" for "broke" or "foots" for "feet."

ovum The female reproductive cell; this egg cell is the largest cell in the human body.

oxytocin A hormone produced by the pituitary glands of both mother and fetus, stimulating labor.

parallel play A form of play in which children play side by side, each intent on his or her own toy; each child may keep up a running commentary that amounts to thinking aloud.

passive genetic influence Influences within the home: both the genes transmitted to the child by his or her parents and the environmental experiences they provide (which are partially determined by the parents' own genes).

perception An important cognitive process involving the transformation of sensations into information.

permissive A style of child rearing in which parents are nonpunitive, accepting, and affirmative. It allows children to regulate their own activities and encourages them to develop their own standards.

perspective In organismic theories, a sense of the self as separate from the world and the realization that one's perceptions, feelings, and reactions are not identical with those of others. In perception, the effect that makes a two-dimensional drawing appear to have depth.

phallic stage The third, highly critical, stage in Freud's theory of psychosexual development; it spans the years from three to six. During this period the genitals are the focus of sensual pleasure.

phenotype Physical or behavioral traits as they appear in the individual, reflecting the influence of both genetic and environmental factors.

phenylketonuria (PKU) An inherited inability to metabolize phenylalanine, a component of some foods.

phonemes The basic sound elements of a language.

phonology The study of the production and comprehension of speech sounds.

placenta A pliable structure of tissue and blood vessels that transmits nourishment and waste between mother and fetus.

placing response The infant's tendency to lift up the foot and place it on top of a surface, a reflex that disappears within a few months.

polygenic Indicates that several genes have an equal and cumulative effect in producing a trait.

practice effect Possible distortion of behavior that may appear in longitudinal studies and that is caused by the repeated study and testing of subjects.

pragmatics The study of language's social purposes.

precedence effect An auditory illusion in which sounds separated by a few microseconds are heard as a single sound, although the sounds come from different directions. This illusion first appears when infants are about five months old.

predetermined epigenesis Development according to preprogrammed maturation, in which genes determine the maturational processes that lead to structural and functional development.

preformation The belief that either the ovum or the sperm contained a preformed human being, which grew larger but did not change in form or feature during the prenatal period.

premature delivery The spontaneous termination of a pregnancy when the fetus is older than twenty weeks but younger than thirty-eight weeks.

premoral level The level of moral reasoning (according to Kohlberg) in which value is placed on physical acts and needs, not on persons or social standards.

preoperational stage The second stage in Piaget's theory; it covers the preschool period and may extend until children are age seven. During this stage, children record experiences symbolically and use language, but their thought is intuitive— not logical.

primary circular reaction The repetition of unlearned behavior (such as sucking, looking, or vocalizing) because of the stimulation it brings. Characterizes Stage Two of Piaget's sensorimotor period.

principled level The level of moral reasoning (according to Kohlberg) in which value resides in self-chosen principles that have a universal logical validity and can therefore be shared.

probabilistic epigenesis Bidirectional development, which begins under the direction of genes, and which can be affected by the functioning of the developing, but not fully established, system.

probability A numerical expression that indicates the likelihood that experimental findings are simply the result of chance.

procedural knowledge "Knowing how"—knowledge that is embedded and that a person normally is not conscious of, such as how to drive a car or how to hit a baseball.

production deficiency The failure to use a skill or capacity that a person possesses.

productivity The ability to combine a finite number of words into an infinite number of sentences; one of language's formal properties.

progressive lateralization The view that the establishment of various functions in one of the brain's hemispheres begins at birth and is not complete until adolescence.

prosocial behavior All actions that promote or benefit another person.

prototype The very best example of a concept, which is surrounded by members of decreasing similarity to it.

proximal development Vygotsky's term for the area in which children, with the help of adults or more capable peers, can solve problems they are unable to handle by themselves.

proximity In Gestalt psychology, the innate perceptual tendency to see as a group elements that are physically close together.

proximodistal development The progression of physical and motor growth from the center of the body to the periphery. For example, a baby learns to control shoulder movements before arm or finger movements.

psychoanalysis A type of psychotherapy devised by Sigmund Freud; it attempts to give a patient insights into his or her unconscious conflicts.

psychodynamic theories Theories of human personality that view behavior as resulting from the interplay of active mental and biological forces with the environment.

psychometrics Mental testing; the branch of psychology that has developed intelligence tests.

psychosexual theory A psychodynamic theory of personality development proposed by Freud; it focuses on the changing seat of libidinal pleasures in the individual.

psychosocial theory A psychodynamic theory of personality development proposed by Erikson; it focuses on the individual's interactions with society.

puberty The attainment of biological sexual maturity.

punishment Any consequence, whether physical pain, harsh words, isolation, or withdrawal of affection, that makes it less likely that a response will be repeated.

quiet sleep *See* non-REM sleep.

reaction range The range of possible responses within which a genetic trait can express itself.

reaction time The interval of time between the instant a stimulus is presented and the individual's reaction to it.

recall The most complex form of memory, in which information is remembered in its absence.

recapitulation theory The theory that from conception to birth, each person's development repeats the evolutionary history of the species.

recessive gene The subordinate member of a pair of alleles, whose corresponding trait fails to appear in an individual who carries the allele.

recognition The simplest form of memory, in which an object is perceived as something that has been perceived in the past.

reconstruction An intermediate form of memory, in which a person constructs a three-dimensional reproduction of an object previously seen.

reflex An unlearned or naturally occurring reaction to a stimulus.

rehearsal An encoding strategy in which a person repeats information that is to be remembered.

reinforcement The presentation or withdrawal of an event following a response; it increases the likelihood of that response occurring again.

reinforcement theory The view that behavior can be explained by the consequences of an organism's actions, that is, by reinforcement and punishment.

releasing stimulus An event that regularly evokes certain behavior in all members of a species and helps to explain regularities in typical behavior.

REM sleep Sleep that is accompanied by rapid eye movements (REM), rapid respiration, and a more even pattern of brain waves; also called active sleep.

replication The repetition of an investigation's essential features and its findings.

representation A model that represents information in memory so that it can be retrieved.

respiratory distress syndrome A lung condition (formerly called hyaline membrane disease) in which the premature infant cannot maintain necessary surfactin levels.

respondent conditioning *See* classical conditioning.

response Any reaction to a stimulus—whether word, deed, or a bodily change such as glandular secretion, brain wave, and variation in heart rate, blood pressure, or the electrical resistance of the skin.

retrieval Removing information from long-term store to short-term store, where it can be used; also called decoding.

reversibility The understanding that irrelevant changes in appearance can be reversed and that such changes tend to compensate one another; reversibility is one of Piaget's concrete operations.

rickets A condition caused by calcium deficiency during infancy and childhood; characterized by softening and malformation of the bones.

role taking The ability to assume the role or point of view of another person.

rooting reflex The infant's tendency to turn the head and mouth in the direction of any object that gently stimulates the mouth; the reflex disappears after about two or three months.

sample Individuals selected for study in any investigation; a good sample accurately reflects the nature of the larger group from which it is drawn.

schemes Piaget's term for patterns of action (banging, sucking) or mental structures (classification of objects) that are involved in the acquisition and structuring of knowledge. In infants, schemes are like concepts without words.

scripts Cognitive frameworks that describe the customary sequence of events for various activities.

secondary circular reaction The repetition of learned actions (such as shaking a rattle) because the events interest the baby. These circular reactions first appear in Stage Three of Piaget's sensorimotor period.

secondary sex characteristics Genetically based characteristics—such as breast development, facial hair, and voice quality—that accompany puberty; these characteristics differentiate the genders but have no direct reproductive function.

self-concept The sum of ideas each person has about him or herself.

self-demand feeding A feeding schedule in which babies are fed whenever they are hungry instead of when an imposed schedule calls for meals.

self-esteem The way a person evaluates him or herself.

self-regulation Carrying out acts freely in order to fulfill an intention.

semanticity The ability to transmit meaning; one of language's formal properties.

semantics The study of meaning in language.

sensitive period A period of development during which an organism is most likely to be susceptible to a particular influence.

sensitivity An empathic understanding of a child's needs, so that babies' signals are interpreted and responded to effectively and older children are encouraged to be autonomous.

sensorimotor stage The first major stage in Piaget's theory; it lasts through most of the first two years of life. During this stage, knowledge derives from the infant's sensations ("sensori") and physical actions ("motor").

sensory register The first form of storage in the memory system, which holds a fleeting record of all stimuli received by the sense organs.

separation distress A baby's negative reaction to being parted from an attachment figure.

sequential design A combination of elements from cross-sectional and longitudinal designs in a single study, whose basic structure may be either a cross-sectional or a longitudinal sequence.

seriation The ordering of objects by size or weight.

sex role The socially prescribed pattern of behavior and attitudes considered characteristic of each gender.

sex-role stereotype A simplified, fixed concept concerning the behavior and traits typical of each gender.

sex-role strain Anxiety felt by a person who does not live up to stereotypical sex roles; sex-role strain can lead to unhealthy personality characteristics such as dependency in women or aggression in men.

shame A negative feeling that results from the disapproval of others.

shape constancy The brain's tendency to perceive objects as having a stable shape despite moment-to-moment changes in the shape of the image cast on the retina.

short-term store Temporary, working memory; holds active information in a person's awareness.

sickle-cell anemia A hereditary condition caused by codominant alleles, in which red blood cells sickle, sometimes leading to severe anemia or even death.

sighting dominance Control over the point on which both eyes focus; exercised by the muscles of the dominant eye.

similarity In Gestalt psychology, the innate perceptual tendency to see as a group elements that are generally alike in form.

size constancy The brain's tendency to perceive objects as the same size despite changes in the size of the image they cast on the retina.

skeletal maturity A measure of developmental age based on the shape and relative position of bones and their degree of calcification.

socialization The process by which an individual acquires the behavior, attitudes, values, and roles expected from its members by a society.

social-learning theory A view of development in which behavioral change results from conditioning, observation, and imitation. Cognitive social-learning theorists believe that cognition also plays an important role, since a person's interpretation of the stimulus—not the stimulus itself—regulates behavior.

social referencing A deliberate search for emotional information in the expression, tone of voice, or gestures of another.

sociometric analysis A method for charting how often a child is chosen by peers as a friend or preferred companion.

sonogram A picture produced by bouncing sound waves off an object. Sonograms are used to detect the presence of twins, fetal abnormalities, and other visible complications of pregnancy.

spermatozoon The male reproductive cell; a sperm.

spina bifida A protrusion of spinal cord nerves through an opening in the back, caused by the failure of the neural tube to close during fetal development.

stage A concept used to explain the orderly relationship among developmental changes in behavior and to indicate that the organization of behavior is qualitatively different from one stage to the next.

state-dependent learning A phenomenon in which details and events occurring when a person is in a particular state (altered by drugs) are difficult to recall unless the person returns to the state in which the material was learned.

stepping response The baby's tendency to straighten out the legs at knee and hip as if to stand when the infant is held with feet touching a surface; disappears within a few months.

stimulus Anything within the body or in the world outside that evokes a response.

strabismus Lack of coordination between the muscles of the eyeballs so that the two eyes fail to focus on exactly the same point.

strategy A technique used to encode or retrieve information, such as scanning, rehearsal, or imagery.

structuralist An approach to cognition that focuses on the qualitative analysis of the structures that underlie intelligence.

sublimation Handling the conflict between social demands and instincts by altering behavior in socially acceptable ways.

subordinate level category Category formed at the most specific level of abstraction: robins, coffee tables, teaspoons.

sudden infant death syndrome (SIDS) An affliction, commonly called crib death, in which apparently healthy infants between two and four months old suddenly die in their sleep.

superego In Freudian theory, an aspect of the self that corresponds to the conscience. It develops in early childhood as a child internalizes parental values and standards.

superordinate level category Category formed at the most abstract level, in which membership is determined more by function than by appearance: animals, furniture, eating utensils.

surfactin A liquid that coats the air sacs of the lungs, enabling infants to transmit oxygen from the air to the blood.

symbolic play Play involving imagination and pretense, in which objects or people stand for something they are not.

synapse The space between neurons in the central nervous system, across which electrical and chemical signals pass.

syntax The structural principles that determine the form of sentences (*see* grammar).

Tay-Sachs disease A hereditary condition caused by recessive alleles, in which the lack of an enzyme renders the individual unable to metabolize certain fatty substances. It results in blindness, paralysis, and death within seven years.

temperament Stable individual differences in the readiness to express emotions and the intensity with which they are expressed.

teratogen Any influence that can disrupt fetal growth or cause malformation in the developing organism.

term The gestational age of 266 days from conception.

tertiary circular reactions Intelligent, systematic adaptations to specific situations; these circular reactions first appear during Stage Five of Piaget's sensorimotor period.

testes The male reproductive glands, which manufacture and release sperm.

theory A set of logically related statements that explain the nature of related phenomena.

tonic neck reflex A neonatal reflex that appears when an infant turns the head: One arm is automatically extended in the direction in which the head is turned.

transitivity The making of logical inferences based on separate related observations; it requires the joining together of two or more abstract relations.

transsexual A person whose gender identity does not correspond with his or her anatomical gender.

trimester A period of approximately three months, often used when discussing pregnancy.

Turner's syndrome A condition resulting from the absence in girls of one female sex chromosome (XO). The girls are generally short, lack secondary sex characteristics, and have mild to moderate mental retardation.

umbilical cord The flexible cord, containing two arteries and one vein, that connects the developing organism to the placenta.

unchanging lateralization The view that the right and left hemispheres of the brain are specialized for basic functions at birth.

underextension A temporary period in which the child's meaning for a word fails to include the entire meaning adults attribute to it, as when a child fails to include "lollipops" in the meaning of "food."

U-shaped behavioral growth A pattern of development in which a response appears, then disappears, to reappear later in development.

variable A factor that can vary in size or strength and that may or may not affect the result of a study.

vernix The white greasy material that lubricates the fetus for passage through the birth canal.

vesicle Small sacs filled with neurotransmitters, which are located on neuronal end fibers at synapses.

visual accommodation The ability to alternate focus for objects at different distances.

vital capacity The capacity of the lungs to hold air.

wariness of strangers *See* fear-wariness system.

working memory *See* short-term store.

Abrahamson, A. A., 296
Abramov, I., 119
Abramovitch, Rona, 411, 444
Abravanel, Eugene, 229
Acheson, Roy M., 154, 156, 157, 163
Ackerman, B., 559
Acredolo, C., 320, 331
Acredolo, Linda P., 215, 227, 239, 320
Adams, A., 331
Adamson, K., Jr., 112
Adelson, Joseph, 454, 561
Adinolfi, A. A., 447
Adler, T. F., 463
Ahammer, I. M., 525
Ahr, P. R., 324
Ainsworth, Mary D. S., 63, 376, 381, 382, 384–85, 386, 391
Albert, M. L., 258
Alcoholics Anonymous, 427
Aldrich, C. Anderson, 115
Aleksandrowicz, D. D., 98
Aleksandrowicz, M. M., 98
Allen, Gary L., 240
Allen, K. Eileen, 451
Allen, Leticia, 520
Als, H., 88, 98
Altura, B. M., 97
Altura, B. T., 97
Alvarez, William F., 415
Amato, S. S., 102
American Cancer Society, 459
American Humane Association, 427
American Psychiatric Association, 199
American Psychological Association, 66
Ames, E. W., 221
Amgott-Kwan, T., 558, 560
Anastasi, A., 345
Anderson, Daniel R., 245, 246, 552–53
Anderson, John R., 287
Anderson, R. B., 116
Andres, David, 415
Andy, O. J., 174
Anglin, Jeremy M., 249, 250
Annett, Marian, 187
Anooshian, Linda J., 239
Antonucci, T. G., 379
Apgar, Virginia, 88
Appelbaum, M. I., 42, 351, 353, 354, 355, 367
Arend, Richard, 396, 409
Ariès, Philippe, 6, 7
Aristotle, 12
Aronfreed, Justin, 509, 510
Asher, Steven R., 438, 447, 448, 450, 451, 452, 453, 460–61
Ashford, J. R., 79
Ashmead, Daniel H., 223
Aslin, R. N., 120, 126, 208, 288, 289
Atkinson, R. D., 254

Ault, R. L., 19
Ausubel, David P., 395

Babson, S. G., 96, 97, 98, 100, 104
Bach, Johann Sebastian, 168
Bacon, Margaret, 459
Bacon, Margaret K., 423, 474
Baer, Donald M., 15, 286, 382
Bahrick, L., 217
Bailey, Margaret M., 463
Baillargeon, Renée, 33, 314, 319, 322, 333, 335
Baker, D. P., 195
Baker, Nancy, 508
Baker, Susan W., 481
Baker-Ward, L., 414
Bakker, D. J., 186
Balaban, T., 478
Baldwin, James Mark, 10–11, 30
Baldwin, L. M., 240
Balfour, G., 296
Ball, S., 366
Ball, William A., 242
Balling, John D., 187
Baltes, Paul B., 46, 60, 61
Bandura, Albert, 15–17, 287, 408, 444, 513, 527, 531
Bandura, Mary M., 192
Banks, M. S., 119, 120, 124, 209, 210, 211, 212, 214, 219
Barbee, A. H., 357
Barnes, I., 209
Barnett, Mark A., 521
Baron, Robert A., 531
Barr, H. M., 97
Barrett, D. E., 530
Barron, F., 358
Barry, Herbert, 423, 474
Bartel, H. W., 460
Bartel, N. R., 460
Bates, Elizabeth, 277, 278, 280, 287
Bates, J. E., 136, 409
Bauchot, R., 174
Baumrind, Diana, 405, 406, 408, 463
Bay, E., 191
Bayley, Nancy, 145, 147, 149, 217, 220, 352, 354, 493
Beach, David R., 260
Beal, Carole R., 556
Beason-Williams, L., 123
Beatty, R. A., 104
Becker, Jacqueline M., 438, 439
Beeghly, M., 541
Beintema, D., 215
Belknap, Beverly, 548
Bell, Richard Q., 512
Bell, Silvia M., 379
Bellugi, U., 272, 304

Bellugi-Klima, Ursula, 302
Belmont, L., 93
Belsky, Jay, 386, 391, 413–14
Bem, Sandra L., 485, 499
Benacerraf, B. R., 86
Benbow, Camilla P., 194, 195, 316
Bereiter, C., 328
Berendes, H. W., 363
Berg, Cynthia A., 353
Berg, K. M., 114
Berg, W. K., 114
Bergman, T., 210
Bergson, Henri, 30
Berndt, Thomas J., 454, 457, 458, 551–53
Bernholtz, Nancy, 299
Bertenthal, Bennett I., 227, 540
Berzonsky, Michael, 334
Bierman, J. M., 363
"Big Blue Marble," 523
Bigi, L., 245
Bijou, Sidney W., 14, 15, 286, 382
Biller, Henry B., 417
Billman, D. O., 350
Binet, Alfred, 30, 341, 348
Bingham, M. T., 359
Bionic Woman, 491
Birch, Herbert G., 132
Birch, Rosemary, 213
Biringen, Z. C., 498, 499
Birnholz, J. C., 86
Birns, B., 364, 365
Bisanz, J., 14, 19
Bizzell, Rondeall, 368
Blank, Marion, 318
Blasi, Augusto, 519
Blau, Z. S., 423
Blewitt, Pamela, 296
Blizzard, R. M., 158
Block, J., 131, 409
Block, Jeanne H., 131, 409, 483, 487, 530
Bloom, F., 360
Bloom, K., 439
Blumberg, S. L., 495
Blurton-Jones, Nicholas, 442
Boccia, M., 385
Boden, M., 347
Bogatz, G. A., 366
Boismier, J. D., 114
Bolton, F. G., Jr., 92
Bond, E. A., 355
Bonney, M. E., 450
Borke, H., 548
Bornstein, M. H., 209, 210
Borstelmann, L. J., 7, 12, 13
Botvin, Gilbert J., 320–21
Bowen, Robert, 542
Bower, G. H., 313

Bower, Thomas G. R., 120, 220
Bowerman, Melissa, 296
Bowes, W. A., 98
Bowlby, John, 22, 27, 376, 377, 382, 391
Boyle, F. M., 320
Boysen, S., 273
Brackbill, Yvonne, 98, 121, 132
Brackney, B., 499
Braddick, O., 119
Bradley, R. H., 364
Brady, J. E., 454
"Brady Bunch, The," 525
Braff, Anne M., 44
Braine, Martin D. S., 300, 323, 329, 330
Brainerd, Charles J., 319, 322, 333
Brannigan, G. G., 497
Bransford, John D., 265
Brasel, J. A., 158
Brazelton, T. B., 88, 98
Brent, Sandor, 337
Bretherton, I., 541
Briars, Diane, 332–33
Bricker, William, 443
Bridger, W. H., 121
Bridges, K. M., 396
Broadbent, Donald E., 18–19
Brody, G. H., 449
Brody, L. R., 127
Brodzinsky, David M., 44–45
Bromley, D. B., 542, 545
Bronfenbrenner, Urie, 59, 392, 399, 415, 424, 460
Bronson, S. K., 419
Brooks, V., 238
Brooks-Gunn, Jeanne, 393–94, 493, 497, 540
Broughton, J. M., 120
Brown, Ann L., 19, 37, 255, 259, 264, 310, 336, 337, 338
Brown, Craig, 152
Brown, Roger, 270, 273, 282, 302
Brozoski, Thomas J., 179
Brück, K., 112
Bruner, Jerome S., 28, 36, 175, 221, 247, 248–49, 256, 274, 275, 280, 281, 282, 287, 292, 295, 326, 441
Bruno, L. A., 127
Bryan, James H., 521
Bryant, B. K., 412
Bryant, Peter E., 214, 218, 322
Bryden, M. P., 187, 192
Buck, S., 210
Bukowski, William M., 448
Bull, D., 208
Bullinger, A., 326
Bullock, Merry, 334, 335
Bullough, V. L., 168
Bunker, Archie, 518
Burgess, R. L., 431
Burke, B., 110
Burton, Roger V., 505
Busch-Rossnagel, N. A., 56
Bushnell, N., 518
Buss, D. M., 131
Bussey, Kay, 484
Butler, N., 98, 363
Butterfield, Earl C., 288
Butterworth, G., 227

Cairns, R. B., 10, 11
Caldwell, B. M., 364
Campbell, J. D., 446
Campione, J. C., 19, 37, 352
Campos, Joseph J., 132, 188, 213, 385, 392, 396, 550
Cane, Valerie, 512
Cannizzo, S. R., 260
Cantor, J. H., 313
Carella, A., 97
Carey, Susan, 236, 296, 298
Carlsmith, L., 418
Carlson, V. R., 213
Caron, Albert J., 213
Caron, R. F., 213
Carpenter, C. Jan, 62–63, 68
Carr, S., 385
Carr, T., 385
Carroll, J. J., 541, 542
Carroll, John, 349
Carter, G. L., 187
Carter-Saltzman, L., 360
Case, R., 254
Catalano, R., 430
Cattell, P., 147
Cattell, Raymond B., 344
Cavanaugh, J. C., 266
Cazden, Courtney, 302
Cermak, L. S., 254
Chabon, I., 89
Chaika, H., 127
Chan, G. M., 93
Chapeskie, T. R., 455
Chaplin, J. P., 343
Chapman, M., 58, 519, 520, 521, 525
Charcot, Jean Martin, 21
Charles, D. C., 10, 11
Charlesworth, Rosalind, 442, 447
Charlesworth, William R., 346–47
Charnov, E. L., 387, 388, 392, 416
Chase, G. A., 102
Chatillon, J.-F., 326
Chaudhari, N., 176
Chen, S.-J., 392
Chess, Stella, 131, 410
Cheyne, J. A., 530
Chi, Michelene T. H., 19, 264
Child, Irvin L., 423, 474, 506
Childs, B., 102
Chinsky, Jack M., 260
Chomsky, C., 305
Chomsky, Noam, 270, 285, 286
Churchill, J. A., 363
Cicchetti, D., 393, 429
Cicirelli, V. G., 412
Cioffi, Joseph, 192
Clark, Eve V., 293, 294, 298, 302
Clark, M. C., 379
Clark, Russell D., III, 137
Clarke, A. D. B., 399
Clarke, A. M., 399
Clarke, Harrison, 164
Clarke-Stewart, K. Alison, 384, 389, 390, 391, 414, 486
Clausen, J. A., 355
Cleaves, W., 212
Clement, J., 367
Clifton, Rachel K., 121, 178
Clingempeel, W. G., 422, 423
Cloutier, R., 328

Clyburn, Andrea, 508
Coates, Brian, 277, 445–46
Cobb, J. A., 526
Cohen, E. M., 256
Cohen, Leslie B., 209, 221, 228, 249
Cohen, R., 240
Cohen, Sheldon, 52
Coie, John D., 452
Colby, A., 517, 518
Cole, Michael, 36, 37, 256, 262, 326
Collins, W. Andrew, 491, 532, 552, 553
Collmer, C. W., 427, 428, 430
Columbia Broadcasting System, 524
Condry, John C., 464
Conel, Jesse Le Roy, 176, 190
Conger, R. D., 431
Connell, D. B., 414
Connolly, J. A., 441
Connor, J. M., 192
Connors, K., 132
Cook, Michael, 213
Cooke, R. A., 66, 67
Cooper, H. M., 466
Cooper, J., 478
Cordura, G. D., 486
Coren, S., 189
Cornell, Claire P., 431
Corsini, D. A., 463
Corson, J. A., 451
Corter, C., 411
Cosgrove, J. M., 556
Costanzo, Philip R., 457, 458, 460
Courchesne, E., 180
Cowan, C. L., 521
Cowan, G., 485
Cowan, W. M., 85
Cowen, E. L., 450
Cox, M., 420, 422, 423
Cox, R., 420, 422, 423
Craik, F. I. M., 254
Cravioto, J., 363
Creche, The, 160
Croft, K., 546
Crook, Charles K., 115, 121
Crouter, A., 430
Crutchfield, R. S., 357
Cummings, J., 424
Cummins, R. A., 194
Curtiss, S. R., 287
Cutrona, Carolyn, 495, 498

Dabbs, J., 385
Dabek, R. F., 516
Daglish, Linda, 486
Daher, M., 121
Damrin, D., 456
D'Andrade, Roy, 462
Daniels, Pamela, 426
Darley, J. M., 516
Darling, Rosalyn B., 153, 154
Darlington, Richard, 366
Darvill, D., 530
Darwin, Charles, 27, 30
Daurio, S. P., 317
Davenport, R. K., Jr., 398
Davidson, R. J., 187
Davis, Janet M., 222
Davison, M. L., 517
Dawe, H. C., 528
Day, Mary Carol, 241, 242

Day, Ross H., 211, 214
Deaux, Kay, 470
Debakan, A., 145
DeCasper, Anthony J., 86, 121, 377
Delia, Jesse G., 279
Delicardie, E., 363
De Loache, Judy S., 209, 221, 337
Delys, P., 421
deMause, L., 8
Dement, W. C., 114
Demorest, Ann, 559
Denenberg, V. H., 398
Dennis, M., 184, 196
Dennis, Wayne, 159, 160
Deutsch, G., 190
Deutsch, Morton, 460
deVilliers, Jill G., 290, 296
deVilliers, Peter A., 290, 296
DeVries, Rheta, 315
Diamond, R., 236
Dick-Read, Grantly, 89
Diener, C. I., 469
Dion, Karen K., 446
Dobbing, John, 154
Dodd, B., 217
Dodge, Kenneth A., 527, 529, 554, 555
Dodge, S. H., 213
Dollard, John, 16, 25–26, 526
Donaldson, Margaret, 296, 318, 324
Dooley, D., 430
Dorval, B., 414
Douglas, Virginia I., 199, 200
Douvan, E., 423, 454
Downs, A. Chris, 487, 488, 489
Doyle, A.-B., 441
Drabman, R. S., 486, 533
DuBois, Louise, 481
Dubowitz, L. M. S., 89
"Dukes of Hazzard, The," 552, 553
Dulit, E., 326
Duncan, P., 189
Dunn, Judy, 386
Dunphy, D. C., 455
Dvir, R., 387, 389, 393
Dweck, Carol S., 447, 464, 467–69, 470
Dwyer, J., 155
Dyan-Hudson, R., 521
Dyer, Sharon L., 464
Dziadosz, G. M., 189

Easterbrooks, M. A., 54, 387, 388, 412, 437, 489
Eccles-Parsons, J., 481
Eckerman, Carol O., 382, 394–95
Edelbrock, C., 488
Eder, Rebecca, 257
Egeland, Byron, 386, 387
Ehrhardt, Anke A., 44, 476, 479, 480, 481, 482
Eichenwald, Heinz F., 155
Eichorn, D., 494
Eimas, P. D., 209, 289
Eisenberg, N., 519
Eisenberg, R. B., 121, 126
Eisenberg-Berg, Nancy, 521, 523
"Electric Company, The," 57
Elkind, David, 236–37, 242, 516, 542
Elliott, Elaine S., 464, 467–68, 470
Elliott, G. L., 419, 420, 422
Elson, Bill, 336

Elster, Arthur B., 93, 426
Emde, Robert N., 152, 180, 385
Emerson, P. E., 386
Emler, N. P., 506
Emmerich, Walter, 436, 477, 478
Endsley, Richard, 531
Engen, T., 122
Entingh, Dan, 179
Entwisle, D. R., 195
Epstein, R., 273
Erikson, Erik, 20, 22–25, 39, 55, 380, 431, 543, 544
Eron, Leon D., 57, 532
Eskimos, 345
Estes, D., 387
Estes, W. K., 18
Evans, Debra, 215, 227
Evans, Mary Ann, 302
Evans, R. I., 459
Eveleth, P. B., 157
Evers, W. L., 451

Fabricus, William, 265, 266
Fagan, Joseph F., III, 210, 219, 222
Fagot, Beverly I., 487, 488, 490
Falbo, Toni, 54, 467
Falkner, F. T., 147, 163
Fantz, Robert L., 124, 210, 211, 219
Farah, M. J., 311, 312
Farber, Ellen A., 386, 387
Farnham-Diggory, S., 47, 198
Farran, D., 414
Farwell, C., 291
"Fat Albert," 524
Faulkender, P. J., 255
Faust, M. S., 166, 494
Feig, E., 418
Fein, D., 507
Fein, Greta G., 389, 390, 414, 442
Feinman, S., 385
Feiring, C., 383
Feldhusen, John F., 317
Feldman, David H., 359–60
Feldman, Shirley S., 495, 498, 499
Felleman, E. S., 550
Fels Research Institute, 353–54, 355, 356
Fenson, L., 188
Ferdinand the Bull, 492
Ferguson, C. A., 281, 291
Ferguson, Tamara J., 529, 546
Feshbach, N., 409
Feshbach, Seymour, 526, 530
Field, Jeffery, 120, 217
Field, Tiffany M., 130, 229, 388, 438, 439
Fielding, J., 92
Fifer, W. P., 126, 377
Finlay, B. L., 178
Fischer, Kurt W., 227, 518, 540, 558
Fishbein, Harold D., 161, 174
Fisher, K., 431
Fishkin, J., 518
Flanery, Randall C., 29, 187
Flavell, John H., 13, 233, 260, 262, 263–64, 265, 266, 323, 528, 539, 546, 555, 557
Floyd, Joanne M., 443
Ford, K., 170
Ford, L. H., Jr., 540

Forgus, R. H., 398
Fowler, W., 311, 313
Fox, G. L., 419
Fox, N., 187
Fox, Robert, 211
Fraiberg, Selma, 220
Frank, Françoise, 275
Frank, L. K., 114
Frankel, G. W., 243
Frankel, K. A., 409
Freedle, R., 365
Freedman, Daniel G., 27, 48, 50, 220
Freedman, J. L., 533
French, Doran C., 449
French, F. E., 363
Freud, Sigmund, 20–22, 39, 133, 382, 397, 399, 506
Frey, Karin S., 478–79, 484
Frías, J. L., 91
Friedl, E., 474
Friedman, S. L., 136, 238
Friedman, Steven, 127
Friedrich-Cofer, Lynette K., 524
Frisch, Hannah L., 486
Frodi, Ann M., 135, 136, 430, 495
Froming, William J., 520
Fry, Dennis, 271
Fry, Peggy Crooke, 155
Fryer, J. G., 79
Fuchs, A.-R., 87
Fullard, W., 383
Furman, W., 65, 443
Furth, Hans G., 252–53, 262, 560–61

Gaensbauer, T. J., 429
Gagné, Robert M., 313–14
Gagnon, John H., 492, 498
Gaite, A. J. H., 490
Gaitonde, M. K., 179
Galin, David, 185
Gallatin, Judith, 561
Gallistel, C. H. Randy, 332, 333
Ganchrow, J. R., 121
Gandelman, R., 90
Ganz, L., 180
Garbarino, J., 430
Gardner, Beatrice, 272
Gardner, Howard, 181, 182, 183, 197, 345, 359
Gardner, Judith M., 124
Gardner, L., 158
Gardner, R. Allen, 272
Gardner, W. P., 393
Garmezy, N., 391, 392
Garn, S. M., 70
Garnica, Olga K., 289
Garvey, C., 296
Garwood, S. G., 447
Gazzaniga, M. S., 184
Gekoski, Marcy J., 112, 129
Gelfand, Donna M., 521, 528
Gelles, R. J., 412, 427, 429, 430, 431
Gelman, Rochel, 33, 279, 314, 319, 320, 322, 332, 333, 334, 335, 556
Gentner, Dedre, 295
George, Carol, 429
Gerard, Harold G., 460
Gerbner, George, 430, 533
Geschwind, Norman, 174, 181, 183, 187, 195

Gesell, A. L., 147
Gholson, B., 38
Gibson, Eleanor J., 212, 213, 214, 216, 220, 235, 237, 238, 241, 245, 266
Gilligan, Carol, 326, 518, 544
"Gilligan's Island," 525
Glass, David C., 52
Glazer, J. A., 447
Gleason, Jean Berko, 281, 282, 287, 304
Gleitman, Lila R., 198
Gluck, L., 83
Glucksohn-Waelsch, S., 104
Gnepp, J., 550
Goetz, T. E., 447
Golbek, Susan L., 256
Gold, Dolores, 415
Goldberg, J., 254
Goldberg, S., 495
Goldberg, W. A., 54, 387, 388
Golden, M. M., 450
Golden, Mark, 364, 365
Goldman-Rakic, P. S., 175, 176, 178, 179, 196
Goldschmid, M. L., 328
Goldsmith, L. T., 238
Goleman, D., 251, 357, 359
Golinkoff, Roberta M., 228, 334
Gombe Stream Chimpanzee Reserve, 341
Gonso, J., 447
Goodenough, F. L., 528
Goodman, Joseph, 510
Goodson, B. D., 414
Gordon, John E., 154
Gottlieb, Gilbert, 80
Gottman, J. M., 447, 448
Govatos, Louis A., 163
Gove, F. L., 550
Graham, Douglas, 505
Granoff, D., 363
Gratch, G., 227
Gray, William M., 543
Graziano, W. G., 449, 461
Green, Richard, 479, 480
Greenfield, Patricia M., 57, 249, 283–84, 326
Greenough, W. T., 194
Greenspan, Emily, 164
Greer, L. D., 491
Greif, E. B., 516
Griffin, Donald R., 342
Griffiths, R., 147
Grill, J. J., 460
Grinder, R. E., 507
Grisanti, G., 479
Gronlund, N. E., 450
Gross, Larry, 533
Grosser, D., 511
Grossman, K., 392
Grossman, K. E., 392
Gruendel, Janice, 285, 294
Grusec, Joan E., 444, 511, 521
Guilford, J. P., 343–44
Gump, P. V., 56
Gunderson, Virginia, 91, 94, 99
Gutteridge, M. V., 161, 162
Guttman, David, 499

Hagen, John W., 19, 243, 244, 254, 257, 258, 261, 266

Hagen, M. A., 238
Hahn, W. E., 176
Haines, A. C., 456
Hainline, L., 210, 418
Haith, Marshall M., 123, 124, 125, 147, 210, 216
Hake, Janet L., 215
Hale, Gordon A., 19, 243, 244
Halford, G. S., 320
Hall, E., 22, 134, 153, 155, 156, 413, 415
Hall, G. Stanley, 10, 11, 110
Hallstrom, J. L., 238
Halperin, Marcia, 228
Hamill, P. V., 156
Hammer, E. F., 499
Hanlon, C., 282
Harari, Herbert, 447, 448
Harding, C., 334
Harlow, Harry F., 65, 378, 391, 437
Harlow, Margaret K., 378, 437
Harris, P. L., 33, 209, 216, 227, 228–29, 394
Harrison, C. W., 456
Hart, R., 487
Harter, Susan, 540, 541, 542, 543, 544
Hartman, E. F., 246
Hartmann, Donald P., 521, 528
Hartshorne, Hugh, 505
Hartup, Willard W., 55, 65, 277, 438, 439, 442–43, 445–46, 447, 448, 449, 453, 454, 455, 456, 457, 458, 460, 494, 528
Harvard University, 14, 24
Haskett, Roger F., 482
Haskins, R., 415
Haugh, S. S., 485
Haviland, J., 396
Hawkins, J., 329
Hay, Dale F., 382, 395, 438, 439
Healy, M. J. R., 163
Hebb, Donald O., 343
Hecaen, H., 258
Hechtman, L., 198, 199, 200
Hecox, K., 120
Hegel, Georg, 35
Heiss, J., 425
Held, Richard, 160
Helson, R., 355
Henderson, Charles R., 415
Henig, Robin M., 103
Henninger, P., 183
Hermelin, Beate, 189
Hershenson, Maurice, 123
Herzberger, S., 431
Herzog, Elizabeth, 418
Hess, E. H., 398
Hess, R. D., 157, 363, 422
Hetherington, E. Mavis, 417, 420, 422, 423
Hevey, C. M., 486
Hewitt, Edith S., 115
Hicks, D. J., 446
Hicks, R. E., 187
Hill, Robert B., 424
Himes, J. H., 169
Hinde, R. A., 27, 28
Hiscock, Merrill, 182, 183, 185, 186, 188, 189, 190, 196, 197, 198, 286
Hitler, Adolf, 24

Hochberg, J. E., 238
Hodgen, Gary D., 98, 103
Hoefkens, M., 186
Hoefnagel-Höhle, Marian, 286
Hoffman, C. D., 485
Hoffman, L. W., 415, 416
Hoffman, Martin L., 137, 503, 507, 509, 512, 513, 514, 518, 521, 522, 549
Hoffman, Robert F., 180, 210
Hogan, R., 507
Hogarty, P. S., 351, 353, 354, 355, 367
Holden, G. W., 489
Holyoak, K. J., 350
Honzik, M. P., 361
Hooker, Davenport, 86
Horn, John L., 344
Horn, Joseph M., 361
Horner, Matina, 464
Horowitz, Frances D., 89, 98
Hoving, K. L., 254
Howard, J. A., 521
Howard, K. I., 493, 496
Howes, Carolee, 439, 449
Hubel, David H., 83, 174, 193
Hudson, Lynne M., 543
Huesmann, L. Rowell, 530
Hughes, Martin, 546
Hulse, F. S., 169
Humphrey, T., 86
Hunt, Earl, 18, 348–49
Hunter, M. A., 221
Huntsman, N., 19
Huston, Aletha C., 408, 478, 485, 486, 487, 490
Huston-Stein, Aletha, 62–63, 68
Huttenlocher, Janellen, 548
Hwang, Carl-Philip, 134, 398
Hyde, J. S., 483
Hyman, I. A., 355
Hymel, S., 450, 451

Ianotti, Ronald J., 551
Illsby, R., 156
"I Love Lucy," 525
Imperato-McGinley, J., 482
Ingram, Dianna, 186
Inhelder, Bärbel, 250, 252, 253, 255, 256, 321, 325, 327, 328
Institute for Personality Assessment and Research, 358–59
Interprofessional Task Force, 89
Iowa State University, 17
Ironsmith, M., 556
Ituri pygmies, 157
Iverson, L. I., 179

Jacklin, Carol N., 190, 482–83, 529
Jacobson, J. L., 281, 381
Jacobson, Lenore, 466
Jacobson, Sandra, 130
James, L. S., 88
Jean Jacques Rousseau Institute, 30
Jensen, Arthur R., 357, 361–62
Jerison, Harry J., 174, 175
Jersild, A., 164
Joffe, J. M., 99
Johansson, G., 241
Johansson, S. R., 474
John, E. Roy, 356–57

Johns Hopkins University, 10, 194–95, 316
Johnson, C., 92
Johnson, James E., 449
Johnson, P., 121
Johnston, F. E., 156
Jones, K. L., 363
Jones, Mary Brush, 459
Jones, Mary Cover, 493, 494
Jones, R. K., 238
Joos, S. K., 97
Journal of Educational Psychology, 342
Julesz, Bela, 211
Junn, E. N., 350
Juraska, J. M., 194
Jusczyk, P. W., 120, 126, 208, 288, 289

Kaczala, C. M., 463, 490
Kagan, Jerome, 16, 209, 219, 227, 346, 365, 381, 392, 414, 421, 514
Kail, Robert V., Jr., 14, 19, 239, 254, 257, 258
Kalnins, Ilze V., 221
Kaltenbach, K., 383
Kamin, L. J., 361
Kandel, Denise B., 454, 458
Kandel, Eric R., 179–80
Kandel, Gillray L., 192
Kanner, Leo, 251
Kantner, J. F., 170
Karana, 492
Karmel, Bernard Z., 356–57
Karniol, Rachel, 516
Kaye, Herbert, 356–57
Kaye, Kenneth, 133, 392
Kearsley, R. B., 126, 414
Keating, D. F., 550
Keating, D. P., 317
Keating, M. T., 70
Keeney, T. J., 260
Kegan, R., 38
Kehl, T., 93
Keller, A., 541
Keller, Barbara B., 512
Keller, Helen, 220
Kempe, Henry C., 429, 431
Kempe, Ruth S., 429, 431
Kendler, Tracy S., 312, 313, 329
Kendrick, Carol, 410
Keniston, A., 518
Kennell, John H., 134–35
Kenney, M. D., 398
Kershner, J. R., 190
Kessen, William, 118, 124, 147, 155, 208
Kidd, K. K., 48, 50, 51, 362
Killarney, J., 92
Kimura, Doreen, 183, 189
King, L. M., 521
King, Suzanne, 481
Kinsbourne, Marcel, 182, 183, 185, 186, 187, 188, 189, 190, 196, 197, 198, 199, 200, 286
Kinsey, Alfred, 497
Kippax, S., 56
Kirasic, Kathleen C., 239
Kirkpatrick, M., 479
Klahr, David, 19
Klaus, Marshall H., 134–35
Kleiman, D., 83

Klima, E. S., 272
Klinnert, Mary D., 385
Klosson, E. C., 516
Kobasigawa, Akira, 263, 264
Koepke, Jean E., 131
Koeske, R. D., 264
Koffka, K., 234
Kohlberg, Lawrence, 336, 476, 477, 478, 479, 484, 485, 504, 515, 516–18, 534
Köhler, W., 237
Kohn, B., 196
Kohn, Melvin, 421
Kolata, G. B., 98, 101, 103, 195
Kolb, S., 118, 158
Konner, Melvin, 26
Koopman, R., 221
Kopp, C. B., 100, 241
Korner, A. F., 123, 131
Kornfeld, Judith R., 292
Kossan, Nancy E., 312
Kosslyn, Stephen M., 248, 256, 311, 312
Krakow, J. B., 241
Krasnor, Linda R., 451, 554, 555
Krawiec, T. S., 343
Krebs, Dennis, 447
Krebs, R. L., 517
Krehbiel, Gina, 452
Kremenitzer, J. P., 124
Kreutzer, Mary Anne, 233, 265
Kriger, A., 495
Kroll, J., 7
Kuczaj, Stan A., II, 301, 303, 304
Kuczynski, Leon, 509–10
Kuhn, Deanna, 326–27
Kulovich, M. V., 83
!Kung San, 26
Kurland, D. M., 254
Kurtines, W., 517
Kutz, K. J., 292

Laboratory of Comparative Human Cognition, 36
Ladd, Gary W., 447
Lagerspetz, K., 532
Lamb, Michael E., 54, 65, 70, 93, 134–35, 136, 153, 379, 380, 385, 386, 387, 388, 389, 392, 397, 398, 400, 405, 406, 409, 412, 415, 416, 417, 419, 426, 429, 430, 436, 476, 489, 495, 540
Lamke, L. K., 499
Lange, Garrett, 255, 256, 263
Langlois, Judith H., 446, 487, 488, 489
Lanza, R. P., 273
LaPlante, M. N., 497
Lasky, R. E., 312
"Lassie," 525
Laurendeau, Monique, 547–48
Lawson, Katherine R., 217
Layzer, J. I., 414
Lazar, Irving, 366–67
Leakey, R. E., 175
Leat, M., 445
Lecours, A. R., 176
Lefkowitz, M. M., 98
Leibel, R. L., 154
Leifer, A., 532
Leiter, M. P., 442
Lemeshow, S., 156

Lemoine, P., 363
Lempert, Henrietta, 305
Lenneberg, Eric H., 147, 185, 196, 285–86, 291
Lennon, Randy, 521
Leonard, Catherine, 233, 265
Leonard, C. O., 102
Lerner, R. M., 38, 499, 543
Lesser, Gerald S., 57, 366, 458
Lester, B. M., 98, 136, 381
Leventhal, A. S., 121
Levin, Harry, 69, 405, 407, 506
Levin, Iris, 330
Levin, Stephen R., 245
Levine, J. A., 387, 388, 416
LeVine, R., 43
Levine, S. B., 479
Levitt, M. J., 379
Lewin, R., 175
Lewis, Michael, 128, 365, 383, 393–94, 540
Lewis, T. L., 209
Lewkowicz, K. S., 387, 389, 393
Liben, Lynn S., 253, 548
Licht, Barbara G., 469
Liebert, D. E., 328
Liebert, Robert M., 328, 531
Lind, J., 135
Lindauer, B. K., 242, 245
Lindberg, M., 264
Lindgren, Gunilla, 157
Lippitt, R., 511
Lipsitt, Lewis P., 46, 110, 116, 121, 122
Little, Stuart, 492
Littman, Richard A., 443
Livesley, W. J., 542, 545
Lloyd, Barbara, 486
Locke, John, 12, 13
Locke, John L., 291, 292
Lomas, J., 189
Lorch, Elizabeth P., 245
Lorenz, Konrad, 27, 525
Lothstein, L. M., 479
Lounsbury, M. L., 136
Lovell, K., 321
Lowell, Amy, 359

McAdoo, John L., 427
McAnarney, Elizabeth, 93, 426
McAra, M. J., 529
McCall, Robert B., 42, 221, 247, 346, 351, 353, 354, 355–56, 367, 368, 370
McCartney, K., 49
McCauley, E. A., 479
McClearn, G. E., 48
McClelland, D. C., 355
McCluskey, K. A., 92
Maccoby, Eleanor E., 54, 69, 190, 405, 406, 407, 408, 409, 410, 482–83, 506, 529
McCormick, N., 497
McCormick, R. A., 67
McDavid, John W., 447, 448
McDevitt, T. M., 363
Macfarlane, Aidan, 122–23, 209, 377
MacFayden, J., 262
McGarrigle, James, 324
McGraw, K. O., 486
McGraw, Myrtle B., 159, 161–62
McGuinness, D., 199

McKain, Kristine, 187
McKenna, J. J., 116
McKenry, P. C., 92
McKenzie, B. E., 214
MacKinnon, C., 518
MacKinnon, D. W., 359
Maclean, Paul D., 174
McMichael, R. E., 507
McQueen, Albert J., 424
Main, Mary, 387, 429
Malatesta, C. Z., 135, 396
Malina, Robert M., 167, 168, 169, 170
Malkin, C. M., 429
Mamay, P. D., 491
Mandler, Jean M., 247, 249, 250
Mans, L., 393
Maratos, O., 131
Maratsos, Michael, 285, 298, 299, 300, 303, 305
March, Jo, 492
Marcia, James E., 543, 544
Marcus, Dale E., 477, 479
Marcus, T. L., 463
Markell, R. A., 448, 451
Markman, Ellen M., 251, 320, 324–25
Markus, G. B., 55
Markus, H., 55
Martin, D. C., 97
Martin, Grace B., 137
Martin, John A., 405, 406, 407, 408, 409, 410
Martin, Marian F., 528
Marvin, Robert S., 549
Marx, J. L., 85
Marx, Karl, 35
Maslin, L. A., 409
Mason, W. A., 398
Masters, J. C., 443, 550
Masur, E. F., 279
Matas, Leah, 383, 396, 409
Matthews, W. S., 497
Maurer, Daphne, 209, 210
May, Mark A., 505
Mayer, J., 155
Meacham, J. A., 541
Mead, Margaret, 89
Means, B. M., 262
Meck, E., 335
Meece, J., 195, 490
Megaw-Nyce, J. S., 241
Meichenbaum, Donald H., 510
Meicler, M., 227
Mellin, Gilbert W., 96
Meltzoff, Andrew N., 130–31, 229
Mendelson, Morton J., 216
Menyuk, Paula, 288, 299
Menzel, E. W., 398
Mercer, J. R., 355
Meredith, Howard V., 148, 168–69
Mermelstein, E., 321
Merten, D., 497
Mervis, C. B., 250, 251
Mezei, L., 445
Michaels, Richard H., 96
Michejda, Maria, 103
Milewski, Allen E., 221
Milgram, J. I., 412
Milgram, N. A., 262
Millar, W. S., 128
Miller, G. A., 262, 276, 297, 298

Miller, Louise B., 368
Miller, Neal E., 16, 25–26
Miller, P. H., 245
Miller, P. Y., 496, 497
Miller, Wick R., 292
Milner, Brenda, 182–83
Milner, J. S., 428
Minkowski, A., 177
Minuchin, Patricia P., 460, 461, 465, 467, 490
Mirabile, Paul J., 186
Miranda, Simon B., 210, 219
Mischel, Harriet N., 504, 508
Mischel, Walter, 422, 504, 508
Miscione, John L., 295
"Mr. Rogers' Neighborhood," 524
Miyake, K., 392
Moely, B. E., 262
Mogford, K., 220
Mohr, Don M., 541
Molfese, Dennis L., 186, 305
Molfese, Victoria J., 186
Money, John, 44, 476, 479, 481, 482, 484
Moore, Bert S., 508, 520
Moore, M. J., 210
Moore, M. Keith, 120, 130–31, 229
Moore, S. G., 447
Morgan, George A., 383
Moro, Ernst, 116
Moss, H. A., 482
Moyer, Karl E., 526
Mueller, W., 154
Muir, D., 120, 216
Mukherjee, A. M., 98
Murray, Ann D., 132
Murray, Frank B., 320–21
Murray, J. P., 56, 525
Muson, H., 518
Mussen, Paul, 494, 523
Musser, L. M., 449
Muzio, J. N., 114
Myers, Nancy A., 255, 256, 257

Nagy, Maria, 336
Najarian, P., 160
Nash, A., 438
Nash, Sharon C., 495, 498, 499
National Center for the Prevention and Treatment of Child Abuse, 431
National Child Development Survey, 156
National Commission for the Protection of Human Subjects of Biomedical and Behavioral Research, 66
National Institute of Mental Health, 531
Naus, M. J., 254, 260
Neimark, Edith D., 326, 328
Neisser, Ulric, 217, 348
Nelson, Katherine, 249, 250, 283, 293, 294, 300
Nelson, K. E., 226, 256, 293
Nesdale, A. R., 529
Nesselroade, J. R., 60, 61
Netley, Charles, 192
Newcomb, Andrew F., 449, 454, 553
Newcombe, Nora, 192
Newman, P. R., 85
Newton, N., 89, 114
New York Times, 426

Nida, S., 264
Nielsen Television Index, 491
Nigro, G., 350
Ninio, A., 282
Norcia, A. M., 180
Novak, J. D., 195

O'Brien, R. G., 556
Ochs, E., 283
O'Connor, N., 189
Oden, M. H., 357
Oden, Sherri L., 447, 452, 453
Offer, D., 493, 496
Office of the Surgeon General, 531
Offir, Carole W., 464, 491
Ogilvie, E., 321
O'Keefe, Barbara J., 279
Oller, D. K., 290
Olsen, M. G., 239
Olsho, L. W., 208
Olson, D. R., 284
Olson, Gary M., 127, 128, 218, 219, 221, 222
Olver, R. R., 249
Olweus, D., 447–48
Oppel, W. E., 93
Orlofsky, J. L., 500
Ornstein, P. A., 254, 260
Ornstein, R. E., 183
Osborn, D. Keith, 531
Osofsky, J. D., 132
Ostrov, E., 493, 496
Overton, Willis F., 13, 28, 477, 479
Owsley, C. J., 217

Palermo, D. S., 305
Palincsar, A. S., 36
Papcun, G., 183
Papert, Seymour, 57, 336
Papini, D. R., 92
Papoušek, Hanuš, 133
Papoušek, Mechthild, 133
Paris, S. G., 242, 245
Parke, Ross D., 388, 427, 428, 430, 511, 512, 525, 529, 530, 532, 533
Parmelee, Arthur H., Jr., 100, 114, 176, 177, 178, 194, 363
Parsons, Jacquelynne E., 462–63, 469, 490
Pastor, D. L., 397
Patterson, Charlotte J., 519, 525, 526, 528, 556
Patterson, Gerald R., 443, 526
Payne, P. R., 154
Pea, Roy D., 337
Pearl, R. A., 522
Pedersen, F. A., 123
Pedersen, J., 438
Peel, E. A., 326
Peeples, D. R., 210
Pepler, D., 411
Percival, Andrew, 103
Perkins, S., 316
Perlmutter, Marion, 222, 223, 254, 255, 256, 257, 260, 264, 266
Perner, J., 559
Perry, David G., 484
Peskin, Harvey, 494
Peter Rabbit, 492
Peters, J., 94

Peters, Kenneth G., 199, 200
Peters, M. F., 424, 427
Petersen, A. C., 163, 165, 193
Peterson, Lizette, 64, 65, 67, 523
Pettersen, L., 212
Pezdek, K., 246
Phelps, Erin, 326–27
Phillips, Sheridan, 481
Piaget, Jacqueline, 277–78
Piaget, Jean, 11, 29–33, 35, 37, 38, 39, 69, 130, 159, 207, 215, 216, 218, 223–24, 225, 226–31, 236–38, 247, 248, 249, 250, 252–53, 254, 255, 256, 276, 277–78, 310, 313, 314–15, 318–39, 342, 345, 346, 347, 350, 359, 367, 504, 515–16, 533, 540, 544–49, 561, 563
Piaget, Laurent, 333
Piazza, Donna S., 188
Pick, Anne D., 200, 243
Pick, H. L., Jr., 239
Pillemer, David B., 258–59
Pinard, Adrian, 547–48
Pisoni, D. B., 120, 126, 208, 288, 289
Pitkin, R. M., 96
Pittman, L., 264
Plato, 12
Pleck, J. H., 387, 388, 416, 419, 492
Plutchik, R., 27
Polansky, N., 511
Pollins, Lynn D., 317
Pollio, H. R., 276
Pollitt, E., 154, 363
Pollock, D., 428
Porac, C., 189
Potts, D., 431
Powell, G. F., 158
Powell, Janet S., 342, 348, 350
Pratt, K. C., 110
Prawat, Richard, 336
Prechtl, H. F. R., 117, 118, 215
Pressley, M., 262
Presson, Clark C., 548
Preston-Martin, S., 94
Pritchard, J. A., 83
Pueblo Indians, 159
Pulkkinen, L., 408
Pulos, E., 210
Putallaz, M., 448

Rader, Nancy, 241, 245
Radin, Norma, 416, 417
Radke-Yarrow, Marian, 58, 136, 519, 520, 522, 525
Ragozin, A. S., 426
Rahe, D. F., 65
Rajecki, D. W., 28
Rakic, P., 85
Ramey, C., 414
Ramey, C. T., 366
Ramsay, Douglas S., 188, 191
Ramsey, P., 67
Rasmussen, B., 447
Rasmussen, T., 182
Rawls, D. J., 456
Rawls, J. R., 456
Reed, E., 220
Reese, Hayne W., 13, 28, 46, 60, 61, 262
Regnemer, J. L., 518

Reichenbach, L., 550
Reinisch, June M., 90, 97, 481, 482
Reisman, J. M., 453
Reiss, Ira, 496, 498
Renshaw, P. D., 450, 451
Resnick, L. B., 342
Rest, James R., 517, 518, 519
Rheingold, Harriet L., 378, 382, 394–95
Rholes, William S., 470, 545
Ricciuti, Henry, 383
Richman, C. L., 264
Ridley, D. R., 195
Riegel, Klaus, 35
Rieser, John J., 215
Rigler, D., 427
Riley, K. P., 85
Rinebold, S., 93
Ripp, Chris, 391, 428, 429
Rissman, M. W., 221
Ritter, K., 263, 265
Rivest, L., 441
Robbins, S., 517
Roberts, D. F. C., 524, 532
Roberts, E. J., 488
Roberts, G. C., 409
Roberts, Ralph J., Jr., 556
Robin Hood, 492
Robinson, Halbert B., 96, 316, 317
Robinson, Mitchell, 333
Robinson, N. M., 96
Robles, B., 363
Roche, Alex F., 156, 168, 169, 170
Rock, I., 214
Rockefeller University, 298
Rodgers, J. L., 55
Rodin, Judith, 155, 156
Roeper, T., 300
Roff, N., 450
Roffwarg, H. P., 114
Rogers, C. M., 398
Rogoff, B., 36
Rohwer, William D., Jr., 46, 262
Roopnarnine, Jaipul L., 438, 439, 443, 449
Rosch, Eleanor M., 249, 250, 251
Rose, D., 258
Rose, R. J., 361
Rose, S., 174, 175, 176
Rose, Susan A., 218, 318
Rosen, Bernard C., 462
Rosen, R., 153
Rosenblith, J. F., 116
Rosenhan, D. L., 521
Rosenthal, Robert, 355, 466
Rosenthal, T. L., 319
Rosenzweig, M. R., 193
Rosett, H. L., 363
Rosner, B. G., 195
Ross, Bruce M., 252
Ross, H. G., 412
Ross, H. S., 439
Rossman, E., 365
Rotenberg, Ken J., 529
Rousseau, Jean Jacques, 13
Rovee-Collier, Carolyn K., 112, 129, 222
Rovet, Joanne, 192
Rovine, M., 386
Roy, R., 479

Royston, A. B., 93
Rozin, Paul, 198
Rubens, Peter Paul, 7
Rubenstein, Judith L., 123, 439
Rubin, Kenneth H., 440–41, 442, 451, 520, 554, 555
Rubin, Robert T., 90, 482, 483
Rubinstein, E. A., 57
Ruble, Diane N., 478, 493, 542, 545–46
Ruff, Holly A., 211, 213, 217
Rule, Brendan G., 529
Rumain, Barbara, 323, 329, 330
Rumbaugh, Duane M., 272, 273
Rushton, J. P., 522
Russell, G., 416
Rutgers University, 44
Rutter, Michael, 251, 389, 391, 392, 420
Ruzskaya, A. G., 235
Ryan, M. L., 296

Sackett, Gene P., 65, 91, 94, 99
Sackin, Steve, 68
Saegert, S., 487
Sagi, Abraham, 137, 387, 389, 392, 416, 514, 549
St. James-Roberts, Ian, 196–97
Salapatek, Philip, 119, 120, 124, 147, 209, 210, 211, 212, 214, 219, 396
Salatas, Harriet, 263–64
Salisbury, D. M., 121
Saltzstein, Herbert D., 509
Sameroff, A. J., 206
Sander, L. W., 363, 393
Santrock, J. W., 419, 420, 422
Savage-Rumbaugh, E. Sue, 273
Savin-Williams, Ritch, C., 456
Sawin, Douglas B., 388, 522
Saxby, L., 187
Sayegh, Yvonne, 160
Scaife, Michael, 281
Scarr, Sandra, 48, 49, 50, 51, 151, 212, 346, 353, 360, 361, 362, 396, 413, 415
Schachtel, Ernest G., 258
Schachter, F. F., 54
Schackman, M., 193
Schaffer, H. R., 131, 386, 391, 393
Schaie, K. W., 60
Schiedel, D. G., 544
Schneider, B., 208
Schneider, Frank W., 520
Schneider-Rosen, K., 429
Schonfeld, William A., 493, 494
Schultz, L. A., 429
Schwartz, G., 497
Schwartz, J., 361
Schwartz, J. C., 451
Schwartz, Joyce, 183
Schwartz, Marcelle, 211
Schweinhart, L. J., 367
Scollan, Ronald, 297
Scott, E. M., 156
Scott, J. P., 378, 397
Scott, Phyllis M., 522
Scribner, S., 37, 256, 262
Scrimshaw, Neville S., 154, 155
Searleman, A., 194
Sears, P. S., 357
Sears, Robert R., 11, 69, 405, 407, 408, 463, 507

Sekel, M., 210
Self, P. A., 89
Sells, S. B., 450
Selman, Robert L., 454, 545, 551
Selye, H. A., 99
Serbin, Lisa A., 192, 489, 491
"Sesame Street," 57, 245, 246, 262, 366
Shankweiler, D., 186
Shantz, Carolyn U., 545, 546, 547, 549, 551, 560
Shapiro, Edna K., 460, 461, 465, 467, 490
Shatz, Marilyn, 279, 280, 282, 284, 556
Shaw, Marvin E., 457, 458, 460
Sherif, Carolyn W. S., 456
Sherif, Muzafer, 456
Sherman, D., 430
Sherman, J. A., 163, 164
Sherman, R. G., 240
Sherman, Tracy, 127, 128, 218, 219, 221, 222
Shiffrin, R. M., 254
Shigetomi, Carol C., 521
Shipstead, S. G., 546
Shoham, R., 387, 389, 392
Shorr, S. I., 453
Short, E. J., 366
Shucard, J. L., 190
Shultz, Thomas R., 335
Siebert, J., 324
Siegel, Alexander W., 7, 11, 239, 240
Siegel, L. S., 324
Siegler, Robert S., 19–20, 207, 320, 328–29, 332–33
Sigafoos, Ann D., 121, 229
Sigel, I. E., 321
Sigman, Marian D., 114, 176, 177, 178, 194, 278, 363
Simon, D. P., 19
Simon, Herbert A., 19
Simon, William, 496, 497, 498
Simpson, Elizabeth L., 518
Simpson, R. L., 491
Sinclair, Caroline B., 161, 163
Singer, Jerome E., 52
Singer, Leslie M., 44
Singer, L. T., 222
Singleton, Louise C., 460–61
Sioux Indians, 24
Siperstein, Gary N., 288
Siqueland, E. R., 129
Skeels, H. M., 361
Skinner, B. F., 14, 39, 273, 286
Skodak, M., 361
Skubiski, Sandra L., 521
Slaby, Ronald G., 478–79, 484, 525, 529, 530, 532, 533
Slattery, M., 178
Slobin, Dan I., 300, 303, 304, 305
Slobin, Heida, 304
Smith, Aaron, 196
Smith, Caroline, 96, 486
Smith, K. V. R., 479
Smith, Peter K., 439, 442, 486
Smith, Robin, 552–53
Smith, Sally B., 530
Smith, S. D., 198
Snow, Catherine E., 281, 286
Sobesky, William E., 506

Society for Research in Child Development, 66, 67
Sonnenschein, Susan, 557
Sontag, Lester, 99
Sorbonne, 30
Sorce, J. F., 385
Sorell, G., 499
Sorenstein, F., 497
Spanier, G., 543
Spear, N. E., 254
Spearman, Charles, 343
Speece, Mark, 337
Speer, James M., 556
Spelke, Elizabeth S., 217–18, 233, 237, 238, 241
Spence, Janet, 499
Spence, Melanie J., 86, 126
Spiegel, F. S., 90
Spiker, C. C., 313
Spinetta, J. J., 427
Springer, S. P., 190
Sroufe, L. Alan, 383, 393, 396, 397, 409, 436
Staffieri, J. Robert, 493
Stanford University, 12, 17
Stanjek, K., 520
Stanley, Julius C., 194, 195, 316
Stanovich, K. G., 258, 261
Starr, M. D., 383
Starr, R. H., Jr., 427
Staub, E., 513
Steele, B. F., 428
Stein, Aletha H., 463, 524
Steinberg, Laurence D., 391, 413–14, 430, 496
Steiner, Jacob E., 121, 122
Steinmetz, S. K., 412, 427, 429, 430
Stenberg, Craig, 385, 396
Stendler, C., 456
Stephan, Cookie F., 447
Stephan, H., 174
Stephens, M. W., 421
Stern, C., 79
Stern, D. N., 281, 393
Sternberg, Robert J., 342, 343, 348, 349, 350, 353
Sternglanz, S. H., 491
Stevenson, H. W., 15, 198, 207, 243
Stevenson, M. B., 238
Steward, M. S., 541, 542
Stewart, Robert B., 549
Stipek, D. J., 470
Stirnimann, Fritz, 124
Stolz, Herbert R., 163, 493
Stolz, Lois H., 163, 493
Straus, M. A., 412, 427, 429, 430
Strauss, M. S., 209
Strauss, Sidney, 118, 158
Strayer, F. F., 28, 455, 526
Strayer, Janet, 28, 455
Streissguth, A. P., 97, 98, 363
Strickland, D. M., 87
Studdert-Kennedy, M., 186
Sturner, W. Q., 110
Sudia, Celia E., 418
Sugarman, Susan, 337
Sugawara, A. I., 488
Suomi, Stephen J., 65–67, 391, 410, 428, 429, 437
Super, C. M., 159

Surber, C. F., 516
Susman, Elizabeth J., 245
Sutton-Smith, B., 54
Swanson, J. M., 187, 198, 199, 200

Tallal, Paula, 183
Tanner, J. M., 99, 151, 154, 156, 157, 158, 162, 163, 169
Tavris, Carol A., 464, 491
Taylor, B., 163, 165
Taylor, D. C., 190
Taylor, D. G., 386
Teller, D. Y., 210
Terman, Lewis, 11, 61, 357, 358, 359
Terrace, Herbert S., 271, 272–73
Thelen, Esther, 68, 159
Thoman, E. B., 123
Thomas, Alexander, 131, 410
Thomas, M. H., 533
Thomson, A. M., 156
Thompson, R. A., 387, 392
Thompson, Spencer K., 476, 489
Thompson, W. C., 521
Thompson, W. P., 99
Thorndike, E. L., 11
Thorpe, L. A., 208
Three Little Pigs, 492
Thurstone, Louis I., 343
Tinbergen, Niko, 49, 131
Todd, Christine M., 257, 260
Tolan, W. J., 386
Tootell, H. E., 214
Trabasso, Tom, 313, 322–23, 325
Tracy, Russel L., 65, 384
Trause, Mary Anne, 384
Trehub, Sandra E., 208, 289
Tremaine, Johnny, 492
Tresemer, D., 464
Tryon, R. C., 48
Tuchmann-Duplessis, H., 95, 96
Tulkin, Steven R., 209, 365, 392
Turing, A. M., 18
Turkewitz, Gerald, 124
Turkle, Sherry, 335, 338
Tutko, Thomas, 164
Tyler, Leona E., 355

Ulian, D. Z., 478
Ullman, C. A., 450
Underwood, Bill, 508, 520
Ungerer, J. A., 278
University of California, 12, 24
University of Geneva, 30
University of Lausanne, 30
University of Washington, 316, 317
Urberg, Katheryn A., 476, 494–95
U.S. Bureau of the Census, 424
Uzgiris, Ina C., 230, 321

Vance, A. K., 56
Vandenberg, B., 442
Van der Vlugt, H., 186
Van Dusen, R., 521
Van Lawick-Goodall, Jane, 341
Van Tassel-Baska, J., 316
Vasta, Ross, 287
Vietze, P., 127
von Frisch, K., 270
von Hofsten, C., 119, 218

Vurpillot, Eliane, 242
Vygotsky, Lev S., 35–38, 275, 276, 352

Waber, Deborah P., 192
Wachs, Theodore, 365
Wahler, Robert G., 443
Waldron, A., 255
Walford, R. L., 50
Walk, Richard D., 212, 213
Walker, Ann, 217, 391, 413–14
Wallace, J. G., 19
Wallach, H., 237
Walters, C. E., 131
Walters, L. H., 92
Walters, Richard H., 16, 445, 511, 512
Wannemacher, J. T., 296
Warshak, R. A., 419, 420, 422
Waterlow, J. C., 154, 155
Waters, E., 383, 397
Watson, John B., 11, 14
Watson, J. S., 129
Watson, Malcolm W., 558, 560
Watusis, 157
Waxler, Carolyn Z., 521, 522
Webb, P. A., 114
Wechsler, David, 343, 351
Weikart, D. P., 367
Weinberg, R. A., 362
Weinert, F., 254
Weingarten, Kathy, 426
Weinraub, K. M., 383
Weinrott, M. R., 451
Weintraub, Sandra, 281, 282, 287
Weir, Anthony, 301
Weir, Ruth H., 301
Weisfeld, G. R., 42
Weisner, T. S., 412
Weiss, G., 198, 199, 200

Weiss, J., 242
Weisz, J. R., 470
Weller, C., 94
Wellman, Henry M., 265
Wells, Anne J., 133
Werner, E. E., 363, 390
Werner, Heinz, 29, 33–35, 39, 147
Werner, John S., 129, 254, 255, 256
Weston, Donna, 389
Whalen, C. K., 199
White, Burton L., 160
White, C. B., 518
White, D. G., 489
White, Edward, 336
White, Sheldon H., 7, 11, 258–59
Whitehouse, R. H., 163
Whitehurst, Grover J., 286, 287, 294, 300, 556, 557
Whiting, John W. M., 16, 506
Whorf, Benjamin Lee, 276
Wickelgren, L. W., 120
Widdowson, Elsie M., 158
Wiesel, Thorsten N., 193
Wiesenfeld, A. R., 135
Wilchelsky, M., 453
Wilkening, Friedrich, 331
Wille, D. E., 381
Wimmer, H., 559
Wine, J. D., 468
Winer, G. A., 324
Winterbottom, Marian, 462
Wippman, J., 397
Witelson, Sandra F., 190–91, 192, 197–98
Wittig, Barbara, 381
Wittig, M. A., 193
Wohlwill, J. F., 352
Wolf, Thomas M., 444

Wolff, Georg, 154
Wolff, P. H., 114, 135, 289
Women on Words and Images, 492
Wonder Woman, 491
Woodlawn, Caddie, 492
Woodson, R. H., 100, 112
Wozniak, Robert H., 35
Wright, J. C., 255

Yakovlev, P. I., 176
Yang, R. K., 482
Yarrow, L. J., 123
Yarrow, Marian R., 446, 520–21, 522
Yeates, K. O., 366
Yendovitskaya, T. V., 266
Yonas, Albert, 212, 238
Young, L., 430
Younger, Barbara A., 228, 249
Youniss, James, 252, 324
Yu, M., 94
Yueok Indians, 24

Zahn-Waxler, Carolyn, 58, 136, 519, 520, 521, 522, 525
Zajonc, R. B., 55
Zanna, M. P., 516
Zaporozhets, A. V., 235
Zarbatany, L., 385
Zavak, Elaine, 164
Zelazo, N., 118, 158
Zelazo, P. R., 116, 118, 127, 158, 414
Zelnik, M., 170
Zeskind, P. S., 136
Zimmerman, B. J., 319
Zimmerman, S. A., 532
Zinshensko, V. P., 235
Zucker, Kenneth J., 480

abortion, 104, 106
accommodation, 29, 31–32, 39, 229, 249, 315
achievement motivation, 461–71
activity, neonate, 130–31
adaptation theories, 13, 26–28, 39
    aggression as viewed by, 526–27
    attachment as viewed by, 382
adaptive change, 34
adolescence:
    conformity pressures in, 458–59
    emergence of, 6, 8–9, 10
    fear of success in, 464
    formal operational thought in, 326, 542–44
    friendship in, 55, 453–55, 551–53
    hyperactivity in, 200
    identity in, 24–25, 55, 543–44, 563
    peer group structures in, 448, 455–56
    physical changes in, 147, 165–70, 492–94, 496
    popularity in, 447
    scapegoats and bullies in, 447–48
    self-concept in, 542–44
    sex-role stereotypes a retreat in, 494–95
    sexual behavior in, 496–98
    sexual maturation in, 165–70, 492–98
    understanding of others in, 545
adoption, 44–45, 361
adulthood, 6–7, 25
    late, 7, 9, 499
affiliative behavioral system, 380, 382
AFP (alpha-fetoprotein), 102
African descent, 157
afterbirth, 87–88, 105
age-normative influences, 46, 71
aggression:
    in abused children, 429
    adaptation view of, 526–27
    behavior-learning view of, 526–27
    causes of, 90, 525–28
    development of, 528–29, 534
    dominance hierarchy and, 28, 526
    information-processing approach to, 527–28
    peer influence on, 443
    popularity and, 443
    in primates, 437–38
    sex differences in, 43–44, 481, 483, 529–30
    among siblings, 412
    socialization and, 526, 528, 553–54
    television violence and, 16, 57, 530–33
aging, 7, 9, 50, 499
alcohol:
    adult and adolescent standards for use of, 448, 459–60

intellectual development and, 362–63
    learning under influence of, 200
    as teratogen, 95
alleles, 77, 78, 79, 105
allergies, 199
alpha waves, 180
altruism, 445–46, 512, 519–25, 534
    defined, 519
    empathy and, 521, 522
    generosity as, 520–22
    giving aid as, 522–23
ambivalent attachment bonds, 382, 384–87
amino acids, 179
amnesia, 258–59
amniocentesis, 101, 106
amniotic fluid, 101
amphetamines, 199
anaglyphs, 211
analogies, 349–50
anal stage, 21–22
androgens, 165
    fetal exposure to, 481
androgyny, 499–501
anencephaly, 101, 118
anesthetics, 98–99, 132
anger, 396, 528
animal studies:
    of attachment, 378–79, 391, 397–98
    of brain functions, 178, 179–80, 181, 187, 193–94, 196
    of child abuse, 428, 429
    genetic, 48–49, 65–67
    of intelligence, 315
    of language and communication, 272–73
    of malnutrition effects, 154
    of parental style, 410
    of peer contact, 436–38, 442
animism, 334, 339
anorexia nervosa, 493
anthropology, 43, 89
antisocial behavior, 525–34
apes, see primates
Apgar scores, 88, 105
aphasias, 181–82, 196
appearance:
    body ideal and, 493
    child abuse and, 137, 429
    peer relationships and, 446–47
approach-avoidance, 429
Asiatic descent, 157
ASL (American Sign Language), 272
aspirin, 97
assimilation, 29, 31–32, 39, 249, 314, 560
association areas, 174, 200
asynchrony, 167, 168
athletes, professional, 164

at-risk babies, 136
attachment:
    child abuse and, 429
    to fathers, 387–89
    function of, 380
    to multiple caregivers, 389–92
    personality and, 392, 396–97
    separation distress and, 380–82, 400
    social skill development and, 393–96
    sociocultural influences on, 381, 388–89, 392–93, 415
    stages of, 376–80
    theories of, 22, 382
    wariness of strangers and, 375, 380, 383–85, 396, 400
    to working mothers, 415
attention:
    auditory, 126
    development of, 219–21, 241–46
    joint, 280, 281
    selective, 219, 230, 242–45
    visual, 123–25, 219–21, 281
attentional inertia, 247
attention deficit disorder, 199
auditory attention, 126
authoritarian parents, 405–6, 427, 431
authoritative parents, 406, 407, 420, 427, 431
autism, 251
autonomy, 22, 395, 400, 421, 499
avoidant attachment, 382, 384, 429

babbling, 191, 287, 289–91, 306
babysitters, 381, 413
baby talk, 281–82
basal metabolism, 163, 165
basic stage, 15
Bayley Scale, 352–53
behavior, defined, 42
behavior-learning theories, 14–18, 286
    aggression as viewed by, 526–27
    attachment as viewed by, 382
behavior modification, social skills taught by, 451–53
Berkeley Growth Study, 352
biographical self-awareness, 394
biological factors, 43
    intelligence and, 346–47, 370
    sex roles and, 480–83
    in transsexuality, 479–80
birth, see childbirth
birth defects, 7, 95, 96–97, 101–3
birthing rooms, 89, 90
birth order:
    height and, 157
    intelligence and, 54–55, 368
    personality and, 410
blacks:
    intelligence tests and, 352

blacks (*continued*)
　sickle-cell anemia and, 93–94
　socialization and, 424–27
blind children, 27, 189, 220, 251
boarding schools, 158
body ideal, 493, 501
bonding:
　adaptation theory of, 26–27
　importance of early contact in, 134–
　　35
　sensitive periods and, 398–99
　See also attachment
books, sex-role stereotypes in, 492
boys:
　achievement motivation in, 462–64
　aggression in, 63, 91
　castration feared by, 22
　with extra sex chromosomes, 90
　fear of success in, 464
　teachers' criticisms of, 468–69, 490
　teachers' reinforcement of stereo-
　　typed sex roles for, 489–91
　transsexual, 479–80
　See also sex differences
Braille, 189
brain, 189
　electrical activity in, 180, 356–57
　evolution of, 174–75
　fetal, 85, 105, 194, 481
　growth and development of, 84–86,
　　173–201, 258
　hemispheric specialization of, 181–93,
　　201, 286
　lateralization of, 185–93, 197–98, 201,
　　286
　learning disorders and, 197–200
　neurochemistry of, 179–80
　plasticity of, 193–97
　sex-related differences in, 190–95,
　　481
brain damage, recovery from, 194–97
brain shunt, 103
brain waves, 180, 356–57
Brazelton Neonatal Behavioral Assess-
　ment Scale, 88
breast-feeding, 114, 133, 135
　by adolescent mothers, 92–93
　by wet-nurses, 8
Broca's area, 181, 183
bulimia, 493
bullies, 447–48
　See also aggression

Caesarean section, 88
caffeine, 94
calcium, 155
canalization, 151, 346
capitalism, 7
caregivers:
　language and, 280–82
　multiple, 389–92
　See also attachment
castration fears, 22
catch-up growth, 99, 100, 151, 154
categorical representation, 228, 247,
　249–52, 312
causality, 333–35
cell death, 85
central learning, 243

central nervous system, fetal, 84–85,
　105
cephalocaudal development, 145, 146,
　170, 177
cerebellum, 154, 174, 176, 178
cerebral dominance, 185
child abuse, 8, 93, 427–31
　infant crying patterns and, 136–37,
　　429
Child Abuse Potential Inventory, 428
childbirth, 86–89, 136
　complication of, 89–100, 363
　methods of, 89, 105–6
child development, *see* development
child-guidance clinics, 11
childhood, historical perspectives on, 6–
　8
childhood mortality, 7–8
child labor laws, 8–9
chimpanzees, *see* primates
chorionic villus biopsy, 101, 106
chromosomes, 77–78, 105, 481
　abnormal, 90–91, 192, 198
　See also genetic factors
cigarettes, *see* smoking
circular reactions, 224–25, 231
class differences, *see* social class; socio-
　economic status
classical conditioning, 14–15, 39, 207
class inclusion, 323–25, 338–39
clinical studies, 64, 69–70, 71
closure, principle of, 235
codominant genes, 79, 106
cognitive development, 206–7
　attention and, 219–21, 241–46
　language and, 277–78, 287, 295, 365
　learning vs., 313
　memory and, 221–23, 233–34, 252,
　　254–67, 336
　perceptual development and, 207–19,
　　234–41
　representation and, 247–54
　self-awareness and, 393
　social-learning theory of, 16
　See also intelligence; social cognition;
　　thought
cognitive maps, 239–40, 266
cognitive social-learning theory, 17–18
cognitive theory:
　gender identity as viewed by, 478
　moral development as viewed by,
　　504, 515–19
　sex roles as viewed by, 483–86
cohorts, 60, 71
color perception, 120, 209–10
common fate, principle of, 235
communication, 278–85, 555–57
　See also language acquisition
competence, 394–95, 514, 523, 524
　achievement motivation and, 461–71
　instrumental, 406–7, 431
computers, 58, 356–57
　impact of, 57
　in information-processing theory, 14,
　　18–20
　as model of the mind, 14, 18–20, 335–
　　36, 338
concepts:
　learning, 310–12
　representation and, 249–50, 267

concrete operational stage, 33, 39, 314,
　318–25, 338, 541–42, 561
conditioning:
　classical, 14–15, 39, 207
　in learning theory, 11, 14–15, 39
conformity:
　parental encouragement of, 421
　peer pressure and, 456–60
congenital abnormalities, 7, 91–94, 95,
　96–97
　diagnosing, 101–2
　preventing, 101–4
conscience, 506–7
　See also morality
conservation, 313, 314, 318–21, 332,
　338
　gender constancy and, 477
conservation of energy, law of, 21
constructionism, 28, 29
context, 283–85, 296, 306
continuity, principle of, 235
control:
　executive, 336, 339, 349
　in experiments, 63–64, 65, 68, 159
　locus of, 395, 421
　self-, 507, 508
conventional level of morality, 517, 534
convergence, 120
convergent thinking, 344
conversation, 280–82
cooing, 289
　as social response, 377, 382
corpus callosum, 184–85, 186, 201
correlation, 70, 71, 341
cortex, 85, 118, 119, 120, 174, 175–78,
　193, 200–201
co-twin control, 159
counting, 332
creativity, 358–60
crib death, *see* Sudden Infant Death
　Syndrome
crib speech, 301
cross-sectional studies, 59–60, 71
crying, 134–37
　child abuse and, 136–37, 429
　as social response, 377, 386
crystallized intelligence, 344–45
cuddling, 131, 379, 386
　cultural influences on patterns of, 392
cultural influences:
　importance of, 35, 57–58
　socialization and, 423
"culture-fair" tests, 345
cytoarchitecture, 177–78, 201

dating, 497, 498
day care, 390–91
　mixed age groups in, 449
　as socialization agent, 413–14
deaf-blind children, 27
deaf children, 251, 272, 290–91
death, understanding, 25, 336–37
deictic words, 295–96, 306
delayed gratification, 380, 422, 423, 508
delta waves, 357
deoxyribonucleic acid (DNA), 77
dependent variables, 64
depression, 391
depth perception, 211–13, 238
DES (diethylstilbestrol), 97

development:
  adaptation theories of, 26–28
  biological vs. social, 6
  of brain, 173–201, 258
  characteristics of, 12
  defined, 5
  determinants of, 41–71
  dialectical theories of, 35–38
  of gender identity, 476–80
  moral, 503–19
  organismic theories of, 28–35
  prenatal, 75–106
  psychodynamic theories of, 20–26
  of representation, 247–54
  of self-concept, 540–44
  of sex roles, 62–63, 473–92
  of social cognition, 540–61
  studying determinants of, 59–71
  of thought, 223–30, 314–30
  of visual perception, 209–19
  See also cognitive development; motor development; social development
developmental age, 149, 170
developmental dyslexia, 197–98, 201
developmental psychology:
  concepts and theories of, 5–39, 206–7
  ecological approach to, 59
  emergence of, 10–12
  historical perspective on, 12–13
dialectical theories, 13, 35–38, 39
dichotic-listening technique, 186–87
diet:
  growth rates and, 154–56
  intellectual development and, 363
  prenatal development and, 92–93, 96–97
diethylstilbestrol (DES), 97
differentiation, 146, 170
disadvantaged children:
  early intervention programs for, 365–67
  IQ scores of, 364–65
discipline:
  abuse justified as, 8, 430
  moral development and, 509–10
  styles of, 405–10, 431
diseases:
  genetic, 91–94
  growth rate slowed by, 156
  prenatal development affected by, 96
  venereal, 96
displacement, as property of language, 270–71, 305
divergent thinking, 344
divorce, 416, 417, 420
DNA (deoxyribonucleic acid), 77
dominance, hemispheric, see hemispheric specialization
dominance hierarchies, 28, 526
  peer relationships and, 444, 455–56
  sex differences and, 164
  social competence predicted by, 456
dominant genes, 78–79, 91, 105
dopamine, 179, 199
Down's syndrome, 91, 101, 106, 152, 241, 393
dreaming, 114
drinking, see alcohol

drugs, 94, 97, 459–60
  See also medication
Dubowitz scoring system, 88–89
dyslexia, 197–98, 201

ear dominance, 185, 186–87, 188
early intervention programs, 365–69
eating disorders, 493
"echo-box" effect, 257
echolocation, 220
ecological approach to development, 59
ecological intervention, 399, 401
ectoderm, 81
education, see schooling
educational psychology, 11
ego, 20
egocentrism, 29, 32–33, 227, 544–45, 547–49, 550
  communication and, 555–56
  generosity and, 521
ego integrity, 25
electrical activity, brain, 180, 356–57
electroencephalographs (EEGs), 113, 114
embryonic period, 80, 81, 82–83, 85, 105
emotions, 395–96
  brain functions and, 183, 187
  inferring of, 550
  self-concept and, 541, 542
  See also anger; fear; shame
empathy, 503, 510, 513–15, 521, 522, 533
  social cognition and, 544, 549–51
  stages of, 513–14, 549
enactive representation, 247–48
encephalocele, 101, 103
encoding, 254, 260–63, 267, 325
endocrine system, 165, 166
endoderm, 81
environmental factors, 51–59
  brain development and, 194
  ecological intervention and, 399, 401
  genetic factors and, 41, 43, 48–49, 50, 51, 71, 79, 176, 360
  growth rates and, 154–58, 170
  intellectual development and, 360, 361, 363–70
  physical, 52
  social, 52–59
epidural anesthesia, 132
epigenesis, 79–81, 105, 193
epilepsy, 184
epistemology, 30
equilibration, 32
estrogens, 165, 166
ethnic factors:
  genetic diseases and, 91–94
  growth rate and, 157
ethology, 26, 39, 376, 382
event perception, 240–41
evoked potential, 180, 201
evolution, 26, 30, 43, 346, 376
  of brain, 174–75
executive control, 336, 339, 349
executive dependence or independence, 395
experimental method, 63, 64–67, 71, 159
exploration, 380, 382, 394–95

eye-hand coordination, 218
eyes:
  dominance in, 188, 189
  movement of, in REM sleep, 113–14
  See also visual perception

facial expressions, 378, 385, 550
  imitation of, 130, 229
  recognition of, 221–22, 236
facial proportions, 147, 149
factor analysis, 343, 348
failure to thrive, 363
fairweather cooperation, 551
Fallopian tubes, 79
families:
  attachment process and, 387–89
  black, 418, 424–27
  historical perspective on, 8
  impact of, 54–55
  as socialization agent, 54, 403–32
  See also parents; siblings
fat cells, 155–56, 163
fathers:
  absent, 416–19
  as attachment figures, 387–89
  family involvement of, 54, 66–67, 387–89, 416, 419, 427
  school success and involvement of, 461
  single, 419
  See also parents
fear:
  of castration, 22
  of heights, 213, 396
  of strangers, 64–65, 375, 380, 383–85, 396, 400
  of success, 464–65
fear-wariness system, 380, 382, 383–84
feeding:
  attachment process and, 378–79, 382
  of newborns, 114–15, 133, 137
  See also breast-feeding
fetal alcohol syndrome, 97, 362–63
fetal development, 52, 81, 83–84, 86
  See also prenatal period
fetal surgery, 103
field studies, 64, 68–69, 71
figurative whole, 237, 266
first-borns, 157, 410
  See also birth order
first words, 291, 292–93
fixations, 21
fluid intelligence, 344–45
food additives, 199
foreclosure, 543, 563
formal operational stage, 33, 39, 314, 315, 325–30, 339, 542–44, 561
friendship, 453–54, 551–55
frustration-aggression hypothesis, 526, 534
frustration tolerance, 380, 397
functional theories of language acquisition, 287–88
future-oriented poor, 425

gametes, 77–78, 90, 105
gender constancy, 477–79, 484–85, 500
gender differences, see sex differences
gender identity:
  ambiguous, 482–83

gender identity (*continued*)
  development of, 476–80
    implications of, 484–86
    sex roles and, 480–92, 500
    transsexual, 479–80, 500
gender schemas, 485–86, 500
generativity, 25
generosity, 520–22
genes, defined, 41, 77
genetic counseling, 102–4
genetic epistemology, 29
genetic factors, 47–51
    active, passive, and evocative, 50, 71
    animal studies of, 48–49, 65–67
    in autism, 251
    counseling on, 102–4
    in developmental defects, 89–94
    environmental factors and, 41, 48–49, 50, 51, 71, 79, 176, 360
    in gamete production, 77–78
    heritability and, 51, 71
    intellectual abilities and, 360–62
    prenatal development and, 77–79
genital stage, 22
genotype, 50–51, 71, 78–79, 105
German measles (rubella), 96
germinal period, 81–82, 105
Gestalt psychology, 234, 236–38
gestation period, 81, 105
girls:
    achievement motivation in, 463
    androgenized, 481
    eating disorders and, 493
    fear of success in, 464
    learned helplessness in, 468, 470
    passiveness in, 63, 195, 463
    penis envy in, 22
    teachers' criticisms of, 468–69, 490
    teachers' reinforcement of stereotyped sex roles for, 489–91
    Turner's syndrome in, 90–91, 192, 481
    See also sex differences
giving aid, 522–23
glial cells, 85, 105, 175
gonorrhea, 96
grammar, 274, 276–77, 285, 286–87, 297, 298–306
grasping reflex, 116–17, 137
gratification, delayed, 380, 422, 423, 508
gravity, 215
growth, *see* physical growth
growth hormone (GH), 158
growth-plate injuries, 164
guilt, 23–24
    management of, 507
    moral development and, 506–7
Gutteridge scale, 161, 162
gyrus, 177

habituation, 127, 138, 180, 221–22
handedness, 185, 187–91, 195, 201
handicapped children:
    autistic, 251
    blind, 189, 220, 251
    deaf, 251, 290–91
    deaf-blind, 27
    with Down's syndrome, 91, 101, 106, 152

family's adjustment to, 152–53
head, 27, 145
    circumference of, 154
Head Start program, 366, 371
health:
    growth rate and, 156, 169
    intellectual development and, 362–63
hearing, 177, 208–9
    in newborns, 120–21, 126, 138, 186
    See also sound
hemispheric specialization, 181–93, 201, 286
hemoglobin, 92
hemophilia, 79
heritability, 51, 71
    See also genetic factors
heroin, 97
herpes simplex, 96
heterozygous offspring, 78
Hex A, 91, 102
hierarchical coding, 325
hierarchic integration, 33, 147
hippocampus, 258
history-normative influences, 46, 60, 71
homosexuality, 479
homozygous offspring, 78
hormones:
    aggression and, 43–44, 481
    brain functions at puberty and, 192, 195
    growth rate and, 158
    sex role development and, 481
    sexual maturation and, 165–66
hostile aggression, 526, 528, 531, 534
hydrocephaly, 101–2, 103
hyperactivity, 198–200, 201
hypnosis, 21
hypocrisy, 522
hypothalamus, 165, 166, 481
hypothesis testing, 313
hysteria, 21

id, 20
identification, socialization and, 408
identity:
    in adolescence, 24–25, 55, 543–44, 563
    as concept, 315–18, 321, 338, 559
    sex roles and, 476–80
    See also gender identity
identity achievement, 543–44
identity crisis, 543
identity diffusion, 543–44
illegitimacy, 7, 424
illness, *see* diseases; health
imagery, 261–62, 267
imaginal representation, 247, 248
imitation, 219–20, 370
    in blind children, 220
    language acquisition and, 277–78, 287
    by newborns, 130–131, 229
    of peers, 444–46
    socialization and, 408, 411
    social-learning theories and, 15–16
    See also models
imprinting, 398
incidental learning, 244
independent variables, 64
indifferent parents, 406, 431
induced abortions, 104

industry, 24
infancy, *see* newborns
infanticide, 7–8
infant mortality, 7, 97, 98, 104
inferiority, 24
inflection, 300–302
influenza, 96
information-processing theories, 14, 18–20, 39, 207, 254–55, 256, 258, 287, 370
    aggression as viewed by, 527–28
    conflict resolution as viewed by, 554–55
    intelligence as viewed by, 348–51
    sex roles as viewed by, 485–486
informed consent, 67
initiative, 23
instrumental aggression, 526, 528, 534
instrumental competence, 406–7, 431
integration, 33, 147
intelligence:
    biological factors and, 346–47, 370
    brain functions and, 175, 356–57
    genetic and environmental influence on, 51
    information-processing approach to, 348–51, 370
    measurement of, 351–52
    modifiability of, 360–70
    nature of, 342–51
    neurometric approach to, 356–57
    Piaget's theory of, 29–33, 224, 254, 342, 346, 347
    psychometric perspective on, 347–48, 370
    structuralist approach to, 346, 347, 370
    See also cognitive development
intelligence tests, 344–45, 370
    in childhood, 353–54
    computerized, 356–57
    cross-sectional studies of, 60
    in infancy, 352–53, 364
    stability and change in scores of, 352–54
    uses of, 348, 351, 355–60
intention, 280
inter- and intraindividual differences, 46, 71
interposition, 212
intimacy, 25, 551–52
intonation, 298–99
IQ score:
    interpretations of, 351
    See also intelligence tests
irritability, 131
isolation, *see* social isolation

Jewish ancestry, 91
jigsaw puzzles, 235
just world hypothesis, 507
juvenile delinquency, 418, 420
    social isolation and, 450

kibbutzim, 387, 389
kinesthesis, 123, 138, 159
Klinefelter's syndrome, 90
kwashiorkor, 155, 363

labor, 87–88, 105, 132
    See also childbirth

Lamaze method of childbirth, 89
landmarks, 239–40, 266
language:
    brain areas controlling, 174, 177, 181–83, 189, 191, 196, 286
    cognitive development and, 277–78, 287, 295, 365
    errors in, 291–92, 296–97, 303–4
    meaning and, 270, 290–98
    playing with, 290–91
    private functions of, 274–77
    properties of, 248–49, 270–71
    public functions of, 278–79
    social foundations of, 274, 279–85
    written, 326
language acquisition, 36
    crib speech and, 301
    in deaf children, 290–91
    sensitive periods and, 285–86
    social class and, 365, 392
    sound and, 191, 208–9, 271, 288–92
    syntax and, 271, 274, 276–77, 286–87, 298–306
    theories of, 285–88
    See also speech, onset of
lanugo, 111
latchkey children, 430
latency period, 22
lateralization, 185–93, 197–98, 201, 286
lead, 94, 199
leadership, 455–56
learned helplessness, 468–70, 471
learning:
    cognitive development vs., 313
    under drug influence, 200, 201
    in newborns, 14, 128–29, 138
    rote, 195, 263
    state-dependent, 200, 201
learning disorders, brain functions and, 197–200
learning theory, 14–18, 46–47
    conditioning in, 11, 14–15
    Freudian theory and, 25–26
lesbian mothers, 479
levels-of-processing approach, 254, 267
libido, 20, 21
limbic system, 174
linguistic relativity, 276
linguistic representation, 247, 248–49, 274–76
locus of control, 395, 421
logical thought, 314, 329–30, 339, 561
longitudinal studies, 60–61, 71
long-term store, 254, 267
love, 25, 496, 497, 543
    withdrawal of, as punishment, 506, 509
lungs, 163, 164
lying, detection of, 559

magnesium, 97
malaria, 94
malnutrition, 154, 363
marital discord, 387, 420
Marxist framework, 35
mass media, see media; television
maternal deprivation, 391
maternal diet, 92–93, 96–97

mathematical ability, 190, 194–95, 462–63
maturation, defined, 159
mechanistic theories, 13–20, 39, 206–7, 286–87
media:
    body ideal in, 493
    impact of, 56–57
    sex-role stereotypes purveyed by, 491–92
    See also television
medication:
    developmental or birth complications following, 94, 95, 97, 98–99, 122
    for hyperactivity, 199–200
meiosis, 77, 90
memory:
    cognition and, 221–23, 233–34, 252, 254–67, 336
    information-processing theory and, 19
    language and, 277
    loss of, 258–59
    neurochemical basis of, 179–80
    in newborns, 127–28
    recall and, 256–58, 267
    recognition and, 255–56, 267
    reconstruction and, 256, 267
    retrieval and, 254, 263–64, 267
    strategies in aid of, 259–64, 267
memory molecule, 179
memory tasks, 260
menarche, 166, 167, 168
menstruation, 166, 168, 419, 493
mental development: see cognitive development; intelligence; memory; mental retardation; social cognition; thought
mental retardation, 153
    alcohol and, 363
    detection of, 353
    genetic factors in, 91
    memory and, 19
    nutrition and, 363
    self-recognition achievement and, 393
mesoderm, 81
metacognition, 335–37, 339
metamemory, 265–66, 267, 336
metapelet, 387, 389–90
methadone, 94, 97
Middle Ages, 6, 7, 8, 12
middle class, growth of, 7
midgets, 158, 394
minimal brain dysfunction (MBD), 199
mirrors, 393–94, 540
miscarriage, 104
mitosis, 77
models:
    gender identity and, 485
    moral development and, 510–13, 522
    social isolation modified by, 451–53
    See also imitation
mongolism, see Down's syndrome
monkeys, see primates
Montessori program, 368–69
morality:
    cognitive approach to, 504, 515–19
    defining, 504
    delayed gratification and, 508
    development of, 503–19

empathy and, 503, 510, 513–15, 521, 522, 533
    inconsistency in, 504–6, 519
    psychoanalytic approach to, 506–7
    social-learning view of, 507–15
morality of constraint, 516, 533
morality of cooperation, 516, 533
moral reasoning:
    behavior weakly linked with, 504–6, 519
    stages of, 515–19
moratorium, 543–44, 563
Moro reflex, 116–17, 137
morphine, 94
Morse code, 183
"motherese," 281
mothers:
    absent, 419
    adolescent, 92–93
    alcoholic, 363
    attached formation and, 376–92
    employed, 414–16
    lesbian, 479
    See also bonding; parents
motivation, moral development and, 513–15
motor development, 148, 158–62
    Gutteridge scale for, 161–62
    sex differences in, 163
multiple-choice tests, 255
mumps, 96
music, 183, 185, 186, 208
myelin, 85, 105, 175–76, 185

naïve realism, 13
names, 447
Native Americans, 24, 159
"natural deprivation," 129
naturalistic observation, 62–63, 68, 71
Neanderthal man, 181
negativistic crisis, 395
neighborhood, 43, 55–56
neocortex, 174, 176
neonate:
    defined, 110
    See also newborns
neural tube defects, 101–3
neurometrics, 356–57
neurons, 85, 105, 175, 176, 179, 194, 195
neurotransmitter, 179, 199, 201
newborns, 109–38, 175
    assessment of, 88–89
    catch-up growth in, 99, 100, 151
    cuteness of, 27
    death of, 7, 104
    egocentricity of, 29
    emotions of, 395–96
    fear in, 64–65
    feeding of, 114–15, 133, 137
    id in, 20
    learning in, 14, 128–29, 138
    oral stage of, 21
    perception and attention in, 123–26, 186
    reflexes in, 116–18, 131, 137, 146, 176, 187, 224
    sensorimotor stage in, 32
    sensory capabilities in, 119–23, 137–38, 186, 209–10

newborns (*continued*)
size of, 84, 89, 92, 96, 99
sleep in, 112–114, 137, 180
smiling in, 27
social relations of, 131–37, 376–77
sucking in, 115
temperament in, 129–32, 133, 138
temperature of, 111–12
trust in, 22
noise, background, 365
nonconformist parents, 406, 431
non-normative influences, 46, 71
norepinephrine, 179, 199
norms:
defined, 147, 170
peer group influence on, 455
nouns, 295, 305
collective, 320, 324–25
novelty, preference for, as indicator of
intelligence, 353
number:
concept of, 331–33
conservation of, 320, 332
nursery school:
peer impact in, 435, 436
sex-role stereotypes reinforced in,
489–90
nutrition, *see* diet

obesity, 155–56
object concept, 226–29, 231, 379
object perception, 234–36
object permanence, 226–29, 379–80,
540
old age, 7, 9, 499
one-way assistance, 551
open schools, 465
operant conditioning, 14, 39
operating principles, 303, 306
operations, cognitive, 315, 338, 343
operative representation, 247, 252–54
operative whole, 237, 266
optic nerve, 119
oral stage, 21
organismic theories, 13, 28–35, 39, 206,
207
organization, 262–63, 267
organizational stability, 34
orgasm, 497
orphans, 158
orthogenetic principle, 33
ovaries, 165
overextension, 293–94, 306
overregulation, 304, 306
ovum, 77, 94, 105, 165
oxytocin, 87

paleomammalian brain, 174, 176
parallel play, 439, 470
parents:
abusive, 8, 427–31
authoritarian, 405–6, 427
authoritative, 406, 407, 420, 427,
431
conflicts with, 22, 25, 395, 496
discipline styles of, 405–10, 431
genetic counseling for, 102–4
of handicapped children, 152–53
homosexual, 479
identification with, 22, 23–24

imitation of, 16
indifferent, 406, 431
memory influenced by, 257
nonconformist, 406, 431
older, advantages and disadvantages
of, 91, 426
peer influence compared to that of,
436
permissive, 406, 431
sex-role development and, 486–88
sex roles of, 498–99
as socialization agents, 405–10
step-, 422–23
transsexual, 479
See also attachment; families; fathers;
mothers
peek-a-boo, 223, 281
peer groups, 455–56
peers:
conformity pressures among, 456–
60
impact of, 55
primate studies of contacts among,
436–38, 442
as role models, 444–46
sex-role development as influenced
by, 488–89
social development and, 435–60
penis envy, 22
perception, 207, 234
perceptual constancies, 213–15, 230,
235
peripheral vision, 119, 209
permissive parents, 406, 431
personality:
attachment and, 392, 396–97
birth order and, 410
early experience and, 397–400
psychoanalytic theory of, 20–21, 397
See also temperament
person permanence, 379–80
perspective, 29, 212
phallic stage, 22, 258
phenotype, 50–51, 71, 78–79, 105
phenylketonuria (PKU), 77, 78–79, 91,
102, 105, 106
phonology, 271–73, 306
physical growth, 143–71
in adolescence, 147, 165–70
environmental influences on, 154–58,
170
maturational trends and, 167–70
motor abilities and, 158–62
norms in, 147–54
sex differences in, 162–70
sexual maturation and, 165–70
socioeconomic status and, 156–57
picture perception, 236–39, 266
pituitary gland, 165, 166
placenta, 81, 87
place perception, 239–40
placing response, 118, 137
planning, in metacognition, 336–38
play, 24, 221, 230
adaptation theory of, 27–28
of blind children, 220
with language, 290–91
peer influence on, 438–42
rough-and-tumble, 388, 437, 442,
480, 481, 483

sex-role development and, 62–63,
486–90
socialization and, 439–42
polio, 96
polygenic traits, 79
popularity:
appearance and, 446–47
names and, 447
personal and social consequences of,
448
reinforcement and, 442–44
social skills and, 442–43, 447–48
stability of, 448–50
poverty, 9, 157, 424–25
practice effect, 61
pragmatics, 271, 274, 287, 306
precedence effect, 120–21, 138
predetermined epigenesis, 80–81
prednisone, 97
preeclampsia, 97
preformation, 80
pregnancy:
teenage, 92–93, 170
termination of, 104, 106
prematurity, 52, 99–100, 104
premoral level, 516, 534
prenatal period:
androgen exposure during, 481
behavior in, 86
development in, 75–106
environmental factors in, 52, 75, 94–
99
growth in, 79–84
maternal diet during, 92–93, 96–97
prematurity and, 99–100
prevention of developmental defects
during, 101–4
preoperational stage, 32–33, 39, 314,
315–18, 338, 541
pretend play, 440–41, 442
primates, 28, 196, 343, 346, 376
studies of, 65–67, 179, 181, 187, 272–
73, 378–79, 391, 397–98, 410, 428,
429, 436–38, 442
principled level, 517, 534
probabilistic epigenesis, 81, 193
probability, 70, 71
problem-solving behavior, 225, 249,
336–38
See also hypothesis testing; thought,
formal operational
procedural knowledge, 247, 267
production deficiency, 260, 262, 267
productivity, as property of language,
270, 274, 305
progressive lateralization, 185, 191, 192,
201
propositional storage, 249
prosocial behavior, 519–25, 534
prostaglandin, 87
protein deficiency, 154–55
prototypes, concepts founded on, 249,
267, 312
proximal development, 36, 352
proximity, principle of, 235
proximodistal development, 145–46,
170, 177
psychoanalytic theory, 20–21, 258,
397
attachment as viewed by, 382

moral development as viewed by, 506–7
psychodynamic theories, 13, 20–26, 39
"psychosocial dwarfism," 158
psychometrics, 347–48, 370
  See also intelligence tests
psychosexual theory, 20–22, 39
psychosocial theory, 22–25, 39
puberty, 8, 171, 192, 492
  biological events in, 165–67
  in daughters of single fathers, 419
  defined, 149
  growth spurt in, 150, 166
  impact of, 496
  trends in onset of, 167–70
pubic hair, 166
punishment:
  guilt and, 506–7
  moral development and, 509–13
  peer use of, 443, 516
  See also discipline

race relations, 424, 460–61
  See also blacks; ethnic factors
rapid eye movement (REM) sleep, 113–14, 137, 180
reaction range, 50–51, 71
reaction time, 161, 171
reading, 47, 49, 50, 195
  learning disorders and, 197–98
  selective attention required for, 245
recall, 256–58, 267
recapitulation theory, 10
recessive genes, 78, 91, 92, 105
recognition, 255–56, 267
  self-, 393–94, 540
reconstruction, 256, 267
reflexes, 116–18, 146, 176, 224
  grasping, 116–17, 137
  Moro, 116–17, 137
  rooting, 116, 137
  Sudden Infant Death Syndrome and, 116
  tonic neck, 187
rehearsal, 260–61, 267
reinforcement theory, 14–15, 39
  See also learning theory
releasing stimuli, 27
replication, 59
representation, 247–54
  categorical, 228, 247, 249–52, 267, 312
  concept building and, 311–12
  enactive, 247–48, 267
  imaginal, 247, 248, 267
  linguistic, 247, 248–49, 267, 274–76
  operative, 247, 252–54
  symbolic, 248–49, 274–76
repression, 258
reptilian brain, 174, 176
respiratory distress syndrome, 83, 101
response, defined, 14
responsiveness, neonate, 131, 180, 376–77
retina, 119
retrieval, 254, 263–64, 267
reversibility, 318, 338
rickets, 155
Ritalin, 199, 200
RNA (ribonucleic acid), 179

rock videos, 531
role models, peers as, 444–46
role-taking, 550–51
rooting reflex, 116, 137
rough-and-tumble play, 388, 437, 442, 480, 481, 483
rubella (German measles), 96
rules:
  learning, 312–14
  linguistic, 302–3
  moral development and, 515–16

sampling, 59
sarcasm, 559
scanning, 210–11, 241–42
scapegoats, 28, 447–48
schemes, 29, 39, 223, 225, 249, 314
Scholastic Aptitude Test (SAT), 194–95
schooling, 460–71
  for academically precocious children, 316–17, 354
  cognitive development effected by, 326
  desegregated, 460–61
  educational psychology and, 11
  emergence of childhood concept and, 7, 8
  impact of, 56, 326
  IQ scores as predictive of success in, 351, 355
  parental expectations and success in, 195, 461–64
  selective attention development and, 244–45
  social class and attitude toward, 423, 463–64
  stages of development initiated by, 15, 24, 326
  teacher expectations and success in, 468–69, 490
scripts, 284–85, 306, 552
search strategy, 124–25
secondary sex characteristics, 165–66
secure attachment bonds, 382, 384–87, 389, 400
selective attention, 219, 230, 242–45
self-concept:
  attachment and, 393–94
  development of, 540–44
  sex roles and, 499
self-consciousness, 542–43
self-demand feeding, 115, 137
self-esteem, 543, 563
self-recognition, 393–94, 540
self-regulation, 337, 519, 534
semanticity, 270, 305
semantics, 271, 273–74, 303, 306
sensitive periods:
  attachments and, 398–99, 401
  language acquisition and, 285–86
sensorimotor coordination, 161, 216–19
  See also motor development
sensorimotor stage, 32, 39, 224–30, 314, 334, 346, 347, 352–53, 540
sensory deprivation, 193–94
sensory registers, 254, 267
separation distress, 380–82, 400
sequential design, 61–62, 71
seriation, 321–22, 331, 338

serotonin, 179
sex differences, 162–70, 171
  in aggression, 43–44, 481, 483, 529–30
  in brain development, 190–95, 481
  in early intervention programs, 368–69
  in friendship formation, 454–55, 551
  in generosity, 521
  genetic determination of, 79
  in identity, 544
  in maternal employment effects, 415
  in moral reasoning, 518
  in parent preferences of infants, 388
  in peer pressure effect on smoking, 459
  prepubertal, 163–64
  in response to parental discipline styles, 405–6
  sex roles and, 481–83, 495–98
  in sexual maturation rates, 163, 165–70, 496–97
sex roles:
  absent fathers and, 417
  development of, 62–63, 473–92
  family life and, 54
  identity and, 476–80
  life span changes in, 498–99
  media influence on, 491–92
  peer influence on, 488–89
  pervasiveness of, 474
  sex differences and, 481–83, 495–98
  in single-father households, 419
  teachers' influence on, 489–91
  working mothers and, 415
sex-role strain, 492, 501
sexual maturation, 492–98
  early vs. late, 493–94
  sex differences in, 163, 165–70, 496–97
shame, 23, 506, 541, 542
shape constancy, 213–14, 230, 235
short-term store, 254, 267
shyness, 541–42
siblings:
  rivalry among, 54, 412
  as socialization agents, 410–12
sickle-cell anemia, 92–94, 106
sighting dominance, 189
similarity, principle of, 235
size constancy, 213, 214–15, 230, 235
skeletal maturity, 149, 162, 163, 170
sleep, 112–14
  REM, 113–14, 137, 180
small-for-gestational age (SGA) babies, 99, 106, 363
smell, in newborns, 121–23
smiling, 27, 152
  as social responsiveness, 210, 220, 377–78, 382
smoking:
  peer pressure and, 459–60
  prenatal development and, 94, 97, 98
social class:
  maternal behavior and, 364, 365, 392
  maternal employment effects and, 415
  socialization and, 421–23
social cognition:
  self-concept and, 540–44
  understanding others and, 544–57

social cognition (*continued*)
    understanding society and, 557–61
    See also social development
social development, 393–96
    attachment and, 376–92
    biological vs., 6
    conformity pressure and, 421
    maternal employment and, 414–16
    parental discipline style and, 405–10
    paternal absence and, 416–19
    peer influence on, 435–60
    sibling influence on, 410–12
    See also personality; social cognition;
        social interaction; socialization; so-
        cial skills
social hierarchies, 164
    See also dominance hierarchies
social interaction:
    between infants, 137, 438
    of newborns, 131–37, 376–77
    peer reinforcement and, 442–44, 451–
        53
social isolation:
    modification of, 451–53
    through peer rejection, 450–51
    primate studies of, 437–38
socialization:
    of aggression, 526, 528, 553–54
    childhood amnesia and, 258
    class and cultural differences in, 421–
        27
    defined, 404, 431
    discipline and, 509
    gender identity and, 479, 482
    play and, 439–42
social-learning theories, 15–18, 39, 287
    moral development as viewed by,
        507–15
social referencing, 385, 550
social roles, 557–60
social skills:
    popularity and, 442–43, 447–48
    taught to isolated children, 451–53
    See also social development
societal stage, 15
society, understanding, 560–62
socioeconomic status:
    child abuse and, 430
    growth rate and, 156–57
    IQ scores and, 364–65
sociology, 43
sociometric analysis, 446, 471
somatomedin, 158
sonogram, 101, 106
sound:
    auditory discrimination of, 181, 183,
        186–87, 288–89
    language acquisition and, 191, 208–9,
        271, 288–92
    sight and, 216–18
    See also hearing
Soviet Union:
    peer group functions in, 460
    socialization in, 392, 424
space perception, 215–16
    brain areas controlling, 183, 187, 189,
        190, 192–93, 197–98
species intelligence, 342–43
speech:
    crib, 301

onset of, 182–83, 191, 276, 289–92
    See also language; language acquisition
speed, concept of, 331
spelling, computer program for, 19–20
spermatozoon, 5, 77, 79, 94, 105, 165,
    166
spina bifida, 101–2, 103
spontaneous abortion, 104
stabilimeter crib, 113
stage theories, 13, 14, 15
    Erikson's, 22–25
    Freud's, 20–22
    Piaget's, 32–33, 224–31
Stanford-Binet Test, 353, 355
state-dependent learning, 200, 201
statistics, interpretation of, 70–71
stepparents, 422–23
stepping movements, 117–18, 137, 158
stillbirths, 96, 97
stimulant drugs, 199–200
stimulation:
    attachment and, 386
    cognitive development and, 365, 398
    cortical development and, 193–94
    deprivation of, 193–94
    excessive, 160
stimuli, 17
    defined, 14
    releasing, 27
strabismus, 120
strangers, wariness of, 64–65, 375, 380,
    383–85, 396, 400
Strange Situation, 375, 381, 393
strength, 160–61
stress:
    growth rate and, 157–58
    in pregnancy, 99
sublimation, 20
success, fear of, 464–65
sucking, 115, 224
Sudden   Infant   Death   Syndrome
    (SIDS), 110, 116, 137
suffixes, 303
superego, 20, 22
superordinate categories, 250–52, 267,
    323, 325, 339
surfactin, 83, 104
sylvian fissure, 181
symbolic representation, 248–49, 274–
    76
synapses, 174, 176, 193–94
syntax, 271, 274, 276–77, 286–87, 298–
    306
syphilis, 96

tabula rasa, 12
taste, in newborns, 121
Tay-Sachs disease, 91–92, 101, 102, 106
teachers:
    expectations of academic achievement
        and, 465–66, 490
    sex-biased criticisms by, 468–69, 490
    sex-role development as influenced
        by, 489–91
television:
    attention and, 245–46
    body ideal in, 493
    children's understanding of, 552–53
    effects of habitual viewing of, 532–33
    impact of, 56–57, 530–31

as   intervention   for   disadvantaged
        children, 366
    prosocial programs on, 523–25
    sex-role   stereotypes   purveyed   by,
        491–92
    as socialization agent, 56–57, 530–31
    violent programs on, 16, 57, 530–33
temperament:
    in newborns, 129–32, 133, 138
    parental style and, 409–10
    See also personality
temperature, of newborns, 111–12
teratogens, 95, 106
testes, 165, 481, 482
thalidomide, 95, 97
theta waves, 357
thought:
    concrete operational, 314, 318–25,
        338, 561
    convergent vs. divergent, 344
    development of, 223–30, 314–30,
        338–39
    formal operational, 314, 315, 325–30,
        339, 561
    language and, 276–77
    logical, 314, 329–30, 339, 561
    precausal, 334
    preoperational, 314, 315–18, 338
    sensorimotor, 224–30, 334, 346, 347,
        352–53
    symbolic, 225
    See also cognitive development
thumb-sucking, 116
time, concept of, 309, 330–31
toilet training, 21–22, 26
tongue protrusion, 130–31, 229
tonic neck reflex, 187
touch, 218
toy industry, 27
tranquilizers, 200
transitivity, 321–23, 338
transsexuals, 479–80, 500
triune brain, 174
troubled poor, 425
trust, 22, 380, 381, 431
tuberculosis, 51
Turner's Syndrome, 90–91, 101, 192,
    481
turn-taking experiences:
    breast-feeding and, 133
    in language acquisition, 273, 281
    self-concept and, 393
twins, 52, 55, 187, 251
    co-twin control studies of, 159, 161–62
    IQ correlation between, 360–61

ultrasound examinations, 101
umbilical cord, 82
unconscious, 258
underextension, 294–95, 306
understanding, 330–35
universal grammar, 285
universal stage, 15
U-shaped behavioral growth, 118, 137,
    158, 296–97, 303, 477

variables, 64, 68
venereal diseases, 96
verbal ability, 353
    See also language acquisition

verbs, 295, 304
vernix, 111
vesicles, 175, 201
violence, *see* aggression
viruses, 96
visual cliff, 212–13
visual perception, 177, 181, 186–87, 188, 189, 209–19, 234–41
  depth perception and, 211–13, 238
  in newborns, 119–20, 123–25, 137–38, 209–10

perception constancies and, 213–15, 235
picture perception and, 236–39, 266
sensorimotor coordination and, 216–19
social cognition and, 546–49
space perception and, 215–16
vital capacity, 163, 171
vitamins, 96, 155
vocabulary, accumulation of, 290–98

walking, development of, 117–18, 158–59, 177
wall-eyes (strabismus), 120
Wernicke's area, 181–82
wet-nurses, 8
withdrawal, 450–53
  See also social isolation
word order, 274, 299–300, 303, 305
words, first, 291, 292–93
working mothers, 414–16
written language, 326